HISTORICAL AND POLITICAL GAZETTEER OF AFGHANISTAN

Vol. 6

KABUL
AND SOUTHEASTERN AFGHANISTAN

Edited by
LUDWIG W. ADAMEC, Ph. D.

AKADEMISCHE DRUCK- u. VERLAGSANSTALT
GRAZ–AUSTRIA
1985

The Afghanistan Gazetteer, printed originally for secret official purposes, is here published with additions and editorial changes by permission of the Controller of Her Majesty's Stationery Office, London, United Kingdom.

The present edition includes the formerly secret Gazetteer of Afghanistan (compiled in 1914) with corrections and additions of maps and considerable new material to take into account developments up to 1978.

© Akademische Druck- u. Verlagsanstalt, Graz 1985

Printed in Austria

ISBN 3-201-01272-6

CONTENTS

Preface VII
Introduction 1
Historical and Political Gazetteer of Afghanistan 9
Glossary of Terms 825
Map Section 849

PREFACE

The sixth volume of the Historical and Political Gazetteer of Afghanistan, covering the provinces of Kabul, Parwan, Maidan (Wardak), Logar, Ghazni, Paktia, Nangarhar, Bamian, Kunar, and Kapisa in eastern and southeastern Afghanistan, provides general information for the layman and specialized data for the scholar, much of which is not available in any other reference source. Scholars in all fields will find it indispensable as a point of departure for specialized research on Afghanistan. Those with a nonspecialized interest will find the Gazetteer useful for locating a particular area or geographical feature, and for obtaining background material of a political, historical, and geographical nature.

This work is based largely on material collected by the British Indian Government and its agents since the early 19th century. In an age of imperialism, Afghanistan became important as the „Gateway to India" and an area of dispute between the British and Russian empires. It is therefore not surprising that much effort was expended by various branches of the British Indian Government to amass information regarding the country's topography, tribal composition, climate, economy, and internal politics. Thus, an effort which began with military considerations in mind has now been expanded and updated with maps and data compiled by both Western and Afghan scholarship to serve the non-political purpose of providing a comprehensive reference work on Afghanistan.

ORGANIZATION AND SCOPE

In the preparation of this volume, I was able to benefit from the comments, suggestions, and criticisms of a wide variety of readers who examined the previous volumes. I depended primarily on written sources for the task of updating the material and could not check my information in the field; but I succeeded in obtaining the most recent statistical data available in Afghanistan, problematical as it may be. New features adapted in the third volume have been continued and expanded.

Geographical Coordinates. Not all entries listed in this work can be located in the Map Section; I placed the letter "m" next to the geographical coordinates of each entry which can be found in the Map Section. For example, "Ak Robat," located at 34–56 67–39 m., can be found; whereas "Akinabad," located at 34–42 70–15, cannot be found on the maps. "Bagrami," located at 34–5 70–13 G., can be found only in the *Qamus-i-Jughrafiya-ye Afghanistan*, therefore the letter "G" was added; and "Adam Khan," located at 34– 68–, could not be located, but lies within the degress of longitude and latitude given. The letter "A" placed after geographical coordinates indicates that the place can be found only in the *U.S. Official Standard Names Gazetteer;* for example, "Kulam," 35–9 70–18 A.

I determined geographical coordinates on the basis of maps published in Kabul at the scale of 1:250,000. If a name could not be located, I referred to maps at the scale of 1:200,000; U.S. world aeronautical charts at the scale of 1:1,000,000; and other cartographic sources. Only degrees and minutes were given because the primary purpose in giving coordinates (and distances) was to enable the reader to locate the entry in the Map Section. In many cases when a place was not indicated on any maps it was nevertheless possible to obtain fairly accurate coordinates. Places were often described as located a certain distance from another, or near some geographical feature, as the bend of a river, a valley, a crossroads, which made it possible to take measurements from the maps to indicate the general location of a place.

To locate an entry in the Map Section, the reader should refer to the degrees of longitude and latitude listed below the entry heading and find the coordinates in the Map Index. For example: to locate the entry "Bamian" in the Map Section, note coordinates 34–49 67–49 m. Next, refer to the Index in the Map Section and you will find the coordinates in grid No. 8 (A,B,C,D,). The minutes 49 and 49 will be located in the upper right section, marked B.

Measures and Weights. It has been suggested that I list all measures and weights in metric units. This could have been done with little difficulty as far as British units are concerned, but I felt it desirable to give Afghan units in their historical terms. Furthermore, the situation is somewhat complex: units of measure identical in name are not necessarily also identical in the quantities measured. It was therefore much simpler to provide the reader with conversion tables which will enable him to make his own computations:

Western Units

Length

1 inch	25.4	mm	1 cm	0.394 inch
1 foot	0.3048	meter	1 meter	3.281 feet
1 yard	0.9144	meter		1.094 yard
1 furlong	201.168	meters	1 km	4,971 feet
1 mile	1,609.344	meters		

Area

1 sq inch	6.4516	sq cm	1 sq cm	0.155 sq inch
1 sq foot	0.092903	sq meter	1 sq meter	10.7639 sq feet

Area

1 sq yard	0.83613	sq meter		1.19599 sq yard
1 acre	0.404686	hectare	1 hectare	2.4711 acres
1 sq mile	2.590	sq km	1 sq km	0.3861 sq mile

Weight

1 ounce	28.3495	grams	1 gram	0.035274 ounce
1 pound	0.4535924	kg	1 kg	2.20462 pounds
1 ton (l.)	1.01605	m ton	1 m ton	0.9842 ton (l.)

Degrees
Fahrenheit to Centigrade

F	C	F	C	F	C	F	C
1	−17.2	36	2.2	71	21.7	106	41.1
2	−16.7	37	2.8	72	22.2	107	41.7
3	−16.1	38	3.3	73	22.8	108	42.2
4	−15.6	39	3.9	74	23.3	109	42.8
5	−15.0	40	4.4	75	23.9	110	43.3
6	−14.4	41	5.0	76	24.4	111	43.9
7	−13.9	42	5.6	77	25.0	112	44.4
8	−13.3	43	6.1	78	25.6	113	45.0
9	−12.8	44	6.7	79	26.1	114	45.6
10	−12.2	45	7.2	80	26.7	115	46.1
11	−11.7	46	7.8	81	27.2	116	46.7
12	−11.1	47	8.3	82	27.8	117	47.2
13	−10.6	48	8.9	83	28.3	118	47.8
14	−10.0	49	9.4	84	28.9	119	48.3
15	− 9.4	50	10.0	85	29.4	120	48.9
16	− 8.9	51	10.6	86	30.0	121	49.4
17	− 8.3	52	11.1	87	30.6	122	50.0
18	− 7.8	53	11.7	88	31.1	123	50.6
19	− 7.2	54	12.2	89	31.7	124	51.1
20	− 6.7	55	12.8	90	32.2	125	51.7
21	− 6.1	56	13.3	91	32.8	126	52.2
22	− 5.6	57	13.9	92	33.3	127	52.8
23	− 5.0	58	14.4	93	33.9	128	53.3
24	− 4.4	59	15.0	94	34.4	129	53.9
25	− 3.9	60	15.6	95	35.0	130	54.4
26	− 3.3	61	16.1	96	35.6	131	55.0
27	− 2.8	62	16.7	97	36.1	132	55.6
28	− 2.2	63	17.2	98	36.7	133	56.1
29	− 1.7	64	17.8	99	37.2	134	56.7
30	− 1.1	65	18.3	100	37.8	135	57.2
31	− 0.6	66	18.9	101	38.3	136	57.8
32	0	67	19.4	102	38.9	137	58.3
33	0.6	68	20.0	103	39.4		
34	1.1	69	20.6	104	40.0		
35	1.7	70	21.1	105	40.6		

Afghan Units: Length

1 gaz-i-shah (Kabul yard)	1.065 meter
1 girah-i-gaz-i-shah	0.066 meter
1 gaz-i-mimar (mason's yard)	0.838 meter
1 gaz-i-jareeb (for land)	0.736 meter
1 jareeb (one side)	44.183 meters
1 biswah (one side)	9.879 meters
1 biswasah (one side)	2.209 meters

Weights

1 nakhud	0.19 gram	
1 misqal	4.4 grams	
1 khurd	110.4 grams	
1 pao	441.6 grams	
1 charak	1,766.4 grams	1.77 kg
1 seer	7,066.0 grams	7.07 kg
1 kharwar	565,280.0 grams	565.28 kg
24 nakhuds	1 miskal	
30 miskals	1 seer	
40 seers	1 man (12 lbs., if wheat 13 lbs.)	
100 mans	1 kharwar (1,200 lbs.)	

British sources in the late 19th and early 20th centuries describe weights in Afghanistan as follows:

Herat:

8 tolas	—	1 Herati seer	—	$1/10$ of a British (Indian) seer.
40 seers	—	1 Herati man	—	4 seers British.
100 mans	—	1 Herati kharwar	—	10 maunds British.

Actually the weights are a trifle more than the stated British equivalent. Moreover, the seer varies locally: thus the Obeh seer has 10 tolas and in Badghis there are two seers, one of 12, and one of 16 tolas. In all cases the man has 40 seers, so that the local weight can easily be calculated, if necessary. Herat weights are more or less recognized throughout the province.

Mazar-i-Sharif: The Mazar-i-Sharif weights differ considerably from those of Tashkurghan, Haibak, etc., but are in more general use, though it is said that Akcha has a system of weights of its own.

1 Mazar seer	—	$1\frac{1}{2}$ Kabuli seers ($11\frac{1}{4}$ British seers).
16 Mazar seers	—	1 Mazar man (4 maunds, 20 seers, British).
3 Mazar mans	—	1 Mazar kharwar (13 maunds, 20 seers, British).

The long measure of the district, and of Afghan Turkistan in general, is:

16 tasa (of $1\frac{3}{4}$ inches)	—	1 kadam, or gaz-i-shari (pace of 28 inches),
12,000 kadam	—	1 sang, or farsakh (5 miles, 5335).

The length of the 'kadam,' or pace, appears to vary in different parts of the country, but a sang in Turkistan, or farsakh in Herat, is always 12,000 kadam.

The 'gaz-i-shari,' (shari means "book") which is the same as the kadam, is used for land measuring. There are, however, three varieties of the gaz-i-shari. One is a tasa longer than the above standard, and therefore $29^{3}/_{4}$ inches, practically the same as the British pace. The other is a tasa shorter than the first, therefore $26^{1}/_{4}$ inches. Besides these three varieties of the gaz-i-shari, there is the gaz-i-shahi, which is the measure for cloth. It is either 3 feet 3 inches, or 3 feet 6 inches. Perhaps both are in use. Another common measure of length is the kulach, or fathom (6 feet). This is supposed to be the furthest stretch between the hands of a full-grown man, extended horizontally, as in measuring a long rope. Land is also measured by jaribs, or 'tanabs,' of so many 'gaz,' or 'kulach' square. They vary much in size. However, 60 jaribs or tanabs appear always to go to the kulba or plough land.

Land is (according to Sardar Baha-ud-din) estimated, and held, by kulbas and paikals. A kulba, or plough, is a common land measure in Afghanistan. It is as much land as can be cultivated by one plough and one pair of oxen. If calculated at 60 jaribs, or tanabs, each at 60 paces square, it is equal to about 144,000 square yards, or 30 acres nearly. The paikal (unit of assessment?) is 4 kulbas in the Hazhda-Nahr, and 2 in Tashkurghan and Haibak. (Baha-ud-din Khan.)

The average produce of grain per kulba in southern Afghanistan in the time of Nadir Shah was 50 Kandahar kharwars (500 British maunds). (Rawlinson.) And it is not likely to be more in Afghan Turkistan.

Money is the same all over Afghan Turkistan. It is as under:

5 Turkistan pul — 1 miri (no coin)   3 tangas — 1 Kabuli rupee
4 miris (20 pul) — 1 tanga   15 Kabuli rupees — 1 Bokhara tilla.

Tashkurghan/Khulm: The Tashkurghan seer is equal to 9 British seers, and the Tashkurghan man is 8 seers: it is therefore equal to 1 maund, 32 seers British. There is no kharwar.

Maimana: Accounts are made out in tangas and Bokhara tillas, but the coins most in use are Herati krans and Kabuli rupees.

3 tangas — 2 krans — 1 Kabuli rupee
20 tangas — 1 Bokhara tilla.

British rupees are accepted as $2^{1}/_{2}$ krans. Russian 5-rouble gold pieces are current as 10 Kabuli rupees, or 20 krans.

Maimana long measure is the common kulach or fathom, of 6 feet, and a gaz of 40 inches. The latter is divided into four charaks of 10 inches each. (DeLaessoe.) Land is measured almost everywhere by the tanab, or jarib, of 60 gaz or 60 kulach, square; while 60 tanabs go to a plough-land. If this holds good in Maimana, and the length of the gaz is correctly stated, it will make the tanabs, and consequently the plough lands, much larger than is usual.

However, DeLaessoe says measures vary in the different subdistricts. So do the weights. According to DeLaessoe, the Almar scale and the Maimana scale are those principally used—the former west of Maimana and the latter east of that place.

Probably Maimana weights are in use over a large part of the Sar-i-Pul district.

Almar:	1 khurd	—	12½ oz.		
	4 khurds	—	1 nimchak, or charak	—	3 lbs. 2 oz.
	4 nimchaks	—	1 man	—	12½ lbs.
	4 mans	—	1 seer	—	50 lbs. (25 Indian seers).
Maimana:	1 pun	—	1½ lbs.		
	4 puns	—	1 nimchak, or charak	—	6 lbs.
	16 nimchaks	—	1 seer	—	95 lbs.
	80 seers	—	1 batman	—	7,680 lbs. (96 Indian maunds).

(Maitland.)

Kandahar: The foundation of all weights is the Indian rupee. There are three scales of weight:

The ordinary or grain scale, known as the 17 Tomani. (A toman in Kandahar means twenty of any rupee; thus 1 toman kulladar—20 Indian rupees, and 1 toman Kandahari—20 Kandahar rupees.)

Grocer's weight, known as the 16 Tomani.

Wood weight, known as 18 Tomani.

Each of these numbers multiplied by 20 gives the number of rupees weight in a man.

Thus in ordinary weight a man	—	340 Rs.
Thus in grocer's weight a man	—	320
Thus in wool weight a man	—	360

or 4¼, 4, and 4½ seers respectively.

The weight of grain is calculated as follows:

	Kandahari	Rupees	Indian Seers	Indian Mounds
1 Kharwar	100 mans	34,000	425	10,625
1 Kandahari man	40 seers	340	425	10,625
1 Kandahari seer		85	10,625	266

The cash revenue is calculated in tomans, hazars or rupees, and dinars, a hazar being one thousand dinars and a toman twenty hazars, or 20,000 dinars.

An ordinary Kandahari toman equals ten Indian rupees, the coined Kandahari rupee being worth eight annas. But revenue accounts are kept in kham or kacha rupees, each of which is worth half a Kabuli rupee, or rather more than 6 annas 8 pies. Thus a kham toman is worth Rs. 8-5-4 or 8½ rupees.

The Kandahari yard contains 41½ English inches.

A tanab is 60 x 60 yards — 4,114 English yards or 85 acres.

Land is assessed in kulbas or ploughs. Of these there are two: tiyali or tauili containing about 75 tanabs, and raiti double that amount. Thus a kulba tiyali contains about 63.75 acres, and a kulba raiti about 127.50.

The grain assessment is made as a rule in galah or mixed grain, to which custom has given the proportion of one-third barley and two-thirds wheat. A certain amount of wheat, or in rare instances barley, was occasionally added in the settlement to make the assessment correspond with the area ordinarily sown with the two grains.
(The following additional notes on the currency, weights and measures used in Kandahar may be conveniently given here):
There are two sorts of rupees in use at Kandahar, the rupee Pukhta and the rupee Kham.
The first is the one actually coined, and the second is the one used for all revenue and other accounts.
The nominal value of the coinage in use is:

1 Indian rupee	— 24 Shahi	1 Kandahar kham	— 10 Shahi
1 Kabuli rupee	— 20 Shahi	1 Abasi	— 4 Shahi
1 Kandahar rupee Pukhta	— 12 Shahi	1 anna Indian	— 1½ Shahi

The following is the relative value in Indian coinage:

1 Kabuli rupee	— 13 annas 4 pie	1 Kandahar kham	— 6 annas 8 pie
1 Kandahar rupee pukhta	— 8 annas 4 pie	1 Abasi	— 2 annas 8 pie
	1 shahi — 8 pies.		

Long and Square Measure. The only standard measure of length at Kandahar is the yard and of this there are two kinds, viz., the "Gaz-i-Shahi" and the "Gaz-i-Raiati or Bana." The Gaz-i-Shahi contains 14 gira, and is used for the measurement of all description of goods and for woodwork.
The Gaz-i-Raiati or Gaz-i-Bana contains 16 gira, and is used for masonry and for land measurements.
The Indian gaz or yard contains 13½ gira, Kandahari.
One gira Kandahari is the breadth of 4 fingers. The tanab is the only fixed used measure and contains 60 Gaz-i-Raiati.

Liquids are sold by weight. (Biscoe.)

Jalalabad:
                    Weights and coins:
There are two systems of computation both in weight and in money.
The one method of computing by money is called "pukhta," and is as follows:
               50 dinars = 1 shahi
                2 shahis = 1 sanar
                2 sanars = 1 abbasi
                3 abbasis = 1 rupee
This rupee, estimated by the weight of silver in it, is worth 13 annas 6 pies of Indian money.

The other method of computing is called "kham," and is as follows:"

      10 dinars = 1 paisa
      5 paisas = 1 shahi
      10 shahis = 1 rupee
      20 rupees = 1 toman

One toman is worth Rs. 16 and 8 shahis pukhta. The kham rupee is merely one of account; it has no tangible existence. All the revenue accounts are kept on this system.

There are also two systems of measuring weights. The one in ordinary use is as follows:

      1 charak = 16 khurds
      4 charaks = 1 seer or dhari
      8 seers = 1 maund
      10 maunds = 1 kharwar

One of these seers is equal to 7 seers and 13.5 chittacks of Indian standard weight; consequently 1 kharwar is equal to 15 maunds 27 seers 8 chittacks of our standard weight.

The other method is called tabrizi, and is that in which the revenue accounts are kept. It is as follows:

      2.5 charaks = 1 maund
      100 maunds = 1 khawar

One of these maunds is equal to 4 seers 14.5 chittacks of our standars weight; hence a tabrizi kharwar is equal to 12 maunds 10 seers 10 chittacks of our weight.

Transliteration and Style. The reader will notice that many entries are taken verbatim from the writing of various authorities. This resulted in a mixing of styles and terminology, which is further aggravated by the fact that names are given from sources, including the maps appended to this volume, which employ different systems of transliteration. There are names in Arabic, Turkish, Persian, Pashtu, and a number of other languages and dialects which cannot easily be written in one system of transliteration. Afghan sources are not consistent in their spellings and often list words according to local or colloquial pronunciation, even though correct literary spellings exist. I have not felt it my task to impose my own system of transliteration in an attempt to bring order and standardization into a somewhat chaotic situation. The problem of transliteration and indexing has therefore been solved in the most practicable manner: terms are written as they appear in non-technical literature, such as newspapers and most scholarly and general publications. Exact transliterations, if they are not easily recognizable to the layman, are cross-listed in alphabetical order and spellings in Perso-Arabic script are given with each entry. Thus it has been possible to satisfy the scholar, who wants exact spellings, without confusing the layman with a complex system of transliteration.

Finally, the reader should keep in mind that vowels are often used interchangeably, depending on the style of transliteration, and "e" and "i" are used (as in Registan or Rigistan), as are "o" and "u" (as in Mohammad or Muhammad). The letter "k" is used for both the equivalent of the English "k" and for Arabic "q" (as in Kandahar and Qandahar). The letter "i" is used rather than "y" in words like Haidar; and the letter "b" becomes "w," as in Shorawak, or "u" as in Au (for Ab). It is not feasible to cross-list all combinations of spellings, therefore the reader should look for an entry under other combinations if it cannot be found under one spelling.

Statistic: One question which requires some clarification is my use of recent Afghan statistics. In previous volumes I indicated that "statistical data used in updating this work was taken from the latest published Afghan sources. It is presented primarily as a means for comparison with statistical data of various periods in the past, and should not be taken as absolutely reliable because Afghan statistics often show considerable variation."

In October 1979, the Hafizullah Amin government announced completion of a census according to which Afghanistan's population amounted to 15,540,000. It is doubtful whether this census was actually carried out, as claimed, between June 15 and July 5; but this figure seems plausible because it comes closest to previous estimates by a number of consulting firms.

I was able to obtain a seven-volume, mimeographed publication by the Central Department of Statistics of Afghanistan (Prime Ministry, Republic of Afghanistan, 1346 and 1352) with detailed data on the population, livestock, crops, and irrigation, compiled on the basis of sources of the Afghan Ministry of Agriculture and Irrigation.

I translated the data and included in this volume six tables each under the entries of Kabul, Parwan, Maidan (Wardak), Logar, Ghazni, Paktia, Nangarhar, Bamian, Kunar, and Kapisa.

Updating of Entries. Most entries have been updated to some extent. Locations were identified as far as they could be ascertained on the basis of available sources. In addition to this, entire entries have been compiled on the basis of material available in 1976. These entries are identified by asterisks; passages contributed by this writer have in past volumes been written in italics. It was not feasible to continue using italics; therefore I have identified such passages with the initials (LWA).

THE SOURCES

It has been suggested by a reviewer of a previous volume of this work that sources and authorities be cited. While it would indeed be useful to include here an exhaustive bibliography I feel that it goes beyond the scope of this work and that it really is not necessary.

The reader will find what he seeks in such bibliographies as Donald N. Wilber's *Annotated Bibliography of Afghanistan,* revised and updated by M. J. Hanifi (1982); the two-volume *Bibliographie der Afghanistan-Literatur 1945–1967* by E. A. Messerschmidt and Willy Kraus, which includes much German material and some recent sources not covered by Wilber; and *A Bibliography of Afghanistan,* by Keith McLachlan and William Whittaker (1983). An important source, especially for German and French is the comprehensive card catalog, "The Bibliotheca Afghanica," produced by Paul Bucherer-Dietschi in Liestal, Switzerland. There is also the Soviet bibliography by T. I. Kukhtina, *Bibliografia Afghanistana: Literatura na russkom iazyka,* and Vartan Gregorian's *The Emergence of Modern Afghanistan,* which includes a bibliography of some 50 pages. For the Area of Nuristan, there is the *The Kafirs of the Hindukush,* by Sir George Scott Roberston, republished in 1974 with an introduction by Louis Dupree. Schyler Jones published *An Annotated Bibliography of Nuristan (Kafiristan) and the Kalash Kafirs of Chitral,* (1966), and *A Bibliography of Nuristan (Kafiristan) and the Kalash Kafirs of Chitral: Selected Documents from the Secret and Political Records, 1885–1900,* (1969).

The reader may want to consult the *Afghanistan Studies* series, published under the auspices of an editorial board composed of Ludolph Fischer (deceased), Karl Jettmar, Rene Koenig, Willy Kraus, and Carl Rathjens. I should mention here as an example, Volume 14, entitled *Aktuelle Probleme der Regionalentwicklung und Stadtgeographie Afghanistans,* by Erwin Groetzbach (ed.), with contributions by Nigel J. R. Allen, Daniel Ballard, Pierre Centlivres, P. Lalande, Xavier de Planhol, Dietrich Wiebe, and others. These scholars have published numerous articles and monographs which are listed in Bucherer-Dietschi's *Bibliotheca Afghanica.*

Appended to this introduction, the reader will find a list of British authorities including such individuals as M. Biddulph, M. Elphinstone, C. M. McGregor, E. Pottinger, A. H. McMahon, and members of the Afghan Boundary Commission (A.B.C.). These and the other names given below are individuals who at some time or other during the past 100 years have participated in campaigns or peaceful missions to Afghanistan and collected data on the area. Many of them published their findings only for secret British government use and their contributions are known only to those who have canvassed British archival sources. As to sources I have found useful in updating this volume I might mention the following specialized publications which are not listed in the above bibliographies:

Important Afghan sources include both the *Qamus-e Jughrafiyaye Afghanistan,* a four-volume, geographical dictionary in Persian, compiled by the Anjoman-e Aryana Da'erat al-Ma aref, published in Kabul between 1956 and 1960, and the Pashtu *Da Afghanistan Jughrafiya-i Qamus.* They are largely, but not completely, identical and therefore both had to be consulted. These works are, however, often incorrect with respect to geographical coordinates and distances given; therefore I have used the Qamus primarily for checking Afghan spellings of place names.

The reader of Persian will want to consult the *Rahnama-ye Kabul*, by Muhammad Naser Gharghasht, and the *Fehrest-i Kutub-i Chapi-ye Dari-ye Afghanistan*, by Husain Na'el.

My most important statistical source was a seven-volume, mimeographed publication by the Central Department of Statistics of Afghanistan, entitled:

1. *Tauhīd-e ʿUmūmī Natāyej-e Iḥṣāʾiya Giri Sarwey Muqaddāmatī-ye Zerā ʿatī-ye Sāl-e 1346;*
2. *Iḥṣāʾiya-ye Nufūs-e Zerāʿatī, Taʿdād-e Zamīndār o Māldār, Sāḥeh-ye Zamīndārī-ye Sāl-e 1346 be Tafrīq-e Woleswālī-hā wa Welāyāt-e Keshwar;*
3. *Iḥṣāʾiyā-ye Sāḥeh-hā-ye Takhta Zarʿ az Manābeʿ-e Mokhtalefeh Ābī, Taʿadād-e Manābeʿe Ābī wa Āsyāb-e Ābī, Sal-e 1346, be Tafrīq-e Woleswālī-ha wa Welyāt-e Keshwar;*
4. *Iḥṣāʾiyā-ye Mawāshi-ye Sāl-e 1346 be Tafrīq-e Woleswālī-ha wa Welāyāt-e Keshwar;*
5. *Iḥṣāʾiyā-ye Sāhe-ha-ye Takhta Zarʿ-e Nabātāt-e Mokhtalefa-ye Zerāʿ atī-ye Sāl-e 1346 be Tafrīq-e Woleswālī-hā wa Welāyāt-e Keshwar;*
6. *Iḥṣāʾiyā-ye Sāḥeh-hā-ye Būrah-ye Mowaqtī, Sāḥeh-ye Zamīndarī, Jangalāt wa ʿAlafchar-e Sāl-e 1346 be Tafrīq-e Woleswālī-hā wa Welāyāt-e Keshwar;*
7. *Iḥṣāʾiyā-ye Taūlidāt-e Nabātāt-e Mokhtalefa-ye Zerāʾatī-e Sāl-e 1346 be Tafrīq-e Woleswālī-hā wa Welāyāt-e Keshwar*. Material from the above source became subsequently available in abbreviated form in the *Majmu'a-ye Ihsa'ivi-ye Afghanistan,* Published in English under the title *Statistical Pocket Book of Afghanistan,* and published by the Department of Statistics, Ministry of Planning, in 1350/1972.

Formerly secret British sources relevant to the area covered in this volume include the oft-quoted *Military Report on the Hazarajat, Routes in Afghanistan: Southeast, Notes on the Nomad Tribes of Eastern Afghanistan,* by J. A. Robinson; *The Pathans: Handbook of the Indian Army,* and *The Tribes of Waziristan,* by C. E. Bruce.

A new and important source was the *National Demographic and Family Guidance Survey of the Settled Population of Afghanistan,* Volume 1, *Demography and Knowledge Attitudes and Practices of Family Guidance;* Volume 2, *Methodology;* Volume 3, *Tables;* and Volume 4, *Folk Methods of Fertility Regulation; and the Traditional Birth Attendant (the Dai),* sponsored by the Government of Afghanistan and Agency for International Development, Government of the United States, 1975; as well as *A Provisional Gazetteer of Afghanistan,* 3 volumes, published in 1975 as part of the above survey. All place names listed in this Gazetteer have been included in this work under the respective woleswalis and alakadaris. A source on the administrative divisions of Afghanistan during the period of King Amanullah is the *Nizam-name-ye Taqsimat-e Mulkiya,* published in 1300/1921 at Kabul.

ACKNOWLEDGMENTS

It is my pleasure and duty to acknowledge my gratitude and thank all those who have been directly or indirectly involved in this project. This includes the officers of the India Office Library and Records of the Foreign and Commonwealth Office in London who permitted the publication of material complied as a result of over half a century of British research. I also want to thank officials of the following Afghan institutions: the Afghan Cartographic Institute; the Afghan Historical Society; the Anjoman-e-Aryana Da-erat al-Ma'aref; the Pashtun Academy; Kabul University; the Department of Planning and Statistics, and the Ministry of Foreign Affairs. In Afghanistan I am obliged to more Afghans and Americans than I am able to mention here. Finally I want to thank Dr. Karl Gratzl and Ing. Leopold Schedl for helping in the assembly of a photo-ready copy, produced by this writer.

L. W. A.

British Authorities quoted in this volume include the following:
A. B. C., Afghan Boundary Commission.
Agha Abbas, of Shiraz, traveller and author, 1837.
Amir Khan, Duffadar, Guides, Afghan Boundary Commission.
Atta Muhammad, Sub-surveyor, Afghan Boundary Commission.
Belew, H., Surgeon, Bengal Army, Kandahar Mission, 1857.
Biddulph, Sir M., General, 2nd Afghan War.
Broadfoot, Lieutnant J. S., Bengal Engineers, 1839.
Burnes, Sir A., Kabul Mission, 1837–38.
Campbell, Major N., D. Q. M. G., 1st Afghan War.
Campbell, Major N. M., R. E. 2nd Afghan War.
Clifford, Major C., 2nd Punjab Cavalry, 2nd Afghan War.
Coldstream, Lieutenant W., R. E., Bajaur Boundary Delimitation Commission, 1894–95.
Collett, Major H., A. Q. M. G., 1884.
Combe, B., Brigade Major, Cavalry Brigade, 2nd Afghan War.
Cotton, Sir Willoughby, Commanding Bengal Division, 1st Afghan War.
Creagh, Major (later General Sir) O'Moore, V. C., 2nd Afghan War.
Davies, R. H., Esquire, I. C. S., 1865.
Dobbs, H. R. C., Esquire, I. C. S., Russo-Afghan Boundary, 1904–05.
Donald, J., I. C. S., Durand Boundary Delimitation.
Douglas, Captain J. A., 2nd Bengal Lancers, 1898.
Drummond, Captain F. H., R., 11th Bengal Lancers Afghan Boundary Commission.
Dutton, Captain, Hon'ble C., A. Q. M. G., 2nd Afghan War.
Edwards, Sir Herbert, 1851.

Elphinstone, the Hon'ble Mountstuart, author of "The Kingdom of Kabul," 1840.
Euan Smith, Major, Political Officer, 2nd Afghan War.
Eyre, Lieutenant Vincent, 1st Afghan War.
Ferrier, General J. P., a French soldier of fortune, 1845–46.
Forster, G., traveller and author, 1778.
Gaselee, Captain (later General Sir) A., D. A. Q. M. g., 2nd Afghan War.
Gerard, Lieutenant-General Sir Montague, K. C. B., K. C. I. E., Pamir Boundary Commission, 1896.
Griesbach, C. L., Esquire, Afghan Boundary Commission, and Geologist to the Amir, 1889.
Griffiths, Dr.
Hastings, Lieutenant-Colonel E. G. G., Political Officer, Kabul.
Havelock, Captain H., 13th Light Infantry, 2nd Afghan War.
Hensman, H., "Pioneer" Staff, author of "The Afghan War of 1879–80."
Hoghton, Captain F. A., Intelligence Branch.
Holdich, Major T. H., R. E., Survey Officer, Afghan Boundary Commission and Pamir Boundary Commission, 1896.
Hough, Major W., 1st Afghan War.
I. B. C., Intelligence Branch Compilations.
Irvine, Major T. N., Medical Officer, Sistan Mission, 1903–05.
Jenkyns, W., Esquire, Bengal Civil Service, 1879.
Johnston, F. W., Esquire, I. C. S., Secretary to Chief Commissioner, North-West Frontier Province, 1905.
Kabul Mission, 1904–05.
Kaye, Sir J. W., 1869.
Keane, Sir John, Commanding Bombay Division, 1st Afghan War.
Kennedy, Dr. H. R., author of "Army of the Indus in Sind and Kabul, 1838–39."
Kinloch, Brigadier-General A. A. A., 1892.
Leach, Captain V. P., V. C., 2nd Afghan War.
Leech, Major R., R. E., 1st Afghan War.
Lumsden, Lieutenant-Colonel H. B., Guides, head of the Kandahar Mission, 1857.
McGregor, Colonel (afterwards Major-General Sir) C. M., 2nd Afghan War.
Maitland, Lieutenant-Colonel P. J., Afghan Boundary Commission.
Malleson, Colonel W., Kabul Mission, 1904–05.
Mason, Colonel A. H., R. E., Intelligence Branch.
Masson, Charles, explorer, 1836–41.
McLean, Captain J. G., 14th Sikhs, 2nd Afghan War.
McMahon, Major (later Sir) A. H., head of the Afghan-Baluch Boundary Commission, 1894–95, and Sistan Mission, 1903–05.
Molloy, Captain E., 5th Gurkhas, 2nd Afghan War.
Moorcroft, W., traveller and author, 1830.
Muhammad Akbar Khan, Duffadar, Afghan Boundary Commission.

Mulla, The, Survey Department Explorer.
Outram, Major J., Political Officer, 2nd Afghan War.
Paget, Lieutenant-Colonel W. H., 5th Punjab Cavalry.
Peacock, Captain W., R. E., Afghan Boundary Commission.
Peart, Captain C. L., 106th Hazara Pioneers.
Pollock, General (afterwards Field Marshal Sir George), 1st Afghan War.
Pottinger, Major Eldred, R. E., Mission to Herat, 1837.
Raverty, Major H. G., 3rd Regiment, Bombay Native Infantry.
Robertson, Sir G. S., British Agent, Gilgit, author of "Kafirs of the Hindu-Kush."
Saiyidulla, Sub-Surveyor, Afghan Boundary Commission.
Shahzada Taimus, Duffadar, Guides, Afghan Boundary Commission.
Shelton, Brigadier-General, 1st Afghan War.
St. John, Major O., Political Officer, 2nd Afghan War.
Stewart, Colonel C. E., Guides, Afghan Boundary Commission.
Stewart, R. McG., R. A., A. Q. M. G., 2nd Afghan War.
Stocqueler, F. H., traveller and author, 1832.
Thornton, E., author of "Gazetteer of countries adjacent to India, etc."
Wanliss, Major C., D. A. Q. M. G., Sistan Mission and Russo-Afghan Frontier, 1904—05.
Warburton, Captain R., Political Officer, 2nd Afghan War.
Wood, Captain J., Indian Navy, author of "A journey to the sources of the Oxus."

INTRODUCTION

The area discussed in this volume comprises what was once the heartland of the "Kingdom of Kabul," later Kabul province, and now includes the provinces of Kabul, Parwan, Maidan (Wardak), Logar, Ghazni, Paktia, Nangarhar, Bamian, Kunar, and Kapisa. (See Figure 1.)
The region is bounded in the west by Zabul, Urozgan, and Ghor, in the north by Jawzjan, Balkh, Baghlan, Takhar, and Badakhshan provinces, and in the east and southeast by the State of Pakistan.
The size of the area is approximately 116,946 square kilometers, comprising 65 districts (woleswalis), 68 subdistricts (alakadaris), and 5,030 villages with a population which has been variously estimated at from 1,998,038 to 2,481,844 as follows:

	Area	Villages	Wols.	Alaq.	Population*
Bamian	17,546	326	4	2	85,108 - 112,342
Ghazni	32,797	783	10	12	314,313 - 414,128
Kabul	4,720		8	4	188,391 - 263,517
Logar	4,409	338	3	3	112,579 - 172,704
Maidan	9,699	870	4	4	113,812 - 148,517
Nangarhar/ Kunar	18,636	825	17	14	469,609 - 496,068
Paktia	17,772	579	11	21	432,285 - 569,537
Parwan/ Kapisa	11,367	477	8	8	281,941 - 305,031

*This includes only the agricultural population (Provisional Gazetteer of Afghanistan and Majmu'a-ye Ihsa'iwi, Sal 1350). Afghanistan has an estimated population of about 15.5 million, and Kabul City had a population of about half a million in the 1970's - which seems to have increased to some 1,500,000 in the 1980's.
For detailed information on the provinces covered in this volume, see individual entries. (LWA)
In 1914, the area was described as follows:
Boundaries. The Province of Kabul, which includes Kafiristan and the Hazarajat, is approximately bounded as follows: On the east by the Indo-Afghan frontier, as defined in the "Durand Agreement" of 1894; on the south by the Kandahar Province and the Zamindawar district of the Farah Province; on the west by the Taimani and Chakhcharan districts of the Herat Province, and on the north by the Provinces of Afghan Turkistan and Badakhshan.
Starting from a point on the Hindu Kush between the Dorah and Mandal passes the boundary runs in a southeasterly and southerly direction along the watershed between the Chitral and Bashgul valleys to the junction of the two rivers, where it crosses the Chitral, or Kunar, river giving the village of Birkot, on the right bank, to Afghanistan and Arnawai, on the left bank, to Chitral. The line then ascends to the watershed between the Kunar and Swat Valleys which it follows in a general southwesterly direction, past the Nawa Sar peak, to the neighbourhood of the Silala pass where it turns southeast and descends to the Kabul river. Crossing the Kabul river the line runs in a general southerly direction and ascends to the crest of the main Safed Koh range near the head of the Bazar valley, in Tirah, and then, turning due west, follows the crest-line to the Sika Ram peak. From Nawa Sar to Sika Ram the line has never been actually demarcated, but from the head of the Bazar valley westwards to Sika Ram the crest-line of the Safed Koh has been accepted by both parties as forming a sufficiently definite boundary, and actual

Figure 1.

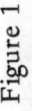

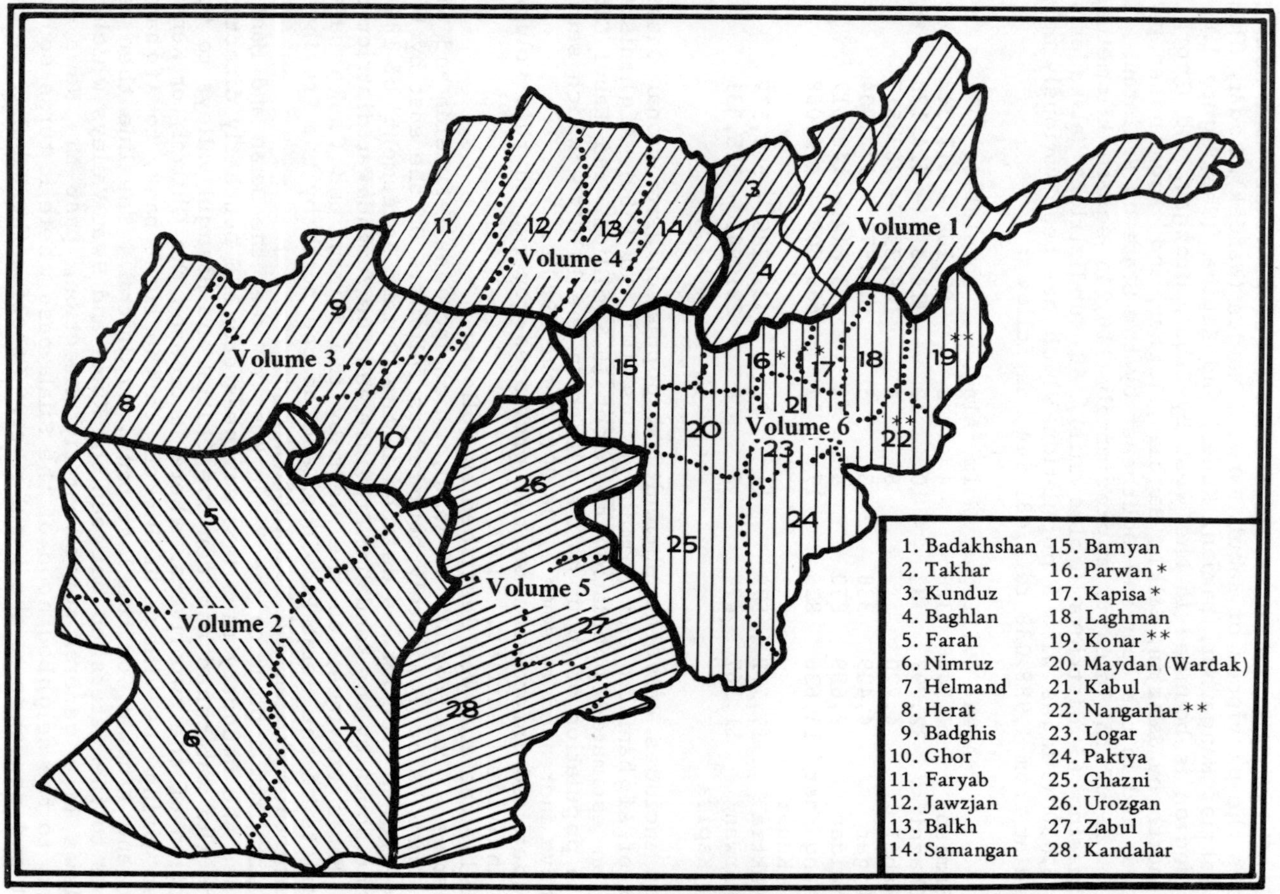

Volume 1
Volume 2
Volume 3
Volume 4
Volume 5
Volume 6
1. Badakhshan
2. Takhar
3. Kunduz
4. Baghlan
5. Farah
6. Nimruz
7. Helmand
8. Herat
9. Badghis
10. Ghor
11. Faryab
12. Jawzjan
13. Balkh
14. Samangan
15. Bamyan
16. Parwan *
17. Kapisa *
18. Laghman
19. Konar **
20. Maydan (Wardak)
21. Kabul
22. Nangarhar **
23. Logar
24. Paktya
25. Ghazni
26. Urozgan
27. Zabul
28. Kandahar

Provinces of Afghanistan

* Kapisa (17) is now part of Parwan (16)

** Konar (19) is now part of Nangarhar (22)

Afghanistan is now divided into 26 (rather than 28) provinces.

demarcation here has been thought unnecessary. From Sika Ram the line runs down to the Paiwar Kotal and then descends in a southeasterly direction to the Kurram river. Crossing the river between the villages of Pathan a Kharlachi (Pathan being on the Afghan side), it ascends to the peak of Khwaja Kurram on the Watershed between the Kurram and Kaitu valleys; it then follows this watershed (leaving Jaji Maidan to Afghanistan), to the neighbourhood of Shabakghar, in Khost; it then turns southwest and crossing the Kaitu river, ascends to Laram peak on the Kaitu-Tochi watershed which it follows for about 40 miles to the Charkhel peak. Here the line turns south and, crossing the Mastoi and Margha streams a few miles above their junction at Dotoi, in Waziristan, ascends to the watershed dividing the Afghan valley of Birmal from the Wazir valley of Shawal which it follows to a point about 40 miles north of Domandi on the Gumal.

Here the boundary of the Kabul Province leaves the Indo-Afghan frontier and runs northwest to the Sarwandi pass in the Sulaiman range, and then follows the crest of this range in a northwesterly direction to about the latitude of the Ab-i-Istada lake, which it crosses, and continuing northwest crosses the Tarnak river and reaches the crest of the hills in the southwest of the Mukur district, near Aghao Jan; the Mukur and Katawaz districts are thus included in the Kabul Province. From this point the line zig-zags in a general westerly direction till it crosses the Helmand river about 35 miles above the junction with the latter of the Tirin, and, about 50 miles further west, meets the eastern boundary of the Herat Province, thus including the Hazarajat in the Kabul Province. It then runs in a general northerly direction, separating the Hazarajat and the Shaikhmiran district of the Kabul Province from the Taimani country of Herat, crosses the main Kabul-Daulat Yar-Herat road at the Lashkar Rah Kotal, 8 1/2 miles east of Daulat Yar, and meets the southern boundary of the Turkistan Province about 25 miles further north. From this point the line makes a bend to the north eventually reaching the Katar Sum pass at the head of the Bamian valley, including the Yakh Walang and Upper Band-i-Amir valleys in the Kabul Province, and giving the Dara Yusuf, Kamard and Saighan valleys to Turkistan. From the Katar Sum pass the line runs to the crest-line of the Hindu Kush, which it reaches just north of the Shibar pass, and thenceforward coincides therewith till it eventually rejoins the Indo-Afghan frontier near the Mandal pass, thus including the whole of Kafiristan in the Kabul Province.

Physical features. The Kabul Province is for the most part mountainous, although it contains numerous fertile valleys. The lofty ranges of the Hindu Kush and Koh-i-Baba rising over 16,000 feet, and the uplands of the Hazarajat with an average elevation of 10,000 feet, form natural barriers on the north and west. The Safed Koh range to the south of the Jalalabad district rises to 15,620 feet and the Paghman range to the northwest of Kabul to 15,440 feet.
The principal rivers are the Kabul, Kunar, Helmand, and Ghazni.
The first-named, with its tributaries, drains the northeastern districts. These tributaries are the Logar, Panjshir, Alishang and Alingar, Surkhab, and Kunar, besides numerous minor streams. The main river rises near the Unai pass, about 40 miles west of Kabul city, and flows through the Maidan district and so on to the capital. From here it flows eastwards to Jalalabad, whence it turns southeast to Dakka. From Dakka it flows northeast, and then turns east and south again, eventually debouching into the Peshawar valley at Michni. Having received the waters of the Panjkora, Swat and Bara rivers, it falls into the Indus at Attock after an entire

course of about 300 miles.

The Kunar river rises in the Hindu Kush near the Karkot pass, and after passing through Chitral forms the eastern boundary of Kafiristan. It joins the Kabul river at Jalalabad.

The Helmand also rises near the Unai pass, but on its northern side, and flows southwest through the Hazarajat. It is described under "Helmand" in Volume 2.

The Ghazni river is formed some 14 miles north of the town of Ghazni, and after passing the latter place, receives from the east the Gardez or Zurmat stream. It then runs through a desolate tract to the Ab-i-Istada lake.

In addition to the above there are several other important rivers which have their sources in the Kabul Province, viz:

The Sar-i-Jangal and Lal, which rise in the Dai Zangi country and are the head-waters of the Hari Rudd—see Volume 3.

The Band-i-Amir, rising north of the Koh-i-Baba and draining Yak Walang—see Volume 4.

The Bamian, which drains the valley of that name and is one of the chief affluents of the Surkhab—see Volume 1.

The Kurram river, also, with its tributaries, the Kaitu (or Shamil) and Tochi, and the Gumal river all have their sources in the Kabul Province, and, crossing the Indo-Afghan frontier, eventually fall into the Indus.

Climate. The climate is as diversified as its physical configuration. In Ghazni the winter is sometimes very severe, while in the Hazarajat it is even more so. In Bamian, when our troops were there in 1840, the thermometer frequently fell to 10 and 12 degrees below zero. Even in Kabul the snow lies for two or three months and 53 degrees of frost (21 below zero) were experienced by the Dane Mission in Kabul in the first week of February 1905. The Koh Daman is considered by the Afghans to be the most favoured spot on earth as regards climate. During summer the heat of an Indian sun is tempered by cool breezes from the adjacent snowy ranges, whilst the rigours of winter are faced in clothing of sheepskins and furs. From July to October, however, fevers and bowel complaints are prevalent even in this favoured region. The heat of the summer throughout the province is everywhere great, except in the most elevated parts. In the confined valley of Jalalabad the heat is intense and is made more trying by frequent storms. The monsoon which deluges India has scarcely any effect west of the Sulaiman range, nor are the falls, either of rain or snow, heavy during the cold season, while in the hot season the rains are for the most part slight and of rare occurrence.

Towns. The towns are few in number, the only places which can be called by this name being Kabul, Ghazni, Jalalabad, Charikar, Istalif, and Urgun.

Population. It would be useless to attempt to give even an approximate estimate of the number of inhabitants of the province; information on the subject is vague, and a large proportion of the population is migratory, a good many, e.g., the Powindahs, coming every year to British India in the cold weather and returning to Afghanistan in the spring. As far as possible the population of each town, village, etc., has been given in the article relating thereto. Generally speaking the eastern portion of the province is inhabited by Kafirs, Mohmands, Shinwaris and Khostwals, the center by Ghilzais, and the western portion by Hazaras. Considerable numbers of Tajiks, Dehgans, Arabs, Safis and so-called Parsiwans are also to be

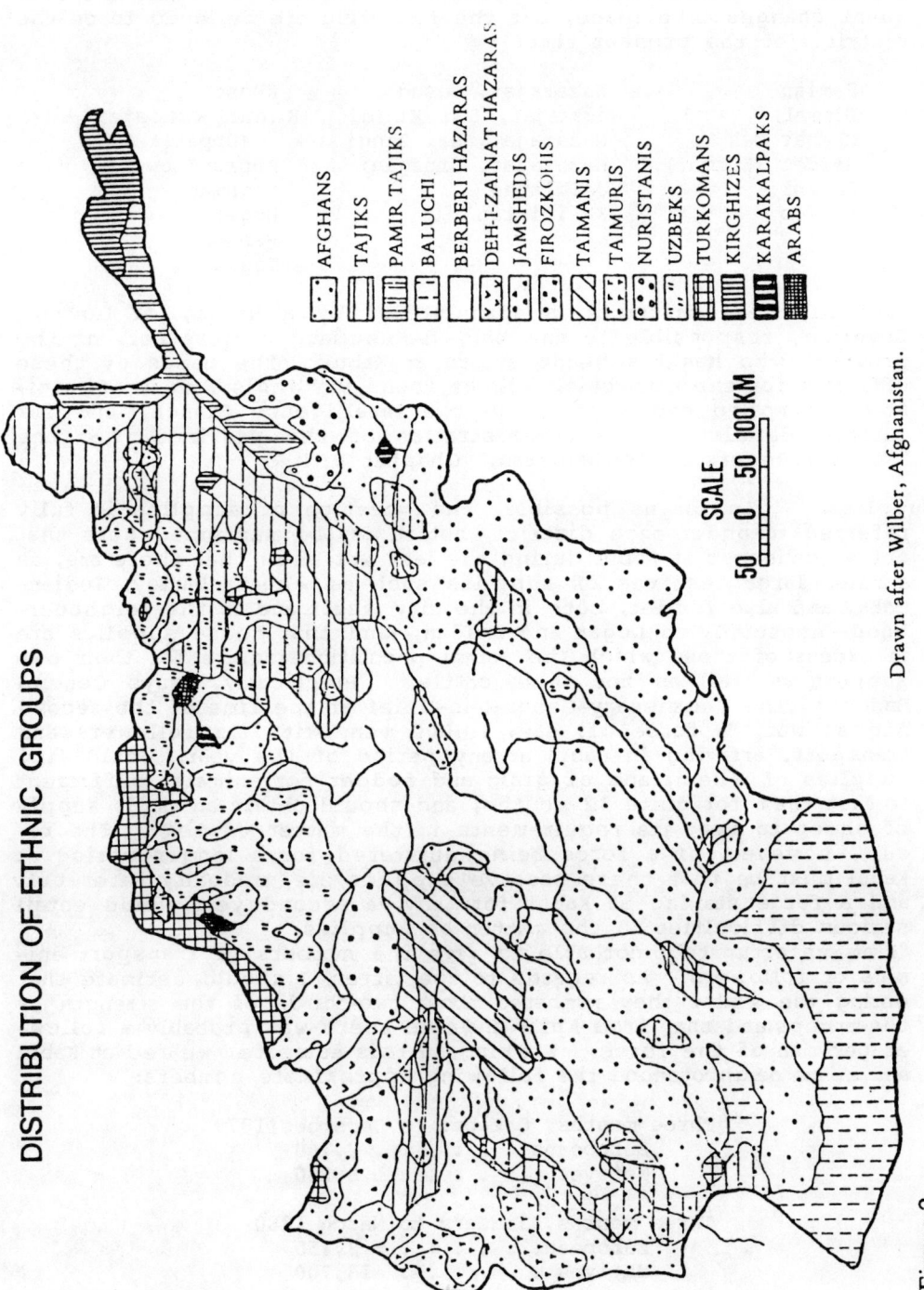

Figure 2.

found, more especially around Kabul and in the Jalalabad district; in the towns, too, and in all the larger villages, there are a number of Hindu shop-keepers. For the distribution of enthic groups in Afghanistan, see Figure 2.

Administration. It is impossible to say exactly how the province is divided for administrative purposes, as authorities differ and frequent changes take place, but the following are believed to be the districts at the present time:

Bamian	Hazarajat, Besud	Khost
Birmal	Hazarajat, Dai Kundi	Kunar Kohistan
Chahar Deh	Hazarajat, Dai Zangi	(Upper)
Gardez (Zurmat)	Hazarajat, Uruzgani	Kunar (Lower)
Ghazni	Jalalabad	Laghman
Hariob	Kafiristan	Logar
		Panjshir
		Tagao

Each of these districts is administered by a Hakim, or District Governor, responsible to the Naib-ul-Hukumat, or Governor, of the province who has his headquarters at Kabul. The names of these officials for the time being will be found in "Who's Who in Afghanistan," compiled and kept up in the Intelligence Branch, and for further details of the administration of the province, see the "Military Report on Afghanistan," Chapter VIII.

Supplies. As far as possible, the question of supplies is fully referred to under each district, but it may be mentioned here that our experiences at Kabul during the last war show that there are, as a rule, large reserves of supplies such as wheat, barley, Indian-corn, and also fodder, both in the city itself and in the neighbourhood--especially in Logar and Maidan,--and that these supplies are in excess of those which the normal population require for their own support as well as for their cattle. "Practically," says General Badcock, the Commissary-General-in-Chief at the time of the second Afghan war, "a force of, say, 10,000 men, with its followers and transport, arriving in Kabul at any period of the year, would find supplies of wheat, and of grain and fodder for animals, sufficient to last them for quite 12 months, and should obtain an ample supply of sheep to meet its requirements in the matter of meat. The result, however, of a force being quartered for a longer period at Kabul must be that these reserve supplies are gradually eaten out, and a force staying at Kabul for, say, a second year would entail serious difficulties in the matter of supplies.
"I am unfortunately not able to give the numbers of transport animals or followers. As regards to the latter, I should estimate that during the winter they numbered about two-thirds of the strength of the troops,and that from April onwards there was probably a follower per man of the force. Working on this estimate, we fed at Kabul and in its neighbourhood the following approximate numbers:

```
        Three months, October to December 1879
            Europeans . . . . . . 2,700
            Natives . . . . . . . 8,250

        Three months, January to March 1880
            Europeans . . . . . . 3,450
            Natives . . . . . .  13,700
```

One month, April 1880
Europeans 4,200
Natives 23,350

Three months, May to July 1880
Europeans 6,120
Natives 35,610

"The above figures give some idea of what the country can and did supply, for, with the exception of some ghi, and perhaps rum and at first tea, we practically obtained all our food and grain supplies locally, and had little or no assistance from India. In salt, tea, and sugar there was a considerable trade from India, and we used to buy from the traders. Dal is not obtainable in the country, and the small supply which was taken with the troops was sold and re-sold as the men did not eat it, chiefly owing to difficulties as regards cooking. Firewood is obtainable in good quantity, but difficulty might arise in respect to this article after the first year, as the expenditure in fuel would be necessarily heavy in winter. (Fuel is now [1910] very scarce in the neighbourhood of Kabul.)

"The supply of vegetables at Kabul is very fine, hardly any potatoes, but the cabbages, turnips, beetroot, and carrots quite surpass anything I have ever seen in India. Similarly there is a large supply of fruit in the season; these commodities enable beneficial changes to be made in the rations.

"There are no horned cattle in the country, except those used for the plough or as transport, and not many of them, so the meat supply has to be obtained solely from the 'dumba' sheep. They are of excellent quality, and average in weight over 40 lbs., when dressed.

"Large supplies of clothing can be obtained in the city of Kabul, barak and other locally manufactured material being utilised. Socks, gloves or mittens, and native shoes are also procurable in good number. Posteens are made in large numbers and of excellent description, the fleece of the 'dumba' being utilised."

Army. Information as to the number of troops in the province is not very reliable, but at the present time (1906) the strength and distribution is somewhat as follows:--

District	Cavalry	Guns	Sappers	Infantry	Khassadars
Kabul	3,600	151(a)	2,400	25,600	6,750
Jalalabad and Asmar	1,850	52(b)	200	13,111	6,410
Khost	500	33(c)	. . .	3,900	3,550
Ghazni and Hazarajat	1,100	29(d)	. . .	7,400	4,838
TOTAL	7,050	265	2,600	50,011	21,548

	Mountain	Field	Heavy	Quick-Firing	Machine
(a)	72	52	13	8	6
(b)	39	. . . .	4	3	6
(c)	18	11	. . . .	. . . .	4
(d)	22	5	2	. . . .	. . . .

For further information on this subject, see the "Military Report on Afghanistan," Chapter IX.

HISTORICAL AND POLITICAL GAZETTEER OF AFGHANISTAN

AB Also see AO

آب

ABADIAN

عبدیان

34- 70-. A village in the Besud division of the Jalalabad district. Inhabitants are Dehgans and Tajiks. (Jenkyns.)

*AB BAND

آب بند

32-51 68-5. Ab Band is an alaqadari in Ghazni province. The alaqadari comprises an area of 1,105 square kilometers and has a population that has been estimated at from 5,159 to 6,239. The alaqadari is bounded in the south by Dila, in the southeast by Jani Khel, in the northeast by Giru, in the north by Qarabagh, and in the west by Muqur. Ab Band has about 51 villages, five of which have more than 500 inhabitants. The villages are listed in the PG as follows: Akhund Khel, Woreshmin Khel, Spin Khulai, Oshlan, Asghari, Chambar-i-Almar, Badam Kacha, Baz Mohamad, Baddar, Barakat, Payendah Khel, Patrah, Pyari, Tari, Jangul, Jalal Khel, Chori, Chawni, Haji Khel, Huwat, Khado Khel, Khwaja Khel, Darya Khan Khel, Darya Khan-Khel Ulya, Du Kohi, Zam Zam, Saqi Khel-i-Ab Band, Saqi Khel-i-Giro, Godah Giro, Akhund Khel-i-Giro, Sar-Faraz, Sahib Zadah, Chahar Qala, Sala Khel, Buzai, Dalani, Qala-i-Khushk, Mula Fateh, Fateh Ab Band, Qandahari, Qala-i-Gudiyan, Mohammad Ghaws, Atak, Kakar, Gand Ab, Landah Khel, Mohammad Nur, Nazuka, Tozhna, Bagai (Bazge), Zarrin Chori, Chambar-i-Satar, Rahman, Ibrahim Khel, Qamaruddin, Qurban Khel, Akhtar Khel, Ato China, Tayak, and Sadozai.

ABBAS KALA

عباس قلعه

34-28 69-15. A village 5 miles southeast of Kabul, on the right bank of the Logar river between Sak and Bagrami. (Kennedy.)

*ABCHAKAN

ابچکان

33-54 69-13 m. A village in Pul-i-Alam district of Logar province with an agricultural population of 2,000.

AB DARA

آب دره

35-14 69-23 G. A ravine which descends northwest and joins the Panjshir valley about 4 miles above Anaba. It contains the following villages: first, Pashar with 60 houses. Above this the ravine forks. In the right branch, known as the Dara Kar-o-ghin about a mile above Pashar, are the two hamlets of Kar-o-ghin containing together 20 houses. Half a mile further up is Burja Khel, with 30 houses. In the left branch, the Dara Ghulbak, are first, Ghulbak village containing 70 houses; next Guna, 30 houses; higher still Kanku, with 40 houses and lastly, the highest village Shufa, 40 houses. Altogether there are 300 houses in this glen and the inhabitants are all Tajiks. There is also cultivation and some little wood on the hills, but it is only buta. From the head of the glen a track leads over the Bolaghan Kotal down another dara to Bolaghan village, and so to the plain of the Koh Daman, but it is said to be only a footpath. (Shahzada Taimus.)

AB DARA

آب دره

33- 68-. Hills lying 2 or 3 miles north of the Gudal-Ghazni road, at a point about 1 mile from Isfidar towards Zana Khan. (Gaselee.)

*AB DARA

آب دره

32-42 69-16 m. A village in Dehsabz district of Kabul province with an agricultural population of about 260.

AB DARA-I-KALAN آب دره کلان
   33-41 68-44 m. A village in Sayyidabad district of Wardak province with an agricultural population of about 600. Other places with this name are located at 33-40 68-1 and 33-41 68-44 m.

ABDUL عبدل (؟)
   33- 68-. A subsection of the Besuds. (See Military Report on Hazarajat, Part II.)

ABDUL AZIZ KALA عبدالعزیز قلعه
   34- 69-. A fort in the Chardeh valley of Kabul, near the village of Kala-i-Fathu. Inhabitants: Tajiks; 15 families. (I.B.C.)

ABDUL BURJ عبدل برج
   34- 69-. A village on the right bank of the Panjshir river, on the road from Kabul to Nijrao, 35 miles north-northeast of the former. (Thorton.)

ABDUL GHAFUR KALA عبدالغفور قلعه
   34- 68-. The principal village in the Langar valley. It is 8 miles west of Shaikhabad. (Dutton.)

ABDUL HAKIM KALA عبدالحکیم قلعه
   34- 69-. A fort in the Chardeh valley of Kabul, included for revenue purposes in Kala-i-Fathu; 7 families of Tajiks. (I.B.C.)

ABDUL KARIM KALA عبدالکریم قلعه
   34- 68-. A village of 40 families of Taimuris lying 4 miles east of the Unai pass on the main Kabul-Herat road. Headman (1904) Ghulam Nabi. The inhabitants possess about 60 head of cattle and 150 sheep and goats. The annual production of wheat and barley averages about 450 Indian maunds. (Wanliss.) Recent maps show a place called Muhammad Karin at 34-26 68-25 m. (LWA)

ABDULLA KALA عبدالله قلعه
   32- 67-. A small Tajik village near Kala-i-Haji Saf, to the west of and close to Deh-i-Mozang. (Kennedy.)

***ABDULLA KHEL** عبداللهخیل
   35-15 69-37 m. A village located on a tributary of the Panjshir, west of the Kuh-i-Gardana, with an agricultural population of about 1,100.

ABDULLA KHEL see HAZARA DARA عبدالله خیل

ABDUL MAJID عبدالمجید
   34- 69-. A small village to the north of the Kabul river, east of Sherpur. Its inhabitants are Tajiks, and it forms one of the cluster of villages composing the township of Yakatut. (q.v.) (Kennedy.)

ABDUL MAJID KHAN KALA عبدالمجیدخان قلعه
   33- 69-. A village about 12 miles northeast of Gardez, on the road thence to the Mirzakai kotal. There is room for a brigade to camp about 1 mile further on near Baladeh. (q.v.) (I.B.C.)

ABDULQADIR KALAY عبدالقادر کلی
   32-12 67-16 m. A village located west of the Sur Ghar, about 10 miles from the Tarnak river.

ABDUL RAHIM KHEL   see MANDRAWAR   عبدالرحیم خیل

ABDUL RAHMAN KALA   عبدالرحمن قلعه
   34-   69-.   A small village on the left bank of the Logar river,
near Bagrami, southeast of Kabul.   (Kennedy.)

ABDUL RAHMAN KHEL   عبدالرحمن خیل
   A tribe of Khost, who inhabit the Matun district of that valley, and
are hence sometimes called Matunis.   They have six sections: 1,
Haji Khan Khel; 2, Sodi Khel; 3, Ahmad Khel; 4, Modi Khel; 5, Kundi
Khel; 6, Mangash.   They are also called Mamuris.   They number about
1,000 fighting men, and are mostly husbandmen.   (Muhammad Hayat,
Norman.)

ABDUL SAMAD KALA   عبدالصمد قلعه
   34-   69-.   A fort in the Chardeh valley of Kabul, included for
revenue purposes in Deh-i-Dana.   Inhabitants: 9 families of Hazaras.   (I.B.C.)

*ABDUL WALI   عبدالوال
   33-19 68-30 m.   A village in Andar district of Ghazni province with
with an agricultural population of about 200.

*ABID KHEL   عابد خیل
   35-54 69-31 m.   A village located on the Dara-i-Khawus, about 5
miles south of Khawus.

AB-I-ISTADA See Volume 5.   آب ایستاده
   32-30   67-55 m.

AB-I-JOSH   آب جوش سفلی
   33-51 68-50 m.   Two villages in Charkh district of Logar province.
The upper village has an agricultural population of about 500.   The
lower village is located nearby at 33-51   68-52 m.   (LWA) In 1914,
this area was described as follows: the name given to the western
entrance to the Charkh valley.   The road is easy throughout, although narrow in the middle.   It derives its name from a   bubbling
spring.   The village of this name is inhabited by the Gada Khel
section of the Sahak Ghilzais.   (McLean.)

AB-I-TALKH   آب تلخ
   A salt rivulet which joins the Gumal river 2 and one half miles from
Sarmargha, on the road from Ghazni to Dera Ismail Khan.   Thornton
Errouneously calls it a village, but there is no village anywhere;
Sarmargha, the nearest halting place, being merely an opening in the
fefile 500 yards wide and a few feet above the river. (Broadfoot.)
This may be located in Katawaz, at 32-10   68-57 G.   (LWA)

AB-I-TAMAGHAN   آب تمغان
   The name given to higher reaches of stream draining a valley of the
same name in the Hazarajat.   (See Military Report on Hazarajat, Part
II.)

ABKHOR See SANG DARA   آبخور

AB KOL   آب قول
   34-52   67-16 m.   Two ravines of this name debouch into the Band-i-
Amir valley above Jafir Kala.   The village of Ab Kol, situated in
the most northerly ravine, was deserted in 1886.   (A.B.C.)

ABLAITO ابليتو (ابلتو)
32-44 67-0. A valley in the Kalandar country draining into the Arghandab river at Saigan. (See Military Report on Hazarajat, Part II.) Recent maps show the spelling Ablatu. (LWA)

*ABPAR آب پر
34-58 67-52 m. A village located north of the Kuh-i-Salonag in the Shibar district of Bamian province. Recent maps show the spelling Awpar. (LWA)

*ABPUSH آبپوش
35-46 68-20 m. A village in Surkh Parsa district of Parwan province with an agricultural population of about 700.

ABRONS آب رونس
35-40 71-23 G. A hamlet on the left bank of the Bashgul river, in Nuristan, 1-1/4 miles about Bragamatal. (I.B.C.)

ABU BAKAR ابو بكر
A section of the Ghilzais. See "Laghman."

*ACHIN اچين
34-5 70-41 m. Achin is a village and a woleswali in Nangarhar Province. The woleswali comprises an area of 463 square kilometers and has an agricultural population that has been estimated at from 34,080 to 48,460. The woleswali is bounded in the west by Deh Bala, in the north by Rudat, in the east by Loye Shinwar, Naziyan, and Dur Baba, and in the South by the State of Pakistan. Achin has some 33 villages, 23 of which have more than 500 inhabitants.
The villages are listed in the PG as follows: Wach Kot, Abdul Khel, Mohmand Rahimdad Khel, Mamand-i-Haidar Khel, Pikha Khol (Dehsarak-i-Jadid), Dehsarak-i-Kohna, Maydanak, Qala-i-Hajum, Paikha, Achin, Kahi, Kostal, Bander, Trili, Gerdi, Batan, Asad Khel, Srah Qala, Landi (Gondi), Maruf China (Maro China), Anzarai, Sanduq, Chehil Gazai, Lokhi (Lur), Bahram Khel, Kundarai Paikha, Abdati Kaidara, and Chand.

*ADAM KALA آدم قلعه
33-33 68-47 m. A village located about 20 miles east of Ghazni and southwest of the Loe Nawe Ghar.

ADAM KHAN آدم خان
34- 68-. A defile and pass in the hills from Wardak into Logar, about 5 miles northeast of Shaikhabad. When the Ghazni Field Force marched from Kandahar to Logar in April and May 1880, the Adam Khan route was thought of and reconnoitred from Shaikhabad, but it was found more practicable to take the guns over the Zamburak pass. (Hervey.)

ADAR ادر
34- 70-. A village lying northwest from Jalalabad, on the Alingar river, consisting of 50 houses. It is included in the Lagman district, and the inhabitants are "Arokis." (Leech, Warburton.)

ADDA See HADA هده

ADHERA Or HADIRA (?) اديره
34- 69-. A pass in the hills between the Lakarai and Hisarak, according to native information. It is said to be low, and easy for the passage of camels. (Gordon.)

ADIA KHEL
A section of the Kharotis.

ADINA
33- 67-. A locality in the Faoladi Hazara country of Malistan. A village with this name and some 250 inhabitants is located in Jaghatu, Wardak, at 33-44 68-19 m. (LWA)

ADIN KHEL Or DILAH
32-36 68-2 m. A village in Katawaz, on the route from Pannah to Dala-i-Kharoti. A few supplies procurable. Inhabitants: Kaisars, at feud with the Jalalzais, both Ghilzai tribes. (Broadfoot.)

*ADO
32-7 67-9 m. A village, also called Sulaimankhel, located in the valley of the Tarnak river, some 9 miles from the river.

*ADOR
34-16 70-16 m. A village on the Kambu Khwar stream, some 15 miles southwest of Jalalabad.

ADRAG BADRAG
39- 69-. Elevation about 4,200 feet. A pass over the northern slopes of the Siah Koh range, leading form the Laghman valley to Kata Sang and the Tezin valley. The road over the pass is practicable for camels, and there would be no difficulty in aligning a good road for wheeled traffic. By using this road from Jalalabad via the Darunta gorge the whole of the Gandamak-Jagdalak portion of the Peshawar Kabul route may be turned. (I.B.C.)

*ADRAK
34-29 69-36. A village 46 miles east of Kabul, between Charbagh and Jagdalak. (Thornton.)

ADRAMZAI
A subdivision of the Ghilzais

AFGHAN, DEH-I
34- 69-. Deh-i-Afghan is a suburb of the city of Kabul, situated on the left bank of the river, and connected with the town by a stone bridge. It stands upon a low eminence overlooking Taimur's tomb. During the investment of Sherpur in December 1879, this suburb, distant from the southwestern bastion about 1,300 yards, was a place of assembly for the Afghans. On the 17th of that month the place was shelled with good effect, and when the enemy finally withdrew a great part of it was demolished. Inhabitants: Tajiks, Tokhi Khel Ghilzais, and Kizilbashis. (I.B.C.)

*AFSAHO Or AFSA, AFSAY
35-46 71-21 m. A village with an agricultural population of about 900 in Barg Matal district of Nangarhar province, located on the Kaligal river, some 7 miles north of Barg Matal.

AFSHAR Or AOSHAR
34-33 69-7 A. A large Kizilbash village in the Kabul district, 4 miles west of Sherpur. Here Macpherson encamped on the 8th and 9th December 1879, leaving his camp on the 10th to fight the action of Karez-i-Mir. It was from this place also that, on the 11th December, the horse artillery and cavalry advanced towards Arghandi, when

they encountered the overwhelming force of Afghans under Muhammad Jan. Immediately to the east of Kala-i-Aoshar is the Nanachi or Aoshar Kotal over which an excellent road now leads. The place is strong, surrounded by bastioned walls from 15 feet to 20 feet high. This village contains 100 houses. (Kennedy, A.B.C.)

*AFZUK   افزوك
35-48 71-16 m. A village with an agricultural population of about 270 in Barg Matal district of Nangarhar province.

*AG   آگ
34-21 67-28 m. A village near the junction of the Darazqul and Kalankhana streams in Bamian province.

AGAM   اگام
34- 70-. Elevation 11,766 feet. A pass over the Safed Koh, leading from the Jalalabad district into Kurram. The crest of the pass lies about 27 miles south-southeast of Gandamak and about 7 miles west of the Papin pass.
The road is practicable for laden mules with the exception of about 1 1/2 miles from the crest downwards on the Kurram side; it could however be made practicable for baggage animals of all descriptions without much difficulty. It is the lowest and easiest of all the passes over the Safed Koh, between the Jalalabad district and Kurram, and the only one of any military importance. It is closed by snow for at least six, and sometimes eight or nine, months in the year. By this route Jallabad is distant 57 miles from Parachinar. (I.B.C.)

AGAM   اگام
34-12 70-17 m. A fortified hamlet in the Chapriar subdivision of the Jalalabad district. It lies at the foot of the Safed Koh on the road leading over the Agam pass into Kurram. There is a force of 400 khasadars permanently stationed here, and in the hot weather the greater part of the Jalalabad garrison is moved up to this neighbourhood. New lines for the troops have recently been built here, consisting of 22 blocks, each containing 12 quarters. The hamlet is about 20 miles northwest of Deh Bala in Pachir Agam district, Nangarhar province. (I.B.C.)'

*AGAR   اگر
33-27 68-10 m. A village with some 400 inhabitants in Jaghatu district of Ghazni province, about 15 miles southwest of Ghazni.

AGARU Or AGRU   اگرو
35-24 71-18 m. A hamlet of 8 or 9 houses on the left bank of the Nichingul torrent, in Kafiristran. It is inhabited by members of the Utah-dari clan of Kam Kafirs who have become Muhammadans. The village is about 3 miles west of Kamdesh. (Robertson.)

AGATSI   اگاتسی (اگاخی)
35-25 71-22 m. Elevation 4,000 feet. A small settlement of Kam Kafirs of the Bilezhedari clan who have become Muhammadans. It is on the left bank of the Bashgul stream, about 1 1/2 miles east of Kamdesh, and comprises only one or two families. (Robertson.)

AGHA ASGHAR KALA   آقا اصغر قلعه
34- 69-. A fort in the Chardeh valley of Kabul. (I.B.C.)

*AGHAIL KHEL-I-AGH ALI KHAN   اغيل خيل اغ على خان
    35-13 69-13 m. A village with some 630 inhabitants in Jabal Saraj
    district of Parwan province. It is located in the Dara-i-Salang on
    the highway from Kabul to Mazar-i-Sharif.

AGHA JAN   آغه جان قلعه
    34- 69-. A village in Logar, southeast of Zargun Shahar, situated
    in the Tangi-Sar-i-Chashma. (Gaselee.) A place called Agho Jan is
    located southwest of Muqur, at 32-44 67-36 m. The name is also
    spelled Ghojan. (LWA)

AGHA JAN KALA   آغه جان قلعه
    A village in the Surkhab division fo the Jalalabad district. (Jen-
    kyns.)

AGHA MUHAMMAD KALA   آغه محمد قلعه
    A fort in the Chardeh valley of Kabul. (I.B.C.)

AGHAO JAN Or GHOJAN   آغو جان
    32-44 67-36 m. A halting place, 59 miles from Kalat-i-Ghilzai, 75
    miles from Ghazni, on a fine open plain, with a high hill on one
    side. Supplies procurable in considerable quantities in the neigh-
    bourhood; water, grass, and camel forage abundant; fuel scarce.
    Many forts and villages near. On the top of one of the conical
    hills near this place two stone pillars mark the site of a pyramid
    of Ghilzai skulls made by order of Nadir Shah after his defeat of
    that tribe. The spot is called "Khak Khana." The following is
    extracted from the diary of Sir D. Steward's march in April 1880,
    when the force halted at Aghao Jan or Ghojan. "Ghogan is the name
    of a district watered by a karez with several ramifying branches.
    On this karez are a group of villages, seven in number, situated to
    the northwest about 2 miles distant. The two to the south are
    called Ghojan or Aghajan; two in the centre, Zabit; and the norther-
    ly ones, Shinkai.
    "They are villages of considerable size, and the district is fairly
    fertile. Encampment upon a fine open plain with its right resting
    on a hill to the east of road. From Shinkai the Otla pass, said to
    be easy, leads to Rassana and thence to the country of the Jaghuri
    Hazaras.
    In Ghojan district the inhabitants are Taraki Ghilzais. (Hough,
    Outram, Garden, etc., I.B.C.)

AGHA SARAI   See AK SARAI   آق سرای

AGHLI KHAN   آغلی خان (اغیل)
    35-13 69-13 m. A village of 40 houses in the Salang dara, about 12
    miles above Parwan. (I.B.C.) This seems to be identical with
    Aghail Khel-i-Agh Ali Khan, listed above. (LWA)

AGHRABAD Or AQ ROBAT   آق رباط
    34-32 70-13 m. One of the principal villages in Laghman, situated
    on the right bank of the Alingar river, east of Mandrawar. Its
    inhabitants are Utkhel Ghilzais. It consists of 16 hamlets, as
    follows:
        1. Kala-i-Haidar   7. Kala-i-Adil
        2. Kala-i-Tajuddin   8. Kala-i-Asad
        3. Kala-i-Muhammad Kasim   9. (Old) Aghrabad
        4. Kala-i-Gul Baz   10. (Old) Lal Muhammad
        5. Kala-i-Nur   11. (Old) Gul Ahmad
        6. Kala-i-Gul Ahmad   12. (Old) Allahdad

13.	(Old) Allahdad II	15.	(Old) Sher Muhammad
14.	(Old) Kahir	16.	(Old) Hashim

(Warburton.) The correct name of the village is probably Ak Robat.

*AHAD احد
33-4 68-19 m. A village in Giro district of Ghazni province with an agricultural population of about 250.

*AHANGARAN آهنگران
35-6 69-2 m. A village with an agricultural population of about 500 in Jabal Saraj district of Parwan Province. It is located on a tributary of the Ghorband river. Other places with this name are located at 34-32 68-37, 33-50 67-7, 34-48 67-55, and 35-37 69-29 A.

AHANGARAN آهنگران
34-48 67-57. A long glen which descends north and debouches into the Bamian valley, 1 1/2 miles above Topchi. The village of Ahangaran contains 40 houses of Tajiks. (Maitland.)

*AHAN KUSHTA اهن کشته
33-6 67-16 m. A village is Malestan district of Ghazni province, located on the Shila-i-Naeb, a tributary of the Arghandab.

AHMADA احمده
A section of the Jaghatu Hazaras.

AHMAD DIWANA احمد دیوانه
35-55 71-19 m. Elevation 8,530 feet. A tract of country, 3 miles or so in length, at the upper end of the Bashgul valley. It has a tower at each end and a defensible homestead in the middle. At its northern limit is a famous shrine of Imra. Forage and firewood are abundant here.
A path from the Lutkuf valley in Chitral via the Zidig pass (14, 850 feet), and another more circuitous route from the same place come in here. The latter is said to be used by Badakshi traders for taking laden animals to Chitral. (Robertson, I.B.C.) Recent maps show a village with the name Diwana Baba. (LWA)

AHMAD KALA احمد قلعه
34- 69-. A small village in the Shakar Dara glen in Koh Daman. (Masson.)

*AHMAD KALAY احمد کلی
32-8 67-29 m. A village in a valley east of the Sur Ghar and west of the Shinkai Ghar.

AHMAD KHAN KALA احمد خان قلعه
34- 69-. A village on the right bank of the Logar river, between Sak and the bridge of Bagrami. (Kennedy.)

AHMAD KHAN KALA احمد خان قلعه
34- 69-. A large village at the eastern end of the Siah Sang ridge, 5 miles east of Kabul. (Kennedy.)

AHMAD KHEL احمد خیل
34- 70-. A large village in the Gandamak valley, Jalalabad district, containing with the neighbouring villages of Pira Khel and Khwaja Khel, 1,000 houses of Wazir Khugianis. (McGregor.)

AHMAD KHEL احمدخیل
33-49 69-37 G. A large group of villages in Hariob situated in a plain about five miles square in the angle formed by the Karaja and Mirzakai streams, about 28 miles west of Pathan. Contains nearly 600 families of Jajis. The best place for a camping ground is on the right bank of the Mirzakai stream, where there is room for a brigade. (I.B.C.)

AHMAD KHEL احمدخیل
33-21 68-19 G. A village 22 miles from Ghazni on the Kandahar road. The village or fort of this name is situated in a little hollow among the hills on the west of the road, and there is a valley or opening in this low range down which runs the bed of a torrent and a line of karez. The plain in the vicinity where the British army encamped in 1893 is for the most part stony and sandy, but there is a good deal of ploughed land and cultivation near. Water is procured from karez in abundance, and forage for camels and horses is also in plenty. There are a number of small forts in the vicinity. Here on the 19th April 1880, the division under Lieutenant-General Sir Donald Stewart, marching from Kandahar towards Kabul, encountered and defeated an Afghan force estimated at 1,000 horse and 12,000 to 15,000 foot. For details of the action see "Official history of the 2nd Afghan War." Other places with this name are located at 33-50 69-39 and 33-52 69-41 A; and 34-6 70-27, 33-21 68-19, and 34-0 69-51 G. (LWA)

AHMAD KHEL احمدخیل
34-0 69-51 G. A village in the Khugiani division of the Jalalabad district, on the slopes of a spur from the Safed Koh range. The inhabitants belong to the Wazir section of the Khugianis. (Jenkyns.)

AHMAD KHEL احمدخیل
A section of the Jajis. Their villages lie principally in the Hazardarakht valley, and extend down the right bank of the latter to the neighbourhood of Ali Khel. Fodder for 400 animals for one day and about 500 maunds of unground grain may be collected from the Ahmad Khel villages:

	Fighting Men				Fighting Men
1.	Dabuzai	300	7.	Alam	200
2.	Sishta	500	8.	Kasim	150
3.	Lodrakh		9.	Oron	100
4.	Ali Khel	200	10.	Zarak	200
5.	Mama Khel		11.	Turkar	100
6.	Landi Wam	200	12.	Chergo	150

(Collett, Johnston.)

*AHMAD KHEL احمدخیل
32-29 68-7 m. A village in Katawaz district of Ghazni province, about 5 miles northeast of Malikdin.

AHMADZAI احمدزی
34-31 70-19 G. A village in Laghman, inhabited by Tajiks. (Warburton.)

*AHMADZAI احمدزی
33-57 69-19 G. A village located some 50 miles west of Qala Ali Khel. Other villages with this name are located at 34-2 69-35 A., and a few miles south of the Panjshir river, near Niazi Geranshakh, at 34-54 69-26 m.

AHMADZAI   احمدزی
   A section of the great Sulaiman Khel division of the Ghilzais. They are pastoral in their habits. Their settlements are at Spiga and in a group of villages at the mouth of the Altimur pass leading into Zurmat, but they drive their flocks from Logar as far east as the hills of Jalalabad. (See Ghilzai.)

AHMADZAI-KATS   احمدزی کټ
   A halting place in the bed of the Gumal river, about 25 miles from its source. (Broadfoot.)

*AILAKA-I-AJAR or YELGAH AJAR   ایلکه اجر
   35-21 67-29 m. A village in Kahmard district of Bamian province, located on the Ajar stream, northwest of Rui Sang.

AISHGHI   ایشغی
   A section of the Jaghatu Hazaras.

AJUM   عجم سنگشانده
   An important valley in the Beed (Behsud?) Hazara country. A village in this area is called Ajam-i-Sang Shanda. (LWA)

AKA KHEL   اکاخیل
   34-11 70-29. A village in the Hisarak division of the Jalalabad district, situated on the right bank of the Hisarak stream, 3 miles south of Mazina. The inhabitants are Shinwaris. (Jenkyns.)

*AKA KHEL   اکاخیل
   34-48 69-40 m. A village in the Tagab district of Parwan province with an agricultural population of about 220. It is is is on the Tagab river, north of the Naghlu dam.

AKA KHEL   اکاخیل
   One of the nomad sections of the Ghilzai tribe, who inhabit a group of villages called Sharana in Gardez. The subdivisions of the section are (i) Miankhan Khel; (ii) Jalal Khel; (iii) Khorojak Khel; (iv) Masti Khel. They are a very poor race, and but few of the men can afford to travel on their own account, so let out their camels to hire to the Mian Khel, with whom they perform the march from Gardez into the Derajat and back. The few who can afford to trade bring down fruits, cloths, etc., and these men, in common with the richer Powindahs, visit the markets of Calcutta and Bonbay. Their kiris are usually pitched in the district of Dera Ismail, far from any villages, and the able-bodied men all work as labourers to eke out a livelihood when away from their own country, leaving a very few men, with the women, in the tents, to tend the camels while grazing.
   The first three sections of Aka Khel all trade with or travel in Hindustan; the Masti Khel, however, confine their operations to Kandahar.

*AKASI   اکاسی (آقاسی)
   33-41 68-23 m. A village on the Ghazni river, aobut 10 miles north of Ghazni.

*AKBAR KHEL   اکبر خیل
   32-57 68-14 m. A village with an agricultural population of about 100 in Giro district of Ghazni province. A place with this name is

some 5 miles northeast of the road from Gardez to Kabul, at 33-49 69-10 m. and another is 5 miles south of Mukur at 32-46 67-46 m.

AKBAR KHEL اکبر خیل
A section of the Ghilzais settled in the country between the Lakarai pass and Aspando Kats. One of their maliks, Mulaim of Stirkala, was killed at Jagdalak in December 1879, when fighting against the British. (Gordon.)

*AKHIZIAN اخیزیان
32-30 67-5 m. A village located a few miles south of the Shahid Mandeh, a tributary of the Arghandab.

*AKHTAR KHEL اختر خیل
32-49 67-43 m. A village with an agricultural population of about 100 in Mukur district of Ghazni province. The village is southwest of Mukur.

AKHUND KALA Or AKHUND KHEL آخند قلعه
33-56 69-13 m. A Ghilzai village at the west foot of the Shutar Gardan pass, between Kurram and Logar. Opposite the village are high Karewah lands, in which are the remains of a large thana. Forage, fuel, and provisions are not procurable here without the greatest difficulty. (Lumsden.)

AKHUND KALA آخند قلعه
34- 70-. A village in the Kama subdivision of the Jalalabad district, about 16 miles east of Jalalabad. (Jenkyns.)

AKHUND KHAISUDDIN آخندغیث الدین (؟)
34- 69-. A village 5 miles east of Kabul, on right bank of the Logar. (Kennedy.)

AKHUND KHEL آخند خیل
33-57 69-13 m. A pass between the Shutur Gardan and Shinkai Kotals. Its difficulties were found by the British in September 1879 to have been over-estimated, although doubtless, if resolutely held, its passage might be attended with difficulty. (Baker.) There is now a village with this name, located north of Gardez. (LWA)

AKHUND KHEL See AKHUND KALA آخند خیل

AKIL JUNI (JANI) اکیل جانی (؟)
35- 69-. A village east of Charikar. Inhabitants: Tajiks. (Shahzada Taimus.)

AKINABAD اکین اباد
34-42 70-15. One of the principal villages in Laghman. Situated on the left bank of the Alingar river, 4 miles north of Shamti. (Warburton.)

AKORI اکوری
34- 70-. A village in the Khugiani division of the Jalalabad district, about 6 miles southwest of Nimla. The inhabitants belong to the Kharbun section of the Khugianis. (Jenkyns.) A village with this name is some six miles east of Qala Sarkari, at 32-52 67-53 G. (LWA)

AKRAM KHAN KALA اکرم خان قلعه
34-29 69-14. A small village on the left bank of Logar, between

Beni Hisar and Bagram, about 3 1/2 miles southeast of Kabul. (Kennedy.)

AK ROBAT آق رباط
34-56 67-39 m. Elev. 10,225 feet. A pass at the head of the Bamian valley, crossed at 111 miles from Kabul by the main Kabul-Mazar-i-Sharif road. On the Bamian side there is a made road, fit for guns, half-way up to the summit, but the remainder requires to be cut out. All round are smooth, low hills, undulating, but rather steep, and covered with grass in spring. The descent into the Ak Robat valley is easy, though the gradient is considerable. (A.B.C.) There is now a village with this name about 15 miles northwest of Qala Sarkari. (LWA)

AK ROBAT آق رباط
Elev. 9,955 feet.

AK SARAI Or AGHA SARAI آق سرای
34-47 69-10 G. A village in the Koh Daman, 22 miles north of Kabul. It contains 200 houses of Tajiks; water from a stream. Burnes describes it as a flourishing place. (Leech, Burnes.)

AKZAR Or AGHZIR آقزیر (اغزیر)
A section of the Chahar Dasta Hazaras.

AK ZARAT آق زرت
34-23 66-36 G. Elev. 10.880 feet. A pass in the Koh-i-Baba range at the head of the Ak Zarat valley. This pass is about 15 miles west of the Qala Pai Kutal. (LWA)

AK ZARAT آق زرت
34-22 66-40 G. A valley in the Dai Zangi country.

ALADAI الله دی
A section of the Chahar Dasta Hazaras paying revenue to Ghazni.

ALAF علف (؟)
34- 67-. A small fort in Bamian, close to Shahidan. (A.B.C.)

*ALAGHZAR الغزار (؟)
32-56 67-32 m. A village located on the stream of the same name, northwest of the town of Mukur.

ALAK الاک
A section of the Dai Kundi Hazaras.

ALAKA (See Military Report of Hazarajat, Part II.) علاقه

ALA KALA اعلی قلعه (الله)
34-14 67-46 m. A village in the Tagao Saiad subdistrict of Yak Walang; 10 houses of Besud Hazaras. (Maitland.) The village is in the Surkhsang area, west of the Kuh-i-Mazar. (LWA)

*ALAKH الاخ
32-38 67-41 m. A village on the Tarnak river, some 12 miles south of Mukur.

ALAKOH الکوه
33- 68-. A peak on the range which throws out a spur running west to Ghazni, and which is crossed by the Tang-i-Sher on the Kabul

road. (Broadfoot.)

ALAM علم
A small section of the Muhammad Khwaja Hazaras paying revenue to Ghazni.

*ALAM KHEL عالم خیل
33-16 68-27 m. A village with a population of about 150 in Andar district of Ghazni province. Another place with this name is in the Tarnak valley, some 5 miles northeast of Mukur, at 32-50 67-51 m.

*ALASAY الله سای (الاسای)
34-53 69-43. Alasay is an alaqadari in Parwan province. The alaqadari comprises an area of 324 square kilometers and has an agricultural population that has been estimated at from 6,998 to 7,234. The alaqadari is bounded in the west by Tagab, in the north and northwest by Nejrab, in the east by Daulatshah and Alishing, and in the south by Sarobi. Alasay includes about 34 villages, of which one has more than 500 inhabitants. The villages are listed in the PG as follows: Gulka Khel, Okrachi, Sultan Khel, Jafar Khel, Lich, Sheraka Khel, Kochi Sheraka Khel, Bahadur Khel, Dawan Khel, Saheb Zada Khel, Darwali wa Ahangaran, Rah Sang-i Shipi, Shado Khel, Warna Kunda, Sangi Khel, Fael, Chora Khel, Mira Khel, Chahi Khel, Setraj, Masum Khel, Sar Godar, Kacha, Gonstur Khel, Qala-i-Iskin, Dawud Khel, Saber Jal, Adina Khel, Poylam, Alla Dost Khel-i-Koti, Lau Luwan, Wali Beg Khel (Koti), and Kochi (Kochi-i-Alah Sai).

ALGUD الگد
34-37 69-3 G. A section of the Jajis settled in villages to the west of Jaji Maidan. (Carr.) There is also a village with this name, about 10 miles southwest of Sarai Khwaja. (LWA)

ALI علی
34-43 67-2. A dara which descends northwest from the Koh-i-Baba and debouches into the Band-i-Amir valley, 4 miles below Firozbahar. For a list of villages, etc. see "Bamian (district)."

ALIABAD علی آباد
34-31 69-8 A. A small village to the west of the Asmai hill near Kabul, which gives its name to the pass over the above - named heights. This spot was the scene of severe fighting on on the 14th December 1879. Kabul University campus is now in this area. (LWA)

ALI BOGHAN علی بوغان (؟)
34- 70-. Elev. 1,580 feet. A village 7 miles southeast of Jalalabad, standing on some rising ground about 1 mile from the right bank of the Kabul river. It contains (in 1904) some 40 families of Saiyids, mostly weavers. They possess about 160 head of cattle, 2,500 sheep and goats, 20 horses and 100 buffaloes. The village is "muaf," i.e., exempt form paying revenue, probably on account of a famous ziarat which exists here.
There is room for a force of any size to encamp, with plentiful good water from the river. Grass is procurable in the vicinity; grain, etc., from the opposite side of the river which can be forded in the cold weather and crossed at other times by ferry about 4 miles below the ford; supplies of all sorts could be collected on due notice. The valley in the vicinity of the river, and esewhere wherever irrigation is available, is richly cultivated.
A post was built here by us in 1879 which was garrisoned by 32 sowars and 150 infantry; the remains of the huts were still visible

Some few trade on their own account, but the majority hire out their camels to the Sulaiman Khel (with whom they travel) at the rate of Rs. 5 to 5-8 a maund from Khorasan to the Daman. (Norman.) According to McMahon the various sections are as follows:

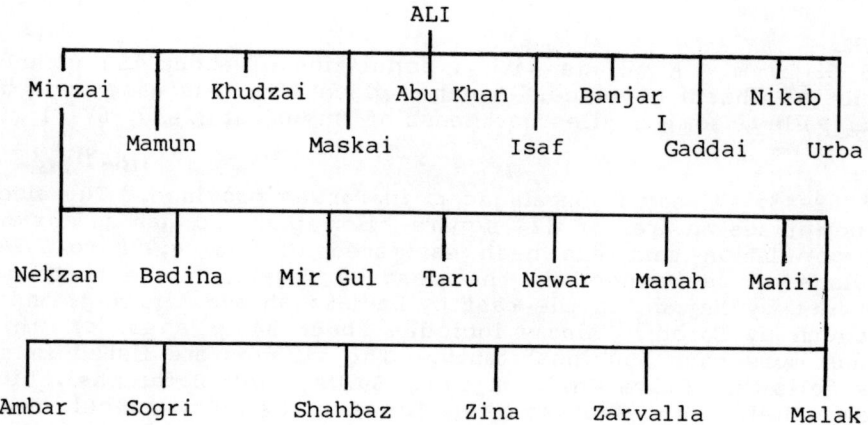

Of the Ali Khel the Minzais and their subsections are the only people with whom we have much intercourse. The following subsections under the following headmen yearly visit Zarmelan, the Girdao plain and other tracts on the British side of the border, i.e.,:

    Nekzan Khel   - Babar Khan, Fateh Khan
    Mir Gul Khel - Haidar Khan, Mehrban
    Badina   - Zaffar Khan, Kaisor Khan

The Taru, Nawar and Mana Khel chiefly live with the Saraz Sulaiman Khel on the Pierak range. The Manir, Ambar, Zina, Sogri, Shahbaz, Zarvalla and Malkak Khels all live in Katawaz. The Malkaks are the most numerous subsection of the <u>Minzais</u>. (McMahon.)

*ALIKOT
33-22 69-20 m. A village in the Kabul district, about 2 miles east of the Sherpur cantonment, in the Yakatut township. (Kennedy.) A village with this name is located at 35-39 67-19 G. (LWA)

ALI MARDAN
34- 69-. A small Tajik village in the Kabul district, about 2 miles east of the Sherpur cantonment, in the Yakatut township. (Kennedy.) A village with this name is located at 35-39 67-10 G. (LWA)

*ALINGAR
34-50 70-21 m. Alingar is a woleswali in Laghman Province. The woleswali, which comprisis an area of 838 square kilometers, has an agricultural population that has been estimated at about 19,000. It is bounded in the north by Nuristan, in the east by Chapa Dara and Dara-i-Nur, in the south by Qarghai and Mehterlam, and in the west by Alishing. The woleswali contains about 57 villages, 9 of which have more than 500 inhabitants. The villages are listed in the PG as follows: Kundah, Rajai (Arjai), Kokhi, Shorawah (Kochi Shoraba), Gadi (Kuchi Kalai), Sakhrah, Shahi, Kachor (Machkor), Salub-i-Sufla (Salab), Salub-i-Ulya, Lokal, Adhar, Waranta, Mango, Wat-i-Jabar Khel (Wat-i-Jabar), Puranah (Paryana), Mandal, Gundah Gul, Parwai, Lajorak (Lajdarak), Chatla (Chetla), Khwaja Khel-i-Sufla, Khwaja

Khel-i-Ulya, Sangar, Qala-i-Taksaw (Qaltak), Stanisaw (Stan Saw), Bealamsaw (Bay Alam Saw), Ishkamash Saw, Yulam-i-Kazhdaka Kalman, Gorjan (Gojan Kalman), Khorak Kalan (Khorak-Kalman), Parch (Parch Kalman), Kundahlam, Ambir-i-Kalman (Jana Mir-i-Kalman), Kahu Kalman, Kota Khel (Kata Khel), Alu Khel, Nim Nani, Shorabad (Shorasaw), Qaltak-i-Niyazi (Qala Tak-i-Niyazi), Tangawor (Tigor), Salingar, Qasaba, Gul Aram Kalman, Tag, Khwajam Kot, Punda Kachi Tag, Sundarwa (Sandora), Oyenaw (Kochi Oye Taw), Sami Saw, Sahur wa Sangarak Kalman (Kalyan-i-Khas Shahungok), Kazhwaka Kalman, Landrutak, Baylem, Balatak, and Aqwam-i-Kajro Khana.

ALINGAR
النگار (علینگار)

34-39 70-14 m. A river which rises in the south slopes of the Hindu Kush, being formed by the junction of the Ramgul and Kulam valleys of Nuristan. In its upper reaches it is known as the Kao. After a course of about 70 miles, it joins the Alishang at Tirgarhi, in the district of Laghman, and then takes the name of Laghman, and after flowing for 8 to 10 miles further throught the abovementioned district it joins the Kabul river some 12 miles northwest of Jalalabad. Though not deep, this river has a rapid current, and its bed is so full of loose boulders that it is always dangerous to cross. No year elapses that some accident does not happen in crossing it. The valley of the Alingar from Tirgarhi is wide and spacious, and trends east, and is described as very fertile in grain. It is inhabited by Ghilzais, Arokis, and Niazis, is amply provided with small forts, but has no considerable village.

Above the Niazis, come the Nimchas, or converted Kafirs, and above these again in the mountains, true Kafirs may be met with. A route up the Alingar valley leads into the very heart of Nuristan. At its head is said to be a pass known as the Pir Panjal, which leads into Badakhshan.

The principal villages in this valley are Zola, Nikara, Badmask, Mian Shak-Panjpai, Kulman, and Gaochak. The population of the whole valley is estimated at 10,000 souls, includes Shahgiris, Randus, Katihis, and Sandus. (Masson, Raverty, Bellew, McNair, I.B.C.)

Colonel Stewart, from native information, gives us a good many details regarding the upper part of the Alingar. He says the upper portion of the valley is more open than the lower. Wheat, barley, and jowar are cultivated and grapes and apricots grow in great profusion. The tribes he mentions as occupying this valley are: the Wamah, Katihi, and Karak Kafirs, who together muster between 7,000 and 8,000 fighting-men. The Katihi Kafirs he places at the head of the valley, the Wamah on its eastern side, and Karak on the western. The following table is given on his authority:

LEFT BANK			RIGHT BANK		
Valley	Inhabitants	Houses	Valley	Inhabitants	Houses
Kanagali	Kathihi	400	Uskin Dara	Katihi	80
Jamagali		800	Gamgata Dara		200
Kulum Dara		500	Pairwal Dara		300
Pegali					
Paragali	Wamah	400	Ghun Dara Korgali	Karak	80
Karegali		2,000	Shamgali		100
Manjagali,			Pashangar Dara		1,000
Masur, Kulatan		100			
Gulcha		60			
Teton Dara		1,000			

(Stewart.)

Some few trade on their own account, but the majority hire out their camels to the Sulaiman Khel (with whom they travel) at the rate of Rs. 5 to 5-8 a maund from Khorasan to the Daman. (Norman.) According to McMahon the various sections are as follows:

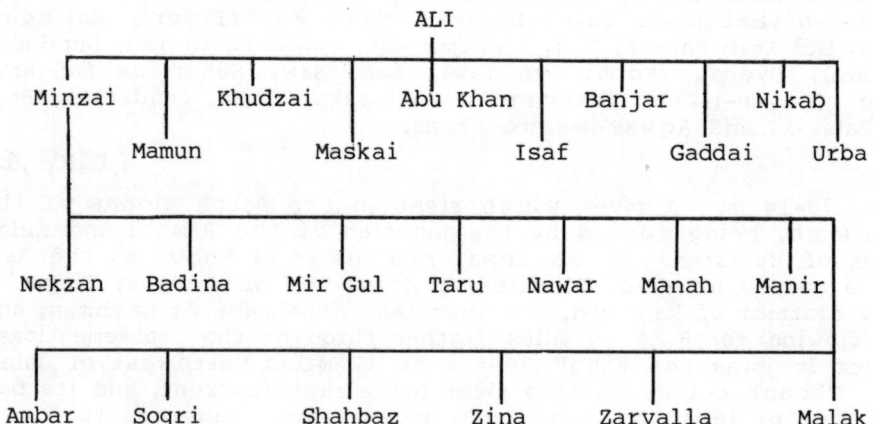

Of the Ali Khel the Minzais and their subsections are the only people with whom we have much intercourse. The following subsections under the following headmen yearly visit Zarmelan, the Girdao plain and other tracts on the British side of the border, i.e.,:

                Nekzan Khel   - Babar Khan, Fateh Khan
                Mir Gul Khel - Haidar Khan, Mehrban
                Badina   - Zaffar Khan, Kaisor Khan

The Taru, Nawar and Mana Khel chiefly live with the Saraz Sulaiman Khel on the Pierak range. The Manir, Ambar, Zina, Sogri, Shahbaz, Zarvalla and Malkak Khels all live in Katawaz. The Malkaks are the most numerous subsection of the <u>Minzais</u>. (McMahon.)

*ALIKOT   علیکوت
33-22 69-20 m. A village in the Kabul district, about 2 miles east of the Sherpur cantonment, in the Yakatut township. (Kennedy.) A village with this name is located at 35-39 67-19 G. (LWA)

ALI MARDAN   علی مردان
34- 69-. A small Tajik village in the Kabul district, about 2 miles east of the Sherpur cantonment, in the Yakatut township. (Kennedy.) A village with this name is located at 35-39 67-10 G. (LWA)

*ALINGAR   النگار (علینگار)
34-50 70-21 m. Alingar is a woleswali in Laghman Province. The woleswali, which comprisis an area of 838 square kilometers, has an agricultural population that has been estimated at about 19,000. It is bounded in the north by Nuristan, in the east by Chapa Dara and Dara-i-Nur, in the south by Qarghai and Mehterlam, and in the west by Alishing. The woleswali contains about 57 villages, 9 of which have more than 500 inhabitants. The villages are listed in the PG as follows: Kundah, Rajai (Arjai), Kokhi, Shorawah (Kochi Shoraba), Gadi (Kuchi Kalai), Sakhrah, Shahi, Kachor (Machkor), Salub-i-Sufla (Salab), Salub-i-Ulya, Lokal, Adhar, Waranta, Mango, Wat-i-Jabar Khel (Wat-i-Jabar), Puranah (Paryana), Mandal, Gundah Gul, Parwai, Lajorak (Lajdarak), Chatla (Chetla), Khwaja Khel-i-Sufla, Khwaja

Khel-i-Ulya, Sangar, Qala-i-Taksaw (Qaltak), Stanisaw (Stan Saw), Bealamsaw (Bay Alam Saw), Ishkamash Saw, Yulam-i-Kazhdaka Kalman, Gorjan (Gojan Kalman), Khorak Kalan (Khorak-Kalman), Parch (Parch Kalman), Kundahlam, Ambir-i-Kalman (Jana Mir-i-Kalman), Kahu Kalman, Kota Khel (Kata Khel), Alu Khel, Nim Nani, Shorabad (Shorasaw), Qaltak-i-Niyazi (Qala Tak-i-Niyazi), Tangawor (Tigor), Salingar, Qasaba, Gul Aram Kalman, Tag, Khwajam Kot, Punda Kachi Tag, Sundarwa (Sandora), Oyenaw (Kochi Oye Taw), Sami Saw, Sahur wa Sangarak Kalman (Kalyan-i-Khas Shahungok), Kazhwaka Kalman, Landrutak, Baylem, Balatak, and Aqwam-i-Kajro Khana.

ALINGAR
الئگار

34-39 70-14 m. A river which rises in the south slopes of the Hindu Kush, being formed by the junction of the Ramgul and Kulam valleys of Nuristan. In its upper reaches it is known as the Kao. After a course of about 70 miles, it joins the Alishang at Tirgarhi, in the district of Laghman, and then takes the name of Laghman, and after flowing for 8 to 10 miles further throught the abovementioned district it joins the Kabul river some 12 miles northwest of Jalalabad. Though not deep, this river has a rapid current, and its bed is so full of loose boulders that it is always dangerous to cross. No year elapses that some accident does not happen in crossing it. The valley of the Alingar from Tirgarhi is wide and spacious, and trends east, and is described as very fertile in grain. It is inhabited by Ghilzais, Arokis, and Niazis, is amply provided with small forts, but has no considerable village.

Above the Niazis, come the Nimchas, or converted Kafirs, and above these again in the mountains, true Kafirs may be met with. A route up the Alingar valley leads into the very heart of Nuristan. At its head is said to be a pass known as the Pir Panjal, which leads into Badakhshan.

The principal villages in this valley are Zola, Nikara, Badmask, Mian Shak-Panjpai, Kulman, and Gaochak. The population of the whole valley is estimated at 10,000 souls, includes Shahgiris, Randus, Katihis, and Sandus. (Masson, Raverty, Bellew, McNair, I.B.C.)

Colonel Stewart, from native information, gives us a good many details regarding the upper part of the Alingar. He says the upper portion of the valley is more open than the lower. Wheat, barley, and jowar are cultivated and grapes and apricots grow in great profusion. The tribes he mentions as occupying this valley are: the Wamah, Katihi, and Karak Kafirs, who together muster between 7,000 and 8,000 fighting-men. The Katihi Kafirs he places at the head of the valley, the Wamah on its eastern side, and Karak on the western. The following table is given on his authority:

LEFT BANK			RIGHT BANK		
Valley	Inhabitants	Houses	Valley	Inhabitants	Houses
Kanagali	Kathihi	400	Uskin Dara	Katihi	80
Jamagali		800	Gamgata Dara		200
Kulum Dara		500	Pairwal Dara		300
Pegali					
Paragali	Wamah	400	Ghun Dara Korgali	Karak	80
Karegali		2,000	Shamgali		100
Manjagali, Masur, Kulatan		100	Pashangar Dara		1,000
Gulcha		60			
Teton Dara		1,000			

(Stewart.)

Surgeon-Major Robertson remarks: "Concerning the Alingar or Kao, the stream which empties itself to the south into the Kabul river, I know nothing except by hearsay. My informants told me that the main western valley of Nuristan was inhabited by the Ramgul branch of the Kafirs, and that it was large and maintained a numeous population. Its river, after receiving many side streams, was joined by the Kulam valley stream from the left, and ended in the Kabul river at Laghman. The Kulam river is probably much shorter than the Ramgul river, for the valley of the former only contains four villages as against the 20 or 30 said to be in the Ramgul country."

ALISANGI علی سنگی
A village in the Lakarai ravine, about half-way between the Paiwar Kotal and Ali Khel. (Kennedy.)

ALISHANG or ALISHING علیشنگ (الیشنگ)
34-38 70-14. A river which rises in the south slopes of the Hindu Kush above the district of Najil, and after running about 60 miles southeast, almost parallel with, and about a few miles distant from, the Alingar, joins that river at Tirgarhi, whence the united stream is known as the Laghman. Though not a deep river, except after rain, it has a rapid current, and its bed is so full of loose boulders that it is always dangerous to cross. The northeastern limit of this valley is prominently marked by the high mountain Koh Karinj, extending from east to west along its entire length. The valley of Alishang is said to be chiefly inhabited by converted Kafirs or Nimchas. Above Najil it is inhabited by Kafirs of the Shahgiri, Pandu and Katihi clans, who possess in all about 2,000 houses, and are constantly a feud with one another. The valley is said to be very fertile. Its principal villages are Atu, Chakala, Yolanai, Sardu, Farajghan, and Bargaon. (Raverty, Masson, Leech, Elphinstone, McNair.)
The above is not reliable: the Alishang cannot be much more than 40 miles in length, and it is by no means certain that any part of the valley is inhabited by true Kafirs. According to Stewart the inhabitants are Hazaras, Panjshirs, Tajiks. Kohistanis, Safis, etc. (Barros, Stewart.)
Up the Alishang valley lies one of the chief routes from the Jalalabad district into Nuristan. (I.B.C.)

ALISHANG or ALISHING علیشنگ
34-47 70-6 m. Alishing is a woleswali in Laghman Province. The woleswali, which comprises an area of 745 square kilometers, has an agricultural population that has been estimated at about 13,700. Alishing is bounded in the north by Daulatshah and Nuristan, in the east by Alingar, in the south by Mehterlam, and on the west by Panjshir and Nejrab. The woleswali contains about 88 villages, 4 of which have more than 500 inhabitants. The villages are listed in the PG as follows: Kohna Pall, Manjan, Najil-i-Khas, Nilo ((Nalo-i-Shamsa Khel), Ghaziabad, Nolam-i-Sufla (Noram-i-Sufla), Kutli (Kotali),Jamshedabad, Watan Gato (Wateka Tu), Saikul, Khud Zangal, Murcha Khalil (Murcha Khel), Bumbi, Shamsi Khel (Shamsa Khel-i-Khas), Kundali (Karandali), Deh Malich (Damlich-i-Najil), Masmut-i-Ulya, Masmut-i-Sufla, Kar Gar, Darweshabad, Paye Khel, Andoral, Shamkat-i-Ulya wa Sufla, Tornaw, Mustafa, Chanaki Shamkat, Kohistan-i-Shamkat, Shegi, Dur Duri (Dawduri), Kandun, Pohanshama Khel, Achekzai, Shamoram (Shamram), Qala-i-Husain, Qala-i-Baiya, Islamabad, Zhain (Dahan), Akhund Sahib, Shakarman, Alnai (Arlin), Chanak-i-Lashti Pul, Hasan Khel, Chaparah, Salabi-i-Ulya, Domiya, Hajiyan, Kachan, Kun-

jnun (Ganjawan), Harwarah, Kasig, Barekzai, Qala Tak, Hasanzai, Kala Khel (Gula Khel-i-Khawabi), Qandau (Qandau Batiyan), Sabrabad, Chawni, Qandali (Qandala Gona Pall), Dara-i-Miyasaheb, Nuri Mil-i-Ulya (Nuri), Tapa Kal (Tapa-Kal-i-Mil), Tili, Shamya, Parmawan, Kamrahi, Kandi, Najil, Andra (Andra-Watan Kato), Qala-i-Gul Ahmad, Tarnak-i-Shamram (Tarnak), Deh Qazi, Qala-i-Khan, Talab-i-Ulya and Sufla, Batiyan, Kurdi, Kota (Kotanjil), Para Dehli (Parado-i-Sayegal), Moma (Moka), Baharandak (Barandak), Taro (Tarho), Tanksho, Doshto (Awarestar), Lut Khando, Sobun, Manjakam (Bachalam-i-Kona Pal), Dawlat Khando, Sherino, Barozi-i-Nau, Chergai-Nau, Sandali, Yegh Nau, Chanar Nau, Shala Kut-i-Kohestan, Patau, Nakundi. In 1914 the village of Alishang was described as follows: Elev. 2,900 feet. One of the principal villages in Laghman, on the left bank of the Alishang river, about 6 miles above Tirgarhi. It consists of the following hamlets, all of which are inhabited by Tajiks:

1. Mazkura
2. Kalaicha
3. Taj Garhi
4. Haji Zargun Shah Tarra Khel
5. Kala-i-Shaghasi
6. Kala-i-Ata Muhammad Khan
7. Deh-i-Mishkati
8. Shakarman
9. Deh-i-Mianji
10. Deh-i-Kazi
11. Deh-i-Safi
12. Deh-i-Hasanzai
13. Kala-i-Kulma Haji Sahib

A force of 200 khasadars is stationed at Alishang. (Washburton, I.B.C.)

*ALISHER Or TERIZI, TRAIZAI   علی شیر (تیریزی)
33-26 70-2 m. A village in Traizai district of Paktya province, a few miles northwest of Bokhan.

ALISHER KHEL   علی شیر خیل
A main division of the Shinwaris.

ALISHER KHEL   علی شیر خیل
32-59 68-14 G. A village in the Ghazni district, near Pannah, inhabited by Andari Ghilzais. The surrounding country is exceedingly bare, and is a series of low swells and hollows. (Broadfoot.)

ALLAH BAKSH   See KHAK-I-ALLAH BAKSH   الله بخش

ALLAH-DAD KHAN KALA   الله داد خان قلعه
34- 70-. A village in the Khugiani subdivision of the Jalalabad district, at the junction of the Marki Khel and Surkhab streams. (McGregor.)

*ALLAH DAD KHEL   الله داد خیل
33-52 68-55 m. A village with some 300 inhabitants in Baraki Barak district of Logar province.

*ALLAH DAD KULAI   الله داد کولی
32-46 68-45 m. A village in the Qajrano Ghar, south of Omna.

ALLAH QULI   الله قلی
A subdivision of the Bachari Ghulam Clan of Dai Zangi. A Village with this name is located in Paghman, at 34-36 68-56 m. (LWA)

ALLAH-UD-DIN Or ALAUDDIN   علاءالدین
34- 69-. A township in the Chardeh valley of Kabul, midway between the Chamchamast and the Kabul, about 2 miles above their junction.

The inhabitants are all Gadi Hazaras.
The following forts compose this township:
1. Kala-i-Mir Akhor Agha Jan
2. Kala-i-Mohib Ali
3. Kala-i-Malik Dost
4. Kala-i-Jan Muhammad
5. Kala-i-Muhammad Riza
6. Kala-i-Ali Riza
7. Kala-i-Sardar Muhammad Sharif Khan
8. Kala-i-Wazir
9. Kala-i-Majnun Shah
10. Kala-i-Sultan Ali
(I.B.C.)

Another place with this name is in Bargai district of Paktya province, west of Nadir Shah Kot, at 33-19 69-32 m. (LWA)

ALLAKAH الاكه (؟)
A section of Uzbaks, who live in the Dahan-i-Marghi in Yak Walang. They are said to have come from Allakah in the Balkh-Ab district of Afghan Turkistan. (A.B.C.)

*ALMAR KHEL المارخيل
32-50 68-5 m. A village on the Ghazni river, near Spina Kala.

ALMERACH or NADIR SHAH KOT المرچ (نادر شاه کوت)
33-18 69-41 A. A village in Khost, said to be the second stage from Matun towards Ghazni, and distant from the former 11 km. The inhabitants are said to be Jajiraons, but who the latter are is not known. (Kennedy, from native information.) Some maps show the name Almera, which appears to be the present Nadir Shah Kot. (LWA)

ALOK الوك
35- 69-. A village in the upper Panjshir valley, situated on the left bank of stream, 6 miles below Bazarak. It has 15 houses of Tajiks. (Shahzada Taimus.)

*ALTAK التك
33-49 69-30 m. A village located on a tributary of the Gardez river, some 20 miles northeast of Ghazni.

ALTAMUR or ALTIMUR التمور
33-48 69-5 m. A village in the Logar valley. Lumsden says: "There is a cross-road from Hisarak to Kurram striking off in a southeast direction; passing through Altimur, crossing the watershed line of the Logar and Kurram rivers into the Zurmat valley, thence through the Mangal village of Kasur, two kos above the junction of the Hariob with the Kurram; but this route is reported difficult, and little frequented, owing to the predatory habits of the tribes through whose country it passes." (H.B. Lumsden, Thornton.)
In the Altimur group of villages there are some belonging to the Ahmadzai Sulaiman Khel. (McLean.)
There is room for a brigade to encamp near the village with a sufficient water-supply. Fuel and fodder are procurable. (I.B.C., Johnston.)

ALTAMUR or ALTIMUR التمور
33-45 69-10 A. Elev. 9,600 feet. A pass over the Machalgu hills leading from Zurmat into the Logar valley. It is crossed by a road which forms an important connection between the Kharlachi-Ghazni road, and the road from Kabul to Ghazni via the Logar valley. It is said to be never closed by snow. There is nothing to prevent field guns from reaching the summit of the pass from the Zurmat side, but the road on the Logar valley side is more difficult and would require a good deal of work. (I.B.C.)

The following is a report furnished by Captain Call, who accompanied a reconnaissance under Lieutenant-Colonel MacLean, 1st Punjab Cavalry, from the Logar valley to the summit of the pass in May 1880:
Altimur pass. I enclose an eye sketch of the approach taken with a clinometer and paced. Our movements were too hurried to admit of much accuracy or detail. On leaving the cultivation, which extends for a breadth of 3 or 4 miles along the Logar river, the road to the mouth of the Altimur pass lies over a gradually rising plateau, showing traces of extended cultivation under favourable conditions of rainfall, and scoured by the boulder and shingle beds of moutain torrents, which, however, nowhere appear to have excavated regular beds for themselves. This plain is everywhere practicable for troops as far as the mouth of the pass, where the nala banks become scarped and the fields begin to be laid out more in terraces. The road passes to the right of a ruined fort, where it is confined between dry stone walls and is very contracted in places. A working party should precede or accompany the guns for the last mile. There is no water between the Logar canal system and Altimur.
From Altimur to the foot of the pass, hard by the Saiyid village of Niasi, is some 5 miles. The road so far is passable for artillery with some petty repairs; but as the track follows the shingly bed of the river for more than half the distance, leavng it only to cross three low spurs to save detours, draught will be very heavy, although the gradients are not excessive.
As regards the pass itself, the total ascent in some 1,900 yards is about 800 feet, giving a gradient of 1 in 7. For the first 1,200 yards the road follows the nala bed, passing at 9 yards through a picturesque little nook called the ziarat, shaded by noble shisham trees of great age and watered by a trickling spring. In this length it is only necessary to clear a wheel track of stones and boulders.
Then the road zig-zags up the face of the hill to the left and passes through a cleft in the rock, which is partly filled with stones; another path encircles the rock, but neither are suitable for guns at present, and as the gradients are bad and the curves awkward, considerable work is required before horses in draught can surmount the ascent.
Although I was only able to make a very cursory examination of the ground, I believe the better plan will be to carry the road up the ravine for another 100 yards, at the expense of some blasting and filling, and then to regain the old track above the rocky promontory by a return, with a slope of 1 in 5, some 40 yards long. The only objection being that the narrowness of the nala will probably prevent the teams from getting round the corner, and it may be necessary to unhook and run the guns up by hand. In any case working parties with drag-ropes will be necessary for the remainder of the ascent.
For the next 400 yards the road is wonderfully good, 17 to 20 feet wide, sloping 1 in 5.5 to 1 in 7, and just rough enough to give foothold. There are two places in this length requiring improvement; a sidelong piece of ground at about 130 yards and a rocky corner at 240 yards.
The remaining 350 feet consist of a series of short zig-zags varying from 14 to 24 paces in length and 18 to 7 in width, ending in a narrow defile 100 feet long. The slope hardly exceeds 1 in 4.5.
It will be necessary to straighten the track as far as possible to allow of the horses working well together in making a final effort, and blasting will have to be resorted to, before the cutting through hard limestone, which forms the saddle, will be passable.

The summit once reached, all difficulty is at an end as far as could be seen. A broad rough track winds down a little ravine with a slope of 1 in 6 to 1 in 9 for 250 yards, passing a spring-head, and then debouches with a grade of 1 in 14 on to a little open plain, beyond which it was impossible to carry out the inspection.

Another pathway leads up the right side of the nala to join the old road just short of the top. This would not be of much service. Probably a portion at least of the baggage would march by Shawaz, to avoid the delay in passing the camels over in single file.

Supposing the pass to be occupied at daylight, guns might be taken over with some difficulty by the afternoon of the following day. Two companies of sappers being employed, one at the top of the pass, the other at the return half-way up, in addition to three companies of infantry working in two reliefs (equal to six companies). Much depends, however, on the progress made in blasting, and it would be safer to give two clear working days. The ground to the left of the pass is favourable to an attack, originating either up the valley to the left of the rocky gorge facing Niasi, or from the village of Shawaz. Guns posted on the Niasi slope would fire with good effect on the kotal with a range of two thousand yards, as well as on the last five hundred yards, of road.

There is abundance of water near the village at this time of the year; while the ground beyond the crest is suitable for small camp and favourable for an active defence. (Call.)

ALTAMUR Or ALTIMUR التمور
33-48 69-5 m. A village at the northern fort of the Altimur pass, 10 miles from its summit. There is room for a brigade to encamp here with sufficient water. This village appears to be identical with the one mentioned above. (I.B.C.)

*ALUCHAKHAN الوچه خان
35-20 69-9 m. A village on the Nawa Bala, tributary of the Koklan, northeast of the Salang pass.

ALUDINI علاءالدینی (؟)
A section of the Jaghatu Hazaras.

*ALU KHEL الو خیل
33-21 69-32. A village with an agricultural population of about 550 in Shamal district of Paktya province.

ALWA KOL الواکول
34- 67-. In the Yakh Walang district. It is one of the villages in the Sari-Kol glen above Firuzabad, and contains 10 families of Yaugur Hazaras. (A.B.C.) Recent maps show the place Alwaqol at 34-27 68-1 m. (LWA)

*AMAD KALAI امدکی
32-31 68-19 m. A small village on the Gwashta stream, northeast of Qadir Khuni in Ghazni province.

*AMANA امانه
32-29 68-16 m. A village located on a path from Gwashta to Monarai in the Katawaz area.

AMAN KHEL امان خیل
33- 68-. A village in Kharwar about 31 miles northeast of Ghazni. (I.B.C.) A village with this name is some 20 miles southwest of Sultan Khel, at 33-46 68-23 G. (LWA)

AMAR KHEL عمر (؟)
34-18 68-41 G. A Ghilzai village 6-1/2 northwest of Jalalabad, lying about 1 mile from the right bank of the Kabul river. There is said to be a powder-factory here. (Malleson, I.B.C.) Another place with this name is located at 33-41 68-52 G. (LWA)

AMARA KHEL امرا خیل
34- 70-. A village in Jalalabad, south of Balabagh. There are several topes here which Moorcroft examined. (Moorcroft.)

AMBAR KHANA امبار خانه
34-17 70-49 G. A collection of 3 Mohmand villages about 28 miles southeast of Jalalabad; it lies on the right bank of the Kabul river, at the junction with the latter of the Mohmand Dara. The villages contain some 300 families: headman (1904), Nur Muhammad. The inhabitants possess about 900 head of cattle, 1,500 sheep and goats, 20 horses, 50 buffaloes and 200 camels. All their flocks and herds are taken up to the Safed Koh in the hot weather. The annual production of wheat and barley averages about 3,000 Indian maunds. In winter Tarazi Kuchis with their camels settle here.
An alternative to part of the main road from Dakka to Jalalabad leaves the latter at Basawal and, keeping to the right bank of the river nearly the whole way, passes through Ambar Khana and regains the main road near Ali Boghan. This route is fit for camels and is much used by kafilas. There is also a new (1905) cross-road, fit for camels, which leaves the main road about 4-1/2 miles east of Basawal and leads direct to Ambar Khana. There is a force of 30 khasadars quartered in Ambar Khana. (Johnston, Malleson, Wanliss, I.B.C.)

AMBAR SAMUCH عبر سموج
34-48 67-35 m. A village in the Shahidan glen, in the district of Bamian. It contains 50 families of Yangur Hazaras. (A.B.C.) Recent maps show a place with this name in the Darwazan glen, further to the south. (LWA)

AMBO KHAK امبو خاک
34- 68-. A village in the Langar, or Khawat, valley, 5-1/2 miles west of Shaikhabad. Supplies are plentiful at all seasons and water is abundant. (I.B.C.)

*AMBORQUL امبر قول
34-6 67-18 m. A village on a stream which debouches on the Helmand near Sinjitak.

AMIN امین
A section of Muhammad Khwaja Hazaras.

AMIN-UD-DAULA KHAN KALA امین الدوله خان قلعه
One of the Rishkhor forts in the Chardeh valley of Kabul, containing 13 families of Tajiks. (I.B.C)

AMIR KALA امیر قلعه
31-46 66-46 G. A village at the southern mouth of the Tangi Wardak defiles, 59 miles from Kabul, 46 miles from Ghazni, situated on the left bank of the Logar river. It consists of three forts which, if held, would very well bar the road. There is some cultivation, but little camel-grass and fuel.
The Ghazni Field Force, marching from Kandahar, encamped here on the

30th April 1880. Sir Frederick Roberts also encamped here in August of the same year, when marching from Kabul on Kandahar.

There is no space for a regular camp of any size, and troops must pitch here and there as the ground serves. Provisions in any quantities can be procured from the Logar villages of Hisarak, Padkao, Kulangar, Baraki, Rajan, etc., but due warning must be given for their collection.

The inhabitants are a mixture of Tajiks, Cholozais, Wardaks, and Ahmadzais. From Amir Kala to Shaikhabad is about 15 miles, by the Adam Khan defile, but that route presents great difficulties for guns,--vide "Adam Khan." (Lumsden, I.B.C.)

*AMIR KHAN KALAI امیر خان کلی

32-16 68-55 m. A village on a tributary of the Gomal river, north of the Paryano Ghar.

*AMREY امری

34-45 70-51 m. A village on a tributary of the Kunar river, some 8 miles north of Khas Kunar.

AMRUTAK امروتك

35-1 66-28 m. A hamlet in Yakh Walang, situated on the left bank of the Rud-i-Band-i-Amir, between the villages of Marghi and Baharak. It contains 10 families of Hazaras. (A.B.C.)

AMZHI امژی (؟)

A village in Nuristan, situated in a gul which debouches into the Pech near the village of Tsaro. (Robertson.)

ANABA Or ANAWA انابا

35-14 69-22 m. A large village in the upper Panjshir glen, distant by road 61 miles from Kabul. It is situated on right bank of the stream and is inhabited by 150 Tajik families. (Shahzada Taimus.)

*ANARGAI انارگی

34-28 69-44 m. A village located about 10 miles south of Sarobi, on the way to Gandomak.

*ANDAI اندی

32-10 68-11 m. A village in the Wazakhwa area, one mile south of Marjana.

*ANDAR اندر

33-19 68-27. Andar is a woleswali in Ghazni province. The woleswali comprises an area of 828 square kilometers and has an agricultural population that has been estimated at from 21,941 to 26,331. The woleswali is bounded in the west by Qarabagh, in the south by Giru, in the southeast by Yusuf Khel, in the east by Sharan, in the northeast by Deh Yak, in the north by Ghazni, and in the northwest by Jaghatu. Andar has about 228 villages, 3 of which have more than 500 inhabitants. The major villages listed in the PG are as follows: Isperah Waghaz, Addin, Atalwal-i-Waghaz, Khar Khasha, Ahmadi Haraktu, Ibrahim Khel, Bar Buzuk, Baz Mohamad, Bakhtiyar, Badwan, Badri Waghaz, Barahu, Baryam, Basan, Jan Khan Waghaz, Jan Nur, Jamal, Jami, Char Dewar-i-Mulla Salim, Char Dewar Kabuli, Chaghari Waghaz, Chambar-i-Mawla Dad, Chehiltan, Hayat Khel, Khanan, Khederwal, Khado Khel-i-Sufla, Khani-i-Sufla and Ulya, Kharoti, Dadai, Duzdan, Dewi, Raz Beg, Rahim Khel-i-Chando, Rustam, Rashid Khel, Zarin, Zakori, Sar Bulagh-i-Chardah Waghaz, Sardar Khel, Sar Deh, Sarferaz, Sulaiman Khel, Sulaimanzai, Sanginak,

*ANIKHANKHEL انیخان خیل
   34-17 70-51 m. A village on the Kabul river, about 2 miles north of the Jalalabad - Torkham highway.

*ANJIRAK انجیرك
   34-37 69-7 m. A village northwest of Kabul, and east of the road to Charikar.

*ANJIRAN انجیران
   34-44 69-40 m. A village on the Tagab river, some 6 miles north of the Naghlu dam.

*AO Also see AB او (آب)

AO BAND او بند
   34-29 68-17 m. A low total crossed by the Kabul-Bamian road northwest of the Unai pass. The ascent commences soon after leaving the hamlet of Jaokul, the summit being reached at 3-3/4 miles from that place. The descent from the kotal is about half a mile in length and is easy.
   A dry nala is next crossed, and then there is a gentle rise of one furlong to the Sanginia Kotal. From this the road descends by an easy gradient for half a mile, when it enters a hollow.
   At 5-1/4 miles from Jaokul it enters a defile, about 10 yards wide. The road through it is rough and indifferent, and does not appear to be practicable for artillery.
   At 7-1/4 miles the road leaves the defile and shortly after crosses the Helmand. (A.B.C.)

AO BAZAK او بازك
   34- 68-. A village in the district of the lower Logar, west of that river in a valley towards Maidan. It consists of eight forts, or hamlets, and is inhabited by Sahak Ghilzais. In 1880 Ao Bazak contained 102 families. Water from a karez. (Euan Smith.)

*AODA اودا
   35-37 69-17 m. A village on the Arzo stream, near its confluence with the Andarab.

*AODAK اودك
   35-10 69-9 m. A village on a tributary of the Salang river, some 6 miles west of the Salang highway.

AO DAKAI اودكی
   33- 68-. A kotal leading over the hills south of Kharwar. It is an easy route for foot travellers, but is seldom used by mounted men or baggage animals, though passable for the latter with some trouble. The track ascends the hill southeast of Ispidar over an exceedingly steep gradient till near the first kotal over the ridge which divides Ispidar from Ergana. It then follows the curves of the spurs, and after passing over another low kotal descends into the upper part of the valley of the Ergana stream. The latter rises in a grassy basin-shaped trough, surrounded by high limestone cliffs and runs northwards through a narrow defile to Ergana.
   There are two paths from Ergana to the Ao Dakai Pass. One crosses the hills south of the village, and joining the route from Ispidar, passes into the upper part of the valley. The other is impassable for horses and ascends the stream via the defile. The basin-shaped valley of the upper Ergana is closed to southward by a rocky ridge, which forms the watershed. Over it lead two routes known as the Ao

Dakai passes. They are very rough on the southern sides. (Griesbach.)

AO DAKAI   اودکی
33-37 68-44 m. A kotal leading from Kharwar to Tera in Gardez. It lies just east of the Altimur pass, and is a very difficult path, only passable by men on foot. (Griesbach.) There is now a village in this area. (LWA)

AO DARA   اودره
34-55 68-1. The rocky gorge through which the Bamian river flows from Shikari to Doab-i-Mekhzari is called the Ao Dara. See "Surkhab." Recent maps show the name Dara Shikari in this area. Villages with this name are located at 33-42 67-48 and 35-10 67-29 G. (LWA)

AO DARA   اودره
34- 69-. A village 12 miles northeast of Kabul, on a feeder of the Panjshir river. It is inhabited by Jabar Khel Ghilzais. (Kennedy.) A village with this name is southwest of the Kuhi-i-Safi, at 34-42 69-19 m. (LWA)

AO DARA ZAGH   See KOH- I- BABA   اودره زاغ

AO DILLA   اودیله
34-25 68-5 G. A tributary of the Helmand, which, rising near the Aoband kotal in the Butland-i-Kash hills, flows northwards and joins the Helmand about 7 miles below Gardan Diwal.

AO GARDAN OR GHAO GARDAN   اوگردان
34-23 67-15 A. A kotal in the east of the Dai Zangi country, crossed by the main road leading from Kabul through the Hazarajat to Herat.

AO KHANA   اوخانه
33- 68-. A pass leading north from Kharwar to the Charkh river. It is a footpath oinly and forms a convenient short cut from Chala Khel. The path branches off the main road from Kharwar to Kharpachak, and ascends the low range which runs south from the Doshakh peak; after skirting the latter on its east side it descends by way of a steep ravine, which joins the Charkh river just below the defile. From that point it is an easy track to Kala-i-Bala, the first settlement of Charkh. (Griesbach.)

AO KOL Or ABQOL   او قول
34-52 67-16 m. A tagao in the Dai Zangi country. There is also a village with this name north of the Band-i-Amir. (LWA)

*AOLAD   اولاد
35-40 69-21 m. A village on the Andarab river, about 6 miles northeast of Banu.

*AONARAI   اونری
33-52 68-37 m. A village on the road from Ghazni to Kabul, about 30 miles northeast of Ghazni.

*AOPAR   اوپر
34-58 67-52 m. A village on a tributary of the Shikar Dara, north of Bamian.

AO PARAN اویران
34-12 69-14 m. A village in the lower Logar valley, east of the river Logar and close under the hills. It contains five forts or hamlets, and 30 families, its inhabitants being Ahmadzai Ghilzais. Water from a karez. (Euan Smith.)

AO SHAHAR-I-THIBA اوشهر (افشار)
34- 69-. A detached portion of the village of Thiba, lying between and latter and Khingot, in the Chardeh valley of Kabul. Inhabitants: Kizilbash. There are 11 forts in the place, viz:
1. Kala-i-Mirza Karb Ali
2. Kala-i-Dost Muhammad
3. Kala-i-Mirza Khan
4. Kala-i-Ghulam Riza
5. Kala-i-Mirza Baba Khan
6. Kala-i-Ghulam Haidar
7. Kala-i-Ghulam Ali
8. Kala-i-Karam Ali
9. Kala-i-Muhammad Hashim
10. Kala-i-Mulla Sultan Ali
11. Kala-i-Mirza Ahad
(I.B.C.)

AO SHAR See AFSHAR اوشار

AO TAKTAK اوتكتك (آب توگك)
34-20 67-12 G. A small village of about 10 houses on the left bank of the Siah Dara, about 11-1/2 miles east of Panjao. The valley is here about 50 yards wide and contains a little cultivation. (Wanliss.) Recent maps show the name Abtugak on the Darazqol, east of Panjao, at 34-23 67-13 m. (LWA)

AO ZANJAN اوزنجان
34-16 69-48 G. A valley between Aspando and Hisarak, west of Gandamak. It is inhabited by the Miran Khel, who are said to number 15,000 fighting-men! From where the waters of these valleys unite with the Ghaoghizah stream, is a distance of 3 miles to the fort at Hisarak, and the united waters fall into the Surkhab river. (Collett.) A village with this name is nearby, at 34-16 69-32 G. (LWA)

*APARAN ایران
32-29 67-36 m. A village located about halfway between the Ab-i-Istadah and the Tarnak river.

APSAI Or AFSAI آفسی
35-46 71-21 m. Elev. 7,230 feet. A fort village in the Katir division of the Bashgul valley situated on Left bank of stream and containing about 200 families. There is a small suburb on the right bank reached by a good bridge. Just inside the river entrance there is an underground passage which opens a few yards further on to the river bank. At this exposed end of the passage there is a rough covered way of planks enabling the villagers in war time to draw their water-supply from the river. Also see Afsai. (Barrow, Robertson.)

ARABS عرب
In the Jalalabad district there is a small colony of Arabs, who suppose they came to it with Timur Lang about four-and-a-half centuries ago. They speak no language but Persian, and apparently have lost all traces of their national character, save that they are courageous and somewhat given to namadic habits. They form the following clans:

        Bahloli   Shutari
        Kunram Khel   Deh-i-Nazar

        Wahteiti   Deh-i-Daulat
        Jamuli   Deh-i-Jani
        Zangui   Iraki

These chiefly reside in Besud and Kunar. The chief is of the Bahloli clan. This is a well-conducted industrious tribe, given to both pastoral and agricultural pursuits, and in the time of the monarchy furnished 100 horsemen. An ancestress of the chief of this tribe was married to Ahmad Shah Durani and was the mother of his son Timur Shah.

These Arabs have also colonized in Bajaur, Peshawar, and Paghman. (MacGregor.)

The following is Jenkyns' account of the Arabs in the Jalalabad district: "Taimur Lang introduced a colony of Arabs into Jalalabad. Similar colonies are to be found in Kabul and Turkistan. There are twelve divisions of them, viz:

1. Miran (in Kala-i-Fazil Beg)
2. Sarbadali (in Karez-i-Shukur Khan)
3. Zinjani (in Besud)
4. Zangoi (in Ghanchak and Bakhtan)
5. Iraki (in Kama)
6. Wilayati (in Wilayat)
7. Pashai (in Kama)
8. Baloi (in Kama)
9. Khuram Khel (in Nahr-i-Shahi)
10. Sikandari (not found in Jalalabad)
11. Zedaulat (in Karez-i-Kabir)
12. Zenazar (in Kabul)

"The Arabs do not give their daughters in marriage to men of other tribes. They are engaged in agrucultural and pastoral pursuits. They keep flocks of camels, sheep, etc., and are, generally, ready to undertake carrying work. They are all kuchis, that is during the hot weather they migrate to Kabul returning to Jalalabad in the winter. Their summer settlements are at Paghman and Besud near Kabul. They number about 1,500 families, in this district. They speak Persian, and have quite forgotten the language of Arabia. In former days the whole of Besud was in possession of this tribe."

The following is Jenkyns' list of the villages in the Jalalabad district, which are wholly or partly occupied by Arabs:

1. Johan-nama alias Kasa-i-Payan (including Kala-i-Ali-Khel, Kala-i-Babari, Kala-i-Arbabha, Kala-i-Fazil Beg)
2. Nahar-i-Shahi
3. Karez-i-Malik Lala
4. Imlak-i-Shahi-Paiwasta-i-Jalalabad
5. Gaomeshbela
6. Kala-i-Saiyid Ahmad
7. Wilayati
8. Ikhlasabad-i-Arabi
9. Zangoi
10. Besud
11. Mirikbela
12. Nurzai-o-Ushturi
13. Jamali-o-Sirbadali
14. Bilangar
15. Pirawar
16. Deh-i-Ghazi
17. Shergar
18. Landabuch and Jam Ali
19. Zarsha-i-Jalaluddin Khan
20. Zakhel-i-Zulfikar Khan
21. Kala-i-Shaikh

(Jenkyns.)

ARCHAGAON   ارچه گون
35-28 70-0. A pass leading into Nuristan from Deg-i-Parian at the head of the Panjshir valley. Archagaon is also the name of a fort in Nuristan having 18 towers. (Leech.)

ARDA ارده
33- 68-. A pass leading south from Kharwar to Shilghar and Ghazni. It is passable for horses and baggage, easy on the Kharwar side, a rapid descent on the other. (Griesbach.)

ARGHACH ارغچ
34-18 70-9 G. A Khugiani village containing about 200 houses about 5 miles southeast of Nimla. Water enough for two brigades. Fodder for about 6,000 animals for one day and about 1,000 maunds of unground grain can be obtained from Argach and neighbourhood. Fuel in large quantities is procurable from Kaja. (Johnston.)

ARGHANDEH ارغنده
34-29 68-54 m. Elev. 7,628 feet. A large village between Kabul and Maidan, 14 miles from the former and 10 from the latter. It consists of two portions, Arghandeh-i-Bala and Arghandeh-i-Pain, the latter lying to the north. It was a place of considerable importance during the British occupation of 1879-80, as it commands the road by which supplies are brought into the city of Kabul from the west and southwest.
The village lies about 2 1/2 miles north of the road, going from Kabul. There is plenty of space for camping ground to the east of the village, with abundant supplies and good water.
Here in 1839 Dost Muhammad abandoned his artillery, consisting of 28 guns, to the British advancing on Kabul.
According to Molloy, Arghandeh is inhabited by the Bazid Khel section of Ghilzais, with whom are intermingled a few Tajik families. There are about 1,500 families in all, and they pay R 5,000 in revenue. The present (1895) headman is Fazl-ud-din Khan. (Molloy, Masson, Hough, Havelock, Campbell, Kennedy, I.B.C.) Arghandeh Pain is located at 34-31 68-56 m. (LWA)

*ARGHU ارغو
33-25 69-45 m. A village on a small stream, northwest of Khost.

ARGU ارگو
35- 70-. Deh-i Argu is a village in the Parian valley, a tributary of the Panjshir, 9 1/2 miles above the junction, and 6 miles below the Archagaon pass into Nuristan. (Leech.)

ARIOH اریو
35-31 69-57 m. A tributary glen of the Parian or upper Panjshir. "From Chahar Deh of Parian there are tow roads into Nuristan the Wariaj and Arioh. Both go up glens of those names and descend by other glens having the same names. The Arioh is the best. Horses have been taken over it. The Wariaj path is used by salt traders. Those from the Panjshir side take the salt half way to the kotal (about 5 miles?), and are there met by the Kafirs who barter for it. The Wariaj is said to be very similar to the Chamar road. The kotal is on the Koh-i-Surkhshal which has a high peak. The peak northeast of the Kotal is Mir Ismail. The Arioh Kotal is southwest of the Surkhshal peak. Wakhe Peak is on the other side of it.
The distance from the Wariaj Kotal to the first settlement of Kafirs is said to be the same as the corresponding distance on the Chamar road, that is, about 14 miles. The first village is Lina, then Purang. The two contain 250 houses of Koreshi Kafirs (so called from the name of the place, which was once inhabited by Koreshi Arabs). There is cultivation, and also orchards. The glen is 200 yards wide, with a narrow bottom and sloping sides. There is a place lower down called Dasht-i-Ayar, where troops might encamp. Below this the glen

becomes a defile called Mukhim Kadao. Lower still is another, Lina, with steep high hills on both sides.
The Arioh road is said to be the best of the three from Parian, and laden yabus can be got over it, though with difficulty. It resembles the others more or less. Some 5 or 6 miles up the western Arioh glen was formerly a village called Arioh, but having been constantly attacked by the Kafirs, it has been abandoned. The Arioh Kotal is said to be 15 miles from Chahar Deh, and the first Kafir village is the same distance beyond. It is now deserted like Arioh; and for a like reason, because it is too exposed to the attacks of the Panjshiris." (Shalzada Taimus.)

ARODA   اروده
34- 70-. A village in the Alishang valley, left bank of that river, 58 miles from Jalalabad on road to Farajghan, from which it is 65 miles south. It has 70 houses of Safis. (Leech.)

AROKI   اروکی
A tribe mentioned by Masson as inhabiting the valley of Alingar. He gives no information regarding them beyond their name. (Masson.) A village with this name is about 4 miles south of Jabal Saraj in Parwan province, at 35-6 69-16 G. (LWA)

ARSALA KHAN KALA   ارسلاخان قلعه
34- 69-. A fort in the Charasia township of Kabul. There are in the place 20 families of Jabar Khel Ghilzais. The fort stands on a ridge between Kala-i-Fathu and Rishkhor. It belonged to the Jabar Khel chief, Mazulla Khan. (I.B.C.) One place with this name is near Bawali, Surkhrud, at 34-24 70-15 G. (LWA)

ARU   ارو
35-23 69-36 G. A village in the upper Panjshir, about 6 1/2 miles above Bazarak. Fifteen houses of Khawanin Zadagan Tajiks, relatives of the Khans of Panjshir. (Shahzada Taimus.)

ARUKI   اروکی
34-59 69-23 m. A village in Charikar, situated some 12 miles below Anaba, on both banks of the Panjshir river. One hundred houses of Ghilzais. (Shahzada Taimus.)

ARZANI   ارزانی (ارزانیان)
35-16 69-13 M. A village south of the Bajgah pass, 9 miles above Nowach; close by is the village of Wawak. (I.B.C.)

ARZBEGI   عرض بیگی
33- 68-. A walled village, about 60 miles southeast of Ghazni. (Campbell.)

ARZBEGI   عرض بیگی
32- 67-. A village near Aghao Jan, on the road from Ghazni to Kalat-i-Ghilzai. There is a karez here, the water of which though not bad, has a slightly insipid flavour, as if it held in solution a small quantity of nitre. (Bellew.) A village with this name is located at 32-40 68-32 G. (LWA)

ARZIA See ZURIA   ارزیه

*ARZIGAI   ارزیکی (ارزل)
35-10 71-30 m. A village on the Kunar river, about 3 miles southwest of Narai in Kunar province.

ARZU   آرزو کوتل

35-26 69-17. A pass leading over the Hindu Kush from the Panjshir valley to Banu in Andarab--See "Khwaja Deh." It is the shortest possible line for travellers from Kabul to Khanabad and Kunduz but it is too difficult to be made much use of. The road is bad, and the pass is said to be very high, though lightly laden camels of the country can get over it.

The descent north is by the narrow Arzu glen, which joins the Andarab valley just above Banu. Its stream is crossed by a rickety wooden bridge on the road up the Andarab. Banu is 16 miles from the kotal. The village of Arzu, about a mile above the mouth of the glen, contains 10 families of Kohzi Hazaras. There is no information on record regarding the closing of this road in winter, but as it is said to be the highest of all the passes, it is almost certainly impassable at an earlier date than the others, and also opened later. (A.B.C.) A village near this pass is about 4 miles south of Banu, at 35-36 69-16 m. (LWA)

ARZU (OR URZU)   ارزو

33-28 68-29 m. A small village 6 miles southeast of Ghazni and 1/2 mile north of Shalez. Inhabitants: Tajiks. for details of the action fought by Brigadier-General Palliser between Aruz and Shalez on 23 April 1880, see "Official History of the Second Afghan War." (I.B.C.)

*ASADABAD   اسد آباد

34-52 71-8. Asadabad is the administrative center of Kunar and a woleswali in the Nangarhar province. The woleswali comprises an area of 480 square kilometers and has an agricultural population that has been estimated at from 9,102 to 12,010. The woleswali is bounded in the west and north by Pich, in the northeast and east by Bar Kunar and the State of Pakistan, and in the south by Sirkai and Narang. The woleswali has about 30 villages, 10 of which have more than 500 inhabitants. The villages are listed in the PG as follows: Dam Kalai, Dosha Khel, Yargul, Karala (Kerhala), Tesha, Nauabad, Danduna, Bacha Kalai (Licha Kalai), Wata Pur, Shingam, Lodam, Karmol, Dagi-i-Karmol, Qamchi, Saparai (Sapari), Katar Qala, Qaru or Qaraw, Karung, Dehwaz-i-Jadid, Gambir-i-Jadid, Gambir-i-Afghan, Katar-i-Afghan, Qatar-i-Jadid (Qatar Qala), Sangar (Shangar), Dehwaz-i-Kuhna, Tus Qala, Hazar Bagh, Maidan-i-Nankata, and Zirani.

*ASAR   اسر

33-23 69-50 m. A hamlet in the hills northwest of Khost.

*ASGHARI   اصغری

32-33 67-28 m. A village on the Tarnak river, northeast of Shahjui.

*ASHAK   اشک

32-16 68-10 m. A hamlet northwest of Marjana in Wazikhwa district of Ghazni province.

ASHKUN   اشکون

An important Kafir tribe. - See "Nuristan." Their country is said to be surrounded by thick forest, practically inpenetrable, and is defended by a very brave people, particularly well armed with matchlocks, who are at war with all the other Kafir tribes, with the possible exception of the Wai. The Pech river is joined by the two Ashkun streams, the upper falling into the Kti river, the lower, which drains the Ashkun valley inhabited by "Shaikhs," joining the

Pech direct. (Robertson.)
There is also a mountain with this name north of Pesh Darrah in Kunar province, at 37-7 70-40 G. (LWA)

ASHLAN Or USHLAN اشلان
32-46 68-9 m. A village on the left bank of the Ghazni river about 20 miles north of the Ab-i-Istada lake. There are two forts here and 20 families of Ghilzais. The Ghazni river flows sluggishly between steep banks, and the country round is completely devoid of brushwood and impregnated with salt. No supplies are obtainable. (Broadfoot.)

*ASHPI اشپی
35-18 71-22 m. A village on the Loy Khwar stream which debouches on the Kunar river near Nishagam.

ASHUK SALI عشق سالی
34- 69-. A pass between the Lakarai and Aspando Kats, 9 1/2 miles from the former and 2 1/2 from the latter. Ascent and descent similar to those of the Paiwar Kotal. (Gordon.)

ASHUR اشور (عاشور ؟)
34- 69-. A small village 4 miles northwest of Kabul, near Deh-i-Kipak. It stands on the western shore of the Wazirabad lake. The inhabitants are Hazaras. (Kennedy.)

ASLAM KALA اسلام قلعه
34- 68-. A village on the main Kabul-Herat road about 9 miles east of the Unai pass and close to another village called Daulat Muhammad Kala. The two together contain about 140 families of Timuris and Tajiks. The inhabitants possess about 200 head of cattle and 200 goats. The annual production of wheat and barley averages about 2,000 Indian maunds. (Wanliss.)

ASMAI آسمائی
34- 69-. Elev. 6,790. A hill forming the northern barrier of the Kabul gorge, and dominating from the west Deh-i-Afghan, the northern suburb of Kabul. Its distance from Sherpur is about 3,000 yards. This hill was the scene of hard fighting on the 14th December 1879. For details see "Official History of the Second Afghan War."

ASMAR اسمار
35-2 71-22 m. A fort, village, and cantonments on the left bank of the Kunar river, distant 77 miles from Jalalabad. At 8 miles from Sihgal on the right bank of the river, the Asmar bridge is reached: a wooden cantilever bridge of about 90 feet span, with small loop-holed block-houses about 15 feet square, guarding it at either end. The roadway 7 feet wide with low (18 inches) wooden railings. In April 1895, the roadway was about 12 feet above the water. The abutments are of dry stone masonry bonded with wooden beams, and as already mentioned, are surmounted by small masonry rooms which serve the double purpose of defence and counterweights to keep the shore ends of the road-bearers in position. Horses have to be led across as the bridge sways a good deal in the centre. Laden mules would have to be unloaded before crossing, as their loads would be certain to catch in the doorways of the blockhouses. On the right bank, just above the bridge and close to the camping ground, which is of rather limited area, is a very dilapidated fortified sarai with loop-hooled towers and gate-way. Except near Shigal and at Asmar there is no cultivation on this march. The valley between

Shigal and Asmar is rather narrow -- about 250 or 300 yards, as a rule, from hillside to hillside. the river flows in a series of S-curves, giving a little fairly level ground alternately on the east and west sides in the bends of the curve.

Half a mile below the bridge there is an outpost on a spur, the road on either slope here being very steep and the zig-zags badly laid out. The shale of which the spur is formed is soft and friable, and a new line could be laid out without much difficulty. From the road at this spur a good view of the Asmar or Karkot Dara, the stream of which separates the cantonments on the south side from the village and fort of the old Khans of Asmar on the north bank. The garrison of Asmar consist of a squadron of cavalry, 3 battalions of infantry, mountain, and 3 machine, guns and 200 Khasadars. The infantry are said to furnish the detachment of 2 companies at the Mirzakai Kotal A small wooden bridge connects the cantonments with the old village, which contains from 150 or 200 houses and is commanded by the fort, a strong place of its kind, about 60 yards square with walls about 20 feet high and towers at two of the angles to provide flank defence. The fort is bisected diagonally by a high traverse wall 18 or 20 feet high. Owing to this traverse, in spite of the fact that the site is commanded nearly all round at ranges varying from 200 to 500 yards, the terrain of the fort is well defiladed. There is aparently no well within the fort itself, but the Asmar stream flows within 12 or 13 paces of its south face, and a portion of the bank is within the outer enclosure wall. Below the fort inside the outer enclosure is a lemon garden. From Asmar there is a fairly good road into upper Bajaur and Dir up the Asmar Dara and over the Binshi pass (9,000 feet) to Janbatai. This road is not as a rule practicable for a couple of months in winter. Another road from Dangam in the Asmar Dara leads over the Trepaman pass (about 10,000 feet) into the Salarzai country.

At the present time Asmar is understood to form a subdivision of the Kunar district -- see "Kunar;" but previous to 1891 it enjoyed a more or less independent position under a chief of its own, its territories extending up the main valley from a point near Chigha Sarai to the vicinity of the north of the Bashgul. Hazrat Ali was chief of Asmar at the time of McNair's visit in 1833, and was killed in 1886 by the acidental discharge of his gun; he was succeeded in the chiefship by his son Tahmasp Khan. The latter was murdered by his Kafir servant in 1890, whereupon several parties, including Umar Khan and Safdar Khan, immediately tried to gain possession of the vacant Khanship. In the spring of 1891 Tahmasp Khan's infant son was expelled from the country by Umra Khan, and the latter appointed Ghulam Khan, the late chief's half-brother, Khan in his stead. These events were followed early in 1892 by the despatch towards Asmar of a large Afghan force under Ghulam Haidar Khan, and on the 18th of March that place was occupied by the Afghan Troops, Umar Khan's nominee fleeing towards Chitral. This change in the aspect of affairs was the cause of much corresponcence between the Government of India, the Amir, and Umra Khan, but by the Kabul Agreement, 1893, the Amir was allowed to retain possession of Asmar -- much to Umra Khan's disappointment and annoyance.

McNair estimated the population of the district at 5,000 Tarkalanis. Rice, wheat, barley, and maize are the principal products of the soil, and suffice for the wants of the population. Iron, butter, skin, wool, timber, walnuts, and honey form the chief exports, while manufactured fabrics, indigo and salt are imported. (McNair, Coldstream, I.B.C.)

ASMATULLAH KHAN عصمت الله خان
34- 70-. A village 13 miles northwest from Jalalabad by the Darunta pass, on the right bnak of the Kabul river. There is only a narrow strip of cultivation round the fort, extending between the road and the river. From Kala Asmatulla Khan to Khairo Khel is about 10 miles up-stream. -(Holdich, Thompson.)

ASPAN اسپن
34-19 69-55. A subdivision of the Khugiani section of the Jalalabad district. It is situated on the right bank of the Surkhab river, to the east of Hisarak and west of Gandamak. Inhabitants: Khugianis. (Jenkyns.)

ASPAN Or ASHPAN اسپن
34-19 69-55 m. The principal place in the Aspan division of the Khugiani section of the Jalalabad district. It stands about 21 miles to the south of Surkhpul. The inhabitants are Sherzad Khugianis. Fodder for 8,000 animals for one day and about 600 maunds of unground grain and a fairly large quantity of ghi may be collected in the village and neighbourhood. Fuel and grazing are plentiful and there is good ground for encampment. Here in 1801 Shah Shuja received a severe defeat from Shah Mahmud, and was obliged to flee from the kingdom. (Thorton, Jenkyns, Johnston.)

ASPANDO KATS اسپندو کچ
34-13 69-43 A. A village between the Lakarai Kotal and Hisarak, about 13 miles from the former and the same distance from the latter. It stands about 2 1/2 miles distance from the top of the Hazro Kotal on the Hisarak side. It is 31 miles from Ali Khel and contains 10 houses. Inhabitants. Akbar Khel Ghilzais. Camping ground with water and wood. The village is in Azru district. (Gordon.)

ASTANA آستانه
35-21 69-34 m. A village in the upper Panjshir valley, containing 80 houses of Tajiks. (Shahzada Taimus.) The village is about 10 miles of Rakha on the Panjshir river. (LWA)

ASTANAZAI آستانزی
A section of the Ghilzais.

ATA اته
A Subsection of the Besuds.

ATA اته
A section of the Jaghuri Hazaras.

ATAK OR HOTAK هوتک
33-1 67-59 m. A large fortified village in Jamrud, 46 miles south-southwest of Ghazni, and 25 miles northwest of lake Ab-i-Istada. Supplies are not very abundant. Water from an irrigation channel. Atak and the hamlets belonging to it are inhabited by Popalzai Duranis. (Campbell, I.B.C.)

ATAMBUR اتمبور
An alternative name for the Altimur Kotal.

*ATAM KHEL آتم خیل
32-16 68-24 m. A village on the Baghlang Mandah, north of Wazakhwa and southeast of Janikhel.

ATASHER اته شیر
35- 69-. A wide ravine which joins the Kaoshan glen from the west at about 8 miles south of the Kaoshan pass. Its mouth is passed on the road leading from Ghorband, by Sherakai and the Kaoshan pass into Khinjan at about 4 miles north of Sherakai. (Maitland.)

ATLAK اتلك (؟)
33- 68-. A village 28 miles northeast of Ghazni. (Thorton.)

*AURAGA اورگا
34-16 67-10 m. A village located on a tributary of the Helmand in Bamian province.

AUZANGIANI اوزنجانی
Probably the same as Ao Zanjan.

*AWAK اوك
34-14 67-10 m. A village located on a tributary of the Helmand in Bamian province.

AZARAI ازری
34- 69-. A valley running in a northern direction from the Sulaiman range towards the Hisarak villages. At its head is the pass of the same name. (Stewart.)

AZHARBAI See DUNGUL اژربای

AZHDA اژده
A rock in the valley of the head waters of the Logar river, Hazarjat.

AZHDAR OR HASHTDAR اژدهار
Elev. about 10,250 feet. A village with this name is located on a tributary of the Dara-i-Julga, at 34-9 67-50 m. (LWA)

AZIZ عزیز
A subdivision of the Daya Faulada.

*AZRO ازرو
34-9 69-38 m. Azro is the name of a woleswali in the Logar province. The woleswali comprises and area of 770 square kilometers and has an agricultural population which has been variously estimated at from 8,630 to 9,510. The woleswali is bounded in the southwest by Khoshi, in the northwest by Mohamamad Agha, in the north by Hesarak, in the east by Shirzad, and in the south by Jaji. Azro has some 32 villages, of which about four have more than 500 inhabitants. The villages are listed in the PG as follows: Gumran, Torah Pana, Qassem Khel, Zaman Khel, Abdul Rahman Khel, Albak Khel, Qarya-i-Babar, Salim Khel, Qarya-i-Akbar Khel, Gandaw, Kharoti, Amrut, Qarya-i-Jani Khel, Tang, Nughlak, Mangal, Arab Khel, Paja Larah, Fateh Khel, Shahin, Osman Khel, Baghak, Musa Khan, Chotra-i-Sufla, Chotra-i- Ulya, Mullayan, Allahdin, Ispando Kats, Kats Wal, Serkai, Reza Khel, and Qarya-i-Zarand.

BABA بابه
A section of the Jaghuri Hazaras paying revenue to Ghazni.

BABAKA بابکه
A subsection of the Besuds.

BABAKAR   بابکر
   35-7 68-18 m. A village located some 30 miles south of Ghazni.

BABAKAR KHEL KALA   بابکر خیل قلعه
   32- 68-. A halting-place on the Gumal route to Ghazni, 64 miles
   above Domandi. There is a fort here which is garrisoned by a small
   guard of khasadars while the Powindah kafilas are moving up and down
   in spring and autumn; at other times the place is uninhabited.
   Camping-grounds for at least two brigades, and possibly more, could
   be found along the bed of the Gumal, above the site of an old tower.
   Above the camping-ground is a graveyard overlooking which is another
   old tower on the spur of a hill. The camping-ground is surrounded
   by hills on all sides, the highest being on the south and west.
   Camel-grazing abundant; water plentiful and good. The main stream
   of the Gumal rises here, several springs uniting close to the fort.
   This place was formerly known as Kala Kharoti. (I.B.C.) A place
   called Babu Khel is in this area, about 16 miles southeast of Mir
   Rasul Khan, Katawaz, at 32-37 68-52 m. (LWA)

BABA KHEL   بابه خیل
   35-48 69-51 m. A village east of Charikar, which, together with
   Mian Shakh, contains 300 Tajik houses. (Shahzada Taimus.) A place
   called Deh-i-Babi is located at 35-1 69-18 m. (LWA)

BABA KUSH KAR Or BABA QASHKHAR   بابه قشقار (قشخار)
   34-40 69-21 m. A large village in the Koh Daman, Lying to the
   north of Sherpur, from which it is distant, by Khwaja Chasht and the
   Zimma pass, about 32 miles; by the Khirskhana pass and Kala-i-Murad
   Beg, about 22 miles.
   The village stands in the midst of thick plantations, most of it on
   the right bank of the Shakardara stream, but a portion of it on the
   left. The inhabitants are Tajiks, Saiyids, Utkhel (Only 10 houses of
   this tribe); and Hindus (50 houses).
   Maitland's diary of October 1886, contains the following: "At 14
   1/4 miles, (from Ziarat-i-Shahid), Baba Kushkar, the fort of Mir
   Bacha, destroyed by a detachment from Sherpur in the last week of
   1879. It did not strike me as looking very much the worse. I
   believe the interior was burnt, but no particular damage done to the
   walls. We passed along one side of it. Road confined, and continued
   to be more or less a narrow lane to 15 miles, when the Baba Kushkar
   Nala was crossed just above its junction with another, which I was
   told was the Siah Ab." (I.B.C., A.B.C.)

BABALI   بابه علی
   Another name for the Khatai Hazaras. See "Bamian."

*BABALI   بابه علی
   35-16 69-41 m. A village and a pass in Parwan, about 20 miles
   northeast of Rakha, Panjshir. Another village with this name is
   east of Charikar, at 35-3 69-20 m.

BABAR   ببر
   34-10 69-38 m. A village of Babar Ghilzais between the Shutur
   Gardan pass and Kushi, about 8 miles from the former. It lies in a
   small plain, about a mile in width, which is used as an encamping
   ground by caravans, and there is room to encamp two or three regiments. The adjacent hills are open and easy of access, but there
   is no grazing for camels. Water and a few supplies are procurable.
   (Hamilton.)

BABAR بابر
A section of the Shaikh Ali Hazaras.

BABAR BADSHAH بابر بادشاه
34- 69-. The tomb of the King Babar, near Kabul. The tomb of the great monarch is accompanied by many monuments of similar nature commemorative of relatives, and they are surrounded by an enclosure of white marble, curiously and elegantly carved. A few 'arghawan' trees, in the early spring putting forth their splendid red blossoms, flourish as it were, negligently aout the structure. Behind, or west of the tombs, is a handsome masjid; also marble, over which is along Persian inscription, recording the cause and date of its erection. The latter was subsequent to the decease of Babar. Again, behind the mosque, is the large and venerable grove which constitutes the glory of the locality. The ground is laid out in a succession of terraces, elevated the one above the other, and conconnected in the centre by flights of ascending steps. At each flight of steps is a plot of plane-trees, and to the left of the superior flight is a very magnificent group of the same trees, surrounding as they overshadow, a tank or reservoir of water. The principal road leads from west to east, up the steps, and had formerly on either side lines of cypress trees, and a few of which only remain. Canals of water , derived from the upper tank, were conducted parallel to the course of the road, the water falling in cascades over the descents of the several terraces. This tank is filled by a canal, noted by Babar himself.
"Its situation is likewise admirable, being without the city, yet conveniently near. Parties from the western portion of the city pass through the Deh Mazang gorge to it. From the eastern portion and the Bala Hisar, it may more speedily reached by crossing the Sher Darwaza hill." In 1879 the tomb was found by the British in a state of great dilapidation. -(Masson, I.B.C.)

*BABASAN باباسان
33-43 68-13 m. A village on the Dara-i-Yusuf, southwest of Wardak.

BABRAK KALA ببرك قلعه
33- 69-. A village in Khost, on the left bank of the Shamil river, about 24 miles west of Matun. (I.B.C.) Recent maps show the name Barak Kalai in Shawak alaqadari, at 33-24 69-23 m. (LWA)

BABU KHEL بابوخیل
A subdivision of the Chakmanis. A village with this name is about 8 miles southwest of Jani Khel, in Katawaz, Ghazni, at 32-43 68-20 G. Other places with this name are located at 32-37 68-52 m. and 32-47 68-58 m. (LWA)

BABULI (not BABALI) بابلی
A subdivision of the Daikhitai Hazaras. It is stated by some that they are not Uruzgani but Daikundi. A village with this name is on the Darazqul stream, near Panjao, at 34-22 67-5 m.

*BABUR بابر
34-42 70-57 M. A village on the Kunar river, about 2 miles northeast of Chawkai. Also a village of the Dara-i-Yusuf, west of Ghazni and one mile south of Gholi Talab, at 33-35 68-2 m.

*BABURDISH بابردیش
35-28 71-32 m. A village on the Majam stream, a tributary of the Kunar, north of Barikot.

BABUS بابوس
35- 69-. A small kotal crossed by the road between Dasht-i-Rewat and the Khawak pass. (I.B.C.)

BABUS بابوس
34-4 68-59 m. A village in the Logar valley, 12 miles southwest of Zargan Shahar. It is inhabited by Painda Khel Ghilzais, and contains two forts. In 1880 the population amounted to 120 families. From Babus to Shaikhabad by the Adam pass is 21 miles. (Clifford, Euan Smith, Hervey.) Recent maps show another Babus nearby, at 34-5 69-1 m. (LWA)

BACHA GHULAM بچه غلام
A section of the Dai Zangi Hazaras, inhabiting the valleys of Sar-i-Jangal, Lal, Kirman, Talkhak, Aghazirat, Tarbulak, Takht and Waras. (Peart.)

BACHA SHADI بچه شادی
A section of Hazaras living in the Turkoman Dara. (Peacocke.)

*BADAI بدی
33-31 70-1 m. A village located near Bak in Paktia province.

*BADAL KALAI بدل کی
33-26 69-48 m. A village some ten miles northwest of Khost.

BADAM ALI بادام علی
34-58 69-23 m. A village in the upper Panjshir glen, containing 30 houses of Ghilzais. It is situated just below Aruki. (Shahzada Taimus.)

*BADAMQUL بادام قول
34-28 68-52 m. A village near Arghandai, about 3 miles from the road from Ghazni to Kabul.

BADAMUK بادامك
35-38 71-20 m. Elev. 6,140 feet. A Katir village of 120 houses on the right bank of the Bashgul river, 3 miles south of Bragamatal (Lutdeh.). It is built in the oblong fort shape against a rocky slope, on a shoulder of which there is a tower. Below that, there are two or three other towers over four stories high. The houses are all two or three stories high, and so built as to form a continuous wall 15 or 20 feet high. (Robertson.)

*BADAR بدر
33-1 67-57 m. A village on the highway from Ghazni to Kabul.

*BADARKHEL بدر خیل
34-11 70-21 m. A village on a tributary of the Kabul river, about 15 miles south of Jalalabad.

BADASIA باداسیا
A fan-shaped plain in the Besud Hazara country. (Wanliss, Dobbs.) One village with this name is about 7 mmiles southwest of Aodala, Behsud, Dai Zangi, at 34-22 68-34 G. (LWA)

BADAWAN بادوان
Another name for Ahmad Diwana. A village called Badwan is located some 10 miles south of Ghazni, at 33-23 68-29 m. (LWA)

BADIABAD   بدی آباد
34-44   70-16 G.   A village in the Laghman district, on the right bank of the Alingar river, about 10 miles above the junction of that river with the Alishang. It consists of the following hamlets:

1. Deh-i-Mulla Nazar   3. Banda-i-Mian Sahib
2. Banda-i-Aba Khel   4. Kala-i-Muhammad Ali
             5. Kala-i-Niaz Muhammad

The inhabitants are Arokis.
Lady Sale says it is situated almost at the top of the valley, and close to the first range of hills towards Nuristan. It is square, each face about 80 yards long, with walls 25 feet high, and a flanking tower in each corner. It is further defended by a fausse braie and deep ditch all round, the front gate being on the southwest face, and the posterior on the northeast, each defended by a tower of bastion. The walls of mud are not very thick and are built up with planks in tiers on the inside. In the centre is a large square space, where is built, surrounded by a high wall, a house, each wing of which contains three apartments 8 feet from the ground. There is no supply of water in the fort, but a small river runs past it at the distance of 1/2 mile on the southeast side, and a little stream or canal about 100 yards outside the walls. It was here that Muhammad Akbar confined the British captives who had been surrendered during the retreat to Jalalabad of the Kabul garrison; they were 119 women, 37 men, and 15 children, and were kept here from 17th January to 10th April 1842, being fairly treated. (Eyre, Sale, Warburton.)

BADPAKHT Or BADPASH   بادپښ
34-38   69-50 A.   A range of hills on the western limits of Laghman. They are an offshoot of the great Chardi range. (Holdich.)
The road to the Badpakht pass branches off due west shortly after leaving Mandrawar; it is very good as far as the foot of the kotal, and practicable for all arms except wheeled artilery. The kotal itself is fit for pack animals, and is constantly traversed by kafilas from Nijrao to Jalalabad. The descent west is to Nagulu on the Kabul river. From Mandrawar to Nagulu the distance is 31 miles. (I.B.C.) There is a pass with this name east of Sarobi. (LWA)

BADPASH   بادپښ
34-38   69-53 m.   A spot in the Jalalabad district, on the road between Bairik and Laghman, remarkable for the strength of the wind which always blows there. On one occasion it is said that Muhammad Akbar passing this place with his troops was caught in a tempest, and they were nearly all blown away. Some perished with their horses. This spot is also called Shaitan Gum. Vide "Badpakht." (Masson.) Recent maps show the name Badpash Kuza Kalam. West of it is Gharbi Badpash, at 34-38 69-50 m.   (LWA)

*BADQOL   باد قول
34-10   68-36 m.   A village located on the stream of the same name, northwest of the Ghazni-Kabul road.

*BADRAZAR   بدرازار
33-13   67-21 m.   A village on a tributary of the Arghandab, northwest of Jaghuri.

BADSHAHI KALA   بادشاهی قلعه
34-   69-.   A fort in the Aspan subdivision of the Jalalabad dis-

trict, about 6 miles west of Gandamak, on the road to Aspan village. The road skirts the southwestern bastion of the fort. (McNair.) One place with this name is 2 miles northeast of Shiwa, Kunar, at 34-36 70-37 G. (LWA)

*BADURZAI باد ورزائی
33-2 67-33 m. A village located on a tributary of the Arghandab, southeast of Jaghuri.

BAGALAK KALA بگلک قلعه
A ruined village in the Siah Dara valley, on the main Kabul-Hazarajat-Daulat Yar road.

BAGALGROM بگلگرام
35- 71-. A Madugal village in Nuristan, consisting of 150 houses and situated on right bank of the Bashgul river. It is the headquarters of the Madugal or Muman tribe, and has cultivation on both banks of the stream. (Robertson.)

*BAGH باغ
35-1 70-50 m. A village located on a pass between the Pich and Waigal rivers, some 6 miles northwest of Nangalam. Other places with this name are located on a mountain, some 5 miles east of the Kunar river, at 34-40 71-2 m., and some 15 miles south of Kabul and east of the Logar, at 34-18 69-16 m.

BAGHAK باغک
35-11 67-58 m. A village in Bamian, situated in the Ao Dara, 6 miles above Doab-i-Mekhzari. The inhabitants are Tajiks, who cultivate the Kaftar Khana and Upper Zarsang valleys. When Peacocke visited it in 1886, however, they had emigrated to the Dara Yusuf on account of the locusts. (Peacocke.) Other places with this name are located at 34-17 68-5 m., 34-8 68-36 m., 33-54 68-36 m., and 33-51 68-33 G. (LWA)

BAGHALAK بغلک
34-47 66-53 m. A rocky glen which joins the main valley of Yak Walang from the north, 3 miles above Deh Surkh. A well-marked road leads up to the Baghalak village, which is said to be distant about 6 miles from the mouth. About 8 miles above the village, at the head of the glen is the Baghalak Kotal. The road leads over this and thence by Sukaluk to Walishan. From Baghalak village to Sukaluk is about 16 miles, thence to Walishan about 33 or 34 miles. (Maitland.)

BAGHAL-I-AFGHANI بغل افغانی
34- 70-. A village in the Surkhab division of the Jalalabad district. Inhabitants Ghilzais. (Jenkyns.)

BAGHARAK باغرک
34- 69-. A village in the Koh Daman between Karabagh and Ak Sarai (or Agha Sarai) on the right bank of the Kahdara stream. There are some 70 or 80 houses of Tajiks in the place. (I.B.C.) A mountain with this name is located southwest of Jaldak, Qalat, at 31-34 66-23 G. (LWA)

BAGHAR DARA بغار دره
34-30 68-25. A tributary of the upper Kabul river which, rising near the Baghar Kotal north of the Unai pass, flows in a southeastter-ly direction and joins the Kabul river at Sar-i-Chashma. (Wanliss.)

BAGHAR DARA بغار دره
A small tributary of the Helmand river.

BAGHAR KOTAL بغار کوتل
34-29 68-23 G. Elev. about 11,000 feet. A pass over the Sanglakh range about 4 miles north of the Unai pass. It is crossed by a road which leaves the main Kabul-Herat road at Sar-i-Chashma and, following the Baghar Dara up to the crest, descends on the western side by the Rama Tala tagao to its junction with the Helmand. From this point, Jaokul, where the main road is rejoined, is distant about 5 miles. This road affords a means of completely turning the Unai pass position, but in its present (1906) condition is difficult in several places for mounted men. It could, however, easily be made fit even for wheeled artillery. (Wanliss.) The pass is about 13 miles east of the Gardan Dival in Behsud. (LWA)

BAGHATAK باغتك
A name sometimes applied to the Siah Koh range.

*BAGHDARA باغ دره
34-54 69-31 m. A village on a hill, overlooking the Panjshir river, southwest of Nejrab.

BAGH-I-ALAM باغ عالم
34- 69-. A village in Kohistan, in the township of Khawaja Khidr, 28 miles from Kabul and 95 from Farajghan. Inhabitants Tajiks and Musazai Afghans. In 1882 there were said to be 9 forts and 400 houses. There are also said to be 20 Hindu families resident at Bagh-i-Alam. (Leech, I.B.C.) There is also a dasht with this name, north of Qarabagh, Parwan, at 34-52 69-9 G. (LWA)

BAGH-I-ALAMGANJ باغ عالم گنج
34- 69-. A large garden in the neighbourhood of Kabul, on the left bank of the river, opposite Chandawal. It is a vegetable garden, and contains an immense ice pit which supplies a great part of the city in summer. (I.B.C.)

BAGH-I-AOGHAN باغ اوغان
This appears to be the name of a portion of the Ghorband valley, commencing 3-3/4 miles below the junction of the Kaoshan Dara and continuing 4 1/2 miles down the valley. About 5 1/2 miles below the mouth of the Kaoshan Dara, the road crosses from the right to the left bank of the stream by a wooden bridge, which is thus described by Peacocke in October 1886:
"This bridge will carry field guns and laden camels. Roadway 11 feet wide in clear between hand-rails. Seven circular road-bearers, 10 inches diameter, covered by 3-inch planking; span 33 feet. Abutments are of rubble stone corbelled out 8 feet on each side of the span, with brushwood and logs. Bridge was built last year; is sound, but very springly. Comparatively roomy approaches on both banks." The Ghorband district ends at the bridge. (Peacocke.)

BAGHIAR بغیار
33-48 69-45 m. A subdivision of Chakmanis. The village is west of Chamkani. Recent maps show the spelling Bagyar. (LWA)

BAGH-I-BALA باغ بالا
34- 69-. A large royal garden in the neighbourhood of Kabul, situated on the slopes of a hill between Shah Mardan and Wazirabad. In 1893 a fine substantial residence was constructed on the top of

the hill, and immediately in front of it is a masonry tank 5 feet deep and thirty yards square. Here the late Amir, Abdur Rahman, suffered his last illness and died. (Clarke, Dobbs.)

BAGH-I-BEGAM باغ بیگم
34-59 69-9. A famous garden in Kohistan, between Charikar and Top Dara. It is full of mulberry and arghawan trees. In the spring there is a great fair held here, which lasts ten days, and vast herds of sheep are on that occasion brought for sale from Turkistan. There is no village, and the buildings in the garden have fallen into decay. (I.B.C.)

BAGH-I-DALA See URETI باغ دله

*BAGH-I-KHEL باغ خیل
33-16 69-57 m. A village located in the valley of the Shamal Khwar, some 6 miles southeast of Khost.

BAGH-I-LANGAR باغ لنگر
34-27 68-35. A village of 60 houses on the right bank of the Kabul river, about 4 1/4 miles west of Jalrez. The inhabitants are Tajiks and possess about 80 head of cattle and 100 sheep and goats. The annual production of wheat and barley averages about 800 Indian maunds. The main Kabul-Herat road here crosses the Kabul river by a wooden bridge of 20 feet span and 15 feet roadway. The whole valley here is full of cultivation, and there are many poplars and orchards of apricots, plums and apples. (I.B.C., Wanliss.)

BAGH-I-SULTAN باغ سلطان
34- 69-. A village in the valley of the lower Logar, on the right bank of the river opposite Mughal Khel. Inhabitants Tajiks. It is celebrated for the excellence of its fruit. (Clifford, Euan Smith, I.B.C.)

*BAGH-I-ZAGHAN باغ زاغان
34-50 69-12 m. A village located east of the Kabul-Charikar road, about 10 miles south of Charikar.

*BAGHUCHAR باغوچار
33-13 67-27 m. A village located on a tributary of the Arghandab, north of Jaghuri.

BAGHUCHARI باغوچاری
One of the main sections of the Jaghuri Hazaras.

BAGHUCHINA باغ و چینه
34- 69-. A village in Hariob, 14 miles northeast of Ali Khel and 8 miles from the top of the Lakarai pass, on the southern side. (Collett.)

BAGHUNDAK باغندك
34- 67-. Two forts in the Khawat glen, in the Besud country.

BAGHUNDAK CHASMA باغندك چشمه
34- 67-. A grassy hollow on the road from Firozbahar to Karghanatu in Bamian. It commences 8 miles from Firozbahar and, with the exception of a short stony bit at first, is very easy, descending gently between very low hills. It joins the Kochinak or Kara Khawal hollow. (Maitland.)

باغوانه

BAGHWANA
34- 69-. A large village in the Chardeh valley of Kabul, 5 miles southwest of Sherpur. Inhabitants Tajiks, whose headman, Muhammad Husain Khan, was hanged at Kabul in December 1879 for having opened fire from his village on the retiring guns and cavalry of the British on the 11th of that month. Close to this village, four guns of F.A., R.H.A., had to be abandoned on that occasion, but were rescued by the Chief of the Staff, MacGregor, with a handful of officers and men, the same evening.
The ground about the village is much cut up by ditches, and the poplar trees along their sides add to the dificulties of the passage of artillery. There were three forts outside of the village, but they were all destroyed by Sir Frederick Roberts. (I.B.C.)

باغوانی

BAGHWANI
34-23 70-12 m. A village in the Surkhab division of the Jalalabad district. It is situated on the right bank of the Surkhab river, between Balabagh and Barina. Inhabitants, Tajiks. The village is about 4 miles southwest of Bawali. (Jenkyns.)

بگی

*BAGI
35-0 70-30 m. A village located some 10 miles south of Kolatan in Laghman.

بگیار

BAGIAR
33-48 69-45 m. A village of 100 houses on the left bank of the Karaia, 15 miles from Karlachi on the road to Ghazni.

بگی خیل

*BAGIKHEL
33-16 69-57 m. A village located in the valley of the Shamal Khwar, some six miles southeast of Khost.

بگینه

*BAGINA
33-41 70-2 m.. A village northwest of Maidan-i-Jaji in eastern Paktia province.

بگرام

*BAGRAM
34-56 69-13. Bagram is a woleswali in Parwan province. The woleswali comprises an area of 470 square kilometers and has an agricultural population that has been estimated by various Afghan sources at from 21,205 to 24,526. The woleswali is bounded in the west by Ghorband, in the northwest by Shinwar, in the north by Charikar and Mahmud Raqi, in the east by Kohe Safi, and in the south by Istalif and Qara Bagh.
Bagram includes about 58 villages, of which 19 have more than 500 inhabitants. The villages are listed in the PG as follows: Qala-i-Malik (Qala-i-Malik Daulatshahi), Tughchi, Aka Khel, Janqadam, Qalan-der Khel, Chinezai, Qaracha, Sayad, Shahkah, Qala-i-Nasro, Yoz Bashi, Qala-i-Khwaja, Deh Meskin, Qala-i-Guli, Nau Deh, Jafar Khel, Yurchi, Durani, Kharuti (Kariz-i-Saifullah), Deh Hazara, Turkman, Khanjer Khel, Saighani Niazi, Daulat Shahi, Qala-i-Nau Daulat Shahi, Ghulam Ali, Nas Dara-i-Jala, Bad Khel (Bahadur Khel), Qureghchi, Khanaqa, Nekah Khel, Niazi Gran-Shakh, Niazi Qala Buland, Char Qala-i-Niazi, Augamati, Qalacha-i-Panjera, Rud Rabat, Chub Bakhsh (Chub Bakhsh Rabat), Jawaz Sang-i-Rabat, Qara Baghi Rabat, Mahigir, Laghmani Kohna, Qala-i-Buland, Qol-i-Asyab, Bakhshi Khel, Qala-i-Amiri, Qala-i-Kotwali, Chaikal, Dasht Chaikal, Deh Mulla (Deh Mulla Daulatshahi), Shahi Deh Mulla, Gujar Khel, Qala-i-Khan Baba, Sufi Baba, Chur Charak, Saighani, Qala-i-Mohammad Rafiq, Mayan Shakh, Baba Khel, and Nazar Mohammad Khan.

BAGRAM بگرام
34-57 69-17 m. A plain in Kohistan, between Charikar and Bagh-i-Alam, forming the grazing-ground in spring for flocks and herds of Safis from Nijrao, and Ghilzais from Laghman. In summer it dries up completely and is deserted. It was formerly the site of a g reat city, the ruined walls of which were found by Masson to measure above 60 feet in breadth, and to have been built of unburnt bricks of unusual size. Masson considers the city of Bagramn as having been the Alexandria ad Caucasum of the Greeks, and to have been destroyed by Jangez, since the historians of Timur make no mention of it in describing his march through the plain of Bagram, from which it may be inferred that it then no longer existed.
This opinion as to the locality of Alexandria ad Caucasum receives some support from Professor Wilson, but on the other hand it may be urged that as Bagram is situated nearly opposite the mouth of the Kaoshan pass (Bagram is understood to be some 10 miles east of the mouth of the Kaoshan glen, somewhere near the confluence of the Ghorband-Panjshir streams.) and as Arrian relates that Alexander crossed the Caucasus in spring, he must have taken the route by Bamian, which is open all the year round: and as, according to the same authority, his march brought him to Alexandria ad Caucasum, we must assign Bamian as its locality. Accordingly we find Ritter, Rennell, Vigne, Gosselin and Burnes of opinion that Bamian was the Alexandria ad Caucasum. With reference to this controversy, it is not unworthy of remark that no traces have been discovered of Grecian architecture in the mud-built ruins of Bagram. The structures of Ghulghulah and Saiyidabad have at least been more lasting."
(I.B.C.) Recent maps show the name Dasht-i-Bagram. (LWA)

BAGRAMI بگرامی
34-29 69-16 m. Bagrami is the name of a village and a woleswali in Kabul province. The woleswali comprises an area of 224 square kilometers and has an agricultural population which has been variously estimated at from 12,502 to 15,820. The woleswali is southeast of the City of Kabul.
Bagrami woleswali includes some 21 villages, of which about 13 have more than 500 inhabitants. The villages are listed in the PG as follows: Husain Khel, Kamari, Qala-i-Adamkhan, Kareza, Qala-i-Rabaz, Shina, Bagrami, Nauabad, Qala-i-Hasan Khan Sufla, Botkhak, Qala-i-Shanan, Shahak, Nauburja, Qala-i-Ahmakdhan, Qala-i-Hasan Khan Ulya, Deh Yaqub, Niazi, Mamozai, Shewaki, Alo Khel, and Welayati. (LWA)
In 1915, the village of Bagrami was described as lollows: a village half-way between Kabul and Butkhak, on the right bank of the Logar river, a quarter of a mile above the masonry bridge. Gough encamped near this place on the 23rd December 1879 when marching to reinforce Sir Frederick Roberts at Sherpur. (I.B.C.)

BAGRAMI بگرامی
34-5 70-13 G. A village in the Surkhab division of the Jalalabad district. Inhabitants Tajiks and Dehgans. (Jenkyns.)

BAGRAMI بگرامی
35- 69-. A village in Charikar, on the right bank of the Ghorband river. It contains 30 houses of Safi Afghans, and is about 4 miles from Charikar. It stands on the bare plain of the Dasht-i-Bagrami. (Shahzada Taimus.)

BAGWANA See BAGHWANA بگوانه

BAHAR-I-BALA Or BAHAR-I-PAYAN بهار بالا
34-17 70-12. Two villages 8 miles west of Chapriar, containing 800 houses inhabited by Khungianis. Water plentiful throughout the year. Fodder for about 6,000 animals for one day and about 1,000 maunds of unground grain may be collected from these villages and their neighbourhood. Feul is abundant. Ghi in small quantities is available and there is good grazing ground for camels and transport animals. (Johnston.)

BAHARAK بهارك
34-55 66-37. A subdivision of Yak Walang--see "Bamian (district)." There are two hamlets of Baharak, about a mile apart, on the left bank of the Band-i-Amir river, opposite Ghorband. The upper one is 8 miles below Marghi. They are both situated at the mouths of large ravines. Baharak and the Ghorband together contain about 50 families, 30 of whom are land-owners. The road up the valley here is pretty good. There is no room to encamp anywhere about. The saiyids of Baharak are hardly distinguishable from the Hazaras, and live in very much the same way. (Maitland.)

BAHAR ROBAT بهار رباط
34-21 67-54. A village on the bank of the Kabul river, 1 mile from Besud. there is a ferry across the river at this point, and the inhabitants wash for gold in its stream. (Masson.)

*BAHAUDDIN بهاؤ الدين
32-47 67-44 m. A village located about 4 miles southwest of Mukur on the highway to Qalat.

BAHI بامی
33-43 67-43 A.   A place in Nawar.

BAHRABAD بهر آباد
34- 70-. A village in the Besud division of the Jalalabad district. It is situated on the left bank of the Kabul river, just above Kasimabad, and the inhabitants are Rikas. (Jenkyns.)

BAHRAM بهرام
A section of the Muhammads Khwaja Hazaras.

BAHRAM KHAN بهرام خان
34- 70-. A fort in Laghman, about 2 miles from the northern foot of the Darunta pass. It lies a little to the north of the village of Fatehabad, and boasts of a small garden of sypresses and palms. (Holdich.) A village called Bahram Khan Kalai is about 2 miles west of Qaria Loe, at 34-12 71-2 G. (LWA)

BAHRAM KHEL بهرام خیل
A village in the Jaji country on the right bank of the Karaja river, beyond Zabardast Kala. (Lumsden.) One village with this name is about 6 miles northwest of Shinwar, at 34-6 70-41 G. (LWA)

BAIAN بایان
A subsection of the Besuds.

BAIAN بایان
35-3 69-9 M. About 3 miles northeast of Charikar is the township of Baian, containing the following villages: Baian-i-Malik, Baian-i-Mughal, Deh Mulla Yusuf Abadi, and Felaji. All together there are 366 houses of Tajiks. About a mile to the left, on or near the

55

right bank of the Ghorband river, is a village called Toghbidi. It contains 60 houses of Afghans and Tajiks mixed. There is the usual abundance of fruit trees, etc., and the whole country is cultivated to the daman of the western hills (Koh-i-Paghman). There is no good place for an encampment just here, the country being too close. Wood, water, and supplies are plentiful. (Shahzada Taimus.) Baian Pain is nearby, at 35-0   69-14 m. Another village called Baian is on the Saighan river, about 8 miles east of Saighan, at 35-11   67-47 m. (LWA)

BAIAT   بایات
A section of the Jaghatu Hazaras.

BAIBOGHA   بای بوغه
A section og the Dai Kundi Hazaras.

BAI KALA   بای قلعه
A Besud Hazara village.

BAILAM   بیلم (؟)
35- 71-. A village on the right bank of the Kunar, some 3 miles below Chandak, containing about 80 houses of Chitralis and Afghans. It is situated amidst fertile fields and used ot be the limit of Chitral authority in the Kunar valley. (Robertson.)

BAILAM, UPPER   بیلم
35- 71-. Appears to be another name for Nurdi.

BAINDARRA, KOH-I See URAZGANI   بایان دره

BAINTAN Or BAINTU   بین تان
A subdivision of the Daichopan Hazaras.

BAJGAH   باجگاه
35-29 69-35 A.   Elev. 12,300 feet. A pass over the Hindu Kush at the head of the Salang dara. It is crossed by a road leading direct from the Panjshir valley into that of Andarab at about 39 3/4 miles from Charikar. The road over the pass, in its present condition, is only just practicable for Afghan camels, but it is reported (1905) that the Amir intends to improve it. (I.B.C.) A village with this name is located at 35-35   69-1 m. (LWA)

BAJINDRA   باجندرا
35-38 71-22 G.   A Katir village of 30 houses, on the left bank of Bashgul river, some 2 miles south of Bragamatal. Most of the houses are perched on the top of a large rock, to reach which a bridge stretching to it from the slope behind has to be crossed. The water-supply can only be obtained at some little distance from the foot of the rock. (Robertson.) Recent maps show the name Bachancha, at 35-38   71-20. (LWA)

*BAK   باك
33-32 70-1.   Bak is an alaqadari in Paktia province. The alaqadari comprises an area of 175 square kilometers and has an agricultural population that has been estimated at from 4,605 to 6,395. The alaqadari is bounded in the west by Jani Khel and Saroti, in the south by Trayzai, in the north by Ja-ji Maidan, and in the west by the State of Pakistan. Bak has some 25 villages, 12 of which have more than 500 inhabitants. The villages are listed in the PG as

follows: Kotgai Sal Kalai, Mohsen Kalai, Palo Khel (Pori Khel), Badai, Gulbad Shahmir, Sadin, Saman Kel (Shaman Khel), Wardgan Kalai, Kotwalay, Ahmad Kalai (Ahmad Ali), Chori Kalai (Chori Kahol), Wazir Kalai, Pahlawan Khel, Haji Gulmat Khan, Mana Kahol, Sperkai, Nangar (Sangar), Mami Kahol (Mari Kahol), Shamal Khel, Pass Kalai Nar (Barkalai Nar), Koz Kalai Nar, Omar Khan, Tutak (Tutak-i-Khurd), and Mangai.

*BAKAS باکس
35-4 68-43 m. A village located in the valley of a tributary of the Ghorband, some 6 miles north of Galian.

*BAKHSHAK بخشك
34-11 68-16 m. A village in the valley of the Dara-i-Jelga, southwest of Miran. Another village with this name is some 10 miles southwest of Ghazni, at 33-30 68-17 m.

BAKHSHI KALAI بخشی کلی
33-20 68-17. A village in the Ghilzai country, 36 miles from Ghazni, and 10 miles from Mashaki. It is a collection of several walled villages inhabited by Tokhi and Andari Ghilzais. Supplies are abundant and cheap. "Salep misri" is found all over the hills near this place. (N.Campbell, Broadfoot.) Another place with this name is located at 31-47 68-23 A. (LWA)

BAKHSHI KALAY بخشی کلی
33- 68-. A village in the Kharwar, containing 50 houses of Yusuf Khel Ghilzais. (Griesbach.)

BAKHTAN KALA بختان قلعه
34- 70-. A village in the Surkhab division of the Jalalabad district, about a mile northwest of Ghaurhak. Inhabitants Tajiks and Dehgans. (Jenkyns.)

*BAKHTANA بختانه
33-27 69-56 m. A village located a few miles southwest of Nakam and north of Khost.

BAKHTIARAN بختیاران
34-36 69-16 m. A village in the Kaubul district, 2 miles north of the small kotal near the village of Deh-i-Yahiya. It is a straggling place. Inhabitants: Ghilzais. Much firewood is collected here (from Deh-i-Sabz, etc.) and sent into the Kabul market. (I.B.C.)

BAKKAK بكك
34-38 66-50. Elev. 11,520 feet. A pass in the Koh-i-Baba range over the watershed between the Band-i-Amir and the Sar-i-Jangal valleys. It is crossed by the main Kabul-Bamian-Daulat Yar road at about 65 miles from Kala Sarkari in Bamian.
The ascent from the east lies up the Bakkak glen, a tributary of the Siah Dara. It is practicable for Afghan camels carrying full loads, but Indian camels would scarcely be able to get up unless very light laden; any considerable train of baggage animals would be necessarily much delayed by it. This ascent is, however, the only really difficult bit for camels on the road between Bamian and Daulat Yar. Once the summit is reached the road is very good, and 3/4 mile further on crosses a spur; this is known as the Shamsher Sang kotal, and is about 30 feet higher than the actual Bakkak watershed. From here the descent to the village of Surkhak, in the Sarma Kol, is

remarkably good and easy on the whole, but the road is liable to become soft and slippery in wet weather.
Another road strikes off from the summit of the Bakkak pass and leads nearly straight down the Kohna Deh ravine to Kala Mirdad, and thence over the Roghani Gardan pass into the Sar-i-Jangal valley. (A.B.C.)

BAKKAK-I-BURNA (Upper Bakkak) بك برنا
34-38 66-48 m. A village in the Bakkak glen, at the eastern foot of the Bakkak pass, and about 1 1/2 miles from its summit. It contains some 25 houses of Takana Hazaras. There is a good deal of cultivation here mostly on the hillsides to the south of the glen. (A.B.C.)

BAKKAK-I-TAIRNA (Lower Bakkak) بك تيرنا
34-38 66-50 m. Elev. about 8,970 feet. A village in the Bakkak glen, about 2 1/2 miles below Bakkak-i-Burna. It contains some 30 or 40 houses of Bacha Ghulam Hazaras. The glen here is some 200 or 300 yards wide, and is cultivated, but 1/2 mile higher up it becomes quite narrow, varying from 15 to 40 or 50 yards in width. (A.B.C.)

BAKSHI KALA بكشى قلعه (بخشى)
31-47 68-23 m. A collection of walled villages in the Jamrud subdivision of the Ghazni district, about 10 miles south of Mashaki. There is much cultivation here; supplies are plentiful and water is abundant. Inhabitants, Andari and Tokhi Ghilzais. (I.B.C.)

BAKSHI KHEL بكشى خيل
35- 69-. A village in the upper Panjshir valley, on the road down from Bazarak to Anaba. 100 houses of Tajiks. (Shahzada Taimus.)

BAKU KHAM See USHTARGIRAN باكو خام

*BAKULSHATA بكولشته
35-27 71-24 m. A village in a glen, some 6 miles northeast of Kamdesh.

BALABAGH بالاباغ
34-24 70-14 A. A walled village in the valley of Jalalabad, 15 miles west of Jalalabad, on the right bank of Surkhab. It is celebrated for its fruits, as well as for its sugarcane, which is here extensively cultivated; more, however, for a sweetmeat than manufacture of sugar. The neighbourhood abounds in topes. From a commercial point of view the village is the most important place in the valley of Jalalabad; it has many Hindu traders and a few bankers resident at it. To the west there is a large regal garden, and the environs to the east are highly cultivated, particu-larly with sugarcane. On the opposite side of the river is the site of the city of Admapur, flourishing in the time of Babar. To the south and west a bleak stony plain extends.
There is a small fort attached, and it is said by Leech to be a picturesque place, exceedingly fruitful, yielding almost every production. The site being more elevated, its climate is less sultry than that of Jalalabad.
The inhabitants of Balabagh are Tajiks, Ghilzais and some 30 families of Sikhs, settled here since 1849, when some refugees from the Punjab took shelter in the district. These Sikhs retain their religion and are generally shopkeepers. (Masson, Leech, I.B.C.)

BALA DEH   بالاده
    34-6   70-28 m. A small fortified hamlet in the Hisarak subdivision of the Jalalabad district at the foot of the Oghaz pass which leads over the Safed Koh to Kurram. there is a company of infantry, detached from Kahi, stationed here and 2 mountain guns. (I.B.C.) Recent maps show the spelling Deh-i-Bala. (LWA)

BALA DEH   بالاده
    34- 68-. A village in Koh Daman, on the hills to the west of Shakardara, and some 4 miles from that place. There is said to be a great deal of cultivation here. (I.B.C.)

BALA DEH   بالاده
    33-38   69-17 m. A large village in Zurmat between Mushkhel and Fakirkhel. Inhabitants: Sulaiman Khel Ghilzais. There is a large fort here. (I.B.C.)

BALA DEH   بالاده
    33-26   70-25. A village in the Surkhab division of the Jalalabad district, about 3 miles west of Jalalabad town. Inhabitants Tajiks. (Jenkyns.)

BALA DEH   بالاده
    33-37   69-17 m. A village a few miles northeast of Gardez on the road thence to Mirzaka kotal. There is room for a brigade to camp here, with sufficient water from the Sapega Rud. The inhabitants are Dehgan Tajiks. (I.B.C.)

*BALA DEH   بالاده
    35-1   70-5 m. A village in a glen, running into the Alishang, east of the Kuh-i-Korangal. Other places with this name are located at 34-31   67-14 m. south of the Kuh-i-Baba; 33-37   69-17 m. a few miles northeast of Gardez; 34-29   68-47 G. and 33-35   69-14 G.

BALAGHIL   بالاغیل
    35- 69-. A village on the Daman of the Paghman range, east of Charikar. Hundred families of Tajiks. (Shahzada Taimus.)

*BALAI   بالای
    33-25   68-39 m. A village located west of the Tapor Dasht and about 20 miles southeast of Ghazni.

*BALA KAREZ   بالاکاریز
    34-38   69-2 m. A village east of the Kabul-Charikar road, about 15 miles northwest of Kabul.

*BALANZAI KHUNE   بلنزی خونی
    35-14   71-15 m. A village located in the valley of a tributary of the Kunar, a few miles northwest of Girdab.

*BALAQALA   بالاقعه
    34-23   67-5 m. A village on the Dara-i-Mur, a few miles east of Panjao.

*BALDARGHAN   بلدرغان
    33-26   67-59 m. A village in the Dara-i-Khush, east of the Kuh-i-Zardnan.

BALINA IRAK   بلینه عراق
    34- 68-. A small fort with about 15 houses of Darghan Hazaras,

situated 8 miles north of the Irak Kotal. (Muhammad Akbar Khan.)

BAL-I-REG بل ریگ
34- 67-. A hamlet in the southeast of Yak Walang, passed on the road leading from Kara Khawal up to the Zard Sang Kotal.
This would be a fairly good place to camp, but no supplies are locally procurable. Grass in spring and summer; buta for fuel.
From Bal-i-Reg a road branches right (south-southwest) up a ravine to Shah-i-Birahna, a place on the other side of the Koh-i-Baba, and said to be 30 miles distant. It is a ziarat. (Muhammad Akbar Khan.)

BALO بلو
34-25 70-19. Deh-i-Balo is a village in the Jalalabad district on the right bank of the Surkhab river at about 3 miles from its junction with the Kabul. Inhabitants: Tajiks. (Jenkyns.)

BALOJ بلوج
33- 69-. A small deserted village in the Ali Khel district, a little over a mile from Ali Khel, on the opposite side of the Karaia stream. (Collett.)

BALTUKHEL بلتوخیل
34- 69-. A village in the northern part of the Koh Daman, north of Kabul. It has a certain amount of cultivation and pasturage. (Kennedy.)

*BALUCH بلوچ
35-1 67-42 m. A village on the Gorgorawa stream which runs into the Saighan.

BALUTAK بلوتك
34- 69-. The name given to a point on the Tezin and Khurd Kabul road, where it is met by a path from Lataband, in the neighbourhood of the Haft Kotal. (Young.)

BAMIAN بامیان
34-49 67-49. A province in central Afghanistan which comprises an area of 17,546 square kilometers and an agricultural population estimated at from 85,108 to 112,342. The province is bounded in the west by Ghor, in the north by Balkh and Samangan, in the east by Parvan/Kapisa, in the southeast by Maidan, and in the southwest by Uruzgan. Bamian province is divided into the four woleswalis of Kahmard, Yakowlang, Panjab, and Waras and into the alaqadaris of Saighan and Shibar, as well as the district of Bamian. The capital of the province is the city of Bamian. (LWA) For woleswali lists from the Department of Statistics of the Ministry of Agriculture and Irrigation see the following six pages. In 1914 Bamian province was described as follows:
This administrative division is the only part of the Kabul province north of the great range of the Koh-i-Baba and Hindu Kush. It comprises: (I) the valley of Bamian and its affluent glens, all draining to the Surkhab (Kunduz river): (II) the considerable district of Yak Walang, which is to the west of Bamian, and is drained by the head waters of the Rud-i-Band-i-Amir, the ancient Balkh-Ab: (III) the northwestern Hazarajat districts, commonly called the Dai Zangi country.
The following statistics of population, etc., and general remarks on the Bamian division, as above defined are taken from Major Maitland's diary Bamian proper being further dealt with under that heading:

Administrative Divisions of Bamian Province

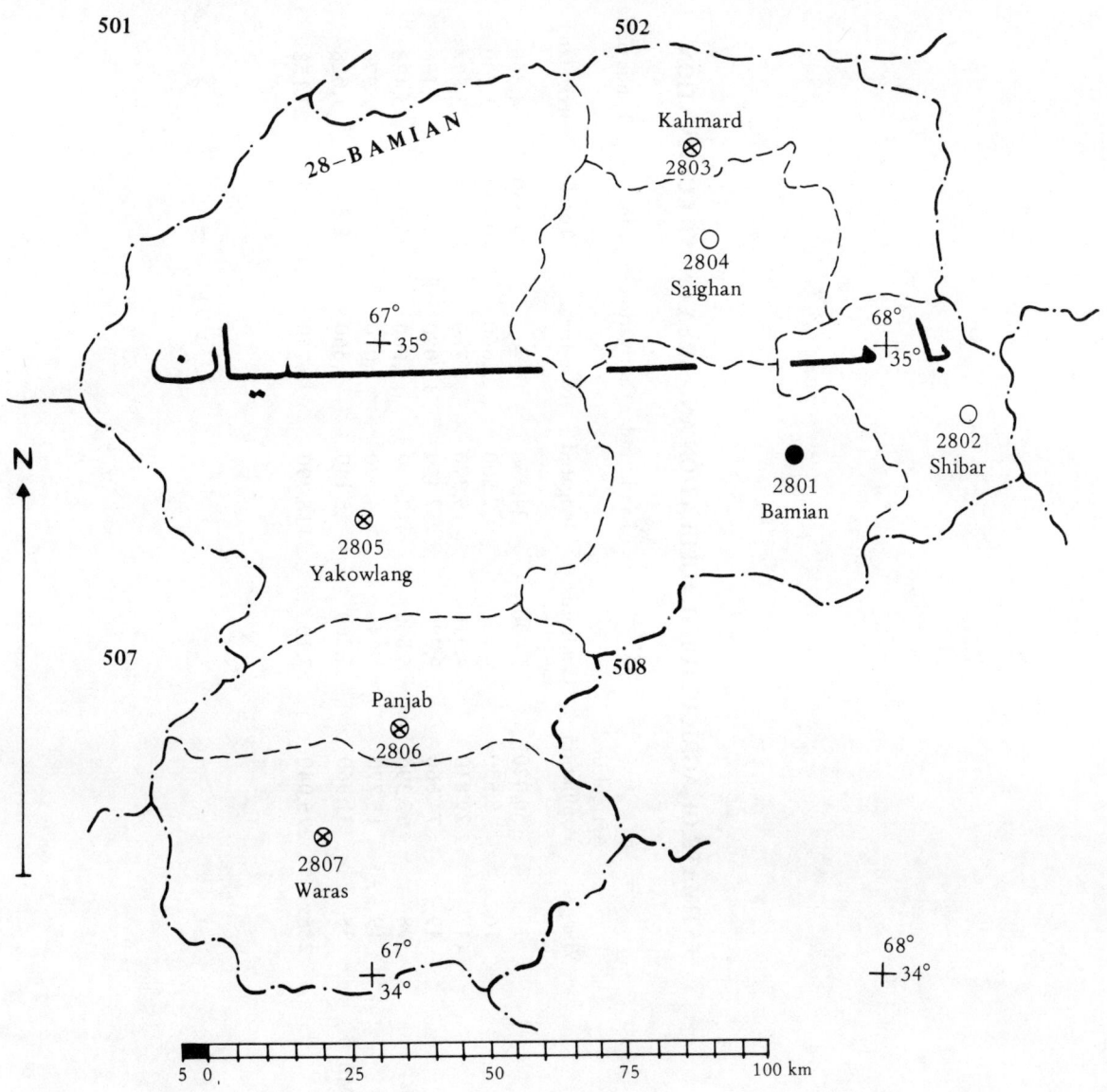

ESTIMATE OF AGRICULTURAL POPULATION AND AREA UNDER CULTIVATION

	Villages	Agricultural Population	Landlords	Lands under Cultivation in Jaribs			Lands under Cultivation in Hectares		
				Irrigated	Non-Irrig.	Total	Irrigated	Non-Irrig.	Total
PANJAB	18	50,920	1,930	24,330	—	24,330	4,866	—	4,866
KAHMARD	16	8,530	890	7,500	2,660	10,160	1,500	532	2,032
BAMIAN	47	29,810	4,310	19,370	2,780	22,150	3,874	556	4,430
WARAS	49	74,660	9,220	37,430	17,020	54,450	7,486	3,404	10,890
YAWKOWLANG	98	63,390	5,850	17,140	5,860	23,000	3,428	1,172	4,600
SAIGHAN	19	15,770	1,640	4,880	2,070	6,950	976	414	1,390
SHIBAR (SHAMBUL)	38	31,960	3,260	5,140	3,360	8,500	1,028	672	1,700
TOTAL	285	275,040	27,100	115,790	33,750	149,540	23,158	6,750	29,908

STATISTICAL ESTIMATE OF LIVESTOCK BY WOLESWALIS AND ALAKADARIS

	Sheep	Karakul Sheep	Goats	Cattle	Buffaloes	Camels	Horses	Donkeys	Mules	Poultry
PANJAB	14,580	—	3,610	15,990	—	—	280	620	—	8,720
KAHMARD	12,650	—	5,580	7,480	—	—	370	1,990	—	900
BAMIAN	59,530	—	12,010	31,780	—	—	2,160	9,000	—	36,520
WARAS	36,240	—	8,480	33,150	—	90	600	4,110	—	16,250
YAWKOWLANG	60,690	—	10,810	35,100	—	30	2,030	12,830	—	22,550
SAIGHAN	30,750	—	5,000	5,360	—	110	250	6,340	—	124,050
SHIBAR (SHAMBUL)	40,940	—	3,550	15,700	—	20	920	3,660	—	26,610
TOTAL	255,380	—	49,040	144,560	—	250	6,610	38,550	—	235,600

PRODUCTION OF AGRICULTURAL CROPS—IN KABULI SEERS

	Grains			Vegetables	Other Crops		Fruits
	Irrigated	Non-Irrig.	Total		Industrial Crops	Other Temp. Crops	
PANJAB	809,760	–	809,760	421,200	–	–	–
KAHMARD	265,860	10,650	276,510	103,680	4,900	24,000	100,020
BAMIAN	705,180	12,000	717,180	129,600	–	316,000	125,310
WARAS	1,344,840	167,100	1,511,940	486,000	–	–	480,810
YAWKOWLANG	675,360	43,050	718,410	239,760	–	58,000	120,570
SAIGHAN	212,100	4,350	216,450	17,820	–	–	24,180
SHIBAR (SHAMBUL)	207,900	16,350	224,250	35,640	–	24,000	14,710
TOTAL	4,221,000	253,500	4,474,500	1,433,700	4,900	422,000	865,600

LAND UNDER IRRIGATION AND SOURCES OF IRRIGATION

	Area in Jaribs					Number of Sources				
	Canals	Springs	Karez	Wells	Total	Canals	Springs	Karez	Wells	Water Mills
PANJAB	14,330	10,000	—	—	24,330	16	12	—	7	121
KAHMARD	6,700	800	—	—	7,500	14	10	—	5	18
BAMIAN	15,540	3,830	—	—	19,370	38	18	—	3	105
WARAS	34,220	3,210	—	—	37,430	6	5	—	3	255
YAWKOWLANG	13,000	2,830	—	1,310	17,140	69	56	—	120	37
SAIGHAN	1,100	3,780	—	—	4,880	16	14	—	2	51
SHIBAR (SHAMBUL)	1,420	2,320	—	1,400	5,140	20	22	—	160	64
TOTAL	86,310	26,770	—	2,710	115,790	179	137	—	300	651

TOTAL CULTIVABLE LAND, BY CROP—IN KABULI JARIBS

	Grains			Vegetables	Industrial Crops	Other Crops	Fruits	Total Cultivated Land
	Irrigated	Non-Irrig.	Total					
PANJAB	19,280	–	19,280	2,600	–	–	–	21,880
KAHMARD	6,330	710	7,040	640	140	120	630	8,570
BAMIAN	16,790	800	17,590	800	–	1,580	790	20,760
WARAS	32,020	11,140	43,160	3,000	–	–	3,040	49,200
YAWKOWLANG	16,080	2,870	18,950	1,480	–	290	760	21,480
SAIGHAN	5,050	290	5,340	110	–	–	150	5,600
SHIBAR (SHAMBUL)	4,950	1,090	6,040	220	–	120	90	6,470
TOTAL	100,500	16,900	117,400	8,850	140	2,110	5,460	133,960

TOTAL CULTIVABLE LAND—IN KABULI JARIBS

	Fallow Lands	Under Cultivation	Forests	Pastures	Total
PANJAB	8,070	24,330	2,460	44,080	70,870
KAHMARD	1,870	10,160	120	26,650	36,930
BAMIAN	4,660	22,150	230	243,130	265,510
WARAS	16,680	54,450	9,260	66,850	130,560
YAWKOWLANG	5,430	23,000	3,740	129,770	156,510
SAIGHAN	1,190	6,950	—	66,360	73,310
SHIBAR (SHAMBUL)	2,160	8,500	190	64,760	73,450
TOTAL	40,060	149,540	16,000	641,600	807,140

I. Bamian
In Bamian are comprised: (1) Bamian proper, that is the valley of Bamian, with the Saiyidabad and Polada glens. (2) The Kalu subdistrict, including Kalu, Irak, and Shibar, etc. (3) Sokhdar or Surkhdar, with some outlying places. (4) Shahidan, with Shibartu. (5) Karghanatu or Karakanstu.

1. The following places belong to Bamian proper:

Villages	Families	Villages	Families
Topchi	100	Gharibabad	100
Ahingaran	40	Deh Wahid	40
Sumara	50	Buri Sunia	60
Sad Masti	60	Sar-i-Asia	20
Lala Khel and Mulla Ayan	60	Jui Sar Bala	40
Jagar Khel	50	Tahbuti	40
		Daudi	50
		Bughlani	50
		Total	760

The two last-named places are the cave-villages about the idols. Bughlani is the upper one, near the sarai.

There is no town of Bamian (now there is-LWA). The Hakim lives in an ordinary mud fort known as Kala Sarkari.

At the foot of the big idol is a large new sarai, where all travellers have to put up, and where toll is taken from kafilas.

The population of these villages is Tajik except for Bughlani where it is mixed.

The next two place are large glens, entering the Bamian valley from the south:

Villages	Tribe	Families	Villages	Tribe	Families
Sayyidabad					
Sayyidabad	Sayyids and	100	Bam Sarah	Sayyids	100
Khushkak	Hazaras	50	Dukani	Sayyids and Hazaras	80
Chap Dara		100			
Ulangash	Hazaras	40			
				Total	470
Faoladi					
Dasht-i-Tikar	Polada Hazaras				500
Dasht-i-Kazan					500
				Total	1,000

The whole population of Sayyidabad glen is said to be Shiah. The villages in the lower part of this glen (Buri Sunia, etc.) are inhabited by Tajiks included in Bamian proper. This lower part is locally known as Tagao Tajik and not as Polada. According to Dafadar Amir Khan, there are also some Tajik villages at the extreme head of the glen.

Mir Baba Beg was chief of the Polada Hazaras in 1885, he was then in confinement at Kabul.

2. Kalu

Kalu, Irak and Bulola are large glens running from the main range on the south and east, to the east end of the Bamian valley and district. The roads to Kabul lie up these glens. Together with their affluent glens, they form the Kalu subdistrict, which is exclusively inhabited by Khatai Hazaras.

Places	Sections of Khatai Hazaras	Families
Shibar and Bulola	Shaikha	300
Ahingaran (Shikari?)	Ahingaran	80
Birgilich glen	Shak	120
Jolah	Gudi	100
Irak glen	Khida	300
Jandargal	Mirdad	40
Kalu valley	Maikadam, Mirdad, Irakhchi, Ahingaran	400
Sabz-Ao	Jan Muhammad	10
Jaokul	Mirdad	30
		1,390

Mir Kalbi Husain, Mirdad Khatai, is chief of the whole clan, and originally the entire revenue of the subdistrict was paid through him. Since the accession of Amir Abdur Rahman, however, Irak and Shibar (or Bulola), with Birgilich and Jolah, have been removed from his jurisdiction, and now pay their revenue direct to the Hakim of Bamian.

The revenue payable by Kalbi Husain was stated by himself to be: 3,000 Kabuli rupees kham (Apparently has no reference to Kabuli "kham" currency, and "pukhta" currency. It is understood to be all reckoned in "pukta.") i.e., in kind, taken in grain, sheep, barak, etc., 2,427 Kabuli rupees pukhta, i.e., in cash.

Kalbi Husain's "muajib" is 25 Kabuli kharwars of grain, etc., and 29 tomans (580 Kabuli rupees) in cash.

He has 12 sowars, of whom 7 are paid by the Amir's Government.

3. Surkhdar or Sokhdar

Villages	Inhabitants	Families
Surkhdar (several forts)	Tajiks	150
Kham-i-Kelak (2 forts below Sokhdar)	Tajiks	20
Bariki (near Shahidan)	Sayyids	20
Sabzak (up the defile)	Tajiks	20
Gumbat	Mixed Hazaras	60
Ak Robat	Mixed Hazaras	40
	Total	310

Surkhdar, or Sokhdar, is the upper part of the Bamian valley, commencing a few miles above the idols. It includes various places, as Ak Robat and Bariki, which are on affluent ravines.

The real name of the place is said to be "Surkhdar," but it appears to be invariably called "Sokhdar."

All the people of Sokhdar are said to be Shiahs.

4. Shahidan and Shibartu

The following places are glens, or upland valleys, draining to the upper course of the Bamian stream, that is the defile above Sokhdar. They are crossed by the road from Bamian to Yak Walang and Daulat Yar. Shahidan and Shibartu are counted as one.

```
Shahidan
    Lado                Yangur Hazaras           30
    Kala Muhammad Ali                            10
    Kala Allah Baksh                              5
    Kala Kadam Shah                              10
    Kala Bakar                                   10
    Ambar Samuch                                 50
    Mumarak             Mumarak Besud  Hazaras   30
    Kala Abdul Rahim    Yangur Hazaras           10
Shibartu
    Kala Ao Bashi       Khubzat section of       20
    Ikhtiaran              Polada Hazaras        30
    Pirdad                                       40

                Total of Shahidan and Shibartu  245
```

Mir Ata Beg is the headman of these two valleys. The revenue is said to be 4,000 Kabuli rupees (all payable in cash?), of which Mir Ata Beg gets 15 tomans (300 Kabuli rupees) and 7 Kabuli kharwars of grain, etc.

5. Karghanatu, or Karakanatu

Villages	Families	Villages	Families
Chahar Chashma	16	Khairkhana	14
Kala Abbas	12	Kala Gadai	10
Deh Muhammad Ali	12	Kohna Kala	17
Deh Bacha Aka Raza	11	Kala Zafar	3
Walangak	13	Shah-rah	12
Tob Ali	16		
		Total	126

Mulla Gadai and Mauladad Sultan were the heads of the Shahgum Beg Takanas of Karghanatu in 1885. The revenue of Karghanatu is said to be 25 tomans (500 Kabuli rupees) in cash, and 30 (600 Kabuli rupees) in kind. All of the above are inhabited by the Shahgum Beg and Takana Hazaras.

```
            Abstract of Population
              Families                      Families
    Bamian       760       Sokhdar             310
    Sayyidabad   470       Shahidan            245
    Polada     1,000       Karghanatu          135
    Kalu       1,390
                           Total of Bamian   4,310
```

The population is divided into the following classes:
```
        Tajiks          900    Khatai           1,390
        Sayyids         270    Yangur             125
        Mixed Hazaras   400    Shahgum Beg
        Polada        1,090      Hazaras          135

                               Total            4,310
```
Except for the Tajiks and the Sayyids, all are Hazaras.

The Tajiks occupy the valley of Bamian proper, and the Sayyids are in close proximity. The whole of the rest of Bamian is peopled by Hazaras.

The revenue of Bamian is unknown, but it probably amounts to about 50,000 Kabuli rupees, without transit dues.

Jan Muhammad Khan, of Barikab near Ghazni, was Hakim of Bamian in 1885-86; but it was then said that he was likely to be relieved before long by Ghulam Haidar Khan, a younger brother of Muhammad Husain Khan, Jawan-Sher Kizilbash, the Hakim of Besud. (Muhammad Ayub Khan, son of Sarwar Khan of Parwan, was Hakim in 1906.)

There are no troops in Bamian except 100 khasadars; but according to Dafadar Shamshuddin Khan, who passed through in 1886, the Amir had ordered quarters for 12,000 men to be rebuilt. There were in 1906 a battery of artillery and two companies of infantry quartered at Kala Sarkari, in addition to 300 khasadars. The roads from Bamian to Kabul have lately been greatly improved by Amir Abdur Rahman.

There is a good deal of cultivation in the valleys and glens of Bamian, but no large amount of supplies is procurable. Wheat and barley are grown. In the more elevated tracts there is no wheat, and the people eat barley bread.

According to the Afghan officials, the following amounts can be collected at the undermentioned places:

At Irak or Kalu, from the Kalu subdistrict: supplies for 2,000 sowars for one day are immediately procurable.

At Bamian itself: supplies for 2 Kabuli cavalry regiments for one month.

At Sokhdar: supplies for 2 Kabuli cavalry regiments for one day.

At Shahidan: supplies (including ata) for 5 Kabuli cavalry regiments for one day.

At Karghanatu: supplies for one Kabuli cavalry regiment for one day.

In the matter of supplies 2 Kabuli cavalry regiments may be taken as equal to 1 Indian native cavalry regiment on Kabul scale.

The above amounts, put into maunds, would be approximately:

	Ata	Barley
Irak or Kalu	50 maunds	200 maunds
Bamian and Sokhdar	400	1,440
Shahidan	60	225
Karghanatu	12	45
Total	522	1,910

A depot at Bamian might be stocked from Dara Yusuf. Grain would be 8 or 10 days coming on pack bullocks. There are sufficient water mills in Bamian and Saighan to grind the wheat.

There are a good many small orchards in the valley of Bamian. Fruit and garden produce would be procurable in season.

Sheep are abundant. Ghi is procurable from Besud.

The pack animals of the district are yabus and bullocks.

There are no camels, though large kafilas are continually passing through, especially in autumn.

The baggage mules of a force would probably find good grazing in the hills to south, but the country has not been seen. There is not likely, however, to be much camel forage at any time of the year.

There is excellent ground for camping on the plateau, known as the Dasht-i-Sarkar, south of Kala Sarkari. The land is Gorvernment property. It is watered by a karez. Lucerne is cultivated there.

II. Yak Walang

The district of Yak Walang contains the following subdivisions:
(1) Yak Walang, comprising the valley of Yak Walang and a number of glens and minor valleys running into it.
(2) Tagao Sayyid, which is the main valley above Yak Walang and various affluent glens.
(3) Sar-i-Kol, a large glen above Tagao Sayyid and Firozbahar, with some outlying places.
(4) Kham-i-Aba (with Baharak), the valley of the river below Yakh Walang and its tributary glens.
The people of Yak Walang are all Hazaras and Hazara Sayyids. Those of the Yak Walang subdistrict are Takanas, a tribe of the Dai Zangi stock.
Their chief is Muhammad Amir Khan, who has the hereditary title of "Ilkhani" by which he is always known. He resides at Deh Surkh in Yak Walang.
The Takanas are said to be divided into the following sections:

>   Kam*-i-Kaka   Nurkah
>   Kam-i-Yarka   Pirkuli
>   Kam-i-Anda   Khwajadad
>   Rustam   Baikah
>   Begal

*Hazara form of "Kaum."

But these divisions have little meaning now-a-days among the Hazaras. The Begal are the "Mir" section, or "Khan-Khel" as it would be called among the Afghans.

1. The Yak Walang subdistrict
The following are the places included in Yak Walang, with their population, etc.:

Villages	Inhabitants	Families
1. Zari		
Kalkhak	Khwajadad Takanas	10
Sang-i-Sulakh	" "	15
Mard Kush	" "	20
Kala Nao. This place is "Khas" Zari	" "	20
Lorcha	Sayyids	20
Lailur	"	11
Kalandaran	Yangur Hazaras	20
"	Sayyids	11
	Total	127

Mir Yusuf Beg, a relative (uncle?) of the Alkhani, is Mir of this subdivision and lives at Kala Nao. His son, Ghulam Husain, resides at Mard Kush.

2. Siah Dara

	Rustam Takanas	50
	Yangur Hazaras	70
	Besud Hazaras	40
	Abdal (Bacha Ghulam Hazaras)	40
	Total	200

Kambar Zawar is chief man in this subdivision, which is the upper part of the Zari glen.

Villages	Inhabitants	Families
3. Sabzak		
Various hamlets	Anda Takanas	100
4. Nurkah		
Nurkah	Nurkah Takanas	20
Chukarnao, etc.	Khwajadad Takanas	20
5. Bakkak		
Bakkak-i-Burna	Baikah Takanas	20
Bakak-i-Tairna	Bacha Ghulam Hazaras	30
	Total	190

Zafar Ali, Mir Hazar, is head of the above.

6. Tagao Sharfak	Baikah Takanas	100
7. Kanak		
Sar-i-Kanak	Anda Takanas	20
Dahan-i-Kanak	Anda Takanas	20
Kanak-i-Shewna	Tajiks	10
8. Chahar Deh		
4 small forts and villages	Kam-i-Kaka Takanas	100
	Total	250
9. Sarmakol		
Surkhak	Tulighali Besud Hazaras	15
Sarmakol	Anda Takanas	10
Noastu	Mukadam Yangur Hazaras	20
Charharkash	Neka Hazaras	10
	Total	55

Samakol is beyond the Bakkak Kotal, but drains to the Kanak glen. Sidik Ali is the headman of the whole.

10. Deh Surkh, or Yak Walang proper		
Deh Surkh (2 forts)	Mixed Hazaras	50
Do-Ai (4 hamlets)	Begal Takanas	20
Dahan-i-Tawa (2 hamlets)	Begal Takanas	30
Utiparghulak	Pirkuli Takanas	7
Sar Takhak	Begal Takanas	10
Sang Ispizak (2 villages)	Rustam Takanas	20
	Total	157
11. Surshuri		
8 small villages	Kam-i-Yarka Takanas	50
12. Tarnuk		
Tarnuk	Baikah Takanas	20
Sar-i-Dasht	Neka Baikah Takanas	20
	Total	90
13. Naitak		
Naitak	Pir Kuli Takanas	50
Kala Tezao	Yangur Hazaras	10
	Total	60

14. Sabz Dara   Kham-i-Aba Hazaras
       Surkhbed   10
       Do-Ao   5
       Dumi Dasht   20
       Miantik   10
       Legu   20
       Mian Deh   5
       Gird Walang   5
       Pitao Kala   5
       Siah Deh   10
       Shahrah   10
                                                        ―――
                                              Total   100

This subdivision properly belongs to Kham-i-Aba. It is under Mir Farz Ali Beg, who lives at Legu. He is of the family of Mehdi Beg of Dahan-i-Marghi (see Khan-i-Aba subdistrict), but is father-i-law of Ilkhani Muhammad Amir, and pays his revenue through the latter. The total population fo the Yak Walang subdistrict, including Sabz Dar is 1,229 families, of whom 10 only are Tajiks, the remainder being all Hazaras.
The Ilkhani's revenue jurisdiction only extends over the subdistrict (1885).

2. The Tagao Saiad Subdistrict

   1. Tagao Saiad
       Tarachi   Hazara   10
       Ghunda Sang   5
       Kham-i-Aftana   10
       Gird-Bed   5
       Naishahar   5
       Kala Kazi   15
       Kala Shah Bunyad   20
       Naiak Pain   50
       Naiak Bala   20
       Kuchkak Akkundan   Mullas*   10
       Kuchkak-i-Saiadan   15
       Gidar Gujui (opposite
       Dehan-i-Band-i-Amir)   Hazara Sayyids   18
                                                   ―――
                                        Total   183

*These people are not Sayyids, nor Hazaras.

   2. Dara Ali
       Siahbumak   Neka Hazaras   8
       Ziarat (1)   "   "   17
       Ziarat (2)   "   "   10
       Sabzju   Besud Hazaras   8
       Nawarju   "   "   16
       Deh Mir   "   "   23
       Utipur   "   "   10
       Sung   Sayyids   8
       Zarab   Besud Hazaras   20
       Kala Shah Akram   Hazara Sayyids   16
       Doburja   "   10
       Jamak   "   15
       Kala Shah Gaohar Ali   "   15
       Kala Shah Mosan   "   20
       Kala Shah Nahang   "   25
       Kala Shah Muhammad Amin   "   5

Pushta	Besud Hazaras	20
Chehil Dukhtaran	Neka Hazaras	10
Ala Kala	Besud Hazaras	10
Sarbulak (1)	Sayyids	20
Sarbulak (2)	Neka Hazaras	20
	Total	306

3. Firozbahar

Rashk	Besud Hazaras	15
Pitao	Neka Hazaras	10
Kala Miana (or Kala Safeda)	Besud Hazaras	20
Ghulam Khwaja	Mixed Hazara Sayyids and Hazaras	20
Firozbahar (2 forts and villages)	Mixed Hazara Sayyids and Hazaras	50
Gaobargi	Hazara Sayyids	30
Namadak	Hazara Sayyids	20
Hauz-i-Shah	Hazara Sayyids	10
	Total	175

4. Band-i-Amir villages

Kupruk	Hazara Sayyids	40
Jarukashan	Hazara Sayyids	15
Kala Sabzal	Hazara Sayyids	30
Deokhana	Hazara Sayyids	10
Gumao	Hazara Sayyids	10
Kutak	Hazara Sayyids	10
	Total	115

Total population of the Tagao Sayyid subdistrict, 779 families, all Hazara Sayyids and Hazaras, except the few "Akhunds" at Kuchkak. Shah Raza Baksh is chief of the Sayyids, and is also responsible for the revenue of the subdistrict. He lives at Naiak in Tagao Sayyid.

3. The Sar-i-Kol Subdistrict

1. Sar-i-Kol and adjacent glens.

Munar (Minar?)	Neka Hazaras	8
Kargar (Kharghar)	Sayyids	12
Larbuzan	Sayyids	20
Urburgat	Neka Hazaras	20
Isfirah	Kham-i-Aba Hazaras	8
Zobak	Sayyids	2
Kata Kala Pain+Bala	Mixed Hazaras	40
Chahar Diwali	" "	15
Kaogan	" "	15
Rahkol	Gaoshak Bacha Ghulam (Dai Zangis)	15
Sehpaksah	Neka Hazaras	12
Doburja	Mixed Hazaras	13
Sagdao	Taraghai Yangurs	15
Joshanak	Neka Hazaras	10
Khakchagir	Yangur Hazaras	15
Alwakol	" "	10
Siahshangak	" "	12

Siahbumak	Besud Hazaras	15
Bedak	Yangur Hazaras	8
Shudosh	Neka Hazaras	25
Ziarat-i-Shah Barhana	Sayyids	6
Nao Dost	Neka Hazaras	8
Zard Sang	" "	30
	Total	334

Outlying places of the Sar-i-Kol subdistrict
1. Tagao Gharak

Ulangak	Neka Hazaras	20
Kaltatop	" "	25
Gharak	" "	20
	Total	65

2. Zardgah (Zard-i-gao of map), northeast of Band-i-Amir

Zardgah (Khas)	Neka Hazaras	30
Khakdao	" "	30
Deh Bebud	" "	12
	Total	72

3. Siahkak

Karakhawl	Neka Hazaras	5
Siahkak	" "	10
	Total	15

The total population of the Sar-i-Kol subdistrict is 485 families, all Hazaras. This does not include two villages in Firozbahar, which belong to Sar-i-Kol.
The chief of Sar-i-Kol is Mir Murtaza Beg, of the Ilkhani's family (a cousin?). He collects the revenue of the subdistrict, and remits it to the Hakim of Bamian.

4. The Kham-i-Aba Subdistrict
This subdistrict, which is on the river below Yak Walang, is principally populated by Hazaras of Dai Zangi stock, who are known as "Kham-i-Abas." Kham-i-Aba is understood to be the name of the district, signifying "bend of the water" (as Kham-i-ab on the Oxus), in allusion to the winding nature of the river. "Kam" on the other hand is the word Kaum, "a tribe," or tribal division, pronounced in Hazara fashion, as bam is always pronounced bum.
They are said to be divided into the following sections:

Kirigu	Kam-i-Sadat	Kam-i-Idah
Halwakhor	Kam-i-Mattal	
Beg Ali	Kam-i-Saburi	

Also, concerning the above, the "Mir" section (Khan Khel), which is subdivided into Kalanni (elder branch) and Khurdakzi (junior branch). Mehdi-Beg, Kurban Beg, etc., belong to the former, and Faiz Ali of Sabz Dara to the latter. Mehdi Beg's own family is called Lukhman Khani, from his grandfather, Lukhman Khan.
The subdistrict properly begins at, and includes, Sabz Dara; but that glen now belongs to Yak Walang, under the personal authority of the Ilkhani.
The following are the villages of Kham-i-Aba, with their population,

etc.:

Villages	Inhabitants	Families
Sachak	Kam-i-Sadat	100
Khwaja Bedak		10
Chahilburj	Saburi	20
Sokhtagi	Mattal	60
Dahan Zulich	Halwakhor	10
Kiligan fort and Kirigu village	Kirigu	30
Dahan-i-Dara Chasht	Gangsu*	10
Siah Dara	Halwakhor	20
Maghspartao	Mingak*	15
	Idah	20
Dahab-i-Marghi	Beg Ali	20
	Allakah Uzbaks**	20
Nobala Marghi: Kham-i-Gumbat	Idad	20
Puza Asia, Khalaf Shir	Beg Ali	35
Do-ai Shah Kadam	Kalanzai	25
Khwaja Kaushah	"	10
Amrutak	"	10
	Total	425

* These are not, properly speaking, Kham-i-Abas. The Mingak Hazaras are mostly in the Balk-Ab district which is next below Kham-i-Aba.
**The people of Allakah in the Balkh-Ab district are Hazaras. The Uzbaks here mentioned may have come from Allakah at some time or other. They are probably the most southern colony of that race.

Mehdi Beg is chief of the Kham-i-Aba subdistrict, but having been contumacious in 1883-84, he was deprived of the greater part of his authority, and now only collects the revenue of Marghi (that is, Dahan-i-Marghi and Nobala Marghi). The other places are said to pay direct to Bamian.

The people of the Kham-i-Aba subdistrict go into "ailaks" every spring and summer, with their flocks. This is not the case in other parts of Yak Walang.

5. Baharak or Ghorband

This is a small Sayyid district next below Kham-i-Aba, of which it may be considered to form a part, and is the last of Bamian in this direction, the Balkh-Ab district of Turkistan commencing below Sulij.

The following is a list of villages, with their inhabitants, etc.:

Villages	Inhabitants	Families
Jaozari	Hazara Sayyids	5
Gawara Sang	" "	15
Ghorband and Baharak	" "	50
Sulij	" "	12
	Total	82

Sayyid Zulf Ali and Saiad Kurban are the chief men, each having about half the subdistrict.

Abstract of population in the Yak Walang district:
   Yak Walang   1,229 Families
   Tagao Sayyid   779

           Sari-Kol   485
           Kham-i-Aba   425
           Baharak   82

                    Total   3,000 Families

These are practically all Hazaras, the very small number of Tajiks, Uzbaks nad Akhunds being not worth counting.

The district is said to have been always quiet and well ordered, and to have paid its revenue without difficulty. The late Ilkhani seems to have been chief and Hakim of the whole, as was also the present Ilkhani, Muhammad Amir Khan, until after the accession of Amir Abdul Rahman, when the district was subdivided, and the Ilkhani is now directly responsible only for his own subdistrict of Yak Walang. Nevertheless he is a person of considerable influence, and in 1885-86 was frequently at Bamian, where he acted as a sort of deputy to the Hakim Jan Muhammad Khan. Of course things may be different with another Governor. As above stated, Shah Raza Baksh collects the revenue of the Tagao Sayyid subdistrict, and Murtaza Beg that of the Sar-i-Kol, while Mehdi Beg would have the charge of Kham-i-Aba, if he had not misconducted himself.

Revenue: Revenue is levied in this district, according to the Hazara custom, on landowners; the dehkans, who are non-landowning tenants and labourers, paying nothing. As a general rule, the assessment appears to be by houses (i.e., families); but the Ilkhani is understood to levy the revenue of his subdistrict on lands.

The proportion of landowners is large, four-fifths or three-fourths of the whole. Thus in the Yak Walang subdistrict there are said to be about 1,000 landowning families out of a population of 1,229 families.

The total revenue of the district is stated to be 18,000 Kabuli rupees. This, however, appears to be exclusive of Kham-i-Aba and Baharak. The revenue of these places is not exactly known, but that of Marghi, for which Mehdi Beg is now alone responsible, is stated to be 20 tomans, or 400 Kabuli rupees, levied at the rate of 14, 15, and 16 krans per house (family?) on landowners. The total revenue of Kham-i-Aba and Baharak may therefore be assumed to be about 2,000 Kabuli rupees.

The Ilkhani's "muajib" is said to have been originally 4,000 Kabuli rupees. This was when he had charge of the whole district. He now gets only 500 Kabulis, paid out of the revenue. The smaller Mirs also used to get something, but now receive nothing, while they have to pay revenue on their lands which were formerly free. It appears to be Hazara custom for all members of the "mir" section, or chief's family, to hold their lands free of any revenue.

The Ilkhani has 300 sowars (for which the old allowance was partly intende?). They are now paid by some small remission of revenue.

Shah Raza Baksh, of Tagao Sayyid, used also to get a large "muajib." He now receives 400 rupees, but is said to have 400 sowars paid in the same way as those of the Ilkhani.

Murtaza Beg is said to have no allowance, and no sowars.

The levy of the district is therefore 700 sowars. They are of little value, except for postal service and the like.

Produce and Supplies: The district grows a considerable amount of wheat and barley in its fertile glens, also a little fruit, and some small quantity of garden produce. The people have a good many small horses and ponies, and also cattle. Sheep are not numerous, except in the Kham-i-Aba subdistrict.

The dark-brown "Dai-Zangi" barak is made in the district (as also by some of the Hazaras of Bamian), and is appreciated at Kabul. The

"gilims" of the district, particularly those of Kham-i-Aba, are famous, and find a ready sale.
The main road from Bamian to Daulat Yar, etc., runs up the Zari and Bakkak glens to the Bakkak Kotal. Supplies can be collected at Kalandran, from Zari, Deh Surkh, Kanak, and Shurshuri, sufficient for one Kabuli cavalry regiment (equivalent to 2 squadrons of our Native cavalry on Kabul scale) for one month. This with ease. Also at Bakkak from Siah Dara, Naitak, Chahar Deh, etc., to nearly the same amount.
From the Tagao Sayyid subdistrict supplies for one Kabuli cavalry regiment for nine days can be collected, and put on the road which runs through it.
At Firozbahar can be collected, from the Sar-i-Kol subdis-trict, supplies for one Kabuli cavalry regiment for eight days.
Down the river, in case of a detachment being required to go by that road, supplies can be collected at the following places.
At Sabz Dara, from Kiligan and Sabz Dara, 60 kharwars of barley and 20 kharwars of wheat. Barley is largely grown at Sabz Dara, and bhusa is said to be more abundant in proportion at Kiligan than elsewhere.
At Sachak, from Sabz Dara and Sachak, 35 kharwars of barley and 15 kharwars of wheat.
At Sokhtagi, 20 kharwars of barley and 15 of wheat.
At Dahan-i-Marghi, 20 kharwars of barley and 15 of wheat.
In other words, a depot might be formed at Firozbahar, Kochinak, (Kochinak or Kohkinak, near Kara Khawal, where the road from Ghazni, over the Zard Zang pass, to Band-i-Amir, and the road from Bamian to Daulat Yar, cross each other.) or Band-i-Amir, containing the following amounts, collected from the whole district:

	Wheat maunds	Barley maunds
From Yak Walang subdistrict	750	2,700
From Tagao Sayyid subdistrict	110	400
From Sara-i-Kol subdistrict	100	360
From Kham-i-Aba subdistrict	1,040	2,480
Total	2,000	5,940

If a force of one British Indian infantry division, with its artillery and cavalry, and an attached cavalry brigade of two regiments, (roughly estimated at 4,000 combatants, 12,000 followers, 2,000 horses, and 5,000 mules and ponies.) were passing through the district, the above amounts would suply rations--for men, for 3 days; for animals, 13 or 14 days.
The amounts are given on the authority of the district officials.
Probably more wheat might be obtained. There are sufficient mills to grind it, if this is done locally, but 15 to 20 days should be allowed for grinding and collection.
Ghi in proportion to ata might be forthcoming from the Kham-i-Aba subdistrict. Deficiencies can be made up from Besud, the country south of the Band-i-Baba--where it is produced in large quantities.
Grass is abundant in the Yakh Walang valley; and baggage animals would find grazing in most parts of the district in spring and summer.

BAMIAN بامیان
34-49 67-49. Bamian, is the name of a town and woleswali in the Bamian province. The woleswali comprises an area of 2,178 square kilometers and has an agricultural population which has been

variously estimated by various Afghan sources at from 13,549 to 14,180. The woleswali is bounded in the west by Yakowlang, and in the north by Saighan, in the east by Shibar districts, and in the south by Oruzgan and Maidan provinces. Bamian has about 58 villages of which about 10 have more than 500 inhabitants. The villages are listed in the PG as follows: Gulestan, Aqrubat, Gunbad, Shahidan (Shaidan), Bariki, Darwaza-i-Shahidan, Ladu, Khwaja Hasan, Jum Qala, Dahan-i-Jaw Palal, Bam Saraye, Bersuna wa Siyah Khak, Paye Kotal (Tikar), Tajek, Tupchi, Cherastughi, Sar-i-Qol, Joye Shahr, Tibuti, Jagra Khel, Haidarabad, Shebertu, Sher Qad (Shew Qad), Fatmasti, Qazan, Qarghanatu, Qafela Bashi, Miyana Qol-i-Surkhjoy (Kata Sang), Katuri (Katwaye), Gorwan, Lala Khel, Mulayan, Miyana Quad (Miyana Qad-i-Tiker), Naurozi, Dahudi, Katuk-o-Tiker (Katuk), Dost Beg (Foladi), Khosh Rak-i-Jadra (Khushkak-i-Chap Dara), Kham-i-Kelak, Khwaja Roshnai wa Bersuna, Khor Lankash (Kholankash), Dahan-i-Ahangaran, Dokani, Dasht-i-Isa Khan, Zekriya wa Borghastun, Sar Asiab, Sar Ahangaran (Ahangaran-i-Kalu), Surkhdar, Sabzak, Somara, Siyah Layak, Sayyidabad, Faqirga, Tangi Bariki, Miyan-i-Wilayat, Zuti, Zawjak, Sultan, Minara, Kamati, and Chardehi. (LWA) In 1914, this area was described as follows:

A district on the north side of the Koh-i-Baba. It consists of a long, deep valley immediately at the foot of the northern spurs of the main range, with all the glens and ravines running into it. North it is bounded by the Doab and Saighan districts; east by Shaikh Ali country; and south by Besud. Its western boundary is the watershed between the Bamian stream and the sources of the Rud-i-Band-i-Amir, which drains the Yak Walang district. Yak Walang, peopled by Takana Dai Zangis, and the whole Dai Zangi country, were under the jurisdiction of the Governor of Bamian in 1886, and are probably still attached to the district. They are separately described under their own headings, while statistics of the population, resources, etc., of Bamian proper. Yak Walang, and the Dai Zangi country will be found under "Bamian (district)."
The climate is severe in winter, the elevation roughly ranging between 7,000' and 11,000' in the inhabited parts. Kala Sarkari is 8,350', Karghanatu 10,845', Ak Robat 9,955', and Kala Darwesh 9,300'. Lower down the Bamian stream, Jalmish is 6,630'.
Forts, or high walled villages, are scattered up and down the valley, but there is no central agglomeration of houses which could be called the town of Bamian. Looking east from the Kham Kotal (11,660 feet) on the Bamian-Band-i-Amir water-shed, Maitland describes the general aspect of the country as bleak and barren, the Bamian valley lying in a deep hollow before him between the snowy heights of the Koh-i-Baba on the right and the Koh-i-Ghandak on the left. The road leading east from the Kotal runs across the drainage of several large inhabited glens, and reaches Kala Sarkari, the centre of Bamian, at 27 miles. 9-1/2 miles lower down, just below the mouth of the Kalu glen, the valley runs abruptly to the north, and becomes a narrow defile, known as the Ao Dara. At Nagara Khana the Bamian and Saighan streams unite, while the Kamard comes in at Doab-i-Mekhzari, the river thus formed being at first known as the Surkhab and afterwards as the Aksarai or Kunduz. Near Kala Sarkari the width of the valley is about half a mile; the stream is shallow in autumn and only a few yards wide.
The most important routes which traverse the district are the main Kabul-Turkistan road, via the Shibar and Katar Sum passes; the Kabul-Hajigak and Kabul-Irak roads; and the Yak Walang road to Daulat Yar. Other roads, from the north, are the Chap Kolak, four difficult paths over the Ghandak Koh, and the Zarsang road; but

south the Koh-i-Baba forms an almost impenetrable barrier, and, with the exception of the Irak, Hajigak, and the Kotal-i-Kafzar in the southeast corner, there is no practicable route. Thus it will be seen that all the roads from the principal passes over the Koh-i-Baba to Kabul unite near Zohak, and the strategic value of the position fully accounts for the ancient prestige of that ruined fortress. The importance of Bamian is therefore due to its position, as a force located there would cover the group of passes mentioned above, and would command the main route from Turkistan to the Afghan capital.

Regarding the inhabitants of Bamian, Maitland gives the following information: "Omitting these (i.e., the Dai Zangis of the Dai Zangi and Yak Walang districts), the population of Bamian proper is four-fifths Hazara, very little beyond the actual narrow valley being held by the Tajiks and Sayyids, who constitute the remainder of the inhabitants. The next district north of Bamian is that of Saighan and Kamard, which belongs to Afghan Turkistan. There are a few Hazaras settled in Saighan, and they graze their flocks all over the hills of the district in summer.

The Khatai, or Darghan, Hazaras of Bamian

The eastern end of the Bamian district is occupied by a tribe of Hazaras who originally lived in Besud, but about a hundred years ago crossed the watershed and established themselves in their present location. To the compiler they spoke of themselves as Khatai, but Peacocke, who saw more of them, invariably calls them Darghan. As a matter of fact, they are the Darghan branch of the Khatai tribe. The Khatai Hazaras are one of the main or original divisions of the Hazaras, and the bulk of them, who are also called Babali, are adjacent to, or partly in, the Kandahar districts of Tirin and Dehrawat (see "Hazaras").

The country of the Darghan or Khatai Hazaras principally consists of the large glens of Kalu, Irak, and Bulola, which lead to Kharzar in Besud and the main road from Kabul to Bamian now passes over the Hajigak although up to the end of 1886 it was by the Irak. Both these roads are closed in winter, and the Shibar is then alone used. Running east from the Shibar is the Dara Shaikh Ali, and north of the watershed of the Bulola glens is Jalmish, also inhabited by Shaikh Alis, so the Darghan Hazaras are to some extent interposed between two of the principal locations of that tribe.

Kalu proper extends from the watershed of the Hajigak and Kafzar Kotals down to Gumbat, and is a fertile valley for the most part, half a miles wide. Being the most thickly populated part of the Darghan Hazara country. It appears to give its name to the whole, which is officially known as the Kalu subdivision of Bamian.

The elevation of the country generally, that is, of the inhabited valleys and glens, is from 8,000 to 10,000 feet. There seems to be a good deal of cultivation considering the mountanious nature of the district, and the people have some orchards. Besides wheat, barley, and the usual pulses, carrots and turnips are grown. The Darghanis also possess flocks of goats and sheep, a few horses, and the average amount of cattle.

They make barak, jhools, khurzins, etc., like most other Hazaras. They live in small forts or walled villages all the year round, and do not go to ailaks to pasture. They do not go to Kabul or elsewhere in winter to obtain employment like many other Hazaras; at least if they do, it is in small numbers. This may be taken as a sign that they are fairly well off. Their dress is much the same as that of their Tajik neighbours, and they appear to be quiet and unwarlike.

The following is a detail of the Darghan Hazaras by their subdivisions:

The Khatai, or Darghan, Hazaras of the Bamian district

Sections	Location	No. of Families	Remarks
Shaikha	Shibar and Bulola	280	These 800 families, all in the Bulola and Irak glens and their lateral ravines, are under Sayad Baksh Khan of the Khida section.
Shakh	Birgilich	120	
Gudi	Dara Jola and Dara Shambol	100	
Khida	Irak, Some in Shambol and Bulola	300	
Markadam	Pai Muri, Jaokol, and Kalu	190	These 270 families under Kalbi Husain Khan.
Ahingaran	Ahingaran (and Sadbarg?)	80	
Thkarachi	Kalu and lateral glens	200	These 330 families under Ghulam Haidar Khan.
Khwaja Jama	Upper Kalu	130	
	Total	1,400	Families

The above follows Subadar Muhammad Husain's list more closely than that at page 412 of Volume 4, and, after carefully collating all the information available, it is believed to be nearly correct. Only the sections are probably more mixed than is apparent from the table.

Kalbi Husain is chief of the whole, and in the time of Sher Ali was responsible for the entire revenue of the subdistrict. But since Abdul Rahman became Amir, he has been deprived of authority over all but a small portion of his people. He appears in fact to have only lower Kalu: Ghulam Haidar Khan has upper Kalu, while a majority of the whole tribe living in Bulola, Irak, etc., are under Sayad Baksh Khan.

According to Subadar Muhammad Husain, the revenue taken from the Darghan Hazaras amounts to 7,000 Kabuli rupees, which is payable in cash not in kind.

Other Hazaras of Bamian: On the south side of the Bamian valley are several large glens running up to the crest of the Band-i-Baba. The largest and most important is the Dara Fauladi, the lower portion of which is known as Tagao Tajik. The latter is inhabited by Tajiks, and the former is occupied by Fauladi Hazaras, no doubt a branch of those of Malistan and Ujaristan elsewhere described. Little is known of them except that they number 1,000 families and that their Chief, Mir Baba Beg, was in confinement at Kabul in 1885-86, and had not been heard of for a long while.

A short distance east of the Dara Fauladi is Tagao Sayyidabad, which contains about 200 families of Hazaras, apparently mixed. About 100 families of mixed Hazaras are also found at Gumbat and Ak Robat, which are at the head of Bamian on the roads leading to Saighan, also over the watershed, in the Saighan district, at Chapkolak, Naorak, Ghorao, etc., are about 125 families of Hazaras, some of whom are Fauladis.

Going westward from Bamian by the main road to Herat via Daulat Yar, which passes through Yak Walang, three valleys are crossed, all of which drain to the Bamian stream. These are Shahidan, Shibartu, and Karghanatu. They are all inhabited exclusively by Hazaras. Those of Shahidan are Yangur Dai Zangis (150 families); those of Shibartu are Khubzat Fauladis (90 families); and those of Karghanatu are Shahgum Beg Hazaras, who are supposed to be Takana Dai Zangis, but have now little to do with the Takanas of Yak Walang.

Finally, about the head of Saighan, at and above Sayyid Baba, in the glens called Khargin or Begal and Ao Dara, are about 80 families of Begal Hazaras, who are also Takanas.

None of the above are of sufficient importance to merit a special description. They dress much like the Tajiks. They all appear very quiet, peaceable folk.

There are no Hazaras settled in Kamard, although many pasture over the hills in summer.

The following table shows the total number of Hazaras in Bamian proper and Saighan:

Total Hazaras of Bamian and Saighan

District	Tribe	Location	Families
Bamian district of the Kabul Province.	Khatai or Darghan Hazaras*	Kalu, Irak and Bulola glens, all east of the Bamian Valley	1,400
Ditto	Polada**	Polada	1,000
Saighan, which belongs to Afghan Turkistan	Polada	Chapkolak and Naorak	25
Bamian	(Kubzat Section)	Shibartu	90
Ditto	Yangur Dai Zangis***	Shahidan	150
Ditto	Shahgum Beg Takana Dai Zangis****	Karghanatu	135
Saighan	Begal Beg Takana Dai Zangis	Khargin and Ao Dara west of Saighan valley.	80
Bamian	Mixed Hazaras	Saiyidabad glen, south of Bamian valley; Gumbat and Ak Robat, west of the same.	300
Saighan	Mixed Hazaras	Ghorao and Surkhshahar, south of Saighan valley.	100
		Total	3,280 Families

*Mir Kalbi Husain was the nominal Chief of the Darghan Hazaras, in 1908. **Mir Baba Beg was Chief of Fauladis, but was in prison at Kabul in 1885-86. ***Total of Fauladis, 1,115 families. Mir Ata Beg was head of both Shahidan and Shibartu in 1885-86. ****Total of Takanas, 215 families.

It will be observed that of the above total of 3,280 families, 3,075 are in the Bamian district and only 205 in Saighan. If to the 3,075 families we add the 1,000 families of Sadmarda Shaikh Alis in Jalmish, it brings up the total to over 4,000 families of Hazaras in Bamian, while the Tajik and Sayyid population of that district is just about 1,200 families.

Bamian is remarkable for some of the most extraordinary relics of antiquity; its colossal idols, its caves, and the ruins of Zohak and Gulghulah. These idols have been described by many travellers whose speculations as to their origin are somewhat at variance. Burnes says: "It is by no means improbable that we owe the idols of Bamian to the caprice of some person of rank, who resided in this cave-digging neighbourhood, and sought for an immortality in the colossal figures which we have now described."

Masson attributes them to the White Huns, who conquered Transoxian and Khorasan about the fifth century of the Christian era, but were subsequently subdued by the Turkish hordes, and finally exterminated by Changiz Khan. He considers the caves to have been catacoombs, and the gigantic images intended to represent illustrious persons deceased.

Moorcroft, familiar with the opinions, faith, prageantry and buildings of the Lamas of Thibet, is of opinion that Bamian was the residence of a great Lama bearing the same relation the Lamaism of the west that the Lama of Lhassa does now to that of the east; "that those excavations, which were con- nected by means of galleries and staircases, constituted the acommodation of the higher orders of the Lama clergy, and that the insulated caves and cells were the dwelling-places of the lower classes of the monastic society, the monks and nuns, and hostels for visitors. The laity inhabited the adjoining city." On the whole, it seems most probable that these relics are of Budhist origin, and this belief is countenanced by their resemblance to fix the date of formation of the idols, of Bamian, it should be borne in mind that they are nowhere described by the Greek historians, who, cursory as their notices on this country generally are, could scarcely have failed to mention such extraordinary objects, if existing during the Macedonian campaigns. Elphinstone, whose opinions seems to be the best supported, attribute the idols and the contiguous caves to the Budhist Princes of Ghor, who ruled the ocuntry between Kabul and Persia in the early centuries of the Christian era. They are noticed by Sharif-ud-din in his account of Timur Lang's campaigns, and this is perhaps the earliest authentic evidence which we have respecting them. They were visited by Maitland and Talbot and the following is Maitland's account of them, writing form Kala Sarkar.

On the north side of the valley the cliffs are tolerably continuous, and average perhaps 300 feet in height, including the broken ground and debris slope at their foot. It is in these cliffs the famous idols, the "Bhut-i-Bamian," are sculptured. They are, moreover, literally honeycombed with caves for nearly half their height. Caves are also found in the debris slope at the bottom. The entrances of the caves are often protected by mud walls, and a straggling sort of village extends all along the base and on the slope. Most of the caves are also inhabited.

Facing the cliff, the larger of the two big idols is to the left, the other to the right. They are about a quarter of a mile apart, and are both undoubtedly Budhas, which once belonged to Budhist monasteries in the adjacent rock chambers. (These gigantic figures are practically identical in design, drapery, and detail with statues of Budha preserved in the Lahore Museum.) These figures are supposed, by the present inhabitants, to be male and female, their heights are respectively 180 and 120 feet. They have names, those given us being the same as were recorded by earlier travellers, Sal Sal for the larger figure and Shah Mama for the other. The Budhas are standing figures, sculptured in very bold relief, in deep niches. Between the two large Budhas are or rather were, two smaller ones also in niches. These are equidistant from the large ones and from each other; that is to say, there is about 150 yards between each of the niches, great and small. The niche nearer to the large figure which I will call No. 3, is the largest; it is about 60 or

70 feet in height, and now empty, though a close inspection shows fragments of the Budha which once filled it. The other niche (No. 4) is still occupied by a sitting figure, which is about 40 feet high, and is locally known as the bacha or child. The general shape of the niches is the same as in all cases as that of the so-called female figure (No. 2) is evidently unfinished, and the shoulders are not marked, nor the edges smoothed off. The depth of the niches of the two large Budhas is about twice the tickness of the figures standing in them. The latter are therefore fairly well protected from the weather, which partly accounts for their excellent preservation, nearly all the damage done to them being due to the hand of man. The whole interior of the niches, and particularly the arches over the heads of the figures, have been marked with what appear to have been allegorical designs. Although much damaged - in fact obliterated wher ever they could easily be got at - enough remains to show the general style of the work, which is exceedingly well executed and forcibly reminds one of what is generally understood as Byzantine art. I set the young native draughtsman at work to copy as much as he could of the fragments, and, ill-situated as they are for the purpose he has succeeded in bringing away some interesting bits.

The Budhas themselves are rather clumsy figures hewn in the tough conglomerate rock, and afterwards thickly overlaid with stucco, in which all the details were executed. The stucco appears to have been painted, or at least paint was used in some places. The features of the figures have been purposely destroyed, though the mouth of the larger one remains. On the other hand, the legs of this figure have been partly knowcked away; it is said by cannon shot fired at it by Nadir Shah. Both idols are draped in garments reaching to below the knee. The limbs and contour of the body show through, and the general effect of muslin is excellently immitated in the stucco. The arms of both are bent at the elbow, the forearms and hands projecting, but the latter are now broken off. The feet have also been battered out of shape.

Narrow stairways, hewn in the interior of the rock, lead up from cave to cave, to the heads of the figures, and even to the summit of the hill. Two of my men actually ascended to the top of the so-called female figure, and we measured its height by letting down a rope. The upper part of the ascent is not, however, very easy. The head of the largest figure is now inaccessible, a portion of the stairway having fallen within the last few years; but it is said the summit of the cliffs can still be gained.

The caves, though so numerous, are not large. By far the great portion of them are chambers 12 or 16 feet square, with domed roofs. I think, as a rule, several chambers open into each other , and have a wide portico in front, by which the light is admitted to the doorways. The latter have generally round arches. There are certainly no pointed arches anywhere, but some of the openings may be quare-headed. The domes are set on the foursided chambers in a remarkable manner, the square being reduced to an octagon by cornices, springing in tiers from the angles, in unmistakeable imitation of brickwork. It is a very curious fact that at Kandahar domes are to this day built on square chambers in exactly the same fashion. We noticed one roof of a different kind: it was flat, and divided in four by deep wide cuts crossing each other in the centre. Small cupolas were hewn in the centre of each of the spaces and at the intersection of the cuts.

The largest cave of all is said to be that whose entrance is between the feet of the Budha; but this, with several other of the most interesting caves, is used as a government store, and was filled with lucerne, etc. We saw no vihara caves, but some are said to exist. As above mentioned, the majority of the caves are inhabited. It is said they all were, a few years ago. Together with the mud huts and houses beneath, they form two contiguous villages called Daudi and Bughlani, the latter being in the neighbourhood of the biggest figure.

The interiors of the caves are plain, without sculptural ornamentation and are now completely smoke-blackened. The whole, however, were plastered with stucco and painted. The stucco remains, and can be chipped off, with fragments of paint still on it. In one of the upper caves, near the head of the so-called female idol, some designs are still visible, and a curious one was copied by the native draughtsman.

A short distance east of this figure (No. 2), in the fields near the foot of the cliff, is a mound which Talbot believes to be the remains of a Budhist "top." He could not, however, find any brickwork in position, so as to settle the matter beyond doubt.

Went to the second largest figure (female idol) this evening and measured it. It is some way up the cliff, the bottom of the niche being on a level with the top of the debris slope. In the many hunderd years that have elapsed since the figures and caves were hewn, portions of the surface of the rock have scaled off, partially destroying the cave openings. This is particularly the case to left of the second figure, where a considerable lump has come down. There are darksome caves at the back of the niche on the ground level, the entrances being between the legs of the figure, and on each side. But these caves are of no size or interest. The design on the arch over the head of the Budha can to a certain extent be made out with a field glass. Within a circle, is a figure in a long robe, armed with a spear, and apparently slaying something. The two upper corners, outside the circle, are filled with figures of angels, or cherubs, waving scarves at each other. They might well date from the last century. On either side is a border, with male and female busts, or half figures, in circles, and all adorned with halos. Outside the central design, of the left hand side, is a very curious figure of a human-headed bird.

Further on Maitland gives the following additional information about the largest figure:

"In the figure itself, and the back and side of the niche, are numerous holes, revealed by the disappearance of the stucco. These we thought must have been sockets for the ends of the beams and poles forming the scaffolding errected for the plastering and painting of the Budhas and its niche. On the ample left shoulder of the monstrous image a pierced wall has been built to some height. It is impossible now to conjecture what this was for, and it is inaccessible, at least I think so. It may be mentioned the only way of getting to this figure is through the sarai newly built in front of it. The old sarai was a little distance to one side. It was disappointing to find that the large cave, the entrance of which is between the feet of the figure was sealed up, and could not be entered.

The rock on the left side (west) of the figure is badly cracked, the cracks extending into the niche. This has been caused, in recent times, by water penetrating from above, and is the reason why the staircase is now impractible. The day is not far distant when there will be an extensive fall of rock here, involving the partial destruction of the niche, which is much to be regretted, thought the figure itself is in no danger, as far as can be seen.

We went here and there, and examined various other caves out of the hundreds in the neighbourhood. There were few we could closely inspect as they are nearly all inhabited, as we did not like to

intrude too much on the domestic life of the people. No one seemed to mind us, however, and the women went on with their occupations, little disturbed by the presence of strangers. This was somewhat remarkable, as the residents in the caves are all Tajiks; and these people seem to seclude their women as jealously as the Afghans. Almost our last visit was to the Jah-i-Jamshed, one of the largest of the caves, and by far the largest of any we saw. It is situated some distance east of the second largest figure. A narrow stair is ascended, after which it is necessary to proceed in a bent attitude along a very narrow path cut in the face of the rock which overhangs it. Another narrow stair in the rock leads up to the spacious portico in front of the cave. In exploring these caves candles should be taken (good reflecting laterns if possible) and a native should be sent first, for the people keep their cattle with them, and one is as likely as not to meet a cow on the staircase. In some places, and in the dark, such a rencontre would be awkward.
Being only lighted through the door, quite a small one, the cave was intensely dark, and the candles we lighted seemed to have no effect in illuminating its cavernous blackness. Nevertheless, at least one family lives in this cave, which is divided by low stone walls into small compartments like old fashioned pews, in some of which goats, cows, and donkeys are installed. We guessed the cave to be some 30 or 35 feet square with a domed roof. As is almost invariably the case, there is a shallow recess, or niche, at the further end.
Being unable to ascent to the head of the largest figure, Talbot took its height by triangulation, and made it as before stated, 180 feet.
On the east side of tagao Saidabad is the fifth idol, or gigantic Budha. It is some way up the cliff, which is pierced with numerous caves like that on the north side of the main valley. The niche appears to be about the size of No. 3 (say 60 feet high), and the figure in it has its head covered with a sort of cap or tiara (common in statues of Budha). There can be no reasonable doubt that the two big Budhas were once adorned in like manner. The tops of their heads are now unnaturally flat, forcibly suggesting the idea that something has been cut off." (Maitland, I.B.C.)

BAM SARAH   بامسرا
34-47 67-52 G. A village in Bamian, situated in the Sayyidabad glen, 100 houses of Sayyids. (A.B.C.)

BANAHAL   بانههل
33-10 68-26 m. A village located northwest of the Jarkana Ghar and south of Ghazni.

BANARAS KHAN KALA   بنارس خان قلعه
34-18 67-54. A village in the Besud division about 3 miles southwest of the Besud village. Inhabitants: Duranis. (Jenkyns.)

BAND   بند
33-18 68-37 m. A Ghilzai village of about 40 houses in the Shilghar division of Zurmat. It lies about 21 miles northwest of Sarafsar and the same distance southeast of Ghazni. Water is plentiful and forage and fuel are available in the village while other supplies may be procured in the neighbourhood.
At Band the road from the Tochi valley to Ghazni, via Urgun is joined by the road from the Kurram valley to Ghazni, via Gardez; Gardez lies about 49 miles northeast of Band. (I.B.C.) Recent maps show the name Sardeh Band. (LWA)

BANDA بنده

34- 70-. A village of 800 inhabitants in the Jalalabad district, about 18 miles W.S.W. of Basawal. there is a good camping ground here with an abundant water supply, and supplies are fairly plentiful. (I.B.C.) Recent maps show the name Bandeh on the Alishang river, at 34-51 70-6. (LWA)

BANDA بنده

34- 69-. A small fort, containing 12 houses, near the north-west angle of the Sherpur cantonment, close to the British burial ground of 1879-80. (I.B.C.)

BANDA-I-HAJIAN بنده حاجیان

34- 70-. A village in the Surkhab division of the Jalalabad district. Inhabitants: Hindkis. (Jenkyns.)

BANDA-I-MIR AKRAM بنده میر اکرم

34- 70-. A village in the Surkhab division of the Jalalabad district. Inhabitants: Sahibzadas. (Jenkyns.)

BANDA-I-MIR SAHIB GUL بنده میر صاحب گل

34- 70-. A village in the Kama division of the Jalalabad district. Inhabitants: Saiyads. (Jenkyns.)

BANDALI بندعلی

A section of the Muhammad Khwaja Hazaras. There is a village called Band-i-Ali some 7 miles south of Gholi Talab and west of Ghazni. 33-30 68-2 m. (LWA)

BAND-I-AMIR بند امیر

35-50 67-13 m. A series of natural dams across the bed of the Band-i-Amir, where the head waters of this river are retained in a succession of large reservoirs.
There are altogether five dams, and each reservoir in succession overflows into the one next below it, the whole series being called Band-i-Amir. They are supposed by the inhabitants to be among the works of Ali, relics of whose doings abound throughout the whole country thereabouts.
Maitland's description of the Band-i-Amir lakes, starting from Kala Jafir, is as follows:
"Now turned to the right up the valley, soon reaching a small lake below the first band. The latter is a natural rocky ledge across the valley. It is known as the Band-i-Ghulaman. Above it is a lake, along the shore of which the road winds. This lake is not very deep, at least near the edges, and it has a few reeds. The water is of remarkable purity, and of the deepest blue. On the further side is the hamlet of Jaru Kashan. At the end of the lake which is perhaps half a mile in length, are rocky slopes and two ledges, with pools of shallow water. This is the Band-i-Kamar. Immediately above is the Band-i-Haidar, a natural dam about 40 feet high. The road now crosses diagonally among the pools, and turns to the right, up an easy rocky slope, covered by a few inches of water running down. This water is so absolutely clear that the rock is seen through it as if it were glass. Luckily the road is not at all slippery. At the top of the slope is the ziarat, 10 miles from our camp at Firozbahar. It is a small domed building of mud brick on the shore of the third lake, just above the Band-i-Haidar. This lake runs up several miles, being bordered, apparently the whole way, by cliffs. Its breadth here, at the lower end, is about 400 yards, and

it continues the same as far as I saw it. A little way above the
ziarat is a deep bay. The water of this lake, as of the others, is
of a most vivid blue. Elevation of the ziarat 9,790 feet.
The country above the cliffs is open and undulating.
There are two other bands above the Band-i-Pamir, and the last the
Band-i-Zulfikar. This is 3 or 4 miles from the Ziarat, and is said
to be much higher than the others. The lake above it is described
as being of great length and from 1 1/2 to 2 miles in breadth. It
is perhaps 6 to 8 miles in length, and at its head the stream issues
from a rock. It is said to be warm.
On the north side of this lake is the large village of Kupruk, said
to be about 7 miles from the ziarat. The Khakdao glen enters the
valley of the lake at this place.
The road leads along the north side of the lake to Kupruk and goes
on up the Khakdao glen to Khakdao village, from which it
leads northeast, over a watershed, into the Ao Dara, which is at the
head of the Saighan drainage. Then down the Ao Dara, through defiles, to Saighan. From thence to Kamard by the ordinary road.
The lakes of the Band-i-Amir are full of fish. At the Ziarat they
are fed by those who visit the place and a large number may always
be seen swimming about under the rocky ledge on which the place
stands, on the lookout for food. We could not determine their
species. The largest were three or four pounds." (Maitland)
The villages of the Band-i-Amir valley are given under "Bamian
(district)."

BAND-I-AZHDAHA بند اژدهار
34- 67-. A rock in the Bamian district. It is crossed by the road
from Shahidan to Kala Sarkari. (Bamian.) Maitland says of it:
"At 8 1/4 miles a low rocky band crosses the hollow. There is a
considerable drop. This is the Band-i-Azhdaha, being supposed to be
the remains of one of various dragons slain in these parts by Ali,
and subsequently turned to stone for the edification of the doings
of Ali, among which I ought to have mentioned the natural dams of
the Band-i-Amir. The outline of the rock, as looked at from above,
bears some resemblance to the body of and immense reptile, but a
certain exercise of the imagination is necessary to see it clearly.
The descent of the steep rock slope of the Band-i-Azhdaha is by no
means easy. The rough, and rather slippery, track runs diagonally
down the face of the rock at a sharp gradient. It is perhaps a
quarter of a mile in length, and the fall is 275 feet in that
distance. It would not be easy to make a gun road here. A built up
road would probably be necessary, and possibly zig-zags might have
to be resorted to.
From the bottom of the Band-i-Azhdaha, the road continues to descend
the ravine which is about 300 yards across, the sides being frequently cliffs of gravel or clay, but not at first more than 150
feet feet in height. The ravine winds to a certain extent, and the
cliffs become higher. They are pierced by numerous caves towards
the lower end of the ravine. The road is very good all the way. At
9 3/4 miles entered the Bamian valley." (Maitland.)

BAND-I-BABA   See KOH-I-BABA بند بابه

BAND-I-BARAN (Or BAIRUN) بند باران
34- 67-. A subsidiary range running between, parallel to the Band-i-Baba and the main Kabul-Hazarajat-Daulat Yar road. (Wanliss.)

BAND-I-DOKAT بند دوکت
34- 66-. Appears to be another name for the Band-i-Duakhan.

BAND-I-DUAKHWAN   بند دواخوان (دو آخند)
   34- 66-.   The name given to the western extension of the Koh-i-
   Baba. Recent maps show the name Band-i-Doakhund, at 34-23 66-20 m.
   (LWA)

BAND-I-SULTAN   بند سلطان
   33-46 68-23 m. A dam formed by Mahmud of Ghazni across a rocky
   valley, to dam up the Ghazni river. It is a wall of masonry, which,
   when complete, must have been 300 yards long, its height varying
   from 20 feet to 8 feet, and its thickness 6 or 7 feet. (Broadfoot.)

*BAND-I-TAL   بند تل
   35-11 66-57 m. A mountain south of the Band-i-Karak in eastern
   Bamian.

BAND-I-WARSANDAN   بند ورسندان
   35-13 68-35 m. The name locally applied to that part of the Hindu
   Kush which lies to the north of Ghorband.

*BANDSANG   بند سنگ
   34-9 67-36 m. A village in the Kamarak area, 2 miles south of
   Kamarak in southern Bamian province.

*BANDUK   بندوك
   34-7 70-34 m. A village located about 10 miles south of Shahikot in
   Nangarhar province.

*BANDUL   باندول
   35-9 70-8 m. A village located on a tributary of the Pashal (Nuristan) river in Laghman province.

*BANG   بنگ
   33-18 68-36 m. A village near the Sardeh Band on the road from
   Sharan to Ghazni.

BANGI   See BARAM KHEL   بنگی

*BANGIQOL   بنگی قول
   34-27 68-2 m. A village located 2 miles south of the Helmand river
   in Maidan province.

*BANGISHAI   بنگی شی
   34-7 68-27 m. A village on the Dara-i-Jelga, east of the Bolibum
   Ghar.

BAPROK   بپرك
   35- 71-. A Katir Kafir village of 40 houses situated up the gul of
   the same name, on the road from the Bashgul to the Mami pass.
   (Robertson.)

BARABAD   برآباد
   34-41 70-58 G. A village in the Kunar district, on the left bank fo
   the Kunar river, about one mile below Pashat, where there is a ferry
   over the river. It lies at the mouth of a dara leading down from
   the Shaunkarai pass in the Kabul Tsappar range, over which goes a
   path into the Mohmand valley of Mitai. (I.B.C.)

*BARA DARGAI   See DARGAI   بره درگی
   A village with this name is located about 10 miles northeast of

Jagdalak, at 34-28 69-52 G.

BARAK برك
35-22 69-31 m. A village on left bank of the upper Panjshir river, 7 miles above Bazarak. It has 20 houses of Tajiks. (Shahzada Taimus.)

*BARAKALA بره كلا
34-24 68-39 m. A village located on a tributary of the Maidan river, about 12 miles west of Nerkh.

BARAKAT بركت
33-39 68-20 m. Said to be a pass over the Gul Koh. It is within 16 miles of Ghazni, and resembles the Gulbauri. (Broadfoot.)

*BARA KHEL بارمخيل
34-3 70-47 m. A village located southeast of Achin and south of Sorubai.

BARAKI بروكى
34- 69-. A large village 1 1/2 miles west of Sherpur, 1/2 mile east of Nanachi. Inhabitants Tajiks. There is a fort here and 65 houses. The inhabitants belong ot the Baraki section of Tajiks, but have lost their peculiar dialect. (I.B.C.) Another village with this name is near Abana, on a tributary of the Arghandab, at 33-17 67-12 m. (LWA)

BARAKI بركى
A tribe of Tajiks who inhabit Logar and part of Butkhak. Mixed with the Ghilzais they differ from the other Tajiks, inasmuch as they form a tribe under chiefs of their own, furnish a good many troops to the Government, closely resemble the Afghans in their manners, and are more respected than any other Tajiks. All traditions agree that they were introduced into their present seats by Sultan Mahmud, about the beginning of the 11th century, and that their lands were once extensive, but their origin is uncertain. They pretend to be sprung from the Arabs, but others say they are descended from Kurds. They are included in the general term Tajik. They accompanied Sultan Mahmud of Ghazni in his invasion of India, and were preeminently instrumental in the abstraction of the gates of the temple of Somnath. There are two divisions of this tribe, the Barakis of Rajan, in the province of Logar, who speak Persian, and the Barakis of Barak, a village near the former, who speak the language called Baraki. Sultan Mahmud, pleased with their services in India, was determined to recompense them by giving them in perpetual grant any part of the country they chose; they fixed on the district of Kaniguram in the country of the Waziris, where they settled. (Elphinstone, Leech.)

BARAKI BARAK بره كى برك
33-58 68-57 m. Baraki Barak is the name of a village and a woleswali in Logar province. The woleswali comprises an area of 329 square kilometers and has an agricultural population which has been variously estimated at from 39,068 to 60,875. The Woleswali is bounded in the west by Sayyidabad, in the north and east by Puli Alam, and in the south by Charkh. Baraki Barak includes some 168 villages, of which about thirteen have more than 500 inhabitants. The villages are listed in the PG as follows:
Qarya-i-Shah Mazar, Qala-i-Abdullah, Ozbak Khel, Qala-i-Abas, Shaikhi Khel, Deh-i-Shah Mazar, Edo Khel, Qala-i-Moh'd Rafiq, Allah Dad

Khel, Qala-i-Shaikh Maulawi, Qala-i-Yusuf Khel, Chalozai, Qala-i-Lalak, Qala-i-Tagab, Char Qala-i-Chalozai, Qala-i-Kalan-i-Chalozai, Baraki Barak, Masjed-i-Shaikhan, Masjed-i-Takya, Qala-i-Gulam Haider, Masjed-i-Qazi, Masjed-i-Kako Saheb, Qala-i-Alef, Qala-i-Wardak, Qala-i-Hafizulla, Qala-i-Taqi, Qala-i-Dad Mohammad, Qala-i-Payendah Jan, Qala-i-Dawud, Qala-i-Chandal, Qala-i-Zaqum Khel, Qala-i-Haji Modh. Shah, Qala-i- Turab, Qala-i-Bajawri, Qala-i-Qadir, Qala-i-Baz Khan, Qala-i-Mirza Abdul Ghafur, Qala-i-Qalich, Qala-i-Shaikhan, Qala-i-Siddiq, Qala-i-Habib, Qala-i-Sar Buland, Qala-i-Pad Khwabi, Qala-i-Nazir Mohd. Ismail, Qala-i-Qazi Mohd. Ishaq, Qala-i-Abdul Samad, Qala-i-Mohd. Omar, Qala-i-Malik Sadat, Qala-i-Shaikhan-i-Mohmand, Qala-i-Jogi, Qala-i-Lalak, Qala-i-Darya Khel, Qala-i-Kohna-i-Mohmand, Qala-i-Mulla Akhtar Mohammad, Deh Shaikh, Qala-i-Topak, Qala-i-Hawas Khel, Qala-i-Sajawand, Qarya-i-Malika, Qala-i-Babi, Khwaja Ahmad, Qala-i-Qeyamuddin, Akhund Khel, Nau Burja, Chowi, Baraki Rajan, Pahn Deh, Mohsin Shah, Kata Paye, Lala Shah, Shahghasi, Faiz Mohammad, Sultan Mohd., Bakoni, Kashmiri, Mulla Mir, Mohammad Jan, Belal, Sangbur, Masjed-i-Karendah, Masjed-i-Hosain Khan, Darwaza-i-Kalan, Qala-i-Morad Khan, Masjed-i-Sayedha, Qala-i-Sayed Afraz, Qala-i-Mir Shahabuddin, Qala-i-Ahmadak, Qala-i-Zarabshah, Qala-i-Shah Abulfatah, Qala-i-Nad-i-Ali, Lal Mohammad, Chehiltan, Sayyidi, Masjed-i-Shah Sekandar, Masjed-i-Kalan, Masjed-i-Nadi Khel, Qala-i-Janak, Qala-i-Mulla Musa, Qala-i-Panj Paye, Qala-i-Ghairat, Qala-i-Mirza Khel, Qala-i-Ata Mohammad, Qala-i-Allahyar, Qala-i-Sangi, Qala-i-Mulla Shirjan, Qala-i-Qazi Mohd. Akbar Khan, Qala-i-Karez-i-Hayat, Qala-i-Sher Khan, Qala-i-Baqa, Qala-i-Mulla Khel, Masjed-i-Mirza Ghaws, Qala-i-Faizulla, Qala-i-Bahu, Qala-i-Durani, Masjed-i-Hazrat-i-Ghaws, Qarya-i-Hayat, Qarya-i-Samandar, Qarya-i-Afghanan, Qarya-i-Mohammad Shah, Masjed-i-Bala Kocha, Qala-i-Shamak-i-Shak, Masjed-i-Khair Khana, Masjed-i-Baqer Shah, Qarya-i-Gagai, Qarya-i-Naqak, Shaikh Neyazulla, Qala-i-Mir Aman, Qala-i-Ziawuddin, Qala-i-Nur Mohammad, Qala-i-Rahmatullah, Qala-i-Nayeb, Qala-i-Rajab Ali, Qala-i-Aminulla, Masjed-i-Shah Qussur, Qala-i-Char Suq, Qala-i-Janlala, Qala-i-Sadat, Qarya-i-Faqir, Qala-i-Din Mohd. Afghan, Qala-i-Gul Mohammad, Rustam Khel, Gagari Khel, Qarya-i-Dastagir, Qarya-i-Bahadur, Qala-i-Nazir, Ibrahim Khel, Qala-i-Yahya, Qala-i-Nurullah, Qarya-i-Hazrat, Qarya-i-Rajan, Qarya-i-Koko Gul, Badni Khel, Qala-i-Qazi, Pad Khwab-i-Roghani, Qala-i-Baburi Roghani, Qala-i-Nau-i-Roghani, Qarya-i-Dawud Shah, Qarya-i-Namdar, Qala-i-Mohd., Qala-i-Tawakul wa Babi, Qarya-i-Tundan, and Qarya-i-Qadir. (LWA)

In 1914, the village of Baraki Barak was described as follows: A large village in the upper portion (southern division) of the Logar valley. The inhabitants are Tajiks, and in 1880 the village contained 500 families.

Baraki Barak stands on the left bank of the Logar river and about 1 1/2 miles to the north of Baraki-Rajan. Surgeon Major Johnston describes the lithological composition of the hills in the immediate neighbourhood of Baraki Barak as follows:

"Pepper and salt trap, spider-veined hornblende, dark-streaked diotite." The inhabitants (vide "Baraki") speak a dialect of their own. Supplies are plentiful at Baraki Barak, and water is abundant. The cavalry and two infantry brigades of the Kabul-Kandahar force camped here together on 11th August 1880. (Clifford, Evan Smith, I.B.C.)

BARAKI RAJAN برکی راجان
33-56 68-54 G. A large village in the upper portion (southern division) of the Logar valley. The inhabitants are mostly Tajiks, and the village, including its outlying hamlets, contained, in 1880,

1,000 families. They speak the Baraki dialect (vide "Baraki"). A larger number of Hindus live here also.

Baraki-Rajan stands on the right bank of the Logar river, about 1 1/2 miles south of Baraki-Barak, and from it roads branch off towards Kabul on the north, towards Charkh on the south, and towards the Tangi Wardak and the Sojawan pass on the west and southwest, respectively. The Hakim of Logar has his headquarters at Baraki-Rajan, and a battalion of infantry is stationed here. (Clifford, Evan Smith, I.B.C.)

*BARAK KALAI   برك كلى
33-24 69-23 m. A village on the road from Waze to Gardez, about 3 miles south of Shewak.

BARAKZAI   باركزى
35- 69-. A village in the upper Panjshir valley, 45 miles from Kabul, consisting of two forts and 40 houses of Barakzais. Water from a stream. Thence there is a pass named Solanah, extremely dangerous, on account of the Durnama and Sigrawir robbers. (Leech.)

BARAKZAI   باركزى
For a description of this Durani clan, see Volume 5.

BARAM KHEL   بارام خيل (بهرام)
A village in the upper Panjshir glen 5 miles above Anaba, twelve houses of Tajiks. Near it is the village of Bangi, also containing 12 houses of Tajiks. (Shahzada Taimus.)

*BARAN KALA   باران قلعه
33-17 68-53 m. A village on the road from Yusufkhel to Gardez, about 30 miles from Gardez.
A village called Barankhel is located at 35-15 69-27 m.

BARAT   برات
A section of the Dai Kundi Hazaras.

*BARAT KHEL   برات خيل
33-1 68-40 m. A village in Yusufkhel alaqadari, about 2 miles southeast of Yusufkhel.

BARBAR   See HAZARAS   باربر

BARBARA   See BOBAR   باربره

BARG   برگ
A tagao in Dai Zangi country.

*BARGAI   برگى
33-19 69-32 m. A village near Alauddin and some 8 miles west of Nadir Shah Kot.

*BARGAM   بارگام
35-8 71-23 m. A village on the Kunar river, some 8 miles north of Asmar in Kunar province.

BARGHAR   برغار
A district inhabited by Dai Zangi Hazaras.

*BARG-I-MATAL or BRAGAMATAL   برگ متال
35-40 71-20 m. Barg-i-Matal is a village and an alaqadari in Nangar-

har province. The alaqadari comprises an area of 1,977 square kilometers and has an agricultural population that has been estimated at from 2,880 to 6,600. The alaqadari is bounded in the south by Chapa Dara and Kamdesh, in the west by Keran or Munjan, in the north by Zibak, and in the east by the State of Pakistan. Barg-i-Matal has about 18 villages, 5 of which have more than 500 inhabitants. The villages are listed in the PG as follows: Barg Matal, Nek Mok, Baddin Shah, Chapo, Awla Gul, Shud Gul, Afsaho (Afsa), Peshawor, Faqirabad, Atayti, Afzuk, Najelshak (Kachla-Kashal), Pachakwam (Pachgeram), Dewana Baba, Shamir Yagam (Sharigam), Papla, Pazhgam, and Dalok (Lolak). For a description of this area before 1914, see Bragamatal.

*BARGUGAR
33-46 68-31 m. A village near Shashgao on the Ghazni-Kabul road.

BARGUL See PASHKIGROM

*BARIGAH
34-8 67-35 m. A village in the Kamarak area, on a tributary of the Garmab river.

*BARIGAO
33-52 67-49 m. A village north of the Dasht-i-Nawar and southeast of the Kuh-i-Surkhgoli.

BARIK
A place in the Jaghuri Hazara country.

BARIKAK
A pass over the Baud-i-Duakhan. Villages with this name are located west of Band-i-Doab, at 34-6 67-49 m., and on the Darazqol, at 34-24 67-11 m. (LWA)

BARIKAO
34- 69-. Elev. 4,900 feet. A village in an open space in the hills between Jagdalak and the Lataband pass. It is distant 11 miles from Jagdalak and 2 miles east from Seh Baba in the Tezin valley. The inhabitants are Kuru Khel Ghilzais. The place is much frequented as a halting place by kafilas and there is a small sarai in the ravine being only about 80 or 100 yards across. The Kabul Mission (about 450 men and 550 animals) had considerable difficulty in finding room to camp here in 1904. In the cold weather there is a certain amount of water in the ravine and there is a fine spring for drinking-water about 1/4 mile above the camping ground. No supplies are to be had nearer than Sarobi, 8 miles north, or Tezin, 10 miles south. (I.B.C.) Other villages with this name, also spelled Barikab, are located at 33-45 68-18 G., and 33-45 69-48 G. (LWA)

BARIKAO
34-19 70-43 m. A village in the Pesh Bolak division of the Jalalabad district, about 6 miles northwest of Ambar Khana. Inhabitants Mohmands and Dehgans. There was a cavalry and infantry post near this, during the war of 1879-80, the water supply of which was good, but liable to be cut off from the south. There is unlimited space for camping grounds at Barikao; barley is procurable as is also grass; other supplies must be procured from Batikot, 4 miles to the southeast, or from Chardeh, 2 1/2 miles to the east. Fuel is obtainable. A squadron of cavalry and a company of infantry are quartered here. Hazarbuz and Hasan Khel Kuchis with about 400 camels come and settle in the vicinity in the winter. In summer this road is not generally

used. The Basawal-Lachipur route is preferred by kafilas. (Jenkyns, Johnston, I.B.C.) Another village with this name is located at 33-52 67-49 A., and a stream is at 34-56 69-27 A. (LWA)

BARIKI باریکی
34- 67-. A village in the Bamian district, situated on an affluent ravine of the main valley, about a mile northeast of Shahidan and close to the main road from the west into Bamian. There are several hamlets and a tower. Bariki is included in the Surkhdar subdistrict of Bamian. It contains 20 families of Sayyids. (Maitland.) Two places with this name are located at 34-15 67-45 G. and 34-49 67-37 G. (LWA)

BARIKI BALA باریکی بالا
34- 66-. A village on the Kabul-Hazarajat-Daulat Yar main road, about 4-1/2 miles east of the Akzarat kotal.

*BARIKJUI باریک جوی
33-17 67-29 m. A village in the upper Arghandab valley, southwest of the Dasht-i-Nawar.

*BARIKOT See BIRKOT بریکوت

BARINA برینه
A village in the Surkhab division of the Jalalabad district. It is situated on the right bank of the Surkhab, and about one mile west of Baghwan. Inhabitants, Astanazai Ghilzais. (Jenkyns.)

BARISHTUGAK بریشتوگک
A dara in the Dai Zangi country.

BARKAR برکار
A locality in Dai Zangi country.

*BARKHANA بارخانه
34-57 68-16 m. A village located on a stream running south into the Ghorband at Dahan-i-Ghorbandak.

*BARKI بارکی
34-53 68-3 m. A village located on the Ghorband river, about 6 miles west of Shebar.

*BAR KONAR برکنر
35-2 71-21. Bar Konar is a woleswali in Nangarhar province. The woleswali comprises an area of 908 square kilometers and has an agricultural population that has been estimated at from 7,096 to 9,919. The woleswali is bounded in the west by Pech, in the south by Asadabad, in the east by Dangam and Naray and the State of Pakistan, and in the north by Kamdesh. Bar Konar has about 65 villages, one of which has more than 500 inhabitants. The villages are listed in the PG as follows: Sangarak (Shangorak), Kanasir (Kanamir), Qol-i-Sarani, Sur Mal (Surmi), Matina (Mattin), Nadib, Sama Lam, Moni, Suri Kalai (Shor Kalai), Madesh-i-Ulya (Madesh), Arnawi Shagal, Madesh-i-Sufla, Helalzai (Helal-i-Ulya), Chunas, Lachin, Shangar Kalai (Shangar), Chaqoli, Ato Kalai, Aman Kot, Khul Kalai, Shingash, Mulla Alam Kalai (Sangi Mulla Alam), Shal, Dab Kalai, Muladiq, Jalala, Badgam, Nawai Kalai, Nesha Gam, Sonak, Dambarai (Dambar), Spin Kai, Asmar, Jaja (Jaj), Qala-i-Wardak, Tangi, Haji Abad, Kassa Gul, Balawlo (Balwalai), Kuhna Kohi, Taisha Aghaz Bagh (Aghaz Bagh), Shal Khol (Qol Shal), Chapak, Nadit-i-Ulya, Nadit-i-Sufla, Islam Zai,

Sawki Khol, La Hussain, Gulai-i-Ulya, Gulai-i-Sufla, Wati, Shangar Gul, Kar Boli, Dagi Ser, Shontala, Pama Lam, Darkalo-i-Sufla, Darkalo-i-Ulya, Kalo Gul, Garwalai, Chama Din, Takhto Khol, Sarko, Toghgan, Fataw Kalaw, and Belal Zai.

BARKOT برکوت
34-40 70-35 G. A valley situated to the west of the Dara-i-Nur. It is inhabited by about 150 families of Safis, who are independent and lawless, and leagued with the people of Kashmund, a village high up in the hills still further to the west. Muhammad Zaman Khan, when Governor of Jalalabad, marched a force against Barkot, but they flooded the approaches to their valley, and he retired after losing many men. (Alim Ullah.)

*BARLA برله
33-9 67-51 m. A village in the Zardalu area, southeast of the Dasht-i-Nawar.

*BARMAL or BIRMAL برمل
32-34 69-11. Barmal is an alaqadari in Paktya province. The alaqadari comprises an area of 1,084 square kilometers and has an agricultural population that has been estimated at from 27,200 to 34,254. The alaqadari is bounded in the west by Sarobi, in the north by Urgun and Gayan, in the east by the State of Pakistan, and in the south by Gomal. Barmal has some 55 villages, 16 of which with more than 500 inhabitants. The villages are listed in the PG as follows: Marah Molai, Tand Shega, Margha, Tora Wale, Kalam, Pyawdad (Pyawzar), Naar Saiki (Naar Samiki), Sardali Khan, Dangarrulgadah (Dangar Lagol), Mohamad Ajan (Marbeka), Ata Gul, Taglai Lwarah (Nazim Khel), Aramal, Kas, Warzah, Mirajan, Mira Khan, Shewaki Ghina, Sherwah, Shararah Sher Khun Khel, Faqiran, Rubat, Dolan, Torah Tangai, Gul Kot, Mangliti, Wacham, Bandari, Shakai (Shaki Khel), Baqi Khel, Gabarai, Yami Khel (Mawi Khel), Suri (Sodi Khel), Meta Khel, Kasskai, Farsin (Kharsin), Ghoshi (Moshi), Totai Khola, War Kalai, Jar Lobi, Miyagan, Korah Khola, Agha Jan Kalai, Faqir Ali, Ari Gul, Saleh Khel, Sharmat Khel, Aref Khan, Sar Puza (Tar Buza), Ghondakai, Tor Khel, Lewagai, Tor Gandi, Baki Khel, Tipi (Moh'd Khan), and Reza Khan. For a description of this area before 1914, see Birmal.

*BARMANAI برمنی
33-44 67-6 m. A village located on a tributary of the Helmand, south of Ahangaran.

*BAR MAZID برمزید
33-21 67-40 m. A village on the Chawak river, about 8 miles southwest of the Dasht-i-Nawar.

*BAR NARANG برنرنگ
34-46 71-4 m. A village on the Kunar river, some 2 miles southwest of Shirkani.

BARU-I-KALAN Or LOE BARU باروکلان
34-16 70-38 m. A village in the Jalalabad district, about 12-1/2 miles west of Basawal. It lies on the right bank of the Hisarak, or Papin stream, and contains about 1,000 families of Mohmands. Fodder for about 3,000 animals for one day and about 500 maunds of unground grain may be collected in the village and neighbourhood. (I.B.C., Johnston.)

BARU-I-KHURD   Or KAM BARU   بارو خرد
   34-15 70-37. A village in the Jalalabad district, about 1 1/2 miles
   southwest of Baru-i-Kalan, containing some 50 families of Mohmands.
   Supplies are procurable here, and there is a good camping ground
   with trees; water in plenty from the Hisarak stream and from karez.
   In winter large numbers of Kuchis camp here, and at that time transport animals would be procurable, as also would meat. (I.B.C.)

BASAWAL   or BATSAWUL   باسول (باخول)
   34-15 70-52 m. Elev. 1,400 feet. A collection of Mohmand villages in
   the Jalalabad district, 10 miles from Dakka and about 29 from Jalalabad on the main Peshawar Kabul road. They contain in all some 1,000
   families of Mohmands possessing about 2,000 head of cattle, 100
   horses and 150 buffaloes. The annual production of wheat and barley
   averages about 90,000 Indian maunds.
   There is room to encamp a force of any size near the main village on
   some grassy fields about 1/2 mile from the river. There is a fair
   amount of supplies available locally and any amount can be got from
   Pesh Bolak (5 miles) and the surrounding country. Fodder for about
   20,000 animals for one day is procurable.
   One mile to the west of the village is a new sarai and an old mud
   fort. The sarai was built in 1905 and is about 80 yards square. The
   fort when seen in 1905, was in poor repair and of slight account
   altogether; it consists of a redoubt 80 yards square, with walls 12
   feet high, and of a much larger horn-work with a small ditch and
   wall 6 feet high, the perimeter of the whole being some 600 yards.
   There is a force of 200 Khasadars quartered here.
   From Basawal there are two roads forming alternatives to portions of
   the main Peshawar-Kabul road which keeps along the river bank
   through Lachipur and Ali Boghan. The first of these leads over the
   Choragali pass and rejoins the main road near Ali Boghan; the
   second leads south through the cantonment of Kahi and then turning
   northwest runs direct to Jalalabad. (Johnston, Malleson, Wanliss.)

BASHGUL Or BASHGAL, LANDAY SIND   بشی گل (لندی سیند)
   35-20 71 32 m. A river which rises in the southern slopes of the
   Hindu Kush, and after a south-southeasterly course of not less than
   60 miles debouches into the Kunar at a point some 45 miles below
   Chitra. The Mandal pass, near which the river takes its rise, has
   an altitude of 15,300 feet, while at its junction with the Kunar the
   elevation is about 3,000 feet. It is known to the Afghans as the
   Landai Sin, and it is sometimes called the Arnawai. The latter name
   is apt to be misleading, as indeed it proved during the delimitation
   of this part of the Indo-Afghan frontier in 1894-95 for the village
   of Arnawai (called Arundu by the Chitralis) is on the left bank of
   the Kunar, a few hundred yards below the Bashgul junction, while the
   Arnawai gul, up which there is a road to Dir, is the local name of
   the valley down which a torrent rushes to join the Kunar, and on the
   right bank of which the village of Arnawai is built.
   In the Bashgul is a village called Bazgul, which may have been the
   origin of the name now given to the whole of that valley by the
   Chitralis. The Kafirs themselves call different parts of it after
   the name of the different tribes who inhabit it, but in no case do
   they call it Bashgul, the latter being purely a Chitrali name. Thus
   the upper part is called Katirgul (Chitrali-Lutdeh or Kamtoz), the
   middle portion Muman (Chitrali-Madugal), and the lower part Kam
   (Chitrali-Kamoz or Kamdesh). However, for the purposes of this
   article, Bashgul will be a convenient designation for the whole
   valley from the Mandal pass to the Kunar.
   Of the three main sources from which the Bashgul draws its highest

waters, the stream coming directly from the Mandal is only the second in volume. As it descends it passes near its source through a lake of considerable size and a tarn, and then receives on either hand bubbling rills, streams, and mountain torrents; of these, the first of importance is the Skorigul, which joins the main stream just above Pshui. The next is the Manangul, which comes in at Bragamatal. The pleasant river then pursues its quiet course, and winds past Badamuk, Oulagul and Purstam, gradually changing its character in its narrowing rocky bed, until at Sunru it assumes many of the features of a cataract. It becomes a raging torrrent in the dark narrow valley, dashes against the huge boulders which obstruct its course, and flings high its spray with deafening uproar. Tree trunks encumber the waterway, jam against the rocks, pile up in confusion, or hurry round and round in the swirl of a backwater. The river races past Bagalgrom, receiving at the village of Urmir the torrent from the Kungani pass and the drainage of the Nichingul valley. Below Kamu it is joined on its left bank by the Pittigul stream, by the Gourdesh stream, and by many others of less importance, ending, as before stated, in the Kunar river opposite to Arnawai.

The population of the valley is roughly estimated by Surgeon-Major Robertson, who traversed the Bashgul from end to end, at 20,000 Siah-Posh inhabitants, all of whom belong to the Katir, Madugal, Kashtan and Kam sections. The villages in the Bashgul and its tributaries from above downwards are:

Katir--

	Ptsigrom	?
	Pshui or Pshowar	Badamuk
	Apsai	Oulagul
	Shidgul	Chabu
	Bragamatal (Lutdeh)	Purstam
	Bajindra	Baprok

Madugal--

	Mungul	Bagalgrom or Muman,
	Susku	and a few hamlets.

Kashtan--

Kashtan and two or three little settlements.

Kam--

	Urmir	Kamu
	Kamdesh	Sarat
	Mergrom	Pittigul
	Bazgul.	

There is a little colony of Siah-Posh Kafirs at Gourdesh, who are said to be very different people from all the other Siah-Poshis and to be in great part a remnant of an ancient people called the Aroms. As regards the lateral communications, the following routes lead from Chitral over the eastern watershed:
 (a) The Zidig, leading from the Upper Lutkho valley
 (Gabar) to Ahmad Diwana.
 (b) The Pshui from the Lutkho valley (Izh) to Pshui.
 (c) The Shawal from the Kalash valley of Bomboret to
 Lutdeh (Bragamatal).
 (d) The Parpit from the Kalash valley of Bomboret to
 the Manjam pass and so to Bragmatal, or by the Pittigul
 valley of the Kam country to Saratgul.
 (e) The Bromni from the Kalash Utzun district to the
 Pittigul valley of the Kam country.

(f) The Patkun from the Kalash valley of Utzun to the
Kafir valley of Gourdesh--the easiest of all.

Westward, the following are the most improtant roads which leave the
valley.

(a) The Skorigul (Luluk), up which are two or three
roads leading over passes to Minjan, and one leading
over a pass into the Wez valley of Presungul.
(b) The Baprokgul, which leads over the Mami pass into
the Wezgul and the Presun valley.
(c) the Nichingul, which leads over the Kungani pass
into the short Uzhamezhal valley, which debouches into
the Wezgul of the Presun valley, and also by roads up
lateralstreams joining it on the right bank of the
Wai country.
(d) The Kamu valley, which divides and has roads, one
over a low ridge into the Birkotgul, the other into a
fine valley which joins the Dungul, and others of less
importance.

The track up the Bashgul itself is "easy" from a Kafir's point of
view; and the Amir is understood to be contemplating the construction of a made road by this route, thus linking the Jalalabad-Asmar
road up the Kunar valley with that said to have been already made
from Faizabad up the Kokcha.
The most recent information regarding Bashgal agrees well with that
given above excepting as regards the population which is estimated
too high. But this may be attributed to emigration.
In 1897, two years after the subjugation of the ocuntry, whilst the
Afghan troops were at Bragamatal, the people revolted and burnt
their own houses, both to show their determination and, perhaps
also,to cause supply difficulties. They also killed the mullahs
told off to each village. At this time many Kafirs migrated to
Chitral. Subsequently the villages were rebuilt and the new ones
are very superior, the houses being excellently constructed. In
many cases too the new villages have been built in the valley instead of on the hillsides. The villages are very strikingly superior to those in Parun. The bridges are also very strong and well
made. The people are now all Mussalman and there is a mullah in
each village, as in Parun. Islam now appears popular, especially
with the younger generation.
By the Amir's orders Bashgul is now to be known as Nuristan, the
place of light, i.e., where the light of religion has penetrated.
The people are very lightly assessed, and revenue may be paid either
in cash or kind. It is frequently paid in ghi. The officials also
do not oppress the people as they are protegees of the Amir, and
particularly of Nasrulla. They consequently find that Islam has
considerable material as well as advantages spiritual. They are
well to do and have many flocks and good cultivation. They engage
in no trade and are not armed. In spite of their social improvement
the women still do all the work. (Robertson, I.B.C., N.I.) A
village called Bashigul is located at 33-19 68-17 G., and Bazgal is
at 35-25 71-32 m. (LWA)

BASI بسی
A small section of the Fauladi Hazaras paying revenue to Ghazni.

*BAST بست
34-53 67-33 m. A village located on a tributary of the Bamian

river, some 20 miles west of Bamian.

BASUTI بسوتی (بهسودی)
The Besudis, or Besud Hazaras, are sometimes designated Basutis.

*BATA BAGU باتاباگو
33-21 68-22 m. A village located some 15 miles south of Ghazni.

BATAI See KHOST باتی

BATAI KANDAO باتی کنداو
33-23 70-19 A. The name by which the Shabak pass is locally kown.

BATA KHEL باتاخیل
One of the subdivisions of the Takhi Ghilzais.

BATIKOT باتی کوت
34-16 70-44. Batikot is an alaqadari in Nangarhar province. The alaqadari comprises an area of 147 square kilometers with an agricultural population that has been estimated at 24,500 to 25,960. The alaqadari is bounded in the north by Kama and Goshta Khwaja Zemar, in the east by Mohmand Dara, in the south by Loye Shinwar and in the west by Rodat. Batikot has about 9 villages, 6 of which have a population over 500. The villages are listed in the PG as follows: Narai Oba, Chardehi, Mushwani, Ghazibad, Galai (Kalkai), Lacha Pur, Bara Anbar-Khana, Kaza Anbar-Khana, and Nader Kot. (LWA) In 1914, this area was described as follows:
A plain between Jalalabad and the Khaibar, south of Chardeh. It is little more than a stony desert, but in the winter affords good pasturage, and the Ghilzais bring great numbers of camels and sheep to graze on it in the autumn, returning in spring. Burnes says the plain of Batikot is famed for a pestilential wind that blows in the hot season. This strikes men and horses, and the flesh of those who fall victims to it becomes so soft and putrid, that the limbs separate from each other and the hair may be pulled out with the least force. This is probably nothing more than sunstroke (heat apoplexy) caused by the exclusive heat of the wind in crossing this arid plain, whether by day or night. (McGregor, Burnes.)

BATIKOT باتی کوت
34- 70-. Elevation 1,850 feet. A village 21 miles southeast of Jalalabad, containing about 800 houses, situated on the plain of the same name. Here there are five or six mud forts, inside which the villagers live. Supplies are procurable, and there is a good encamping ground. It is famed for the Ziarat of Akhund Musa, who is said to have made the snakes on the Markoh harmless with a word.
Ample water throughout the year. Fodder for about 8,000 animals for one day and unground grain about 1,000 maunds from Batikot and neighbouring villages within 4 miles procurable. Fuel obtained in small quantities.
An alternative route branches off from here, leading to Nimla via Chapriar. It is used by Kuchi convoys to escape impressment of camels at Jalalabad. The inhabitants of Batikot are Tirahis. (Masson, Burnes, Leech, MacGregor, Jenkyns, Johnston.)

BAWALI بوالی
34- 70-. A large camping ground, 12 1/2 miles west of Jalalabad on the road to Gandamak, close to the village of Rozabad. Water ample from Surkh Rud. Fodder for 10.000 animals for one day about 2,000 maunds of unground grain procurable from neighbourhood. There is

sarai here, built in 1905. (I.B.C., Johnston.)

BAYAZID بایزید
A place in the Besud country.

BAZAN KHEL بازانخیل
33-59 69-52. A village in the Jaji country, just west of the Paiwar pass. It is a scattered mountain hamlet, and contains some 20 or 30 detached little forts stuck upon projecting rocks all over the hillside. (Bellew.) This place seems to be called Bazai Khel generally, i.e., the name of a Ghilzai subdivision. (I.B.C.)

*BAZAR بازار
33-21 70-5 m. A village on the Lakan river, southeast of Lakan.

BAZARAK بازارک
34-33 70-33 m. A village in the Kunar valley, on the right bank of a stream. It is a well walled-in village of 300 houses. (Masson.) Another village with this name is located at 35-20 69-30 m. (LWA)

BAZARAK See KACHU بازارک

BAZARAK (Pass) See PARANDEV بازارک

BAZARI بازاری
34-48 69-9. A village in the Koh Daman of Kabul, on the left bank of the Ak Sarai stream, about 1 1/2 miles from Ak Sarai. In 1882, it contained forts -- one belonging to a Kizilbash, one to a Kharo- ti, two to Tajiks. Apart from the forts, there are said to be 60 houses in the place, all inhabited by Tajiks. (I.B.C.)

*BAZGAI بازگی
32-58 67-56 m. A village located some 15 miles northeast of Mukur on the highway to Ghazni.

*BAZGAL بازگل
35-25 71-32 m. A village located about 2 miles north of the Landai Sin (Kunar) river, east of Ormol.

*BAZGULKHEL بازگلخیل
34-20 68-39 m. A village located on a tributary of the Maidan river, some 10 miles west of Nerkh.

BAZID KHEL بازیدخیل
34- 70-. A village in the Kama Division of the Jalalabad district. Inhabitants: Mohmands and Wardaks. (Jenkyns.)

BAZ MUHAMMAD KHAN باز محمدخان
34-29 69-15. A small Tajik village on the left bank of the Logar river, southeast of Kaubl and between Beni-Hisar and Bagrami.

BED بید
In the Shaikh Ali country.

*BEDAK بیدک
35-8 66-42 m. A village northwest of the Kuh-i-Laghband and north of Tusri. Other places with this name are located on a path leading to Qomaghai on the Darazqol river, at 34-19 67-2 m.; on the Helmand river, some 10 miles west of Qash, at 34-29 68-4 m.; near Chehel Dukhtaran, some 15 miles south of Kabul, at 34-21 69-4 m.; and,

west of the road from Ghazni to Kabul, at 33-53   69-2 m.

BEDAK بيدك
34-39 67-13 m. A hamlet in the Sar-i-Kol subdistrict of Yakh Walang.

BEDAK بيدك
34-44 69-2 m. A village in the Koh Daman of Kabul, between Bezati and Kahdara, about 23 miles northwest of Kabul. It is described by Masson as romantically situated on an eminence, and surrounded by gardens, vineyards, and orchards. Inhabitants: Tajiks (150 houses and Kizilbashis (50 houses). Here and at Istalif are grown the punja-chinar trees, the timber of which is sent to Kabul for the manufacture of gun-carriages. Walnut-timber is also sent in for rifle-stocks.

BED DARA بيد دره
A section of the Chahar Dasta Hazaras. There is also a village with this name on the Kabul river, across from Basawul, at 34-16   70-55 m. (LWA)

BEDKUL بيد قول
34-53 68-17 m. A dara which joins the Ghorband valley from the south, about 3 miles east of the Shibar pass. It is in the Shaikh Ali country.

BED MASHK Or BEDMUSHK بيد مشك
33-44 68-23 m. A village in the Sar-i-Ab valley, about 16 miles northwest of Ghazni. It contains about 100 houses of Besud Hazaras. At about 1 miles northwest of Bed Mashk the Sar-i-Ab stream is crossed by a wooden bridge, passable for camels, but not strong enough for field guns. (I.B.C)

*BEGAL بگل
35-11 67-30 m.   An area in the upper valley of the Saighan river, near the village of Irgana.

BEGAM KALA بيگم كلا
33-40 68-51 G. A village in Kharwar; 30 houses of Ghilzais. (Griesbach.)

BEGRAN Or BEGARA بگران
35-12 69-22 m. A village in the upper Panjshir glen situated some 2 miles below Anaba. It has 150 houses of Tajiks. (Shahzada Taimus.) Another village with this name is located at 34-58   69-17   A. (LWA)

BEG SAMAND بيگ سمند
34- 68-. A collection of thirteen forts, on the road between Maidan and Wardak.
The place is surrounded on all sides by hills, and is said to be about 14 miles west of Shaikhabad. Rice, wheat, jowar, and Indiancorn are grown in the valley, which is watered by the Dai Mirdad stream from the Hazara hills. Inhabitants: Piaru Khel Ghilzais, Wardaks, and Hazaras. (I.B.C.) A glen with this name is located at 34-10 68-37 G.   (LWA)

BEGTUT Or BEKTUT بيگ توت
34-33 68-56 m. A collection of eight forts between Paghman Arghandeh, 11 miles west of Kabul. It is full of orchards, and there is little other cultivation.

Inhabitants: Tajiks and Kizilbashis of the Farasha subdivision. It was to this point that Macpherson followed the retiring Afghans on the 11th December 1879, after the cavalry and horse artillery had retired to Sherpur. (I.B.C.) The name is also spelled Bektot. (LWA)

BEGTUT بیگتوت
34- 69-. A village included in the Chandawal quarter of Kabul city. Inhabitants: Kizilbashis. (I.B.C.)

BEHAR See BAHAR بهار

BEHBUD بهبود
A subsection of the Besud. There is also a village with this name, northwest of the Ab-i-Istada, at 32-33 67-46 m. (LWA)

*BEHSUD See BESUD بهسود

BEHUDA بهوده
34-59 68-35 G. A dara draining south from Band-i-Warsandan and entering the Ghorband valley 7-1/2 miles west of Pin-Sehwak. Here the main valley widens out to 1/4 mile; but its bed is uneven and its slopes steep. Cultivation in occasional patches.
At the mouth of the Dara Behuda there is a small hamlet, with a few trees; and up the dara live 60 families of Babar Hazaras, owning 10 flocks and 200 head of cattle. A bad footpath leads up the dara to the Taori Kotal on the Band-i-Warsandan. (Peacocke.)

*BEHZADI بهزادی
34-42 69-2 m. A village located northwest of Kabul and west of the road to Charikar.

BELUCH بلوچ
32- 69-. A halting-place on the road from Shakin to Urgon, 13 miles south of the latter and 2 miles north of the Spidar Narai. It is the site of a small temporary village of about 20 houses.
Water is available and a little grazing, but no other supplies. (I.B.C.)

BELUT See BILUT بیلوت

BEMARU See BIMARU بیمارو (بی بی مهرو)

BENI BADAM See BIN-I-BADAM بینی بادام

BENI HISAR See BIN-I-HISAR بینی حصار
34-29 69-13 m. A village located about 4 miles south of Kabul.

BENINGA بنینگا
34- 70-. A village in the Besud division of the Jalalabad district, close to the southern entrance of the Paikob defile. It is probably identical with the Binigah of Jenkyns. If so, the inhabitants are Mohmands.
It was at Beninga that Doran defeated a body of fighters under Mulla Khalil in May 1889. (I.B.C.)

*BESARAK بیسرك
33-24 67-59 m. A village located near the Qolyaqol stream, southeast of the Dast-i-Nawar.

BESUD or BEHSUD   بهسود

34-27 70-27.   Behsud is an alaqadari in Nangarhar province. The alaqadari comprises an area of 220 square kilometers and has an agricultural population that has been estimated at about 12,500. The alaqadari is bounded in the north by Kauz Konar, in the east by Kama, in the south by Surkh Rud, and in the west by the State of Pakistan. Behsud has about 41 villages, 17 of which have more than 500 inhabitants. The villages are listed in the PG as follows: Buland Ghar, Shaghali, Chahar Mora, Qala-i-Mirza, Banda Mohabat, Hazar Mishi, Bini Gah, Kakaran, Pirawar, Miran, Qasaba-i-Nahr-i-Shahi, Char Asiab, Zangoy, Welayati, Ekhlasbad, Nahr-i-Shahi, Karez-i-Kabir, Gerdi Kaj, Hada-i-Sharif, Mirak Bela, Qala-i-Janan Khan, Abdian, Samar Khel (Shar Khel), Qasembad, Qala-i-Shahi, Chamyar, Du Bila-i-Ulya, Khush Gunbad , Tangi Tukhchi, Bahrabad, Qala-i-Muqam Khan, Tamirat, Saracha-i-Ali Khan, Arbha-i-Saracha, Saracha, Naqdi Saracha, Arabha-i-Pataw, Jamali, Sardaran, Behsud Khas, Nahr-i-Massi. (LWA) In 1914 this area was described as follows: A division of the Jalabad district comprising all that portion of the latter lying to the north of the Kabul, and west of the Kunar rivers. It is officially called Rud-i-Kashkot (for revenue purposes), but takes its popular name from the village of Besud. It has a mixed population of Arabs, Dehgans, and Tajiks.

The following is a list of the villages contained in Besud, drawn up by Jenkyns in 1879:

Village	Inhabitants	Village	Inhabitants
Bahrabad	Rikas	Mirga Bela	Tajiks, Arabs
Kasimabad	Dehgans, Tajiks, Afghans	Nurzai-o-Ushturi	Tajiks, Arabs
		Jamali-o-Sirbadali	Tajiks, Arabs
Banaras Khan	Duranis	Kazi Muhammad Shah	
Gaomesh Bela	Arabs		Tajiks
Nahar-i-Masi	Dehgans, Tajiks	Bilangar	Arabs, Tajiks, Dehqans
Abadian	"	"	
Dubela (2)	"	"	Bininga	Mohmands
Sayyid Ahmad	Arabs	Pirawar	Arabs
Wilaiti	"	Tokchi	Tajiks, Barkazais
Ikhlasabad	Tajiks, Arabs	Nurkhel	Dehqans
Zangui	Arabs	Daulatshahi	" "
Besud	Tajiks, Arabs		

Besud is described by Brigadier-General Doran as bounded on the north by a range of hills separating it from the plain called the Dasht-i-Gamberi, and from the rich valley of the Kunar river. There are three main tangis, or passes, through these hills--the Maruf on the west, the Tokchi on the east along the right bank of the Kunar, and the Paikob, about 2 miles west of the Tokchi and separated from it by a high hill, running north and south and about 4 miles in length. The Tokchi Tangi is passable by infantry in single file, and cavalry can lead through it, though with some risk, as the path at one place is along a wooden aqueduct 4 feet wide, over-hanging the Kunar river. The Paikob pass presents no difficulties. The

Kunar after passing through the hills joins the Kabul river about 4 miles below Jalalabad and forms the eastern boundary of the district. The only portions of Besud in which troops can act are strips on the banks of the two rivers and the slopes at the foot of the range of hills. The whole of the centre of the district is, at the season when the operations took place (May), under rice cultivation, and forms an expanse of standing water and marsh intersected by numerous deep watercourses, with ditches branching from them in all directions.

In the month above mentioned in 1880, a column was sent by Lieutenant General Bright from Jalalabad into Besud, to operate against a priest, Mullah Khalil by name, who was raising the tribes there against the British. The mullah was routed near Beninga. (Jenkyns, Doran, Coldstream.)

BESUD   بهسود
A section of Hazaras.

*BESUD   بهسود
34-21 67-54. Markaz-i-Behsud is a woleswali in Wardak (Maidan) province. The woleswali comprises an area of 2,198 square kilometers and has an agricultural population that has been estimated at from 30,935 to 40,154. The woleswali is bounded in the west by Panjab, in the north by Bamian, in the east by Behsud 2 and Day Mirdad, and in the south by Nawar. Markaz-i-Behsud included 303 villages. The villages are listed in the PG as follows: Koh-i-Birun, Mir Bacha, Gharghara, Maidan, Sukhta, Bid Qol, Sar Jarya Khana, Nau Rah, Zarnala, Girdolang Mir Shadi, Siroq-i-Mir Shadi, Balder Ena, Behbud, Sanginak, Sayed Bacha Qala, Sayed Bacha Muka, Chap Nau, Khak Badak, Nau Balaye, Irgin, Sayed Qol-i-Kushta, Khushk Qol, Qarukh Nau, Shiberak, Sar Bulaq, Miyan Qol, Sabzah, Dasht-i-Koh-i-Birun, Shiberak Mir Bacha, Dewar, Sar Sang-Parida, Kajak-Sar Sang, Dahan Sar-i-Sang-i-Parida, Shibar-i-Kalanzai, Nurak Kalanzai, Kalanzai, Ajam, Lundha, Dasht-i-Mir Bacha, Shibar, Hesar, Hujra-i-Kalanzai, Paye Kajak, Sanginak-i-Kalanzai, Dasht-i-Rast, Khurdakzai, Qarya-i-Ewaz, Ghawchak Ewaz, Shirum, Dashtak, Nawer Subh, Qarya-i-Zaryafta, Shirum wa Baba Khan, Sirah Qol, Lal Bak, Jan Qarah, Jambud, Maghak, Zaghcha, Obaye, Altar Ankak, Qol-i-Khurdak, Khushk Ab, Sar Qol, Bed Qol, Sabz Sang, Sabz China, Qash, Shag Qol, Ab-Dar, Bum, Mirshadi, Kotal-i-Mula Yaqub, Menj Kora, Seb Joy, Joy-i-Namud, Gardan Qara, Ajum Kotal, Paye Qol Kotal, Jalil Kotal, Shar Jalil, Jaw Qol, Gurdam-i-Band Shoy, Dahan Reshqa, Band Shoye, Kalan Khana, Surkhbad, Terabad, Tuli Qol, Dewali, Nau Rah, Paye Koshek, Kutak, Tai Rashk, Delka, Dewal Qol, Sar Band, Kushk, Dasht-i-Saqi, Ramoz, Qobi Bahi, Warni Tagab, Sar Jangal Bahi, Qala-i-Sultan, Qala-i-Kata, Sar-i-Qol Bahi, Seyah Kharak, Barik Joy, Karezak, Dahan Bahi, Haq Dad, Chob-i-Shanda, Payeki, Jangalak, Mangasak, Janqara, Payendah Qadam, Sar Ulyad, Zar Joy, Baghak, Sar Qol Baghak, Khak Pahenda, Qichak, Qol-i-Nokerr, Wardak-i-Ulya wa Sufla, Zeratak, Nawur Ghaibi, Wagaw Murda, Qawda-i-Dal, Gidar Go, Daman, Seyah Nahur, Nau Joy, Bai Ramoz, Petab-i-Deh Murdagan, Kata Khaki, Raba Dahan, Seyah Khak, Moshak, Bayazid, Hoqi, Safed Sang, Mandalyad, Qol-i-Juwali, Giro, Qarya-i-Marg, Qara Qol, Mir Bacha, Shekh Dawlat, Jar-i-Ali, Qawm, Berimak, Qebcherak, Nala-i-Dehqan, Seyah Qol, Gawhar, Kamarak, Khar-Qol, Sangi-Shanda, Sar Zirat, Paye-i-Zirat, Qol Ikhtiyar, Sar-i-Top-i-Ojai, Qol-i-Banda, Ajdar, Joye Zang, Miyana Deh, Qol-i-Mirak, Ajam, Mazar Gardan, Hasht Darakht, Shina, Baraki, Siyah Sangak, Surkh, Surab Goshak, Du Abi, Qambar Ali Helmand, Shina, Baba, Ghujur, Dam Ghajur, Halwa Qol, Sar Iska, Ali Dad ya Sar Iska, Shah Qadam-i-Para Shak, Naudal-i-Khedr, Khedr, Sher Dad, Helmand, Abagha,

Tokhak, Shah Sultan Ata, Shukur, Oba Chorah, Shina Qurban, Durna
Joy, Shad Mohamad, Tokhak, Qambar Ali-i-Kajab, Pewand, Bughundak,
Abagha, Dawlat, Giroy, Baba, Sadat-i-Kajab, Kajab, Juma Ali, Khurdi,
Ab Paye, Arab, Toman, Damarda, Dopushta, Qalandar , Khalil Murda,
Sarbad-i-Asyab, Qarqatak, Khar Qol, Shash Burja, Khan Mula, Arab-
Kajab, Raqol, Zard Sang-i-Dost, Iska, Shahrak, Shaitan, Gidar Gejo,
Rashk, Gardel, Tala Qol, Barghasang, Khalil wa Khwaja Hasan, Qarya-
i-Khalil, Choli-i-Daman, Aptak Khalil, Kohna Deh-i-Zerat, Zar Sang,
Safed Dewar, Sabz Samuch, Qarya-i-Marg Omarak, Chuli, Dewar Qol,
Safed Sang, Bum, Babaka, Deljam, Juma Ali, Nadri, Miyan Qol, Kata
Sang, Naurist, Bahadurka, Ojai, Jayl Baz, Koh Shak, Qala-i-Zangi,
Sabz Sangak, Koti-i-Sangak, Tala Deh, Bulghak, Chaw, Seyah Qeta,
Dahan Sinak, Band Dali, Surab-i-Choli (Sar-i-Suhrab), Ata-i-Pul-i-
Afghanan, Qurukh, Safed Dewar, Bad Asyab, Abtak-i-Juma Ali, Miyana,
Awribab, Panji Qala, Khar Qol-i-Panji, Sar Qol, Khak Afghan-i-Ghaib,
Sarbad Asyab, Juma Ali, Da Murda, Safed Sang Ata, Darwishan, Omar
Khan, Sabz Darakht-i-Toman, Safed Bed, Seh Qala, Seh Sarah, Ghaib
Ali, Sadat Khurdi, Dasht-i-Bud Bad, Bad Syab), Khurdi, Qorah, Qarya-
i-Panji, Seh Qaum, Gardan Burida, and Ghawas, Wazirbad (Sahib).

*BESUD بهسود
34-30 68-15. Hesa-i-Awal Behsud is a woleswali in Wardak province.
The woleswali comprises an area of 1,327 square kilometes and has an
agricultural population that has been estimated at from 13,722 to
14,257. The woleswali is bounded in the west by Markaze Behsud, in
the north by Shibar and Surkh Parsa, in the east by Jalrez, and in
the south by Day Mirdad. Hesa-i-Awal Behsud includes 100 villages,
11 of which have more than 500 inhabitants. The villages are listed
in the PG as follows: Qarya-i-Dostdar, Qol-i-Bangi, Toba-Kahi, Qol-
i-Faqir, Dahan-i-Tanor, Tak Parida, Oba-i-Sayed, Topak, Pir Mohamad,
Seya Buta, Qarya-i-Shirdad, Shirdad-i-Kalanzai, Shirdad-i-Khurdak-
zai, Shirdad Abdara wa Fara Khulm, Shirdad Lal Beg, Seyah Sang,
Qezel Bashia, Tibar wa Gandah Qol, Sar Ulum, Shaikh Chal, Dost Qul,
Zarkharid, Qala-i-Nau, Qol-i-Kalan, Lata Band, Oba-i-Zafar wa Sharak
Zafar, Chokana, Dasht-i-Utman, Lorah, Dasht-i-Qala, Sabz Darakht,
Sabz Kelk, Gardan Dewar, Qash Qargho, Ahangaran, Jaw Darak, Qarya-i-
Tezak, Khar Bedak, Gardan Tala, Bidak, Demorad, Shahr Daye-Mirdad,
Sag-i-Zayida, Abpa, Dahan, Qala-i-Murad Khan, Kota-i-Serak, Qala-i-
Sayed, Sebak, Yurtop, Daye Mirdad Hesa-i-Awal, Qol-i-Khushhal, Sur-
khak-i-Qol, Chol-i-Qol, Edak Hessar, Kah Khana, Khan Mohd., Shina,
Shah Qol, Dasht-i-Shina, Zard Qol, Burghistan, Dahan-i-Hesar, Miya-
na, Dahan-i-Lakhshan, Ujurak, Wari Kabk, Kharzar, Shah Mazid, Sar
Qol, Cholail, Lakhshan, Charshanba, Surkhak, Abdul Khaleq, Seh Kota,
Jo Qol, Garm Ab Topak, Garm Ab Qol-i-Chakar, Garm Ab, Dahan Garm Ab,
Yordjo Qol, Yord Dozd, Jo Qol-i-Bala, Jo Qol-i-Pain, Darweshan, Pang
Asyab, Mir Bacha, Tanor, Qirghoy, Bepsarak, Barghasang, Titar, Da-
han-i-Abdala, Paitab, Abdala, Safed Bed, Panjpai, Nayak, Dahah-i-Ab
Dara, Zargaran, Kahmaro, Hesar, Farjam, Kakakzara, and Gul Mazar.

BESUD بهسود
A Darghan Hazara hamlet of 10 families in the Kalu glen.

BESUD OR BESUT بهسوت
34-27 70-28. The principal village in the subdistrict of the same
name. It is situated about 5 miles from Jalalabad on the left bank
of the Kabul river. Inhabitants Tajiks and Arabs. (Jenkyns)

BESUDI (not BESUD) بهسودی
A subdivision of the Daya Polada Hazaras.

BEZATI بیزاتی
34-42 69-2 m. A village in the Koh Daman of Kabul between Baba Kush Kar and Bedak. The inhabitants are all Tajiks, and there are about 100 houses in the place, It is celebrated for its vinegar, which is manufactured from mulberries, raisins and grapes. (I.B.C.)

BIAN KHEL Or BAYANKHEL بیان خیل
33-57 69-45 m. A village midway between the Paiwar Kotal and Ali Khel, on the right bank of the Karaia stream. The village is situated on a ravine of the same name. A camp was formed here in the early part of 1879 for a portion of the Kurram Field Force. (I.B.C.)

BIAR (BAR AND KUZ) بیار
34- 70-. A group of villages on the right bank of the Wazir Rud, about 12 miles east of Gandamak. There is a Kuchi camping ground here. (I.B.C.)

BIBI MAHRU KALA بی بی مهرو قلعه
34- 70-. A village in the Chapriar division of the Jalal-abad district, dituated on the left bank of the Chapriar stream, opposite Deh-i-Gar. Inhabitants: Tajiks and Dehgans. (Jenkyns.) A place with this name is located 34-33 69-12 A. (LWA)

BIBI MARU   See BIMARU بی بی مهرو

*BIDAD KALAI بیداد کلی
35-1 71-23 m. A village located on a tributary of the Kunar river, three miles southeast of Asmar.

BIDIWA بدیوا
35-13 70-51 A. A halting-place on the left bank of the Virun (or Pech) river, about 66 miles above Chigha Sarai. No supplies procurable except fuel and grass. (I.B.C.)

BIHAR-I-SUFLA بهار سفلی (؟)
34-18 70-14. A village in the Khugiani division of the Jalalabad district, situated about 5 miles south of Fatehabad. The inhabitants belong to the Kharbun section of the Khugianis. (Jenkyns.)

BIHAR-I-ULYA بهار علیا
34- 70-. A village in the Khugiani division of the Jalala-bad district, about 4 miles southeast of Bihar-i-Sufla. Inhabitants: Kharbun Khugianis. With this village that of Surma is included in one township. (Jenkyns.)

*BILA بیله
34-16 70-52 m. A village on the Kabul river, across the river from Basawul.

*BILANDI بلندی
35-5 69-9 m. A village located on the Ghorband river, a few miles north of Charikar.

BILAND KALA بلند قلعه
34-59 69-15 G. A small village, situated at the northwest corner of the plain of Bagram, north Kabul. A few Hindu traders reside here, who have considerable intercourse with the neighbouring hill tribes. (Masson.)

BILANGAR Or BOLAND GHAR بلندغر
34-37 70-30 G. A village in the Besud division of the Jalalabad district. Inhabitants: Arabs, Tajiks, and Dehgans. (Jenkyns.)

*BILANGASH بلنگاش
33-52 68-34 m. A village located west of the Ghazni-Kabul road, near Ao Narai.

BILEL KHEL بلیل خیل
34- 70-. A village in the Khugiani division of the Jalala-bad district, 2 miles south of Akori. Inhabitants: Kharbun Khugianis. (Jenkyns.)

BILUT OR BELUT بلوت
33- 69-. A group of 3 hamlets on the left bank of the Lalidar stream, about half-way between the Paiwar Kotal and Ali Khel. They contain some 50 houses of Jajis. From Bilut two roads lead, respectively, via the Lakarai Kotal to Safed Sang, 54-1/2 miles, and via the Kharshatal Kotal to Khurd Kabul, 48 miles. Both these roads are said to be practicable for camels, and form lateral communications between the Khaibar and Paiwar Kotal main routes to Kabul. (I.B.C.) Recent maps show the spelling Bar Belawut at 33-59 69-50 m. (LWA)

BIMARU OR BEMARU, BIBI MAHRU بی بی مهرو
34-33 69-12 A. A village at the north east corner of the Sherpur cantonments. Inhabitants: Tajiks and Khwajas. The ridge, at the eastern end of which the village stands, called in the old war the "Bimaru heights," forms the north side of the Sherpur enclosure, and was a feature of much military importance both in 1841 and in 1879; and in the last campaign the village itself was turned to account, first as a defensive post, and subsequently as the trasport headquarters. The place is called, at length, Bibi Maru, after the sister of holy man of Persia, who was at Kabul in Babar's time. Both brother and sister have shrines; the brother's, a little to the south of the ridge, was destroyed in December 1879 by the British, when holding Sherpur; but the sister's shrine, just above the village was not injured. Both shrines have a great repute; that of the brother, Sayyid Mehdi, for both sexes, and all religions--Hindu, Sunni, and Shiah; that of the sister, for women only, but for women of every faith. (I.B.C.)

*BIMAT بمت
33-31 68-8 m. A village located on a tributary of the Ghazni river, some twenty miles southwest of Ghazni.

BINARUM بنارم
35-24 71-20. A Kafir hamlet on about the same level as, and one and half miles distant from, Kamdesh. It consists of not more than a dozen houses, standing on the right bank of the Bashgul, but bears signs of having been formerly of greater importance than it is at present. To reach Binarum from Kamdesh the torrent to the east which turns the water-mills has to be crossed. (Robertson.)

BIN-I-BADAM بینی بادام
34-18 68-37. A village in the Maidan district, on the Wardak border, situated between Kala-i-Durani and Sar-i-Top. Inhabitants: Ghilzais of the Adramzai and Ahmadzai divisions. There are only about 100 houses on the plain, but on the hillside there are 3 or 4 forts belonging to the place. The main road from Kabul to Ghazni

runs past Bini Badam, which is about a mile to the west of it, at a point nearly midway between Kala-i-Sher Muhammad (or Durani) and Top. The Langar road passes through the village. (I.B.C.)

BIN-I-GAH   See BENINGA   بینی گاه

BINIGAO   بینی گاو
The name applied to the lower portion of the Khurdak Takhta, before its junction with the Panjao. There is also a mountain with this name. A village with this name is located at 34-15 66-43 m., and a stream with this name is located 34-14 66-54 m.   (LWA)

BIN-I-GAO-GIR   بینی گاوگیر
34- 69-. A cattle toll station in Logar, on the direct road from Kabul to Kushi, due east of Kuti Khel. The toll is said to be worth Rs. 12,000 per annum. (I.B.C.)

BIN-I-HISAR   بینی حصار
34-29 69-13 m. A large irregular village in the Kabul dis-trict, 2 miles south of the Bala Hisar on the Logar road, which runs through it. It stands at the foot of a long spur running down from the Takht-i-Shah. The village has about 400 houses on well-cultivated land, which is watered by a canal (Nahr-i-Damgah) from the Logar river. It possesses many orchards and gardens, and the Bagh-i-Sarkari, a royal garden constructed by Amir Sher Ali, stands to the south of the walls. Near this garden Sir Frederick Roberts' force bivouacked on the 7th October 1879, the day after the action of Charasia. It was by the Bin-i-Hisar spur that the 92nd Highlanders advanced on the 18th December 1879 when the Takht-i-Shah was carried, and here Lieutenant Forbes of the regiment fell.
The inhabitants of Bin-i-Hisar are Kizilbashis and Tajiks (the former preponderating). (I.B.C.)

BININGA   See BENINGA   بنینگا
33-40 68-24 m.

*BINISANG   بینی سنگ
33-46 67-33 m. A village on the Nawa-i-Batur, near the village of Barakjui. Another village with this name is located on the Ghazni river, some 8 miles north of Ghazni, at 33-40 68-24 m.

BIN-I-SEHWAK   Or SHEWAK   بینی سیوك
34-56 68-29 A.   Elevation 7,340 feet. A small village in the Shaikh Ali country.

*BIN-I-SIASANG   بینی سیاه سنگ
34-7 67-23 m.   A village near the source of a tributary of the Helmand river, in southern Bamian province.

BIN-I-YAR   بین یار
A village which appears to be situated in a branch of the Kol-i-Yer, a glen which joins the main Ghorband valley from the north at Dahan-i-Kaoshan. (Maitland.)

BIRGALICH   بیرگالج
35-1 67-58. A valley in the eastern part of the Bamian district draining southwards from the Jalmish Kotal to the main Shibar glen, which it joins about 7-1/2 miles west of the Shibar pass. For the first 4 miles of its course it is known as the Rah Kol; here it is joined from the left by the Jaozar Dara and, a mile lower down, by

another wide glen leading from the Sangandao Kotal. At its head the Rah Kol has a width of about 50 yards, increasing gradually as it approaches the point of junction of the Jaozar Dara. From this point down to Kala Yadgar (6-1/2 miles from the Jalmish Kotal) the Birgalich valley is some 200 yards wide, well cultivated, with occasional grassy chamans and a good stream. A short distance below Kala Yadgar it contracts suddenly and for the remainder of its course flows through a narrow, rock-bound gorge, enclosed by lofty perpendicular cliffs, and known as the Tangi Kablantu. This gorge is not more than 50 yards wide in the broadest parts and frequently contracts to about 30 feet.

A good camel road (Northeast Afghanistan) leaves the main Shibar-Bamian road about 4-1/2 miles west of the Shibar pass and, running north east, enters the Birgalich Dara at Kala Yadgar and continues up it to the Jalmish Kotal at its head. A difficult camel track runs up the Tangi Kablantu and joins this road at Kala Yadgar.

The Birgalich Dara belongs to the Kalu subdistrict but pays revenue directly to the Hakim of Bamian. It contains about 120 families of Khatai Hazaras. (Maitland, Peacocke.)

BIRJAMA بیر جامه
A village in the upper Panjshir glen, 5 miles above Marz, 20 houses of Tajiks. (Shahzada Taimus.)

BIRKOT Or BARIKOT بریکوت
35-18 71-32 m. On of the five Gabar villages of the Kunar valley, on the right bank of the river, opposite to, and 1,000 yards south of, Arundu (Arnawai) as the crow flies. The houses, about 60 in number, are closely fitted together in the form of a square and surrounded by an 18-foot wall, with a tower at each corner. The eastern face of the wall is in a dilapidated condition. The houses are built up against the wall. The centre of the village is an extremely filthy farmyard, where extremely narrow lanes converge. The entrance to the village is by a gate in the south wall. There is here a garrison of one infantry regiment and two mountain guns, whose lines, together with the married quarters, are outside the walls to the south and southwest, and not fortified in any way.

The ground round Birkot is highly cultivated, chiefly with rice and a little Indian corn. The valley at Birkot, from the river to the hills on the right bank, is about 1/2 mile wide. The river banks are very high and the river flows very rapidly. From bank to bank is about 100 yards and in autumn the water is about 60 yards wide. There is no bridge or ferry here, and the river is crossed by inflated skins. The hills are wooded. One mile above Birkot are the ruins of an old bridge. The river is very narrow here and the site is a good one for a bridge. (Robertson, I.B.C., N.I.)

BIRMAL Or BARMAL برمل
32-34 69-11. An administrative district of the Kabul Province, lying between the Ghazni district on the northwest, and west, and Waziristan on the east. It consists of the valleys of the Margha and Mastoi streams which, flowing roughly northeast, cross the Indo-Afghan frontier and unite at Dwa Toi to form the Tochi river. The average elevation of the district is considerable, probably nearer 6,000 than 5,000 feet. The inhabitants are mainly Kabul Khel Wazirs and Kharoti Ghilzais, though in Urgun there are also some 1,200 families of Tajiks. The Wazirs permanently resident in Birmal (chiefly of the Saifali and Paipali sections of the Kabul Khel, Utmanzai, Darwesh Khel), are said to number 10,000; in addition,

many other Kabul Khel Wazirs annually migrate from their territory within the British border to Birmal for the hot weather.

The chief place of the district, Urgun, is situated in the upper Mastori valley, and constitutes the official headquarters of the Hakim, or Governor. This office is at present (1906) held by Shahgassi Dost Muhammad Khan, a relative of the Luinaib Khushdil Khan. The only other places of importance inthe district are Pir Koti, 400 houses, on the Mastoi and Marghan, a Waziri village of 300 houses in the valley of that name.

The southern, or upper, portion of the district is described as being very open, the ground sloping gently down from the foot of the lofty range on the east, along whose crest runs the Indo-Afghan boundary. The range itself is well wooded with pines and deodars, and grazing is everywhere plentiful, while the upper portion of the sloping daman at its foot is also covered with chilgoza trees; lower down it is bare with the exception of small patches by the banks of side streams. The valleys of the Mastoi and Margha themselves are studded with villages throughout, and form almost continuous strips of cultivation.

The main road from Bannu to Ghazni, via the Tochi valley, crosses the frontier at Piyaodin and passes through Margha and Urgun. It is fit for camels. Another road, also fit for camels, leads from the head of the Kazha valley through Pir Koti and joins the first-mentioned road at the Kotanni Kotal, about 12 miles beyond Urgun. A third road runs northward from Shakin to Urgun. In addition to these three main lines of approach to Birmal from the east there are numerous tracks leading across the watershed from Shawal, in Waziristan, thus opening up an easily accessible haven of refuge to any Mahsuds, or others, who may have incurred the displeasure of the British Government. (Anderson, Douglas, Donald, Kemball.)

*BISHKUL بشكول
 35-7 71-31 m. A village on a tributary of the Kunar river, near the Pakistan border.

BISRAM بسرام
 A village in Laghman; inhabitants Arokis. (Warburton.)

BOBAR Or BARBARA بوبر
 A village on the road from Bilut to Kabul by the Kharshatal pass. It is situated in a gorge nine miles beyond Khotki, and is about 23 miles from Bilut. The inhabitants are Ghilzais. (Kennedy.)

*BODA بوده
 33-29 67-59 m. A village east of the Dasht-i-Nawar, near Katakhak.

*BODAK بودك
 34-17 68-16 m. A village on the Dara-i-Jelga, northwest of Miran.

BOGARA بگره
 A locality in the Polada Hazara country.

*BOGHRI بوغری
 35-2 66-38 m. A village on the Dara-i-Chasht, southwest of Azad Kuh.

BOKAN بوكان
 33-57 68-5 G. A glen draining northward into the Khawat valley which it meets at the point where the latter makes a marked bend from southeast to northeast. At the head of this glen is a kotal of the same name; it is crosssed by the Ghazni-Yak Walang road at about

38 miles from Ghazni; the road after crossing the kotal continues down the Bokan glen to its junction with the Khawat. The road over the kotal is not difficult for laden camels, but would require mending for wheeled guns. It is said to be closed by snow from the beginning of December till the beginning of March. (I.B.C.)

BOKAN   بوکان
33-58 68-2 m. Elevation 9,570 feet. Two fortified hamlets in the glen of the same name and about 5 1/2 miles north of the Bokan Kotal. They lie on either side of the small stream which flows down from the Bokan Kotal and contain between them some forty families of Besud Hazaras. Here resided in 1905 Wali Muhammad Khan, Chief of the Bul Hasan Besud Hazaras, and a man of considerable local influence. The inhabitants possess about 300 head of cattle and 800 sheep and goats.
The Bokan glen is here about 700 yards wide and is uncultivated, the cultivation, as is usual in these parts of the country, being all on the hillsides. There would be room for 6,000 men to camp here, but supplies are scanty, sufficient for about 1,000 men might perhaps be procured locally. A certain amount of grass is to be found in spring; small bushes, only, are available for fuel and then not within a mile or two of the camping ground. (I.B.C.)

*BOKHAN   بخان
33-25 70-5 m. A village on the Khost river, near its confluence with the Lakan.

*BOKHANKHEL   بوخان خیل
33-3 68-40 m. A village in Yusufkhel district, about 1 mile northeast of Yusufkhel.

BOKHARA-I-NAWAR   بخرای ناور
A place in the Nawar district.

*BOLAGH   بولاغ
34-3 68-25 m. A village northwest of Katagai Ghar, on a tributary of the Dara-i-Jelga.

BOLAGHAN Or BOWLAGHAYN   بولاغان
35-7 69-25 A. A village situated 18 miles east-northeast of Charikar, in an open plain which stretches east from the Panjshir river. There is a footpath to the village from the upper Panjshir valley, leading south up the Ghulbak Dara and over the Bolaghan Kotal. It leaves the Panjshir valley two miles above Anaba. (Shahzada Taimus.)

BOLAN   بولان
A village in the Laghman district. The inhabitants are Ghilzais of different sections, including Jabar Khel and Nasari. The following are the hamlets included in the place:

    1. Kala-i-Sultan Muhammad   4. Kala-i-Ahmad Khan
    2. Deh-i-Azim Khan   5. Ghundi
    3. Khwajawadan   (Warburton.)

*BOR   بور
33-22 68-31 m. A village located some 15 miles southeast of Ghazni.

BORI   بوری
34- 69-. A collection of three villages in the Kabul district, 1 1/2 miles west of Deh Mazang. Inhabitants are Tajiks. (Kennedy.)

*BOSTAN بوستان
34-47 69-4 m. A village on the Kabul-Charikar road, a few miles south of Istalif.

BOTIAN بوتیان
34-55 68-22 m. A large valley in the Shaikh Ali country, which joins the upper valley of the Ghorband river, from the north about six miles to the east of the Shibar pass. A road, fit only for pack animals, leads up it to the Kharzar Kotal on the Band-i-Warsandan. The valley appears to be called Botian near the mouth of the Dara Botian. The Dara Botian is about 200 yards wide at the Junction. (Peacocke.) Recent maps show Dahan-i-Botian. (LWA)

BRAGAMATAL Or BARG-I-MATAL برگ متال
35-40 71-21 m. The chief village of the Katirs of the Bashgul valley, and called sometimes Lutdeh. It consists of two parts: a larger portion on the left bank and the smaller on the right, with a good bridge connecting them. The smaller or west village is built partly on rock close to the water's edge, and partly on the level ground to the southwest, where many houses and the dancing place are situated. On the left bank the houses are arranged on a low hill in the form of a half hexagon open to the south. In the semi-enclosed space are the gromma, the dancing place, and a few detached groups of houses. The total number of houses in the whole village is probably 700. On a hill to the west of the west portion of Bragamatal are the ruins of several walls marking the site of the old village, which seems to have been formerly on the right bank, one above, the other in the present position of the west village. Bragamatal is visited by traders from Minjan, Badakhshan, and Chitral. There are 200 Khasadars quartered at Bragamatal. (Robertson, I.B.C.) For a description of this area in 1980 see Barg-i-Matal.

BUBAK بوبك
A subdivision of the Bacha-i-Ghulam clan of Daizangi. (Peart.)

BUBAK بوبك
A section of the Muhammad Khwaja Hazaras. This name is also applied to a tribe of Hazaras, which is now scattered, but is said to have come originally from the neighbourhood of Ghazni. (Maitland.)

BUBAK See PARIAN بوبك

BUBAN KHEL بوبان خیل
33- 69-. A village on the left bank of the Gobarak stream, a quarter of a mile north of Niazak in the Chamkmani valley. (Kane.)

BUDAKHEL بود اخیل
34- 70-. A village near Chaknaur, five miles northeast of Basawal. (Wanliss.)

BUGHLANI Or BUGHTANI بغلانی
34-50 67-48. A cave village in the Bamian valley near the idols. It is in the neighbourhood of the biggest figure, near the sarai, and is the upper of two contiguous villages, Daudi being the lower one. The inhabitants dwell chiefly in caves though some are in mud huts below them. The village has a mixed population of fifty families. (Maitland.)

*BUGHUND بوغند
33-57 67-35 m. A village in the Garmab area, on the Dara-i-Chagai.

BULAND QASH بلند قاش
A kotal over the Koh-i-Korkhui. (Peart.)

*BULBUL بل بل
33-27 68-13 m. A village on a tributary of the Ghazni river, southwest of Ghazni.

BUL HASAN بوالحسن
A main section of the Besud Hazaras.

BULOLA Or BOLOWLEH بلوله
34-53 68-5 m. A large valley which starts near the Shibar pass and joins the main Bamian valley at its eastern end, at the village of Shikari. It is inhabited by Darghan Hazaras. The upper part is the Shibar valley, but after its junction with the Birgalich Dara it is called Bulola. At the junction of the two valleys it is fifty to eighty yards wide, shut in on both sides by rugged rock cliffs 200 to 300 feet high and quite inaccessible. The bed of the gorge is stony, but fairly level. A quarter of a mile lower down is the Tangi Sang Nawishta where the road is very bad. Below this the valley again opens out and at Kala Bulola is 400 yards wide. It is cultivated in terraces and a stream winds through it. The road here is good for camels. Four miles below the junction of the Birgalich and Shibar valleys the main road leaves the Dara Bulola and goes up the Dara Irak, but a camel road to Shikari continues down the valley, which here commences to contract into a rocky defile, 100 yards in width. (Peacocke, Maitland.)

BULOLA بلوله
34-53 68-5 m. A group of small mud fortlets in the Bulola valley, the principal (Kala Bulola) being about three miles below the junction of the Birgalich and Shibar glens. There are about 100 houses of Darghan or Khatai Hazaras. Below the forts there is good camping ground for several divisions. No grass; no camel grazing; no fuel, except the standing fruit trees. A small amount of supplies is procurable.
Kala Bulola affords a good rear-guard position facing west close to the main road. It is of course turned by the alternative road from the Irak valley over the Kotal-i-Khushkak and Kotal-i-Jolah, but it is sufficiently advanced to close access to that road by the Dara Khushkak and the Dara Jolah. Kala Bulola is an irregular star-shaped mud-walled fort, with an outlying mud wall on its west. It lies in the center of the valley, with a clear range to its front down the valley over open sloping cultivation; and behind its left is a flat terrace at the mouth of the Dara Khushkak, capable of accommodating a battery which could fire over, and at the side of the fort. The hills on both sides of the valley are inaccessible.
Below the first of the Bulola forts the main road crosses the Bulola stream to the left bank, the road on the right bank below this point becoming a mere foot track. The Bulola stream is here twelve feet wide and only a few inches deep. It is said never to rise more than another foot. (Peacocke.)

BURG برگ
34-5 69-14 m. A village in the valley of the lower Logar, five miles southeast of Zargan Shahar, and ten miles east of the Logar river, where that stream washes the village of Purak. The inhabitants are Ahmadzai Ghilzais. In 1880 the village contained four forts with separate hamlets, and the total number of fammilies was 100. Water is obtained from a karez. (Clifford, Euan Smith.)

BURHAN برهان
One of the two main divisions of the Ghilzai tribe, Turan being the other. See Ghilzais. This division has also been called Ibrahim.

BURI SUNIA بوری سونیا (سینا)
34-48 67-47 G. A village in Bamian, situated a mile or two from the mouth of the Polada glen. A road from Buri Sunia strikes the Bamian - Daulat Yar main road about four miles from Shahidan. The village contains sixty families of Tajiks. (Maitland.)

BURJIGAI برجی گی
A section of Besud Hazaras.

BURJ-I-GULJAN برج گلجان
35-3 69-4 m. Elevation 5,600 feet. A small Shinwari hamlet in the Ghorband district, close to the mouth of the Kaoshan Dara. It is on the main road from Kabul via Charikar through Ghorband, seventeen miles from Charikar and thirteen from Siah Gird. There is good camping ground close to the road. Supplies exist in small quantities from the village. Water from the river. Firewood is fairly abundant. (Peacocke.)

BURJISTAN برجستان
A tributary glen of the Turkoman Dara.

BURLAK Or BARLAK برلک
32-40 68-30 m. A village in the Ghilzai country, half-way between Pannah and Kala-i-Kharoti. It is known as Burlak of the Shukhel Jalozai. (Broadfoot.)

BURMAIN برمین
One of the four sections of the Kalanzai division of the Dai Kundi Hazaras. (Brereton.)

*BUMAK بومک
34-29 66-59 m. A village northeast of Shinia in the southeastern part of Bamian province.

BURU KHANA برو خانه
34- 67-. A village eleven miles southwest of the Koh-i-Baba mountains, and fifty miles southwest of Bamian. (This is probably Barakhana, lamb-shed. These barakhanas are places dug out in the ground and roofed with reeds for the protection of ewes and lambs in severe weather, and are common throughout Hazara country. Mud huts are built beside the barakhana for the shepherds.) (Thornton.) Recent maps show the name Koh-i-Boro, at 34-36 67-24. (LWA)

*BUSAGH بوساغ
33-17 67-53 m. A village near Qaria-i-Baian, southeast of the Dasht-i-Nawar.

*BUSHTI بشتی
34-47 69-54 m. A village near Arawu on the Wuzbin Khwar, northeast of Sarobi (Sorubay).

BUTAO بت او
A subsection of the Polada Hazaras.

BUTKHAK بت خاک
34-30 69-22 m. A small subdistrict of Kabul, whose western boundary

is Kala-i-Tajkhan, the eastern being Gazak. It is watered from the Chinari Dara, and is included, for revenue purposes in Kabul, although Bagrami between it and the city is in the Logar daftar.

BUTKHAK بت خاك
34-30 69-21 m. A village in the subdistrict of the same name, about eight miles from Kabul. Inhabitants are Lakan Khel Gilzais, Tajiks, and a small number of Khugianis. Three roads go from here to Gandamak: one by the Lataband pass, one by the Khurd Kabul defile, and one by the Chinari Dara. Water is plentiful. Fodder for 12,000 animals for one day and 1,600 maunds of underground grain may be collected from Butkhak and its neighborhood. The massacre of the British garrison from Kabul in 1842 began between Butkhak and Bagrami.
In the occupation of Kabul in 1879-80 there was a post established here which was withdrawn during the investment of Sherpur. The garrison was quartered in two forts lying to the north of the village and connected by a sunk road. The larger or southern fort was of the following dimensions: Walls - North and south faces 90 yards; east and west faces 80 yards; height 36 feet.
The smaller or northern fort was as follows: Walls - Length of faces 40 yards; height 36 feet.
The towers of the larger fort, Kala-i-Shahgai, were six in number, 46 feet in height; the towers of the smaller fort, Kala-i-Abdullah Khan or Kohna Kala, were four in number, 36 feet in height.
The village contained between 400 and 500 houses. The country toward Kabul is low and level, much cut up by small watercourses, one rise, the Kotal-i-Yak-Linga, occuring on the road where the latter crosses a spur from the Siah Sang.
Sultan Mahmud of Ghazni is said to have brought some idols with him from Somnath to this place, when he was asked by a deputation of Hindus, who offered him a large sum of money for the images which they desired to carry back. Sultan Mahmud thereupon had the idols ground to powder, and forced each Hindu in his camp to swallow some of it; hence the name but-khak, idol earth.
The place is a center of religious hostility, being the residence of a disciple of the Adda Mullah, Najam-ud-Din. (I.B.C.)

*BUZAK بزك
32-57 67-54 m. A village on the Mukur-Ghazni road, about 15 miles northeast of Mukur. Another village with this name is on the Ghazni-Kabul road, about 15 miles northeast of Ghazni, at 33-43 68-29 m.

BUZUNG KOL بزنگ قول
A place in the Dai Kundi country.

*CHABNAO چبنو
34-34 67-22 m. A village located near Qarkhnao, southwest of the Kuh-i-Boro.

CHABU Or CHAPU چپو
35-35 71-19 m. A Katir village on the right bank of the Bashgul river, about a mile below Oulagul, and double that distance from Badamuk. It consists of 55 houses terraced on the slope, with fields and Pshals about its base. There is a good bridge over the river at this point. (Robertson.)

*CHAGALAI چگلی
34-46 71-5 m. A village on the Kunar river, some 8 miles southwest of Asadabad.

CHAGHAN SARAI See CHIGA SARAI چغه سرای
34-52 71-9 m.

*CHAGHARA چغره
34-17 68-52 m. A village east of the road from Ghazni to Kabul and south the village of Andara.

*CHAH چاه
34-14 67-12 m. A village near Awak, on a tributary of the Helmand.

*CHAHARASIAB چهارآسیاب
34-24 69-9 m. A village south of Kabul, and southwest of Khairabad. Another village with this name is located on a tributary of the Qol-i-Khish, near Qala Para, at 34-44 68-21 m.

CHAHAR ASMAN چهارآسمان
35-10 67-2 G. A pass on the road which goes north from Jafir Kala (Band-i-Amir) to Dara Yusuf. The road, on the south side, ascends a narrow ravine for about 7 furlongs to the foot of the kotal. The ravine is between high rocky cliffs, and, for part of the way at least, is only 15 feet wide. The road is bad and rocky, and fit only for mules and yabus. From the head of the ravine is a steep rocky ascent to the kotal, 3 furlongs further on. At the top of the kotal the road from Yakh Walang, by the Baghalak glen and pass, joins. The descent is very easy down a large nala, and practicable even for guns. (Amir Khan.)

CHAHAR BAGH See CHAR BAGH چهارباغ

CHAHAR BAGH چهار باغ
33-46 68-18 G. A village about 17 miles north-by-west of Ghazni, containing 40 houses of Andari-Ghilzais. It lies on the left bank of an affluent of the Barikao stream. The surrounding country is said to be open and undulating, and there will probably be fair ground for encamping. Supplies are procurable from the Barikao villages, but fuel is said to be scarce. (I.B.C.) Other places with this name are located at 34-32 70-18 and 35-58 69-38 G. (LWA)

CHAHAR BURJA See NAO KALA چهار برجه

CHAHAR BURJAK چهار برجک
34-22 66-53 G. A village on the main Kabul-Hazarajat-Daulat Yar road, about 6 miles west of Panjao.

CHAHAR CHASHMA چهارچشمه
34-41 67-24 G. A fort village in the upper part of the Karakanatu or Karghanatu valley in the Bamian district. Sixteen families of Takana Hazaras. (A.B.C.) Another place with this name is located at 35-50 67-42 A.

CHAHARDAR چهاردر
35-9 68-51 m. Elevation 13,900 feet. A pass over the Hindu Kush leading northwards out of the Ghorband valley. it is crossed by the most direct route from Kabul to Haibak, in Afghan Turkistan at about 90 1/2 miles from Kabul. There is a made road over the pass which is said to be practicable, though probably only with considerable difficulty, for wheeled guns. Once over the pass, however, the road as far as Chahardar village, 21 1/2 miles from the summit, must be condidered as impracticable for any form of wheeled traffic. This

pass is also known as the Hindu Kush pass. (I.B.C.) A village with this name is located on the Payandeh stream, at 35-24 68-37 m. (LWA)

CHAHAR DASTA چهار دسته
A tribe of Hazaras.

CHAHAR DEH Also see CHARDEH چارده

CHAHAR DEH چارده
35-1 68-47. Elevation 6,470 ? feet. A group of villages in the Ghorband valley near the mouth of the Parsa Dara and the residence of the Hakim of that district. A terrace, 150 to 200 feet high with steeply scarped sides, projects across the valley from the hills on the north, and forces the river through a narrow gorge between its extremity and the rocky hillsides on the south side of the valley. It is called the Kotal Sakha.
Peacocke says: "Three of the lager Chahar Deh villages are situated on the top of the terrace, and others are perched on smaller, but equally high terraces, which form a line of broken, steep cliffs on the left side of valley below the first terrace. The villages are all of a substantial character, and many of the houses are three-storied buildings. The valley where it widens out again to the east of the terrace is thickly timbered, and is a close mass of gardens, orchards, and rich cultivation. There are 600 families in all in Chahar Deh; two thirds are Tajiks, and the remainder are Afghani Koishki. They own 600 gardens, 8 water-mills, and 1,000 head of cattle. Cultivation of fruit is the main employment."
There is good camping ground in the cultivation about one mile below Chahar Deh. Supplies procurable at Chahar Deh and at Gazar. Fuel scarce throughout valley. Camel grazing and grass scarce all down the valley below Nirkh. (Peacocke.) Another village with this name is located at 35-32 67-13 A.

CHAHAR DEH چارده
34-43 66-49 G. Elevation 8,360 feet. Four small fort villages lying up a small glen of the same name which joins the Bank-i-Amir valley from the south. The mouth of the Chahar Deh hollow is about 2 miles west of Dahan-i-Kanak. The high slopes at its head are all cultivated. The mouth is so swampy that the road down the main valley has to go a little way up to get round the bog, but about half a mile up there is room for several battalions to encamp, partly in the hollow, and partly on a small plateau on the left bank of the stream. The ground, however, is mostly cultivated.
The villages together contain 100 families of Takana Hazaras. (Mait-land.) Other villages with this name are located at 34-23 67-11 m. near Pestalak; about 10 miles southwest of Bamian, at 34-46 67-44 m., and north of Kota-i-Ashro, 34-29 68-48 m. (LWA)

CHAHAR DEH چارده
33-11 68-7 G. A group of villages on the Ghazni-Kandahar road, inhabited by 200 families of Chahar Dasta Hazaras. It is situated on the right bank of the stream coming from the Jangalak glen of the Gul Koh, where the little valley of this brook is crossed by the main road above mentioned. The other side of the valley belongs to Muhammad Khwaja Hazaras. The principal place in Chahar Deh, known as Chahar Deh Bebud to distinguish it form numerous other localities of the same name, is a large and very strongly walled village. In shape it is a parallelogram of 150 yards x 100 yards, and is surrounded by a wet ditch. Strong bastions are built at intervals

along the face of the wall, and each entrance is guarded by a traverse. (I.B.C.)

CHAHAR DEH-I-BEBUD چارده بهبود
A section of the Chahar Dasta Hazaras. (Peart.)

CHAHAR DEH-I-GHORBAND چارده غوربند
35-0 68-44 G. A village located 3 miles north of Ghorband.

CHAHAR DEH KHAK چارده خاك
A settlement of the Karakul-Daghi clan of Sehpai Daizangi. (Peart.)

CHAHAR DIWALI چهار ديوالى
34- 66-. A village in the Karzi-Kol subdivision of the Yak Walang district. Fifteen houses of mixed Hazaras. (A.B.C.)

CHAHAR KASH چهار كش
34- 66-. A village in the Yak Walang district, containing 10 families of Neka Hazaras. (A.B.C.)

CHAHAR KICHGHU چهار كچگو

CHAHAR SHAMBA See KOH-I-BABA چهار شنبه

CHAHAR SHINIA چهار شينيه
A locality in Hazarjat.

CHAHARTUT SEE CHARTUT چارتوت

CHAH-I-AHU چاه آهو
34- 67-. The name given to a portion of the upper course of the Bamian stream. It is just below the defile where the Karghanatu stream joins, about 3 miles above the Pul-i-Faringi. Chah-i-Ahu means "deer's well" (Maitland.)

*CHAHIKHEL چهيخيل
34-58 69-47 m. A village located on a tributary of the Tagab, some 12 miles northeast of the village of Tagab.

CHAHKAORI چهكورى
34- 70-. A village 3 miles north of Hazarnao, Jalalabad district; good grass and bhusa are procurable here. (Hough.)

CHAIKAL چيكل
34-56 69-10 m. A large village in Kohistan, between Karabagh and Charikar, nearer to the latter than the former, and situated on the east of the road, close to it. There are said to be 200 houses of Tajiks in the place, and a few of Hindu shop-keepers. On the opposite (west) side of the road is the shrine of the nephew of Shah Nakhshband. Water from the Ghorband river. Four roads from Kabul meet here. (I.B.C.)

*CHAINAK چاينك
34-11 67-4 m. A village east of the Band-i-Zirak in southern Bamian province.

CHAJ-I-HAZARA چاج هزاره
34-33 68-40. In 1904 Major Wanliss, when exploring the Kotal-i-Baghar to the north of the Unai pass, was told by his guides that the source of the Helmand lay at a place named Hazar Kash (thousand

119

clefts), at the head of an uninhabited valley known as Chaj-i-Hazar, formed by the Koh-i-Baba with the Sanglakh range and about 25 miles northeast of the Unai pass. This valley is said to the the original home of the Gurkhas of Nepal.

*CHAKA چاکه
33-3 67-45 m. A village lying east of the Kuh-i-Surkhlang and southwest of Zardalu.

CHAKANOR چکنور
34-16 70-52. Some caves on the left bank of the Kabul river, opposite Basawal, in the Jalalabad district, attributed to the Kafirs. The name seems identical with that of Chiknaur, a village whose situation corresponds with that given above. (Masson, Burnes.)

*CHAKAO چکاو
34-23 68-18 m. A village located on a tributary of the Dara-i-Jelga, southwest of the Kuh-i-Qalandaran.

CHAKAR چکر
A bridge over the Arghandab.

CHAKARI چکری
34-20 69-26 m. Elevation 8,030 feet. A large village about 5 miles southeast of Khurd Kabul commanded by a fort on a hill. It lies in a plain, or basin, in the hills about 10 miles square. The inhabitants are Ghilzais and Dehgans. Supplies are fairly plentiful.
The village was once the residence of a famous Ghilzai robber, by name Wali, a Khairo Khel, and after him of his son and son-in-law, Sadu and Dadu. These two were notorious freebooters, and came to terms with the British, on General Roberts' first occupation of Kabul, in December 1879, however, they fled, took to the hills and were afterwards present with the Afghan army at the investment of Sherpur. When the Afghans retired, Sadu and Dadu again took to the hills, and gave great trouble by hanging about the road between Lataband and Kabul with their followers, attacking small convoys, cutting and carrying off telegraph wire, etc. After the British evacuation the pair continued their marauding practices, and Amir Abdur Rahman sent a body of cavalry against them in 1881, under the then Kotwal of Kabul, Parwana Khan. Sadu, his family, and the family of Dadu were taken and made prisoners at Kabul, but Dadu himself escaped. A quantity of booty, valued at Rs. 100,000, was recovered, and, and all the property of the robbers was confiscated, but the fort was not destroyed. Chakari is reached from Musai, in Logar, by the Guldara pass, from Kabul by the Yakh Dara, from Butkhak by the Gosfand Rah, and also by the Khurd Kabul defile. The latter is the only route by which wheeled guns could be taken to Chakari; the Yakh Dara route is fit only for men on foot; the other two (Guldara and Gosfand Rah) are fit for camels.
On the heights above Chakari is a lofty obelisk which can be seen from Kabul. (I.B.C.)

*CHAKAWUR چکور
35-22 70-4 m. A village located on the stream of the same name, one mile west of Busaidur.

*CHAK-I-WARDAK چک وردك
34-6 68-35. Chak-i-Wardak is a woleswali in Wardak province. The woleswali comprises an area of 1,192 square kilometers and has an

agricultural population that has been estimated at from 11,700 to 14,627. The woleswali is bounded in the west by Day Mirdad, in the north by Nerkh, in the east by Sayyidabad, in the southwest by Nawa, and in the south by Jaghatu. Chak-i-Wardak includes 142 villages, of which four have more than 500 inhabitants. The villages are listed in the PG as follows: Unbo Khak, Allah Sang, Langar wa Alisha (Chob Dara-i-Alisha), Shaikh Yassin, Lala Khel, Khalili (Khalili Khawat), Bambai, Ali Hemat, Qala-i-Baba, Qarya-i-Chak, Nur Khel, Barghesun, Mehtar Khel, Ali Shing, Bayanan, Kachagho, Seyab, Gangar-i-Araban, Nekpaye Qol, Dewalak, Paiwand, Karam Ali, Naborja, Omarzai, Faqiri, Sayyidan-i-Muli Khel Alisha, Mado, Moza Khel-i-Goda, Chojan, Zarsang, Jalil Beg, Qala-i-Mohammad Husain Beg (Qala-i-Mohd Husain Khel), Hejrak-i-Shuja Beg, Urdu Beg, Sarfaraz Beg, Mohammad Yar Khel, Zaman Khel, Kaka Khel, Shah Qalandar, Langar, Godi, Jahuz, Qader Khel, Kot Mughul (Kota Mughul), Peshgar, Darband, Bayakzai, Tapur Khwat (Tapur), Haidar-i-Araban, Khwaja Angur-i-Ulya, Charshanba, Chorak Khel (Shorak Khel), Shali, Mushak, Miraka, Bum, Sang Baba, Shina, Char Murdeh, Gul Sang, Qarya-i-Ghulam, Qala-i-Mahumud, Qala-i-Sarposh, Zulfeqar Goda, Landaa Khel, Ali Khel, Gul-i-Hazar Bagh, Bulandi, Nura Khel, Zulfeqar Beg Samand, Bad Qol Beg, Saya Naw, Palizak, Allah Khel, Panah, Sani Khel, Rashidan, Ghani Khel, Jawar Khel, Dawran Khel, Mando Khel, Mohammad Khel, Monki, Nangi, Adam Khel, Kodi Bahadur, Ibrahim Khel, Sewak, Qurbani, Mahkum Khel, Qala-i-Safed, Kabutar, Nala, Mawrus Khel, Fazel Khel, Ahmad Khel, Kunj-i-Jaghatu, Sangin Araban, Sharif Khel, Qala--i-Surkh, Manjar Khel, Cheshma, Qarqat, Kot (Kod), Tar Mama, Shina Khel, Sokhta, Kodi Gharaban (Kodi), Khwaja Angur-i-Sufla, Saida-i-Araban, Nokar Khel, Shahbaz Khan Khel, Marsangi, Bahadur Khan, Khwaja Ahmad, Kodi Sufla, Qala-i-Safed, Khankhel-i-Seyab, Taja Seyab, Mulla Gul Khel Seyab, Afzal Khel, Sufi Khel, Kodi-i-Ulya, Qajir Khel-i-Godah, Mulla Emran Khel, Qala-i-Khwaja, Omarzai-i-Ulya, Zarlak, Goda-i-Ulya, Goda-i-Sufla, Zoya, Hakim Baba Khel, Gharak, Gulab Khel, Shakardad-i-Baghlan, Bangesh, Zarif Khel, Makhdum, Mir Ahmad Khel, Berana, Hakim Khel, Bahram Khel, Chilgari, Pas Koh, Ab Guzar, Jawandi, Araban, Qulang, Saleh Khel, Gudan, Goran, Beg Samand, Godah, and Nawa-i-Masya.

CHAKMAK چکمك
A locality in Ujaristan.

CHAKMANI or CHAMKANI چکمنی (چمکنی)
33-48 69-49 M. Part of the Karaia, or upper Kurram, valley above Kharlachi, and some of its side glens, are inhabited by people calling themselves by this name. From their geographical situation it would be natural to suppose that they are a branch of the Chamkanis who inhabit the hills to the east of Parachinar, on the British side of the Durand Line. They themselves, however, claim to be a branch of the Sulaiman Khel Ghilzais and say that they came from the Logar valley and wrested the land they now occupy from the Chamkanis (British) and that, on their taking up their residence in the district, the name Chamkani, or Chakmani, stuck to them.
Among their subdivision are the Mada Khel, Kamzai, Babu Khel, Darman Khel, Sulaiman Khel, Baghiar and Hisarak. (Donald, I.B.C.)

CHAKMANI چکمنی
33-47 69-48 A. A valley seaprated from the Mukhbil valley on the east by a range of hills and bounded on the north by the Kurram river. It drains in a northeasterly direction, debouching into the Kurram about 22 miles above Kurram fort. The valley, and the collection of villages therein, are also known as Isarak. The road up

the Chakmani passes between the two mud forts of Salim and Saleh at about 1 mile; then the village of Alim is passed, while Saleh Khan fort is reached at 2 miles. The valley now narrows from 700 yards to about 200 yards at Niazak and Buran Khel. The path gradually becomes more difficult crossing the rocky ends of projecting spurs separated from one another by stony ravines. At about 6 miles, to the southeast, is a narrow valley giving difficult access to Khost. A party of 200 cavalry under Major-General Roberts reconnoitred for 7 miles up the Chakmani in 1879, and came to the conclusion that "the passage of troops through this valley, if seriously opposed, would be a matter of extreme difficulty, owing to the numerous towers and half-fortified villages on commanding points which line the route, as well as the contraction of the valley in many places bringing both sides within easy musketry range one of the other.
"It would be imperative to move in two columns, one on each side of the Gobarak (Chakmani) stream, in order to capture simultaneously the villages on both banks. A third column (of cavalry and mountain guns) might possibly find a route along the bed of the stream, if its waters are not swollen by rain or melted snow.
"Distance (from the mouth of the valley), approximately, to the boundary of the Mangal country, 8 miles. (See "Mangal.")
"Time, on horseback, at a walk, without halting, 2 hours." (Kane, I.B.C.)
The valley is south of Qala Chamkani, called Lador Kholeh in its upper regions. (LWA)

CHAKRI   See CHAKARI

CHAKSAK
34-28 66-11 A.   A small Dilapidated fort in the Dai Zangi country.

*CHAKULAI
35-1 71-16 m.   A village on the Segal Khwar which runs into the Kunar river at Aman Kol.

*CHAKULAK
35-1 71-25 m.   A village located on a stream which runs into the Kunar at Asmar.

*CHAL
34-31 68-2 m.   A village on the Helmand, south of the Kuh-i-Baba and west of Bidak.

*CHALAWAK
34-28 67-10 m.   A village located on the Tarapas stream, about 2 miles northeast of Watapur. Another village with this name is some 6 miles southeast of Behsud, at 34-19 67-59 m.

CHALMA
A section of the Muhammad Khwaja Hazaras.

CHALMADAK
A place in the Jaghuri Hazara country.

CHALOZAI
A section of the Ghilzais -- See "Cholozai." A village with this name is about 10 miles west of Baraki Barak in Logar province, at 33-58 68-52 m. (LWA)

*CHAM چم
    34-46 69-30 m. A village located northeast of the Koh-i-Safi and west of the Sur Ghar.

CHAMAL See KHWAJA DEH چمال

*CHAMAN چمن
    35-22 70-35 m. A stream which runs into the Pich near the village of Khost. A village with this name is located on the Dara-i-Kantiwa, at 35-14 70-49 m.

CHAMAR چمار
    35-31 70-3. A ravine which drains west and debouches into the Parian Dara, at the head of Panjshir, just below the village of Parian. A difficult footpath leads up it into Kafiristan. It is enclosed by high hills, is not very narrow, and there are places where a few troops might encamp. The people of Parian get their firewood from Chamar, where there is abundance of willow. The distance from the Parian to the Chamar Kotal is some 10 miles. The descent is down a similar glen equally difficult. At 14 miles the first Kafir settlement is reached. It is called Atati. The next is Poshal, then Lashta Gham, and then Larha Pachha. The latter is a fort said to have been built by Amir Timur (-i-Lang). Below Pachha are Gadu, Chatur, and Madul. At the latter place the eastern Arioh and eastern Wariaj glens unite. (Shahzada Taimus.)

*CHAMBAR چمبر
    33-9 67-45 m. A village located south of the Dasht-i-Nawar, and northwest of Taqchin. Another village with this name is on the Ghazni river, near Abdul Rahman, at 32-41 68-8 m.

*CHAMBARA چمبره
    32-57 67-30 m. A village located south of the Bala Kuh.

*CHAMBO چمبو
    34-8 69-14 m. A village located on a tributary of the Logar, between Mazgin and Shahtut.

CHAMCHAMAST or CHAMCHEH MUST چمچه مست
    34-30 69-9 A. A stream in the Chardeh valley of Kabul, formed by drainage from the western hills from the Surkh Kotal to the Korogh mountain, and joining the Kabul at Guzargah. In its course through the valley, it washes the villages of Unchi, Bagwana, and Deh-i-Bori. Its name is said to have been given to it from the fact that it is formed by such numerous small contributions, i.e., spoonfuls. It is dry for a month or so at midsummer. Many attempts have been made to bridge the Chamchamast in the neighbourhood of (above) Deh-i-Bori, but a sudden rise of the waters has always swept away the bridge. (I.B.C.)

CHAMKANI چمکنی
    33-48 69-49 A. A small vilage near the Mirzakai Kotal: 10 or 15 Khasadars are stationed here. (I.B.C.)

CHAMKANI see CHAKMANI چمکنی

*CHAMKANI چمکنی
    33-48 69-48. Chamkani is a woleswali in Paktia province. The woleswali comprises an area of 264 square kilometers and has an agricultural population that has been estimated at from 8,149 to 12,833.

The woleswali is bounded in the west by Hasan Khel and Lajmangal, in the south by Jani Khel, in the east by Dand-wa-Patan and Dareh Darang, and in the north by Jaji. Chamkani has about 71 villages, one of which has more than 500 inhabitants. The villages are listed in the PG as follows: Garmai (Garami), Darak (Daraka Khoroti), Mangyar, Orgor, Darza Khel, Hesarak-i-Sufla (Ster Kalai Hesarak), Safed Kot (Spin Kot, Safed Koh), Khandan Khel (Akhund Dad Khel), Sulaiman Khel (Sulaiman Kalai), Hakimzai (Piran-i-Hakim Zai), Gerami Khurd (Kamkai Gerami), Morgho Manki, Sar Angur, Tana, Andar, Maidani, Tser Dalai, Chenargai, Tiyoshi (Toshi), Abdurahman Khel, Hesarak-i-Ulya (Julga-i-Hesarak), Alam Kalai, Miyana, Sultanzai (Sultangai), Bangash, Lato Kalai, Ghundi Kalai (Ghundi), Shogi Kalai (Leski), Wish Kalai, Muzdi Kalai (Murdi Kalai), Warah Kalai (War Kalai), Landi Ragha-i-Sar Angur, Taghoshti, Saqi Khel, Mir Ghozarkai (Waghozai), Surai Khola (Saroy Khola), Nozi Khola, Tani, Shenkai, Khwaja Mehrab, Alam Kalai, Spir Kalai, Kotkai, Bamos Kalai, Botowalai, Natsapa Kalai, Taru Kalai, Jayo Kalai, Sahibzadagan, Mirzabeg, Badur Kalai, Haider Khel, Koto Kalai, Woti Kalai, Keterah, Jangai Kalai, Chandakh, Draykahol, Mahkam Kalai, Sher Khan Kalai, Abdur Rahman Kalai, Bakhtawar Kalai, Kolyarai, Nawai Kalai, Maidah Kalai, Ap Khel, Ster Kalai (Hakimzai), War Kot, Mangal, Lagozai, Nargess, Darka-i-Kharoti, Sar Negun, Babu Khel, Mada Khel, and Bagyal.

*CHAMRI چمری
34-8 68-29 m. A village located in the Chak-i-Wardak area, on the Dara-i-Jelga. Another village with this name is near the Ghazni river, 3 miles southeast of Spina Kala, at 32-49 68-7 m.

CHANDAK چندك
35- 71-. A Shaikh village in the Kunar valley, just below and on the opposite (right) bank to the Gabar village of Sao. It consists of 18 houses, one of which is detached and surrounded by a high wall looking like a fort or a masjid, but declared to be merely a dwelling-house. The fields about the village are prosperoud looking. (Robertson.) Recent maps show the name Chunek, at 35-10 71-25. (LWA)

*CHAO چاو
34-24 67-50 m. A village located south of the Helmand, about 5 miles northwest of Behsud.

*CHAOGAI چوگی
32-9 68-38 m. A village in the Wur area, northwest of Alakzi.

*CHAOGAM چوگام
34-55 71-18 m. A village lying between the Kunar river and the Afghan border, near the village of Lemgai.

CHAOKUNI See CHOKANA چوکی

*CHAONI چونی
34-15 67-51 m. A village located some 8 miles southwest of Behsud in Maidan province. Another village with this name is located 34-19 68-1 m.

*CHAPA DARAH چپه دره
34-58 70-54. Chapa Darah is an alaqadari in Nangarhar province. The alaqadari comprises an area of 2,297 square kilometers and has an agricultural population that has been estimated at from 8,398 to 11,393. The alaqadari is bounded in the south by Dara-Nur and Nur

Gul, in the east by Chauki, Pech, and Kamdesh, in the north by Keran o Minjan and Bargai Matal, and in the west by Alingar and Nuristan. Chapa Darah has about 50 villages, 7 of which have more than 500 inhabitants. The villages are listed in the PG as follows: Kundi, Kharah, Qala, Gul Sang, Gozcham Wama, Susam Parun, Bastala (Batala), Watla, Karangul, Digul, Marchal, Sarigul, Qarya-i-Saydar, Machura, Qalachi, Ghondi, Tango, Handurak-i-Ulya, Handurak-i-Sufla, Chambarak, Seh Kot, Surmara, Goshalam, Warsak, Kotkai, Badgah, Bahadur Kalai, Karbori, Mohabat Kalai, Hazar Mirgul, Nakora, Sayyid Khel, Sartur, Katak, Sulaimanshah, Zemakoh, Wama, Muncham Wama, Kanit Wa, Kushtakay Parun, Pronsparun, Ishtoye, Diva Parun, Peshaki Parun, Kordar, Achno, Kanitwa-i-Ulya, Kanitwa-i-Sufla, Purchaman, Pascham Wama.

*CHAPARHAR   چپر هار
34-17 70-21 m. Chaparhar is an alaqadar in Nangarhar province. The alaqadari comprises an area of 185 square kilometers and has an agricultural population that has been estimated at from 16,965 to 19,390. The alaqadari is bounded in the north by Surkh Rud, in the east by Rodat, in the south by Pachir Aqam, and in the west by Khogiani. Chaparhar has about 29 villages, 10 of which have more than 500 inhabitants. The villages are listed in the PG as follows: Godara Arokal (Godara), Dago, Sholana, Banda, Lunga Pur, Hidya Khel (Sandi Khel), Gratak, Masti Khel, Char Qala, Mano, Dawlatzai (Dawan Zai), Bibi Mahro, Lukhi, Qala-i-Shaikh, Fatiri, Ghorabad, Qala-i-Surkh, Qala-i-Deh Kazi (Ghazwa Kalay), Karez-i-Akhund-Dada, Lalma, Kundi Bagh, Trili, Taraki, Tsaparai, Masjid-i-Safed, Gulam Dag, Sangina, Mander Khel, Hafezan, and Afghan.

*CHAPARI   چپری
33-48 68-5 m. A village on the Shemeltu stream, south of the Sang-i-Aoparan.

*CHAPARQOL   چپر قول
34-30 67-12 m. A village on the Dara-i-Mur, south of the Kuh-i-Baba in Bamian province.

CHAPCHI   چپچی
35- 69-. The first village passed on the road leading from the Khwak pass into the upper Panjshir valley. It is about 6 miles east of the kotal and contains 20 houses of Tili Hazaras. (Shahzada Taimus.)

*CHAPDARA   چپدره
35-7 69-5 m. A village on a tributary of the Ghorband river, northwest of Charikar.
Another village with this name is located on a tributary of the Panjshir, northeast of Charikar, at 35-7 69-28 m.

CHAPDARA   چپدره
35- 68-. A pass leading over the Hindu Kush, northeast of the Chahardar Kotal. Approaching from the southeast, the track leads up the Hazar Kuch ravine which joins the Nimakao at Khurd Barg, crosses the Chapdara Kotal, and then down to Chapdara itself (distant about 14 or 15 miles), joins the Chahardar road at the junction of the Pareshan and Chapdara streams. (I.B.C.)

*CHAPKOL   چپقول
34-58 68-59 m. A village near Dumba, east of the Kuh-i-Khushkak.

CHAPKOLAK چپكولك
34-59 67-36 A. A pass over the hills separating the Bamian valley from that of Saighan. Judging from Dafadar Sahibdad Khan's description it is easier than the Katar Sum Kotal, though the latter is considered the main road. Gumbat can be reached in one march from Bamian. Thence over the Chap Kolak Kotal. Halt would be at Naorak, about 10 miles from Gumbat, where there is plenty of room in the defile. Thence to Dahan-i-Karaoua below the large village of that name, is about the same distance. Here the defile joins the Tagao Saiyid Baba--that is, the upper part of the Saighan valley, the name Saighan being applied from this point downwards. In general character the road resembles that by the Katar Sum but it appears to be more easily made practicable for artillery. (Sahibdad Khan.)

CHAPRIAR or CHAPRIHAR چپریار (چپرهار)
34-17 70-21. A stream which, rising in the Safed Koh, flows northeast and falls into the Kabul river about 2 miles north west of Ali Boghan. It washes the village of Agam and gives its name to the portion of the Jalalabad district through which it flows. (I.B.C.) Some sources show the name Chapliar Khwar at 34-24 70-33. (LWA)

CHAPRIAR چپریار
34-17 70-21 m. A large valley containing about 2,000 houses of Tajiks and Mohamands about 16 miles west of Sharshahi. Water is plentiful throughout the year. Fodder for 12,000 animals for one day and about 2,500 maunds of unground grain can be collected in the neighbourhood. Fuel also is procurable. There is good grazing ground for camels and transport animals. Amar Khel, Daulatzai Kuchis with about 200 camels encamp here in the winter at which time of the year ghi in large quantities may be obtained. (Johnston.)

CHAPRI KOL چپری قول
A village in the Sar-i-Jangal valley. Ruins are located 20 miles west of Sarmaqul, in Garmab district, at 34-36 66-25 G. A village with this name is located on the Dara-i-Pich, some 8 miles south of Wama in Kunar province, at 35-3 70-42 m. (LWA)

CHARAH چاراه
A village in the Muhammad Khwaja, Hazara country.

CHARASIAB or CHARASIA چارآسیاب
34-24 69-9 m. Charasiab is an alaqadari in Kabul province. The alaqadari comprises an area of 261 square kilometers and has a population which has been variously estimated at from 12,989 to 13,365. The alaqadari is south of the City of Kabul. Charasiab includes about 73 villages, of which about 9 have more than 500 inhabitants. The villages are listed in the PG as follows: Chel Dukhtaran, Elyas Khel, Lako, Mohammad Wais, Andar Ha, Haji Elyas Khel, Qala-i-Ghaffar, Qala-i-Bawar, Tangi Sayedan, Kakariha, Qala-i-Khan, Formoli Ulya, Formoli Sufla, Jalal Tangi, Rahmatabad, Alu Khel, Deh Kalan, Qarya-i-Luqman, Shah Aziz, Siyah Joy, Shad Khana, Sur Yawand, Kata Sang, Mia Khel, Qarya-i-Khanan Khel, Payendahkhel, Haji Khel, Qarya-i-Charsuq, Ahangaran, Qala-i-Abdul Rauf, Moin Khel, Sayed Khel, Qeshlaq, Abbas Quli, Qala-i-Kohna, Dashtak Ulya (Tangi Dashtak), Gorgab, Qarya Pachi, Qarya Tajeka (Tajikia), Qarya Gulzar, Qala-i-Naim, Qala-i-Rashid, Qala-i-Jafar, Haq Dad, Bala Koh, Bala Qala, Kanwala (Kandolah), Qala-i-Malik, Charsuq Charasiab, Qala-i-Jarnel, Qala-i-Nau, Khairabad, Nau Niyaz, Shah Tut, Rish Khor, Qala-i-Taghan (Qala-i-Tufan), Qala-i-Ata, Yahya Khel, Qala-i-Tarin, Tangi Deh Kalan, Haji Malang, Lalundar, Ushturparidah, Tangi Lalundar,

Sahibzadaha, Karez, Asman Qala, Qala-i-Aslam, Mirakhor, Qala-i-Muhammad Aziz wa Ahmadzai, Qarya Afghania, Qala-i-Muhammad Din, and Tahir Khel. (LWA) In 1914, the area was described as follows:
A subdivision of the Kabul district containing, according to Molloy, about 10,000 families; all Tajiks. The village of Charasia lies to the south of Kabul and distant from it, by the Sang-i-Nawishta route, about 10 miles. It is situated on a small plain enclosed by hills on all sides, except the southwest. The Logar river cuts throught the eastern range and makes its exit at the northeast corner of the plain through a gorge called the Sang-i-Nawishta. Three roads lead from the Charasia plain towards Kabul. The main, and most easterly, road leads through the Sang-i-Nawishta along the river, and so northwards by the village of Bini Hisar to the Bala Hisar of Kabul. Immediately to the south of the gap is a semi-detached hill on the left bank of the river, and joind to the heights on the west by a low neck, over which the road passes. Another road strikes off from the first, and crossing a comparatively low part of the hills due north of Charasia, leads to Indaki, a village in the Chardeh valley close under the range which lies immediately to the west of Kabul, and on an easterly spur of which the city and Bala Hisar are situated. A third road leads from Charasia itself straight over the hill, in a westerly direction, into Chardeh.

The Charasia group of villages consisting of about 1,200 houses of Afghans and Tajiks is surrounded by orchards and walled enclosures. Fodder for 10,000 animals for one day and about 1,000 maunds of unground grain would be obtainable at any time.

The locality is now historical as the scene of Sir Frederick Roberts' victory over the Afghan army on the 6th October 1879, when marching on Kabul to avenge the massacre of the British embassy in the preceeding month. For details of this action and of that of the 26th April 1880, see the "Official History of the Second Afghan War."

CHARBAGH   چارباغ
34-32 70-19 m. A village in the Surkhab division of the Jalalabad district, situated about 6 miles west of the town of Jalalabad. Inhabitants: Tajiks. (Johnston, Jenkyns.) This village may be identical with the one below. (LWA)

CHARBAGH   چارباغ
34-32 70-18 A. A large village in Laghman, situated 2 miles north of the confluence of the Alingar and Kabul rivers. It was formerly well known as a place where swords and gun-barrels werre manufactured. The Emperor Babar made a royal garden at Charbagh. A squadron of cavalry is quartered here.
The inhabitants are Tajiks. The following are the hamlets composing the Charbagh township:

1. Kala-i-Ghulam Jan
2. Kala-i-Muhammad Akram
3. Kala-i-Muhammad Akbar
4. Kala-i-Saidan
5. Lalapur
6. Kala-i-Saiyid Ali
7. Deh Kuz Kulalan
8. Deh Bar Kulalan
9. Kala-i-Mufti
10. Kala-i-Kazi
11. Banda-i-Baba
12. Kala-i-Ibrahim
14. Kala-i-Sardar Mahmud Yahiya
15. Kala-i-Bostan
16. Kala-i-Mahmud Akram Khan
17. Kala-i-Mulla Haidar
18. Kala-i-Gul Badshah
19. Kala-i-Haji
20. Kala-i-Kalatak
21. Kala-i-Arwa
22. Kala-i-Haji Rasul Khan
23. Kala-i-Kazi Imamuddin
24. Kala-i-Rahim
25. Banda-i-Akhunzada

13. Kala-i-Mulla Idris   26. Kala-i-Mian Nur
(Moorchoft, Masson, Warburton, I.B.C..)

CHARDEH   چارده

34-32 69-0. A valley, or rather a plain, lying to the west of Kabul, and forming a subdivision of the Kabul district. Its boundaries may be thus roughly defined: north the hills (an offshoot from the Paghman range) running from the Surkh Kotal to Aoshar; south the Korogh mountain; east the Asmai, Sher Darwaza, and Haft Kotal heights; west the hill known as the Koh-i-Chonghor, and a spur to the north of it, running down from the ridge east of the Surkh Kotal. The valley is, as nearly as possible, 6 miles square, and is very fertile. It is watered by the Kabul river and its tributary the Chamchamast, and also by numerous karez.

The whole of this plain is covered with small villages and forts, surrounded with orchards, willows and poplars, and is one mass of cultivated fields. It is traversed by a number of roads, the principal ones being that running westwards to Arghandeh (the main Kaubl-Herat road), where another branches off to the southwest to Ghazni, over the Kotal-i-Takht; another runs southwards along the left bank of the river of Rishkor where it crosses the river by a stone bridge and eventually joins the main Ghazni road north of Kala Durani; yet another branches off to the north from Arghandeh and running between the Asmai and Aoshara hills eventually joins the main Kaubl-Charikar road. These roads are all well made, and practicable for wheels, but owing to the cultivation and to the number of fortified villages, orchards, etc., the intervening country is difficult even for the passage of infantry. Chardeh has a population of some 12,000 families, and the production of wheat, barley, rice and maize, which are almost the only crops grown, must be very great. None of the land is allowed to lie fallow, a considerable amount of lucerne and shaftal (a species of clover) being grown as alternative crops to wheat and barley.

The name is said to have been originally Chahar-dar-Chahar, i.e., "the square," and to have been corrupted to Chardeh. The following is a list of the Chardeh villages and forts:

	Villages	Inhabitants
1.	Aliabad	Barakzais and Tajiks
2.	Allah-ud-din	Gadi Hazaras
3.	Aoshar	Kizilbashes
4.	Aoshar-i-Thiba	Kizilbashes
5.	Bagwana	Tajiks
6.	Deh-i-Bori	Tajiks
7.	Deh-i-Kalandar	Tajiks
8.	Deh-i-Mozang	Tajiks and Kizilbashes
9.	Deh-i-Miskin	Tajiks
10.	Deh-i-Murad Khan	Tajiks
11.	Gaokhana	Hazaras and Tajiks
12.	Guzargah	Tajiks and Kizilbashes
13.	Inchu	Tajiks
14.	Indaki	"
15.	Jangalak	"
16.	Kala-i-Abdul Aziz	"
17.	Kala-i-Abdul Hashim	"
18.	Kala-i-Abdulla Khan	"
19.	Kala-i-Agha Asghar	Kizilbashes
20.	Kala-i-Agha Jan	"
21.	Kala-i-Agha Muhammad	"

22.	Kala-i-Ali Mardan Kul	Barakzais
23.	Kala-i-Amin-ud-daula Khan	"
24.	Kala-i-Fatu	Hazaras
25.	Kala-i-Fazil Beg	Tajiks
26.	Kala-i-Ghaibi	"
27.	Kala-i-Haji Yusuf	Kizilbashes
28.	Kala-i-Jabar Khan	Barakzais
29.	Kala-i-Jafir Jan	Kizilbashes
30.	Kala-i-Iltifat	Tajiks
31.	Kala-i-Karim Khan	Kizilbashes
32.	Kala-i-Kazi	Tajiks
33.	Kala-i-Muhammad Karim Khan	Barakzais
34.	Kala-i-Muhammad Umar	Tajiks
35.	Kala-i-Mir Akhor Agha Jan	Kizilbashes
36.	Kala-i-Mir Akhor Ali Muhammad Khan	Hazaras
37.	Kala-i-Mir Akhor Kasim	Tajiks and Barakzais
38.	Kala-i-Mir Ghaza	Popalzais
39.	Kala-i-Mirza Ahmad Khan	Baluchis
40.	Kala-i-Mirza Ghulam Sidik	Tajiks and Baluchis
41.	Kala-i-Mirza Jafir	Tajiks
42.	Kala-i-Mirza Jawat	Kizilbashes
43.	Kala-i-Mohib Ali Khan	"
44.	Kala-i-Munal	Barakzais
45.	Kala-i-Nazir Ali Muhammad	Tajiks
46.	Kala-i-Safdar Ali Khan	Kizilbashes
47.	Kala-i-Samandar Khan, or Chonghor	Tokhis
48.	Kala-i-Sardar Muhammad Amin Khan	Tajiks
49.	Kala-i-Sardar Wali Muhammad Khan	Gadi Hazaras
50.	Kala-i-Shah Mardan Kul	Tajiks
51.	Kala-i-Shams-ud-din Khan	"
52.	Kala-i-Shukur Ulla Khan	Barakzais
53.	Kala-i-Sultan Ali	Kizilbashes
54.	Kala-i-Sultan Jan	Hazaras
55.	Kala-i-Surkh	Tajiks
56.	Kala-i-Wazir	Hazaras
57.	Kala-i-Zaman Khan	"
58.	Khingot	Ahmadzai Ghilzais
59.	Murghigiran	Adramzai and Ahmadzai Ghilzais
60.	Musai	Tajiks
61.	Rishkor-i-Pain	"
62.	Sarasia	"
63.	Teba	"

The Revenne of Chardeh is said to amount to about two lakhs of rupee (Kabuli?).
For an account of the action on the Chardeh plain on 11th December 1879, see the "Official History of the Second Afghan War." (Molloy, Wanliss, I.B.C.)

CHARDEH چارده
34- 70-. Elevation 1,822 feet. A large walled village in the Pesh Bolak subdivision of the Jalalabad district. 7 1/2 miles northwest of Basawal. It contains (in 1904) some 400 families of Barakzais, possessing about 1,200 head of cattle, 1,500 sheep and goats and 50 buffaloes. The annual production of wheat and barley averages

about 22,000 Indian maunds. Fodder for about 3,000 animals for one day is procurable from Chardeh and its neighbourhood. Mandezai Kuchis with about 250 camels come and settle here in the winter. There is grazing ground for camels and mules. There is a force of 400 khasadars stationed here. (Wanliss, Johnston, I.B.C.)

CHARDEH چارده
34- 70-. A large village, or rather township in Laghman, situated on the right bank of the Alingar river, about 8 miles above the junction of that stream with the Kabul. The inhabitants are Umar Khel Ghilzais.
The following forts and hamlets are included in Chardeh:

1. Kabil-i-Mulla Jan Dad
2. Kabil-i-Yunis Akhunzada
3. Banda-i-Pahlwan
4. Kala-i-Sher Gul
5. Kala-i-Ghulam
6. Hasan Khel
7. Kala-i-Muhammad Rahim
8. Kala-i-Abdul Rahim
9. Kala-i-Sher Gul
10. Kala-Miran
11. Ghundi Khudadad
12. Kala-i-Akhunzada
13. Mullayan
14. Pajagi
   (Warburton.)

*CHARDEH چارده
32-55 67-30 m. A village in Ghazni province, northwest of Mukur. There is also a village with this name located at 34-43 66-49 A.

*CHARDEHI چاردهی
34-28 69-8. Chardehi is a woleswali in Kabul province. The woleswali comprises an area of 140 square kilometers and has an agricultural population which has been variously estimated by Afghan sources at from 31,314 to 48,325. The woleswali is bounded in the west by Paghman, in the north by Shakar Dara and Deh-Sabz, in the east by Bagrami and in the south by Charasiab. Chardehi includes about 46 villages, of which about 41 have more than 500 inhabitants. The villages are listed in the PG as follows: Qala-i-Wazir, Qala-i-Jafar, Qala-i-Akhund, Bangsidar, Diwan Begi, Deh Mubarak, Qala-i-Jawad, Afshar-i-Nanakchi, Spin Kalai, Qala-i-Morghgiran, Qarya Alawuddin, Qarya Khwaja Mulla, Qala-i-Shadah, Gulkhana, Afshar Darul-Aman, Deh Murad Khan, Qala-i-Muslem, Sar Asyab, Qala-i-Bakhtiyar, Qala-i-Jabar, Qala-i-Alimardan, Chehil Sutun, Qala-i-Fatu, Qala-i-Qazi, Qala-i-Nau, Rishkhor-i-Sufla, Chahar Qala, Qala-i-Bahadur, Saber, Chahar Qulba, Aqa Ali Shams, Deh Dana, Waselabad, Qala-i-Ghaibi, Jangalak, Fazel Beg, Niaz Beg, Deh Qalander, Unchi Baghbanan, Yusuf Bangi, Qala-i-Khashef, Qala-i-Musa Chardehi, Qala-i-Khwajaha, Dehburi wa Pul-i-Sokhta, Doghabad, Qala-i-Wahed, Qala-i-Nazar, and Qala-i-Maruf.

CHARDI چاردی
34- 70-. A lofty mountain range to the north of Laghman, piled up between the Alingar and Alishang rivers. The Badpakht hills are an offshoot from this range. (Holdich.)

CHARDU KOL چاردو قول
34- 70-. A place in the Besud country.

CHARGO Or CHERGO چرگو
33- 69-. A village on the right bank of the Karaia stream, about 5 miles east on Ahmad Khel. Inhabitants: Ahmad Khel Jajis. The place is said to contain 150 fighting men. (Collett.) A well called Chargo Chashma is about 13 miles south of Ali Mardan in Parwan province, at

35-34 67-12 G. (LWA)

*CHARGOSHA چارگوشه
34-28 67-46 m. A village located on a tributary of the Helmand, about 4 miles north of its confluence with the Helmand.

CHARIAK چاریک
Two villages in the Rah Kol valley.

CHARIKAR چاریکار
35-0 69-10. Charikar is a woleswali in Parwan province. The woleswali comprises and area of 189 square kilometers and has an agricultural population that has been estimated at from 28,928 to 30,519. The woleswali is bounded in the west by Shinwar, in the north by Jabal Saraj, in the east by Mahmud Raqi, and in the south by Bagram. Charikar includes about 70 villages, of which 25 have more than 500 inhabitants. The villages are listed in the PG as follows: Senjed Dara, Kariz Ulya, Deh Guchak, Deh Rais, Deh Aftab, Deh Neshar, Deh Gholaman, Qala-i-Sifalan, Qala-i-Ali Khan, Kulalan, Qala-i-Najarha, Karizak Sufla, Qala-i-Sharif, Peshian, Khwaja Sayaran-i-Ulya, Qala-i-Mulla, Qala-i-Lal Mir Khan, Qala-i-Khwajaha, Deh Qazi, Toghberdi, Qala-i-Mirza, Dolana, Nahya-i-Awgal-i-Seh Guzer, Guzer-i-Aqai, Guzer-i-Charsuq, Nahya-i-Dum-i-Seh Guzer, Guzer-i-Khalifa, Naimguzer Khan Mohammad Khan, Guzer-i-Sultani, Nahya-i-Sewum, Guzer-i-Haqdad, Charmgari, Guzer-i-Sayed Ali, Totum Dara-i-Sufla, Dogh Abad, Khwaja Sayaran-i-Sufla, Laghmani, Meyanshakh, Baba Khel, Abdibay, Qala-i-Nau-i-Abdibay, Sadullah, Baran Ulya, Tup Dara, Qala-i-Safed, Qala-i-Khalifaha, Shamaq, Baltukhel, Hofyan-i-Sharif, Dasht-i-Hofyan-i-Sharif, Qala-i-Mir-Kalan, Totum Dara-i-Ulya, Qala-i-Sahra, Sayadan, Qalacha-i-Sokhta, Jamshed Khel, Qala-i-Zaman, Akhtchi, Deh Molla Yusuf, Qala-i-Nau, Qala-i-Badal, Qala-i-Faqirshah, Bayan-i-Sufla, Khala Zai, Choney Sadozai, Kangal Sadozai, Rahasht, and Shahr-i-Nau. (LWA) In 1914, the area was described as follows: A subdivision of Kohistan. It consists of the town of Charikar and its neighbourhood, and is said to be under Jalal-ud-dun, Kandahari. The following is a list of the villages on the daman of the Paghman range, with their populations, as given in 1886 to Shahzada Taimus at Charikar, but it is not known whether they all belong to the Charikar subdivision:

Villages	Number of Houses	Inhabitants
1. Tutamdara	200	Tajiks
2. Oplam	300	Tajiks
3. Khwaja Siahran Aolia	300	Tajiks
4. Top Dara	300	Tajiks
5. Shahmak	50	Mohmads
6. Sinjit Dara	1,000	Tajiks
7. Khalazai	100	Afghans

Sinjit Dara comprises the following: Kala-i-Mir, Akbar Khan, Deh Pitao, Deh Ghulaman, Deh Nishar, Asiawanan, Kulalan, Deh Ghaochak, Deh Rais, Karezak-i-Pain, and Karezak-i-Bala.

East of Charikar are the following villages:

Villages	Number of Houses	Inhabitants
1. Baba Khel and Mian Shakh	300	Tajiks
2. Daulat Shahi	200	Tajiks
3. Khwaja Siahran Sufla	250	Tajiks

4.	Laghman and Sujian	400	Tajiks
5.	Pashaian	500	Tajiks
6.	Daulana	400	Tajiks
7.	Kalacha-i-Sokhta	100	Tajiks
8.	Deh Mulla Yusuf	120	Tajiks
9.	Balaghil and Akil Juni	100	Tajiks
10.	Kala-i-Zaman	100	Tajiks
11.	Deh Kazi	400	Tajiks
12.	Deh Saijad	500	Tajiks
13.	Toghbidi	400	Tajiks
14.	Darashah Khel	200	Tajiks

Farther east or southeast, toward, or along, the Panjshir river are:

1.	Khwaja Khizri	1,000	Tajiks
2.	Robat	2,000	Tajiks

(Shahzada Taimus.)

CHARIKAR چاریکار

35-1 69-11 A. Elevation 4,920 feet. A town at the mouth of the Ghorband valley, 40 miles north of Kabul, the residence of the Governor of Kohistan.

It is said (1882) to contain 3,000 houses inhabited by Tajiks (900 houses), Uzbaks, Kizilbashes, Hazaras, and Hindus (150 houses). The latter, some of whom are Sikhs, are all traders and shopkeepers. Iron-ore is brought here in great quantities from the Ghorband mines, and is worked up for the Kabul market.

Transit dues are, or were, charged at the rate of Rs. 5 per camel or pony-lead, Rs. 3 per donkey-load, Rs. 5 per horse or camel, Rs. 3 per donkey, Rs. 3 per head of cattle, Rs. 1 per 6 head of sheep coming from Turkistan.

The dues on goods are the same going upwards as downwards, but unladen animals returning are not charged for.

There are several mud forts in the town and more in the immediate neighbourhood. Within the walls the largest fort is Kala-i-Kazi; outside the place the principal one is Kala-i-Khwaja Abdul Khalik. There are a number of orchards at Charikar which extend for some distance north and south along the road.

The position of Charikar is of great strategic importance, as the roads over the Hindu Kush proper unite in its neighbourhood. There is a road from Charikar which goes over the hill by Opian to Tawakal in the Ghorband valley. (See "Chetak.")

In 1839 Charikar was the seat of a British Political Agent, and the station of Shah Shuja's Gurkha regiment. When the insurrection broke out, the postion was attacked by the warlike Kohistanis, and after some days' severe fighting, and the supply of water being cut off, a retreat was made on Kabul, which ended in the destruction of the greater part of the garrison, Major Eldred Pottinger, Lieutenant Haughton, and one Gurkha only escaping, although 165 men, survivors, were afterwards collected by the latter officer on the advance of General Pollock's army.

The valley of Charikar, says Pottinger, offers every advantage for the cantonment of troops; it abounds in supplies of all kinds; labour is cheap, and the forage for horses and camels excellent and the climate is milder than that of Kabul. (A.B.C., I.B.C.)

*CHARK Or CHARQ چرق

34-5 67-11 m. A village located at a bend of the Helmand river, north of the Pitaoqol.

*CHARKALA   چار قلعه
33-45 68-10 m. A village located on a tributary of the Ghorband, south of Shibar.

CHARKH or CHERKH   چرخ (څرخ)

CHARKH   چرخ (څرخ)
33-48 68-56 m. Charkh is the name of an alaqadari in the Logar province. The alaqadari comprises an area of 760 square kilometers and has an agricultural population which has been variously estimated at from 13,758 to 21,463. The alaqadari is bounded in the west by Sayyidabad and Zenakhan, in the north by Baraki, in the northeast by Pul-i-Alam, and in the southeast by Gardez and Zurmat. Charkh includes some 63 villagesx, of which about nine have more than 500 inhabitants. The villages are listed in the PG as follows: Garmaba, Bandoka, Shash Qala, Bakhshi Kharwar, Mango Khel, Khumari Khel, Shamshir Khel, Hush Khel, Saido Khel, Balo Khel-i-Kharwar, Omar Khan Kharwar, Khani Khel, Jawzi, Chalak Khel, Bazi Khel, Kunj Qala, Kotagai, Charkhi, Qarya-i-Karez, Qala-i-Naft, Zard Sang, Abjosh-i-Sufla, Qala-i-Nau Shahr, Pinsgram, Abjosh-i-Bala, Qala-i-Nau, Qarya-i-Homai, Bibi Sholgar, Mirgat, Qol-i-Jalal, Argana, Warsang, Ghurfan, Khak, Qol-i-Sabz, Gadol, Khwaja Angur, Ashi Khel, Qala-i-Shaikhan Sadat, Haibat Khel, Delbar Alu, Begum Kharwar, Tawus Khel, Mochi Khel, Kandel, Bahadur, Arzokhel, Dabar-i-Rahim Ali, Dabar-i-Khwajaha, Khushk, Dasht, Azuk Khel, Mani, Karez-i-Mohd. Rasul, Yar Gul, Ali Jan Khel, Qarya-i-Safedar, Tughyani, Dawlat Khel, Apakhan-i-Kharwar, Qarya-i-Rustam-i-Masudi, Asiyab, Kunji Khel, Qarya-i-Mane, Kata Sang, Baba Khel, Shaykhan Shamsher, Kotaki-i-Shamsher, Zardak Khel, Daftak Khel, Kodoli, Qarya-i-Kharwar, Takhtak-i-Charkh, Jaw Darakht, Pagram, Panj Paye, Kunj Darah, Qala-i-Yar Gul, Shaikhan and Allah Khan. (LWA) In 1914, this area was described as follows: A subdivision of the Logar district. The Charkh, or Cherkh, valley is formed by a recess in the range dividing Logar form Kharwar, and shut out from the former by some low hills running for 9 miles nearly east and west.
The valley contains 4 villages.
        1. Kala-i-Nao   2. Pingram
        3. Garmao   4. Nao Shahar

The above villages contained, in 1880, 1,000 Tajik families, and the head men then were Kutab-ud-din and General Ghulam Haidar, the late Sipah Salar. The valley, being well-watered by a stream rising in Kharwar, is highly cultivated: Wheat appears to be the principal crop. It abounds in vineyards and fruit gardens, whilst poplar, chinar, and ash are very numerous.
In the background the hills are dotted with wild almond trees. The Tajik inhabitants are divided into two factions, which are constantly at war with each other. Further information regarding the upper portion of the Charkh is given under "Kharwar." See also "Logar."
A squadron of regular cavalry and 150 khasadars are quartered in Charkh. (I.B.C., McLean, Euan Smith.)

CHARKHEL   چارخیل
33-5 69-33 m. The western extremity of a lofty range of hills which divides Khost form the Tochi valley and rises to an elevation of 9,900 feet. On the southern slopes the forest consists of oak below and pines above; on the west there is a dense forest of chilgoza and other pines; on the northern slopes the chilgoza disappears, but there is an equally dense forest of other pines and deodar. The

summits of the peaks are steep, but the range is not precipituos as a rule. There is excellent grazing in the valleys.

On the north and west side of Charkhel runs the Mir Tsappar valley which is bounded by the Mir Tsappar hills. This valley is some 3 miles broad, and here and there in it are extensive clearings.

The highest peak of Charkhel is also known as Charkiaghar, or Khar Kamar. On this peak was placed, in 1895, pillar No. 1 of the Charkhel-Laram and Charkhel-Khwaja Khidr sections of the Indo-Afghan boundary. The summit of the Charkhel ridge forms the boundary for about 15 miles east from this pillar, and along the watershed runs an old road, known as the "Badshahi Lar." This road, which is supposed to have been made by Mahmud of Ghazni and to run all the way from Ghazni to Khost, though in bad repair in parts, is still a good mule road throughout.

*CHAR QARYA (HESA-I-AWAL) چار قریه (حصه اول)
35-23 69-40. Char Qarya is an alaqadari in Parwan province. The alaqadari comprises an area of 2,113 square kilometers and has an agricultural population that has been estimated at from 14,199 to 17,586. The alaqadari is bounded in the west by Panjshir and Andarab, in the north by Khost o Farang and Warsaj, in the east by Keran 0 Munjan and Nurestan, and in the south by Dara Hazara. Char Qarya includes about 19 villages, of which 10 have more than 500 inhabitants. The villages are listed in the PG as follows: Kor Pitab, Shal Kacha, Jeshta, Kojan, Shah Niz, Deh-i-Parian, Koh-i-Sur, (Koh Sur-i-Parian), Qala-i-Parian, Peshghor, Tule (Tole), Khawak, Khinj, Purchaman, Daht-i-Zewat (Albut), Safid Chehr, Omar Khel (Omarz), Zina-i-Omarz, Raghak Ghoza (Ghorar), Kharo, Chinzai, Ibrahim Khel, Khumari Khel, Awal Khel, Rutam Khel, and Gadi.

CHARTUT چارتوت
34-17 69-52 m. A village in the Jalalabad district, about 10 miles west of Gandamak, on the left bank of the Surkhab river, and about 5 miles above the Surkhpul bridge. The road from Gandamak to Tezin passes through this place. It contains about 300 houses inhabited by Ghilzais. Fodder for 3,000 animals for one day and about 400 maunds of unground grain may be collected in the village and neighbourhood. Fuel is abundant and there is good ground for encampment. (McNair, Johnston.) Another place with this name is near Kalakan, east of the Kabul-Charikar road, at 34-48 69-12 m. (LWA)

*CHARU چارو
35-22 69-39 m. A village on the Panjshir river, about 1 mile northeast of Barak.

*CHARWAZAI چاروزی
33-24 69-9 m. A village southwest of Ghazni in the Zurmat area.

CHARWAZAI چاروزی
34- 69-. A village in the Jalalabad district. It stands between the Narioba and Hisarak streams, about 2 miles southwest of Yaghiband. Inhabitants, Shinwaris. (Jenkyns.) Another place with this name is located southeast of Kabul, at 34-19 69-19 m. (LWA)

*CHARWAZGAI چاروازگی
34-9 70-26 m. A village south of Jalalabad and 2 miles northwest of Haska Mina.

CHASHMA DUZDAN See DANDAN SHIKAN. چشمه دزدان

CHASHMA HUSAIN See HUSAIN چشمه حسین

CHASHMA-I-ALI MALANG چشمه علی ملنگ
34- 69-. A spring and shrine near Kabul, between Indaki and Babar's tomb. (I.B.C.)

CHASHMA-I-CHONGHOR Or KALA-I-SAMANDAR KHAN چشمه چنغر
34- 69-. A fort in the Chardeh valley, Kabul district, about 2 miles north of Kala-i-Ghulam Haidar Khan. There are, in all, about 30 families in the place, Tajiks and Ghilzais.

CHASHMA-I-KHIDAR چشمه خضر (؟)
34- 69-. A spring and shrine near Kabul, below the road (south side) between the Bala Hisar and the Sher Darwaza hill. On Fridays the shrine is visited by crowds of city people, both Musulmans and Hindus. (I.B.C.)

CHASHMA-I-MUKU چشمه مکو
33- 69-. A village in the Ali Khel subdivision of the Ghazni district, situated on the main road from Kandahar to Ghazni. (Hastings.)

CHASHMA-I-MURGHAN چشمه مرغان
34- 69-. A spring in the southern slopes of the Korogh montain, near Kabul, between Shahtut and Lalandar. It is well known as a favorite resort for hill-partridges which are here trapped in great numbers. (I.B.C.)

CHASHMA-I-PANJA-I-SHAH چشمه پنجه شاه
34- 69-. A spring and well-known shrine in the Kabul district, situated on the eastern slope of the Takht-i-Shah mountain, about 1 mile above Kala-i-Hashmat Khan. (I.B.C.)

CHASHMA-I-PANJAK چشمه پنجک
A halting place in the Ghazni district, at some springs 2 miles to the west of the Tarnak river. About 1 mile on the left bank of the river is Kala-i-Jafir Khan, and there are several large villages on either side of the river. Firewood procurable, and grass and camel forage are plentiful. This point marks the southern boundary of the Ghazni district. (Hough, Outram, N. Campbell, Hastings.)

*CHASHMAO چشماو
35-14 69-18 m. A village on the Shotul stream, a tributary of the Panjshir.

CHASHMA PALU See PALU چشمه پالو

CHASHT چشت
34-58 66-32. A glen in the northwest of Yak Walang. It drains from the northeast and debouches into the Rud-i-Band-i-Amir at 3 miles above Marghi. It is three or four hundred yards across where it joins the main valley, and it is said to be a long march to the head of it. There are roads from it to Dara Yusuf and Bamian, and probably also to Saighan and Kamard. A considerable stream comes down the glen. At its mouth there are two neat little walled hamlets, with 10 families, and a few apricots and willows. (Maitland.)

*CHATUR Or CHOTUR چتور
35-19 70-12 m. A village on the Nuristan river, 4 miles southwest of Gadwal.

CHAUKI Or CHAW KAI چوکی
34-42 70-55 m. Chauki is a woleswali in Nangarhar province. The woleswali comprises an area of 249 square kilometers and has an agricultural population that has been estimated at about 8,900. The woleswali is bounded in the west by Chapa Dara and Nur Gul, in the southeast by Khas Konar and in the east by Sirkanay, and in the north by Narang, Chapa dara, and Pech. Chauki has about 31 villages, 5 of which have more than 500 inhabitants. The villages are listed in the PG as follows: Shaluti, Kalmani, Gato Qala, Khadi Khel (Khan Khel), Babur, Kandal (Kanawar), Masud Chawki, Garbuz-i-Chawki, Tarnaw, Garigal, Chambel (Jamil), Karboli (Karbola), Plar Darah, Khadah, Qala, Kagzai (Kagizai), Badinzai, Sulaimanzai, Pahosari (Pahlu wa Sari), Andar Lachak, Murcha Khel, Bad Gol, Safedar, Chalas Kalani, Nori Chalash, Shirgul Chalas, Amri (Amrawi), Gombal, Nassafa (Nasapa), Islam Khana, and Kundi. (LWA) In 1914, the area was described as follows: At 34 1/2 miles from Jalalabad the road up the Kunar valley passes through cornfields across the Chauki basin (3/4 mile from hills to river). The largest Chauki village is situated at the mouth of the Chauki Dara, 1/2 mile from the road at the foot of the hills. There are several other villages near the road. The inhabitants are Safis. Opposite and about 4 miles below Chauki, between the river and the Kabul Tsappar range, there is a curious, conical, isolated hill rising some hundreds of feet out of the fields. The villages on the downstream side of this hill are apparently called Kunar, and those on the upstream side Tanna (Coldstream.)

*CHAUNI چونی
33-52 69-9 m. A village located northwest of Gardez, about 5 miles east of the Gardez-Kabul road.

CHAUSH چوش (؟)
A section of the Dai Kundis.

*CHAWAK چوك
34-5 67-32 m. A village located east of Kushk, near the Garmab river.

CHECHENEH (CHICHINA?) چیچنه
34-36 69-50. A village in the Laghman district, at the confluence of the Panjshir and Kabul rivers. (Thorton.)

CHEHIL BACHA GUM چهل بچه کم (بچگان)
33-30 68-24 G. A place of pilgrimage in the Ghazni district, 6 miles southwest of the town of Ghazni, on the Kandahar road. (Thorton.) Afghan Gazetteers show the name Bachagan. (LWA)

CHEHIL BURJ چهل برج
34-55 66-37 m. The remains of a fortress in the Band-i-Amir valley, in the west of the Yak Walang district. The fortress originally consisted of three lines of walls running completely round the semi-isolated hill on which it stands. The walls are flanked by loopholed towers at very short intervals. These towers are of considerable diameter, though not very high, and many of them are still nearly perfect. This is particularly the case at the east end of the fortress where the towers and curtain wall of the second line of defence are both in remarkably good preservation. Maitland estimated the height of the latter at 50 or 60 feet. The whole is of unburnt brick. The loopholes are of noticeable shape, having three triangular openings above the long slit. The walls were built on a

foundation of rounded stones, set in mud or mortar. The river is in a deep broad channel, on the further side of which steep reddish hills rise to a great height. (Maitland.)

CHEHIL DUKHTARAN چهل دختران
35-10 68-47 G. Two miles south of the Chahardar pass are the springs of Chehil Dukhtaran. Here there is space on level open flats in terraces for at least a battalion. Water good and abundant. Firewood obtainable a little way down ravine (bushes and scrub). Supplies procurable from Deh Tangi villages (and others lower down), distant 4 miles. (Drummond.)

CHEHIL DUKHTARAN چهل دختران
34-23 69-7 m. A large village, 2 miles south of Charasia. With the villages in its vicinity it forms one of the subdivisions of the Kabul district. Inhabitants: Barakzais, Tajiks, and Umar Khel Ghilzais. (I.B.C.)

CHEHIL MATI چهل متی
34- 70-. A village in the Laghman district, omitted from all maps, but probably identical with leech's Chehlmati, said by that authority to be in the valley of the Alingar, 46 miles northwest of Jalalabad, and to consist of 70 houses of Tajiks. Leech says it is "on a road to Kashkar." Warburton, without defining its geographical position, gives the following particulars regarding the place. The inhabitants are Tajiks, Shamsher Khan Khel, and Mahmud Khel. The following are the hamlets which make up the township:

1. Deh-i-Mahfuz
2. Miangan
3. Kala-i-Rahimdad
4. Kala-i-Abdullah
5. Kala-i-Baz Muhammad
6. Kala-i-Mir Sarak
7. Kala-i-Malik Nur
8. Kabil-i-Muhammad Khel
9. Deh-i-Baghlak
10. Kala-i-Langar Khan
11. Kala-i-Pir Muhammad
12. Kala-i-Shao Khan
13. Kala-i-Khal Muhammad
14. Kala-i-Sarfi Khan
15. Deh-i-Fathullah
16. Banda-i-Mulla Saleh
17. Band-i-Sadullah

(Leech, Warburton.)

*CHEHILSUTUN چهل ستون
34-27 69-10 m. A village located some 8 miles south of Kabul, and east of Dehdana.

CHEHILTAN چهل تن
34-31 69-0 G. A village about 6 miles west of Kabul, situated on the Chamchamast stream to the north of the Chonghor hill. The inhabitants are Kizilbashes (of the Arab section), Tajiks and Gadi Hazaras. There are about 15 houses in the village itself, but the name Chehiltan includes 11 forts and hamlets. There is a shrine here on the hillside, that of Khwaja Musafir, and the place is otherwise well-known for its apple orchards. When the apples are ripe, crowds of people flock here from the city and make holiday. (I.B.C.) Other places with this name are located at 34-44 67-37 m. and 35-18 68-5 G. (LWA)

*CHEMAR KHOLEH چمار خوله
35-8 69-3 m. A village located on a tributary of the Ghorband, northwest of Charikar.

CHERGO See CHARGO چرگو

CHERKH See CHARKH چرخ

CHETAK or CHIRTAK چیتک
35-5 69-12. A dara which descends north and joins the Ghorband valley at about 3 miles above Tutam Dara. It is inhabited by Salang Parsiwans, who until lately robbed all travellers by this road. It is a narrow, rocky ravine, and a footpath, difficult for laden yabus or bullocks, leads up it and across a kotal at its head to Charikar, striking the Koh Daman at the village of Opian. (Peacocke.)

CHIGAR SARAI See CHIGHA SARAI چغه سرای

CHIGHA SARAI Or ASADABAD چغه سرای
34-53 71-9 m. Elev. 2,800 feet. Three villages on the right bank of the Kunar river, at the junction with the latter of the Pech Dara. The largest of the villages lies on the left bank of the Pech, 57 miles from Jalalabad. There are three old forts, one on the right bank of the Pech and two on the left bank, about 1/4 mile from the village; the two last mentioned are (1895) in ruins. The inhabitants are Shinwaris.
From Chigha Sarai a road leads up the Pech dara and forms the chief entrance of the Waigul valley of Nuristan. The Pech Dara is crossed, about 3/4 mile above the village, by a bridge over which goes the Jalalabad-Asmar road. The roadway is only about 6 feet wide, there are no railings and the centre portion sways considerably. The piers are of dry stone masonry bonded with wood. Horses, mules and camels can be led over it. The Pech is a very rapid stream and is here unfordable in the hot weather, from April onwards. The bridge described above is said to remain standing all year round, and in the cold weather there is also a foot-bridge, with a roadway about 10 inches wide, about 3/4 mile lower down. A battalion of infantry and 300 khasadars are stationed at Chigha Sarai (Coldstreeam, I.B.C.) For a recent description of this area, see Asadabad. (LWA)

CHIKNAK چکنک
A bridge over the Arghandab.

*CHINA چینه
34-1 68-20 m. A village south of Mirzabele in Maidan province. Other villages with this name are located south of Jalalabad on the road to Chapriar, at 34-19 70-24 m.; south of Zardalu, on the edge of the Sagi Dasht, at 33-5 67-40 m.; on the Tagab river, north of the Band-i-Naghlu, at 34-41 69-42 m.

*CHINAGAK چینه گك (چین گك)
34-50 69-32 m. A village in the Panjshir valley, some miles west of Tagab.

CHINAKI چینکی
A village in Panjshir.

*CHINAR چنار
34-37 70-27 G. A place located 13 miles northwest of Shiva in Kunar province. Other places with this name are located on the Hindu stream, a tributary of the Kunar, southeast of Asadabad, at 34-51 71-14 m. Sixteen miles southeast of Basul in Shinwar province, at 34-5 70-59 m. Near Darin, some 4 miles east of the Kunar river, at 35-6 71-25 m. Near Aodara, northeast of Kabul, at 34-43 69-19

m. On the Wuzbin Khwar, which runs into the Kabul river northeast of Sarobi, at 34-41 69-49 m. Southwest of Shartan, Asmar, at 34-50 71-13 G. South of Numla in the Khugiani district, at 34-11 70-5 G.

CHINAR چنار
34- 70-. A pass leading from the Parian glen of Panjshir into Nuristan. (Leech.) Probably the same as Chamar. (LWA)

CHINARI چناری
34-31 69-28 G. A glen in the Kabul district, running from south to north between Lataband and Khurd Kabul; its waters supplying the fields of Butkhak, and falling into the Kabul river near the Pul-i-Charki. (I.B.C.)

CHINARI چناری
34- 69-. A pass over a low ridge between Lataband and Khurd Kabul. (Young.)

*CHINGAI چینگی
34-42 71-0 m. A village located on the Kunar river, about 5 miles southwest of Narang.

CHINGAK چین گک
33-44 69-27 G. A village at the source of the Zurmat river, consisting of 40 houses of Ahmad Khel Jajis. (Hastings.)

*CHINO چنو
34-16 71-14 m. A village near the Kambu Khwar, some 15 miles south-southwest of Jalalabad.

CHIPRIHAR See CHAPRIAR چپریار

*CHIRG چرگ
33-59 69-38 m. A village on the Ruqyan Tuq, about 2 miles west of Ruqyan.

*CHIRGAKAI چرگکی
33-46 69-32 m. A village located on a tributary of the Patan Tuy, 2 miles south of Ghundai.

CHIRTAK See CHETAK چیرتک

CHOGAI چوگی
35-0 71-19 G. A village located about 7 miles southwest of Asmar. Another village with this name is located about 12 miles north of Kunar, at 34-41 70-55 G.

CHOGAI چوگی
33- 68-. A village in Kharwar, 80 houses of Andaris. (Griesbach.)

CHOKANA چوکنه
A section of the Daulatpai Besudis.

CHOL چل (چول)
35- 71-. A camping ground on the right bank of the Pech, or Presun, river, about 37 miles above Chigha Sarai. The river is crossed here by a "good" wooden bridge. No supplies are to be had here except fuel and grazing. (I.B.C.) Other places with this name are located at 35-35 67-38 G. and 35-11 70-48 G.

139

CHOLI چولی
34-28 68-43 m. A village on the Maidan river, some 7 miles northwest of Kota-i-Ashro.

CHOLOZAI چلوزی
A section of the Ghilzais, whose head-quarters appear to be in the Logar valley, between the village of Baraki-Rajan and the Sojawan pass. In winter they go to Laghman with their camels for the grazing there. Lumsden says they are a subdivision of the Ibrahim Ghilzais. (I.B.C.)

CHOLOZAI چلوزی
33- 68-. A village in the upper Logar valley (southern division), midway between Baraki-Rajan and Sojawan. It has nine forts inhabited by Cholozai Ghilzais.
Clifford and Euan Smith say the inhabitants are Sulaiman Khel, but the Cholozais, who are the sole residents cannot be referred to that division of the Tribe, and are more probably Ibrahim Ghilzais, as Lumsden says. (I.B.C.)

*CHONAR چنار
34-52 68-50 m. A village on a tributary of the Ghorband river, east of the Kuh-i-Yakhdara.

*CHONESH GHAR چونش غو
35-7 71-12 m. A mountain located north of Segal Khwar. The village with this name is further southeast at 35-5 71-13 m.

CHORA چوره
A subsection of Daikundi Hazaras. It is stated by some that they are not Uruzgani but Daikundi.

CHORAGALI چوره گلی
37- 70-. A pass over the Surki Diwal hills crossed by a road forming an alternative to the main road from Basawal to Ali Boghan. The pass is easy for camels and could, with little difficulty, be made fit for wheeled traffic. (I.B.C.)

CHOWKI See CHAUKI چوکی

CHUKARNAO چوکرنو
A village in the Yak Walang subdistrict, containing 20 houses. (A.B.C.)

CHUKATU چوکتو
More probably Choghatu; a pass in the hills west of the Logar valley between the Adam Khan pass and the Tang-i-Wardak defile. It is steep on the eastern but easy on the western side. (Harvey.)

CHULA KUR Or CHILLA KHOR چوله کور
A tribe of Hazaras.

CHULI چولی
A section of Besudis.

*CHUMI چومی
34-25 67-52 m. A village on the Helmand river, northwest of Behsud.

CHUNDAK See CHANDAK چندك

CHUNDUK چندك
34-43 70-9. A village in Laghman on the left bank of the Alishang, about 5 miles above the confluence of that river and the Alingar. It stands midway between the village of Alishang and Tigri. Inhabitants: Dehgans. The village comprises three hamlets: Banda-i-Fakir Muhammad, Banda-i-Mirza Sayyid Muhammad, Kamdah. (Warburton.)

CHUNDUK See PARIAN چندك

*CHUQA چوقا
33-12 67-42 m. A village on the Nawa-i-Barik, south of the Dasht-i-Nawar.

*CHURA چوره
33-56 67-35 m. A village on a stream, some 4 miles east of Giruqala.

*CHURKA چورکه
34-3 68-0 m. A village south of the Katar towers and east of Godol.

*DAB داب
35-6 71-21 m. A village on the Kunar river, some 6 miles north of Asmar.

*DABA دابه
34-59 70-27 m. A village near Kolatan Dara, north-northeast of Alingar.

DABELI دبلی
34- 69-. Elev. 5,600 feet. A pass in the Jalalabad district, on the northern road from Jalalabad to Sang Toda, 6 miles from Dargai, and estimated at 5,600 feet high. There are no villages in the neighbourhood, and the ground between Dargai and Sang Toda offers numerous defensive positions to a force opposing an advance in that direction. (Young.)

*DAB KALAI داب کی
35-13 71-17 m. A village located on a tributary of the Kunar river.

DABUZAI دبوزی
33-51 69-38 m. A village in the Kurram valley, about 6 miles southwest of Ali Khel, on the right bank of the Kurram river, and 1 1/2 miles distant from it. The village lies in a well-cultivated valley, surrounded and commanded on all sides, except the west, by low, bare hills. The inhabitants are Ahmad Khel Jajis, and can turn out 300 fighting men. (Collett.)

DAD داد
33- 68-. A village in the Ghilzai country, 30 miles southwest of Ghazni, containing two forts and 200 houses, situated in a fertile and well-populated district belonging to the Sulaiman Khel Ghilzais. Water is procurable from springs. (Davies.)

*DADA داده
33-48 69-40 m. A village on the Kuram river (Patan Tuy), about 10 miles west of Chamkani.

DADA KHEL داده خیل
35-20 69-32. A village in the upper Panjshir glen, 2 miles above Bazarak, on the right bank of the stream, containing 30 houses of Tajiks. (Shadzada Taimus.)

*DADIKHEL دادخیل
    34-7 69-44 m. A village located on a tributary of the Azro river, southeast of Azro and west of the Spin Ghar range.

DADO KHEL دادو خیل
    34-5 69-6 m. A village in the northern portion of the upper Logar valley, 2 miles due east of Purakh. It consists of two hamlets with a population in 1880, of 100 families. The inhabitants are Ahmadzai Ghilzais. (Clifford, Euon Smith.) Other places with this name are located south-southwest of Miran, at 34-9 68-15 m.; 3 miles north of Mota Khan, at 33-14 68-52 m.; east of the Ghazni-Kandahar road, at 33-7 68-4 m.; and southeast of Dila, at 32-27 68-6 m. (LWA)

DAHANA DRANG دهانه درنگ
    33- 68-. A pass leading from Kharwar to Zurmat. It is formed by a rather wide valley, or rather a low watershed, dividing two wide valleys. The valley of the Kharwar side is an open dasht, formed by an extensive fan sloping down to Panjpai. The ascent is scarcely noticeable and the road is good. The watershed is marked by two or three willow trees, and the old double ziarat of Bai Badshah and Khwaja Buk Shah-i-Wali. From there the road follows a stream which drains the southeastern side of the hills dividing Kharwar from Zurmat. The route is nearly straight and the undulating area of the watershed commands a full view of the entire distance down to the much lower plain of Zurmat and its scattered villages. There is a little water in the Dahana Drang stream. (Griesbach.)

DAHANA GAI دهانه گی
    34- 69-. A place on the Jalalabad-Kabul road, between Seh Baba and the top of the Lataband. There are some caves and a chauki of 2 or 3 sowars. There is also a spring which supplied sufficient water to give General Gough's brigade a drink all round in 1879, but the weather was cold and neither men nor horses were thirsty. (A.B.C.)

*DAHANA-I-ASHEQ دهانه آشق
    34-47 68-35 m. A village near Asheq on the Dara-i-Turkoman.

*DAHANA-I-BARIK دهانه باریک
    34-48 68-40 m. A village in the Gumbad area on the Shila-i-Parsa.

DAHAN-I-BARKAR دهان برکر
    A ford over the Helmand in the Hazarajat. (Peart.)

*DAHAN-I-BOTIAN دهان بوتیان
    34-55 68-22 m. A village on the Ghorband, between Shebar and Shaikh Ali.

*DAHAN-I-GHORBAND دهان غوربند
    34-55 68-16 m. A village on the Ghorband river between Shebar and Daha-i-Botian.

DAHAN-I-GULI دهان گلی
    34-51 66-42. A large watercourse, formed by the united nalas of Suchak and Sabz Dara, which issues through a gorge and joins the Band-i-Amir river at about 17 miles above Marghi in the Yak Walang district. On this stream are the Kiligan hamlets, containing about 30 families of Kirigu Kham-i-Aba Hazaras. There is a small fort on the left bank, and a number of caves used for storing grass, corn, etc., and as houses. (Maitland.)

DAHAN-I-JALMISH See JALMISH   دهان جلمش

DAHAN-I-KANAK   دهان كنك (كانك)
   34-43 66-52 A. A village in the Yak Walang district, situated in the Kanak glen and containing 20 families of Takanas. (Maitland.)

DAHAN-I-KHUSHNAO   دهان خوشنو
   A village, containing about 20 families of Dai Zangi Hazaras, on the main Daulat Yar-Kabul road.

DAHAN-I-KOL   دهان كول
   34- 66-. The western defile into the Ghizao valley, through which runs the Helmand to the south. (Brereton.)

DAHAN-I-MARGHI See MARGHI   دهان مرغی

DAHAN-I-SHOR   دهان شور
   A village in the Dai Zangi district of Lal. There is a place with this name at 34-36 66-31 G., and a watercourse at 34-27 66-11 G. (LWA)

DAHAN-I-TARNAK   دهان ترنك
   34- 66-. A wide and stony glen, with a very broad marshy mouth in the northwest of the Yak Walang district. It drains northeastwards to the Rudi-i-Band-i-Amir, and is crossed by the road down the Yak Walang valley at about 8 miles southeast of the Sabz Dara. In the middle of it is a hamlet of 20 houses; and down the glen to the right, several houses are seen in the main valley. Up the glen, at the edge of cultivated plateau, on the left hand is the village of Sar-i-Dasht, 20 houses. (Maitland.)

DAHAN-I-ZALIKAN See ZALIKAN   دهان زلكان

DAHLA See POLADA   دهله

DAHLA   دهله
   33- 67-. At the head of the Mahshan valley, where the Arghandab rises.

DAIAK Or DEHYAK   دايك
   35-17 69-12 m. A village of 30 houses in the Salang Dara, about 18 1/4 miles above Parwan (I.B.C.).

DAI CHOPAN   دای چوپان
   One of the original main divisions of the Hazaras.

DAI KALAN   دای كلان
   A section of the Shekh Ali Hazaras. (q.v.)

DAI KUNDI   دای كندی
   35-57 67-33 A. A district of Hazarajat.

*DAI MIRDAD   دای ميرداد
   34-13 68-18. Dai Mirdad is an alaqadari in Wardak (or Maidan) province. The alaqadari comprises an area of 1,357 square kilometers and has an agricultural population that has been estimated at from 4,140 to 7,069. The alaqadari is bounded in the west and south by Nawar and Markaze Behsud, in the north by Behsud 2, in the east by Jalriz,

Nerkh, and Chak-i-Wardak. Dai Mirdad includes 143 villages two of which have more than 500 inhabitants. The villages are listed in the PG as follows: Anka, Sado Khel, Nazuk Khel, Changa-i-Ulya, Dalan, Miran (Maydan Jelga), Bakhshak, Hajka (Kajika), Badol, Moka (Moka Jelga), Shah Kadam, Karinga, Kunj, Foladi, Mohd. Khel, Ahmad Khel, Paye-i-Bulaq, Khumari, Ali Jan Khel, Rashid, Ormal (Armir), Ibrahimzai (Maryamzai), Dado Khel, Safed Dewar, Qol-i-Zangi, Kodi (Kadi), Ozbaki, Kushqol, Barkhanjoye (Barkhanjo), Sang-i-Shanda (Qarya-i-Sang Shanda), Nahurjoye, Panj Qeshlaq, Sarkhanto, Mohd. Yar Khel, Lalandar, Kadgak, Shah Mansur, Lashkari, Pirah, Chatu, Dawrani, Karez, Guli, Shar Toghi (Sher Toghi), Fekr (Pekar), Bahak, Garm Ab, Kota-i-Khayat, Kota-i-Sayed Ali, Kota-i-Darak, Siah Khawal, Bodak, Dawlat Sha (Dawlat Shah), Gidargo, Kota-i-Faiz, Qarya-i-Sadat, Tangi Saidan (Tangi Sadat), Safed Qadah, Dasht-i-Nau, Baghalak, Nakhshin (Naqchin), Qarqat, Kota-i-Asha, Dam Qarq, Sur Sing (Qarya-i-Sur Sing), Khar Khel, Qutun-i-Ulya, Qutun-i-Sufla, Saya Chagar, Kotal-i-Sufla, Kotal-i-Ulya, Badragha, Dasht-i-Qader, Shah Yar, Qala-i-Mulayem, Chak Khor-i-Sufla, Gard Bed, Bulagh-i-Husaini, Bari Qol, Jor Sang (Jossa Sang), Jaw Qol, Kota-i-Jaw Qol, Zardak, Surkhi, Ulyatak, Qol Dada (Qol Dadi), Qol-i-Mughul, Sar Jangal, Qol-i-Rah, Kota-i-Sulaiman Shah, Qol-i-Nemat, Sar-i-Qol, Takht, Nari (Bari), Bekh-i-Koh, Shadi Murdah, Kota-i-Sar-i-Sang (Kota-i-Jang), Sang Pul (Sang-i-Pul), Fakhrah, Fakhcha Qala (Pakhcha Qala), Qarya-i-Tara (Tarah), Sokhta, Kota Kharida, Gardan Hesar, Daraz Samuch, Qol-i-Wali, Qol-i-Banu, Dahan Erakank, Kota-i-Juma, Shaban, Sar Qash, Yak Roya, Qol-i-Banu-i-Ulya wa Sufla, Kutub Khel, Ormal Kutub, Hakim Khel, Ocha Nahorjoye, Chardewal, Par Qala, Karez-i-Folad, Dewal, Qash-i-Sayedan, Tangi Dewar, Qarya-i-Jar, Ghajorak, Kadol, Qol-i-Gholi, Chaka Khor-i-Ulya, Kota-i-Ali Mohd., Safed Nawah, Garm Ab-i-Ulya, Garm Ab-i-Sufla, Kota-i-Sufla, Gidargo-i-Sufla, Qarqat-i-Sufla, Sel-i-Dastam Nil-i-Rustam, Ab Paranak, Shahi Khel, Seyah Chaghar-i-Ulya, Toyaka, Kulakh, Changa-i-Sufla, Sultan Khel, Hazarah, Kota-i-Nazar Ali, Qurdun-i-Naser, Qol-i-Afghan Gul, Band Qol, Pesh Tolak, and Seyahkak.

DAIZANGI داى زنگى
A district of Hazarajat.

*DAKARI دكرى
34-57 69-7 m. A village located some 6 miles southwest of Charikar and west of the road to Kabul.

DAKKA (LOE) لويه دكه
34-13 71-3 m. Elevation 1,300 feet. A village in the Jalalabad district, 12 1/2 miles from Landi Kotal, on the road to Kabul. It stands on the right bank of the Kabul river, in a cup-shaped basin enclosed on the west, south and east by hills, and on north by the river. There is, however, a gap between the river and the hills on the south, and through this gap comes the road from the Khaibar Pass, the distance from the western exit of the latter being about 3 miles.
The village contains about 120 families of Mohmads and Shinwaris; head man (1904) Mir Ali Mohmand. The inhabitants possess some 300 head of cattle and 700 sheep and goats. The annual production of wheat and barley averages about 5,000 Indian maunds. Land-tax is assessed at the rate of 2 maunds in cash, and 20 maunds in kind, per jarib. A force of 200 khasadars, armed with Lee-Metford rifles, is stationed here, under a Sarhang. In winter Usmanzai Kuchis, with 350 camels and Lalpura Ghilzais with about 250 camels settle in the neighbourhood.

The valley at Dakka is about 1 mile across, the hills on the left bank coming close down to the river's edge. The river runs in several channels separated by low-lying islands: its bed is, altogether, about 400 yards wide. The main channel was found in June 1904 to run under the right bank, here about 30 feet high. In the cold weather a bridge of boats is kept up betwen Dakka and Lalpura; it consists of 16 boats with a plank roadway 12 feet wide; it is generally either washed away, or dismantled, when the melting snows cause the river to rise in the spring.

A mud-walled serai was built in 1905, nearly opposite the southern end of the bridge; it is completely commanded at short range.

One mile to the west of the village stands an old fort, built in 1876 by Amir Sher Ali but now (1905) in ruins and unoccupied. The fort is rectangular, about 400 yards by 500, with walls 15 feet high. It has a circular bastion at each corner and three semi-circular bastions on each face. There are several wells in the interior. It stands close to the right bank of the river and on the opposite bank, at a distance of 1,300 yards from the northeast corner of the fort, is the town of Lalpura. The interior of the fort is completely commanded by the low spurs of the hills to the northwest and southwest within 400 yards.

The fort was occupied by us during the second Afghan war the normal garrison being 2 guns, 1 company British Infantry, 1 squadron, Native Cavalry, aand 1 battalion, Native Infantry. The place proved most unhealthy to our troops, pneumonia being the most fatal disease. No oposition was offered to our occupation of the place which is of some importance owing to its position opposite Lalpura and to its being at the junction of several routes from the Peshawar valley. The walled enclosure which used to exist on the southern side of the fort and was used by us during the war as a commissariat yard has now entirely disappeared.

Camping ground for a force of any size is to be found to the west of the fort. There is an unlimited supply of good drinking water from the river and at Bagh, also there is a very large supply of water which could easily be led down towards Dakka. Supplies (about 1,000 maunds of unground grain and fodder for 10,000 animals for one day) are obtainable.

The ground in the vicinity is covered with an effervescence of soda for some distance from the river, and is in consequence very damp. There is good grazing ground for camels and transport animals. Fuel is procurable.

All travellers have to obtain rahdaris, or passports, and pay customs dues here. (Johnston, Malleson, Wanliss, I.B.C.)

DAKKA دکه
34-43 69-6 A. Elevation 3,800 feet. A village in the Koh Daman district, situated 3 1/2 miles south of Baba Kush Kar at a mile's distance form the left bank of the Shakar Dara stream. The place is said to contain 200 houses. Inhabitants: Tajiks. (Kinlock, I.B.C.)

*DAKUI دکوی
34-43 69-5 m. A village north of Kabul, about half way to Istalef.

*DALAI دلی
33-9 69-23 m. A village in the Sultankhel area, east of Ziruk.

DALAN دالان
32-48 67-37 G. A village in the Mukur district, 6 miles from Ghojan

(Aghao Jan), and south of Ghazni. It is inhabited by Ali Khel Ghilzais, and has supplies of forage. (Leech.) Another place with this name is located on the Dara-i-Jelga, some 5 miles east of Miran, at 34-13 68-22 m. (LWA)

*DALASHI دلاشی
35-4 69-38 m. A village on the upper Tagab river, northeast of Bazar-i-Badakhshi.

DALNA دلنه
33- 68-. A village in the Ghazni district. 36 miles southwest of Ghazni. (Thorton.)

DALTAMUR دلتمور
A small Hazatra tribe unconnected with any other subdivision, who appear to have come into Afghanistan with Timur Lang. (Peart.)

*DALWAZI KALAI دلوزی کلی
34-37 69-39 m. A village located where the Kabul river runs into the Naghlu lake, a few miles south of the confluence of the Panjshir.

*DAM دم
33-37 69-30 m. A village in the Usmankhel area, east of Ghazni.

*DAMAI دمی
34-12 68-37 m. A village on a tributary of the Dara-i-Jelga, 2 miles north of Badqol.

DAMAN دامن (دامان)
34-21 67-45 m. A village in the Rah Kol valley. (See Rah Kol). Another village with this name is on the Alingar river, some 10 miles southwest of Alingar. (LWA)

DAMARDAH دامرده
A section of the Besuds (q.v.) A section of the Jaghuri Hazaras also bears this name. A place with this name, also spelled Damurda, is located on a tributary of the Helmand river, southeast of Khushqol, at 34-9 67-22 m. (LWA)

DAMINJ دامنج
34- 70-. A valley to the west of the Dara-i-Nur, a tributary of the Kunar river. It is inhabited by Safis and contains rather more than 150 families. (Masson.)

DANA دانه
34-27 69-8 m. Deh-i-Dana is a village in the Chardeh valley, on the left bank of the Kabul river, between Thiba and Indaki. Inhabitants: Tajiks, Khwajas and Kizilbashes. There are ten forts included in the village, and the whole population numbers 300 families. The forts are as follows:

       1. Kala-i-Ghulam Sidik (Tajik)
       2. Kala-i-Mirza Muhammad (Tajik)
       3. Kala-i-Samand (Tajik)
       4. Kala-i-Barat (Tajik)
       5. Kala-i-Khwaja Khan (Tajik)
       6. Kala-i-Mulla Yusuf Ali (Kizilbash)
       7. Kala-i-Khwaja Ahmad (Tajik)
       8. Kala-i-Nasir Gul Muhammad (Kizilbash)

  9. Kala-i-Asia -i-Butat (Tajik)
  10. Kala-i-Mirza Jafar (Kizilbash) (I.B.C.)
Another place with this name is south of Bazar-i-Yakowlang, at 34-28 66-56 m. (LWA)

DAND   دند
32-37 67-49 m. A Sulaiman Khel Ghilzai village, consisting of 30 houses and a fort on the main Dera Ismail Khan-Ghazni road. It lies 238 miles from Dera Ismail Khan and 51 miles south of Ghazni. It has some 150 acres of cultivation, but there is no water to be had nearer than Dihsai, 4 miles northeast or Nani, 4 miles southwest. Camel grazing is procurable, (I.B.C.)

DAND   دند
32-57 68-23 G. A village 30 miles south of Ghazni, on the road to the Gumal pass, inhabited by Sulaiman Khel Ghilzais, in a fertile and well-populated district. Water from springs. (Leech.)

*DANDA   دنده
33-48 69-56 m. A village on the Kuram river, about 8 miles east of Chamkani.

*DANDAB   دنداب
34-4 67-42 m. A village northwest of the Kuh-i-Mir and southeast of the Garmab river.

DANDAK   دندك
33-6 68-50 m. A village in the Zurmat district, near Patanai, on the direct road from Ghazni to Dawar. It stands in low, rolling hills. (MacLean.) Other places with this name are located at 33-52 68-37 G. and 33-20 68-53 G.

DANDAN   دندان
33- 68-. A kotal at the head of the northeastern part of the Kharwar valley. A track ascends the Kawaja Angur valley to the small village of Dandan, and then up a narrow ravine to the kotal at an easy gradient. The descent into the Altimur valley from the top of the pass is rocky and difficult, but passable for horses. (Griesbach.)

DANDAN SHIKAN   دندان شكن
35-16 67-37 A. A pass over the Kajkamar, or Kamarzard hills at the head of the Dara-i-Yusuf in Afghan Turkistan. (See Volume 4.) It is crossed by the road from Maidan-i-Pai Kotal to Mazar-i-Sharif. The road over the pass is very steep, so much so as to be difficult even for yabus, but there would be no difficulty in making a graded road down the open slopes on either side of the summit, the soil being earth mixed with loose stones. At the summit the road crosses the boundary between the Provinces of Kabul and Afghan Turkistan. (I.B.C.)

DANDUR   دندور
34-32 70-16. A village in Laghman, on the left bank of the Alingar river, and about 3 miles above its junction with the Kabul. It is about 2 miles west of Charbagh. (Warburton.)

*DAND-WA-PATAN   دندوپتان
33-49 69-55. Dand-wa-Patan is an alaqadari in Paktia province. The alaqadarei comprises an area of 163 square kilometers and has an agricultural population that has been estimated at from 2,040 to

7,097. The alaqadari is bounded in the west by Chamkani, in the south by Jani Khel, in the sutheast by Jaji Maidan, in the north by Dareh Darang, and in the west by the State of Pakistan. Dand-wa-Patan has some 46 villages, 2 of which have more than 500 inhabitants. The villages are listed in the PG as follows: Patan, Dand, Kagina Kalai (Gagina), Mutwarukh, Landi Kalai, Narai Wuraza (Narai Worazay), Istiya (Seliya), Tsaprai Qara-i-Akhzari, Dag, Sharif Kalai, Sayed Shah Kalai, Hujri Kalai, Abdullah Kalai, Yaro Kalai, Malik Mira Jan, Moh'd Ayaz-Kalai, Mulla Kalai-Dandi, Nabi Kalai, Malik Din Moh'd, Algad Walo Kalai, Shapola Khola, Kawlah, Hassan Khel, Wocha Algada, Tirulgada, Gorandi, Narai, Ghonzai, Surgai, Kot Kalai, Seti Kalai, Chenai Kalai, Asko Mato Kats, Mana Mila, Zandah, Seron Ulgadah, Mazr-i-Ulgadah, Saltak, Guldarah, Tori Khel, Ghwawo Kalai, Taraki Khel, Patan-i-Ulya, Patan-i-Sufla, and Qala-i-Momen.

*DANGA   دنگه
34-16 67-50 m. A village southeast of the Kuh-i-Badurka, on a tributary of the Dara-i-Jelga.

DANGAK   دنگک
34-49 66-18 m. A pass over the northern watershed of the Sar-i-Jangal valley leading into the valley of the Rud-i-Band-i-Amir. It is crossed by a road leading from Daulat Yar to Mazar-i-Sharif and Balk via Katlish and Isfi Maidan. The road on the southern side of the pass is said to be easy, but on the northern side it is difficult, over loose slopes of shale and shingle, and the pass can only be considered as practicable for mule traffic. The watershed crossed here forms part of the boundary between the provinces of Kabul and Afghan-Turkistan. This pass is sometimes spoken of as the Kashan Kotal, from the name of the glen which runs down from the northern side of the pass to the Band-i-Amir. (I.B.C.) A ravine by this name is located at 34-36 66-14 G. Recent maps show the Band-i-Dangak at 34-49 66-17.

DANGAK   دنگک
34-43 66-18. A halting-place, in a glen of the same name, near the southern foot of the Kangak Pass. The glen is said to be 300 yards wide here and there is room for troops to encamp. There is a certain amount of cultivation, and supplies can be arranged for. There is no grass but Bhusa is fairly plentiful. Brashwood is available for fuel, and there are also some willows growing along the stream in the glen. (I.B.C.)

*DANGAM   دانگام
34-59 71-25. Dangam is an alaqadari in Nangarhar province. The alaqadari comprises an area of 236 square kilometers and has an agricultural population that has been estimated at from 5,023 to 8,940. The alaqadari is bounded in the west by Bar Konar, in the north by Naray, and in the east and south by the state of Pakistan. Dangam has about 17 villages, 4 of which have more than 500 inhabitants. The villages are listed in the PG as follows: Dangam-i-Ulya, Bidad Kalai, Tanga, Mesha (Mabandi-Maikha), Warakoti Garigah (Khora Garigah), Loy Garigah, Derai, Sayan (Nayan), Kharah, Karkot, Bar Sur Kamar-i-Ulya, Kuz Su Kamar-i-Sufla, Kachli, Qasem, Rawul-i-Kohna (Barawul-i-Kohna), Sabandi (Siyah Bandi), Dangam-i-Sufla, and Brun Gar.

*DANGANA   دنگانه
35-21 69-30 m. A village on the Dara-i-Parandeh, about 2 miles north of its confluence with the Panjshir.

*DANGAR   دنگر
33-40 69-47 m. A village one mile north of Janikhel Mangal woleswali seat, south of Chamkani.

*DANGDANG   دنگدنگ
33-53 69-43 m. A village on the Aryobster Tuy, south of Chawnai.

DARA   دره
33- 69-. A pass leading from Zurmat to the Jaji country. Near this is a plain inhabited by Sahak Ghilzais. (Broadfoot.) Recent maps show a place southeast of Gardez on the road to Shiwak, at 33-31 69-19 m. (LWA)

DARA   دره
34- 69-. Elevation 10,200 feet. Deh Dara consists of two small villages situated about 6 miles south of the Zard Sang Kotal on the Ghazni-Mazar-i-Sharif road. Other places with this name are located west of the Kuh-i-Boro, at 34-36 67-23 m.; on a stream in the Pitaw area, at 34-32 70-58 m.; 2 miles north of the Maidan river, northwest of the Kota-i-Ashro, at 34-29 68-45 m.

DARAFSHAN See URAZGANI   درفشان

DARAGALI   درگلی
34- 70-. A village in the Kama division of the Jalalabad district, situated about half a mile northwest of Bazid Khel. Inhabitants: Tajiks and Dehgans. (Jenkyns.)

DARAGARH   دره گړ
34-39 70-13. A village in Laghman, situated on the right bank of the Alinshang river, opposite Tigri. It consists of the following hamlets and forts:

        1. Kala-i-Samandar   4. Banda-i-Shahabad
        2. Kala-i-Kashmir   5. Bela-i-Rustam
        3. Lal Muhammad   6. Banda-i-Bushai

The inhabitants are Mamozai and Malla Khel Ghilzais. (Warburton.)

*DARA HAZARAH (HESA-I-DUWWUM)   دره هزاره (حصۀ دوم)
35-17 69-40. Dara Hazarah is an alaqadari in Parwan province. The alaqadari comprises an area of 707 square kilometers and has an agricultural population that has been estimated at from 5,445 to 6,180. The alaqadari is bounded in the west by Panjshir, in the north by Char Qarya, in the east by Nuristan and Daulatshah, and in the south by Najrab. Dara Hazarah includes about 14 villages, of which 6 have more than 500 inhabitants. The villages are listed in the PG as follows: Tum Bana, Pujada, Malima, Keraman, Pasgaran (Bazargaran), Tun Kho, Abdullah Khel, Baba Ali, Dost Ali, Jar-i-Ali, Sangi Khel, Qolandawer, Istaeder Kalan, and Gulab Khel (Gulda Khel).

*DARA-I-DARANG   دره درنگ
33-53 69-53. Dara-i-Darang is an alaqwadari in Paktia province. The alaqadari comprises an area of 57 square kilometers and has an agricultural population that has been estimated at about 2,000. The alaqadari is bounded in the west by Jaji, in the south by Chamkani and Dand-wa Patan, and in the east by the State of Pakistan. Dara-i-Darang has some 6 villages, three of which have more than 500

inhabitants. The villages are listed in the PG as follows: Qimati (Qemshi), Gondai, Mir Hasan, Bagh Lagrah, Bagh Algadah, Bagh Lagar, Khargai, Tsaparai Kalai, Khaman, and Kharot (Kharoti).

DARA-I-JAKUNI دره جاکونی
34- 68-. A valley in the Kabul district, west of Rustam Khel. (Wood.)

DARA-I-LAM دره لم
A Village in Laghman, comprising the hamlets of - 1. Banda Badi, 2. Wali, 3. Abdul Salam.
Inhabitants: Tajiks and Utkhel Ghilzais. (Warburton.)

DARA-I-NUR دره نور
34-41 70-35. Dara-i-Nur is an alaqadari in Nangarhar province. The alaqadari comprises an area of 331 square kilometers and has an agricultural population that has been estimated at from 11,020 to 14,270. The alaqadari is bounded in the north by Chapa Dara, in the east by Nur Gul, in the south by Kauz Kunar, an in the east by Alingar districts. Dara-i-Nur has about 25 villages, 10 of which have more than 500 inhabitants. The villages are listed in the PG as follows: Wigal, Safar Qala, Sutan, Qala-i-Shahi, Machgandol, Lamatak, Chuwal, Sar Galak, Otran, Kandak, Shamal, Bamba Kot, Shakya-lai,
Omar Qala, Shahgahi, Du Darak, Panjo Qala, Keshmand Qala, Alma, Jumja Pur, Shiram Qala, Janishgul, Lamgandah, Laghyak, Sarwar (Sarwar Qala), Nikyan, and Sarghalak. The village of Dara-i-Nur is located at 34-37 70-36 m. (LWA) In 1914 the area was described as follows: A valley tributary to the Kunar river, joining it from the north at a point some 15 miles from Jalalabad, where the road up the main valley crosses it is a short, steep descent and ascent of about 30 feet to and from the nala bed.
It is inhabited by a people calling themselves Safis, speaking their own peculiar diaclect, and not understanding the Pashtu language. They are a straightfoward, manly race with florid complexions, light eyes and hair. They have many peculiar customs, and retain many vestiges of ancient arts. For instance, they have bee-hives, unknown to the inhabitants of the plains. Their valley is most celebrated amongst their neighbours as being the native soil of nargis (narcissus). It is affirmed that here is a variety of the flower with black petals. Their hills yielding grapes, quantities of wine and vinegar are made by the inhabitants. Babar states that the inhabitants of this valley were in his time Kafirs.
The Dara-i-Nur used to be the route by which Kafir slave-girls were brought down by the Laghmanis to the Jalalabad markets. (Masson, Coldstream, Holdich.)

DARA-I-ROBAT دره رباط
34-58 68-32 G. A valley located about 9 miles west of Ghorband.

DARA KALA دره قلعه
34-26 70-16 A village in the Surkhab division of the Jalalabad district, a mile to the west of Kala-i-Lala. Inhabitants: Ghilzais. (Jenkyns.)

DARAKH درخ
34- 66-. A hamlet at the mouth of the Sang Dara pass lying on the right front of the entrance and 300 yards off. It contains five houses on the slope of the hill. There is a good spring of water here. (Gaselee.)

DARASHAH KHEL دره شاه
35- 69-. A place lying east of Charikar. It is said to contain 200 families of Tajiks. (Native information.)

DARA YUSUF دره يوسف
The head-quarters of the Dai Mirdad subsection of Hazaras.

*DARAZ دراز
34-28 66-39 m. A village north of Asgharat, on a tributary of the Lal Dara.

*DARAZGAR درازگر
34-12 67-13 m. A village on a tributary of the Helmand, 4 miles west of its confluence with the Qol-i-Tsuitaman.

DARAZ GIRD درازگرد
35-0 68-53 m. A group of four small forts in the Ghorband valley, situated 2 miles below Siahgird, on the left bank of the river. The inhabitants are Shinwaris. The valley here is 2 miles wide, with gardens and trees. The river bed is of gravel, 400 to 800 yards across. (Peacocke.)

DARAZ KOL دراز قول
34-23 67-18 m. A valley in the Dai Zangi Hazara country. Recent maps show a stream with this name. (LWA)

DARBAND See FIRAJ دربند

*DARBAND دربند
35-17 67-56 m. A village on the Kahmard river, about 3 miles northwest of Doab-i-Mikh-i-Zarin. Other places with this name are west of Sangdari Ghar and southeast of Kabul, at 34-17 69-23 m. and on the Shamshad Ghar, at 34-6 71-4 m.

DARBAND دربند
A pass over a spur of the Safed Koh called the Talkha Guzar mountain.

DARBAND دربند
35- 69-. A village at the head of the Tagao valley, 12 miles from Farajghan, 135 miles northeast of Kabul, inhabited by (Nimcha) Kafirs, who act as brokers and bargainers in time of peace between the Kafirs and Muhammadans. (Leech.)

DARGAI درگی
34-28 69-56 m. There are two halting places designated respectively, "Bara" and "Chota" Dargai by officers employed in 1880 in reconnoitring the route from Jalalabad to Sang Toda by the Adrag Badrag pass. "Chota" Dargai is at the eastern foot of the Adrag Badrag, about 14 miles west of Khairo Khel; and "Bara" Dargai is about 6 miles further west at the opposite base of the pass, near the junction with the Kabul river of the Dargai Oba stream (q.v.). "Chota" Dargai is a small piece of level ground near a stream, commanded on all sides by high barren hills. "Bara" Dargai has less than a dozen houses and no supplies; nothing but water and water-cresses, coarse grass and holly, "mistletoe and boulders." (I.B.C., Ross, Thompson, Dutton.) Recent maps show the names Kam Dargai and Loy Dargai, the latter at 34-27 69-52 m. (LWA)

DARGAI OBA   درگی ابه (اوبه)
34-30 69-54 A. A tributary of the Kabul river, rising in the Siah Koh range and joining the Kabul river about 16 miles west of Jalalabad. The river road from Jalalabad to Kabul crosses this stream by a wooden bridge about 1 mile above its junction with the Kabul river. (I.B.C.) Recent maps show the name Dargai Khwar. (LWA)

DARGEH   درگه
33- 69-. A village in Khost, 12 miles southwest of Matun. It is the principal place of the Tani section of the Khostwals. (I.B.C.)

DARGHAN HAZARAS   See BAMIAN (PROPER)   درغان هزاره

DARI   دری
33- 69-. A wide plain on the west of the Kurram valley and Jaji country inhabited by Sahak Ghilzais. (Broadfoot.) A fort with this name is 5 miles southeast of Asmar, at 35-47 71-28 G. (LWA)

DARKHINJ   See KHINJ   درخنج

DARMAN KHEL   درمان
A subdivision of the Chakmannis (q.v.).

DAROGH   See DARGEH   دروغ

*DARSUDYAR   درسودیار
34-35 68-43 m. A village on a tributary of the Maidan river.

*DARU   دارو
33-29 68-9 m. A village located on a stream southwest of Ghazni.

DARUNTA   درونته
34-28 70-22 A. A small subdivision of Jalalabad, on the left bank of the Kabul river, opposite the junction of the Surkhab. There is an old fort of Darunta about 2 miles above the confluence of the rivers. A force of 450 khasadars is quartered here. (I.B.C.)

DARUNTA   درونته
34-29 70-22 A. A difficult gorge through which the Kabul river flows between the Jalalabad district and Kats Laghman.
It is reached at 7 1/2 miles from Jalalabad and on the left bank of the Kabul river stands the old Darunta fort mentioned in the preceding article.
A steel suspension bridge built by Messrs. Burn & Co., Howrah, and completed early in 1909 spans the gorge near this point. The bridge is 306 feet long, with a 10 feet roadway and is contructed to carry a load of 120 lbs. per square foot.
The Tangi Gharu road crosses the spur on the right bank by zig-zags. Wheeled vehicles have been taken over it with difficulty. (I.B.C.)

DARWAZA   دروازه
34- 68-. A pass over the eastern end of the main Koh-i-Baba range, crossed by a road which leaves the Ghorband valley at about a mile below Bin-i-Sehwak. Here the hills on the south sink into a series of gentle rounded ridges and spurs projecting from the Koh-i-Darwaz. The main range of the Koh-i-Baba, which runs like a wall from the main Irak Kotal to abreast of this point, here end in the Koh-i-Darwaz. Behind the Koh-i-Darwaz lies the large Turkoman Dara, and beyond that again lies the range of the Paghman mountains. (Peacocke.) A village with this name is located at 34-44 67-31 m. and

another is at 35-43 69-42 A. (LWA)

DARWESH   درويش
35- 67-. A square mud fort in the Birgalich Dara, passed on the road leading north from the Shibar valley over the Jalmish Kotal to the Ao Dara (Bamian river).
There is a fairly good camping ground along the sides of the Birgalich valley, but the centre of the valley is waterlogged by the stream and irrigation channels. Suplies procurable. There is no wood, and a thorny weed, which grows in the shape of a large close circular tuft on all the hills and is called kirpi, is burnt by the inhabitants. Grass is to be found stored in all the forts and hamlets. (Peacocke.) A village with this name is on the road from Gardez to Kabul, about 3 miles southeast of Mangokhel at 33-57 69-1 m. (LWA)

DARWESHABAD   درويش آباد
A village in Langman (Laghman?), containing the following hamlets: 1. Kalagai, 2. Kala-i-Akhundzada, 3. Dera-i-Mirza Sahib. The inhabitants are Tajiks. (Warburton.)

DARWESH ALI   درويش علی
A section of the Besudis.

*DARWESHAN   درويشان
35-9 67-42 m. A village on a stream, about 2 miles south of Saighan. Another place with this name is northwest of Khair Kot, at 32-59 68-20 m.

DARWESH KALA   درويش قلعه
34-28 68-37. A village on the left bank of the Kabul river, 4 miles west of Jalrez. Close by is the village of Nawab Kala. (Wanliss.)

*DARZAKHEL   درزاخيل
33-47 69-49 m. A village on the Kuram (Patan Tuy) opposite Chamkani.

*DASHT   دشت
33-11 67-50 m. A village on the Chashma-i-Aghlar near Zardaluy. Another place with this name is north of the Kuh-i-Charband, a tributary of the Helmand, at 34-28 67-23 m.

DASHTAK   دشتك
34-18 69-13 m. A village in the valley of the lower Logar, i.e., north of the Tangi Waghjan pass. The inhabitants are Hasan Khel, and in 1880 the village contained five hamlets and 40 families. It lies to the east of the Logar river and close under the hills. Water from a karez. (Clifford, Euan Smith.) This place is also called Loy Kalai and is some 10 miles south of Kabu. Another place with this name is on a stream running north into the Bamian near the town of Bamian, at 34-46 67-49 m.

DASHT-I-REWAT   دشت روات
35-29 69-49 A. Elevation 6,970 feet. A small plain in the upper Panjshir valley, on the right bank of the stream, crossed by the Khawak pass road at about 11 miles above Marz. It is from 400 to 700 yards wide, and is about 2 miles in length. Numerous small hamlets and groups of huts are strung along the right bank of the stream, and are surrounded by extensive orchards through which the road passes. In places the trees are so thick as to impede baggage animals, and in others the rough stone walls of the orchards have

fallen down, obstructing the narrow road. There are said to be 130 families in the Dasht-i-Rewat hamlets, who are all Tajiks.
Up the Dara Rewat is a footpath leading into Kafiristan. It crosses the Wakhe Koh and then joins the Arioh road.
On the left bank of the main stream rises the Koh-i-Buzmal, while the hill on the other side of the plain is the Koh-i-Iskabun.
Camping ground for a division might be found on the Dasht-i-Rewat, but it would be mostly on cultivated ground. Supplies are not abundant. Enough for one battalion for 3 or 4 days might be procurable. The width of the stream is here 20 yards and its depth 2 1/2 feet. It is fed by numerous little streams coming down every glen and ravine on either side. Its bed is 50 yards across. (Shahzada Taimus.) Recent maps show the name at 35-27 69-49.

DASHT-I-SARKAR   See BAMIAN (DISTRICT)   دشت سرکار

DASHT-I-TALKHGUZAR   دشت تلخ گذر
33- 68-. A plain in the Ghazni district, between the Sher Dahan pass and Robagh. (I.B.C.)

DASHT-I-TIKAR   دشت تکار
A place in the Faoladi glen.

DASHT-I-TOP   دشت توپ
34- 68-. A plain in the district of Kabul, between Zarnai and Kala-i-Durani. It takes its name from the village of Top, which stands in it. (I.B.C.)

DASHT-I-ZIARAT   دشت زیارت
34-32 70-2 G. A plain in Laghman, extending from the Kabul river, near its junction with the Badpakht stream in a northeasterly direction to the Alishang. The route from Tigri towards Badpakht and Kabul passes over this plain, which slopes very gently up to the base of the hills, and is covered with coarse grass. All the western portion of the dasht is good grazing-ground for sheep, and very large flocks belonging to Tigri are grazed on it. (Young.)

*DASHT KOLA   دشت کوله
34-7 67-58 m. An area in northern Ghazni province, north of Shahr-i-Khawat.

DAUDI   See   BUGHLANI   داودی

*DAUDKHEL   Or   DAWUDKHEL   داودخیل
34-54 69-51 m. A village located on a tributary of the Tagab, north-northeast of Sarobi.

DAUDZAI   داودزی
34-49 69-10 G. A village in the Koh Daman of Kabul, about midway between Bazari and Karabagh. It contains eight forts, and has a population of some 300 Daudzai families who possess many camels and do a great deal of carrying between Kabul and Peshawar, and Kabul and Turkistan. They are in no sense, however, Kuchis. (I.B.C.)

DAULANA   دولانه
35- 69-. A village in Kohistan, between Baian and Tokhwirdi. It stands on the left bank of a rivulet known by the name of Ajmil, a cut from the Ghorband river. It has 60 houses of Tajiks. The lands of this village are fertile, producing much wheat, cotton, jowar, rice, etc. Of fruit trees, mulberries and vines are plentiful. There

are here many head of cattle, but few sheep. Shahzada Taimus mentions a village of this name as being situated east of Charikar, and containing 400 families of Tajiks. (A.B.C., I.B.C.) A village with this name is located at 35-22 69-25 G.

DAULANA دولانه
35- 69-. A village in the Parendev Dara, about 9 miles above its junction with the Panjshir. Close by is another village called Kund, the two together containing some 10 families of Tajiks. (I.B.C.) Other places with this name are located at 32-57 67-46 G. and 34-21 67-32 G.

DAULAT KHAN دولت خان
A subdivision of the Daya Polada.

*DAULAT KHAN دولت خان
32-36 67-58 m. A village on the Ghazni river, some 6 miles northeast of the Ab-i-Istadeh.

DAULAT KHAN دولت خان
33-31 68-48 m. A village on the road between Ghazni and Kalalgu in Zurmat. (Broadfoot.)

*DAULAT KHAWANI دولت خوانی
32-52 68-42 m. A village located some 6 miles southeast of Yahyakhel in southern Ghazni province.

DAULAT MUHAMMAD KALA   See ASLAM KALA دولت محمد قلعه

DAULATPAI دولت پای
A main section of the Besuds.

DAULAT SHAH دولت شاه
34-57 70-4 m. Daulat Shah is a village and an alaqadari in Laghman province. The alaqadari which comprises an area of 703 square kilometers, has an agricultural population that has been estimated at from 3,774 to 8,414. Daulat Shah is bounded in the north by Panjshir and Nuristan, in the east and south by Alishing and in the west by Alsai and Nejrab districts. The alaqadari contains about 32 villages 5 of which have more than 500 inhabitants. The villages are listed in the PG as follows: Sel (Suhail), Chakla, Wala (Nala), Kalai, Atuk, Rasami (Ranami), Kunda Kuri, Dalangi (Dalangi-Balal), Manan Gul (Monawar Kalai Gul), Gadyala (Kalyala), Daulat Shah, Munjaghan, Chashidar-i-Fereshghan, Pitak-i-Fereshghan (Wataypak-i-Freshghan), Nilkhan (Tel Khan), Kasuk (Kashwak-i-Najil), Ratuk (Darah Tu), Khandan-i-Mir Afghan (Chandal), Khandok (Gamtarak), Aluk-i-Najil, Nurah Daulat Shah, Wez (Waiss), Murah, Tombala (Tanbala), Meyo (Meyo Fereshghan), Mushkandi (Mash Kondi), Mangal Pur, Noya (Qarya-i-Noyaye), Noya-i-Ulya, Noya-i-Sufla, Qarya-i-Dogelan, Rakarak, and Fereshghan. The village of Daulat Shah is on the upper Alishang river, some 10 miles north of Alishang. (LWA) In 1914, the village was described as follows: A village of 80 houses in the Alishang valley, about 70 miles from Jalalabad. The dialect spoken about here is known as Pashi and is different from the Laghmani dialect. (I.B.C.)

DAULAT SHAHI دولت شاهی
34- 70-. A village in the Besud division of the Jalalabad district. Inhabitants: Tajiks and Kazi Khel. (Jenkyns.)

DAULAT SHAHI دولت شاهی
34-57 69-10 m. A village in Kohistan, between Baian and Charikar, about 3 miles from the latter, on the right bank of the Charikar stream, opposite Mian Shakh. About 200 houses of Tajiks. The village is khalisa, i.e., the property of the State, and its lands are fertile producing grain of all kinds (including rice), and every sort of fruit. (I.B.C., A.B.C.)

DAULATZAI دولت زاى
34-18 70-23 m. A group of fortified hamlets, surrounded by cultivation in the Chapriar subdivison of the Jalalabad district. It lies on the left bank of the Chapriar stream, about 9 miles south of Jalalabad, on the road from that place to the Kurram valley via the Agam pass. Supplies and water plentiful. Two hundred khasadars are stationed here. (I.B.C.) The village is some 3 miles northeast of Chapriar, on the way to Jalalabad. Other places with this name are located at 34-36 69-39 G., 33-36 69-11 G., and 33-35 69-9 G.

DAYAH داية
The largest subdivision of the Polada Hazaras. (See Military Report on Hazarajat, Part II.)

DAYAH داية
A section of the Besudi Hazaras. (See Military Report on Hazarajat Part II.)

DAYAK   See DAIAK داياك

DEBEH دبه
34- 70-. A gorge about 1 mile west of Kats Muhammad Ali, in Laghman, through which flows the Kabul river. No track whatever exists, and it is necessary to leave the river at this point, where it is about 2,200 feet above sea-level, and rise gradually over the Adrag Badrag. The whole difficulty of the Laghman valley route to Kabul from Jalalabad may be said to lie in its two ends, viz., th Darunta and the Debeh defiles. (Holdich.)

*DEHAK دهك
33-28 68-39 m. A village located some 4 miles south of Ramak and southeast of Ghazni.

DEH BACHA AKA RAZA ده بچه اقارغا
34- 67-. A small village in the Karghanatu glen of Bamian. (A.B.C.)

*DEH BALA ده بالا
34-7 70-27. Deh Bala is a woleswali in Nangarhar province. The woleswali comprises an area of 479 square kilometers and has an agricultural population that has been estimated at from 23,940 to 46,840. The woleswali is bounded in the north by Rodat, in the east by Achin, in the south by the State of Pakistan, and in the west by Pachir Agam. Deh Bala has about 36 villages, 22 of which have over 500 inhabitants. The villages are listed in the PG as follows: Ghokhadrah, Sara Qala, Eshpola, Khum-i-Eshpola (Khum-i-Kalai), Kota Wal (Kot Wal), Murgai, Dawlat Khel, Shaikh Maidan, Gorgori (Gargari), Charwazi, Marez, Rud Khana, Narai Oba, Suna Khel, Shabi, Guzara, Oghaz, Kassu, AhmadKhel, Ganja, Khar Kanai Sufla, Khar Kanai Ulya, Gagra, Kamki Papin, Tangi Deh Bala, Ghalnai (Gharani), Sharmukhi, Yaghiband, Shaghala, Jaudara, Rawagai, Loy Papin, Haram Qatra, China, Gana, Min Kats, Okan, and Aska Mina.

DEH BARKA ده برکه
A subdivision of the Daya Polada. (See Military Report on Hazarajat, Part II.)

DEH BEBUD ده بهبود
A village in Yakh Walang, situated in the Zardigao glen, and containing 12 families of Neka Hazaras. (A.B.C.)

DEHGAN دهگان
33- 69-. A village in Khost, about 7 miles southwest of Matun. (Collett.)

DEHGAN دهگان (دیگان)
A tribe settled in the Kunar valley, and scattered also over the districts of Jalalabad and Laghman.
In the Jalalabad district Dehgans are found principally in Pesh Bolak, Kandibagh, Hisarshahi, Deh-i-Tahir, Lawangapur, and Mast Ali, but the present home of the race is Kunar and in the Dara-i-Nur and some parts of Laghman.
The Dehgans are often confounded with the Tajiks by the people of the country, but they are quite distinct. While the Tajiks invariably speak Persian, the Dehgans have a peculiar language of their own, called Laghmani or Kohistani. This language seems to be comprised of Sanskrit and modern Persian, with some words of Pushtu, and a very large admixture of of some unknown root. Jenkyns, in 1878, from comparing their language with that of Nuristan, came to the conclusion that the Dehgans and Kafirs were one race. He says: --"The Dehgans are Kafirs converted to Muhammadanism, probably within the last three or four centuries. From intermarrying with the Tajiks and other races, their appearance is not now very different from the other inhabitants of the plains, except that they have no resemblance to the Afghans. They are wholly engaged in agriculture. Their Afghan neighbours affect to look down on them."
McGregor says they form six divisions, viz., Dumeh, Chaguni, Kuli, Buzurg, Debazai, and Malikzai, and that the four last are found chiefly in Kunar and the Safi valleys. (Elphinstone, McGregor, Jenkyns.)

DEHGAN KALA دهگان قلعه
34- 68-. A village in the upper Kabul river valley, about 2-1/4 miles above Jalrez. The inhabitants are Tajiks. (Wanliss.) Recent maps show the spelling Diwgan at 34-27 68-37 m. (LWA)

DEHGAZ دهگز
34-18 70-25 m. A village in the Chapriar division of the Jalalabad district, situated on the right bank of the Chapriar stream, about 12 miles due south of the town of Jalalabad. Inhabitants: Mohmands. (Jenkyns.) Recent maps show the spelling Degaz. (LWA)

DEH-I ده
Places the names of which begin with the word Deh followed by the Persian izafat are usually described under the second word of their designations.

*DEH-I-DAULAT ده دولت
33-32 68-11 m. A village located some 10 miles west of Ghazni and south of Shahbidak.

*DEH-I-KHODAIDAD ده خدائی داد
   33-31 68-27 m. A village located about 3 miles southeast of Ghazni.

*DEH-I-MULLA ده ملا
   33-33 68-19 m. A village located about 5 miles west of Ghazni.

*DEH SABZ ده سبز
   34-32 69-12. Deh Sabz is a woleswali in Kabul province. The woleswali comprises an area of 648 square kilometers and has an agricultural population which has been estimated at about 18,500. Deh Sabz is located north of the City of Kabul and includes about 48 villages, of which about 18 have more than 500 inhabitants. The villages are listed in the PG as follows: Tarahkhel, Puli Sangi, Qala-i-Haji Mohmmad Afzal, Char Qala-i-Wazirabad, Qala-i-Musa, Deh Khudaidad, Deh Yahya, Khwaja Bughra, Khwaja Chasht, HutKhel, Wazirabad, Paye Minar, Bakhtyaran, Qala-i-Shah Muhammad, Shahi Qala, Kota Ha, Deh Sabz-i-Khas, Qabil Bay, Kata Chah, Shaikho, Sang Ab, Bandi Khana, Jaru, Ab Dara, Bar Abdara (Ab Dara-i-Ulya), Abdara-i-Sufla, Nawah, Qala-i-Rustam, Qala-i-Ghulam Qader, Shorab, Tang-i-Gharu, Kata Khel, Yaka Darakht, Pul-i-Charkhi, Khwaja Rawash, Baba Quchqar, Hazara-i-Baghal, Ali Khel, Qala-i-Miran, Qala-i-Gagar, Sayed Hasan Kharoti, Surgai, AKh Bulandi, Akhal, Khwaja Ghar, Qala-i-Gul Muhammad, Qala-i-Mirza Zahid, and Qala-i-Mirza Ahmad.

DEH SARAK ده سرك
   A group of villages containing about 80 or 90 small hamlets, between Pesh Bolak and Kahi in the Jalalabad district. (I.B.C.)

*DEHYAK Or DEYAK ده یك
   33-31 68-38. Dehyak is the name of a village and an alaqadari in the Ghazni province. The alaqadari comprises an area of 736 square kilometers and has an agricultural population which has been variously estimated at from 10,895 to 24,294.
   The alaqadari is bounded in the west by Ghazni, in the north by Zena Khan, in the southwest by Andar, in the southeast by Sharan, and in the east by Zurmat. De Yak has about 53 villages, of which 11 have more than 500 inhabitants. The villages are listed in the PG as follows: Wolunger, Alo Khel, Ata Moh'd Alo Khel, Miran, Balai, Paye Loch, Pana Khoshk, Tason, Janabad, Deh Yek, Zaker, Ramak, Tanfer, Robat, Rahmdel, Rostam, Ibrahimzai, Rozi, Sar Andaz, Sanger, Sayed Nazim, Shah Tur, Shah Khok, Shahabuddin, Qarya-i-Ebad, Qala-i-Haji Torabaz, Qala-i-Seterni, Qala-i-Shadi, Qala-i-Shuko, Qala-i-Sher Buz, Qala-i-Sadu, Qala-i-Usman, Qala-i-Alam, Qala-i-Ali, Baruk, Yahya, Qala-i-Mulla, Qala-i-Mehtar, Qala-i-Hadah, Karim Dad, Kondur, Kena Gonbad, Kodwal (Gadol Aziz), Leghbat (Laghwat), Pajak, Mustajer, Mulla Jani, Nasrat Ibrahimzai, Niyaz Baba, Tapur, Manak, Khashik, Qashang, Warunger, Qala-i-Manak, Mohamad Hasan, and Nagi.

DERA-I-JAGARAON دیرای جگرون
   33- 69-. A village in Khost, on the road from Matun to Ghazni. Its inhabitants are said to be "Jagaraons" and it is said to be 8 kilometers from Almerach and 7 kilometers from Dhara. (Kennedy.)

DERAO دیراو
   34- 69-. A small village at the western end of the Abkhor defile which lies to the east of Burg in the Logar valley. A stream of excellent water comes in here from the northeast. (Collett.) Recent maps show the name Dara at 34-8 69-17. (LWA)

DEVERGROM   See DIOGROM ديوگرام

DHANI Or DANI داني
   33-36 70-6 m. A valley in the hills north of Bak, in Khost, and southwest of Jaji Maidan. It is open, and in it are some 13 villages of the Dhani Jajis. The villages are without towers, and the houses are of stone. (Carr.)

DHARA داره
   33- 69-. Said to be a halting place, 4 kilometers from Dera-i-Jagraon towards Gardez, on the road from Matun in Khost to Ghazni. (Kennedy.)

*DIBA ديبه
   33-21 67-21 m. A village located on a tributary of the Arghandab, southwest of the Dasht-i-Nawar.

*DIDAK ديدك
   33-39 68-38 m. A village northeast of Ghazni about halfway to Nawa-i-Kharwar.

DIHSAI Or DISI ده سي
   33-1 68-25 m. Alarge Andari Ghilzai village lying about 50 miles south of Ghazni. Water procurable. (I.B.C.)

DILA ديله
   32-36 68-2 m. A fort in the Ghazni district, on the left bank of the Ghazni river, near its confluence with the Ab-i-Istadah lake. It is inhabited by a few families of Kuduzais, who own a strip of cultivation and a well of good water. (Broadfoot.)

*DINARKHEL دنار خيل
   33-37 68-52 m. A village located some 6 miles south of Nawa-i-Kharwar. Another place with this name is located on the Wur Khwar, about 6 miles northeast of Wur, at 32-10 68-42 m.

DIOGROM Or DEVERGROM ديوگرم (ديوگرام)
   35-23 70-59 G. Elevation 8,480 feet. A half-moon shaped walled village of 60 houses on the left bank of the Presungul in Kafiristan, about 79 miles above Chigha Sarai. The river, close at hand, runs in a shallow tranquil stream fordable everywhere; it is about 18 yards broad, and is spanned by a good bridge with concave parapets made out of a single large tree trunk. There is a tower on the left bank a short distance from the village wall. The village is built in the usual half subterranean Presun way and has many pshals, especially on the south face. (Robertson.)

DIPI See MANDRAWAR دي

DIRAZ KOL See DARAZ KOL دراز قول

*DIWAL ديوال
   33-47 68-1 m. A village near the Shemeltu stream, 2 miles south of Tukrik. Another village with this name is located on a stream north of the Kuh-i-Chaharband and south of the Kuh-i-Baba range, at 34-28 67-21 m.

*DIWALAK ديوالك
   34-31 67-16 m. A village southwest of Qash and northeast of Baladeh. Other villages with this name are located on the Nawa-i-Surkh-

jui, north of Waras, at 34-16 66-55 m.; on the Gardez-Kabul road, some 6 miles north of Kolangar, at 34-10 69-5 m.; north of Nauruzi and south of the Khwaja Dur Khwaja Faqir mountain, at 33-3 67-47 m.; 2 miles north of the Dara-i-Jelga at 34-58 68-16 m.; and at 34-31 67-16 m., 34-58 68-14 m., 34-32 68-13 m., and 34-58 68-16 m.

DIWAL BOLA   See   SHIBAR   ديوال بوله

DIWAL KOL   ديوال قول
34-2 67-55 G. A long tagao in the Besud country.

*DIWANA   ديوانه
34-40 71-1 m. A village near Bagh, southwest of Narang in Paktya province.

*DIWANA BABA   ديوانه بابا
35-54 71-19 m. A village on the Dara-i-Penghar, some 8 miles northwest of Peshawur in Kunar province.

*DIWLAK   ديولك
33-38 68-4 m. A village on the Dara-i-Yusuf, northeast of Gholi Talab.

DIZGI DARA   دزگی دره
34- 68-. A tributary of the upper Kabul river, which it joins from the south about 9 miles east of the Unai pass, being crossed just above the junction by a wooden bridge of 15 feet span and 12 feet broad, over which goes the main Kabul-Herat road. The stream is here about 6 feet broad and 6 inches deep. The bridge is practicable for field guns. (Wanliss.)

*DOAB   دو آب
34-2 68-46 m. A village on the Ghazni-Kabul road, about 40 miles northeast of Ghazni.

DOABA   دو آبه
34-36 69-38 G. A valley lying to the east of Goga Manda, through which the Kabul river flows just before receiving the waters of Panjshir and Tagao. (Holdich.)

DOABA   دو آبه
34- 68-. A village at the northern mouth of the Tangi Wardak defile, a little to the southeast of Shaikhabad. Inhabitants: Wardaks. (I.B.C.)

DOABA   دو آبه
35-5 69-14 G. A village in the Kohistan of Kabul, at the junction of the Panjshir and Ghorband rivers. It is generally known as Doab-i-Abdul Karim Khan. About 40 houses. Inhabitants: Sufis. There is a ferry at the junction of the streams. (I.B.C.)

*DOABI   دو آبی
34-46 67-46 m. A village on a tributary of the Dara-i-Sialaiak, southwest of Bamian. Another village with this name is on the Dara-i-Qiagh, about 5 miles south of Ghar, at 34-1 66-40 m.

DOAB-I-SHAH KADAM   دو آب شاه قدم
34-57 66-32. A collection of hamlets in the west of the Yak Walang district, near Marghi, collectively containing about 25 houses. (A.B.C.)

DOAB KALA دوآب قلعه
Three small forts, with some cultivation and gardens in the bed of the Ghorband valley, 8 miles above Chahardeh. Here the valley is about 1 mile in width, and is for the most part occupied by the broad gravel beds of the Loling and Ghorband rivers, which unite just below Kala Doab. (Peacocke.)

DOAI دوای
34- 66-. Four hamlets in the Yak Walang district, situated near Deh Surkh on the Rud-i-Band-i-Amir, and containing 25 families of Hazaras. (A.B.C.)

DOAKAN   See   BAND-I-DOAKAN دواخان

DO-AO دواو
35-20 69-7 G. A dara which joins the Salang Dara from the northwest at about 7 miles south of the Bajgah pass. At the junction there is plenty of room to encamp on some cultivated ground; grass and water plentiful, but fuel, other than fruit trees, is scarce. (I.B.C.)

DOBANDI دوبندی
33-56 69-16 m. A village at western foot of the Shutur Gardan pass, inhabited by a few families of Ghilzais who, like the huts they dwell in, are the picture of all that is forlorn and wretched. It lies on the right bank of a nala and on the road. There is no camping ground for any force of more than one regiment and the position is a very bad one for any body of troops to halt in at all. Supplies, forage and fuel are not procurable without great difficulty, but water is plentiful. (I.B.C.) A stream with this name is located at 33-57   69-20 m., and a village at 33-57   69-19 A. (LWA)

*DOBUKA دبوکه
34-28 67-17 m. A village northwest of Ishar and southwest of Shinia in Bamian province.

*DOBURJA دوبرجه
34-17 66-40 m. A village on the Nawa-i-Shagdiz, south of Asgharat. Another village with this name is near Raqol on a tributary of the Band-i-Amir, at 34-40   67-11 m.

*DODAMAST دودامست
34-34 69-1 m. A village one mile northwest of the Band-i-Qargha, on the way from Kabul to Paghman.

*DOGHA دوغه
33-2 67-46 m. A village northeast of Kaftarkhana and west of Nauruzi.

DOGHABAD دوغ آباد
34- 69-. A small walled village 2 miles from the Bala Hissar of Kabul, on the east side of the Charasia road. The wall-faces measure 300 feet and the place contains 30 houses. Inhabitants: Kizilbashes. (Kennedy, I.B.C.)

DOGHOR   See   JUI MIR HAZAR دغور

DOKAN دکان
34-40 67-53. A pass over the Band-i-Baba at the head of the Saidabad Tagao, which runs north to Bamian. (Maitland.)

161

*DOKANI دوكانی
34-44 67-51 m. A village on the Dara-i-Kakrak, some 6 miles south of Bamian.

DOKUI دوكوی
33- 68-. A village situated 40 miles south of Ghazni, and in the elevated and mountainous tract lying between that place and Lake Ab-i-Istadah. (Thornton.)

DOKUI دوكوی
32-53 68-6 m. A fort in the Ghilzai country, on a road from Pannah to Adin Khel. It is a fort of the Shinukzais. (Broadfoot.)

DOLA دوله
A subdivision of the Bacha-i-Ghulam clan of Dai Zangi.

DOLAI دولی
35- 71-. A pass in the Uchiri range, over which a path leads from Nari, in the Kunar valley, into Baraul. (I.B.C.)

*DOLANA دولانه
33-5 67-28 m. A village located on a tributary of the Arghandab river, a few miles southwest of Jaghori.

*DOQAD دوقد
34-33 67-7 m. A village on the Tarapas stream, a tributary of the Dara-i-Mur, southeast of the Kotal-i-Gharghara.

DOSA دوسا
A section of Jirghai Besudis.

DOSHA دوشا
34-10 70-37 G. A village in the Pesh Bolak division of the Jalalabad district, 6 miles to the southwest of Batikot. The inhabitants are Tirais. (Jenkyns.)

*DOSHANAI دوشنی
32-20 68-17 m. A village east of the Shinkai Ghar and west of Balawri.

DOSTAM KHEL   See FIRAJ   دوستم خيل

*DOSTBEG دوست بيگ
34-46 67-44 m. A village on the Dara-i-Sialaiak, some 7 miles southwest of Bamian.

DOSTDAR دوستدار
A section of the Daulatpai Besudis.

DOSTDAR دوستدار
34- 68-. A village on the right bank of the Helmand, about 3 miles above Farakhulm. (Wanliss.)

DOTANI دوتانی
A tribe of Powindahs, divided into the following sections:
    1. Madu Khel   4. Sado Khel
    2. Ibrahim   5. Hasan Khel
    3. Badin Khel   6. Bana Khel
    7. Usmanzai   8. Sankizai
              9. Nuso Khel

This is one of the richest Powindah tribes; they chiefly bring silk "pashm," carpets, and "charas." They are sometimes spoken of as Lohani.

The Dotanis are said to be able to muster some 2,500 fighting men, but of this number at least 1,000 are either permanently, or semi-permanently, settled within the British border, and of the remainder nearly all pass through the Gumal twice a year with kafilas to and from Afganistan.

It is to be noted that for peace or war the Dotani and Sulaiman Khel are one. Several hundreds of Sulaiman Khel have been killed fighting the battles of the Dotanis against the Ahmadzai Wazirs over the Wano lands amongst them the father of Muhammad Akram, one of the leading Sulaiman Khel maliks of these parts. As late as October 1894 the allied army of the Powindahs including 1,800 Dotanis and 19,000 Sulaiman Khel, collected at Warshak with the intention of ravaging Wano and then attacking the Mahsuds.

To understand the relations between the two parties that gave rise to this projected torah it will be necessary to go back a little in the history of the tribes chiefly concerned. In bygone times the Wano valley was in possession of the Dotanis. About 1840 the Ahmadzais, who were then a nomad tribe moved from their settlements in Margha and Birmal to Wano and obtained a footing in the valley, partly by force and partly by occupying land in the capacity of mortgages. In the course of time almost the whole valley had come into their hands. Some 30 years later the Dotanis, with the aid of the Sulaiman Khel, who themselves claimed grazing rights in Wano, made a desperate attempt to recover possession of the valley. A fierce fight ensued, in which the invaders were worsted and lost heavily. The scene of the fights, old Dotani Kot has been a ruin ever since. After this there was a chronic dispute between the Ahmadzais on the one hand and the Dotanis and Sulaiman Khel on the other, about the possession of landed and grazing rights in Wano. In the autumn of 1893 a dispute arose between the Ahmadzais and Dotanis respecting the right to a certain "karez" known as Mir Khan. In the fight which ensued the Ahmadzais killed a number of Dotanis and demolished their fortified village (new Dotani Kot).

In consequence of this the Dotanis and Sulaiman Khel determined to make a joint attack on the Ahmadzais of Wano on their way back to Khorasan. On receiving information of this the Civil authorities in Dera Ismail Khan, summoned a jirga of Sulaiman Khel, Dotani and Ahmadzai Maliks, with a view to preventing reprisals and bringing about if possible an amicable arrangement between the hostile tribes. The Ahmadzais ultimately agreed to pay bloodmoney or compensation for the Dotanis they had killed and to rebuild the village they had demolished. On receiving a satisfactory assurance of this the Dotanis and Sulaiman Khel promised to refrain from further hostilities. In the summer of 1894, however, the Dotanis were again attacked by the Ahmadzais at Tatai on the Wano Toi, where they had halted on their return to their summer quarters. In this raid the Dotanis lost seven men killed and had 120 cows looted as well. The Dotanis thereupon determined to exact revenge for this unprovoked attack, and accordingly approached their allies, the Sulaiman Khel, with a view to their taking joint action against the Wanowals during the ensuing cold weather.

The Sulaiman Khel not only agreed to support them, but determined to get up a coalition of all the Powindah tribes for the purpose. The torah collected in October, as stated above, but the British Commissioner with the Afghan-Wazir boundary delimitation party warned the allied army against committing hostilities in Wano, which was then under our protection and was shortly to be occupied by our troops.

The projected attack was accordingly checked and the hostile gathering shortly afterwards dispersed. This matter is further referred to under "Powindah." (Carr, King.)

DOZAN دوزن
35- 69-. A fort in the Kohistan of Kabul, on the right bank of the Barikab stream. (Pottinger.)

DRE KALA Or DRE KHOLE دری کلا (خوله)
34-1 69-39 m. A village at the mouth of the Hazardarakht defile about 9 miles northwest from Ali Khel, and 6 miles northeast from Jaji Thana. There is room for a brigade to bivouac here, but no supplies are procurable.
From Dre Kala a track said to be practicable for horsemen and laden mules, leads over the Mula Khak pass into the Surkhab valley. (I.B.C.) Recent maps show the spelling Dre Khole. (LWA)

DRE PLARA دری پلاره
A valley situated at the head of the Kurram river, between Hazardarakht and the Shutur Gardan pass. It is said to be 6 kilometers long, and to contain two forts with 120 houses and 400 fighting men. If there is a valley of this name, it seems strange that Lumsden does not mention it, as he went from Hazardarakht over the Shutur Gardan pass. (Agha Abbas.)

DUBELA دوبله
34-27 70-30. Two villages in the Besud division of the Jalalabad district on the left bank of the Kabul river, nearly opposite Jalalabad. Inhabitants: Dehgans and Tajiks. (Jenkyns.)

DUKANI دوکانی
34- 67-. A village in the Bamian district, situated in the Saiyidabad glen, and containing 80 families of Sayyids and Hazaras. (A.B.C.)

DULGHA دلغه
34- 67-. A pass over the Band-i-Baba.

*DUMBA دمبا
34-57 68-58 m. A village near Chapqol, on a tributary of the Ghorband.

DUMB-I-USHTAR دنب اشتر
35- 67-. A pass crossed by the Maidan-i-Pai Kotal—Mazar-i-Sharif road at about 10 miles south of the Dandan Shikan pass. The road for a short distance of either side of the summit is too steep for camels. (I.B.C.)

DUNAI دونی
34-46 71-5 m. A place opposite to Narang in the Kunar valley. (Coldstream.) Another village with this name is on the Nuristan stream, about 7 miles south of Mandol, at 35-13 70-10 m. (LWA)

DUNGANA Or DANGANA دنگانه
35-21 69-30 m. A village in the Parandev Dara about 3 miles above its junction with the Panjshir. It contains some 8 families of Tajiks. (I.B.C.)

DUNGUL دونگل
35-17 71-22. A valley descending south and debouching into the Kunar a short distance below Chandak.
From Kamdesh (6,020 feet) in the Bashgul valley a road runs south for 3 miles to the top of a pass (10,300 feet) at the head of the Dungul, and then winds down the latter by an extremely rough road, the slopes of the hills being thickly covered with deodars and pines. At 8 3/4 miles are the ruins of a Kafir fort called Azharbai, and here the Azharbai valley brings its torrent down from the east. A track to Kamu is said to lead up it. At 10 miles the road runs through an extraordinary narrow defile, with precipitous cliffs nearly 1,000 feet high. To the west runs a gorge a few yards wide, from top to bottom of the mighty cliffs it pierces. "The lower part of the Dungul is said to be easier than the upper part. It could not well be worse. The whole valley is extraordinarily strong, abounding in defensive positions and the dense forest which Kafirs love to war in.
"To the west of the Dungul valley, a mountain ridge was shown me, beyond which the Waigul was declared to be." (Robertson.) A stream with this name is located at 32-6 69-26 G. (LWA)

DUNNI   See   KHOST   دنی

*DUNNI   See   DUNAI   دنی

*DURAN   دوران
32-48 69-17 m. A village southeast of Urgun and east of Sarobi in Paktia province.

DURANI   دورانی
For a description of this tribe, see "Volume 5."

DURANI KALA   Or   DORANAY   دورانی قلعه (درانی)
34-17 68-49 m. A village on the right bank of the Kabul river, about two miles south of the bend which that river makes northwards towards Laladar. It is 29 miles from Kabul on the road to Ghazni. There is plenty of space for a camping ground here, and ample good water from a stream near by. About 2 1/2 miles below the village the Kabul river is crossed by an easy ford, 18 inches deep in April; here also there are the remains of a masonry bridge. A road comes in at Durani Kala from Hisarak, via the Surkh Bedak pass, 23 miles. (I.B.C.)

*DUR BABA   دور بابا (در)
34-2 70-45. Dur Baba is a village and an alaqadari in Nangarhar province. The alaqadari, which comprises an area of 427 square kilometers, has an agricultural population that has been estimated at from 2,875 to 12,800. The alaqadari is bounded in the west by Achin and Naziyan, in the north by Loye Shinwar and Mohmand Dara, in the east and south by the State of Pakistan. Dur Baba has about 31 villages, 9 of which have more than 500 inhabitants. The villages are listed in the PG as follows: Lal Mandi, Lalmi Kalay, Baru Khula, Dwa Nazian Khula, Karmo Khel, Ali Koh, Kara Pa, Tsapari, Badin Kalay, Munda Ti, Nakhtar Naw, Sholgar, Surkando, Torlala, Tora, Dur Baba, Omar Khel, Pakha Mina, Shinkai Gerdi, Qasaba, Sofi, Chenar, Sasobi, Zala Darband, Khosa Changai, Darbi China, Tawda China, Inzar, Galoko, and Noargossi.

*DURKOTKI   دور کوتی
33-17 69-51 m. A village in Khost, about halfway between Tani and Matun (Khost).

165

DUR NAMA در نامه
35-29 69-50 m. A dara or ravine which runs into the Panjshir from the northwest at 2 miles above Dasht-i-Rewat. The road to the Khawak pass turns up this dara for a short distance, and there is a path practicable only for men on foot, which leads up the dara and over the Wakhe Koh into Nuristan. (I.B.C.) A place with this name is located at 35-4 69-30 m. (LWA)

*DURRANI درانی
33-40 69-24 m. A village east of the road from Gardez to Mirzaka, about halfway between the two places. A mountain with this name is located near Ibrahimkhel, northwest of Baraki Barak in Logar province, at 33-59 68-53 m.

*DUZDQOL دزد قول
34-27 68-52 m. A village on a path from Kota-i-Ashro to Arghandeh, about halfway between the two places.

DWA GUMAL See GUMAL دوه کومل

EHSIAR احسیار
A small tributary of the Turkoman Dara.

EJAN (Or EJRAN) ایجان (اجران)
35- 69-. A dara draining eastwards into the Salang Dara which it joins about 12 1/4 miles above Parwan. A road runs up the Ejan Dara, over the Salang Kotal, into the Khinjan valley. (I.B.C.)

EJRAN See EJAN اجران

EMILAH امیله
34- 69-. A village in the Koh Daman of Kabul, one mile from Istalif. The principal fighting in General MacCaskill's storming of Istalif took place at this village, most of the enemy retiring to it and making a bold stand within it. (Stacy.) Recent maps show the name Mahala, at 34-50 69-6 m.

*ENAM انعام
34-6 68-54 m. A village about 1 mile southeast of Shulak and some 4 miles northwest of Babus.

ERGANA Or YERGANA ایرگنه
33-39 68-2 m. A small village in Kharwar, containing 20 houses of Ghilzais. See "Ao Daka (1)." (Griesbach.) Another place with this name is about 12 miles west of Saighan, at 35-11 67-28 m. (LWA)

*ERGANAK ایرگنک
34-14 66-47 m. A village north of the Nawa-i-Waras, west of the village of Waras.

*ERGIN ارگین
34-35 67-23 m. A village southwest of the Kuh-i-Boro, and southeast of Dara.

EWAZ·KALA عوض قلعه
A village in the Surkhab district of the Jalalabad district, about a mile northeast of Sultanpur. Inhabitants: Ghilzais. (Jenkyns.)

EZDARI عزداری
A dasta, or subdistrict, of the Jaghuri Hazaras.

*FAIZI فیضی
34-17 67-16 m. A village on the Tagab-i-Sagsukhta, at its confluence with the Qol-i-Tsuitaman.

*FAKIRAK فقیرك
34-46 68-25 m. A village located on a tributary of the Qol-i-Khesh, southwest of Asheq.

*FAKIRAN فقیران
34-9 67-44 m. A village on a tributary of the Garmab, southeast of Qaraqol. Another place with this name is on the Margharud, 2 miles north of Dandai, at 32-44 69-17 m.

FAKIR KALA فقیر قلعه
33- 68-. A fort in Zurmat, between Gardez and Kalalgu, four marches from the former. It is a large walled village with six towers. Inhabitants: Sulaiman Khel Ghilzais. There are here all kinds of supplies necessary for an army. It is watered by the Kalalgu stream, and has also three karez. (I.B.C.) Other places with this name are located at 32-38 67-26 G. and 32-42 68-35 A.

FAKIR KHEL فقیر خیل
34- 69-. A village in the Hisarak subdivision of the Jalalabad district. The inhabitants are Shinwaris. (Jenkyns.)

FARAJ See FIRAJ فراج

FARAJGHAN فراج غان (فرجه غان)
35-12 69-41 G. A village at the head of the Alishang valley, 123 miles northeast of Kabul.
It lies at a great elevation, and cultivation is carried on with difficulty. It is about 94 miles from Jalalabad by the Alishang valley. It is the mart of western Nuristan, and consists of 400 houses of Hazaras, situated in the plain. Water abundant from streams. Intercourse between the Kafirs and Musalmans is carried on by the Nimchas of Darband.
Farajghan can be reached by three routes from Kabul:

       1. Via the Pachigan valley
       2. " the Nijrao and Dara-i-Fota
       3. " Ghani and Ishpi

The above distance has, Colonel Stewart thinks, been overstated. It cannot be more than 75 or 80 miles, as the journey is done in four days by horses and in six days by bullocks. (Leech, Stewart.) The pass with this name is located at 35-5 69-50 A. (LWA)

FARAKHOLAM See FARAKHULM فراخلم

FARAKHULM فراخلم
34-29 68-6. Two Besud Hazara villages on the right bank of the Helmund, about 6 1/2 miles below Gardan Diwal.

FARAKSHA فراخشاه
One of the four valleys of Nijrao, inhabited by Tajiks and "Pashais."

FARASH	فراش

A section of the Jaghatu Hazaras paying revenue to Ghazni. A village with this name is located at 34-28 66-29 m.

FARINJAL	فرنجل

34-59 68-42 A. A village in the Ghorband valley, 6 1/2 miles west of Chahar Deh. It contains about 80 families of Tajiks possessing some flock and 400 head of cattle, and is surrounded by walled enclosures, gardens, orchards, etc. There is room to encamp on the left bank of the stream, and from the opposite bank a flat terrace projects on top of which is the small village of Khal Beg Kala. This terrace affords a good, though small, position for closing the valley, and could be held by one or two brigades.

About 2 1/2 miles west of Farinjal is a lead mine, which had not been worked for so long a period that its existence was unknown to the neighbouring inhabitants, until rediscovered by Dr.Lord. The ore is very abundant and valuable, being a rich sulphurate of lead. Lord observes that the shaft descended 100 feet perpendicular before it reached the ore, and that "the galleries have been run, and the shafts sunk with a degree of skill that does no little credit to the engineering knowledge of the age." He further remarks that the dialling (as a Cornishman would call it) "showed an acquaintance with the lie of the mineral and the level at which they had arrived, that could scarcely be exceeded in the present day." So extensive were the workings that Lord employed three hours in exploring them, yet without ascertaining their full extent. In 1886 there was a colony of 300 workmen here in huts: Turkomans and Parsa Hazaras. The ore is smelted at site, firewood being brought from the Dahn-i-Turkoman: the entire Ghurband valley is destitute of any timber for fuel, except fruit trees. (Peacocke, Lord, I.B.C.)

FARINJAL DARA	فرنجل دره

35- 68-. A glen draining southwards from the Tawa Kotal, in the Hindu Kush, to the Ghorband valley, which it joins about 2 1/2 miles to the west of Farinjal village. It is a narrow glen, issuing from among very broken clay hills, and is some 18 or 20 miles in length. A path leads up the glen and over the Tawa Kotal; in the glen the path is said to be easy for pack-animals, but the kotal itself is only fit for men on foot. (I.B.C.)

*FARMAN	فرمان

34-40 69-49 m. A village on a stream, north-northeast of Sarobi.

*FARMANKHEL	فرمان خیل

34-32 70-13 m. A village near Aghrabat (Mehterlam) in Laghman province.

FAROBAL	فروبل

35-18 69-30. A village in the upper Panjshir glen, situated on the left bank of the stream, some 2 miles below Bazarak, and inhabited by 80 families of Tajiks. (Shahzada Taimus.)

FARUKHSHAH KHEL	فرخ شاه خیل

34- 70-. A village in the Jalalabad district, about 12 miles southwest of Batikot. The inhabitants are Tirais. (Jenkyns.)

FARZA	فرزه

34-46 69-3 G. A large village 22 miles northwest of Kabul, 4 miles south of Istalif. It is situated at the eastern base of the Paghman range, on the right bank of the Farza ravine. The headman of this locality was Mir Arab Shah, Tajik, brother-in-law to Mir Bachha, the notorious chief who showed such determined hostility to the British in 1879-80, and afterwards became a refugee with the Shinwaris. Mir Arab Shah was himself most active in his hostility towards us, and brought every available man with him from Farza for the attack on Sherpur. The lands are very fertile, everything in the shape of field-produce, and fruit thriving, with the exception of grapes, which do not grow here. A road, fit only for foot passengers and horsemen, runs up the Farza Dara to the Kachin Kotal and then down the Findukistan Dara to the Ghorband valley. (A.B.C., I.B.C.)

FATEHABAD فتح آباد
34- 70-. A village in Kats Laghman, about 1 1/2 mile from the northern foot of the Darunta pass. A little beyond the village is a small garden laid out with much care and taste, near the fort of Bahram Khan. This village is also known as Kala-i-Fateh Muhammad. The ground on which the village stands is well cultivated and apparently open and traversable, but in reality so deeply intersected by watercuts for irrigation as to be almost impracticable for cavalry. A force of 200 khasadars is quartered in the village. (Holdrich, I.B.C.)

FATEHABAD فتح آباد
34-22 70-14 m. Elevation 2,550 feet. A village of 300 houses, about 15 miles southwest of Jalalabad. The inhabitants are Tajiks, possessing (in 1904) about 1,000 head of cattle. There are 1,400 jaribs of land under cultivation, yielding an annual produce of about 50,000 Indian maunds of wheat and barley; cotton, rice and many pulses are also grown. Land-tax is assessed at the rate of 15 krans per jarib. Water ample from springs, ravines, etc., throughout the year. Fodder for 7,000 animals for one day is procurable from Fatehabad and neighbourhood. Fuel also obtainable.
Fatehabad is the place where the six out of the seven last survivors of the Kabul massacre were killed in 1842, and in its neighbourhood an action was fought on the 2nd April 1879, between the British and the Khugianis, in which Major Wigram Battye, of the Guides Cavalry, was killed. For a detailed account of this action see the "Official History of the Second Afghan War." (Wanliss, Johnston.)

FATEH KALA فتح قلعه
33- 69-. A village 1 1/2 miles northeast of Mirzakai Kotal, on the road to Kurram. (I.B.C.)

FATEH KHEL فتح خیل
33- 69-. A village in the upper Logar valley close to the village of Mangu Khel. These two villages are inhabited by Astanazai Ghilzais and between them number 100 families. Situation between the villages of Hisarak and Unisaiadam. (Clifford, Euan Smith.) A village with this name is located at 33-28 69-3 G. (LWA)

FATHU KALA فتو قلعه
34-26 69-8 m. A large village in the Chardeh valley, standing on the right bank of the Kabul river, between Indaki and Rishkhor. Inhabitants: Gadi Hazaras. About 100 houses. (I.B.C.)

*FATHU KATS فتو کٹ
34-20 70-3 m. A village 2 miles south of the Surkhrud, near Shaikhan.

FAULADI Or POLADA فولادی
One of original tribes of Hazaras.

FAZIL BEG KALA فاضل بیگ قلعه
34-32 69-6. A village in the Chardeh valley, about 2 miles southwest of Aoshar. There are only 60 houses in this village. (Kennedy.)

*FAZLI TANA فضلی تانه
33-58 69-30 m. A village on a stream west of Alikhel.

FINDUKISTAN فندقستان
34-59 68-51 G. A valley tributary to the Ghorband. Its name means "the place of filberts." See Siahgird.

*FIRADOLI فرادلی
34-48 70-2 m. A village on a tributary of the Alishang, northwest of Alishang.

FIRAJ Or FARAJ فراج
35-12 68-21 G. At half a mile below Anaba the road down the Panjshir glen crosses to left of the stream, and then ascends the Garda Chatha, winding up the low hills bordering the glen. The top is reached at 1 1/2 miles from Anaba, then there is a rather bad descent to a ravine, up which the road turns to the left.
This is the Dara Firaj and it runs into the main glen about 1 3/4 miles lower down. Immediately below, where the road enters, is the village of Mukhtiar Khel, 20 houses of Tajiks. Up the glen, about half a mile on the left, is Begran which has 150 houses of Tajiks. About a mile higher are Dostam Khel and Firaj containing together 30 houses of Tajiks. The whole glen is filled with a mass of orchards among which the houses of the above named villages are scattered in groups. It is about half a mile wide, but there is little room to encamp on account of the trees, though perhaps a battalion and a few squadrons might find space. The hill at the head of the glen is called Tara Koh, and is wooded principally with archa (Juniper). The ravine narrows a good deal below the road, and where it runs into the main glen is a mere gorge about 80 yards wide. The road in it is hardly practicable for horses. It is really a sheep track, and not used by travellers.
The road soon takes to the hillsides and ascends the glen gradually, in a southerly direction, for about three-quarters of a mile. It is good for all pack animals. At 2 1/2 miles (from Anaba) the top of the spur is reached and there is a steep descent over a very bad road for about a quarter of a mile. Having crossed a rocky ravine the road winds upwards for about 2 miles, when the stones cease and the slopes are gentle. There are springs and some cultivation with about a dozen huts scattered here and there. The road continues to ascend for another mile to the top of the Kotal-i-Darbad where there is a karachgir (tool station) and the ziarat of Khwaja Ibrahim Darbandi. Elevation 7,380 feet. From this spot there is a path branching to the right, but it is only practicable for men on foot. The main track, bending to the left, descends very gently at first. At 6 1/2 miles it divides. The left branch leads to the village of Sanjan, and the other is the main road, known as the Rah-i-Top-Kash, and descends rapidly, winding down for 3 miles, when the bottom of the hills is reached. (Shahzada Taimus.)

*FIROZAI فیروزی
34-57 69-38. A village on the Tagab river, some 8 miles north of Tagab.

FIROZBAHAR فیروز بهار
34-43 67-3. Elevation 8,945 feet. A division of the Tagao Sayyid subdistrict of Yak Walang, containing some 180 families of Hazaras. Firozbahar, properly so called, consists of a village and two forts, containing 50 families of Hazaras. One of these forts, the larger one, is known as Kala Sayyid Saidulla. The Band-i-Amir valley is half a mile wide here, and there is ample room to camp; but it is nearly all cultivated, and mostly irrigated.
From Kala Sarkari in Bamian to Firozbahar proper the distance is 46 miles. (Maitland.)

FIROZ KHEL فیروز خیل
33- 69-. A village about 22 miles northeast of Gardez, on the road thence to the Mirzakai Kotal. Inhabitants: Amazai Ghilzais. (I.B.C.) A village with this name is located at 34-45 69-40 G. (LWA)

FORT BATTYE
34- 70-. Elevation 2,900 feet. The name given to a fortified post established by the British during the war of 1879-80 on the Khaibar-Kabul road at a point 8 miles northeast of Safed Sang (Gandamak), in the Khugiani subdivision of the Jalalabad district.
Its name was bestowed on the post owing to its proximity to the spot where Major Wigram Battye of the Guides Cavalry was killed in action on the 2nd April 1879.
On the 26th March 1880 a night-attack was made on Fort Battye by a mixed body of Shinwaris and Khugianis. The normal garrison of the post had been 100 rifles 4th Madras Native Infantry, and 40 sabres 4th Bengal Cavalry, but on the night of the attack a detachment of the 31st Punjab infantry, 148 strong, under Lieutenant Angelo, with a few details of British Infantry, had arrived and halted, and this accidental accession of strength was fortunate.
The attack was beaten off, with loss to the assailants, but the casualties among the defenders were heavy. Lieutenant Angelo was shot through the head when standing on the parapet; 5 sepoys and 2 dooly-bearers wounded, most of the casualties being from sword cuts. Fort Battye has not been used since the British evacuation of the country: probably the Afghans recognise its unsuitability as a defensive position. Only the solid stone walls now remain. (I.B.C.)

FRINJAL See FARINJAL فرنجل

FULADI See FAULADI فولادی

FULGIRD فلگرد
A cavern situated at the head of the Ghorband valley, and 2,000 feet above it. (Lord.)

FURMUL فرمل
32-34 69-11. An alternative name for Birmal.

GABAR گبر
35-8 to 35-19 71-2 to 71-33. The Gabar villages in the Kunar valley are five in number, namely, Arundu (in Chitral territory), Birkot, Nari or Narsat, Sao, and Palasgar. They are inhabited by people said to have been originally fire-worshippers who were expelled from Persia, and after many wanderings at length found a home in the Kunar valley. They speak a language different to that spoken by any of their neighbours.

The dress of the men is indistinctive. The women dress in loose trousers and shirts to the knees of a very dark blue, nearly black, which fall naturally into graceful folds. They are fond of white metal or brass neck and wrist ornaments. They wear a close fitting blue cloth skull cap, from beneath which two long plaits hang down behind. The tout ensemble is picturesque and pleasing. Of the different villages the Sao women are the best dressed.

Amongst the Gabars generally the most notable point is their strongly Semitic cast of countenance, which is at times so exaggerated that certain of the people look like the Jews of burlesque or caricature. The Gabars are called Satrs, and the villages Satrgrom by the Kafirs, while th Chitralis classify them all as Narsatis. They are poor fighters, bullied by Afghans, Chitralis, and Kafirs indiscriminately. It is from the Gabars that the Kam Kafirs obtain most of the clothing, gunpowder, and other articles they import. (Robertson.)

GABAR گبر
33- 69-. A section of the Mangals settled in the Chakmani valley. Their principal village is Mamoh Kandi, which is well cutivated and shaded by many trees. (Kane.)

GABAR MANGAL گبرمنگل
33- 69-. A village in the Gabar hills in the Mangal country. There is a permanent dtachment here of 1 squadron of cavalry from Matun, and in the hot weather nearly all the infantry of the Matun garrison move up here. (I.B.C.)

*GABRAI گبری
32-49 69-23 m. A village on the Margha river, southwest of Nizamkhel.

*GABRU گبرو
32-45 67-44 m. A village located some six miles east of Ghojan and southwest of Mukur.

GACH گچ (گوچ)
34-27 70-33 m. A village in the Kama division of the Jalalabad district, situated about 2 miles from the left bank of the Kunar river, and northeast of Deh-i-Ghazi. Inhabitants: Sayyids and Wardaks. (Jenkyns.) Recent maps show the name Goch. (LWA)

*GADAI گدای
33-59 68-35 m. A village located on a stream, southwest of Sayyidabad.

GADAI KHEL گدای خیل
33- 68-. A village in Kharwar, about 27 miles northeast of Ghazni. There is room for a brigade to camp here with sufficient water from streams. (I.B.C.) Recent maps show a place with the name Gidarkhel, at 33-41 68-39 m. (LWA)

*GADA KHEL گداخیل
33-17 68-19 m. A village west of Kalakhel, near the highway to Ghazni.

*GADALI گدلی
32-14 68-19 m. A village located northwest of Waza Khwa and west of Tarwukai.

GADIALI   گدی علی
    34- 70-. A halting place in the Alishang valley, on the road from Jalalabad to Farajghan. It is about 83 miles from the former, and 11 miles from the latter. (I.B.C.)

*GADO CHINA   گدو چینه
    34-40 69-41 m. A village on the Tagab river, a few miles north of the Naghlu lake.

*GADOL   گدول
    35-8 71-12 m. A village located near the source of the Shegal Khwar, north-northeast of Mena.

GAGRA (or GOGRA)   گگرا
    34- 70-. A village in the Hisarak subdivision of the Jalalabad district. Inhabitants: Shinwaris. (Jenkyns.)

GAHIK   گاهك
    34- 70-. A village in the Kama subdivision of the Jalalbad district. Inhabitants: Mohmands. (Jenkyns.)

*GAIAN   گیان
    32-58 69-22. Gaian is an alaqadari in Paktia province. The alaqadari comprises an area of 276 square kilometers and has an agricultural population that has been estimated at from 9,390 to 10,459. The alaqadari is bounded in the west by Urgun, in the north by Sperah, in the east by the State of Palestan, and on the south by Barmal. Gaian has some 33 villages, 5 of which have more than 500 inhabitants. The villages are listed in the PG as follows: Mayen Kalai, Kamal Kalai, Moin (Mana Kalai), Magal Kalai, Stor (Lestur), Inzarkai, Khan Moh'd Khel, Aka Kalai, Fodikai, (Podilkai), Wochekai Rowata, Badi Kalai, Sterah Gayan, Birak Wakil, Qamargai, Kajir, Salat Kando Kalai, Chapakai Kalai, Tsalowatta, Salah Shah, Khanuddin, Landakai-Mzaka, Wara Kalai Wochkai (Wachke Karez), Alizar, Woghost Kalai (Waghoz-Kalai), Turghowagai, Galai Kalai, Kanderai (kandorai), Miyama, Dur Badana, Migarr, Momen Kalai, Durgar, Fateh Khel Kalai, and Aga.

GAIGRUZ   گیگروز
    34- 70-. Said to be a village on the road from the Hariob valley to Jalalabad, 12 or 15 miles from Hisarak, containing 120 houses and inhabited by Ghilzais. (Kennedy.)

GAJAN   گجان
    34- 70-. A village in the Hisarak division of the Jalalabad district, containing 200 houses of Shinwaris. (McGregor.)

GAJURBASH   See GHUJARBASH   گجور باش

*GALA   گله
    34-44 71-5 m. A village on the right bank of the Kunar river, some 3 miles southeast of Narai.

*GALIAN   گلیان
    34-59 68-45 m. A village on the Ghorband, some miles west of Siahgerd.

*GALUCH   گلچ
    34-42 69-55 m. A village some 12 miles northeast of Sarobi.

*GAMBEL کبیل
   34-16 70-22 m. A village near Chapriar, southwest of Jalalabad.

GAMBERI Or GAMBERAY کمبری
   34-33 70-23 m. A desert plain between Laghman and Kunar, about 8 miles east to west and 6 miles north to south in extent. (Dutton.)

GAMBIR کمبیر
   35-1 70-6 m. A village in Nuristan on the Kunar frontier. It is said to be situated on the crest of a tableland and to contain a thousand houses. This also appears to be the name of one of the Kafir subdivisions living north of Laghman. There is a clan of this name living on the west side of the Pech Dara. (Masson, Turner, Barrow.)

GANDA گنده
   34- 69-. A large village in the Khugiani subdivision of the Jalalabad district, situated about 2-1/2 miles southwest of Gandamak. There is a considerable amount of cultivation hereabouts. (I.B.C.)

*GANDAB See GANDAO گنداب

GANDA BAGHAL گنده بغل
   34-23 67-40 G. A fort in Besudi country. (See Military Report on Hazarajat, Part II.)

*GANDABARA گنده باره
   35-8 71-29 m. An area located south of the bend of the Kunar river, east of Gawi and south of Satu.

GANDAMAK گندمک
   34-18 70-2 A. Elevation 4,150 feet. A village of 200 houses in the Jalalabad district. It lies on both banks of the Gandamak stream, about 29 miles from Jalalabad. The inhabitants are Sherzad Khugianis; headman (1904) Pir Dost, Khugiani. They possess about 300 head of cattle and 40 horses. Land under cultivation amount to 1,500 jaribs, the annual production of wheat and barley being about 34,000 Indian maunds. Land-tax is assessed at only 4 krans, 3 shahis per jarib, but the inhabitants have to furnish free rations, etc., to all troops and Government officials passing through. There is a small sarai in the village and several mud forts and walled orchards in the vicinity. Fodder for about 5,000 animals for one day is obtainable from Gandamak and the neighbourhood. Fuel also is procurable.
The plain in which the village lies is some 5 miles from north to south, being bounded on the north by the Siah Koh and on the south by the Safed Koh, the lower slopes of which are covered with pine forest.
The Gandamak stream is a tributary of the Surkhab river; it rises in the northern slopes of the Safed Koh, and, joining the Marki Khel stream about 2-1/2 miles north of Gandamak village, falls into the Surkhab 2-1/2 miles lower down, close to the village of Allah Dad Khan. Near the village it is (in August) some 6 feet wide and 6 inches deep; it is joined 300 yards north of the main Jalalabad-Kabul road by the Anian (or Nian) stream, which contains about the same volume of water.
There is room for a division, even two, to encamp to the west of the village, on the site of the old British camp, with a plentiful water-supply. There is good camel-grazing and a fair amount of

supplies are procurable; fuel, bhuta and pine boughs from the Safed Koh.

The vicinity of Gandamak has been made famous by the numerous actions which took place between our troops and the Afghans in the of 1839-42.

On the march between this and Jagdalak, Sale's force was here strongly opposed by the Ghilzais, and lost over 100 men killed and wounded. Sale then halted here for a fortnight before going to Jalalabad.

On the retreat from Kabul of the British army in 1842, Gandamak was the scene of the massacre of the last surviviors of that force, viz., 20 officers and 45 British soldiers. The numbers of this party were as one to a hundred, most of them already wounded but they were resolute not to lay down their arms whilst a spark of life remained. The enemy mustered round them and called on them to give up their arms. The refusal of these brave men was followed by a violent attempt to disarm them, which brought on a hand-to-hand contest. The infuriated mob then overwhelmed the little party of Englishmen and cut them up almost to a man. Gandamak has given its name to the treaty of peace signed there on the 2nd May 1879 by Lord Lytton's plenipotentiary, Major Cavagnari, and Amir Yakub Khan; the right, or Khaibar column, having reached the place in April. the site selected for the encampment of the British force in both advances to Gandamak, in the year 1879, was on the right bank of the river,. about 1-1/2 miles east of the village, at a spot known as Safed Sang. Here a fortified enclosure protected the store of ammunition and provisions on some rising ground. On the first withdrawal in May, a large quantity of commissariat store was left in this enclosure for the Amir, as there was difficulty in transporting it. This store of grain, flour, etc., remained untouched until a few hours before the second occupation, when the villagers helped themselves to it and carried away an immense quantity before the head of the column arrived. (Malleson, Wanliss, Johnston.)

*GANDAO or GANDAB گنداو
32-40 68-8 m. A village located northwest of Khushamand. Other places with this name are located south of Shahjui, at 32-25 67-26 m.; some 8 miles north of the Kabul river and west of Tirgari, at 34-39 70-1 m.; north of Dopushta, at 34-20 68-5 m.; and some 4 miles west of Surkho Parsa, on a tributary of the Ghorband, at 34-54 68-36 m.

GANDAO or GANDAB گنداو
34- 66-. A tributary of the Guzrah tagao, which it joins, from the north at about 4 miles east of the junction of the Guzrah and Akzarat streams. The Gandao stream is about 3 feet broad and 6 inches deep at its mouth (in June). (Wanliss.)

GANDAO See SIAH DARA گنداو

GANGA KHEL گنگه خیل
34- 70-. A village in the Khugiani division of the Jalalabad district, about 5 miles southeast of Gandamak. The in- habitants are Kharbun Khugianis. (Jenkyns.) One place with this name is located at 34-14 70-2 G. Another also called Gangikhel is north of De Pash Khune, at 32-36 69-19 m. (LWA)

GANJAWAN or GANJUN گنجون
34-46 70-6. A village in Laghman, on the right bank of the Alishang

river, nearly opposite to, but rather lower than, the village of Alishang. Inhabitants: Uria Khel Ghilzais. The following hamlets are included in Ganjawan:

1. Kala-i-Malik Sherdil
2. Deh-i-Shakarabad
3. Kala-i-Saadat Khan   (Warburton.)

Recent maps show the spelling Ganjun. (LWA)

GAOCHAK See GHUCHAK   گاوچك

*GAOHARDISH   گوهردیش
35-24 71-35 m. A village on a tributary of the Kunar river, northeast of Kishur.

GAO KHANA   گاو خانه
34- 69-. A village in the Chardeh valley, on the right bank of the small southern tributary to the Chamchamast stream, 4 miles west of Kabul city. It contains six forts, and has in all some 300 houses. Inhabitants: Gadi Hazaras and Tajiks. It is a place of some prosperity the chief industry being the manufacture of mustard oil, the seed being brought in great quantities from the Hazarajat. (I.B.C.)

GAOMESH BELA   گاومیش بیلا (بالا؟)
34-26 70-30. A village in the Besud division of the Jalalabad district, situated on the left bank of the Kabul river about 3 miles southwest of the village of Besud. Inhabitants: Arabs. (Jenkyns.)

*GAOMISHAK   گاومیشك
33-9 67-55 m. A village located southeast of Zardalu in Ghazni province.

*GAOMURDA   گاومرده
33-6 67-29 m. A village located on a tributary of the Arghandab, south of Jaghuri.

*GAOPUR   گاو پور
34-6 70-35 m. A village southeast of Jalalabad, at the foot of the spin Ghar.

GAOSHAK   گوشك
A subdivision of the Bacha-i-Ghulam Dai Zangis. (See Military Report on Hazarajat, Part II.)

*GARA   گاره
32-59 67-53 m. A village located some 2 miles west of the Mukur-Ghazni highway, northeast of Mukur. Another place with this name is near the northwest edge of the Ab-i-Istada, at 32-31 67-50 m.

*GARAI Or GARI   گاری
32-39 67-41 m. A village located some 8 miles southeast of Ghojan and northwest of the Ab-i-Istada. Other villages with this name are located on the Tagab river, a few miles east of Nejrab, at 34-58 69-49 m.; near the Nawarud and southeast of Chahartut, at 34-16 69-49 m.; and southwest of Alingar and west of Kanda, at 34-47 70-16 m.

GARBAND KAI   گاربندکی
34-28 69-49 G. A place on the river route from Jalalabad to Sang Toda, at which alternative roads diverge. One goes by the Dabeli Kotal; the other goes by the ruby mines to Jagdalak. The gradients

of this latter route are easy, and it is perfectly practicable for pack camels without any improvement being necessary. It is about 3 miles longer than that by the Dabeli Kotal. (Ross, Thompson.)

GARDAN   گردن
33- 66-. A locality on Ujaristan. (See Military Report on Hazarajat, Part II.) Other places with this name are located west of the Dasht-i-Barikak and north of the Kuh-i-Mir, at 34-6 67-44 m. and southeast of Behsud, at 34-16 67-55 m. (LWA)

*GARDANAK   گردنک
34-3 67-23 m. A village located west of Garmak and north of the Dara-i-Garmab.

GARDAN CHATHA See FIRAJ   گردن چتحه

*GARDANDEH   گردن ده
34-6 67-15 m. A village located northeast of Pitaoqol.

GARDAN-I-MASJID   گردن مسجد
33-55 68-25 G. A halting place in the Sar-i-Ab valley about 30 miles northwest of Ghazni. There is room for a large fort to camp here, with sufficient water. (I.B.C)

GARDEZ   گریز
33-36 69-14 m. Gardez is town and a woleswali in Paktia province. The woleswali comprises an area of 653 square kilometers and has an agricultural population that has been estimated at from 21,980 to 35,390. The woleswali is bounded in the west by Zormat, in the northwest and north by Charkh and Pul-i-Alam in the east by Sayed Karam, and in the south by Shawak. Gardez has some 42 villages, 20 of which have more than 500 inhabitants. The villages are listed in the PG as follows: Dara-i-Mulla Qudrat, Karmashi, Melan, Za Aw, Hutamani Sepahi-Khel, Bala Deh Gardiz, Tirah, Salo Khel, Robat, Chawni, Ibrahim Khel, Aslat Beg Khel, Ahangaran, Bazari Kohna, Motafereqa Bayn-i-Bazar, Qarya-i-Ziyari, Khanaha-i-Shahr Pahlu-i-Bala Hesar, Shakar Khel, Hasan Khel, Sar-i-Sang, Nayeb Khel, Dawlat-zai, Shaikhha, Malek Khel, Kochi Khel, Habib Wa Hajian, Habib Wa Melan, Hamri-i-Bala Deh, Khetaba-i-Gardez, Khwaja Gardez, Darah, Fathullah Khel, Sayyidha-i-Shah-Afzal, Muqarab, Doaba-i-Melan, Hajian, Najaran, Sadat, Arjal Khel, Banuzi, Dakhel-i-Hawza-i-Shahr, Famil-ha-i-Shahri-Nau, Shozai, Rojan Khel-i-Gardiz, Sayed Khel, Momen Khel, Jamaluddin Kala, Baloch Khel, Bayak Khel, and Salam Khel. (LWA) In 1914, the area was described as follows: The chief place, and the Civil head-quarters of Zurmat. It is 6 marches (about 70? miles) from Kharlachi on the road from the Kurram valley to Ghazni and about 14 miles southeast of the Altimur pass. Over the Altimur pass a good camel-road leads into the Logar valley and so to Kabul. This forms an important lateral communication between the main routes leading from the Kurram valley to Kabul and Ghazni respectively.
Gardez is a town of about 3,000 houses, the inhabitants being mostly Tajiks with a few Ghilzais; there is a large bazar here. A great deal of grain of all sorts is produced here and taken to the Kabul market; ghi is also sent to Kabul in large quantities. Of livestock only a few head of cattle go to Kabul, but great flocks of sheep are sent in. In return Kabul sends raisins, mulberries, tobacco, onions, and cotton cloth. There is a good deal of horse-breeding from Waziri stock done in the neighbourhood.
There are two forts outside the town, the older of which is occupied

by khasadars, while the newer is held by regular troops. The whole garrison of Gardez consists of 1 squadron cavalry, 2 battalions infantry, 4 mountain guns and 300 khasadars.
There is room to encamp a division at Gardez, with sufficient water; forage is available, but other supplies should have to be collected. In addition to the Kharlachi-Ghazni road mentioned above, a road goes from Gardez to Kabul over the Altimur pass. Afghan field batteries are said to use this route constantly, but the northern descent from the summit of the Altimur pass appears to require some improvement to make it really fit for wheeled traffic. Another road, said to be fit for field-guns, goes from Gardez to Mukur, via Shilghar. (I.B.C.)

*GARGAO گرگاو
34-13 69-15 m. A village located about 8 miles east of the Logar river and south of Kabul.

GARGARH گرگرح
A village in Laghman, containing two hamlets, viz., Kansigar and Kala-i-Sarfaraz Khan. Inhabitants: Safis. (Warburton.)

GARI Or GARAI گری
34-47 70-16 m. A village in the Hisarak division, Jalalabad district, containing 300 houses of Mohmands. (McGregor.) Another place with this name is located northwest of Chegha Sarai, at 34-47 70-56 G. (LWA)

GARI گری
One of the main clans of the Jaghuri Hazaras. (See Military Report on Hazarajat, Part II.)

GARMAB گرماب
33- 68-. A village at the head of the Charkh valley, south of the Logar district, and one of the most important places in the valley. Inhabitants: Tajiks. (MacLean, Euan Smith.)

GARMAK گرمک
34- 68-. A village of 20 families of Taimuris, in the Sar-i-Chashma valley, about 6 miles east of the Unai pass. Headman (1904) Daulat Muhammad. The inhabitants possess about 30 head of cattle and 40 sheep and goats. The annual production of wheat and barley averages about 375 Indian maunds. (Wanliss.) Other village with this name are located west of Shahr-i-Khawat, at 34-5 67-55 m.; and south of the Kuh-i-Ghulparida, at 34-3 67-27 m. (LWA)

GARMAO گرم او
34- 67-. A place in the Besud country. (See Military Report on Hazarajat, Part II.) Another place with this name is located at 34-21 68-6 m. (LWA)

GARMAO گرم او
34- 66-. A subdivision of the Sar-i-Jangal district. (See Military Report on Hazarajat, Part II.)

GARMAO گرم او
A large Dai Zangi village on the Daulat Yar-Kabul road. (See Military Report on Hazarajat, Part II.)

GARMAO-I-JIRGHAI گرم او جیغی
A river in Hazarajat. (See Military Report on Hazarajat, Part II.)

*GARMILA گرمیله
    34-34 70-47 m. A village located a few miles south of Nurgal and the Kunar river.

*GAWI گوی
    35-8 71-22 m. A village located on the Kunar river, opposite Bargam.

GAZA Or GHAZA غازه
    34-38 68-59 m. A village in the Koh Daman, 15 miles northwest of the city of Kabul. In its vicinity are abundant mounds or tumuli. The population is Tajik, and 1880 there were 100 houses in the place. (Masson, Kinloch.)

GAZAK گزك
    A place in the Hazarajat. (See Military Report on Hazarajat, Part II.) Other places with this name are located southeast of Jagdalak, at 34-22 69-54 m.; on the Shemeltu stream, at 33-40 68-8 m.; and south of Surkhshahr, at 35-16 67-45 G. (LWA)

GAZAR گزر
    34- 69-. A village in the Logar district, between Kuti Khel and Deh-i-Nao. It has two karez, and the land is well cultivated. Grain plentiful. No sheep. Inhabitants: Ahmadzai Ghilzais. (I.B.C.)

GAZ DARA گز دره
    32-54 68-25 m. A range of hills in the Ghilzai country. (Broadfoot.)

GAZIK گزیك
    34-30 69-26. A dak and customs post about 5 miles east of Butkhak, on the main Peshawar-Kabul road. (Wanliss.)

*GAZ-I-ULYA گز علیا
    34-47 69-50 m. A village located about 2 miles from the Wozbin Khwar, northeast of Sarobi.

GEHAR گهار
    A section of the Mangal tribe occupying the villages of Taghan, Langar, Kala, Sirkot, and Nasir Muhammad, in a valley on the northern slope of the Safed Koh, tributary to the Surkhab river. (Collett.)

GERI گیری
    A section of the Jaghuri Hazaras. (See Military Report on Hazarajat, Part II.)

*GHADAKI غدکی
    34-3 67-31 m. A village on the Dara-i-Garmab in the Safidab area.

GHAF غف
    34-9 66-54 G. A locality in Dai Zangi. (See Military Report on Hazarajat, Part II.)

*GHAIBANA غیبانه
    33-59 69-32 m. A village in Paktia province near the Logar border.

GHAIBI غیبی
    34- 69-. A village in the Chardeh valley, on the right bank of the Kabul river, between Guzargah and Indaki. There are about 80 fami-

lies of Tajiks in the place, which is walled with six towers and only one gate on the western face. (I.B.C.)

*GHAIBKHEL غیب خیل
32-17 67-41 m. A village in the Sikanderkhel area, southwest of the Ab-i-Istada. Another village with this name is located a few miles northwest of Yahyakhel alaqadari seat, at 32-27 68-38 m.

GHAIN-GRAIJAN غین
34- 69-. A village situated on a tributary of the Panjshir valley, called the Pahna river, 54 miles northeast of Kabul, containing 100 houses, inhabited by Pashais. · (Leech.)

GHAIN-I-BALA غین بالا
34- 69-. A village in Panjshir valley, 65 miles from Kabul, consisting of 30 houses of Pashais. Water plentiful from a stream. Ghain-i-Pain, near it, contains 100 houses. (Leech.)

GHAJI غاجی
35- 69-. A village in the upper Panjshir glen, some 8 miles above Anaba, inhabited by 40 Sayyid families. (Shahzada Taimus.)

GHALANG غالنگ (غرنگ)
33-27 69-50 A. A glen in Kush, lying to the northwest of Matun, which latter is watered by the stream flowing from the Ghalang defile. The inhabitants are Mangals, and gave some trouble to General Roberts in the beginning of 1879. (I.B.C.)

*GHALGHO غلغو
34-8 67-7 m. A village on a tributary of the Helmand in the south of Bamian province.

*GHALIKHEL غالی خیل
33-17 68-46 m. A village near the Rud-i-Jelga-i-Janubi, east of the Sardeh Band.

GHANDAI غندی
33- 69-. A village lying to the east of the Istiar Kotal. Another place with this name is located at 33-5 68-2 m. Recent maps show the name Ghunjay, at 33-40 69-59 m. (LWA)

GHANDAK غندك
34-59 68-1 m. A high hill also called Koh-i-Gulistan, running along the north side of the Bamian valley and separating the latter from Saighan. It is a long, rounded, rocky mass, and its head, though far lower than the peaks of the main range to the south of the valley, was well covered with snow in October 1885. The spurs of the Koh-i-Ghandak, to the south, are rocky, but its upper slopes are very easy. However, only one or two difficult paths lead over it to Saighan (See note to stage 11, route 32, North-East Afghanistan). The main road goes up the valley, westward, and then to the north turning the highest part of the hill. (Maitland.)

GHAND-I-URA-KHEL غند اریاخیل
34- 70-. A village in the Laghman district, on the right bank of the Alishang river, about 1 miles west of Deh-i-Ziarat. Inhabitants: Uria Khel Ghilzais. (Warburton.)

*GHANIKHEL غنی خیل
34-12 70-49 m. A village southwest of Basawul, about 4 miles south

of the Jalalabad-Torkham road.

*GHAOCH غوچ
34-4 67-39 m. A village east of the Kuh-i-Khushkak on a tributary of the Garmab.

GHAO GARDAN See AOGARDAN غوگردن

GHAO GHIZA See GHAUGHIZA غوغیزه

*GHARA غاره
33-8 67-37 m. A village located on a tributary of the Arghandab in Ghazni province. Another place with this name is located northwest of Shahr-i-Khawat in northern Ghazni province.

GHARAK غرک علیا
34-22 67-11 m. An easy-looking kotal which is crossed by a road leading from the Karghanatu Tagao, in the west of the Bamian district, to the Tabarghan Kol in Yakh Walang. (A.B.C.) This is Gharak-i-Ulya. Recent Maps show the spelling Qharak, at 34-43 67-19 m. (LWA)

GHARAK غرک
34- 67-. A halting place on the left bank of the Khawat river, about 53 miles northwest of Ghazimand 20 miles southeast of Diwal Kol. There is room for a brigade to camp here, with ample water from the river, which is here about 30 feet wide and 2 feet deep, with a swift current. There is a wooden bridge across the river here, but it is also fordable. (I.B.C.) One place with this name is located at 34-8 68-24 m. (LWA)

GHARAK غرک
33- 69-. A fairly large village about 26 miles northeast of Gardez, on the road thence to the Mirzaka Kotal. Inhabitants: Amazai Ghilzais. There is room for a brigade to encamp here with sufficient water, but supplies are scarce. Camel-grazing is abundant. (I.B.C.) Another place with this name is located 34-11 66-51 m. (LWA)

GHARGHA غرغه
A rocky dara which falls into the Kalu glen about 13 miles above Zokak. At the junction is the village of Dahan-i-Ghargha, 13 families of Darghan Hazaras; fair camping-ground. (Amir Khan.)

GHARGHAR غرغر
34-18 66-15. A fort village of about 50 Dai Kundi houses, 3 miles east of Talpech. (See Military Review on Hazarajat, Part II.)

GHARGHARA غرغره
34-36 67-31 m. A village of about 30 houses situated in Daraz Kol in the east of the Dai Zangi country. (See Military Report on Hazarajat, Part II.) Another place with this name is located at 34-19 66-16 A. (LWA)

GHARGOTAK غرگتک
34- 67-. The head-quarters of the Governor of the Besud District of the Hazarajat, Sayyid Jafer Khan. (See Military Report on Hazarajat, Part II.)

GHARIB غريب
A locality in the Faoladi Hazara country.

*GHARIB RAH غريب راه
33-1 67-26 m. A village on a tributary of the Arghandab river in Ghazni province.

GHARIGI غرگي
A pass over the western continuation of the Safed Koh, between the Shutur Gardan and Lakarai Kotals. Over this pass a path is said to go direct to Kabul from the Hariob valley, thus turning the road through the Logar valley. (I.B.C.)

*GHARSANG غرسنگ
33-15 67-13 m. A village on a path connecting the Amrestan and Arghandab valleys.

GHARU See TANGI GHARU غارو

*GHATKAI غتکی
32-32 67-39 m. A village located about halfway between Shahjui on the Tarnak river and the Ab-i-Istada lake.

GHAUGHIZA Or GHAWAY GUZA غوايگوزه
34-2 69-34 m. A valley between Hisarak and Aspando Kats on the Lakarai route from Safed Sang to Hariob. It is about 9 miles in length, and at its head is the Ghaughiza Kotal; this is difficult but is said to be practicable for camels. The Ghaughiza valley belongs to Nasir Khel Ghilzais. (I.B.C.) Recent maps show a village with the name of Ghaway Guza. (LWA)

*GHAWAS غواص
34-31 67-27 m. A village on the Dara-i-Shorshori, southwest of Gharghara.

*GHAZA غازه
34-38 69-0 m. A village northeast of Paghman and northwest of Kabul.

*GHAZABI غضبی
34-25 70-56 m. An area northeast of Goshta and north of Basawul.

GHAZI غازی
34-28 70-33. A village in the Kama division of the Jalalabad district, situated on the left bank of the Kunar river, about 2 miles above its junction with the Kabul. Inhabitants: Arabs and Safis. (Jenkyns.) Another place with this name is located at 34-38 69-0 m. (LWA)

GHAZIABAD غازی آباد
34-19 70-46 m. A large walled village in the Pesh Bolak subdivision of the Jalalabad district; it lies 1-1/2 miles southeast of Chardeh and 7 miles northwest of Basawul. It contains some 500 families of weavers, possessing (in 1905) about 1,500 head of cattle, 1,200 sheep and goats, and 200 buffaloes. There is no cultivation. (Malleson, Wanliss.) Another place with this name is located at 34-43 70-46 A. (LWA)

GHAZIABAD غازی آباد
34-57 70-3 G. A village in Laghman, on the left bank of the Alishang river, about 55 miles from Jalalabad. Eight houses, inhabited

by Pashais. (Leech.) Other places with this name are located at 34-43 70-46 m. and 34-18 70-46 G. (LWA)

GHAZI BABA غازی‌بابه
34- 70-. A shrine near the confluence of the Alishang and Alingar rivers, and close to the fortified cantonment of Kalut-us-Seraj.

*GHAZIKHEL غازی خیل
34-24 68-39 m. A village located on a tributary of the Maidan river, northwest of Nerkh.

GHAZNI غزنی
33-33 68-35. A province in southeastern Afghanistan which comprises an area of 32,797 square kilometers and an agricultural population estimated from 314,313 to 414,128. The province is bounded in the west by Zabul, Oruzgan, and Bamian, in the north by Maidan (Wardak), in the east by Paktia, and in the south by the State of Pakistan. Ghazni is divided into the wolewalis of Nawar, Jaghatu, Malestan, Ghazni, Jaghuri, Andar, Moqur, Qarabagh, Sharan, Katawaz, Nawa, and Wazakhwa, and into the alaqadaris of Wol-Mamai, Jani Khel, Omna, Sultan Khel, Giru, Ab Band, Gilan, Khwaja Omri, Zena Khan, Deh Yak, and Yusuf Khel. The capital of the province is the city of Ghazni. (LWA) For woleswali lists from the Department of Statistics of the Ministry of Agriculture and Irrigation, see the following six pages
In 1914 the area was described as follows: The Ghazni district is bounded north by Maidan and Besud, south by the districts of Mukur and Katawaz, east by Logar, Kharwar and Zurmat, and west by the Pas-i-Koh and other semi-independent Hazaras. It is watered by the Ghazni, upper Logar, and Gardez streams.
The western portion of the district is hilly; the Wardak subdivision is a long valley between Logar and the Hazara hills; the remainder of the district is said to be generally an irregular plain, well irrigated and cultivated in many parts, with here and there tracts of waste, diversified by undulations, and by low, stony, and bare hills. To the south and west is a range of lofty mountains called the Gul Koh; to the west the principal peaks in this range are the Maku, the Koh-i-Sabz-nala, the Shahtus, and the Siah Koh; to the east are mountains known as the Koh-i-Jaoz, the Siah Koh, the Allah-Koh, and the Baba Abdul.
The main roads are to Kandahar via Kalat-i-Ghilzai, and to kabul via Maidan or via the Logar valley. These roads have all been traversed by troops of all arms. There is also a road to Yakh Walang said to be practicable for baggage animals; and lastly, there are the roads to India via the Tochi and Gumal, both of which are practicable for everything except wheeled traffic.
The elevation of the inhabited portions of the district ranges roughly between 6,500 and 9,000 feet. Ghazni itself is 7,279 feet, Sayyidabad on the Logar is 8,630 feet and Mashaki is 6,900. The Hazara country has, however, a considerably higher elevation than the Ghazni district proper, its altitude being guessed at from about 6,000 to 11,000.
For revenue purposes Ghazni is, according to the second edition of this gazetteer, divided into eight subdivisions, following the tribal distributions:
Divisions. (1) Tajik, occupied chiefly by Tajiks. This subdivision includes the town of Ghazni. (2) Wardak, occupied by the Wardak clan; the long valley mentioned above. (3) Dai Mirdad, lying due north of Ghazni town, between Wardak and Besud: occupied by a miscellaneous population of Wardaks, Hazaras, and Kizilbashis. (4) Hazara, includes the western portion of the district; occupied by

Administrative Divisions of Ghazni Province

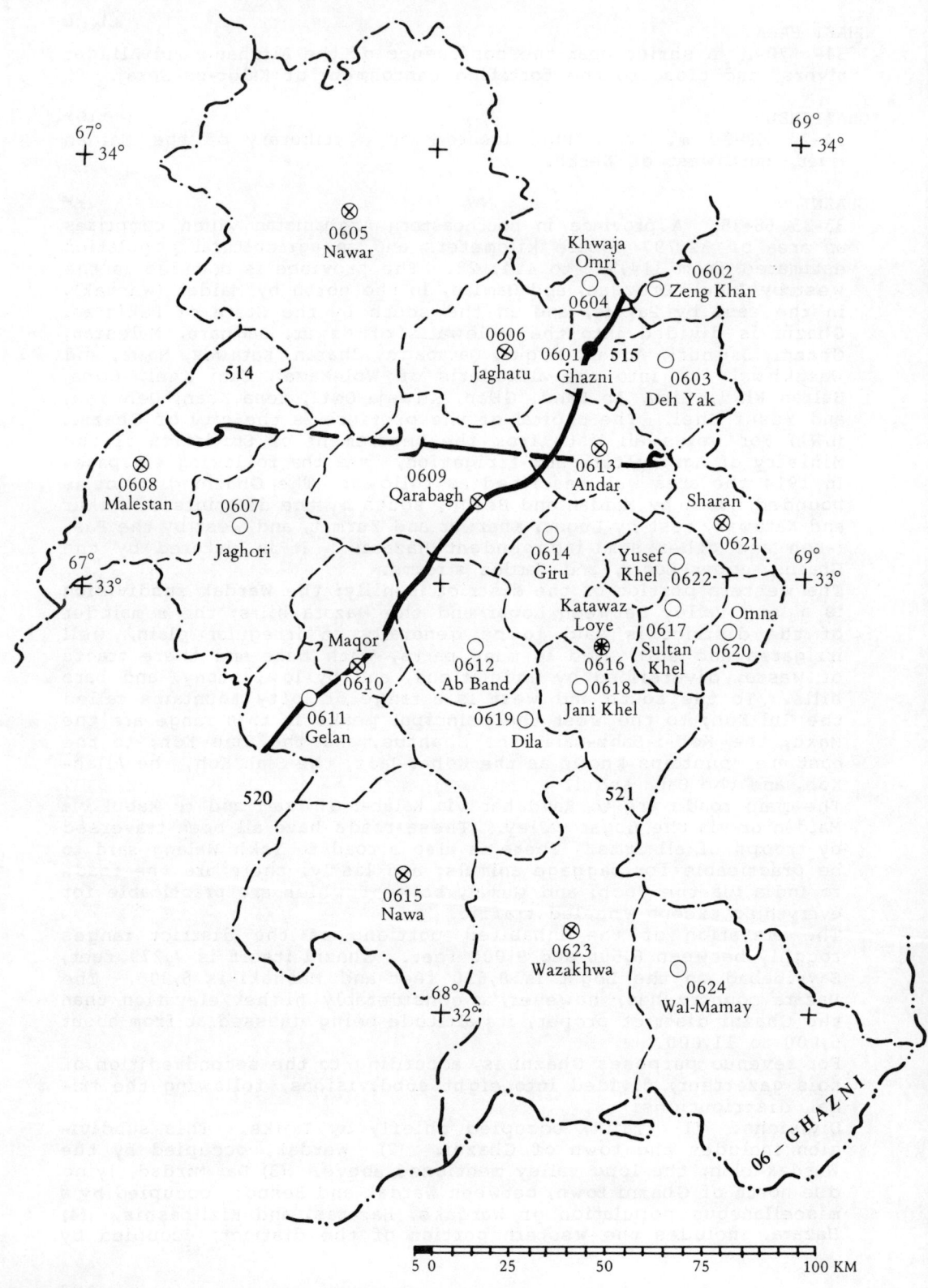

ESTIMATE OF AGRICULTURAL POPULATION AND AREA UNDER CULTIVATION

	Villages	Agricultural Population	Landlords	Lands under Cultivation in Jaribs			Lands under Cultivation in Hectares		
				Irrigated	Non-Irrig.	Total	Irrigated	Non-Irrig.	Total
OMNIA	78	28,340	3,580	61,160	3,490	64,650	12,232	698	12,930
ANDAR	213	86,360	4,400	73,470	20,990	94,460	14,694	4,198	18,892
JAGHORI	65	98,800	8,260	39,470	1,880	41,350	7,894	376	8,270
JAGHATU (WAIZ)	287	62,460	4,200	75,840	6,410	82,250	15,168	1,282	16,450
SHARAN	74	15,890	880	11,350	22,780	34,130	2,270	4,556	6,826
QARABAGH	303	88,570	11,200	97,920	10,860	108,780	19,584	2,172	21,756
MALESTAN	95	66,460	5,600	44,340	4,490	48,830	8,868	898	9,766
KATAWAZ (ZARGUN SHAR)	9	4,020	430	3,140	18,450	21,590	628	3,690	4,318
MOQUR	80	30,360	4,510	37,950	31,600	69,550	7,590	6,320	13,910
NAWA	54	30,140	2,440	8,580	—	8,580	1,716	—	1,716
NAWOR (NAHUR)	257	53,430	5,220	31,270	9,000	40,270	6,254	1,800	8,054
WAZAKHWA	89	11,930	1,300	2,900	21,120	24,020	580	4,224	4,804
AB BAND	51	14,730	1,590	5,140	5,320	10,460	1,028	1,064	2,092
UMNA*	21	2,490	260	720	1,040	1,760	144	208	352
JANI KHEL	28	5,380	640	4,740	5,620	10,360	948	1,124	2,072
KHWAJA OMRI	30	14,180	1,210	23,970	1,070	25,040	4,794	214	5,008
KHOSHAMAND (DILA)	37	7,670	800	6,970	32,160	39,130	1,394	6,432	7,826
DEH YAK	50	54,250	3,550	12,340	14,650	26,990	2,468	2,930	5,398
ZANKHAN*	33	4,830	530	1,860	4,280	6,140	372	856	1,228
GIRU ANDAR (KIRO)	45	18,180	1,420	8,540	18,450	26,990	1,708	3,690	5,389
WOL-MAMAY	39	4,850	560	1,020	—	1,020	204	—	204
GILAN	70	19,280	2,260	14,400	9,270	23,670	2,880	1,854	4,734
YAHYA KHEL (SULTAN KHEL)	21	8,770	460	13,020	7,040	20,060	2,604	1,408	4,012
YUSUF KHEL	10	8,840	530	7,290	9,480	16,770	1,458	1,896	3,354
TOTAL	2,039	740,210	65,830	587,400	259,450	846,850	117,480	51,890	169,370

STATISTICAL ESTIMATE OF LIVESTOCK BY WOLESWALIS AND ALAKADARIS

	Sheep	Karakul Sheep	Goats	Cattle	Buffaloes	Camels	Horses	Donkeys	Mules	Poultry
OMNIA	32,440	—	1,110	12,790	—	—	130	5,090	—	13,620
ANDAR	64,380	—	670	18,240	—	60	230	7,510	—	31,320
JAGHORI	136,650	—	7,190	31,430	—	—	180	6,850	—	28,980
JAGHATU (WAIZ)	61,140	—	1,860	14,450	—	—	160	5,440	—	12,590
SHARAN	27,860	—	80	9,280	—	30	110	2,580	—	11,790
QARABAGH	56,160	—	2,960	31,260	—	20	160	6,850	—	21,760
MALESTAN	80,110	—	6,860	16,710	—	—	150	5,710	—	22,380
KATAWAZ (ZARGUN SHAR)	10,820	—	190	8,140	—	110	20	1,330	—	2,240
MOQUR	34,630	—	1,790	4,540	—	160	70	3,960	—	24,960
NAWA	17,550	—	630	11,320	—	—	30	2,370	—	14,200
NAWOR (NAHUR)	75,270	—	5,320	32,240	—	—	450	11,130	—	52,000
WAZAKHWA	50,880	—	3,910	8,940	—	950	30	6,020	—	6,430
AB BAND	21,630	—	850	9,390	—	—	40	1,880	—	13,640
UMNA*	6,540	—	1,120	10,460	—	170	—	990	—	930
JANI KHEL	10,710	—	540	7,750	—	—	30	1,250	—	2,680
KHWAJA OMRI	8,390	—	130	9,050	—	—	50	1,550	—	5,720
KHOSHAMAND (DILA)	38,990	—	780	8,460	—	110	90	1,660	—	13,590
BABAK* (DEH YAK)	46,950	—	1,560	13,780	—	—	70	4,190	—	31,260
ZANKHAN	3,180	—	790	380	—	—	—	260	—	1,910
GIRU ANDAR (KIRO)	20,600	—	180	8,800	—	—	50	1,950	—	20,340
WOL-MAMAY	9,190	—	380	8,360	—	90	—	—	—	1,500
GILAN	29,950	—	1,090	10,450	—	—	80	3,440	—	22,360
YAHYA KHEL (SULTAN KHEL)	28,830	—	1,220	9,590	—	—	50	1,280	—	2,100
YUSUF KHEL	14,750	—	1,290	7,880	—	100	20	1,630	—	3,600
TOTAL	887,600	—	42,500	302,690	—	1,800	2,200	84,920	—	361,900

PRODUCTION OF AGRICULTURAL CROPS—IN KABULI SEERS

	Grains			Vegetables	Other Crops		Fruits
	Irrigated	Non-Irrig.	Total		Industrial Crops	Other Temp. Crops	
OMNIA	1,775,470	38,550	1,814,020	1,836,320	—	—	1,408,910
ANDAR	1,812,020	143,250	1,955,270	394,740	54,390	1,764,000	1,723,600
JAGHORI	2,002,510	14,250	2,016,760	208,980	—	316,000	348,240
JAGHATU (WAIZ)	2,878,850	61,650	2,940,500	197,370	—	1,820,000	151,760
SHARAN	382,270	47,100	429,370	—	9,500	364,000	—
QARABAGH	3,967,180	78,900	4,046,080	311,540	22,050	1,566,000	503,190
MALESTAN	2,072,600	48,750	2,121,350	187,700	—	—	—
KATAWAZ (ZARGUN SHAR)	147,060	126,000	273,060	—	—	100,000	140,580
MOQUR	1,243,130	240,300	1,483,430	476,010	—	608,000	159,740
NAWA	371,950	—	371,950	—	—	138,000	—
NAWOR (NAHUR)	854,410	58,950	913,360	19,350	—	650,000	28,760
WAZAKHWA	111,370	178,350	289,720	—	—	92,000	—
AB BAND	184,900	37,350	222,250	—	1,400	82,000	79,870
UMNA*	73,960	7,800	81,760	—	—	12,000	—
JANI KHEL	155,660	42,300	197,960	—	9,300	76,000	—
KHWAJA OMRI	521,590	8,700	530,290	127,710	—	382,000	143,770
KHOSHAMAND (DILA)	181,030	256,200	437,230	—	7,200	56,000	—
DEH YAK	445,910	119,400	565,310	77,410	6,900	198,000	79,870
ZANKHAN*	67,080	46,500	113,580	48,380	—	54,000	6,610
GIRU ANDAR (KIRO)	228,330	124,500	352,830	152,870	15,840	—	134,190
WOL-MAMAY	70,090	—	70,090	—	—	16,000	—
GILAN	540,510	67,500	608,010	77,400	—	346,000	57,510
YAHYA KHEL (SULTAN KHEL)	501,810	51,600	553,410	19,350	—	208,000	127,800
YUSUF KHEL	213,710	72,600	286,310	—	14,480	118,000	—
TOTAL	20,803,400	1,870,500	22,673,900	4,135,130	141,150	8,966,000	5,094,400

LAND UNDER IRRIGATION AND SOURCES OF IRRIGATION

	Area in Jaribs						Number of Sources			
	Canals	Springs	Karez	Wells	Total	Canals	Springs	Karez	Wells	Water Mills
OMNIA	40,000	8,000	10,000	3,160	61,160	50	12	42	165	35
ANDAR	51,000	3,470	17,000	2,000	73,470	60	5	240	16	46
JAGHORI	31,910	3,860	2,200	1,500	39,470	12	46	37	13	115
JAGHATU (WAIZ)	17,170	12,340	42,830	3,500	75,840	12	190	205	58	62
SHARAN	3,610	1,000	2,840	3,900	11,350	16	1	69	104	171
QARABAGH	90,190	2,300	3,930	1,500	97,920	187	58	204	4	141
MALESTAN	36,850	4,890	1,200	1,400	44,340	45	35	1	3	94
KATAWAZ (ZARGUN SHAR)	840	270	1,300	730	3,140	6	3	65	47	10
MOQUR	21,250	4,350	12,350	—	37,950	14	4	75	—	29
NAWA	6,730	290	1,560	—	8,580	56	2	147	—	18
NAWOR (NAHUR)	10,040	19,830	1,400	—	31,270	197	129	9	—	43
WAZAKHWA	910	650	580	760	2,900	—	30	66	198	—
AB BAND	1,740	—	3,400	—	5,140	14	—	72	—	13
UMNA*	—	300	420	—	720	—	19	13	—	8
JANI KHEL	1,540	2,000	1,200	—	4,740	3	20	12	—	9
KHWAJA OMRI	19,470	1,300	3,200	—	23,970	—	20	22	4	30
KHOSHAMAND (DILA)	1,770	1,800	1,200	2,200	6,970	16	5	6	—	6
DEH YAK	3,640	3,400	4,300	1,000	12,340	13	6	14	8	40
ZANKHAN*	290	400	350	820	1,860	34	10	18	10	11
GIRU ANDAR (KIRO)	6,000	—	2,540	—	8,540	34	—	75	—	24
WOL-MAMAY	120	—	900	—	1,020	2	—	12	—	5
GILAN	10,820	1,000	2,580	—	14,400	22	4	83	—	39
YAHYA KHEL (SULTAN KHEL)	11,220	—	1,800	—	13,020	13	—	22	—	7
YUSUF KHEL	4,470	1,200	700	920	7,290	12	5	7	6	38
TOTAL	371,580	72,650	119,780	23,390	587,400	818	604	1,516	636	994

TOTAL CULTIVABLE LAND, BY CROP—IN KABULI JARIBS

	Grains			Vegetables	Industrial Crops	Other Crops	Fruits	Total Cultivated Land
	Irrigated	Non-Irrig.	Total					
OMNIA	41,290	2,570	43,860	9,490	—	—	8,820	62,170
ANDAR	42,140	9,550	51,690	2,040	2,270	8,820	10,790	75,610
JAGHORI	46,570	950	47,520	1,080	—	1,580	2,180	52,360
JAGHATU (WAIZ)	66,950	4,110	71,060	1,020	—	9,100	950	82,130
SHARAN	8,890	3,140	12,030	—	400	1,820	—	14,250
QARABAGH	92,260	5,260	97,520	1,610	920	7,830	3,150	111,030
MALESTAN	48,200	3,250	51,450	970	—	—	—	52,420
KATAWAZ (ZARGUN SHAR)	3,420	8,400	11,820	—	—	500	880	13,200
MOQUR	28,910	16,020	44,930	2,460	—	3,040	1,000	51,430
NAWA	8,650	—	8,650	—	—	690	—	9,340
NAWOR (NAHUR)	19,870	3,930	23,800	100	—	3,250	180	27,330
WAZAKHWA	2,590	11,890	14,480	—	—	460	—	14,940
AB BAND	4,300	2,490	6,790	—	60	410	500	7,760
UMNA*	1,720	520	2,240	—	—	60	—	2,300
JANI KHEL	3,620	2,820	6,440	—	390	380	—	7,210
KHWAJA OMRI	12,130	580	12,710	660	—	1,910	900	16,180
KHOSHAMAND (DILA)	4,210	17,080	21,290	—	300	280	—	21,870
DEH YAK	10,370	7,960	18,330	400	290	990	500	20,510
ZANKHAN*	1,560	3,100	4,660	250	—	270	40	5,220
GIRU ANDAR (KIRO)	5,310	8,300	13,610	790	660	—	840	15,900
WOL-MAMAY	1,630	—	1,630	—	—	80	—	1,710
GILAN	12,570	4,500	17,070	400	—	1,730	360	19,560
YAHYA KHEL (SULTAN KHEL)	11,670	3,440	15,110	100	—	1,040	800	17,050
YUSUF KHEL	4,970	4,840	9,810	—	600	590	—	11,000
TOTAL	483,800	124,700	608,500	21,370	5,890	44,830	31,890	712,480

TOTAL CULTIVABLE LANDS—IN KABULI JARIBS

	Total	Pastures	Forests	Under Cultivation	Fallow Lands
OMNIA	575,100	509,450	1,000	64,650	13,970
ANDAR	184,850	90,390	—	94,460	25,190
JAGHORI	163,900	122,550	—	41,350	8,730
JAGHATU (WAIZ)	122,530	40,280	—	82,250	17,270
SHARAN	68,770	34,640	—	34,130	23,560
QARABAGH	161,000	52,220	—	108,780	14,810
MALESTAN	154,180	105,350	—	48,830	7,010
KATAWAZ (ZARGUN SHAR)	31,620	10,030	—	21,590	9,800
MOQUR	73,000	3,450	—	69,550	23,200
NAWA	30,040	21,460	—	8,580	1,200
NAWOR (NAHUR)	148,380	108,110	—	40,270	14,600
WAZAKHWA	95,600	71,580	—	24,020	11,140
AB BAND	38,460	27,000	1,000	10,460	2,700
UMNA*	10,450	8,690	—	1,760	650
JANI KHEL	39,400	29,040	—	10,360	3,760
KHWAJA OMRI	35,270	10,230	—	25,040	9,330
KHOSHAMAND (DILA)	654,930	615,800	—	39,130	17,470
BABAK*	230,960	60,970	143,000	26,990	7,750
ZANKHAN*	14,280	8,140	—	6,140	1,410
GIRU ANDAR (KIRO)	57,510	30,520	—	26,990	11,090
WOL-MANAY	11,390	10,370	—	1,020	100
GILAN	61,230	37,560	—	23,670	5,300
YAHYA KHEL (SULTAN KHEL)	53,330	33,270	—	20,060	6,120
YUSUF KHEL	37,570	20,800	—	16,770	6,020
TOTAL	3,053,750	2,061,900	145,000	846,850	242,180

various sections of Hazaras. The Hazaras who pay tribute to Ghazni are the Dai Mirdad, Jaghatu, Muhammad Khwaja and the Chahar Dasta. (See Military Report on Hazarajat, Part II.) (5) Ali Khel, occupied by the Ali Khel section of the Ghilzais. (6) Taraki on the southern border: occupied by Taraki Ghilzais. (7) Andari, the southeast corner of the district; occupied by Andar Ghilzais. (8) Kharwar, inhabitants Yusuf Khel and Gadai Khel Ghilzais. (According to Griesbach, only the western division of Kharwar pays revenue into the Ghazni treasury.)

Ghazni is a flourishing district, fertile, well watered, and well cultivated. Its yearly revenue was said in 1880 to average 9 lakhs kham,. or Rs. 6,50,000 British.

Climate. Rain usually falls in March and April, and is generally preceded by a north wind. The chief characteristics of the climate are the severe cold of winter and the mildness of the summer heat. The Ghazni winter, which commences in November and ends in March, is more severe than the Kabul one: There is always a great deal of snow. During the months of May and June there is often a strong wind from the Wardak direction, which brings with it violent and disagreeable storms of dust; it is destructive to the fruit. Fever prevails in the autumn, and cholera makes its appearance at the same season, and generally after it has appeared in India.

Population. The Population is made up mainly of Ghilzais (for the most part belonging to the Andari, Taraki, and Ali Khel sections), Wardaks, Tajiks, and Hazaras. There are besides a few Duranis and Hindus. The main divisions of the Ghilzais in Ghazni have separate tracts of country known by the name of the tribe or section occupying it.

The villages are usually made up of a group of forts, or walled enclosures which collectively bear a common name. In most villages, there are usually families of hereditary servants and artizans, such as the lohar (blacksmith), najjar (carpenter), hajam (barber), dum (musician). They receive their wages by a share of the produce at harvest time. The few Hindus there are, chiefly reside in Ghazni.

The inhabitants are divided into "Jais" and "Kuchis:" the former include the settled portion of the population and tillers of the soil; the "Kuchis," or nomads, are only to be found at their tribal homes in the summer. The Andari, Taraki, and Ali Khel sections of the Ghilzais; the Wardaks, including the Gadai Khel, the Tajiks, Hazaras, and Duranis, are chiefly "Jais" or settlers. The "Kuchis" with the exception of the Dotanis are all Ghilzais and belong mainly to the sections known as Kharotis, Mian Khel, Nasirs, Mulla Khel, and Mianis. Many of the "Kuchis" come donw to British territory in the winter, and are known as Powindahs. Except among Tajiks and Hazaras, the Pushtu language is generally spoken. All but the Hazaras are Sunnis.

Chief imports and exports. The following goods are imported: salt, drugs, cotton and woollen goods, sugar, copper, and damani sheep brought from Multan and the Derajat chiefly; they are imported for the sake of their skins, from which the best kinds of postins are manufactured. In exchange, the following goods are exported; oil, ghi, wool, apricots, almonds, zira, majit, carpets, drugs, and sword-belts.

Wheat and barley are exported to Kabul, and supplies for a large force are obtainable in the neighbourhood of Ghazni itself.

Afgriculture. The land is, according to the presence or absence of artificial irrigation, called abi or lalmi. The irrigated or abi land it further distinguished as yakfasli (single crop) and dufasli (double crop). There is a third kind of soil called chilki; this is the worst description.

The chief products of the spring harvest are: wheat, barley, gram, mustard masur, lucerne and clover. The autumn crops are: rice, Indian-corn, moth kanghi, and tobacco.

The best wheat crops in a good year are said to be raised on the lalmi lands. They are sown in the spring after the snow has melted. The spring crops on irrigated lands are sown in the autumn.

Besides the crops above mentioned, there are turnips, cucumbers, melons and carrots. There are also vegetable gardens round Ghazni and other large villages. Large quantities of fruit are raised, grapes, plums, mulberries, apricots, apples, pears, peaches, almonds, pomegranates, quinces, etc.

A proprietary body exists; they either cultivate the land themselves, or by means of Dehkans (or tenants). If the tenants provide the cattle for the plough and find half the seed, they receive one third share of the produce; but in the event of the cattle and seed being found by the proprietor, quarter share is received.

Land is sold and mortgaged; the selling price of good land is said to be Rs. 20 Kabuli for land which requires one seer of seed. Seven seers of séed land--1 jarib, the average selling price of which is 7 tomans, or Rs. 140.

There appears to be a plentiful supply of water except in June and July. For those months it is usually found necessary to appoint a Mirab (lord of the water) to regulate its distribution in the Sehkot-paying villages. Lots (kurre qur'a andazi) settle the order of turns; when once the turns are settled no fresh casting of lots to start a new rotation can be made for a month. For the Tajik division, a day's water-supply is allowed to irrigate a kulba of land.

In the jamabast, or village with fixed revenues, the regulation of the water distribution is managed by the maliks and proprietors.

Revenue system. The revenue year commences on Naoroz, corresponding to the 21st March. There are three kinds of assessments--(1) jamabast, (2) sehkot, (3) khalsa.

Under "jamabast" the revenue is paid partly in cash and partly in kind. The amount is a fixed quantity. This is the assessment most agreeable because it saves the interference which is necessitated when a share of produce is taken.

The sehkat assessment, as the name implies, represents one-third share of the produce, The villages under this assessment are usually farmed.

The khalsa assessment is for khalsa lands considered Government property: half share of the produce is taken. This revenue is also usually farmed. The khalsa lands appear to have escheated to the State at some former period, owing either to the failure of heirs, or difference between the occupants of khalsa villages and ordinary villages is the higher rate of revenue paid. The State in khalsa lands recovers what we should call a superior proprietary right above the usual revenue. There is apparently no interference with any of the rights and privileges which attach to proprietors.

Fruit trees, mustard, lucerne (reshka), clover (shaftal), tobacco, and vegetables pay at a cash rate of Rs. 5 kham per jarib.

Other income besides land revenue. Besides the land revenue the following taxes are also levied. They are divisible under three heads, and include all the income but that which comes under land revenue:--

Wajuhat or Taxes

(1) "Sayer," or custom duties. These are transit duties levied on merchandise passing throgh the district at the rate of Rs. 2 per load (camel), and Rs. 1 for every 40 rupees' value, arbitrarily settled by the Hakim's representative when the goods reach Ghaz-

ni. The income was said to be Rs. 46,333 in 1879.

(2) "Zarb Khana," or mint-tax. The farmer's income is made by calling in the copper coinage twice in the year and re-stamping it; when called in to be re-stamped, six pice are reckoned as equal to one shahi; when re-issued five pice (the ordinary value of a shahi) are paid. The tax was farmed for Rs. 1,100 in 1879. (It is probably now extinct.)

(3) Tobacco License Tax. The sale of licenses to sell tobacco realized Rs. 200 in 1879. Only persons with licenses are permitted to sell tobacco.

(4) "Dalali Bazar," or Agent's Tax. The dalals, or agents are entitled to a commission at the rate of 1.8 per cent. The State is entitled to half of this. The tax is usually farmed: it realized Rs. 400 in 1979.

(5) "Kala Dagh," or literally, the head stamp. This is a tax on meat killed and brought into the city for consumption. The tax is, like the others farmed; the income was Rs. 1,166 in 1879.

(6) "Resham Faroshi," or license for the right to sell silk. This tax fetched Rs. 216 in 1979.

(7) "Tarazudari" or tax for the right to weigh grain. Liense entitles the holder to weigh grain where the revenue is collected in kind; the weighman receives a certain amount for the trouble of weighing. The tax fetched Rs. 410 in 1879.

(8) "Kotwali Tax." This tax is recovered from the fees paid to Kotwals on their appointment. It is made good by the Kotwal from fines, forfeitures and bribes. It realised Rs. 500 in 1879.

There is besides an income from "Asnaf," or taxes on every trade and profession, which bring from Rs. 30 to one-third per annum, in accordance with the profits of the trade or profession. They realised Rs. 484 in 1879.

There is another imposition known as "Sarghala," which is a tax on sheep and cattle in the city and some seventeen villages, and in the suburbs where the tax is not included in the revenue.

The total of all these taxes is said to have been Rs. 55,530 during the year 1879. Most of the foregoing which relates to taxation has ben taken from the 1882 edition.

Civil administration. The civil administration of the district is in the hands of a Governor or Hakim appointed from Kabul. His headquarters are at Ghazni. In 1879 there were also Hakims in the Wardak, Ali Khel, and Taraki divisions; they received their pay and the proportion on fines and forfeitures in their own district. They were under the Ghazni Hakim in revenue and criminal matters, in so far that Ghazni was the capital of the district and the head office for accounts. Appeals against oppressions were also made to him. The duties of the governor appear to have been to receive revenue and decide small criminal cases in which the punishments were usually fines. Civil cases went to the kazi.

Criminal cases of a serious kind were, and no doubt still are, reported for orders to Kabul.

In each tappa there was a Diwan or Mirza by whom the revenue collections were superintended and the account kept. They were paid in proportion to the revenue recovered.

The revenue acounts were according to the kham and tabrizi systems of computing money and measuring by weight. (Hastings, I.B.C.)

GHAZNI غزنى
33-33 68-25. Ghazni is the name of a town and a woleswali in the Ghazni province. The woleswali compromises an area of 328 square kilometers and has an agricultural population which has been variously estimated at from 13,540 to 26,432.

The woleswali is bounded in the west by Jaghatu, in the north by Khwaja Omri and Zena Khan, in the east by Deh Yak, and in the south by Andar. The woleswali includes 85 villages of which 18 have more than 500 inhabitants.
The villages are listed in the PG as follows:
Qala-i-Ahangaran, Gadol-i-Ahangaran, Rawza-i-Sultan, Bahlol Sahib, Shams Sahib, Hakim Sahib, Mugulan, Kushk, Mir Moh'd Kan (Qala-i-Amir Moh'd), Pas Hesar, Shaliz, Qala-i-Shir-Moh'd Shaliz, Arzo, Gadol Malik Moh'd, Amir Shabaz, Zargar, Mangal (Mangor), Khwaja Ahmad, Gadol-i-Raiyat, Mushakan, Kala Ghach, Kala Ghach-i-Ulya, Kala Ghach-i-Sufla, Zay Waj (Zaywjat), Naka, Qarya-i-Qarah-Baghi, Ali Lala, Arbabaha, Hindu Guzar, Gadol-i-Jabar, Gadol-i-Wahshi, Gadol-i-Akhtar, Gadol-i-Mulla Abdurrahim, Gadol-i-Parwiz, Qala-i-Ashrat, Qala-i-Mudir-Sahib, Qala-i-Kalantar, Pirzad, Char Qala-i-Niyazi, Qala-i-Qadam Khan, Saray-i-Arbab, Qala-i-Arbab, Masjed-Kard-Gari, Qarya-i-Malik Kunjak, Qala-i-Mufti (Masjed-i-Mufti), Qala-i-Niyazi, Niyazi-i-Ulya, Niyazi-i-Sufla, Qarya-i-Mushak, Bakawol-i-Saydan (Bakawol), Qala-i-Azad Khan, Qala-i-Nau-i-Khwaja Rushnai, Deh Khudaidad, Nokhi (Noghi) Zelzela, Qalati, Lashmak, Jelaugir, Laghari, Qala-i-Qazi, Masjed-i-Baba-Ali Sahib, Masjed-i-Khutbi, Mahala Qarah, Darwaza-i-Sanai (Guzar-i-Sanai Sahib), Qala Nau-i-Sar Reg (Qala-i-Nau-i-Sarakak), Qala-i-Yaqub, Qarya-i-Mirza-Ataullah Wa Sardar, Masjed-i-Kulali, Mahala-i-Rais, Masjed-i-Darwaza-i-Miri, Khwaja Baqal Sahib, Gadol-i-Ata Moh'd, Qarya-i-Ahmadi, Qarya-i-Shakhtak (Sinjetak), Gheyab Qalandar (Ghaib Qalandar), Qala-i-Khanjar, Qala-i-Jawz, Isfandeh, Qala-i-Amu, Qala-i-Wali Postin Doz, Qarya-i-Mohammad Ali, Masjed-i-Babaji Sahib, Masjed-i-Utaq-i-Shah, Masjed-i-Shah Abulfateh, Alizai, Qala-i-Shukurkhan, Qala-i-Amir Sahib, Qala-i-Darakhshan, Asfakha, Imalistan Sahib, and Gomali (LWA).
In 1914 Ghazni was described as follows: Elevation 7,279 feet. The principal place in the Ghazni district, distant 89 miles from Kabul via Maidan, 221- 1/2 from Kandahar via Kalat-i-Ghilzai and about 190 from Bannu via the Tochi. It is a decayed town of no miliary strength, and contains only about 1,000 inhabited houses. It is situated on the left bank of the Ghazni river on the level ground between the river and the termination of a spur which here runs east and west from the Gul Koh range: and it may be described as an irregular square, having a total circuit of about 2,175 yards, exclusive of the wall of the citadel. It is surrounded by a high wall (about 30 feet high) built on the top of a mound, in part natural and in part artificial. The wall is partly of stone and brick masonry laid in mud, and partly of clay built in courses in a manner common in Afghanistan. It is flanked at irregular intervals by towers.
The Citadel is perched on the top of an abrupt detached knoll on the north side of the city. It is 150 feet above the plain, and commands the city completely. Its defences are a high masonry wall, loop-holed and provided with a parapet, but no rampart, save the natural hill. There are four towers at the angles, but these are small and insignificant. The citadel has no other strength than that afforded by its commanding situation and formidable slopes; the area of the summit of the knoll is so confined, and the buildings so ill-adapted to withstand shells that when the outer or town wall is carried, a garrison would be able to make but a short defence, if vertical fire were brought into play against them.
The supply of the water in the citadel is very bad, there being only one well inside it, which is generally dry.
The town and citadel are both commanded by the hills to the north, but the former is in a measure sheltered by the citadel rock.
The city itself is composed of dirty irregular streets of houses

several stories high. Round the foot of the citadel rock on the east and west sides, there is a small open space varying from 100 to 50 yards, but on the south side the houses come close up to the scarp of the rock. The streets are very irregular, but from the Kanah gate to the Kandahar gate a street runs with some pretentions to uniformity of breadth and directness of course. Another street leads northeast to the open space on the west of the citadel rock, and from the Kabul gate to the others there is communication by several narow and irregular streets. The houses are built of mud, and have flat roofs in most cases, but in some they are domed.

As a city, Ghazni will not bear any comparison with Kabul or Kandahar, and a previous visit to the Bazars of either would disappoint one in visiting the darkened narrow streets and small "Chaharsu" of Ghazni. However, it posesses snug houses and capital stabling, sufficient for a cavalry brigade, within its walls and in the citadel; particularly the squares and residences of its leading men are in many instances spacious, and even princely in their style and decorations.

The inhabitants are composed of Afghans, Hazara labourers, and perhaps 50 families of Hindu shop-keepers, bankers, and traders. Bellew says they have a look of wretchedness and poverty, and are remarkable only for their ignorance and superstition. They are a very mixed community; the Hazaras here are more numerous than anywhere else in the country, and the Hindus are a thriving race.

The Hindus are required to wear tight trousers instead of loose ones, and a black cap for a turban, and to pay a small tax as infidels. For these concessions they receive protection and even consideration, and are allowed to practise their idolatries in secret; their strange dress and dirty habits are very unlike the Hindus of India, but they are still the same quiet, money-making people.

The chief trade of the place is in corn and fruits and madder all of which are largely produced in the district. Sheep's wool and camel's hair cloth are brought into the market from the adjoining Hazara country. But the trade of Ghazni is not nearly so great as it might be, and this is attributed by Bellw to various circumstances, of which the principal are a want of liberal encouragements on the part of the rulers of the country and the unfavourable situation of the city as well as its severe climate. There are no manufactures carried on at Ghazni, except that of sheepskin coats. (postins).

Water is supplied to the city from the river of Ghazni, and the facility with which it can be turned into the ditches precludes the possibility of its being cut off.

Supplies should be procurable in Ghazni in considerable quantity, especially wheat and barley, as it furnishes Kabul with these articles; and as there are magnificent pastures near it, grass should also be abundant. The food supplies normally available in Ghazni are:

Atta	800 maunds	Wheat	4,000
Dall	50	Barley	5,000
Ghi	200	Rice	500
Salt	80		

Ghazni is celebrated for the excellence of its apples and melons, both of which are supplied to th Kabul market in great quantities, together with apricots and corn. The madder grown in the vicinity is almost all exported to Hindustan. Tobacco and corn are grown only for home consumption; so is the castor-oil plant on account of its oil, which is generally used for domestic, and in a measure even, for culinary purposes. On the capture of Ghazni by the army of the Indus, 500,000 lbs. of wheat and barley and 79,080 lbs. of flour were found in the place.

The climate of Ghazni for several months of the year is very cold. Snow is said to lie on the ground from November to February, but when Lord Cruzon was at Ghazni early in December 1894 there was no snow at all. In summer the heat is said not to equal that of Kabul or Kandahar, though it is rendered disagreeable and injurious by constant dust-storms, whilst the bare rocky heights of Balai (Hisar?) that rise immediately to the north of the city radiate their heat into it and render the night-air close and oppressive.

During the summer and autumn months, fevers of typhoid or bilious type are said to be very prevalent and fatal, whilst in winter the mortality among the people is greater than in other cities of Afghanistan, owing to the severity of the cold and the scarcity of fuel. Wood is not usually to be had for fuel, and its place is supplied by thorny shrubs that grow in the surrounding country though every availabel combustible is also used by the poor.

The view from the citadel is extensive, but by no means inviting; the plain is but indifferently furnished with villages, but there are very many shrines, 197 being the number given. These are for the most part surrounded by orchards, vineyards, and cornfields. Excepting along the course of its river, to the vicinity of which the cultivation and villages are mostly confined, the plain of Ghazni has an empty and bare aspect. The lines of karez cross the road at intervals of 8 or 10 miles on their way to the few villages that are widely scattered over the plain country.

The distant hills extend in low ranges of bare rock, and the country skirting them is a raviny waste, wandered over by a vagabond secton of the Ghilzai tribe, whose immense flocks of goats, sheep, and camels share the pasture with herds of wild deer, which, with wolves, foxes, and hares, are the denizens of this wilderness, in which also tortoises and several species of lizard abound. The black hair tents ("Kizhdi") of these Israelites of the desert are seen dotting the country at frequent intervals, and always occupying the sheltered hollows in its surface for protection from the keen blast of the west wind, which blows with considerable violence during the spring, and, till the sun be well risen, is very bleak and numbing in its effects, and injurious to the eyes from the force with which it drives particles of dust before it. A stunted brushwood, seldom exceeding 3 feet in height, and usually not so high, is scattered over the dreary waste.

The site of the old city, destroyed by the Prince of Ghor, lies 2 1/2 miles to the northeast and is now occupied by the village of Roza.

Probably the earliest authentic notice which history affords of Ghazni is of the date 976, when it was made the seat of government by Abustaken, an adventurer of Bokhara. He was, after a short interval, succeeded by Sabaktagin, the father of the renowned Mahmud, the destroyer. Few pursued the career of conquest with more perseverance or success than Mahmud, whose empire extended from the Tigris to the Ganges, and from the Indian Ocean to the Oxus. It fell to pieces on his death; and in 1151 his capital, Ghazni, was stormed by Allahuddin, Prince of Ghor, who massacred the inhabitants on the spot with the exception of those of rank; these he conveyed to Ghor, and there butchered them, using their blood to moisten the mortar with which he constructed fortifications.

At the time of the first British invasion of Afghanistan, Sir John Keane, moved by the reports he had heard as to the weakness of the defences of Ghazni, left behind all siege guns at Kandahar. On arrival at Ghazni it was closely reconnoitred by the Quartermaster-General and Field Engineer, and found to be very much stronger than they had been led to expect; the obstacles to either mining or escalading were said to be insurmountable, and as there was no siege artillery with the force the only resource left was to attempt a coup-de-main by blowing in the Kabul gate. Here the road to the gate was clear, the bridge over the ditch unbroken; there were good positions for artillery within 300 yards of the walls on both sides of the road, and it was the ony gateway not built up. It was accordingly determined to make the attempt.

"It was arranged that an explosion party, consisting of three officers of Engineers, Captain Peat, Lieutenants Durand and McLeod, 3 sergeants, and 18 men of the sappers in working dress, carrying 300 lbs. of powder in 12 sand bags, with a hose 72 feet long, should be ready to move down to the gateway at daybreak.

"At midnight the first battery left camp, followed by the other four at intervals of half an hour. Those to the right of the road were conducted to their positions by Lieutenant Stuart; those to the left by Lieutenant Anderson. The ground for the guns was prepared by the sappers and Pioneers, taking advantage of the irregularities of the ground to the right, and of some old garden walls to the left.

"The artillery was all in position and ready by 3 A.M. of the 23rd and shortly after, at the first dawn, the party under Captain Peat moved down to the gateway, accompanied by six men of Her Majesty's 13th Light Infantry without their belts, and supported by a detachment of the same regiment, which extended to the right and left of the road. When they arrived at the ditch they took advantage of what cover they could find, and endeavoured to keep down the fire from the ramparts, which became heavy on the approach of the party, though it had been remarkably slack during the previous operations. Blue lights were shown which rendered surrounding objects distinctly visible, but luckily they were burned on the top of the parapet instead of being thrown in to the passage below.

"The explosion party marched steadily on headed by Lieutenant Durand; the powder was placed, the hose laid, the train fired, and the carrying party had retired to tolerable cover in less than two minutes. The artillery opened when the blue lights appeared, and the musketry from the covering party at the same time. So quickly was the operation performed, and so little was the enemy aware of the nature of it, that not a man of the party was hurt.

"As soon as the explosion took place, Captain Peat, although hurt by the concussion, his anxiety preventing him from keeping sufficiently under cover, ran up to the gate, accompanied by a small party of Her Majesty's 13th Light infantry, and ascertained that it was completely destroyed. There was some delay in getting a bugler to sound the advance, the signal agreed on for the assaulting column to push on, and this was the only mistake in the operation.

"The assaulting column, consisting of four European regiments (Her Majesty's 2nd Regiment, Bengal European Regiment, Her Majesty's 13th Light Infantry, and Her Majesty's 17th Regiment) commanded by Brigadier Sale, the advance under Lieutenant-Colonel Dennie, accompanied by Lieutenant Stuart, Engineers, moved steadily through the gateway, through a passage inside the gateway in a domed building, which opening on one side rendered everything very obscure and rendered it difficult to find the outlet into the town. They met with little opposition; but a party of the enemy seeing a break in the column, owing to the difficulty in scrambling over the rubbish in the gateway, made a rush, sword in hand, and cut down a good many men, wounding the Brigadier and several other officers. These swordsmen were repulsed, and there was no more regular opposition; the surprise and alarm of the governor and sardars being so great, when they saw the column occupying the open space inside the gate and firing upon them, that they fled, accompanied by their men, even the garrison of the citadel following their example. Parties of the Afghans took refuge in the houses, firing on the column as it made its way through the streets, and a good deal of desultry fighting took place in consequence, by which some loss was sustained. The citadel was occupied as soon as daylight showed that it had been abandoned by the enemy, and the whole of the works were in our possession before 5 A.M.

"We lost 17 men--6 Europeans and 11 Natives killed, -- 18 officers and 117 Europeans and 30 Natives wounded: total 182. Of the Afghans, more than 514 were killed in the town (that number of bodies having been buried and, and about 100 outside by the cavalry; 1,600 prisoners were taken but there was no means of estimating the number of their wounded. After the capture of this place, a garrison of a detachment of artillery, one regiment of infantry (16th Bengal Native Infantry) and 200 cavalry of the Shah's force, was left in it.

"This was afterwards changed, and at the time of the outbreak in 1841, the 27th Bengal Native Infantry was in garrison, but no repairs had been made in the citadel, nor had any steps been taken to lay in provisions. On the 20th November the enemy appeared, and on the 16th December, aided by the townspeople, they got into the city, forcing the garrison to retire to the citadel. The garrison began to suffer considerable hardship. they were all told off into three watches. The thermometer sank to 14 degrees below zero, two pounds of wood was all that could be allowed for cooking or warmth, and the garrison was put on half rations. 'The sepoys' says officer of the garrison, 'became useless, and if the enemy had had pluck to make a rush, they could have carried the works any day after Christmas Day.' The garrsion held out till the 6th March, when having no longer the snow to rely on for a supply of water, and their provisions being exhausted, they evacuated the citadel. They were then quartered in the town, but on the 7th December they were treacherously attacked by the enemy, and the houses carried and all who were found murdered. On the 10th all the survivors were collected in two houses into which the enemy fired round shot. On that night they surrendered themselves to Shamsh-ud-din Khan; the officers were most brutally treated, the sepoys were sold into slavery or murdered, but when General Nott advanced and occupied Ghazni 327 of the sepoys were recovered."

On the occasion of General Nott's advance, the enemy evacuated Ghazni without fighting, except in a skirmish the day before the town was to have been attacked; but as General Nott proposed to have attacked the city at a different point to that used by Sir J. Keane, it will be useful and interesting to give an extract from the report of Major Sanders, the Engineer in charge of the proposed attack: -- "The guards," he says, "required for the protection and general duties of the camp absorbed so many men that but few were available for the duties of a siege. The General therefore determined not to invest the place in form, and directed the engineer to concentrate the resources at his disposal at one spot, where protection might be most conveniently afforded to the siege operations.

"With advertence to these instructions the engineer proposed to establish a battery on the ridge of the hill north of the town in advance of the village of Balal, and distant about 350 yards from the nearest point of the walls. From this battery it was expected that the four 18-pounder guns would lay open the thin flank wall connecting the citadel on the west with the town wall in a few hours. The defences of the citadel could be swept from the same point by the light artillery, and the lines of loop-holed wall which would bear on the advance of the storming party, were all viewed in enfilade from the site selected for the battery. The advance of the party to the assault would have been greatly facilitated by the existence of a thick dam of earth across the ditch immediately opposite the point marked out for the breach.

"It was further proposed that the principal assault should be supported by two other attacks, one an attempt to blow in the Water gate (both the others having been strongly built up, and the causeways in front of them out through), another to escalade a weak point near the Kabul gate, which would have been greatly aided by the fire of the artillery from the hill.

"This project met with the General's approval, and at dusk on the evening of the 5th September a working party, composed of the sappers and of 160 men from the regiments occupying the hill, commenced work on the battery. By 4 A.M. on the 6th September, cover for the party had been secured across the ridge of the hill, and so much progress made in the execution of the work, as to lead to reasonable expectations that the four 18-pounder guns and two 24-pounde howitzers would be established in position, and ready to open their fire during the day.

"Early on the evening of the 5th, a brisk matchlock fire was kept up from the citadel on the hill, but this gradually slackened, and at 10 P.M. had entirely ceased. The enemy's infantry had been observed at dusk crossing the river near the Water gate, with the intention, it was supposed, of attacking the working party during the night; but towards the morning of the 6th there was ground for believing the fort was evacuated. At daylight this was ascertained to be the case by Lieutenant North, of the Engineers, who took possession at that hour of the Water gate without opposition."

General Nott then gave orders for the destruction of the citadel--a measure which was carried out by Major Sanders.

Ghazni was twice visited by a British force in 1880, viz., in April by Sir Donald Stewart, on his march from Kandahar to Kabul, and in August by Sir Frederick Roberts, on his march from Kabul to Kandahar. On the former occasion an Afghan force was defeated in the vicinity of the town; on the latter, our army was unopposed.

Owing to its being commanded within range from the northwest Ghazni would never be able to resist the attack of a modern European army; yet its position is of strategical importance, whether considered as part of a line of defence against an enemy advancing from the west, or as a position giving an invader from the east a dominance over all the country of Afghanistan. I shall therefore make no apology for lengthening this article by the introduction of the following report drawn up in April 1880 by Captain Larminie, R.E., attached to Sir Donald Stewart's staff:--

"Taking into consideration that full accounts already exist regarding the position and situation of Ghazni in a geographical and descriptive point of view, it appears unnecessary to make any further remark beyond stating that its height above sea-level appears to have been over-estimated by several hundreds of feet, and that the perimeter or total circuit of walls given in former reports as 1,750 yards, inclusive of the citadel wall, is, after careful measurement, found to be 2,115 yards, without the wall of the citadel being included. With a few slight exceptions to be noted hereafter, nothing whatever, either in the shape of repairs or new buildings, appears to have been done since the date of our last occupancy, nearly forty years ago; hence the whole has fallen into a state of ruin and decay. A ruined citadel, broken and useless parapets, cracked and tumbled-down towers, crumbling curtain walls, and a silted-up ditch, are all that remain of the once famous stronghold of Ghazni.

"At the present moment a breach exists, extending from the terre-plein of the citadel to the main ditch on the western front; and in two places in the southern face gaps caused by the falling down of portions of the curtain walls have been so feebly repaired and are so accessible, that a party of sappers could, with crowbars and other tools, form practicable breaches in the course of a few minutes, and that without any loss, as the flanking towers are here utterly broken down and useless. Even were these points non-existent, there are but comparatively few of the curtains capable of withstanding the explosion of a few bags of powder, without falling down and forming more or less practicable breaches. Indeed, such is the wretchedly feeble condition of some of these walls that a battery of field artillery would probably be able to breach them with but a very small expenditure of ammunition.

"The original brick and stone facing has, speaking generaly, stripped and fallen off the walls and towers, leaving the earthen backing exposed to the weather, resulting in a considerable diminution of the original thickness, and the consequent weakness has been further increased by portions of the wall and rampart having been hollowed out behind to serve as dwelling-places for some of the city people.

"The Mur de rondes or fause braie, as it was termed in former reports has, with the exception of that one front, almost entirely disappeared, and has, apparently with the upper portion of the scarp, slipped or been washed down into the ditch, which has consequently become shallow, and of little value as an obstacle.

"No further demolition would render Ghazni less important than it is as a fortress, and taking into consideration its very defective construction, and the fact that from its situation a command of fire and observation will always be attainable over the whole of it, no amount of repair could give it any real importance, or cause any loss of time in reducing it.

"Northern face.--Has suffered less from decay than any of the others. The Mur de rondes is in a good state of preservation and the ditch has not silted up. The parapet also is still in fair order, but inside the rampart has fallen away from it in many places, leaving it without banquette, and in others houses have been built up so as to render it useless. The Kabul gateway appears to have been cleared and to a certain extent repaired, since it was blown in by us, and the screen wall is also in fair order. The walls of this face are decayed but not entirely stripped of the outer facing, and some of the towers are fairly perfect; but owing to the ruinous state of the rampart on the inside this front has no real strength so far as the wall is concerned.

"Eastern face.--Here the Mur de rondes has disappeared, and the slopes of the ditch become more easy. The Kandahar or Bazar gateway in this face consists of a domed building with gates opening straight through, and not as the Kabul gateway, where the inner gate is at right angles to the first or outer. There is a broken down tower and screen wall in front of that Kandahar gateway, but not of a sufficient height to serve its purpose. The ditch in front of this gateway has been filled up for a length of about 15 yards. The walls of this front are much damaged, and a partial gap has been repaired by a wall, which, though carried up to nearly the origial height, is thin and constructed of broken bricks, small stones, and rubbish without any binding material.

"The large tower or bastion between this face and the southern is, perhaps, the best preserved portion of the whole fortress, and was apparently added after the original design of Ghazni had been completed. The brickwork is still in great part perfect, but as the upper portion is merely a thin wall with rooms inside, the strength of this tower is more apparent than real.

"Southern face.--Is in a miserable condition as regards defensive power. Two of its curtains have had large gaps filled to a height of 15 or 20 feet, with mere apologies for walls. The Mur de rondes has entirely disappeared and the ditch, which is here at a considerable distance from the walls, has become a mere shallow puddle, and as the foundations of the walls are here but little above the level of the edge of the ditch, it is a perfectly easy slope from the ditch to the wall. The towers on this side are much split and fallen down, and the Kaneh or Water gateway, has lost one of its towers, has no screen wall, and, like the Kandahar gateway, opens straight into the town, whilst in front, and for many yards on each side, the ditch has been filled up. The outwork which formerly existed on the right bank of the Ghazni river, protecting the approach to the bridge in front of this gateway has nearly disappeared, only a mound about 6 feet high and 40 feet by 26 feet, with a couple of wing walls, now remains.

"Western face.--Derives any strength it may possess from the steep slope upon which the wall is built, as there is no rampart whatever, and the wall is pierced by many openings serving as windows to the houses built against the interior. In this face is the breach already a spoken of, as extending from the citadel downward.

"Citadel.--A house with courtyard, occupying in all an area of 90 feet by 150 feet, has been built on the terre-plein, otherwise nothing has been done since the towers, etc., were blown down in 1842. The new building has no loopholes or other means of defence. One of the towers at the end has a balcony and glass windows.

"Well.--The well is lined with brick, is 4 feet 6 inches in diameter, has a depth of 73 feet, and has at present 2 feet of water in it.

"Magazine.--A rectangular enclosure with walls about 20 feet in height and 2 or 3 feet thick, with a building inside consisting of a series of domes of but little strength. The amount of ammunition, etc., found was but small.

"Guns.--The guns found were ten in number, all brass or bronze; four about 3 inches average diameter, and six 3-pounders.

"City.--Is merely an assemblage of wretched houses with nothing deserving the name of street."

The British camp of April 1880 was about a mile northeast of the town. There is a bridge over the river close to the west angle of the town, and another lower down southwest of the town, by which the Kandahar road crosses. The former is described as being a well-built structure, capable of carrying guns. The garrison of Ghazni at the present time (1906) is believed to be 1 Regiment of Cavalry, 15 guns (mountain and field) 3 batteries of infantry and 400 khasadars. (1882 edition, Curzon, I.B.C.)

GHAZNI (RIVER) غزنی رود

A river formed in a little valley 14 miles N. N. W. of Ghazni from three rivulets which formerly met and flowed through different channels fertilizing a few fields and then being lost. These streams are:--Gardan-i-Masjid from the northeast; Barikao (i.e., the Sar-i-ab) from the southwest; and the Shimiltu from the northwest. According to Broadfoot, "Mahmud of Ghazni dammed up all but one outlet, and thus caused the present river. It issues from here a stream in the dry season, 20 feet wide, 2 feet deep and with a velocity of 5 feet per second. In spring it is much larger. The Band-i-Sultan, by which this is effected, is a wall of masonry closing a rocky valley. The dam when complete must have been 300 yards long, its height varying from 20 to 30 feet, and its thickness from 6 to 7. In autumn, when the ploughing is over, and the water no longer required, the outlet is shut, and a lake fills the valley 600 yards wide with a greatest depth of about 30 feet. In spring, when cultivation begins, the orifice is opened and the stream rushes out in several cascades giving the whole water of the year in the season it is required. From the city of Ghazni the river passes between Shilghar and Nani, sending off many irrigation cuts, till the water, after 10 or 12 miles, becomes much less, and its bank too steep. It next runs west of Pannah and Khogh Hilal between Dokuvi and Abband; in this desolate tract it is strongly impregnated with salt, and falls into the Ab-i-Istada lake, where a curious circumstance occurs. The fish brought by the stream fromt he upper parts, on entering the salt part, sicken and die, so that they may be taken by the hand in all stages of sickness." (Broadfoot, I.B.C., Johnston.)

GHAZNI HAZARAS   (See Military Report on Hazarajat, Part I.)   غزنی هزاره

*GHILZAI   غلزی (غلجی)
33-30   69-21 m.   A village northwest of Shewak and some 10 miles southeast of Ghazni. Another place with this name is located in the Tutakhel area, northeast of Gardez, at 33-42   69-29 m.

GHILZAI   غلزی
The Ghaljai (plural Ghalji) as he calls himself--Ghilzai, as strangers call him--is a numerous and widespread people who may roughly speaking, be said to inhabit the country bounded by Kalat-i-Ghilzai on the south, the Gul Koh range on the west, the Sulaiman on the east, and the Kabul river on the north. In many places they overflow these boundaries, as to the east they come down into the tributaries of the Gomal, and on the north they, in many places, cross the Kabul river and extend to the east, along its course, at least as far as Jalalabad. This country is about 300 miles long, and 100 miles broad in its south portion, and 35 miles in the north.
All travellers agree in putting the southern boundary of the Ghilzais on the Kandahar road at a stone bridge at Asia Hazara, 12 miles south of Kalat-i-Ghilzai. We know also that Maruf belongs mostly to the Barakzais, though it is very close to the Ghilzai frontier. On the route from Quetta to Ghazni, Poti is the last village mentioned as inhabited by Barakzai Duranis. Beyond this there appear to be no villages for some miles. A line, therefore, drawn from Asia Hazara to just north of Maruf, and thence north of the Lowana country to the Kandil-Kundar confluence, and then along the Kundar to Domandi will give us the approximate south boundary.
From Domandi the boundary line runs north and northeast including all the Kharoti country about the sources of the Gumal. Thence it continues along the crest of the Sulaiman range, skirting the Jadran and Mangal country except in one place, viz., Dara, a pass leading from Zurmat to the Jaji country where it encroaches rather on the Mangals.
On the Kurram route, Jaji Thana marks the boundary between the Ghilzais and Jajis, and thus the boundary again oversteps the main range.
From this the wave which has come down to Jaji Thana recedes to the crest of the Safed Koh, whence the stream of Ghilzai encroachment turns east, keeping for the most part pretty high up on the north

slopes of the Safed Koh as far as Jalalabad, whence one body of the Ahmadzai section crosses the Kabul river and stretches into the Kunar valley for a short distance; whilst another body crosses the Kabul river between the junction of the Alingar and Tagao river.
Near Jagdalak the limits of the Ghilzais come down to near the Kabul river, indeed almost to its banks, and follow the south bank of the river to its source in the Sanglakh range, whence to the parallel of Asia Hazara it follows the crest of the range called the Gul Koh, and thence it descends to the stone bridge on the Kandahar road from whence we started. I do not mean to say that the whole of this space is inhabited exclusively by Ghilzais for numerous other tribes, as Wardaks, Barakzais, Hazaras, Tajiks, etc., occasionally occupy lands within it; yet in these limits Ghilzai influence and power reign supreme, except, of course, within Kabul itself.
The Ghilzais, whose limits have thus been approximately defined, are described by Captain (now Major Sir A.H.) McMahon as follows:
"The Ghilzais are descendants of "Ghalzoe," i.e., the 'son of a thief' or 'illicit son' of Shah Husain, a Tajik, Chief of Ghor, and Bibi Mato, the daughter of Bait or Baitani, so called from the fact of his birth within three months of the marriage of his parents. (Shaikh Baitan, or Batan, was the second son of Kais, the great ancestral progenitor of the Afghan nationality. Bibi Mato had a second son, who was named Ibrahim, and he was surnamed Loe, or "Great"--see "Lohana.") Authorities differ as to the genealogy of the various branches of the vast tribe who claim descent from Ghalzoe. The following genealogies are the result of a course of enquiries extending over the last five years from numerous trustworthy and intelligent members of the tribe. I have been obliged to restrict my researches to the sections of the tribe who reside nearest the border of present British territory. Regarding the more distant sections, who have little connection with our border, I have been able to add but little information to that already recorded in Gazetteers.
"From Ghalzoe are descended the two main divisions of the tribe named Turan and Burhan with their main branches as follows:

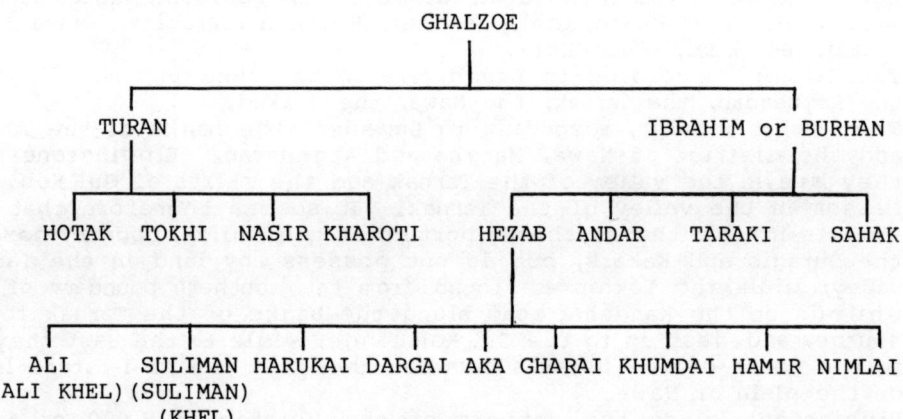

"Much doubt exists as to whether the Nasirs and Kharotis are pure Ghilzais. They themselves claim to be so, but the other Ghilzais deny this claim. It is more probable that the founders of those tribes were originally only hamsayas of the Turan tribes, Hotaks and Tokhis."
The Sulaiman Khel are the largest and most important of all the Ghilzai sections, while they and the Ali Khel are the most important of the Burhans. A full account of the several sections will be found

203

under their respective headings, the Hotakis, Tokhis and Tarakis being dealth with in "Volume 5" as they are more or less connected with the Kandahar province. Lumsden divides the Turans thus:
Ohtak, subdivided, 1 Sakzai, 2 Tunzai, 3 Satkhel, 4 Shagri; but according to Leech they are divided as follwos; viz., Malizai; Khadzai; Tadzak; Baratzai; Ramzai; Umarzai; Tunzai; Thari; Satkhel; Yusufkhel; Marufzai; Utmankhel; Isakzai; Akazai; Baizai; Babazai; Saghazdai; Alizai; Polad. The Isakzai he again subdivides into Katizai, Kadinzai, Kandalzai, Hadizai, Umarzai, Maudin Khel.

Lumsden gives no division of the section he calls Hotaki, and as no one else but him gives the division Ohtak, it is probable that Ohtak and Hotaki sections are one and the same, and this belief is confirmed by comparing some of Lumsden's divisions of the Ohtaks, viz., Sakzai, Tunzai, Satkhel with Leech's of the Hotakis, in which the same divisions appear, viz., Isakzai, or Sakzai, Tunzai, and Satkhel.

Lumsden says the Ohtaks occupy all the ocuntry of Kalat-i- Ghilzai, and south until they meet the Kakars and Tarins. Broadfoot also agrees with him, saying they dwell north from Maruf, as does Leech, who says they are found in Margha, which is in the extreme south of the Ghilzai country. Masson, however, and Elphinstone place them north of the Tokhis.

The Tokhis are thus subdivided by Lumsden: 1, Shah Alam Khel; 2, Shah-ud-din Khel; 3, Kalu Khel; 4, Miranzai; 5, Jalalzai; 6, Bakarzai; 7, Pir Khel; 8, Likaki; 9, Amu Khan.

Leech however, gives the divisions of the Tokhis thus: 1, Kishyanis; 2, Bata Khel; 3, Jalalzai; 4, Parozai; 5, Baso Khel; 6, Ayubzai; 7, Miranzai; 8, Nur Khel; 9, Muhammadzai; 10, Akazai.

The Jalalzai section he again subdivides into Firoz Khel, Bahram Khel, Najo Khel, Nano Khel, Sizai, Bahlol Khel.

The Pirozai are probably the same as Lumsden's Pir Khel, he subdivides -- Sayyid Khel, Ashozai, Iraki, Surezai.

The Miranzai, a section also given by Lumsden, are subdivided by Leech into Nuradin, Akazai, Uhwazai, Sen Khel, Moghalzai; and the Muhammadzai into Pirak Khel, Kalu Khel, Isezai, Fakirzai, Babri, Burhan Khel, Patozai, Musazai, Karmu Khel, Bahlozai, Natozai, Pirwali Khel, Shah Hasan Khel, Adamzai, Hotakzai, Arabizai, Musa Khel, Saizai, Bazikzai, Khan Khel.

The Tokhis, according to Leech, are to be found in the valleys of the Arghandab, the Tarnak, the Nawa, the Khakad.

The Tokhis inhabit, according to Lumsden, the banks of the Tarnak and the district of Nawa, Margha and Arghastan. Elphinstone says they live in the valley of the Tarnak and the skirts of Gul Koh, and Masson in the valley of the Tarnak. It seems, therefore that the Hotakis inhabit the southeast portion of the Ghilzai country next to the Duranis and Kakars, but do not possess any land in the Tarnak valley; while the Tokhis are found from the southern boundary of the Ghilzais on the Kandahar road along the banks of the Tarnak to its source, and west up to the Gul Koh range, while to the east they go to the north of the Hotakis between them and the Ab-i-Istada lake, on the plain of Nawa.

Elphinstone gives the numbers of the Hotakis at 5,000 or 6,000 families, and of the Tokhis at 12,000. Broadfoot agrees in this estimate. Molloy estimates the Hotakis at 7,000, and the Tokhis at 20,000 families. Leech says the Hotakis furnished 500 horsemen and the Tokhis 2,000 to the king in former days. Masson says the latter are more numerous than the former, and, lastly, Lumsden estimates them together at 60,000 souls.

According to the second edition of the Gazetteer, the Ibrahim or Burhan division appears to be divided as follows: 1, Zabar Khel; 2,

Sulaiman Khel; 3, Alikhel; 4, Andaris; 5, Tarakis. Besides these, Lumsden has the Umar Khel, Adamzai, Chalozai, Chinzai sections, which are not mentioned by any one else. The Khojaks are mentioned by Outram, Broadfoot, and Lumsden.

Zabar Khel, given by Lumsden, are not mentioned by any other authority.

Sulaiman Khel are subdivided by Elphinstone into Kaisar Khel, Samalzai (Shah Momalzai of Lumsden), Astanazai, Ahmadzai, Babikar Khel. Of these the Babikar Khel are subdivided by Lumsden into Sherpai and Sak (probably the Serpai of Elphinstone and the Sahak of him and others). These again are divided into Uria Khel, Utkhel, Utman Khel, Kharoti, Mir Ali Khel, Edu Khel, and Umar Khel; these generally occupy the lands about Gandamak, Tezin, and Jalalabad, and are chiefly engaged in pastoral pursuits, with the exception of the Utkhel and a few fellow-spirits from among the others, who are notorious throughout Afghanistan as a pack of plundering villains, adepts at cattle-lifting and burglary. Many of the most daring robberies committed in the former days at Peshawar were known to have been the handiwork of these miscreants. The Kaisar Khel are given by Elphinstone as a division of the Sulaiman Khel, who inhabit the southeast of Ghazni, sharing Zurmat with the Ali Khel, and moving in the winter to Wano. Lumsden merely mentions them as a section of the Ibrahim division, and says they move about the district of Ghazni, Daba, and Maidan. They number about 5,000 families. The same may be said of the Samalzai or Ismailzai, as Elphinstone terms them, or Shahmomalzai according to Lumsden. They are found, according to Leech at Shibar, Halatagh, Setz, and Mandan.

The Kalandar Khel is a branch of this section.

The Astanazais are given by Elphinstone as a division of the Sulaiman Khel and though Broadfoot does not say so, he implies that he so considers them. Lumsden does not state that they are connnected with this division, nor does he say anything to the contraray. They have 21 subdivisions, and inhabit Logar and Maidan north of the Wardaks. Their numbers are not given, though Elphinstone states them to be more numerous than the Ahmadzais.

The Ahmadzais hold the Shutur Gardan Kotal, and they inhabit during summer the mountains of Surkhel and Safed Koh, while in winter they are found in Kurram and Tezin.

The Kaisar Khel and Samalzai are given at 5,000 each; it is therefore probable that the Astanazai or Sultanzai number 15,000 and the Ahmadzai 12,000 families.

The Babikar Khel of Lumsden are probably the same as the Babakarzais of Leech. The latter says they are found at Swadzai Jangir, Sar-i-Asp, Shah Mardan and Nawa.

Elphinstone says the Sherpai are not a clan, but an association formed out of all the clans and number 6,000 men.

The Sahaks are not mentioned at all by Lumsden, though they are by Elphinstone, Broadfoot, Gerard, and McMahon. They occupy one third of Kharwar and two-thirds of Paghman, and also, according to Broadfoot, a part of Dara. They number 5,000 ot 6,000 families.

The Ali Khel inhabit the northeast portion of Zurmat, according to Elphinstone and Broadfoot, though Lumsden places them about Mukur. They are agricultural in habits, and number perhaps 5,000 families. Elphinstone is uncertain where to place the Kharotis, but Lumsden includes them in the Ahmadzais.

The division of the Andaris occupy the side district of Shilghar and Zurmat, and are also found in Dehsai and parts of Pannah. They number 12,000 families according to Elphinstone and Broadfoot. Lumsden says they are a powerful division, and Leech gives the number of their horsemen at 600. They are both agricultural and pastoral in their habits.

The Tarakis are subdivided by Leech into Babadinkhel; Sakkhel; Firozkhel; Isoikhel; Garbazkhel; Nakhel.

It is difficult to reconcile the localities said to be occupied by this tribe. Elphinstone says they have Mukur and the country south of it as far as the southern boundaries of the Ghilzais. Masson says they also border on the frontiers of Kandahar, and are east of the Tokhis, and also in Mukur and Karabagh. Broadfoot says they stretch from Gilan and Lalizai to Karabagh; and Lumsden says they lie west of Ghazni, between the Ab-i-Istada lake and the mountains of Nur. They appear to be scattered: some are to be found in the district of Nawa, south of lake Ab-i-Istada (Broadfoot, N. Campbell), some in the north of Mukur and south of Karabagh (Gerard), others north of Ab-i-Istada, between Zazgai and Dila (Broadfoot), and others in Tirwah. The Tarakis are pastoral and are known as the most respectable and well-disposed of their race. They move in the winter into the Durani country, and some of them into the Derajat. Elphinstone estimates them at 12,000 families, and Broadfoot agrees with him. Lumsden says nothing of their number, and Masson says they are less numerous than the Tokhi, a statement in which Leech impliedly agrees, stating that the number of horse required from them is only 600. Lastly Molloy computes them at 25,000 families.

The Umar Khel occupy Maidan and the country drained by the Surkhab.

The Adramzai, says Lumsden, are all shepherds, and herd their flocks in Gumran, Safed Sang and the lower portions of the Logar valley.

McGregor, writing of the Ghilzais who swell in the district of Jalalabad, says they are of the Adramzai, Manuzai, and Utkhel branches. They seek their livelihood by theft, plunder, and burglary. The Manuzai are to be found in a hilly tract of country at a place called Taran in the Kama district. The Adramzai at Mir-i-obi near Mazina in the Shinwari country, and the Utkhel in Darunta, Lahak, Kotaki, and Sangin.

The Chalozai, mentioned by Lumsden only, hold the Sojawan hills between Logar and Ghazni.

The Chinzai are one of Lumsden's division, but they are not mentioned by any one else. They occupy Bini Badam, with grazing grounds in Maidan, and on the east slopes of the Paghman hills.

Elphinstone does not mention the Khojaks, though Broadfoot and Lumsden do, placing them among the Sulaiman Khel. No one mentions their exact locality, but Outram attached one of their forts in the Koh-i-Jadran, 20 miles east of Kalalgu; so it is not improbable that they inhabit the west slopes of those mountains and east portion of Zurmat.

It will be observed that the above accounts differ considerably from Captain McMahon's division of the tribe, but as it is desirable to have all available opinions on a subject which may be of great importance, and about which we at present know really very little, I have given them for what they may be worth.

The total strength of the Ghilzais is estimated by various authorities as follows:

Elphinstone	99,000 families
Masson	35 to 50,000 fighting men
Broadfoot	100,000 families
Lumsden	200,000 souls

From these it is quite impossible to choose with any certainty; Broadfoot is, perhaps, our best authority on this subject. He travelled more amongst them than anyone else, who has given us the benefit of his experience, and he is a very accurate and careful writer.

Lumsden is of opinion that 30,000 good fighting men is the total defensive strength of the Ghilzais: but as they never can be united owing to the endless feuds amongst them, he thinks more than 3,000 or 4,000 could not be got together for offensive operations out of their own country. This, however, must be taken cum grano, for though it might be impossible to collect more than 3,000 or 4,000 Ghilzais to obey one chief for his own ends, there can be little doubt the prospect of plunder would place the whole fighting strength of the clan at the disposal of anyone who could satisfy them of his power to furnish them with such delights.

Besides the above regular clansmen, there are several mixed families of Ghilzais settled in the Herat and Farah provinces, who are supposed to be descendants of those families who were transported from Kandahar by Nadir Shah to make room for his Persian followers. These are roughly calculated at 18,000 houses. In the Obeh district alone there are some 2,000 families.

Elphinstone says there are some Ghilzais still settled in Persias at Khabis in Nurmashir, probably the descendants of some of the Ghilzai conquerors of Persia.

Masson remarks that the Ghilzais, although considered and calling themselves Afghans, and moreover employing the Pushto or Afghan dialect, are undoubtedly a mixed race. The name is evidently a modification or corruption of that of Khalji or Khilichi, that of a great Turki tribe mentioned by Sharafudin in his history of Taimur, who describes a portion of it as being at that time settled about Savah and Kum, in Persia, and where they are still to be found. It is probable that the Hotak and Tokhi families particularly are of Turki descent, as may be the Taraki and Andari, and that they were located in this part of the country is evident from the testimony of Ferishta, who describing the progress of the Muhammadan arms, calls them Ghilji and Khiliji, and notes that in conjunction with the tribes of Ghor and of Kabul, they united, A.H. 943, with the Afghans of Bangash and Peshawar to repel the attacks of the Hindu princes of Lahore.

The testimony of Ferishta, while clearly distinguishing the Ghilzai tribes from the Afghans, also establishes the fact of their early conversion to Islam; still there is a tradition that they were at some time Christians of the Armenian and Georgian churches. It is asserted that they relapsed or became converts to Muhammadanism from not having been permitted by their pastors to drink buttermilk on fast days--a whimsical cause, truly, for secession from a faith; yet not so whimsical but that, if the story be correct, is might have influenced a whimsical people. This tradition is known to the Armenians of Kabul, and they instance, as corroborating it, the practice observed by the Ghilzais of embroidering the front parts of the gowns or robes of their females and children with figures of the cross; and the custom of their housewives, who previous to forming their dough into cakes, cross their arms over their breasts, and make the sign of the cross on their foreheads after their own manner.

Referring to the Afghan account of the origin of the word Ghilzai, or "Ghal Zoe," Bellew remarks:--"it seems to point to an early mixture of the original Ghilji with some tribe of Ghor, perhaps of Persian descent, though the name Batan sounds of Indian origin (the Sanskrit name of Brahman priests being Bata), and the title of Shaikh being the one usually applied in India to converts from Brahmanism to Islam."

The Ghilzais were originally a pastoral race, and many sections of the tribe still retain their nomadic habits, for as surely as the spring and autumn come round, they will be found packing up their worldly goods and chattels and moving off to more congenial climes.

On these occasions the sheep are sent on a month before, and followed at intervals by the cattle and camels, the women, children, and baggage being carried on the latter. The grazing grounds of these tribes, both in the hills and plains, are apportioned off, and are as well known, even in the wildest country, as the gardens and fields of more civilized races; and as a Ghilzai is always buried close to the encampment in which he may happen to die, it becomes a point of honour among these tribes never to give up an inch of ground which the clan has once occupied, as it may be the last resting place of some of their ancestors, and it is easy to imagine that this feeling alone leads to frequent and bloody feuds.

The Ghilzais neither dwell in cities nor practise any handicraft or trades, procuring their living by agriculture or pasturage. Their country, without the heat and rains of India, requires more for a harvest than scratching the soil and scattering the seed. Necessity has forced them to make irrigation canals from the rivers and "karez" from every spring. They are rewarded for their toil by good crops and neat farms. Unlike the Tajiks, they cultivate no fruit, but occasional melons. But the wheat for their own food, and barley, lucerne, and clover for the cattle, are of excellent quality and grown only for home consumption. Madder is much produced to barter for cloth to the trading tribes.

The fields belong to the head of the family, who, with seven or eight houses or relations, inhabits a little fort above his cultivation. The fort is an enclosure 40 or 50 yards square, the mud wall is 3 feet thick below, and at top at each angle has round towers with loopholes. The houses are generally 9 feet high and about 12 feet square, the walls of mud, and the roofs of brushwood hurdle covered with clay; to the south the roofs are made of little arches of unburnt brick. The houses being generally built round the fort, the roofs serve as a rampart from whence a loophole fire can be brought to bear. The space in the centre serves for cattle, and the towers for storehouses of forage and grain. These forts are intended to keep off enemies without cannon or scaling ladders and they answer the purpose simply and well.

A large proportion of the Sulaiman Khel and some others are pastoral; they live in rude tents, made of two rough poles supported by hair ropes, on which they hang coarse blankets of their own making. Each family possesses its own flock and a few camels, a tent, two or three iron cooking pots and wooden bowls, with a few sacks of flour. When several families move and live in concert, they form a "khel." While the men watch the flocks with arms by their sides, the women make "kurut" and cheese for winter; buttermilk and bread for the daily consumption. On the march they help to lead the camels and pack the tents; they are decently dressed in a brown petticoat and veil, but seldom cover their face unless impudently stared at. Their features are regular, but somewhat masculine, and their figures tall and good. They marry late and keep their looks a long time. The father of a young man, who wants a wife, proposes for his son to the bride's father previously feeling his way carefully, as a refusal may cause a feud; then, ensues a long scene of bargaining, at last ended by an agreement, that the bridegroom shall give a feast and certain presents of clothes, sheep, and cattle; this is not a bargain for the girl, but to satisfy the neighbours that her friends will not give her to a beggar. The expense of a marriage is about Rs. 100 in the poor classes, hence men are often 35 or 50, and generally 28 or 30, before they can afford the money. The obstinacy of the custom prevents the price being lowered, though many fathers would be happy to give their daughters for nothing were they not ashamed. The desire to get married makes the Afghan sometimes trade and oftener plunder. When all is arranged, he is admitted to see her once or twice (alone and at night) before the ceremony; if the young couple forget themselves, it is not enquired after by her friends, but the mother rates the girl soundly and calls her a "bad-zat;" but should the male relations actually hear of it, a bloody feud is the result. The fear of death makes them chaste in general. This curious custom is not intended to prevent people marrying who do not like each other, as the bargain is fixed before the lover is admitted, but seems a childish experiment in the strength of virtue under temptation.

The pastoral Ghilzais are all robbers; when stimulated by idleness or hunger, they sally out on foot and carry off the cattle of some weak tribes or look out for traveller on a road. There is no calculating on half barbarians, sometimes they spill his blook like water, at others they only rob him; if he is well dresssed, they exchange his fine clothes for their filthy rags, and send him away in the dress of a beggar; this is thought nothing of. Occassionally they give him a blanket when they find him naked. Unless stimulated by despair or to defend their families, the pastoral Ghilzais seldom show much courage, but fight at long range and against weaker parties. If they return laden with spoil, their wives receive them with new affection, and the children are decked with plunder. In the Sulaiman range, Broadfoot saw several ruffians with their children and their horses decked out with necklaces of the new Company's rupees, which as well as the "gutki" of Bokhara, are admired for the image; there was no mistaking how they had got them.

The Ghilzais generally are wealthy in flocks, but have no manufactures except coarse carpets and felt, sacking, and other rough articles for domestic use prepared from wool and camel hair.

They have no weights or measures; one shepherd settles with another, how many of his handfuls equal a Kabul seer, or how many of some peculiar wooden bowl.

Each of the tribes is divided into numerous khel, and each khel into a few families. The natural head of each family is implicitly obeyed. The oldest by descent of these heads of families is usually, not always, the malik of the khel, with a power but little obeyed. It is understood that the head of the senior khel is chief of the tribe. He dare not collect any income from his tribe, living on the produce of his own lands, and appropriating by fraud part of the duties on infidels and merchandise, and on the obedient tribes part of the royal taxes. Among the eastern tribes he uses his influence to head plundering expeditions and procure a good share in the spoil. His seniority in birth makes the Afghans pay him the respect of an elder brother, but nothing more. If his character is disliked, he has not even that; the lowest of his tribe eat, drink, and smoke with him. In urgent danger the Khan is often set aside and a "khelwashti" or leader is chosen, and while the danger lasts is pretty well obeyed.

The Ghilzais had kings when they were conquering Persia, and were not taxed for their support. They say they had them before; if so, they were merely nominal ones. The Ghilzais then appear to be a nation of families, or a little federation of men connected by blood, submitting to their natural heads, union among these societies is their common language and descent from one stock; they are in a transitory state from pastoral to agricultural life, and low in the scale of civilization.

The Ghilzais do pay some attention to the code of customs known as the Pakhtun Wali, the grand precepts of which are hospitality to stangers, obedience to parents and elders, and revenge for the injuries of kindred. No allusion is made to paying taxes and following kings. Their injunctions clearly point back to a nomad state of society, where a man depended on his immediate relations, not on laws, for protection, and when to refuse hospitality was equivalent to murder. These precepts are most closely followed by the more barbarous tribes.

On a visit of importance a sheep is killed, made into "kababs" on a ramrod, and served on cakes of leavened bread. The guest and his followers sit on the best carpets, and eat according to their station out of dishes, pewter or wooden bowls. The host stands behind pressing them respectfully to eat. After washing the hands and smoking the "chilam," a horse or camel is brought for the guest's acceptance. The horses of the stranger are all amply fed. In this manner, says Broadfoot, I have been entertained several times; the common people confine their attentions to a hearty welcome and profusion of their own coarse food.

The revenging of wrongs is the worst part of Pakhtun Wali, and encourages feuds more than it punishes aggressions. Two men quarrel in a field, and one strikes or wounds the other; the relations take it up. They meet on some occasion fight and kill a man; from that moment the quarrel is deadly; if of different tribes and the quarrel important, the whole tribes go to feud. Once in Zurmat, Broadfoot saw a fort shut by rolling a stone against the door instead of with the usual heavy chain; on enquiry as to the cause of such carelessness, the malik a fine old man with a plump, good-humoured face, stretched his arm out towards the line of distant forts and said--"I have not an enemy." It was a pleasing exception to the rule; feuds are a system of petty warfare carried on by long shots, stealing cattle, and burning crops. Samson burning his neighbour's crop acted just like an Afghan. When the harvest is nearly ripe, neither party dare sleep. When the enemies are distant, the feud often lasts for generations; but when they are neighbours, it becomes an intolerable nuisance. Pakhtun Wali devises a remedy. This is to let both parties fight till the same number are killed on each side, then their neighbours step in and effect a reconciliation called "nanawat." the party who first draws blood is looked on as the aggressor whatever may have been his provocation: he pays the expense of a feast, and gives some sheep and cloth as an atonement to the others. But in case this ideal of equal justice cannot be procured by one party having more killed than others, the price of the reconciliation is much higher; but it never exceeds a feast and a few virgins. These girls are not given as concubines but are married and well treated. The expense of marriage being so heavy, to get so many of their young men well married without expense is a great object and a real money compensation. The other party do not like it however, as to give Afghan virgins without getting presents is thought a want of spirit.

A fertile source of dispute is the right to water. In Katawaz is a spot called Khuni Karez, or the bloody spring. It has been claimed and stoutly contested by two tribes. One party would occupy it and bring crops nearly to perfection. Then a constant skirmishing began, on one side to destroy the grain, on the other to preserve it; but the first is more easily done than the latter, and the cultivation was always laid waste. In these combats the water was often stained with blood; hence its name. It now has not a trace of cultivation. The respect for their elders is a trait in the Afghan character; and the reason for this is, the young people are as ignorant as beasts, they know nothing but their genealogies and the confession of faith. Without any means of education but their individual experience, they for many years plough the earth, and then commit crimes and excesses. By degrees their wild independent life makes them rely on their own judgment, and gives them an acquaintance with human nature, at least in its Afghan form. As they get old, they are constantly employed about reconciling feuds, or arranging marriages in which they have to reason with some, flatter others, and browbeat a third; their fine climate and temperate habits preserve their faculties for a long time. They are much superior to the young or middle-aged men, and respected accordingly. Pakhtun Wali, though a code good enough for wandering shepherds,— for when land and water were abundant for all, it tended to foster the best virtues of barbarians and probably produced a simple, hospitable, spirited race,—has not kept pace with increase of population, its present influence on the Afghan character being bad. These feuds cannot be carried on without falsehood, treachery, and meanness, and their skulking guerilla warfare is not favourable to courage. The hospitality daily tends to a mere worthless form. All this is very observable in the Ghilzai country.

The old system of taxation among the Ghilzais was a very bad one. The Khan directed the khel to bring their quota, and presently lots of rotten sheep and toothless camels arrived at his gate. These were bought on the king's account at high prices, and sold at what they fetched. Blankets, grain, and a little money made up the remainder. There was always a deficiency in the amount, and the Khan usually took half of what he received, and gave the king the rest with an apology; sometimes the king allowed him to take a certain share. This kind of thing has no doubt been placed on a far different footing by the present Amir.

The people of Katawaz, with all their discord, have united more than once. Some years ago, says Broadfoot, a son of Dost Muhammad, Afzal Khan, tried to reduce Zurmat; his troops penetrated by Kalagu along the western line of the forts of the Andars. Some he destroyed, others he passed; but at Nushkhel, he was met by nearly all Katawaz, and was defeated. Again, when our army approached Ghazni, the Sulaiman Khel, allured by reports of our wealth and effeminacy, and excited by Dost Muhammad speaking of the nang-da-pakhtana (Afghan honour), and the Mullas promising heaven to those killed by infidels, came in a tumultuous rush from all quarters; but the head of the throng being promptly charged, the whole dispersed. Again when the force with Captain Outram arrived at Misal Khel, many of the tribes burned their grain and forage to prevent us entering katawaz, and he had to go round by Panna and Ashlan.

The following instance of a foray of the Ghilzais is extracted from Broadfoot's journal, and will give an idea of how these raids are conducted:--

"Mehtar Musa is the son of Yahia Khan, and head of the Sultan Khel, of Sulaiman Khel. He is a shrewd, plausible man, and has acquired more influence than any other man of the tribe, and as he has an Ulus of his own, he is a formidable enemy. In want of some livestock a few years ago, he despatched his family drummer to every khel in Katawaz to announce that on the third day he would head a chapao. The rendez-vous was Burlak; several thousands assembled with every sort of weapon from a rifle to a club, and some on horses, some on foot, poured in a disorderly torrent over the pass of Sargo and fell upon the lands of the Wazirs, surprising their flocks and camels in great numbers. The Wazirs occupied the gorges and crests of their mountains and saw their country ravaged. But at night signal fires were lighted on the hills, and the whole tribe came, tolerably armed and eager for vengeance.

"The Sulaiman Khel had attained their object; some carried their plunder home, and I believe part, under Mehtar Musa, passed into

Daman to collect a little more. The Wazirs formed a bold resolution. They crossed the hills by paths known only to themselves, and pounced on Katawaz while their enemies were absent, guided to the flocks and herds by one of the Sulaiman Khel, and then returned home richer than before. The Sulaiman Khel were greatly vexed at being so outwitted, and had no resource but negotiation, as entrapping the Wazirs twice was hopeless. After much swearing on 'Korans' and giving to each other some unfortunate Sayyids as pledges of their faith, all the cattle were restored on both sides, except those bona fide eaten, or over-driven on the march. The Sulaiman Khel made up for lost time by plundering a weaker tribe, and the Wazirs by attacking the Lohanis. These anecdotes are characteristic."

In general forays are on a smaller scale, sometimes they are mere thefts. They seldom plunder near their own houses, and have an understanding with other predatory tribes by which the cattle taken are passed along by secret paths. When Afghans are robbed and cannot help themselves by force, they negotiate. Ten or fifteen rupees will generally redeem a camel worth Rs. 40 or 50.

The Ghilzais are a remarkably fine race of men, being unsurpassed by any other Afghan tribe in commanding stature and strength. They are brave and warlike, but have a sternness of disposition amounting to ferocity in the generality of them, and their brutal manners are unfortunately encouraged by the hostility existing between them and their neighbours; while they are not discountenanced by their chiefs.

"The Ghilzais of the west," says Elphinstone, "as far nearly as to the meridian of Ghazni, bear a close resemblance to the Duranis. This resemblance diminishes as we go eastward. The Hotaks and Tokhis in dress, manners, and customs, and in everything which is not connected with their mode of government, exactly resemble the neighbouring Duranis."

The Tarakis, though more similar to the Duranis than to any other tribe, mix something of the manners of the East Ghilzai, and this most in the south part of the Taraki country. The Andars resemble the east clans in everything except their government. The internal government of the Ghilzais is entirely different from that of the Duranis. The chiefs of the former have now lost the authority which they possessed under their own royal government. There is great reason to doubt whether that authority ever was so extensive as that which has been introduced among the Duranis on the Persian model. It is more probable that the power even of the king of the Ghilzais was small in his own country, and that the tumultuary consent of his people to support his measures abroad was dictated more by a sense of the interest and glory of the tribe than by any deference to the king's commands. Some appearances, however, warrant a supposition that his power was sufficient to check murders and other great disorders. Whatever the power of the king may have been formerly it is now at an end, and that of the aristocracy has fallen with it; and though it has left sentiments of respect in the minds of the common people, yet that respect is so entirely unmixed with fear that it has no effect whatever in controlling their actions. No khan of a tribe, or malik of a village, ever interferes as a magistrate to settle a dispute, or at least a serious one; they keep their own families and immediate dependents in order, but leave the rest of the people to accommodate their differences as they can. The degree in which this want of government is felt is not the same throughout the tribe. Among the people round Kabul and Ghazni, the power of the Amir's governor supplies the place of internal regulation. With the Hotaks, the Tokhis, and generally with the Ghilzais on the great roads, the authority which the chiefs derive from the central government, and perhaps the respect still paid to their former rank, enables them to prevent general commotion, though they cannot supress quarrels between individuals; but among the southern Sulaiman Khel these disorders rise to feuds between the subdivisions of a clan, and even to contests of such extent as to deserve the name of civil wars; yet even in the most unsettled tribes, the decision of an assembly of Mullas is sufficient to decide disputes about property, and one great source of quarrels is thus removed. Among the East Ghilzais, and especially among the Sulaiman Khel, the power of a chief is not considerable enough to form a tie to keep the clan together, and they are broken into little societies which are quite independent in all internal transactions (like the Yusufzais).

Notwithstanding their domestic quarrels and feuds with other tribes, they are by no means a violent or irritable people. They generally live in tolerable harmony, and have their meetings and amusements like the Duranis, undisturbed by the constant alarm, and almost as constant frays, of the Yusufzais.

Instead of the Persian "kaba" of the Duranis, or the original "kamis" of the Afghans (which is here ony worn by old men), the generality wear the Indian dress of white cotton. Their dress is also distinguished from that of the tribes further west by the use of white turbans. They also wear a cap like that of the Duranis, but much higher.

Their arms are the same as those of the Duranis, with the addition of a shield of buffalo's hide, or, when it can be procured, of the skin of rhinoceros.

Most men have a strip shaved in the middle of their heads like the Duranis' but those who set up for professed champions let all their hair grow: it is customary with each of those, when he is just about to close with the enemy, to drop his cap, and rather to give up his life than retreat beyond the spot where it is fallen.

Several of the Ghilzai clans are almost wholly engaged in the carrying trade between India and Afghanistan and the northern states of Central Asia, and have been so for many centuries to the exclusion almost of all the other tribes of the country. From the nature of their occupation they are styled "Powindah."

HISTORY

It is unnecessary to attempt to trace the history of the Ghilzais further back than their great strike for liberty in 1707. Mr. Wais, son of a descendant of Malakhi, a powerful Ghilzai who as at that time a leading man in Kandahar, was seized by the Persian governor and sent to Ispahan on pretext of conspiracy, but he turned his visit to so good account that he was reinstated. On his return he raised a rebellion, and having defeated and killed the Persian leader, made himself governor of Kandahar. The Persians sent three armies against him, but he defeated them all, and in 1715 he died after having ruled Kandahar for eight years.

He was succeeded by his son Mir Mahmud who at first temporised with the Persians, but at last, in 1720, undertook the invasion of Persia. He first moved on Kirman with 12,000, men, 5,000 of whom perished amid the intervening deserts; the town soon surrendered, and the Afghans gave themselves up to plunder and every imaginable excess for four months, when they were attacked and put to flight by the Persian General Lutf Ali Khan and Mir Mahmud escaped with a few followers.

Taught by this bitter experience, Mir Mahmud raised another army 28,000 strong, in 1722, and commenced the campaign by rapidly crossing Seistan to Bam, which having stored with provision, he advanced once more on Kirman. The town surrendered but the citadel held out, and the garrison declaring their intention of never capitulating, he was induced by a bribe of 18,000 tomans to raise the siege. He then marched on Yezd, and having failed signally in gaining it by assault, he left it also in his rear and marched on Ispahan regardless of communications. He arrived within 10 miles of that place with 23,000 men worn out with fatigue and hunger, with scarcely any ammunition and in rags. After great delay caused by indecision in their councils, the Persians marched out to attack the Afghans, but, being badly commanded, their assault was unsuccessful and ended in their complete defeat. Mir Mahmud then advanced and laid siege to Ispahan; the Shah strove by a large bribe to buy him off, but this of course only exposed his fear and weakness, and Mahmud pressed the blockade the more, and cut up every Persian attempting to escape or bring provisions into the city. At last after enduring the siege for eight months, Shah Husain entered Mahmud's camp and abdicated the throne in his favour and delivered up the city to him. Mahmud then ordered a massacre of the troops who had defended the city.

Up to this point the conduct of Mahmud had at least been distinguished for courage, energy, and intelligence, but now his nature quite changed; he became morose, suspicious, and cruel. He laid seige to Kasvin, and, having taken it, gave it up to three days' indiscriminate slaughter,--an act which so roused the inhabitants that they rose, massacred in their town nearly half the Afghans, and drove the remainder from the city. Mahmud then massacred all the chief nobles and leading men he could secure, believing that terror alone would keep the Persians from revolt. Meanwhile his Afghan troops were fast becoming reduced in numbers, and he was forced to recruit his army with Kurds and other Sunni tribes. In 1724 he reduced Irak and Fars, and took Shiraz after a siege of eight months. But becoming more and more insanely cruel, more and more insatiate for blood, he was at last put to death by his chiefs, and Mir Ashraf, his relation, raised to the throne.

The prince found enough to do; the Russians had taken Gilan, the Turks were advancing from the west, and Tahmasp, the son of Shah Husain, was at large with an army. He first marched against and defeated the Turks near Burujard, and having induced them to acknowledge him, he next advanced against Tahmasp, defeated him too, and took Kasvin and Ispahan. But this was the last of his successes; a greater than he had now arisen in the person of Nadir Kuli Khan, who, once a robber chief, had now been appointed to the command of Tahmasp's army. Mir Ashraf advanced to meet him, but the tide had turned, and at the battle which ensued near Damghan, he was totally defeated, and leaving 12,000 of his soldiers dead on the field, he fled to Ispahan. Here he raised another army and again advanced to meet Nadir, and entrenched himself 24 miles north of Ispahan; but with no better success than before, for Nadir turned and stormed his entrenchments and 4,000 more Afghans were left dead. Mir Ashraf then fled to Shiraz, and again having recruited his forces he advanced to meet Nadir, but with no better success, for he was again defeated and again driven to Shiraz and his soldiers, being now sick of stemming the tide that would not be turned, made terms with Nadir. Mir Ashraf, hearing this, fled with 200 devoted horsemen, but the pursuit was so close that on arriving in Sistan he had only two servants left, so that the Baluch chief of that country found little difficulty in murdering him. This ended the Ghilzai dynasty of Persia, a dynasty which, though it lasted but seven years, cost Persia a third of its population.

After this Nadir, having taken Herat and Farah, advanced in 1737 on Kandahar with 100,000 men. This city was governed by Mir Husain,

Ghilzai, brother of Mir Mahmud, and garrisoned by many of his tribe, who were still imbued with the gallantry which had enabled them to achieve such conquests in Persia, and they held out for 18 months, and at last only gave in on favourable terms to Nadir. After Nadir's death arose the Durani dynasty; the Ghilzais, probably bereft of all their best and bravest by the wars of the last 30 years, made no show against this assumption of what they to this day consider their rights, and are very little heard of in Afghan history till the final struggle between Mahmud and Zaman, grandsons of Ahmad Shah. This, occurring in the heart of the Turan Ghilzai country, appears to have encouraged them to revolt and reestablish a Ghilzai dyansty. Abdul Rahim Khan, Hotak, was declared king, and Shahabudin, Tokhi, was appointed his wazir, but the troops of the Duranis at once advanced from Kabul and Kandahar, and totally defeated the Ghilzais on every occasion, and at last the rebellion was put down.

From the date of this attempt nothing more is recorded of the Ghilzai history, till we come to their connection with the events of the British occupation fo Afghanistan. The Ghilzais did not perhaps actually fire the first shot against us in that campaign, but they certainly undertook the first serious attack on our troops, when they advanced to attack the shah's camp near Ghazni, the day before the assault on that fort, viz., 22 July 1839. They were, hewever, beaten off with a loss of 30 or 40 killed and wounded and 50 prisoners. After the entry of the British into Kabul, the Ghilzais, not having made their submission to Shah Shuja, Captain Outram was sent to reduce them to order, his instructions being "to disperse, and, if possible, to arrest, the refractory Ghilzai chiefs, Mehtar Musa Khan, Abdur Rahman Khan, Gul Muhammad Khan, and the Mama, and to establish the newly-appointed Ghilzai governors, Mir Alam Khan, Zaman Khan, and Khalil Khan; and lastly to reducte the forts of Nasir-ud-Daulah, should they still be held by his adherents." The cold-blooded murder of Colonel Herring having been also reported, he was further directed to punish the perpertrators of that atrocity.

The detachment placed under his orders for this purpose was composed of a wing of the Shah's 1st cavalry, a Gurkha battalion, and a battery of 9-pounders from Kabul, which were to be reinforced from Kandahar by a regiment of the Shah's infantry, half of the Shah's 2nd regiment of cavalry and a brigade of horse artillery. One thousand Afghan cavalry were also to have accompanied him thence; but in consideration of the difficulty that would be experienced in foraging so large a force, as well as in restraining them from plunder, the number was reducd, at his own request, to 500, the whole under the command of Muhammad Usman Khen, a nobleman of great consideration and uncle to the king.

Starting on the 6th September 1839, he reached Kala Ali Jah on the 12th. On the 17th he entered the Zurmat valley, where many of the leading men gave in their submission. On the 18th he was joined by a wing of infantry. On the 20th he conducted a smart affair against the Khojak Ghilzais killing 16 and taking 112 prisoners, with a loss of a few killed and wounded. On the 25th he went to Shorkach; 26th to Chalak; 27th to Musa Khel, where Mehtar Musa, the leader of the attack at Ghazni, surrendered; 29th to Malinda; 30th to Pannah; 1st October to Ukori; 2nd to Ushlan; 4th to Dila and mansur; 5th to Firoz; 6th to Kala-i-Margha, the fort of the principal Ghilzai chief, son of Abdur Rahman, Hotak, who headed the rebellion against the Duranis; on the 17th Kala-i-Margha was taken and destroyed, and on the 18th he joined General Willshire's camp.

Thus it will be seen that Outram with 2 1/2 regiments of infantry, 1 1/2 regiments of cavalry, a battery of artillery and 500 irregular horse, marched all through the Ghilzai country from one end to the other, and was only once opposed, though the country was studded with forts in every direction.

During the ensuing winter the Ghilzais remained quiet, but on the return of spring, they immediately began raising their tribes and harrassing the communications between Kandahar and Kabul. General Nott sent Captain Anderson, of the Horse Artillery, with 4 guns, 500 cavalry, and one regiment of infantry to clear the road. Anderson met the Ghilzais at Tazi and after a fight, in which the enemy behaved with great gallantry, charging down on to the bayonets of our infantrry, they were defeated leaving 200 men killed.

Sir William Macnaghtan now proposed to pay Rs. 30,000 per annum to the Ghilzais for keeping this road open, but this plan was not more successful than the more forcible argument of the bayonet, and the Ghilzais still went on plundering.

Again in the spring of 1841 the Ghilzais became restless, and a force of two regiments of infantry some cavalry and guns, moved out to Kalat-i-Ghilzai under Captain Macan. They were sent immediately on their arrival to attack a small Ghilzai fort in the vicinity; this they effected with small loss, the chief of the Ghilzais being killed with some of his men. This tended to irritate the Ghilzais, and it was therefore determined to place the fort of Kalat-i-Ghilzai in a state of repair. The Ghilzais then surrounded the fort, and attempted to harass the working parties. Colonel Wymer was now sent out to reinforce the post with 406 bayonets, 2 guns, and some cavalry. On his way he was attacked by 5,000 Ghilzais who came on in the most gallant and determined manner, sword in hand, to the very bayonets of Wymer's men. Again and again they came on, and again and again were they beaten back by the fire of Hawkins' guns and of the 38th Infantry. For two hours they continued the fight, but at last they gave way. They left many dead on the ground, and all night long the moving lights announced that many more, both of killed and wounded, were carried off to their camp.

The Eastern Ghilzais now rose, and Colonel Chambers was sent from Kabul with a force to punish them; but before he got up to them, a charge of the 5th cavalry had scattered them in disastrous flight.

A force was sent in September 1841 into Zurmat to reduce that country once more to obedience. All the forts were found evacuated and were destroyed.

At this time came the resolution of the Indian Government to curtail the expenditure in Afghanistan, and consequently the allowances given to the Ghilzais were amongst others withdrawn. They at once rose, occupied the passes towards Jalalabad, plundered a kafila, and entirely cut off communication with Peshawar. Sale's brigade, returning to India, was commissioned to stifle the insurrection en route. On the 9th October 1841, Colonel Monteith's force was attacked by them at Bukhak, and 25 men were killed and wounded. On the 12th they occupied the Khurd Kabul defile, but after a smart fight the pass was cleared. On the 14th the Ghilzais made a night attack on the camp in the Khurd Kabul valley, which, aided by treachery, was in a measure successful. Sale then made a move forward, and was again attacked with great persistency and considerable gallantry in the defiles of Jagdalak, losing more than 100 men killed and wounded. After this they skirmished more or less with Sale till his entrance into Jalalabad, and it is probable that a great portion of the force wich afterwards beseiged him were Ghilzais.

But the grand opportunity of the Ghilzais was to come. On the 6th January 1842, the British authorities at Kabul took the fatal step of retreating, during an Afghan winter, with a disorganised army, and in the face of a treacherous foe. From Butkhak, till the last man of that force was killed or taken prisoner, the Ghilzais surrounded them, attacking, plundering, massacring all that came to hand; 3,000 souls went down before their merciless hand in the Khurd Kabul; at Tezin the number was raised to 12,000; at Gandamak 20 muskets were all that could be mustered, and in a few hours more of these too were gone. The Ghilzais indeed drank their fill of British blood.

Again, on the occasion of General Pollock's advance at Jagdalak, on 8th September 1842, the Ghilzais appeared crowning the heights. "Large bodies of Ghilzais," says Kaye "were clustering on the heights. The practice of our guns was excellent, but the Ghilzai warriors stood their ground. The shells from our howitzers burst amongst them; but still they held their posts, still they poured in a hot fire from their jezails. The flower of the Ghilzai tribes were there under many of their most renowned chiefs, and they looked down upon the scene of their recent sanguinary triumphs. But they had now other men to deal with. The loud clear cry of the British infantry struck a panic into their souls, and they turned and fled." Nevertheless, they again appeared to attack and molest McCaskill's advance to join Pollock. Again, on the 13th September at Tezin, they joined Akbar Khan, fighting with great gallantry and perseverance, but again in vain, being in the presence of better men.

Now we turn to the southern Ghilzais, who displayed the same determined hostility as did their northern brethren.

Captain Woodburn, proceeding just before the outbreak at Kabul from Ghazni to Kabul with a detachment of 130 men, was set upon by a party of Ghilzais, and all but six were killed.

The Ghilzais attacked Ghazni on the 20th November 1841, but confined themselves to keeping up a blockade, shooting everyone who appeared. At last in March 1842 the garrison surrendered. Many of the sepoys were massacred by the Ghilzais in attempting an escape by themselves.

Kalat-i-Ghilzai was also besieged by the Ghilzais. They arrived on 9th December 1841, but did not attempt anything serious till April, when they began to collect in great numbers, and by May had completely surrounded the place. At last, hearing that General Nott had sent a force to relieve Kalat-i-Ghilzai under Colonel Wymer, the Ghilzais determined to anticipate the relief by making a desperate assault. Accordingly they prepared a number of sealing ladders and gallantly mounted to the assault. Thrice they came boldly on, planting one of their standards within a yard of the muzzle of one of the guns and thrice they were driven back with discharges of grape and hot fire of musketry. They also attempted to get in at the embrasures and over the parapets in the most determined manner. They fired little, but came on sword in hand with their matchlocks slung. The assault lasted from twenty minutes to half an hour. Every one was astonished at the boldness and determination of the attack. They left 104 dead bodies at the foot of the defence, and within a few days after the assault, it was found that the number of killed and wounded men, who died within a few days after the action, considerably exceeded 400. Their number were computed at 6,000 men. Undismayed by this defeat, they again joined Shams-ud-din Khan at Ghazni to oppose Nott's advance, and this force is described by Nott as having behaved in a most bold and gallant manner.

Again they joined Shams-ud-din in opposing General Nott at Bini Badam.

Again the Ghilzais assembled on the retirement of Pollock's force and attacked it at Tezin, Haft Kotal and Jagdalak.

Thus, it may be said, with perfect truth, that in this campaign the Ghilzais were the first to attack us and the last to oppose us.

They were engaged in every fight of any consequence during the whole campaign, and in all they showed a most determined gallantry and a most untiring hostility to us.

The Ghilzais all execrate the Duranis, whom they regard as usurpers, and sullenly pay obedience to the Kabul Government. In the beginning of 1849 the northern sections revolted. It appears that Muhammad Akbar Khan had taken the oath of brotherhood with Muhammad Shah Khan Ghilzai, (Of Badiabad renown, and father of Faiz Muhammad Khan—see "Laghman.") which act under the Muhammadan law placed them on the footing of brothers. Accordingly when Muhammad Akbar died, Muhammad Shah not only claimed to inherit his property, but demanded possession of his widows and the post of Wazir. These pretensions Muhammad Shah was prepared to enforce by arms, and the Ghilzais responded in large numbers to his appeal. Dost Muhammad sent an army to reduce him, but it proved insufficient for the purpose. At length in April 1849 he raised an army of 25,000 veteran Abdalis, who had been brought up in hatred of the Ghilzais, and soon compelled Muhammad Shah to surrender at discretion, and to give up certain treasures he had seized. Ghulam Haidar Khan, the heir-apparent, was then placed in charge of the Ghilzais. They again rebelled under Muhammad Shah, but Ghulam Haidar being sent against them, they were once more reduced to obedience.

Ismatulla Khan, Jabar Khel, a devoted friend of Yakub Khan, was head of the Ghilzais during the last Afghan war. He gave a great deal of annoyance during the whole of the period that the British army remained in Afghanistan, and during the investment of Sherpur he attacked Norman near Jagdalak and was defeated. In the end of 1881 he was discovered intriguing with Ayub Khan, and was consequently imprisoned at Kabul. After being kept in confinement for some time by Amir Abdur Rahman he was privately hanged (October 1882), and his body given to his relatives. His eldest son Muhammad Hashim was also killed by Amir Abdur Rahman, whilst two others are said to be in Kafiristan (Nuristan), and the youngest, Abdur Rahman, is with other Afghan refugees in Rawal Pindi.

Another powerful chief of the Ghilzais was Arsala Khan, Jabar Khel. He was a staunch supporter of Amir Sher Ali, and suffered greatly in that sovereign's cause. On Sher Ali's return to power he was made Governor of Kurram and Zurmat. In 1870 he was appointed one of the chosen councillors, and received the post of Foreign Minister in November 1873. He died some six months before the war with England broke out—see "Jabar Khel."

In 1882 the acknowledged chief of the Ghilzai tribe was Khar Muhammad Khan, Jabar Khel, son of Muhammad Khan. He was then an old man of over 70 year of age.

1886 saw the Ghilzais once more in open rebellion against the Ruler of Afghanistan. This time the revolt appears to have had its origin in the oppressive taxation imposed on the tribe by Amir Abdur Rahman. The first overt act was an attack between Mukur and Ghazni on a newly raised Durani regiment marching unarmed from Kandahar to Kabul with treasure; the regiment being defeated and the treasure looted. This happened about the 20th of October. The rebels chiefly consisted of Andaris, but they were joined by others, especially the Sulaiman Khel; the revolt was led by the sons of our old opponent, Mushk-i-Alam. The Amir at once despatched a force from Kabul consisting of 3 regiments of infantry, 1 of cavalry, and 1 battery of artillery, under Ghulam Haidar Khan, Orakzai. The rebels by this time were said to number 20,000 men of all sections. No decisive action took place till the 11th November, when the rebels were atacked and dispersed.

During the winter perfect quiet prevailed, but his was chiefly due to the season. In March 1887 the outbreak was renewed, apparently by the Hotaks, Tokhis, Andaris and Tarakis, assisted by the Jaghuri Hazaras. After gaining some slight success they seem to have met with two defeats near Mukur, at the hands of Ghulam Haidar, but in the Maruf district they in their turn appear to have defeated some Kandahar troops under Sikandar Khan. The rebellion continued to spread, the Nasirs, Kakars, and certain sections of the Hazaras making common cause with the Ghilzais. Owing to this increase in their numbers, Ghulam Haidar played a waiting game and after some indecisive fighting marched south and effected a junction with the Kandahar force.

The Amir's difficulties were further enhanced at this time by disturbances in the Shinwari country, which broke out about the end of April and continued throughout May and June.

The Ghilzai insurrection consequently assumed still more formidable proportions, and a large number of Tokhis and Tarakis, said to have amounted to 30,000, men assembled in Nawa near the Ab-i-Istada, whilst another body collected in Mizan, between the Tarnak and Arghandab. On the other hand, the gathering in Maruf dispersed and thus set free a portion of the Amir's troops for operations in Nawa. Leaving Sikandar Khan in Maruf to watch the Hotakis, Ghulam Haidar therefore moved northwards against Nawa, Muhammad Husain Khan, with another force advancing on the same district from Ghazni.

About the middle of July, Ghulam, Haidar appears to have received some reinforcements, and on the 26th of that month he came up with the Nawa insurgents at Shiri Kotal, also called Kotal Dab, and gained a somewhat decisive victory.

This appears to have disheartened the malcontents, and they were about to disperse, but on hearing of Ayub Khan's escape from Teheran they began to gather again, and continued to commit depredations by night near the military camps, retiring to the hills by day. The Amir desirous of conciliating them, allowed Ghulam Haidar to expend Rs. 50,000 in granting khillats, etc., and soon afterwards the revolt died out. In December the Amir issued a proclamation calling on the Andaris to return to their homes, and extending pardon to all insurgents, except Mulla Abdul Karim, son of Mulla Mushk-i-Alam, Sher Jan Khan, Taraki, and Muhammad Shah Khan, Hotaki.

Each family possesses its own flock and a few camels, a tent, two or three iron cooking pots and wooden bowls, with a few sacks of flour. When several families move and live in concert, they form a "khel." While the men watch the flocks with arms by their sides, the women make "kurut" and cheese for winter; buttermilk and bread for the daily consumption. On the march they help to lead the camels and pack the tents; they are decently dressed in a brown petticoat and veil, but seldom cover their face unless impudently stared at. Their features are regular, but somewhat masculine, and their figures tall and good. They marry late and keep their looks a long time. The father of a young man, who wants a wife, proposes for his son to the bride's father previously feeling his way carefully, as a refusal may cause a feud; then, ensues a long scene of bargaining, at last ended by an agreement, that the bridegroom shall give a feast and certain presents of clothes, sheep, and cattle; this is not a bargain for the girl, but to satisfy the neighbours that her friends will not give her to a beggar. The expense of a marriage is about Rs. 100 in the poor classes, hence men are often 35 or 50, and generally 28 or 30, before they can afford the money. The obstinacy of the custom prevents the price being lowered, though many fathers would be happy to give their daughters for nothing were they not ashamed. The desire to get married makes the Afghan sometimes trade and oftener plunder. When all is arranged, he is admitted to see

GHILZAO غلزاو
   34-7 66-45. In the Dai Kundi country. (See Military Report on Hazarajat, Part II.)

GHOGAZAI Or GHAWAY GUZE غوغیزای
   34-2 69-35 m. A village at the head of the Hazardarakht defile, near the Karshatal Kotal. (Barton.) A place called Ghogizai is located at 34-18 69-45 G. (LWA)

GHOJAN See AGHAO JAN غوجان
   32-44 67-36 A.

*GHOLAM Also see GHULAM غلام

*GHOLAM BANDEH غلام بنده
   35-11 71-25 m. A village located on a tributary of the Kunar, north of Tsunek.

*GHOLAM KHAN KALAI غلام خان کلی
   33-7 70-1 m. A village located south of Mashi Kalai, near the Pakistan border.

*GHORAO غوراو
   35-1 67-43 m. A village located on a tributary of the Saighan river, south of Saighan.

GHORBAND غور بند
   35-6 68-10 m. Ghorband is a woleswali in Parwan province. The woleswali comprises an area of 1,504 square kilometers and has an agricultural population that has been estimated at about 21,500. The woleswali is bounded in the west by Shaikh Ali, in the north by Tala wa Barfak, in the east by Shinwar and Bagram, and in the south and southwest by Surkh-i-Parsa. Ghorband includes about 43 villages, of which 21 have more than 500 inhabitants. The villages are listed in the PG as follows: Surkhi ya Qalacha, Miana Deh, Do Ab, Bagh-i-Khum, Muli Khel, Yakhdara, Rahim Khel, Dara-i-Tang, Tai Khan, Qol-i-Khol, Qol-i-Luch, (Qol-i-Luch-i-Chardeh) Taylor-i-Chardeh, Luch-iChardeh, Sar Dara-i-Fanduqestan, Rangab, Farah Gerd, Joye Dukhtar, Maker Khel, Qala-i-Nau Qumchaq, Hesar-i-Qumchaq, Gardana-i-Qumchaq Chilan, Faranjel, Janbut Khel-i-Qumchaq, Janbut Khel-i-Saidan, Alam Khel, Kara Khel (Magar Khel), Kana Khel, Shahi Khel, Bala Ghal, Faraz Khel (Waz Ghar), Seyah Gerd, Tangi Bala-i-Seyah Gerd, Seyah Gerd, Deh Nau-i-Siyah Gerd, Mazanah, Payan Deh (Payan Qarya), Chardeh Langar (Chardeh), Kaliyan, and Saqab-i-Chardeh. (LWA) In 1914 the area was described as follows: A valley drained by the Ghorband river, and lying between the Hindu Kush on the north and Koh-i-Baba and the Paghman ranges on the south. Above Kala Doab it is known as the Dara Shaikh Ali. Its total length by road from the east foot of the Shibar pass to the Tutumdara is about 60 miles. Its breadth varies greatly, as will be seen from the detailed description given below. The elevation of the valley ranges between 8,420 feet at the foot of the Shibar and 5,600 feet at Burj-i-Guljan.
The houses of the inhabitants are flat-roofed; in summer many of them live in black tents. There is excellent pasturage on some of the surrounding hills, but the chief subsistence of the people is from agriculture. The valley is enclosed between cliffs of slate and quartz occasionally interrupted by basaltic rocks, amygdaloid volcanic ashes, sulphate of lime, and other indications of igneous action. It abounds in minerals, and at Farinjal a mine of very rich

lead ore is worked to a great extent and with remarkable skill. Iron ore occurs so abundantly in the hills that Lord did not think it necessary to particularize its localities. Lapis-lazuli is believed to exist near Fulgird, and zinc, sulphur, sal-ammoniac, ochre, and nitre are found, as is salt. In 1905 coal was discovered near Siah Gird, but it appears to be of poor quality and the output is so small that the workings will probably be stopped before long (1906).

At the present time (1906) the Hakim of Ghorband is said to be one Shah Daula Khan. He resides at Chahardeh.

The following note is by Captain Drummond. It must be remembered, however, that the Ghorband district, properly so called, extends only from Kala Doab to the Bagh-i-Aoghan bridge, 7 miles below Burj-i-Guljan, whereas this note appears to include all the valley down to Tutamdara. Above Kala Doab to Kala Pai Kotal-i-Shibar the valley is under the Shaikh Ali Hakim, whose district also includes the Turkoman and Parsa Daras.

"Revenue--1-1/2 lakhs (Kabulis).

"Land revenue (all irrigation).--76,000 rupees, levied at 6 rupees (Indian) per 'jarib.'

"Poll tax.--4 Kabuli rupees per head (for male adults only).

"Sheep tax.--One sheep out of every forty, or 8 rupees instead.

"Goat tax.--4-1/2 rupees for every 40 goats.

"According to the Amir's ruling, taxes should be levied in Kabuli rupees. The Government officials, however, line their own pockets by making the people pay at the rate of full rupees.

"There are not very many sheep in the Ghorband valley. The largest owners are the Shinwaris, who inhabit some of the ravines between the Shekh Ali river and the Paghman mountains.

Toll tax.--Per donkey load at various places in the district, according to the description of article carried.

"The chief trade is pistachios, 'buzghurj' (a dye) and salt (from Turkistan).

"Tax on pasturage for nomads, 5 Kabuli rupees per flock of 200 or 300 sheep.

"There are no camels in this district, except with the Shinwaris, who have about 1,000. The Shinwaris number about 500 families.

"There is grazing for about 10,000 camels near Farinjal. Very little came grazing on the hills near Siah Gird.

"The transport of the district is chiefly donkeys, numbering 100 or more per village.

"In the Afghan official records the carriage in donkeys of the whole district is laid down at 2,000. Oxen are not much used. There are roughly 10,000 head of cattle. Horses nil. Ponies very few.

"Crops.--Wheat, barley, Indian corn, and little cotton in the lower valleys. There is only one crop per annum.

"Vegetables.--Beet-root, carrots, turnips, lucerne.

"Fruits.--Grapes (the celebrated Husaini black, and Dahmurgh species. The Husainis are much prized and exported in large quanitities as raisins.) Apricots (excellent), almonds (for export), pears, apples, pomegranates (scanty), quince (abundant), walnuts (abundant).

"Firewood--Plentiful in the lower valleys of both the Paghman and Hindu Kush ranges. The roots of bushes are largely used, and are said to be excellent. Formerly there were a great number chinar trees, but 70,000 of them have been cut down by the Amir's orders and sent into Kabul for building purposes. There are now hardly any left. There are no pistachios or junipers and but few poplars. Willows are plentiful. All the big trees with thick trunks have been cut down and sent to Kabul, and the supply of wood is officially recorded for the lead mines at Farinjal. (The entire Ghorband valley is destitute of any timber for fuel, except fruit trees. Peacocke.)

"The district of Ghorband consists of 18 valleys, as follows:--

1.	Deh Tangi	?	families	Tajiks, etc.
2.	Shaikh Ali	5,000	"	Hazaras
3.	Dara-i-Saiadan	2,000	"	Kheshgi Afghans
4.	Findukistan	300	"	Tajiks
5.	Wazghur, Darzgird	200	"	?, Shinwaris
6.	Ustarshahar	100	"	1/2 Tajiks,
7.	Kakshal	100	"	1/2 Shinwaris and 1/2 Turki-speaking Tajiks.
8.	Kaoshan	40	"	Shinwaris
9.	Mir-i-Ashwa	40	"	Sayyids
10.	Kol-i-Yer	40	"	Shinwaris
11.	Istama	40	"	"
12.	Kol-i-Kol	100	"	Nek Pai Hazaras
13.	Kol-i-Lich	50	"	"
14.	Mazara	300	"	Shaikh Ali Hazaras
15.	Behuda	20	"	Tajiks
16.	Kol-i-Parsa	500	"	Hazaras
17.	Kol-i-Shingaran	50	"	Shaikh Ali Hazaras
18.	Darwaz	300	"	"

"The above is a very rough estimate. The total population of the district may be put down at 46,000 souls."
Further information regarding the Shaikh Ali portion of the valley is given under that heading.
In 1886 a made road, 15 to 30 feet wide, generally practicable for wheeled carriage, led up the Ghorband as far as the mouth of the Kipchak glen, and information has since been received to the effect that this road has now been completed as far as Bamian, and also up the Kipchak and over the Chahardar Pass.
The following detailed description of the valley from above downwards is taken from Peacocke's Diary, 1886:
Descending east from the Shibar pass, the head of the Ghorband valley is entered at 2-3/8 miles from Diwal Bolak. The valley at and below this point is most generally known as the Dara Shaikh Ali. It takes its rise in the Koh-i-Jaolangah, and as far as this point is known as the Dara Sangandao. This latter dara issues close to the foot of the descent through a narrow, rocky gorge, below which the valley bends eastward and at once expands to a width of 200 yards. A road, fit for pack animals, runs up the Dara Sangandao to either the Kotal-i-Kharzar or the Kotal-i-Sangandao.
At 1/4 mile (distances from the point where the valley was entered) is Kala Pai Kotal. Two small mud forts of 10 families of Kara Malli Shaikh Alis. The bed of the valley here becomes dry, and the stream is now confined in a regular watercourse. There is good camping ground about the forts. Cultivation commences, and continues down the valley occasionally interspersed with small grass chamans and trees.
At 1/2 mile a small ravine called Dara Ghorbandak joins on the right, and by it an alternative road joins from Diwal Bolak over the Shibar watershed. In heavy snow this road is used in preference to the main road, and is cleared of snow by the men of Diwal Bolak if

troops should then have to march. Snow rarely falls at Kala Pai Kotal deeper than 2 feet. The valley now increases in width to about 400 yards, and at 1-1/4 miles is joined on the right by a large dara called Bedkul, up which is a difficult road to the crest of the Koh-i-Baba and thence to Kala Hissar in Besud.

From here downwards kishlaks and small fort villages are passed in the bed of the valley at short intervals, none of any particular name, except Bed Kala Nirkh and Bin-i-Sehwak. The others are known by the names of the particular lateral valley that happens to join close by, all of which have well-known names.

At 2-1/2 miles up the Tangi Taidu Kul occurs the only difficult bit of any importance in this stage. There is an old, unsound, masonry foot bridge called Pul-i-Sangi below Taidu Kul, where the river gully is only 10 feet wide. The Sagpar valley that joins here from the south runs up to the Koh-i-Baba, thus giving access to Gulak in Besud.

At 3 3/4 miles the Dara Botian joins on the left, and at 4 1/2 the Dara Kajak comes in from the south. Roads lead up both, and over the main ranges.

At 6 3/4 miles the Sabz Kotal is crossed. It is a low, flat spur projecting across the valley from the hills on the left and confining the river to a bed 20 yards wide. The kotal is only about 70 feet high, and presents no difficulty to guns.

The Dara Jarf joins on the right at 9 1/2 miles, and the Dara Nirkh at 11 miles. Both are large, well-cultivated valleys with their head in the main Koh-i-Baba range. The road up the Nirkh is passable by camels.

The village of Pin-i-Sehwak is reached at 12 miles.

At 12 1/2 miles Kala Kazi Nawi is passed; 10 families of Naiman Shaikh Alis, owning 2 flocks and 50 heads of cattle. The Naiman taifa ends here, and from here to Dahan-i-Taori belongs to the Kalluk taifa, of which there are 500 families in all in the valley, owning 6 watermills, and 200 flocks and 700 head of cattle. Sixty more families of this taifa live up the Dahan-i-Taori.

Below Kala Kazi Nawi the valley opens out to a breadth of 1 1/2 miles and is well cultivated, with numerous villages and gardens. This broad portion is called Nawi. The hills on the right of the valley now sink into a series of gentle rounded ridges and spurs projecting from the Koh-i-Darwaz. The main range of the Koh-i-Baba, which runs like a wall from the Irak Kotal to abrest of this point, here ends in the Koh-i-Darwaz. Behind Koh-i-Darwaz lies the large valley called Dahan-i-Turkoman, and beyond that again to the south lie the Paghman mountains.

At 13 1/2 miles the valley contracts to 150 yards, and is mainly occupied by the gravelly bed of the river. About here the Dara Shingarian joins on the left. Up it runs a road to Sai Kazi.

At 15 miles the end narrows, and the valley becomes 3/4 mile wide, and is filled with a large, level, grassy haman dotted with habitations, walled gardens, and orchards. The chaman is called Gazar, and forms a good camping ground.

At 15 3/4 miles the wide and fertile Dara Jangalak joins on the right. A road goes up it for the Turkoman Dara. At 16 1/2 miles the Robat Dara comes in on the left. It gives access to the Zak Kotal. Just below its mouth the main valley bends to the left, and contracts seriously for the first time to form the tangi called Khak-i-Ghulam Ali. The steep, rocky precipices of the rugged, rocky hill called Koh-i-Ghafrah abut on the right bank of the river, and the left bank is closely lined with broken high ground, through which a number of ravines and daras discharge great heaps of stones and boulders. Habitations and cultivation now almost entirely cease, and the road becomes hilly for the next 4 miles.

At 17 1/2 miles a road branches up a ravine named Dahan-i-Sai, and leads by the Sai Kotal to Loling and the Dahan-i-Turkoman. It is said to be easy.

Here the tangi is further contracted by a flat terrace, 70 feet high, which projects across it from the hills on the left, and confines the river to a small gully 80 yards wide. This terrace forms a good position to bar the road, and could be held by two battalions.

At 18 miles the Dara Taori joins on the left, issuing from among broken steep clay hills. A bad footpath leads up it and over the Kotal-i-Taori to Dasht-i-Ghabar at the head of Dara Margh for Tala. The tangi now bends sharply to the right round the foot of the cliffs of the Koh-i-Ghafrah, and for the next mile widens out to 200 to 300 yards, with a wide strip of level but stony ground on the left bank of the river. The Dara Saraj joins on the left, and a path leads up it to the main range; but nothing could be learned about it. It is little used and little known.

From the commencement of the Tangi Khak-i-Ghulam Ali to Farinjal the population is very scanty, and there is little or no cultivation. Some 10 families of Ali Jam live just below Taori; 10 more live at Kala Shah Nazar; and another 10 at Kala Khal Beg---owning in all 10 flocks and 200 head of cattle. The only other habitations in this section are Kala Doab, 10 families Tajiks, and a small hamlet at the mouth of the Dahan-i-Behuda. Tajik population commences regularly at Kala Doab.

At 19 1/2 miles the Dara Behuda joins on the left, and here the main valley widens out to 3/4 of a mile. 1 1/2 miles further on the Turkoman Dara stream issues through the Tangi Loling and as large as the main stream. Here at Kala Doab, the Tangi Khak-i-Ghulam Ali may be said to cease.

The valley, which is 1 mile wide at Doab, contracts at 22 1/2 miles to half a mile in width, and thence to 24 3/4 miles is a good easy road over the plain or sloping dasht. Kala Shah Nazar is passed at 23 1/2 miles, and a little further on are the Farinjal lead mines, while at 24 3/4 miels the Dara Farinjal joins on the left.

For the next mile the road runs round the foot of a flat terrace about 70 feet high, which projects across the valley from the broken hills on the left. This terrace forms a good, but small position to close the valley, and could be held by one or two brigades. After rounding the end of the terrace, the valley opens out into a flat, gravelly bay, quite 1 mile in width. The village of Farinjal lies on the left.

At 27 1/2 miles the small village of Kala Khan, 10 families of Sayyid Tajiks, lies close on the right.

At 28 1/2 miles another terrace, 150 to 200 feet high, with steeply scarped sides, projects across the valley from the hills on the left, and forces the river through a narrow gorge between its extremity and the rocky hill sides on the opposite side of the valley. This terrace is called Kotal Sakha.

Chardeh is reached at 29 1/2 miles. Here the steep and narrow Dara Parsa joins on the right. Up it a camel road leads to the Kah Dara Kotal for Kabul. On the left is the narrow Kol-i-Lich, up which is a track over the main range to Dara Paiandeh.

At 32 miles Dara Jui Dukhtar joins on the left. There is a village of the same name at its mouth; while up the dara live 150 famiales of Afghan Koishki, with 3 water-mills, 10 flocks, and 500 head of cattle. A road runs up the dara to the Chahardar Kotal.

At 32 3/4 miles is the small village of Deh Rangar, and here the main road from the Chahardar pass joins down the Dara Kipchak past

Deh Tangi. One thousand families of Tajiks are said to live up the Dara Kipchak, owning 50 flocks, 1,000 head of cattle and 12 watermills.

At Deh Rangar the road crosses to the right bank of the river by a wooden bridge of two spans -- one of 15, the other of 2 feet. Roadway 14 feet wide in the clear, and capable of carrying field guns. River 30 yards wide and fordable in October.

At 34 1/2 miles easy descent at 1 in 15 to 1 in 12 for 250 yards into Farahgird. Here the hills on the right bank break back, and from behind them on the south the Pahgman range of hills is now seen approaching the river. This range has a harsh, irregular outline, and is of a rugged, impracticable nature; from here downwards it forms the south side of the Ghorband valley. The Saidan Dara joins at this break, and the main valley becomes 1 mile wide, being studded with habitations, gardens, and orchards; the river trough is level and half a mile wide.

At 37 miles is Siahgird. Here the Dara Findukistan joins on the right while the Wazghar comes in on the left. Opposite the mouth of these two daras the river trough is 1 mile wide, the valley opens out to a width of 5 to 6 miles, and a broad, gravelly dasht on the right bank slopes down from the foot of the Paghman range to the river trough, abutting on it in gravel cliffs 150 feet high.

At 38 3/4 miles is Darazgird; a group of four small forts on the left bank, peopled by Shinwaris. The valley is 2 miles wide, with gardens and trees.

At 40 miles Kala Chaman Nasir Khan, in the centre of a level, grassy chaman extending along the roadside for some 2 miles.

At 41 3/4 miles thre is a good position to close the valley facing west along the right bank of the Shuturshahr Nala. The latter joins on the right side and from its mouth a flat terrace, 80 feet high with sides scarped at 45 degree projects entirely across the valley. Along the top of this rise are a line of trees and gardens and stone walls, with a small mud fort in the centre. On the left at the mouth of the ravine with its back to inaccessible hills forming the south side of the main valley there is a series of low, narrow terraces; but they are commanded by the position. In front of the centre lies the open valley with uninterruped range up it. In front of the right and across the river the Dahan-i-Nimakao joins. It is enfiladed from the position, which also enfilades the river bend and commands it where it winds around the right of the position.

The main defect of the position is a knoll, 1,300 yards in front of the right, at the end of the west side of the mouth of the Nimakao ravine. The knoll is very small. Its crest commands the position, but is a knife-edged ridge. Steep, inaccessible rocks form its west side, and steep slopes its east side. On the west side it is only accessible by the narrow neck connecting it with the inaccessible hills on the north side of the valley. The knoll would have to be held by infantry, who would only have to guard this neck. In front of the left, up the main valley, there is also a small terrace with a command over the position, but it is out of effective artillery range and would only be of advantage to the enemy as a post of observation. The position would be suitable for occupation by a division.

The road ascends on to the position by an easy ramp of 1 in 7 for 150 yards, and then crosses the gravelly terrace, with the river on its left sunk 150 feet in a trough half a mile wide. The trough is bordered by steep hills on the left bank, and contains many villages, gardens and trees. The population are Turks, who came originally from Samarkand, and have been long established here.

At 43 1/2 miles Khak-i-Sanga, a group of villages, trees, and gardens. The inhabitants here and up the Dara Sinjit are also Turks. Cultivation now ceases, and the river trough is wholly occupied by the broad, gravelly river bed. The trough gradually contracts to half a mile, then to a quarter mile, and then to 200 yards wide at the Tangi Khakshall. Road remains good and level, is 18 feet wide, and overhangs the river bed 20 feet below.

At 46 miles the mouth of the Dara Sinjit is crossed. This is a small, stony ravine, and a road runs up it to Kotal-i-Sinjit on the Paghman range, said to be difficult, but practicable for laden camels. The valley again opens out to 2 miles wide, with cultivation, villages, and gardens and trees, called Khakshall. From here downwards inhabitants are Shinwaris.

At 48 miles a good camping ground on the Chaman on the river bank at the commencement of Bagh-i-Guljan.

At 49 miles the large Istaman ravine joins on the right. A bad track leads up it to the Paghman range.

The valley changes character at Burj-i-Guljan; and below it becomes a large ravine from half to quarter mile wide with broken, rugged bed and steep, rocky hills at sides.

At 50 1/2 miles the Dara Kaoshan joins on the left. Patches of poor cultivation and large walnut trees line the bank of the river, and an occasional stone hamlet is perched up the hillside.

At 54 miles the valley contracts permanently to a width of one-quarter mile. Road runs along the foot of the high rocky hill, rising at times to 50 feet above the river. There are several sharp turns here and one short, steep pinch (ascent and descent) at 1 in 4 for 50 yards, all requiring careful driving. At 54 1/2 miles Burj-i-Guljan ends and Bagh-i-Aoghan begins.

At 56 1/2 miles is the wooden bridge of Bagh-i-Aoghan, and the road crosses by it to the left bank. It will carry field guns and laden camels. Roadway 11 feet wide in clear between hand-rails. Seven circular road-bearers, 10 inches diameter, covered by 3-inch planking; span 33 feet. Abutments are of rubble stone corbelled out 8 feet on each side of the span with brushwood and logs. Bridge was built in 1885; is sound but very springy. Comparatively roomy approaches on both banks.

The Ghorband district ends here.

At 57 1/2 miles the Chirtak Dara joins on the right. The river is here 1 1/2 feet deep (October), with sound, gravel bottom.

At 59 miles Bagh-i-Aoghan ends, and the valley bends sharply to the right and from here downwards is called Tutamdara. Its inhabitants are all Tajiks. For the next 300 yards the road is only 10 feet wide, and has been built up from the river bed along the foot of the high hill on the right. It is substantially constructed of stones and wooden staking, but would be likely to suffer injury when the river is high. It is all at a low level 6 to 10 feet above the water, except in its last 50 yards, where it ascends through a 10 feet wide cutting through a projecting reef of rock, and ends with a short descent for 30 yards at 1 in 4.

At 59 1/4 miles the valley contracts to 80 yards, and the road could be easily blocked by a few blasting charges in this or the next bend.

At 60 miles the valley is again forced to bend to the right by a rocky spur projecting from the hill on the left. From here to its mouth the valley contracts to the mere breadth of the river channel with high cliffs on each side. The road therefore leaves the valley to avoid this gorge, and, ascending over the neck of the spur called the Kotal-i-Matak, descends into the Tutamdara plain.

The ascent of the Kotal-i-Matak is very steep, and for 300 yards the road zig-zags at a gradient of 1 in 4 (in a few places 1 in 3) up to the neck of the spur. There is a 15 to 20 feet wide roadway, but guns would have to unhook and be got either up or down by dragropes, and the returns of the zig-zags require widening. The road could be easily improved, as the soil is partially clay, and what rock there is, is not hard. The ascent, though steep, is very short, but would occasion a block in any train of wheeled carrriages or baggage animals. On reaching the top of this main ascent the road for another 300 yards continues to ascend gradually along an open slope to what is true kotal. Total rise from where valley was left, 340 feet. The descent is very gradual and is a broad, easy road leading down over open gravelly slopes to the plain. Here at the foot of the descent the hills are finally left, and the road, bending to the right, crosses the river at 60 1/4 miles to the Tutamdara village and then runs over the open daman that stretches along the foot of the Paghman hills, passing just clear of the line of villages and cultivation, which lie close on the left all the way to Charikar.

There is a wooden bridge where the river is crossed at the Tutamdara. The span is 35 feet, but otherwise the bridge is similar to that of Bagh-i-Aoghan, and can take field guns and laden camels. The volume of water is here much reduced by the four large canals which take off from the river on the right bank near the mouth of the valley.

The Kotal-i-Matak enfilades, looking westwards, the last bend but one of the Ghorband, and a small force posted on it could bar the road down the valley.

The top of the rise on to the daman at Tutamdara on the right bank of the river again is an excellent position to close the exit from the valley. It has an easy slope to the front down to the river, which flows at its foot 75 feet below it, and the three large canals run along the slope parallel to the river. On its left is the large village of Tutamdara, consisting of a compact group of about 100 houses, and all along the crest of the rise extends a chain of ruined walls, buildings, and trees. The fourth canal runs along inside the crest of the rise. The banks of the river in front are covered with large mulberry trees suitable for abattis. The position would be suitable for a division. It is, however, turned in the direction of Charikar by the Chirtak pass and by the other passes leading from the valley over the Paghman hills down to the Koh Daman.

These passes, as well as could be ascertained by Peacocke, are as follows, in order from Tutamdara westwards:—

(1) Kotal-i-Chirtal.—A mere footpath; difficult even for bullocks, or yabus; leads from near Pul-i-Bagh-i-Aoghan to Opiam.

(2) Kotal-i-Istamah.—Mere footpath; impracticable for laden pack animals; leads from near Burj-i-Gulzan.

(3) Kotal-i-Sinjit.—Fairly good road; is used by laden camels; leads from Khakshal to Kala Mir Akbar.

(4) Kotal-i-Istarghij.—Difficult foot track.

(5) Kotal-i-Istalif.—Difficult, but is used by laden camels; leads from Siahgird up Dara Findukistan, past Makhan Khar at the head of that dara, to Istalif; is only really fit for laden yabus and bullocks.

(6) Kotal-i-Garza.—Is the road mainly used; is good and much frequented by camel kafilas; runs from the Kala Sarim in the Dara Findukistan to Sikandar Kala at Farza.

(7) Kotal-i-Kah Dara.—A fairly good road; is used by laden camels; leads from Siahgird by Dara Koishki and Dara Saidan.

(8) Sahkar Dara.—A good road.

(7) and (8) can be reached from Kala Doab and Chahardeh in

Ghorband through Parsa by one and the same road, which forks beyond Parsa at Wan Hazara to the two passes.
Some 5 miles to the east of the mouth of the Ghorband valley is the mouth of the Dara Salang, down which leads the road over the Hindu Kush by the Bajgah Kotal.
The Ghorband river unites with the Panjshir some 8 miles southeast of Tutamdara near the ruins of the ancient city of Bagram.
The construction of a railway from the crest of the Shibar Kotal down the Ghorband valley would present no difficulty whatever as far as Burj-i-Guljan. From Burj-i-Guljan to the mouth of the valley at Tutamdara the cost of construction per mile would be heavy, as the line would almost throughout have to be cut out of the hillside. Otherwise however, there are no physical difficulties. The gradient of the valley is gentle, and little or no extra widening would be requisite. The rock, too, for the most part is of crumbly, shaly nature, easily worked. (Peacocke, Drummond, I.B.C.)

GHORBAND Or BAHARAK غوربند
A small Sayyid district in Yak Walang, see "Bamian (district)."

GHORBAND غوربند
34- 69-. A pass on the route from Belut to Khurd Kabul between the Ghilzai village of Rogun and the Dehgan village of Chakari. (I.B.C.)

*GHORBANDAK غوربندك
34-55 68-16 m. A village and a Dahana, running into the Ghorband river.

*GHOSHTARA غوشتره
34-8 70-28 m. A village near Haska Mina, south of Jalalabad.

GHOST KHOR, DARA-I- دره غوست خور
On the Helmand river. (See Military Report on Hazarajat, Part II.)

*GHOZAI غوزی
32-20 67-17 m. A village 2 miles east of the Tarnak river, south-southwest of Shahjui. Another place with this name is in the area of Zarghun Shahr, at 32-52 68-4 m.

GHUCHAK غچك
34- 69-. A village adjoining and forming part of Deh-i-Afghan in the Kabul district. Inhabitants: Tajiks; one hundred families. The people are called Tasma by their neighbours, as the land on which the village stands was granted by Timur Shah to the extent that a cow hide cut into strips (tasma) would encircle. (I.B.C.)

GHUCHAK غچك
34-26 70-25. A village about 3 miles west of Jalalabad. Inhabitants: Tajiks. About 120 houses. This is evidently the Gaochak of the map. (I.B.C.)

GHUJARBASH غوجرباش
A village in the northwest corner of the Dai Kundi country. (See Military Report on Hazarajat, Part II.)

*GHUJUR غجور
33-25 67-22 m. A village located southeast of Ajrestan.

*GHUJURAK غجورك
33-21 67-27 m. A village southwest of the Dasht-i-Nawar. Other

places with this name are located norhtwest of Ghazni, at 33-43 68-4 m.; on the Ghorband river, southwest of Shibar, at 34-52 68-10 m.

*GHULAM Also see GHOLAM غلام

GHULAM ALI غلام علی
A subdivision of the Bacha-i-Chulam clan of Dai Zangi. (See Military Report on Hazarajat, Part II.)

*GHULAM BANDEH See GHOLAM BANDEH غلام بنده

GHULAM HAIDAR غلام حیدر
34-30 69-2. A village on the north side the Ghazni road, nearly opposite Kala-i-Kazi, about 8 miles west of the city of Kabul. (I.B.C.)

GHULAM MUHAMMAD MUKHTAR غلام محمد مختار
Another name for Aliabad, in the Chardeh valley fo Kabul.

GHULGHULAH غلغله
34- 67-. A ruined city in the valley of Bamian, regarding which Maitland makes the following remarks:
"The road (from Kala Sarkari) goes for a few hundred yards up the Tagao-i-Shahar, and then, turning left, gains the plateau at the foot of the hill, on the northeastern side. There are mounds and hollows at the base of the hill, showing it was strongly entrenched on the side of the plateau. The hill is very steep, too much so for horses. Its shape is that of a sharp pointed cone, the apex being (by aneroid) about 500 feet above the valley at its foot, and perhaps 400 above the plateau, on the edge of which it stands. The hill is surrounded with the remains of several lines of walls and towers, all of unburnt brick. Previous travellers appear to have so described the place as to leave the impression that the ruins are of burnt brick; but this is not the case. The extreme summit appears to have been occupied by the palace, or principal residential buildings. A mass of inferior houses occupies a portion of the southwest slope of the hill, within, I think, the second line of defences, counting from the bottom. The general style of the buildings and walls resembles those of Chehil Burj (on the Band-i-Amir in Yakh Walang); but the towers are less massive, and Ghulghulah strikes me as being on the whole, the less interesting of the two. Possibly this is because I expected more of it. If not aware that it had been destroyed by Changez Khan, I should have thought it almost a modern place.
"On the plateau to the south, between Tagao-i-Shahar and Tagao Saidabad, is Kala Dukhtarah (not Dukhtaran). It is a large high-walled fort, said to be co-eval with Ghulghalah, and to have been the residence, or possession of the daughter of the sovereign whose stronghold Ghulghulah was. West of the Tagao-i-Shahar, on the portion of the plateau between it and Tagao Tajik is Gaokush, the ruins of which look rather imposing at a distance. The Dasht-i-Sarkar is south of Gaokush. The remainder of the plateau, to its edge, is all cultivated.
"Descending the hill, we rode round Kala Dukhtarah. The high walls are in very tolerable order, but have been so often reparied that it is uncertain how much of the ancient structure may be still remaining. I noticed here loopholes, resembling those of Chahil Burj, except that the upper hole was wanting. The fort now contains a village.
"From thence westward, across the Tagao-i-Shahar, the ruins of

Gaokush, on the Dasht-i-Sarkar portion of the plateau. They are not particularly interesting. Some of the arches are pointed."
Apart from their antiquity and associations, neither Zohak nor Ghulghulah are worth going a quarter of a mile to see, and as architectural remains are absolutely insignificant, beside the magnificent forts, palaces and tombs which abound in India. (Maitland.)

*GHUNDAI غوندی

34-13 70-2 m. A village south of Godar and southwest of Jalalabad. Other places with this name are located on a tributary of the Dara-i-Pich in Kunar province, at 34-54 70-41 m.; southeast of Tsawkay in Kunar province, at 34-35 70-58 m.; northwest of Khost, at 33-23 69-44 m.; on the Gardez river, northeast of Mirzaka, at 33-48 69-32 m.; on the Lazha Khwar, northeast of Gardez, at 33-45 69-38 m.; some 15 miles east of Gardez, at 33-36 69-28 m.; northeast of Chamkani, near the Pakistan border, at 33-53 69-52 m.; and Ghundai Kalai, southeast of Khost, on a tributary of the Shamal Khwar, at 33-18 69-56 m.

*GHUNJAI غونجی

33-40 69-59 m. A village southeast of Chamkani and north of the Tangi Tuy. Another place with this name is on the Gardez river, northeast of Mirzaka, at 33-48 69-31 m.

*GHUZBA غوزبه

33-47 68-16 m. A village located some 4 miles north of the Band-i-Sultan.

*GHWASHTEH غواشته (كواشته)

32-27 68-21 m. A district placed by Elphinstone south of Katawaz and near Ab-i-Istada. A stream with this name is northeast of Waze Khwa, at 32-13 68-24 G. (LWA)

*GIDARGU گدرگو

33-33 67-57 m. A village near the Qol-i-Surkhab, east of the Dasht-i-Nawar.

GIGI GOSHTA گیگی گوشته

34-32 70-21. A plain in the Jalalabad valley, on the north of the Kabul river, nearly opposite Chardeh and at the skirt of the hills. It affords excellent pasturage of which the pastoral Ghilzais take advantage, bringing a great number of camels and sheep in the autumn, and returning to Kabul in the spring. (McGregor.)

GILAN گیلان

32-44 67-38. Gilan is an alaqadari in Ghazni province. The alaqadari comprises an area of 1,041 square kilometers and has an agricultural population that has been estimated at from 10,695 to 20,600. The alaqadari is bounded in the south by Nawa, in the east by Dila, in the north by Muqur and Jaghori, and in the west by Shahjui. Gilan has about 80 villages, 14 of which have more than 500 inhabitants. The villages are listed in the PG as follows: Ozbak (Ozang), Qarya-i-Ahmadi, Akhto Khel, Ispin Tak, Agho Jan, Alakh, Awtala, Shirak, Bakhtiyar, Behbud, Balahir Wa-Mastan, Petab, Purdel, Fatehshi, Qarya-i-Taj, Qarya-i-Tas (Tes), Jabar, Jahangir, Jalim, Chala Jawak, Chamber-i-Sayed, Qarya-i-Hasan Khan, Khatak, Khanan, Dana Khel, Rasna, Qarya-i-Jabar, Dand, Spin (Safid) Ghondi, Safidar, Sujamand (Shuja Ahmad), Shoko, Mirza Khan, Shah Murad,

Shinki, Shela, Shamalzai, Ghulam Khel, Ghulam Moh'd Khan, Qala-i-Azad, Qala-i-Akhtar Moh'd, Qala-i-Tut, Garri, Qala-i-Ghazi Khel, Qala-i-Moh'd Ali Khan, Karez-i-Nau, Katal, Kerbuddin, Kochal, Kawdi, Gohar (Gawhar), Latif, Baru (Mehro) Khan, Qala-i-Mustana, Muqarab Khel, Mulla Janan, Muryani, Minzai, Naburhu, Wala, Qala-i-Wahab, Hotak, Lawar Khel, Yahya Khel, Saleh Khel, Zabet, Chambar-i-Khairuddin, Lawang, Qarya-i-Reza, Sahib Zadah-Khel, Chamberi-Shah Mohammad, Darband-i-Maryani, Nau-Khuni, Mal Khel, Kasem Khel, Holi Khel, Moteh, Ali, Malik Shinkai, Yunus Khel, Kakai, Egani, Tonak, Qala-i-Rona, Shamak Khel, Goyan, Waya Khel, and Atal. (LWA) In 1914 the area was described as follows: A district in the Ghilzai country, situated between the Ab-i-Istada lake and Mukur, and next to that district. It is very fertile, and is inhabited by Taraki Ghilzais and a few Duranis. (Broadfoot.)

*GIRDAB گرداب
34-9 68-42 m. A village on a stream, some 5 miles west of the Ghazni-Kabul highway.

GIRDAO گرداو
34-24 70-43 m. A village in the Kama division of the Jalalabad district, on the left bank of the Kabul river, nearly opposite Lachipur. Inhabitants: Mohmands. (Jenkyns.)

*GIRDAO گرداو
34-17 71-7 m. A village on the Kabul river, a few miles north of Kama Daka. Another place with this name is on a tributary of the Kunar river, northwest of Nishagam, at 34-14 71-17 m.

GIRDBED گردبید
34- 67-. A locality in the Besud country. (See Military Report of Hazarat, Part II.) Other places with this name are located north of Jaghuri in Ghazni province, at 33-14 67-26 m., on a tributary of the Dara-i-Jelga in Maidan province, at 34-22 68-18 m.; at 33-34 67-9 G., 34-44 66-55 G., and 34-52 66-59 G. (LWA)

*GIRDI گردی
34-49 68-43 m. A village in the Gumbad area, southeast of Surkho Parsa. Another village with this name is located on a tributary of the Kabul river, southwest of Ghanikhel, at 34-6 70-40 m.

GIRDI گردی
34-14 70-59 m. A village on the right bank of the Kabul river, about five miles west of Dakka. It contains some 700 families of Mohmands; headman (in 1904) Muhammad Azim, Sadbashi of khasadars. The inhabitants possess about 1,600 head of cattle, 1,200 sheep and goats, and 100 buffaloes; the annual production of wheat and barley averages about 90,000 Indian maunds; land revenue amounts to about 10,000 krans per annum. There is a shrine here of a famous saint who was said, among other divine properties, to be able to dive into the river at Girdikand to come up again at Attock. There is a force of 200 khasadars stationed at Girdi. The village is completely commanded by two small isolated hills to the west.
From Girdi a good road leads direct to Painda Khak, in the Khaibar, passing the Gurakki Obo spring on the way; it is fit for all classs of transport animals and could easily be made into a cart-road. (Malleson, Wanliss.)

GIRDI KACH گردی کچ
34-30 70-6 G. A small village on the right bank of the Kabul river

to the west of Khairo Khel and to the north of the Waragali pass, in the Laghman country. It consists of merely a few huts. It is said (1907) that the Amir intends to build a bridge over the Kabul river at this point. (Young.)

GIRDI KATS Or KACH گردی کٹ (کٹس)
34-23 70-40 m. Elevation 1,520 feet. A village surrounded by a considerble amount of cultivation, on the right bank of the Kabul river, 3 1/2 miles below Jalalabad. It contains some 160 families of Mohmands and Dehgans; headman (1904) Mir Afzal, Mohmand. The inhabitants possess about 500 head of cattle, 100 goats and 50 buffaloes. Land under cultivation amounts to 700 jaribs, the annual production of wheat and barley being about 28,000 Indian maunds. Land-tax is assessed at the rate of 9 kabuli rupees cash, and 16 kabuli seers grain, per jarib. The village lies about 3/4 mile from the river bank and the whole of the intervening ground is under cultivation, the crops being very rich. The principal crops are wheat, barley, jowar, rice, cotton, and pepper. There is a sarai, builty in 1905, at the west end of the village; it is completely commanded by the hills to the south.

There is room for a division to encamp on the stony plain to the south of the village, but the position is commanded by the semi-circle of hills to the south. Supplies are procurable on 1 or 2 days' notice. Fodder for about 5,000 animals for one day and about 500 maunds of unground grain may be collected from Girdi Kats and Kama. Fuel is obtainable. Water from an irrigation channel running through the village, or from the river. (Malleson, Wanliss, Johnston.)

GIRU گیرو
34-22 66-31 G. A small village on the right bank of the Nalgis stream. (See Military Report on Hazarajat, Part II.)

*GIRU گیرو
33-6 68-18 A. Giru is an alaqadari in Ghazni province. The alaqadari comprises an area of 877 square kilometers and has an agricultural population that has been estimated at from 6,000 to 12,767. The alaqadari is bounded in the west by Qarabagh, in the southwest by Ab Band, in the southeast by Jani Khel and Katawaz, in the east by Yusuf Khel, and in the north by Andar. Giru has about 56 villages, 6 of which have more than 500 inhabitants. The villages are listed in the PG as follows: Ahad, Idriskhel, Adina, Ereski, Akbar Khel, Bator, Baghgai, Badai, Bahadur Khel, Parcha, Pana, Tor Kosai, Jahangir, Chambar Abdulla, Khar Chosh, Khwarakai, Daysi, Spin Panay, Shagul Khel, Shokur, Shela, Safar Wal, Azmat, Alisher Khel, Anbar Khel, Qala-i-Arsala, Qala-i-Hakim, Qala-i-Surkh, Qala-i-Shorab, Qala-i-Abdulla, Qala-i-Musali-i-Safarwal, Qala-i-Sulaiman, Qarya-i-Tamir, Muy Bulagh, Matakhan-i-Sufla, Matakhan-i-Ulya, Mazar, Musa Khel, Milanai, Milaw, Nakam, Nani Ghund, Nazar Khel, Nemati, Qarya-i-Shal, Manaki, Ahmad Khel, Bahar, Kolagi, Zhazhgh-i-Rustam Khel, Qalagi, Koda, Qala-i-Irbahim, and Khata Khel. Other places with this name are located on a tributary of the Maidan river, north of Jaliz, at 34-31 68-39 m.; east of Behsud in Maidan province, at 34-21 67-59 m.; southeast of Bughra in Ghazni province, at 33-18 67-22 m.; northwest of Bughra in Ghazni province, at 33-21 67-20 m.; on a stream near Dasht in Bamian province, at 34-29 67-23 m.

*GIRUQOL گیرو قول
34-7 67-17 m. A village located on a tributary of the Helmand river in Bamian province. Another place with this name is on the Garmab

river, southwest of Qaraqol, at 34-5 67-34 m.

GOBARAK See CHAKMANI   گبرک

GODA   گودا
34-12 68-30 m. A village about 55 miles north of Ghazni and 32 miles northwest of Shaikhabad, on the direct road thence to Bamian. It is a small village situated in a confined but fertile valley. Here Outram bivouacked on the evening of his first march in prusuit of Dost Muhammad in 1839. (Outram.)

*GODALI   گدلی
33-3 68-15 m. A village near Dabar in Ghazni province. Another place with this name is located between Ghunday and Wazir in Nangarhar province, at 34-11 70-6 m.

*GODAN   گدان
34-9 68-44 m. A village located on a stream, southwest of top Kalai and the Ghazni-Kabul road.

*GODAR   گدر
34-14 70-1 m. A village in the Gandomak area, north of Wata. Another place with this name is northeast of the Shutur Gardan in Logar province, at 33-59 69-27 m.

*GODARA   گداره
34-18 69-41 m. A village located on a stream west of Doaw. Another village with this name is located on the Panjshir river, northeast of Astana, at 35-22 69-38 m.

GODARAN   گداران
35-21 69-29 m. A village in the Parandev Dara, 6 miles above its junction with the Panjshir. It contains some 15 families of Tajiks. (I.B.C.) Recent maps show the spelling Gudran. (LWA)

GODARMAN   گودرمان
35-9 68-58 G. A place in the Kaoshan glen about 12 miles above its junction with the Ghorband valley, on the road (North-East Afghanistan route No. 28) leading over the Kaoshan pass into the Khinjan valley. The glen, which just below Godarman is very narrow and confined, opens out here, and walled fields extend for some 2 miles up the glen. This would be the best halting-place between Burj-i-Guljan and the foot of the Kaoshan pass.

GOGAMAND Or GUGAH MANDAH KALAI   گوگامند مکی
34-35 69-35 m. A village of about 70 houses on both banks of the Kabul river, at the eastern end of the Tangi Gharu route. The valley here is fairly open, but there is a little cultivation and few supplies except ghi are available. Fuel however is procurable. There is room for 3 battalions to camp on the right bank, with water from springs and from the river. (I.B.C., Johnston.)

GOGHAI, AB-I See URAZGANI   گوغی

GOGRA See GAGRA   گگرا

*GOLA   گوله
34-1 67-28 m. A village near the Garmab river, east of Safidab in southern Bamian province.

*GOLAB KHUNE گلاب خونی
    32-49 68-50 m. A village located some 7 miles southeast of Omna in eastern Ghazni province.

GOLAI گلی
    34-12 70-46 m. A valley in the Jalalabad district, 2 miles west of Pesh Bolak. It contains numerous forts, 25 of which were destroyed by Brigadier Monteath in 1842. This officer describes the country as very favourable for troops, being very open and high, having abundance of the best water, plenty of good grass and forage for camels and horses, and much bhusa. In the valley are also 10 or 12 mills, and wheat is procurable in some quantity. (Monteath.)

GOMAIN گومین
    34-40 70-13. A township in Laghman, about 2 miles above the confluence of the Alishang and Alingar rivrs. It consists of the following hamlets:

    1. Kala-i-Amir Khan   8. Ziarat-i-Sultan Ghazi
    2. Kabela-i-Aziz Khan   9. Banda-i-Abdulla
    3. Kabela-i-Sultan Mahmud   10. Banda-i-Zafar
    4. Kabela-i-Pir Muhammad Khan 11. Banda-i-Haji
    5. Kabela-i-Purdil   12. Banda-i-Tar
    6. Kabela-i-Sufi   13. Kala-i-Sarwar Khan
    7. Kabela-i-Mulla   14. Banda

    The inhabitants are all Tajiks. (Warburton.)

GOMAL See GUMAL گومل

*GOMALI گمالی
    33-24 68-30 m. A village northeast of Mirai and southeast of Ghazni.

GONDI گندی
    34-16 70-10. A village on the right bank of the Kabul river, about 16 miles above Jalalabad. There are two fords across the river here through which runs a road to Mandrawar. The water at these fords, at any rate in the cold weather is not deep, and they are wide and safe. (I.B.C.)

*GOSHAK گوشک
    34-10 67-48 m. A village located on a stream east of Qaraqol.

GOSHA KALA گوشه قلعه
    A place in the Jaghatu Hazara country. (See Military Report on the Hazarajat, Part II.)

GOSHTA گوشته
    34-22 70-47 m. Goshta is a village and a woleswali in Nangarhar province. The woleswali comprises an area of 545 square kilometers and has an agricultural population that has been estimated at about 8,930. The woleswali is bounded in the north by Nur Gul and Khas Konar, in the east by Pakistan and Lalpur, in the south by Mohmand Dara and Bati Kot, and in the west by Kama. Goshta has about 12 villages, 4 of which have over 500 inhabitants. The villages are listed in the PG as follows: Khwajazai, Kundah Ghor, Goshta, Ragha, Arkhi, Sar Band, Sordak, Bila-i-Ulyam Bila-i-Sufla, Orsak, Wartak, Khar Bandi, and Banda. (LWA) In 1915 the area was described as follows: A village in the Jalalabad district on the left bank of

the Kabul river, nearly opposite Chardeh. Inhabitants: Mohmands. It is a large village with some open cultivated country round it. Between it and Kama there are a few hamlets with little strips of cultivation round them; but the greater part of the neighbouring country is barren and hilly, though practicable for laden animals. From Goshta, 5 miles to Chiknaur, the sides of the Bedaulat hill fall abruptly to the very brink of the river, quite impracticable for laden animals. Mules are taken from one village to the other by the Kulalas, a rough route crossing a rugged pass at the back of Bedaulat.

Teh Khan of Goshta is, or was Mughal Khan, the chief of Baizai Mohmands.

Khadi Khan is the ancestor of this house. Its minor branches have been portioned off in Kama and at Girdao, and enjoy the villages of Mayar, Gahik, Mama Khel, Safedbini, Girdao, Kala Yamin Khan, and Bazid Khel as jagir.

The principal line is now represented by the Khans of Goshta and of Chardeh. Khalik Khan, fifth in descent from Khadi Khan, was the last to hold the whole estate of the Khans in his hands. He lived during the first Afghan war, and was able to do service to Sir R. Sale at Jalabad. At his death his posessions were divided: Sayyid Amir, Azim Khan, and Bahram his sons by his first wife taking the villages on the right bank of the river, and Taj Muhammad Khan with his brothers, the sons of the second wife, settling at Goshta on the left bank. The sons by the third wife are of no account.

Taj Muhammad Khan died about 1880, and was succeeded by his son, Mughal Khan, a man of some energy and force of will. He was steadily hostile to the British in the war, and popular with his tribe. He held Goshta, Girdao, and Deh Tahir in jagir, receiving in cash Rs. 1,900, and in kind about Rs. 18,000 worth of produce, -- Total Rs. 20,000. He also arranged for the transit of Mohmand Kuchi caravans from Goshta via Bohai and Gandao to Peshawar levying tolls at the ferry near Goshta. The transit dues on this route were reported to be Rs. 3 per camel, divided equally among Baizai, Khwaizai, and Halimzai. One-half of the Baizai share was taken by Mughal Khan. (Jenkyns, Scott, Merk.)

According to another, and more reliable, acount, Mughal Khan was removed from the chiefship in November 1882 and replaced by Akbar Khan of Girdao. The following professes to be a genealogical table of this family:

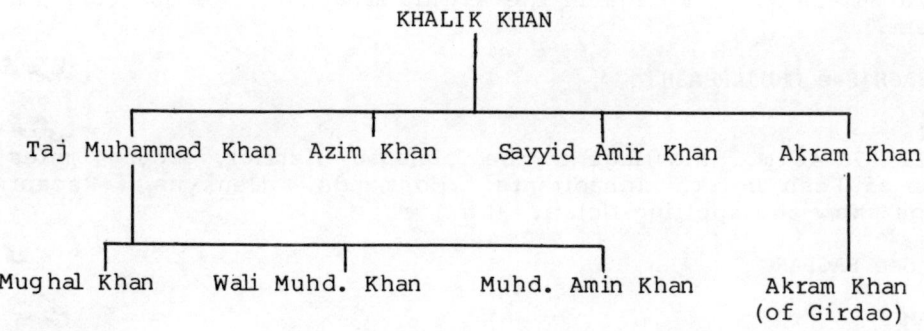

GOSPAND

34- 69-. A pass between Kabul and khurd Kabul over the same spur as the Khurd Kabul pass. It was used by General Pollock to turn the Khurd Kabul, by which means the passage of the latter was secured without molestation. (Stacy.) Recent maps show a place with the name Gosfanddara in this area, at 34-27 69-24 m. (LWA)

*GOTKAI گوتکی
33-31 70-3 m. A village located southeast of Bak in eastern Paktia province.

GOURDESH Or GAWHARDESH گاوهردیش (گوردیش)
35-24 71-35 m. Elevation 4,130 feet. A Kafiristan village, called also Istorgats by the Chitralis, and Ishtrat by the Kafirs, situated at the lower part of the Gourdesh valley, about 3 miles from the Bashgul river. Its inhabitants are of mixed descent, and do not belong to the Kam tribe. The village is built on the rocky knife-edge of a narrow spur which projects into the valley nearly at right angles to it, and forces the river to take a pear-shaped course round its base. Owing to the limited space available for building, there are not more than 25 houses, all of which are greatly over-crowded. On the south side of the spur is a precipice two or three hundred feet high; on the north side it is difficult of approach. The way to get to the village is along the neck of the spur which is narrow and well-defended.
There are plenty of cultivated fields along the river bank. Roads lead from Gourdesh to the Patkun pass and to Bazgul. (Robertson.)

GUDA گودا
A section of the Sahak Ghilzais settled in Kharwar and Paghman, and also in Logar at Ab-i-Josh in the Bibi Shilghar pass. (McLean.)

*GUDAH گوده
32-46 68-24 m. A village in the Ghanikhel area, southwest of Zarghun Shahr.

GUDAH See KHURDAK TAKHTA گوده

GUDAL گودل
33- 68-. A place in Kharwar, said to be 9 miles north of Ispidar, on the road from Kharwar to Ghazni. (Gaselee.) A village with this name is located on a lake near Shahr-i-Bala-i-Khawat in northern Ghazni province, at 34-5 67-59 m. (LWA)

*GUDAL PITAO گودل پیتاو
33-20 67-58 m. A village in the Asghir area, south of the Qolyaqol stream.

GUJARBASH See GHUJARBASH گوجربش

GULAHI گولائی
34-12 70-46 m. A village in the Jalalabad district, about 4 miles west of Pesh Bolak. Inhabitants: Mohmands. (Jenkyns.) Recent manps show the spelling Gula'i. (LWA)

GULAK See SAGPAR گلک

*GULARAM گل آرام
34-41 70-20 m. A village located east of Mehterlam at the foot of the Amber Ghar.

GULBAHAR گلبهار
35-8 69-18 m. A large village in the Charikar district, situated on the right bank of the Panjshir stream. It contains 300 houses of Tajiks, and there is a wooden bridge over the stream, practicable

for horsemen and yabus, etc., but not for camels. (Shahzada Taimus.)

GULBAURI گلبوری
A pass leading west form Ghazni into the Hazara valley of Jarmatu over the Gulkoh range. (See Military Report of Hazarajat, Part II.)

*GULDAD گلداد
32-46 68-25 m. A village in the Janikhel area, southwest of Zarghun Shahr.

*GULDAG گلداک
34-16 70-58 m. A village on the Kabul river east of Basawul and on the opposite bank of the river.

GUL DARA See KAH DARA گل دره

*GULDIN KALA گلدین قلعه
33-41 69-23 m. A village in the Tutakhel area, northeast of Gardez.

*GULHAMID گل حمید
34-16 69-17 m. A village on a path leading west to the Logar valley in the Gumaran area.

*GULIBANDA گل بنده
35-1 71-28 m. A village on a tributary of the Kunar river, between Asmar and the Pakistan border.

*GULIKHEL گلی خیل (گلو)
34-18 69-46 m. A village on a stream northwest of Chahartut.

GUL-I-ROBAT گل رباط
34-41 66-59. A pass over the Koh-i-Baba, west of the Zard Sang. It is reached from Siah Bumak at the head of Sar-i-Kol in the Yak Walang district. On the south side of the kotal is Sar-i-Bulak Targhai, not the same as the Sar-i-Bulak south of the Zard Sang pass. It is said to be a better pass than the Zard Sang, and about the same as the Bakkak. (Maitland.)

GULJATNI گل جتنی
34- 68-. Said to be a village near the south side of the Hajigak pass. It is inhabited by Hazaras.

GULKARIA گل قریه
34-40 70-11. A village in Laghman, on the left bank of the Alishang river, about 2 miles northwest of Tigri. The inhabitants are Musa Khels. (Warburton.)

GUL KOH گل کوه
33-16 67-49 m. A range of hills which starts from the Paghman range about Lat. 34, Long 68, and runs south forming the watershed between the Arghandab and Tarnak rivers, and bounding Ghazni on the west. (See Military Report on Hazarajat, Part II.) There is also a village in this area with the name Erma-i-Gul Koh. (LWA)

GULKOHI گل کوهی
A section of the Chahar Dasta Hazaras. (See Military Report on Hazarajat, Part II.)

*GULMIRZA KHEL گل میرزاخیل
   35-8   69-16 m.   A village on the Panjshir river, northeast of Charikar.

GUL MUHAMMAD گل محمد
   A village marking the eastern extremity fo the Surkhab Tangi in the Logar valley. See "Sang Dara."

GULRAZ گلراز
   33- 69-.   A village on the left bank of the Karaia stream, about 3 miles east of Ahmad Khel and opposite the junction with the Karaia of the Lajha nala. There is a customs post here with 10 khasadars. (I.B.C.) Another place with this name is located at 35-28   66-52 G. (LWA)

GULZAR گلزار
   32-43 67-13 G.   A place in the Hazarajat. (See Military Report on Hazarajat, Part II.) Another place with this name is located south of Kabul at 34-23   69-10 m. (LWA)

*GUMAL گومل
   32-30 68-51. Gumal is a woleswali in Paktia province. The woleswali comprises an area of 4,072 square kilometers and has an agricultural population that has been estimated at from 10,359 to 16,781. The woleswali is bounded in the west by Omna, Janikhel, and Wazakhwa, in the north by Sarhawza, Sarobi, and Barmal, in the east by the State of Pakistan, and in the south by Wol Mamay. Gumal has some 60 villages, 6 of which have more than 500 inhabitants. The villages are listed in the PG as follows: Bahadur Khel, Hawas Khel (Koshi Khel), Shah Gul Berimi, Khumaruddin Kalai (Mulla Khumaruddin), Mirza Kala (Qarya-i-Mirza Payendah Khan), Ali Zai (Mulla Rahim-i-Ali Zai), Dawud Khel, Mohamad Jan Khel, Mulla Sultan Kala (Mulla Sultan Sayed Khel), Sinzela, Moshagai, Bazo, Eid Mohammad, Pir Mohammad, Dabar, Jangai Khan, Nawab Kalai (Ali Nawab), Kherman Zai (Kherman Dargai), Esagai, Zangi Khel, Musa Khel, Sharki Haibati, Duchar Baran-i-China Kalai (Tor China), Shaikh Karimdad, Sulaiman Khel, Ya Khel (Yahya Khel Dost Mohamad), Shir Gulai, Kheder Khel, Srah Darga, Shadi Khan Kochi (Shad Gul-i-Kochi), Baghgai, Bang, Zawli Khel, Sayed Khel Mulla Rasul (Sayed Khel Kochi), Karim Khan, Bacho Khel Kochi, Kundah Khel Kalai (Kundah Khel Kochi), Kakelzai, Khwajagai, Rozi Khan, Mir Ahmad, Musa Kalim, Nabi Khan, Khan Shirin, Maghreb, Ya Khel Kalagai (Yahya Khel-i-Kalagai), Nemat Khan, Paroti, Gul Khan, Mir Azam, Shadizai-i-Kochi, Zawli Khel, Roz Sayed Khel (Sayed Khel Sufla), Bobi Sayed Khel, Khado, Payendah Khel, Tor Babu Khel, Khalifa Gumal (Khalipa Gumal), Amand Khel, Tabut, Ahmad Kheli-Ulya, Ahmad Khel-i-Sufla, Alzai, Kherkai, and Chamber Dara-i-Star.

GUMAL گومل
   A river which rises in the slopes of the Sulaiman range in two branches. The first, which, for the purposes of this article is taken as the main stream, rises near the fort of Kala-i-Babakar in the Kharoti country from several small springs which join near the fort, whence it flows in a general southerly direction to Domandi about 90 miles from its source, being joined at this place by the Kundar from the southwest. From Domandi the joint stream runs for 32 miles in an easterly direction through British territory to Khajuri Kats. Here the Gumal and Zhob rivers unite: below this point the course of the combined stream is too well known to require description.
   Broadfoot is our best authority regarding the course of the Gumal as

far as Domandi. According to his account, the stream rapidly increases below Kala-i-Babakar, till at 6 miles it is 12 feet wide 6 inches deep, and runs 4 feet per second. The banks here, 3 feet high and 200 yards wide, show that river is considerable in March. The channel winds in tortuous curves all down the valley to the foot of the Waziri Maranu ranges, which then confine the river into a narrow space between higher rocks with more frequent curves. At 14 miles from its source it joins the other branch or the Dwa Gumal. This rises in the hills southeast of Sarafsar, and flows through the Kharoti country, draining the Waziri and Kohnak ranges. It is of the same size as the other branch. Thence for 6 miles to Sarmargha, where there is an open space 500 yards wide; thence at 2-1/2 miles the river is joined by the salt rivulet Ab-i-Talkh. Thence the channel is narrow, and winds to every point of the compass in bends at every 300 yards yet never less than 30 yards wide. At 3-1/2 miles further is Mamatsile, a large white rock in the centre of the pass, whence the valley becomes wider and straighter to Staghai. But from this for 5 miles it again winds very much so that the road down it crosses very frequently. It is here 20 feet broad and 1 foot deep. Thence for 24 miles, Broadfoot makes no mention of the river, but it is probable that it runs during this distance between steep cliffs, as the road leaves the river altogether and takes to the hillsides. Kafilas, however, sometimes prefer to follow the river-bed between Staghai and Domandi.

Looking up from Domandi, the river is seen to be locked in by high hills; going down it, however, the banks gradually diminish in height, till at 2 miles below the Kundar junction the valley opens out to nearly a mile broad, and is here known as Maricho Kats. After passing the latter the valley narrows again, and at 3 miles is only 150 yards broad. On the left is the Zarmelan plain, and on the right Manzaraguna. At 4-1/2 miles the valley begins to open again, and at 5 miles Gul Kats is reached. It is about 4 miles long, and at its widest part 1 mile broad. Below the further side of Gul Kats the road leaves the Gumal, crosses the Khajuri Kotal, and again strikes it at Kotkai, or Dobandi. From this place to Khajuri Kats is 12 miles. The road follows the river sometimes along its bed, sometimes along its banks, in places very high and rocky. At its junction with the Zhob the Guma flows between precipitous banks 30 feet high, and its bed is about 200 yards broad. (Broadfoot, Masson, I.B.C.)

*GUMBAD Or GUNBAD گمبد (گنبد)
34-41 67-59 G. A village located about 22 miles southeast of Bamian. Nearby is Gumbad Thani, located at 34-54 67-37 G.

*GUMBADAK گمبدک
34-12 67-21 m. A village on the Helmand river, northeast of Khushqol. Another place with this name is on a tributary of the Ghorband river, at 34-59 68-39 m.

*GUMBADI گمبدی
34-22 67-3 m. A village on a stream northeast of Panjao in Bamian province.

GUMBAT گمبت
34- 67-. A village in the Surkhdar subdistrict of Bamian, situated on the upper course of the Bamian stream and containing about 50 houses of Neka Hazaras. The valley runs from northwest to southeast; it is 300 to 400 yards wide, and well-cultivated.
From Gumbat a road goes up the valley, which turns north. It leads

over the Chap Kolak Kotal, and thence down a long ravine to Karaona in Saighan, Taking a line generally parallel to that of the main road by Ak Robat. There are also roads to Karghanatu and Shahidan. They are, however, indifferent, and laden camels can only traverse them with difficulty. They are tolerable bridle tracks. (Sahibdad Khan.) Two places spelled Gunbad are located at 34-54 67-37 G. and 34-41 67-59 G. (LWA)

GUMBAT گمبت
34- 68-. A group of three villages in the Kalu Dara, in the southeast of the Bamian district, containing in all 30 families of Daraghan Hazaras. (Amir Khan.) Two other places with this name are located southeast of Ghazni, at 33-23 68-35 m. and 33-24 68-55 m. (LWA)

*GUMBAZA گمبذه
34-22 69-14 m. A village in the Logar valley, south of Kabul.

*GUMBAZI گمبذی
34-12 67-56 m. A village on a stream, south of Behsud in Maidan province.

GUMRAN گمران
34-17 69-9 m. A village on both banks of the Logar river, about 2-1/2 miles below Sayyidabad, or Zahidabad, where the main road from Kurram crosses the river. Inhabitants: Adramzai Ghilzais and Tajiks; headman (1906) Sultan Muhammad Khan. The four fortified hamlets of which the village was then composed contained in 1880, 150 families. The country all round is richly cultivated. Tracks, fit for camel transport, lead down either bank of the river from Gumran to the entrance to the Sang-i-Nawishta gorge, where the main road to Kabul is re-joined. There is a rude country bridge across the river at Gumran itself. (I.B.C.)

*GUNDALAM گند هلام
34-42 70-22 m. A village northwest of the Kuh-i-Kashmund and south of Alingar.

*GUNGI گنگی
34-13 67-52 m. A village on a stream south of Behsud in Maidan province.

*GURAND گورند
32-16 67-51 m. An area northwest of Nawa and south of the Ab-i-Istada.

GURBAZ گرباز
A tribe who live in the hills south of Khost. They are descended from Khadri, son of Wazir, and consequently are a branch of this clan. At first they resided to the north of the Mahsud territory. About 200 years ago they attacked the Batannis, and drove them from the Gabar mountain; but the Batannis, assembling their tribe, regained the hill and the Gurbaz were gradually driven to the hills mentioned above. They then appear to have recovered strength and, being a warlike tribe, took some land from the Khostwals. They are now under the governor of Khost. In manners and customs they are similar to the Khostwals, but in appearance they are like the Wazirs. They have now no feelings of clanship with the latter, though they acknowledge the relationship. They are supposed to number about 1,500 fighting men, and are principally employed in agricul-

ture, trading, and furnishing escorts to merchants. (Muhammad Hyat.)

"The Gurbaz extend from the (Indo-Afghan) boundary now demarcated to the watershed into Khost. It is a country of lowish hills and is covered with a network of valleys. The Gurbaz do no build houses, but live all the year round in grasshuts. There is fair grazing on the hills. They work as carriers in addition to cultivating and grazing. Two-thirds of them live in Khost, and those on this (the Tochi) side of the watershed have much intercourse with Khost. They have paid revenue to the Governor of Khost for the last two years. The chief valleys of the Gurbaz on the west are the Zanshora, the Shadiaka and Mughalgai. The last two join the Zanshora, and the united stream which runs into Dandi is called Sanjala, and lower down Kanibogh. The main valley of the eastern part of the country is named Charkhai. Its chief tributaries are the Musha and the Sir Khobi. The southern slopes of Laram are drained by the Goreshta, which falls into the Kaitu. (Anderson.)

For a fuller description of the Gurbaz see "Military Report on Waziristan, 1905," pp. 124-126.

GURBAZ See SAFI گرباز

GURBED گوربید
33-36 68-42 G. A kotal leading over the hills southwest of Kharwar. The ascent to the watershed is easy and the track good. The descent to Robat is sudden and would be impassable for wheeled guns. This is the principal route to Shilghar from Western Kharwar. (Griesbach.)

*GURBUZ گوربز
33-17 69-54. Gurbus is an alaqadari in Paktia province. The alaqadari comprises an area of 385 square kilometers and has an agricultural population that has been estimated at from 6,561 to 13,665. The alaqadari is bounded in the west by Tani, in the northwest by Mandozai, in the east by Khost, and in the south by the State of Pakistan. Gurbuz has some 32 villages, 7 of which have more than 500 inhabitants. The villages are listed in the PG as follows: Izhdan (Izhnwal), Bagi Khel, Mangala, Mullayan (Mulayan Kalai), Shahid Kalai, Ghondi Kalai, Tawdah China, Shaikh Amir Kalai (Sher Gul Kalai), Ghulam Khan, Padsha Kalai, Mashi Kalai (Mesher Kalai), Sargalai (Sar Kalai), Kegai, Lagai Khel, Zin Sherah (Zen Shorah), Zhawaruna (Zhawar Kalai), Natsay Khel (Zalai Khel, Manzai Khel), Shodika (Shudyak), Katskai (Kajakai), Gulak Khel, Khandir (Khander Kalai), Mir Akbar, Shaykhan, Kodi Khel (Kozbori Khel), Bori Khel (Barbori Khel), Khan Kotkai (Kotgai Khan), Patlan, Kotkai Shaikh Amir Lashra, Lalizha, Keptan Kalai, Walo Kalai, Balai (Barai), Natori, Mazi, Zhasir Kalai, Dala Kalai, Nyazi Khel, Kod Khel, Razhd Twan, Narali, and Nai-Shin Kalai.

*GURDUM گوردم
34-19 67-29 m. A village near the Helmand river, south of Shewqol Karez in Bamian province.

*GURGI گرگی
33-49 68-8 m. A village on the Shemeltu river, southwest of Gazak.

GURGI-MAIDAN گرگی میدان
34- 69-. An extensive plain to the east of the Surkhao-Mazgin valley in Logar. It contains one fort. (I.B.C.) A village with this name is northeast of Zarghun Shahr and one mile north of Randa-

khel, at 34-14 69-23. (LWA)

*GURG KUSHTA گرگ کشته
33-55 67-57 m. A village north of Okak (Nawur) in Ghazni province.

GURGURI گرگی
34- 70-. A village in the Hisarak division of the Jalalabad district, situated on the northern slopes of the Safed Koh. Inhabitants; Shinwaris. (Jenkyns.)

GURSALAK گرسالک
35-1 70-51 G. A village of 120 houses in Kafiristan, situated on the left bank of the Presungul, about 29 miles above Chigha Sarai. Supplies are plentiful here. (I.B.C.)

GUZARA گذرا
A village on the Kabul-Hazarajat-Daulat Yar road. (See Military Report on Hazarajat, Part II.)

GUZARGAH گذرگاه
34-30 69-7 G. A village in the Chardeh valley, on both banks of the Kabul river, 1-1/2 miles south of Deh-i-Mozang. The two portions are connected by a good brick bridge wide enough for field-guns. On the right bank the villagers are Tajiks; on the left, Kizilbashis and Sayyids. The former have some 300 to 400 houses, the latter about 200. (I.B.C.)

GUZAR-I-MAMA-KHATUN گذر ماماخاتون
34- 69-. A village in the Koh Daman of Kabul, between Baba Kush Kar and Kala-i-Murad Beg. It has 15 forts and some 400 houses in all. Inhabitants: Tajiks, Rikas, Ghilzais, and a few Sikh traders. (I.B.C.)

*GWASHTEH See GHWASHTEH گواشته

*HABIB KALAI حبیب کلی
32-27 67-37 m. A village located west of the Ab-i-Istada, and east of the Qalat-Ghazni road.

HADA Or ADDA هده
34-22 70-29 m. A village in the Chapriar subdivision of the Jalalabad district, about 6 miles due south of Jalalabad. It is a place of considerable trade and contains some 400 families of Mohmands. It is known as having formerly been the residence of the late Najam-ud-Din, generally known as the "Hada Mulla," who was a great power among the Mohmands and always very hostile to the British. Mir Sahib Jan Badshah, and other pupils of the "Hada Mulla," now reside here. (I.B.C.) Recent maps show the spelling Ada. (LWA)

HADIA KHEL عدیه خیل
34- 70-. A village in the Chapriar subdivision of the Jalalabad district, about 12 miles west of Mazina. Inhabitants: Shinwaris. (Jenkyns.) Recent maps show the spelling Adadkhel, at 34-16 70-13 m. (LWA)

*HAFIZA حافظه
34-14 67-12 m. A village on the Qol-i-Tsuitaman, a tributary of the Helmand.

HAFIZ KALA حافظ قلعه
34-17 70-22. A village of 9 houses in the Chapriar subdivision of the Jalalabad district. It lies near the left bank of the Chapriar stream, about 1 mile west of Kandibagh on a road from Basawal to Safed Sang. A small stream from the Safed Koh runs by the village. Inhabitants: Ghilzais. (I.B.C.)

HAFIZULLA KALA حفيظ الله قلعه
34- 69-. A small hamlet on the left bank of the Logar. The inhabitants are Astanazais. There were only four families living in this hamlet in 1880. (Clifford, Euan Smith.)

HAFT ASIA هفت آسيا
33-50 68-37 m. A halting place 21 miles from Ghazni, 64 miles from Kabul, near some low hills and in the midst of ten to twelve walled villages surrounded by cultivation. Supplies and water, sufficient for three brigades, are available. Water is procured from karez. Camel forage and short grass, straw and lucerne are procurable. The inhabitants are Wardaks. (Campbell, I.B.C.)

HAFT CHAH هفت چاه
34- 71-. A small stone fort, 8 miles from Landi Kotal and 5 miles from Dakka. It is garrisoned by 50 khasadars, armed with Lee-Metfords, and is well posted on the top of a conical hill, about 100 feet high, 1 mile from the western exit of the Khaibar pass. The "Seven Wells," after which the fort is named, have long since been stopped up, and the nearest water-supply is now a spring about 1,000 yards to the east of the fort. There is also a good spring of water on the northern side of the Gara ridge; over this ridge a camel-pass leads due north to Kam Dakka; parties using this route should be provided with a guide, as it may easily be mistaken, as was done once in 1879. (Mallesone, I.B.C.)

*HAFT GODI هفت گدى
34-19 67-20 m. A village on the Tagab-i-Sagsukhta, south of the Kuh-i-Shar.

HAFT KOTAL هفت كوتل
34- 69-. A pass on the route from Jalalabad to Kabul, between Tezin and Khurd Kabul. The name signifies "seven passes" though Hough reckoned eight, and remarks "an enemy might dreadfully annoy a column moving down this last descent, as they would have a flanking fire on it;" and in fact in this defile, about 3 miles long was consummated the massacre of the British force in the disastrous attempt to retreat from Kabul at the commencement of 1842. Here, also, in September of the same year, the Afghans, after their defeat at Tezin, attempting to make a stand, were in turn utterly routed with great slaughter by General Pollock's army. (I.B.C.)

HAFT KOTAL هفت كوتل
34-26 69-9. A spur of 7 peaks thrown off to the southwest from the Takht-i-Shah mountain at Kabul. It separates the Chardeh valley from that of Charasia, and is separated from the Korogh mountain by the Kabul river. At its northern base it has the villages of Kala-i-Fathu, Rishkhor, and Kala-i-Ali Muhammad; on its southern slopes it has Kala Arsala Khan; and at the edge of its southern skirts stand the villages of Charasia and Chehil Dukhtaran.
The best road over the spur is from Indaki, leaving Kala-i-Fathu to the west. This, however, is only fit for mule batteries to cross. (I.B.C.)

HAGAH هگا
   34- 70-. A village in the district of Jalalabad, at the foot of the Safed Koh. It is situated on the southern road between the Khaibar pass and Kabul, and 75 miles southeast of the latter place. The adjacent country is watered by numerous streams descending from the Safed Koh, and is remarkable for picturesque beauty. (Thornton.)

*HAIBAT هیبت
   33-8 68-43 m. A village located 3 miles south of Sharan and east of the mountain of the same name.

*HAIBATI هیبتی
   32-44 69-3 m. A village located 4 miles southwest of Sarobi in Paktia province.

*HAIBAT KHEL هیبت خیل
   34-50 69-42 m. A village located about 2 miles southeast of Tagab alaqadari seat and north of Sarobi. Another place with this name is southwest of Gardez, at 33-32 69-2 m.

HAIDAR حیدر
   A subdivision of the Polada Hazaras of Ujaristan, (See Military Report on Hazarajat, Part II.)

HAIDAR حیدر
   A section of the Jaghuri Hazaras. (See Military Report on Hazarajat, Part II.)

HAIDAR BEG حیدر بیگ
   A section of the Dai Kundis. (See Military Report on Hazarajat, Part II.)

HAIDAR KHANI حیدرخانی
   34-36 70-13 m. A village in Laghman, 4 miles to the north of Mandrawar on the right bank of the Alingar river. The following is a list of the forts and hamlets composing the township:

   1. Banda-i-Fakir   8. Kala-i-Nao
   2. Kala-i-Muhammad Sayyid   9. Kala-i-Nazir Turabaz
   3. Kala-i-Hameshabahar   10. Kala-i-Muhammad Jan
   4. Banda-i-Tajo   11. Karaho
   5. Kala-i-Ayub   12. Kala-i-Shahghasi
   6. Banda-i-Ali Ahmad   13. Kala-i-Mullayan
   7. Kala-i-Nao   14. Kala-i-Mirza

   The inhabitants are Tajiks. (Warburton.)

*HAIDAR KHEL حیدرخیل
   34-9 70-37 m. A village on a tributary of the Kabul river between Haska Mina and Ghanikhel.

HAIDAR KHEL حیدرخیل
   33-57 68-42 m. Elevation 7,647 feet. A village 33 miles from Ghazni, 54 miles from Kabul, in the Takia district situated in a beautiful valley between low hills, watered by a feeder of the Logar, and richly cultivated. There is a fort here on the east of the road and 1 mile on the west a number of villages with much cultivation. This village is notorious for the audacity and skill of its robbers. It was here that Fateh Khan, the Afghan king-maker, was murdered by Shah Mahmud and his son Kamran, a crime which had

the unexpected result to the perpetrators of ending the Sadozai dynasty.

A good camping ground exists to the west of the road with room for 2 infantry brigades, and another for a similar force can be found about 1 mile to the south, between Haidar Khel and a place called Takin, or Takia. Supplies and water are available for 1 cavalry and 3 infantry brigades. (I.B.C.)

HAIDAR KHEL   حیدرخیل
33-19 69-51 A. A village on the right bank of the Shamil, or Kaitu, river, about 12 miles west of Matun. There is room for a division to camp here on uncultivated ground, with a sufficient supply of water. (I.B.C.)

*HAIDARKHUNE   حیدرخونه
32-28 68-26 m. a village on the Wech Khwareh, southeast of Khushamand.

HAIDAR (KOL-I)   قول حیدر
A ford over the Helmand in the Hazarajat. (See Military Report on Hazarajat, Part II.)

*HAJELLAH   حجلاه
34-4 67-21 m. A village on a tributary of the Garmab river, east of Pitaoqol.

HAJI   حاجی
A subsection of the Polada. (See Military Report on Hazarajat, Part II.)

*HAJI   حاجی
33-19 67-14 m. A village located on a stream, one mile southwest of Lalchak.

*HAJIABAD   حاجی آباد
35-0 71-23 m. A village located about 3 miles north of Bargam on a tributary of the Kunar river.

*HAJIAN   حاجیان
34-24 68-49 m. A village about 4 miles south of Kota-i-Ashro and north of Nerkh in Maidan province. Another place with this name is on the Maidan river southeast of Nerkh, at 34-20 68-58m.

*HAJI BAK GHAR   حاجی بك غر
35-19 71-14 m. A mountain located northwest of Bargam in Kunar province.

HAJIBINI   حاجی بینی
A subdistrict of the country of the Jaghuri Hazaras. (see Military Report on Hazarajat, Part II.)

*HAJIGAK   حاجی گك
34-4 67-17 m. A village located on a tributary of the Helmand river, east of the Pitaoqol area.

HAJIGAK or HAJI KHAK   حاجی گك
34-39 68-5 m. Elevation 12,000 feet. A pass over the Koh-i-Baba range, leading from the valley of the Helmand into the Bamian valley. It is crossed by the main Kabul Mazar-i-Sharif road (North-East Afghanistan route No. 32) at about 13-1/2 miles northwest of

Gardan Diwal, where the road crosses the Helmand. The ascent from the Helmand side, though steep, is practicable for laden animals; the descent on Bamian side is very steep, but the road is otherwise good, leading over open clay slopes, and would be practicable for wheeled guns with the aid of drag-ropes. The ridge forming the actual kotal is a fairly broad and gently rounded saddle, and there is a good extent of level and smooth ground on either side of the road where it crosses the crest. To the right of the road (going towards Bamian) the slopes on both sides of the kotal are moderate and open, and can be traversed with ease by cavalry and infantry. The soil is clay mixed with rock. Theses slopes could be well swept by rifle fire from the crest of the pass. In any attemp to hold this pass, except as a delaying, or rearguard, position, it would apparently be necessary to hold also the Khafzar Kotal to the south. There is no direct communication between the Hajigak and the Irak passes except back through Kharzar, a village 22 miles southeast of the former. The Hajigak pass is said to be considerably lower than the Irak, but even the Hajigak is closed by snow during January, February, March and April. Formerly the main road used to be over the Irak pass, but the Hajigak now appears to be always used in preference thereto. (I.B.C.)

*HAJI GHULAM RASUL CHINA حاجی غلام رسول چینه
32-6 68-34 m. A village located west of Wur and southeast of Wazakhwa.

*HAJIGUL MINA حاجی گل مینه
32-54 69-1 m. a village located southwest of Urgun in Paktia province.

*HAJI JANSHAH KALAI حاجی جانشاه کلی
32-14 68-13 m. A village located northwest of Wazakhwa and southeast of Shinkai Ghar.

HAJI KALA حاجی قلعه
34- 69-. A fortified village in the Koh Daman, about 13 miles north of Kabul. Inhabitants: Tajiks and Hazaras. It is the first stage on the most easterly of the three roads leading northwards from Kabul. It lies in the valley of a small stream which, running northwards for about 1-1/2 miles beyond the village, joins the Kara Dushman stream, a tributary of the Panjshir. Supplies procurable at Kala Haji; water abundant. From Kala Haji a road leads westwards through Kara Dushman to Kala Murad Beg, thus forming a lateral communication with the other two roads from Kabul towards Charikar. It was at Kala Haji that Sir Lepel Griffin, with General Gough's brigade, encamped to meet Abdur Rahman when the latter arrived from Turkistan in July 1880, to be installed as Amir of Kabul. (I.B.C.)

HAJI KALA حاجی قلعه
34- 69-. A village 7 miles west of Kabul, on the Ghazni road. The surrounding country is an expanse of groves, gardens, and orchards, watered by channels drawn from the Kabul river.

*HAJI KHEL حاجی خیل
32-59 67-58 m. A village northeast of Bazgai and east of the Mukur-Ghazni road.

HAJI MIR ALI حاجی میرعلی
A fort on the east side of the Kabul-Charasia road, 22 miles from the Bala Hisar. The faces of the fort, which is square, are 60

yards long, the walls high, with bastions at the angles. The inhabitants are Kizilbashis. (Kennedy.)

*HAJI MOQAM حاجی مقام
33-1 67-37 m. A village north of Siyah Deh in Ghazni province.

HAJI MUHAMMAD KHAN حاجی محمد خان
33-39 68-24 G. A village 9 miles north of Ghazni, containing 60 houses of Besud Hazaras, Wardaks, and Tajiks. (Muhammad Akbar Khan.)

*HAJI MULLA GOLAN KALAI حاجی ملاگلان کلی
32-14 68-15 m. A village northwest of Wazakhwa in southern Ghazni province.

HAJIPAIK حاجی پیک
34-42 69-3 m. A village in the Koh Daman of Kabul, 4 miles north of Karez-i-Mir, containing 80 houses. Inhabitants: Tajiks. (Kinloch.)

HAJI SAF KALA حاجی صاف قلعه
34- 69-. A square fort in the Kabul district, 1 miles west of Deh-i-Mozang, inhabited by Tajiks. (Kennedy.)

HAJI SHAKUR KHAN حاجی شکور خان
34- 70-. A village in the Surkhab division of the Jalalabad district. Inhabitans: Rikas. (Jenkyns.)

HAJI YUSUF KALA حاجی یوسف قلعه
34- 69-. A fort in the Chardeh valley of Kabul, about 1 mile west of Deh-i-Mozang to the north of the Ghazni road. There are 30 families of Gadi Hazaras in the place. (I.B.C.)

*HAKDAD حق داد
34-22 67-44 m. A village in the Helmand valley, west of Behsud.

HAKIMABAD حاکم آباد
34- 70-. A village in the Jalalabad district, 10 miles southeast of Nimla. Inhabitants: Khugianis. (Jenkyns.) Recent maps show a place with this name at 34-42 70-16 m. (LWA)

HAKIM KALA حاکم قلعه
34- 69-. A village in the upper Logar Valley which, together with Kala-i-Yakub and Khalilabad, forms a township. All three are inhabited by Hazaras. (Clifford.) Recent maps show a place with this name at 32-43 68-28 m. (LWA)

*HALMA حلمه
34-38 70-36 m. A village located on a tributary of the Kunar river, north of Dara-i-Nur.

*HALQABELO حلقه بیلو
33-18 67-16 m. A village on a stream, southeast of Lalchak.

*HALWAQOL حلواقول
34-39 67-14 m. A village in the Kuh-i-Baba range, east of Sariqol.

*HAMANAG همنگ (همه نگ)
34-58 69-40 m. A village on a tributary of the Tagab river, southeast of Nejrab.

247

*HAMZA   حمزه
    33-32 67-18 m. A village in the Amrestan valley, about 5 miles east
    of Ajrestan.

*HANGARA   هنگره
    35-11 69-10 m. A village on a tributary of the Salang river, north
    of Charikar.

*HANITWAL   حنیتوال
    33-16 68-46 m. A village southeast of Sardeh Band and northwest of
    Motakhan.

HANUR KALA See MAIDAN-I-PAI KOTAL   هنور قلعه

HAOZ   حوض
    Elevation 10,500 feet. A kotal crossed by the Bamian-Daulat Yar
    road soon after entering the Dai Zangi Country. (See Military
    Report on Hazarajat. Part II.)

HARIOB Or ARYOBSTER   هریوب (اریوبستر)
    33-56 69-42. A district inhabited by the Jajis, and comprising the
    valley of a stream which rises in the Sikaram and joins the Upper
    Kurram. Ali Khel, about half-way down the valley, has an elevation
    of 7,565 feet. The villages of this district are of peculiar con-
    struction, seldom consisting of more than four or five houses,
    usually situated on commanding eminences or in retired little glens.
    Those in the latter situation are provided with a detached tower of
    observation, in some instances supported on poles of pine wood, and
    ascended by a ladder. Each house is detached and forms a little
    fort of itself. The thick walls of stone and mud are pierced by
    numerous holes that serve the threefold purposes of ventilators,
    chimneys, and loopholes for firing through. The strong wooden door
    occupies the centre of one side, whilst the flat roof communicates
    by a trap-door and ladder (formed of the trunk of a tree, notched so
    as to form steps when the wood is fixed in a standing position) with
    the interior, an open space sunk below the level of the ground, and
    with galleries all round that shelter the family as well as their
    cattle, consisting of a few cows, goats, and horses, together with
    stores of grain, fodder, and fuel. Rice is the chief crop of this
    district. Bronchocele is not an uncommon disease among the Jaji
    inhabitants. The valley is exceedingly cold in the winter, but
    delightful during the summer months. The main road from the Paiwar
    Kotal to Kabul passes through the Hariob district. Two other roads,
    both said to be fit for camels, lead northwards from Bilut by the
    Lakarai Kotal to Gandamak, and by the Kharshatal Kotal to Khurd
    Kabul. From Ali Khel in Hariob a camel-road leads down the valley
    of the Karaia to Ahmad Khel on the Kurram route to Ghazni.

HARMUL   هرمل
    A village in Laghman, consisting of the following hamlets of mixed
    tribes:
                    1. Kala-i-Akram
                    2. Kabil-i-Akram
                    3. Ali Asghar   (Warburton.)

*HASAN   حسن
    32-40 76-40 m. A valley south of Ghojan (Aghojan) in the Tarnak
    valley.

HASANAK حسنك
A place in the Dai Kundi country. (See Military Report on Hazarajat, Part II.)

HASAN KHAN حسن خان
34- 69-. A small village in the Kabul district, on the left bank of the Logar river near Bagrami. (Kennedy.) Recent maps show the name Hasankhel, at 34-29 69-18 m. (LWA)

HASAN KHEL حسن خیل
33-52 69-41 A. A section of the Jajis. They have three large and four small forts containing 300 houses. Their number of fighting men is 1,000. There is much garden cultivation in their valley. Lumsden calls them the Husain Khel. (Agha Abbas.)

HASAN KHEL حسن خیل
33-53 69-40 G. A Jaji village about 8 miles from Ali Khel containing about 200 houses. Water is abundant throughout the year. No supplies available. (Johnson.)

*HASAN KHEL (AHMAD KHEL) حسن خیل
33-50 69-37. Hasan Khel is an alaqadari in Paktia province. The alaqadari comprises an area of 198 square kilometers and has an agricultural population that has been estimated by various Afghan sources at from 1,805 to 6,474. The alaqadari is bounded in the west by Sayed Karam, in the north by Jaji, in the east by Chamkani, and in the south by Lajmangal. Hasan Khel has some 24 villages, 3 of which have more than 500 inhabitants. The villages are listed in the PG as follows: Mokhi Kalai Hazar Darakht. Bekarai, Ali Khel, Merazi, Mesharai (Meshrai Khola), Mama Khel, Moshaka, Kabuli, Wom Hasan Khel, Da Hasan Khel-Loy Kala, Khelal Khel, Mani Khel, Deh Khwara, Sheshta, Ishkawa-i-Sekandar-Khel, Moti (Mokhi), Dray Khel, Ghundi, Kharzon (Kharzana), Salimi Kalai, Shaikho Kalai, Sikander Khel, Wodam-i-Ahmad Khel, Shawat, Shabad Khel, and Sprot-i-Hazar-Darakht.

*HASAN KHEL حسن خیل
33-55 68-41 m. A village located on the Ghazni-Kabul road, 4 miles southwest of Sayyidabad. Other places with this name are located on a tributary of the Tagab river, northeast of Nejrab, at 35-0 69-41 m., and on a tributary of the Alishang river, west of Feradoli, 34-46 69-59 m.

HASAN KHEL حسن خیل
An Afghan pastoral tribe who reside in the summer in the Hazarajat and in the winter in Laghman. They possess many camels, horses, asses, bullocks, and sheep. They are said to be a subdivision of the Sulaiman Khel Ghilzais. (Masson, I.B.C.)

*HASANZAI حسنزی
34-50 69-22 m. A village north of the Kuh-i-Safi and east of Istalif.

HASHIM KHEL هاشم خیل
34-15 69-59 A. A village containing about 100 houses, 1-1/4 mile east of Gandamak, in the Jalalabad district. It is inhabited by Kharbun Khugianis and is situated on the Marki Khel Stream which is here spanned by a stone and wooden bridge (see Marki Khel). Water abundant. Fodder and supplies procurable in small quantities. Vast ground for encampment. There is a customs post in the village.

(Jenkyns, Wanliss, Johnston.) Recent maps show the spelling Hasim Khel. (LWA)

HASHMAT KHAN حشمت خان
34-30 69-12. A village at the eastern base of the Takht-i-Shah and between Bini Hisar and the city of Kabul. It is situated 500 yards southwest of the Kabul-Charasia road, and to the north of the village is a marsh. (Kennedy.)

HASHTALAI هشت علی
One of the principal districts of the Dai Kundis. (See Military Report on Hazarajat, Part II.)

HASHTDAR See AZHDAR هشت دار

HASHT DARAKHT هشت درخت
Elevation 10,200 feet. The sixth stage on the road leading from Ghazni through the Besud country to Band-i-Amir. (See Military Reportoon Hazarajat, Part II.)

*HASKA MINA هسکه مینه
34-8 70-28 m. A village north of Spin Ghar and south of Jalalabad.

*HASTI هستی
32-42 68-21 m. A village located east of Khushamand and southwest of Janikhel, in Deh Bala Woleswali.

*HAUZ حوض
34-23 67-24 m. A village located on the Darazqol, north of the Kuh-i-Siahkhar.

HAUZ-I-KHAS حوض خاص
34-3 69-54 G. A pool and shrine on a spur of the Paghman range above the Koh Daman of Kabul. It is frequented by the Hindus of Kabul, Koh Daman, and Kohistan, who believe that it connects itself by a subterranean passage with the Ganges river. (I.B.C.)

HAUZ-I-MAHYA See SAR-I-CHASHMA (3) حوض ماهیه

*HAUZ-I-SHAH حوض شاه
34-46 67-8 m. A village located southwest of the Band-i-Amir lakes in Bamian province.

*HAYAT KHAN KALAI حیات خان کلی
34-6 69-13 m. A village located some 8 miles east of Kolangar and southeast of Mazgin.

HAZARA DARA هزاره دره
35-21 69-37. A large glen draining nearly due north, and entering the upper Panjshir valley about 3 miles below Marz. The first village, about one mile up is Tambanah (Tamana), containing 30 houses. At 2 miles are Pojawah and Malimah on either side of the stream, with 40 houses. The glen is said to be 200 yards wide here. At 4 miles is Malik Khel, 100 houses. At this village the glen forks, the right branch being the Abdulla Khel Dara, while the left is the Hazara Dara proper. Up the former, 5 miles from the main glen, is Bazgiran, containing 80 houses. At 6 miles is Tundkhu on the right bank of the stream. It has 60 houses. At 8 miles is the Abdulla Khel group of Hamlets on both sides of the glen, containing in all 200 houses. The glen is said to be here from 400 to 450

yards wide, and is well cultivated. There are no trees, and the people use buta for fuel. No good place to camp. The kotal at the head of the glen is called Nijrao; the road over it is said to be too dificult for pack yabus unless with very light loads. After descending into Nijrao the road is said to be good. The inhabitants of all the foregoing villages are Tajiks.
Ascending the left-hand branch of the glen, that is the Hazara Dara, the first village is Baba Ali, 8 miles from the main glen (4 miles from the fork). It has 60 houses of Gawi Hazaras. Here the glen again forks. Up the right branch, known as the Dara Jar Ali, at 9 miles (1 mile from last fork) is Jar Ali village, containing 60 houses of Gawi Hazaras. Up the left branch, the Hazara Dara, at 10 miles from the main glen and 2 miles from the last fork, is Sang-i-Khan, containing 100 houses of Gawi Hazaras. At 11 miles are the village of Gulab Khel and Dost Ali, containing together 60 houses of Gawi Hazaras. Four miles further up (15 miles) is Astana Kalan on the left bank of the stream. It has 30 houses of Musalman Kafirs of the "Koresh" tribe or section. The road, as far as this place, is practicable for horsemen and yabus with light loads. Onwards from Astana Kalan are two tracks over the hills. The one to the right leads to Farajghan, Najil and Laghman. It is said to be merely a footpath impracticable for horses. The left-hand path leads into Kafiristan, and is equally bad, being only fit for foot-men. (Shazada Taimus.)

*HAZARA, DEH-I- ده هزاره
34-57 69-12 m. A village located east of the Kabul-Charikar road, south of Charikar.

HAZARAJAT Or HAZARISTAN هزاره جات
(A full description of the district is given in the Military Report on the Hazarajat, from which the following is extracted.)
The Hazarajat is the name given to the great central mountainous region of Afghan occupied by the Hazara race. It must be considered a geographical rather than an ethnographical expression, for there are tracts exclusively inhabited by Hazaras which do not appear to be considered within the Hazarajat. Its exact limits cannot be defined, but the term appears to be applied to the country south of the Band-i-Baba, between the watershed of the Helmand and the Wardak country on the east and the Taimani country on the west. On the south it may be said to be bounded by the Baghran and Khunai subdistricts of Zamindawar, by the Kandahar districts of Dehrawad and Tirin and by the Nawa-i-Arghandab, a subsection of Kalat-i-Ghilzai. On the southeast is Ghazni in the Kabul District.
On the northern side of the Hazarajat the country of the Shaikh Alis together with Bamian mostly populated by Hazaras, and Yakh Walang to the west of Bamian which is exclusively Hazara, are not in the Hazarajat, although many Hazaras maintain that Yakh Walang is included. No Hazara inhabited country north of these places is included. But Lal and Sar Jangal, between Yak Walang and Daulat Yar, are in the Hazarajat. The area, elevation and history of the country are all dealt with in the Military Report, whilst the inhabitants, the various sections of the Hazaras, will be found under "Hazaras" and under their own special headings.

HAZARAS هزاره
A detailed description of the Hazaras is given in the Military Report on the Hazarajat whilst a description of their various tribes is also given under their several headings, namely:
Dai Kundi, Under this heading has also been included the Dai Zangi

tribe, not because they are one, but because they have been intimately connected both geographically and administratively and are nearly always spoken of together.
Besud
Dai Mirdad
Ghazni Hazaras. These comprise the Jaghatu, the Muhammad Khwaja and the Chahar Dasta Hazaras.
Jaghuri
Polada of Malistan and Ujaristan
Urazgani
Shaikh Alis, the Hazara inhabitants of Bamian and those of Yak Walang, will be found under their respective headings, whilst the Hazaras of Kala Nao are fully described in the Gazetteer of the Herat Province.)

HAZARA THANA   هزاره تانه
33- 69-. A square building, sides 150 feet in length, passed at the 12th mile from Dre Kala twoards the Shutur Gardan pass, close to the camping-ground of Kasim Khel.
The position is badly selected, as the hills at the back command and look into it. The Shutur Gardan pass is rather more than 2 miles further on. (Spratt, I.B.C.)

HAZAR CHASMA See KAJKAMAR 35-18 66-59 A.   هزاره چشمه

HAZARDARAKHT   هزاره رخت
33- 69-. Elevation 9,382 feet. A camping-ground of Ghilzais to the east of the Shutur Gardan pass, on the road from Kurram to the Logar valley. It is a plateau which is buried under snow for about half the year, but which forms the summer grazing ground for the Ghilzais, who collect here in large numbers with their families and flocks, from April to August, for the sake of the pasturage -- a short sweet grass and a stunted growth of artemisia, both of which are grazed indiscriminately; exept at the above-named season there is no food for man or beast for 20 or 30 miles round.
There is no village here, and though it is the broadest place in this elevated glen, there is but just room for the encampment of one regiment. Any force in camp here would have to be greatly scattered, and it would be a nasty place to be attacked in, but no better ground is to be had. (Lumsden.)

HAZARADARAKHT   هزار د رخت
33- 69-. A narrow winding defile, at the head of the stream of the same name, a tributary of the Kurram river. The road from Kurram towards the valley of the Logar ascends through this defile for 16 miles from the village of Rokian. The heights bounding the defile on either side are formed mainly of limestone, except where the defile branches off in little glens, that, winding north between the hills, convey their drainage into the main channel. The opposite heights are nowhere more than 600 or less, than 80 yards apart whilst their steep, and in many places perpendicular sides are thickly covered to the very bottom with trees. The interval between forms the stony bed of a mountain torrent, which has little water in it at times, but at others is of extreme violence. The defile is ended by a short sharp ascent by the Surkai Kotal to the plateau of Hazardarakht. (Lumsden.)

HAZAR KASH See CHAJ-I-HAZARA   هزار کش

*HAZARKHEL هزارخیل
33-24 68-57 m. A village on the road from Gardez to Ghazni, about 22 miles west of Gardez.

HAZAR KUCH See KHURD BARG هزار کچ

HAZAR NAO هزارنو
34-14 70-54 m. A large straggling village on the main Peshawar-Kabul road, 3 1/2 miles east of Basawal. It is one of the busiest and most populous places on this route containing about 900 families of Mohmands, headman (1904) Shakar Khan. The inhabitants possess about 2,500 head of cattle, 1,500 sheep and goats, 100 horses and 200 buffaloes. The annual production of wheat and barley averages about 170,000 Indian maunds; land revenue is said to amount to 30,000 krans per annum. The hills to the south are intersected by numerous ravines, draining into the Kabul river, which give the village its name. There is a good camping ground here, with plenty of grass and camel-grazing and an abundance of water from channels from the river. There is a force of 600 khasadars stationed here. (Malleson, Wanliss, I.B.C.)

HAZAR NAO هزارنو
33-38 68-57 m. A range of hills, being a parallel ridge to the Jadran range. It reaches a height of about 2,500 feet above the plain of Ghazni and is bare and rugged in its aspect. It is a southern spur of the range of mountains which connects the Paghan with the Safed Koh, and is sometimes called Ghar Koh. (Broadfoot.)

*HAZARNAO هزارنو
34-37 71-4 m. A village located on a tributary of the Kunar river, southeast of Narang. Nearby is another village with this name, at 34-38 71-4 m.

HAZRAH هزره (ازرو)
Elevation 13,458 feet. A halting place 2 miles west of the Shutur Gardan pass. There is a small fort here, which is the limit of the Ghilzais in this direction. The country around Hazrah stretches away to the northeast in a succession of tolerably level plateaux of considerable length, though of no great breadth, and forms an elevated table-land, which for half the year is more or less covered with snow. In the summer months this region is resorted to by various nomad tribes of the Ghilzais, who here find sustenance for their flocks and refuge for themselves from the heat of the plains. It abounds with wormwood and orchids; lilies and tulips are strewed about in every direction. No supplies are procurable here, but water can be procured from springs, the sources of the Surkhab. The ground for encamping is good, there being commanding heights all round which could be held. It is sometimes called Ucha Margha. (Lumsden.) Recent maps show the name Azrow at 34-11 69-39 A.

HAZRAH هزره
34- 69-. A pass between Taghan and Aspando Kas, on the road from the Lakarai Kotal to Hisarak. This pass is steep on both sides, but the soil is not difficult to work and could be easily cleared for the passage of troops. (Collett.)

HAZRAT LUT حضرت لوط (؟)
34- 70-. A shrine in the Jalalabad district, within a mile of Tatang in a valley of the Safed Koh. It is said to be the grave of Lot, and is 33 yards in length, enclosed by a wall rudely

253

constructed of stones. It is surrounded with poles surmounted with flags and a rich collection of stones thrown down by devotees. (Masson.)

HELMAND   See Volume 2.   هلمند

*HEMAT   همت
   33-48 67-43 m. A village north of the Dasht-i-Nawar and east of the Qarabayn mountain.

HERAT KHEL   هرات خیل
   33- 68-. A village, about 16 miles northeast of Ghazni, on the road to Kharwar. (I.B.C.)

HERDAH   هرده (؟)
   34- 70-. A village in the valley of Jalalabad. (McGregor.)

HIDA Or ADA   هده
   34-22 70-29 m. A village 5 miles south of Jalalabad. It is remarkable for several topes, mounds, and caves--the relics of a people of whom no other memorial exists. The topes may be described as structures of rude masonry, having generally a cylindrical base surmounted by a hemispherical dome. They are solid, and the fact that they have been found in most instances to contain small cases, the depositories of relics, cannot be considered to negative this proposition. Those which have been opened have been ascertained to contain ashes, bones, and other decayed animal matter, metallic and earthen vessels, gold and silver ornaments, and many gems and coins; to quote the words of Masson --"the major part silver Sassanian, but also several gold ones, of which, singular to relate, are five of Roman emperors, two of Theodosius, two of Leo, and one of Marcianus." As these emperors reigned between A.D. 408 and 474, there is thus conclusive evidence that the structures in which these coins have been found must have belonged to an era not earlier than the fifth century; and as they are by the best judges regarded as unquestionably Buddhist monuments, they cannot be referred to a later period than the eighth century, at which period Muhammadanism became predominant in Afghanistan. (Thorton.) Also see Hadda (LWA).

HIDWANI   هدوانی
   34-11 70-38 G. A village in the Jalalabad district, about 7 miles southwest of Batikot. Inhabitants: Tirais. (Jenkyns.)

*HILALKHEL   هلال خیل
   33-2 67-48 m. A village south of the Dasht-i-Nawar in Ghazni province.

HILAZAI   هلازی (هلازی؟)
   A section of the Sulaiman Khels.

HINDKI   هندکی
   The name given to the Hindus who live in Afghanistan. They are Hindus of the Khatri class, and are to be found all over Afghanistan even amongst the wildest tribes. They are wholly occupied in trade, and form an important and numerous portion of the population of all the cities and towns, and are also to be found in the majority of large villages. This enterprising people transact much of the banking business of the country, and by these means they prove useful to the Afghans, who, indeed, could not get on without them. The Hindkis, on their part, though they appear to thrive and live

happily, nevertheles labour under many disabilities and restrictions of their liberty, the endurance of which is a proof of the profit they extract from those amongst whom they dwell as exiles. Besides paying a high capitation tax, termed "jizia," they are denied many privileges enjoyed by other races in the country who profess the Muhammadan religion. They are not allowed to perform or observe any of their religious ceremonies in public, nor are they allowed to give evidence in a court of justice, nor to ride on horse-back, unless barebacked, etc. They are rarely converted to Muhammadanism, and are remarkable for a quiet and steady perseverance in the acquirement of wealth under the most varying, and often trying, circumstances. Their position in Afghanistan is somewhat analogous to that of the "heathen" in the cities of the ancient Israelites. They number about 300,000 souls, Amir Habibulla Khan is believed, since his accession, to have mitigated to a certain extent the disabilities under which Hindus formerly laboured in Afghanistan. The important post of Accontant-General at Kabul is held by a Hindu, Niranjan Das, who has also been granted the rank of Civil Colonel. (Bellew, I.B.C., 1906.)

HINDU هندو
34- 70-. A village in Laghman, on the right bank of the Alingar river, 50 miles northwest of Jalalabad. Inhabitants: Tajiks. Twenty houses. (Leech.)

HINDU هندو
34- 69-. A village in the Koh Daman of Kabul, about 6 miles west of Shakardara. Inhabitants: Tajiks. There are only 15 or 16 houses, but on Hindu festivals the people of that race assemble here from the contry around, and go on in bodies to Hauz-i-Khas, a shrine in the hills some 15 miles off. (I.B.C.)

HINDU هندو
33- 68-. A village in the Ghazni district, about 4 miles south of Rozabagh. Inhabitants: Tajiks. Thirty houses. (I.B.C.)

HINDU KUSH هندوكش
35-0 71-0 A. A range of lofty mountains which, with its continuation the Koh-i-Baba, runs like a great vertebral cord through the heart of Afghanistan. The Hindu Kush (The name Hindu Kush, though applied by us to the whole range, is only locally applied to what is described below as the Western section.) has its origin in the southwestern corner of the Pamirs, in about longitude 74' 38'E. and extends in a general westerly direction to about longitude 68'15' E, forming between these points the watershed between the Oxus on the north and the Indus on the south. From near the western extremity of the Hindu Kush the Koh-i-Baba runs nearly due west for a further distance of about 100 miles. This range has been spoken of above as a continuation of the Hindu Kush, but it is doubtful if this term can be properly applied to it for the one range is not an actual prolongation of the other ; the ends of the two do not meet, they overlap, and are connected by a rather flat and open watershed known as the Shibar pass.
For purposes of geographical description the Hindu Kush range may be conveniently divided into three sections, the Eastern, Central and Western. The Eastern section stretches from the point of origin of the range to the Dorah pass; the Central section from the Dorah to the Khawak pass; and the Western from the Khawak to the termination of the range near the Shibar pass. Of these sections only the two latter, the Central and the Western, will be dealt with here; the

Eastern section will be found described in the Gazetteer of Afghanistan, Volume 1, Badakhshan.

The Central section forms the northern boundary of Kafiristan, and divides this part of the Kabul Province from the Province of Badakhshan on the north. Little is known of this part of the range, and even the direction of its main water shed is uncertain. It seems probable, however, that the latter instead of running in a straight line between the Dorah and Khawak passes makes a deep dip southwards into the heart of Kafiristan between the Presun, or Pech, and the Ramgul valleys, reaching down to about latitude 35.30' N. Sir George Robertson, in 1890-91, reached two of the passes over this section, the Mandal (15,300) and the Kamah (15,500 feet). The former, which lies at the head of the Bashgul valley of Kafiristan, must be considered as impracticable for baggage animals, though ponies are said to have been taken over it. The latter is crossed by a road leading from the Presun, or Pech, valley of Kafiristan to Faizabad, in Badakhshan; it is said to be practicable for laden mules and to be much used by traders when not closed by snow, i.e., from July to September. The only other pass in this section of the range which is known to be practicable for animals is the Nawak, or Parian, which lies about 15 miles northeast of the Khawak pass. It leads from the head of the Panjshir valley into the Anjuman valley of Badakhshan, and is said to be practicable for laden camels.

The country lying immediately to the north of this section is practically unknown to us, but from the neighbourhood of the Nawak pass a long spur is believed to run in a north-northeasterly direction for some 80 or 90 miles, separating the valley of the Kunduz river from that of the upper Kokcha. This spur is sometimes known as the Khwaja Muhammad range.

To the south the main range throws off a succession of spurs separating the deep and precipitous valleys of Kafiristan one from the other, and to the west of these a great spur runs down dividing Kafiristan from the Panjshir valley and terminating in a peak, 13,890 feet high, not more than 20 miles north of Nagalu on the Kabul river.

The general elevation of the main range in this section may be taken as between 14,500 and 17,00 feet, while there are numerous peaks of over 20.000 feet high. The range is a true sierra, being everywhere jagged precipitous and arid. It is destitute of trees, and there is but little grass or herbage of any description. Above 15,000 feet snow is perpetual. A more inhospitable, desolate region it is difficult to imagine, but the scenery is often sublime.

The Western section, from the Khawak pass to the termination of the range near the Shibar Pass, though slightly lower in general elevation than either the Eastern or Central sections, is still a formidable obstacle to direct communication between the country lying to the north of Kabul and the Provinces fo Badakhshan and Afghan Turkistan. It is, however, crossed by now fewer than 19 recognized passes, viz.:

1. Khawak (11,640)
2. Regak
3. Til (11,700')
4. Zuria*
5. Shahbah
6. Parandev
7. Arzu
8. Sardara*
9. Bajgah (12,300')
10. Salang
11. Kaoshan (14,320')
12. Walian
13. Chapdara*
14. Chahardar (13,500')
15. Kol-i-Lich*
16. Tawa*
17. Zak*
18. Tunkhana*
19. Kharzar*

Of these passes those in asteriscs can only be considered as footpaths, impracticable for baggage animals of any description; the remainder are all fit for laden mules while the Khawak, Regak, Chahardar and Salang are practicable for camels. The Khawak is the only one of the group, which, in ordinary winters, remains open all the year round.

An important point to note in connection with the Hindu Kush is that this range, in conjunction with the Sanglakh and the Sulaiman ranges, forms one great watershed which separates the whole of the drainage of the Iranian plateau (of the Oxus and the Helmand) from that of the Indian river system (see articles on Sanglakh and Sulaiman).

In 1886 five routes over the Hindu Kush were reconnoitred by the combined Intelligence and survey Parties of the Afghan Boundary Commission, without counting the Shibar pass, viz; --the Khawak, Bajgah, Kaoshan, Walin (half), and the Chahardar.

The following extract relating to this portion of the range has been taken from a lecture delivered in 1889 by Colonel Maitland at the United Service Institution, Simla:

"The general character of all the passes appears to be much the same. The paths ascend narrow glens on the south side of the range to the lofty and desolate crest, with its splintered granite peaks and patches of perennial snow. The scenery here is not in the least like that of ordinary Afghan mountains, but rater resembles that of the higher Grampians. Northward, the descent is down longer and less narrow glens, at an easier gradient. These glens have a very Scotch look about them, and the lower parts are fairly well wooded. Towards the mouths of the glens, on both sides, are masses of orchards, with strips of cultivation, and more or less scattered villages, some of them of considerable size.

"The Hindu Kush is passable for about seven months in the year, from May to November inclusive: but on account of the difficulty of crossing the unbridged streams during the early part of the season the roads are not considered fully open until about the end of June.

"The Hindu Kush is here a single range, not a mountainous region (It must be explained, however, that notwithstanding its being a single range, distinctly limited on its northern side by the Andarab valley and the deeply sunk course of the Surkhab stream, hills actually extend for a considerable distance northward, in fact to within a few marches of the Oxus.), and although of considerable elevation, the passes averaging about 13,000 feet, it can be crossed by any of the routes in four or five marches. Most of the roads are, no doubt, rough, bad, and steep in places, but they are rarely dangerous.

"Some of the most successful of the invaders of India from the north crossed the Hindu Kush in their path of conquest. Amir Timur, known in our histories as Timur Lang, not only passed over it with a large army, but went out of his way to invade Kafiristan in passing. Both Babur and his son Humayun, in their internal wars passed it repeatedly with considerable forces. All the principal passes are mentioned as having been used on different occasions, and it may surprise some here to learn that the route by Bamian was never resorted to except when the lateness of the season necessitated recourse being had to the Shibar, which is never completely closed.

"Coming down to later times, Aurangzib's passage of the Hindu Kush by the Chahardar pass is still talked of in the country.

He is said to have had a numerous artillery, which was transported on camels. Still more recently, and in our own times, the various disputants for the throne of Kabul have again and again crossed and recrossed the Hindu Kush with troops and guns. Indeed, to read the history of those wars, as of the earlier campaigns of Babur and

Humayun, one would almost imagine from the light way in which such and such a leader is said to have marched across the mountains to attack somebody on the other side, that the Hindu Kush was but a trifling obstacle.

"Trifling it is not: but on the other hand it is not so formidable as has generally been supposed. The reason I have thus drawn attention to the frequency with which the range has been crossed by armies, is to impress on you that the roads which really connect the political and strategic centre at Kabul with Afghan Turkistan and Badakhshan, and therefore with the Russian frontier, are those over the Hindu Kish and no others."

At its western end the Hindu Kush abuts on the deep gorge of the Surkhab river (here called the Ao Dara), and its main axis is deflected southwards, forming a depression which is the terminal western watershed of the Ghorband valley. This depression is, as above mentioned, the Shibar pass. Thence the axis of the watershed again turns westwards, and becomes known as the Koh-i-Baba. (Maitland, Barrow, Peacocke, Cockerill, Robertson.)

HINDU KUSH   هندوکش
The only name locally applied to the Chahardar pass.

*HISAR   حصار
35-10 69-20 m. A village located north of Gulbahar and east of the Panjshir river. Other places with this name are at the Nawa-i-Khoda-i-dad, at 33-12 67-35 m., and on the Gandamak river, near the village of Takhumi, at 34-7 67-37 m.

*HISARAK   حصارك
33-59 69-2 m. A village near Mangokhel on the Gardez-Kabul road. Other places with this name are located southwest of Khost and south of the Shamal river, at 33-14 69-42 m.; a few miles west of Chamkani, at 33-48 69-47 m.; in the Logar valley, some 6 miles south of Kolangar, at 34-1 69-2.; in the Panjshir valley, east of Anawa, at 35-14 69-30 m.; and an area southwest of Ukak and northeast of the Dasht-i-Nawar in Ghazni province, at 33-51 67-55 m.

HISARAK   حصارك
34-15 69-52. Hisarak is a woleswali in Nangarhar province. The woleswali comprises an area of 642 square kilometers and has an agricultural population that has been estimated at from 6,674 to 17,680. The woleswali is bounded in the east by Sherzad, in the north by Sarobi, in the west by Khak-i-Jabar, and in the south by Jaji and the State of Pakistan. Hisarak has about 48 villages, 18 of which have more than 50 inhabitants. The villages are listed in the PG as follows: Jaw Kan, Nargosi, Shaikhan-i-Ulya, Arab Khel, Dawran Khel (Doran Khel), Shaikhan-i-Sufla, Lachgar, Ghogizah, Garri Karr-Kacha, Siab-i-Sufla, Chin Zai, Chartut, Farjina, Katsai, Sarando, Zarif Khel (Roz Zarif Khel), Nawar, Tamnai, Manai, Garrai, Gazak, Kulali (Kulala), Yaghi Band, Zangani, Qader Khel, Jamal Khel, Kafur Khel (Kafar Khel), Lahor Khel, Kok Darah, Uzbak Khel, Wattai, Ghundah Sarrai, Sharif Khel, Tsaparai, Nasser Khel, Bahawali, Mansur China (Rochashma-i-Mansur), Alam Kats, Mohamadi (Mohmandi), Halim Khel, Golu Khel, Langar Khel, Muin Khel, Ragha, Seyab-i-Ulya, Gango Khel, Chor Chang, Khanjar, and Salim Khel. (LWA) In 1914 the area was described as follows: A division of the Jalalabad district consisting of the valley of the Hisarak Rud. The following is Jenkyns' list of the Hisarak villages in 1879:

Village	Inhabitants
1. Ughar g	Shinwaris
2. Dehbala	"
3. Mahrez	"
4. Papin-i-Kalan	Mians
5. Papin-i-Khurd	"
6. Charwazai	Shinwaris
7. Sangota	"
8. Gagra	"
9. Gurguri	"
10. Yaghiband	"
11. Tarnao	"
12. Tsandalai	"
13. Shpola	"
14. Nari	"
15. Akakhel	"
16. Fakirkhel	"
17. Mazina	Sayyids, Dehgans
18. Hisarak	Mohmands, Dehgans
19. Kala-i-Mirzi	Sayyids
20. Kala-i-Zaino	Duranis
21. Kadd-i-Roghani-o-Banda	"
22. Hisarshahi	Dehgans
23. Baru-i-Khurd	Tajiks, Dehgans
24. Baru-i-Kalan	Mohmands, Tajiks, Dehgans, Kuchis
25. Kuchi-i-Hazarbuz	Kuchis
26. Tirelai-i-Miran	Sayyids
27. Barikab	Mohmands, Dehgans
28. Lachipur	Dehgans, Tajiks, Ghilzais
29. Chardeh and Mishwani	Tajiks, Mohmands, Ghilzais
30. Zangokach	Mohmands
31. Kahan-i-Tajiki	Tajiks, Dehgans
32. Kahan-i-Khalsa	Mohmands
33. Kaltarghar	Tirais

The valley has many orchards, vineyards, and cornfields on the banks of its river. Supplies of all sorts are procurable. The valley is famed for its production of the seedless pomegranate. (Hough, Wood, Jenkyns, I.B.C.)

HISARAK حصارك
34-13 70-30 G. A village in the Hisarak subdivision of the Jalalabad district. It lies on the left bank of the Hisarak Rud, about 15 miles southwest of Chardeh. There is a garrison here consisting of 1 squadron cavalry (detached from Jalalabad), 2 battalions infantry and 100 khasadars. (I.B.C.)

HISARAK حصارك
34- 69-. A village situated south of the road from Jalalabad to Kabul, about 12 miles from Gandamak southwest, and the same south-east from Jagdalak.

HISARAK حصارك
34- 69-. A large collection of villages in the Ghilzai country, 16 miles west of Gandamak. The inhabitants are Jabar Khel Ghilzais. The village stands on the left bank of the Surkhab river. Here there are

fruit trees in abundance, whilst the country above and below is bare, with the exception of bushes and stunted trees. The inhabitants occupy themselves in the fruit trade with Hindustan. (I.B.C.)

HISARAK حصارك
34-1 69-3 m. Elevation 5,140 feet. A village in the upper portion of the Logar valley, standing to the north of what is called the Hisarak pass, at a distance of 12 miles in a southwesterly direction from Zargan Shahar. The principal village stands on the right bank of the Logar river, whilst its hamlets are situated on both banks. In the village itself are 100 families of Tajiks and Liasi Khels (a branch of the Astanazi Ghilzais). Attached to Hisarak are:

4 hamlets of Liasi Khels	45 Families
2 hamlets of Tajiks	20 "
1 hamlet of Kizilbashis	15 "
3 hamlets of Popalzais	40 "

(Clifford, Euan Smith)

HISARAK See ISARAK (2). حصارك

HISARAK KALA-I-SAIADAN حصارك قلعه سيدان
A village in Hisarak division, Jalalabad district, containing 100 houses of Tajiks. (McGregor.)

HISARAK RUD حصارك رود
34-22 70-30 G. A tributary of the Kabul river. It rises near the foot of the Papin pass in the Safed Koh and joins the Kabul river near Lachipur. In its upper reaches it is known as the Papin, or Mazina, Dara. It gives its name to a subdivision of the Jalalabad district. (I.B.C.)

HISAR SHAHI Or SHAHI KOT حصار شاهی (شاهی کوت)
34-16 70-34 m. A village in the Hisarak division of the Jalalabad district, about 6 miles northeast of Mazina. Inhabitants: Dehgans. (Jenkyns.)

HISHPI هشپی
35- 69-. A village in the valley of Nijrao, inhabited by "Pashais." It is the largest in the valley, and round it are numerous orchards well stocked with walnut, mulberry and pomegranate trees and vines. The mountains round are covered with "chilgoza," pine and holly trees.
Hishpi, or Ishpi as it is sometimes called, is said to be 60 miles from Kabul. (Masson.)

HOTAK هوتك
A main division of th Turan Ghilzais (See Volume 5.)

HOTAK KALA See ATAK هوتك قلعه

*HUJRA حجرا
34-27 67-19 m. A village located on a stream, about 5 miles southwest of Giru in Bamian province.

HUKMAT حكمت
33- 69-. A village about 16 miles northeast of Gardez, on the road thence to the Mirzakai Kotal. Inhabitants Amazai Ghilzais. (I.B.C)

HURAN KATRA حوران قطره (؟)
34- 70-. A large village in the Hisarak division, Jalalabad,

containing 2,000 houses of Shinwaris. (McGregor.)

HUSAIN حسین
35-6 68-59 G. A hamlet 13 1/2 miles south of the Kaoshan pass; it lies at the junction, from the west, with the Kaoshan glen of the Husain Dara. Up this dara a track leads to Chashma Husain and over the kotal of same name; it then leads down the Talkhak ravine into the Nimakao glen which it joins nearly opposite the mouth of the Zalikan ravine. (Maitland.)

HUSAINABAD حسین آباد
A village in Laghman. Inhabitants: Abdul Rahimzais. The following are the hamlets it contains, viz:

       1. Lamatai Sulaiman Khel   4. Deh-i-Akhunzadagan
       2. Wattapur   5. Kala-i-Umar
       3. Bahrabad   6. Banda-i-Sherdil
                                                         (Warburton.)

HUSAIN ALI حسین علی
A subsection of Daikhitai Hazaras. (See Military Report on Hazarajat, Part II.)

*HUSAIN KALA حسین قلعه
32-50 68-46 m. A village located about 6 miles south of Omna in eastern Ghazni province.

*HUSAIN KHEL حسین خیل
34-29 69-18 m. A village located east of Bagrami and southeast of Kabul.

*HUSAIN KOT حسین کوت
34-41 69-5 m. A village located on the Kabul-Charikar road, about one mile south of Haji Payk.

*HUSAIN NIKEH حسین نکه
31-52 69-15 m. A village located on the Kundar river in southeastern Ghazni province and near the Pakistan border.

*IBAD KHEL عباد خیل
34-55 69-37 m. A village on the Tagab river, about 6 miles southeast of Nejrab.

IBRAHIM See BURHAN ابراهیم

*IBRAHIM KALA ابراهیم قلعه
32-30 68-13 m. A village located about 3 miles south of Monarai in the Katawaz area, Ghazni province.

IBRAHIM KHAN ابراهیم خان
34- 69-. A fort 3-1/4 miles southeast of the southeast bastion of Sherpur, and on the right bank of the Kabul river. During the British occupation in 1880 this fort was occupied by half a battalion of infantry for the protection of the bridge then constructed. (I.B.C.) One place with this name is near Khwaja Sarai, at 34-44 69-6 G. (LWA)

IDAR KHEL ایدر خیل
34- 70-. A village in the Jalalabad District, about 7 miles southwest of Batikot. Inhabitants: Tirais. (Jenkyns.)

IKHLASABAD اخلاص آباد
   34- 70-. A village in the Besud Division of the Jalalabad district. Inhabitants: Tajiks and Arabs. (Jenkyns.)

IKHTIAR اختيار
   A section of the Muhammad Khoja Hazaras. (See Military Report on Hazarajat, Part II.)

*ILDUDAR الدودر
   34-44 66-52 m. A village located on the Band-i-Amir, some 6 miles west of Yakawlang in western Bamian province.

ILIAS الياس
   A small section of the Jaghatu Hazaras. (See Military Report on Hazarajat, Part II.)

*ILSHAFI ايلشفى
   35-16 69-53 m. A village located some 2 miles northeast of Astana, near the source of the Panjshir river.

ILTIFAT التفات
   34-40 69-8 G. A village 1-1/2 miles southeast of the Mama Khatun Pass. It is about 12 miles north of Kabul, and by the road about half as much again. It is inhabited by Tajiks and Hazaras, and is a place of importance from its position, which watches the road from the Paiminar pass into Koh Daman by the Mama Khatun pass, as well as the road to Zimma. (I.B.C.)

*IMENDAO ايمنداو
   35-8 67-56 m. A village located on a tributary of the Shekari river, southwest of Doab-i-Mikh-i-Zarin in Bamian province.

IMLAK-I-ARBABHA املاك اربابها
   34- 70-. A village in the Surkhab division of the Jalalabad District. Inhabitans: Tajiks and Dehgans. (Jenkyns.)

IMLAK-I-SHAHI املاك شاهى
   34- 70-. A village in the Surkhab division of the Jalalabad District. There seem to be two villages of this name in the Surkhab, one of which is inhabited by Tajiks, Ghilzais, and Dehgans; the other by Tajiks, Arabs, and Dehgans. (Jenkyns.)

INAL عنال (؟)
   A subdivision of the Daya Polada. (See Military Report on Hazarajat, Part II.)

INAYATULLA KHAN عنايت الله خان
   A village in the Jalalabad district. Inhabitants: Mohmands. (Jenkyns.)

INCHU or UNCHI انچو
   34-30 69-4 G. A large village in the Chardeh valley of Kabul, 3-1/2 miles west of Deh-i-Mozang. Inhabitants: Tajiks. Two hundred houses. The people are employed in the timber trade chiefly, and bring in beams and planks to the city for sale. (I.B.C.)

INCHU انچو
   35- 69-. A village in the Kohistan of Kabul, between Gulbahar and Parwan. There are about 200 houses in the place, and 20 forts are included in it.

Inhabitants: Tajiks, who bring fish (from the Panjshir river) and game to the Kabul market. (I.B.C.)

INDAKI اندکی
34- 69-. A village in the Chardeh valley, situated on the right bank of the Kabul river, at the southwestern foot of the Takht-i-Shah hill, 4 miles south of the city.
It is one of the most important of the Chardeh villages, and includes in the township 16 forts and small hamlets. Inhabitants: Tajiks. This place played an important part during the investment of Sherpur in December 1879. (I.B.C.)

INGAN انگان
34- 69-. A Mangal village on the northern slope of the Lakarai pass, 3 miles from the crest in the Hisarak direction. The road to it from the top is one long, easy descent. (Gordon.)

*INJIRAI انجیری
34-32 69-42 m. A village located near Ganda Khasarai, some 6 miles south of Sarobi.

IRAK عراق کوتل
34-42 68-6 G. Elevation 13,000 (?) feet. A pass leading over the Koh-i-Baba from the Helmand valley to that of Bamian. It lies about 7 miles north of the village of Kharzar, the 8th stage from Kabul on the main road to Mazar-i-Sharif.
Up to the end of 1886 the Kabul-Bamian main road used to go over the Irak, but it now passes over the Hajigak. Both these, however, are closed in winter, and then the Shibar route alone is used.
At 6 miles from Kharzar there is an ascent of a mile to the Kotal. It is steep, so much so as to be difficult for camels, but the road is smooth and good. The soil is soft, and there are no stones. The crest of the kotal is the boundary between Besud and Bamian. The descent is about a mile and a quarter long, steep and rather stony, and the road is not very good. Some way down there is a ravine on the left, and the road on the edge of this is narrow. The road has to be re-made whenever guns are taken over it, as it is always damaged by the snow of winter. It is not, however, difficult for camels when unrepaired. (I.B.C.)

IRAK See KHUSHKAK عراق

*IRAKA ایراکه
34-16 67-25 m. A village located on a tributary of the Helmand, some 2 miles from its confluence with the Helmand.

*IRAQ-I-SUFLA عراق سفلی
34-51 68-2 m. A village located on a tributary of the Ghorband river. Two miles south is another village with this name, at 34-50 68-2 m. Iraq-i-Ulya is another village nearby, at 34-50 68-3 m.

IRGANA See ERGANA ارگانه

*IRGIN ایرکین
34-23 66-46 M. A village located near the junction of two streams east of Asgharat, in western Bamian province.

IRO MANZIL ایرومنزل
34-24 69-39. Elevation 9,350 feet. A pass in the Karkacha range leading from Jagdalak to Tezin. The following is a report on the

route by Lieutenant-Colonel Stewart of the Guides:
"The true Iro-Manzil route leaves the road from Surkhpul to Jagdalak about 4 miles before reaching Jagdalak, at about 1 mile to the eastward of the Jagdalak or Chishmakai Kotal. It then goes through a mass of ravines, and ultimately ascends a long spur which leads up to the summit of the pass about 9,000 feet high. Between Surkhpul and Tezin this is the most direct route, and is reported to be very easy, the road via Jagdalak, Kata Sang, and Seh Baba being about 11 or 13 miles longer.
"From Jagdalak, however, there is another easy road leading to the Iro-Manzil pass, and up this it was that the reconnoitring party of the Guides under the command of Lieutenant-Colonel Jenkins, C.B. went on the 8th November 1879. Leaving the encampment at Jagdalak, the party went by the village of Jagdalak, about a mile to the south up a ravine. It then crossed a piece of level plateau-land, and descended into the ravine which runs down to the Jagdalak encamping-ground (the road by the ravine is really the shorter of the two); a slight ascent up a narrow ravine led to the top of a spur, from whence was a short descent into the bed of a stream which runs down to the village of Dabali. Here is situated a small village called Walai occupied by Ahmadzai Ghilzais who cultivate the little level land about the place. The road now ascends this nala almost to its source being bounded on either side by high rounded spurs and hills of an average height of 100 or 150 feet above the stream, which trickles down the whole way. The slopes of the hills are covered with holly bushes, and the surface is strewn with rounded boulders, the under strata, exposed here and there by the cutting of the stream, being of a soft white sandstone.
"To a point at two-thirds of the distance from Jagdalak to the crest, the road is up the bed of the stream, and has a very steady ascent; so much so that, were it not for the boulders, a carriage might be drawn up without difficulty; but the bed of the stream is one mass of boulders and very difficult walking for infantry.
"After this point is a steep ascent of 500 feet which zig-zags up a spur, which then slopes gently to the summit of the pass. The top of the spur is well rounded, broad, and smooth, having a rich, soft and rather friable soil free of stones, on which wheat is cultivated in the summer months. The poor inhabitants of Walai manage to reap some 50 or 60 maunds of wheat from these high lands.
"The summit of the pass is so level and soft on the top that horses could gallop without fear, the edges of the ravines only being steep and rugged. Water is procurable close under the summit, which is quite bare of trees, there being only holly bushes in the slopes of the ravines. This part of the range was, in the memory of men now living, once covered with deodar and other fine trees, which have been all cut down and burnt for charcoal, and on the higher portions of the Karkacha range to the south, where pines are yet plentiful, the same destruction of trees is now going on, to supply charcoal to the inhabitants of Kabul.
"Iro in Pushtu means ashes, ergo Iro-Manzil would mean 'the stage of ashes.' Ashes may at some time or other have been strewn over the hill and given the name to the route. It is a probable derivation. From the summit is a most extended view. Northwards are seen the lofty peaks of the Hindu Kush and the valleys of Tagao and Uzbin sloping down to the Kabul river. On this side is the village of Sarobai, and on the other side is the village of Naghalu. The river itself cannot be seen anywhere, as it flows in deep channels.
The whole of Laghman is distinctly visible, and to the eastward lies the long valley of Jalalabad. To the south are the low breaks in

the Safed Koh range, through which lie the Lakarai pass and the pass called the Katru leading to Pegai. To the west lie the well-cultivated valley of Tezin, with its several villages, and the whole of the country up to the Khurd Kabul hills. A road called the Balutak road leading to the Chinari pass is clearly distinguishable, and the Tangi Gharu, where the Kabul river runs through steep and lofty hills.

"From no point in the Jalalabad district, can such an extended view be obtained from east to west, and further up the range to the south, towards the Karkacha route, the view would be even better.

"Hisarak, Jagdalak, and Tezin are all within easy distance of this commanding position, and it would make a most suitable summer encampment for a small body of troops, equipped with carriage for their own supplies, as from the heights they would overawe the Ghilzais on all sides.

"It could only be occupied during the summer months, as the winter colds are said to be very severe; even on the day of the reconnaissance (8th November 1879), the streams in the shade were frozen at 3 in the afternoon, and the wind on the top, coming from the westward, was so cutting and cold that one could scarcely stand against it." (Stewart.)

ISA KHEL عیسی خیل
33- 69-. A village in Hariob, 12 miles northwest of the Istiar Kotal. (Kane.)

ISARAK Or HISARAK احصارك
35-15 69-28. A dara which joins the left bank of the Upper Panjshir, 3-1/2 miles below Bazarak. It contains the following villages: Dar Khel at its mouth; next Dostan Khel or Deh Bilandi, with 20 houses; above is Maristan with 80 houses; and lastly Isarak, with 20 houses; all Tajiks. From this glen there is a direct road across the spurs of the hills to the Dara Hazara. It is a good footpath, but is hardly practicable for horses. (Shahzada Taimus.)

ISARAK Or HISARAK احصارك
33-48 69-47 m. A group of Chakmani villages on the left bank of the Kurram river, about 12 miles west of Pathru. Supplies procurable. The Hakim of Hariob and Chakmani has his headquarters here. The inhabitants belong to the Spin Gund faction and are thus opposed in politics to the neighbouring Mangals, Jajis, and Mukbils, who are Tor Gund. They would, therefore, probably be friendly to us. (Burton.)

ISFIBED اسفی بید
A kotal crossed by the Kabul-Hazarajat road about 30 miles west of Jalrez. (See Military Report on Hazarajat, Part II.)

*ISFI DAQ اسفی داق
34-20 66-43 G. A village located 6 miles southwest of Pai Kotal.

ISFI SANG Or SAFED SANG, ISPI SANG اسفی سنگ
35-1 67-58 m. A dara in the west of the Besud country. (See Military Report on Hazarajat, Part II.) A village called Ispi Sang is located in this dara. (LWA)

*ISHANHA اینانها
35-13 67-46 m. A village located on the Saighan river, northeast of Saighan.

ISHKARABAD اشکرآباد
A settlement of the Qaraqul Daghi clan of Sehpai Dai Zangi. (See Military Report on Hazarajat, Part II.)

ISHMAILZAI اشماعیلزی
Said to be a section of the Ibrahim division of Ghilzais which Elphinstone also calls Samalzai, and Lumsden, Shah Memalzai.

*ISHPAN Or ASHPAN اشپان
34-19 69-54 m. A village located in Shirzad district, about one mile south of Shaikhan in Nangarhar province.

ISHPI اشپی
34- 70-. A valley 93 miles from Kabul, 30 miles from Farajghan, containing 3,000 houses in all. (See 'Hishpi.') Water is procured from a small stream. Thence there is a road leading to Alishang and Tirgarhi. (Leech.)

*ISHTOYE Or ESHTWI اشتوی
35-27 70-56 m. A village located on the Paron stream, some 3 miles north of Poruns in the Chapa Dara district.

*ISHTURMURDA اشترمرده
34-46 68-49 m. A village located near Wand on a tributary of the Ghorband river.

*ISKA اسکه
34-31 67-56 m. A village located on a tributary of the Helmand, 2 miles southwest of Sar-i-Iska in Bamian province.

ISKA اسکه
A subdivision of the Daya Polada. (See Military Report on Hazarajat, Part II.)

ISKAN اسکن (عسکان)
A settlement of the Miramur clan of Sehpai Dai Zangi. (See Military Report on Hazarajat, Part II.)

ISKAN اسکن
A place on the Helmand. (See Military Report on Hazarajat, Part II.)

ISKANDARAI اسکندری
A section of Jirghai Besudis. (See Military Report on Hazarajat, Part II.)

*ISKANDO اسکندو
35-8 70-11 m. A village located on a path over the Kuh-i-Tamarai, southeast of Bandol in Laghman province.

ISLAMBAD اسلام آباد (اسلام باد)
34-48 70-6 G. A village in Laghman, inhabited by Mixed tribes, and containing three hamlets, viz:
         1. Haidar Khani
         2. Kala-i-Faiz Muhammad Khan
         3. Girdi. (Warburton.)

ISLAMABAD اسلام آباد
A village in the Kunar valley, inhabited by Sayyids of Kunar. It is small but walled in. (Masson.)

*ISLAM KALA اسلام قلعه
   34-30 68-57 m. A village located east of Arghandai and about 14 miles west-southwest of Kabul.

ISLAM KALA اسلام قلعه
   A village in the Mukur district, 60 miles from Ghazni on the road to Quetta. Supplies and forage are abundant. (Campbell.)

ISMAIL اسماعیل
   A subsection of the Bacha-i-Ghulam Dai Zangi. (See Military Report on Hazarajat, Part II.)

ISMAIL KALA اسماعیل قلعه
   34-37 69-29 m. A small walled village, 2 miles to the eastward of Bimaru, near Kabul. Inhabitants: Tajiks. (Kennedy.)

ISMAIL KHEL اسماعیل خیل
   A section of the Khostwals.

ISPANDI اسپندی
   33-28 68-24 A. A halting place between Ghazni and Nani on the Kandahar road, 7 miles from Ghazni, 7 miles 1 furlong from Nani. (Gaselee.)

ISPIBED اسی بید
   A kotal over the Koh-i-Kirghui, southwest of Uchak. (See Military Report on Hazarajat, Part II.)

ISPIBED See ISFIBED اسی بید

ISPIDAK JU اسی داك جو
   34-22 66-56 G. A village on the right bank of the Nalgis stream. (See Military Report on Hazarajat, Part II.)

ISPIDAR اسپیدر
   33-41 69-1 G. A village in the northeast of Kharwar, containing 15 houses of Kharotis. From here a road ascends the rather steep ravine in which the village is situated, and following it ascends the hills by a difficulty foot-path to the Ispidar Kotal. Thence the descent into the Charkh valley after crossing a spur of the Koh-i-Kalar is said to be very difficult. This pass is only used by shepherds and men on foot. (Griesbach.)

ISPIDAR اسپیدر
   33- 68-. A village in the southwest of Kharwar, inhabited by 80 families of Ghilzais. (Griesbach.) Recent maps show the spelling Spidar at 33-38 68-44. (LWA)

ISPI DIWAL (See Military Report on Hazarajat, Part II.) اسی دیوال

ISPINGAR, AB-I آب اسپنگر
   A tributary of the Helmand. (Military Report on Hazarajat, Part II.)

ISTALIF استالف
   A large village in the Koh Daman, 20 miles north-northwest of Kabul. If is built on the side of the hills in the form of a pyramid, the houses rising one above the other by terraces, and the whole being

crowned by the magnificent chinars which denote the shrine of Hazrat Eshan, whilst far below in a deep glen rushes a foaming yet clear and rapid brook over a bed of rocky boulders, on both sides of which the valley is covered with the richest orchards, and vineyards. Every one agrees as to the beauty of Istalif. Masson says, "Istalif is one of the most picturesque spots that can be conceived; all that a natural combination of beauties can achieve we here behold in perfection; their effect being rather augmented than diminshed by the rude appearance of the houses of the town. The scenery of the country is extensive and grand, in happy unison with the whole picture. Looking down the stream, the dale gradually opens out and presents to the eye a vast plain, rich in trees and verdure, and dotted over with innumerable forts; beyond all this, rocky mountains are seen, and over these again tower the eternal snow-clad summit of the Hindu Kush. The scene is as sublimely grand as it is beautiful and enchanting. The people of the country have a proverb that he who has not seen Istalif has seen nothing, and certainly it may be allowed that he who has seen Istalif is not likely to see many places to surpass it and few to equal it." Nearly every householder of Istalif has his garden or orchard. In most of these is a tower, to which, as soon as the fruits ripen, the families repair, closing their houses in the town. The inhabitants are Tajiks and, contrary to the usual habits of these people are among the most turbulent set in the country. They have the reputation also of being the best foot-soldiers in Afghanistan, and are a healthy, handsome race, alike fond of sport and war. The natives of Kohistan gravely set down their turbulent and desperate characters to their heating diet of mulberries, which is their general food. Besides the town of Istalif, the district comprises the adjacent villages of Gudara, Pargana, Shonaki, Khwaja Hasan, Malla, Hasan, Hasan Kucha, and Shorawar. The whole is reckoned to contain together 3,000 houses, which would give a population of from 15,000 to 18,000 souls to the district. The revenue from it is said to amount to Rs. 4,000. A great part of the population of the town is of the weaver class, and quantities of coarse cloths, "lungis" and "susi" are manufactuared, and a trade in them is maintained with Turkistan.
Istalif was carried by assault by the troops under the command of Major-General Sir John McCaskill on the 29th September 1842, and totally destroyed on account of its having harboured several chiefs implicated in the murder of Sir A. Burnes at Kabul, and in the massacre of the garrison of Charikar. The loss of the British on this occasion was very slight, only a few killed and wounded.
The inhabitants are Tajiks, Hassan Khel Ghilzais, Kizilbashis, and about 50 families of Sikh shop keepers. There are also a few families of Rikas. (Masson, Wood, Burnes, McCaskill, IB.C.)

ISTALIF استالف
34-53 69-1. A pass over the Paghman range. It is reached by a road from the village of Istalif, which ascends the Makhan Khar Dara to the watershed, thence descending to Siahgird in the Ghorband valley by the Findukistan Dara. The kotal is said to be difficult, but is used by laden camels. (Peacocke.)

ISTAMAH استامه
34-46 68-49. A large ravine draining north from the Paghman range and debouching into the Ghorband valley immediately above Burj-i-Guljan. A path runs up it to the Kotal-i-Istamah for Charikar; but it is impracticable for laden pack animals. (Peacocke.)

*ISTARAB استراب
34-2 67-4 m. A village located on a tributary of the Helmand, west of Waras in southern Bamian province.

ISTARGHIJ استرغج
34-53 69-6 G. Two adjoining villages in the Koh Daman of Kabul, about 6 miles north of Istalif. Inhabitants: Tajiks. The land is highly cultivated, and celebrated for grapes, and the inhabitants are notoriously turbulent. (I.B.C.)

*ISTAWAI استاوى
32-41 69-9 m. A village located on a path from Barmal to Sarobi in Paktia province.

ISTIAR Or STYA استيار (استيا)
33-54 69-50 G. Elevation 9,700 feet. A pass in the range forming the water-parting between the Hariob and the Kurram valleys, distant from the Paiwar Kotal by a path, about 9 miles, and from Ali Khel 10 miles. The Istiar Kotal is the most notable saddle of this ridge; its rocky surface is almost bare of trees; towards the Kurram river the descent is apparently easy, the path following the right slope of the ravine, of which the bottom and sides are covered by a dense forest; the ground at its outlet is more open where the village of Ghandai is seen lying in a cultivated patch. Beyond is the village of Istiar concealed by a projecting spur said to be two to three hours' journey on foot from this kotal. The southern slope is the steeper one. (Kane.) Recent maps show the spelling Stya, at 33-51 69-55. (LWA)

ISTIAR استيار (استيا)
33- 69-. A ravine running from the Istiar pass to the plain of the same name and falling into the Karaia stream opposite Ali Khel at a point 1/2 mile distant from the latter.
This ravine, which runs in a southeast direction, is one of the main roads used by the inhabitants of the Hariob and Ali Khel for communication with the Istiar villages and the lower portion of the Kurram valley. The road runs along the bed of the ravine, and is only a well-worn track; no steps have been taken to improve it artificially, but it is a fair hill road, and as the gradient up the Istiar ravine is slight (1-1/2 or 2 degrees), it may be considered a good road for laden animals, both camels and mules. In the upper portion the road is not so good as it is nearer the mouth of the ravine, and it continually crosses and recrosses and winds from one bank to the other. About a mile from the point where the Drakal Algad joins the Istiar ravine the road passes between high and rocky cliffs, and at this point the ravine is not more than 20 to 30 yards wide; at other points the average width of the valley is about 100 yards. About 3/4 of a mile from the mouth of the Istiar ravine, on the south bank, is situated the ruined hamlet and tower of Baloch Kot which has been built at the junction of a large ravine which joins the Istiar from the south at this point. From this point a clear rushing stream of good water continues along the remainder of the Istiar, but it disappears into the ground at Baloch Kot, and the portion near its mouth is dry.
The Istiar is commanded on both sides by hills covered with dense forest, of pine trees, which would afford a great amount of cover both to a force advancing and to an enemy opposing an advance. The hills on the north side are higher and more precipitous than those on the south, which are more undulating and gradual in slope, but on both sides the heights could be crowned and the pass thus rendered

secure. The density of the pine forests on both sides, the whole way along the nala, is the most objectionable part of this route for military purposes, and the road itself often passes through wood and jungle. The road could with little trouble be made available for all the dismounted branches of the service, and for laden camels and mules if ever required.

The Istiar ravine, at the point where the Drakal Algad ravine joins it, is 8,400 feet high, and is here rather wider than at any other point; it continues on in an easterly direction to the Istiar Kotal, which is distant about 2 miles. (Manners Smith.)

ISTIAR Or STYA استیار (استیا)
33-51 69-54 m. The names of two villages (Bala and Pain), 4 miles apart in the Istiar valley. They are said to contain 40 families of Hasan Khel Jajis, and 30 families of Mangal hamsayahs. (Kane, Barton.)

ISUMTUMUR اسمتومور (؟)
One of the main sections of the Besud Hazaras. (See Military Report on Hazarajat, Part II.)

*IZA ایزه
32-34 69-19 m. A village located near De Pash Khuneh and the Pakistan border in Paktia province.

JABA جابه
34-12 70-39 A. A group of villages, the largest of which contains about 100 houses, in the Jalalabad district, 9 miles west of Kahi cantonment. (I.B.C.)

*JABA جبه
33-39 70-2 m. A village located northwest of Jaji Maidan on the way to Chamkani in Paktia province.

*JABA KALAI جبه کی
35-12 71-30 m. A village located on the Kunar river, about 2 miles south of Narai in Kunar province.

*JABAR Or JABBAR جبار
32-40 67-41 m. A village located southeast of Ghojan and south of Gilan in Ghazni province.

*JABAR KALAI جبار کی
32-8 68-9 m. A village located west of Wazakhwa in southern Ghazni province.

JABAR KHAN جبار خان
34- 69-. A fort in the Chardeh valley, on the right bank of the Kabul river, between Indaki and Kala-i-Fathu. The place contains 30 families of Tajiks. (I.B.C.)

JABAR KHEL جبار خیل
A section of the Ghilzai tribe occupying the country between the Siah Koh range and the Surkhab river, and scattered over the greater portion of Laghman.

The following is a note on the Jabar Khels of Laghman by Captain Warburton, written in 1880:

"We will first deal with Aziz Khan, head of the Jabar Khel Ghilzais. His father, Ahmad Khan, was in the service of Wazir Fateh Muhammad Khan and secured Masti Khel in lieu of pay; also Rawat, Gondarzai,

Waliabad, Amnabad, for feed of his horses. A sister of his married Amir Dost Muhammad Khan, and through him he secured immense influence amongst the Ghilzais; also two thirds of the paternal estate on the death of his father, whilst merely one-third went to his step-brother Karim. The tract of land immediately south of the Kabul river, and opposite Charbagh, was named after him, Kats-i-Aziz Khan.

"On his death he left six sons, of whom the eldest, Niamatulla, was murdered by Hamid Khan over a quarrel arising on account of the distribution of the paternal estate.

"It has always been a policy of the Amirs of Kabul to secure on their side the chiefs of the Ghilzais, through whose limits the main road from Kabul to Gandamak passes. On this account Asmatulla, a younger brother of Niamatulla, was taken into high favour; and being liked by the late Amir Sher Ali Khan, he bestowed on him the title of Hashmat-ul-Mulk. For services performed at the taking of Herat, he received in jaghirs Surkhakan, Khairo-Khel, Girdi Kats, Kaja-Kats and Ormur.

"When Sardar Muhammad Yakub Khan was plotting against his father at Herat because Abdulla Jan had been appointed heir to the Kabul throne, Asmatulla Khan, Arsala Khan, and the late Mir Akhor, Mir Ahmad, were deputed by Amir Sher Ali Khan to Herat, with the object of bringing in to Kabul, by every promise, Sardar Muhammad Yakub Khan. Their promises and oaths were successful; the son, trusting to his father's word, appeared at Kabul, and was immediately cast into prison. Whether Asmatulla Khan suffered in influence amongst his people for his treacherous participation in this act, does not appear. We find him figuring next about the commencement of the Afghan war of 1878-79, and again in an act of treachery. Amir Sher Ali Khan, after the repulse of the Chamberlain mission at Ali Masjid, was forced to realise, in spite of the assurances of certain of his advisers, that not ony was it possible, but very probable, for the British troops to advance into Afghanistan, and avenge the insult offered to the mission. He directed certain of the Ghilzai chiefs to collect local levies, and proceed with them for the defence of the Khaibar. Amongst them was Asmatulla, who received 200 rifles for arming his men, and sum of Rs. 12,000 or Rs. 14,000 for equipping them in necessaries. He was on his way from Kabul, and had reached Seh Baba, when he met the discomfited troops of the Amir escaping from the Khaibar and carrying with them the Jalalabad arsenal, which had been moved away to prevent its falling into our hands. He promptly attacked them with his Ghilzais, secured more rifles and property, and quietly moved off to Kashmund and lodged his gains in the hands of his Hindu bankers. Here he remained till Amir Sher Ali fled to Mazar-i-Sharif; and Sardar Yakub Khan had not forgotten either of the two episodes mentioned above; and whilst he treated Faiz Muhammad (who had not only acted loyally and bravely, but had also suffered at his father's hands for friendship towards him about the time he was cast into prison) with the utmost consideration and respect, he gave to the other a cold shoulder. Vexed at the attention shown his enemy, Asmatulla went back to Laghman and sulked for a time. Hearing that Sardar Yakub Khan was coming to Gandamak, and had actually reached Jagdalak, he came in to Sir Louis Cavagnari's camp just two days before the ex-Amir arrived there.

"After the treaty of Gandamak, Asmatulla rose against the Governor of Laghman, and eventually had his fort seized and a portion of it burnt. During December 1879 he attacked our communications at Jagdalak; and, his gathering having been broken up by Colonel Norman's force he has led a wandering life ever since, and bears the

reputation amongst his clansmen of being a great liar and a notorious coward."
(He--Asmatulla Khan--and his eldest son, Muhammad Hisham were killed by Amir Abdur Rahman. Two other sons are said to be in Kafiristan and the fourth and youngest, Abdur Rahman Khan, is with other Afghan refugees in Rawal Pindi.)
"As the acknowledged head of the Jabar Khel Ghilzais, he has been made a great deal more of than his character deserves. During November or December 1879 he, Hamid Khan, Fateh Muhammad Khan, and Bahram Khan swore at the ziarat of Mehtar Lam to let their private feuds remain in abeyance, pending the troubles that their country was undergoing. Hence one saw in 1880 the combination that was not in existence at the commencement of last year, when General Sir Sam Browne's force was in the Jalalabad district. Fateh Muhammad Khan has in Kats-i-Aziz Khan two, and Bahram Khan eight, villages,--Bahram Khan is reputed to exceedingly wealthy.
"Arsala, son of Muhabat Khan, first came into notice when Sher Ali Khan, defeated at Shaikhabad, was forced to take refuge Kandahar, and Afzal Khan, Azim Khan, and Abdur Rahman had secured their hold on Kabul. Arsala fled to Hisarak, and sent his family to the Dara-i-Ab-i-Zangi. Azim Khan had, as his wazir, or agent, amongst the eastern Ghilzais, Sarfaraz Khan Sahakzai, a great and firm friend of Arsala, whom he often saved from Azim's vengeance by telling him that Arsala in reality was not opposed to the party in power, but had fled to save his own credit, since he was supposed to belong to Sher Ali's faction. Arsala kept up a correspondence with Sher Ali Khan at Kandahar, and eventually joined him; and when the Amir returned from Umballa in 1869, he appointed him wazir, and to the charge of Zurmat, where he amassed considerable wealth. Later on he was sent with Asmatulla Khan and the Mir Akhor to Herat, to deceive and bring down Sardar Yakub Khan to Kabul.
"When Naoroz Khan rose in rebellion against Sher Ali, the Amir directed Shah Murad Khan, Governor of Jalalabad, and Arsala Khan to proceed with troops to Lalpura, and force the Mohmands into order. To overawe Lalpura completely, he directed a fort to be built at Dakka, and troops permanently located there. The contract for building this was handed to Arsala Khan; and he is said to have made enough on it to build his present fort, known to us as Rozabad, and called by him Kala-i-Arsala Khan. He died in 1876 or 1877, leaving four sons--

1. Mazulla Khan 3. Nur Khan
2. Sayyid Khan 4. Taj Muhammad Khan

"The first was in Hisarak, and gave endless trouble on the road between Safed Sang and Jagdalak from the commencement of December 1879."
The Jabar Khels are distributed as follows:

In Laghman

Karghai	Kamalpur	Lam	Kats-i-Muhammad Ali Khan
Dandar	Lara Mora	Kaga-Kach	Kats-i-Aziz Khan
Polan	Negar	Shahmangal	Kats-i-Ilias

In Surkhab

Mast-i-Khel	Kala-i-Nao
Kala-i-awaz	Kala-i-Mokim
Khudpur	Kala-i-Lala
Seh-Mahal (1/2)	Kala-i-Jamadar

Bazid-Khel	Deh-i-Saiyidan-i-Arabi
Wattapur	Deh-i-Saiyidan.

In Hisarak

Chartut	Ghwaghiza
Ganji-Khel	Maruf Khel
Ab-i-Zangi	Jokan.
	(Warburton.)

In 1882 Muhammad Khan was head of the Jabar Khel section and indeed of the whole tribe of Ghilzais.
Of the four sons of Arsala Khan, Mazulla Khan joined Abdur Rahman in 1880, and was for some time one of his confidential advisers. Subsequently the Amir placed him in confinement, but released him again in March 1881, presented him with a khilat, and promised to make him governor of Zurmat. In spite of these promises Mazulla Khan left Kabul secretly and tried to stir up disturbances amongst the Ghilzais. At the Amir's request he eventually returned to Kabul, but as his brother, Taj Muhammad Khan, and cousin, Muhammad Karim Khan, had not come in, the Amir again imprisoned him. He was released in 1882, and went to the Hisarak country. The Amir again threw him to prison in 1883. It is not clear what happened to Mazulla Khan after this.
Taj Muhammad commanded troops in the battles fought by Ayub Khan against us, and afterwards accompanied Ayub to Persia. In 1882 Sayyid Khan was a youth of about 18 years, and was living at Jalalabad. Nur Khan, then a lad of about 12 years, was living at Arsala Khan Kala, near Charasia. (I.B.C.)

*JABAR KHEL   جبارخیل

33-5 68-55 m. A village located near Madu Kach, about 10 miles south of Motakhan in Paktia province.

JABAR-O-MITRANI   جبار مترانی

34-11 70-38 m. A village consisting of two hamlets in the Jalalabad district, about 5 miles southwest of Batikot. Inhabitants: Tirais. (Jenkyns.) Recent maps show only the name Metrani. (LWA)

JABIR KALA   جبار قلعه (؟)

33- 68-. A village in the upper Logar valley (southern division). Inhabitants: Astanazi Ghilzais. In 1880 the village contained 200 families. (Clifford, Euan Smith.) This should probably be Jabar Kala, at 33-32 69-42 G. (LWA)

JABL-US SARAJ   جبل السراج

35-5 69-15. Jabl-us Saraj is woleswali in Parwan province. The woleswali comprises an area of 194 square kilometers and has an agricultural population that has been estimated at from 21,384 to 27,178. The woleswali is bounded in the west by Shinwar, in the north by Salang, in the east by Panjshir and Kohistan, and in the south by Charikar. Jabl-us Saraj includes about 95 villages, of which 17 have more than 500 inhabitants. The villages are listed in the PG as follows: Mamo Khel, Niazak Khel, Qader Khel, Meyana Guzer, Akbar Khel, Qala-i-Surkh (Qala-i-Sarak), Taglar (Tagla), Qala-i-Sahra, Matak, Ashaba-i-Sharif, Deh Bala, Deh Mir Khan, Nur Mohammad Khan Khel, Chinkai Ulya, Seh Burja-i-Incho, Bala Deh Incho, Aghur Sang Incho, Qala-i-Safid, Mulla Sher Khan, Dinar Khel, Mahmud Khel, Barut Saz-i-Incho, Fateh Khan Khel, Chingai Sufla, Tajekan, Meyan Joy, Hessar, Nasrullah Khel, Khwaja Mohammad Khel, Madad Khel, Malikjan Khel, Munara-i-Hessar, Eshqabad, Abed Khel, Qader Khel (Bed Khel), Rasuldad Khel, Zarif Khel (Harif Khel), Hamza Khel, Haibat

Khel, Khwajagi, Khan Jan Khel, Shabdar Khel, Ibrahim Khel, Luqman Khel, Akhtaj, Chuqur Khel, Jan Nessar Khel Gulbahar, Nahr-i-Gulbahar, Sabz Khel, Pai Mazar-i- Gulbahar, Tursan Khel, Lugar-i-Gulbahar, Mir Khan Khel, Qala-i-Bala (Gulbahar), Sahra-i-Gulbahar, Guzar Payan, Ezat Khel, Bain Baghha, Abdul Khel, Ushturgar, Shinwari, Chawar Khel, Kohna Qala, Shaikh Ali, Ashraf Khel, Mulla Habib Khel, Aziz Khel, Bahadur Beg Gulbahar, Hamid Khel Gulbahar, Gul Mirza Khel, Bulaq-i-Gulbahar, Panjah Khana, Deh Nau, Kocha-i-Payan, Sar-i-Bazar, Sangi Khel, Khwaja Khel, Mohammad Khan Khel, Mohammad Khan Khel Gulbahar, Sherullah Khel, Baqi Khel, Hashem Khel, Kaman Gar, Munarah, Qala-i-Bala, Shutul, Sayed Khel, Incho, Zeba (Zerbia), Char Burj, Mirza Khel, Sufi Khel, and Sayed Khel. (LWA) In 1914 Jabl-us Saraj was described as follows: A large fortified cantonment now (1906) in course of construction near Parwan, north of Charikar. It has been decided to build here a citadel, or "arg", to contain a palace for the Amir and quarters for the Ardal troops, as well as a fortified cantonment for 12,000 men. Owing to the scarcity of fuel in Kabul the Amir proposes to remove the workshops from Kabul to Jabl-us Saraj, and to connect the two places by a railway. (I.B.C.)

JADRAN جدران
33- 69-. A village in the Jaji country, on the right bank of the Karaia stream and in the district of Hariob. (Lumsden.)

JADRAN Or ZADRAN خدران (جدران)
A tribe inhabiting the east slopes of the Sulaiman range, east of Zurmat. On the north and east they have the Mangals; on the north and west, Ghilzais; on the east, Khost and Dawar; south and east, the Wazirs; south and west, the Kharotis; and west, the Ghilzais. How far they extend down the slopes of the Sulaiman range is not known, but it certainly cannot be far, as Broadfoot says they are confined to one ridge. They are probably a very small tribe. Elphinstone says their manners, etc., resemble the Wazirs, and Broadfoot, those of the Kharotis, from which we must infer they are utter savages, and, as Elphinstone says more like mountain bears than men. They live in very small villages; some of them cultivate the little land they have, but they appear chiefly to depend on their flocks for subsistence. They live, some in houses and some in tents. They are great robbers, and their country was formerly a refuge for bad characters. It is said to be very difficult, and one of their forts, Kala Nak, is described as exceedingly strong. Their hills are covered with pines in the higher parts and in the lower with other trees. They go to Gardez to sell their wool and cheese, and get in return cloth and corn. They appear to have some intercourse with the Jajis, and it is possible they may have something of the same origin. No one says whether they are Shiahs or Sunnis, or whether Persian or Pushtu is their language. They are of no importance whatever, and only in the case of the Dawar route being used to Ghazni could they ever become so. It may be noted that one of the Jaji villages is called Jadran.
During the time the British troops remained in Khost in 1879, they were kept on the qui vive by constant reports of the assembly of the then two independent tribes. Mangals and Jadrans, who occupy the mountains northwest and west of the district. Both tribes did come together in considerable numbers, but probably, from being alarmed for themselves, to act chiefly on the defensive. If the Jadrans had any intention of attacking the camp, as was sometimes stated, they were probably deterred therefrom by the cavalry reconnaissance which visited the villages along the Jadran border in January.

In 1882 some desultory fighting took place between the Jadrans and the Amir's troops. Information received on the subject was extremely vague, but it appears that the Jadrans were quickly and thoroughly subdued, and that three Afghan posts were afterwards established in their country. (I.B.C., Elphinstone, Broadfoot.)

JADRAN
33-23 69-26. Jadran or Waze Jadran is a woleswali in Paktia province. The woleswali comprises an area of 427 square kilometers and has an agricultural population that has been estimated at from 6,100 to 18,590. The woleswali is bounded in the west by Orma, in the north by Shawak, Musa Khel and Qalandar, in the east by Nader Shah Kot and Shamal, and in the south by Sperah, Zeluk, and Neka. Jadran has some 44 villages, 12 of which have more than 500 inhabitants. The villages are listed in the PG as follows: Ayo Khel, Laka Tiga Dari-Khel, Sargoli-i-Sari-Khel, Lota Dari Khel, Ghorka Khola Mangat Khel, Bakht Kahol-i-Dari Khel, Tangi Bari, Hawas Khel, Miti Darikhel, Ali Moh'd Khel, Shahid Khel Kalai, Shalam Dari-Khel, Ghorka Ayo-Khel, Moti (Mita), Khelwati, Matka (Mastaka), Tsapruna, Asmani Mozi (Asmani), Kajakai Mozi (Zamarai Kats), Darwol Mozi (Darwol), Plangi, Kheng Mozi (Khengi), Qarya-i-Fakhri, Star Kalai, Jakhi Karezgai, Kha Khel, Soran, Khan Gul Kot, Shnay Gul Kot (Shnay Kotgai), Oji Khel-i-Mozi (Roji Khel), Aboshtai Mozi (Abokhti), Khal Khel Mozi, Tori Khel, Ewaz Khel, Sori Khel, Katskai Dari-Khel, Kalezha Khola, Spaye Khel, Aboshtai, Surgori, and Lota.

*JADRAN KALA
33-23 69-5 m. A village located on the way to Gardez, about 4 miles south of Zurmat.

JAFAR
A halting place, on the road from Pannah to Kala Kharoti. There is a spring here. (Broadfoot.)

JAFFAH
A small section of the Muhammad Khwaja Hazaras. (See Military Report on Hazarajat, Part II)

JAFIR JAN
34- 69-. A fort in the Chardeh valley of Kabul, between Aoshar and Kala-i-Fazil Beg. Inhabitants: about 20 families of Gadi Hazaras. (I.B.C.)

JAFIR KALA
34- 67-. Elevation 9,600 feet. A group of small forts and villages at the lower end of the Band-i-Amir lakes in the Yak Walang district. The largest fort is on the left bank of the river. There are about 70 families in all, and a little cultivation is carried on. Several easy roads connect Jafir Kala with the Bamian-Yak Walang road, and a road goes north through Dara Yusuf to Mazar-i-Sharif. (Maitland.)

JAFRA See SAFRA

JAGDALAK Or JEGDALAY
34-26 69-46 A. Elevation 5,420 feet. A village on the left bank of the stream of the same name; it lies on the eastern slopes of the Karkacha range, just south of the entrance to the Pari Dara gorge; it is 47 miles from Kabul, and 52 miles from Jalalabad, by the main road. It contains, in conjunction with another village about 3/4

mile to the west, some 120 families of Astanazai Ghilzais. All the village lands are khalsa, or State property, and the State takes half of the annual produce. The land is very fertile and the produce of grain is about forty-fold.

There is a dak-post in the village, and on a ridge about 600 yards to the north are an old fort, garrisoned by a company of infantry, and a new sarai. The water-supply of the fort is obtained from a small stream which joins the Jagdalak stream just north of the village; the water is led into a tank in the centre of the fort by an aqueduct, and the supply could therefore be easily cut off. The fort lies about 350 yards off the main road, and could accommodate 200 infantry. There is a squadron of cavalry quartered in the village.

At Jagdalak room can be found to encamp about three battalions of infantry and a regiment of cavalry, but the valley is very narrow and cramped, and units would have to be scattered about. Rather more than a mile to the south, towards the Jagdalak Kotal, there is room for a brigade to encamp, with water supply close by, sufficient for 5,000 men and animals; there is also a good spring for drinking water in the nala 100 feet below the fort. Suplies are only available with difficulty and there is little grazing; fuel is plentiful. Just to the north of Jagdalak the stream enters the famous Jagdalak (or Bari Dara) defile.

It is entered immediately after leaving the village of Jagdalak, and continues for 3 1/2 miles along the bed of the stream. It is very narrow and stony; it winds several times almost at right angles. The average width is about 40 or 50 yards, but there are three places where it is less than 10 feet, and in one it is only 6 feet. The almost perpendicular cliffs on both sides appear as if threatening destruction to the traveller. A small party of armed men would stop the passage of any force which had entered it. This difficult pass is in some repects not unlike the defile of the "valley of hell" between Neustadt and Friburg. Hough finishes this account by saying it was more difficult than anything he had seen in all Afghanistan, adding "it beggars description." Havelock calls it "another terrific defile, the rocks of which said to be granite and sandstone, are piled one upon the other in dark frowning strata, sloping down on either side towards a mountain rivulet for which they hardly leave room to flow."

The name of this defile is well known to history, as the spot where the last remnants of the British army retreating from Kabul in 1842 were destroyed. Kay thus geographically describes the closing scene:

"The enemy were crowning the heights; there was no possibility of escape. Shelton, with a few brave men of the rear-guard, faced the overwhelming crowd of Afghans with a determined courage worthy of British soldiers, and fought his way to Jagdalak. Almost every inch of ground was contested. Gallantly did this little band hold the enemy in check, keeping the fierce crowd from closing in upon the column, but suffering terribly under the fire of their 'jezails,' they made their way at last to the ground where the advance had halted, behind some ruined walls on a height by the roadside. Their comrades received them with a cheer. The cheer came from a party of officers who had extended themselves in line on the height to show an imposing front to their assilants. The enemy seemed to increase in number and in daring. They had followed the rear-guard to Jagdalak, and they now took possession of the heights commanding the position of their victims.

"The hot fire of the enemy's 'jezails' drove the survivors of the Kabul army to seek safety behind the ruined walls near which they had posted themselves. Withdrawn from the excitement of the actual conflict, these wretched men now began to suffer in all their unendurable extremes the agonies of hunger and thirst. They scooped up the snow in their hands and greedily devoured it. But it only increased their torments. There was a stream of pure water near at hand, but they could not approach it without being struck down by the fire of the enemy.

"The men lay down in the snow to snatch a little brief repose after a long vigil of thirty hours, when the enemy poured in volley after volley upon their resting place, and compelled them in wild confusion--soldiers and camp-followers again huddled together--to quit the enclosure in which they had bivouacked. Individual sets of heroism were not wanting at this time to give something of dignity even to this melancholy retreat. A handful of the 44th Regiment here made a gallant rush at the enemy and cleared al the ground before them. But the little party was soon recalled to the main body, which again retired behind the ruined walls; and again the enemy returned to pour upon them the destructive fire of their terrible 'jezails.'

"All night long and throughout the next day the force halted at Jagdalak."

"It was about eight o'clock on the evening of the 12th that the few remaining men, now reduced to about 120 of the 44th and 25 artillerymen, prepared to resume their perilous march. The curse of camp-followers clung to them still. The teeming rabble again came huddling against the fighting men; and the Afghans, taking advantage of the confusion, stole in knife in hand amongst them, destroying all the unarmed men in their way, and glutting themselves with plunder.

"They did not this time escape. The soldiers turned and bayonetted the plunderers, and fought their way bravely on. But there was a terrible fate awaiting them as they advanced. The Jagdalak pass was before them. The road ascends between the steep walls of this dark precipitous defile, and our wretched ment struggled onward, exposed to the fire of the enemy, till, on nearing the summit, they came suddenly upon a barricade, and were thrown back in surprise and dismay. The enemy had blocked up the mouth of the pass. Barriers, made of bushes and the branches of trees, opposed the progress of the column, and threw the whole into inextricable confusion. The camp-followers crowded upon the soldiers, who, in spite of the overwhelming superiority of the enemy, fought with a desperate valour, worthy of a better fate. The Afghans had been lying in wait for the miserable remnant of the British army and were now busy with their cruel knives and their unerring 'jazails.' The massacre was something terrible to contemplate. Officers, soldiers, and camp-followers were stricken down at the foot of the baricade. A few, strong in the energy of desperation, managed to struggle through it. But from that time all hope was at an end. There had ceased to be a British army."

On the occasion of Sale's march to Jalalabad, the Ghilzais had occupied the kotal of Jagdalak in force, but were driven off by turning columns, not, however, before we had lost 1 officer and 28 men killed, and 4 officers and 87 men wounded.

On the advance of Pollock's force, the Ghilzais again held the kotal, but were again driven off with comparative ease by turning columns, though they are said to have been 5,000 in number. Our loss on this occasion was 1 officer and 6 men killed, and 1 officer and 57 men wounded. Recent maps show the spelling Jegdalay. Sar-i-

Jagdalak is located at 34-24   69-44 m.   (LWA)

JAGDALAK KOTAL   جگدلک

34-24   69-44. Elevation 6,200 feet. A pass over a spur of the Karkacha range, its summit lying about 3 miles southeast of the village of Jagdalak. It is an important strategical point, forming the watershed between the Kabul and Surkhab rivers and being the highest point reached by the road between Safed Sang and Seh Baba. During the second Afghan war there was a small fort on the kotal which was usually garrisoned by 130 British infantry; it is now (1905) in ruins. The water-supply, which was only just sufficient for the garrison, was obtained from two springs about 600 yards to the southeast of the fort, and drinking-water from springs at the foot of a round conical hill about a mile below the kotal, known as "Pudding Hill." This hill completely commands the northern side of the pass, of which a considerable part can be enfiladed. Firewood is obtainable close to the fort; grass and supplies with difficulty from the neighbouring villages.

In 1880 signalling communication was maintained with Pezwan, Jagdalak and Lataband from a hill (7,050 feet) 1,500 yards northeast of the fort; the fort itself was only in direct communication with Pezwan. The descent from the kotal towards Jagdalak is very steep. (I.B.C.)

*JAGH   جاغ

33-2   67-2 m.   A village located south of the Kuh-i-Dadi in northern Ghazni province.

*JAGHAIN   جاغین

34-26   68-35 m.   A village located on a tributary of the Maidan river, about 5 miles southwest of Jalriz.

JAGHATU   جغتو

A main section fo the Hazaras. (See Military Report on Hazarajat, Part II.)

*JAGHATU   جغتو

34-48   68-23. Jaghatu is the name of an alaqadari in Wardak province. The alaqadari comprises an area fo 622 square kilometers and has an agricultural population which has been estimated at about 7,700. The alaqadari is bounded in the west by Nawar, in the north by Chak-i-Wardak, in the east by Sayyidabad, and in the south by Jaghatu and Khwaja Omri. Jaghatu includes about 107 villages, of which about six have more than 500 inhabitants. The villages are listed in the PG as follows: Dahana, Sadat Khel, Abtala, Hanzal Khel, Mohamad Quli, Adina, Riyab-i-Kalan, Qala-i-Wazir, Aslam Khel, Batawak, Qala-i-Munar, Riyab-i-Khurd, Ghozia, Barikab-i-Durani, Shaikh Ali, Murad Khan, Khalai, Bed Mushk, Qala-i-Rabat, Kamal Khel, Seper Gin, Abdul Rahim Khel, Mahala, Sabz Sang, Kunj-i-Jaghatu, Dewalak, Shah Butak, Khudran, Se Deh, Chashma-i-Kalan, Chashma-i-Khurd, Dulana, Kharr, Mardla, Bangi, Zarin Khurd, Surkh Qol, Lalaki, Kalandeh, Folad Beg, Taki, Tangi, Qol Perak, Kaj Qala-i-Abtala, Kohi, Buland Khel, Sadat Sar Band, Mesri Khel, Chopan, Laghari, Khalifa Baba Khel, Ali Khel, Alana-i-Bala, Alana-i-Pain, Akhtum, Babur Khel, Champarak, Zarin Kalan, Azim Khel, Shishak Khel, Koshaki, Ma Mah, Piyadarah, Delawar Khel, Lali, Choka, Qala-i-Alim (De Alam Kali), Nuri Khel, Qol-i-Bakot (Qulba Kot), Kodi Abatala (Kaday), Mangli, Saleh Khel, Bocha Khel, Khwaja Ab, Qol, Saleh Khel, Chacha, Abtala-i-Khona, Mirza Beg, Mir Khan Khel, Lagai Khel, Sar Tabib Khel, Zarif Khel, Sar Mast Khel, Lar Khan Khel, Gardan, Moka,

Fazilat, Shahnurullah, Mulla Hafez, Siyah Qol, Hajum, Shirdagh, Chakol, Akhtar Khel, Chaworchi, Qala-i-Kako, Saydal Khan, Mohammad Akbar Khan, Kohna Deh-i-Ahangaran, Karez, Qala-i-Halim, Hamzah, Qala-i-Nau, Se Deh, Gandah Qol, Spin Qala, Bad Mushak, Ruy Ab-i-Khurd, Ruy Ab-i-Kalan, Kalan Deh, Akhter Khel, and Barikab.

*JAGHATU جغتو

33-34 68-11. Jaghatu is a woleswali in Ghazni province. The woleswali comprises an area of 1,265 square kilometers and has an agricultural population that has been estimated at from 22,456 to 25,212. The woleswali is bounded in the north by Jaghatu (Wardak) and Khwaja Omri in the east by Ghazni, in the south by Andar and Qarabagh, and in the west by Nawar. Jaghatu includes about 294 villages, one of which has more than 500 inhabitants. Villages with over 100 inhabitants are listed in the PG as follows: Adam Khel, Agar (Agar Kakrak), Ahangaran, Bakhtiyar, Qarya-i-Bubul Gulan, Bocha Khari Qala, Band -i-Ali, Qala-i-Bed Darah, Bed Shaki, Payendah Khel, Piraka Ulya, Patya-i-Rahim Beg, Talkhak-i-Sarab, Tangi, Jaja, Chadah, Chalma, Hoj Tarkan, Qarya-i-Haji Khan, Hussain Khel, Haidara, Khashah, Qarya-i-Khandaq, Khosh Abdal, Khwaja, Khosh Ali, Deh Ahan-i-Turkan, Deh Ahin, Deh Dawlat, Deh Ramzi, Deh Ali Gul, Deh Esa, Deh Mulla, Deh Mir khan, Rahim Beg, Qarya-i-Sarban, Sar Bed (Sobed), Surkhdeh, Sulaiman (Rashida), Sang-i-Zaidah, Seyah Qol (Kakarak), Seyah Qol (Turkan), Sayedan-i-Balkhi (Sadat-i-Balkhi), Sayda, Shahzadagan, Shamsuddin, Shaikh Aka(Shaikh Gah), Qarya-i-Sher Khan, Safar Kushta Bulbul (Safar Pushta), Taleb (Tullab) Begum, Ashur, Moh'd Ali Khan, Ali Khan Khel, Alyat, Faqir Shah, Qala-i-Adrowaz (Adro Khan), Qala-i-Surkh Hakimabad, Qala-i-Sadat Khan Qala-i-Sayed Alam, Qala-i-Shamsher, Qala-i-Karim, Qala-i-Mulla, Qala-i-Nazar Qayaq, Qalandar, Qul Janan, Zaman Khel, Qala-i-Moh'd Khan, Qol-i-Jina, Qol-i-Bayan, Qol-i-Shorah, Qol-i-Gurg, Qarya-i-Moh'd Kazim Khan, Qarya-i-Kochi, Gosha-i-Turkan, Gosha-i-Jurmtu, Kohna Deh, Kula Khel-i-Waez, Kula Khel-i-Ulya, Gadoli-Shamsher, Gandab-i-Sufla, Qarya-i-Lali, Deh Lalandar, Ilyas, Mama, Musa Khel, (Kakrak), Mohmand, Nau Deh (Qarya-i-Yusuf), Nekzai, Qarya-i-Wali Moh'd Khan, Qarya-i-Haft Asayab, Huta (Qayaq), Qarya-i-Laghari, Kula Khel-i-Sufla, and Seh Qala.

JAGHURI جاغوری

A main section of the Haaras. (See Military Report of Hazarajat, Part II.)

*JAGHORI جاغوری

33-8 67-27. Jaghori is a woleswali in Ghazni province. the woleswali comprises an area of 1,855 square kilometers and has an agricultural population that has been estimated at from 35,136 to 39,565. The woleswali is bounded in the east by Qarabagh and Muqor, in the south by Gilan, Shahjui and Arghandab, in the west by Malestan, and in the north by Nawar. Jaghori has some 127 villages, of which about 70 have over 500 inhabitants. The villages are listed in the PG as follows: Asiyab Khurd, Sokhta, Hashem Bakht, Alqoy-i-Haider, Gaw Murdah, Kamarak-i-Almeto, Ulum-i-Qada Bu Said, Abudal, Gunbad-i-Anguri, Chaka, Baba Qol, Meta Baba, Baba Kamal Bagh-i-Ahangar, Shaikh Chagho, Darwishan, Murgh Lana, Sabz Sang, Beg Barik, Paye Julga-i-Loman, Paye Julga-i-Haider, Tabarghanak-i-Mirdad, Tabarghanak Wa Khwaja Ali, Qambar Jala, Chob-i-Bu Said, Chel Baghtu-i-Oqi, Qala-i-Khan, Khak Bada-i-Pusht-i-Bum, Mirza Khel-i-Dawud, Barga-i-Dawlat Shah, Deh Murda-i-Gulzar, Zirak, Sabz Chob-i-Sufla, Zangab, Sabz Sang-i-Haider, Sar-i-Loman, Tarmala, Sang-i-Shanda, Sang-i-Masha, Toghi, Chambar, Dolana, Nau-Deh, Deh Gholi, Amaliyat, Pusht-i-Chob, Kata Sang, Sang-i-Surakh, Sar Qol-i-Jala, Asp-i-Khwaja, Dolana, Toghi, Mirtani Sang, Manga, Ali Said Ahmad, Shah Khwaja-i-Loman, Shash Par, Shughla, Shar-i-Zahidah, Ulya-To-i-Khudaidad, Bator, Qarah, Qalandari, Qoghzar, Gardan, Goshai-i-Safed Rish-i-Sang Masha, Khundel Qash-i-Sang-i-Masha, Ghujor, Gula Beg-i-Baba, Giro-i-Baba, Tilom-i-Baba, Maska, Soya Allahyar, Chob-i-Khushk, Tab Qawas-i-Sarab, Khar Kas, Ambulaq, Dala, Qari, Dang Rozi-i-Allah Yar, Gharib Rah-i-Allah Yar, Miyana Loman, Muhajerin-i-Bu-Said, Allah Dad-i-Ud-Qul, Geran Sang, Hicha, Takhtak, Darwaz Qul, Mawla Dad-i-Siyah Zamin, Lakhshak Haider, Sar Qol-i-Jala, Sang-i-Surakh, Jawdari, Sabz Chob-i-Ulya, Qash Hajat Khwaja-Ali-i-Sabz Chob, Qash Muqam, Mamadak, Siyah Zamin, Joy-i-Sultan, Surkh Ab, Geran Sang, Sabqal, Mitar Khel, Wakil Khel, Razi, Sokhta-i-Qalandari, Beg, Khudaidad, Qarah Qul, Lala Khel, Khar Tezak, Mitar Khel-i-Haji Bini, Tam Khel, Chob Jumak, Deltamur-i-Dawud, Maidan-i-Pataw, Bini Barik, Qotaq-i-Bala, Belaw Dawud, Aza-i-Kula Beg, Namak Dawlat Shah, Aqel Beg-i-Ud Qul, Tabqus-i-Allahyar, Qena Pataw, Suk-i-Pataw, Karez-i-Patau-i-Sar Qol, Khwa Buta, Qotaq-i-Pain, Dam Joy-i-Shah Dawlat, Abroshan, Taqul, Sar Sadiq, Sang Joye, Seh Paya, Qaltar Ghoy-i-Haider, Qumagh-i-Haider, Fato, and Ghajor.

*JAHANGIR KALAI
32-41 67-46 m. A village located east of Jabbar and south of Mukur in Ghazni province.

*JAHANGIR KOT
33-19 69-10 m. A village located 3 miles south of Shahi Kot in Paktia province.

JAHAN NUMA
34- 70-. A collection of villages forming a suburb on the north and west of the town of Jalalabad. They are four in number, viz.:

1. Kala-i-Ali Khel
2. Kala-i-Babari
3. Kala-i-Arbabha
4. Kala-i-Fazal Beg

The inhabitants are Tajiks, Mughals, Kashimiris and Arabs. (Jenkyns.)

*JAINIMA
35-19 69-9 m. A village located on the Koklam stream, east of the Salang tunnel.

JAJAH
A locality in the country of the Muhammad Khwaja Hazaras. (See Military Report on Hazarajat, Part II.)

JAJI
A tribe inhabiting the valley of the Hariob (affluent of the Kurram) and of its tributaries, the Karaia and Hazardarakht rivulets, stretching from the Palwar pass to near that of Shutur Gardan. They are estimated at about 5,000 families and divided into numerous smaller sections; there are 8 divisions, called "wands," as follows:—1, Lehwani; 2, Ada Khel (tribe of the chief); 3, Petla, which is coupled with the Allisemgeh; 4, Ahmad Khel, who combine with the Bayan Khel; 5, Ali Khel; 6, Jamu Khel; 7, Husain Khel; and 8, Karaia Ahmad Khel, It is said that the Jajis and Turis are descended from a common ancestor, and judging from the similarity between the two tribes, Donald thinks this is not at all unlikely; but while the Jajis are of the Sunni sect, the Turis hold Shiah tenets. At the

same time it is a very usual thing in Kurram and its neighbourhood to find two brothers, one of whom is a Sunni and the other a Shiah. The Jajis make excellent labourers, and all the buildings in the Kurram station of Para Chinar have been made by them. As a tribe they are greatly weakened by internal feuds, and most of their villages are divided accordingly into numerous separate parts to suit these factions, while rival towers shoot up side by side in every direction.

The houses of the jajis are of peculiar construction, which is indicative of the life of contention they lead. Each house is a detached tenement built in a square form. In the centre of one side is the entrance by a large door of stout pine plants, which are often closely studded with broad mushroom-headed nails. The floor, which occupies the whole of the interior space, is sunk a little below the level of the ground outside. The walls are built of unhewn stones, cemented together by a plaster of clay and chopped straw and rise 2 or 3 feet above the level of the flat roof, which during fine weather is the resort of the family, who here bask in the sun and perform their toilette in its genial warmth.

The roof communicates with the interior of the house by a trap-door and ladder. The latter is formed of a fir pole notched at intervals and fixed in a slanting position between the trap-door and the floor. The interior of the house is an open space that shelters the entire family, their cattle, poultry, etc., and contains also stores of wood, grain, and fodder; for the Jajis are liable to frequent blocades, not only by their enemies, but by the snow also which sometimes, it is said, covers the ground to a great depth. The walls all round are pierced with a series of apertures, in two or three rows, near the upper part. These serve the threefold purpose of ventilators, chimneys, and loop-holes for shooting through. In some of the houses galleries run round the walls inside, and are used for the shelter of the family, and storing fodder, wood, grain, etc., whilst the space on the ground floor is allotted to the cattle, goats, mules, etc. The Jajis are a very prolific race, if one may judge from the number of children to be seen about every village but they have barely culturable land sufficient to produce subsistence for them; wheat, barley, rice and peas are produced from the irrigated lands, but their chief stock is goat. Timber, fuel, and fodder are abundant, and some provisions are exported to Kabul, to which they also send some planks of pine about 6 or 7 feet long. Some honey also is exported, especially from the village of Rakian. The Jajis wear the lungi or turban, and Bellew, who saw them in their own homes, says they are mostly dressed in loose shirts and trousers of cotton dyed blue, and over one shoulder they carry a matchlock with a forked rest, whilst from the other depends against the back a large circular shield of camel's or buffalo's hide; around their waist are suspended by leather straps three or four powder-flasks of uncured sheep skin, together with a host of other paraphernalia belonging to the matchlock, such as tinder box, flint and steel, hammer, picker. Those not armed with the rifle carry an Afghan knife (chura). They wear their hair long. Their skins are tinged a deep brown colour from constant exposure to the sooty smoke of the pine-wood they use as fuel, aided by their aversion to the use of cold water. These people, as their dress and dwellings indicate, are very poor, and depend for support entirely on the produce of their cattle and crops. They breed, however, numbers of mules, which are much esteemed and greatly in demand at Kabul. The Jajis have, or had, a blood feud with the Turis. When Lumsden's mission passed through their country it was with the greatest difficulty they were prevented from attacking it. Bellew's description of the scene of excitement which occurred on this occasion is as follows:

"Of their proximity, indeed, there was no doubt, for we could hear the sounds of their drums ('nagara') and pipes ('surnai'). The sound of the latter very much resembled that of the Scotch bagpipe. These sounds rolled along from valley to valley, and seemed to acquire fresh impetus from each projecting spur and opposing hill, whilst the loud and shrill yells, into which the Jajis burst every now and then, were echoed along in the same way, and told us of the excited state of the tribes. Before our party, headed by the officers of the mission, had fairly emerged from the forests bordering the summit of the hill, our road was obstructed by a party of some fifty or more Jajis, who with 'Chura' (Afghan knife) in hand, were capering about and gesticulating in a wild fashion to the exciting notes of a war-song chanted by the leaders of the band, and in the chorus of which the whole party joined with a sonorous 'Woh-ho, Ah-ha' repeated several times in a deep bass voice, and followed by a peculiar shrill yell, during which the actors leapt about like mad men over the intervening rocks, till they approached our advancing party to within 8 or 10 yards, and equally wonderful was the agility with which the Jajis bounded about from rock to rock up the faces of the hill with the ease and nimbleness of monkeys. A few hundred yards lower down the hill we were met by a similar though larger party of Jajis, among whom were several armed with the long Afghan rifle, or 'jezail.'

"We were disturbed during the whole day until nightfall by these villainous Jajis who, with war-songs and dances, accompanied by a constant beating of drums, worked themselves up to a pitch of excitement barely restrainable, their scattered parties on the hill tops around following each other in a succesion of defiant shouts and yells, and such like exhibitions of hostility.

"Their war-dance was a most exciting performance, and as far as I could make out from watching the proceedings of a crowd occupying an eminence, some 300 yards off, was conducted somewhat in this fashion; some dozen or fifteen men of their number, after divesting themselves of their rifles, shields, etc., uncovered their heads, and tied the 'pagri,' or turban round the waist; each man then unsheathed his 'chura,' and took his place with his fellow, the whole together forming a circle. They then commenced chanting a song, flourishing their knives overhead, and stamping on the ground to its notes, and then each gradually revolving, the whole body moving round together and maintaining the circle in which they first stood up. Whilst this was going on, two of the party stepped into the centre of the ring and went through a mimic fight, or a series of jumps, pirouettes, and other movements of a like nature, which appeared to be regulated in their rapidity by the measure of the music, for towards the close of the performance the singing ceased, and the whole party appeared twirling and twisting about in a confused mass, amidst the flashings of their drawn knives, their movements being timed to the rapid roll of their drums. It was wonderful they did not wound each other in these intricate and rapid evolutions with unsheathed knives. On the conclusion of the dance, the whole party set up a shrill and prolonged yell that reverberated over the hills, and was caught up by those on the neighbouring heights and thus prolonged for some minutes. (The Turis perform a similar dance--Donald.)

"Whilst all this was going on upon the heights around our camp, several parties of armed Jajis ranged in columns, three or four abreast and eight or nine deep, followed each other in succession round and round the skirts or our camp, all the time chanting an impressive and passionate war-song in a very peculiar sonorous tone that seemed to be affected by the acoustic influences of the locality, which, as already mentioned, was a deep basin enclosed for the most part by bare and rocky eminences and hills. This effect was most marked in the chorus 'Woh-ho, Ah-ha,' the slowly repeated syllables of which were echoed back in a continuous and confused reverberation of rumbling noise. At the conclusion of the war-song, they all leapt simultaneously into the air, and on again alighting on terra firma, the whole party together took a leap, or skip, forwards, at the time yelling and screaming like fiends. The excited apearance of these men and the wild antics they performed are hardly credible."

The Jaji country can be entered from the Logar by the Shutur Gardan pass and perhaps others; from Zurmat through the Mangal country; from Kabul by the Gharigi road; from the Jalalabad district by a road leading from Marki Khel, south of Gandamak; and from Kurram either by the Paiwar Kotal or the bed of the Kurram and Chamkani. (Bellew, Donald, I.B.C.)

*JAJI (ALI KHEL)   خاخی (علی خیل)

33-56 69-43. Jaji (Ali Khel) is a woleswali in Paktia province. The woleswali comprises an area of 617 square kilometers and has an agricultural population that has been estimated at from 27,852 to 31,526. The woleswali is bounded in the west and north by Azro, in the northeast by Shirzad, in the east by the State of Pakistan, and in the south by Dareh Darang, Chamkani, Hasan Khel, and Sayed Karam. Jaji has some 47 villages, 25 of which have more than 500 inhabitants. The villages are listed in the PG as follows: Kharmana, Kotkai, Kuz Shaga (Shege), Bar Shega (Shegai Ulya), Sorani Khel, Meri Khel, Katskai (Katsaki), Mina Khel, Roqiyan (Oqyan), Qarya-i-Mulla Fateh, Hasan Ulgada (Hasan Laka), Deray Kholay, Ali Khel, Khwazi Khel (Khozikhel), Ghonzai Ahmad Khel, Bayan Khel, Ali Sangi, Petla, Kharshatal, Bar Belawat (Belawat-i-Ulya), Mir Khel, Sor Gul, Ahmad Khel-i-Safed Koh, Gul Ghondi, Kotgai, Sharif Kalai, Lar Belawat (Belawat-i-Payan), Zadran Kalai, Lal Lewanai (Lewan Khel), Khwazi Khel (Khwaja Khel), Jono Mandai, Choryan, Jabar Khel, Barets Khel, Shah Mohamad, Teri Kona, Tsaparai, Ghogosai, Khalwati, Badali Mangal, Kata Sang, Istiya, Maram, Obakhti, Hotaki, Soye Kalai, Mosin, Lar Bozi, and Jelam-i-Sharif.

JAJI MAIDAN   خاخی میدان

33-37 70-7 m. Jaji Maidan is a woleswali in Paktia province. The woleswali comprises an area of 395 square kilometers and has an agricultural population that has been estimated at from 7,737 to 18,628. The woleswali is bounded in the west by Dand-wa-Patan and Jani Khel, in the south by Bak, and in the east and north by the State of Pakistan. Jaji Maidan has some 74 villages, 5 of which have more than 500 inhabitants. The villages are listed in the PG as follows: Skandarah, Aka Kahol, Derai Mela, Inzar Pela, Bagina, Hasan Khel, Korkori (Kokari), Shamtai (Shamshai), Bedad Kalai, Jaba-i-Ulgada, Landai Rogha, Chughan, Shaikhan, Smutkai (Satkai), Ister Kalai (Ster Kalai), Sarra Pela (Sar Pela), Shaweya, Spai Warzah, Hashim Khel-i-Dani, Taghari, Ali Sangi, Qazi Tangai, Manjo, Zhel Pan, Sami Kalai, Hesar Kalai, Shagai, Bar Abbas Khel (Abass Khel), Suwaki, Ghaza Ghundai, Sur Watakai, Ata Khel, Wazgarai, Khal Kot, Kotkai Ulgadah, Sro Kalai, Khan Kalai, Kochukan, Bari Qala (Bori Mughol Khel), Guli Kalai, Pass Kalai, Muchai Kalai, Kama Ghunzai, Tayaki (Asl-i-Tayaki), Mandita (Mandata), Bokarai, Chengai, Borrai, Miya Khun Jaba, Wala Kalai (Wala), Munzi Zani Khel, Koti Kalai, Hashim Khel-iQala-i-Mughol-Khel, Hashim Kalai, Bar Kalai-Hashim,

Mazari Kamar, Oga, Sara Nisara, Loti Kalai, Tiyakizai Kalai, Pir Mila, Takhi Koy Kalai, Dedar Kotkai, Loya Ghonzai, Jaba Dani, Khelwati Kalai, Kortso Kalai, Nangrosi Kalai, Nangrosi Bagh Kalai, Katski Kalai, Almawrizai Kalai, Deshi Payli Kalai, Mazrin Kats, Kuz Kalai-Abbas Khel, Bar Kalai Moghul Khel, Bar Kalai, and Kotkai-i-Moghul Khel. (LWA) In 1914 the area was described as follows: A collection of villages on the route from Hazir Pir into Khost. This route goes over the Duni pass to Yakubi. (Collett, I.B.C.)

JAJI THANA خاجی تانه

33-30 69-58. A small square fort with two towers flanking it, but commanded itself by hills on all sides. It is 5 miles from Dredkala up the Hazaradarkht defile, on the road to the Shutur Gardan. (Collett.)

JAKOUL جاوظ

34-44 68-2 m. There appear to be two small daras of this name which drain to the Kalu Glen in the Bamian district, inhabited by Darghai Hazaras. (Amir Khan.) There are also two villages, one at the above location, the other at 34-40 68-2 m. (LWA)

JALALA جلاله

35-6 71-23 G. A small village on the right bank of the Kunar river, 6 miles above Asmar. Just below the village the road from Asmar up the Kunar valley crosses the river by a bridge, the abutments of which are well above the stream on the low rocky cliffs which here bound the river; the bridge is thus probably a permanent one, and is not washed away by the spring floods. The roadway is about 3 or 4 feet wide; horses and unladen mules can be led across it, if quiet, but it is impossible for camels. (I.B.C.)

JALALABAD (DISTRICT) جلال آباد

34-26 70-28 m. This district is now part of Nangarhar province. See Nangarhar and Ningrahar. (LWA) Boundaries - general description: the district of Jalalabad is about 80 miles long from east to west, and on an average 35 miles broad from north to south. To the east it extends to the western end of the Khaibar pass and to the Bazar valley. On the south it is bounded by the Safed Koh ranges. The western boundary is a lofty spur from the Safed Koh, called Karkacha, between the valleys of Gandamak and Jagdalak. The Karkacha range, after running northwards to the latitude of Jagdalak, turns eastwards and forms the northern boundary of the Jalalabad district (separating it from Laghman) to the point where the Kabul river enters the plain. The eastern portion of the Karkacha range is usually known by the name of Siah Koh. The remaining northern boundary of the district is defined by the low hills north of Besud to the Kunar, and by the Mohmand hills from the Kunar valley to Lalpura.

The general surface of the district is diversified by long spurs thrown out by the Safed Koh in a northerly direction reaching to within a few miles of the Kabul river; and by two short isolated ranges of hills--one to the south of Ambar Khana; and the other running from Ali Boghan to Lachipur. The Kabul river enters the district at Darunta--the eastern termination of the Siah Koh range--and flows in an easterly direction through the whole district, dividing it into two parts. That to the north is a narrow strip between the river and the mountains, called Besud, to the west of the Kunar river, and Kama to the east of that river up to the point where the mountains come down close to the Kabul river. Eastward of this point where the mountains come down close to the Kabul river.

Eastward of this point lie Goshta and Chiknaur. South of the Kabul river the district of Jalalabad may be described as an irregular, undulating tract, enclosing a few small plains, e.g., Jalalabad, Chardeh, Pesh Bolak, Batikot, etc., covered with low, bare stony hills, and intersected by numerous streams issuing form the Safed Koh, and flowing towards the Kabul river. These streams depend upon the melting snow for their supply of water, and sometimes run entirely dry.

The Surkhab, which rises in the Safed Koh and flows along the eastern and southern foot of the Karkacha and Siah Koh ranges is a considerable stream. When in flood, its waters are of a bright red colour, whence its name of "red" river. On the left bank of the Kabul river the only tributary worthy of mention is the river of Kunar, which joins at a point 4 miles below Jalalabad, with a volume of water which is probably not less than that of the Kabul river itself.

The principal streams that intersect the district south of the Kabul river are --Gandamak, Karasu, Chapriar, Hisarak, Kot, and Mohmand or Mahman Dara.

The district of Jalalabad is thus seen to be entirely surrounded by mountains. The view from the town of Jalalabad in the winter is very fine, in whatever direction the eye is turned. Most impressive is the splendid range of the Safed Koh, towering to a height of 15,000 feet, and forming a magnificent wall of snow between Kurram and Jalalabad. Due north, at a distance of about 20 miles, rises the massive mountain of Kund--about 14,000 feet high, overlooking the whole of Kafiristan, and the head of which, it is fabled, was the resting place of Noah's ark after the deluge. Beyond Laghman to the northwest some glittering peaks of the Hindu Kush are visible and to the northeast stretches away a rolling sea of mountains towards Bajaur and Kunar.

The southern portion of the district, lying along the skirts of the Safeh Koh, is popularly known by the name of Nangarhar or Ningrahar (the present name of the province LWA).

The elevation of the inhabited parts of the district varies from about 6,500 feet to 1,250 feet; Jalalabad itself is 1,950 feet, Gandamak is 4,500 feet. Dakka is 1,300 feet, while high up on the spurs of the Siah Koh and Safed Koh are villages situated at an altitude of over 6,000 feet.

Two main roads traverse the district from east to west, forming portions of the main line of communication between Peshawar and Kabul. One runs from Dakka along the right bank of the Kabul river to Jalalabad; from Jalalabad one branch goes southwest up the Surkhab valley to Gandamak, while another continues along Kabul river through the Darunta hills. The other main road leaves that just mentioned at Basawal, and runs thence almost due west to Gandamak. Both the above are good camel-roads, and would require little work to render them passable by wheeled traffic.

From Jalalabad roads run southwards up the valleys of the various streams running down from the Safed Koh, and cross the latter by several difficult passes; while to the north roads lead up the Kunar valley and, crossing the Kabul river at the lower end of the Darunta gorge, into Laghman and Kafiristan.

Jalalabad is generally supposed to be the Nysa of Arrian, and Vigne ("Personal Narrative," 232) would, consequently, identify the Safed Koh with Mount Meros. The modern name of the district and town is from Jalaluddin, one of the names of the Emperor Akbar, by whose direction the town was built in 1570.

Subdivisions of the district.--According to Jenkyns (1879), the district of Jalalabad is divided into the following subdivisions:--

(1) Khugiani, which occupies the southwestern corner of the district, and is inhabited almost entirely by the tribe of Khugianis.

(2) Surkhab, on both banks of the Surkhab stream, and including the town of Jalalabad.

(3) Kashkot, which is popularly known as Besud. It comprises all that portion of the district which lies north of the Kabul river and west of the Kunar river.

(4) Kama, the portion of the district north of the Kabul river, east of the Kunar river, as far as Chiknaur.

(5) Chapriar, the country watered by the Chapriar stream, excepting a few villages at the head of the stream, which are attached to Khugiani.

(6) Hisarak, which adjoins the Hisarak stream. The head of this stream is occupied by the Mandozai Shinwaris.

(7) Kot, the subdivision occupied by the Tirahi tribe. It is watered by the Kot stream.

(8) Mohmand (Mahman) Dara, which includes the southeastern corner of the district.

Further details of the above are given under their respective headings.

Climate. The climate of the plains of Jalalabad bears a general resemblance to that of Peshawar. After the Sikhs took Peshawar from the Afghans, Jalalabad, on account of the mildness of its climate compared with that of Kabul, was the favourite winter residence of the Kabul rulers. But for two months in the summer the heat on the plains is excessive. The wide stony waste or "dasht" of Batikot is dreaded from a pestilential wind or simoon which blows over it in the hot weather.

Rain usually falls in moderate quantities in the months of December, January, and February. Snow rarely, if ever, falls on the plains east of Gandamak. During the winter, from November to May, the wind steadily blows from the west, often bringing violent and disagreeable storms of dust. The west wind is generally the rain-bringing wind.

As the spring crop is getting ripe, this wind frequently causes much loss by shaking and bending down the heavy ears of grain.

This wind blows most severely in the immediate neighbourhood of the town of Jalalabad, which may, perhaps, be attributable to the situation and configuration of the Siah Koh range to the west. From May to November the wind blows from the east.

The valleys of the Safed Koh and the heights of Gandamak afford cool and healthy retreats in the hottest weather.

The unhealthy season in Jalalabad, as in the Punjab, is autumn. Fevers are very common. Small-pox annually carries off large numbers of children. Vaccination is unknown, but the native method of innoculation is practised. In the hot season eye diseases are frequent.

Cholera is as familiar as it is in India.

During winter shocks of earthquake are often felt.

Inhabitants. The inhabitants of Jalalabad belong to various tribes and races.

Kama, Chiknaur, and Lalpura are mostly occupied by the Khwaezai and Baezai Mohmand; but numerous small communities of Arabs, Dehgans, Tajiks, Saiyids, Pirachas, Hindkis, Lodias, etc, are also found in this part of the district. Crossing the Kunar into Besud, we find a very mixed population of Arabs, Dehgans, and Tajiks. On the western side of the district we come upon the great Ghilzai tribe. The strip of country between the Surkhab and the Siah Koh and Karkacha mountains is mostly in the hands of the Ghilzais. They have encroached upon the lands of the Khugianis west of Gandamak, and several villages, eg., Hisarak, Jokan, etc., formerly in possession of the Khugianis, are now held by the Ghilzais. They are also found scattered in other parts of the district. They belong chiefly to the Jabar Khel and Babakar Khel sections of the tribe.

The whole of the southwestern corner of the district is occupied by the Khugiani tribe.

East of the Khugianis come the Shinwaris, who inhabit the whole of the skirts of the Safed Koh to the eastern limit of the district.

The central portion of the district along the right bank of the Kabul river, including Dakka, Hazarnao, Basawal, Chardeh, etc. is occupied by Mohmands of the same sections as those on the opposite side of the river. Most of the Kot division is inhabited by a peculiar tribe called Tirahis, who were expelled from Tirah by the Afridis and Orakzais. They speak a peculiar language in their homes, which seems to be of Sanskrit origin.

The inhabitants of the Surkhab valley are mostly Tajiks. In the Chapriar and the Hisarak divisions the population is mixed, containing Mohmands, Dehgans, Shinwaris, Tajiks, Sayyids, etc., etc. The Tajiks invariably speak the Persian language, and are devoted to agriculture.

The other races, as a rule, speak Pushtu, but some of them, as has been stated, have peculiar dialects of their own.

A few Hindus are found in every large village. In Balabagh they form a considerable community. Other tribes, e.g., Rikas, Arabs, etc., are found here and there. Respecting these and the other races and tribes mentioned, further information is given under their own headings.

A class of people called Kuchis deserve separate mention. The word "Kuchi" literally means a person who migrates, and it is applied to all the nomadic tribes who visit this district in the winter, and remove to colder climates in the summer. Amongst the Kuchis are found Arabs, Mohmands, Ghilzais, etc. The Arabs and Nomad Ghilzais bring their flocks of camels and sheep down to the Jalalabad plains to graze during the winter, but remove to the hills towards Kabul in the summer. Some of the Kuchis live in tents, others have permanent houses. They are purely pastoral in their pursuits, keeping large flocks of sheep, goats, and camels. They are ready to take carrying contracts, and were largely employed as carriers during the last Afghan war.

Principal towns and other places of note. --The district of Jalalabad contains no town of note. The capital itself is a miserable, squalid place, and, with the exception of the Amir's new palace, possesses not a single edifice of any architectural pretensions. Some villages have a local celebrity as being the resting-places of noted saints. Amongst these is Ali Boghan, which contains the shrine of Mian Ali, where lunatics and demented persons are cured of their malady. At Batikot is the ziarat of Akhund Musa, which is famous for the cure of snake-bite.

Papin has the shrine of Akhund Yar Muhammad.

Akhund Abdullah - a celebrated saint - rests in Kama.

Other villages have received a name from the beautiful royal gardens that used to adorn them. Of these the garden at Nimla was celebrated. It was made by the Emperor Babar. Nimla is further noted as the scene of Shah Shuja's final defeat at the hands of his brother, Shah Mahmud, in 1809.

Several villages and localities posses great archaelogical interest; but to these further allusion will be made in a subsequent paragraph.

Trade and manufactures. Silk worms are reared in the Khugiani division, and, to a less extent, in Chapriar. At Kailagu, in Khugiani, there are some silk factories, where silken stuffs, e.g., gulbadan daryai, kanawez, etc, are made and exported; but, with that exception, there are no manufactures worthy of mention.
Iron and wheat in moderate quantities are imported from Bajaur.
Salt comes up from the Kohat salt mines.
Pomegranates and other fruits from the Khugiani country are exported in large quantities.
Gold-washing is carried on at the mouths of the Kunar and Laghman rivers, and at Bahrabad on the Kabul river, but is not very remunerative.
Elphinstone mentions the existence of lead-mines in the Shinwari country, and there is an unworked ruby mine near Jagdalak.
Rafts of wood are floated down the Kunar river to Peshawar, but the wood of the Safed Koh is too distant to be utilised in the same way. The trading classes are Hindus, Pirachas, and Tajiks. Bullocks are the animals chiefly used for carriage. Some of the Shinwaris possess mules, which they hire for carriage. Horses are few, and of an inferior breed. The Kuchis keep large droves of camels.
Agricultural products. Compared with the total extent of the district the area under cultivation is small. The plains of Basawal, Chardeh, and Jalalabad, the low-lying lands of Besud and Kama, and the banks of the Surkhab are all highly cultivated. For the rest the cultivation is confined to the banks of the streams that descend from the Safed Koh, where a breadth of from 1 to 2 miles is carefully cultivated. In these secluded valleys abound the mulberry, pomegranate, and other fruit trees, while the banks of the small streams that meander through them are edged with a fine sward enamelled with wild flowers and fragrant with aromatic herbs. The lowest ridges and spurs of the Safed Koh that intersect the district are bare and unculturable; but the higher mountains of Kashmund, Karacha, and Safed Koh, are clothed with thick forests of pine, almond, and other trees, where bears (both black and brown), panthers, wild sheep and goats, foxes, jackals, etc., are to be found.
Wells are not used for irrigation. A few are to be seen in villages for drinking-water, or in front of mosques for purposes of ablution, but not elsewhere. Irrigation is effected by the karez and by cuts and canals from streams and rivers. The Nahar-i-Shahi is a canal taken out of Kabul river at Kala-i-Mulla Bashir, which, after passing through the royal gardens, irrigates the plain as far as the village of Kush Gumbaz. A much larger canal leaves the Surkhab at Barina, and waters Baghwani, Balabagh, Kushkak, etc. Another larger canal is taken out of the Kunar river, and it irrigates all the Kama villages. One leaves the Kabul river at Bahrabad and flows through Besud. Others exist at Shamsapur and Kotapur.
The area of cultivation could be considerably extended by the construction of irrigation canals from the Kabul, Kunar, and Surkhab rivers, especially near Jalalabad and in Besud; but there is little room for further cultivation in the vicinity of the smaller streams. (The Amir is believed to have extensive schemes of irrigation under consideration at the present time, 1906.) The water-supply of the district depends upon the fall of snow on the Safed Koh and other mountains to the west; when less than the usual amount of snow falls in the winter, scarcity sometimes approaching to famine, is experienced.
Where water is abundant two crops are obtained in one year. The chief products of the spring harvest are:

Wheat	Opium
Barley	Mustard
Masur	Linseed
Peas	Aori (a variety of mustard).

In the autumn harvest the principal crops are:

Rice	Cotton
Bajra	Jowar
Mash.	

The best wheat is produced on "lalmi" lands in a good year, e.g., on the plain of Batikot. Gandamak is also celebrated for its wheat.
Opium is raised on the Surkhab to a small extent.
Most of the cotton is produced in the Hisarak and Chapriar divisions.
There are several sorts of rice. Distinguishing by colour there are two descriptions, white and red. The grains of the red rice are large, hence it is also called luk. The white rice is of two sorts--thin, called barik; and thick, called luk. Most of the rice is raised in Kama.
Besides the crops already mentioned, melons, cucumbers, pumpkins, turnips, etc, are produced. This sort of cultivation is called palez.
A small quantity of tobacco is raised in the Khugiani division, but it is not of good quality. A sort of trefoil, called shaftal, and lucerne are cultivated for fodder, which in general, is not plentiful.
The usual garden stuffs are sown near Jalalabad and other large villages.
In the Khugiani division large quantities of fruit are raised, e.g., grapes, apricots, pomegranates, quinces, plums, mulberries, walnuts, oranges, limes, etc. Although the fruits cannot be compared with those of Kabul, they are good of their kind, and some of them are superior. The seedless pomegranates of Kaja are famous.
Wheat and jowar are the staple food of the people. Barley is given to horses. Bajra, which is not much grown, is given to the cattle.
The agriculturists possess bullocks (which are used for the plough), cows, sheep, goats, and asses in large numbers. Buffaloes are less common.
Land of the first class will sometimes fetch Rs. 300 a jarib (2 jaribs-1 acre, approximately). Good average land, with a sufficient supply of water will fetch Rs. 200 a jarib. Inferior, unirrigated land sells at from Rs. 30 to Rs. 50 a jarib.
The ancient custom of vesh, or redistribution at stated intervals of time of all the lands of a community, which is found to exist in some parts of our trans-Indus districts, still survives in a few places in Jalalabad. It seems to possess most vitality in Girdi Kats, where the lands are reallotted every three years. It exists also in the Basawal and Hazarnao group of villages--the period being twelve years.
Revenue system. The general principles of revenue administration prevailing in the district of Jalalabad (in 1879), were introduced and fixed in the second-half of last century by Ahmad Shah Abdali. The Government, as a general rule, professed to take one-third of the gross produce as revenue. This principle is known under the name of seh-kot (three parts). Originally the whole revenue was taken in kind, but the difficulty of realising it from distant and turbulent tribes led, in many cases, to the substitution of a fixed cash assessment based on the seh-kot principle.
In cases where the proprietorship of the land belongs to the State,

one half of the gross produce is usually taken as the share of the Government, if the cultivator furnished seed, cattle, and implements of agriculture; but if the cultivator did not supply seed, cattle, etc. or supplied only some of these necessaries, the State took five-sixths or two-thirds of the gross produce. In the first case the revenue was called nim-kot (two shares); in the second case it was called shash-kot (six shares).

The principle of seh-kot prevails in the Kashkot, Surkhab, Chapriar, and Hisarak divisions. It applies to all descriptions of the agricultural produce. Khasil is charged with revenue, as well as ripened crops. All fruit trees appear to be charged with revenue on the same principle.

A large part of Kot pays only one-fourth share of the gross produce as revenue. This light assessment is called char-kot (four shares), and was granted by Timur Shah on account of the assistance he derived from the men of Kot during one of his expeditions.

In Khugiani every village, with the exception of five, pays a fixed cash assessment called Jama-i-Kalandar Khan, after a revenue administrator of Ahmad Shah, who first introduced it. Originally calculated to represent one-third of the gross produce, it now falls very much below that.

In Kama, Mohmand Dara, and Kot, most of the villages pay a fixed revenue assessment either in cash or kind.

With one or two exceptions the Ghilzai villages do not pay any revenue to the Jalalabad authorities. (This has probably been changed since 1879) The account of their revenue is kept in Kabul; but such revenue as is imposed is commonly remitted in favour of the Ghilzai Maliks.

The Sipai and Sangu Khel (including a portion of the Alisher Khel) Shinwaris have never paid any revenue to Government. (But they almost certainly do so now, see "Shinwari"). Their brethren, the Manduzai Shinwaris, are assessed at a total sum of Rs. 10,314 cash on the whole section.

The wandering pastoral tribes pay a fixed revenue in cash or in roghan (butter) and kurut (cheese).

The revenue year commences on Nauroz, the new year's day of the Persian calendar, corresponding to the 21st of March. Where the assessment is fixed it is generally realised in full within one or two months of the beginning of the year; but where it is a seh-kot or other fluctuating revenue it is paid in two instalments—one after the spring, and the other after the autumn harvest.

Other revenue besides land revenue. The other sources of revenue, in addition to the land revenue, will now be enumerated, and it will be seen that, while professing to appropriate only one-third of the gross produce of the country, the Government, by means of a multiplicity of vexatious cesses, in reality receives very much more.

(1) A tax called jaribi is put upon horticulture as follows:

	Rs.
On sugarcane	10 per jarib
On melons, poppy and vegetables	3 " "
On tobacco	6 " "
On hinna	5 " "

(2) From the pastoral tribes, one out of every forty sheep or goats is taken. This is called chilyak-i-gosfandi. From the permanent population one shahi is taken for every female sheep or goat possessed.

(3) Shakh shumari is a tax of one rupee (kham) on every buffalo. Cows are exempted from this tax.

(4) Asia or tahuna is the tax on flour-mills taken either in cash or kind. There is no fixed rate.
(5) Asnaf if the tax on trades, varying from Rs. 7 to Rs. 2.
(6) Jezia is a poll-tax levied from Hindus of Rs. 5 (kham) each.
(7) Dudi, a house tax of one rupee (kham) on each house.
(8) Naukar is a tax levied as commutation for service. The Arabs of Jalalabad are specially taxed in this way to the amount of Rs. 723 per annum.
(9) Kadkhudai is a tax on marriages. There is no uniform rate, but it falls very heavy on a Muhammadan who marries a Hindu.
(10) Mihmani--This exaction was taken originally on the pretext of furnishing supplies for the King's table during his winter stay in Jalalabad, but the collection of it is now continued as an ordinary item of revenue. It yields Rs. 9,835 per annum.
(11) Rasum-i-Daftar are the dues that were formerly levied by the Diwans of the district as their personal remuneration, but for many years they have been appropriated by the State. They bring in Rs. 2,350 yearly.
(12) Kimarkhana, or gambling tax. This is usually granted in farm. The farmer appoints a house in which alone gambling is permitted to be carried on. He or his agent superintends the game, and is entitled to a certain percentage on all the winnings.
(13) Zarbkhana, or mint-tax. This, too, is generally given in farm. The farmer is allowed to call in all the copper coin as often as he likes and to re-stamp it, charging a small sum for the stamp. Only coin impressed with the latest stamp is permitted to circulate. This absurd process is generally repeated three or four times a year, but the farmer is only prevented from doing it more frequently by the outcry of the trading classes.
(14) Ghoza-i-abresham is a tax on silk-worms. It is levied in Khugiani and Chapriar. The rate is Rs. 3 on every building in which silk-worms are reared.
(15) Sayer, or customs duties at Jalabad, Gandamak and Basawal. These are transit dues on merchandise passing through the district. They yield on an average Rs. 66,000 a year.
(16) Similar duties are taken separately at Dakka, and amount to Rs. 10,000 per annum.
(17) Tolls on rafts of wood floated down the Kabul river, and dues upon merchandise exported or carried by the river, are other sources of revenue.
(18) Salt brought up from Kohat is taxed at Pesh Bolak.
(19) In the town of Jalalabad the asnaf and jezia yield separately about Rs. 380 per annum.
(20) Fines and forfeitures are another considerable source of income. In 1878 Rs. 20,000 were collected under this head.
(21) Kotwali is a fee paid by Kotwals on the occasion of their being appointed to office.
Fixed expenditure.--The permanent local obligations on the Government of Jalalabad may be classed under five heads:
(1) Wazafas.--These are allowances in cash and grain made to men of the priestly and religious classes, e.g., Sayyids, Ulama (i.e., learned men, Mullas, Kazis, Muftis, etc.), Sahibzadas, Khwajazadas, and Fukara (i.e., beggars and mujawirs at shrines).
The total amount given away under this head is Rs. 56,621 per annum. Every learned and religious person in the district appears to be in receipt of a wazifa, a fact which fully accounts for the determined hostility of these classes to a British occupation of the country.
(2) Malikana.-- These are small allowances in cash, or kind granted to the headmen of the villages. They amount to Rs. 16,521 per annum, and would have to be kept up under any administration.

(3) Takhfif.—Is the name applied, locally, to remissions of revenue, or payments on account of diluvion, etc. In 1879 the amount so paid was Rs. 3,614.

(4) Jagirs. These are remisssions or assignments of revenue in favour of certain Khans, Sardars, and Maliks residing in the district. They amount to Rs. 15,585.

(5) Tankhwah-i-Waliyati.—Under this peculiarly named heading are included all the allowances made to independent and semi-independent tribes, e.g., Afridis, Shinwaris, Mohmands, etc.; also the salaries granted to the officials and chief men of the district. They amount to Rs. 1,67,715.

Revenue and expenditures compared.

The summary of the revenue of the whole district is as follows:

I-Land Revenue

1.	Khugiani	Rs. 56,872
2.	Surkhab	1,40,513
3.	Kashkot (Besud)	38,413
4.	Kama	92,000
5.	Chapriar	49,817
6.	Hisarak	71,766
7.	Kot	41,585
8.	Mohmand (Mahman)	42,403

II.—Other Revenue

1.	Mihmani	9,835
2.	Razum	2,350
3.	Kimarkhana	783
4.	Zarbkhana	1,333
5.	Kotwali	250
6.	Ghoza-i-abresham	728
7.	Customs, etc.	66,000
8.	Transit dues (Dakka)	10,000
9.	Rafts of wood	50,000
10.	Tolls at Dakka	6,840
11.	Dues on merchandise exported on rafts	1,300
12.	Salt dues	790
13.	Asnaf and jezia in Jalalabad	380
14.	Fines and forfeitures	20,000
	Total Rs.	6,97,038

The total fixed expenditure is as follows:

1.	Wazifas	56,621
2.	Malikana	16,521
3.	Takhfif	3,614
4.	Jagirs	15,585
5.	Tankhwah	1,67,715
	Total Rs.	2,60,056

After deducting the fixed charges, there thus remains a balance of Rs. 4,36,982.

Since 1879 many changes have no doubt been introduced into the system of revenue then prevalent, but the information given above will serve, for the want of better, as a rough approximation to the system now in vogue.

Civil Administration. The civil administration of the district is carried on by a Governor, called the Hakim. He is appointed from Kabul, and resides at Jalalabad.

The pay of the Hakim was fixed nominally at 8,000 kham rupees per annum, which he realised from any revenue-paying village in the district. He also divided with the Diwans and Daftaries one-tenth of all fines and forfeitures—the Hakim taking three-fourths, and the others one-fourth. It was usual for the Hakim himself to take the farms of several villages in his district, and by this and many other means he illicitly realised very much more than his nominal salary. The pay of the Hakim at the present time is not known.

Under the Hakim were three revenue accountants called Diwans (if Hindus), or Daftaris (if Muhammadans). They kept the revenue accounts, and, under the Hakim's directions, managed generally the whole revenue administration. They used to be remunerated by the rasum-i-daftar; but this cess is now credited to Government, and the Diwans and Daftaris receive a fixed salary.

In each division there is probably a Naib Hakim.

Weights and coins:

There are two systems of computation both in weight and in money.

The one method of computing by money is called "pukhta," and is as follows:

        50 dinars = 1 shahi
        2 shahis = 1 sanar
        2 sanars = 1 abbasi
        3 abbasis = 1 rupee

This rupee, estimated by the weight of silver in it, is worth 13 annas 6 pies of Indian money.

The other method of computing is called "kham," and is as follows:"

        10 dinars = 1 paisa
        5 paisas = 1 shahi
        10 shahis = 1 rupee
        20 rupees = 1 toman

One toman is worth Rs. 16 and 8 shahis pukhta. The kham rupee is merely one of account; it has no tangible existence. All the revenue accounts are kept on this system.

There are also two systems of measuring weights. The one in ordinary use is as follows:

        1 charak = 16 khurds
        4 charaks = 1 seer or dhari
        8 seers = 1 maund
        10 maunds = 1 kharwar

One of these seers is equal to 7 seers and 13.5 chittacks of Indian standard weight; consequently 1 kharwar is equal to 15 maunds 27 seers 8 chittacks of our standard weight.

The other method is called tabrizi, and is that in which the revenue accounts are kept. It is as follows:

        2.5 charaks = 1 maund
        100 maunds = 1 kharwar

One of these maunds is equal to 4 seers 14.5 chittacks of our standars weight; hence a tabrizi kharwar is equal to 12 maunds 10 seers 10 chittacks of our weight.

Archaeology. From an archaeological point of view few districts are more interesting than Jalalabad. Although it has been occupied by Muhammadans for more than a thousand years, there still remain abundant traces of an ancient Indian population. Certain spots are still considered sacred by the Hindus of the country, and are visited by pilgrims from India.

The perennial springs of Sultanpur are said by the Hindus to have gushed forth at the command of Baba Nanak, to whom the place is still sacred. Charbagh and Pesh Bolak are also looked upon with veneration by Hindus; the former contains the shrine of Gaddi Bramdas, and the latter that of Darbarra Sinh. Numerous mounds, caves, etc., are found near Pesh Bolak. The shrine called Gaddi Surya, in Jalalabad, is also very sacred to the Hindus. The caves of Chiknaur, on the left bank of the Kabul river, and the many ancient vestiges at Basawal, on this side of the river, are interesting evidence of the ancient population.

There are, however, three localities where these remains are found in great profusion. At Darunta, where the Siah Koh range meets the Kabul river, and along the skirts of the hills as far as Balabagh, numerous ancient buildings are found. On the left bank of the river opposite to Darunta similar remains exist. The plain to the east of Jalalabad as far as Sultanpur -- especially along the low ridges of conglomerate that bound the plain on the south, and on the banks of the river near Bagrani and Chiknaur--is full of evidence of ancient Hindu civilization.

The third archaeological interest attaches to three descriptions of buildings, viz., topes, tumuli, and caves.

Few topes have been found in this district with a greater circumference than 160 feet, or with a greater height than 60 feet. They are found to consist of two topes, one within the other. The smaller or interior tope contains a small chamber in which the relics are deposited. The favourite situation of a tope is on the skirt of a hill on an elevaton overlooking the plain. Water is always found near them, and at Hada there are traces of water having been brought in aqueducts from a distance at much labour and expense.

There is no dispute that these monuments are peculiar to the Buddist religion; and the most probable theory as to their meaning is that they are large dagobas, or shrines, erected for the protection of some relic of the great Buddha, Sakya Muni, or of some local Lama of note. Many of them contain vases of stone, and caskets of gold, silver, or copper, in which are often found coins, pearls, ornaments, rings, beads, etc., etc.

In one of the Hada topes, opened by Mr. Masson 53 years ago, five gold coins of the Lower Empire -- viz., solidi of Theosius, Marcian, and Leo-- were discovered. Eighteen similar coins were more recently obtained from a tope overlooking Jalalabad. Sassanian and old Hindu coins have also been found; but no coin of a Greek prince of Bactria has ever been seen in a tope. From the coins found it would appear that these topes were built during the first seven centuries of the Christian era, when the country had again come under the domination of the Indians, after the disappearance of the Greek and Scythian invaders, and when the religion of Buddha was spread over all Northern India and the adjacent countries. The Muhammadans commenced to encroach on Afghanistan in the end of the 7th century, so that the erection of these topes cannot be put later than that period.

The tope which is in the best state of preservation is one called Nandara or Khayasta (meaning "beautiful") in Darunta. It still preserves many of the mouldings, arches and pilasters that adorned its outer surface.

Tumuli are distinguished from topes in general in dimensions, and in not having a distinct cylindrical body between the base and the dome. It is also found that fragments of bones and ashes are found in tumuli in considerable quantities, while in topes they are sparingly found. As a rule the tumuli are destitute of relics. They may be seen isolated; but wherever there is a tope, it is accompanied by a number of tumuli. This has given rise to the idea, which is a very probable one, that these tumuli are the tombs in which the ashes of devoted Buddhists are deposited under the shadow of the sacred receptacle of some holy relic.

Caves are always found in the neighbourhood of topes and tumuli. Some are large and crowned with a cupola; these were probably temples or viharas. The others were the abodes of the monks or priests, or recluses who formed the establishment connected with the sacred edifice. The caves at Darunta are of great dimensions, and are known by the name of fil-khana (elephant- house.)

Burnes, Masson, and M. Court consider that topes are regal sepultures, and this is the notion of the people of the country.

All these buildings are spoken of by the present Muhammadan inhabitants of the valley as Burja-i-Kafir (infidels' fort). We know that at the time of the invasion of Afghanistan by the Muhammadans, Hindu Rajas reigned in Kabul and Jalalabad. So late as the time of Babar, Kafirs occupied the mountains of the north boundary of Besud; and to this day the ruined police-posts, erected for the protection of the low country on the Kabul river from the Kafirs by the Mughal rulers, are to be seen within 6 miles of Jalalabad.

Amongst other traces of the old inhabitants may be mentioned the city of Adinapur, which was flourishing in the time of Babar, on the left bank of the Surkhab, opposite Balabagh; and the Kala-i-Rajputana on the site of the present Tatang-i-Jabar.

At Marki Khel, under the Safed Koh, traces of another sort are found. Masson (Travels 1,225) says that there "human bones are so abundant on the soil that walls are made of them. There is every reason to suppose it a sepulchral locality of the ancient Gebers; and as if to leave no doubt of it, coins found in some number there, are invariably of a Geber line of princes and have a distinguished fire-alter on them." At Nokurkhel, in the same locality, entire skeletons are often found, which have trinkets, coins, etc., tied round their ankle bones. Of Muhammadan antiquities might be mentioned many of those graves of extraordinary dimensions (called chilgazi) which occur in the valleys of Ningrahar and other places. The most famous of them is the grave of Hazrat Lut (the patriarch Lot) near Balabagh. It is about 383 yards long, and is held in veneration by both Hindus and Muhammadans. In connection with it may be mentioned the celebrated ziarat of Mehtar Lam in Laghman, to which at the ripening of the autumn harvest crowds of the Jalalabad people repair to pay their devotions. Mehtar Lam is the patriarch Lamech, the father of Noah, whose name is also connected with this country, for the ark is fabled to have rested after the deluge on the Kund mountain and the valley now called Dara-i-Nur was originally called Dara-i-Nuh, or the vale of Noah.

History. The following summary of the history of Jalalabad is by McGregor:

"As far back as A.D. 977, we find that Ningrahar was the scene of contention between Sabaktagin, the Tartar, who assumed the title of Nasir-u-din and Jaipal, the Brahmin prince. History mentions that their armies came in sight of each other on the confines of Limgan, now called Laghman, and the present village of Fatehabad is said to mark the spot where a victory was gained by Sabaktagin over the Hindu prince.

"In the year 1570, Jalaladin Muhammad Akbar Badshah, when proceeding from Kabul to India, desired Shamshudin Khaffi to build the towns of Jalalabad and Atak, and these were completed in two years. His son Salim (Jahangir) was for some time acting Governor of Jalalabad.

"During Shah Jahan's reign, that monarch made some additions to the town. An inscription on a marble slab, taken from an old fort, and placed in the principal 'masjid' of the town, shows that the fort was built by Itimam Khan in Shah Jahan's reign, A.D. 1638.

"In A.D. 1735, Nadir Shah sent Sulaiman Yesawal (stick-bearer) from Kabul at the head of a mission to Muhammad Shah of Delhi. On the fifth day Sulaiman and his party reached Jalalabad. Abidulla, the son of Mir Abbas of Kunar, whose power extended over the whole of Ningrahar, desired Sulaiman to be slain, and he was killed with much cruelty. Nadir Shah, on hearing of the treatment that Sulaiman had met with, immediately left Kabul with his army and marched to Gandamak via Charikar, Nijrao, and Tagao; thence he sent on to Jalalabad Sardars Jillayer and Niaz with the vanguard; Abidulla evacuated Jalalabad and fled to Kunar; he was pursued by the Sardars and fled to Swat. Many of his followers were slain, and his sister and women made prisoners and brought to Nadir Shah.

"The monarch with his main army went from Gandamak to Behai, thence to Jalalabad, where he remained only 31 days, his Sardars meanwhile having captured Kunar and Bajaur. He proceeded via Chura to Peshawar, where Nasir Khan, the Governor, submitted without making any defence.

"To enumerate all the important events which have taken place in this district since that period would take up too much space. I will only briefly allude to a few of them.

"On the 10th of September 1801, Shuja-ul-Mulk marched from Peshawar to attack Kabul.

"At Ishapan he found Mahmud's force, consisting of 3,000 men, drawn up, the Surkhurd being in their front.

"Elphinstone thus describes the battle: 'Shuja had at this time at least 10,000 men, but they were Barduranis, and though accustomed to the battles of their clans, they were strangers to discipline and to regular warfare. Shuja's arms were at first victorious, but his Bardurani troops, eager to profit by the confusion, quitted their lines as soon as they thought the victory decided, and began to plunder the royal treasures, which Shuja had imprudently brought into the field. Fateh Khan seized this opportunity and charging at the head of his Barakzais, completed the confusion in Shuja's army; the battle was now decided, and Shuja escaped with some difficulty to the Khaibar.

"In A.D. 1809, June 29th, Shah Shuja sustained another defeat at Nimla, when opposed to Mahmud Shah and his minister Fateh Khan. Akram Khan, Shah Shuja's prime minister, was slain in this battle. Shah Shuja fled over the mountains south of the Khaibar pass to Hisarak.

"On Zaman Shah's defeat near Sar-i-Asp, he fled to the Jalalabad valley, and stopped at Mulla Ashak's fort, which is on the Chapriar rivulet, about 14 miles from the town of Jalalabad, near the Safed Koh.

"The Mulla received them hospitably, but took means to prevent their escape, and sent off a messenger to Mahmud Shah. Shah Zaman, during his confinement, secreted the Koh-i-Nur with some other jewels in the wall of his apartment, which were afterwards found on Shuja's accession. The poor monarch was blinded on his road to Kabul by piercing his eyes with a lancet.

"On Shah Shuja being restored to this throne, the first step he took was to release his brother Shah Zaman, and soon after Mulla Ashak, who had betrayed him, was apprehended, and suffered the punishment of his perfidy and ingratitude.

When the Barakzai Khan gained the ascendancy over the Saduzai monarchs, Azim Khan placed his nephew Nawab Zaman Khan in the government of Ningrahar, and from the time of Azim Khan's death 1823, until the year 1834, the Nawab enjoyed the entire government of Ningrahar. Dost Muhammad insisted upon a portion of the collections of the province being made over to him; this the Nawab refused. The Amir collected a force and marched against him, and on his approach, the Nawab withdrew his guns to Kama, and there took up a position near Abdul Rahman's fort; negotiations took place between the contending parties. The Nawab having made some slight sacrifice of his interests, Dost Muhammad returned to Kabul.

"The Nawab then commenced fortifying the town of Jalalabad; the old fortifications were nearly on a level with the ground; a great number of people were collected for the purpose; the work advanced rapidly; but ere a month had elapsed the Amir was again on his march to Jalalbad, and the fort was still incomplete. The Nawab, however, determined to defend it. After three days' resistance a mine was sprung, the town was taken by assault, and it was given up to plunder. The Nawab was taken prisoner and displaced from power, and Sultanpur and the transit duties of Kabul were made over to him for his maintenance. Dost Muhammad's brother, Amir Muhammad, remained a short time in charge of the province. He was succeeded by the Amir's son, Muhammad Afzal, who was recalled after a few months, and succeeded by his younger brother, Akbar; he continued in charge until the arrival in 1839 of the British troops. Mirza Agha Jan, Kizilbash, was then, on the part of the Shah, appointed Governor. Since the evacuation of Afghanistan by the British, Jalalabad has been governed by members of the Barakzai family." (MacGregor, Jenkyns, etc.)

JALALABAD (Town) جلال آباد
34-26 70-28 m. This city is now the capital of Nanagarhar province. The city and its outskirts now comprise an area of 20 square kilometers. (LWA) In 1912 this town was described as follows:
Elevation 1,950 feet. The civil headquarters of the Jalalabad district, and the only town therein. It lies on the right bank of the Kabul river, and is distant 83 3/4 miles from Peshawar and 98 from Kabul by the main road. It is an irregular quadrilateral, with a perimeter of 2,100 yards, enclosed by a mud wall. It is divided into four irregular parts by streets running from the four gates, one in each face of the perimeter. The walls are in good order but would form a very poor defence against heavy artillery; they are about 20 feet high and at the gateways, 16 inches thick. They appear to be badly loopholed and consequently have much dead ground in front. With modern artillery the town could be rendered quite untenable from a position to the south. The town itself is a miserable place, and can only be compared to a very third-class walled village in the Punjab. The shops in the town are mostly kept by Hindus, but there are few signs of trade or prosperity. The permanent population does not exceed 2,000 souls (mostly Hindus, Tajiks and Afghans), but in the cold weather it is very largely increased by the influx of the tribes from the hills to the south who bring their flocks and herds down to Jalalabad for the sake of its warmer climate. The river here runs in two channels of which the southern is the larger; in the winter of 1904-05 the water in the main channel was found to be from 8 to 10 feet deep; the current was of moderate strength and the river was said to be fordable at several places in the neighbourhood. In the same year there was a rope-ferry across the river with one large boat, capable of accommodating about 30 men, in each channel. These two channels are each about 100 yards wide. During the Second Afghan War an efficient service of rafts was maintained for some time between Jalalabad and Dakka as a supplement to the land transport.
About a mile to the east of the town a fort (Fort Sale) with a large horn-work was built by us 1879, intended to accommodate 2,835 men and some 5,000 animals. The horn-work, when seen in 1905, was in ruins, but the barracks inside the fort are kept up by the Amir and would accommodate about one battalion.
Just outside the eastern gate of the town is a walled sarai, built in 1905.
About 1/2 miles to the west of the town is a garden, and a palace, of the Amir; this is called the Wazirbagh; there are two large tanks

in the garden and the place would form an ideal head-quarters in the event of the occupation of Jalalabad.

There is room for a force of any size to encamp to the south and southwest of Fort Sale, but there is no shade here and it would probably be a most unhealthy camping ground owing to the amount of irrigation close by. Good watersupply from the river (1/4 mile from the fort) and from a spring on the river-bank. Supplies are to be had here in large quantities; the surrounding country is fertile and there should be no difficulty in maintaining a force of 5,000 men for some time. Near the Wazirbagh, also, there is a shady camping ground for about 2,000 men. An approximate estimate of food supplies normally available in Jalalabad city is as follows:

Atta	100 maunds	Wheat, unground	1,500 maunds
Ghee	25	Barley	2,500
Dall	20	Rice	200
Salt	15	Maize	600
		Black sugar	150

Jalalabad is one of the chief cantonments in Ningrahar; the garrison is reported to consist of 2 squadrons of cavalry, 6 guns and 3 battalions of infantry, besides 300 khasadars. In the cold weather the infantry of the garrison are quartered in Fort Sale and in a grove of Shisham trees, known as the Shishambagh, between the fort and the town; in the hot weather nearly the whole garrison is moved to the neighbourhood of Agam, near the head of the Chapriar stream.

Jalalabad lies at the junction of two roads from Kabul via Gandamak and the Tangi Gharu respectively (Southeast Afghanistan routes Nos. 1 and 9); another road (Southeast Afghanistan route No. 8) leads up the Chapriar valley to the Agam pass over the Safed Koh, and a fourth (Southeast Afghanistan route No. 6) leads southwest to the cantonment of Kahi and thence to Basawal. North of the river roads lead up the Alingar, and Alishang, valleys into Kafiristan (Northeast Afghanistan routes Nos. 7 and 8), and up the Kunar Valley (Northeast Afghanistan route No. 2) to Chitral and Badakhshan. The place is thus advantageously situated for trade which consists for the most part in the export to Peshawar to fruit, chiefly pomegranates, and of timber from the pine-forests of Kunar.

In the neighbourhood of Jalalabad is the shrine of Shah Mardan, held sacred under the supposition that Ali rested there, and in the temple is exhibited a large black stone showing an impression of the hand of Ali. A garden is attached to the shrine, and a fair held there every Thursday to which crowds resort.

The town of Jalalabad is chiiefly known to English readers on acount of the siege which a British force under Sir Robert Sale stood during the period of the Kabul disasters. The following is a brief summary of that event from Sale's dispatch: On the 13th of November 1841, Sale's brigade took possession of Jalalabad; the walls were in a state which might have justifies despair as to the possibility of defending them. The enceinte was far too extensive for the small force, embracing a circumference of upwards of 2,300 yards. Its tracing was vicious in the extreme; it had no parapet excepting for a few hundred yards, which was not more than 2 feet high. Earth and rubbish had accumulated to such an extent about the ramparts that there were roads in various directions across and over them into the country. There was a space of 400 yards on which none of the garrison could show themselves, excepting at one spot; the population within was disaffected, and the whole enceinte was surrounded by ruined forts, walls, mosques, tombs, and gardens, from which a fire could be opened upon the defenders at 20 or 30 yards.

The garrison took full possession of the town in this state on the morning of the 15th of November, and in the course of the day the plain and detached hills by which on one side it is commanded were surrounded and surmounted by a force of not fewer than 5,000 insurgents. A general atack on the 14th of November rid the garrison of these enemies, and a similar array brought against them a fortnight afterwards was dissipated by a second sally on the 1st of December. But they had seized the town, having in their possession not quite two days' provision, and corn for their men and horses, and with the arduous task before them of striving to render the works defensible, and collecting supplies for their magazine from the midst of a fanatical and infuriated people with very narrow means in the way of treasure to purchase them.

On the 9th of January 1842, the garrison was summoned by the leaders of the Afghan rebellion to give up the place in fulfilment of a convention entered into by the political and military authorities at Kabul, but as the British General, Sir Robert Sale, was fully assured of the bad faith of his enemies he refused to do this. Works had in the meantime been completed, which rendered the place secure against the attack of any Asiatic enemy not provided with siege artillery. But on the 19th February a tremendous earthquake shook down all the parapets built up with so much labour, injured several of the bastions, cast to the ground all the guard-houses, demolished a third of the town, made a considerable breach in the rampart of a curtain in the Peshawar face, and reduced the Kabul gate to a shapeless mass of ruins.

The troops turned with indefatigable industry to the reparation of their walls, but at the moment of the great convulsion, Sardar Muhammad Akbar Khan, Barakzai, the assassin of the late Envoy and teacherous destroyer of the Kabul force, having collected a body of troops, had advanced to Markhel, within 7 miles of the gates. He attacked the British foraging parties with a large body of horse on the 21st and 22nd, of February, and soon after establishing his head-quarters to the westward, 2 miles from the place, and a secondary camp to the eastward, about 1 mile distant, invested the town and established a rigorous blockade. From that time up to the 7th of April the reduced garrison was engaged in a succession of skirmishes with the enemy, who, greatly superior in horse, perpetually insulted the walls by attacks and alerts, and compelled the garrison daily to fight at a disadvantage for forage for their cattle. The most remarkable of these affairs were those of the cavalry under Lieutenant Mayne, commanding detachment Shah Shuja's 2nd Cavalry and Jamadar Dina Sing, 5th Light Cavalry; a sally under Colonel Dennie, C.B., to defeat a suspected attempt of the enemy to drive a mine on the 11th of March; the repulse of an assault upon the transverse walls to the northward of the place on the 24th of the same month by detachments under Captain Broadfoot (who was severly wounded) and Captain Fenwick, Her Majesty's 13 light Infantry; the capture of bullocks and sheep by Lieutenant Mayne on the 30th and 31st of January; and the seizure of large flocks of the latter, in the face of Muhammad Akbar's army, by a force of Infantry under Captain Pattison, Her Majesty's 13th light Infantry, and of cavalry under Captain Oldfield, on the 1st instant. These successes were crowned by Providence by the issue of the brilliant and decisive attack on the camp of the Sardar on the 7th April.

In addition to the troops a large body was formed from the camp followers and armed with pikes and other weapons. On all occasions of assault and sally these men were available to make a show upon the curtains.

From the time that the brigade threw itself into Jalalabad, the native troops were on half, and the followers on quarter, rations, and for many weeks they were able to obtain little or nothing in the bazars to eke out this scanty provision. The troops, officers, and men, British and Hindustani, of every arm, remained fully accoutred on their alarm posts every night from the 1st March to 7th of April. The garrison was then relieved by General Pollock, though Muhammad Akbar raised the blockade after his defeat on the 7th April. The loss of the garrison throughout the siege was one officer and 24 men killed, 7 officers and 131 men wounded. The defences of the city were afterwards destroyed. (I.B.C., Johnson.)

JALAL KOL جلال قول (کور)
33- 68-. A village in Kharwar; 24 families of Gada Khel Ghilzais. (Griesbach.) Recent maps show the name Kor Jalal at 33-37 68-48. (LWA)

*JALALU جلالو
33-47 69-22 m. A village located northeast of Gardez and west of Mirzaka in Paktia province.

*JALAM جلم
32-37 67-40 m. A village located on the Tarnak river, 10 miles south of Ghojan.

*JALAT KALAI جلات کی
32-3 68-40 m. A village located near Patan Kalai, southeast of Wur in southern Ghazni province.

JALGAH جلگه
A fort 16 miles from Charikar. It was unsuccessfully assaulted by a British force, 5th October 1840, under Sir Robert Sale, with a loss of some 25 killed and wounded; the enemy, however, evacuated it during the following night. (Sale.)

*JALIL جلیل
34-9 68-38 m. A village located near Chak-i-Wardak and west of Top Kalai in Maidan province.

*JALIL SHAR جلیل شار
34-31 67-40 m. A village located on the Bum-i-Abd-i-Ulum, south of the Gardan-i-Qada.

JALMISH جلمش
35-1 68-4. Elevation 6,630 feet. A place in the Aodara, or defiles of the Bamian river between Shikari and Doab-i-Makhzarin.
The inhabitants of Jalmish and the Dahan-i-Jalmish are Shaikh Ali Hazaras of the Sad Marda section. The main number of them live up the Dahan-i-Jalmish. In 1886 they numbered over 1,000 families, though quite half as many more had recently emigrated on account of the locusts. A large quantity of wheat, jowar, and some rice is grown; and a considerable amount of supplies would be procurable. The inhabitants also own flocks and herds. There is good camping-ground at Jalmish proper, with abundance of fuel and some grass. Dried grass cut on hillsides is also stored in quantities at every hamlet.
There used to be a track down the Aodara to Baghak; but it has been destroyed by the river, and now only men on foot can make their way down, and they have at one place to clamber over a smooth sloping sheet of rock. Another road to the Surkhab valley goes northwest by

the Khoja Kashmir and the Tajdin Kotal. There is no track up the river to Shikari, as the valley contracts to an impassable gorge at the mouth of the Kara Sirkhoshak, a short distance above the mouth of the Dahan-i-Jalmish. Besides the path by the Kotal-i-Jalmish (described below), the only other path leading south from Jalmish is a foot track by the Dara Ghandak and over the mountains to Bamian, passable only by cragsmen.

From Jalmish proper the road to Birgilich, via the Jalmish Kotal, ascends the Aodara for 1-1/3 miles until it meets the mouth of the Dahan-i-Jalmish.

The latter is about 200 yards wide at its mouth, and its bed for the first 2 miles is a level water-logged chaman; but there is a good dry roadway, 6 to 8 feet wide, along the side. It then becomes closely cultivated, and habitations are strung out all up it as high as the Pai Kotal village. At 3 miles the valley opens out to 400 yards, and at 3-1/2 miles the large village of Sar-i-Polak is passed with trees, fields, and grassy chamans.

At 4-1/2 miles the valley makes an abrupt bend; and perched on the rocks and guarding the valley are two picturesque ruined castles, one on each side and about 300 yards apart, build of brick and stone, and called Kala Khak-i-Sabur. These castles have been fine buildings, are said to be very ancient and to have been built by a chief called Kakaha.

Habitations, fields, and trees continue to 7th mile. Then the valley contracts, and there is a steep rise of 70 feet in its bed, down which the stream falls in a cascade. The road ascends this rise by an easy track. Two hundred yards further on the valley contracts to 40 feet between high rocks, forming a short gorge called Tangi Kul-i-Agha. Above this tangi the valley is only 100 yards wide, and cultivation is less continuous. Small hamlets are, however, met with at short intervals, and every available patch of fertile ground is tilled up to the head of the valley.

Pai Kotal-i-Jalmish, 9 miles, is the highest hamlet in the valley. Good camping ground. Supplies procurable. No fuel. Altitude 9,760 feet.

From it a path leads by Dara Karnala and over the hills to Girdaneh, where it hits the difficult foot-track which leads from Doab-Mikhzarin by the Dara Purkaf and over the Kotal Kharzar on the main range of the Hindu Kush into the Dara Sangandao. Laden yabus use it, and it is said that camels also could travel by it to Girdaneh.

Half a mile above Pai Kotal village the Birgilich road bends to the right up the hillside, and commences the ascent to the Jalmish Kotal.

The ascent is about 1-3/4 miles long (it took 40 minutes to ride up it). For the first mile the path zig-zags up a projection in the hillside at a gradient of 1 in 6 and for the remainder of the distance ascends diagonally across the sloping hillside at 1 in 10 to 1 in 12. During this latter part of the ascent the path is exposed to rifle fire from the kotal, and the hillside is too steep to allow of infantry leaving the pathway. The path itself is quite safe, varying in breadth from 2 to 4 feet; but a false step would be fatal to man or beast. It is practicable for yabus and mules; and were it not for the length of the ascent might be pronounced practicable for clever hill camels, if lightly laden.

The summit of the kotal is open and rounded, and troops could extend with ease right and left along it. In the face of even a company of rifles on the top, it would be impossible for infantry to storm the kotal in daylight. Altitude 11,767 feet.

The ridge on which the kotal is situated, is a main spur of the Koh-i-Jaolangah, which is the most westerly eminence of the main range of the Hindu Kush, and further westwards becomes very broken and rocky, until it finally abuts on the Aodarah. Besides this kotal, the only other pathway over it is a track, difficult even for the native mountaineers, which leaves the Dahan-i-Jalmish at Tangi Kul-i-Agha, and leads into the head of the Dara Kariak.

Southwards from the top of the kotal, a hill footpath leads to Jaozar and the Kotal-i-Sangandao.

The descent on the south is much easier. A fall of 900 feet, and about 1 mile long (it took 25 minutes to lead a horse down it), leads into the head of a valley, about 50 yards wide and with a level smooth bed, called Rah Kol. The zig-zags of the descent slope at 1 in 8 to 1 in 6, and soil is easy clay or gravel; no rocks. There is a good easy mule track.

There are a number of springs in the head of the Rah Kol, which would afford water for any troops occupying the kotal, and the road is easy going for all arms down the Rah Kol and the Dara Birgilich to Kala Darwesh, 16-1/2 miles from Jalmish.

With respect to the feasibility of using the road above described, as a means of communication between the Surkhab valley and the Shibar pass, Peacocke makes the following remarks:

"The ascent of the Kotal Salati, the descents of the Tajdin and Pandanao Kotals and both ascent and descent of the Jalmish Kotal are all very steep. Their main descents and ascents all average a height of from 1,000 to 1,400 feet, and have mere mountain tracks up or down them. The descent into the Aodara at Jalmish is also a very bad rocky gorge below Muhammad Kichah, and one climbs down the narrow rocky watercourse between lofty cliffs, at one place only 5 feet apart, and a led horse descends its lower 2-1/2 miles with difficulty. Elsewhere the going is for the most part easy for pack animals along good paths running up or down fairly open valleys. The two greatest elevations reached on the route are the Kotal-i-Pandanao 11,260 feet, and the Kotal-i-Jalmish 11,767 feet.

No force of troops of any magnitude could venture to march by this path from Doab-i-Mekhzarin to the Shibar. A lightly-equipped column of infantry could, no doubt, if unopposed, traverse this route in single file, and would find supplies at Jalmish, and in ordinary years at the head of the Dara Zarsang; but the attempt would be dangerous in the extreme. A few charges of gun-cotton would hopelessly block the path in the defile below Muhammad Kichah, where there is no alternative path available, and a small detachment could hold the Kotal-i-Jalmish, against enormous odds. Checked below Muhammad Kichah, or at Kotal-i-Jalmish, such a force would find themselves in a cul de sac, with no outlet of escape, except the steep mountain road by which they had come.

Considered as a continuation of the Surkhab road, this path may be disregarded by the foot-runners of the Badakhshan-Kabul post in winter, when the Chahardar road is closed by snow. A small detachment on the Jalmish Kotal would close it if it came within the sphere of operations.

The roads up the Kamard and the Saighan valleys are the only directions in which there is a practicable outlet for troops out of the head of the Surkhab valley." (Peacocke.)

*JALOKHEL   جلوخیل
 32-20 67-56 m. A village located south of the Ab-i-Istada and 2 miles northeast of Nawa.

*JALRIZ   جلریز
 34-28 68-38. Jalriz is an alaqadari in Wardak province. The alaqadari comprises an area of 1,139 square kilometers and has an agri-

cultural population that has been estimated at from 10,931 to 15,644. The alaqadari is bounded in the west by Behsud 1 and Day Mirdad, in the north by Surkh Parsa, in the east by Maidan Shar and Nerkh, and in the south by Day Mirdad. Jalriz includes 104 villages. The villages are listed in the PG as follows: Qarya-i-Mamaki, Zeyolat, Zaimani, Deh Mirdan Zaimani, Ismail Khel, Qala-i-Tajek, Qala-i-Musa, Mohd. Nur Khel, Qol-i-Butum, Dara-i-Zeyarat, Jaitun, Kharuti Ulya wa Sufla, Khani Khel (Khana), Fateh Khel, Mir Gul Khel, Qala-i-Mansur, Qala-i-Negar, Qala-i-Surkh, Dur Khan Khel, Qarya-i-Jalriz, Markaz-i-Jalriz, Fazel, Yadgar, Behbud, Shah Rukh, Pas Shoy (Shawi), Sanglakh, Dahan-i-Raqol, Pul-i-Shah, Dur Saray, Dahan Qolak, Koti Qazi, Khushk-i-Berzej, Qala-i-Zir Chenar, Khairullah, Seyah Sang, Surkh Qala, Qala-i-Sari-Sang, Petab Qala, Qala-i-Sayed Khan Shirin, Qala-i-Shah, Qala-i-Abgha, Qala-i-Giro, Qala-i-Shah Alam, Seh Qala, Dahan Armo, Daridah, Qala-i-Mirza Khan, Bala Koh, Qala-i-Qutugh, Kota-i-Sukhta, Dara-i-Hesar, Qala-i-Sayed Mirza, Koti Postin-i-Doz, Koti Hukumat, Qala-i-Malik, Bala Qala, Qala-i-Bangi, Ahangaran, Dara-i-Shukur, Dara-i-Zaker, Kota-i-Ali Akbar, Qala-i-Burjak, Sayed Khel, Gardana, Dara-i-Lak Khana, Qala-i-Rajab, Ta Qala, Pain Qala, Qala-i-Masum, Shakhal Zar, Qala-i-Mohd. Ali Shah, Qala-i-Ismail, Dara-i-Baqab, Kharulang, Dewlan, Takana-i-Ulya wa Sufla, Siyah Petab, Deh Qalandar, Qala-i-Petab, Bagh-i-Langak, Jaghin, Qam Khalak, Qala-i-Malik, Tandorah, Qol-i-Dost, Dewgan, Qala-i-Jan Mohammad, Toghri, Tanglich, Dahan Tangi, Burjak, Qala-i-Karez, Qala-i-Akhund, Dara-i-Masjed, Qala-i-Jamil (Jamal), Qol-i-Nali, Qol-i-Nati, Sarcheshma, Qala-i-Sabz, Pushta-i-Mazar, Dar Kota, Qala-i-Aslam, Qala-i-Kuhna, and Honi.

JALREZ Or JALIZ   جلريز
34-28 68-38 m. A large village on the main Kabul-Herat road, about 33 miles west of Kabul. It lies on the left bank of the Kabul river, immediately above the junction with the latter of the Sanglakh Dara. It contains (in 1904) some 450 families of Tajiks and a few Hindu shop-keepers. The inhabitants possess about 500 head of cattle, 700 sheep and goats and 100 horses. The annual production of wheat and barley averages about 16,500 Indian maunds. The valley here is not less than a mile in width, and is well wooded, chiefly with poplars and willows. A great deal of timber is cut here and floated down the river to Kabul, where it is used as fuel in the Government workshops.
The Kabul river valley from Sar-i-Chashma village down to Jalrez is inhabited by Tajiks. On every side are prosperous valleys and the cultivation is very rich especially in the neighbourhood of Jalrez, where irrigation channels have been led far up into the hills on either side of the valley. The principal crops are wheat and barley, besides which the bakuli (horse-bean) and red clover are largely grown. There are many mulberry, walnut and apricot trees. Grapes and melons do not ripen as high up as Jalrez but the climate is much milder than in the Hazarajat. In 1904 the barley had already been harvested in the first week of July.
From Jalrez down to Kot-i-Ashru, the valley, known at first as the Zaiman and later as the Manduka, is inhabited by Ghilzais. The cultivation, though still extensive, is distinctly inferior to that in the upper portions of the valley occupied by Taimuris and Tajiks. (Wanliss.)

JAMADAR KALA   جمدار قلعه
34- 70-. A village in the Surkhab subdivision of the Jalalabad district. Inhabitants: Tajiks and Ghilzais. (Jenkyns.)

JAMA-I-ALI جمعه علی (؟)
A section of the Bul Hasan Besud Hazaras. (See Military Report on Hazarajat, Part II)

*JAMAIN جمین
35-6 69-35 m. A village located near the source of the Tagab river, on a path running north to the Panjshir valley.

JAMAL جمال
A section of the Muhammad Khwaja Hazaras. (See Military Report on Hazarajat, Part II) A village with this name is west of Mushakai, Ghazni, at 33-14 68-7 m. (LWA)

*JAMALAGHA جمال آغه
35-4 69-18 m. A village located northeast of Charikar and south of Gulbahar in Parwan province.

JAMALI-O-SARBADALI جمالی و سربدعلی
34- 70-. A village in the Besud division of the Jalalabad district, situated near the confluence of the Kabul and Kunar rivers, between both. The inhabitants are Tajiks and Arabs. (Jenkyns.)

JAMROGHA See DAIMIRDAD جمروغه

JAMBUD جمبود
A section of Naoroz Besud Hazaras, numbering 100 families and residing near Pai Kotal of Shibar. (See Military Report on Hazarajat, Part II.)

JAMI جامی
A section of the Dai Kundis Hazaras, numbering 300 families. (See Military Report on Hazarajat, Part II.)

JAMIAT جمعیت
A small district, distant 12-1/2 miles from Oba and 2 miles south of Karabagh. There are a great number of square forts scattered over the plain, which is highly cultivated, having much lucerne and clover. Supplies of all sorts are procurable here, except that camel-forage is not very plentiful. (Garden.) A village with this name is located at 32-14 67-43 m. (LWA)

JAMRUD OR JAN MURAD جمرود
33-8 68-5 G. A halting place between Mukur and Ghazni, 26 miles from the former and 38 from the latter. The inhabitants are Chahar Dasta Hazaras. It is fortified, owing to its close proximity to villages to the Andari Ghilzais. (Gaselee.) (See Military Report on Hazarajat, Part II.)

JAMSHIDABAD جمشید آباد
A village in Laghman. Inhabitants Tajiks. (Warburton.)

*JANA جانه
33-25 68-8 m. A village located on a stream, northwest of Ranakhel in Ghazni province.

*JANABAD جان آباد
33-24 68-36 m. A village located 2 miles east of the Sardeh Band-Ghazni road, about 14 miles southeast of Ghazni.

*JANBAZKHEL جانبازخیل
    34-17 70-14 m. A village located west of Chapriar and southwest of Jalalabad.

*JANDA جانده
    34-18 69-34 m. A village located on a stream north of Tiza, on a path running between Chakarai and Chahartut.

*JANDAD جانداد
    34-7 67-33 m. A village located on a tributary of the Garmab river, near Gardandeh in southern Bamian province. Another place with this name is about 4 miles south of Behsud in Maidan province, at 34-19 67-54 m.

JANDARGAL جندرگل
    34-46 68-2 m. A village in the Kalu subdistrict of Bamian. (See Military Report on Hazarajat, Part II.) Recent maps show the name Jandargal-i-Ulya. (LWA)

*JANGADAM جانگدم
    34-57 69-15 m. A village located west of the Dasht-i-Bagram and southeast of Charikar.

*JANGAL جنگل
    35-23 67-54 m. A village located on a tributary of the Kahmard, about 4 miles from its confluence with the Kahmard.

JANGDALAK جنگلك (جنگدلك)
    34-54 68-31. A wide and fertile dara which joins the Ghorband valley from the south at about 4 miles east of Bin-i-Sehwak. A road runs up it to the Kotal-i-Jangalak for the Turkoman Dara. (Peacocke.) Recent maps show the spelling Jangalak. (LWA)

JANGALAK جنگلك
    35-11 67-44 m. Two hamlets in the Dai Zangi district of Lal. (See Military Report on Hazarajat, Part II.) The area is a few miles east of Saighan. (LWA)

*JANGALAK جنگلك
    33-17 68-5 m. A village located some 2 miles east of Kuhna Deh and west of Qalat-Ghazni road. Nearby is another village with this name at 33-19 68-4 m. Other villages with this name are located on the Taranpas stream, on a path leading from the Dara-i-Mur across the Kuh-i-Baba, at 34-32 67-7 m. On the Saighan river, some 5 miles east of Saighan.

JANGALAK جنگلك
    34-29 69-9 A. A village in the Chardeh valley, on the right bank of the Kabul river between Guzargah and Kala-i-Ghaibi. About 100 houses, Inhabitants: Tajiks. (I.B.C.)

*JANGALKAI جنگلکی
    34-4 70-7 m. A village located north of Spin Ghar on a stream running north into the Surkhrud in Nangarhar province.

JANGAL MURDA جنگل مرده
    34-30 67-34 G. (See Military Report on Hazarajat, Part II.) The 8th stage on the Ghazni--Band-i-Amir road, 88 miles north-northwest of the former place, and just east of the Jangal Murda Kotal.

*JANGHARIQ جانغرق
    34-18 67-27 m. A village located on a stream, about 3 miles from its confluence with the Helmand river. Another village with this name, also called Janghariq Jui, is in the Charburja area, west of Tor Band.

*JANGI KHAN KALA جنگیخان قلعه
    32-41 68-52 m. A village located on a road running north from Gomal, east of Metar Khune.

*JANGJAI جنگجای
    34-31 67-33 m. A village located on the Katakhak stream, about 4 miles northwest of Katakhak.

JANGO جنگو
    A stream draining to the Talkhak valley.

*JANGRIGH جنگریغ
    34-19 67-30 m. A village located near Shawqol Karez on the Helmand river. Also see Janghariq.

*JANGUL KALA جانگل قلعه
    32-46 68-46 m. A village located east of the Qajirano Ghar and south of Amna in eastern Ghazni province.

*JANI KHEL جانی خیل
    32-18 68-18 m. A village located west of the Loy Ziri Ghar, on the way north from Wazakhwa. Another village with this name is located at 32-46 68-24 m.

JANI KHEL جانی خیل
    33-39 69-46. Jani Khel is a woleswali in Paktya province. The woleswali comprises an area of 294 square kilometers and has an agricultural population that has been estimated at from 13,725 to 20,909. The woleswali is bounded in the west by Lajmangal, in the north by Chamkani and Dand-wa-Patan, in the east by Jaji Maidan, and in the south by Bak, Saroti, and Musa Khel. Jani Khel has some 87 villages, 11 of which have more than 500 inhabitants. The villages are listed in the PG as follows:
Chelam, Robat, Nagar Kalai (Dangar Kalai), Raghosh Kalai, Almar Khel (Lmar Khel), Tabulzai (Bulzai), Barkahol (Bar Kalai), Srah Bulzai, Moti, Sawaki, Ghundi Kalai, Mezay, Mana, Sti Khel (Stan Khel), Khalil (Khalilan), Dwa Mandi, Bazi Khel, Surokai, Paro Khel, Wasti (Westo Ghundi), Darwaza Kalai, Mya Khel, Wocha Khola, Mushi, Ster Kalai, Hasanzai (Senzai), Bashti (Obukhti), Alghor (Wargol Kalai), Mogai-i-Ulya (Bar Mogai), Mogai-i-Sufla, Darghakai Mogai, Mogai-i-Sarmasti Kahol, Kotkai, Bora Khel, Shero Khel, Fazel Kahol, Agal Kahol, Kamar Khel (Lmar Khel), Alech Kahol, Khoy Kahol (Khi Khel), Suri, Wocha Khola, Shagi Kahol, Azo Kahol, Mundata, Zhawrona, Khandmang (Khadang), Khar Kot, Dar Kahol (Darro Kahol), Taraki Balkhel, Derendah Bar Khel, Khoni Kahol, Galarzai (Glizhan Barkhel), Lagada (Algadah Bar Khel), Shah Khel (Dara-i-Shah Khal), Mandi Khola (Monda Khel), Ghonzai, Tanga, Tandah, Bad Nagha (Bogh), Lalmi, Mad Khan Kalai, Chinargai (Senari), Managai (Mandagai), Landi Ragha, Meshi, Shagi, Chali (Charri Bazi Khel), Jani Khel (Maidan Khola), Togha Kalai Bar Khel, Bar (Barkho Kalai), Koz Khangi, Bar Khatgai, Tangi (Tangi Shakhal), Pelwa, Garshin (Barsha Barr Khel), Manzulgadah, Bor Bulzai (Bor Kahol Bulai), Tor Bulzai, Madkhi, Ishkeri, Lwarrah, Zargon, Worzoki, Khal Kahol, Khabi Kahol, Apkhel, and Mag Kahol.

JANI KHEL   جانی خیل
   32-46 68-23. Jani Khel is an alaqadari in Ghazni province. The
   alaqadari comprises an area of 983 square kilometers and has an
   agricultural population that has been estimated at from 3,766 to
   4,051. The alaqadari is bounded in the west by Ab Vand, in the
   southwest by Dila, in the south by Wazakhwa, in the east by Gomal,
   and in the north by Katawaz, Sultan Khel, and Omna. Jani Khel has
   about 48 villages, one of which has more than 500 inhabitants. The
   villages are listed in the PG as follows: Jalalzai, Jafar Kala Khel,
   Kala Khel, Chambar-i-Faqir, Malang Khel-Wa-Shadi-Khel, Gadol-i-Shir
   Khan, Chambaran, Sher Ali, Guldar, Qala-i-Sado, Mohammad Ayub, Shin
   Chah, Dawud, Karim Khan, Ali Khan, Qalandar, Malik Khel, Qala-i-
   Ahmadi, Chambar-i-Mohammad Nazar, Mohammad Amin, Shak Khel, Hasti,
   Qala-i-Haji Yaqub, Masjed-i-Mami Chambar, Qala-i-Kohna, Kala Khel-i-
   Muchak, Babu Khel, Shatori, Khanjaki, Mohammad Ali, Chuni, Kola-i-
   Hakim, Kandari, Kanizak, Barlak, Faqiran, Naim Gul, Kok Mandi,
   Qarya-i-Mahtar, Zalgaray, Qalandar Khel, Rasul Khan, Qarya-i-Tor,
   Jaye Shinya Mullahir, Marzak, Tirah, Jegan, Qarya-i-Baluch, Jan
   Khel, and Kala To.

JAN MUHAMMAD   جان محمد
   A village in Laghman. Inhabitants Kohistanis. (Warburton.)

*JAODUDI   جاودودی
   34-26 67-13 m. A village located on a path connecting the valleys
   of the Dara-i-Mur and Darazqol in Bamian province.

*JAODURA   جاودوره
   34-9 67-25 m. A village located near the source of a tributary of
   the Helmand river in Bamian province.

*JAODURI   جاودوری
   33-7 67-23 m. A village located on a tributary of the Arghandab
   river in Ghazni province.

JAO KALA   جاو قلعه
   (See Military Report on Hazarajat, Part II.)
   A village in the Kolani glen in the Dai Zangi Hazara country.

*JAOKAR   جوکار
   34-21 68-13 m. A village located south of Birnaidi, on a tributary
   of the Dara-i-Jelga in Maidan province.

*JAOKUL or JAWQUL   جوقول
   34-44 68-2 m. A village located on a tributary of the Shikari
   river, about 2 miles southeast of the Sawzaw in eastern Bamian
   province. Other places with this name are located on the Shikari
   river, southeast of Gumbad, at 34-40 68-2 m.; on a tributary of the
   Ghorband, about 2 miles from its confluence with the Ghorband, at
   34-54 68-23 m.; and on the Shemeltu stream, about 2 miles northeast
   of Bari Qol, at 33-52 68-10 m.

JAOKUL   جوقول
   34-24 68-18 m. (See Military Report on Hazarajat, Part II.) A
   fortified village, and a sarai, on the main Kabul-Herat road, 56
   miles west of Kabul and 6 1/2 miles west of the Unai pass. Another
   place with this name is located at 34-29 68-17 m. (LWA)

JAOLANGAH KOH   جولنگر کوه (جوانگاه)
Is the most westerly eminence of the main range of the Hindu Kush, which further westwards becomes very broken and rocky, until it finally abuts on the Aodara. Besides the Jalmish Kotal, there is a pathway over it, difficult even for native mountaineers, which leaves the Dahan-i-Jalmish at Kul-i-Agha and leads into the head of the Kariak Dara, and so on to the Brigilich valley; and another via the Sangandao Kotal, which crosses one of its southern spurs, thus forming a communication between the Ghorband valley and the Birgilich Dara. The prolongation of this same spur forms the watershed of the Shibar Kotal. (Peacocke.)

*JAOPALAL   جوپلال
34-35 68-14 m. A village located on a tributary of the Helmand, east of the Siasang area. Other places with this name are located south of the Kuh-i-Tabaqsar and 2 miles north of the Dahana-i-Jaopalal, at 34-54 67-31 m.; in the Kuh-i-Baba, north of the Kuh-i-Sar-i-Ghar, at 34-36 67-44 m.

*JAORSANG   جورسنگ
34-22 68-16 m. A village located near a tributary of the Dara-i-Jelga in Maidan province.

*JAOZAI   جوزی
33-40 68-59 m. A village located on the upper Logar, southeast of Nawa-i-Kharwar.

*JAOZAR or JAOZZAR   جوزار
33-46 69-1 m. A village located some 4 miles west of the Gardez-Kabul road, north of the Kharmurda mountain. Other places with this name are located near a tributary of the Ghorband, north of Shibar, at 34-27 68-11 m.; and on a tributary of the Ghorband, east of the Kuh-i-Yakhdara, at 34-53 68-48 m.

JAOZAR   جوزار
34-20 67-11 m. See Military Report on Hazarajat, Part II. A village in the east of the Bamian district.

*JARCHIAN   جارچیان
33-59 68-38 m. A village located some 6 miles southwest of Sayyidabad in Maidan province.

JARF   جرف
34- 67-. A large, well cultivated valley, draining north from the main Koh-i-Baba range, and debouching into the Ghorband valley about 3 miles west of Bin-i-Shewak. A road leads up it to the Nirkh Kotal for Karezak. (Peacocke.)

*JARK   جرك
34-3 67-11 m. A village located in the Pitaoqol area, northwest of Sar-i-Jark in southern Bamian province.

*JARKANA   جرکه (جرخانه)
33-5 68-30 m. A village located east of Jarkana Ghar and about 30 miles south of Ghazni.

JARKHANA or JARKANA   جرخانه
33-5 68-25 m. The name of a ridge to the east of the Ghazni river in the Ghilzai country. Broadfoot connects it with the range above Kharwar; but this must be a mistake, as the Gardez river runs be-

tween the Jarkhana and Kharwar hills. (Broadfoot.)

*JARMATOI جرمتوی
34-6 69-46 m. A village located south of the Spin Ghar mountain range, southeast of Azro in Logar province.

*JARUKASHAN جاروکشان
34-49 67-10 m. A village located on the Band-i-Amir, west of the lakes in Bamian province.

JASHA جاشه
A section of the Dai Kundi Hazaras. (See Military Report on Hazarajat, Part II.) A village with this name is located east of the Tor Band and southwest of Mazar in Ghazni province, a 33-15 67-8 m. (LWA)

JAUZ KHEL جوزخیل
33-40 68-54 G. A village in Kharwar, 40 houses of Gada Khel Ghilzais. (Griesbach.)

JAWARI CHINI جواری چینی
34- 70-. Elevation 5,300 feet. A pass in the Siah Koh range, leading from Jalalabad into the Laghman valley. (I.B.C.)

*JAWUL KHEL جاول خیل
31-59 68-50 m. A village located about 5 miles south of Mamai (Sharak) in southern Ghazni province.

*JEDACHEL جداچل
34-49 67-17 m. Two villages located about 5 miles southeast of the Band-i-Amir lakes in Bamian province.

JELAL KHEL جلال خیل
A main section of the Nasirs. A village with this name is located at 32-20 68-38 G. (LWA)

JELAL KHEL جلال خیل
A section of the Sulaiman Khels.

JEZKA جزکه
34- 67-. A place in the Besud country. (See Military Report on Hazarajat, Part II.)

*JIJAN-I-BALA جیجان بالا
34-4 67-2 m. A village located northwest of Kajalak, on a tributary of the Helmand river in Bamian province.

*JILAN جیلان
33-9 68-12 m. A village located some 5 miles east of the Qalat-Ghazni road in Ghazni province.

*JILGA جلگه
33-7 67-5 m. A village located north of the Kuh-i-Nawa and southeast of the Kuh-i-Pai Jilga in western Ghazni province.

JILGA See MURSAL جلگه

JILGA Or JILGU جلگه
33-18 68-42 m. A name given to the river formed by the junction, southwest of Gardez, of the stream flowing from the Altimur pass

with the Spin, or Sapega Rud which flows from the direction of the Mirzakai pass. The Jilga eventually falls into the Ghazni river some distance below Ghazni. Recent maps show the spelling Rud-i-Julga-i-Janubi.

*JIMATI جیتی
34-38 68-2 m. A village located near the Kotal-i-Hajigak, on the border of Bamian and Maidan provinces.

*JIM QALA جیم قلعه
34-51 67-32 m. A village located on the Achaqol-i-Shahidan, some 20 miles west of Bamian.

JINGAN See BAGHAL-I-KANDU جنگان

JINJAM جنجم
35- 71-. A Kam hamlet, of some dozen houses, in Kafiristan perched high up on the right bank of the torrent which flows down to the east of Kamdesh. (Robertson.)

*JIRALI جیرعلی
35-14 69-41 m. A village located on a tributary of the Panjshir, about 2 miles south of Babali in Kapisa province.

JIRGHAI جیرگی (جیرغی)
A large section of the Besud Hazaras. (See Military Report on Hazarajat, Part II.)

JIRGHAI USI MUHAMMAD جیرغی اوسی محمد (جرگه؟)
A section of Besud Hazaras. (See Military Report on Hazarajat, Part II.)

JIRIA KHANA جیریه خانه
34- 67-. A pass over the Koh-i-Baba range, crossed by a track which leaves the Ghazni-Bamian main road at a place about 1 1/2 miles east of Jangal Murda village. The track leads up a ravine, which is doubtless the main branch of the
Kata Khak glen, to the Siah Reg Kotal. The top of the pass would be about 10 miles from where the track leaves the main road. Jiria Khana is understood to be a place on the north side of the Koh-i-Baba, at the head of the Shahidan glen. However, the Siah Reg road proper appears to lead direct to Bamian by the Fauladi glen, and there is reason to suppose another pass exists, west of the Siah Reg, which is known as the Jiria Khana. On the other hand, Jiria Khana may be only another name for the Siah Reg. The latter is said to be a high and rather difficult pass. It is, however, practicable for laden mules and yabus. If there is a Jiria Khana Kotal it is worse than the Siah Reg, but neither of them are so good as the Zard Sang. Another road to the Siah Reg pass appears to lead from Kala Ghawas, a place about 9 miles west of Jangal Murda. (A.B.C., from native information.)

JIRMATU جیرمتو
A stream in the Jaghatu Hazara country. (See Military Report on Hazarajat, Part II.)

*JISH جیش
34-4 67-15 m. A village located on a tributary of the Helmand river, east of Pitaoqol.

*JISHPAL جشپال
35-25 70-20 m. A village located on the Nurestan river, some 6 miles southwest of Atati in Laghman province.

*JISKA جیسکه
34-6 67-27 m. A village located on a path from Garmab to the Helmand valley in southern Bamian province.

*JIWAZAK جوازک
34-43 68-23 m. A village located on the Qol-i-Khesh, about 1 mile from Dahan-i-Khakriz in Parwan province.

JOGA جوگه
33-15 68-23 G. A village in Shilghar district of the Ghilzai country, 27 miles from Ghazni on the road to Pannah. Broadfoot describes it as a cluster of forts. (Broadfoot.)

*JOKAK جوکک
34-58 68-1 m. A village located on the Shikari river, some 6 miles north of Shikari in eastern Bamian province.

JOKHAN or JOKAN جوکن
34-16 69-52 A. A village in the Khugiani country, southwest of Jalalabad. (McNair.) Recent maps show the spelling Cakan (Tsakan). (LWA)

JOLAH جوله
34-53 68-3. A dara draining north from the Koh-i-Baba to the Shibar valley here called the Bulola Dara. At its debouchure into the latter, 2-1/4 miles below the mouth of the Kablantu Tangi, it is 400 yards wide. A road leads up it to Kala Jolah (3 miles), and continues on the "Kala Hisar" in Besud by the Kotal-i-Sabzab, said to be a difficult road, but practicable for laden animals. From Kala Jolah a road also leads over the Kotal-i-Jolah to the mouth of the Dara Shumbal on the one hand, and on the other over the Kotal-i-Khushkak past Khushkak village and over the Irak Kotal (Not to be confused with the pass of that name on the main range to the south—"Khushkak.") to the Irak valley, which it joins about 3/4 mile above the junction of that valley with the Dara Jandargal. This road forms an alternative to the main Shibar road between the Kashka Kotal and the mouth of the Dara Shumbal.
According to reports the main route is actually half a mile shorter than the Jolah road, but in the latter the distances appear to be exaggerated, and perhaps a mile and a half may be taken off. Still the saving cannot be sufficient to compensate for having to cross three high kotals. As an alternative road it is good for everything but artillery and heavily laden camels, and might be employed to relieve pressure on the main route.
The road from the Bulola up the Jolah is thus described by Peacocke (October 1886):
"The lower 2 miles of Dara Jolah is a difficult path, even for pack animals. The dara is here 75 yards wide and very rocky, and the path climbs along the foot of the hillside, constantly crossing and recrossing the narrow rocky gully in which the Jolah stream flows. It would be a fairly heavy bit of work to make it passable for guns. At 2nd mile the dara opens out to 500 yards, and the slopes of the high hills at both sides become smooth and rounded. From here upwards, as far as could be seen, the dara is well cultivated, with a few trees in the bed of the valley, though all the hillsides are quite bare. Habitations now commence, there being in all seven fort

villages with three watermills grouped around the main village of Kala Jolah at 3rd mile. Each fort is of about 15 to 20 families (Darghanis); and each fort owns about one flock of 500 sheep and some 500 head of cattle. At Kala Jolah I joined the alternative road from Irak, which here bends to the left up the long hillside slope to the Jolah Kotal."

His account of the road from Kala Jolah over the Jolah pass ot the Shibar valley is as follows:

"The ascent is a steady gradient of 1 in 6 to 1 in 4 for one mile. There is a good road for baggage animals, except over the last quarter mile, which would require cross levelling even for baggage animals, the hillside is so steep. It is quite impracticable for a battery, owing to its combined steepness and length, and is a very heavy climb for laden camels. The total rise to the top of the ascent from the point where the Dara Jolah (8,785 feet) is left is 1,120 feet. The hillside is quite open and smooth--soil a light clay-- and except for the length it would not be difficult to make a road up it. To allow of a gradient of 1 in 15, such a road would be some 3 miles long. The top of the kotal is an open grassy dasht draining in deep undulations towards the Dara Shumbal. The descent to the Shumbal is, owing to its steepness, quite impracticable for guns. It is in all 1 1/4 miles long, and the total fall is 1,060 feet. For the first half mile the gradient is easy, and the road good down a hollow. It then becomes very steep, varying from 1 in 4 to 1 in 3. There is, however, a 10 foot wide road all the way, which is practicable for laden camels and all troops, except artillery."

"The Dara Shumbal is an open roomy valley about 700 yards wide; its bed is level and well-cultivated and studded with villages. It contains in all 11 villages, with 7 watermills and 270 families of Darghan Hazaras. A good stream flows down it in a broad gravelly bed, and a road leads up it and over the Kotal-i-Zirak at the head in the main range ot Kala Hissar (This place has never been located.) in Besud. The Kotal-i-Zirak is very high and difficult, and is said to be fit only for pack yabus and bullocks. At its mouth a minor valley joins on the west called Dara Gharjarak, containing a couple of small forts and a small area of cultivation.

"There is good camping ground for a large force in the Shambal. No grass or fuel, but supplies are procurable.

"Crossing the Shumbal stream, the main Shibar road which had been left at Bulola was joined at 4 12 miles above Kala Bulola, and close under the towering crags on the left called Sangi-Shibar. Below this point the Shumal stream flows at the foot of these crags in a dep, narrow, wall-sided gorge to the mouth of the Dara Birgilich. This gorge is about 70 yards wide, and cliffs at each side are 200 to 400 feet high, without any break, and quite inaccessible. The bed of the gorge is stony, but fairly level; and there is a good road, easy for guns, down it to the mouth of the Birgilich ravine 1 1/2 miles lower down.

"Crossing the mouth of the Dara Shumbal, the main road (to Shibar pass) passes through a deep rocky gorge, about 40 yards wide, for 3/5 mile (viz., to 4 7/8 mile above Kala Bulola). At the entrance to this small gorge the road is blocked by large boulders. There is a good camel track through them; but to remove boulders and improve a few other rocky bits for guns would take 50 men three days. This gorge affords a good point for blocking the main road by a few blasting charges; and the high cliff forming the descent from the Jolah Kotal as well as the gorge down which the main road runs to the junction of Dara Birgilich, is a good position to bar the main road. It can, however, be turned by the Tangi Birgilich and Kala Shah Darwesh; and, if occupied, that tangi should be blocked at Kablantu, or the low rise be held between Kala Shah Darwesh and the Shibar valley. The position, however, would only be tenable on the assumption that artillery could not be brought into action against it on the Jolah Kotal. Emerging form this short gorge, the road enters the Shibar valley, which is a broad, shallow hollow about 300 yards wide, with low accessible side." (Peacocke.)

JOLGA See JULGA (Military Report on Hazarajat, Part II.) جلگه

*JORKANI حرکنی
35-5 69-59 m. A village located about 3 miles northeast of Deh-i-Kalan, on the upper source of the Alishang river in Laghman province.

*JOROBAI حروبی
34-21 69-37 m. A village located on a path leading from Jagalak to Butkhak and Kabul, about 8 miles southwest of Jagdalak.

*JOSHAN جوشان
33-34 67-40 m. A village located west of the Dasht-i-Nawar and south of Sabz Nala in Ghazni province.

JOSHANAK-KHAK-I-CHAGIR

*JOSHANAK جوشانک
34-39 67-11 m. A village located north of the Kuh-i-Baba in the Sar-i-Qol area in Bamian province.

*JOSHI جوشی
33-53 68-24 m. A village located about 20 miles north of Ghazni in Maidan province.

*JUBAGAI جوبگی
34-48 70-53 m. A village located north of Tsawkai on a path leading from the Kunar to the Pich valley in Kunar province.

JUGAR KHEL جوگرخیل
A village with a fort, in the Bamian valley, inhabited by 50 families of Tajiks. (Maitland.)

*JUGIAN جوگیان
31-58 68-51 m. A village located about 7 miles south of Mamai in southern Ghazni province.

JUI AHIN جوی اهین
33- 68-. A place in the Jaghatu Hazara country, some 16 miles northwest of Ghazni, situated at the junction of the Sar-i-Ab and Jarmatu streams. (A.B.C.)

JUI BADAL جوی بدل
A village on the right bank of the Lal stream, about 32 miles east of Daulat Yar. (Wanliss.)

JUI BAR جوی بار
34-42 69-13 m. A village in the plain, north of the Paiminar Kotal, some 8 miles from the latter. One of the best routes from Kabul to Koh Daman passes through this village; the road being fit for wheeled artillery. (Kinloch.) Another place with this name is on

313

the Tagab river, about 2 miles north of Tagab, at 34-52 69-38. (LWA)

JUI DUKHTAR جوی دختر
35-1 68-47 m. A dara which joins the Ghorband valley from the north at a point some 2 3/4 miles east of Chahardeh. There is a village of the same name at its mouth, and here and up the dara live 150 families of Afghan Koishki, with 3 water-mills, 10 flocks, and 500 head of cattle. A road runs up the dara to the Chahardar kotal; but the main road to that pass leaves the valley at a point 2 miles lower down. (Peacocke.)

JUI FAULADI جوی فولادی
34- 68-. A village and fort in the Sar-i-Chashma valley, west of Kabul, near the source of the Kabul river. It has some land attached to it. (Masson.)

JUI MIR HAZAR جوی میر هزار
34- 66-. (See Military Report on Hazarajat, Part II.) A tagao in the west of the Dai Kundi country, draining in a general south-easterly direction from the Karodil Kotal to the Helmand.

*JUI NAO جوی نو
34-2 66-53 m. A village located on a tributary of the Helmand river, south of the Espighaw area in northern Ghazni province. Another village with this name is located north of the Kuh-i-Baba range, on a path leading to the Band-i-Amir in Bamian province, at 34-41 67-13 m.

*JULAGAN جولاگان
34-14 70-27 m. A village located southwest of Shahi Kot and south of Jalalabad.

JULGA-I-KAJAO See SANG-I-SHANDA جلگه کجاو

JULGA-I-KAJAO جلگه کجاو
34- 67-. A considerable plain to the south of Besud. (See Military report on Hazarajat, Part II.)

JULGA or JOLGA جلگه
33-7 67-19 A. Apparently the name given to the lower part of the Sar-i-Ab valley in Jaghatu Hazara country. (See Military Report on Hazarajat, Part II.)

JULGAI RAOTI جلگه روتی
Said to be a large valley in the Ujaristan district. (See Military Report on Hazarajat, Part II.)

JULGAI ZAOLI جلگه زولی
Said to be a large valley in the Ujaristan district. (See Military Report on Hazarajat, Part II.)

*JULUZI جولوزی
34-19 70-21 m. A village located on the Kambu Khwar, some 10 miles southwest of Jalalabad.

*JUMJUMI DASHT جمجمه دشت
32-37 68-22 m. An area southeast of Khushamand and south of Jani-khel in Ghazni province.

*JUNIA جنیا
35-7 70-16 m. A village located near the Dara-i-Poshal, about 2 miles northeast of Gada in Laghman province.

JURA جورا
33- 69-. A village in Khost, 7 miles from Sabari, towards the Sterkual ravine. (Spratt.)

JURAB KALA جوراب قلعه
34- 69-. A small Tajik fort, on the left bank of the Kabul river, to the east of Sherpur. It is comprised in the township of Yakatut. (Kennedy.)

JUYAK Or JOYAK جویک
A village in the upper Logar valley, containing 40 families of Kizilbashis and a few Afghans of various tribes. (I.B.C.)

KABAR-I-JABAR قبر جبار
34-24 69-30 m. A tomb 24 miles east of Kabul. It is that of Jabar, the first of the Jabar Khel Ghilzais. Its position on the Khurd Kabul-Tezin road is very wild, and exposed to the weather and to the wolves.
There is a saying at Kabul--
  Gurg dar Kabar-i-Jabar.   Wolves of Kabar-i-Jabar.
  Khunuk dar Kabar-i-Jabar. Frost at Kabar-i-Jabar.
  Duzd dar Kabar-i-Jabar.   Thieves at Kabar-i-Jabar.
  Atish dar Kabar-i-Jabar. Fire at Kabar-i-Jabar. (i.e., burn the accursed place.)
Here many of the British, retiring from Kabul in 1842, died. (I.B.C.) Recent maps show the name Khak-i-Jabar Bala. Kabar should be spelled Qabr. (LWA)

KABAZAN قابضان
35-16 69-28. A village in the upper Panjshir glen, 5 miles below Bazarak, situated on the left bank of the stream, and containing 200 houses of Tajiks. On the opposite side of the stream in Bangi, a small place of 12 houses; and to the right of the latter is Baram Khel, also with about 12 houses.
The Hakim of Panjshir was living at Kabazan in 1886. (Shahzada Taimus.)

*KABCHERAK قبچیرك
34-13 67-29 m. A village located on the Qol-i-Beremak, a tributary of the Helmand river in southern Bamian province.

*KABILA قبیله
34-57 68-54 m. A village located on a tributary of the Ghorband, about 4 miles south of Siagird in Parwan province.

*KABIR KAREZ کبیر کاریز
34-22 70-31 m. A village located southeast of Jalalabad and 1 mile southwest of the Jalalabad - Torkham road.

KABLANTU See BIRGALICH کبلنتو

*KABRATU کابرتو
34-43 69-47 m. A village located west of the Wuzbin Khwar and northeast of Sarobi in Kabul province. Another village with this name is nearby, north of Sarobi and northeast of the Naghlu lake, at 30-43 69-44 m.

*KABR-I-AFGHAN قبر افغان
   34-48 67-22 m. A village located on the road from Bamian to Yakaw-lang, southeast of the Band-i-Amir lakes.

KABRISTAN قبرستان
   34-29 66-1 m. A small village on the main Kabul-Hazarajat—Daulat Yar road on the right bank of the Lal stream, about 21 miles from Daulat Yar. Recent maps show the name Nawe Qabrestan.

KABUL کابل
   34-31 69-13 m. The capital city and a province in eastern Afghanistan which comprises an area of 4,720 square kilometers and an agricultural population estimated at from 188,391 to 263 517. The province is bounded in the west by Maidan and Parwan, in the north by Kapisa, in the east by Laghman and Nangarhar, and in the south by Logar. Kabul is divided into the woleswalis of Qara Bagh, Mir Bachakot, Shakar Dara, Paghman, Deh Sabz, Sarobi, Chardehi, and Bagrami, and into the alaqadaris of Istalif, Kalakan, Charasiab, and Kahak-i-Jabar. For woleswali lists from the Department of Statistics of the Ministry of Agriculture and Irrigation see the following pages. (LWA) In 1914 Kabul district was described as follows: The home district of Kabul, i.e., the land immediately around the capital is very fertile and populous, its principal subdivisions are Paghman, Chardeh, Butkhak, Charasia, and Chehil Dukhtaran; and within those limits there are numerous townships and villages. The district is watered by the Kabul and Logar rivers, and by several streams from the west, which unite and fall into the Kabul at Guzargah, under the name of the Chamchamast. Irrigation by means of karez is extensively practised, and the natural streams are thereby much reduced in volume.

Wheat is the chief product, and after it barley. The poorest clases consume a considerable proportion of barley and jowar, and animal food is abundantly used by all who can afford it. Corn is imported from the Ghazni and Logar districts; rice from Logar, Jalalabad, Laghman and Kunar. In years of scarcity Bamian sends a little corn, but, as a rule, the quantity of imported grain bears a small proportion to that produced in the district, and provisions are rarely dear. The chief supply of ghi is from Bamian, the Hazarajat, and the nomadic Ghilzais. From Turkistan and the Hazarajat come cattle and sheep, whilst horses and ponies are imported from the former, as well as bred in the district itself. Timber is brought chiefly from the head of Kurram, fruit from the Koh Daman, and there is, as well, a considerable cultivation of fruit on the spot, whilst willows and sycamores grow in profusion. Vegetables of all kinds abound in the neighbourhood, and clover and lucernce are grown everywhere.

For carriage, bullocks are used chiefly in the valley; traders to the north use camels; to the east and south, camels, mules and ponies; to the Hazara country, mules and ponies.

The town and province, however, and indeed all Afghanistan, are dependent on India chiefly for tea, sugar, and cotton fabrics. From Turkistan silk fabrics, sheep-skins for postins, and considerable numbers of camels and horses reach the capital.

With regard to the subdivisions of the Kabul district a very brief description is all that is required.

Chardeh.--The Chardeh valley lies west of the city. It is as nearly as possible six miles square, and is very fertile. Further information is given under "Chardeh."

Paghman.--The villages of this subdivision are located to the west of the Chardeh valley in the glens running down from the Paghman range.

Administrative Divisions of Kabul Province

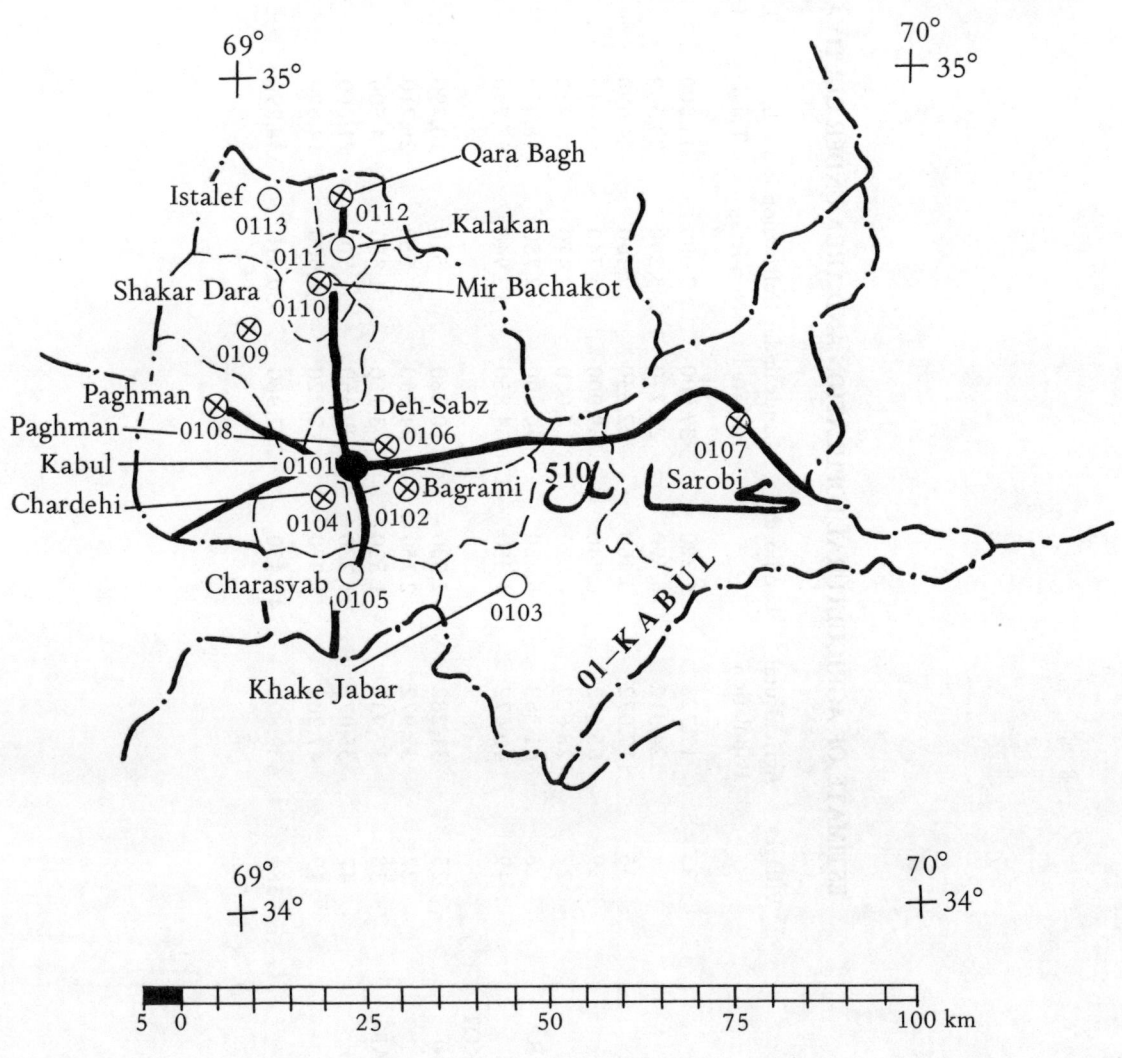

ESTIMATE OF AGRICULTURAL POPULATION AND AREA UNDER CULTIVATION

	Villages	Agricultural Population	Landlords	Lands under Cultivation in Jaribs			Lands under Cultivation in Hectares		
				Irrigated	Non-Irrig.	Total	Irrigated	Non-Irrig.	Total
BAGRAMI	23	17,728	4,220	37,000	7,000	44,000	7,400	1,400	8,800
PAGHMAN	27	124,312	6,590	29,770	3,590	33,360	5,954	718	6,672
CHARDEHI	35	117,072	3,460	22,530	2,160	24,690	4,506	432	4,938
DEH SABZ	39	65,572	6,240	39,900	13,740	53,640	7,980	2,748	10,728
SAROBI	27	28,622	4,820	7,060	2,420	9,480	1,412	484	1,896
SHAKAR DARA	28	61,562	5,250	46,200	2,750	48,950	9,240	550	9,790
QARA BACH	49	40,472	4,350	34,850	12,940	47,790	6,970	2,588	9,558
MIR BACHAKOT (KOHDAMAN)	25	31,282	2,530	10,280	510	10,790	2,056	102	2,158
ISTALEF	27	32,972	2,750	24,660	550	25,210	4,932	110	5,042
KHAK-I-JABAR	38	37,932	1,530	3,150	1,350	4,500	630	270	900
CHARASYAB	47	35,072	1,720	20,360	700	21,060	4,072	140	4,212
KALAKAN	19	47,202	1,970	12,220	2,600	14,820	2,444	520	2,964
TOTAL	384	639,800	45,430	287,980	50,310	338,290	57,596	10,062	67,658

STATISTICAL ESTIMATE OF LIVESTOCK BY WOLESWALIS AND ALAKADARIS

	Sheep	Karakul Sheep	Goats	Cattle	Buffaloes	Camels	Horses	Donkeys	Mules	Poultry
BAGRAMI	—	—	—	4,410	—	—	280	6,510	—	15,840
PAGHMAN	18,330	—	210	5,110	—	110	—	1,140	—	15,350
CHARDEHI	660	—	100	2,440	—	—	400	3,670	—	14,470
DEH SABZ	8,390	—	550	6,220	—	—	250	6,370	—	15,080
SAROBI	5,730	—	3,660	3,020	—	—	—	1,360	—	14,460
SHAKAR DARA	3,680	—	610	5,180	—	—	—	1,530	—	11,980
QARA BAGH	2,530	—	930	4,340	—	20	120	4,470	—	9,720
MIR BACHAKOT (KOHDAMAN)	8,310	—	70	3,170	—	—	50	2,690	—	10,350
ISTALEF	9,020	—	770	5,530	—	—	120	2,750	—	11,820
KHAK-I-JABAR	3,360	—	1,950	2,810	—	20	—	2,280	—	11,760
CHARASYAB	3,830	—	310	4,360	—	—	—	3,360	—	10,060
KALAKAN	240	—	—	1,810	—	—	20	1,410	—	3,930
TOTAL	64,080	—	9,160	48,400	—	150	1,240	37,540	—	144,820

PRODUCTION OF AGRICULTURAL CROPS—IN KABULI SEERS

	Grains			Vegetables	Other Crops		Fruits
	Irrigated	Non-Irrig.	Total		Industrial Crops	Other Temp. Crops	
BAGRAMI	1,745,550	38,400	1,783,950	1,523,610	13,300	94,400	190,000
PAGHMAN	1,153,350	22,800	1,176,150	286,740	28,820	188,800	520,000
CHARDEHI	511,200	6,240	517,440	1,368,090	—	177,000	540,000
DEH SABZ	668,250	91,200	759,450	3,873,420	—	224,100	200,000
SAROBI	343,350	3,120	346,470	70,470	3,240	103,800	46,000
SHAKAR DARA	1,752,300	13,200	1,765,500	369,360	—	245,400	402,000
QARA BAGH	1,190,250	98,400	1,288,650	313,470	—	481,400	440,000
MIR BACHAKOT (KOHDAMAN)	366,300	2,400	368,700	191,970	—	129,800	196,000
ISTALEF	880,650	3,840	884,490	468,990	—	269,000	384,000
KHAK-I-JABARA	167,850	9,600	177,450	—	—	33,000	40,000
CHARASYAB	761,850	2,160	764,010	957,420	—	153,300	122,000
KALAKAN	440,100	9,840	449,940	114,210	—	—	380,000
TOTAL	9,981,000	301,200	10,282,200	9,537,750	45,360	2,100,000	3,460,000

LAND UNDER IRRIGATION AND SOURCES OF IRRIGATION

	Area in Jaribs					Number of Sources			
	Canals	Springs	Karez	Wells	Total	Canals	Springs	Karez	Wells	Water Mills
BAGRAMI	35,000	—	1,000	1,000	37,000	11	—	11	150	46
PAGHMAN	26,120	2,000	1,650	—	29,770	12	4	19	—	75
CHARDEHI	17,440	510	4,580	—	22,530	17	7	27	—	53
DEH SABZ	21,400	2,700	15,800	—	39,900	19	10	38	—	36
SAROBI	2,590	1,930	1,540	1,000	7,060	14	17	8	100	70
SHAKAR DARA	34,350	3,500	8,350	—	46,200	28	12	30	—	85
QARA BAGH	7,680	—	27,170	—	34,850	21	2	61	—	25
MIR BACHAKOT (KOHDMAN)	5,690	400	4,190	—	10,280	11	8	46	—	36
ISTALEF	20,470	4,070	20	100	24,660	12	3	1	24	46
KHAK-I JABAR	900	700	1,150	400	3,150	7	10	18	61	47
CHARASYAB	19,950	—	410	—	20,360	14	4	12	—	72
KALAKAN	2,800	690	7,930	800	12,220	11	4	50	101	25
TOTAL	194,390	16,500	73,790	3,300	287,980	177	81	321	436	616

TOTAL CULTIVABLE LAND, BY CROP—IN KABULI JARIBS

	Grains Irrigated	Non-Irrig.	Total	Vegetables	Industrial Crops	Other Crops	Fruits	Total Cultivated Land
BAGRAMI	38,790	3,200	41,990	6,270	370	400	950	49,980
PAGHMAN	25,630	1,900	27,530	1,180	800	800	2,600	32,910
CHARDEHI	11,360	520	11,880	5,630	—	750	2,700	20,960
DEH SABZ	14,850	7,600	22,450	15,940	—	950	1,000	40,340
SAROBI	7,630	260	7,890	290	90	440	230	8,940
SHAKAR DARA	38,940	1,100	40,040	1,520	—	1,040	2,010	44,610
QARA BAGH	26,450	8,200	34,650	1,290	—	2,040	2,200	40,180
MIR BACHAKOT (KOHDAMAN)	8,140	200	8,340	790	—	550	980	10,660
ISTALEF	19,570	320	19,890	1,930	—	1,140	1,920	24,880
KHAK-i-JABAR	3,730	800	4,530	—	—	140	200	4,870
CHARASYAB	16,930	180	17,110	3,940	—	650	610	22,310
KALAKAN	9,780	820	10,600	470	—	—	1,900	12,970
TOTAL	221,800	25,100	246,900	39,250	1,260	8,900	17,300	313,610

TOTAL CULTIVABLE LANDS—IN KABULI JARIBS

	Total	Pastures	Forests	Under Cultivation	Fallow Lands
BAGRAMI	44,510	510	—	44,000	10,900
PAGHMAN	35,260	1,900	—	33,360	7,750
CHARDEHI	25,110	280	140	24,690	5,080
DEH SABZ	54,990	1,350	—	53,640	14,850
SAROBI	12,280	2,320	480	9,480	1,620
SHAKAR DARA	50,230	1,280	—	48,950	10,610
QARA BAGH	48,980	860	330	47,790	15,440
MIR BACHAKOT (KOHDAMAN)	11,830	990	50	10,790	2,290
ISTALEF	25,700	490	—	25,210	5,200
KHAK-I-JABAR	5,480	980	—	4,500	1,300
CHARASYAB	23,040	1,980	—	21,060	4,220
KALAKAN	14,880	60	—	14,820	3,440
TOTAL	352,290	13,000	1,000	338,290	82,700

Butkhak.—This subdivision lies to the east of Kabul. Its largest village, known as Butkhak, is occupied by 400 to 500 families of Ghilzais, Tajiks, and a few Khugianis.

Charasia.—Consists of a group of hamlets lying about 10 miles to the south of the city, situated on a small plain enclosed by hills on all sides, except the southwest.

Chehil Dukhtaran.—Includes the country in the neighbourhood of the large village of that name about two miles south of Charasia.

Kabul itself is fully described in the next article. (I.B.C.)

KABUL CITY

کابل

34-30 69-13 m. Kabul City is the capital of Kabul province and of the State of Afghanistan. The city has grown in size from an estimated population of some 140,000 at the time of Amir Sher Ali in 1876 to about 600,000 in the 1970's, and - with the influx of people from the provinces in the early 1980's - is estimated to have a population of about a million and a half. In the early 1980's the city has been considerably developed with the construction of multi-storied apartment buildings. Because of the fact that few western scholars have visited Afghanistan since 1980, it is difficult to have a clear picture of recent urban development in Kabul. (LWA)

In 1912 the city was described as follows: Elevation 5,895 feet. The capital of Afghanistan is situated on the right bank of the Kabul river, six miles above its junction with the Logar. North of the city, on the left bank of the river, stand the suburbs of Deh-i-Murad Khani, Andarabi, and Deh-i-Afghan, and beyond these lies the military cantonment of Sherpur, 3/4 mile from Deh-i-Afghan, backed by the Bemaru hill. South of the walls are the Sher Darwaza heights, whilst to the east are the Bala Hisar and the Siah Sang ridge. On the west the Kabul river flows through the gorge formed by the Asmai and Sher Darwaza hills.

Kabul is distant from:	Miles
Bamian (Kala Sarkari) via the Unai and Hajigak passes	98
Mazar-i-Sharif via the Unai and Hajigak passes, Haibak and Tash Kurghan	318
Jalalabad	98
Peshawar	181
Ghazni via Maidan	89
Kandahar	310
Herat by the Hazarajat-Dulat Yar road	490

The city is 3 1/2 miles in circumference, and is no longer walled although traces of a wall remain. Only one gate of the original seven stands. This is the Darwaza-i-Lahori on the eastern face.

The old residence of the Amirs of Kabul used to be in the Bala Hisar, but the Amir moves about from one to another of the various country residences that he has built on favourable spots in the neighbourhood of the city.

The lower Bala Hisar has been completely dismantled. The Upper Bala Hisar is kept up as as grain store, and the huts built by us for the Gurkhas are kept up also.

The climate of Kabul may be pronounced a healthy one. The great lake of Wazirabad, north of the town, and the low-lying marshy meadows, or chamans, in the immediate vicinity, give rise to malaria and consequently to fevers, but with proper drainage, and good shelter from the vigours of winter and the midsummer sun, the place would, no doubt, be well suited to European constitutions. But

British and Native troops at Kabul in the winter of 1879-80 suffered a good deal from pneumonia, due to constant exposure at all hours in the snow, with sometimes insufficient clothing; and after months of ocupation, the cantonments of Sherpur began to show symptoms of being foul, which, under the conditions of December's investment, was to be expected.

On the whole, the climate would be thought a fine one in any part of the world. The city itself, wedged in as it is between two hills, its confined streets, want of proper drainage and proximity to extensive marshes, would seem to labour under strong disadvantages, but, in compensation, it has the benefits of a fine atmosphere, excellent water and provisions, with delightful environs. During summer and autumn the phenomenon of the khakbad, whirlwing or "dust devil," is common in the afternoons. The complete obscuration of the atmosphere announces its formation, and a furious blast and sudden fall of temperature gives warning of its immediate approach, and it is sometimes attended by a few drops of rain. Fine particles of dust brought with the whirlwind, penetrate through closed doors and windows, but the duration of the blast is short.

The range of thermometer at Kabul, from the 6th to the end of August 1839, was recorded as being 46 degrees to 74 degrees at 4 p.m. and 72 to 96 at 3 p.m.

The following are the meteorological reports of Sherpur cantonment drawn up from observations taken in the Quarter Master General's Department there in the year 1880. These are unfortunately incomplete:

Meterological report of the cantonment of Sherpur from the 16th January to the 12th February 1880:

Date	A.M. 9:30	P.M. 4:30	Maximum	Minimum	Remarks
January					
16	42	56	61	25	Cloudy.
17	38	34	59	32	Ditto. Slight snow. Heavy snow at night.
18	40	36	41	30	Morning, cloudy; fine afternoon.
19	37	35	43	21	Fine clear sky.
20	31	28	48	21	Ditto.
21	31	31	48	17	Ditto.
22	36	38	54	19	Ditto.
23	35	38	59	17	Ditto.
24	35	40	53	20	Ditto.
25	38	41	55	24	Ditto.
26	43	43	53	26	Ditto.
27	39	42	58	27	Ditto.
28	41	39	57	30	Cloudy; inclined to snow
29	35	36	48	30	Cloudy all day; heavy snow at night.
30	36	36	42	32	Snowing morning; cloudy all day.
31	43	40	47	29	Cloudy morning
February					
1	36	34	56	32	Snowing all day
2	34	33	38	32	Cloudy; strong northeast wind.
3	22	23	35	11	Ditto.
4	22	24	35	9	Fine.
5	23	26	35	12	Do.

6	32	28	43	13	Do.
7	35	32	41	22	Cloudy. Snowing afternoon. Heavy snow at night.
8	34	33	39	26	Cloudy all day. Light wind from west.
9	33	36	43	26	Fine clear sky. Ditto, southeast.
10	31	33	48	18	Ditto. Ditto. Ditto, west.
11	33	34	40	14	Ditto. Ditto. Ditto, south.
12	27	29	37	9	Ditto. Fresh ditto. Ditto.
13	27	30	37	17	Cloudy. Snowing. Light wind from southeast.
14	37	31	37	25	Ditto all day. Ditto, south.
15	32	32	42	17	Fine clear sky. Ditto, west.
16	31	30	45	15	Ditto.
17	27	34	43	19	Cloudy morning. Clear sky afternoon. Light wind from west.
18	29	29	45	15	Fine clear sky. Fresh wind from southeast.
19	32	32	43	15	Ditto. Snow at night. Calm.
20	34	36	41	18	Ditto. Light wind from south.
21	35	36	44	18	Ditto. Ditto, southeast.
22	36	42	51	21	Ditto. Ditto, west.
23	32	32	52	27	Heavy snow all day. Calm.
24	32	36	40	28	Snowing. Calm.
25	36	34	47	28	Fine clear sky. Strong wind from south.
26	30	36	43	18	Ditto. Light wind from southeast.
27	28	32	41	8	Ditto. Strong wind from southeast.
28	28	43	43	13	Ditto. Ditto.
29	34	43	49	21	Ditto. Calm.
March					
1	33	45	55	22	Ditto. Light wind from south.
2	34	42	60	30	Ditto. Ditto, west.
3	38	44	56	26	Ditto. Strong ditto, west.
4	39	42	50	29	Ditto. Calm.
5	42	43	53	36	Cloudy. Slight rain afternoon. Calm.
6	50	38	52	36	Fine clear sky. Light wind from west. Rain afternoon.
7	43	43	54	35	Sky cloudy all day. Calm.

8	46	50	57	38	Ditto. Light wind from south.
9	48	43	55	38	Ditto. Rain afternoon. Calm.
10	53	52	70	36	Fine sky. Light wind from west.
11	57	58	70	37	Ditto. Ditto, south.
12	50	60	72	40	Ditto. Calm.
13	56	60	66	40	Fine sky. Calm.
14	58	63	78	40	Ditto. Ditto.
15	54	64	75	40	Sky cloudy, morning. Fine afternoon. Light wind from west.
16	62	55	74	44	Sky clear. Strong wind from west.
17	58	60	72	37	Ditto. Light wind from north.
18	64	64	75	40	Ditto. Ditto.
19	66	66	77	40	Ditto. Calm.
20	62	58	68	45	Ditto. Strong wind from east.
21	58	64	77	35	Ditto. Light ditto.
22	60	72	77	37	Ditto.
23	66	77	80	42	Ditto. Calm.
24	71	70	79	43	Ditto. Light wind from north.
25	67	64	83	48	Ditto. Ditto.
26	66	70	72	44	Ditto. Calm.
27	63	70	80	46	Ditto. Do.
28	66	56	77	40	Ditto morning. Rain afternoon.
29	64	58	77	41	Ditto, ditto. Strong wind from west.
30	66	68	77	44	Ditto.
31	70	66	83	45	Ditto. Light wind from northeast.

April

1	68	69	75	44	Sky clear. Strong wind from west.
2	70	68	80	45	Ditto. Slight ditto southeast.
3	70	62	73	44	Ditto.
4	69	67	79	45	Ditto. Slight wind from west.
5	71	67	80	44	Ditto. Ditto.
6	72	68	81	40	Ditto. Ditto.
7					
8					
9					
10					
11					
12					
13					
14					
15					
16					
17					

The readings between these dates are of no use. The site on which the thermometers were placed during the period was unfortunately exposed to the direct rays of the sun, and the mat shelter was insufficient.

18				
19	65	68	70	44
20	66	69	72	45
21	65	68	71	44
22	64	67	72	44
23	67	69	72	44
24	66	68	72	45
25	67	68	73	44
26	65	68	72	43
27	64	67	71	42
28	67	68	70	41
29	66	68	72	42
30	66	68	72	43

Register of meteorological observations taken at Kabul from the 4th to the 31st July 1850.

Date July	9 A.M. Max.	Min.	3 P.M. Max.	Min.
4	85	45	97	62
5	82	43	91	56
6	90	42	95	59
7	92	50	94	60
8	97	49	99	61
9	97	49	99	61
10	95	48	97	69
11	91	47	101	67
12	91	47	101	66
13	90	45	101	63
14	99	46	99	68
15	90	53	104	68
16	94	53	105	70
17	102	57	101	63
18	96	57	104	57
19	90	52	102	73
20	103	52	100	70
21	97	50	93	65
22	92	50	93	65
23	92	50	97	56
24	93	57	90	65
25	93	57	97	65
26	92	58	97	65
27	90	57	91	63
28	88	61	92	63
29	85	62	90	65
30	not given			
31	90	58	89	62

General Babcock's estimate of supplies available in 1880 will be found in the Introduction.

The water-supply of the capital is good, and is derived from wells and also from an excellent canal (amongst several others) called the Jui Sher which is brought from the Paghman hills and joins the Kabul river near Chandawal.

The bridges across the river at Kabul are:

    I. Pul-i-Mozang. This was built by the Emperor Babar, and was broken in Amir Sher Ali's reign. The bridge is a brick one.

    II. Pul-i-Shah-i-Dushamshira. This is a brick bridge leading to Chandawal. It was built by Shah Jahan, and is rather narrow.

    III. Pul-i-Khishti. A brick bridge connecting Deh-i-Murad Khani with the city.

IV. Pul-i-Mahmud Khan. A stone bridge on the road leading from Sherpur to the Bala Hisar.

V. Pul-i-Kala-i-Muhammad Umar. A wooden bridge on the road leading from the southeast of Sherpur cantonment to the Butkhak road, north of the Siah Sang hill. Was renewed and enlarged by the British in 1879-80.

In 1880, II, III, IV and V were fit for the passage of guns.

The situation of Kabul marks it out as the natural capital of Afghanistan, but the city has in it neither external nor interior evidences of grandeur. It is built of bricks, burnt or sun-dried, and of mud. The houses of burnt brick are of old standing. The general want of substantiality of the buildings does not prevent their being conveniently arranged, and the quarter of Chandawal especially shows taste.

The city is divided into quarters (mahalas) and streets (Kuchas). The latter are closed by small gates, which, on occasions of war or tumult, are built up, and the place becomes then a collection of small fortresses. This mode of defence is called "Kuchabandi."

The following is a list of the streets as they existed in 1880:

1. Ashikan-i-Arifan
2. Kucha-i-Kazi
3. Barana
4. Murdashoi
5. Kucha-i-Jangalak
6. Khwab Gah
7. Teri Guzar
8. Chob Faroshi
9. Sang Tarashi
10. Kucha-i-Ali Riza Khan
11. Bala Joi
12. Rika Khana
13. Bagh-i-Nawab
14. Bagh-i-Ali Mardan Khan
15. Kucha-i-Lahori Darwaza
16. Islamabad
17. Sih Dukan
18. Mahala Achakzai
19. Kucha-i-Mir Waiz
20. Ganda Kucha
21. Kucha-i-Damgah
22. Kucha-i-Darwaza-i-Sardar
23. Kucha-i-Wazir
24. Kucha-i-Misgari
25. Kucha-i-Ahingari
26. Pain Chauk
27. Bala Chauk
28. Mandai
29. Mahala-i-Jatan
30. Shor Bazar
31. Char Chata

The principal streets are the two last named, which are the chief bazars of Kabul. The former extends east and west from the Bala Hisar to the Ziarat-i-Baba Khudi, a distance of 3/4 mile. The Char Chata consists of four covered arcades at the western end of Lahori Darwaza street, and is the pride of the inhabitants. It was originally built by Ali Mardan Khans, was destroyed by Pollock in 1842, and restored by Amir Dost Muhammad about the year 1850. Its shops are tenanted by silk mercers, jewellers, furriers, cap and shoemakers, fruiterers, money-changers, etc., whilst beneath the shop-counters are the stalls of cobblers and other handicraftsmen.

The four principal mosques are--

1. Masjid-i-Safed, built by Timur Shah.
2. Madrasa, built for a college by Shah Jahan.
3. Masjid-i-Pul-i-Khishti, built by Shuja-ul-Mulk.
4. Masjid-i-Bala Chauk, built by Babar.

The principal sarais are--

1. Sarai Amir Sher Ali Khan
2. Sarai Zardad
3. Sarai Jabar Khan
4. Sarai Madar-i-Wazir
5. Sarai Muhammad Kumi
6. Sarai Aziz
7. Sarai Mir Waiz
8. Sarai Mir Haji

There are many public baths, the best being--

        1. Hamam-i-Wazir   4. Hamam-i-Pain Chauk
        2. Hamam-i-Nao   5. Hamam-i-Latif.
        3. Hamam-i-Pul-i-Khishti

The Bazaars of Kabul, by Dr. C-J Charpentier.
"Bazaars in contemporary Kabul are numerous and scattered in clusters all over the city, both in Shahr-e Nau and in the old section, the latter part being Kabul's traditional centre of commerce.
"In the old section, which roughly consists of the area between the mountains and the river, shops and workshops are still dominating the streets. In this part of Kabul the old covered bazaar once was located before its destruction in 1842. In those days the bazaar probably comprised the area between Bala Hissar and the corner of Jad-e Maiwand Street and Nadir Pashtoon Street towards Pul-e Khisti having its centre most likely in today's Shor Bazaar.
"Today the principal bazaars follow both sides of Jad-e Maiwand and adjacent streets to the river and the southern part of Murad Khan Quarter. Most of the buildings in this area were erected in the beginning of this century following the construction of new streets. Thus there are hardly any real old commercial houses left in Kabul. Houses in the bazaar area are generally three or four stories high with residential quarters above the shops and closed courtyards in the back.
"The traditional structure can, however, still be observed. Commercial streets are lined with shops with one side open to the street, craftsmen and shopkeepers still tend to operate in specialized clusters although there are hardly any specialized streets left. At the outskirts of the bazaars one finds the more "bulky" trades such as sellers of wood, charcoal, wickerwork, metal junk, etc. as well as wholesale-enterprises, <u>sarays</u> where cars and lorries are repaired, and transport companies.
"Today, selling activities dominate and true traditional craftsmen constitute a decreasing minority. Several crafts have disappeared as a result of modernization and increased import of foreign commodities. Thus there are e.g. hardly any weavers left, specialized blacksmiths and founders are few, potters have moved to the outskirts, likewise many of the remaining tanners; coppersmiths are decreasing in number and many traditional daily artifacts such as woodwork, ropes, hardware, coarse cloth, etc. are brought to town from the provinces.
"Following the extinction of several traditional crafts, new trades have entered the bazaars, mainly tinsmiths (<u>halabi saz</u>), furniture makers, various repair shops (watches, radios, bicycles, cars, electric utensils, etc.), and shops where old materials such as waste metal and tires are recycled.
"Following the Jad-e Maiwand from west to east one finds, among others, sellers of wood, wicker and charcoal in Chandaul; salt, soap and cloth in Bagh-e Umumi; tailors, shoemakers, blacksmiths, clothsellers and furniture makers in Shor Bazaar; and on the Bagh-e Mardan side, finally sellers of household utensils and cloth, coppersmiths, leatherworkers and butchers. At the eastern end of Jad-e Maiwand lie the car repair shops and <u>sarays</u> where lorries are decorated, as well as several <u>mandawis</u> where food stuffs are sold.
"On both sides of the river one finds furmakers and tailors, silversmiths, carpet sellers and tinsmiths, the latter making white metal suitcases and stoves, as well as several <u>sarays</u> where imported commodities are sold. In a special market facing the river moneychangers and bankers, usually of Indian descent, throng together

with large scale merchants.
"Around Pul-e Khisti, knives and scissors from Charikar are sold together with hardware and daily commodities, and in this area there are several engravers and barbers operating outdoors.
"In a triangle from the river to Pashtunistan Square and Muhammad Jan Khan Watt, cloth and modern imported articles and capital goods are sold; in this area there is also a market for second-hand western clothes close to the Khiaban bazaar which was partly torn down after the Saur revolution.
"To conclude, there are probably more than 3,000 shops in old Kabul, the sale of food and cloth dominates.
"In the middle of Shahr-e Nau, bazaar streets have grown during the last decade. Most shops supply the Afghan middle class, resident foreigners and tourists. Antique and curio dealers are numerous as well as sellers of "typical" Afghan-style clothes. The transformation of "Chicken Street" in a few years into a hippie and budget-traveller's haven constitutes a good example of this recent development in Shahr-e Nau.
"But not only salesmen were attracted by the tourist trade in Shahr-e Nau. Several craftsmen opened workshops in this section manufacturing leather bags, belts, shoes, boots postins and clothes. Old residential houses were overnight turned into hotels, tea houses and restaurants.
"The commercialization of Shahr-e Nau reached its peak during the Daoud regime and faced a decline after 1978."
Outside the city are the tombs of Babar and Timur Shah, and there are many shrines and gardens in the neighbourhood.
The burial places are all outside the town, and the principal ones are those of Ziarat-i-Khidari, Ziarat-i-Panja-i-Shah-i-Mardan, Darwaza-i-Shah Shahid; Ashikan-i-Arifan and Darwaza-i-Lahori. The above are Sunni Burial-grounds, the Shiahs having their own separate place of sepulture on the Khwaja Safar and Asmai hills. East of the city, on the slopes of the Tapa-i-Maranjan, Jews are buried and Hindu corpses are burnt. The Armenians have their own walled-in cemetery amongst the Muhammadan graveyards of Khwaja Khidar.
The Muhammadan tombs vary little, except in position, from ordinary Christian ones. They are placed from north to south. They have the same shaped headstone, generally of marble, either of the costly kind imported from eastern countries, or of the native alabaster procured in the quarries of Maidan. The headstone also bears an inscribed epitaph, and is ornamented, if not with faces of angels and cherubs, with sculptured flowers and other fanciful devices. It is no uncommon circumstance among the graves of the Shiah tribes to see shields, swords and lances engraved on the tombs, commemorating the profession of the deceased, a practice observed in various parts of Persia, particularly in Kurdistan.
On the Asmai hill a neglected stone, distinguished by a sculptured mitre, denotes the place of rest of a Georgian bishop, who, it would seem, died at Kabul three or four centuries ago. In the Armenian cemetery, likewise, a mitre on one of the stones points to the rank of the person deposited beneath, although tradition is silent as to him or to his age.
Close to the Ziarat-i-Shahid there stood an English tombstone bearing the inscription in Roman characters: "Here lies the body of Joseph Hicks, son of Thomas Hicks and Edith, who departed this life the eleventh of October 1866." The stone was broken by the Afghans in December 1879, when the British force was shut up in Sherpur.
The Amir's fortified palace, or Arg as it is locally called, is situated in extensive grounds (not less than three quarters of a mile by half a mile in area) north of the city between Alamganj and

Sherpur. It occupied 5 years in building and is from a design prepared entirely by Abdur Rahman himself. Mr. E.H.S. Clarke, a member of Sir Mortimer Durand's mission, 1893, says of it: "The cost of the whole is estimated, apart from the contents of the palace and store-rooms, at twenty lakhs or ruppes. A considerable portion of the grounds is laid out in fuit and flower gardens; part is merely enclosed by an iron garden railing, and part by a wall. There are two gateways--one facing Alamganj, the other facing east towards Siah Sang. Round the walls of the outer enclosure, and facing inwards, are the different Government offices--some twenty or thirty large rooms, all crowded with officials, mirzas and suiters. Bundles of records, neatly tied between boards were seen arranged in racks up to the roof, and it is clear that the work of the State is carried on in a much more methodical manner than one would have supposed. These Government offices are now under the control of Sardar Nasrulla Khan; but their organization is entirely the work of the Amir himself.

"Our carriages drove through the east gate and as we alighted near the moat which surrounds the fortified Arg. The latter is a massive structure about 250 yards square; the width of the ditch from the edge of the roadway to the same level on the fortifications is not less than sixty feet, the actual breadth of the water at the bottom of the ditch being about half as much. The Arg rises to a height of some fifty feet from the bed of the moat, and has three bastions on each face, upon which guns are mounted. The walls are of immense thickness and loop-holed for musketry. At the top, built into the wall, and on the inner side, are store-rooms and the barracks of the Orderly and Shahi regiments which alone garrison the fortress.

"Though the appearance of the Arg from the outside is that of a strongly fortified position, once inside there is little to convey such an impression. Crossing a bridge over the moat (a solid masonry work, not a drawbridge), and passing through the main entrance, which consists of a large domed porch with spiked wooden gates, we entered a garden of old mulberry trees; and proceeding along a pathway for some forty or fifty yards, we found ourselves confronted by the outer wall of yet another enclosure. Turning to the left, we entered this through a handsomely carved and inlaid wooden doorway. This doorway is an unusually fine piece of work: it is made from sheesham and other hard woods of Afghanistan, and is entirely of local labour.

"We now retraced our steps along the outside of this enclosure, until we came to a line of 25 Kabul-made guns, which we examined. Three were of a large bore, probably 32-pounders; the remainder screw-guns (in three pieces) for mountain artillery. Entering a narrow staircase, we next mounted to a room used apparently as a sort of exhibition of arms. It contained every description of gun and rifle from the oldest 'jezail,' fastened to its stock by a piece of raw cow hide, to the latest magazine rifle and sporting express; also swords, daggers, knives, revolvers, pistols, etc. On a table in the centre were the insignia of the G.C.S.I., and the sword presented to the Amir by Lord Dufferin at Rawalpindi; also a diamond-mounted dagger and sheath of great value, with other jewellery.

"From here we strolled to the public Darbar Hall in the outer enclosure. It is a somewhat plain building, the inside measurement of which is 190 feet long, 60 broad, and 30 high. There are probably few halls in India which can boast these dimensions. It is heated by hot air pipes, and the ceiling is supported by two parallel rows of seven pillars. To the left of the entrance are some handsomely furnished reception rooms in two stories. From the

balcony of the upper storey we obtained a good general view of the Arg, which, it may be remarked, is kept in perfect repair."
The present Amir, Habibulla, like his father, shows a remarkable interest in developing on his own account many branches of industry, and the workshops erected by Sir Salter Pyne, are a very striking feature of modern Kabul. These shops are situated on the left bank of the Kabul river, right in the Deh-i-Mozang gorge. The Kabulis work in great numbers in the shops, being taught by the English engineers, who have from time to time been in the service of His Majesty, and by the Hindustani mistris who have been introduced from Lahore and Bengal. Not only is war material produced in the workshops, but various handicrafts are practised there. One body of men do leather work, copying English and Russian boots of various kinds, and making saddles and bridles, belts and cartridge-pouches, portmanteaux and mule trunks. Then there are the workers in wood from those who manage the steam-saws to those who produce beautiful carved work for cabinets and chairs. There are workers in brass who make vases, candelabra, door handles, lamps, and many other things, both useful and ornamental. The most artistic are perhaps the workers in silver. Their work, however, is at present rarely original. The Amir shows them a drawing, or gives them a good English model to copy from. In November 1893, when the officers of Sir Mortimer Durand's mission visited these workshops, every branch of machinery was in motion. Martini-Henry cartridge making was proceeding at a great pace, minting was going on, guns and rifles were being bored, shells cast, the steam hammer was at work on a nine-pounder gun cast in the shop, and the new powerful rolling mill was set in motion. The steam saw mills, boot factory, candle and soap factory, harness and tailoring shops were inspected, and the small steam engine took the British Commissioner and Sipah Salar for a run down to Deh Afghan, a distance of a little under half a mile.
The population of Kabul, according to the census taken by order of Amir Sher Ali in the year 1876, was stated at about 140,000. The official who superintended the census operations, Kazi Abdul Kadir, gave the following as the result:

Duranis	3,000	Kashmiris	3,000
Tajiks	12,000	Saifis	4,000
Ghilzais	2,000	Hindus	4,000
Parachas	3,000	Armenians*	100
Kizilbashis	6,500	Jews*	50
		Kabulis	103,050
		Total	140,700

*It is doubtful whether there are any now (1910) left in Kabul.
The last named division of the population is a race containing probably the elements of each wave of invaders that has passed over the capital since the Indo-Scythian period. Resembling the Tajiks a good deal, and being, like them, Sunni Muhammadans, they are yet classed apart. There are some 20,000 of those Kabulis par excellence to be found outside the town and its suburbs. Away from Kabul, they call themselves Tajiks, and are apparently tolerated in the villages by the latter as inferior and mongrel kinsmen. The Tajiks take their daughters in marriage, but seldom reciprocate in that matter. On the other hand, the Kizilbashis give their daughters in marriage to the Kabulis, who, in their turn, decline to reciprocate with any Shiah tribe. The Kabulis seldom rise to any position of eminence in the State. Some of them are officers in the army, but none have risen to high military rank, and they are chiefly to be found engaged in petty merchandise and as handicraftsmen.

The blacksmiths, carpenters, and shoe-makers of the capital are generally Kabulis, but there are no great merchants among them. They furnish, however, from city and district nearly 2,000 soldiers, and are, taken as a whole, a useful, hard-working section of the community. (The other tribes composing the population are treated of in their own places.)

Kabul was first made the capital of Afghanistan by Timur Shah, and it continued so throughout the whole of the Sadozai dynasty; on their overthrow it remained in the hands of Dost Muhammad, who, gradually increasing his power, was crowned Amir, and since then it has always been considered the capital town of Afghanistan.

It was on the 7th August 1839 that Shah Shuja, escorted by the British, made his state entry into Kabul. Through that year and the next the British troops remained without hindrance.

Lieutenant Durand, of the Engineers, drew up a report soon after the arrival of the force on the defences of the place, which showed clearly that it was essential 'that the garrison should have military possession of the Bala Hisar, that being the proper place for lodging the troops.

This was, however, not done, and the troops were permitted to take up a position in the plain below, an idea of which cannot be better given than in the words of Lieutenant Vincent Eyre:

"To render our position intelligible, it is necessary to describe the cantonment or fortified lines, so called. The credit, however, of having selected the site for the cantonments, or controlled the execution of its works, is not a distinction now likely to be claimed exclusively by any one. But it must always remain a wonder that any government, or any officer, or set of officers, who had either science or experience in the field, should, in a half-conquered country, fix their forces (already inadequate to the services to which they might be called) in so extraordinary and injudicious a military position. Every Engineer Officer who had been consulted since the first occupation of Kabul by our troops, had pointed to the Bala Hisar as the only suitable place for a garrison which was to keep in subjection the city and the surrounding country; but, above all, it was surely the only proper site for the magazine, on which the army's efficiency depended. In defiance, however, of rule and precedent, the position eventually fixed upon for our magazine and cantonments was a piece of low swampy ground, commanded on all sides by hills or forts. It consisted of a low rampart and a narrow ditch in the form of a parallelogram, thrown up along the line of the Kohistan road, 1,000 yards long and 600 broad, with round, flanking bastions at each corner, every one of which was commanded by some fort or hill. To one end of this work was attached a space nearly half as large again, and surrounded by a simple wall. This was called the 'Mission Compound;' half of it was appropriated for the residence of the Envoy, the other half being crowded with buildings, erected without any attempt at regularity, for the accommodation of the officers and assistants of the mission, and the Envoy's body-guard. This large space required in time of siege to be defended, and thus materially weakened the garrison; while its very existence rendered the whole face of the cantonment to which it was annexed, nugatory for purposes of defence. Besides these disadvantages, the lines were a great deal too extended, so that the ramparts could not be properly manned without harassing the garrison. On the eastern side, about a quarter of a mile off, flowed the Kabul river in a direction parallel with the Kohistan road. Between the river and cantonments, about 150 yards from the latter, was a wide canal. General Elphinstone on his arrival in April 1841, perceived at a glance the utter unfitness of the cantonment for purposes of protracted defence, and when a new fort was about to be built for the magazine on the south side, he proposed to purchase for the Government a large portion of the land in the vicinity, with the view of removing some very objectionable enclosures and gardens which offered shelter to our enemy within 200 yards of our ramparts; but his proposal was not sanctioned, nor were his representations on the subject attended with any good result. He lost no time, however, in throwing a bridge over the river, in a direct line between the cantonments and the Siah Sang camp, and in rendering the bridge over the canal passable for guns; which judicious measure shortened the distance for artillery and infantry by at least 2 miles, sparing, too, the necessity which existed previously of moving to and fro by the main road, which was commanded by three or four forts, as well as from the city walls; moreover, the Kabul river being liable to sudden rises and almost always unfordable during the rainy season (March and April), it will easily be understood that the erection of this bridge was a work of much importance. But the most unaccountable oversight of all, and that which may be said to have contributed most largely to our subsequent disasters, was that of having the commissariat stores detached from cantonments, in an old fort which, in an outbreak, would be almost indefensible. Captain Skinner, the Chief Commissariat Officer at the time when this arrangement was made, earnestly solicited from the authorities a place within the cantonment for his tores, but received for answer that no such place could be given him. The Envoy himself pressed this point very urgently, but without avail. At the southwest angle of cantonments was the bazar village surrounded by a low wall, and so crowded with mud huts as to form a perfect maze. Nearly opposite, with only the high road between, was the small fort of Muhammad Sharif, which perfectly commanded our southwest bastion. Attached to this fort was the Shah Bagh, or King's Garden, surrounded by a high wall, and comprising a space of about half a square mile. About 200 yards higher up the road, towards the city was the commissariat fort, the gate of which stood very nearly opposite the entrance of the Shah Bagh. There were various other forts at different points of our works, which will be mentioned in the course of events. On the east, at the distance of about a mile, was a range of low hills dividing us from the Siah Sang camp; and on the west, about the same distance off, was another somewhat higher range, at the northeast flank of which, by the roadside, was the village of Bemaru, commanding a great part of the 'Mission Compound.' In fact, we were so hemmed in on all sides that, when the rebellion became general, the troops could not move out a dozen paces from either gate, without being exposed to the fire of some neighbouring hostile fort garrisoned, too, by marksmen who seldom missed their aim. The country around us was likewise full of impediments to the movements of artillery and cavalry, being in many places flooded, and everywhere closely intersected by deep water cuts."

On the 2nd November 1841 the rebellion broke out and found the British troops occupying the position above described. At first there was some desultory fighting. On the 4th the enemy took possession of Muhammad Sharif's fort and thus effectually prevented any communication between the cantonment and the commissariat fort. They then surrounded this last fort, and drove back three detachments sent from cantonments to the assistance of its garrison with heavy loss. During the night of the 4th it was arranged to try and seize Muhammad Sharif's fort, but on the morning of the 5th, just as a party got ready for the purpose, the garrison of the commissariat fort arrived at cantonments, having evacuated their post. Thus were all the supplies of the garrison lost, there being at that time only two days' rations in the cantonment.

During the 5th an attempt was made to carry Muhammad Sharif's fort, but failed, owing to the officer commanding the infantry not advancing at the proper moment.

On the 6th this fort was carried after a breach had been made, and an attemp to dislodge the enemy from the Shah Bagh, close to it, was defeated with heavy loss. On the 8th the enemy attempted to mine Muhammad Sharif's fort, but failed.

On the 9th General Shelton, who till this had held the Bala Hisar, withdrew there from with his garrison. On the 10th the enemy received some reinforcements from the Ghilzais, and seized the Rika Bashi fort, 400 yards from the northeast angle of the cantonments. A party was then detached under General Shelton to capture it. Captain Bellew blew in the gate, the storming party advanced, and Colonel Mackerell and Lieutenant Bird with a few man got in; but at this moment a party of Afghan cavalry charged round the corner of the fort, and the rest of the party gave way, only being saved from utter destruction by the Gallantry and firmness of General Shelton. Meanwhile the small party who had got in drove the enemy out and shut the gate by which they went, but on the above disaster occurring the enemy came back in overwhelming numbers, and soon killed all but Lieutenant Bird and one sepoy. These two retreated to a stable and closed the door, and there stood at bay keeping up a hot fire for quarter of an hour, when, having then only five cartridges left between them, they were rescued having killed upwards of 30 of the enemy during that time. The rescue was effected by the entrance of General Shelton with a storming party. Our loss was 200 killed, and wounded, but the enemy evacuated all the forts in the neighbourhood, and left 1,400 maunds of grains in our hands. Only half of this, however, was secured, the rest being taken off by the enemy, in consequence of no guard being left in charge of it.

On the 13th the enemy occupied the heights of Bemaru, and a strong force, consisting of 2 guns, 4 squadrons cavalry, and 17 companies infantry, went out to dislodge them. This movement was successful, and the enemy's guns were captured, but we lost two of our best officers—Major Thain and Captain Paton wounded.

This was the last success gained by the British till the end of the siege.

On the 15th Major Pottinger and Lieutenant Haughton came in, having escaped from Charikar.

On the 19the a futile attempt was made to drive the enemy off the height, off Bemaru, which they had occupied.

On the 23rd another force, consisting of one horse artillery gun, 3 squadrons cavalry, and 19 companies infantry, was sent to drive the enemy of the same heights, but they received reinforcements to the extent of about 10,000 men and surrounded the British detachment. The Afghans behaved with gallantry; the British troops do not appear to have emulated them, except in the case of the officers, whose conduct was beyond all praise. After the whole day had been spent in doing nothing, General Shelton, seeing the troops were in bad heart, retired. On this the enemy followed, slaughtering as they went, the British force being saved from utter destruction by a gallant charge of Lieutenants Hardyman and Walker of the cavalry, and the forbearance of the enemy. The British loss was tremendous. After this all heart seemed to go out of the men; several attempts were made to induce the authorities to move out and seize the Bala Hisar, but all were frustrated by objections which can only be accounted for by the proverb Quem Deus vult perdere, prius dementat. On the 27th the enemy proposed terms, which could not be accepted. On the

1st December the enemy made an ineffectual assault on the Bala Hisar, which was gallantly defeated by Major Ewart.

On the 4th December the enemy moved to the Bemaru heights and fired into the cantonment, but without doing much damage, and during the night they tried to carry the gate of Muhammad Sharif's fort.

On the 6th December the garrison of this fort, consisting of one company British and one company Native infantry, fled though scarcely attacked at all.

On the 8th December talk of retreat commenced; the garrison had now 600 wounded and only three days's supplies half-ration.

On the 11th Sir William MacNaghten, accompanied by Captains Lawrence Mackenzie, and Trevor, went out to meet Akbar Khan and certain other chiefs for the purpose of arranging the terms of surrender.

On the 13the the troops in the Bala Hisar evacuated it and came into cantonments.

The next days were spent in negotiations, and Sir William MacNaghten on the 21st December again met Akbar Khan on the plain towards Siah Sang. On the 23rd, Akbar Khan having proposed separate terms to Sir William by which he was to be made Wazir, and troops were to be admitted into Muhammad Khan's fort and to the Bala Hisar, the Envoy again went out to meet him. But a plot had been arranged, and at a given signal the four English officers were seized, and Sir William MacNaghten was shot by Akbar Khan and hacked to pieces immediately, his escort all running away at once.

From this day till the 6th January the negotiations went on, and at last on that morning the garrison, numbering still 4,500 fighting men (of which there were 690 British, 970 Native cavalry, and 2,840 Native infantry) and 12,000 followers, marched out. Their fate is well known: of all that number, Dr. Brydon was the only man who reached Jalalabad, besides 95 prisoners, men, women, and children, who were recovered afterwards.

On the 15th September 1842, General Pollock arrived at Kabul with an army, and took possession of the Bala Hisar without any opposition, and the British forces remained till 12th October, when the city was evacuated.

Previous to the departure of the army, the great bazaar, the Char Chata, was destroyed by gunpowder as a retribution for the murder of Sir William MacNaghten and the indignities offered to his remains on this spot.

After General Pollock's departure from Kabul in 1842 no Englishman ever visited the place until 1879, although a Russian Mission had been received there in the previous year, the last members of which accompanied Amir Sher Ali Khan in his flight from Kabul to Afghan Turkistan in December 1878.

For an account of the operations, etc., in the neighbourhood of Kabul in 1879-80 see the "Official History of the Second Afghan War."

The change in the external aspect of Kabul since its evacuation by the British in 1880 is not so great as might be expected. As stated above, Amir Abdur Rahman had built himself a fine fortified residence before his death and the place can now boast of some other good houses which contrast favourably with the old mud buildings of former days. One or two broad roads lined with rows of trees have been constructed, and one sees a few wheeled vehicles about Kabul, but the roads are still very bad. The various forts built by us during our occupation on the Asmai heights, the Siah Sang, and elsewhere, appear to be carefully kept up and occupied by troops. The Sherpur cantonment is full of troops, and looks just as it did during the war, except that the parapets and portions of the wall are somewhat out of repair. The walled garden called Shah Bagh has been removed. Muhammad Sharif's fort and the remains of the cantonment of 1842 are in the same state as they were 15 years ago. The British cemetery at Sherpur is in fairly good order. It is surrounded by a six-foot wall, and the interior is clean and neat. The place is visited daily by one of the sowars of the British Agency, and the Agent himself visits it from time to time. (Lieutenant Durand, Eyre, Kazi Abdul Kadir, Sir Mortimer Durand, Elles, Clark, I.B.C.)

KABUL (RIVER) كابل دريا

The Kabul river rises in the eastern slopes of the Sanglakh range near the Unai pass, about 45 miles west of the city of Kabul. Under the name of the Unai, or Sar-i-Chashma, stream it flows in an easterly direction for about 12 miles to the village of Jalrez where it is joined from the north by a larger stream known as the Sanglakh Dara and, under the name of the Zaimani, or Manduka stream, continues eastwards for another 10 miles to the village of Kot-i-Ashru. Down to this point the river is followed, almost from its source, by the main Kabul-Herat road. At Kot-i-Ashru it is deflected by the Korogh spur of the Paghman range and flows in a south-southeasterly direction, through what is locally known as the Maidan valley, for about 8 miles to the point where it is crossed by the main Kabul-Kandahar road, just north of the village of Kala Durani. In this section of its course it receives from the west the stream which drains the Nirkh valley. Where crossed by the Kabul-Kandahar road there were, in 1895, the remains of a masonry bridge over the river, and it is believed that this bridge has been recently reconstructed. The river is, however, easily fordable here, there being only about 18 inches of water in April. From this point the river makes a sharp bend and flows northeast, through the Lalandar valley, to the Deh Mozang gorge, just west of Kabul city, where it emerges on to the Kabul plain.

Passing between the city of Kabul and Sherpur it flows eastwards through an open plain for about 15 miles when its bed becomes suddenly contracted into a narrow gorge called the Tangi Gharu. Before entering this gorge its volume has been more than doubled by the junction from the south, at about 6 miles east of Kabul city, of the Logar river. Above this junction the Kabul river may be considered to be fordable anywhere, except during an actual spate; below only at a few places and then only in the cold weather.

On emerging from the Tangi Gharu near the village of Gogamand the river is deflected in a northeasterly direction by a long spur running down from the Safed Koh; rounding this spur it bends again to the southeast and continues in this direction for some 12 miles till it reaches the neighbourhood of Dargai. During this part of its course the river flows for the most part in a narrow bed, the hills, as a rule, coming close down to its banks on either side, but occasionally receding to form small maidans which are in every case richly cultivated.

From Dargai it flows nearly due east for about 20 miles to Jalalabad with the spurs of the Siah Koh running close down to its right bank and the open Laghman plain on the left. From Jalalabad it flows east-southeast in an open valley, to Dakka, shortly after passing which place it crosses the British frontier.

The principal tributaries of the Kabul river are:
Right bank. The Logar, the Tezin, and the Surkhab.
Left bank. The Panjshir, the combined Alingar-Alishang, and the Kunar.
Each of these tributaries form natural roads leading to the mountainous regions at their sources. A description of each will be

found under the article relating thereto.
Bridges. There are five bridges over the river at Kabul itself (see Kabul City). Between Kabul and the British frontier the only bridges are three (one of wood and two of brick) in the Tangi Gharu, a steel suspension bridge at Darunta, and a bridge of boats between Dakka and Lalpura. This last is only maintained in the cold weather. At Pul-i-Charkhi, 9 miles below Kabul, part of an old bridge (stone piers and arches) remains but the river has cut away the alluvial soil on the right bank and the bridge now ends in the air.
Fords and ferries. Below Kabul fords are known to exist at the following points: Dakka, Ali Boghan, Jalalabad, Gondi (16 miles above Jalalabad), Khairo Khel and Sarobi.
There are masak-raft ferries at Ali Boghan, Jalalabad and Kajurai, and a ferry of boats at Dakka which is used when the bridge of boats has been dismantled or washed away. The fords are for the most part only practicable during the cold weather when the river is low. At Khairo Khel the water was found to be up to a man's chin in August 1904. The actual positions of the fords change from year to year, and they should therefore never be attempted without the assistance of a local guide who should be made to cross over first.
With the exception of the ferry between Dakka and Lalpura no boats are to be found on the river west of the British frontier. It may, however, be considered as navigable by boats of light draft, and by rafts as far up as Kats Muhammad Ali, 30 miles above Jalalabad. An efficient service of rafts was organized in July and August 1880 between Jalalabad and Dakka as a supplement to the road transport. (I.B.C.)

KABUL BAI کابل بای
34- 69-. The name given to a collection of villages near Kabul, lying 2 miles east of Sherpur on the left bank of the Kabul river and immediately east of Yakatut.
Kabul Bai comprises the following hamlets:

    (1)   Kala-i-Wazir
    (2)   Kala-i-Zanabat
    (3)   Kala-i-Mustaufi

The inhabitants are all Tajiks. (Kennedy.) Recent maps show the village of Zanabad at 34-31 69-18. (LWA)

*KABULI کابلی
34-55 69-6 m. A village located on a path about halfway between Istalif and Charikar, some 3 miles west of the highway. Another place with this name is located west of the Mukur-Ghazni highway, some 8 miles southwest of Ghazni, at 33-27 68-21 m.

*KABULIAN کابلیان
34-18 70-13 m. A village located near Janbazkhel and southwest of Jalalabad.

KABUL TSAPPAR کابل څپر
34-34 70-56 A. A range of hills forming in part the watershed between the Kunar and Panjkora rivers, and separating the Kunar district from Bajaur and Mohamand country--see "Kunar." Recent maps show the name Bar Tsaparai at 34-33 70-52 m. (LWA)

*KABZAR قبزار
34-3 67-32 m. A village located in the Safidab area, near the Garmab stream in southern Bamian province.

KACHAK کچك
34-44 66-58 G. Two hamlets in the Band-i-Amir valley, 5 miles below Firozbahar. (Maitland.)

*KACHAKHEL کچاخیل
34-36 70-57 m. A village located northwest of Ghundai on a tributary of the Kunar river, southeast of Khas Kunar. Another place with this name is located on a path leading from Ghazni to Nawa-i-Kharwar, about 10 miles west of the latter, at 33-41 68-42 m.

KACHAN کچان
34-44 69-2. Elevation not less than 12,000 feet.
A pass over the Paghman range, crossed by a road leading from Deh-i-Nao, a village near Farza in the Koh Daman, distant 20-1/2 miles from Kabul direct to Siahgird in the Ghorband valley. It appears to be also known as the Kah Dara. It is stated that there are two tracks from the Koh Daman valley to the Kachan Kotal; one up the Shakar Dara, and over a ridge into the Kah Dara; and the other up the Kah Dara itself. The former is passable for laden camels. From what could be seen of the Kah Dara ravine from the kotal (October 1886) it seemed fairly easy. The crest of the kotal is a neck in the actual watershed of the main Paghman range. On the northeast the hills rise to a peak somewhat higher than the kotal and are very rocky, but accessible to infantry. On the southwest, rising close above is the peak of Saiyidan. This too, is rocky and precipitous, but accessible to infantry.
From the Kachan Kotal a most magnificent view is obtained both of the Ghorband valley and of the Koh Daman, and indeed up to Kabul itself, the end of the Wazirabad lake, north of the latter, being plainly visible.
The whole of the descent from the kotal into the Saiyidan Dara may be considered a tough job for any laden animals; but the pathway could be improved without much labour by lengthening the zig-zags. The soil is, as a rule, shingly and easy, though, here and there, there are short rocky bits which would give a little extra trouble. After a mile of descent a pathway joins from the Findukistan Dara on the right, the whole extent of which, up to where it debouches into the Ghorband valley, is visible from this point. The pathway down it is said to be only passable for footmen, but it does not appear to be any worse than the road down the Saiyidan ravine. From Deh-i-Nao to Siahgird the distance is about 28 miles. (Drummond.)
Another place with this name is located at 33-10 69-37 G. (LWA)

*KACHARA کچره
34-22 70-5 m. A village located on the Surkhrud, southwest of Jalalabad, and another at 34-16 70-6 m.

KACH-I See KATS-I کچ (کڅ)

KACHRA کچرا
34- 70-. A village in Laghman, on the left bank of the Alingar river, about 5 miles north of Mandrawar. Inhabitants Ghilzais. The village contains a fort called Kala-i-Tarra Khel. (Warburton.) Other places with this name are located 34-15 70-3 G. and 34-32 70-35 G. (LWA)

KACHU کچو
34- 70-. (Also known as Bazarak, or Rahman Khel.) A village in

the Panjshir valley. It lies on the right bank of the river, 72 miles from Kabul on the Kabul-Khawak-Khanabad road; it contains some 40 families of Tajiks. On the opposite bank near the mouth of the Tulkhah Dara, is the village of Tulkhah, containing about 60 families of Tajiks.

There is a good deal of cultivation near Kachu, and room for troops to encamp on the fields. The glen is here from 600 to 700 yards wide; the hills on either side are not very high, being the ends of spurs running down from the mountains, but those on the left bank are almost inaccessible, even to active infantry; those on the right bank are less steep, and there is a path leading up them, practicable for cavalry. The hills on the right bank are known locally as the Koh-i-Khwaja Khan Sayyid, and those on the left as the Koh-i-Tulkhah. The people in the neighbourhood of Kachu go up the Parandev Dara to pasture in summer.

Supplies locally procurable at Kachu would probably suffice for a battalion of infantry, and 3 squadrons, for one week; if the whole of the valley were laid under contribution 5 or 6 time this amount might be collected.

One mile above Kachu the Parandev Dara joins the Panjshir from the east. (I.B.C.)

*KACHU کچو
34-1 70-30 m. A village located at the source of a stream in the Spin Ghar (Safid Kuh) mountains which runs northeast into the Kabul river.

*KACHUGHU کچوغو
34-0 68-31 m. A village located north of Ghazni and some 12 miles west of Sayyidabad in Maidan province.

KACHUR کچور
34-50 70-18 m. A village in Laghman. Inhabitants Kohistanis. (Warburton.)

KADAB کداب
34-14 70-31 G. A small group of villages, containing some 69 families of Dehgans, in the Jalalabad district, about 21 miles west-southwest of Basawal. (I.B.C.)

KADAKH کدخ
A section of the Jirghai Besud Hazaras. (See Military Report on Hazarajat, Part II.)

*KADALAI کدلی
34-10 68-42 m. A village located north of Langar on a stream in the Wardak area in Maidan province.

*KADAL کدال
34-56 68-21 m. A village located on the Ghorband river, west of Dahan-i-Botian.

*KADALAK کدلک
34-6 67-26 m. A village located near Jiska on a tributary of the Garmab river. Other places with this name are located south of Kadirkhel on a tributary of the Ghorband, at 34-55 68-49 m.; southwest of Ghazni a few miles northwest of Ranakhel in Ghazni province at 33-27 68-8 m.

341

KADAM   قدم (کدم)
   33-22 70-11 m. A village in Khost, 9 miles from Sabari, towards the
   Sterkual Nala. The village contains 40 houses and a large walled
   enclosure, 150 feet square, that could be thrown into a good state
   of defence. (Kennedy.)

*KADAM TANA   کدم تانه
   33-23 70-17 m. A village located near the Pakistan border, east of
   Alisher in Paktia province.

KADIR KHAN   قدیرخان (قادر)
   34- 69-. A small Durani fort in the Yakatut township.

*KADIRKHEL   قدیرخیل
   34-56 68-47 m. A village located north of the Kuh-i-Yakhdara, on a
   tributary of the Ghorband.

*KADIR KHUNE   قادرخونه
   32-29 68-23 m. A village located about halfway between Janihel and
   Wazakhwa in Ghazni province. Other places with this name are located about 15 miles north of Wazakhwa, at 32-23 68-21 m.; and east
   of Janikhel, at 32-45 68-34m.

KAD-I-ROGHANI   قدروغانی
   34- 70-. A village in the Hisarak division of the Jalalabad district. Inhabitants Duranis. (Jenkyns.) Recent maps show the name
   Roghani, at 34-14 70-31 m. (LWA)

*KADIR TANGA   قادرتنگه
   32-34 68-30 m. A village located northwest of the Tor-i-Tangarai
   and about 20 miles south of Zarghun Shahr in Ghazni province.

*KADUL   کدول
   34-4 67-44 m. A village located near Altan at the source of the
   Dara-i-Jelga in Bamian province.

KADULA   کدوله
   34-46 69-3 m. A village in the Koh Daman, 26 miles northeast of
   Kabul. (Masson.) Another village with this name is located north
   of Istalif on a path to Charikar, about 3 miles west of the highway
   in Parwan province, at 34-55 69-6 m. (LWA)

*KAFAK   ققق
   34-33 67-22 m. A village located on a tributary of the Bum-i-Yakhak
   south of the Kuh-i-Baba in Bamian province.

*KAFAR KOT GHAR   کفارکوت غر
   33-42 68-58 m. A mountain located some 6 miles east of Nawa-i-
   Kharwar in Logar province.

*KAFFARI   کفاری
   32-52 68-32 m. A village located some 5 miles east of Zarghun Shahr
   and south of Malakh in Ghazni province.

*KAFILABASHI   قافله باشی
   34-48 67-46 m. A village located on a tributary of the Bamian
   river, about 5 miles southwest of Bamian.

KAFIR   کافر
   33- 68-. A village at the western foot of the Zana Khan pass, on

the road from Kharwar to Chazni, and about 18 miles northeast of the latter place. (I.B.C.)

KAFIRISTAN   Now called NURISTAN   کافرستان (نورستان)

35-30 70-45 A. Kafiristan was conquered by Muslim Afghan forces in 1895-6 and the Kafirs were subsequently converted to Islam. A considerable body of scholarly literature has been published since the following article, see bibliographies, especially by Schyler Jones, and Bucherer-Dietschi. Mr. Ahmad Ysuf Nuristani, Ph.D. candidate at the University of Arizona, read the following entry and made some valuable corrections and comments which are marked with his initials. (LWA)

This region, although it is inhabited by tribes of different origin using different languages, all more or less inimical to one another, and among whom a primitive Pagan (But see also last paragraph of this article.), religion affords no bond of common union, is yet known, and has been known for centuries, by the single title, Kafiristan, which literally means "the land of the infidel." This name, for want of a better, and to prevent confusion, must be still adhered to. Its inhabitants willingly accept the designation of Kafir, although it is a word they cannot properly pronounce. They themselves appear to have no single designation for the whole country, but call different parts of it after the name of the different tribes who inhabit it.

Our reliable knowledge of Kafiristan is so limited that whatever is written here is liable to modification. Before Surgeon-Major Robertson's visit to the country in 1889 and again in 1890-91, no European, with one single exception had every penetrated there. The exception referred to was Colonel Lockhart's mission, which, in September 1885, crossed from Chitral into the upper part of the Bashgul valley, remained there a few days, and then withdrew into Chitral by another road. McNair, it is believed, never entered the real Kafir country at all; he only succeeded in reaching some of the Kalash villages of Chitral, which he mistook for the true Kafiristan. Surgeon-Major Robertson traversed the whole of the Basghul, and many of its subsidiary valleys, from end to end, and crossed from it to the top of the Munjan valley of Badakhshan. He also examined the Kunar valley, and many of its side valleys, from Mirkani to Bailam. Finally, he penetrated into one of the inner valleys of Kafiristan, called Viron or Wiron by Muhammadans, and Presun by the Kafirs. In accomplishing this very limited amount of travel he expended more than a year. Tribal jealousies were so great, and his position was often times so difficult, that it was frequently a question, not of his being able to get on, but of his being able to maintain himself in the country at all; while on one occasion the uncomfortable suggestion was fiercely debated if it would not be advisable for the tribe to keep him a close prisoner for three years, and compel him during that period to send to India for as much money and as many rifles as his proposed custodians should see fit to demand.

Thus it will be understood that the actual extent of country Surgeon-Major Robertson was able to explore was not very great. He is, however, by far our best authority, and the following information has therefore been for the most part taken from a report recently furnished by him.

Boundaries. The geographical position of Kafiristan is all included between latitude 34-31' and latitude 36 and from about longitude 70 to longitude 71-30'. The western frontier being practically unknown and somewhat ill-defined it is difficult to estimate accurately the size of the country. Its greatest extent is from east to west at latitude 35-10', its greatest breadth is probably at longitude 71. Its map area may be put down as somewhere about 5,000 square miles. Its boundaries are the Hindu Kush on the north; the eastern watershed of the Bashgul on the east; the Kunar valley and Afghanistan proper on the south; and on the west the ranges above the Nijrao and Panjshir valleys of Afghanistan. On the north, Surgeon-Major Robertson believes, the Munjan valley of Badakhshan dips down, so to speak, into the heart of Kafiristan. He bases his opinion on native information, and on certain deductions which seem to him not unreasonable.

General description. Kafiristan consists of an irregular series of main valleys, for the most part deep, narrow and tortuous, into which a varying number of still more difficult, narrower, and deeper valleys, ravines, and glens pour their torrents. The hills which separate the main drainage valleys, the one from the other, are all of them of considerable altitude, rugged and toilsome. As a consequence, during the winter, Kafiristan is practically converted into a number of separate communities with no means of intercommunication. Take, for example, the Bashgul valley. During the time the hills are under snow, the only way to reach the Katir people, who inhabit the upper portion of the district, is to travel from the Kunar valley through the territory, first of the Kam and then of the Madugal tribe. Supposing either of these two tribes be at war with the Katirs, the last-named are then completely isolated from the rest of the world, until the passes open in the spring. The inhabitants of Viron, or Presun, (Today non-Nuristanis call this valley Parun and its inhabitants Paruni. The letter "n" in Presun is not pronounced. The Katir and Kam call the valley Prasuzgal and the people Prasuz while the people from Waigal valley call it Pazigal and its people Pazai [AYN]), are similarly cut off from the surrounding tribes, for the only entrance, to their country, when the passes are closed, is up the river which flows into the Kunar at Chigha Sarai. All the passes which lead from Badakhshan into Kafiristan are certainly over 15,000 feet in height. On the Chitral side the roads over the enclosing ranges, although somewhat less elevated, are still very high, and are completely closed by snow in the winter. There is one low ridge, 8,400 feet between the Kalash village of Utzun and the Kafir village of Gourdesh, but even that is impassable for two or three months every winter. Some of the ravines up which regular roads run are of most picturesque and romantic description, others are bare rocky glens.

There would appear to be three main drainage systems; that of the Kao or Alingar, the Pech, and the Bashgul. What I have called the Pech is the river which joins the Kunar just below Chigha Sarai, but both Bellew and Lumsden refer to this river as the Kamah, a very good name inasmuch as it flows from the important Kamah pass (The name Kamah, as applied either to the river or the pass, appears to be quite unknown locally.). Robertson speaks of it as the Presungul as well as the Kamah. All these rivers find their way into the Kabul river, either directly to the south as in the case of the Alingar, or after mingling their waters with those of the Kunar at Birkot and at Chigha Sarai. Of the valleys to the extreme west nothing is known except by hearsay, but it is believed that the Ramgul and Kulam torrents join together to form the Alingar which reaches the Kabul river through Laghman. The next valley to the east, the Kti, joins its waters with those of the Pech valley, and afer receiving the Wai (or Waigal) river, flows into the Kunar at Chigha Sarai. The Ashkun rivers probably also joins the Kti and Pech torrents, before they empty themselves into the Kunar.

(The Ashkun river does not join the Kti and Waigal, but rather runs into the Kulam which become the Alingar river and runs into the Kabul river - AYN). The Bashgul river, with its various tributaries, the largest of which are the Skorigul, the Nichingul, and the Pittigul streams, joins the Kunar just above the Gabar village of Birkot. The rivers, as they descend the corkscrew valleys and are fed by subsidiary streams from the ravines, glens, or mountain recesses, increase in velocity until they become raging torrents, dashing against the huge boulders which obstruct their course, and flinging high their spray with deafening uproar. In many places where the tortured water foams and lashes itself against the rocks on its margins, or in its bed, the river almost assumes the nature of a cataract, and is indescribably beautiful. The trunks encumber the waterway, jam themselves against the rocks, pile up in picturesque confusion, or hurry round and round in the swirl of a backwater. To lovers of wild scenery many parts of Kafiristan could not be surpassed anywhere.

It would not be right to assume that the above description, which chiefly refers to Eastern Kafiristan and the Pech valley, necessarily applies to the western districts; yet it is more than probable that in the varying scenery met with in the Bashgul, the Kunar valley, and in the Pech, we have specimens of the kind of country to be met with in Kafiristan beyond those limits.

Geology. The main ranges are probably of granite, overlaid by various metamorphic strata, such as gneiss, amygdaloid trap and slate with schists and shales, while sandstone and limestone probably constitute the lower ridges. Gold is said to be found in the country, but apparently in no great quantity. Lead is certainly found.

Fauna and flora. Almost every kind of mountain scenery is to be met with, from silent peaks and naked ridges, snowfields and glaciers, to thickly wooded slopes, and wild vine and pomegranate thickets. At the lower elevations the hill sides are well covered with wild olives and evergreen oaks; very many kinds of fruit trees, walnuts, mulberries, apricots, grapes, and apples are met with, while splendid horse-chestnuts and other shady trees afford pleasant resting-places from the sun in the hot months. At somewhat higher elevations, say from 5,000 to 8,000 or 9,000 feet, dense pine and cedar forests abound. They are composed of magnificent trees, which, with a snow background, afford most delightful prospects. Higher still, the pines cease; the hills become almost bare, rocky, shaly, etc.; while the willow, birch, and juniper cedar are the chief trees met with. Higher still--say over 13,000 feet--there is no vegetation of any kind, except rough grasses and mosses. Numerous wild flowers are met with at different altitudes. The rivers teem with fish which, however, no Kafir can be persuaded to eat. Immense numbers of "chikor," the red-legged partridge, as well as pigeons and doves are to be seen, and large numbers of "manal" pheasants. The chief wild animals are the "markhor," the "urial," leopards and bears.

Climate. The climate naturally varies with the altitude, but it is very hot in the summer months at all elevations, and in high valleys the winter is certainly very rigorous. During the winter of 1890-91 at Kamdesh (6,100 feet) there was an excessive amount of snow, but the thermometer never showed a lower temperature than 17 degrees F., below the freezing point. In some of the valleys the absence of wind is quite remarkable, and on this account low temperatures can be borne without discomfort. The rainfall is probably greater than in Chitral, but is insufficient for the requirements of the crops, and has to be supplemented by irrigation.

The following table of meteorological observations is taken from

Surgeon Major Robertson's report:

Date 1981	Place	Temperature (Deg.) 7 AM	3 PM	9 PM	Remarks
Jan. 1,	Charadgul	...	48	31	The Charadgul
Jan. 7,	" "	...	34	43	joins the
Jan. 9,	Birkot	...	...	43	Bashgul 4 mi-
Jan. 17,	Kamdesh	32	38	28	les above the
Jan. 19,	"	17	27	24	latter's mouth.
Jan. 29,	"	18	32	21	
Feb. 1,	Agatsi	35	35	34	
Feb. 9,	"	17	34	25	
Feb. 28,	Kamdesh	34	36	31.5	
Mar. 1,	"	35	47	36	
Mar. 31,	"	50	69	45.5	
Apr. 18,	Birkot	54	81	61.5	
Apr. 30,	Kamdesh	54	69	54	
May 15,	"	61	76.5	...	
May 31,	Badawan	45	65	45	
June 15,	Bragamatal	54	66	56	Camp 11,300 feet
June 30,	Kamdesh	66	83	67	
July 15,	"	76	88	62	
Sept. 5,	"	59	84	71	After thunder
Sept. 30	Diogrom	39	64	50-5	
Oct. 2	Satsumgrom	41	47	41	
Oct. 9	Shtevgrom	31	49	--	
Oct. 21	Kamdesh	48	52	45	

Communications. The main roads of communication, if roads they can be called, are almost invariably along the river-banks, so narrow and so steep are the valleys. Although they vary very greatly, the one from the other, they have this quality in common, that they are almost always extremely difficult. That part of the Bashgul valley above Chabu, as well as nearly the whole of the Presungul, is quite easy when you once get into those districts; but all other known Kafiristan roads are simply abominable. Perhaps the worst of all are those on the left bank of the lower part of the Bashgul river and those in the Dungul valley. There it is rare to find even a couple of hundred yards of moderately level ground and in marching it is one incessant clamber along rough, stony tracks, which run over spurs and bluffs, or by means of frail wooden galleries across the faces of low precipices. Sometimes it is most difficult to get over the smooth rock surfaces; indeed, in some positions, where the ground is of this character, the inexperienced or badly shod traveller may only be able to proceed at all by edging himself along in a sitting posture. Dogs cannot get over these places without assistance.
The bridges over the rivers are sometimes extremely well built, but are high above the water, and often not more than 18 or 20 inches wide in the middle, with parapets only a few inches high, so that the whole structure looks far more like an irrigation trough than a bridge. If this is the case with the good bridges, it may easily be conceived how extremely bad the inferior ones are. Sometimes a broken tree hanging across a narrow stream is utilized as a bridge, and the traveller has to run along the tree-trunk at an angle dependent on the height at which the tree partially broke away from the parent stem. Yet there are pleasant and safe ways over the torrent when compared with certain rickety old bridges which groan and sway under you at every footstep. In many instances the bridges simply

consist of a single pole or two poles placed side by side; it then requires a good head to cross them. The rope or rather twig bridge common in Chitral and Kashmir is never met with. In the Presun country the bridges are remarkably good. They are made on the principle of the dug-out boat from large tree-trunks, and are both easy and safe. They are often elaborately ornamented by the carved heads of animals placed at the end of long poles stuck at intervals along the parapet on both sides. Another point which makes travelling in Kafiristan difficult is the frequent necessity for wading. Some of the wading places are of considerable extent and easy enough, except for the sharp stones in the river bed, which are apt, if you are wading with naked feet, to pain you into a stumble and a ducking; but others are actually dangerous both from the force of the water and from its depth. At all the wading places, particularly during the snow-melting season, the current is strong, and great caution has to be observed.

None of the mountain passes are easy. They must be tackled according to their altitude, the amount of snow upon them, the season of the year the time of day, etc.

No horses can be used in any known part of Kafiristan, except in the upper Bashgul and the Presungul valleys.

Setting aside the route up the Alingar, which doubtless exists, but about which we know nothing, and the mountain tracks known to few and seldom used, there remain the following, of which something more or less definite may be said:

1. From Chitral, viz.:
    (a) Lutkho valley to Ahmad Diwana
    (b) Lutkho valley to Pashui (?Ed.)
    (c) Bomboret by the Shawal pass to Lutdeh
    (d)   "   "Parpit and Manjam passes to Lutdeh
    (e)   "   " Parpit pass to Pittigul
    (f) Utzun by the Patkun pass to Gourdesh

2. From the Kunar valley:--
    (a) The Bashgul--an "easy" road. (According to recent reports the Amir's new road up the Kunar has reached the mouth of the Bashgul, whence it has been continued as far as Kamdesh limits.)
    (b) The Dungul (q.v.)--difficult.
    (c) The Pech.

Between these main roads are many others, which are fit only for herdsmen and sportsmen.

3. From Badakhshan:
    (a) The Mandal
    (b) The Kamah
    (c) A road leading straight from Munjan over a pass into the Kti valley.
    (d) A road going west from Munjan, and over a pass into the Ramgul country.
    (e) A road west from Munjan into the Kulam valley.

The last three unnamed passes are all said to be higher than the Kamah (15,500 feet) and more difficult. There is said to be a road, between the Khawak and Dorah, in the "Khilti" country; and between it and the Khawak, but nearer to the latter, is another pass, locally known as the Nimcha Dur.

4. From the Panjshir glen:
    (a) By the Parian and Chamar glens

    (b) From Chahardeh of Parian by the Wariaj and Arioh glens.
    (c) By the Rewat Dara
    (d) By the Darkhinj Dara.

Also there must be tracks leading from the Tagao valley.
Besides the above routes into Kafiristan, the following are the most important roads in the country itself:

  1. From the Bashgul (q.v.):
    (a) The Skorigul   (d) The Oulagul
    (b) The Manjam   (e) The Nichingul
    (c) The Baprokgul   (f) The Kamu.

  2. From the Dungul valley there are difficult hill paths to the west which lead into the Wai country.

  3. From Presungul (Pech):
    (a) Valleys leading to the Wai country
    (b) A valley near Shtevgrom which gives access to the Kti valley and also to the Ramgul.

Of the routes with which we are best acquainted, perhaps the most interesting is that form the Munjan valley over the Kamu pass, and along the course of the Pech river. This route is certainly practicable for mules and yabus, and is much used by traders from Badakhshan.

Villages, etc. Kafir villages are built in various ways according as they are liable to attack by a numerous enemy or by small raiding detachments. The fort village is peculiar to the Kafirs. These villages are built in an oblong figure, the houses two or three stories high, surrounding a centre courtyard which is partially occupied by a dancing place and rude altar, while the dancing house, or gromma, which is used in bad weather, is close by. There is usually only one entrance gate, which is capable of being quickly and effectively closed. The villages are, as a rule, built on the bank of a river, and when besieged the inhabitants obtain their water from the river by means of a tunnel which leads to the river edge, and ends in a covered way made of timbers. The houses which form the four sides of the oblong figure have low cellars underneath them, into which the cattle are driven when an attack is imminent. The corners of the villages are strengthened by towers, and in some instances one or two detached three-storied towers are built up the hill side as an additional security. All the villages appear to be greatly overcrowded.

The simplest form of house consists of one apartment, measuring some 18' x 18', and is usually well built of timber and rubble stones embedded in mud mortar. They have flat roofs, made of boards covered with beaten down earth, and not even moderately watertight. The better class of house consists of three storeys, the top floor being the living place, the middle storey being the store room, while the bottom floor serves as a cow stable or wood store. Many of these houses are much embellished by carving and elaborate decorations in wood.

The houses of the Presungulis differ in many respects from those described above, the most obvious and striking peculiarity arising from the fact that their accommodation is principally underground.

The "Nirmali" house or lying-in hospital and women's periodic retreat, is a building peculiar to all Kafir villages. It is always placed on the outskirts of a village, and sometimes is outside altogether. It has no windows, and is a squalid looking place, blackened by smoke and disfigured by having two or three abominable sheepskins fastened to a pole and stuck on the roof.

Another class of buildings is the "pshal." The word pshal means a stable, but it is used to designate a dairy farm and grazing ground, as well as the buildings in which the herdsman confines his flock and watches them by night.

As regards household appliances it may be mentioned that large wooden tubs are to be seen in most well-to-do-houses; the bedstead is similar to the "charpoy" of India; the tables are small and as a rule not more than a foot high; while the stools for which the country is famous, are usually about 9 inches from the ground, with a square top. The large oblong box called the "sheni," besides being used as a coffin, is also employed as a receptacle for the storage of grain and other property. Clumsy long handled cups are used for skimming pots; wine is handed round in shallow bowls made of tin or walnut wood; flour and grain are carried about in shallow wicker baskets. Cooking vessels are either made of clay or of a peculiar soft stone obtained in various parts of the country.

Origin and history of the Kafirs. The next point for consideration regarding this strange and interesting people is their origin and history.

Some authorities trace back the Kafirs to the Arab tribe of Koresh others find a connection between some of their customs and the Gabars of Persia; and some do not hesitate to suppose that they are the descendants of the Greek soldiers of Alexander. Lumsden is of opinion that they are neither more nor less than the aborigines of the plain country driven into the mountains they now occupy by fanatical professors of Islam. As will be noticed hereafter, their language bears no affinity to Arabic, or Persian or Turkish, but to Sankrit.

Biddulph supports Lumsden's view. He says:

"The Siahposh traditions, however, point to their having been driven into their present narrow limits from a much wider extent of country than they now occupy, and they say that the art of writing was once known among them. There seems to be no doubt that the Kalash tribe of the Siahposh once occupied the south part of the Kashkar valley about Asmar, and the upper part as far as the junction of the Mulkho valley."

Bellew studies the subject with his usual critical care, and he too came to the conclusion that the Kafirs are but a remnant of a people who once occupied a far greater area than that which they now hold. In fact, both he and Biddulph incline to the view that the Kafirs are, after all, but an unconverted branch of what may be broadly called the Dard race. He identifies them more particularly with the Gandhari, that is to say, the former inhabitants of what is now known as the Mohmand country.

Lastly, we have the result of Robertson's enquiries on this subject: He says:

"It seems probable that eventually the view will be accepted that, to speak broadly, the present dominant races of Kafiristan, the Katirs, the Kam, and the Wai, are mainly descended from the old Indian population of Eastern Afghanistan who refused to embrace Islam in the tenth century, and fled for refuge from the victorious Moslems to the hilly countries of Kafiristan. There they probable found other races already settled, whom they vanquished, drove away, or enslaved, or with whom they amalgamated.

"It is possible that part of the present slave population, also the Jazhis and the Aroms, are remnants of these ancient peoples, while the Presuns are probably also a more or less aboriginal race, who either successfully resisted the new comers, or were driven from more fertile regions and milder altitudes to their present valley.

"As there are no rock inscriptions, no ancient books, nor any literature of any kind to be found in Kafiristan, and as the tradition of the people themselves give such small help in forming any opinion regarding their origin, the only hope which remains that the Kafirs may be eventually assigned their proper place in the general history of the world is from a comparative study of their language, their manners and customs, and their religious ceremonies, as well as from their cranial measurements, and other anthropometric observations. That they are made up of different races appears certain; that they have no admixture of Tartar blood sems obvious; that they came from the west, at least the great majority of them, is their own fixed idea, and is more than probable."

The first notice of the Kafirs is in 1339, when Timur Lang being in Andarab, the inhabitants complained to him that they were grievously oppressed by the Siahposh.

It was asserted by the complainants that the Saihposh extorted excessive sums of money from them, calling it a tribute and kharaj, and in default of payment killed their men and caried off their women and children. Timur Lang selecting nearly a third part of his army (or three out of every ten soldiers), marched against the Siahposh. He reached Perjan (Parian), said to be a town of Badakhshan, two days from Andarab, whence he detached a large force to the left, or north, while he proceeded himself to Khawak, where, finding a demolished fortress, he ordered it to be rebuilt. From Khawak, Taimur made the ascent of the mountains of Katur; and this notice would seem to imply that the country to the east of Panjshir was at that time called Katur or Katawar. The passage was difficult, from snow, but when the army had surmounted it, they descended upon a river, that of Najil, where there was a fortress on the western bank. This was abandoned by the Siahposh, who crossed the river and occupied the summit of a high hill.

The infidels are described as "strong men, and as large as the giants of Aad. They go all naked; their kings are named Oda and Odashush. They have a particular language, which is neither Persian, nor Turkish, nor Indian and know no other than this." Timur passed the river and attacked the Siahposh position, which, defended with singular obstinacy, was at length carried. The males of the infidels, whose souls are said to have been more black than their garments, were put to the sword; their women and children were carried away.

Timur ordered the history of this action to be engraved upon marble. It happened in the month of Ramazan, in the year of the Hijra 800 (June 1398), and he added the particular epochs which this people used, that their posterity might have some knowledge of the famous pillar of the ever-victorious Timur. This pillar so inscribed gave the greater pleasure to the Emperor, in that these people had never been conquered by any prince in the world — not even by Alexander the Great.

The large detachment sent by Timur to the left met with signal disgrace and discomfiture. It is pretended that a reinforcement partly retrieved it, but it is clear that the success of the Emperor himself was rather equivocal, and whithout attempting to maintain a position in the country of the warlike infidels he hastily returned to Andarab and rejoined the rest of his army.

From this time it appears to have been the practice of the Muhammadan princes of Turkistan occasionally to make inroads upon the Siahposh, not so much with the view of reducing them, as of gaining for themselves a reuputation, and of meriting the ilustrious title of Ghazi, or Champion of the Faith. History notes many such crusades as that of Sultan Muhammad Mirza of Bokhara in 1453 A.D., who won the honourable title, whatever may have been the fortune of his arms. It has, however, occurred that combinations of Muhammadans princes have been made against the independence of the Siahposh, and that armies from different quarters have entered their country. But these have been invariably repulsed, unable to overcome its natural obstacles, and the gallantry of the mountaineers who defended it.

The celebrated Babar in his Memoirs repeatedly mentions the Siahposh under the designation of Kafirs; yet, as his notices are incidental, they impart no light upon their history, religion, or other important points connected with them; still, they are extremely interesting, both as concerns them on minor details and the neighbouring contries and people to the south, the activity of the observant prince having led him to make frequent excursions amongst the latter. The lapse of a century and a quarter had brought about no change in the nature of the relations between the Siahposh and the people of Panjshir and Andarab, whose ancestors had claimed Amir Timur's protection. Babar, describing Panjshir, notes:—

"It lies upon the road, and is in the immediate vicinity of Kafiristan. The inroads of the robbers of Kafiristan are made through Panjshir. In consequence of their vicinity to the Kafirs - the inhabitants of this district are happy to pay them a fixed contribution. Since I last invaded Hindustan, and subdued it (in 1527), the Kafirs have descended into Panjshir, and returned after slaying a great number of people and committing extensive damages."

Babar had previously noted that in 1514 A.D., the year in which he took Chigha Sarai, "the Kafirs of Pech came to their assistance;" and adds, "So prevalent is the use of wine among them that every Kafir has a khig or leathern bottle of wine, about his neck. They drink wine instead of water." At an earlier period, in 1507 A.D., he had led a plundering expedition against their rice fields in the valley of "Birain," which he thus describes:

"Some persons who were thoroughly acquainted with every part of the country informed us that up the river of Alishang the Kafirs sow great quantities of rice, and that probably the troops might there be able to lay in their winter's corn. Leaving the dale of Ningrahar, therefore, and pushing speedily forwards, we passed Saigal and advanced up the valley of Birain. The troops seized a great quantity of rice. The rice-fields were at the bottom of the hills. The inhabitants in general fled and escaped, but a few Kafirs were killed. They had posted some men in a breast-work, on a commanding eminence in the valley of Birain. When the Kafirs fled, this party descended rapidly from the hill, and began to annoy us with arrows. We stayed one night in the Kafirs' rice-field, where we took a great quantity of grain and then returned to camp."

Here is the narration of a cool exploit; yet Babar nowhere speaks of the Kafirs whith particular ill-feeling, or discovers the slightest ambition to win, at their expense, the title of Ghazni, of which Amir Timur had been so proud. Their jovial habits, so much in keeping with his own, may have somewhat prepossessed him in their favour. In 1520 A.D., he mentions having sent from Badrane (in the present Tagao) one Haldar Alamdar to the Kafirs. This man on his return met him below the pass of Badi (the present Badpakht) and was "accompanied by some of their chiefs, who brought with then a few skins of wine." The present probably explains the nature of the mission.

It is singular that Marco Polo, who, if the statement transmitted to us in the twenty-fifth chapter of his first book, as given by Marsden, be implicitly credited, resided for a year in Balashan or Badakhshan, should not have particularly noticed so interesting a people as the Kafirs.

In 1603 A.D., Benedict Goez, a Jesuit, crossed the Hindu Kush by the

Bajgah pass to Andarab. He heard of the Siahposh tribes, and being told that they were not Muhammadans, and that they drank wine and arrayed them selves in black, inferred that they were Christians. The fanciful notions of the zealous missionary are not more ludicrous than those of later Europeans, who have imagined them to be Arabs.

In the reign of the Emperor Jahanagir, we find the Afghans taking their wives and children prisoners, and at the same time remark that the infidels of Dara Lamghan, Dara-i-Pech, Dara Kunar, belonging to Kabul and Jalalabad, together with Talash, Panjkora, Chamla, Buner, Damtawar, Pakli, and other places, dependencies of Peshwar and Langarkot, were in this manner made converts of Islam. (The foregoing sketch of Kafir history has been taken from Barrow's "Gazetteer of the Eastern Hindu Kush.")

Physique and appearance. The physique of the Kafirs is magnificent of its kind. They are light built men, who almost always seem to be in hard training. Fat men are unknown altogether. Very few of the older men in Kafiristan are even what might be called stout. Their average height is between five feet, five and a half, and five feet six. As a rule, the men of medium height are not only the most active, the fastest runners, the most enduring travellers, but generally the most physically powerful also. The women, with some few exceptions, are of low stature. Very many are weakly looking, yet their powers of endurance are simply marvellous. They often make extememly long marches, carrying loads.

Speaking generally, the Kafirs are by no means fair, although they are equally removed from the black races. They are darker than many Badakshis and Chitralis. Their colour is that of the average inhabitant of the Punjab. The lower classes and slaves are of much darker in tint than their betters; their features also are coarser. Red-haired people or those of a more or less albino tint, are less than one percent of the total population The usual type of feature is distinctly good--purely Aryan. The nose in particular is extremely well shaped. The degraded kinds are either the bird of-prey type, or, as in many of the slaves, a flattish nose and coarse features. In some of these lower forms, the hair of the scalp reaches nearly down to the eyebrows, and gives its possessor a most forbidding appearance. Amongst the more important families, some of the men have singularly well-formed heads, and look as if, under favourable conditions, they might become statesmen, philosophers, or scientific men. The chief drawback to the more intelligent faces is the furtive, stealthy look they sometimes have which is suggestive of shiftness and insincerity; but the majority are sufficiently frank and bold looking in their own country. The women are for the most part singularly unlovely. Little girls are often quite pretty, but the hard field-work and the exposure to all weather the women undergo, makes their complexions rough and dark. They are often also appallingly dirty.

The appearance of both men and women is frequently spoilt by small-pox and its results, and by a terrible ulceration, which eats away the bridge of the nose, the cheeks, or the lower eyelids; also in the Bashgul valley, by goitre, which seems ot be almost exclusively confined to women.

Kafirs have little or no medical knowledge. Firing is their remedy for pains of every kind, while wounds and sores are treated by being packed up tightly in dirty fragments of half cured goat-skins.

Kafir character. The most striking mental peculiarities of Kafirs are their extreme cupidity, their extraordinary jealousy of one another, and the intensity of their inter-tribal hatred. Their cupidity is, indeed, a marvellous sight to witness. A Kafir will come into your house, or tent, sit down on a chair, or stool, and talk quietly until he begins to cast his eyes round the place. You may then notice in many cases the man's eyes half close, his face flush, and his whole demeanour become an extraordinary example of extreme covetousness. Their inter-tribal hatred is so intense that a tribe is always ready to beg the help of its most inveterate Muhammadan enemy and introduce him into its territory in order to aid in the chastisement of some other Kafir tribe.

There is nothing like religious intolerance among the Kafirs. At the foot of the Kamdesh hill there are two hamlets, one to the north called Agatsi, the other to the west called Agaru. These tiny settlements are peopled by Kafirs hwo have changed their religion to Muhammadanism. Their family connections amongst the kafirs would be just as ready to avenge the killing of one of these renegades as they would be to avenge the blood of a co-religionist of their own family. It is blood and race that the Kafir clings to; about religion he is comparatively indifferent.

The Kafirs are by no means simple in character; they can intrigue, concoct secret plots, and then carry them out with the secrecy and subtlety of the average Oriental.

They are boastful, and their want of veracity is most marked, for they, like so many other wild people, evidently hold the belief that telling the truth, merely because it is the truth, must necessarily be harmful to them. It is as natural for a Kafir to thieve as it is for him to eat; while the mere killing of an individual is looked upon as a small affair, provided that he does no belong to the tribe or to another tribe with which it is at peace. Adultery and fornication are looked upon as natural acts, and any one caught in adultery and compelled to pay the customary penalty is merely considered unlucky and a subject for laughter.

On the other hand, the Kafir is kind to all children, extremely sociable, wonderfully brave, has a great sense of personal dignity, and in spite of his avarice, is most hospitable.

In the Kafir's opinion, a "good" man must possess the following attributes: he must be a successful homicide, a good hill man, ever ready to quarrel and of an amourous disposition. If he is also a good dancer, a good shot with bow and arrows or matchlock, so much the better. These qualities constitute a fine man, but to be really influential in the tribe, an individual must also be rich.

Language. "As regards the language or dialect spoken by the Siahposh, there can be no doubt," says Masson, "but that they have one which, as Sharifudin has recorded, is neither exactly Persian, nor Turki, nor Hindi. It is remarkable that on the southwestern and southern borders of the Siahposh country, or in those points where it connects with the actual limits of the Kabul and Jalalabad territories, there ar four distinct dialects spoken independenty of the more prevailing ones of Persian, Afghani, Turki, and Hindi. The dialects in question are called Parancheh (Parachi?), Pashai, Laghmani, and Kohistani. It is said, and with every appearance of probability, that these several people are able to hold converse with Siahposh.

"On a comparison of their dialects, although they by no means coincide there is sufficient similarily to authorize the assumption of their affinity and the conjecture that they are the remains of some old language, once general in this country, before the introduction of Persian, Arabic, and Turki, and that they have a close resemblance to that spoken by the Siahposh."

Dr. Trumpp considers the Kafir language "a pure Prakrit dialect, separated form its sister dialects since the eruption of Muhammadan power in the 10th century of our era," and , as such, he considers

it of the greatest importance to Indian philology.
Lumsden also thinks that the Kafir language is evidently of Sanskrit root, and Elphinstone says:
"There are several languages among the Kafirs, but they have all many words in common, and all have a near connection with the Sanskrit. They have all one peculiarity, which is, that they count by scores, instead of hundreds, that their thousand (which they call by a Persian and Pushtu name) consists of 400, or 200 score."
Robertson alludes to this subject as follows:
"In Kafiristan proper there are certainly three entirely distinct languages besides many dialects. The language spoken by the greatest number is that used by the Siahposh people, so called because they affect dark-coloured, nearly black, clothing. All the Siahposh, however, are not of the same tribe; but although there are dialectic differences in the languages used amongst them, yet they all understand one another readily, and their language may consequently be called Siahposh tongue, a definition which, if not absolutely correct, is at least convenient. The other chief languages in Kafiristan are those spoken by the Wai and by the Presun people, which differ both from one another, and from the language spoken by the Siahposh. On this point many Bashgul Kafirs have assured me that many of their number who go to the Was valley young enough, can easily learn the speech of that people, while no one under any circustances, and no matter how young, can ever learn the Presun language."
Tribal divisions. Kafiristan at the present day is divided among certain tribes who differ from one another in language, dress, manners and customs. Indeed, the only connexion which they have one with another is in the fact that the greater number are non-Muhammadan. Even this peculiarity is gradually disappearing under the spread of Islam.
The old division of Kafiristan into the districts held by the Siahposh, and that inhabited by the Safedposh, was more convenient than scientifically correct. The Siahposh, or black-robed Kafirs, are made up of several different tribes some of which have been at war with one another from time immemorial, but they appear in spite of this fact to have a good deal more in common than merly a resemblance in dress. As above mentioned - they do not all speak the same language, but the difference seems to be more a difference of dialect than a radical distinction of language. However, if this is true of the Siahposh, it is far different when we come to consider the so-called Safedposh, or white-robed Kafirs. Among these tribes, of which two stand out as of chief importance, the Wai and the Presun, there is no similarity in dress appearance, or language; they cannot converse without the aid of interpreters. Indeed the Wai and Presuns (Virons.) are most dissimilar form one another than they are from the Siahposh.
A convenient classification would be to divide all Kafirs into (1) Siahposh; (2) Waigulis (3) Presungulis. There is another important tribe called the Ashkun, of whom very little is known. They are probably allied to the Waigulis. Although the classification given above might be found very convenient, it is necessary to aim at more exactitude by enumerating all the tribes by their local names. But as every valley in Kafiristan has more than one designation, so every tribe is spoken of in a particular way by different people. The names given below are those heard by Robertson in the Bashgul valley or in Chitral:

(1) Katirs
(2) Madugal

(3) Kashtan or Kashtoz   All Siahposh
(4) Kam
(5) Istrat or Gourdesh
(6) Presun, or Viron
(7) Wai
(8) Ashkun

It is probable that numerically considered the Katirs are more important than all the remaining tribes of Kafiristan put together. They inhabit various valleys as Siaposh communities entirely independent of one another, but acknowledging a common origin and a general relationship each to the other.
They are divided into the following groups:

(a) The Katirs of the Bashgul valley, also called Kamoz and Lutdehchis. This people inhabit the Bashgul from Ahmad Diwana down to Sunra on the Madugal border: 12 villages. (There are now more than 12 villages. [AYN])
(b) The Kati or Karwar, a small section who live in the Kati valley, 2 villages.
(c) The Kulam, living in the Kulam country: 4 villages.
(d) The Ramgulis or Gabariks, the most numerous section among the Katirs. They live in the most western part of Kafiristan, and probably inhabit several side tracts besides the main valley from which they take their name: 24 villages.

Of the other Saihposh tribes, the chief is the Kam, inhabiting the Bashgul and its lateral valleys from the Madugal country to the Kunar valley. The villages are: Umir, Kambrom, Kamdesh, Mergrom, Kamu, Sarat, Pittigul, and Bazgul.
The Muman or Madugal come next in general and numerical importance. They occupy the short tract of country between the Kam and the Katirs of the Bashgul. They possess Bagalgrom or Muman, Sasku, Mungul, and a few hamlets.
The Kashtan tribe, with the exception of one or two little settlements, are all located in the village of Kashtan.
Lastly, there is a little colony of Siahposh Kafirs at Gourdesh, who are said to be very different people from all other Siahposhis.
We now come to the Presun, Wai and Ashkun tribes.
The former, also called Viron by their Muhammadan neighbours, inhabit the Presungul. They are remarkable for their more peaceful disposition, and their inefficiency as fighting men. They are a simple people, very industrious, and, with few exceptions, meek and poor-spirited. Their principle villages are: Shtevgrom, Prontzgrom, Diogrom, Kstigigrom, Satsumgrom, Pashkigrom.
The Waigulis have 10 villages in the valley which gives them their name : Runchi, Nizhai, Jamma, Amzhi, Chimion, Kegili, Akun or Akum, Mildesh, Bargul, and Pranita. (According to Ahmad Yusuf Nuristani, these places should be called Runchigul, Nishigram, Jamech, Ameshdesh, Akun, Kegul. Chimion, Akun or Akum are names of the same village. Bargul and Pranita should be Bergali and Panita and are both together called Waigal; they were two villages on both sides of the river which have merged into one. The natives call the upper village Waramdesh and the people are called Panita. The lower village is called Baramdesh and the people are called Bergali. LWA) They are a brave, high-spirited race, remarkable for their hospitality, and for their proneness to quarrel.
Of the Ashkun the small total of our information amounts to this: that they speak a language similar to the Waigulis; that their country is separated from the Kulam valley by a range of mountains;

and that they have two large villages, one on a river which flows into the Kti, the other (Muhammadan) on the bank of a torrent which falls directly into the right bank of the Pech. (According to Ahmed Yusuf Nuristani, the entry on Ashkun is totally incorrect. LWA)

The slave population, as previously stated, are probably the remnant of an ancient people subjugated and enslaved by the present dominant tribe. There is very little traffic in slaves. Female children of slave parents are sold and sent away to neighbouring Muhammadan tribes. The slave population is very limited in number, and as it comprises all the artificers of the village, it would be inconvenient to the tribe if such men were always liable to be sold. Nevertheless, it is believed that the community lays no claim to a common property in the slaves; they all belong to their respective masters, to be sold or retained as each thinks best.

The above account of Kafir tribal divisions has been taken entirely from Robertson's report. To it may be added the following remarks by Biddulph:

"As far as can be ascertained, they are separable into three main tribes conforming to the natural divisions of the country. These are--(1) the Ramgalis or Lamgalis (Laghmanis?), who inhabit the upper parts of the valleys which run down from the Hindu Kush in a southwesterly direction, where they come into contact with the Afghans of Kabul. This tribe also extends, apparently, to the north side of the mountains. The people of Laghman are probably of this stock converted to Islam in comparatively recent times; (2) the Waigalis, who inhabit the valleys extending southeast from the Hindu Kush, which join the Kunar valley at Chigha Sarai; and (3) the Bashgalis, who inhabit the valleys extending from further north in a south-southeasterly direction, and joining the Kunar valley at Birkot. These, again, are subdivided into smaller clans, of which the Waigalis alone furnish eighteen. In the Dara-i-Nur and other valleys joining that of Kunar from the north below Chigha Sarai are portions of the Waigali tribe who have been recently converted to Islam. Many of these still retain the distinctive black garments.

"Besides these main tribes there are several broken or detached clans, such as the Kalashis, who are subject to Chitral, but are claimed by the Bashgalis as their slaves, and the Kittigalis, or Wirigalis, a small tribe who dwell either on the north side of the Hindu Kush, or in the northern-most part of the Wai country on the south side. This last clan is called Safed-posh from their wearing white garments, and the race is said to be very small.

"The principal tribe of the Bashgali country is divided into Kamoz (Upper Kam) and Kamtoz (Lower Kam) (the lower part is Kamoz, the upper is Kantoz. AYN). The Siahposh employ these names amongst themselves when speaking of a tribe as the people inhabiting such and such a country, and employ the clan names when closer specification is necessary, but there is no recognised term known amongst them to distinguish the Kafirs collectively."

Population. The total population of Kafiristan is probably not over 60,000 souls, excluding all Kafirs who have turned Muhammadans and live on the fringes of the country. A rough estimate by Robertson is as under:

```
    Bashgul valley         20,000
    Presun     "            5,000
    Kti        "            1,000
    Kulam      "            3,000
    Ramgul     "           18,000
    Wai        "            5,500
                Total      52,500
```

He had no means of estimating the numbers of the Ashkun tribe.
Internal organization of the tribes. Although the Ramgul, the Kulam, the Kti, and the Katirs of the Bashgul valley, have all been considered as belonging to one great tribe--the Katir, yet each of these divisions is to all intents and purposes a separate tribe. These tribes are again split up into families or clans, and the individual importance of any single Kafir depends entirely on the numerical strength of the clan he belongs to, and upon his position in that clan. The chief clans of the Kam are--

    Utahdari   Waidari
    Demidari   Lanandari
    Garakdari   Kanardari
    Sukdari   Gutkechdari
    Bilezhedari   Batardari

And those of the Bashgul Katirs are--

    Jannahdari   Mutadawadari
    Barmedari   Charedari
    Shakldari   Shtukdari
        Sowadari

Of the subdivisions of the other tribes we have no information.
The affairs of a tribe are nominally arranged by the consultation together of the headmen, who are called "jast," but as a matter of fact, in ordinary times the business of a tribe falls very much into the hands of four or five grey-beards, who are distinguished beyond their fellows for sagacity, or valour, but who must also be the possessors of considerable wealth. Indeed, the importance of worldy possessions is very strongly, perhaps too strongly, recognised in Kafiristan. A man may be brave, devoted, and sagacious; he may have spent the whole of his flocks and herds and other property in becoming a "jast;" he may also be of good family; yet, if he be not possessed of considerable personal wealth, his weight in the tribal council is comparatively small, except in the case of an orator, when, to a certain extent, he may atone by fervid speeches for lack of wealth.
A man can only become a "jast," by going through a prescribed ceremony which lasts nearly three years with the Kam tribe; amongst the Katirs its duration is somewhat shorter. During that period he has to banquet the whole of his tribe on eleven different occasions, and entertain his brother "jasts" with ten separate feasts. He has to do this in conjunction with a woman who may or may not be his wife. She generally is not, for the expense of two people going through the ceremony at the same time is so great that none but the richest families can afford it. The usual plan is for the husbands to make a private arrangement among themselves, by which the wife of one man goes through the ceremonies with another individual, whose wife in her turn will reciprocate by distributing food in conjunction with the husband of the first woman. The woman's sole reward seems to be that she is permitted to attend one or two particular dances, and has also the privilege of wearing "markhor" hair round the tops of her dancing-boots. The man, on the other hand, becomes an exalted personage, one of the great men of the tribe. The complete ceremonies for becoming a "jast" are elaborate and complicated. They would be tedious to read in detail. In the depth of winter the man grows a miniature field of wheat in his won living room, and this is remarkable amongst the Kam tribe as the only occasion on which a man interests himself or actually works in

agricultural pursuits. He has also to wear a particular uniform on appropriate occasions, to make certain sacrifices, appear at the prescribed dances, sleep out at particular shrines, and for one period consisting of several weeks is never permitted to leave his village. It is a very curious custom that, although once a "jast," always a "jast," yet a very wealthy man is practically compelled by public opinion to keep on going through this ceremony again and again, or else he must make his sons and nephews, however young, headmen one after another. Unless he does this he is certain to fail in maintaining his influence and popularity with his fellow-tribesmen. Sumptuary laws are very stringent. No one but a "jast" would dream of wearing a bright-coloured robe at religious dances, nor a gaudy Oriental turban, unless in the case of a well-known warrior of good family, who might be invited to join the dance to complete the number of performers, in which case he also would be decorated something after the fashion of the others.

There is a sort of inner circle amongst the "jast," who, by further banquetings, are allowed what is considered the nearly royal privilege of seating themselves on four-legged stools outside a house. In the Kam tribe there were only five men and one woman entitled to this exclusive privilege. Anybody--men, women, children, slaves--may sit on these stools indoors, or on ordinary wooden benches outside, but to be permitted to sit on these queer little four-legged stools in the open air is only allowable to such as are considered "Mirs" in the tribe, although their royal function begins and ends with the four-legged stool.

The Ur Jast is an official elected annually, who holds an important position in the tribe.

To recapitulate, a Kafir clan, such as the Kam, is composed of the following social grades:

(1) The Mirs and the Priest.
(2) The "Jast" and the "Ur Jast." } All members of the same class
(3) Members of important clans.
(4) Members of very small clans or groups of families.
(5) Poor freemen, patsas or shepherds.

The family is the unity of the Kafir body politic. As the importance of a clan is dependent upon the number of families of which it consists, so the importance of a family is similarly dependent upon the number of adult males it can produce to support the head of the house in all his contentions.

Government and social laws. (But see also last paragraph of this article.) The ruling authority in ordinary times consists of three Jasts, who use their power tactfully and always know the bent of public opinion. For the management of internal affairs of secondary importance there is a kind of elective magistracy, consisting of thirteen persons, who are changed annually. Their chief is known as the "Ur Jast," and is a very important personage indeed. The remainder of the number are merely his satellites, and slaves even are elected. The business of these men is to regulate the supply of water to the different fields, and to see that grapes and walnuts are not picked before the appointed time, while their chief is also responsible for the lighting of the fires at the dancing house every Wednesday night, the commencement of a kind of Kafir sabbath. The elected thirteen punish disobedience and other irregularities by fines, which, as they expressively put it, they eat themselves. On appointment their chief has to entertain the whole village. He is also expected to entertain public guests, but as he receives certain contributions in the shape of flour, etc., his office is believed to be as lucrative as it certainly is honourable. In every circumstance in which a man is in any way exalted above his fellows, he has to pay for the honour.

Disobedience to the Jast in council is punished by burning down the offender's house, and destroying his property. The penalty for theft is, theoretically, a fine of seven or eight times the value of the thing stolen, but such a punishment in ordinary cases would only be inflicted on a man of inferior rank, unless it were an aggravated offence. Murder, justifiable homicide, and killing by inadvertence in a quarrel are all classed as one crime. Extenuating circumstances are never considered.

There are no blood feuds amongst the Kafirs such as those so fatally common amongst their Afghan neighbours. The penalty for killing a fellow-tribesman is, however, extremely severe, Kafirs are continually quarreling amongst themselves, and the danger to his family of one man killing another is so well recognised and understood, that men, women, even children are prepared at all times to throw themselves recklessly between the combatants and try to separate them. It is considered an act of virtue to do this. In these incessant quarrels dagger-wounds are very common, but they are almost invariably inflicted on the hands of those who are trying to separate the quarrellers, and who rush between fighting men with the greatest intrepidity. If a Kafir kill another, he must at once leave his village and become a "chile" or outcast. His house or houses are burnt by the dead man's family or clan, and his property plundered. He must never more return to his native village except by stealth, and whenever he encounters any member of the dead man's family, he is obliged at once to hide himself in bushes or behind doors, etc. The stigma applies not only to the man but to this direct descendants and to his children-in-law. There are several villages which may be called cities of refuge in Kafiristan, where slayers of their fellow-tribesmen reside permanently. They can only be released from their outcast condition by paying down a heavy ransom to the dead man's family. The ransom is so heavy, that it is very rarely paid. Indeed, to pay it shows so much wealth and honour, that the man himself and his descendants, when they return to their village, always afterwards carry a specially shaped axe to indicate their social importance. Concerning this question of men killing one another, Robertson frequently asked Kafirs what would be the result if a man were to slay a fellow-villager, while defending his own life from an attack? The answer was invariably the same. The homicide--justifiable homicide as we should call him--becomes at once a "chile." On his attempting to argue the justice of this, they always made the same reply: the man should have defended his life without killing the other man. This way of avenging a murder is extremely suitable to the small Kafir communities, where the life of every single man is of the utmost value as a factor in the fighting strength of a family or a tribe. For it is obvious that if the custom, "a life for a life," prevailed, the tribe would lose two fighting men instead of one whenever a man was killed in a domestic or village quarrel.

The punishment for a murderous assault is decided by the Jast.

The ordinary punishment for a man caught in adultery is a fine in cows varying from three to six. As a consequence the women often try to entangle men in order to get cows for their husbands.

When it is desired to take an oath of a very binding character, the custom is to sacrifice a cow to Imra, and the persons concerned each put a foot in a pool of the animal's blood. Ordinary vows may be made by killing a goat. Similarly, men may be released from a vow in a precissely similar manner.

The law of inheritance starts with the assumption that a woman cannot hold property. She has no rights of any kind, and cannot inherit. The eldest has his share increased by some single article of value, for instance, a cow, while the youngest inherits his father's house. The inheritance is strictly confined to legitimate sons by free mothers. Slaves' sons do not count. If there are no children the deceased's brothers take all the property. In the failure of the immediate near male relations, the estate falls to distant male relations, and in failure of all such, to the clan.

Women and marriage. Kafir women are practically slaves, and to all intents and purposes they are bought and sold as household commodities. In most cases the entire work of agriculture is in their hands, as well as all carrying work, except the very heavy kinds for which they have no strength. They are rarely actively illused however; they are merely despised. Young women are very immoral, not because their natural average disposition is either better or worse than that of women of other races, but because public opinion is all in favour of what may be called "gallantry." A Kafir guest always expects to have a female companion provided for him by a thoughtful host.

There is little or no ceremony about a Kafir marriage. A man who is enamoured of a young woman, or wishes to get married, sends a friend to the father of his would be bride and asks her price. It is nothing more than that. If he is an ordinary poor man, he will have to pay eight cows, while, if richer, he may give as many as twelve or sixteen. If the father entertains the proposal of the suitor, he sends back word to that effect, and the man immediately goes to the woman's home where a goat is sacrificed, and that constitutes the whole of the ceremony. They are then considered married, but the woman remains in her father's house and works for her father only, until the last penny of her price is paid by her husband.

Divorce is easy. It appears to simply consist in a man selling his wife to some other man.

Kafirs are polygamous, and usually have from one to four, or at the utmost five, wives.

When a man dies, his wives revert to his family, and are either sold or retained by his surviving brothers.

The family life of Kafirs is kindly on the whole. A well-to-do man with several wives may have two or three different homes. The women seem to get on very well together.

Dress and arms. The commonest dress of the poorer classes of the Siah-posh is a goat-skin confined at the waist by a leather strap which also supports the inevitable dagger. The favourite dress of the fairly well-to-do Kafir male of the eastern valleys is a coarse cotton shirt and trousers, a brown Chitrali or a black Minjani robe, brown soft leather boots, and perhaps also footless Chitrali stockings. The national garment, however, is a budzun or tunic, which all women wear without exception, and many men as well. It is made of thick dark brown woollen cloth, and in women reaches from the shoulders to the knee; a wedge-chaped piece of the body in front and behind is exposed owing to the peculiar shape of the garment. It is girdled at the waist by a long dark red flat cord about an inch and a quarter broad, ending in tassels. It has a red edging round the bottom; there are no sleeves, but the upper part of the garment is so fashioned that the wearer often looks, if viewed from the front or the side, as if she were wearing an Inverness cape. The men never bind this tunic tightly to the person as the women do, but simply wear it thrown loosely over the shoulders. The Presum people wear very thick loose grey blanketing clothes, which give them a cumbrous, awkward appearance. The Wai people wear cotton clothes, and affect bright colours whenever they can get them. The Siahposh women wear square cotton caps at the back of the head, while the girls confine their locks with a double thread fastened round the head at the level of the brows. Kafir weapons are the dagger, bow and arrow, spear and matchlock. The bows are feeble looking, but a skillful man will shoot with fair accuracy up to 80 yards. The matchlocks are purchased on the frontier; none are of home manufacture. Shields also are all imported, and are more for ornament than use.

Warfare. It is probable that there is no single tribe of Kafirs which is at peace with all the other tribes. Some of these wars, if wars they can be called, have continued for generations. The commonest cause of an outbreak is robbery. One tribe knows that another tribe has fine flocks and herds, and thereupon decides to make a raid. Another cause is the general excitement of a tribe seeking to find an outlet for its energy.

The most common plan of carrying on hostilities is for small parties, two or more, to penetrate into the enemy's country and kill sleeping people or form small ambuscades, and then, if successful, hurry back at full speed to dance to the god "Gish." On such expeditions the Kafirs exhibit the most extraordinary courage and powers of endurance, their wonderful walking powers enabling them to travel distances which seem almost incredible.

When attacked by foreigners they usually adopt purely defensive tactics. They hold positions, form little ambuscades and so forth; then, when the enemy, from a cumulated loss, lack of supplies, or other cause, begins to retreat, dogged resistance turns into furious bravery, and the light-footed Kafirs attack them on all sides like a swarm of locusts.

It is not quite clear how Kafirs come to an end of hostilities with a Muhammadan people, but they no doubt send and receive messengers, and the Kafirs ratify their promises by sacrificing a goat. Among themselves matters are probably arranged in the first place by some neutral tribe friendly to both parties. The ratification of the necessary preliminaries depends to a great extent upon the peace offerings suggested, which the stronger tribe receives, giving little or nothing in return.

Religion. The religion of the Kafirs is a somewhat low form of idolatry, with an admixture of ancestor worship and some traces of fire-worship also. Imra is the creator of all things, and there are a large number of secondary deities, both male and female, who are described as "prophets." Of these, Moni appears to be the most ancient and Gish, the war-god, the most popular. (But see also last paragraph of this article.)

There are large numbers of other minor deities also, who preside over women and children, who must be sacrificed to for wealth, and who give fruitful harvests, etc. Special animals have to be sacrificed to particular gods: thus, Imra receives cows; Gish, male goats; Dizane (a goddess), sheep, etc. Imra's temples are in every valley, the chief temple being at Kstigigrom in Presungul, which is undoubtedly the most sacred village in the whole of Kafiristan. Gish is believed by the Kafirs to have been created in a miraculous way by Imra. He was a marvellous warrior and slayer of men. He has shrines in every true Kafir village, and the corners of his small temples are not unfrequently ornamented with war-trophies stuck on the end of poles. The object worshipped is either a plain stone, or a wooden head and face carved in a conventional manner. On these the priest cast flour, etc., and the blood of the sacrifice. If you wish to compliment a Kafir you compare him to Gish; while the prettiest thing you can say to a Kafir woman is to call her "Gish Istri," which means Gish's wife. Besides gods, the Kafirs believe in fairies, and also in devils, who have to be propitiated in order that the crops may not be destroyed. In Kafir theology there appears to be both a heaven and a hell. It divides the universe into Urdesh, the world above; Michdesh, the earth; and Yurdesh, the nether world. The aperture which opens into Yurdesh is guarded by a custodian named Maramalik, who permits no one to return to the upper world.

Wooden effigies, or a long single stone placed on end, are erected to the memory of dead relations, and although ancestor-worship is denied by the people, these effigies and monoliths are to be seen sprinkled with the blood of sacrifices offered by those of the same family who were suffering from sickness, while at a particular festival food is presented to the family effigies, and placed round the house for the use of departed shades.

There are no human sacrifices under any circumstances in Kafiristan, except that prisoners taken in war are sometimes stabbed in front of the coffins to satisfy the indignant ghost of a dead warrior. Kafirs are never melancholy, and suicide is not only unknown amongst them, but when they are told about it they are unfeignedly surprised.

There is nothing in the shape of prayers; the substitutes are religious dances, sacred songs, and sacrifices.

The sacrifices are carried out by the "utah," or priest: the "debilala," the singer of the praises of the gods, and the "pshur," who is supposed to be temporarily inspired on all such occasions; but no goat or other animal is ever killed for food in Kafiristan except in the orthodox way, and with the appropriate ceremonies. At such times any one may officiate.

The priest--the Kamdesh priest is the seventh of his line in regular descent--is a very important personage. He is allowed to sit on the stool in the open air, whether he has gone through the necessary banqueting or not. He is always a man of wealth, and the head of a clan. He gets a double share of each animal whose sacrifice he presides over, and has other rights and perquisites. On the march and elsewhere, he takes precedence of every one. For some particular reason he must not go near the receptacles for the dead, nor even traverse certain paths which lead to those places. Slaves may not approach the hearth of any house he may possess, nor come too near any of the shrines.

The "debilala" is also a man held in high respect; he recites the praises of the god in whose honour the sacrifice is being made, and at the great religious dances in the spring time he has a special place assigned him in the centre of the performers, and alongside of the priest. He also is debarred from using certain pathways supposed to be impure.

The "pshur" is the individual who becomes temporarily inspired during sacrifices and on other occasions, when he frequently behaves most violently and is sometimes not soothed before some of the headmen have specially appealed to Imra on his behalf. He is on the whole despised by his fellows, who believe that although he is sometimes really inspired, yet at other times he is simply a liar, as they put it in their charmingly direct way. Besides the functionaries above described, there are others who perform certain subordinate duties in relation to the gods. For instance, supposing there is excessive snow or rain, the people collect together in some particular house, and one of the "jast," who alone can perform the ceremony, binds a piece of cloth turbanwise round his brows, takes a bow in his hand, and after purifying it by the sprinkling of water, proceeds to discover which of the gods is willing to receive a sacrifice. He finds this out by rapidly running over the names of the gods until the bow begins to swing backwards and forwards. The name of the god on his lips when the movement begins is the name of the god desirous of being sacrificed to.

The mode the Kafirs have of disposing of their dead is peculiar. They are not buried, nor burned, but are deposited in large boxes, placed either on the hill side or in some more or less secluded spot. In some few places, notably in Lutdeh, these coffers for the dead are placed just above and close to the village on the level ground and alongside the road. When the wind blows from that particular direction the result is simply appalling. The boxes are very large and usually body after body is put into them, as long as the wood resists the natural decay due to time and the weather. Certain great men are occasionally given a box all to themselves. The lid generally has several largish stones placed on it, possibly to prevent its warping and exposing the contents of the coffer. Ornaments, sliver earrings, etc., and bright coloured clothing are sometimes deposited with the dead, as are also wooden bowls containing bread broken up in clarified butter. When through age the wood-work decays, the bones of the dead are exposed and very little attention is paid to the circumstance.

Miscellaneous manners and customs. Children are always born in a "Nirmali" house on the outskirst of a village. The way they are named is very peculiar. An old woman runs rapidly over the names of the baby's ancestors or ancestresses, as the case may be, and stops at the instant the infant first begins to feed; the name on the reciter's lips when that event occurs being the name by which the child will thenceforth be known during its life. As a consequence of this peculiar custom, it not unfrequently happens that more than one member of a family is compelled to bear the same name. In such cases the children are distinguished from one another in speaking of them by the prefix junior or senior, as the case may be. Kafir men and women are known by their own particular name affixed to that of their father: thus, Chandlu Astan means Astan the son of Chandlu. In the case of very popular names, the grandfather's cognomen has frequently to be employed also to distinguish the various individuals: thus Lutkam Chandlu Merik means Merik the son of Chandlu, the son of Lutkam. Occasionally, though rarely, the mother's name is used along with the father's: so Bachik-Sumri Shaiok means Shaiok the child of Bachik and of Sumri. There is no objection in Kafiristan to a child bearing the same name as its father, as there so commonly is throughout the East; indeed you constantly hear of Merik Merik, Gutkech Gutkech and similar instances of father and son bearing identical names.

Dancing enters greatly into the inner life of the Kafirs. It is a religious exercise, a spectacular performance, and an amusement, but it is possible that there is no such thing as purely secular dancing.

The chief games of the Kafirs are "shil" (the throwing of an iron ball), archery, rolling walnuts, a kind of "touch," and "aluts" (exactly like quoits, flat stones being used instead of the Quoit). Young men occasionally display their activity in running, jumping, and such like athletics, while swimming is an amusement, as well as a necessary part of a Kafir's education.

Trade. The greater part of the external trade of Kafiristan is carried on through the Muhammadan villages on the frontier. There is a certain amount of trade also done in the Chitral Bazar. Pedlars, bringing small wares and ornaments from Peshawar or Badakhshan, also enter Kafiristan to ply their vocation. The Minjanis travel into all Kafir districts, the Ramgul Kulam, Kti, and the Bashgul, and also trade in the Presungul, but they never visit the Kam or the other Siahposh tribes. The Western Kafirs sell young female children to the Minjanis, but of late years this traffic has decreased.

Imports. The Minjanis bring in black woolen robes, coarse cotton cloth wooden combs, trinkets, and salt. Other imports are cheap stuffs for dancing dresses, cotton cloths, needles, thread, beads, thimbles, iron, lead, gunpowder and matchlocks.

Exports. These consist chiefly of ghi, hides, wool, goats sheep, honey and walnuts in the order named.

The Kafirs are well skilled in many of the ordinary trades. They make good foot-coverings, ropes are twisted from goat hair, potter's vessels are well made while the silver and brass workers are decidedly clever. The best carpenters and wood carvers in Kafiristan are to be found in the Presungul, the best iron workers in the Wai country, and the best leather workers in Bashgul. The women weave woollen cloth on upright looms identical in principle with those seen in India.

Agricultural and other products. The chief crop is a kind of millet called in the Punjab "tehina." Others are wheat, barley, and Indiancorn. Millet is the staple food, wheat being considered a luxury. The amount and duration of the snowfall naturally determine the dates of the spring sowings. Robertson says: "Kamdesh village is between 6,000 feet and 7,000 feet above the sea level. On April 4th, 1891, ploughing began in that village, while on October 2nd, 1890, I had witnessed the Indiancorn crop being harvested. In the same place on September 7th, 1891, the wheat and millet crops were cut."

The Kafir cattle are inferior to good English breeds, but reach the average of those seen in Kashmir. Some varieties are humped. The goats are a fine breed, but the sheep are very poor. Butter is churned in goat-skins. The ghi is made in the usual way, and is of excellent quality. The so-called Kafir wine is poor stuff, more like vinegar than wine. Kafir cheese is not bad being very like what we call cream-cheese.

Referring to the political and strategic importance of Kafiristan, Robertson remarks:

"Owing to the comparative scantiness of its food supplies which would be altogether insufficient for anything more than a very moderate addition to its present population, Kafiristan could be neither reinforced to any considerable extent nor for any length of time by an ally, nor could it long afford sustenance to an enemy numerous enough to conquer it."

Currency and measures. Among the Kafirs themselves all business is done by barter. A cow is a standard value being reckoned at 20 Kabuli rupees, a goat is three rupees, and a sheep one. It does not necessarily follow that these animals can be obtained at the prices mentioned.

Grain and flour are measured in shallow wicker baskets for which there are three particular sizes. Rough scales and weights are in common use, the usual weights being a fragment of stone.

Calendar. The Kafir year, at least in the Bashgul, is divided into 360 days and marked by special festivals. The festivals are 12 in number and start with Giche, the first day of the new year. The following list gives all these particular days and the dates on which they occurred in 1891:

Giche	January 16th	Diran	May 9th
Viron	February 3rd	Gerdulow	June 5th
Taska	February 18th	Patilo	June 30
Marnma	March 8th	Dizanedu	July 9th
Duban	March 19th	Munzilo	August 17th
Azhindra	April 4th	Nilu	Sept. 17th

After Nilu there is a long interval--120 days, it is said--until the next Giche. For the purposes of the calendar only three seasons are enumerated, namely, Wazdar (summer), Sharwar (autumn), and Zowar (winter), each of which is computed at 120 days.

In addition to the holidays given above there is a series of weekly rest days, or sabbaths, which occur every Saturday during the time field work is in progress. These rest-days are called Agars. In 1891 the first Agar was on April 3rd, the last on September 17th. (Ro-ertson, Barrow, Masson, Biddulph, Bellew, Lumsden.)

The above article has been produced in its entirety from the third (1895) edition of the Gazetteer, as we have practically no more recent information of a reliable nature, and no European has visited the country since Sir George Robertson. We know, however, that in 1895-96 the then Amir conducted a campaign against the Kafirs who up to that time had been virtually independent of Kabul. This campaign is briefly referred to in "The Life of Abdur Rahman", Vol. I, page 290 thus: "In the winter of 1895, therefore, orders were one day issued for the four columns of the army to surround and simultaneously attack Kafiristan from all directions. This was successfully accomplished, and within forty days the whole country of Kafiristan was conquered." The country is believed to form now one of the regularly administered districts of the Kabul Province, though to what extent the Amir has really consolidated his authority there is not known. After the conclusion of the campaign just referred to many thousands of Kafirs were deported from their own country and settled in the Koh Daman to the north of Kabul, where they are said to have been given grants of land, etc. A large number of the inhabitants are said to have been converted, more or less forcibly, to the Muhammadan religion at the same time, but it is probably only in the more westerly of their valleys, where they come more into contact with the Prophet and that, in the interior of the country they still retain their primitive modes of worships."

In 1906 the Amir re-named the country "Nur-ul-Islam" and ordered the use of the name "Kafiristan" to be discontinued.

*KAFQUL   قف ظل
    34-29 67-13 m. A village located on the Dara-i-Mur, near the village of Surkhsang in Bamian province.

*KAFSHANDAZ   کفش انداز
    34-52 68-3 m. A village located north of Iraq-i-Sufla, on a tributary of the Ghorband river in northern Ghazni province.

KAFTAR KHANA See ZARSANG   کفترخانه

*KAFTAR KHANA   کفترخانه
    33-48 69-3 m. A mountain located west of Altamur on the road from Gardez to Kabul.

*KAFTAR KHANA KALA   کفترخانه قلعه
    35-9 67-54 G. A village located about 20 miles east of Saighan in Bamian province.

KAFZAR   کفزار
    34-38 68-5. A pass over the Koh-i-Baba, south of the Hajigak (see "Kalu"). The track to it is understood to leave the main road a little below Siah Sang, and rejoin it at Sarichal, some 3 miles beyond the crest of the Hajigak. (A.B.C.) Also see "Siah Reg."

KAGGA See KAJA   کجه

KAHAN کن (کاهان)
34-17 70-31 m. A village of 400 houses, in the Jalalabad district, about 16 miles southeast of Jalalabad. (I.B.C.) Recent maps show the name Kan. (LWA)

KAHAN-I-TAJIKI کاهان تاجکی
34-17 70-30 A. A village in the Hisarak division of the Jalalabad district. Inhabitants: Tajiks and Dehgans. This village appears to be also known as Kahan-i-Dehgan. (Jenkyns.) Recent maps show the names Kan and Degan. (LWA)

KAH DARA کاه دره
34- 69-. A village in the Koh Daman of Kabul, 25 miles northwest of Kabul. It is a large village, and has abundance of gardens and vineyards, and is the chief place of a subdivision. There is a considerably rivulet here of the same name which drains into a longer tributary of the Panjshir river to the east.
During Sale's operations in the Kohistan in 1840, a party of 500 rebels from this place made a night attack on his camp at Ak Sarai, 4 miles distant, but did little damage, and on his moving to attack them the village of Kah Dara was found evacuated--a circumstance attributable to the cowardice alone of the inhabitants, for the position is a very strong one, and is thus described by an officer who was present:
"On examining the position which the enemy (800 or 1,000 in number) had not ventured to defend, it became immediately apparent that their want of courage had spared us the loss of probably one half of our men, to say nothing of the possibility of an unqualified defeat. The difficulties presented by the ground to an enemy assailing the village cannot be adequately described; vineyards and gardens, forming a succession of terraces one above the other on the steep hill-side, garden walls without number, and trees of all sorts closely planted, were obstacles to be surmounted ere the village itself could be attained; and the village was of considerable extent, containing about 800 flat-roofed houses, the streets so narrow that only one horseman could pass through the best of them, and only two or three lanes giving entrance from beyond the walls of the place, which was built on a steep ascent, house rising above house like a series of irregular steps. Had the enemy defended this ground with resolution, it was the opinion of some officers that it would have been scarcely possible for us to have carried the village. The road proved to be impracticable for guns, and that arm could have given but little assistance to the assailants from any position to which it could have attained in the course of the morning." (Masson, Sale.)

KAH DARA کاه دره
34- 69-. A dara which descends east from the Paghman range and joins the Shakar Dara near Ak Sarai. A road leads up it to the Kachan Kotal, 11 miles from Deh-i-Nao. Of this road little is known, but see "Kachan." It is stated that the Amir has officially altered the name of the Kah Dara to Gul Dara, i.e., "the valley of roses." (I.B.C.)

KAHI کاهی (کائی)
34-8 70-42 m. A village and fortified cantonment, in the Jalalabad district, 9 miles south-southwest of Basawal. The village contains about 150 families of Shinwaris. There is a bazar of about 15 shops in the cantonment, and the garrison consists of 2 squadrons cavalry, 2 battalions infantry, 14 mountain, 4 heavy, 3 quick-firing, and 3

machine guns, and 50 khasadars.
There are several good perennial springs in the bed of the nala, opposite to the cantonment. (I.B.C.) Recent maps show the spelling Ka'i. (LWA)

*KAHKASH   کاه کش
33-8 68-2 m. A village near Amugai, about 2 miles west of the Qalat-Ghazni highway.

*KAH KATS   کاه کج
34-29 70-3 m. A village located on the Kabul river, on the road from Jalalabad to Kabul in Laghman province.

*KAHKHANA   کاه خانه
34-42 68-12 m. A village located northeast of Hajigak, on a tributary of the Qol-i-Khesh.

*KAHMARD   کهمرد
35-19 67-38. Kahmard is the name of a woleswali in the Bamian province. The woleswali comprises an area of 1,640 square kilometers and has an agricultural population which has been variously estimated at from 4,090 to 4,725.
The woleswali is bounded in the west by Yakowlang, in the north by the provinces of Samangan and Baghlan, in the east by Baghlan, in the south by Shibar and in the southwest by Saighan.
Kahmard has about 23 villages of which about 3 have more than 500 inhabitants. The villages are listed in the PG as follows: Andarab, Baj Gah, Pain Bagh, Darband Wa Tangi Muyak, Dara-i-Ajar, Khargoshak, Deh Tajek, Deh Myana, Ailaka-i-Ajar, Dodari, Dasht-i-Safid, Do Shakh-i-Olang (Do Shakh), Do Ab-i-Mikh-i-Zarin, Ashposhta, Doraw, Surkh Shar, Ruy Ghinak wa Qaghur (Ruy Sang), Deh Khoshhal, Laghaki, Kaluch, Banaq, Lolunj, and Madar.

*KAHU   کهو
34-41 70-23 m. A village located on a stream running into the Alingar river, southeast of Gundalam.

KAILAGU   کیلغو
34-17 70-9 m. A village in the Jalalabad district, 13 miles southwest of Bawali and 6 1/2 miles due south of Fort Battye, belonging to the Kharun section of Khugianis.
The hamlets composing the village are enclosed by walls, with towers. A good deal of fruit is grown, and silk-worms are bred in great numbers on the mulberries. Water from a ravine is good and sufficient. Bhusa, rice-straw, etc., are procurable in considerably quantities. There are five families and a few Hindu shopkeepers in the place. (Massey, I.B.C.) Recent maps show the spelling Kilaghu. (LWA)

KAIRAN DARA   کیران دره
35- 69-. A small valley traversed by the road between Dasht-i-Rewat and the Khawak pass, just before commencing the ascent of the later. (I.B.C.)

KAITU   کیتو
33- 70-. The name given to the lower portion of the Shamil river in Khost. (I.B.C.) A village with this name is located at 33-10 70-33 A.

KAJ Or KAJJRUD کج (کجرود)
32-55 65-30 A. (See military Report on Hazarajat, Part II.) A large affluent of the Helmand.

KAJA Or KAGGA کجه
34- 70-. A village in the Khugiani division of the Jalalabad district, 5 miles southeast of Nimla, It is healthy, and a British regiment was quartered here on that account in the summer of 1840. Inhabitants Kharbun Khugianis, Barakzais, and 30 families of Hindus (Sikh traders). It contains 400 houses, and there are 21 forts belonging to it outside. (I.B.C.)

KAJAK See SAGPAR کجك

KAJAK کجك
34- 67-. (See Military Report on Hazarajat, Part II.) Three villages in the northwest of the Besud country. A village with this name is located on a tributary of the Qol-i-Kesh, southeast of Dahan-i-Khakriz, at 34-41 68-25 m. Another village with this name is about 12 miles northwest of Mashak, at 34-29 67-30 G.

*KAJAKI کجکی
34-54 68-21 m. A village located on a tributary of the Ghorband, south of Dahan-i-Botian.

KAJAK TALKHAK کجك تلخك
34- 67-. (See Military Report on Haxarajat, Part II.)

*KAJALAK کجلك
34-3 67-3 m. A village located near Qolak, on a tributary of the Helmand river in southern Bamian province.

KAJAO کجاو
34-13 68-5 G. A village in the Kajao valley. There is said to be a company of infantry stationed here. (Wanliss.) A stream with this name is located at 34-5 68-32 A. (LWA)

KAJAO (VALLEY) کجاو
34- 67-. Information regarding the Kajao valley is still very meagre, and what little can here be said about it is mainly the outcome of a reconnaissance made by a Native officer who accompanied Mr. Dobbs and Major Wanliss on their journey from Herat to India, via Kabul, in 1904, amplified by the results of personal enquiries made by Major Wanliss hmself.
The Kajao is a tributary of the Logar river and rises somewhere in the Sang-i-Shanda range. It flows at first east and then northeast almost to the foot of the Koh-i-Kalandar (a peak in the Buland-i-Quash range northeast of Badasia); it then sweeps away to the south, and southeast, eventually uniting with the Khawas stream some distance above the junction with the latter of the Barikao, these three streams together going to make up the Logar river.
The valley, where seen by the reconnoitrer (i.e., east of the Buland-i-Qash from Badasia), is richly cultivated and full of villages surrounded by trees. The village of Kara Katta is situated in the Kajao valley. (See also Military Report on Hazarajat, Part II.)

*KAJGAL کجگل
34-57 71-6 m. A village located on a tributary of the Kunar, northwest of Asadabad (Chigha Sarai) in Kunar province.

*KAJI کجی
   34-35 67-29 m. A village located on the Dara-i-Shorshori, at the southern foot of the Kuh-i-Baba range.

*KAJIR GHAR کجیرغر
   33-2 68-35 m. A mountain located southwest of Yusuf Khel in Ghazni province.

*KAJIR KALAI کجیرکلی
   33-21 69-57 m. A village located a few miles northeast of Matun (Khost) in Paktia province.

KAJKAMAR Or KAMARZARD کج کمر (کمرزردکوه)
   35-23 67-15 G. A high range of hills which runs east and west and forms the watershed between the drainage going east to the Kamard stream, and flowing north through Walishan to Dara Yusuf and the Band-i-Amir river. It may be considered the westerly continuation of the Kara Kotal range, and is part of the same watershed. It is the boundary between the Yak Walang district of Bamian, which belongs to the Kabul province, and the Walishan district of Dara Yusuf, which is part of Afghan Turkistan. To the west of the Dandan Shikan Kotal the range rises to a great height, and is called Koh-i-Hazar Chashma. It bends southwest, and then south, enclosing all the Kamard drainage. On the slopes of these mountains are many springs and much grass in summer. They are resorted to by nomads for grazing particularly, it is said, by Firozkohis, who are of lawless character, and make the road unsafe for small parties. Chashma Duzdan, as the name implies is noted for the robberies that have taken place in its neighbourhood. (A.B.C.)

*KAJKOL کجکول
   34-11 67-57 m. A village located near Sar-i-Tob, southeast of Behsud in Bamian province.

KAJURAI کجوری
   34- 70-. A village in the Jalalabad district, about 1 mile from the right bank of the Kabul river, opposite the junction with the latter of the Alingar. It is 14 miles from Jalalabad and contains about 200 houses, with a good deal of cultivation. Large quantities of supplies can be obtained form the Alingar valley, the Kabul river being crossed on rafts. (I.B.C.)

*KAKA CHINA کاکه چینه
   33-51 68-42 m. A village located west of the Ghazni-Kabul road, about 6 miles east of Haftasia.

KAKA KATZ کاکاکج
   34- 70-. A vilage in Laghman, on the right bank of the Kabul river, 1 1/2 miles southeast of Urmur. It belonged to Ismatulla Khan, Jabar Khel Ghilzai. (Warburton.) Recent maps show the spelling Kah Katz (Kac) at 34-30 70-3 m. (LWA)

KAKA KHEL کاکاخیل
   34- 70-. A village in the Surkhab division of the Jalalabad district, situated on the left bank of the Surkhab river, opposite Barina. Inhabitants: Ghilzais. (Jenkyns.)

*KAKAI ککی
   32-50 68-41 m. A village located east of Zarghun Shahr and southeast of Yahyakhel in eastern Ghazni province.

*KAKAL کاکی
   34-52 69-11 m. A village located on the Kabul-Charikar highway northeast of Istalif.

*KAKAR کاکر
   32-3 68-57 m. A village located on a stream, some six miles east of Mamai in southeastern Ghazni province.

*KAKARA کاکره
   32-58 68-8 m. A village located about one mile southwest of Sakikhel in Ghazni province.

*KAKAR KALAI کاکر کلی
   32-4 68-7 m. A village located near Abdullah Kala, southwest of Wazakhwa in Ghazni province.

*KAKRAK کگراك
   34-48 67-50 m. A village located on the Dara-i-Kakrak, about two miles south of Bamian.

KAKRAK کگراك
   33-21 68-25 A. A glen in the Jaghatu Hazara country. (See Military Report on Hazarajat, Part II.) Other places with this name are located at 33-26 68-15 G and 33-21 68-24 G. (LWA)

*KALA قلا
   34-32 67-26 m. A village located near the Dara-i-Shorshori, southwest of Gharghara in Bamian province. Other places with this name are located near Kawras, south of the Kuh-i-Baba range, at 34-33 67-18 m.; north of the Band-i-Zirtak and south of the Band-i-Takhak, at 34-13 67-2 m.; a few miles south of Darazqol, at 34-19 67-2 m.; on a tributary of the Ghorband, northeast of the Kuh-i-Khushkak in Parwan province, at 34-58 68-58 m.; some miles east of Arghandeh on the road to Kabul, about 13 miles from the latter, at 34-29 68-59 m.; northwest of Naser on a path to Loy Dergai in southwest Laghman province, at 34-25 69-58 m.; about 6 miles west of Khak-i-Jabar on a path leading to Kabul, at 34-25 69-21 m.; northwest of Chigha Sarai (Asadabad) and east of Katar in Kunar province, 34-58 71-7 m.; near Kalakhel, about 5 miles southwest of Barlak in Ghazni province, at 32-39 68-25 m.; and about 2 miles east of Khenkai and 3 miles north of Mamai in southern Ghazni province, at 32-4 68-49 m.

KALACHA قلاچه (کلاچه)
   34- 69-. An irregular shaped village 2-1/2 miles from the Bala Hisar, on the east side of the Kabul-Charasia road. Frontage of village 150 yards. Inhabitants: Ghilzais. (Kennedy.) Another place with this name is on the Tagab river, about 10 miles north of Tagab in Kapisa province, at 34-59 69-35 m. (LWA)

KALACHA قلاچه
   34- 66-. A glen in the Dai Zangi Hazara country draining south into the Lal valley. It is crossed by the main Kabul—Hazarajat-Daulat Yar road about 3 miles above its junction with the Lal, at about 24 1/2 miles east of Daulat Yar. Down this glen runs a track which, crossing the Lal valley and going over the Band-i-Doakan, leads to Shinia Takht. (Wanliss.) Another place with this name is at 35-30 67-43 A. (LWA)

KALACHA-I-SOKHTA قلاچه سوخته
35- 69-. A village east of Charikar, inhabited by 100 Tajik families. (Shahzada Taimus, from native information.)

*KALAGAI کلاگی
34-14 69-58 m. A village located on a tributary of the Surkhab river in the Gandomak area. Another place with this name is located on the Kunar river, southwest of Kauz Kunar (Shiwa) in Nangarhar province, at 34-33 70-34 m.

KALAGU Or KOLALGU کلاگو
33-27 68-53 m. A village in Zurmat on the road leading from Gardez to Ghazni. It has 100 houses inhabited mainly by Tajiks, and is situated about 30 miles southeast of Ghazni. (Broadfoot, I.B.C.)

*KALAI کی
34-46 70-22 m. A village located near Aramkhel, on a tributary of the Alingar river in Laghman province. Other places with this name are located about 4 miles northwest of Dila and southwest of Khoshamand in Ghazni province, at 32-38 68-1 m.; some 14 miles south of Omna and southwest of Sayyidkhel in western Paktia province, at 32-40 68-45 m.

KALA-I قلعه
Places the names of which begin with the word Kala followed by the Persian izafat, are described under the second word of their designations.

KALAJAT کلاجات
34- 70-. A village in the Kot division of the Jalalabad district, about 1/2 mile north of Kala-i-Saadatmand. Inhabitants: Tirais. (Jenkyns.)

KALAJAT-I-SHINWARI کلاجات شنواری
A village in the Mohmand Dara division of the Jalalabad district. Inhabitants Shinwaris. (Jenkyns.)

KALAJAT-I-WAHAB KHAN کلاجات وهاب خان
34- 70-. A village in the Chapriar division of the Jalalabad district, including Kala-i-Shah Pasand Khan and Kala-i-Miangan. Inhabitants: Barakzais and Mian Khels. (Jenkyns.)

*KALAKAN ککان
34-47 69-9 m. Kalakan is a village and an alaqadari in Kabul province. The alaqadari comprises an area of 42 square kilometers and has an agricultural population that has been estimated at from 9,198 to 19,490. The alaqadari is bounded in the west by Istalef, in the north by Qara Bagh, in the east by Deh Sabz and in the south by Mir Bachakot. Kalakan includes about 24 villages, of which about 10 have more than 500 inhabitants. The villages are listed in the PG as follows: Zema, Quchi (Kochi), Obaidullah (Ebadulah), Kalakan, Karendah, Mushwani Sufla, Sofian Karenda, Buy Naqara, Chartut, Agha Sarai, Bazari, Qala-i-Khwaja, Qalam Chaq, Qala-i-Perak, Qala-i-Ahmad Khan, Dubari, Baposh, Qala-i-Farhad, Joybar, Mushwani Ulya, Qala-i-Pakhchak, Sadbad, Mughul Beg, Qanat-i-Sadat, Qanat-i-Khudi Nazar and Joy Shadi.

*KALAKHEL كلاخيل
33-16 68-17 m. A village located on the Qalat-Ghazni highway, about 20 miles southwest of Ghazni. Other places with this name are located some 8 miles south of Janikhel in Ghazni province, at 32-39 68-25 m., and about 8 miles southeast of Zarghun Shahr in Ghazni province, at 32-43 68-31 m.

KALA KOT كلاكوت
34-35 70-13 m. A village in Laghman, on the right bank of the Alingar river, 1 mile south of Haidar Khani. It is composed of the following hamlets, all inhabited by Dehgans:

(1) Kohna Kala Kot
(2) Deh-i-Kazian
(3) Massi Khel
(4) Ziarat-i-Chilgazi Baba
(5) Banda-i-Akhunzadagan. (Warburton.)

The village is about 3 miles south of Mandarawur. (LWA)

KALAN كلان
One of the four valleys of Nijrao, inhabited by "Pashais" and Tajiks. (Leech.)

KALAN كلان
33-44 68-54 G. The kotal of this name forms one of the main routes from Charkh to Kharwar. From Charkh the road runs along the right bank of the river, gradually ascending to a very narrow defile, through which the Kalan stream comes. This ravine forms really the only bad part of the route. There appear to be three kotals: that to west is the Maulana (9,140'), the centre one is the principal route (8,970'), the eastern one is an alternative branch to the centre kotal (9,020'). From the top of any of these three kotals the road to Muchi Khel is very good and easy. (Griesbach.)

KALANDAR قلندر
A main section of the Jaghori Hazaras. (See Military Report on Hazarajat, Part II.)

*KALANDAR قلندر
33-31 69-41. Kalandar is an alaqadari in Paktia province. The alaqadari comprises an area of 151 square kilometers and has an agricultural population that has been estimated at from 1,793 to 4,122. The alaqadari is bounded in the north, west, and east by Musa Khel, and in the south by Jadran and Nadir Shah Kot. Kalandar has some 22 villages, one of which has more than 500 inhabitants. The villages are listed in the PG as follows: Khost Maga (Khost Mela), Surunai, Malawgai, Tor Sharah, Aligah, Asman Kot (Sulaiman Kot), Bigalai, Mazari Darah (Faraye Darah), Mashal (Mul), Landay, Waragha, Punga, Gusnai, Star Kot, Landar, Shinkay, Darwishi, Kamran, Qarya-i-Manah, Miya Khel, Kotkai, Sharifi, Rez, Meni Khel and Khanagi.

KALANDAR قلندر
34-28 69-9. A village in the Chardeh valley of Kabul, on the left bank of the river, between it and Deh-i-Dana. About 40 houses, Inhabitants: Tajiks. (I.B.C.)

KALANDAR قلندر
A large section of the Pas-i-Koh Hazaras. (See Military Report on Hazarajat, Part II.)

KALANDARAN قلندران
34- 66-. A village in Yak Walang, a few miles west of Firozbahar, near the mouth of the Kalandaran Tagao, i.e., the lower part of the Zari glen. Thirty houses. (Maitland.)

*KALANDAR GHAR قلندرغر
33-30 69-37 m. A mountain located southwest of Zurkot in Paktia province. Nearby is a stream with the same name, at 33-29 69-44 m.

*KALANDAR KHEL قلندرخیل
33-34 68-14 m. A village lcoated on a path running west from Ghazni to Babur on the Dara-i-Yusuf, about 10 miles west of Ghazni.

KALANDAR KHEL قلندرخیل
32-41 68-19 m. A Sulaiman Khel Ghilzai Village in Katawaz. The village is about 5 miles east of Khushamand in Ghazni province. (LWA)

KALAN DEH کلان ده
(See Military Report on Hazarajat, Part II.) A place in the Besud Hazara country. Two villages with this name are located at 34-24 67-50 G. and 33-13 67-41 G. (LWA)

KALANGAR See KULANGAR کنگار

KALANZAI کلانزی
A section of the Polada Hazaras of Ujaristan. (See Military Report on Hazarajat, Part II.)

KALAO کلاو
34- 70-. A small village in the Jalalabad district, about 1 mile east of Pesh Bolak, and separated therefrom by a large nala running towards the north. On the right bank of this nala is a small post held by 2 companies of infantry and 50 sowars. (I.B.C.)

KALAT قلات
35-20 69-30. A village in the Parandev Dara, about 1 mile above its junction with the Panjshir. It contains some 10 families of Tajiks. (I.B.C.) Other places with this name are located at 32-0 67-15, 32-7 66-54 A., 35-8 67-55 G., and 34-9 67-7 m. (LWA)

KALATAK See NOACH کلاتک

KALBISAT Or KHULBESAT خلبسات
33-29 70-0 m. A village in Khost, between Bak and Khubi, towards Matun. (Carr.)

KALMANAI کلمنی
34- 70-. A village 33 miles from Jalalabad, on the Kunar river, consisting of 36 houses of Tajiks. (Leech.)

KALTAGARAI See KALTARAGHA کل تره غه

KALTARAGHA Or KALTAGARAI, QATRAGHAI کل تره غه
34-17 70-31 m. A group of hamlets, containing some 200 houses in all, about 16 miles southeast of Jalalabad. Inhabitants: Tajiks. (I.B.C.)

KALTARI کلتری
35- 69-. A village in the Parandev Dara about 4 miles above its

373

junction with the Panjshir. It contains some 10 families of Tajiks. (I.B.C.)

KALTARI کتری
35- 69-. A village in the Parandev Dara about 4 miles above its junction with the Panjshir. It contains some 10 families of Tajiks. (I.B.C.)

KALU کالو
34-39 68-3 A. A glen running downwards from the Hajigak pass to the Bamian valley, debouching into the latter near Zohak, about 17-1/2 miles from the top of the Hajigak pass. It forms a subdistrict of Bamian. The main Kabul-Bamian road runs down the glen from the Hajigak pass to Gumbat, 6-1/4 miles; it then leaves the Kalu glen and crosses the Panjfilan Kotal into another glen which joins the Bamian valley at Kala Topchi. Another more difficult road continues down the Kalu glen to Zohak.
The Kalu stream at its junction with the Bamian valley is a rapid mountain torrent, 20 feet wide and 1 foot deep. Its bed is stony and it is shut in by high hills on either side.
The glen contains altogether about 115 families of Darghan Hazaras. Fairly good camping grounds are said to exist from Gumbat upwards; supplies are probably available in small quantities from hamlets scattered up and down the glen; water is abundant and firewood probably sufficient for cooking purposes. The lower part of the Kalu glen, from Gumbat to Zohak, is also known as Pai Muri. (Amir Khan.) Also a village.

KAM کم
The chief tribe of the Siahposh Kafirs, See "Kafiristan." A village with this name is located 35-16 71-24 G. (LWA)

KAM کم
Many of the names of the subdivisions of the Dai Zangis are prefixed by "Kam-i". Kam is understood to be the same as "Kaum," a tribal division, pronounced in Hazara fashion, as bam is always pronounced bum.

KAMA کاما
34-25 70-38. Kama is a village and woleswali in Nangarhar province. The woleswali comprises an area of 174 square kilometers and has an agricultural population that has been estimated at from 14,897 to 27,610. The woleswali is bounded in the west by Surkhrud and Behsud, in the north by Kauz Konar and Mur Gul, in the east by Goshta Khwaja Lemar and in the south by Bati Kot and Rodat. Kama has about 46 villages, 12 of which have more than 500 inhabitants. The villages are listed in the PG as follows: Sangar Saray, Sangar, Must Ali, Guj, Darbang, Kakal Wa Bajawri, Landah Buch, Sada-i-Abdullajan, Safdari (Safdarah), Bazid Khel, Khakhi (Shaikhi), Chuna Kach, Jamali, Deh Taher, Kandahari, Mama Khel, Kandak-Mama-Khel, Mirzai, Deh Ghazi, Zarshoye, Mirza Khel, Shir Garr, Shir Garr Abdul Jalal, Shir Garr-Gul Mohd., Shilam Khanaha, Gahik, Jama Mohd.-Siddiq Khan, Kama-i-Khass, Shilam Ulya (Rayati), Gerdab, Zakhel, Qala-i-Akhund, Warasa-i-Faqir-Khan Saheb, Nau Abad, Bela Yari, Kundiha, Kundi, Sada-i-Shir Ali Khan, Arbapan, Dar Gul-i-Ulya, Deh Gan, Dar Gul-i-Sufla, Qala-i-Sardar (Sardaran), Qala-i-Sardar Fateh Mohd. Khan, Kundi Mir Lalan, Pir Zai, Khair Zai, Katar Khel, and Mata Khel (LWA). In 1914 the area was described as follows: A subdivision of the Jalalabad district, lying to the north of the Kabul river and east of the Kunar river, and extending eastwards as far as Chiknaur.

The inhabitants are Mohmands, but the territory contains many small communities of various races, such as Arabs, Dehgans, Tajiks, Sayyids, Pirachas, Hindkis, Lodins, etc.

The following is a list of the villages in this subdivision, as drawn up by Jenkyns in 1879:

Village	Inhabitants
Deh-i-Ghazi	Arabs, Safis
Mast Ali	Dehgans, Hindkis
Kala-i-Akhun	Mohmands, etc.
Fateh Khan	Hindkis, Dehgans, etc.
Haji Nazar	Lodins
Mamakhel	Mohmands, Wardaks
Bazidkhel	Ditto Ditto
Baragali	Tajiks, Dehgans
Shahalam-i-Afghani	Mohmands
Landabuch	Arabs, Pirachas, etc.
Mir Abdulla	Lodins
Mir Khwaja Jan	Saiyids
Kandahari	Lodins
Mir Lala	Saiyids
Deh-i-Tahir	Dehgans
Sangai Sarai	Pirachas
Gahik	Mohmands
Muhamad Sadik Khan	Hindkis, Tajiks
Shahalam-i-Tajiki	Tajiks
Mayar-i-Akbar Khan	Mohmands
Shergarh	Hindkis, Arabs, etc.
Safedbini	Mohmands
Kama Yamin	Ditto
Sada-i-Ghulam Jan	Saiyids
Zarshoi-i-Arbabha	Mughals
Nawaji	Saiyids
Zarshoi-i-Jalaluddin Khan	Hindkis, Arabs, etc.
Zulfikar Khan	?
Girdao	Mohmands
Goshta	Ditto
Khwaizai	Ditto
Chiknaur	Ditto
Guch	Saiyids, Wardaks
Mirzai	Ghilzais, etc.
Shaikh Misar	Sahibzadas

*KAMA DAKA
  34-13 71-3 m. A village located at the northern bend of the Kabul river, near the Pakistan frontier in Nangarhar province.

KAMAH (Or KAMAR) BIDA Or WERAN
  35-13 70-51 G. Elevation 15,500 feet. A pass leading from the head of the Virun (Presun, or Pech) valley, in Kafiristan into the Minjan valley, in Badakhshan. There is a small circular lake, 80 yards in diameter, on the southern side of the pass, about 2 miles from the summit. The pass is practicable for laden mules, and is much used by traders. There is a force of 200 khasadars stationed near this pass. From the lake a small stream flows into the Pech just below Shtevi. (I.B.C.)

KAMA-I-YAMIN
  34- 70-. A village in the Kama division of the Jalalabad district. Inhabitants: Mohmands. (Jenkyns.)

*KAMA JARKANA كمه جركه
33-4 68-30 m. A village located about 2 miles south of Jarkana and north-northwest of Yusufkhel in eastern Ghazni province.

KAMAL KHEL كمال خيل
34-8 70-36 G. A village in the Kot division of the Jalalabad district, about 8 miles southwest of Batikot. Inhabitants: Tirais. (Jenkyns.)

*KAMAL KHEL كمال خيل
34-5 69-3 m. A village located on the Logar river, about 2 miles south of Kolangar in Logar province.

KAMAL KHEL كمال خيل
A division of the Mangal tribe; see Mangal.

KAMALPUR كمال پور
34- 70-. A village in Laghman, on the left bank of the Alingar stream, just above its junction with the Alishang. It consists of 2 hamlets occupied by Jabar Khel Ghilzais. (Warburton.)

*KAMALUDDIN KHEL كمال الدين خيل
32-51 68-31 m. A village located about 3 miles east of Khairkot (Zarghun Shahr) in the Katawaz area.

KAMANDI كندى
34-52 68-3. A narrow tangi on the stream running northwards from the Irak pass to the Bulola Dara, about 1/2 mile above its junction with the latter. The tangi is short but very narrow, the stream being confined between two rocky cliffs only 10 feet apart. The cliff on the left bank is of great height but that on the right bank is only about 100 feet high, being a spur projecting from the main hill. The road from the Ghorband valley to the Kashka Kotal leads over this spur by a steep and dangerous track, which is however said to be practicable for hill camels. In October, 1886, large gangs of men were at work on this bit of the road so it may now be less difficult. (A.B.C.)

*KAMAO كاو
34-23 68-1 m. A village located near Shika in Maidan province.

*KAMAR كمر
33-59 68-2 m. A village located about one mile north of Naoqala on the Okak stream in northern Ghazni province.

KAMAR BIDA See KAMAH BIDA كمر بيدا

KAMARI كمرى
34-29 69-17 m. A collection of 3 hamlets in the Kabul district, on the right bank of the Logar river, opposite Bagrami, and about 3/4 mile distant from that village. Inhabitants: Parsiwans. (Kennedy.)

KAMARZARD See KAJKAMAR كمر زرد

KAMBAR ALI كبر على
A section of the Besud Hazara. (See Military Report on Hazarajat, Part II.)

*KAMBO کبو
    34-12 70-13 G. A village located about 16 miles southeast of Nimla in the Khugiani area.

KAMBO KHWAR کبوخوار
    34-17 70-16 m. A tributary of the Kabul river, rising in the northern slopes of the Safed Koh and joining the Kabul river in the neighbourhood of Jalalabad. (I.B.C.)

KAMCHAK کچك
    A village or villages in the Ghorband district, passed on the road leading up to the Chahardar pass. Three hundred to 400 houses of Tajiks and Afghans (Drummound.)

KAMDESH کامدیش (لندی سین)
    35-24 71-20 m. Kamdesh is a woleswali in Nangarhar province. The woleswali comprises an area of 1,744 square kilometers and has an agricultural population that has been estimated at from 5,360 to 7,670. The woleswali is bounded in the west by Chapa Dara, in the south by Pech, Naray, and Bar Konar, in the north by Bargey Matal, and in the east by the State of Pakistan. Kamdesh has about 27 villages, none of which has more than 500 inhabitants. The villages are listed in the PG as follows: Kamdesh, Bala Deh-i-Kamdesh, Payan Deh-i-Kamdesh, Paprestan, Jamjoz, Banoz, Keshtwar (Keshtoz), Dagro (Agro), Ormar, Mandgar, Mandagul-i-Sufla, Charsoko (Chasko), Bar Madangar, Barmandagul-i-Ulya, Pilok (Paprok), Pul-i-Rustam, Mahr Desh, Kamar (Kamo), Shawit (Sarit), Patigul, Baz Gul, Kodpesh (Gawhar Desh), Gawhardesh-i-Hawla, Khomar Gul (Khomari Gul), Qala-i-Koti (Kotya), Darin, Akatsi, Nan Gul, Chenar Khor, Tang Bandah, and Arsan. (LWA). In 1914 the area was described as follows: Elevation 6,020 feet. The chief village and the tribal headquarters of the Kam Kafirs. It is high up on a great spur which runs down in an undulating manner from the Arakon range, 4 miles to the south of the village, and which is bounded on one side by the Nichingul and on the other by a second huge spur, on which the hamlets of Binarum and Jinjam are built, and which is divided from the Kamdesh spur by the torrent which turns the village water mills. It is divided into three main portions, the upper, the lower, and the east village, of which the upper is probably as large as the other two parts put together. The whole village is on a slope, which is at places extremely steep, except a portion of the upper village which is built along a moderately level ridge. The only other really level spots are the contiguous house roofs. Kamdesh is about 2,000 feet above the right bank of the Bashgul river, down to which there is a very steep road. It numbers about 600 houses, which are quite sufficient for the inhabitants. There are no defences or fortifications of any kind, with the exception of a picturesque tower which stands close to the highest houses in the village. There are 100 khasadars quartered at Kamdesh. (Robertson, I.B.C.)

*KAMKAY IRYAB ککی اریاب
    33-50 68-26 m. A village located about 2 miles east of Jaghatu-i-Wardak to the north of Ghazni.

KAM KHOST کم خوست
    A stream in Khost formed by several small tributaries from the north, east, and west, which, under the common name of Kam Khost, flow into the Shamil river from the northwest, about 12 miles below Matun. (Carr.)

KAMPAR ..... کمپر
A tribe of Siahposh Kafirs, who dwell in the valley of the Kunar river somewhere north of Nurgul. They retain their ancient faith. (Raverty.)

*KAMRAN ..... کمران (کامران)
33-29 69-38 m. A village located near Darwishi, south of the Kalandar Ghar in Paktia province.

KAMU ..... کامو
35-24 71-3 G. A gul in Kafiristan, which descends north and joins the Bashgul 6 miles below Kamdesh. There is a road over the hills into the Birkot Gul, and so on to Birkot village in the Kunar valley. At a little over 2 miles from its mouth it gives off a large branch, which runs a little west of south. Up this branch is a track which crosses a pass and then descends into the Azharbai valley. (Robertson.)

*KAMUSH ..... کموش
34-49 69-47 m. A village located on a tributary of the Tagab, about 8 miles southeast of Tagab in Kapisa province.

KAMYABA ..... کمیابه
A section of the Dai Zangi Hazaras. (See Military Report on Hazarajat, Part II.)

KAMZAI ..... کمزی
A subdivision of the Chakmanis.

KAMZAN ..... کمزن
Probably the same as Kimsan.

*KANAI ..... کنی
33-23 69-42 m. A village located on the Ster Lgad, northwest of Khost (Matun) in Paktia province.

KANAK ..... کانک
34-40 66-50 m. (See Military Report on Hazarajat, Part II.) A small glen in the southwest of the Yak Walang district. Recent maps show the name Sar-i-Kanak. (LWA)

KANDA ..... کنده
34-47 70-19 m. A village in Laghman, on the right bank of the Alingar river, about 2 miles? north of Mandrawar.
The following are the hamlets composing the village, all the inhabitants of which are Dehgans:

        (1) Banda-i-Malik Shuja
        (2) Duppi
        (3) Sapparha. (Warburton.)

Another village with this name is located on a tributary of the Kunar river, at 34-44 70-43 m. (LWA)

KANDA ..... کنده
34-36 70-44 G. A village in Laghman mentioned by Warburton as consisting of two hamlets; viz, Kala-i-Zargaran and Kala-i-Mosam. Inhabitants: Arokis. (Warburton.)

*KANDAHARI KALA کندهاری کلا
   32-41 68-28 m. A village located some 12 miles south of Khair Kot (Zarghun Shahr) in Ghazni province.

*KANDAK کندک
   34-43 70-36 m. A village located near the source of the Dara-i-Nur stream, about 8 miles north of Dara-i-Nur in Nangarhar province.

*KANDALAI کندلی
   34-54 70-56 m. A village located on the Kugal Rud, about 4 miles from its confluence with the Dara-i-Pich.

*KANDAO کنداو
   34-2 69-17 m. A village located southeast of Zarghun Shahr in Logar province. Other places with this name are located northeast of Sarkani and southeast of Asadabad in Kunar province, at 34-50 71-11 m.

*KANDAO GHAR کنداوغر
   34-5 69-20 m. A mountain located east of Zarghun Shahr in Logar province.

*KANDO KALAI کندوکی
   33-24 69-20 m. A village located southwest of Shwak and northwest of Wazi in Paktia province.

*KANDAR قندر
   34-23 68-18 m. A village located on a tributary of the Dara-i-Jelga, southwest of the Kuh-i-Qalandaran. Other places with this name are located on a path leading from the valleys of the Dara-i-Pich to the Kugar Rud in Kunar province, at 34-55 70-51 m.; and on a stream running north to the Dara-i-Pich in Kunar province at 34-53 70-46 m.

KANDESI قندسی
   33- 69-. A ravine in the Hazardarakht defile, which is passed about the 5th mile from Drekala towards the Shutur Garden. This ravine runs down from the Hasan Khel country.

KANDIBAGH کندی باغ
   34-17 70-23 m. A village of about 1,000 inhabitants in the Chapriar subdivision of the Jalalabad district; it lies on the right bank of the Chapriar stream, at about 21 miles east of Gandamak on the direct road from that place to Basawal. Supplies and water are fairly plentiful here, and grazing is abundant. (I.B.C.)

KANDI-I-FATEH KHAN کندی فتح خان
   34- 70-. A village in the Kama division of the Jalalabad district, about 1/2 mile south east of Kala-i-Akhund. Inhabitants: Hindkis, Dehgans and Tajiks. (Jenkyns.)

KANDI-I-HAJI NAZAR کندی حاجی نظر
   34- 70-. A village in the Kama division of the Jalalabad district situated midway between Kandi-i-Fateh Khan and Kandi-i-Mir Khwaja Jan. Inhabitants: Lodis and Afghans. (Jenkyns.)

KANDI-I-KANDAHARI کندی کندهاری
   34- 70-. A village in the Kama division of the Jalalabad district. Inhabitants: Lodis. (Jenkyns.)

KANDI-I-MIR ABDULLA کندی میر عبدالله
    34- 70-. A village in the Kama division of the Jalalabad district.
    Inhabitants: Lodis. (Jenkyns.)

KANDI-I-MIR KHWAJA JAN کندی میر خواجه جان
    34- 70-. A village in the Kama division of the Jalalabad district,
    situated on the left bank of the Kabul river, about 1 mile southeast
    of Kani-i-Haji Nazar. Inhabitans: Sayyids. (Jenkyns.)

*KANDUN کندون
    34-49 70-2 m. A village located northwest of Alishang in Laghman
    province.

*KANG کنگ
    34-4 67-7 m. A village located on a tributary of the Helmand, a few
    miles west of Pitaoqul in Bamian province.

*KANGARAN کنگران
    34-19 67-59 m. A village located about 5 miles southeast of Behsud
    in Maidan province.

*KANGUR کنگور
    34-59 67-54 m. A village located on a tributary of the Shikari
    river, northeast of Bamian.

KANJAR KALA کنجر قلعه
    34- 69-. A village in the Daman, north of Kabul, containing 100
    houses. Inhabitants solely Ghilzais. (I.B.C)

KANKRAK کنکرک
    34- 70-. A village in the Surkhab division of the Jalalabad dis-
    trict, situated on the right bank of the Surkhab, 6 miles northeast
    of Nimla. Inhabitants: Astanazai Ghilzais.
    Kankrak-i-Tajiki lies 2 miles northeast. Inhabitants: Tajiks.
    (Jenkyns.)

KANTOR کنتور
    A Kafir clan, divided into Kainigul and Gada. The Kainigul is again
    subdivided into the Bairkama, Pimichgram, and Atergam. According to
    Gardner they live high up among the mountains, and are much fairer
    than the tribes of the south. (Lumsden, Gardner.) A village with
    this name is located at 35-34 70-18 G. (LWA)

KAO کاو
    A name by which the Alingar river is sometimes known.

KAOSHAN Or DARA-I-KAFSHAN دره کفشان
    35-3 69-4. A large glen draining southwards from the Kaoshan pass
    in the Hindu Kush to the Ghorband valley which it joins near Burj-i-
    Guljan, 22-1/2 miles from the summit of the pass and 16-1/2 miles
    from Charikar. It is traversed throughout its length by a road
    leading from the Ghorband valley, over the Kaoshan pass; into the
    valley of Khinjan. A considerable stream flows down the glen; this
    stream has to be repeatedly crossed and recrossed and, when swollen
    by the melting snows in spring, renders the road in the lower part
    of the glen impassable. There is however, a road, practicable for
    laden mules, along the crest of the high ridge which bounds the glen
    on the west, and there are several cross-tracks leading out of the
    Kaoshan into the Nimakao glen on the west, and the Kol-i-yer and
    Salang on the east (see notes to stages 2 and 3, North-East Afghani-
    stan route No. 28). (I.B.C.)

KAOSHAN کشان

35-3 69-4. Elevation 14,340 feet. A pass over the Hindu Kush at the head of the Kaoshan glen. The old Kabul-Khinjan main road over this range was that by the Kaoshan, but his has now been superseded by the Chahardar. The Kaoshan route (North-East Afghanistan, No. 28) is, however, still much used by kafilas, with fully laden camels, but would not be practicable for camels of the Punjab. It is customary to repair the road when troops, or an important official, are about to travel over it, the work being carried out by local labour and under local arrangements. The last time this was done apears to have been in 1884 since when the road has doubtless fallen into a very bad condition. Information obtained by Maitland's party, regarding the time when the pass may be considered closed, varies very considerably. In 1885 it was closed at the beginning of November, and Talbot heard an account, which appeared to be true, of several people having lost their lives in trying to get over it when too late. But all accounts agree in saying that there is no certainty as to when the pass mayclose. It may be in October or it may be about the middle of November. It opens about the end of April, but the streams are not down till about the middle of July. The road is completely open for 3 to 2-1/2 months. Of the three main roads over this portion of the Hindu Kush--the Chahardar, the Kaoshan, and the Khawak--the Kaoshan opens last and closes first. The Kaoshan Kotal itself, however, is by no means difficult. The worst parts of the road are the lower half of the Kaoshan glen, and a great part of the upper half of the Khinjan.

The following estimate of the time and labour required to make a road by the Kaoshan from the Khinjan valley to that of Ghorband practicable for British division, with baggage on the Kabul scale, and mule carriage only gives a good idea of the state of the road in 1886:

(1) From Khinjan to Gorsokhta, 11 miles.
"From Khinjan to where the defile (Khinjan Tangi) commences is about 3 miles, of which about 2 miles altogether needs improvement. To do this in one day, 1,000 men would be required: 600 with picks, 50 with crowbars, the remainder with shovels.
"Thence to toll-bar (Sang-i-Lasham) is 3/4ths of a mile. For this piece it would be necessary to have: two companies of sappers, with their blasting equipment and gun-cotton, and about 500 infantry, the latter with 50 crowbars, 100 picks and 100 shovels. The sappers and part of the infantry would be required for two days, and one piece, where a high retaining wall appears necessary, might take three days to finish.
"From Sang-i-Lasham to the mouth of the Chandaran ravine is 1/2 a mile: 100 infantry with 20 crowbars, 40 picks and 40 shovels would be required here.
"Thence to first bridge (Pul-i-Siah Sang) is 1/2 a mile, and to improve the existing line of road would be very troublesome: one company of sappers with their blasting equipment and 400 infantry with picks, shovels and crowbars, would be required for two days on this portion.
"But possibly a better road could be made nearer the stream, through the orchards, in one day, with 1/2 a company of sappers and 200 infantry, one-fourth of the work only being apparently required. In this case some axes must be provided, in addition to the above mentioned tools.
"For bridge (Pul-i-Siah Sang) and its approaches a separate party would have to be provided. The piers would have to be cut down about 2 feet and fresh road bearers cut and placed. Also roadway

and approaches made. For the latter the boulders would have to be smoothed as much as possible and filled in with small stones, and, if possible, they should be covered with earth. There is 100 yards of boulder approach on the right bank.

"The span of the bridge is from 20 to 25 feet. The piers of rough stone and brushwood will probably do as they are, if cut down. Roadway now just wide enough for one baggage animal to go over at a time with tolerable safety, say 4 feet.

"Half a company of sappers and 200 infantry, with 50 crowbars (if possible), 50 picks and 50 shovels would be required for the bridge and approaches. They should also be provided with 10 sand-bags, or something of that nature, for carrying earth and stones; also a supply of iron spikes, if possible. This piece of work might be done in a day if the timber, which is close at hand, can be got ready in that time, but it might be necessary to fell and shape it the day before.

"From the bridge to where the road begins to ascend the hillside is about 3/4ths of a mile; only some clearing away of boulders would be required. In this piece 50 infantry with 10 crowbars, 20 picks and 20 shovels would suffice.

"For the ascent along the hillside, and descent to Bagh-i-Bai hamlet, a new line, about 30 feet below the present road, would probably be the best: 500 infantry, half with picks and half with shovels, would be required for three days, and some blasting might also be necessary.

"The second bridge is of the same character as the first, but the piers do not require cutting down, as it stands low. The approaches are, however, bad; a ramp would have to be cut and embankment made up to it; 1/2 a company of sappers, 50 infantry with 5 crowbars, 10 picks and 10 shovels could do the work in one day. There is wood close at hand for road-bearers, etc.

"Beyond the bridge, on the right bank, the road is bad for 300 yards, and blasting would be necessary: 1 company of sappers with blasting equipment for 3 days and 100 infantry with picks and shovels for the same time would be required. It might, however, be possible to keep along the base of the slope on which the road runs, when little but clearing of boulders would be necessary. In this case 200 infantry with 50 crowbars, 100 picks and 50 shovels might do the work in one day. Some sappers with gun-cotton to smash the boulders might be wanted. Levers can be cut from trees close to the road.

"Thence to Takhta Sang is about 700 yards. The road is pretty good, and requires little doing to it.

"Close to Takhta Sang there is some ground with large boulders protruding; here the road wants blasting and filling in; 10 sappers would be required for the work.

"Thence for 1/2 mile the road is pretty good, but 200 yards beore reaching the third bridge (Pul-i-Malkhan) it requires remaking: a company of sappers and 100 infantry, with crowbars, picks and shovels, as before, might do the work in 4 to 6 days. It is useless to cross this bridge, as the road on the left bank is practically impossible to make for guns in a reasonable time. It would, therefore, be necessary to follow the Salang road which keeps up the right bank. It was not gone over, but looks much easier than that on the left bank.

"From the bridge up to opposite the Gorsokhta camping-ground is 2 1/2 to 2 3/4 miles. The road would require some making, paricularly where it crosses the mouth of the Gorsokhta ravine, distant 1 1/2 to 1 3/4 miles. As far as can be seen 1,000 men might do it in one day." (Talbot.)

(2) Gorsokhta to Kata Sang, 10 to 11 miles.
Maitland says: "In the present (1886) state of the road it would take all day (say 10 hours) to get 4,000 mules and ponies over the 10 miles between camp Gorsokhta and camp Kata Sang. In fact, it would very likely take longer, as the animals would probably get jammed and throw their loads in crossing the ravines.
"It would therefore be necessary to improve almost the whole of the latter half of the road for baggage animals in case of the advance of troops, and following the line of the present road, this would probably take 2,000 men two days.
"To make a gun road crossing from right to left bank about 2 1/2 miles above Gorsokhta camp, and then up the latter, might take 3,500 infantry and three or four companies of sappers a week or ten days. This is, of course, ony a rough guess, as no examination of the road was possible. It is not unlikely that it would prove advantageous to take the road all the way along the right bank."

(3) Kata Sang to Sherakai, 181/2 miles.
No estimate was made of that part of the road from Kata Sang to Maidan-i-Khuni, but of that portion lying between the latter place and Sherakai, Maitland says:
"Talbot is of opinion that it would be practically impossible to make a road betweeen this place and the Maidan-i-Khuni fit for artillery on wheels, the gradients being so severe and the glen so narrow. Talbot also declined to make any estimate of the time and labour required to make the road practicable for the mule carriage of a British division. No doubt the difficulty of such a task would be considerable, but I am not sure that it is quite so great as appears at first sight. Putting aside the actual roughness of the existing road, there are two great difficulties; first, the steepness of the gradient; secondly, the number of times the stream has to be crossed. With regard to the first, it would be impossible to make any material improvement. If the distances and elevations are correct, the existing track has an average rise of not less that 1 in 10 from Sherakai to the Maidan-i-Khuni, a distance of 7 1/2 miles. As to the second, it is probable that, with a certain amount of blasting, almost all the crossings might be avoided. Even now there is said to be a practicable camel track up each side of the glen, for kafilas begin to travel when the stream is still unfordable, and are obliged to keep to one bank or the other. It is true the camels are Kuchi camels, which can carry loads over ground that no Punjabi camels would attempt unladen; still they are hardly as active or sure footed as mules, and I am inclined to think that, with a little blasting and a couple of bridges, a very fair four foot path might be carried up the glen as far as Maidan-i-Khuni in less than a week, if a battalion of pioneers and two companies of sappers were available. Whether the objects to be gained would be worth the time it would take to carry out the work is a matter for separate consideration.
"In its present condition the road may be considered practicable for an infantry brigade, with ammunition mules only, and one mountain battery. Working parties should, however, be sent on, if possible, to improve the worst places. Half a battalion of pioneers so employed, for even one day would make a considerable difference."

(4) From Sherakai to Burj-i-Guljan, 10 miles.
The road is as bad in many places as that in the last stage. Maitland says:
"Where it runs along hillsides it is 4 to 6 feet wide, but even here leaves much to be desired, while in the bed of the stream it is

often very bad.
"I think a 6-foot path, practicable for the mule transport of a division (Kabul scale), might be made without much difficulty, but the stream would have to be crossed a good many times, and any work done to its bed would need constant renewal." (Maitland, Talbot.)

*KAPAR KHUNE کپر خونه
32-7 68-47 m. A village located east of Wur and northwest of Mamai in southern Ghazni province.

*KAPISA کاپیسا
35-0 69-21. Kapisa, once a province in east-central Afghanistan, is now the northeastern part of Parwan province. (See Parwan). Kapisa is divided into the woleswalis of Mahmud Raqi, Kohistan, Tagab, Panjshir, and Nejrab, and into the alaqadaris of Char Qarya (Panjshir 1), Dara Hazara (Panjshir 2), Durnama, and Alahsai. The capital of the province was Mahmud Raqi. For woleswali lists from the Department of Statistics of the Ministry of Agriculture and Irrigation, see tables on the next six pages.

KAPTASAN کپتسان
A main section of the Besud Hazaras. (See Military report on Hazarajat, Part II.)

*KAPZAR قاپزار
34-40 68-26 m. A village located on a tributary of the Qol-i-Khesh, west of the Kuh-i-Chaji in Parwan province.

KARBAGH Or QARABAGH قره باغ
33-11 68-6. Karabagh is a woleswali in Ghazni province. The woleswali comprises an area of 1,799 square kilometers and has an agricultural population that has been estimated at from 28,875 to 73,512. The woleswali is bounded in the west by Jaghori, in the north by Nawar and Jaghatu, in the east by Andar and Giru and in the south by Ab Band and Moqor. Qarabagh has about 371 villages, 33 of which have more than 500 inhabitants. The major villages listed in the PG are as follows: Ibrahim Khel, Akhtar Khel, Haji Akhtar Moh'd, Akhto Wal, Ahan (Ayin), Bayram (Barim), Begi Khel, Baluch Khel, Bayram Bedarah (Bedarah), Yaraki Khel, Tamaki, Warqa, Qol, Tochi, Kohna Deh, Jan Murad Wa Qala-i-Jabar Khan, Jan Murad-i-Sufla, Jan Murad-i-Ulya, Jamal Khel-i-Taraki (Qarya-i-Jamal), Chergi, Khan Mahmud (Mamur), Khado Khel, Khandan Jangalak, Nau Deh Jangalak, Dado Khel, Deh Badai, Darya Khel, Kashi, Hamogai, Zard Alu, Qala-i-Husain-Arbab, Kohna Deh-Zardalu, Nau Deh-i-Zardalu, Zarak, Sar Buland, Sar Sota, Sangi, Surkai Khel, Shah Gholai, Shah Karez, Shakai Noka, Shamada, Sherabad, Sher Turki, Ali Niyazi, Eidi, Ghurghurak, Ghundi, Fateh Moh'd, Fati, (Fateh Moh'd -Sangi), Qaracha, Qala-i-Roshan, Qala-i-Tor, Qala-i-Kakash, Qala-i-Niyaz Khan (Niyaz-Moh'd Kharoti), Qalander Khel, Quluch (Luch), Atal, Ayrma, Bini Ghar, Siya Deh, Ghawch Deh, Qash, Takhun, Qolya Qol (Paywand Goshta), Kata Deh, Karim (Qala-i-Karim Khan), Adam, Kalbi, Kalbi Khel (Kalbi-Khel Jan Murad), Gaw Murdah, Gaw Meshak, Gadol-i-Behbud, Buland Deh, Qala-i- Maidanak, Gerdah, Gurgab, Gul Koh, Bagh-i-Atar, Mir Joye, Mir Zaka, Nau Deh-i-Gul Koh, Ganki (Ganki-Rana Khel), Mado (Mulla-Mado Khan), Masum (Chambar-i-Moh'd Masum), Malang Khel, Basarak, Bam Qash, Jamji, Chogha-i-Bala, Roha, Qeshlaghak, Maluk (Maluk-i- Sangi), Mochi Monsaki (Mochi), Moryani Sufla, Moryani Ulya, Musa Wal, Mulla Khel, Qala-i-Gul Akhund, Nau Deh, Miyantu, Khar Bulaq, Miran (Chambar-i-Mulla Miran,) Mir Hassan Khel, Mir Alam, Qarya-i-Mirak, (Mir Wayez), Natar, Takhel-i-Sufla-i-Jan Murad,

KAPISA — ESTIMATE OF AGRICULTURAL POPULATION AND AREA UNDER CULTIVATION

	Villages	Agricultural Population	Landlords	Lands under Cultivation in Jaribs			Lands under Cultivation in Hectares		
				Irrigated	Non-Irrig.	Total	Irrigated	Non-Irrig.	Total
PANJSHIR	50	98,520	9,330	22,260	—	22,260	4,452	—	4,452
TAGAB	34	54,020	6,130	10,780	—	10,780	2,156	—	2,156
KOHISTAN	40	66,740	6,890	42,400	—	42,400	8,480	—	8,480
MAHMUD RAQI (KAPISA)	50	34,960	3,270	40,860	2,480	43,340	8,172	496	8,668
ALLAHSAY	25	25,430	4,960	3,720	—	3,720	744	—	744
KOHBAND (DURNAME)	28	15,890	1,790	3,240	—	3,240	648	—	648
NAJRAB	132	92,160	10,590	69,680	—	69,680	13,936	—	13,936
CHAR QARYA (PANJSHIR 1)	10	57,200	4,700	4,600	—	4,600	920	—	920
DARAH HAZARA (PANJSHIR 2)	12	15,890	2,120	2,170	—	2,170	434	—	434
TOTAL	381	460,810	49,780	199,710	2,480	202,190	39,942	496	40,438

KAPISA — STATISTICAL ESTIMATE OF LIVESTOCK BY WOLESWALIS AND ALAKADARIS

	Sheep	Karakul Sheep	Goats	Cattle	Buffaloes	Camels	Horses	Donkeys	Mules	Poultry
PANJSHIR	3,820	—	3,520	4,770	900	—	40	8,210	—	25,080
TAGAB	4,850	—	1,990	4,960	1,000	—	30	1,910	—	7,290
KOHISTAN	17,010	—	5,170	11,650	700	10	710	2,830	—	24,550
MAHMUD RAQI (KAPISA)	15,120	—	6,190	12,980	—	20	500	4,160	—	30,670
ALLAHSAY	410	—	5,480	910	1,000	30	10	1,410	—	6,810
KOHBAND (DURNAME)	3,120	—	2,290	900	—	—	—	1,640	—	9,900
NAJRAB	30,750	—	22,670	17,620	700	10	150	6,260	—	47,580
CHAR QARYA (PANJSHIR 1)	10,110	—	3,290	1,920	500	—	300	2,180	—	9,610
DARAH HAZARA (PANJSHIR 2)	1,190	—	3,170	910	800	—	30	1,930	—	6,710
TOTAL	86,380	—	53,780	56,520	5,600	70	1,770	30,530	—	168,200

KAPISA

TOTAL CULTIVABLE LAND, BY CROPS—IN KABULI JARIBS

	Grains			Vegetables	Industrial Crops	Other Crops	Fruits	Total Cultivated Land
	Irrigated	Non-Irrig.	Total					
PANJSHIR	17,680	—	17,680	110	—	500	1,780	20,070
TAGAB	7,410	—	7,410	100	—	490	1,730	9,730
KOHISTAN	32,080	—	32,080	560	1,370	950	3,450	38,410
MAHMUD RAQI (KAPISA)	32,550	1,200	33,750	3,370	3,590	540	3,710	44,960
NAJRAB	51,830	—	51,830	2,100	—	2,470	11,610	68,010
ALLAHSAY	2,880	—	2,880	100	—	100	680	3,760
CHAR QARYA (PANJSHIR 1)	3,360	—	3,360	230	—	230	820	4,640
DARAH HAZARA (PANJSHIR 2)	1,340	—	1,340	50	—	50	360	1,800
KOHBAND (DURNAME)	2,270	—	2,270	70	—	70	270	2,680
TOTAL	151,400	1,200	152,600	6,690	4,960	5,400	24,410	194,060

LAND UNDER IRRIGATION AND SOURCES OF IRRIGATION

KAPISA	Area in Jaribs					Number of Sources			
	Canals	Springs	Karez	Wells	Total	Canals	Springs	Karez	Wells	Water Mills
PANJSHIR	22,260	—	—	—	22,260	50	6	—	—	78
TAGAB	5,130	4,970	680	—	10,780	9	12	6	2	15
KOHISTAN	42,400	—	—	—	42,400	13	—	—	82	78
MAHMUD RAQI (KAPISA)	40,290	570	—	—	40,860	50	2	—	—	93
NAJRAB	57,050	9,100	3,280	250	69,680	98	33	38	92	193
ALLAHSAY	3,400	320	—	—	3,120	25	11	—	—	55
CHAR QARYA (PANJSHIR 1)	4,600	—	—	—	4,600	15	—	—	—	66
DARAH HAZARA (PANJSHIR 2)	2,170	—	—	—	2,170	12	—	—	—	11
KOHBAND (DURNAME)	1,680	1,090	470	—	3,240	13	8	5	—	49
TOTAL	178,980	16,050	4,430	250	199,710	285	72	49	176	638

PRODUCTION OF AGRICULTURAL CROPS—IN KABULI SEERS

KAPISA	Grains Irrigated	Grains Non-Irrig.	Total	Vegetables	Other Crops Industrial Crops	Other Crops Other Temp. Crops	Fruits
PANJSHIR	742,560	—	742,560	20,790	—	105,000	299,040
TAGAB	311,220	—	311,220	18,900	—	102,900	290,640
KOHISTAN	1,347,360	—	1,347,360	105,840	47,950	199,500	579,600
MAHMUD RAQI (KAPISA)	1,367,100	14,400	1,381,500	636,930	125,650	113,300	623,280
NAJRAB	2,176,860	—	2,176,860	396,900	—	518,700	1,950,480
ALLAHSAY	120,960	—	120,960	18,900	—	21,000	114,240
CHAR QARYA (PANJSHIR 1)	141,120	—	141,120	43,470	—	48,300	137,760
DARAH HAZARA (PANJSHIR 2)	56,280	—	56,280	9,450	—	10,500	60,480
KOHBAND (DURMANE)	95,340	—	95,340	13,230	—	14,700	45,360
TOTAL	6,358,800	14,400	6,373,200	1,264,410	173,600	1,134,000	4,100,880

TOTAL CULTIVABLE LANDS—IN KABULI JARIBS

KAPISA	Total	Pastures	Forests	Under Cultivation	Fallow Lands
PANJSHIR	25,270	2,870	140	22,260	5,180
TAGAB	14,580	3,710	90	10,780	2,310
KOHISTAN	55,330	12,750	180	42,400	10,210
MAHMUD RAQI (KAPISA)	55,560	11,120	1,100	43,340	7,390
NAJRAB	102,610	21,440	11,490	69,680	14,440
ALLAHSAY	12,090	570	7,800	3,720	180
CHAR QARYA (PANJSHIR 1)	11,820	7,220	—	4,600	360
DARAH HAZARA (PANJSHIR 2)	3,880	1,710	—	2,170	150
KOHBAND (DURNAMA)	5,750	2,510	—	3,240	920
TOTAL	286,890	63,900	20,800	202,190	41,140

Takhel Ulya, Nawroz Khel, Naso Khel, Naudeh, Neyal Khan (Nehal Khan), Nau Kurdak-i-Raba Khel, Nauy Kurdak, Nai Qala, Alma Shahr, Bulaqi, Dah Bakhsh, Dah, Sayed Khan, Sargha Wa Gosha, Sartalan Shadawla (Shad Wa Diba), Ghar, Ghafto-i-Sufla, Gafto-i-Ulya, Kash Kawa-i-Nekzar, Malakhi, Wata Pur, Wali Jan Murad-i-Nauabad, Wali Dad, Harun Khel-i-Jan Murad), Hamza Khail, Laghar Joye, Lala, Layeq, Khan Zaman Khel, Gul Akhund Zadah, Mir Khan, Khunian, Qaburgah, Khartoghi, Baldar Ghan, Jamal, Safra, Safir (Asfjar), Beni Qala, Surkai Khan, Sayed Khan, Toramai, Sinja, Sulaiman Khel, Barakai, Safar Khel, Moshki, and Nala. (LWA) In 1914 the area was described as follows:

Elevation about 7,000 feet. A district crossed on the road from Kalat-i-Ghilzai to Ghazni, and lying mainly to the west and northwest of the road. It is first entered about 90 miles northeast of Kalat-i-Ghilzai between Oba Karez and Jamrud. In this district, or at any rate in the portion of it crossed by the road, Afghan and Hazara villages are found side by side. In 1880 the valley was a scene of desolation in consequence of the Hazaras having attacked some Afghan villages when the men belonging to them were away at Kabul in January 1880 during the investment of Sherpur.

This led to retaliation on the part of the Afghans, but in April 1880, on the advance of Sir Donald Stewart's force to Ghazni, the Hazaras burnt all the Afghan villages; the result was, as regards the country about Jamrud and Chahardeh Bebud (Behsud?), complete devastation. This was most marked in August 1880, when the country was again traversed by Sir F. Roberts' force proceeding to Kandahar. The inhabitants of the large Hazara village of Chahardeh Bebud (about 2 miles from Jamrud) were released by the advance of the force from an investment of some months; had it not been for this chance they would probably all have been killed by the Afghans, who were much exasperated at their previous behavior in the spring.

The main district of Karabagh is separated from the plain over which the Kalat-i-Ghilzai--Ghazni road passes by a low range of hills which terminated before reaching Jamrud; it is remarkably fertile, well cultivated, populous and productive.

The inhabitants are mainly Hazaras of the Chahardasta and Muhammad Khwaja tribes. (See "Ghazni.") They probably can muster about 2,000 fighting men.

Two roads start from Chahardeh into Hazara territory. At or near Zardalu they diverge, one taking a northerly turn, and the other and most direct road going through Tamaki. At Loman in the Jaghuri district, which is not more than four marches via Tamaki from Chahardeh, both roads meet. As far as Loman both are said to be easy,--practicable, that is, for field-guns and any laden animals. Beyond Loman the country is much more difficult. From Loman a road goes north to the Besud territory, and another runs south, following the course of the Arghandab.

Molloy says: "The Karabagh Hazaras comprise about 7,000 families and pay in revenue Rs. 40,000. This does not include the Aldai section, who do not number more than 100 faimlies; their revenue, amounting to Rs. 600, was made over by Amir Dost Muhammad Khan as a grant to the estate of Mirza Muhammad Husain Khan, a Kizilbash Sardar." The district of Karabagh is under the Hakim of Ghazni. (Molloy, Gaselee.)

KARABAGH قره باغ
33- 68-. Elevation 7,426 feet. A village 37 miles south of Ghazni. There is a large fort here to the east of the road, and three others near it. Water is plentiful from karez; forage is abundant, and fuel also. It is also called Chahardeh-i-Hazara, and is inhab-

ited by both Afghans and Hazaras of the Bubak tribe. There are 100 Khasadars quartered at Karabagh. (Masson, Leech, Campbell, Broadfoot, I.B.C.) Recent maps show the spelling Karabagi, at 33-25 68-25.

KARABAGH قره باغ
34-51 69-9. Karabagh is a woleswali in Kabul province. The woleswali comprises an area of 111 square kilometers and has an agricultural population that has been estimated at from 16,970 to 18,821. The woleswali is bounded in the east by Istalef, in the north and east by Bagram, and in the south by Deh Sabz and Kalakan. Karabagh includes about 56 villages, of which about 40 have more than 500 inhabitants. The villages are listed in the PG as follows: Qarya-i-Langar, Allah Rahim, Alar, Qala-i-Faiz, Qala-i-Gudar, Qala-i-Qazi, Qara Bagh-i-Yusufi, Qarya-i-Karez, Qala-i-Shahi, Nahr-i-Kalan, Qalacha, Qala-i-Jafar, Bagh-i-Aroq-i-Sufla, Qarya-i-Mashur Khel, Qanat Baz, Qala-i-Baz, Sardar Beg, Qara Qul, Sabz Sang, Miana Joy, Dinar Khel, Qala-i-Akhund, Bagh-i-Areq-i-Ulya, Qala-i-Nawruz, Petawa, Esterghech, Tajekan, Khwajaha, Qaria-i-Pashi, Qala-i-Sher, Aghelak, Khoja Shahab, Logari, Jarchi, Bagh-i-Alam, Dama-i-Khwaja, Mir Khan, Urya Khel, Qarya-i-Musazai, Qala-i-Saman, Ashraf Khel, Qala-i-Diwana, Chawni, Bagh-i-Zaghan, Haji Mirullah-i-Bakhshi, Chashma-i-Kharoti, Qaryai-Dawudzai, Qala-i-Kohna-i-Mohammadzai ya Dawudzai, Qarya-i-Sofian, Qarya-i-Pahlawan, Emlake Khairullah, Qarya-i-Kakara, Qarabagh Bazar, Batni bot, Qala-i-Musa, Nahr-i-Bala, Akakhel, Taherian, and Tazian Chenar ya Qazian Chenar. (LWA) In 1914 the area was described as follows: A large group of villages about 22 miles north of Kabul. Kafilas usually make this the second stage from Kabul on the Khawak route. (I.B.C.)

*KARABAGHI قره باغی
33-25 68-25 m. A village located some 10 miles south of Ghazni and about 3 miles north of Shelger.

KARACHAH قره چاه
A section of the Muhammad Khwaja Hazaras. (See Military Report on Hazarajat, Part II.)

*KARACHAH قره چاه
34-59 69-19 m. A village located about 2 miles west of Panjshir and southeast of Charikar. Another place with this name is located on the Dara-i-Garmab, some 6 miles south of Jiska in southern Bamian province, at 34-2 67-26 m.

KARA DUSHMAN قره دشمن (دانشمند)
34-39 69-9 A. A village in the Kabul district, 6 miles northwest of the Paiminar Kotal and close to a pass in the hills (to the westward) leading into the Koh Daman. This gorge, which takes its name from the village of Kara Dushman, is passable for all pack transport. The path leads along the edge of a deep ravine, and is in some places very narrow with sharp angles to turn, but it is practicable for camels and baggage mules. Masson describes Kara Dushman as a plain 12 miles north of Kabul, but omits mention of the village. The inhabitants are Tajiks and Gadi Hazaras. Water from stream flowing through the gorge. Supplies available in small quantities. (I.B.C.) Recent maps show the name Daneshmand. (LWA)

KARAGHAYA See KARGHAI قره قیه

KARAGHOI   قره غوی
   34-29 68-15 m. A fortified hamlet, situated in a tagao of the same
   name, about 3 1/2 miles west of Jaokul on the main Kabul-Hazarajat-
   Dulat Yar road. (See Military Report on Hazarajat, Part II.)

KARAIA   کرایه (؟)
   33-48 69-45. The name applied to the upper Kurram river, between
   Ali Khel and the Frontier at Kharlachi.

KARA KATTA   قره که
   34- 67-. A village in the Kajao valley. (See Military Report on
   Hazarajat, Part II.)

KARA KHAWAL   قره خوال
   34- 67-. Elevation 9,800 feet. The third halting-place on the
   road leading from Kala Sarkari in Bamian to Daulat Yar. The camping
   ground lies in a wide, cultivated hollow on the right bank of a
   stream running from the Tabarghan Kol, and is close to the village
   of Kochinak, or Kokinak. Hardly any supplies are procurable, but
   water and fuel are abundant and there is probably grass in summer.
   About 1 mile to the southeast is a smoke-blackened khawal, or cave,
   in which a post of dak sowars is established, and from which the
   camping ground takes its name.
   The Ghazni--Mazar-i-Sharif road passes near the camping-ground,
   crossing the kotal known as Kara Khawal. The approaches to this
   pass, though slightly undulating, are quite easy. From the crest,
   elevation 11,630 feet, another road runs almost due east via the
   Tabarghan Kol to Sar-i-Karghanatu. (Muhamad Akbar Khan, I.B.C.) A
   place with this name is located at 34-45 68-14 G. (LWA)

*KARAKHEL   قره خیل
   33-13 68-46 m. A village located about 5 miles northeast of Sharan
   in eastern Ghazni province.

*KARAKUL   قره قول
   34-10 67-43 m. A village located on the source of the Garmab river,
   southeast of the Kuh-i-Khalta. Another place with this name is
   located southwest of the Kuh-i-Khalta, on a tributary of the Garmab
   river in southern Bamian province, at 34-11 67-40 m.

KARA-KUL-DAGHI See DAI ZANGI   قره قول داغی

KARAM ALI   کرم علی
   A section fo Shaikh Ali Hazaras.

*KARAM ALI   کرم علی
   34-12 68-31 m. A village located on the Dara-i-Jelga, about 2 miles
   north of Azadkhel in Maidan province.

*KARAMKOL   کرم قول
   34-14 68-38 m. A village located on a tributary of the Dara-i-
   Jelga, about 1 mile north of Suja in Maidan province. Another place
   with this name is located on a tributary of the Garmab river in
   southern Bamian province, at 34-1 67-20 m.

KARASU   قره سو
   34-22 70-14. A stream which rises in the Safed Koh, and runs
   through the valley of the Wazir Khugianis, passed Kaja, Bahar, and
   Fatehabad, and flows into the Surkhab close to the town of Balabagh.
   (MacGregor.)

KARASUF قره صوف
A section of the Jaghatu Hazaras. (See Military Report on Hazarajat, Part II.)

KARATIGA کراتیگا
33- 69-. A walled sarai on the left bank of the Hazaradarkht stream, about 9 miles southwest of Dre Kala on the Paiwar Kotal-Kabul road. Near here, on 22nd September 1879, a combined attack was made by Mangals and Ghilzais on a telegraph party bringing up poles to the Surkai Kotal: for details, see the "Official History fo the Second Afghan War." (I.B.C.)

*KARAWAL Or KARARWAL قرووال
32-51 68-46 m. A village located some 5 miles south of Omna in eastern Ghazni province.

KAREZ کاریز
33- 68-. A halting place 112 miles from Kalat-i-Ghilzai, 32 miles from Ghazni, in a level well-cultivated country. Numerous forts and villages are scattered all over the plain. Supplies procurable, and water, grass, forage for camels and fuel and abundant. (Gardner.) One place with this name is located at 32-58 67-22 A. (LWA)

*KAREZ کاریز
34-28 67-44 m. A village located north of Obah, on a tributary of the Helmand river in Bamian province. Other places with this name are located 3 miles west of Chamri in Maidan province, at 34-9 68-26 m.; on the Dara-i-Maidan southwest of Kabul, at 34-23 69-1 m.; about 2 miles south of Jaghatu-i-Wardak, some 20 miles north of Ghazni, at 33-48 68-24 m.; northwest of Nadir Shah Kot, on the road to Gardez in Paktia province, at 33-20 69-33 m.; and at 34-37 69-2 G., 33-43 69-24 G., 34-50 69-10 G., 34-41 69-15 G., 33-11 67-29 G., 32-53 67-4 G., and 33-29 69-56 G.

KAREZ کاریز
33- 69-. A halting place at the western foot of the Mirzaki Kotal, and about 1 miles from the summit. There is room for a brigade to encamp here, with sufficient water. (The latest report (1906) makes no mention of the halting-place referred to in this article but gives a collection of hamlets known as Karez, 5 miles to the west of the Mirzakai Kotal. The country hereabouts is, however, open and largely watered by means of karez, or underground water channels, so that the name might be applied to a number of different spots in the neighbourhood.) (I.B.C)

KAREZAI کاریزی
35-2 68-48 m. A village in the Ghorband valley, 20 miles east of its head, consisting of 800 houses contained in several forts, and inhabited by Hazaras. (Leech.) One village with this name is located at 34-59 69-24 G. (LWA)

*KAREZAK کاریزك
34-9 67-2 m. A village located on the Sultan Robat stream in southern Bamian province. Other places with this name are located about 8 miles west of Behsud in Bamian province, at 34-21 67-46 m.; about 6 miles southwest of Shahr-i-Khawat in Bamian province, at 34-1 67-56 m.; on the Dara-i-Turkoman, about 2 miles southwest of Asheq in Parwan province, at 34-47 68-3 m.; northeast of Arghandai on the road to Kabul, about 12 miles from the latter, at 34-31 68-59 m.; some 12 miles northeast of Ghazni on the highway to Kabul, at 33-41

68-30 m.; and north of the Karezak Ghar and northwest of Wazakhwa in southern Ghazni province, at 32-12 68-11 m.

*KAREZ FULAD کاریز فولاد
34-20 68-16 m. A village located about 1 mile west of Jakakhor on a tributary of the Dara-i-Jelga.

*KAREZGAI کاریزگی
34-51 69-20 m. A village located north of the Kuh-i-Safi and west of Qarabagh. Another place with this name is some 13 miles northeast of Gardez on the way to Alikhel, at 33-45 69-24 m.

KAREZHA-I-SHAHMARD KHAN کاریزهاشاهمرد خان
34- 70-. A village in the Surkhab division of the Jalalabad district, about a mile south of Jalalabad town. Inhabitants Dehgans and Afghans. (Jenkyns.)

KAREZI کاریزی
35- 69-. A large township in the Charikar district, southeast of Ushtargiran, said to contain 1,500 houses of Tajiks. The leading families are all Khwajas of the family of Abubakar Sadik. The different villages are Kizsaiyidi, Aftawachi, Reg-Rawan, Sherak, Parak, Kala Khwaja Sayyid, Saru, Deh Muzaffar, and Karez-i-Kohna. They are surrounded by masses of orchards and also by open cultivation. (Shahzada Taimus.) Recent maps show the spelling Karezak, at 35-0 69-26. (LWA)

KAREZ-I-ALAM کاریز علم
34-10 69-4 G. A village in the lower or northern portion of the Logar valley and on the left bank of that river, 5 miles north of Tangi Waghjan. Inhabitants Astanazai Ghilzais. In 1880 there were 10 families only resident in the village. (Clifford, Euan Smith.) Recent maps show the place Karez-i-Guli, at 34-14 69-12 m.

KAREZ-I-BASHER کاریز بشیر
34- 69-. A village in the northern division of the Logar valley. Inhabitants: Painda Khel and Sulaiman Khel Ghilzais. In 1880 the village, which consisted of two hamlets, had a population of only 10 families. (Clifford, Euan Smith.)

KAREZ-I-DAULAT کاریز دولت
34- 69-. A village of 10 houses in the northern portion of the Logar valley, on the right bank of that river. It is situated on the east of the Kabul road, halfway between Mirza and Zargan Shahar. The inhabitants are Niazis and Ahmadzais. (Euan Smith.) Recent maps show the name Qala-i-Daulat, at 34-11 69-8 m.

KAREZ-I-GHULAM MUHAMMAD Or GUL MUHAMMAD کاریز غلام محمد
34- 70-. A village in the Surkhab division of the Jalalabad district, about 1/2 mile southeast of Karezha-i-Shahmard Khan. Inhabitants: Barakzais. (Jenkyns.) Recent maps show the name Karez-i-Gul Muhammad at 33-42 68-50 A.

*KAREZ-I-GULI کاریز گولی
34-14 69-12 m. A village located about 5 miles southeast of Gomaran near Niazgul.

KAREZ-I-MALIK LALA کاریز ملک لاله
34- 70-. A village in the Surkhab division of the Jalalabad district. Inhabitants: Arabs. (Jenkyns.)

KAREZ-I-MIR کاریز میر
34-38 69-3 m. A village at the southern extremity of the Koh Daman, consisting of two portions, the upper and lower (Bala and Pain). The upper village contains 60 houses and the lower 100. It was on the low hills to the south of this village that Macpherson, advancing from Aoshar on the 10th December 1879 defeated a large body of Kohistanis under Mir Bacha, who were advancing to join the people of Maidan in the combined attack on Sherpur which took place a few days later. Inhabitants: Tajiks, Kizilbashis and Hindus. (I.B.C.)

KAREZ-I-MIRWAL کاریز میروال
34- 69-. A village of 10 houses in the northern portion of the Logar valley. Inhabitants: Ahmadzai Ghilzais. (Euan Smith.)

KAREZ-I-MIRZA AHMAD کاریز میرزا احمد
34- 69-. A village in Logar, between Dadu Khel and Purak; 12 houses of Ahmadzai Ghilzais. (I.B.C.)

KAREZ-I-OBA See OBA کاریز اوبه

KAREZ-I-PIARO KHEL کاریز پیاروخیل (؟)
34- 69-. A village in the northern portion of the Logar valley. Inhabitants: Piaro Khel and Sulaiman Khel Ghilzais. (Clifford, Euan Smith.)

KAREZ-I-RAHMATULLA کاریز رحمت الله
33-59 69-15. An encamping ground, 1 mile southeast of Kushi, on the road to the Shutur Gardan. (I.B.C.)

KAREZ-I-SAIYIDAN کاریز سیدان
34- 69-. A village of 8 houses in the northern portion of the Logar valley. Inhabitants: Sayyids. (Euan Smith.)

*KAREZ-I-SURKH کاریز سرخ
34-18 68-36 m. A village located about 3 miles north of Sewak and southwest of Nerkh in Maidan province.

KAREZ-I-USMAN KHAN کاریز عثمان خان
33- 69-. A village about 25 miles south of Ghazni. Near this, on his advance to Ghazni, General Nott's rear-guard was attacked by a party of the enemy who were, however, dispersed by Christie's horse. (Nott.)

*KARGA قرغه
34-40 67-9 m. A village located north of the Kuh-i-Baba range, near Sar-i-Qol in Bamian province.

*KARGAI کرگی
32-13 68-8 m. A village located south of the Shinkai Ghar and northwest of Wazakhwa in southern Ghazni province.

*KARGAN کارگان
33-25 68-14 m. A village located near Bagai, some 15 miles southwest of Ghazni.

KARGHA قرغه
34-33 69-3 m. A village in Paghman, half-way to Kabul from Paghman village. It is very fertile, and the land belongs to Kizilbashis,

with a few Gadi Hazara settlers. There are four forts. (I.B.C.) Another place with this name is on the east bank of the Helmand, south of Khushqol, at 34-9 67-17 m. (LWA)

قرغه

*KARGHA
33-56 68-11 m. A village located on the Shemeltu stream, about 1 mile north of Taybum in Ghazni province.

قرغه ئی (قرهقایه)

KARGHAI (KARAGHAYA)
34-33 70-15 A. Karghai is a woleswali in Laghman province. The woleswali, which comprises an area of 276 square kilometers, has an agricultural population that has been estimated at from 17,703 to 29,653. It is bounded in the north by Mehterlam and Alingar, in the east by Dara-i-Nur and Kauz Kunar, in the south by Kats Aziz Khan, and in the west by Sarobi. The woleswali contains 99 villages, 17 of which have more than 500 inhabitants. The villages are listed in the PG as follows: Qarya-i-Charbagh, Shamshirabad, Kar Parah, Kulalan, Qala-i-Mufti, Tarnak, Qala-i-Zaman Khan, Qarya-i-Hada Pur, Dehmanchi (Damanji), Sur Sangi (Surkh Sangi), Qala-i-Qazi, Kachari, Mahi Giran, Najaran, Qala-i-Pacha (Qala-i-Padshah), Qala-i-Hajiha, Qala-i-Akhund, Kargarha, Baghban Kocha, Shar-i-Char Bagh, Qarya-i-Surati, Deh Mazang-i-Qarghai, Mandrawar (Mandawor), Kamalpur (Kamalpur-i-Yaumapur), Mushina, Ferozabad, Kuna Ghar, Bandah Mehr-Del, Bela Fathulla, Mansur Kalai, Kajurah, Deh Mirak Kalai, Deh Mulla Sahib Kalai, Baghal Bandah, Logarlam, Lamtak, Barakat Khan, Abdurahim-Zai (Abdurahim), Sangari (Sangur), Husainabad, Ghundi-i-Abdurahimzai (Qarya-i-Ghundi), Zangora-i-Abdurahimzai, Nau Deh Mardah (Nau Deh-i-Mala), Qabila, Mulla Khel, Bolan-i-Sufla, Bolan-i-Ulya, Dara-i-Ghar (Dargha), Andud, Dara-i-Lam, Baluchabad, Lamti Sulaiman Khel, Lamti Sahak, Aghrabad-i-Khas, Sangar Khel, Addin Khel, Tarnag, Shahi Khel, Ibrahim Khel, Nur-i-Aghrabad, Char Qala, Abbas Khel, Qala-i-Haji Gul Dad-i-Aghrabad, Ambar, Band-i-Payan, Zarina-i-Sufla (Zerani), Zarina-i-Ulya, Qarya-i-Sarferaz Khan, Qala-i-Taj Moh'd Khan, Dandar (Dahandar), Kharoti, Tarah Khel, Fatur Gamba (Patogobah), Kakats, Zara Qala, Farman Khel, Sar Kando Baba (Kaj-i-Moh'd Ali Khan), Qala-i-Malik (Qala-i-Tak), Aminabad, Utra Gul, Shahidan, Nauabad-i-Musa, Kaj-i-Miya Khan, Khairo Khel, Surkhakan, Nasser, Qala-i-Rahim, Lal Khanabad, Kutub Khel-i-Kundah, Chora Khel-i-Kundah, Dopi Kunda, Kundah, Qala-i-Qazi Mandrawol, Miya Khel, Farman Khel, Safar Khel, Kashmand, Zangora-i-Ilyas Khel, Serkai Tsaparai, Qasemabad, Nahr-i-Karim, Shahbab, Kampurah, Kaj-i-Aminabad, Kamsun, Bacha-i-Siyab, Nasir, and Kaj-i-Rokai. (LWA) In 1914 Karghai was described as follows: A village in Laghman, on the left bank of the Alingar river, about 16-1/2 miles from Jalalabad. It is situated on a mound, exactly opposite the village of Mandrawar and about 1-1/2 miles therefrom. The inhabitants are Tajiks and Jabar Khel Ghilzais. At Karghai the Alingar river is crossed by a road leading from Jalalabad to Farajghan. The water at the ford is said to be of no depth, and there is a rude bridge for foot passengers and also a masak raft ferry. The Amir is said (1906) to be building a pucca bridge here. (I.B.C.)

قارغان

*KARGHAN
34-50 71-5 m. A village located on a tributary of the Kunar, some 7 miles southwest of Chagha Sarai in Kunar province.

KARGHANATU قرغنه تو
34-47 67-23 m. A glen draining north-northeast from the Koh-i-Baba to the Bamian valley. The halting-place of this name (elevation 10,845'), on the Bamian-Daulat Yar road, is near the point where the glen is formed by the junction of three tagaos. Looking towards them, the centre one is Sar-i-Karghanatu; that to the left is Walangak; the one to the right is Nobala Sokhta. There are said to be, in all, eleven villages in the Karghanatu and its tributaries. (See "Bamian District"). Several are visible, and within a short distance. On the main stream, and close to it, is Khair Khana. Beyond, on the Walangak water, are the two adjacent hamlets of Kala Kohna. Up Walangak is the fort of the same name. Up the Sar-i-Karghanatu are the forts of Kala Abbas and Chahar Chashmal. Near the mouth of the same glen is Tob Ali. Lower down the main glen, and on the opposite side, is Kala Zafar Naib; but it is deserted, or nearly so.
Below this place the glen is shallow, and about a mile wide. Lower down it contracts to a defile and there is no road down it.
From the top of Sar-i-Karghanatu there is a road over the main range by the Dulgha Kotal to Sar-i-Bulak. This pass is higher than the Zard Sang and was blocked by snow in October 1885. (Maitland.)

KARGHANI کرغانی (قرغنی)
A section of the Jaghatu Hazaras. (See Military Report on Hazarajat, Part II.)

*KARGHANI قرغنی
33-39 68-6 m. A village located on the Dara-i-Yusuf, about 1 mile north of Nadri in Ghazni province.

KARHI کرهی
33- 69-. A hamlet in the Istiar valley, 8 miles northwest of the Istiar pass. The village stands on high ground. (Kane.)

KARIAK See BIRGALICH قریك

*KARIA KULI قریه قلی
34-29 67-8 m. A village located on the Tarapas stream, a tributary of the Dara-i-Mur in Bamian province.

*KARIA JALIL قریه جلیل
33-35 68-10 m. A village located about 12 miles west of Ghazni on the way to Babur over the Kotal-i-Jalil.

*KARIGAR کارگر
34-8 70-21 m. A village located north of Spin Ghar, some 6 miles west of Haska Mina in Nangarhar province.

KARIM DAD KHEL کریم داد خیل
A tribe regarding which Masson has the following note: "To the north of the plain of Bagram, it has an abrupt descent into the cultivated lands and pastures of the Baltu Khel and Karim Dad Khel families." (Masson.)
This tribe is said to be a section of the Jaghatu Hazaras. (I.B.C.)

KARIM KHAN کریم خان
34- 69-. A fort of Aoshar, in the Chardeh valley of Kabul. Four towers. The place contains 40 families--all Kizilbashis of the Aoshar section. (I.B.C.)

*KARIMKHEL کریم خیل
    34-16 69-43 m. A village located on a stream about 2 miles south of Doao and south of Sarobi in Nangarhar province.

KARINDA کارینده
    34-45 69-9 G. A village in the Koh Daman, 2-1/2 miles south of Ak Sarai. In 1880 this village contained 400 houses. Inhabitants: Tajiks. The headman of the village, Rustam Khan, is said to have been shot by Cavagnari just before the latter fell, in September 1879. (Kinloch, I.B.C.)

KARINJ کرنج
    34-46 70-13 m. A mountain range which separates the Alishang and Alingar valleys. It probably forms the western boundary of Kafiristan. Its highest peak is over 14,000 feet. Recent maps show the spelling Karanj Ghar. (LWA)

KARKACH Or KAH KATS کارکچ (کاه کچ)
    34-29 70-4 m. A village in Laghman, on the right bank of the Kabul river, 2 miles west of Girdi Kats and 6-1/2 miles west of Khairo Khel. Karkach is an insignificant village, but has a small fort with two towers of no strength. (Young.)

KARKACHA کرکچه
    34-20 69-39 m. A spur from the Safed Koh which cuts across the extreme west of the Jalalabad valley. It is the last and highest of the ridges which are crossed on the road to Kabul from Jalalabad, the streams from its east face falling into the Surkhab, while those of the opposite side join the river of Logar. Its direction is roughly N.N.E. and S.S.W. and its width about 8 miles. The passes leading over it, commencing from the south, are Karkacha, Iro Manzil, and Lataband.
    The summit of the Karkacha pass lies 8,000 feet above the sea. It is crossed by a subsidiary road, difficult for mules, leading from Gandamak to Butkhak. The hills are of blue slate capped with limestone, and are bare of grass. A fine deodar forest existed formerly, but it has long since been destroyed by charcoal-burners. Within 200 feet of the summit are the ruins of what must once have been a very strongly-built brick fort. (Wood, Jenkins.)

*KARKANAI کرکنی
    34-38 70-21 m. A village located on a stream running south to Charbagh in Laghman province. Another place with this name is located on a stream some 8 miles southwest of Ghanikhel, at 34-5 70-39 m.

*KARKOT کارکوت
    35-0 71-27 m. A village located about 2 miles east of Dangam in eastern Kunar province.

*KARLAI کارلی
    34-59 68-57 m. A village located on a tributary of the Ghorband, southeast of Abgird in Parwan province.

KARLUK کرلوک
    A section of the Shaikh Ali Hazaras.

*KARMA کرمه
    33-20 68-51 m. A village located about halfway between Motakhan and Kolalgu in western Paktia province.

KARMANA خرمنه
33-54 69-39 m. A village in the Hariob, 2 miles south of Ali Khel; 25 houses, and a fair amount of Cultivation. Here the road to Sapri branches off. (I.B.C.) Recent maps show the spelling Khermana. (LWA.)

KARNALA (See Military Report on Hazarajat, Part II.) کرناله
33-2 68-31 G. A large glen draining northeastwards into the Khawat valley.

KARNALA (See Military Report on Hazarajat, Part II.) کرناله
33-55 68-6 G. Two kotals over the Siah Reg hills, crossed by the Ghazni-Yakh Walang road.

KARNALA (See Military Report on Hazarajat, Part II.) کرناله
33-55 68-6 G. A small fortified hamlet in the Karnala glen, about 4 miles north of the northern kotal of the same name.

KARODIL کرودیل
34-18 65-37 A. A kotal on the watershed separating Dai Kundi from Taimani country. It is described in Volume 3.

KARSHATAL See KHARSHATAL کرشتل

*KARTATUT کرته توت
34-3 70-39 m. A village located on a stream running northeast to Ghanikhel in Nangarhar province.

*KARUNG کرونگ
34-59 71-4 m. A village on a stream running southeast into the Kunar at Chagha Sarai in Kunar province.

KARYA YUSUF (See Military Report on Hazarajat, Part II.) قریه یوسف
A range of mountains which lies to the west of the Gul Koh, and extends from Sar-i-Ab to the Wardak country.

KASABA قصبه
34- 70-. A village in the Surkhab division of the Jalalabad district. Inhabitants: Tajiks, Dehgans and Kizilbashis. This village consists of the two hamlets Banda-i-Ambar Shah and Banda-i-Mufti Sultan. (Jenkyns.) One place with this name is located north of Jalalabad on the Alingar river, at 34-44 70-17 m.

*KASAN کاسان
34-28 68-39 m. A village located about 1 mile southeast of Jaliz on the Maidan river in Maidan province.

KASH (See Military Report on Hazarajat, Part II.) کش
A locality in Ujaristan.

KASHAR KATS کشر کټ
34- 70-. A village on the right bank of the Kabul river, on the road from Jalalabad to Jagdalak by the Darunta and Adrag Badrag passes, 3 miles west of Girdi Kats, and about 2 miles southeast Urmur. It possesses about 100 houses and a small square mud fort with 40 yard faces, the road running through the middle of the village and under the fort walls. (Holdich.)

KASHIF KALA كشيف قلعه
34- 69-. A fort in the Chardeh valley of Kabul, between Kala-i-Fazil Beg and Baghwana. Four towers. Inhabitants: Tajiks; 30 houses. (I.B.C.)

KASHKA كشكه كوتل
34-46 68-2. Elevation 8,900 feet. A pass over a spur of the Koh-i-Baba separating the Irak glen from the Bamian valley. It lies about 19 miles north-northwest of the Irak pass, and is crossed by the road leading from Kabul to Bamian via the Irak pass. This road is joined, on the top of the Kashka Kotal by another leading from the Shibar pass and the Ghorband valley. The Kashka Kotal is practicable for camels. Peacocke, who went over the road leading up to the kotal in 1886, says:
"The Kashka Kotal, it is suggested, would be a good position, facing west along the crest of the dasht or saddle, to close at one and the same time both the Irak and Shibar roads. I have not seen the drop from the kotal towards Zohak, but it is said to be fairly steep, and to be capable of being swept by fire from the crest. The crest is quite 2 miles long, with rugged and inaccessible hills rising on each flank. The only road turning its left flank is the path leading from the Kalu valley at 1 mile above Kala Pai Muri and down the Dara Jandargal--a most difficult path except for single men on foot, and easily guarded. On the right flank the only line by which it can be turned is the bad foot-path down the Bamian river to Shikari, and then up the lower end of the Dara Bulola--a path also easily obstructed and guarded. There is water close by in the Irak valley, and both the Irak and Shibar route would be available for a retreat. The site would appear to recommend itself strongly as being just the place where a fort or entrenchment might be judiciously employed, and I would advocate the construction of a strong work at this point. The passage of troops over the Kashka Kotal is restricted to, at best, the open 2 miles of kotal, and a single work on the centre of this broad open crest would close all passage, except at night, and would bar both the Irak and Shibar roads from the direction of Bamian, the only direction practically from which they can be approached. Such a work by securing the northern exit of the Shibar and Irak passes, the two best (Since this was written the road over the Hajigak pass has been improved and is now better than that over the Irak.) passes over the Hindu Kush, would give to a Kabul force the means of initiating operations in Turkistan, would give a feeling of security to any Kabul force advanced towards Haibak, and would cover any possible retreat. The only objection to the site is the absence of water on the kotal; but, judging from the bold manner in which water has been conducted over the Khushkak Kotal to Khushkak, there would be no difficulty in conducting water to the Kashka Kotal by a jui from the Dara Jandargal.
In the rear of the Kashka Kotal any position in the Bulola valley as high up it as the Dara Shumbal is turned by the road from Kala Irak by Khushkak and the Jolah Kotal, and nothing further could be attempted there than blocking the road (easily done at any time at Tangi Kamandi and at Tangi Sang Nawishta). Kala Bulola affords facility for defending the Bulola valley, but can be turned by the Irak-Jolah road, and is only useful for a rear-guard action." (Peacocke.)

KASHKOT كش كوت
34- 70-. A stream of the Jalalabad district, giving its name to the subdivision otherwise known as Besud.

KASHMUND کشمند
34- 70-. A stronghold in the mountains north of the Dasht-i-Gamberi, between the Safi and the Ghilzai country. The position of this collection of forts is described as impregnable, and the place is the refuge of all the bad characters in Afghanistan.
Some of the forts belong to the Ghilzais, some to the Safis, and the mountains on which they stand are known as the Koh-i-Kashmund--see "Kunar."
The family and adherents of the Ghilzai chief Ismatulla Khan fled to this sanctuary on the arrest of Ismatulla Khan in the end of 1881. Kashmund is said to be two marches from Chigha Sarai in the Kunar valley. (I.B.C.) A mountain with this name is located at 34-40 70-25m. And a village is about 14 miles northwest of Shiva in Kunar, at 34-38 70-27 G. (LWA.)

KASHTAN کشتان (کشتوز)
35-23 71-18 G. Elevation 5,960 feet. A large Kafiristan village situated a short distance up the Nichingul torrent on the right bank of which it is built high above the water. It is the headquarters of a small tribe of Kafirs from which the village takes its name. The Kashtan formerly held the village of Dungul in the valley of the same name, but were driven thence by the Afghans. Kashtan village contains about 200 houses, and must be greatly overcrowded. It has a small suburb above, and a short distance from the main village, which is entirely undefended. The cultivable ground is sufficient for the people. (Robertson.) Recent maps show the name Kushtoz in this area, at 35-23 71-19 m. (LWA.)

KASI See KASSI کاسی

KASIM قاسم
33- 69-. One of the Ahmad Khel villages on the right bank of the Hazrdarakht stream, southeast of Ali Khel. It is situated in a small valley, and is said to contain 100 fighting men. No supplies are available. (I.B.C., Johnston.) A village with this name is located northeast of Gardez in Paktia, at 33-36 69-26 G. (LWA.)

KASIMABAD قاسم آباد
34-27 70-27 G. A village in the Besud division of the Jalalabad district, situated on the left bank of the Kabul river, about 1/2 miles below Bahrabad. Inhabitants: Dehgans, Tajiks and Afghans. (Jenkyns.)

KASIM KALA قاسم قلعه
34- 69-. An old deserted fort, 13 miles from Kabul, on the Ghazni road, situated in a beautiful and highly cultivated valley near the bank of a feeder of the Kabul river. A place called Kasim Kola is located a few miles southwest of Yahya Khel, at 32-54 68-36 m. It is on the road from Zarghunshahr to Gardez.

KASIM KHEL قاسم خیل
33-57 69-26 A. A halting place on the Paiwar-Kabul route, in the valley between the Surkai and Shutur Gardan kotals. There is room for an excellent camping ground for 10,000 men, with a good water-supply. There is fair grazing in the summer, and fuel is procurable at a short distance. (I.B.C.)

KASMABAD قاسم آباد
A village in Laghman, occupied by Dehgans, and consisting of four hamlets, viz.:

1. Sanjir
2. Banda-i-Malik Hamid
3. Banda-i-Mulla Badshah Gul
4. Banda-i-Tuti. (Warburton.)

KASSI كاسى
34-18 69-53 G. A village on the right bank of the Surkhab river, 2 miles southwest of Surkhpul, and the same distance west of Asphan. Also a mountain in Katawaz, Ghazni, at 31-51 68-18 G. (LWA.)

KATA DARAKHT كته درخت
34-23 66-36 G. A village of 30 houses in the Dai Zangi district. (See Military Report on Hazarajat, Part II.)

KATAGHAN قطغان
A large section of the Jaghatu Hazaras. (See Military Report on Hazrajat, Part II.)

KATA KALA كته قلعه
34-42 67-9 m. Kata Kala Pain and Kata Kala Bala are two villages in the southeast of the Yak Walang district, situated in the Sar-i-Kol glen, together containing 40 families of Hazaras. (A.B.C.) A fort with this name is located at 34-22 66-57 G.

*KATA KALA كته قلعه
34-19 67-50 m. A village located about two miles south of Behsud in Maidan province. Another place with this name is located near Alaqala in the Surkhsang area, southwest of Behsud, in Maidan province at 34-14 67-45 m.

KATA KHAK كته خاك
34-29 67-35 m. See Military Report on Hazarajat, Part II. Three villages, Vis., Sar-i-Kata Khak, Kata Khak proper, and Pain-i-Kata Khak, in the Besud country. The village of Kata Khak is located on the stream of the same name, about 20 miles northwest of Behsud. (LWA.)

*KATA KHEL كته خيل
34-31 68-52 m. A village located some 4 miles northwest of Arghanday in Kabul province. Another place with this name is northeast of Kabul, and some 5 miles north of the Kabul-Sarobi road, at 34-37 69-21 m.

KATAL Or KATAR كار
34-5 68-1 m. At 7-1/2 miles north of Bokan the Ghazni-Besud road passes between two forts. That on the left is called Katal. The other, about 500 yards off, is called Doburja. Another village with this name is about 10 miles northwest of Asadabad (Chaghasarai), at 34-58 71-5 m.

KATAR Or KATIR كتر
A tribe of Siahposh Kafirs, who, according to Raverty, inhabit the valley of Nurgul, which they are said to have held in Babar's time. Stewart, however, places them east of the eastern watershed of the Alingar. Robertson says the Katirs are probably more important, numerically considered, than all the remaining tribes of Kafiristan put together. See "Kafiristan." (Raverty, Stewart.)

KATAR SUM or QATAR SUM قتارسم
35- 67-. Elevation 10,920 feet. A pass leading into the Saighan valley from the south. It is crossed by the main road from Kabul to Mazar-i-Sharif at about 4-1/4 miles north of the Ak Robat Kotal. (The Katar Sum is sometimes spoken of as the second, or northern, Ak Robat Kotal.) The ascent from the south is not difficult; wheeled guns would most easily reach the summit by keeping in a water-course which runs up a hollow to the left of the road. The descent on the northern side is more difficult, but 200 men could make it fit for taking wheeled guns down by hand by clearing away stones. To make a proper gun-road a new alignment would have to be adopted, probably along the slope to the east of the present road. As far as can be judged this would not be difficult. (I.B.C.) A village with this name is on the road from Bamian to Qurgan, northwest of the former, at 35-0 67-40 m. (LWA.)

KATA SANG کته سنگ
35- 69-. Elevation 11,480 feet. A halting place 6-1/2 miles north of the Kaoshan Kotal.

KATA SANG کته سنگ
35- 69-. A post at the foot of the Surkhai Kotal which marks the boundary between the Jajis and the Ghilzais at the head of the Kurram valley. (Lumsden, Bellew.)

KATA SANG کتهسنگ
34-29 69-43 m. Elevation 4,750 feet. A halting place on the Rud-i-Kata Sang, 7-1/2 miles from Jagdalak and 58-1/4 miles from Jalalabad. Water plentiful; surrounding country barren. No supplies available. Fuel abundant. The camping ground used in the campaign, 1870-80, was in the bed of the stream, about 3 miles west of Sang Toda. From Katar Sang, a road branches off to Sarobi where it joins the Jalalabad-Kabul road via the Tang-i-Ghora. (Johnston, I.B.C.)

KATA SANG کتهسنگ
34-20 69-12 m. A village of 40 houses in the northern portion of the Logar valley, and on the right bank of the river off the main road. (Euan Smith, Clifford.)

*KATA SANG کته سنگ
34-55 68-26 m. A village located in the Ghorband valley, some 5 miles southwest of Shaikh Ali in Parwan province. Another village with this name is southwest of Baraki Barak and north of Abjush-i-Bala in Logar province at 33-52 68-50m.

KATAWAZ کتواز
32-51 68-27. Katawaz is a woleswali in Ghazni province. The woleswali comprises an area of 277 square kilometers and has an agricultural population that has been estimated at from 6,740 to 8,666. The woleswali is bounded in the west by Giru, in the south by Jani Khel, in the east by Sultan Khel, and in the north by Yusuf Khel. Katawaz has about 17 villages, seven of which have more than 500 inhabitants. The villages are listed in the PG as follows: Zarghun Shahr, Balu Khel, Gadol Ya Chambar Haji Pahlawan, Khair Kot, Moh'd Hasan, Payenda Khel, Moh'd Dost, Seh Gana, Malizai, Zafar Khel, Haji Abdul Shah (Gadol-i-Moh'd Shah), Mamor Khel, Sha Gul Qala, Omar Khan Qala, Omari Qala (Gawdal), Baki Khel, Magi, Shah Wali Moh'd, Spina, and Zawaka. (LWA) In 1914 the area was described as follows: A district of the Ghilzai country, about which hardly anything is known. Its length is said to be about 48 miles, breadth 24 miles.

The plain is level and open, bounded on the east by the Kohnak mountains and west by lower hills of Katasang and Zhera. To the north it reaches Zurmat, and south is ended by Luluzai and the Ab-i-Istada lake. The valley is entered on the east by three passes, which meet at Kala Kharoti, and on the west by the passes of Gazdara and Kharbi. This district belong entirely to the Sulaiman Khel; the settled tribes living in the centre of the valley, and the nomads wandering about the foot of the moutains. The Powindah route from Ghazni to the Punjab via the Gumal runs through the district, and is used by the Powindahs in their annual migrations.
The villages are generally groups of five or six forts, each containing 10 to 60 houses. These are from north to south, Mishkhel, Sultankhel, Paindakhel, Mittakhel, Malazai, Shakikhel, Shatkhel, Kalandarkhel, Adinkhel and Nasukhel; beyond is Luluzai of the Tarikis. When caravans passing through Katawaz are too strong to be overpowered without loss, they are only required to pay a small tribute to the tribe whose lands they pass; when they are weaker, the impost is a little higher, and if only a few individuals, they are, or were, usually plundered. The general tax is Rs. 1, or 10 yards of coarse cloth, for every eight loaded camels. Infidels pay more. Traders always choose their road through Katawaz with reference to their relations with the tribe. (Broadfoot, I.B.C.)

KATIHI
Raverty mentions a tribe of Siaposh Kafirs of this name, but Robertson does not.

KATIR See KATAR

KATLISH Or QATLISH
34-40 66-18 m. A village in Sar-i-Jangal. (see Military Report on Hazarajat, Part II.)

KATS-I-AZIZ KHAN
34-29 70-17 m. A village in Laghman about 10 miles from Jalalabad on the left bank of the Kabul river consisting of the following five hamlets:

(1) Waliabad
(2) Tiragar-Kanderzai
(3) Rawat
(4) Kala-i-Ismatulla Khan
(5) Aminabad.

The inhabitants are Jabar Khel Ghilzais, Chinzais, and Dehgans. Fodder for 10,000 animals for one day and about 1,000 maunds of unground grain is obtainable. There is a sarai. The camping ground is good. Fuel is procurable. (Warburton.) Recent maps show the spelling Azizkhan Kac. (LWA.)

KATS-I-MIAN KHAN
34- 70-. A village in Laghman, on the left bank of the Kabul river, 2-1/2 miles southwest of Zerana, and 4-1/2 miles southeast of Kach Muhammad Ali Khan.

KATS Or KACH LAGHMAN
34-29 70-10. That portion of the Laghman district which lies on the right bank of the Kabul river, having as its southern boundary the Siah Koh range, its eastern the Darunta pass, and its western the

Adrag Badrag pass. (I.B.C.) A village with this name is about 5 miles north of Chuki in Kunar in Nangarhar province, at 34-44 70-52 G. (LWA.)

KATS MUHAMMAD ALI KHAN کټ محمدعلی خان
34-31 69-59. A village in Laghman, on the left bank of the Kabul river, 2 miles east of the junction of the Badpakht stream with that river. Inhabitants Jabar Khel Ghilzais and Tajiks. Fodder for about 2,000 animals for one day and about 150 maunds of wheat, barley and maize are obtainable. Fuel also is procurable in abundance. Camping ground is very cramped. An alternative route branches off from here to Kata Sang via Darga Kotal and from Kata Sang rejoins the Tangi Gharu road at Sarobi. (Young, Johnston.)

KATTAL کټال (؟)
A village in Laghman. Inhabitants: Babakar Khel and Muhammad Khel. (Warburton.)

KATWAR See KTI کتوار

KATWAR کتوار
35- 70-. A large village and fort belonging to the Katwar or Kti, Kafirs, one day's march southwest (?) of the Kamah pass. The village is said to contain 100 families and to have many orchards, etc. (I.B.C.)

KAUM-I-ALI قوم علی
A section of the Dai Kundi Hazaras. (See Military Report on Hazarajat, Part II.)

KAUM-I-BARFI قوم برفی
A subdivision of the Bacha-i-Ghulam clan of the Dai Zangi Hazaras. (See Military Report on Hazarajat, Part II.)

KAUM-I-DEHKAN قوم دهکان
A section of the Kaptasan clan of the Besud Hazaras. (See Military Report on Hazarajat, Part II.) A village with this name is located near the Kuh-i-Sai, a few miles south of the Helmand, at 34-11 67-25 m.

KAUM-I-MIRZA قوم میرزا
A subdivision of the Bacha-i-Ghulam clan of the Dai Zangi Hazaras. (See Military Report on Hazarajat, Part II.)

KAUM-I-MURAD قوم مراد
A subdivision of the Yanghur clan of the Dai Zangi Hazaras. (See Military Report on Hazarajat, Part II.)

KAUM-I-SULTAN قوم سلطان
A subdivision of the Yanghur clan of the Dai Zangi Hazaras. (See Military Report on Hazarajat, Part II.)

KAUM-I-YARI قوم یاری
A subdivision of the Bacha-i-Ghulam clan of the Dai Zangi Hazaras. (See Military Report on Hazarajat, Part II.)

KAUN Or KAHUN GHAR کاون
34-52 69-55 m. Elevation 10,690 feet. A mountain range lying to the north of the Kabul river. A main spur from this range runs down into Laghman between the valleys of the Alishang and Uzbin, subsid-

ing in the Dasht-i-Ziarat, between Mandrawar and the Badpakht stream; another spur running down similarly and subsiding between the Badpakht stream and Nagalu. (I.B.C.)

KAUZ KUNAR   کوز کنر
34-34 70-35. Kauz Kunar is a woleswali in Nangarhar province. The woleswali comprises an area of 327 square kilometers and has a population that has been estimated at from 11,728 to 25,425. The woleswali is bounded in the north by Dara-i-Nur, in the east by Nur Gul and Goshta Khwaja Zemar, in the south by Kama and Behsud, and on the west by Qarghai. Kauz Kunar has about 32 villages, 16 of which have more than 500 inhabitants. The villages are listed in the PG as follows: Gurik, Kata Snag, Shigi, Belawri, Bangab, Huz Bagh, Hawz Bagh, Sar Band, Qala-i-Padshahi, Bazarak, Kachrah, Qalah-i-Shad Khan, Koti, Taran, Qala-i-Tak (Qala-i-Atak), Qala-i-Zargaran, Qala-i-Khuram, Sadergak, Kashkot-i-Ulya, Kashkot, Nau Joy, Abdul Khel, Kohna Deh, Kashkot-i-Sufla, Islam Pur, Shewah, Shewa-i-Kauz Kunar, Atawar, Malikzai, Lamtak, Budyalai, and Suruch.

KAWAL   کوال
A small nondescript tribe, who have no fixed land of their own, but mostly wander about the Paghman mountains, and are well known as fortune-tellers and thieves. (Bellew.)
The Kawals are said to be an inferior section of the Tajiks. (I.B.C.)

*KAZAN   قازان
34-44 67-43 m. A village located some 10 miles southwest of Bamian.

KAZI   قاضی
33-30 68-24 G. A village located about 3 miles south of Ghazni. Another place with this name is located about 14 miles south of Ghorband in Parwan province, at 34-56 68-27 G.

KAZI DEH   قاضی ده
35- 69-. A village in the Charikar district, lying east of the village of that name, and inhabited by 400 families of Tajiks. (Shahzada Taimus, from native information.)

KAZI KALA or QALA-I-QAZI   قاضی قلعه
34-29 69-3 m. A village 7 miles west of Kabul, on the Ghazni road, from which it is about 3/4 mile south, at the northern foot of the Korogh range. To the east of the village lies the Chardeh valley, in which district Kala-i-Kazi is included. The inhabitants are Tajiks, and the number of houses is 200. The farthest point reached by the Horse Artillery guns in the Cavalry and R.H.A. engagement on the 11th December 1879 was a little to the northeast of Kala-i-Kazi. Supplies are plentiful here, and there is a good water-supply, but camping ground would be difficult to find owing to the amount of cultivation. (I.B.C.) A fort with this name is about 2 miles southeast of Charbagh-i-Laghman in Nangarhar province, at 34-31 70-17 G. (LWA.)

KAZI KALA   قاضی قلعه
34- 69-. A village and fort 20 miles north of Kabul, southeast of Istalif. (Thornton.)

KAZI KALA   قاضی قلعه
34- 69-. A village and fort 3 miles southwest of Kabul. It is enclosed with a wall, and is surrounded with orchards, and is sit-

uated on an eminence. The inhabitants are Tajiks. Water is plentiful both in "karez" and springs; and firewood, grazing and forage are procurable. (Masson, Campbell.)

KAZI MUHAMMAD SHAH قاضی محمد شاه
39- 70-. A village in the Besud division of the Jalalabad district. Inhabitants: Tajiks. (Jenkyns.)

KEHMA SOKI کهماسوکی (؟)
34- 69-. An old fort in ruins, about midway between Pezwan and Jagdalak. (I.B.C.)

KEJAK کجک
34- 66-. Elevation 11,690 feet. An easy pass over the main watershed between the Hari Rud drainage and that of the Rud-i-Band-i-Amir, crossed by the main Bamian-Daulat Yar road at about 64 miles east of Daulat Yar. From the Kejak pass the tagao of the same name runs in a southwesterly direction forming one of the head waters of the Surkh Bum, as the upper portion of the Kirman, or Lal valley, is known. A good camel-road runs down the Kejak Tagao passing Kejak village at 3 miles. Two miles below the village it leaves the tagao which here makes a bend to the southeast, and crossing three small kotals descends the Altarghan Tagao to the Kirman valley. This road is of some importance as giving direct communication between the two main roads from Kabul to Daulat Yar, viz., that via Bamian and that via the Hazarajat. (I.B.C.) Recent maps show the name Kuh-i-Kejak at 34-32 66-41 m. (LWA)

KERGAH قرگاه
34-31 70-17. A village in Laghman, on the left bank of the Kabul river, at its junction with the Alishang. It is a small village romantically situated on a rocky eminence at the west extremity of a line of hills generally designated by its name. (Masson.) A place named Kergo is located on the Uzbin (Wuzbin) stream, about ten miles northeast of Sarobi, at 34-46 69-53 m. (LWA)

KERIA قریه (؟)
34-0 69-50. A river in the Jaji country, which rises in the south slopes of the Sikarams peak of the Safed Koh mountains, and flows west of the Paiwar to its junction with the Hazardarakht rivulet, whence the combined stream is called the Hariob. (Lumsden.)

KERMU کرمو
34-26 66-30 A. A pass in the Koh-i-Baba range, see Ak Zarat. (See Military Report on Hazarajat, Part II.)

*KHADAL خادل
32-55 68-48 m. A village on the stream of the same name, about 1 mile northeast of Omna.

*KHAGAK خگک
34-32 67-37 m. A village located about three miles west of the Gardan-i-Qada, on a tributary of the Bum-i-Abd-i-Ulum, which runs into the Helmand river.

KHAIDAD KALA (KHODAIDAD?) خدایداد
34- 68-. A village of 50 families of Taimuris in the Sar-i-Chashma valley, about 6 1/2 miles east of the Unai pass. Headman (1904) Daulat Muhammad. The inhabitants possess about 60 head of cattle and

80 sheep and goats. The annual production of wheat and barley averages about 400 Indian maunds. (Wanliss.)

KHAIRABAD خیرآباد
34- 70-. A village in the Jalalabad district, on the right bank of the Surkhab river, about 2 miles south of Balabagh. Inhabitants are Ghilzais, Tajiks and Dehgans. This village is also known as Tatang-i-Usman Khan. (Jenkyns.)

*KHAIRABAD خیرآباد
32-12 68-26 m. A village located some 4 miles east of Khizar Khel and northeast of Wazakhwa in Ghazni province. Other places with this name are located in the Surkhrud area, at 34-23 70-15 G., and in the Khugiani area, at 33-15 69-52 G.

KHAIRABAD خیرآباد
34-25 69-11 m. A village 1 1/2 mile northeast of Charasia. From this village there are two roads to Kabul, viz., one (the eatern) by the Sang-i-Nawishta defile, and the other (the western) by Indaki and Deh-i-Mozang, both fit for all traffic, but the western road would probably always require an hour or two's work with two small working-parties (say 50 men each), before wheeled artillery could pass with ease. The Sang-i-Nawishta defile, however, is very confined and would prove troublesome for the passage of large bodies of troops and transport. (I.B.C.) Another village with this name is located some 8 miles north of Ghazni, at 33-39 68-23 m.

*KHAIRAK خیرک
34-27 67-1 m. A village located some 3 miles north of Bum-i-Afshar on a tributary of the Dara-i-Mur in Bamian province.

*KHAIRKHANA خیرخانه
34-8 67-46 m. A village located west of the Band-i-Doab and north of Tarbolaq in northern Ghazni province.

*KHAIRKOT خیرکوت
32-51 68-27 m. A village located near Zarghun Shahr (Katawaz) in Ghazni province.

KHAIRODANGAR خیرودنگر
32- 69-. A halting place in the bed of the Gumal river, 55 miles from its source. There is a road thence to Wano. (Broadfoot.)

KHAIRO KHEL خیروخیل
34-30 70-9 m. A village on the right bank of the Kabul river in Kats Laghman. It contains about 300 houses with a considerable amount of cultivation reaching down to the bank of the river. It is 12 1/2 miles from the Darunta pass, and 11 miles from Kats-Muhammad Ali. The inhabitants are Nasir Khel Ghilzais. Camping ground for a large force is to be found to the west of the village with water from a canal. The Kabul river is said to be usually fordable opposite Khairo Khel, though the water was found to be up to a man's chin in August 1904. (Holdich, I.B.C.)

KHAISAR خیسار
A main section of the Sulaiman Khel.

KHAJURI خجوری (خاجوری)
A division of the Mangal tribe; see Mangal.

KHAKDAO خاكداو (خاكدو)
34-57 67-16 m. A village in the east of the Yakh Walang district, containing 30 houses of Neka Hazaras. (A.B.C.) The village is located on a stream running into the Band-i-Amir in Bamian province. (LWA)

KHAK DARWESH خاك درويش
34- 67-. A dry, bare, stony valley in the Bamian district, running in a general northeasterly direction to the Bamian valley. The road from Kala Sarkari to Daulat Yar enters the Khak Darwesh at 7 miles. Immediately below this point the valley turns north, and is an impracticable defile, but above it runs up west, is 400 yards wide, and enclosed by bare and rounded hills accessible to cavalry and infantry. A quarter of a mile up a road comes in from the left rear from Buri Sunia in the Fauladi glen. After a mile the valley forks, both branches curving round to south. The road, however, keeps straight on westwards. (Maitland.)

KHAK HAZARA خاك هزاره
33-42 69-11 G. A village of 60 houses about 16 miles from Gardez, on the road to the Altimur Kotal. Inhabitants: Amazai (Ahmadzai?) Ghilzais. (I.B.C.)

KHAKI خاكى
34- 68-. A hamlet of 20 families of Darghan Hazaras in the Kalu glen. (See Military Report on Hazarajat, Part II.)

KHAK-I-ALLAH BAKSH خاك الله بخش
(See Military Report on Hazarajat, part II.)
A pass in the Dai Zangi country, crossed by the Kabul-Hazarajat-Daulat Yar main road.

KHAK-I-CHAGIR (CHEGHEL) خاك چغر
34-35 67-11 m. A pass leading over the Koh-i-Baba from Firozbahar to Panjao. The ascent is by the Sar-i-Kol valley for some miles, and then up the Joshanak Tagao for about 8 miles. Here turn west and ascend the Kotal Gul-i-Yakhak. The ascent is about 600 yards and steep. Descent about the same to a glen (apparently one of those at the head of the Dara Ali). A mile or so southwest up this is the village of Khak-i-Chagir (say 15 miles). It consists of 25 houses of Yangur Hazaras. Half a mile above the village the foot of kotal is reached. The ascent is about three-quarters of a mile in length by a zig-zag road, not very steep. Both ascent and descent are said to be better than those of the smaller Gul-i-Yakhak, but both passes are said to be practicable for laden mules. At or near the foot of the descent is the village of Do Kad, 15 houses of Saiyids. Thence the road is good all the way by the Tagao Barg, or one of its branches, to Panjao, 33 miles from Firozbahar proper.—(A.B.C.) Recent maps show the name Khak-i-Cheghel in this area, and the pass with this name. (LWA)

KHAK-I-GHULAM خاك غلام
34- 68-. At 4 5/8 miles below Bin-i-Shewak the road down the Ghorband valley enters the Tangi Khak-i-Ghulam, and continues in it till Kala Doab is reached. See "Ghorband."

*KHAK-I-JABAR خاك جبار
34-24 69-30 m. Khak-i-Jabar is the name of a village in the alaqadari of the same name in Kabul province. The alaqadari comprises an area of 876 square kilometers and has an agricultural population

which has been variously estimated at from 4,949 to 16,220. The alaqadari is located southeast of Kabul. Khak-i-Jabar alaqadari includes about 28 villages of which six have more than 500 inhabitants. The villages are listed in the PG as follows: Chakari, Malang, Qala-i-Gulmalang, Rojan, Baghgai, Charwazi, Qala-i-Khodayar, Khurd Kabul, Gorg Maidan, Batu Khel, Jalghozi, Taghar-i-Ulya, Shamamzai, Ghazgai, Darband, Malik Khel, Kharoti, Taghar-i-Sufla, Duran Khel, Qanat-i-Mulla Akhter, Karo Khel, Khak-i-Jabar, Zendan, Qala-i-Wali, Abdullah Khel, Chalu, Chenari, Mulla Omar, Natu Khel, Sarw Khel, and Tegari.

*KHAK-I-KARA
34-4 68-5 m. A village located northeast of Podina in northern Ghazni province.

KHAK-I-SANGA
35-1 68-57 G. A group of villages, trees, and gardens in the Ghorband valley, 6 3/4 miles below Siahgird. (Peacocke.) Recent maps show the name Khak-i-Sang. (LWA)

KHAKSHAL
35-2 69-0. The name given to that part of the Ghorband valley lying about 3 miles above Burj-i-Guljan. (Peacocke.)

*KHALACHAK
34-7 67-1 m. A village located a few miles west of Sultan Robat in southern Bamian province.

KHALAJ (See military Report on Hazarajat, Part II.)

KHALAJ, AB-I
A stream joining the Helmand from the east at Chahar Shinia. (See Military Report on Hazarajat, Part II.)

*KHALAMAD
34-5 67-31 m. A village located in the Kushk area on the northern bank of the Garmab river in Bamian province.

*KHALAQ LAM
34-58 70-50 m. A village located on the Dara-i-Pich in Kunar province.

KHALASABAD
34- 70-. A village in the Besud division of the Jalalabad district, situated about 2 miles from the left bank of the Kabul river. Inhabitants: Arabs and Tajiks. (Jenkyns.)

KHALAZAI
35- 69-. A village on the daman of the Paghman range, situated near Charikar, and inhabited by 100 families of Afghans. (Shahzada Taimus, from native information.)

KHALIK
A section of the Besud Hazaras. (See Military Report on Hazarajat, Part II.)

KHALILABAD
A village in the southern division of the Logar valley. In 1880 the population consisted of 110 families, all Hazaras. (Clifford, Euan Smith.)

*KHALILAN خليلان
 33-46 69-29 m. A village located in the Mirzakai area, on the road from Gardez to Ali Khel.

KHALIL KHEL خليل خيل
 34-31 70-9. A village in Laghman, on the left bank of the Kabul river, opposite Khairo Khel. A fair amount of supplies is obtainable here. (Young.) Recent maps show the name Ziranj in this area. (LWA)

*KHALWATI خلواتی
 33-17 69-34 m. A village located on the road from Khost to Gardez, some 6 miles west of Nadir Shah Kot.

*KHAM خم
 34-23 67-1 m. A village located south of Panjaw on the Dara-i-Mur in southern Bamian province.

KHAM خم
 34-47 67-18 G. Elevation 11,660 feet. A kotal in the east of the Yak Walang district, crossed by the Bamian-Daulat Yar road. The ascent commences soon after descending from the Kotal; it is about a mile in length, and easy; rise 130 feet. The descent, which is steep, is by an excellent road to the Kham hollow half a mile from the kotal; fall 255 feet. This kotal is the highest point on the road between Zari and Bamian. From the ridge near the kotal a wide view over the great plateau is obtained. To the northward the cliffs of the Band-i-Amir lake, about Kupruk can be traced, the Band-i-Amir valley being a deep gash in the undulating surface of the country. The general aspect of the scene is bleak and barren, and would be monotonous but for the snowy height of the main range to the south. To the east one looks down the deep hollow of the Bamian valley, between the main range of the Koh-i-Baba on the right and the Koh-i-Ghandak on the left, but the bottom of the valley is too deep to be seen from here. (Maitland.)

KHAM-I-ABA خم آبه
 34- 67-. A subdivision of the Yak Walang district inhabited by Khami-Aba Hazaras of Dai Zangi stock.

KHAM-I-KALAT خم قلات
 34- 67-. Two forts in the Bamian valley, below Surkhdar, with a population of 20 families of Tajiks. (Maitland.)

KHAM-I-ZARDGAR خم زردگر
 35-7 69-20 m. A township in the upper Panjshir glen, situated 2 miles east of Ushturgiran and containing 500 houses of Tajiks. There are two villages or divisions, the houses being scattered in groups among the orchards. (Shahzada Taimus.)

*KHANA خانه
 34-12 69-54 m. A village located near Kharoti in southern Nangarhar province.

KHANAMULLA خانه ملا
 34-28 69-15. A small village, with forts, on both banks of the Logar river, 2 miles southwest of Bagrami, and 5 miles southeast of the Kabul Bala Hisar. The inhabitants are Barakzais. (I.B.C.)

*KHAND خند
   33-26 69-29 m. A village located southeast of Gardez and 5 miles north of Laka Tiza in Paktia province.

KHANIZ خانيز
   35-18 69-30 m. A scattered village in the upper Panjshir glen, situated on the right bank of the stream, distant some 10 miles above Anaba, and containing 60 houses of Tajiks. (Shahzada Taimus.)

*KHANJAR خنجر
   34-17 69-50 m. A village located about 2 miles east of Chahartut on the way to Araban in southern Nangarhar province.

KHAN KALA خان قلعه
   A village of 700 houses in the Koh Daman. (Kinloch.)

KHAORO خاورو(؟)
   33- 69-. A village in the Charkh valley, in the southern division of the Logar district about 9 miles southeast of Baraki Rajan. There is room for a brigade to camp here with sufficent water from karez. (I.B.C.)

KHAPAR خپر
   A section of the Muhammad Khwaja Hazaras. (See Military Report on Hazarajat, Part II.)

*KHAR خار
   33-45 68-34 m. A village located about 1 mile east of Shashgaw on the road from Ghazni to Kabul.

*KHARABA خرابه
   34-58 68-31 m. A village located in the Ghorband valley northeast of Shaikh Ali in Parwan province.

KHARAN خران
   34-15 70-6 G. A village of 80 houses in the Khugiani division of the Jalalabad district, about 5 miles southeast of Nimla. It lies on the right bank of a tributary of the Surkhab, called the Shagai Rud, containing plenty of water. The inhabitants belong to the Kharbun section of the Khugianis. (Jenkyns, I.B.C.)

*KHARBID خربيد
   34-53 68-37 m. A village located southwest of Surkh o Parsa, on a tributary of the Ghorband river.

*KHARBOLAQ خربلاق
   33-17 68-9 m. A village located north of the Qalat-Ghazni highway, about 7 miles northwest of Mushakai.

KHARKAI خارکی
   33-47 69-43 G. A hamlet on the left bank of the Karaia, at the junction with the latter and the Mangiar Khula, about 18 miles from Kharlachi on the road to Ghazni. (I.B.C.)

KHARKOL خرقول
   34-26 67-42 m. A kotal crossed by the main Kabul-Hazarajat-Daulat Yar road about 2 1/2 miles west of Maidan-i-Pai Kotal. (Wanliss.) (See Military Report on Hazarajat, part II.) Other places with this name are located on a tributary of the Helmand, at 34-10 67-31 m.; and in southern Bamian province, at 34-5 67-23 m. (LWA)

KHARKOL See ROGHANI GARDAN خرقول

KHARKOL خرقول
(See Military Report on Hazarajat, Part II.)

KHARKUL خرقول
34- 68-. The last of four low kotals crossed by the road from Kharzar to Khesh in the northeast corner of the Besud country, 5 1/2 miles from the former village. (See Military Report on Hazarajat, Part II.)

KHARLACHI خرلاچی
33-49 69-58. A village located about one mile east of Patan near the Pakistan border.

KHARLANG خرلنگ
34-28 68-38. A village in the upper Kabul river valley, about 3/4 mile west of Jalrez. It contains (in 1904) 20 families of Tajiks, possessing about 30 head of cattle and 50 sheep and goats. The annual production of wheat and barley averages about 360 Indian maunds. (Wanliss.)

KHAROTI خروتی
"The Kharotis" says McMahon, "claim to be Turan Ghilzais, and are divided into three main sections:

Zakho Khel	about 2,000 men
Adia Khel	2,000
Yahya Khel (Ya Khel)	1,500

"Zakho Khel. The chief of the tribe is said to be Ghulam Rasul, son of Khan Muhammad Khan, Zakho Khel. He lives at Karabagh in the summer and at Paharpur in the Derajat in the winter.
"Adia Khel. Headman Babu Khan, son of Samandar.
"Yahya Khel. Headman Muhammad Gul, Son of Kasim Khan.
"All the Powindah portion of the tribe appear to live in Karabagh near Ghazni in the summer and near Paharpur in the Derajat in the winter.
"A portion of the tribe, numbering some 2,000 men, of all three sections, however, own lands and live throughout the year in Saroza and Sarobai and the neighbourhood of Shakin. These claim the Gumal river from Sarwandai to Khairo Dangar."
According to the second edition of this Gazetteer, "the Kharotis are divided into Ahmad Khel, 700 tents; Yia Khel, 200; Pasani, 250; Hudia Khel, 300 Narik, 50; besides a few families residing in Kabul. All the foregoing are engaged in trading.
"Besides there are two divisions, the Marakzai, 600, and Kokalzai, 400 who are engaged as shepherds, and occupy the vicinity of the Jadran country.
"Broadfoot has two divisions—the Zak Khel and Adi Khel.
"There are the following agricultural divisions also:
"Umarkhel residing in Aspana with 140 houses; Saind Khel in Gumal, 80; Yak Khel in Gumal, 80; Haibat Khel in Gumal, 30; Zaku Khel in Babi Khel, 40; Sarobi Khel in Sarobia, 100; Yazi in Yazd, 30; Langi Khel, Yazar Khel, Tumkhel, all reside in the Sarobia Nala and number 500 houses. Elphinstone estimates them at 5,000 or 6,000 families. The Yia Khel is the division that trades with India. They soon acquire wealth and with it a taste for fine clothes and good food and a general dislike to their former habits.
"The climate of the Kharoti contry is very severe in winter, and the

inhabitants are shut up by snow for four months in the year. But the greater part of them go down into warmer country to the Derajat and elsewhere.

"The Kharotis have some sheep, cows, asses, and mules, but horses are not known among them; their whole wealth consists of flocks of goats which feed on the bare peaks, or in ravines covered with pines. The trading sections have large herds of camels.

"Notwithstanding the hardships of their severe climate, they are a healthy robust race; but even for Afghans they are very dirty. Elphinstone says some he saw had acquiline noses and Jewish features, and many were quite fair.

"The Kharotis are hospitable and kind; they seldom attack tribes unprovoked, but have fought more successfully with the Wazirs than any of their neighbours. A traveller is safe in their country, and, as far as a milk diet goes need never want food.

"Their chiefs have no power over them. When two men have a dispute, they sometimes fight it out; but their neighbours and the mullas generally interfere and endeavour to compose the difference. Should one party refuse to abide by the decision, his neighbours give up speaking to him, which soon induces him to give in. When they are threatened with an attack, a council (jirga) is called, and all the armed men obey its orders. They sometimes make, but in general they buy, their own powder.

"Any portion of level ground is carefully cultivated, yet the cultivators are not one-fiftieth of the tribe. Right to soil is only thought of in cultivated spots; a piece of grazing land, however, long occupied by a family, is intruded on by a man even of a different tribe without ceremony.

"One of their chief amusements is deer-stalking.

"Their dress is a shirt of black blanket made by their wives, and sandals of goat-skins nearly raw; sometimes they have a bit of a blanket for a cap or, if lucky, procure for their wool a coarse turban.

"Though they are very poor, they have still fine matchlocks and good swords.

"In spring they live entirely on milk, which is abundant as the kids are then born. Ghi, krut and cheese are made in large quantities, and sold in Katawaz and Zurmat in exchange for flour. In the winter they eke out on their milk diet by a small portion of bread. The pines of their hills furnish a seed called "chilgoza," which is a principal part of their winter food, added to cheese and an occasional bit of bread.

"The Kharotis live in small villages, which are situated on little knolls or on sites cut out of the hill sides. The shepherds live in blanket tents or in rude huts cut out of the hill. Their houses have nothing in them but a rug and an iron pot. They have no weights or measures, and no means of estimating time and distance.

Lumsden says that the Powindah Kharotis must not be confounded with the Kharoti Ghilzais, as they are a perfectly distinct tribe. Yet in his account of the Ghilzais, he gives no such section as Kharoti. Elphinstone certainly devotes a separate account to them, but he does not mean to separate them amongst the Ghilzais. However, whether they are connected in blood with the Ghilzais or not, they are now practically a distinct tribe, and there is ony one tribe of Kharotis whether they are classed with the Powindahs or the Ghilzais. (Lumsden, Elphinstone, Broadfoot, McMahon.)

Further information regarding the strength and possession of the Kharotis is given in a statement under "Powindah."

*KHAROTI خروتی
33-5 68-7 m. A village located about a mile south of Walai and 5 miles east of the Mukur-Ghazni highway. Other places with this name are located north of the Kuh-i-Safi on the path from Qala Yuzbashi to the Panjshir valley, at 34-52 69-23 m.; about 1 mile southwest of Zamankhel in the Azre Dara, at 34-1 69-27m.; southeast of Kabul, on the path from Bagrami to Chakarai, at 34-23 69-20 m.; one mile north of Arabkhel and east of Azraw, at 34-9 69-42 m.; one mile north of Mendrawur on the Laghman river in southern Laghman province, at 34-33 70-12 m.; near Khana, on a tributary of the Nawer Rud in Nangarhar province, at 34-12 69-53 m.

KHAROTI (BALA AND PAIN) خروتی
34-29 68-38 m. Two Ghilzai villages on the main Kabul-Herat road, about 1 1/2 miles east of Jalrez. (Wanliss.)

KHARAPARCHAK Or KHAR PICHAK خراپرچک (خرپیچک)
33-45 68-52 A. Elevation 8,530 feet. A pass over the hills north of Kharwar, crossed by the principal route leading from the Charkh valley. The Kharparchak valley north of the pass is a wide waterless trough with a few patches of rain land. The ascent is very gradual and the road good enough for artillery until the head of the valley is reached. There several ravines unite, every one of them very narrow, blocked up with huge rocks and at first sight seemingly impossible as a road. A ravine which joins from the southwestern side forms an exceedingly difficult ascent, passable only for travellers on foot. The track ascends this ravine and on gaining the ridge joins the main road of the Kharparchak pass. The latter ascends the easternmost ravine which runs down from the Doshakh peaks. It is only a narrow sheep path, well trodden out and passable for laden animals, though very difficult, and then only with considerable risk. With some blasting the track could be made considerably more easy. The pass is completely commanded from the top of the range, two points on opposite sides sweeping the entire ravine. The descent into Kharwar on the south side of the pass is very easy; the road looks made, and with very little trouble could be made into a driving road. Griesbach says that the Cherkh people prefer this road to the Kotal-i-Kalan further east, though the latter is perhaps the better track. The principal route to Ghazni from the Logar, Altimur and Cherkh leads over the Kharparchak pass. It is said that in former days it was the favourite hunting ground for the Kharwar robbers, and no one ventured to cross it without at least 20 jezailchis. (Ghiesbach.)

KHARPOSH خارپوش
34-21 67-5 A. A kotal crossed by the main Kabul-Hazarajat-Daulat Yar road. (See Military Report on Hazarajat, Part II.)

KHARPOSH خارپوش
34-17 67-10 m. Two small villages at the western foot of the Kharposh Kotal, in the Da Zangi country. (Wanliss.)

KHARSHATAL خرشائل
33-59 69-46 m. Elevation 10,000 feet. A pass over the western extension of the Safed Koh on the road leading from Bilut, in the Hariob valley, to Khurd Kabul, Its summit lies 16 miles from the Paiwar Kotal, and about 6 1/2 miles southwest of the Lakarai Kotal. It is said to be practicable, though difficult, for cavalry and lightly laden mules. (I.B.C.)

KHARWAR خروار

33-43 68-55 m. A district northeast of Ghazni, south of Logar, and west of Zurmat. It is a poor country; guns cannot easily cross it, and troops would find little forage. Outram marched through it with troops, including cavalry and a batter of 9 pounders. Its elevation ranges between 7,500 and 10,000 feet. The following has been culled from a report supplied by Griesbach, who visited Kharwar in 1888:

Kharwat is a mountainous region drained by the headwaters of the Charkh stream, one of the tributaries of the Logar.

Geographically it forms a well defined area. It is an elevated tract, in the shape of a plateau of irregular oval shape surrounded by a rim of high mountains over which a number of passes lead down into the surrounding districts, all of them lying considerably below the level of the lowest portion of Kharwar.

Rivers, etc. Kharwar belongs to the Charkh drainage, but there is practically only one stream which lasts the whole year, i.e., the stream which drains the Upper Khwaja Angur valley (northeast Kharwar); it traverses the most fertile part of the district, and escapes through the Tangi Doshakh or Tangi Maulana to Charkh. It is at all times a considerable stream, and though largely used for irrigation purposes and divided into numerous canals, it still has a large volume of water when it finally flows through the Tangi down to the low level of Charkh. Near the group of villages of Chala Khel it receives the drainage coming from Chaghai and the ravines south of it, but there was very little water in this stream in August when I surveyed Kharwar.

The large tributaries of the Sang ab, coming from the Ispidar and Robat valleys (southeast Kharwar) and the streams which drain the western side of Kharwar are great torrents in the spring, but dry up completely after the summer has set in.

Water would unquestionably be found underground everywhere, for all the numerous streamlets drawn in the map exist all the year round and are plentifully supplied with clear and particularly good water near their sources, but they all disappear long before reaching the main channels.

The basin of the Kharwar valley is filled with horizontally bedded deposits of post-tertiary date chiefly consisting of sandstone, clay, and towards the top, conglomerates; below the latter the surface water generally disappears and collects on the impervious strata, the clays. Where the latter are exposed, springs of clear and deliciously cold water are found in great numbers. In fact I have hardly ever been in any valley so well supplied with water.

Contour, etc. As said above, Kharwar forms, as it were, an elevated plateau surrounded basin-fashion with a rim of high ranges. Originally forming an elevated basin formed of highly contorted stata of Mesozoic and Eocene age, it has, in common with all the valleys of this part of Afghanistan been filled by the fresh water strata of post-tertiary times, which form such enormous deposits in the Logar valley and towards Ghazni. The result is that, the central portion of the Kharwar basin forms as it were a sunken plateau. The main mass of the elevated Kharwar area consists of highly contorted strata of sedimentary rocks from the Rhoetic to Eocene groups, many of them greatly altered by intrusive masses of granites, syenites and traps. Kharwar can, therefore, strictly speaking, not be called a plateau.

It is surrounded by high hill ranges, which form a more or less complete rim round the central portion. The only place where the Kharwar area actually communicates with the lower levels is by way of the Tangi Maulana between the Kalan and Kharparchak passes, through which defile the Kharwar drainage escapes down to the Charkh. But this defile is simply a narrow slit eroded out of the hard syenitic granite which makes that part of the hills quite impassable to man or four-footed beasts. About half way down the defile the stream falls down a fine precipice, forming a most picturesque waterfall some 80 or more feet high which may be seen from a point a little in advance of the Kotal-i-Ao Khana west of the gorge.

It is worth noting that this surrounding rim of hills descends much more suddenly down to the lower levels of the adjoining districts than towards the inner side. Only near the northeastern corner and the southwestern portion other elevated tracts approach sufficiently near to be in some sort connected with the Kharwar area. In the northeastern corner the hill ranges run into the elevated region of Gardez, though divided from it by difficult ranges and near the southwestern corner the low hills lying northeast of Ghazni form as it were some sort of approach to the Kharwar district. But structurally the Zanakhan valley formed by these hills belongs really to Kharwar, although the valley is drained by a separate system.

The largest portion of Kharwar is a slightly undulating, on the whole inward-sloping terrain, formed by the more or less horizontally bedded post-tertiary clays and conglomerates above mentioned, fringed by widely extended fans which extend from the outer rim of Kharwar.

This outer rim of hills is crossed by the following passes:
North side. Zukhagak; Piadara; Bibi Shighar; Kharparchak; Ao Khana; Kalan; Ispidar; Jauzar; Dandan; Khwaja Angur; Altimur and Ao Dakai.
East side. Zak and Dahana Drang.
South side. Kuti Khel; Shinkai; Zintega; Jalal; Ao Dakai Gurbed; Arda and Satarnai.
West side. Zanakhan; Peani; Chandrai and Pakaghai.

Roads. With the exception of the Dahan Drang, Zinteg and Zankhan routes all the roads which lead into Kharwar from the surrounding districts are bad and more or less difficult for laden animals. But the tracks which lead to the passes on the Kharwar side are more or less easy and many of them remarkably good, and I imagine they must have been made at some period or another. Perhaps the best road is the one which leads from Chala Khel to Kol-i-Sabz. It crosses a nameless very low kotal about 3 miles west of Chala Khel. Over most of the way one might drive a four-in-hand coach, if it were not for deep furrows caused by flooded streams in the spring time.

Amir Abdur Rahman had once taken possession of Kharwar during his fights with Sher Ali Khan and had occupied the western portion of Kharwar. It is possible that these remains of good roads date from that time.

Villages. The following is a list of all the villages in Kharwar:

Name of Village	Number of Houses	Tribe
1. Ao Dakai, in ravine at head of Khwaja Angur valley.	5 or 6	Niazai (Kuchi)
2. Ispidar, in Khwaja Angur valley	15	Kharotis.
3. Dandan	13	Ahmadzais (Ghilzais)
4. Khwaja Angur	100	Ditto.
5. Panjpai	80	Yusuf Khel

6. Jauz-i-Khel	70	(Ghilzais) Ditto
7. Kala-i-Malikhan	15	Ditto
8. Bakshi Kala	50	Ditto
9. Kala-i-Umar Khan (Umar Khan)	20	Ditto
10. Arzu Khel	13	Nuria Khel (Ghilzais)
11. Muchi Khel	60	Ditto
12. Khwaja Khel or Maruf Khel	55	Ditto
13. Chalak (Chala?) Khel	11	Gada Khel (Ghilzais)
14. Kala-i-Godal	20	Ditto
15. Kala Patak Khel (Shekhana)	15	Ditto
16. Kala-i-Mulla Gulzar	14	Ditto
17. Karez Gul Muhammad	--	-----
18. Appa Khan (Khel)	15	Gada Khel (Ghilzais)
19. Kala-i-Begam	30	Ditto
20. Azak (Azu) Khel	20	Ditto
21. Mani Khel	7	Gada Khel (Ghilzais)
22. Kol-i-Jalal	24	Ditto
23. Niamatal	15	Ditto
24. Ursuk	15	Ditto
25. Jauz Khel	40	Ditto
26. Dinar	12	-----
27. Irgana	20	Gada Khel (Ghilzais)
28. Chogai	80	Andar (Ghilzais)
29. Iwaz Khan	10	Ditto
30. Ispidar (southwest Kharwar)	80	Ditto
31. Sera Kala (ditto)	15	Ditto
32. Shahi (southwest Kharwar)	4	Andar (Ghilzais)
33. Shaikhan	15	Ditto
34. Gurbed	--	-----
35. Sangab	2	Ditto
36. Mahmudi Kala (Nos. 30 to 36 are villages in the Sangab valley, the route to Robat, etc.)	2	-----
37. Rashid	10	Andar (Ghilzais)
38. Kotal	40	Andar (Ghilzais) and Gada Khel
39. Aman	--	-----
40. Pakhagai or Pashagai	15	Andars and Gada Khels
41. Kol-i-Sabz	120	Andars
42. Khawra	12	Gada Khel
43. Urfan or Orpan	20	Ditto
TOTAL	1,180	

As the Zanakhan valley is so closely connected with Kharwar, the list of its villages are also given:

Name of Village	Number of Houses	Tribe
1. Kala-i-Alam	--	Andar
2. Paindeh Khel	--	Do.
3. Dado Khel or Rahat Khel	--	Do.
4. Farid Khel	5	Do.
5. Kala-i-Khwaja	--	Do.
6. Haibat Khel	--	Do.
7. Deduk Khel	--	Do.
8. Yasin Khel	--	Do.
9. Sar Kol	--	Do.
10. Kala-i-Pardil	--	Do.
11. Kush Abdal	--	Do.
12. Mamosh Kala	--	Do.
13. Fakir Kala	--	Do.
14. Dadu	--	Do.
15. Gogar	--	Do.
16. Zarak Kala	--	Do.
17. Lola Kala	--	Do.
18. Godali	--	Do.
19. Kala-i-Mia Dad	--	Do.
20. Kala-i-Mast	--	Wardakis
21. Girdar Khel	--	Do.
22. Bayanai	--	Do.

Divisions. Kharwar is divided for administrative purposes into two division. The eastern portion, from Iwaz to the spur of hills which runs south from near the Koh-i-Surai as far as the Altimur passes, pays revenue direct to Kabul. The western division, including the rest of Kharwar, belongs to the Ghazni district.

Revenues, Eastern Division. There are various taxes levied. The revenue derived from rain-lands (lalmi) is levied in the following manner in the eastern division: The harvest is either divided into ten equal portions, of which one belongs to the Amir or else the amount is estimated and the revenue on rain-lands has been farmed out at the rate of 120 kharwars (Tabrizi), the Tabriz kharwar being equal to 62-1/2 Kabul seers, about 750 maunds (Indian).

The revenue on irrigated lands in the eastern (Kabul) division of Kharwar amounts to R 30,000. From irrigated land a fixed tax is levied at the following rates. Lands irrigated by stream water at the rate of R 4 per jarib; if irrigated by springs at the rate of R3 per jarib, but if watered from Karez at R 2 per jarib.

Besides this there are various minor items of revenue. As for instance: Sar-i-Charb-i-Bibi ("fat for the Queen's hair")--a tax as jagir to the Queen: one and-a-half kharwars of ghi.

Darwazagai (duty on doors)--amounting to about R 800.

Poll-tax--about R 3,000 a year.

Tax on ploughs--used in the cultivation of rain lands, at the rate of 6 annas per plough, which amounts to about R 1,000 (Kabuli).

Sar Ramagi--R1 on 3 sheep (4 annas per sheep), and R1 per 4 goats, amounting to about R 2,000 a year.

Western Division. In years of plentiful rainfall, the revenue on lalmi is fixed at the rate of one-tenth of the actual produce, and it comes to about sixty Tabrizi kharwars. But this portion of the revenue is usually farmed out. The revenue on irrigated land amounts to about 50 tomas Kabuli (R 1,000). (Griesbach.)

KHARZAR	خارزار
34-38 68-6 G. Elevation 11,000 (?) feet. A village in the Besud Hazara country, 2-1/2 miles southeast of the Hajigak, and about 7 miles south of the Irak pass. It forms the 8th stage on the main Kabul--Mazar-i-Sharif road. It contains some 100 houses of Daulat Pai Besuds, of Mir Tahmasb subdivision. The road from Kabul divides here, the branch to the right going up a tagao to the Irak pass, while that to the left, the main road, goes up a ravine to the Hajigak. A little way above the village, towards the Irak pass, the tagao is from 100 to 150 yards wide, and uncultivated, and troops might encamp here; grass is abundant, but fuel is scarce and consists of brushwood only; water from the Kharzar stream. In summer this part of the valley is full of kuchis, who come here for the grazing. (I.B.C.)

KHARZAR	خارزار
35-2 68-14 A. A pass leading over the main range of the Hindu Kush from the Ghorband valley to that of the Surkhab, and situated between the Koh-i-Jaolangah and the Koh Deh-i-Warsandan. It can be reached from the south either by the Sangandao Dara and Kotal, or by the Botian Dara; both of which afford routes practicable for pack animals. At the kotal the road again divides into two. The right hand track goes north by the Narkoh and Pajman Daras to Barfak; the other goes to Girdaneh and down the Purkaf Dara to Doab-i-Mekhzari. The latter is so difficult that it may be disregarded as impracticable. (Peacocke, from native information.) Recent maps show a village with this name located on a tributary of the Ghorband, about 10 miles south of Siagird, at 34-52 68-52 m. (LWA.)

KHARZARI	خارزاری
(See Military Report on Hazarajat, Part II.) A Dai Zangi village on the main Kabul--Hazarajat--Dalat Yar road.

*KHARZUN	خرزون
33-51 69-36 m. A village located on the Aryobster Toy, about 2 miles northwest of Bikarai in Paktia province.

*KHAS KUNAR	خاص کنر
34-38 70-52. Khas Kunar is a woleswali in Nangarhar province. The woleswali comprises an area of 330 square kilometers and has an agricultural population that has been estimated at from 5,106 to 6,520. The woleswali is bounded in the west by Chawki and Nur Gul, in the south by Goshta Khwaja Zemar, in the north by Sirkanai, and inthe east by Pakistan. Khas Kunar has about 21 villages, 12 of which have more than 500 inhabitants. The villages are listed in the PG as follows: Shamkar (Shamka), Hakimabad, Dak Kalai, Akhundzadagan, Arazi-i-Ulya, Arazi-i-Sufla, Tonar (Shanal), Banday, Kulalano Bandai, Kunar-i-Khas, Karmota, Chand Rawi (Chand Rawul), Kawil, Juba, Sana Khel, Chanchan, Mangwal, Daghai, Chamyari, Lutan, Banday Hakimbad, Bailam, and Tai.

KHATAI Or BABALI	خاتی
A tribe of Hazaras; the chiefs are Khatais, said to have come from Khotan, and the mass of the people are Babalis, the tribe being known indifferently by either name. It is not improbable that the Babalis may have been Tajiks which would account for the very partial admixture of the Mongol type in the features of the men.
The Katais own the country nearest Kandahar immediately north of the Darafshan valley, which they formerly owned. (St. John.)
See "Bamian Proper" and also Military Report on Hazarajat, Part II.

*KHATAK ختك
 32-2 68-48 m. A village located about 3 miles west of Mamai on the way to Wur.

*KHATA KHEL خاتاخيل
 32-55 68-13 m. A village located on the Makhi stream, on the road from West to Pana in Ghazni province.

KHATI KHEL خاتی خیل
 34- 70-. A village in the Khugiani division of the Jalalabad district, about 4 miles northeast of Khidar Khel. Inhabitants: Khugianis of the Kharbun section. (Jenkyns.)

KHAT KHAN خت خیل
 33- 69-. A village on the right bank of the Hariob stream 1-1/2 miles south of Ali Khel. It has only 12 houses and little cultivation. (I.B.C.)

KHAWAK خواك
 35-42 69-31 A. Elevation 11,650 feet. A pass leading over the Hindu Kush, crossed by the Kabul-Khanabad road; it is 115 miles from Kabul. Parties of khasadars are stationed at intervals along the road over the pass to keep it clear of snow, and it is thus practically always passable in ordinary years. In February 1905, when the Dane Mission was at Kabul a large camel caravan arrived in Kabul which had crossed the pass in the first week of February, there being at the time 53 degrees of frost at Kabul accompanied by heavy snow-storms. It is said (1905) that the Amir has given orders for parts of the road over the pass to be covered in with corrugated iron pent roofs as an additional precaution against the snow. (I.B.C.)

KHAWAK خواك
 35-38 69-54. A village, and an old fort, near the junction of the Chapchi and Sipi Daras, at the eastern foot of the Khawak pass. There is a garrison here consisting of one regiment of cavalry, one batter of artillery, 2 battalions of infantry and 300 khasadars; of these last some are quartered in huts on the road over the pass itself. (I.B.C.)

KHAWAL, AB-I See URAZGANI خوال

KHAWANICH خوانچ
 A pass in Khost over the range separating the two valleys, northern and southern, composing the district. (I.B.C.)

KHAWAS خواص
 A river rising in the Kuh-i-Berun and flowing into the Helmand from the north. (See Military Report on Hazarajat, Part II.)

KHAWAT خاوات
 34-4 68-0 m. A district in the south of the Besud country. (See Military Report on Hazarajat, Part II.) There is also a village at 34-4 68-33 G. (LWA.)

KHAWAT, AB-I خاوات
 34-5 68-45 A. A river in Besud. (See Military Report on Hazarajat, Part II.)

*KHAZAN خزان
32-59 68-34 m. A village near Malakh, northwest of Yahyakhel in Ghazni province.

*KHAZAN-I-CHINA خزان چینه
32-13 68-35 m. A village located in the Kamkai Wazakhwa area on the way south to Wur.

KHAZAR خزر
A section of the Muhammad Khwaja Hazaras. (See Military Report on Hazarajat, Part II.)

*KHEDRAN خدران
33-49 68-18 m. A village located some 15 miles north of Ghazni and west of Jaghatu-i-Wardak.

KHENJ See KHINJ خنج

*KHENKAY خنکی
32-4 68-48 m. A village located some 10 miles southeast of Wur in southern Ghazni province.

*KHERANAY خیرانی
33-45 69-42 m. A village located some 8 miles southwest of Chamkani in Paktia province.

KHERI TAISANG خیری تیسنگ
34-0 68-42. A village in Wardak, on the left bank of the Logar river, opposite Shaikhabad, and included in that place. Inhabitants Wardaks. (I.B.C.)

KHESH خیش
(See Military Report on Hazarajat, Part II.) A district in the northeast corner of the Besud country.

KHESH خیش
A section of the Daulat Pai Hazaras. (See Military Report on Hazarajat, Part II.)

KHIDA خیده
A section of the Khatai Hazaras of the Bamian district. (A.B.C.)

KHIDAR خیدر
(See Military Report on Hazarajat, Part II.) A place in the Dai Kundi country.

KHIDAR KHANI خیدرخانی
34- 70-. A village in the Jalalabad district, about 1 mile southwest of Batikot. Inhabitants: Tirais. (Jenkyns.)

KHIDAR KHEL خیدرخیل
34- 70-. A village in the Khugiani division of the Jalalabad district, about 10 miles southeast of Gandamak. The inhabitants belong to the Kharbun section of the Khugianis. (Jenkyns.) Another village with this name is located north of Wazakhwa, at 32-13 68-22 m. (LWA)

KHIDDI Or KHANDI GHAKHI خیدی
33-26 69-21 G. Elevation about 10,100 feet. A pass over the range lying to the west of Khost leading from the head of the Shamil

valley on to the Koshin plain. It is crossed at about 16 miles short of Gardez by the main road leading from Matun to Gardez and so to Kabul or Ghazni.

The ascent to the pass from the Khost side is very steep and would, in its present condition, be very difficult for camel transport. The soil however is soft and it would be easy to make a road with easier gradients. Wooded hills rise on either side of the track, but flanking parties could move along them without difficulty. The descent to the Koshin plain is easy leading gently downwards over open spurs and undulations.

The summit of the pass is open, the hills on the right (going from Khost) rising only slightly above the level of the road. On the left they rise to a great height, some 2,500 feet above the pass. The range is well wooded, chiefly with chilghoza trees. Snow is believed never to lie very deep on the pass, and Ghilzai camels are said to be able to cross throughout the winter. (I.B.C.)

KHILTI   خلتی

A Kafir clan mentioned by Girdlestone on the authority of Colonel Gardner. He talks of the Hindu Kush between the Khawak and Dorah passes as being inhabited by Khiltis. According to him the Khiltis prefer to build their houses in a clearing in the heart of some forest. Their houses are seldom less than two storeys high, with side staircases on the outside. The supreme deity of the Khiltis is called Dogan. They also pay special respect to the North Star. (Gardner.)

KHINGOT   خنگوت

34- 69-. A village in the Chardeh valley of Kabul, about 2 miles south of Teba, at the eastern base of the Korogh mountain. It contains about 100 families of Ahmadzai and Adramzai Ghilzais. (I.B.C.)

KHINJ   خنج

35-26 69-44 m. A village in the upper Panjshir glen, situated on the right bank of the stream 6 miles above the village of Marz, and containing 100 houses of Tajiks. On the left is the mouth of the Dara Darkhinj up which a foot-path leads into Kafiristan. A ravine opening on the right bank near Khinj village is called Jarwesh. It has a hamlet of 10 houses at its mouth. A stream issues from each ravine.

One and a half miles lower down is the village of Birjaman, which has 20 houses of Tajiks under the headman of Khinj. (Shahzada Taimus.)

*KHINJ KOT   خنج کوت

32-56 69-27 m. A village located in the Tangi Lgad, about 3 miles west of the Pakistan border.

KHINJUKAK   خنجوكك

34-22 68-33. A halting place at a ruined fort of the Sulaiman Khel Ghilzais, on the road from Panah to Kala Kharoti. There is a karez here. (Broadfoot.)

*KHIR KAREZ   خیر کاریز

34-8 68-57 m. A village located about 5 miles north of Babus in Logar province.

*KHIR KHEL   خیر خیل

33-43 69-25 m. A village located in the Tuta Khel area, about 15 miles northeast of Gardez on the road to Ali Khel in Paktia province.

*KHIRMANA خیرمنه
33-54 69-39 m. A village in the Jaji area, about 5 miles southwest of Ali Khel in Paktia province.

KHIRSKHANA خرس خانه
34-22 68-33. A pass in the hills, about 6 miles south of Sar-i-Chashma. The road to Ghazni (Via Dai Mirdad) goes over this pass, which is fit for mule-traffic but difficult for camels. (I.B.C.)

KHIRSKHANA خرس خانه
34- 69-. Elevation 6,210 feet. A pass leading from Kabul into the Koh Daman 6 1/2 miles northwest of the former. Approaching from the north, the rise is so gradual that the highest point of the road is reached unexpectedly, as it is west of the hills through which the road descends.
The road over the pass, when seen by some members of the Dane Mission in 1905 was found to be good and easily traversable by wheeled guns, except for a distance of about one mile on the summit, where it was out of repair and stony. (I.B.C.) A place called Khir Khana or Khair Khana is located at 34-34 69-6 A. (LWA)

KHIRS KHWAR خرس خوار
34- 68-. A tributary of the upper Kabul river, which it joins from the south about six miles east of the Unai pass. (Wanliss.)

*KHOGAI خوگی
34-13 70-16 m. A village located southwest of Chapriar and northwest of Agam in Nangarhar province.

KHOJA See KHWAJA خواجه

KHOJAK خوجك
A section of Ghilzais who inhabit the east of the Ghilzai country next to the Jadrans. Broadfoot says they are chiefly of the Ahmadzai section of the Sulaiman Khel. On the occasion of the first British advance to Kabul, Colonel Herring, of the 37th Bengal native infantry, was murdered by a party of marauders, afterwards found to be Khojaks. A force was accordingly sent under Captain Outram to attack them in their own stronghold, near Kalagu, in Zurmat. Outram's troops consisted of a wing of infantry and some 350 cavalry; he found the Khojaks strongly posted at the foot of a range of mountains of bare rock, and immediately attacked them, and though they behaved with some gallantry, speedily and utterly defeated them, killing many and taking the rest of them prisoners, 120 in number. Broadfoot says that on this occasion even the women took part in the fight throwing down incessant showers of stones, and handing their husbands powder and ball with the greatest coolness. (Havelock, Outram, Broadfoot.)

KHOJAL KHEL خوجل (خواجه) خیل
33-39 68-38 A. A village about 14 miles northeast of Ghazni on the road to Kharwar. There is room for a brigade to camp on the right bank of the stream on which the village stands. (I.B.C.)

*KHOLA خوله
34-17 67-34 m. A village located some 6 miles west of Surkhabad in Bamian province.

*KHONA خونه
32-21 68-13 m. A village located some 6 miles southeast of Marefkhel and north of Shinkai Ghar in southern Ghazni province.

KHONINDA خنینده
A section of the Polada Hazaras. (See Military Report on Hazarajat, Part II.)

*KHORAM خرم
34-52 68-13 m. A village located in the Shumbul area on a tributary of the Ghorband.

*KHORAMAI خورمی
33-25 70-7 m. A village located some 3 miles southeast of Terezai (Alisher) in eastern Paktia province.

*KHOSHAMAND See KHUSHAMAND خوشامند

KHOST خوست
33-20 69-55. Khost is a woleswali in Paktia province. The woleswali comprises an area of 420 square kilometers and has an agricultural population that has been estimated at from 27,042 to 42,612. The woleswali is bounded in the west by Musa Khel, Nader Shah, and Mandozi, in the south by Gurbuz, on the east by Trayzai, and southeast by the State of Pakistan, and in the north by Saroti (Zambar). Khost has about 111 villages, 23 of which have more than 500 inhabitants. The villages are listed in the PG as follows: Darash Kalai, (Dash Kalai), Qarya-i-Latak, Tani Kalai, Karam Saray, Ayub Khel, Bali, Goriyan, China Kalai, Bakhtawar Kalai, Baddi Khel, Bada Khela, Dolan, Babur (Babar), Sarkai Khel Boli, Piran Shamal Niyazi, Cholan, Qarya-i-Khan (Khan Kalai Latak), Qarya-i-Behsus (Behsudi), Qarya-i-Khalifa, Landi Kalai, Qarya-i-Gulbad Khan, Qarya-i-Mohamad Omar Khan (Omar-Kalai), Kotolai Matun, Wardah Khel, Dari Khel-i-Matun, Torah Wari, Patarah, Niyaz Gul Kalai, Qarya-i-Kajiri, Chaghi (Choghi), Toryan, Qarya-i-Habash Khel, Kot Kai Kalai, Dar Koti, Mando Khel, Wati Kalai, Mina, Shakarah Matun, Khatakai Kalai, Koriyan Matun, Wargha, Gharombai, Matta China, Mashin Latak, Mardi Khel, Kheder Piran, Tandi Piran, Khalesa-i-Matun, Landai Matun, Malkondai (Malo Mondi), Manai, Penzaya-Shamal, Negzai, Keramat Khel, Rasul Mohamad Kalai, Khan Hawas Kalai, Madi Khel, Qarya-i-Magass, Kundi, Welgai, Ali Shirai, Qala-i-Sakhi Khan, Malizai, Qala-i-Wazir, Nurzai, Mer Mandai, Qarya-i-Tabi (Tabi Lakan), Mahmud Khel, Bangi Bagh, Arnam-i-Hendu, Qala-i-Henduwan, Zerai Terkha, Asar, Matkai (Patak), Marzghor-i-Kalan, Ster Mazghor, Kamkai, Qarya-i-Qader Khan (Qader Mangal), Khandar, Qarya-i-Wazyan, Qarya-i-Alidaya, Qarya-i-Kotal, Zar Ghali Latak, Dandayan, Kharsin, Qarya-i-Sahib Zadah Kotai, Amin Gul, Daru Gheljai Kalai, Parangi Zadran Kalai, Dirri Gheljai, Husain Kot, Mamur Janat Gul (Khan Kalai), Mollayan-i-Piran, Fazluddin Pir Kalai, Shenkai Kalai, Gul Ahmad Shah, Dayri Piran, Mollayan-i-Lakan, Qarya-i-Tang (Tang Lakan), Nukut Khel, Sahebzadah Segai, Pas Koriyan, Bar Koriyan, Khodizai, Shir Bazar, Kamar Sar, Choprai, Shah Pol Kalai, Mari Khel, Lakan Tar, Khundai Kalai, Qala-i-Nakam, Qarya-i-Qardat, Qarya-i-Lanu, Moqbel, and Azmati Qala. (LWA) In 1914 the area was described as follows: The district of Khost comprises the upper portion of the valley of the Shamil or Kaitu river. It is bounded on the north, northeast, and northwest by Kurram and Zurmat, and by the Turi, Jaji, Mangal, Mukhbil an Jadran tribes; on the east and southeast by the Dawesh Khel Wazirs, west by the Jadran country, and south by Dawar. It is said to be 40 miles long, and is watered by three streams, the most important of which

is the Shamil. It contains no very large villages, but a vast number of small ones. Matun, besides its fort, consists of a group of some thirty hamlets. It is the usual residence of the Afghan Hakim (Mansur Khan in 1907), and has an elevation of 3,982 feet. The climate of Khost is warmer than that of Kurram.

The inhabitants of the upper portion of the valley are called Khostwals while the lower portion is occupied by Wazirs, with whom the former are always ready to combine in attacking their Turi neighbours. The divisions of the Khostwals are--(i) Ismail Khel, said to number 3,000 men, and reside at the head of the valley next to the Jadrans; (ii) Matun, who number 1,000 men and inhabit the vicinity of the Amir Chaoni (cantonment); (iii) Mandozai, 1,000, next below the Ismail Khel; (iv) Shamil, 1,000 men, below Madozai; (v) Lakkan, 1,000, who inhabit the valley of the Landar Sadak, a stream which joins the Kaitu from the north. Other sections are: Mali, 2,000; Tarwizai, 500; Sabari, 2,000; Bakir Khel, 800; and Tani, 3,000. The Khostwals call themselves Pathans, but they are probably a mongrel race like the Bannuchis. They are divided into Tor Gundi and Spin Gundi factions.

The valley of Khost is said to be nowhere so broad as that of Kurram; it has, however, a greater breadth of cultivation, but the most of it is unirrigated, and dependent on rain; the soil is very fertile when irrigated from the streams. The three streams come down in a southeasterly direction, the most northern, the Jaji Algad, from Shabaras; the middle one, Landu, from the borders of Zurmat, while the most southern, called the Sadik Kaitu, falls into the Kurram river. The chief product is rice. The mountains which confine Khost on all sides afford plenty of timber, fuel and pasturage. Cows, buffaloes and goats are the chief stock. The Khostwals take tobacco, rice, ghi and namdas to Bannu for sale, and bring back salt, indigo, iron and leather goods and cloth. The Khostwals buy their salt from the Wazirs, who bring it from Bahadur Khel, and they are entirely dependent on this source of supply.

According to Donald the revenue paid by Khost is:

Bakir Khel	4,000 R	Kagdam	500 R
Ismail Khel	6,000	Lakkan	10,000
Matun	8,000	Landar	500
Sabari	3,000	Sadik	2,000
Mandozai	6,000	Aran Khel	1,000
Ali Sheri	3,000	Malli	3,000
Sewaki	2,000	Khabast	400
Khudazai	500	Gulbaz	1,000
Khalsen	500		

Total Rs. 51,400 Kabuli1 = to about Rs 29,000 British.

The district was occupied during the month of January 1879 by the British who defeated the Khostwals with considerable loss on the 7th of the month in the neighbourhood of Matun, with a loss of only 2 killed and six wounded on the British side. During the temporary occupation, the only chiefs who showed any disposition to be friendly belonged to the Spin faction.

Khost can be entered by several routes from the Kurram Tochi valleys.

The following is an extract from some notes on Khost furnished, in 1898, by Mr. J. G. Lorimer, at that time Political Officer in the Tochi valley.

"The seat of Government is Matun in the cold weather, and Gabar in the hot. There are four Sub-Governors, or Hakims, one in Jaji Maidan, one in the Mangal country, one in the Zadran country and one in the Tani country.

"A yearly tax of Re. 1 is collected everywhere, and every fortieth animal of the flocks, herds and camels is appropriated annually by the Government. This latter tax is known as 'Chihilyak.' Fruit trees, including mulberries, are taxed at one shahi a year each; a shahi is worth about 3/4 anna. Kharch, or commission, at various rates is also taken by Government on the sale of grain and animals, but not of land; this resembles registry fees in British India, and the transaction is publicly recorded when kharch is paid. Rs. 10-8 is paid to Government on account of every marriage. The unit for the calculation of land revenue is the jarib of 60 steps (or about 50 yards) square with an area of somewhat more than half an acre. The Jajis, Khostwals, Mangals and Zadrans pay revenue at Re. 1-4 a jarib, per annum; the revenue is collected in two equal instalments. It is brought by the maliks to the treasury. Irrigated land on the Shamil and Matun streams pays Re. 1-8. The Tanis pay Rs. 2 per plough instead of paying by the jarib, and the Sabaris, whose land is unirrigated, pay tithes in kind. A very large proportion of the cultivable land in Khost belongs to Government and is called khalisa; it is farmed out to cultivators.

"In the administration of justice all cases are either decided by the Governor himself or are sent to the Kazi for a decision according to Muhammadan law. There is no such thing as trial by jirga. The Governor of Khost has not the power of life and death." (Kane, Donald, Lorimer, I.B.C.)

*KHOST META   خوست میته
33-31 69-41 m. A village in the Qalandar Toy area east of Kalander Ghar in Paktia province.

KHOSTWAL See KHOST   خوست وال

KHOTKI   ختکی
34- 69-. A village on the road leading from Bilut, in Hariob, to Khurd Kabul. It is about 10 miles from Bilut, just beyond the Kharshatal pass. Inhabitants: Ghilzais. (I.B.C.)

KHUBI   خوبی
33- 69-. A township consisting of 12 villages in Khost, 6 1/2 miles from Bak and 12 1/2 miles from Matun. To the north of the place lies an uncultivated salt plain, but Khubi itself is well cultivated, and both water and forage are good and plentiful. The name of this place appears to be occasionally rendered as Akhubi or Ukubi. (I.B.C.) Recent maps show the name Yaqubi, at 33-27 69-59 m. (LWA)

KHUD Or KAJ   خود (کج)
A large affluent of the Helmand river. (See Military Report on Hazarajat, Part II.)

KHUDADAD   خداداد
33- 68-. A village about 11 miles northeast of Ghanzi, on the road to Kharwar. (I.B.C.) Recent maps show the name Kod Ali, at 33-39 68-34 m. (LWA)

*KHUDADAD KALA   خدای داد قلعه
32-44 68-29 m. A village located southeast of Omna and southwest of Urgun in Paktia province.

*KHUDAI   خدای
32-2 68-58 m. A village located east of Mamai in southern Ghazni province.

KHUDAIDAD   خدای داد
34-32 69-14 m. A village in the Kabul district, consisting of four small hamlets close together, at the northern foot of the Siah Sing hill, about two miles from Sherpur. Inhabitants: Tajiks and Rikas. It may have been 100 and 200 houses. (I.B.C.)

*KHUDA-I-NAZAR KALA   خدای نظر قلعه
32-44 68-29 m. A village located southeast of Janikhel and some 8 miles north of Barlak in Ghazni province.

*KHUDA-I-NAZAR KOR   خدای نظر کور
32-16 68-22 m. A village located northeast of Marjana in southern Ghazni province.

KHUDA NAZAR KHAN   خدا نظر خان
33-43 68-23 G. Three fort villages conjointly containing 45 houses of Wardaks, situated in the Sar-i-Ab valley, 10 miles north by west of Ghazni. (Muhammad Akbar Khan.)

KHUDI   خودی
A large section of th Dai Kundi Hazaras. (See Military Report on Hazarajat, Part II.)

KHUDOZAI   خودوزی
A subdivision of the Ghilzais, owning about 3,000 houses in the Ghazni district. (Hastings.)
They are apparently the same as McMahon's Khuidad Khel. See "Sulaiman Khel."

KHUDPUR   خودپور
34- 70-. A village in the Surkhab division of the Jalalabad district, situated on the left bank of the Surkhab river, nearly opposite Wattapur. Inhabitants: Ghilzais. (Jenkyns.)

*KHUGIANI   خوگیانی
34-15 70-11. Khugiani is a woleswali in Nangarhar province. The woleswali comprises an area of 581 square kilometers and has an agricultural population that has been estimated at from 26,663 to 40,245. The woleswali is bounded in the north by Surkh Rud, in the east by Chaparhar and Pachir Agam, in the south by Pakistan, and in the west by Sherzad. Khugiani has about 76 villages, of which about 63 have more than 500 inhabitants. The villages are listed in the PG as follows: Khwaran, Baghcha, Dag Shuja, Darga (Daga), Mankai (Malkai), Arghech, Se Koti-i-Tatang (Sar Koti), Ilyas Khel, Kaj-i-Kotwal, Kaj-i-Almar (Kaj-i-Aljar), Angur Tak, Kaj-i-Yusuf, Kaj-i-Babi, Khwaza Khel, Kheder Khel-i-Zawa, Ibrahim Khel-i-Zawa, Kudali Zawa, Shagi (Shapgi), Memla, Khani Khel, Bazar-i-Kaja (Roshan Koat), Kandwalo, Hamzah Khel, Shaker Khel, Bandah Surma, Qala-i-Sad-Bashi, Lagdi, Nahia-i-Awal, Nahia-i-Dowom, Bandah Arghech (Bandarghech), Qala-i-Karim Khan, Qala-i-Sardarha, Maidan Kani, Bazid Khel, Banda-i-Sardaran and Maidan Kaja, Lokhi, Mundah Chenar, Saqawa Lokhi (Saqawa Mawji), Bahar-i-Sufla, Shirgarr, Kala Khel (Kalai Khel), Darb Gai, Degan, Kamboy-i-Khuskh (Kubra Khubeshak), Janbaz Khel, Chashma-i-Bahar-i-Ulya, Sandalai, Khugai, Hashim Khel, Qala-i-Nazar Mohd., Pirah Khel (Pera Khel), Ahmad Khel, Mirza Khel, Pirghundai, Bulbul Khel (Balal Khel), Kheder Khel-i-Margai Khel, Tangai Miyagan,

Skandarah, Qaligho (Qalgho), Hakim Abad, Odai, Chapar-i-Ahmad Khel, Lalok Chapar (Lalok Char), Kambo-i-Khwaz-Khel, Nekarr Khel, Ganga Khel, Habibulla Khel, Chapar-i-Siyah Koh (Chapart Koh), Bang Sher Ulya, Battnai, Miran (Miran-i-Chapar), Garwandah, Abadi, Shakar Khel, Chambari-Ahmad-Khan, Mirgantai, Mirali, Khumati Khel, Kharoti Parastakar, Koprai Premzo, and Karam Chirako.

KHUGIANI   خوګیانی

A tribe settled principally in the Jalalabad district, although some of its members are found in Laghman, and some also are said to be met with in Kandahar.

This tribe remained in so sullen and unfriendly a mood during the British occupation of Jalalabad that it was not possible to obtain many details regarding them.

They form one of the divisions of the Durani tribe, and are themselves supposed to be divided into three chief clans, viz.:

    (1) Wazir
    (2) Kharbun
    (3) Sherzad

These clans are further subdivided as follows:

Wazir	Sirki, Motik
Kharbun	Najibi, Kharai
Sherzad	Panjpai, Dopai

The Khugianis of Jalalabad occupy the skirts of the Safed Koh in the southwestern corner of the district.

The following list of villages contained in the Khugiani subdivision was prepared by Jenkyns in 1879:

Sherzad Section

Ishapan	Kudi Khel
Petla	Marki Khel
Tutu	Gandamak
Mama Khel	

Kharbun Section

Hashim Khel	Kharan
Nukur Khel	Bazid Khel
Khwazi Khel	Argach
Khidar Khel	Kajja
Bilel Khel	Kailagu
Gang Khel	Hakimabad
Zawa	Bihar-i-Ulia and Surma
Khati Khel	Bihar-i-Sufla
Akori	Nimla

Wazir Section

Ahmad Khel	Agam
Pira Khel	Nani Khel)
	Pachir
Khwaza Khel	Rani Khel)

In 1879 Muhammad Sharif and Haidar Khan, of Gandamak, were the most influential men in the whole tribe.

Although their country is not difficult of access, the Khugianis have always been able to give a good deal of trouble to the Governors of Jalalabad; and probably in consideration of that they are, or were permitted to enjoy a very light revenue assessment, which is fixed in cash.

They have feuds with their neighbours, the Ghilzais on one side and the Shinwaris on the other.

In March 1879 the Khugianis, incited by the Ghilzai chief Ismatulla Khan, assembled to oppose the British and to attack the Ghilzai tribes which had been friendly to the latter. They were attacked and defeated on the 2nd of April at Fatehabad. (Jenkyns, I.B.C.)

KHUKJJA خوکجه (؟)
Said to be a village southwest from Fatehabad. Probably identical with Kaja. (I.B.C.)

*KHUKKUSHTA خوک کشته
34-54 68-11 m. A village located in the Shibar area, some 5 miles northwest of Shibar.

*KHULAI خولی
33-48 68-18 m. A village located north of Ghazni and west of Jaghatu-i-Wardak.

*KHULBESAT خلبسات
33-29 70-1 m. A village located a few miles east of Karezuna in Paktia province.

*KHUMRI خمری
33-19 68-35 m. A village located some 3 miles northwest of Sardeh Band, on the way to Arzo and Ghazni.

KHURD خورد
(See Military Report on Hazarajat, Part II.)
There is abundant grass in the summit plateau, and many flocks pasture there in summer.

KHURDAK TAKHTA خورد تخته
(See Military Report on Hazarajat, Part II.)

KHURDAKZAI خورد کزی
A section of the Polada Hazaras of Malistan. A village with this name is located at 34-45 68-20 m. (LWA)

KHURDAK ZAIDAD خورد ک زیداد
A subsection of the Daichopan Hazaras. (See Military Report on Hazarajat, Part II.)

KHURDAK ZAIDAD See POLADA خورد ک زیداد

KHURD BARG خورد برگ
35- 68-. A halting place in the Nimakao glen at the southern foot of the Walian pass and about 5 1/2 miles from the summit. There are no habitations here, the spot is marked by a tree. There is very little room for encampment, but water is abundant as also is a species of grass known as jaobarabar which is said to make good forage. At Khurd Barg the Nimakao glen is joined from the northwest by a large ravine called the Hazar Kuch; this ravine contains more than the main glen, and up it a track leads to the Chapdara pass. (I.B.C.)

KHURD KABUL خورد کابل
34-23 69-23 A. Elevation 7,220 feet. A village 17 miles from Kabul, 4 1/2 miles east of the Khurd Kabul defile situated under the hills on the bank of the stream. It contains 150 houses of Tajiks and is a

431

halting place for kafilas coming from Kabul. Water is abundant. Fuel is obtainable in small quantities. Supplies are not procurable unless specially arranged for. There is fair ground for encampment. (Johnston.) Recent maps show the spelling Khurkabul. (LWA)

KHURD KABUL   خورد کابل

34-23 69-23. A defile on the road between Kabul and Jalalabad. It commences 10 miles east of Kabul, and 1 1/2 mile from the village of Butkhak, and consists of a defile, down which runs a river, confined by high hills on either side, in a very narrow channel. The length of the defile is about 6 miles, and the width, not more than from 100 to 200 yards, the road crossing the river twenty-three times. The mountains approach so closely that the sun seldom penetrates to the roadway, and they are of the most barren description of basalt and ironstone broken into precipices and crags without a particle of vegetation on them. On leaving the defile, there is a slight ascent over the ridge and a descent to Khurd Kabul village. From a military point of view this defile is a very formidable object to the march of an army, the path used by kafilas being, in Hough's opinion, impracticable for an army, and the passage easily disputed, while there is no point in it where a flanking party could crown the heights. There is a road to the north of this by the Lataband pass, which turns this defile.

On the occasion of the withdrawal of Sale's brigade to India in 1841, it had to pass through this defile: but notwithstanding the superior strength of Sale's force, 200 Ghilzais stoutly contested the passage; and though it was forced, Sale lost 67 men, killed and wounded, in the operation.

The passage of the defile was also contested on the retreat of the British force from Kabul on 8th January 1842. This spot chosen was at the head of the defile. Here the Ghilzais opened fire on the helpless mob of soldiers, followers and women. A panic speedily ensued, and all pressed on in one "frightened mass, abandoning baggage, arms, ammunition, women and children, regardless of all but their own lives." It is supposed that 3,000 souls perished in this defile.

When Sir George Pollock advanced through this defile on the 14th September 1842 he took the precaution to crown the heights, and consequently no opposition was attempted by the enemy. And this was likewise the case on the occasion of the retirement of that General. (Masson, Hough Sale, Kaye, Pollock.)

KHURD KHAIBAR   خورد خیبر

34-12 71-2. A defile in the Jalalabad district, between the villages of Hazarnao and Dakka. It is very narrow, in some places not admitting of two horsemen going abrest, and about 3/4 mile long. It is merely a deep, narrow ravine with high banks in some parts. The road through it is good, and the descent in it is not difficult, but an enemy occupying the heights could stop the advance of any force till they were dislodged. (Hough.)

KHUSHAK   خوشک
A section of the Dai Kundi Hazaras.

KHUSHAL   خوشال (خوش حال)
A section of the Muhammad Khwaja Hazaras.

KHUSHAMADI (See DAI-KUNDI)   خوش آمدی

*KHUSHAMAND (DILE) خوشامند
32-41 68-14. Khoshamand (Dile) is a village and an alaqadari in Ghazni province. The alaqadari comprises and area of 1,344 square kilometers and has an agricultural population that has been estimated at form 2,706 to 9,165. The alaqadari is bounded in the west by Gilan, in the southwest by Nawa, in the south and southeast by Wazakhwa, in the east by Jani Khel, in the north by Ab Band and in the northwest by Muqor. Khoshamand (Dile) has about 46 villages, 11 of which have more than 500 inhabitants. Teh villages are listed in the PG as follows: Nakam-i-Nau, Nakam-i-Kohna, Panagir, Zabto Khan, Qala-i-Kalan, Chambar-i-Moh'd Yar, Watu Khel, Mulla Samand, Mamur Khel Kohna, Mamur Khel Nau, Dawlat Khan, Abdur Razaq, Akan-i-Nezan Khel, Khodzai, Sherkai, Shamo Khel, Mulla Abdul Wahab, Abdul Shah, Mahmud Khan, Nur Mohamad, Atagai, Jani Khel, Khushamand, Shah Tori, Dost Moh'd Nezam Khel (Dost Khan), Jumjuma, Manari, Omar Khel, Ibrahim Khel, Amani, Zamak, Saydan, Maruf Khel, Deldar, Balu Khel, Shahbaz, Qala-i-Sorkh, Dad Khel, Gwashta Ahmad, Pazgai (Pazgai Weski), Chori, Israil, Haji Jamal, Haji Rabani, Ona Kan, Sperah Gereh, Guldar, and Abdur Rahman.

KHUSH GUMBAZ خوش گمبذ
34-25 70-31 m. A village on the right bank of the Kabul river, 2 1/4 miles east of Jalalabad. It contains 50 families of Tajiks, possessing (in 1904) about 120 head of cattle. The annual production of wheat and barley averages about 2,700 Indian maunds. Fodder for about 1,500 animals for one day is procurable. All the village lands are state property. (Wanliss, Johnston.)

*KHUSHI خوشی
33-59 69-12. Khushi is the name of an alaqadari in Logar province. The alaqadari comprises an area of 477 square kilometers and has an agricultural population which has been estimated at from 6,904 to 11,491. The alaqadari is bounded in the west and south by Pul-i-Alam, in the north by Muhammad Agha, in the east by Azro, and in the southeast by Sayyid Karam. Khushi includes some 15 villages of which five have more than 500 inhabitants. The villages are listed in the PG as follows: Payan Deh, Miyana Deh, Bala Deh, Qarya-i-Dubandi, Gando, Darkh, Karez-i-Gul Muhd. Khel, Karez-i-Mochan, Karez-i-Sultan Khel, Barg wa Gazi, Mani, Karez-i-Darya Khan, Karez-i-Fateh Khel, Akhund Khel-i-Dubandi, Saraghundi, Lotak, Chenari, Barim, Lanai, and Abtak.

KHUSHK خشک
33-36 68-25 m. A large fort 3 miles north of Ghazni, with high walls, but apparently no towers. It contains 300 houses of Tajiks and Hazaras. (Muhammad Akbar Khan.)

KHUSHKAK خشکک
34-46 67-49 G. A village in the Saiadabad Tagao in the Bamian district. Another place with this name is 2 miles north of Giru, at 34-30 67-24 m. (LWA)

KHUSHKAK خشکک
34- 70-. A village in the Surkhab division of the Jalalabad district. Inhabitants: Tajiks. (Jenkyns.)

KHUSHKAK خشکک
34-46 68-2. A kotal leading over a spur of the Koh-i-Baba, crossed by a road alternative to the main route from the Shibar pass to Bamian via Bulola. Approaching from the southwest, the road leaves

the Irak valley 3/4 miles above the junction of the Dara Jandargal, and ascends a small nala. The gradient of this nala is gentle; but it is too narrow for guns. It could be easily widened, and the road up it is otherwise good.

At 1 3/4 miles (mileage from the mouth of Dara Jandargal) the road leaves the nala, and ascends the open hillside to the Irak Kotal, the top of which is reached at 3rd mile. The first mile of this ascent is a gentle slope easy for guns, and a road is good; but the last quarter mile before the top of the kotal is reached is very steep and impracticable for guns either up or down, without handling. (This kotal must not be confused with that of the same name leading over the main range of the Koh-i-Baba.)

    Foot of ascent to Irak Kotal   9,143 Feet
    Top of Irak Kotal   9,473

From the kotal an easy descent leads into the Khushkak Dara reached at 4th mile. The first 3/4 mile of this descent is over an open upland dasht. The last quarter of a mile is steeper; but there is a good road, easy for guns all the way.

There is a path down the Khushkak dara to Kala Bulola on the main road, but it is probably bad, as the lower part of the glen is very narrow and rocky.

Crossing the Dara Khushkak, an easy ascent of 3/4 mile leads to the Khushkak Kotal. The gradient is easy for guns; but a few stones in its lower quarter mile would require to be removed. The Khushkak Dara where crossed is 60 yards wide, but widens out to 200 yards a quarter mile lower down at Kala Khushkak (8,923 feet.)

There is no stream, and water is conducted in a jui to Kala Khushkak from the Jolah stream over the Khushkak Kotal.

At 4 3/4 miles the descent from Khushkak Kotal into the Dara Jolah commences. It is 1 3/4 miles long in all, and is a good easy road for baggage animals, but would require considerable improvement for guns over the first quarter mile, where it is much broken by nalas, and also over the last quarter mile. Its general character is a succession of descents and ascents as it winds down projecting under-features of the hillsides. Soil, a light clay. Fall estimated at 800 to 1,000 feet. (Peacocke.)

*KHUSHKAK   خشكك
    34-28 68-36 m. A village on the Maidan river, about 2 miles west of Jaliz in Maidan province. Another place with this name is located north of Paghman and east of Haji Paik in Kabul province, at 34-31 67-24 m.

*KHUSHK DARA   خشك دره
    34-51 67-35 m. A village located south of the Mian Band-i-Khushkdara, some 15 miles west of Bamian.

KHUSHKI See KUSHI   خشكى

KHUSHKIN   خوشكين (كوچكين)
    34-39 69-4 m. A hamlet in the Koh Daman district, northwest of Kabul, and 2 miles northeast of Karez-i-Mir. Contains only 10 houses. (Kincloch.) Recent maps show the spelling Kochkin. (LWA)

KHUSHK KHAK   خشك خاك
    A place leading from the Logar valley into Maidan, between the Tai Taimur and the Abdara passes. (Bishop.)

*KHUSHKOL خوش قول
34-3 68-12 m. A village located east of Panjpitao in northern Ghazni province. Another village with this name is located on the Helmand at the confluence of the Qal-i-Qaitamun in Bamian province, at 34-11 67-18 m. (LWA)

*KHUSHKNAW خشک نو
34-51 68-12 m. A village located some 4 miles southeast of Shibar on a tributary of the Ghorband.

*KHUSHMAND خوش مند
33-35 69-44 m. A village located some 4 miles north of Zurkot woleswali seat.

KHUSHNAO TAGAO See SURKH خوش نو تگاو

KHUSHRUD See Military Report on the Hazarajat, Part II. خوش رود

*KHUT KANDI ختکندی
32-22 68-18 m. A village located on the road from Wazakhwa to Khoshamand in Ghazni province.

KHWAJA خواجه
A small section of the Muhammad Khwaja Hazaras.

*KHWAJA AHMAD خواجه احمد
34-5 68-28 m. A village located east of the Bolibum Ghar and 1 mile north of Zur in Maidan province.

KHWAJA AHMAD KOHI خواجه احمد کوهی
A local name for the Koh-i-Kirghui.

KHWAJA ALI خواجه علی
A subsection of the Dai Khitai Hazaras.

*KHWAJA ALI خواجه علی
34-46 68-31 m. A village located on the Dara-i-Turkargan near Qumri in Parwan province.

KHWAJA ANGUR خواجه انگور
A large village in the east of Kharwar. 100 houses in Ahmadzai Ghilzais. (Griesbach.)

KHWAJA ANGUR خواجه انگور
33-42 69-2 m. Elevation 8,810 feet. A pass over the hills northeast of Kharwar. It has two branches. The western one is a path fit only for sheep or goats. The main eastern track leads into the upper Altimur valley. This road is easily passable for horses and baggage animals. The pass is also known as the Altimur. (Griesbach.) There is also a stream with this name located about 12 miles southeast of Juz Khel in Logar province.

KHWAJA BUGHRA خواجه بوغره
34-34 69-12. A small village in Kabul district, on the northern shore of the Wazirabad lake and about 3 miles southwest of the Paiminar pass. The inhabitants are Tajiks and Hazaras. (I.B.C.)

KHWAJA BULGHAR خواجه بلغار
33-32 68-28. A hill 4 miles long and of inconsiderable height,

south of Ghazni. Its northern slopes run down to the city. No cultivation or water on the hills. (Hastings.)

KHWAJA CHISHT خواجه چشت
34-39 69-14 m. A village 10 miles northeast of the city of Kabul. Inhabitants: Tajiks, Ghilzais, and Hazaras. (I.B.C.)

KHWAJA DAD خواجه داد
A section of the Takana Hazaras. See "Bamian (District)."

KHWAJA DEH خواجه ده
35-15 69-27 m. A village in the upper Panjshir glen, between Bazarak and Anaba. It has 30 houses of Tajiks. There are many orchards about, but open fields in places would allow of troops encamping. Supplies for 2 battalions and 1 cavalry regiment for 4 or 5 days could be collected from the immediate neighbourhood. The Arzu Kotal road into Andarab branches off here from the main Kabul-Khanabad road. It is described as a mere foot-path, impracticable for horses, though possibly a horseman might get over it by leading his animal. The hills on both sides of the road are bare of trees and bushes, but are covered with grass in spring and summer. (Shahzada Taimus.)

KHWAJA GARH خواجه گرج
A village between Kabul and Farajghan, 18 miles from the latter, (Stewart.)

KHWAJA GHAR خواجه غر
34- 67-. Elevation 9,742 feet. A hamlet in the north of the Bamian district, situated at the head of the Zarsang glen, and passed on the road leading from Jalmish via Khwaja Kashmir to Daob-i-Mekhzari. There is a track south to Chankak and Bamian, only passable for men on foot. It descends to the Bamian valley by a ravine called Khwaja Ghar, not far east of Kala Sarkari and the idols. (A.B.C.) A mountain with this name is located at 34-55 67-56 m. (LWA)

*KHWAJAGIAN خواجه گیان
34-45 69-7 m. A village located on the road from Kabul to Charikar, about 3 miles south of Kalakan.

*KHWAJA HASAN خواجه حسن
34-47 67-35 m. A village on the Dara-i-Darwaza, about 2 miles south of Ambar Samuch in Bamian province.

KHWAJA HILAL خواجه هلال
A peak on the range between the river of Ghazni and that of Katawaz. (Broadfoot.)

KWAJA JAMA خواجه جامه
A section of the Khatai Hazaras of the Bamian district. (A.B.C.)

KHWAJA KASHMIR See ZARSANG خواجه کشمیر
35-7 67-56 G. A well located about 22 miles southeast of Saighan.

*KHWAJA KHALAN Or AZIZABAD خواجه خلان
33-42 68-30 m. A village located some 10 miles northeast of Ghazni on the highway to Kabul.

KHWAJA KHEDERE See KHWAJA KHIDAR خواجه خدر

*KHWAJA KHEL خواجه خیل
34-54 69-9 m. A village located on the road from Kabul to Charikar, about 8 miles south of Charikar.

KHWAJA KHEL خواجه خیل
A village in the Gandamak valley, Jalalabad district, containing, with the two other villages of Ahmad Khel and Pira Khel, 1,000 houses of Wazir Khugianis. (McGregor.)

KHWAJA KHEL خواجه خیل
33- 68-. A village in Kharwar, containing 55 houses of Ghilzais. (Griesbach.)

KHWAJA KHIDAR خواجه خدر
A village – 40 miles from Kabul and 83 miles from Farajghan, on the Panjshir river, consisting of 60 houses of Tajiks. (Leech.)
N.B. See next article. A village called Khwaja Khadir is located at 33-4 66-11 A. (LWA)

KHWAJA KHIDAR خواجه خدر
35-2 69-16. A small district near the junction of the Panjshir and Ghorband streams, said to be inhabited by 1,000 Tajik families. The names of the villages are:
Toghchi Erchi, Kala Biland, Jamshed Khel Turkoman, Khan Kadam, Shahgag, Kala-i-Ghulam Ali, Maiogor, Laghmani Kohna, Kala-i-Gulai, Bakshi Khel, Mushum Khel, Kata-Khel, and Uaodeh. (Shahsada Taimus.)

KHWAJA KUSHKAR خواجه قشقار
34-42 69-19. A village close to Aodara, 12 miles northeast of Kabul. (I.B.C.)

*KHWAJA KUT خواجه کوت
33-21 69-31 m. A village located on the Saidkhelo Lgad, on the road from Khost to Gardez in Paktia province.

KHWAJA MIRI خواجه میری
A section of the Jaghatu Hazaras.

KHWAJA MUHAMMAD See MANDRAWAR خواجه محمد

KHWAJA MULLA خواجه ملا
34- 69-. A village in the Kabul district, on the left bank of the river, between Deh-i-Murad Khan and Guzargah. About 35 houses of Tajiks. (I.B.C.)

*KHWAJANUR ZIARAT خواجه نور زیارت
33-13 68-27 m. A ziarat located on the southern banks of the Sardeh Rud and south of Ghazni in Ghazni province.

KHWAJA OMARI خواجه عمری
33-41 68-24. Khwaja Omari is an alaqadari in Ghazni province. The alaqadari comprises an area of 174 square kilometers and has an agricultural population which has been estimated at from 4,580 to 9,456. The alaqadari is bounded in the west by Jaghatu, in the north by Jaghatu and Sayyidabad, in the east by Zena Khan, and in the south by Ghazni and Jaghatu. Khawa Omari has about 35 villages, of which 10 have more than 500 inhabitants. The villages are listed in the PG as follows: Aqasi, Bini Sang, Pya Darah, Taqa Doz, Torami, Chahar Burja, Chehil Gunbad, Deh Haji, Deh Daraz (Deh Darad), Deh Hamzah (Deh Zamta), Deh Dawlat, Dal Quli (Deh Quli), Deh

Niyal (Deh Nehal), Barakat, Aliabad-i-Sayyedan, Qala-i-Nau (Nau Balla), Karez, Karez-i-Aliabad, Gandol-i-Qandahari, Kadwal-i-Khalifa Abdul, Mar Qol, Nawah Gak (Nawahgai), Nau Burja-i-Sayedan, Gadol-i-Tamai, Gadol-i-Toras, Qarya-i-Abdul Salam, Qala-i-Dost Mohamad, Qala-i-Mullayan, Qala-i-Nau-i-Khwaja Omari, Pa-ye Mast Ali, Taqa Doz-i-Hazarah, Barat-i-Barakat, Qala-i-Nawila, Deh Barakati, and Qala-i-Nuri.

*KHWAJAR خواجر
32-18 68-9 m. A village located at the Shinkai Ghar, southeast of Malekdin in southern Ghazni province.

*KHWAJA RAHIM DASHT خواجه رحیم دشت
33-20 69-45 m. A dasht located north of Shamal Khwar and northeast of Nadirshahkot in Paktia province.

KHWAJA RAWASH خواجه رواش
34-33 69-13 m. A village in the Kabul district, 2 miles northeast of Sherpur. it has a high tower, which can be seen from a great distance, and a canal from the Kabul river runs close by it: The land surrounding the village is very fertile. Inhabitants: Tajiks. The side is on an artificial mound. (Kennedy.)

*KHWAJA ROSHANI خواجه روشنی
34-46 67-42 m. A village located on a tributary of the Bamian river, about 8 miles southwest of Bamian.

KHWAJA SARAI خواجه سرای
34- 68-. A halting place on the right bank of the Kabul river, about 1 mile north of Durani Kala.

KHWAJA SARAN خواجه سران
A village in the Koh Daman; 50 houses. (Kinloch.)

KHWAJA SHAWAB خواجه شواب
A village in the Koh Daman; 40 houses. (Kinloch.)

KHWAJA SIAHRAN ULIA خواجه سیاران علیا
35-1 69-4 m. A village near Charikar, containing 300 families of Tajiks. Khwaja Siahran Sufla contains 250 houses of Tajiks. (Shahzada Taimus, from native information.)

KHWAKKHI See KUSHI خواکئی

KHWARO KATS خوارو کڅ
32- 68-. A halting place on the Gumal route, close to, and to the east of, Kala Babakar Khel. It is pretty open. Water and camel forage plentiful. (Broadfoot.)

KHWAZAI خوازئی
34- 70-. A village in the Kama division of the Jalalabad district, on the left bank of the Kabul river, 4 miles northwest of Ambar Khana. Inhabitants: Mohmands. (Jenkyns.) A fort with this name is northwest of Shakut, at 34-20 70-48 m. (LWA)

KHWAZA KHEL خوازاخیل
34- 70-. A village in the Khugiani division of the Jalalabad district, about 12 miles southeast of Nimla. Inhabitants: Wazir Khugianis. (Jenkyns.)

KHWAZI KHEL خوازی خیل
34- 70-. A village in the Khugiani division of the Jalalabad district. It is situated about 3 miles southeast of Gandamak. Inhabitants: Kharbun Khugianis. (Jenkyns.) A place called Khwazi is located at 34-21 70-47 m. (LWA)

KIAGH کیاغ
33- 68-. A glen draining east of the Ghazni plain, and occupied by Jaghatu Hazaras. (See Military Report on Hazarajat, Part II.)

*KILAGHU کلاگو
34-15 70-9 m. A village near Mankai, about 20 miles southwest of Jalalabad. Another village with this name is located at 33-20 68-47 G.

KILDEH کده
A part of the Arghandab valley. (See Mlitary Report on Hazarajat, Part II.)

KILIGAN Or KELIKAN کلگان (کلی کان)
34-52 66-41 m. A collection of hamlets in the Yak Walang district situated about opposite the point where the united Sachak and Sabz Daras debouch into the Rud-i-Band-i-Amir through the Dahan-i-Guli. They contain about 30 families of Khan-i-Aba Hazaras. There is a small fort on the left bank of the Dahan-i-Guli watercourse, and a number of caves used for storing grass, corn, etc., and as cowhouses. (Maitland.)

*KILOKAS کلوکس
34-16 69-41 m. A village located on a tributary of the Surkhab, about 2 miles southwest of Karim Khel in Nangarhar province.

KIMLUT کملوت
A section of Jaghatu Hazaras, who number 400 families and reside in the Jirmatu Dara, and at Momand and Sar-i-Bed.

KIMSAN Or KIMSUNG کسان
Believed to be a locality of Ujaristan.

KIMSAN-I-AYA کسان آیه
A subsection of Dai Khitai Hazaras.

KIMSAN-DANGULA کسان دنگوله
A subsection of the Polada.

KINCHAK کنچک
35-0 68-42 G. A village in the Ghorband valley, near the mine of Farinjal. At the back of the village is a hill, from which antimony is procured in abundance. (Lord.)

KIPAK کپک
34- 69-. A village 4 miles northwest of Kabul, between the Khirskhana and Nanachi Kotals. Through the village runs the road from Kabul to Karez-i-Mir in the Koh Daman. Inhabitants: Tajiks. (Masson, I.B.C.)

*KIRALA کیراله
34-53 71-9 m. A village on the Kunar river, near Asadabad in Kunar province.

*KIRASU کراسو
34-29 69-44 m. A village located some 10 miles south of Sarobi in Kabul province.

KIRGHU قرغو
34-29 68-15 m. A village and three forts in the country of the Besud Hazaras, south of Kharzar. (Masson.) The village is located at the southern bank of the Helmand, one mile from Qash in Maidan province. (LWA)

KIRGHUI KOH-I کوه قرغوی
An offshoot of the Sangakh range.

KIRMAN کرمان
The name applied to the upper Lal valley. There is also a village with this name, located southeast of Lal, at 34-28 66-29 G. (LWA)

KIRPITAO See PARIAN کیرپیتاو

KIRZA کرزا
A village in the Jalalabad district. (MacGregor.)

*KISAR DAKA کسردکه
34-44 70-25 m. A village located on a tributary of the Alingar, some 4 miles southeast of Aram Khel in Laghman province.

KISHAI کشای
A stream joining the Helmand from the west at Chahar Shinia. It flows through Afghan territory. (Peart.)

KISHAN کیشان
34-10 69-5. A village in the valley of the lower Logar, i.e., in the division north of the Tangi-Waghjan. It stands on the right bank of the Logar river, and in 1880 it contained 30 families, all Hazaras. (Clifford, Euan Smith.)

KISHANI کیشانی
A cluster of villages, 117 miles from Ghazni, and 178 from Quetta, belonging to Hotak Ghilzais. (Campbell.)

KISMISHABAD See MANDRAWAR کشمش آباد

KITTI See DAIKUNDI کتی
33-33 65-42 A. A village in Nuristan, 2 miles north of Aramtel.

*KIZHAKAI کیژکی
33-33 69-33 m. A village located in the Musakhel area, east of Gardez in Paktia province.

KIZIL قزل
34-28 66-1 m. A village in the northwest of the Dai Zangi Hazara country, passed on the main Kabul-Hazarajat-Daulat Yar road.

KIZILBASH قزل باش
A Mughal Persian tribe settled in different parts of Afghanistan, and especially in Kabul and its neighbourhood.
When Nadir Shah marched for India in 1738, he left at Kabul a "chandawal," or rear guard, of this tribe, whose name is derived from the red caps they once wore, i.e., kizil bash. After the death of Nadir Shah they remained at Kabul as a military colony, and their

descendants still occupy a distinct quarter of the city, which is called Chandawal. They hold their ground in Afghanistan as a distinct Persian community of the Shia persuasion against the native Sunni population. They constitute an important element in the general population of the capital, and exercise a considerable influence in local politics. Owing to their isolated position and antagonism to the Afghans, they are favourably inclined to the British. Indeed the overture which Burnes reports to have been made to him by Naib Muhammad Sharif shows this. He says that "the Kizilbashis were then dangerously placed, as their quarter, the Chandawal, being completely commanded, they could easily be overpowered by an infuriated population; but if a piece of ground could be got for them at a distance, they would build a fort on it bridle the ruler whoever he might be and prove of eminent service to any power who might purchase their good offices. That besides their own military strength, which amounted to 5,000 cavalry, they could reckon on the aid of the Hazaras, who were also Shias, and the Ghilzais, who were decidedly inimical to the Duranis."

During the British occupation of Sherpur in 1879-80, the kizilbashis were, as a rule, friendly, and in December 1879, when Sir Frederick Roberts' force was besieged in Sherpur, the Kizilbash quarter in Kabul was in like manner beleaguered, but the inhabitants were able to keep off their assailants, and were amply provisioned, as it is the traditional custom of every Kizilbash family, however poor, in Chandawal, to keep one year's supply of food in hand.

When their military employment ceased, many of the Kizilbashes were forced to seek employment as secretaries, stewards, etc., although a portion of them have always remained in the service of the Amir. Their military influence having thus declined, they have turned their attention to adding to their strength by intrigue, and there is no doubt that their power in this way has consequently increased rather than diminished, for every Afghan of rank has Kizilbashis as his secretaries, and thus, all the home and foreign correspondence being in their hands, their influence has opportunities of spreading in every direction. Dost Muhammad, from his mother being of this tribe, was at first inclined to coquet for their support; but finding that it would have made him exceedingly unpopular, he never gave himself much into their hands.

The following is a list fo the divisions of the tribe, in the order of their relative importance:

1. Jawansher
2. Shah Samand
3. Aoshar
4. Kuchari
5. Nabari
6. Kabari
7. Siah Mansur
8. Shah Mansur
9. Kurd
10. Khafi
11. Jami
12. Shirazi
13. Kirmani
14. Arab
15. Baiat

Of the above, Nos. 1,2,3,4,5,6,8 and 9 were originally Turkish; Nos. 7,10,11,12,13, and 15 were Persian; No. 14 was Arab. The different races have now been thoroughly mixed by free intermarriage, and the distinctions are those of name only, although each subdivision has its own hereditary chief, and at Chandawal only, its particular quarter.

The Kuchari section was originally Sunni, but became Shia on arrival at Kabul. In the fort and village of Murad Khani (On the left bank of the Kabul river, opposite the city) the population is entirely Kizilbash of the Kirmani, Aoshar, and Jami sections, and this fact has led some writers erroneously to suppose that the name Murad Khani is applied to a division of the tribe itself.

In appearance the Kizilbash is remarkably handsome, with a fair complexiona and vivacious manners. He is manly, of a hardy frame, and possesses many martial qualities. The bulk of the Afghan cavalry and artillery is Kilbash, and members of the tribe are frequently to be found in regiments of Bengal and Punjab cavalry, where they have the character of being smart and intelligent soldiers, and excellent horsemen.

The Turki language has nearly disappeared from amongst the Kizilbashis of Afghanistan, and Persian has taken its place. The village of Aoshar, in the Kabul district, is an exception to this statement; there the language spoken is exclusively Turki, although of course the inhabitants understand Persian as well. (Elphinstone, Burnes, Bellew, I.B.C.)

KIZILBASH KALA   قزلباش قلعه
34- 68-. A fortified hamlet in the upper Helmand valley.

KIZILBASH KALA   قزلباش قلعه
34-28 68-36 G. A village on the main Kabul-Herat road, about 2 miles west of Jalrez. The inhabitants are Tajiks. (Wanliss.)

KOCHI   کوچی
34- 67-. A village in the Jaji country, consisting of 3 forts, 150 houses, with numerous gardens. It can turnout 400 fighting men. (Agha Abbas.) A village with this name is north of the Koh-i-Baba, at 34-36 67-1 m.

KOCHINAK See KARA KHAWAL   کوچنک

*KOHBAND   کوه بند
35-3 69-29. Kohband is an alaqadari in Parwan province. The Alaqadari comprises an area of 193 square kilometers and has an agricultural population that has been estimated at from 5,225 to 6,658. Kohband includes about 32 villages, of which 3 have more than 500 inhabitants. The villages are listed in the PG as follows: Gayawa-i-Ulya, Gayawa-i-Sufla, Durnama, Malekagar, Turbat, Khum, Shiram (Shirin Khel), Muqam Khel, Shamadad Khel, Rahmat Khel, Kotali, Malang Khel, Shawaq, Shufachi, Chap Dara, Manawar Khel, Arab Khel, Fateh Khel, Jaro Khel, Haji khel, Zarghonat, Aram Kot, Qala-i-Mirza Mir, Qala-i-Ata Khan, Kolalan Arab Khel, Ghairat Khel (Ghair Khel), Sultan Khel, Nauruzkhel, and Jan Khan Khel.

KOH DAMAN   کوهدامن
35-0 69-15. The district of Koh Daman is about 30 miles in length, and varies from 4 to 12 in breadth. It extends along the foot of the Paghman range, which forms its western boundary. Its southern limit is a low range jutting out nearly at right angles from the Paghman range, and separating the Koh Daman from the Chardeh valley. On the east it is bounded by a range separating the Koh Daman from the Chardeh valley. On the east it is bounded by a range separating it form the Safi country. To the north Koh Daman merges into Kohistan somewhere in the vicinity of Tutamdara. The average elevation of the daman proper may be estimated at about 5,000 feet.

The southern part of the district, entered at about Kala Sayyid Mirza, was several times traversed by our troops in 1879-80, but the existence of the great plain of the northern Koh Daman seems to have been hardly recognized. Even with regard to this comparatively small southern end, the information on record does not seem to be very complete or satisfactory.

Eastward from Tutamdara the whole country is like a garden. It is all orchards and fields, with scattered fruit trees, intersperced with numerous villages and hamlets. In fact, it resembles the suburbs of one of the larger towns of Afghanistan. The country hereabouts is traversed by many irrigation canals and their branches and would be difficult for the movement of troops. There is an irrigation canal on the left of the road all the way from Tutamdara to Charikar, sometimes close, and sometimes as much as 150 yards off. It is of varying size, according to the dimensions of its spoil banks, but always impassable for artillery without ramping.

On the right of the road is the open, gently-sloping daman of the Paghman range. It is about a mile wide, gravelly or stony, with no large nalas. Troops of all arms could march over it on a wide front. There is some camel-thorn on this daman.

Tutamdara is at the northwest corner of the Koh Daman. The plain here, at its upper end, is at least 12 miles across. It does not taper to any great extent, but the corners are rounded. The whole plain has an aspect of peculiar richness, partly due to the neatness of the cultivation and number of trees thickly scattered over it, and partly no doubt to the background of magnificent, though bare, mountains. Maitland particularly noticed that no land seemed to be lying fallow; as far as he could make out, it was all actually under cultivation.

The Ghorband river enters the Koh Daman at its northwest corner; that of Panjshir issues from a defile on the north. Between them, but nearer to the Ghorband, and not more than a couple of miles northeast from the Tutamdara villages, is the gap of the Parwan Dara, through which the Salang water escapes. The later soon joins the Ghorband, but the Ghorband and Panjshir do not unite for some 8 to 10 miles after leaving the hills. The ruins of the ancient city of Bagram (the Kabul of the successors of Alexander?), where so many thousands of coins have been found, is situated somewhere about the junction of the rivers. The united river is known as the Panjshir, and goes away southeast across the plain to a great gap in the hills. Thence down a long valley, and finally through various defiles to the Kabul river. In 1886 the Amir was said to be having a new road made along the line of the Panjshir to Jalalabad, which will bring that place into direct ocmmunication with Charikar and the upper Koh Daman. This road was reconnoitred by explorers specially sent from India in 1887 and again in 1906. It is probably a good camel-road.

On the west side of the upper Koh Daman the end of the Paghman range is low, and can be easily crossed by infantry at almost any point. Between the foot of the range and the cultivation is an open, gently sloping daman along which the Istalif road runs. It is a mile or more wide and on this troops can advance on a broad front and manoeuvre with facility.

On the north side of the plain are flat-terraced undulations rising to the base of the hills. They are entirely cultivated.

On the east side of the Koh Daman, above the cap of the Panjshir river, several large glens open into the plain. There seems to be a daman on that side also, with some large villages, one of which is Bolaghain.

At Karabagh the Koh Daman proper is only 7 or 8 miles wide, and it narrows gradually to about 4 miles at Shakar Dara. The eastern part of it, which was traversed by the Afghan Boundary Commission in 1886, is a very close country, with numerous villages and forts imbedded in masses of orchards and high-walled enclosures. The general surface of the ground appears to be undulating, and in such open spaces as exist, the fields are banked or terraced, and roads frequently sunk beneath the general level. The western half of this tract is comparatively open, but not nearly so much so as further north. It appears to be undulating, with a deal of cultivation, and big villages at the mouth of every glen, the watercourses of which may not be very easy to cross.

From the base of the Paghman range much debris, splintered rocky fragments, and heavy boulders are strewed over the plain, having been loosened by the winter's frost from the granite peaks above. The sides of these mountains are split by numerous ravines, down which come tumbling rills of the purest water. The slopes of their rugged channels are thickly planted with the mulberry, and every moderately level spot is clad with fruit trees or the vine.

According to Maitland, "the population of the Koh Daman is said to be 200,000 souls, turning out 50,000 men. It is probable that fully 25,000 men all with firearms of some sort might be easily collected, and in so close a country they would offer considerable resistance to any troops making war in the mild fashion which we practise, and which costs us so many lives." Molloy computes the population at 20,000 families at least, "of which about 17,000 are Tajiks and the rest Ghilzais". The present Hakim is said to be one Latif Khan, a Muhammadzai of Kandahar. The district has not been disarmed like Kohistan; but the carrying of arms is prohibited.

The greater portion of the fruit brought by traders into Upper India is from the Koh Daman. Here are grown grapes of a dozen different kinds, apricots of six sorts, mulberries of as many, besides endless varieties of apples, pears, peaches, walnuts, almonds quinces, cherries, and plums.

Mountain streams pouring down from Istalif, Shakar Dara, and Istarghij unite their waters in the centre of this district, and afford facilities for irrigation, which, as above mentioned, have been by no means neglected.

Koh Daman is a favourite country residence of the wealthy inhabitants of Kabul, and is almost as thickly studded with forts as with gardens. They are strongly built, and are, in fact, mimic representations of the old baronial residences in Europe.

Babar, when he conquered Afghanistan, located a number of his countrymen in the Koh Daman, the descendants of whom are now among the most prosperous in the valley.

The following is from a report on the Koh Daman drawn up in 1880 by Lieutenant-Colonel Kinloch, Deputy Assistant Quartermaster-General, who, in July of that year, accompanied Sir Charles Gough's brigade during the temporary occupation of the district:

General description. "The Koh Daman may be considered the garden of Kabul, the greater part of the cultivated land being taken up by orchards and vineyards. There are two pretty well-defined belts of cultivation, one extending along the foot of the hills, where the mouth of each valley is occupied by a large village, or town, surrounded by extensive and well-watered gardens; the other where cornfields alternate with vineyards stretching along the centre of the main valley on the left bank of the Ak Sarai river. The villages in this lower tract are more scattered, and none of them are of such size and importance as those on the higher slopes.

"Along the skirts of the hills the most important towns are Ghaza, Shakar Dara, Bezati, Kahdara (including Bedak and Deh-i-Nao), Farza, Istalif, and Istarghij.

"In the lower valley lie Karez-i-Mir, Baba Kushkar (which is the name of a district as well as a village), Haji Kaik, Karinda, Ak Sarai and many smaller villages.

"Between the two cultivated strips lies a considerable expanse of gently sloping open and stony ground, intersected by ravines, and it is across this that the main road to Charikar lies, thus enabling a

and vineyards, at least in the plain rather fewer. Lucerne (beda) force to ¹advance on a tolerably wide front, instead of threading the narrow and tortuous paths which lead through the strongly enclosed vineyards and gardens.
Approaches and roads. "The Koh Daman can be entered from the direction of Kabul by several passes: 1st by the Siah Bini Kotal on the southwest. This is an easy pass but with no well-defined road; it is however, practicable for baggage mules and ponies.
"2nd--The Surkha Kotal. This is on the main road from Arghandi to the Koh Daman, through the Paghman valley. It is practicable for camels.
"3rd--The Khirskhana Kotal, leading from Deh-i-Kipok in the Kabul valley proper to Karez-i-Mir. This is also a good road, with easy gradients, but it is said to be rough and stony in places. It did not reconnoitre this road, but it was constantly used. (This is the main road. It is a made road, fit for all arms.)
"4th-- The road through the Kara Dushman gorge. This is nearly level, and leads across open country, except through the gorge itself. There the path leads along the edge of a deep ravine, and is in places very narrow, with sharp angles to turn, but it was used by all arms, with camels and baggage mules.
"5th--the Mama Khatun Kotal. This is steep and rough, and, although baggage mules might cross it with difficulty, it is not advisable to send them by this route.
"6th--The Zimma Kotal. Several roads, as will be seen in the map, lead from Kabul across the Kala-i-Haji and Iltifat plain, and converge at the village of Zimma, whence there are easy approaches over open ground to Baba Kushkar or Ak Sarai. The best for all arms, including wheeled artillery, is via Kala-i-Haji and Ju-i-Bar, through Kala-i-Sayyid Husain, passing through the opening in the hills to the east of Ju-i-Bar instead of going through the rocky gorge which contains the drainage of the plain.
"7th--The Rah-i-Gosfand. Instead of turning west on reaching Kala-i-Sayyid Husain, an easy road may be taken through the gorge to the north.
"There may be said to be only one main road through the Koh Daman leading past Karez-i-Mir through Kala-i-Murad Beg and Haji Kaik, and then skirting the western side of the vineyards of Baba Kushkar. This road is usually in fair order and practicable for all arms and baggage animals, with the exception of wheeled artillery, but as it crosses numerous nalas and water-cuts obstructions could easily be made at such places. As, however, timber is plentiful, bridges could always be rapidly constructed.
Products. "The Koh Daman is chiefly famous for its grapes and other fruits, on which the peoplelargely subsist, besides exporting immense quantities. The grapes are of many different varieties, and are cultivated with great care. Many of the houses are built with interstices in the walls for the purpose of drying the grapes and converting them into the 'kismis' which appears to be one of the staple articles of food in Afghanistan. The walls thus built present the apearance of having been strongly loopholed for defensive purposes.
"The apricot is the commonest fruit, and there are many different kinds varying considerably in colour and flavour; perhaps one of the best is a white fleshed variety called 'kaisi.' Peaches and cherries are also excellent, and large numbers of melons and watermelons are grown where the soil is suitable.
"Wheat and barley are grown rather sparingly in the southern part of the valley, being succeeded by maize in the autumn.
Towards the north the cornfields appear to be more numerous,

and clover (shaftal) are grown in moderate quantities, but after five weeks' occupation by Brigadier-General C. Gough's brigade, with two cavalry regiments, it became rather difficult to procure forage in sufficient quantities.

(Molloy says, "the revenue of Koh Daman amounts to six lakhs of Kabul rupees, of which four lakhs are realised from arbabi and two lakhs for Khalsa land.")

Towns and villages. "The most important towns and villages have been already enumerated; of those whose position I had leisure to fix at all accurately are shown in the map. They are all substantially built of mud with thick walls, and the majority have towers, giving flank defence, and more or less extensively loopholed.

"Most of them are rather difficult to approach in consequence of their being surrounded by vineyards with high walls, which completely shut in the roads and paths. These are, however, occasionally an advantage, as they form covered ways which conceal the movements of troops as well as afford them protection from fire. Without preparation these walls give no advantage to the defenders as they are usually much too high to fire over.

Population. "A large majority of the inhabitants of the Koh Daman are Tajiks, the chief exceptions being the villages of Kala-i-Khanjar and Siah Sang, which are inhabited by Afghans only, and Sarai Murak, which is Hindu.

"The population of Farza is partly Afghan and partly Tajik. I found it difficult to obtain reliable information regarding the numbers of the inhabitants of the towns and villages, but I give the statement made to me by a man who was supposed to be well acquainted with the country for what it is worth:

Names of Villages	No. of houses
Karez-i-Mir Bala	60
Ghaza	100
Kala-i-Khanjar	100
Dolana	10
Kala-i-Mir Kolab	10
Surkh Bulandi	60
Ayub Shaikhu	50
Sarai Murak	20
Deh-i-Chakrak	40
Bakhteri	30
Yakub	50
Loku	100
Bezati	300
Jalwani	30
Bedak	200
Deh-i-Nao	300
Farza	700
Istalif	1,200
Khwaja Shawab	40
Istarghij	400
Chaikal	80
Khwaja Saran	50
Opian	60
Tutamdara	55
Karez-i-Mir Pain	100
Kala-i-Murad Beg	100
Haji Kaik	80

Siah Sang	50
Khush Kin	10
Siab	100
Sufian	30
Dhaku	200
Guzar	30
Mama Khatun	40
Baba Kushkar	300
Kuchi	100
Kala Khan	700
Balao	30
Lucha Khan	80
Karinda	400
Ak Sarai	100
Total	6,495

"Or, roughly, 6,500 houses, exclusive of Charikar (Charikar is said to contain 3,000, and Parwan 1,500 houses, but neither of these places are believed to be in the Koh Daman district properly so-called; they are more probably included in the Charikar subdivision of Kohistan. Maitland, as mentioned above, estimates the population at 200,000 souls, while Molloy computes it at 20,000 families.), and Parwan, which are represented as being very large places. Taking an average of 1.5 men per house, this would give a fighting strength of about 10,000 men.

Manufactures. "As far as I could learn, there are but few manufactures in the Koh Daman; coarse cotton cloth is, as usual, woven is most of the villages.

"In Kala-i-Murad Beg there seems to be a considerable trade in pottery which is made there.

"Bezati is famous all over the country for the excellence of its vinegar." (Wood, Masson, Lord, Elphinstone, Kinloch, Maitland, Molloy.)

KOH DILAN   کوه دلان
   A high mountain in the Siah Koh range.

*KOH-I-AB--I-REG   کوه آب ریگ
   34-43 68-41 m. A mountain northwest of the Paghman range, northeast of the source of the Helmand.

KOH-I-BABA   کوه بابا
   34-41 67-30. A long mountain range stretching from east to west across the centre of Afghanistan, and forming part of the great backbone of the whole country. It is usually spoken of as a continuation of the Hindu Kush, and it is so in fact, as well as in name, but there is this peculiarity (not uncommon in such cases) that the one range is not a simple prolongation of the other, without break. The ends of the ranges do not meet, but overlap, and are united by a rather flat open watershed known as the Shibar pass. (See "Hindu Kush.")
The Koh-i-Baba proper extends from the Koh-i-Darwaz in the Shaikh Ali country to the neighbourhood of the Bakkak pass south of Yakh Walang. Here the hitherto well-defined range breaks up into three. The southern-most branch may be considered the real main range. It is called the Band-i-Duakhwan, Band-i-Baian, and by other names, and continues along the south of the Hari Rud valley to the immediate neighbourhood of Herat, where it is called the Koh-i-Safed. The centre branch runs along the north side of the Hari Rud, parallel to

the first, and is the watershed between the Hari Rud and the Murghab. The northern branch strikes northwest, enclosing the basin of the Upper Murghab, and dividing it from the deep valley and gorges of the Rud-i-Band-i-Amir. Branching right and left, it forms the mass of mountains which are the natural boundary of this part of Afghan Turkistan. The western half of these mountains is called the Band-i-Turkistan. The eastern half has no one name.

The Koh-i-Baba bears considerable outward resemblance to the Hindu Kush, being a sierra, of which the highest peaks rise to over 16,000 feet. The passes are from 12,000 feet to 13,000 feet high. They are therefore not much lower than the Hindu Kush passes, and appear to be closed for much about the same time. But there is this difference between the Koh-i-Baba and the Hindu Kush proper, that while the latter is practically a single range like the Alps between France and Italy, the Koh-i-Baba has a wide tract of mountainous country on either side of it, and the difficulties of the roads are by no means confined to crossing the main range. To the south of the Koh-i-Baba is the Besud district of Hazarajat, a hilly region of great elevation, through the upper end of which lies the road from Kabul to Bamian by the Unai pass. Further west Besud country is succeeded by that of the Dai Zangis.

North of the Koh-i-Baba is the great plateau of Afghanistan, extending for some 140 mile in the direction of the Oxus.

The passes leading over the Koh-i-Baba proper are in order from the east as follows:

Darwaz	Fauladi
Nirkh	Siah Reg
Sagpar	Jiria Khana
Zirak	Dulga
Sabzab	Zard Sang (1)
Irak	Gul-i-Robat Zard Sang (2)
Hajigak	Khak-i-Chagir
Kafzar	Shahtu
Dokan	Kharkol.

The Irak, Hajigak and Zard Sang are the only ones of which reliable and recent information exists. It is not quite clear whether the Bakkak is on the main range or not. Maitland, who crossed it, speaks of it as being so, but from the map it would appear to cross its northern branch. A great branch of the Koh-i-Baba is a range which takes off from the latter at Akzarat and runs southwest through Waras and Takht, turning gradually west and running through the Sehpai country down to the Helmand at Sheran. Its principal names are Koh-i-Chark, Koh-i-Jaokol, Chahar Shamba, Aodarazagh, and Largar. It is comparatively low near the Koh-i-Baba and increases in height as it approaches the Sehpai country. (Maitland, Peacocke, Peart.)

*KOH-I-BADAM   کوه بادام
34-29 68-32 m. A mountain located north of the Maidan river and east of Jaliz.

KOH-I-BIRUNI   کوه بیرونی
A subsection of the Besud Hazaras.

*KOH-I-BORO   کوه برو
34-36 67-25 m. A mountain located south of the Koh-i-Baba range and southwest of Bamian.

*KOH-I-CHAPDARA کوه چپدره
    34-41 67-47 m. A mountain located north of the Koh-i-Baba range and
    some 10 miles south of Bamian.

KOH-I-CHARK See KOH-I-BABA کوه چرك

*KOH-I-DOSHAKH کوه دوشاخ
    34-57 67-20 m. A mountain located northeast of the Band-i-Amir, at
    the source of the Dara-i-Tarikak.

*KOH-I-GHULPARIDA کوه غول پریده
    34-5 67-28 m. A mountain located west of Kushk in Bamian province.

*KOH-I-GIRU کوه گیرو
    34-18 68-7 m. A mountain located east of Baghak in Bamian province.

*KOH-I-GOLI کوه گلی
    34-35 67-6 m. A mountain in the Koh-i-Baba range, north of the
    Kotal-i-Gharghara in Bamian province.

KOH-I-JAOKAL See KOH-I-BABA کوه جوکل

KOH-I-JAUZ کوه جوز
    33- 68-. One of the principal mountains in the range east of
    Ghazni. (Hastings.)

KOH-I-KALANDARAN See KOH-I-SHAITUS کوه قلندران
    34-25 68-21 m. A mountain located southwest of Jalriz in Logar
    province.

KOH-I-KARINJ کوه کرنج
    Elevation 14,337 feet. A peak on a ridge which separates Laghman
    from the Kafir country. From its summit is a most extensive and
    commanding view of this region. It is sometimes covered with snow,
    but is below the snow line, and is covered with forests. The Kafirs
    roam over the north slopes of this hill. (Masson.)

KOH-I-KOHAND کوه کوهند
    A peak on the range which separates the Panjshir valley from that of
    Tagao. It is due north of Tagao, and is probably at the head of the
    above named range as it is in the country of the Kafirs. It is
    covered with snow for a greater part of the year. (Masson.)

KOH-I-KURT کوه کرت
    A range of hills in the Hazarajat.

*KOH-I-MAGU کوه ماگو
    34-29 67-3 G. A well known mountain in the Hazarajat.

*KOH-I-MASAMUT کوه ماسموت
    34-52 70-13 m. A mountain located northeast of Alishang and south-
    west of Alingar in Laghman province.

*KOH-I-MIR کوه میر
    34-2 67-46 m. A mountain located south of Barikjoy in Bamian
    province.

*KOH-I-NAYAK کوه نایك
    34-28 68-31 m. A mountain located north of the Maidan river at
    Sarchashma in Maidan province.

*KOH-I-QAJIR کوه قجیر
   33-50 68-5 m. A mountain located northwest of the Shemeltu stream in Ghazni province.

*KOH-I-RAWZA کوه روضه
   33-36 68-28 m. A mountain located some 4 miles north Ghazni.

KOH-I-SABZNALA کوه سبز ناله
   33- 68-. A mountain to the east of Ghazni. (Hastings.)

KOH-I-SAFI کوه صافی
   34-44 69-22 m. A hilly tract, situated between the valley of Tagao and the Panjshir river, and so called from the Safir tribe who pasture their flocks on it. (Masson.)

*KOH-I-SAFI کوه صافی
   34-51 69-23. Koh-i-Safi is an alaqadari in Parwan province. The alaqadari comprises an area of 701 square kilometers and has an agricultural population that has been estimated at from 4,690 to 5,250. The alaqadari is bounded in the west by Qara Bagh and Deh Sabz, in the northwest by Bagram, in the north by Mahmud Raqi and Nejrab, in the east by Tagab, in the south by Sarobi, Khak-i-Jabar, and Deh Sabz. Koh-i-Safi includes about 37 villages, of which 2 have more than 500 inhabitants. The villages are listed in the PG as follows: Angur Darah, Shergai, Pacha Khak, Lala Baba, Paitab, Sayyid Ali, Khushk Qol wa Qandi Qol, Khak Khur, Landa Khel Juzak, Mulla Ahmad Khel, Hasanzai Sufla, Karizgai, Hasanzai Ulya, Ali Khwaja, Jurghati Ulya, Adin Khel (Adina Khel), Qala Khel, Askendara, Senjetak, Trili, Dander (Dandara), Islam, Baba Ghumbaki, Nili, Bakhti, Chanari, Dewana Khel, Jurghati Ziarat Sufla, Basi Khel, Gadai Khel, Naman Khel, Ahmadzai, Ghafur Khel, Siah Sang, Jauzak, Meya Khel, Ismael Khel, and Mardan Khel.

KOH-I-SHAITUS کوه شیتوس
   A mountain range in the Hazarajat.

*KOH-I-SHANASANG کوه شانسنگ
   34-53 67-2 m. A mountain located south of the Khushkdara stream, and northwest of the Band-i-Amir in Bamian province.

KOHISTAN کوهستان
   35-7 69-18. Kohistan is a woleswali in Parwan province. The woleswali comprises an area of 171 square kilometers and has an agricultural population that has been estimated at from 20,827 to 28,734. The woleswali is bounded in the west by Kapisa, in the north by Panjshir, in the east by Durnama, in the southeast by Charika, and in the south by Mahmud Raqi. Kohistan includes about 104 villages, of which about 27 have more than 500 inhabitants. The villages are listed in the PG as follows: Aftabachi, Pana Khel, Baku Khel, Ghaffar Khel, Baghcha Lalo-i-Karim Khel, Karam Khel-i-Khum-i-Zargar, Baghcha-i-Lalo-Zargar, Kanko, Pufdam (Pughla), Korawa, Qala-i-Shada, Toghak-i-Ushturgram, Tishi Dara (Tal Sheda), Shir Khan Khel, Hazrat Khel, Penja Koti, Deh Nau, Jaldak Qalandar Khan, Jamal Agha, Deh Qurban-i-Qala-i-Regi, Sarband-i-Jamal Agha, Yarow Khel, Malik Khel, Qala-i-Regi, Jamal Agha-i-Ulya, Chashma-i-Mazullah (Chashma-i-Sadullah), Cheghchi Dasht, Sefatullah (Hafizullah Khel), Chashma-i-Allahdad, Khum-i-Roba, Derashan (Deh Perashan), Werashan Ulya, Werashan Sufla, Murad Khwaja, Nur Khel, Deh Payake Dasht, Deh Muzafar, Deh-i-Bulbul, Reg-i-Rawan, Sanjan, Sangburha (Sangaran), Shirak Pirak, Ezat Khel, Qazi Khel, Kocha-i-Sanglakh Qala-i-Mihr,

Qazaq, Qala-i-Sahra, Qala-i-Sahra-i-Ushturgram, Qala-i-Sahra-i-Dasht, Bala Kocha, Qala-i-Nau-i-Dasht, Qalacha-i-Mir Sahib, Kalota, Karezi, Keshketan (Kashkestan), Kala Banan, Kulalan Tapa-i-Malikan, Tapa-i-Kulalan, Tapa-i-Malekan, Kuhna Deh, Mulla Khel (Mulla Khalil), Shokh Chiyan, Waseh Khel, Deh Khum-i-Zargar, Hasan Khel, Pul-i-Ashuq, Pul-i-Gow Kush, Qadam Khel, Char Asyab, Pul-i-Mughulan, Anwar Khan Khel, Poza Dazri, Afghan Beg Khel, Zobaid Khel, Qorban Beg Khel, Khwaja Mir Khel, Nabi Khel, Hamzulla Khel, Tapazar, Latif Khel, Ghulam Khel, Kashaw, Nasser Khan Khel, Faqir Khan Khel, Sher Mohammad Khel, Adel Shah Khel, Karam Khan Khel, Suratbeg Khel, Qul-i-Jamal-i-Khum-i-Zargar, Muri Khum-i-Zargar, Qara Sayyidi, Tajo Khel, Mir Khel, Padshah Khel, Nazam Khel, Kohna Khel, Kohna Qala, Arbab Khel, Sharbat Khel, Char Asyab, Gul Ghundi, Ushturam Khel, Ushtur Khel, Qarya-i-Kayada-i-Sufla, and Qarya-i-Kayada-i-Ulya. (LWA) In 1912 this area was described as follows:

"A district of Kabul, situated north of Kabul, and consisting of the valleys of Tagao, Nijrao, Panjshir, Ghorband, and Charikar, with the minor valleys which open into them." But according to Molloy, "Reza-i-Kohistan comprises that portion of Kohistan which lies between the Koh Daman and Panjshir. The Kotal-i-Darband leading to Panjshir is on the northern border line. West are spurs of the Hindu Kush. On the eastern border are the following independent villages situated on the slopes of the hills which shut off the Nijrao valley, viz., Bulaghain, Sanjan and Durnama. The two districts of Koh Daman and Reza-i-Kohistan together make up what the Afghans mean when they talk of Kohistan. On this point my informant speaks positively. Ghorband, Panjshir, Tagao and Nijrao are looked on as separate districts, and are always so spoken of. They are never, that is included in Kohistan." For the purposes of this article Kohistan will be considered as being subdivided thus: Tagao, Nijrao, Panjshir, Charikar; and further information regarding these subdivisions will be found under their respective headings.

The coup d'oeil presented by Kohistan, when viewed from the plain of Bagram, is most magnificent; the winding courses of the rivers, the picturesque appearance of the gardens and forts, the verdure of the pastures, the bold and varied aspect of the environing hills, crowned by the snowy summits of the Hindu Kush, form a landscape which can scarcely be conceived but by those who have witnessed it. Kohistan is only cultivated in the neighbourhood of the streams, but this portion bears but a small proportion to the mountains which are high, steep, and covered with firs. The cultivated parts yield wheat and some other grains, but the chief subsistence of the people is from their numerous and extensive plantations of mulberry trees. Some grain is imported from the Koh Daman and the returns are made in cheese. There is, however, but little trade, internal or external, and the people live much to themselves. The Kohistanis live in flat-roofed houses and those who attend the livestock to the mountain in the summer do not use tents. The villages are small but numerous, and the population is, according to Elphinstone, 40,000 families. (This refers to Kohistan as defined in the second edition.) The country is very strong for defense, from its unproductiveness and the facility with which the inhabitants can retreat to the mountains.

In their personal character the Kohistanis are bold, violent, and unruly and so much given to war that they reckon it a disgrace for a man die in his bed. They make excellent infantry, particularly among hills, but their courage is generally wasted in internal dissensions. They have seldom disputes between tribes or villages, but many quarrels and assassinations among individuals. Disputes between villages, when they do happen, are more serious in their consequences than elsewhere, since it is almost as easy to fell a plantation of mulberry trees as to reap a field of corn, and the damage is far more difficult to repair. At the present time the Kohistanis are understood to possess but few arms, Amir Abdur Rahman having disarmed them to a large extent.

Their dress is a close jacket and trousers of coarse, black, woollen cloth, a pair of short half-boots, and a small silken cap.

They are all Sunis, and bear more than ordinary hatred to the Persians and to all other Shiahs.

They are under different Khans, and these chiefs, though they cannot control their domestic feuds, are able to direct their foreign operations, particularly when assisted by any religious prejudice.

Masson has the following remarks on the antiquities of Kohistan:

"The Kohistan of Kabul abounds with vestiges of its ancient inhabitants; they are chiefly, if not exclusively, of a sepulchral character, but their greater or less extent, with the numbers and varieties of the coins and other relics found at them, may authorise us to form an estimate of the importance of the places which, we infer, were situated near them. Admitting such criteria, a city of magnitude must have existed at Parwan, about 8 miles bearing north, 19 west, from Bagram, consequently that distance nearer to the great range of Caucasus under whose inferior hills it is in fact found. Coins are discovered there in large numbers, and there is also a cave remarkable for its dimensions.

At Korahtas, east of the famed hill and ziarat Reg Rawan, and on the opposite side of the river to Bagram, from which it is distant about 6 miles bearing north, 48 east, numerous coins are found, and we have the usual tokens of mounds, fragments of pottery, etc., with remains of works in masonry about the hills, which, bearing now the appellations of Kala-i-Kafir, are in truth sepulchral repositories."

During the campaign in Afghanistan in 1840, the Kohistan was the scene of several engagements, vix., at Tutamdara, Parwan, Jalgah, Kahdara, Charikar, and Istalif. A corps of Kohistanis was raised under Lieutenant Moule, but they appear to have been eminently untrustworthy throughout their short service, and at last they broke into open mutiny on the outbreak of the rebellion at Kabul.

During the British invasion of Afghanistan in 1879-80 the Kohistanis took a very prominent part in opposing us, and are said to have sustained the heaviest losses of all our opponents at Sherpur and elsewhere, one of their chiefs, Mir Bachcha, being especially active in his hostility. Towards the end of the investment of Sherpur, they were much disgusted with their treatment by the other tribes, who, they said, always assigned the post of danger to them, whereas they themselves carried off the lion's share of plunder.

In January 1880, Mir Bachcha was punished by the destruction of his forts, orchards and vineyards in the Koh Daman. (Masson, Pottinger, Elphinstone, I.B.C.)

KOH-I-SULTAN کوه سلطان

34-9 69-23 m. A high mountain lying to the southeast of Kabul and to the east of Zargan Shahr in Logar. It is approached from the Logar valley by the Abkhor defile. (I.B.C.) Recent maps show the spelling Koh-i-Sultan Sahib. (LWA)

KOHNA DEH کهنه ده

34- 70-. A village in the Kunar valley close to the village of Kalatak, or about 56 kos from Jalalabad. It has 60 houses is enclosed, and situated on an eminence. Behind it is a small but very perfect tope, the basement and cylindrical superstructure of which are very entire. In the hills behind it are a number of caves proving the spot to have been a monastery (vihara), as there are more than would have been necessary in simple connection with the monument. (Masson.)

KOHNA DEH   کهنه ده
A small crude fort, surrounded by the huts of a Hazara village, situated in the Garmao valley.

*KOHNA DEH   کهنه ده
33-16 68-2 m. A village located on the Zarak Mandeh, about 6 miles northwest of Daftani in Ghazni province. Other places with this name are located near Qarghanatu in Bamian province, at 34-46 67-25 m; and some 6 miles north of Kota-i-Ashro in Maidan province, at 34-31 68-49 m.

KOHNAK   کونک (کهنک)
32-42 68-42. The name applied to the range of hills running north and south along the east side of the Katawaz district. (I.B.C.)

KOISHKI See SAIYIDAN   کویشکی

KOJAK See SAGPAR   کوجک

KOJI   کوجی
A locality in the Besud Hazara country.

KOJJIN   کوچکین
34- 69-. A village in the Koh Daman, 10 1/2 miles from Kabul on the road to Charikar via the Khirs Khana Kotal. It lies about 1/2 miles to the west of the road, and a roomy camping ground can be found between the village and the road. Supplies and water are abundant. (I.B.C.) Recent maps show the name Kochkin, at 34-39 69-4 m. (LWA)

KOKHAR AB   کوخر آب
A river which drains the eastern part of the Dai Kundi country.

KOKINAK See KARA KHAWAL   کوکینک

*KOLAK   قولک
34-3 67-3 m. A village located on a tributary of the Helmand, near Kajalak in Bamian province. Another place with this name is located near the Helmand in the Warash area in Bamian province.

KOLANI   قولانی
34- 66-. A tagao, or glen, running down in a northerly direction from the Band-i-Duakhwan to the Lal valley.

KOLIAN   قولیان
A tribe of independent Hazaras.

KOL-I   قول (کول)
Places, the names of which begin with the word Kol followed by the Persian izafat, are described under the second word of their designations.

KOMAGHAI   قومغی
34-20 67-1 m. A village, with a sarai in the Kirman valley, passed on the Kabul-Hazarajat-Daulat Yar road 7 miles before reaching Kala Safarak. Another village with this name, also spelled Qowmghi, is

located at 34-28 66-31 A., and a mountain at 34-26 66-26 m. (LWA)

KORABA Or KORAWA کوربه
35-12 69-19 m. A village in the upper Panjshir glen 3 1/2 miles below Anaba. It contains 35 houses of Tajiks. (Sahazada Taimus.)

KORA KANDAO کوره کنداو
35- 69-. A pass which connects Nijrao with the head of the Tagao valley. (Stewart.)

KOROGH Or KORAKH کورغ
34-26 69-3. Elevation 10,509 feet. A lofty hill to the southwest of Kabul. It forms the end of a long spur running down in a southeasterly direction from the Paghman range. Arghandi and Kala-i-Kazi lie to the north of the mountain, and the Ghazni road passes over its western slopes by the Kotal-i-Takht. (I.B.C.)

KOT کوت
34- 70-. A stream of the Jalalabad valley, which rises in the Safed Koh and flowing north by Batikot and Chardeh falls into the Kabul river near the latter place. It gives its name to the subdivision of the Jalalabad district lying between the Mahman and Hisarak subdivisions. The following is a list of the villages as drawn up by Jenkyns in 1879:

Lagharjui	Idar Khel
Farukhshah Khel	Hidwani
Shaista Khel	Changar
Andarani	Spergar
Sipai	Dosha
Kamal Khel	Khidar Khani
Madok Badok	Manjuni
Saadatmand	Jaba-o-Mitrani
Kalajat	Zerbachha-i-Miran
Batikot.	

The inhabitants are Tirais, with the exception of Zerbacha-i-Miran occupied by Sayyids. (MacGregor, Jenkyns.)

KOT کوت
35- 69-. A glen of the upper Panjshir, which debouches into the right of the main valley some 8 miles above Anaba, and contains some villages and cultivation. The first settlement is Shast, 100 houses. A mile above are Kot and Kanda, on opposite sides of the glen; together they have 40 houses. Still higher is Garwashi with 40 houses. Inhabitants: Tajiks. Opposite the Kot glen, on the left bank of the main stream, is the mouth of a ravine known as the Isarak Dara. (Shahzada Taimus.)

*KOTAGAI کټگی (کوتگی)
34-37 69-33 m. A village located some 4 miles north of the Kabul river and west of the Naghlu dam. Another place with this name is a few miles south of Sarobi in Kabul province, at 34-32 69-45 m.

*KOTAK کټک
34-49 67-6 m. A village located on the Band-i-Amir, some 3 miles west of Jarukashan in Bamian province. Another place with this name is near the Koh-i-Adera, northwest of Shaikh Ali in Parwan province, at 34-58 68-26 m.

*KOTAL کوتل
33-25 68-7 m. A village located east of the Siahkoh and about 20 miles southwest of Ghazni.

KOTAL کوتل
Elevation 8,750 feet. A village in Kharwar. Forty houses of Ghilzais. (Griesbach.)

*KOTAL کوتل
34-1 70-6 m. A village located on the Garmab stream in southern Bamian province.

KOTALI کوتلی
34-48 70-6 m. A village in Laghman consisting of the following hamlets:

1. Ghaziabad
2. Kala-i-Muhammad Abid
3. Manjan
4. Shamsi Khel

Inhabitants: Dehgans. (Warburton.)

KOTAL-I کوتل
Passes the names of which begin with the word Kotal followed by the Persian izafat, are described under the second word of their designations.

KOTANNI NARAI کتنی نری
8,000 feet. A pass over the hills leading from Birmal into the Zurmat valley. It is crossed by a road from the Tochi valley to Gardez at about 14 miles beyond Urgun. Camels are said to be able to cross the pass in winter both the ascent and descent being reported as very easy. It would apparently not be difficult to make the road over the pass fit for wheeled traffic. (I.B.C.)

KOTAPUR-I-AFGHANI کته پور (کترپور) افغانی
34-24 70-15 m. A village in the Jalalabad district, situated on the left bank of the Surkhab river opposite Balabagh. In it is included the hamlet of Kota-i-Muhammad Shah, both being under the headmen of the Kaka Khel. Inhabitants Ghilzais. There is also a Kotapur-i-Tajiki mentioned by Jenkyns which is probably in the same township. Jenkyns says that the inhabitants are Tajiks and Ghilzais. (Jenkyns.) Recent sources give the spellings Katapur and Kotarpur. (LWA.)

KOTGAI کوتگی
A village, 93 miles from Jalalabad, 36 miles from Farajghan, in the Alishang valley, consisting of 18 houses of "Pashais." The valley here narrows into a defile only accessible to horsemen dismounted. (Leech.)

KOTGAI (in Kunar) See KOTKAI کوتگی

KOTGAI کوتگی
34-7 70-26 G. A large scattered village in the Hisarak subdivision of the Jalalabad district. It lies on the right bank of an affluent of the Papin river, about 7 miles south-by-west of Mazina, on the road from that place to the Oghaz pass. (I.B.C.)

455

*KOTGAI کوتگی
    34-12 68-47 m. A village, also called Khwaja Kotgai, located on the Ghazni-Kabul road, some 2 miles north of Top Kalai. Other places with this name are located some 10 miles east of Kolangar in Logar province, at 34-5 69-15 m.; near the Pakistan border, east of Sarkani in Kunar province, at 34-46 71-13 m.; on the Tangi river, some 3 miles northeast of Spera in Paktia province, at 33-14 69-33 m.; on the Lador Khole, some 3 miles west of Janikhel Mangal in Paktia province, at 33-39 69-44 m.; in Katawaz, Ghazni, at 32-8 69-10 G.; south of Ali Khel, Paktia, at 33-54 69-42 G.; south of Waza in Paktia, at 33-14 69-27 G.; Southeast of Matun, Khost, at 33-18 70-11 G.; northeast of Ali Khel, Paktia, at 33-58 69-50 G.

KOTGAI-I-O-SANGINA کوتگی سنگینه
    34- 70-. A village in the Chapriar division of the Jalalabad district. Kotgai stands on the left and Sangina on the right bank of the Chapriar stream. About 3 miles southwest of Hadia Khel. Inhabitants Shinwaris, Tajki Kakars and Mian Khels. (Jenkyns.)

KOT-I-ASHRU کوت عشرو
    34-27 68-48 m. The district capitol of Maidanshahr woleswali in Maidan province. In 1912 the area was described as follows (LWA): A village on both banks of the Kabul river, about 23 miles west by south of Kabul. It is situated at the point where the main road from Herat to Kabul leaves the Kabul river, the latter here making a great bend to the south. The village contains (1904) some 400 families of Ghilzais possessing about 500 head of cattle, 3,000 sheep and goats and 50 horses. The annual production of wheat and barley averages about 3,200 Indian maunds. Land-tax is assessed at the rate of 12 krans per jarib.
    The valley at this point is about 1/2 mile wide and is highly cultivated. The crops consist mostly of barley (harvested early in July), wheat, rice, and bakuli (horse-bean). The river here is about 20 yards across and 2 feet deep. Room for a brigade to encamp is to be found on the left bank, near the sarai. Supplies are plentiful and fuel is fairly so, but there is no grazing to be had. Just south of Kot-i-Ashru, in the Sadmarda range, is the quarry whence all the white marble used in the Kabul workshops is obtained. (Wanliss.)

KOTKAI ککی
    34-43 71-1. A group of villages in the Kunar district on the right bank of the Kunar river, about 43 miles from Jalalabad. At the most northerly village of the group there is a ferry across the river to Pashat. Near the same village stands an old fort with thick massive walls and bastions, but these are in bad repair. (I.B.C.)

KOTKI ککی
    34- 69-. Elevation 8,290 feet. A village about 1/4 miles from Belut on the road thence to Khurd Kabul via the Kharshatal Kotal. Inhabitants: Ghilzais. (I.B.C.)

KRUL کرول
    A tagao in the Dai Zangi Country.

KSTIGIGROM کستی گی گرام (کشتگرام کشتوز)
    Elevation 8,300 feet. A Kafiristan village, built on a slope on the right bank of the Pech river, about 76 miles above Chigha Sarai. It consists of about 90 houses. It is probably the most sacred place in the whole of Kafiristan, on account of its great Imra house, its

mystic hole in the ground, its iron bar placed in its present position by Imra himself, and its sacred stones believed to have on them divine handwriting. It is undefended, and was a short time ago destroyed by Wai Kafirs and Afghans acting together. The inhabitants, like the feeble folk they are, seek refuge in troublous times in a large cave high up in the rocks. (Robertson.) Recent maps show the name Kashtuz. (LWA)

KTI

35-22 70-49 G. The Kti or Katwar Kafirs are a small subdivision of the Kafirs who live in the Kti valley. They have but two villages. They are roughly estimated to number 1,000 souls. The Kti stream joins the Pech near Tsaro. (Robertson.) Another place with this name is about 20 miles southwest of Kunar, at 34-30 70-36 G.

KUCHANGI See SHIBAR
A place on the Helmand.

*KUCHI
34-36 67-1 m. A village located north of the Koh-i-Baba and 3 miles west of Bairi in Bamian province.

KUCHI
A village in the Koh Daman containing 100 houses. (Kinloch.)

KUCHI See JALALABAD (DISTRICT)

KUCHIAN
34- 70-. A village in the Mahman Dara subdivision of the Jalalabad district. The inhabitants are Kuchis. (Jenkyns.)

KUCHIAN-I-DAULATZAI
34- 70-. A village in the Chapriar division of the Jalalabad district. Inhabitants Kuchis. (Jenkyns.) A place called Daulatzai is located at 34- 18 70-23 m. (LWA)

KUCHI-I-HAZAR BUZ
34- 70-. A village in the Hisarak division of the Jalalabad district. Inhabitants: Kuchis. (Jenkyns.)

*KUCHKAK
34-57 67-3 m. A village 3 miles north of Khurjinbolaq-i-Bala on the path from Band-i-Amir valley north to the Dara-i-Ajir in Bamian province.

*KUDAI
32-57 68-18 m. A village located some 10 miles northwest of Zarghunshahr in Ghazni province.

KUDI KHEL
34-14 69-57 m. A village in the Khugiani country, 8 miles south of Gandamak. The inhabitants belong to the Sherzad section. The village stands on the right bank of the Nian Rud, and almost at the entrance of the defile where the water issues from the hills. The country is very confined in the neighbourhood, and the cultivation-terraces are narrow and steep, with great drops from one to the other; the watercuts are many and at different levels. Fruit-trees line the banks of the streams on either side; mulberries, apricots, cherries, pomegranates, pears and vines being the principal varie-

ties. In the vicinity there are good sites, at an elevation of 5,000 feet, for the encampment of small bodies of troops, and shady groves on both banks of the stream would afford agreeable shelter from the heat of the sun. (Jenkyns, Stewart.) Another place with this name is located at 32-36 67-38 G. (LWA)

KUHIR KAREZ   کوهیر کاریز
34- 70-. A village in the Jalalabad district, 5-1/2 miles east of Jalalabad. It contains some 120 families of Tajiks, possessing (in 1904) about 200 head of cattle. The annual production of wheat and barley here averages about 18,000 Indian maunds. Revenue is assessed in kind at the rate of 10 per cent. (Wanliss.)

KUJU   کجو
34- 70-. A village about 7 miles southeast of Jalalabad. It is famed for its pomegranates. There are many Sikhs here, who have a temple. Though hot in summer, it is cooler than Jalalabad, and is therefore sometimes chosen as a retreat for some of the garrison of that place from its excessive heat. (Burnes.)

KULALA   کلاله (کلالها)
34-22 69-50 m. A tributary of the Surkhab, which it joins about 3 miles north of Surkhpul. (Wanliss.)

KUL ALI   قل علی
A section of the Jirgha Besud Hazaras.

KULAM   کولم (کولاتن)
35-9 70-18 A. Said to be a tributary of the Alingar. The Kafir tribe of this name are said to possess four villages, and to roughly number about 3,000 souls. (Robertson.) Recent maps show the name Kulatan Dara at 35-2 70-25 m. (LWA)

KULANGER Or PUL-I-ALAM   کنگار
34-6 69-3. Kulangar is the name of a village and a woleswali in the Logar province. The woleswali comprises an area of 1,056 square kilometers and has a population which has been variously estimated at from 23,860 to 48,415. The woleswali is bounded in the west by Baraki and Chak-i-Wardak, in the north by Mohammad Agha, in the east by Khoshi, in the southeast by Sayyid Karam and Gardez, and in the southwest by Charkh. Kolangar has about 129 villages, of which about thirty-one have more than 500 inhabitants. The villages are listed in the PG as follows: Bahram Khel, Qala-i-Safed, Peyado Khel, Mulla Inam, Mirwal, Qarya-i-Kaji, Qala-i-Shadi Khan, Mango Khel, Rah-i-Khoshi, Qala-i-Shakar, Tator, Paye Khel, Qala-i-Musa, Qala-i-Leyas Khan, Hud Khel, Kutub Khel wa Marbutat, Neyazi, Qala-i-Khwaja Akbar, Qala-i-Bocha, Qala-i-Ali Khan, Dawud Khel, Qala-i-Sadat Khan, Qala-i-Mirza Abdur-rahman, Babus, Qala-i-Sayed Habibullah, Qarya-i-Darak, Qala-i-Mir Alam, Shash Qala, Khal Karez, Hunai Sufla, Abchakan, Baydak, Qala-i-Nakam, Qala-i-Nau, Deh-i-Mughulan, Bakhshabad, Qala-i-Ibrahim Khan, Pad Khwab-i-Shana, Seyah Koh, Qarya-i-Alozai, Meyanur, Qala-i-Wazir, Qala-i-Malik Nur Mohd, Qala-i-Rahmatullah, Qala-i-Sayed Hasan, Qala-i-Ahmad, Qala-i-Sabzak, Qala-i-Khwaja Baba, Deh Kulangar, Qarya-i-Joyak, Qala-i-Mulla Abdullah, Malik, Qala-i-Shahi, Purak Shaghasi, Qala-i-Sarfi, Altamur, Jawazar, Gharb Khel, Aspasit, Honi Saydan, Sayedha, Hesarak, Qala-i-Mamai wa Doshanba, Namida, Ata wa Dah Doshanba, Qala-i-Ahmad Khan wa Ata, Qala-i-Zardad, Qala-i-Sar-i-Sang, Dughabad, Kamal Khel, Balut Khel, Harun Khel, Kunjak, Muhajer, Zard Gul, Qala-i-Arab Khan, Qala-i-Hakim, Shah Hakim, Qala-i-Juma, Gadaye

Khel-i-Qala-i-Ghaffar, Shuluk, Qala-i-Mir Taqi Shah, Qala-i-Ahmad Shah, Qala-iQezel Bash, Qala-i-Mir Saleh, Qala-i-Sayed Husain, Qala-i-Mir Qader Shah, Qala-i-Darab, Qala-i-Sayed Nur, Qala-i-Hafizulla, Qala-i-Baba Khan, Qala-i-Khwaja Fazel Ahmad, Qala-i-Sultan Ahmad, Qala-i-Sari-i-Khaka, Qala-i-Taza Gul, Qala-i-Khairulla, Qala-i-Abdulla Jan, Qala-i-Mir Sayed Mahmud, Qala-i-Sayed Ahmad, Qala-i-Tahir, Qala-i-Mirulla, Qala-i-Sardar, Qala-i-Mir Sayed Hasan, Qala-i-Saber, Qala-i-Mahand, Qala-i-Baz Gul, Qala-i-Mirza Nazar Mohammad, Qala-i-Malik Ayub, Qala-i-Mir Azimulla, Qala-i-Sher Ali, Qala-i-Sher Jan, Qala-i-Kotagai, Kodali, Qala-i-Hamid Khan, Qala-i-Akhund Zadeh, Kham-i-Hindu, Qala-i-Haji Sayed Gul, Pas Ab, Qala-i-Mohd Sarwar Khan, Qala-i-Nau-i-Kulankar, Deh Nau-i-Kulankar, Qala-i-Sakhidad, Qala-i-Ghulam Mirak, Qala-i-Bashir, Deh Nau-i-Aminulmulk, Qala-i-Abdul Aziz, Qala-i-Jalal, Kotad, Ashinur, Chuwi, and Qater. (LWA) In 1914 the village was described as follows: A large village in the southern division of the Logar district, situated on the left bank of the Logar river, at about 18 miles south of Saiyidabad (Zahidabad). It includes several detached fortified hamlets, with nearly 1,000 houses in all, inhabited by Khwajas (Hazaras), Tajiks and Saiyids. In 1905 Muhammad Rasul Khan, Mulla Khel, Powindah, was Naib-Hakim of Kulangar and the Maliks of the village were Mulla Khwaja Afzal, Abdul Rasul, Abbas and Muhammad Rasul. There is a fine open plain on the left bank of the river which would afford unlimited space for camping, with water from the river; supplies are abundant. (I.B.C.)

KULMAN
A village in Laghman. Inhabitants: Kohistanis. (Warburton.)

KULUJ
A section of the Chahar Dasta Hazaras.

*KUMARKHEL
34-18 6J-50 m. A village located on a tributary of the Surkhab in western Nangarhar province.

KUMRAKH
34-39 66-17. A glen draining north and debouching into the Sar-i-Jangal valley at Katlish.

KUNAI
34-35 70-40 A. A small village on the right bank of the Kunar river, about 18 miles from Jalalabad. There is a squadron of cavalry quartered here. (I.B.C.)

KUNAR
From the 1960s to the 1970s a province in eastern Afghanistan which has since been merged with Nangarhar, forming its northern portion. Kunar is divided into the districts of Chagha Sarai (Formerly Kunar and now Asadabad), Bar Kunar (formerly Asmar), Pich, Chawki, Khas Kunar, Sirkannai, Kamdesh, Bargey Matal, Naranj/Badil, Chapadara, Narai, Nur Gul, and Dangom. For a view of the district map, see Nangarhar entry. For district lists compiled by the Afghan Department of Statistics of the Ministry of Agriculture and Irrigation see the following six pages. (LWA) In 1914 the area of Kunar was described as follows: The Kunar district consists of the valley of that name. It is bounded on the east and southeast by the Kabul Tsappar range, northwest by the Kashmund range, west by Laghman, and south by Jalalabad. These boundaries are, however, not accurately defined, and in a map furnished by the ex-Badshah of Kunar (Sayyid

ESTIMATE OF AGRICULTURAL POPULATION AND AREA UNDER CULTIVATION

	Villages	Agricultural Population	Landlords	Lands under Cultivation in Jaribs			Lands under Cultivation in Hectares		
				Irrigated	Non-Irrig.	Total	Irrigated	Non-Irrig.	Total
CHAGHA SARAY (KONAR, ASADABAD)	24	29,980	2,910	5,690	2,580	8,270	1,138	516	1,654
BAR KONAR (ASMAR)	23	27,260	2,695	6,350	550	6,900	1,270	110	1,380
PICH	25	32,710	3,604	26,330	390	26,720	5,266	78	5,344
CHAWKI	26	24,530	3,545	11,240	—	11,240	2,248	—	2,248
KHAS KONAR	11	12,070	1,475	1,880	20	1,900	376	4	380
SIRKANAY	11	13,550	1,660	7,570	1,590	9,160	1,514	318	1,832
KAMDESH	22	21,810	3,637	10,620	1,750	12,370	2,124	350	2,474
BARGEY MATAL	17	8,180	2,077	1,780	4,170	5,950	356	834	1,190
NARANJ/BADIL	19	16,350	3,447	5,990	560	6,550	1,198	112	1,310
CHAPA DARA	33	21,270	1,960	12,640	530	13,170	2,528	106	2,634
NARAY	23	13,630	570	8,280	3,010	11,290	1,656	602	2,258
NUR GUL	16	28,980	3,132	14,240	100	14,340	2,848	20	2,868
DANGOM	15	10,900	988	3,960	320	4,280	792	64	856
TOTAL	265	261,670	30,700	116,570	15,570	132,140	23,314	3,114	26,428

STATISTICAL ESTIMATE OF LIVESTOCK BY WOLESWALIS AND ALAKADARIS

	Sheep	Karakul Sheep	Goats	Cattle	Buffaloes	Camels	Horses	Donkeys	Mules	Poultry
CHAGHA SARAY (KONAR, ASADABAD)	2,341	—	1,752	577	424	7	7	1,166	—	512
BAR KONAR (ASMAR)	7,680	—	1,444	2,940	326	—	1	1,730	—	2,240
PICH	6,357	—	8,710	9,365	—	32	100	1,251	—	5,619
CHAWKI	4,277	—	8,570	8,635	345	3	40	1,164	—	7,314
KHAS KONAR	1,105	—	—	2,680	507	—	—	1,440	—	940
SIRKANAY	1,807	—	2,075	2,005	371	—	—	1,121	—	1,912
KAMDESH	6,205	—	33,960	5,360	—	—	164	1,835	—	11,130
BARGEY MATAL	15,590	—	4,610	3,210	—	—	570	1,910	—	3,640
NARANJ/BADIL	3,000	—	3,575	3,325	510	—	35	1,192	—	4,605
CHAPA DARA	5,617	—	5,506	5,311	—	4	80	1,162	—	7,158
NARAY	3,610	—	13,585	4,522	—	—	52	1,690	—	3,259
NUR GUL	3,950	—	3,800	8,290	327	30	58	1,128	—	5,741
DANGOM	4,331	—	4,703	4,230	—	64	83	141	—	2,540
TOTAL	65,870	—	92,290	60,450	2,810	140	1,190	16,930	—	56,610

PRODUCTION OF AGRICULTURAL CROPS—IN KABULI SEERS

	Grains Irrigated	Grains Non-Irrig.	Total	Vegetables	Other Crops Industrial Crops	Other Crops Other Temp. Crops	Fruits
CHAGHA SARAY (KONAR, ASADABAD)	267,200	12,480	279,680	72,000	87,670	44,000	114,400
BAR KONAR (ASMAR)	303,600	2,760	306,360	164,250	340,900	22,000	63,360
PICH	1,295,200	2,040	1,297,240	330,750	48,910	44,000	253,440
CHAWKI	511,600	—	511,600	139,500	448,150	11,000	211,200
KHAS KONAR	90,800	120	90,920	22,500	24,350	33,000	36,960
SIRKANAY	350,400	7,800	358,200	191,250	48,710	13,200	75,680
KAMDESH	516,000	14,640	530,640	132,750	—	33,000	107,360
BARGEH MATAL	86,400	20,040	106,440	22,500	—	15,400	45,760
NARANJ/BADIL	283,200	2,880	286,080	76,500	—	8,800	117,920
CHAPA DARA	595,600	2,760	598,360	159,750	—	28,600	248,160
NARAY	61,200	24,480	85,680	18,000	—	11,000	36,960
NUR GUL	663,200	840	664,040	180,000	73,150	55,000	274,560
DANGOM	195,600	1,560	197,160	47,250	—	11,000	40,480
TOTAL	5,220,000	92,400	5,312,400	1,557,000	1,071,840	330,000	1,626,240

LAND UNDER IRRIGATION AND SOURCES OF IRRIGATION

	Area in Jaribs					Number of Sources			
	Canals	Springs	Karez	Wells	Total	Canals	Springs	Karez	Wells	Water Mills
CHAGHA SARAY (KONAR, ASADABAD)	5,690	—	—	—	5,690	15	5	—	—	33
BAR KONAR (ASMAR)	6,346	—	—	4	6,350	11	—	—	3	35
PICH	26,330	—	—	—	26,330	26	8	—	—	81
CHAWKI	7,630	3,590	—	20	11,240	26	12	—	4	52
KHAS KONAR	1,875	—	—	5	1,880	5	2	—	2	25
SIRKANAY	7,570	—	—	—	7,570	11	5	—	2	15
KAMDESH	10,620	—	—	—	10,620	16	13	—	—	111
BARGEY MATAL	1,780	—	—	—	1,780	10	5	—	—	34
NARANJ/BADIL	5,990	—	—	—	5,990	19	2	—	—	35
CHAPA DARA	12,640	—	—	—	12,640	32	—	—	—	58
NARAY	8,280	—	—	—	8,280	21	—	—	—	37
NUR GUL	14,240	—	—	—	14,240	16	6	—	—	76
DANGOM	3,959	—	—	1	3,960	15	9	—	2	89
TOTAL	112,950	3,590	—	30	116,570	223	67	—	13	681

TOTAL CULTIVABLE LAND, BY CROPS—IN KABULI JARIBS

	Grains			Vegetables	Industrial Crops	Other Crops	Fruits	Total Cultivated Land
	Irrigated	Non-Irrig.	Total					
CHAGA SARAY (JIBARM ASADBAD)	6,680	1,040	7,720	320	180	200	650	9,070
BAR KONAR (ASMAR)	7,590	230	7,820	730	700	100	360	9,710
PICH	32,380	170	32,550	1,470	100	200	1,440	35,760
CHAWKI	12,790	—	12,790	620	920	50	1,200	15,580
KHAS KONAR	2,270	10	2,280	100	50	150	210	2,790
SIRKANAY	8,760	650	9,410	850	100	60	430	10,850
KAMDESH	12,900	1,220	14,120	590	—	150	610	15,470
BARGEY MATAL	2,160	1,670	3,830	100	—	70	260	4,260
NARANJ/BADIL	7,080	240	7,320	340	—	40	670	8,370
CHAPA DARA	14,890	230	15,120	710	—	130	1,410	17,370
NARAY	1,530	2,040	3,570	80	—	50	210	3,910
NUR GUL	16,580	70	16,650	800	150	250	1,560	19,410
DANGOM	4,890	130	5,020	210	—	50	230	5,510
TOTAL	130,500	7,700	138,200	6,920	2,200	1,500	9,240	158,060

TOTAL CULTIVABLE LANDS—IN KABULI JARIBS

	Total	Pastures	Forests	Under Cultivation	Fallow Lands
CHAGHA SARAY (KONAR, ASADABAD)	84,450	2,860	73,320	8,270	2,810
BAR KONAR (ASMAR)	729,130	20,980	701,250	6,900	1,530
PICH	45,700	15,490	3,490	26,720	5,780
CHAWKI	68,040	52,490	4,310	11,240	2,660
KHAS KONAR	5,920	1,570	2,450	1,900	390
SIRKANAY	21,170	10,160	1,850	9,160	2,670
KAMDESH	551,000	7,390	531,240	12,370	2,690
BARGEY MATAL	173,440	18,560	148,930	5,950	3,060
NARANJ/BADIL	27,230	18,190	2,490	6,550	1,560
CHAPA DARA	38,240	22,480	2,590	13,170	2,890
NARAY	66,460	12,190	42,980	11,290	870
NUR GUL	60,310	20,490	25,480	14,340	3,060
DANGOM	74,350	68,450	1,620	4,280	1,040
TOTAL	1,945,440	271,300	1,542,000	132,140	31,010

Mahmud) in 1892, the boundaries of the Kunar district (as it was in his time) only include the low spurs and valley on either side of the river. It then extended as far up the valley as Chigha Sarai. The Kunar river rises in a glacier on the south side of the Hindu Kush, northeast of the Darkot pass. From its source to Mastuj, it is known as the Yarkhun, thence to Chitral as the Mastuj thence to about Asmar as the Chitral or Kashkar, and finally as the Kunar. This article deals only with that portion of the stream which runs wholly or partly through Afghan territory--that is, from the mouth of the Bashgul to the Kunar-Kabul confluence near Jalalabad. Within these limits the elevation of the valley ranges between 3,000 and 1,900 feet.

The description given below has been adapted from a report furnished by Lieutenant W. Coldstream, H.E., who accompanied the British party of the Afghan-Bajaur Boundary Delimitation Commission, 1894-95. Previous to that time we knew very little regarding the Kunar valley properly so-called, as it does not appear that any Englishman had every before visited it above Kunar itself:

"In giving a general description of the valley it will be as well to consider it in two portion, an upper and a lower, which differ considerably in characteristics and resources. The two portions however merge into one another and are not very clearly defined. The terms upper and lower valley are not used by the inhabitants.

"Narang, 47 miles by road from Jalalabad, may be considered as the point of division.

"Lower valley--The general width of the lower valley is about 1-1/2 miles bays of fertile level ground alternating with narrower portions where the spurs from the hills on either side run down to the river, which flows in several channels and is unconfined by high banks. Towards the south the valley is very fertile and thickly populated, the roads are very fair and the fields are irrigated by a regular system of canals and rajbahas. The general appearance of the country is much the same as that of the more fertile portions of the Jalalabad plain or the Peshawar valley. Trees, Mostly tamarisks, mulberries, walnuts and chinar, are numerous round the villages and on the roadside. The inhabitants are Safis and although this portion of the valley is said to be very feverish in autumn, they appear healthy and well developed. (Another account describes the inhabitants of the lower valley thus: "the Kunari is a rice-eater, with poor physique, and is probably not a great fighting man. He wears a long coat buttoned down the front, and a pair of very baggy trousers; he does not a wear a kulla...he talks Pashtu.") Arms are not generally carried, and there is an air of prosperity about the crowded villages. On the left bank of the river the country is not so populous as on the right bank, the hills rise from within half a mile of the river and communications are probably bad, as the main route to the villages on that side is by the road on the right bank and ferries.

"The river is said to be fordable in winter in places where it spreads out in numerous channels, but no fords were pointed out to the Delimitation Commission of 1894-95, and the existing ones must be seldom used. Ferries are numerous and consist of the ordinary country boat or a raft of masaks running on a cable. (The Amir is said (1907) to be building bridges over the river.

"The paris, or places where the valley is blocked by spurs running down to the river on either side, are a characteristic feature of the lower valley. They are generally good defensive positions and command the ground on either side of the river. At the points where the road crosses these paris there is always a tower held by an Afghan post of 9 men.

"The chief villages in this portion of the valley are: the groups of Shigal and Shewa villages in the fertile plain one march from Jalalabad, the two or three Nurgal villages (26 miles from Jalalabad), the Chowki villages (37 miles from Jalalabad), the Kunar villages on the left bank of the river (about 32 miles from Jalalabad), the Kotkai and Naran villages (43--47 miles from Jalalabad), and the old town of Pashat with its royal residence and pleasure gardens opposite Kotkai on the left bank. Except where otherwise stated the above places are on the right bank of the river.
"The hills bounding the valley on the northwest side are known as the Kashmund range, which rises to nearly 14,000 feet and presents a very wild and craggy appearance; the summits are snow clad for the greater part of the year, and the higher slopes are covered with deodar and oak forests. In the narrow valleys which penetrate far into the recesses of the range are said to be numerous villages and patches of cultivation.
"The Mohmand hills (called by us the Kabul Tsappar, but the name is not locally recognised.) bounding the valley on the southeast which rise gradually as the valley is ascended till they culminate in a peak between 8,000 and 9,000 feet high above Kunar, are of a different nature. Devoid of trees, except in the sheltered ravines, the features and slopes are generally rounded and covered with grass. Passes over this range into the Mohmand country are said to be fairly numerous and easy. Higher up the valley there is an easy pass called the Nawa Kandao from Dunai opposite Narang to Nawagai in Lower Bajaur. The crest of this pass is just under 6,000 feet in height, and the road is passable for mules all the year round and is in constant use.
"The fighting strength of the lower valley may be taken at between 4,000 and 5,000 men at a rough approximation.
"The Upper valley. A few miles above Narang the valley contracts to a narrow gorge in and above which the river flows in one deep, narrow channel with rocky banks. Cultivation is only found in the valleys of the tributary streams and on the level ground at and near the mouths of these valleys. In many places, even where there is a considerable expanse of fairly level ground there is no cultivation owing to the scarcity of water. Especially is this the case on the plain between Narang and the gorge above mentioned. Here there are the traces of an ancient canal which appears not to have been used for some generations. The Afghans are at present (1895) constructing a new canal which will bring water from the Pech river, which enters the Kunar at Chigha Sarai, about 10 miles above Narang. The width of the valley above Narang is seldom over a quarter of a mile, and in many places the hills rise directly from the river banks. Trees are very scarce: only a few mulberries and chinars.
"The principal villages are: Chigha Sarai, a group of large villages with a fort at the affluence of the Pech river (57 miles from Jalalabad); the Shigal village on the Shigal stream (68 miles from Jalalabad); Marawara a large village of Mamunds on the left bank of the river opposite Chigha Sarai; the Shurtan villages, Mamunds and Salarzais, at the mouth of the Shurtan Dara opposite Shigal; and the town and cantonments of Asmar at the mouth of the Asmar Dara on the left bank of the river (77 miles from Jalalabad). Here there is an old fort formerly the residence of the Khans of Asmar. In the cantonments were quartered (1894 and 1895) a force of 7,000 Afghan regular troops, the object of which before the Chitral expedition was to hold the main road from Bajaur (by the Binshi pass up the Asmar Dara), and to be in readiness to act against Umra Khan's forces on the Bajaur side or the Kafirs on the north and west.

"Above Asmar the principal villages are Bargam, Nawa Kala and Nashagam (82, 83 and 85 miles, repectively, from Jalalabad), Chundak (87 miles), Sao (89 miles), Nari and Arnawai (99 miles from Jalabad). The last three places lie on the left bank. A short way above Arnawai the Bashgul river enters the Kunar, and above this point the valley forms part of Chitral. (On the right bank of the Kunar the eastern watershed of the Bashgul valley forms the Afghan-Chitral boundary while on the left bank the southern watershed of the Arnawai is the dividing line.)

"Above Narang the river is not fordable; there are ferries at the principal villages and bridges at Asmar, Jalala (5 miles above Asmar), Sao and Arnawai. A bridge is said (1907) to be under construction at Sarkani also.

"Exclusive of the army, the fighting strength of the valley above Narang to the frontier may be roughly estimated at 2,000 men; this includes small colonies of Shinwaris, forcibly settled by Abdur Rahman after his Shinwari campaigns at different points to act as a border militia and prevent raiding from Bajaur on one hand and Kafiristan on the other. Above, Asmar the inhabitants appear to be of the same race as the Chitralis; as a rule they are small and emaciated. The languages in use in this portion of the valley are Chitrali, Pushtu and Kafir. Pushtu appears to be generally understood.

"The hills on the north and west side of the valley rise to over 15,000 feet; the summits are covered with snow all the year round, and the range is clothed with deodar, oak and pine forests. Markhor are numerous; pheasants and chikor are fairly abundant. On the other side of the river, below Asmar the hills are like the Mohmand hills already described, while above Asmar is the Uchiri range (13,000'), of much the same character as the Kafir moutains, but on a much smaller scale. The watershed on this side runs parallel to the river and is 4 to 8 miles from it; that on the right bank is distant 10 to 20 miles. The climate of the uper portion of the valley is one of extremes, in winter snow lies occasionally in the bottom of the valley itself, while in summer the heat is said to be very great. Asmar is very unhealthy, especially in the fever season (autumn), but this is probably due as much to defective sanitation and over crowding as to climate."

General. From Jalalabad a good camel-road runs up the right bank of the river to Asmar where it crosses the river and continues thence along the left bank to Birkot.

Lateral communications from the right bank in a westerly direction are few and difficult, being confined as far as we know, to a road leading from Chigha Sarai up the Pech Dara and over the Kama Bida pass into Badakhshan, and another from Birkot up the Bashgul to Kamdesh and the Mandal pass. The former is known to be fit for mules; of the latter little is known, but it is believed to be fit for mules at any rate as far as Ahmad Diwana, 60 miles from Birkot.

From the left bank a number of tracks cross the watershed into Mohmand country and Bajaur; these are, however, for the most part mere footpaths, unfit for laden mules.

According to the second edition of this Gazetteer, the valley, exclusive of Asmar is said in unfavourable seasons to yield a revenue amounting to about R60,000, and in favourable years to yield one reaching R80,000.

Formerly the valley was under the rule of a family of Sayyids, but Sayyid Mahmud, known as the Badshah of Kunar, who is the present representative of the family, rebelled against Abdur Rahman in 1882, and being expelled by him sought refuge in British territory. In 1905 he was permitted to return to Afghanistan by the present Amir, but has not been restored to any of his former power in Kunar. The history of these Sayyids is thus summarised by MacGregor:

"From the time of Hamayun up to the commencement of the reign of Shah Shuja-ul-Mulk, the Sayyids of Kunar held undisturbed possession of the province, and would in all probability have continued to enjoy the same place had not Sayyid Najif espoused the cause of Shah Mahmud, when he was contending with his elder brother Shah Zaman for the kingdom of Afghanistan.

"The treachery of Ahmad Khan Nurzai, as is well known, gave an unhappy turn to the fortunes of Shah Zaman, who was in consequence deserted by his army at Karabagh (near Ghazni) and compelled to make a hasty retreat to Jalalabad, with a few followers only, where he commenced collecting his troops with a view of making another effort to regain his kingdom; but on Sayyid Najif leaving Pashat with a large army, intending to attack His Majesty, the monarch fled to Pesh Bolak and took refuge in the fort of Ashur Shinwari, where he was betrayed, imprisoned, and subsequently blinded.

"This conduct on the part of Sayyid Najif towards His Majesty's ill-fated brother induced Shah Shuja-ul-Mulk, in the commencement of A.D. 1803, to send an expedition against him, which he placed under the command of Arz Begi, Akram Khan, Popalzai. The expedition had scarcely reached 'Kuli-gram,' a village distant from Pashat a few miles only, when Sayyid Najif with his family fled to the neighbouring hills and took refuge in the valley of Denagul.

"Adram Khan and the Sayyid had long been on friendly terms with each other, and this led to an intrigue between them, which defeated in a great measure the object of this expedition. Akram Khan accepted from the Sayyid a bribe of R5,000 to withdraw the troops from Kunar; but it became necessary in doing so that His Majesty should be made satisfied, and the Sayyid accordingly gave up one of his sons (Mohi-ud-din) as a hostage to ensure in future his loyalty and good conduct. Akram Khan returned to Jalalabad and the Sayyid to his capital. Subsequently, on the ascendancy of the Barakzai brothers, Muhammad Zaman Khan was appointed Governor of Jalalabad, and shortly afterwards he required of Sayyid Najif that the district of Shewa should be annexed to that of Jalalabad; this the Sayyid disputed. Both parties assembled troops on their respecive frontiers, an engagement took place, and on Muhammad Zaman being wounded in the shoulder by a cannon shot, which fortunately for him first struck the ground, he withdrew his troops and retreated to Jalalabad.

"In A.D. 1821 Muhammad Azim Khan, the eldest of the Barakzai brothers, was moving with an army from Kabul to Peshawar, and took this opportunity of proceeding against the rebellious Sayyid. On the approach of Muhammad Azim, Sayyid Najif fled to Chigha Sarai with his family and property, but he was there overtaken, imprisoned, and stands of arms valued at R85,000 were taken from him, besides camels, horses, and household furniture. The Sayyid and his family were placed on rafts and conveyed to Peshawar. Muhammad Azim Khan left his son Akram Khan to be assisted by Mirza Agha Jan, Governor of Jalalabad, in charge of the province of Kunar; he then proceeded on his return to Jalalabad, and thence to Peshawar, where he remained during the winter months, the deposed Sayyid and his family also remaining with him. In vain Muhammad Azim attempted to conciliate Sayyid Najif. He offered to place at his disposal territory yielding R40,000 annually, but the offer was declined, the Sayyid soliciting only to be permitted to visit at Kunar the tomb of his ancestor, Sayyid Ali. This request was at length complied with, and the Sayyid pursued his pilgrimage. On reaching Kunar, he went thence to Bajaur, and crossed over the hills into his own valley; there he raised his own standard, and was shortly surrounded by numerous adherents, and commenced besieging young Akram and Mirza Agha Jan, who had taken up a position in the fort of Sayyid Ahmad which they bravely defended until reinforcements reached them from Kabul, headed by Nawab Jabar Khan and Habibulla Khan (the eldest son of Muhammad Azim Khan). Peace was effected between the contending parties on the conditions that Sayyid Najif was to be reinstated in his government, his son Baha-ud-din to be his Lieutenant, and the district of Shewa to be henceforth annexed to the Jalalabad Government. Sayyid Najif and his son thus sharing in the rule of the country, an ill-feeling was engendered between them, which Muhammad Azim hearing of did not fail to work upon. He desired therefore that Baha-ud-din sould seize and imprison his father, or incur his (Muhammad Azim's) serious displeasure. The son accordingly seized and confined his father but at the same time treated him very kindly, and after a few months gave him his release. The father, however, not forgiving this injury, united with all his sons to punish Baha-ud-din, who fled into Sayyid Ahmad's fort, where he stood a siege for three months aided by Fathulla Khan, Mohmand, but finding that the opposing party was too strong for him he fled with his family to Goshta.

"About A.D. 1824 Mir Alam Khan of Bajaur threatened to invade the territory of his cousin, Amir Khan of Nawagai, when the latter applied to Sayyid Najif for assistance, which was readily granted, and the Sayyid proceeded to Nawagai with a large force. Mir Alam Khan, hearing of this movement, withdrew his troops to Bajaur. It was at this period, and at Nawagai, in presence of a large assembly of chiefs at which his father presided, that Sayyid Fakir stabbed and killed his brother Mohi-ud-din. Jealousy of his brother's merits is said to have actuated this atrocious deed. Sayyid Fakir was seized and confined, but shortly afterwards released. Sayyid Najif after this circumstance felt anxious to remove some distance from him not only Sayyid Fakir, but also his three brothers, Sayyids Amir and Abbas (whom he recalled from Kalmanai and Nurgul) and Sayyid Shahbad from Kash Kot, all sons of a sister of Mir Alam Khan, and sent them in charge of the districts Chigha Sarai, Shigar, Sarkani and Dunai. Sayyid Najif then placed his sons Sayyid Husain in charge of Nurgul, Hashim at Kash Kot, and recalling Baha-ud-din from Goshta, placed him in authority at Kunar.

"Sayyid Fakir had not been long at his new post when he commenced, intriguing with his uncle Mir Alam Khan, and also with Amir Khan of Nawagai, offering to give up to the former Chigha Sarai and Shigar, and to the latter Sarkani and Dunai, if they would assist him in displacing his father in favour of himself. The contending parties entered into this engagement, but Mir Alam and Amir Khan, becoming possessed of the places above named, failed to afford that assistance to Sayyid Fakir which they promised him, and he and his three brothers then fled to Kotkai.

"Sayyid Najif, on hearing of the treachery of his sons, sent troops to invest the fort wherein they had taken up a position, but the river face of the fort at all times afforded them a means of escape and Sayyid Fakir was not slow in opening a communication with the townspeople of Pashat, and having induced a party of them to agree to throw open the gates for him, he and his followers left Kotkai at night, entered the town and seized and imprisoned his father. Sayyid Najif's troops, on hearing of his imprisonment, dispersed immediately, and Sayyid Fakir assumed the reins of the government of Pashat.

"A few weeks only had elapsed when the people of Pashat sent a message to Baha-ud-din, who was at Kunar, inviting his assistance and promising that they would release his father and reinstate him in power if he (Baha-ud-din) would unite with them; this plot soon reached the ears of Sayyid Fakir who immediately caused his aged father to be suffocated, and had the effrontery to expose his corpse to the populace, assuring them that he met with a natural death. The people either believed the parricide, or thought it expedient to do so, for he continued in power for a long time afterwards. His father had reached the advanced age of 80 years, during 57 of which he had ruled in Kunar.

"During the year 1826 Sayyid Fakir sent his brother Abbas to the Dara-i-Nao and the Dara-i-Nazar to collect troops in those valleys, and to attack Sayyid Husain, who was then at Nurgul. He succeeded in assembling a force. Sayyid Hashim sent his nephew Ahai-ud-din, son of Mohi-ud-din, to the assistance of Hussain. An engagement took place, Sayyid Husain was killed, but Sayyid Abbas sustained a defeat, his troops dispersed and fled to the hills, and Sayyid Ahai-ud-din remained Governor of Nurgul until Sayyid Fakir was displaced from power by Dost Muhammad in A.D. 1834.

"Baha-ud-din shortly afterwards advanced from Kunar to attack his brother; a contest ensued near Kunar without any very decided advantage having taken place on either side, but the latter retreated before Baha-ud-din as far as Bartad, a village within a mile and a half of Pashat. Near this village the opposing parties raised bastions and continued hostilities for the prolonged period of eight years; each brother collecting the revenues of that part of the country where his own troops held the supremacy. In the year 1834, Dost Muhammad at length interfered and consigned to the charge of Baha-ud-din the whole of the disputed teritory, on his agreeing to pay him R19,000 annually. Sayyid Fakir was called to Jalalabad, and the gardens of Charbagh were made over to him for the maintenance of himself and followers.

"During the early part of A.D. 1839, a Monsieur Carron was on a visit to Nawab Jabar Khan, who was then at Kabul. Dost Muhammad Khan, suspecting him of being employed by the British Government as a news-writer, meditated apprehending him, but through the good offices of the Nawab, Monsieur Carron, in company with Qudus Khan, Barakzai, effected his escape from Kabul and took refuge in Pashat, where he was kindly received and treated by Baba-ud-din. Dost Muhammad hearing of this despatched a messenger to the Sayyid, desiring him to deliver up Monsieur Carron. The Sayyid denied his presence in his country; the Amir again applied to him, and pointed out the fort and house wherin Monsieur Carron was concealed and again Baha-ud-din denied any knowledge of him. This gentleman continued in concealment for a short time in the village of Narinj, and went thence to Peshawar via Kafiristan and Bajaur. Dost Muhammad finding that Sayyid Baha-ud-din would not attend to his orders, addressed a letter to his son, Akbar Khan, who was at this time Governor of Jalalabad, desiring him to possess himself of the person of the Sayyid, and to effect this object under any pretence whatever. Emissaries from Muhammad Akbar were accordingly sent to Baha-ud-din, requesting his presence at Jalalabad, and on his making assurances after the most sacred manner that he intended in no way to injure him, the Sayyid unwillingly obeyed the summons, and immediately on his arrival at Jalalabad was imprisoned. Akbar then proceeded with a force of Pashat to attack Baha-ud-din's two sons, Nizam-ud-din and Husain-ud-din, the former being in possession of the fort of Sayyid Ahmad, and the latter that of Kotkai. Akbar first attacked Nizim-ud-din's stronghold, and brought an 18 or 24 pounder to bear upon one of the bastions, which it fired upon for three days and breached partially. Terms were then effected through the medium of Sadat Khan Mohmand and Amir Khan of Nawagai on the following conditions, viz., that Nizam-ud-din and his followers were to have free egress from the fort, but all their property to devolve to Muhammad Akbar. Nizam-ud-din fled to Hinduraj, thence across the hills, and joined Shahzada Taimur at Peshawar, by whom and by Colonel Wade he was received with every consideration. Husain-ud-din still remained at Kotkai, and with him not only his own but all his father's family, and also the bulk of his father's property. He saw, however, that it was hopeless to contend against Muhammad Akbar's force. The same terms that had been accepted by his brother were offered to him, and, readily availing himself of them he evacuated the fort. He had proceeded as far as Sarkani when Muhammad Akbar broke faith; for notwithstanding his engagement with Husain-ud-din, he sent a party in pursuit of him, and he was overtaken and seized with his women, forcibly placed on rafts, and conveyed to Jalalabad. The women were subsequently transferred to Abdul Ghani Khan, and Husain-ud-din and his father were sent under charge of an escort to Kabul; the former was released in the course of two months, and the latter remained a prisoner until Dost Muhammad's departure for Turkistan on the arrival of the British troops at Maidan.

"The property which Muhammad Akbar thus became possessed of is said to have amounted to nearly one lakh of rupees.

"Sayyid Hashim was summoned from Kash Kot and placed in charge of the government of the province, he promising to pay the Amir R28,000 annually."

In the month of January 1840, Baha-ud-din was reinstated in his government through the assistance afforded him by the British Government, his son Nizam-ud-din having been some months in arms, in support of his father's cause, without having gained any decided advantage over Sayyid Hashim's adherents.

According to another account the two sons of Baha-ud-din were respectively named Hissam Badshah and Mahmud Badshah. The eldest being disinherited, the younger brother succeeded to the chiefship on his father's death in 1866. In 1868 Mahmud Badshah revolted against the power of Azim khan, who was then nominally Amir. However, soon after the return of Sher Ali to power the district was regranted to him on payment of R20,000 per annum as nazar. He was friendly to the English during the last Afghan war, and it was principally due to his influence that no serious gathering of the tribes took place in that part of the country. In 1880 he paid a visit to Amir Abdur Rahman, and was confirmed in the position he held under Sher Ali, but he was not particularly well treated. When he left Kabul he was informed by the Amir that he might retain the nominal possessions, while he must remit all the revenue to Kabul, the Amir paying the cost of holding the country. Owing to this and other causes his relations with the Amir became gradually unfriendly, and in 1882 the Sayyid was in open revolt; but when the Amir's troops advanced on Kunar he fled to Mitai and joined Mughal Khan of Goshta and other malcontents. In 1884 the Government of India offered him R2,000 per mensem, on condition that he would reside at a place selected by the Government, and would abstain from intriguing against the Amir. He hung about the Amir's borders for some time in hope that the Amir would come to grief, but in January 1886 he apparently lost heart and came to India accepting the conditions of the Government.

During the Anglo-Afghan war of 1879-80, a fanatic priest, by name Mulla Khalil, created some excitement by preaching a religious war in Kunar. In May 1880 he crossed into Besud, and the rabble he had collected was dispersed on the 19th of the month near Beninga. (McGregor, I.B.C.)

KUNAR خاص کنر
34-39 70-54. A group of villages on the left bank of the Kunar river, about 27 miles from Jalalabad. There is a ferry (flying bridge) across the river here to Patan on the main Jalalabad-Arnawai road. There is a garrison at Kunar consisting of 100 cavalry (detached from Jalalabad), 2 battalions infantry and 300 khasadars. (I.B.C.) Recent maps show Khas Kunar and Kuz Kunar, at 34-35 70-35 m.

KUND کند
A high snow-capped peak overlooking the Laghman valley from the region of Kafiristan. It is on the summit of this mountain that Noah's ark is supposed to have rested after the flood. (Holdich.) N.B. The name appears to be further applied to the whole range of hills bordering Laghman on the north.

KUND کند
35- 69-. A village in the Parandev Dara, about 9 miles above its junction with the Panjshir. Close by is another village called Daulana, the two together containing some 10 families of Tajiks. (I.B.C.)

*KUNDA منده
34-52 69-49 m. A village near Sarai on a tributary of the Tagab river, Kapisa province.

*KUNDI کندی
34-59 69-49 m. A village near Chahikhel on a tributary of the Tagab in Kapisa province.

KUNGANI See NICHINGUL کنگنی

KUNIGAO کنی گاو
33-57 67-58 G. A hamlet in the northeast of the Dai Kundi country.

KUNTGUL کنتگل
35-17 71-31. A valley which descends east and joins the Kunar one mile below Birkot. From it more or less difficult mountain paths lead to the Birkotgul, the Azharbai valley, the Dungul valley, and the Chandakgul. It contains the ruins of two Kafir villages. (Robertson.)

KUPRUK کپرک
34- 67-. A village in the Yakh Walang district, situated on the norhtern shore of the Bandi-i-Zulfikar (the uppermost of the Band-i-Amir lakes), distant 7 or 8 miles from Jafir Kala, and containing 40 families of Takana Hazaras. (Maitland.)

*KURA قوره
34-1 67-38 m. A village located south of the Koh-i-Khushkak, on a tributary of the Garmab in Bamian province.

KURAK کورک
A clan of Kafirs occupying the western side of the Alingar valley above Badiabad; according to Steward they muster about 2,000 fighting men. (Stewart.)

KURAM کرم
34-22 70-8. A village in the Surkhab subdivision of the Jalalabad

district, situated on the southern slopes of the Siah Koh range, about 7 miles west of Fatehabad, on a road across the Siah Koh range from Fatehabad to Kats Laghman. Inhabitants: Nasir Khel Ghilzais. (I.B.C.)

KURBAN GUSHTA قربان گشته
A place in Nawar, inhabited by mixed sections of the Muhammad Khwaja Hazaras.

KURGAH کورگاه
33-55 67-57 A. A place in the Dai Kundi country, occupied by 400 families of the Khushak section. Recent maps show the name Gurg Kushtah.

*KURGAI کورگی
33-17 69-34 m. A village between Nadirshah Kot and Bargai on the road from Khost to Gardez in Paktia province.

KURGHAN کرغان
An ancient town in Ujaristan.

*KURKOT کرکوت
34-45 69-50 m. A village on the Wuzbin Khwar, southeast of Tagab in Kabul province.

KURRAM کرم
33-49 69-57. For a description of the Kurram river see "Military Report on the country between the Kabul and Kurram rivers. Part I."

KURSHATAL See KHARSHKA خرشاتل
A wide glen with a dry stony watercourse, which debouches into the left of the Band-i-Amir some 24 miles below Firozbahar. (Maitland.)

*KUSHA کوشه
33-16 69-41 m. A village located a few miles south of Nadirshah Kot in Paktia province.

KUSHANGI کوشنگی
Said to be a valley in the Dai Kundi country.

KUSHI Or KHUSHKI, KHWAKKHI کوشی (خوشکی)
34-0 69-13 m. Elevation 7,829. A village 40 miles from Kabul on the left bank of the Dobandi stream being the fifth stage from the Paiwar Kotal on the Shutur Gardan route to Kabul. It contains 300 houses in numerous walled enclosures or forts, and is embosomed in extensive orchards that occupy the bed of a wild ravine opening into the Logar plain. There is a good encamping ground here; provisions of all sorts are procurable in abundance for man and beast; water is plentiful, though not very good; grazing for camels, however is scarce. The principal trade of the place is in preserved apricots and madder, though wheat, barley, clover and lucerne are also extensively cultivated.
Kushi was the first point in the plains were the troops were asembled on the march from Ali Khel to Kabul in September 1879, and here Sir Frederick Roberts was joined by Amir Yakub Khan, his eldest son, Sardar Yahiya Khan, Daud Shah, and other notables. On the 2nd October the final advance was made towards the capital from this place. (Lumsden, Bellew, Agha Abbas, I.B.c.)

*KUSHK كشك
 34-36 68-23 m. A village located some 4 miles north of Ghazni, off the road to Kabul.

KUSHK كشك
 34- 66-. A subdivision of the Sar-i-Jangal district. There is a mountain with this name west of Lal, at 34-28 66-1 G. (LWA)

KUSHK كشك
 34-6 67-30 m. A grassy glen in the west of the Dai Zangi country.

KUSH NAO See SURKH كشنو

KUSSAM كسام
 33- 69-. A valley some 10 miles south of Ali Khel, inhabited by Ahmad Khel Jajis.

KUSTAKI GROM See KSTIGIGROM كستكی گرام

KUTANAI كوتنی
 33-3 69-4. A village in the Ghazni district between Sultani and Shahtori, on the road to Dawar. (McLean.)
 N.B. this place may perhaps be near the Kotanni pass.

*KUTI KHEL کی خیل
 33-16 68-52 M. A village 3 miles north of Meta Khan on the road to Ghazni.

*KUTI KHEL کی خیل
 33-18 69-31 m. A village southwest of Bargai and some 6 miles west of Nadir Shah Kot in Paktia province.

KUTI KHEL کی خیل
 34-13 69-2 G. A village in Logar, on the right bank of the river, 9 miles north of Zargan Shahar. The inhabitants are Astanazai Ghilzais, and in 1880 they numbered 300 families, located in twelve detached forts and hamlets.

*KUTI KHEL کی خیل
 34-24 69-55 m. A village located on a path leading from the Surkhab to the Kabul river.

KUTI KHEL کی خیل
 A pass leading from eastern Kharwar into the upper valley of the Dahana Drang. It is passable for men on foot only. (Griesbach.)

*KUZA کوزه
 33-50 69-54 G. A village located some 20 miles southeast of Khost, Paktia province.

KUZA BAK کوزه بك
 32- 67-. A plain on the road form Kalat-i-Ghilzai to Gahzni, a few miles north of Mukur. It is covered with small villages.

*KUZ JANGJAI کوز جنگجای
 33-46 68-36 m. A village located 3 miles east of the Ghazni-Kabul road in Ghazni province.

*LACHIKHEL لجی خیل
33-56 68-49 m. A village located on the Jar-i-Sejawand and southwest of Baraki Barak in Logar province.

LACHIPUR لجی پور
34-21 70-43 G. Elevation 1,480 feet. A village in the Jalalabad district, 12 3/4 miles northwest of Basawal; it lies near the right bank of the Kabul river at the eastern end of the Surkh Diwal range. The village contains 140 families of Tajiks possessing (in 1904) 500 head of cattle, 700 sheep and goats, and 120 buffaloes. The annual production of wheat and barley averages about 13,500 Indian maunds.
A small post, designed for a garrison of 40 cavalry and 150 infantry, was built by us at Lachipur during the second Afghan war; it is not used, or kept up, by the Amir and was in very bad repair when seen in 1905.
Camping ground for a force of any size exists between the fort and the river with water from the river or from a good spring close to the fort; animals can be conveniently watered at a nala to the south of camp; forage is plentifull. The surrounding country is level and suitable for all arms, though highly cultivated on either side of the road. (Malleson, Wanliss.)

*LADABAGH لده باغ
34-12 69-59 m. A village located a few miles south of Shamalkhel in Nangarhar province.

LAGHANA لغنه
35- 69-. A village on the upper Panjshir stream, near Bazarak. It contains 20 houses of Tajiks. (Shahzida Taimus.)

*LAGHAR لاغر
33-23 68-11 m. A village located north of Ranakhel and southwest of Ghazni in Ghazni province.

*LAGHARAK لاغرك
34-56 68-11 m. A village located on a tributary of the Ghorband, some 4 miles southwest of Shibar in Parwan province.

*LAGHARI لاغری
33-46 68-12 m. A village located on a tributary of the Dara-i-Yusuf, northwest of Ghazni in Ghazni province. Another place with this name is located northwest of Ghazni on the way to Jaghatu in Ghazni province, 33-38 68-23 m.

*LAGHAWAT لغوات
33-28 68-32 m. A village located southeast of Ghazni on the way to Arzo.

LAGHMAN لغمان
35-59 66-6 A. A village east of Charikar, containing, with Sujjan, 400 Tajik families. (Shahzada Taimus.)

LAGHMAN لغمان
35-0 70-15 A. A province in eastern Afghanistan which comprises an area of 7,227 square kilometers and an agricultural population estimated at from 80,606 to 124,264. The province is bounded in the west by Kunar, and in the south by Nangarhar provinces. Laghman province is divided into the woleswalis of Daulatshah, Nurestan,

Alishang, and Qargha'i and into the central district of Mehterlam (Tirgarhi). For woleswali lists from the Department of Statistics of the Ministry of Agriculture and Irrigation see the following pages. (LWA)

In 1914 Laghman province was describes as follows:

The district of Laghman is about 26 miles from east to west, and on an average 32 miles from north to south. It may be said to begin near Darunta and, skirting the northern base of the Siah Koh, extends in a westerly direction up to Badpakht. The valley takes a northern direction at Mandrawar, and proceeding straight up to Tirgarhi, bifurcates into two portions-- one going up the Alingar, and the other up the Alishang valley. Its boundaries on the north are the Kafiristan mountains, on the east the hills of Kashmund, on the south the Siah Koh range, on the west the Usbin river, separating Laghman from the Safis of Tagao. On the eastern side a chain of spurs runs down from the Kashmund range, terminating in the Ambir hills just above Charbagh. The aspect of the country in this direction is dreary to a degree, and consists of sandy hillocks without any cultivation or vegetation on them, till they are finally lost in the Gamberi desert. The southern end of the valley, though it has some cultivated lands and flourishing villages, has nothing to boast of in the way of beauty; and the same remarks may apply to the western portion, but nothing can equal or surpass the beauty and grandeur of its northern parts. Looking northwards from Tirgarhi, the eye rests on the beautiful Alishang valley, with its numerous villages, forts, and river. In the distance can be seen the snow peaks of Koh-i-Kaon and the spurs of the Hindu Kush and mountains of Kafiristan. To the northeast extends the Alingar valley, with its villages and forts belonging to the different Ghilzai chiefs, the whole bounded by a mass of snowy mountains, to which chain the natives give but one name, viz., Koh-i-Kund. Well wooded spurs run down and meet both these valleys, whilst, dividing them, stands, a mass of hills known as Karinj. But little information regarding the elevation of Laghman is forthcoming, but it may be mentioned that Alishang village is 2,900 feet, and the general elevation of the inhabited portions of the district probably ranges between 2,200 and 9,000 feet.

The Kabul river flows from the direction of Badpakht, on the west through the southern parts of Laghman, and, running almost due east, passes south through the Darunta gorge into the Jalalabad district.

The Alishang river, flowing in a south-easterly direction, joins the Alingar a little below Tirgarhi; its feeders are streams that run down from the Kaon and Karinj mountains.

The Alingar stream flows from the mountains of Kafiristan, and joining the Alishang, flows on and combines with the Kabul river close to Charbagh.

Numerous small canals are taken off from all these streams to irrigate the land on their banks.

Laghman, according to the fabulous acounts given by the natives, owes its name to Lamech, father of Noah, whose ark is said to have rested on the Kund mountains after the deluge. After having fought against and conquered all his enemies, he took possession of the country, which came to be called Lamech an Lamakan, and in process of time Laghman. It is entirely surrounded by mountains; the Kund, overlooking Kafiristan, cannot be less than 14,000 feet to 15,000 feet in altitude in some of its peaks. The western spurs of the Kafiristan range, Kaon and Karinj, are also very grand.

Climate. The climate of the southern portion of the Laghman valley is somewhat similar to that of Jalalabad, but more bracing and healthier. The heat during the summer must be excessive, but there

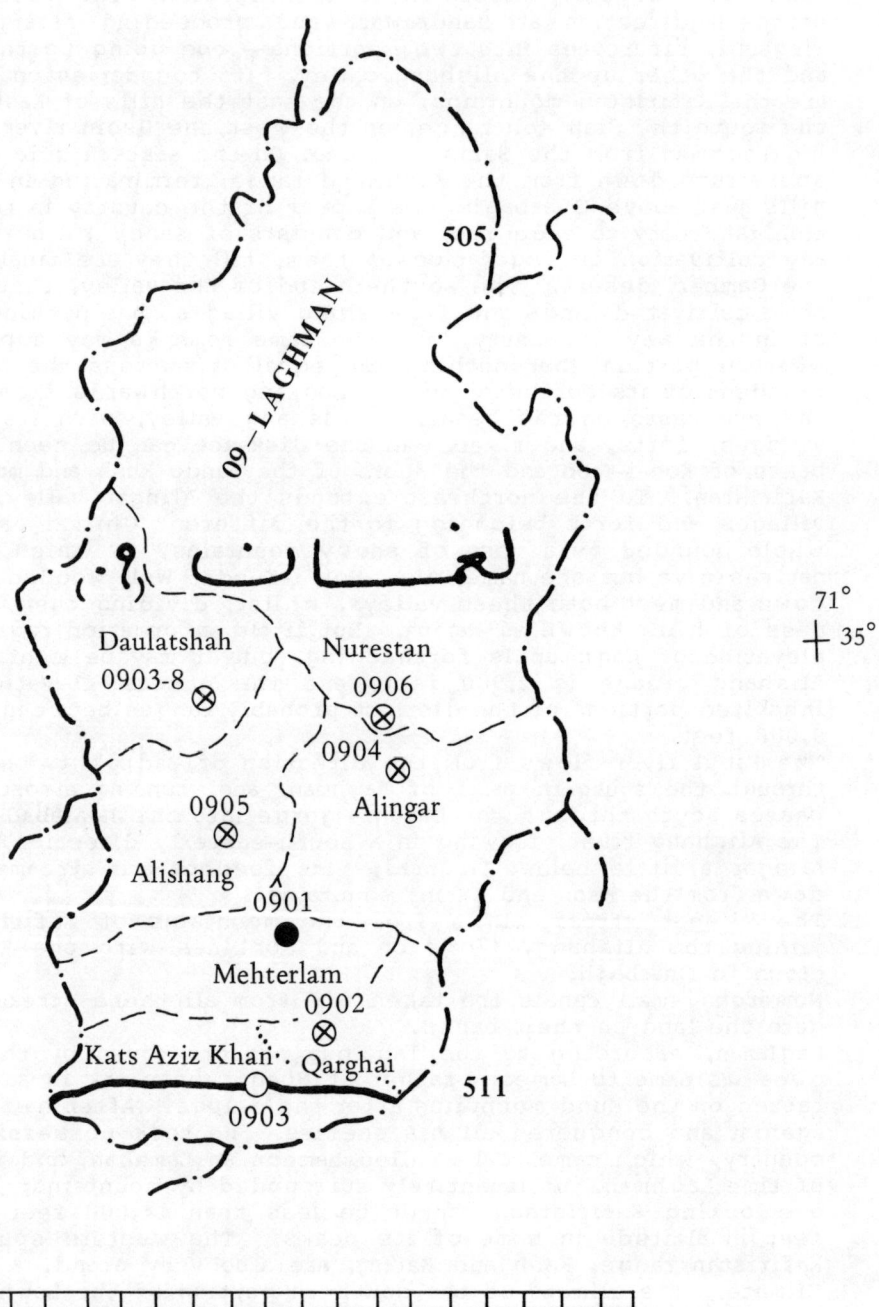

ESTIMATE OF AGRICULTURAL POPULATION AND AREA UNDER CULTIVATION

	Villages	Agricultural Population	Landlords	Lands under Cultivation in Jaribs			Lands under Cultivation in Hectares		
				Irrigated	Non-Irrig.	Total	Irrigated	Non-Irrig.	Total
ALISHING	62	35,450	7,610	26,360	—	26,360	5,272	—	5,272
ALINGAR	50	43,200	9,100	41,130	—	41,130	8,226	—	8,226
QARGHAI	30	21,500	2,500	13,200	—	13,200	2,640	—	2,640
MEHTERLAM	35	22,240	6,390	14,400	—	14,400	2,880	—	2,880
KATZ AZIZ KHAN	10	9,110	1,270	2,400	700	3,100	480	140	620
NURISTAN	35	30,410	3,180	20,420	6,800	27,220	4,084	1,360	5,444
TOTAL	222	161,910	30,050	117,910	7,500	125,410	23,582	1,500	25,082

STATISTICAL ESTIMATE OF LIVESTOCK BY WOLESWALIS AND ALAKADARIS

	Sheep	Karakul Sheep	Goats	Cattle	Buffaloes	Camels	Horses	Donkeys	Mules	Poultry
ALISHING	13,230	–	4,800	9,340	–	–	–	4,360	630	36,260
ALINGAR	9,820	–	16,200	8,800	–	100	310	6,490	420	35,390
QARGHAI	6,830	–	11,000	4,500	–	350	940	3,940	150	17,400
MEHTERLAM	4,920	–	3,860	7,800	2,800	–	300	3,730	200	24,520
KATZ AZIZ KHAN	3,670	–	770	640	2,230	150	60	1,490	–	20,510
NURISTAN	9,930	–	18,500	4,650	–	260	120	3,030	50	23,420
TOTAL	48,400	–	55,130	35,730	5,030	860	1,730	23,040	1,450	157,500

PRODUCTION OF AGRICULTURAL CROPS—IN KABULI SEERS

	Grains			Vegetables	Other Crops		Fruits
	Irrigated	Non-Irrig.	Total		Industrial Crops	Other Temp. Crops	
MEHTERLAM	752,950	—	752,950	1,440,000	305,770	198,000	214,720
ALISHING	1,943,150	—	1,943,150	864,000	63,620	112,200	529,760
ALINGAR	2,693,900	—	2,693,900	913,500	42,170	66,000	651,200
QARGHAI	1,357,400	—	1,357,400	443,250	1,017,150	88,000	269,280
NURISTAN	1,835,900	40,800	1,867,700	450,000	369,040	55,000	461,120
KATZ AZIZ KHAN	535,700	4,800	540,500	128,250	52,720	37,400	133,760
TOTAL	9,119,000	45,600	9,164,600	4,239,000	1,850,470	556,470	2,259,840

LAND UNDER IRRIGATION AND SOURCES OF IRRIGATION

	Area in Jaribs					Number of Sources			Water Mills
	Canals	Springs	Karez	Wells	Total	Canals	Springs	Karez	Wells	
ALISHING	26,240	120	—	—	26,360	14	1	—	—	184
ALINGAR	41,130	—	—	—	41,130	11	—	—	—	65
QARGHAI*	13,200	—	—	—	13,200	3	—	—	—	73
MEHTERLAM	14,400	—	—	—	14,400	4	—	—	—	135
KATZ AZIZ KHAN*	2,400	—	—	—	2,400	3	—	—	—	18
NURISTAN	20,240	180	—	—	20,420	10	2	—	—	86
TOTAL	117,610	300	—	—	117,910	45	3	—	—	561

*now merged into the Qarghai district.

TOTAL CULTIVABLE LAND, BY CROPS—IN KABULI JARIBS

	Grains			Vegetables	Industrial Crops	Other Crops	Fruits	Total Cultivated Land
	Irrigated	Non-Irrig.	Total					
MEHTERLAM	13,690	—	13,690	6,400	580	900	1,200	22,790
ALISHING	35,330	—	35,330	3,840	120	510	3,010	42,810
ALINGAR	48,980	—	48,980	4,060	80	300	3,700	57,120
QARGHAI	24,680	—	24,680	1,970	1,930	400	1,530	30,510
NURISTAN	33,380	3,400	36,780	2,000	700	250	2,620	42,350
KATZ AZIZ KHAN	9,740	400	10,140	570	100	170	760	11,740
TOTAL	167,800	3,800	169,600	18,840	3,510	2,530	12,840	207,320

TOTAL CULTIVABLE LANDS—IN KABULI JARIBS

	Total	Pastures	Forests	Under Cultivation	Fallow Lands
MEHTERLAM	24,700	7,300	3,000	14,400	2,190
ALISHING	82,760	50,500	5,900	26,360	5,630
ALINGAR	93,420	28,690	23,600	41,130	7,390
QARGHAI	122,170	52,470	56,500	13,200	2,860
NURISTAN	249,310	32,690	189,400	27,220	7,820
KATZ AZIZ KHAN	19,850	6,750	10,000	3,100	1,490
TOTAL	592,210	178,400	288,400	125,410	27,380

are no dust-storms like those which render existence unbearable there. During the period General Bright's force was encamped by Asmatulla Khan's fort, terrific gusts of wind, accompanied by rain at times, were experienced, but very little or no dust, except just on the banks of the Kabul river. Further north at Tirgarhi, and up the Alishang and Alingar rivers, the heat during the most oppressive season of the summer is said to be bearable; and the climate during February is certainly all that one could desire. The daras which run down from the high ranges have splendid spots where the people can resort to for the purpose of escaping the hot weather during the worst period, viz., from 20th June to end of August.

Inhabitants. The accounts given by the people note that Laghman was occupied by infidels about the period that the ark rested on Kund, and Mehtar Lam or Lamech and Nur Lam appeared on the scene to fight and drive them out of the country. Chitral came with a post of men from Hindustan to assist Alingar and Alishang, two chiefs of Siah-posh Kafirs against Mehtar Lam, and a battle took place in the country between Karghai and the present site of Ziarat. Lamech was killed, whilst the Kafirs suffered a severe defeat, and were driven to the hills by Nur Lam, said to be Lamech's brother. He was also killed in the pursuit at a place called Manda in the Chittas Dara where he was buried, and his grave is visited now by pilgrims whilst Mehtar Lam found a resting place in the spot above; his present tomb lies at ziarat. Since then the Kafirs have not been able to regain the country once owned by them. Sultan Mahmud of Ghazni is reported to have seen the saint in a dream, and journeying under his instructions to Laghman with ready-prepared bricks to erect a ziarat, hunted for the spot where Lamech had been buried. Another dream disclosed to him the fact that the spot where his lance was struck into the ground was the grave he was searching for; he had the earth removed and soon came on the body with its wounds, fresh as on the day they were inflicted, and the cuts filled with 'Sargarai' gras. Sultan Mahmud erected a tomb over the body, and named the country Lamak-an, after Noah's father. Such is the story repeated and fully believed by the people in the present day. The more probable account seems to be that, previus to the movements of the Afghans into these parts, the inhabitants of the valley were mostly Tajiks. Gradually in process of time the Ghilzais aided by the rulers of Kabul and their Governors in Laghman, secured a good footing, and driving out the peaceful Tajiks from their lands, gradually spread themselves all over it.

At the present moment we find the Ghilzais occupying the country on both sides of the Kabul river, and their forts and villages are scattered throughout the Alingar valley.

The Tajiks occupy chiefly the villages in the Alishang valley and extend to Tirgarhi, Mandrawar, Haidar Khani, Charbagh, etc. Safis are to be found to the northwest of the district. The residents of Niazi are chiefly Afghans. A small colony of Rikas is established in Rikagan.

Hindus are to be found in all the villages. Kuchis visit the district during winter and return with their camels, flocks and herds at the approach of summer to colder regions.

There are no statistics on which to base an accurate calculation of the numbers who inhabit Laghman, but Dutton says they may perhaps be set down at about 25,000.

The most important sections of the Ghilzais in Laghman are the Jabar Khel and the Abu Bakar Khel. The former are fully dealt with under the heading "Jabar Khel" while the following extract from a note written by Warburton in 1880 gives some account of the Abu Bakar Khel. ... "But although the chiefs of the Jabar Khels are nominally the heads of the Ghilzais on the Jalalabad and Laghman borders, a greater interest surrounds the chiefs of the Abu Bakar section--a minor branch of the family--owing to two men of note, who have appeared or risen from its ranks during the last forty years. These notables are Muhammad Shah Khan, of Badiabad renown; and his son Faiz Muhammad Khan. Muhammad Shah Khan, son of Muhammad Khan, was a man of considerable importance during the first Afghan war, not only by reason of his own abilities, which were considerable, but by having Wazir Muhammad Akbar on his side, to whom he had given a daughter in marriage. After the retreat from Kabul and the disasters of the Khurd Kabul, Tezin and Jagdalak passes, the hostages and captives secured by Muhammad Akbar were sent into Laghman, and detained at Muhammad Shah Khan's fort in Badiabad, which he had named Akal Tamian. When Muhammad Akbar Khan was routed at Jalalabad, and the advance of General Pollock's army prevented finally any further attempts against Sir R. Sale's force, the captives were removed from Badiabad across the Badpakht pass towards Kabul, and finally obtained their release. Muhammad Shah Khan, in process of time, secured sway over nearly all Laghman, until his castles in the air were knocked down by the Dost. He was seated one day at Shewakti, a fort and village close to Kabul, with Gul Muhammad Khan, Khuda Baksh Khan, Malik Hamid Abdul, Katumzai, and Malik Shergul, when a horseman was seen urging his steed at fullspeed towards the fort from the direction of Kabul, who on near approach turned out to be Aziz Khan, Jabar Khel. Dismounting quickly, he appeared; and, taking Muhammad Shah Khan aside, informed him that Amir Dost Muhammad Khan had arranged to make prisoners of all the Ghilzai chiefs then present in Kabul. The assembly broke up quickly, and the chiefs made off towards Laghman, where they all joined Muhammad Shah Khan; whilst he removed his family to Usbin and then to Dara-i-Saigal, just above Salab and below Koh-i-Kaon.

"They were left in peace for a short time, as Wazir Muhammad Akbar Khan was engaged in suppressing a rising at Marki Khel in the Khugian country. Succeeding in this, he was returning to Kabul when he died on the march, and his remains were carried to Afghan Turkistan and buried there. The Dost then led his troops in person towards Laghman, and surrounded Muhammads Shah Khan and his family in Dara-i-Saigal. Being satisfied, however, with the surrender of his fort at Badiabad, he demolished it, and let the Abu Bakar Khel chief go. Muhammad Shah Khan then moved up to Dara-i-Najil; and, with the permisssion of Atta Muhammad Khan and the people of Farajghan, commenced building a new fort there.

"He soon began to make himself unpleasant to his neghbours; they complained to the Dost, whose orders were to turn him out. By humbling himself, however, before the Amir, and declaring that he intended coming in to tender his submission, he was provided with carriage to bring his family to Maujuma. But, instead of proceeding to Maujuma, he fled with his family to Adhar. He was pursued by Muhammad Azam Khan, who six months later, with the assistance of others, brought Muhammad Shah Khan to Kabul, where he eventually died, and his remains were interred in Mehtar Lam's ziarat. But Muhammad Shah Khan during his lifetime had made many and numerous powerful enemies, who would not leave him in peace when dead. His grave was opened the first night, and the body exhumed and left exposed. It was thereupon re-interred; and after this for several months a guard was kept night and day at his tomb to prevent a repetition of the occurrence.

"The imprisonment that our captives underwent at his fort at Badiabad, which was revisited by General Bright's force on the 19th

February 1880, attaches a peculiar interest to the name and action of the man.

"His son Faiz Muhammad is also much respected, both as a chief and soldier. His famous interview with Sir Louis Cavagnari at Lala China below Ali Masjid during September 1878 when he was in command of the Ghilzai levies, is too well known and too fresh to all to be repeated here."

Principal places of note. The district of Laghman contains no town of any note. Charbagh, which is the largest place in it, is more like a village with many hamlets than a town. In Babar's time there were some famous gardens in it; but there is not the least sign of them in these days. Mandrawar is another large and flourishing village, with a good Hindu trading community within its walls. Tirgarhi was also flourishing, until a severe flood in the two rivers overthrew its hamlets and ruined its environs. Of ziarats, Laghman is pretty full.

(1) Ziarat-i-Mehtar Lam, situated in the Maira Potai or Dasht-i-Ziarat, named after Noah's father, whose fabulous death has already been noted above. It is a rectangular enclosure, pretty crowded with grapes which seems to be enlarged at the will of the "Mujawirans" to fill their purses. The water is brought down through the desert from a cut in the river by Arora, Ganjawan, Manozai, to the ziarat, and fills a large covered reservoir. Mehtar Lam's tomb is close to the western end of the enclosure and seems always full of rapacious mullas; and beyond its length and reputed sanctity, there is nothing extraordinary about it. A short distance from it towards the north lies the grave of Taimur's wife, mother of Shah Shuja, and that of his son Shahzada Muhammad Akbar, both covered with a neat dome; almost touching it, in a ruinous condition, lies the tomb of Wazir Nizam-ud-Daula and that of some of his family. About the 11th or 12th of Rabi-ul-Sani every year a large fair is held here, to which thousands gather from all parts of the country, while every Friday it is visited by hundreds of mullas; and talibs.

(2) Ziarat of Pir Babaji in Lora Mora, which cures men afflicted with rheumatism.

(3) Sultan Ghazi Baba in Deh-i-Malakh, for fever.

(4) Babaji Baba in Hasanzai, for small-pox.

(5) Abdul Karim Baba in Noa Ram, Pir of the Mohmands. And about fourteen others in different parts of the country.

Subdivisions. Dutton divides the Laghman district into (1) Kats Laghman; (2) Laghman proper; (3) Alishang and Alingar valleys; (4) Dasht-i-Ziarat. The area of these combined is, he says, from 750 to 600 square miles, about one-tenth of which is cultivated. But for revenue purposes, according to Warburton, the district has two subdivisions: (1) Laghman-i-Afghania, which embraces all the Afghan villages from Darunta to Tirgarhi, and then goes up the Alingar valley to Kulman, Chittas, and Niazi; (2) Laghman-i-Tajikia, which includes all the Tajik villages to Tirgarhi, and then runs up the Alishang valley to Shamahat Salab and Najil. The following is a list of the villages as given by Warburton:

List of villages of Laghman-i-Afghania:

VILLAGE	TRIBES	VILLAGE	TRIBES
I. SWATI	Nasir Ghilzais	Ghundi	Abdul Rahimzai Ghilzais
Kala-i-Abdul Hamid	"		
Banda-i-Kazi	"	IV. BOLAN	Jabar Khel, etc.
Daulatabad	"		
Ghundi	"	Kala-i-Sultan	

Kala-i-Malik Rustam	"	Muhammad	"
Kala-i-Muhammad Yusuf		Deh Azim Khan Khojawadan	Dehgan Dehgan and Ghilzais
Deh-i-Muhammad Amin	"	V. DARA LAM	Dehgan
Banda-i-Mian Nur	"		
Kala-i-Muhammad Azim Khan	"	Banda Badi	"
Deh Saiyid Ahmad	"	Wali	"
Kala-i-Arab Khan	"	Abdul Salam	Ut Khel
Kala-i-Sherdil	"		
		VI. KAMALPUR	Jabar Khel, etc.
II. KARGAI	Tajik and Jabar Khel	Banda Bahram Khan	"
Kala-i-Muhammad Azim Khan	"	Ditto	"
Kala-i-Aziz Khan	"		
Kala-i-Dandar	"	VII. LAMATI SAHAK	Dehgans and Ghilzais
Surkhakan	"		
Kala-i-Muhammad Shah Khan	"	Kala-i-Sahrab Sadar Din	" "
Kala-i-Mamwai	"	Banda Hawar	Uria Khel
		Beyat Badro	Mixed tribes
III. AGHRABAD	Ut Khel Ghilzais	VIII. KASAMABAD	Dehgran
Kala-i-Haidar	"		
Kala-i-Tajuddin	"	Sangiri	"
Kala-i-Muhammad Kasim	"	Banda-i-Malik Hamid	"
Kala-i-Gul Baz	"	Banda-i-Mulla Badshahgul	"
Kala-i-Nuro	"		
Kala-i-Gul Ahmad	"	Banda-i-Tuti	"
Kala-i-Adil	"		
Kala-i-Asad	"	IX. HUSAINABAD	Abdul Rahimzai
Old Aghrabad	"		
Old Lal Muhammad	"	Lamatai Sulaiman Khel	"
Old Gul Ahmad	"	Wattapar	"
Old Allahdad	"	Bahrabad	"
Old Allahadad, II	"	Deh-i-Akhun-	
Old Kahir	"	zadagan	"
Old Sher Muhammad	"	Kala-i-Umar	"
Old Hashim	"		
Kala-i-Ahmad Khan	Abdul Rahimzai Ghilzais	Banda-i-Sherdel	"
X. DARAGHAR	Mummozai Ghilzai	Kohna Kala Kot Deh-i-Kazian	Dehgan ?
Kala-i-Samandar	"	Massi Khel	Dehgan
Kala-i-Kashmir	"	Ziarat Chilgazi Baba	"
Lal Muhammad	"		
Banda-i-Shahabad	"	Banda-i-Adhunzadagan	"
Bela-i-Rustam	"		
Banda-i-Bushai	Mullah Khel & above	XVIII. KACHRA	Tara Khel Ghilzais
XI. ANDAR	Mian Khel & Dehgan	Kala-i-Tara Khel	....
XII. RIKAGAN	Rika	XIX. SAYA KANDA	Tara Khel Ghilzais
Kala-i-Baluchabad	Rika & Mian Khel	XX. CHARDEHI	Umar Khel
Kala-i-Abdul Rahman	"	Kabil-i-Mulla Jan	
Banda-i-Baz Gul	"	Dad	Umar and

			Rika
		Kabil-i-Unus Akhundzada	"
XIII. NAODA MORA	Jabar Khel	Banda-i-Pahalwan	"
Kabil-i-Sarbiland Khan	"	Kala-i-Sher Gul	"
		Kala-i-Ghulam	"
Kohna Lora Mora Mashina	Weavers Mohammad	Banda Kolilan	Dehgan
Kabil-i-Nasiri	Nasir	Kala-i-Abdul Ahmad Ibrahim	Dehgans, Khel, etc.
Ziarat Babaji	Mojawiran	Banda-i-Sappo Khel	"
XIV. LOGAR LAM	Jabar Khel	Banda-i-Mian Khel Karimabad	Mian Khel Mixed
Kotlaha-i-Afzal Khan	"	Kala-i-Miran	tribes and
Kala-i-Afzal Khan	"		Rika
Kala-i-Sikandar Khan	"	Ghundi Khodadad	"
		Kala-i-Akhundzada	"
Kala-i-Mir Alan Khan	Jabar Khel	Mullayan Pajagi	" "
XV. LAMATAK	Dehgan	XXI. DEHZIARAT	Sabak and Shaikhan
Banda Musa Dado	"	Banda-i-Wali Muhhammad	"
Fakiran	"	Banda-i-Shaikhan	"
Ziarat Pir Sabz Baba	"	Banda-i-Sadulla Khan	"
XVI. KANDA	Dehgan	XXII. TUNDI	Tara Khel
Banda Malik Shuja	"	XXIII. SHAMANGAL	Tajik and Jabar Khel
Duppi	"	Deh-i-Kamal Khan	"
Sapparha	"		
		XXIV. SHAMATAI	Shamsher Khan Khel
XVII. KALAKOT	Dehgan		
Nilawat	Shamsher Khan Khel	XXVIII. BISRAM	Aroki
Banda Fateh Khan	"	XXIX. BADIABAD	"
Ghandi Taria Khel	"		
Deh Sahibzada	"	Deh-i-Mulla Nazir	"
Lakari Akhunzada	"	Banda-i-Aba Khel	"
Kala-i-Jalal Khan	"	Banda-i-Mian Sahib	"
Kala-i-Yar Muhammad	"	Kala-i-Muhammad Ali	"
Banda-Mamo Khan Kachur	"	Kala-i-Niaz Muhammad	"
Hakimabad	"	XXX. KANDA	
Bela Par-i-Daria	"		
		Kala-i-Zargaran	"
XXV. CHILMATAI	Shamsher Khan Khel, Mahmmad Khel and Tajiks	Kala-i-Mosam	Aroki
		XXXI. KALA-I-RAJAI	"
Deh-i-Mahfuz	"	Kala-i-Shigi	
Miangan	"		
Kala-i-Rahimdad	"	Kala-i-Kokhi	"
Kala-i-Abdulla	"	Kala-i-Shahi	"
Kala-i-Baz Muhammad	"	Kala-i-Sakhra	"
Kala-i-Mir Sarak	"	Kala-i-Kukur Mangai	"
Kala-i-Malik Nur	"	Kanda Shahdad	"
Kabil-i-Muhammad			

Khelha	"	XXXII. ADHARAND WARNATA	Aroki
Dehi Baghlak	"		
Kala-i-Langar Khan	Shamsher Khan Khel	Kala-i-Akbar	"
Kala-i-Pir Muhammad	"	Kala-i-Baz Khan	"
Kala-i-Shao Khan	"	Kala-i-Hakim	"
Kala-i-Khal Muhammad	"	Kala-i-Malikdin	"
Hasan Khel	Umar and Rika		
Kala-i-Muhammad Rahim	Umar and Rika	XXXIII. LOKARH	Aroki
		Kala-i-Jan Muhammad	"
Kala-i-Abdul Rahim	"		
Kala-i-Sher Gul	"	XXXIV. DEH-I-TAG	Kohistani
XXVI. HARMAL	Mixed tribes	XXXV. KACHUR	Kohistani
Kala-i-Akram	"	Kala-i-Safi Khan	Shamsher Khan
Kabil-i-Akram	"		
Ali Asghar	"	Deh Fatehulla	"
		Banda-i-Mulla Saleh	"
XXVII. KATTAL	Dehgan	Banda-i-Sadulla	"
Kala-i-Shah Nur	Babakar Khel	XXXVI. SALAB	Kohistani
Kala-i-Mir Akhor	"		
Kala-i-Sher Ahmad Khan	"	XXXVII. KALA-I-JAN MUHAMMAD	Kohistani
Banda-i-Abl Khan	"		
Banda	"	XXXVIII. WATTI JABAR KHEL	Jabar Khel
Kala-i-Makam Khan	Muhd. Khel		
Kala-i-Manjuma	"		
XXXIX. NIAZI KHEL	Niazi Khel	XLVI. KAGAKACH	Mamozai
Kala-i-Ghulam Jan	Khadani	Kala-i-Kaza Khan	"
Kala-i-Nur Muhammad	Ghilzai	Kala-i-Sultan Muhammad Khan	"
Kala-i-Saiyid Ahmad	"	Chaparha	
Kala-i-Amir Muhammad	"		
Kala-i-Azundin	"	XLVII. KACH-I-ILYAS	
Kala-i-Rinda Gul	Ghilzai		
Kala-i-Tingawar	"		
Kala-i-Hazrat Nur	"	Band-i-Mulla Gulbaz	Ilyas and Khairo Khel
Kala-i-Malik Jahid	"		
Kala-i-Tak	"		
Kala-i-Fakir Muhammad Akzan	"	XLVIII. SURKHAKAN	Nasir
Kala-i-Sharfuddin	"		
Kala-i-Hasan	"	Banda-i-Din Muhammad	"
Banda-Sharfuddin	"	Banda-i-Fatehulla	
Kala-i-Sharfuddin	"		
Kala-i-Ahmad Khan	"	XLIX. GULKABI	Musa Khel
Kala-i-Umra	Khoza Khel		
Kala-i-Malik Adam	Kota Khel	L. KACH-I-AZIZ KHAN	Jabar Khel
Kala-i-Abdul Kadir	Khoza Khel		
		Waliabad	"
XL. DARA-I-SAO	Kohistani	Tiragar Kandarzai	"
XLI. KULMAN	Kohistani	Rawat	Chinzai
		Kala-i-Asmatulla Khan	Jabar Khel
XLII. ZEBANI/ZARANI	Kohistani Uria Khel	Aminabad	Dehgan

Kotlahai Azam
Banda-i-Abdulla   "
  Khan
Banda-i-Murad Khan   "
Banda-i-Mulla Azam   "
Kaj Mian Khan   "

XLIII. SAHRDAN   Kuchis

Kala-i-Damardin   "
Banda-i-Muhammad   "
  Islam
Banda-i-Shahabuddin   "
Deh-i-Dur Muhammad   "

XLIV. KACH MUHAMMAD Jabar Khel
    ALI KHAN

XLV. URMUR   Mamozai

Banda-i-Bahauddin   "
Banda-i-Din Muhammad   "

   Lists of villages in Laghman-i-Tajikia.

VILLAGE	TRIBES	VILLAGE	TRIBES
I. CHARBAGH	Tajik	Kala-i-Hamesha-dahar	Tajik
Kala-i-Ghulam Jan	"	Banda-i-Tajo	"
Kala-i-Muhammad Akram	"	Kala-i-Ayab	"
Kala-i-Muhammad Akbar	"	Banda-i-Ali Ahmad	"
Kala-i-Saiyidan	"	Kala-i-Nao	"
Lalpur	"	Kala-i-Nao	"
Kala-i-Saiyid Ali	"	Kala-i-Nazir Turabaz	"
Deh-i-Kuz Kulalani	"	Kala-i-Muhammad Jan	"
Deh-i-Bar Kulalani	"	Karaho	"
Kala-i-Mufti	"	Kala-i-Shahghasi	"
Kala-i-Kazi	"	Kala-i-Mullayan	"
Banda-i-Baba	"	Kala-i-Mirza	"
Kala-i-Ibrahim	"		
Kala-i-Mulla Idris	"		
Kala-i-Sardar Muhammad Yahya	"	IV. TAJIKIA GUNKAR	Tajik
Kala-i-Bostan	"	Kala-i-Rahim	"
Kala-i-Muhammad Akram Khan		V. TIRGARHI	Tajik
Kala-i-Mulla Haidar	"		
Kala-i-Gul Badshah	"	Bagh-i-Bibi Sahiba	"
Kala-i-Hazi Arbab (Kazi?)	"	Shigi	"
		Kala-i-Jaji	"
Kala-i-Kalatak	"	Kala-i-Sher Muhammad	"
Kala-i-Arwa	"	Kala-i-Hasan	"
Kala-i-Haji Rasul Khan	"	Kala-i-Khala Khel	"
		Deh-i-Ziarat	"
Kala-i-Kazi Imamuddin	"	Deh-i-Sherulla Khan	"
Banda-i-Akhunzada	"	Banda-i-Abdul Ahmad	"
Kala-i-Mian Nur	"	Kala-i-Shah Baz	"
		Sang Toda	"
II. MANDRAWAR	Tajik	Deh-i-War	"
		Deh-i-Sultan	"

Dippi	"	Muhammad Khan	
Kishmishabad	"	Mariam Kora	"
Kala-i-Kazai	"	Kala-i-Muhammad Khan	"
Kala-i-Khwaja Muhammad	"	Kala-i-Wali	"
Abdur Rahim Khel	"	VI. PASHAI	Tajik
III. HAIDAR KHANI	Tajik	Deh-i-Malakh	"
		Deh-i-Hashim	"
Banda-i-Fakir	"	Banda-i-Fakiran	"
Kala-i-Muhammad Saiyid	"	VII. GOMAIN	Tajik
Kala-i-Muhammad Saiyid	"	Kala-i-Amir Khan	"
Kabil-i-Aziz Khan	Tajik	Deh-i-Mianji	Khel
		Deh-i-Kazi	"
Kabil-i-Sultan Muhammad	"	Deh-i-Safi	"
		Deh-i-Hasazi	"
Kabil-i-Pir Muhammad Khan	"	Kala-i-Kulma Haji Sahib	Mixed Tribes
Kabil-i-Purdil	"		
Kabil-i-Sufi	"	XII. SHIMRAM	Kohistani
Kabil-i-Mulla	"		
Ziarat-i-Sultan Ghazi	"	XIII. GARGAR	Safi
Banda-i-Abdulla	"		
Banda-i-Zafar	"	Kansigar	"
Banda-i-Hazi	"	Kala-i-Sarfaraz Khan	"
Banda-i-Tara	"		
Kala-i-Sarwar Khan	"	XIV. KOTALI	Dehgan
Banda	"		
		Ghaziabad	"
VIII. MARIAM	Dehgan	Kala-i-Muhammad Abid	"
Muhammadpur	"	Manjan	"
Kala-i-Mulla Afzal	"	Shamsikhel	"
Kala-i-Mir Badshah	"		
Kala-i-Kasim	"	XV. NAJIL	Tajik
Kala-i-Sufian	"		
Kala-i-Malik Lang	"	XVI. SHERGARH	Mixed Tribes
Kala-i-Mullayan	"		
Banda-i-Malik Shuja	"		
Malik Jan Muhammad	"	Ganji Najabuddin	"
Kala-i-Mansur Khan	Tajik	Deh-i-Aiaz	"
		Deh-i-Mulla Ashraf	"
IX. CHUNDKU	Dehgan	Banda-i-Sadulla	"
		Banda-i-Mulla Ashraf	"
Banda-i-Fakir Muhammad	"	Deh-i-Abdulla	"
		Khairabad	"
Banda-i-Mirza Saiyid Muhammad	"	Kala-i-Sher Gul	"
		Banda-i-Lalai	"
Kanda	"	Banda-i-Mulla Rahim	"
		Banda-i-Sikandar	"
X. NAWAR LAM	Mixed Tribes	Banda-i-Muzi	"
		Banda-i-Majid	"
		Banda-i-Malik Sher Muhammad	"
XI. ALI SHANG	Tajik		
		Banda-i-Ghulam	"
Mazkura	"	Bnada-i-Hamid	"
Kallicha	"	Banda-i-Addo Khel	"

Taj Garhi	"	Kala-i-Fateh Muhammad	"
Haji Zargun Shah Tara Khel	"	Banda-i-Kalandar	"
Kala-i-Shahghasi	"	Banda-i-Isakzai	"
Kala-i-Ata Muhammad Khan	"	Farozai	"
		Kala-i-Haji Sahib	"
Deh-i-Mishkati	"	Deh-i-Muhammad Akhunzada	"
Shakaiman	Khel		
Deh-i-Mirzajan	Mixed Tribes	Andarwan	Tajik
Deh-i-Zargaran	"	XXV. PALA KHEL	"
Kala-i-Shah Muhammad	"		
Deh-i-Dost Muhammad	"	XXVI. NAORAM	"
XVII. PULWATA	Tajik	Hajiabad	"
		Duburja	"
Kala-i-Ohadadar	"	Krandali	"
XVIII. AHMADZAI	Tajik	XXVII. DARA NAJIL	"
XIX. GHUNDI	Uria Khel	Sih Khandeh	"
		Kalwata	"
Banda	"	Kala-i-Ata Muhammad	"
		Kotah	"
XX. GANJAWAN	"	Kaswak	"
		Mandul	"
Kala-i-Malik Sherdil	"	Daratui	"
Deh-i-Shakarabad	"	Shahi	"
Kala-i-Saadat Khan	"	Dakawaito	"
		Naora and Ulwak	"
XXI. ISLAMABAD	Mixed Tribes	Dwa Shakh	"
		Dun Kroh	"
Haidar Khani	"	XXVIII. JAMSHIDABAD	Tajik
Kala-i-Faiz Muhammad Khan	"	XXIX. MANJAN	Kohistani
Girdi	"	XXX. REHAN	Safi
XXII. DARA SALAB	Dehgan	XXXI. SHAMSI KHEL	Dehgan
Kala-i-Allaram	"		
Kala-i-Shah Nur	"	Watangatu	
Kala-i-Halim	"	Nalu	
Banda-i-Muhammad Azim Akhundzada	"	Krandali	
Tangi	"		
Kotki	"		
Dakian	"		
Ghundi-i-Barakzai	"		
Sharbat-Khel	"		
XXIII. DARWESHABAD	Tajik		
Kalagai	"		
Kala-i-Akhunzada	"		
Dera-i-Mirza Sahib	"		
XXIV. MORCHA KHEL	"		
Kala-i-Mian Sahib	"		

Trades and manufacturers. The only trade in Laghman is that of rice of which no less than four different sorts are raised in the country and exported on rafts to Jalalabad, or taken by Kuchis to Kabul. Iron is imported from Bajaur, and salt from Peshawar. Grapes and mullberries are cultivated in abundance; the other fruits are not worth recording.

Agricultural products. With the exception of the desert just due north of Kats-i-Aziz Khan and the Dasht-i-Ziarat, the district of Laghman is extensively cultivated, having three rivers and thirty-eight irrigation canals. The inhabitants of the valley have brought under crop every bit of land wherever they can manage to carry any quantity of water; on this account the lands are all abi and very valuable, and very little lalmi or dependent entirely on rain. Wells are few, and are to be found only here and there in certain masjids, and used for purposes of ablution.

The chief products of the spring harvest are wheat and barley. The autumn crops produce cotton, jowar, mash, rice of four sorts, and sugarcane (small quantities). The best wheat is grown in Kats-i-Aziz Khan, Mandrawar and Charbagh.

Palezi refers to cultivation of cucumbers, pumpkins, turnips which are grown in abundance.

The fruit produced in Laghman is not to be compared to that raised in Jalalabad.

Speaking generally, the cultivation is of a high class, and there is no doubt that a large amount of supplies is forthcoming.

Revenue System. The revenue system of Laghman is similar to that of Jalalabad.

Other revenue besides land. The different taxes as realised in 1879-80 may now be given.

(1) Jarabi, a tax on horticulture:

	R	a		
On sugarcane	10	0	per	jarib
On melons, vegetables (palezi)	4	0	"	"
On tobacco	7	0	"	"
On cotton	8	0	"	"
On tamhil	1	8	"	"

(2) Asia (each mill)   R 7 to 3
(3) Asnaf is a tax on trade

Weavers	1 to 3
Dyers	1 to 3
Smiths	1 to 4
Sword-makers	1 to 3
Telis	2 to 5
Goldsmiths	3 to 4
Fruit-sellers	2 to 5
Bazaz	2 to 5
Faludapaz	8
Kolals	1 to 3
Bakers, two shops pay	100 per annum
Shali Koh of Charbagh only	20 to 5 shahis

(4) Shakh Shamars merely in Charbagh pays R2 to 4 on each she-buffalo.
(5) Jizia is a tax levied on Hindus from 3 to 4 shahis.
(6) Dudi, a house-tax of R1 and 2 shahis on each Hindu's shop in Charbagh and Alishang.
(7) Kadkhudai is levied merely in Tirgarhi and Alishang on the marriage of Hindus at the rate of R5 to 10.
(8) Mehmani is included in the revenue.

(9) Rasum-i-Dafar is collected merely in Laghman-i-Tajikia.
(10) Sayer or Chabutra is levied in Charbagh, Alishang, Tirgarhi.
(11) Soap tax in Charbagh only.
(12) Kotwali in Charbagh, Tirgarhi, Alishang.
(13) Kahbaha is included in the revenue, and means the value paid to the State for its share of bhusa and missa bhusa, not required for the use of Government.
(14) Tarazudari is the sum paid by the farmer of Dharwais dues, which are usually 4 seers of grain from each kharwar of village produce.
(15) Nawadi is a tax realised by some former hakim at his will and pleasure from Dara-i-Lam, Andar, Kanda, Dandar, at the rate of R5 to R12.
(16) Chaudharana is paid to masullis for cleaning grain at Khirman, who in return hand a share of R5 to R20 to the State.
(17) Dallak is the tax paid by barbers, who receive a small share from the village for their services.

Fixed expenditure. (1) Wazifa is the allowance in cash and grain paid to the priestly and religious classes, which include Sayyids, Ulama, Sahibzadas, Khojazadas, Fukaras, etc.

The learned and religious persons in Laghman as well as in Jalalabad are in receipt of a wazifa. These men are kept contented by the rulers of Kabul to suit their own purposes, and many of them have rendered good services in return by stirring up the fanaticism of the hill tribes against us. In every rising that has taken place since November 1878 the leaders have always been mullas like Mushk-i-Alam of Ghazni, and Khalil of the Mohmand hills, and numbers of others of inferior note.

(2) Malikana is the allowance paid to headmen in the Tajikia subdivision of Laghman only for services rendered by them; in Laghman-Afghania it is termed tankhwah-i-wilayati.
(3) Takhfif means remission of revenue for diluvion, etc.
(4) Tankhwah-i-wilayati is the allowance paid to different chiefs and notables for their services; this custom is said to have been inaugurated first in the days of Ahmad Shah, Abdali, who wished to reward men for their gallant behaviour in Hindustan, and originated this custom on his return.

Amil and Zabit is the allowance paid to the daftaris and faujdars of Laghman.

Warburton furnishes (1879-80) the following account of the revenues and expenditure. The calculations are based on Kabuli rupees:

NATURE OF INCOME	QUANTITY				VALUE		
					R	a	p.
(1) DARA-I-TAJIKIA							
Cash	....				38,448	10	0
Wheat	801	kh.	65 1/2	seers	48,109	0	0
Barley	56	"	46	"	2,542	8	0
Ghalla	43	"	51 1/4	"	2,182	0	0
Jowar	166	"	4 1/4	"	5,226	6	0
Masur	11	"	3 1/4	"	552	1	0
Kangni	20	"	6 3/4	"	502	3	0
Sarson	42	seers			28	0	0
Mash	4	kh.	15	seers	188	8	0
Til	15 1/2	seers			15	8	0
Mustard	6 3/4	"			4	8	0
Takhur-i-Palak	1 3/4	"			3	0	0
Brinj-i-bara Peshawari	47	kh.	66 1/4	seers	3,826	10	0
Shali Kunar	507	"	23 1/4	"	20,291	10	0
Shali Luk	1,368	"	74 1/2	"	47,422	0	0

Shali Bara Laghman	847	"	5 3/4	"	33,882	14 0
Shali Bara Peshawari	48	1/4 seers			24	2 0
Shali Karnal	1	kh.	17 1/2 seers		54	8 0
			Total		203,304	0 0

(2) DARA-I-AFGHANIA

					R	a p.
Cash					49,054	9 0
Ghalla (wheat and barley)	63	kh.	20 seers		3,162	8 0
Wheat	573	"	35	"	34,406	4 0
Barley	47	"	7 1/2 seers		2,119	2 0
Jowar	305	"	40	"	13,747	8 0
Masur	17	"	4	"	852	8 0
Kangni	13	"	63 1/2	"	345	0 0
Mash	7	"	79 1/2	"	359	13 0
Peas	55	"	37 1/2	"	1,664	0 0
Sarson	19	1/2 seers			12	0 0
Til	5		"		5	0 0
Mustard	26		"		16	0 0
Shali Kunar	330	kh.	7 1/4	seers	13,203	12 0
Shali Luk	1,891	"	4	"	66,186	12 0
Shali Bara	47	"	19	"	1,889	8 0
Shali Karnal	1	"	69	"	83	12 0
TOTAL					187,108	0 0

OTHER REVENUE OF LAGHMAN-I-TAJIKIA

NATURE OF INCOME	R	a p.
Jama Kalandar Khani	10,219	10 0
Asnaf	2,691	0 0
Koh Khosha	53	0 0
Tawachi	127	0 0
Kahbaha	76	0 0
Chabutra	3,450	0 0
Chungarana	384	0 0
Tarazudari	1,782	0 0
Asiab	25	0 0
Rasum	276	0 0
Tahmil	8,563	0 0
Cotton	8,146	0 0
Palezi	2,656	0 0
TOTAL	38,448	10 0

THER REVENUE OF LAGHMAN-I-AFGHANIA

NATURE OF INCOME	R	a p.
Jama Kalandar Khani	38,031	9 0
Mehmani	1,297	0 0
Kahbaha	474	0 0
Kharj Jamai	85	0 0
Asiab	149	0 0
Koh Khosha	91	0 0
Koh Mash	57	0 0
Tarazudari	1,434	0 0
Cotton	6,174	0 0
Palezi	1,029	0 0

Chungarana		151 0 0
Namad		34 0 0
Asnaf		48 0 0
TOTAL		49,054 9 0

FIXED CHARGES ON THE REVENUE

NATURE OF PAYMENT	QUANTITY	VALUE
(I). WAZIFAS		R a. pi
Cash	.....	3,299 4 0
Ghalla	81 kh. 10 seers	4,056 4 0
Shali	154 " 50 "	5,427 8 0
TOTAL		12,783 0 0
(II). MALIKANA		
Cash		3,904 10 0
Ghalla	66 kh. 70 seers	3,343 12 0
Shali	111 " 15 "	3,894 6 0
TOTAL		11,142 12 0
(III). TAKHFIF		R a. p.
Cash	.....	1,315 2 0
(IV). TANKHWAH-I-WILAYATI		
Cash	.....	28,246 9 0
Ghalla	170 kh. 10 seers	8,506 4 0
Shali	722 " 60 "	25,296 4 0
Mash	60 seers	43 12 0
Jowar	31 kh. 40 seers	1,417 8 0
Kangni	7 "	175 0 0
TOTAL		63,685 5 0
(V). AMIL AND ZABIT		
Cash	.....	6,500 0 0
Ghalla	60 kh. 55 seers	3,034 6 0
Shali	139 " 60 "	6,978 8 0
TOTAL		16,512 14 0

REVENUE AND EXPENDITURES COMPARED

DETAIL	AMOUNT
LAND REVENUE	
	R a. p.
Dara-i-Tajikia	2,03,304 0 0
Dara-i-Afghania	1,87,108 0 0
TOTAL	3,90,412 0 0

The total expenditure is--   R a. p.

1.	Wazifas	12,783 0 0
2.	Milikana	11,142 12 0

3. Takhfif	1,315	2 0
4. Tankhwah	63,685	5 0
5. Amil and Zabit	16,512	14 0
	1,05,439	1 0
BALANCE	2,84,972	15 0

Civil administration. The civil administration of Laghman is carried on under a Governor appointed from Kabul. He usually resides at Tirgarhi. Sardar Abdul Majid Khan, Muhammadzai, is said to be Hakim at the present time (1907). It will be of interest to enter into a brief account of the few Governors that have been appointed subsequent to 1842.

The authority about the time that our troops evacuated Kabul is said to have been vested in the hands of Muhammad Shah Khan, Abu Bakar Khel Ghilzai. That chief fell into disgrace about the period that the Peshawar district came into our hands. Amir Dost Muhammad Khan returning to Kabul, bestowed the revenues of the Tajikia portion of Laghman on his brother Sultan Muhammad Khan, valued at 3 lakhs of rupees. Sardar Sultan Muhammad Khan divided this between his descendants, Sardar Sultan Muhammad Khan divided this between his descendants, Sardar Yahia Khan securing R48,000 for himself and R12,000 per annum for his wife.

On the death of Sardar Sultan Muhammad Khan, the Tajikia, subdivision was bestowed on his son, Sardar Yahia Khan, except Mandrawar, Islamabad Salah, Sabrabad, valued at R25,000 per annum, which had come to Sardar Zakaria Khan. When Amir Sher Ali Khan turned against and imprisoned his son Sardar Yakub Khan, who was married to a daughter of Sardar Yahia Khan, the latter, exciting the suspicion of the Amir by this relationship, and having his jagirs seized, fled to Kashmir with his sons, Sardars Asaf Khan and Yusuf Khan.

The Amir then appointed Sardar Abdulla Khan, son of Sultan Jan, Hakim of all Laghman, who remained in office until the advance of the British troops into the Jalalabad district about the commencement of 1879, when Ismatulla Khan rising up against the Amir's authority, Sardar Abdulla Khan fled to Kabul.

Sardar Yahia Khan was sent up with his sons by our Government to assist Major Cavagnari in his negotiations with Sardar Muhammad Yakub Khan; and when the treaty of Gandamak was signed, Sardar Asaf Khan was appointed to the vacant Governorship of Laghman. In October 1879 Yahia Khan was arrested at Kabul by order of Sir F. Roberts who considered him one who would be sure to use his influence against us. He was subsequently deported to India (with Zakaria Khan), and for nine months remained a State prisoner at Ajmere. Immediately before the evacuation of Kabul (August 1880) the whole of Yahia Khan'a family were also sent to India, and remained at Lahore and Amritsar with Yahia Khan, who had in the meantime ceased to be a State prisoner. In March 1881 Yahia Khan was granted a fixed monthly allowance of R600, exclusive of R1,000 per mensem paid to his two sons, Asaf Khan and Yusuf Khan. In May 1881 the family moved to Dehra. The family tree will be useful here, beginning with:

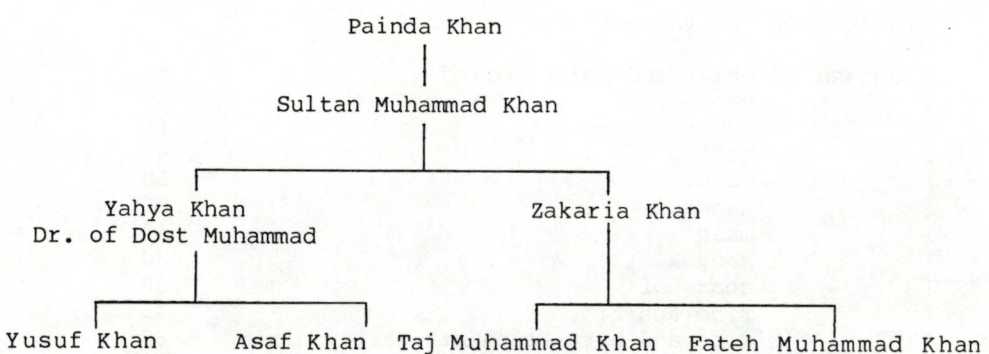

The other sons of Sultan Muhammad Khan, who are said to have numbered no less than 70, have been omitted.

It has always been a difficult undertaking for the Governor of Laghman to realise not only his own jagirs, but the different "barats" issued from Kabul on Laghman Afghania by the Amir of Kabul, from the troublesome Ghilzai chiefs, who swarm in that quarter of Afghanistan, and invariably set the Hakim's authority at defiance.

Currency, etc. There are in Laghman as well as in Jalalabad two systems of computation, both in weight and in money. The one method of computing by recovering is called "them pukhta," and is as follows:

```
50 dinars   = 1 shahi
2 paisas    = 1 sanar
2 sanars    = 1 abbasi
3 abbasis   = 1 rupee.
```

This rupee, estimated by the weight of silver in it, is worth 13 annas and 6 pies of our money.

The other method of computing is called "kham," and is as follows:

```
10 dinars   = 1 paisa
5 paisas    = 1 shahi
10 shahis   = 1 rupee
20 rupees   = 1 toman.
```

One toman is worth R16 and 8 shahis "pukhta." The "kham" rupee is merely one of account; it bears no tangible existence. All the revenue accounts are kept on this system.

```
        Measuring weights
1 charak   = 16 khurds
4 charaks  = 1 seer
8 seers    = 1 maund
10 maunds  = 1 kharwar.
```

The seer equals 7 seers and 13-1/2 chittacks of British Indian standard weight; consequently one kharwar comes to 15 maunds 27 seers and 8 chittacks of our standard weights.

The Tabrizi method in which the revenue accounts are kept is as follows:

```
2-1/2 charaks = 1 maunds
100 maunds    = 1 kharwar.
```

One of these maunds is equal to 4 seers 14-1/2 chittacks of our standar weight; hence a "Tabrizi" kharwar is equal to 12 maunds 10 seers and 10 chittacks of our weight.

In computing the value of the revenue--

		R
1 kharwar of wheat and barley mixed		50
1	wheat	60
1	jowar	45
1	barley	45
1	masur	50
1	kangni	25
1	mash	45
1	sangak	30
1	sharshaf	100
1	rice Kunari	45
1	rice and bara Peshawari barley mixed	80
1	rice and bara Laghman " "	50
1	rice and Harrial " "	40
1	rice and Luk " "	35

Communications. The following are the principal roads running through the district:
From Jalalabad, along the right bank of Kabul river past Khairo Khel and Dargai Oba, to Sarobi and thence to Kabul by the Tangi Gharu. A good camel road, and will probably soon be fit for wheeled transport.
Crossing the Kabul river at Jalalabad a good mule-road runs northwest to Mandrawar and thence north to Tirgarhi.
From Mandrawar a good mule-road leads west over the Badpakht pass to Nagalu.
From Tirgarhi mule-paths lead up the Alingar and Alishang valleys.
In 1908 a steel suspension bridge was built by a Calcutta firm across the Kabul river near Darunta; it is said also that a masonry bridge is being built over the Alingar-Alishang river at Karghai, opposite Mandrawar. It is therefore, probable that, when these bridges are completed, a new and important line of communication will be opened up keeping north of the Kabul river the whole way from Jalalabad to Kabul. (Warburton, Dutton, I.B.C.)

LAGHMANI   لغمانی
34-40 69-21. A village in the Koh Daman on the left bank of the Shakar Dara stream about 1 mile east of Bab Kushkar. Inhabitants: Tajiks. Fifty houses, of which 4 belong to Hindus. (I.B.C.)

LAGHMANI   لغمانی
34-59 69-9 G. A village 3 miles south of Charikar. Inhabitants: Tajiks and Khwaja Khels. It was at this village in November 1842 that Pottinger was treacherously attacked and Lieutenant Rattray, his assistant, killed, he himself escaping with part of the Gurkha garrison to Charikar in the night. (Eyre, I.B.C.)

LAGHRI   لغری (لاغری)
A small section of the Jaghatu Hazaras.

LAGZI   لغزی
A subsection of the Yanghur clan of Dai Zangi.

*LAHUR   لاهور
34-51 71-9 m. A village located a few miles south of Chagha Sarai (Asadabad) in Kunar province.

*LAHURI   لاهوری
34-17 69-39 m. A village located near Sharifkhel on a tributary of the Surkhab in Nangarhar province.

*LAJGAN لاجگن
34-15 69-50 m. A village located on a tributary of the Surkhab, 3 miles south of Alikhel in Nangarhar province.

LAJHA OR LAJHI لجه (لجهی)
A stream in the Mangal country, falling into the Karaja river at about 7 miles east of Ahmad Khel. Its course, which is northeast, is about 17 miles in length, and up its bed runs an alternative route to Gardez. Near its junction with the Karaia is the village of Lajha or Lajhi. (Kane, I.B.C.)

*LAJ (Or LAJA) MANGAL لجه منگل
33-47 69-40. Laj Mangal is an alaqadari in Paktia province. The alaqadari comprises an area of 258 square kilometers and has an agricultural population that has been estimated at from 2,141 to 4,370. The alaqadari is bounded in the west by Sayed Karam, in the south by Musa Khel, in the southeast by Jani Khel, in the east by Chamkani, and in the north by Hasan Khel. Laj Mangal has some 19 villages, one of which has more than 500 inhabitants. The villages are listed in the PG as follows: Kharkai, Haram, Tot Nargai, Doda, Kaja Khola, Zar Kol, Pataka (Patak), Chergo Kalai, Khiranai Khola, Shigalay Khola, Toshang (Toshang Khola), Shara Beg, Sala Kahol, Gosani, Shah Zaman Gondi, Sozi Khola (Sorwi), Todi Tak, Maranj Kalai, Shinkai Khola, Lal Kalai and Lalak Kahol.

*LAKAI KALA لکی قلعه
32-19 68-21 m. A village located near Janikhel, east of the road from Wazakhwa to Khushamand in Ghazni province.

*LAKAN لکن
33-22 70-3 m. A village located south of Alisher in eastern Paktia province.

LAKARAI لکړی
34-4 69-47 A. Elevation 10,400 feet. A pass over the western continuation of the Safed Koh, its crest lying about 12 miles northwest of the Paiwar Kotal. It is said to be the easiest of all the passes over the Safed Koh, being only closed by snow for about 3 months in the year, and even then it is nearly always practicable for men on foot. Over this pass goes a road from Bilut to Safed Sang. This road is said to be practicable for laden camels and forms a lateral communication between the Paiwar-Kabul and the Peshawar-Kabul routes. (I.B.C.)

LAKHI لخی
34-21 69-52. A pass in the Siah Koh range. See "Waragali."

LAKHI-I-TAJIKI لخی تاجکی
A village in the Surkhab division of the Jalalabad district. Inhabitants: Khugianis. (Jenkyns.)

LAKHSHAN لخشان
Said to be a kotal at the head of the Turkoman Dara--see "Shaikh Ali Hazaras."

LAKKAN لکن
33-22 70-3 m. A village, or district, in Khost, a few miles east of Matun. (I.B.C.)

LAL   لال (لعل)
34-25 65-56 A. A stream which is formed north of the Akzarat Kotal, by the confluence of the Surkh Bum and Siah Bumak. The former, known higher up as the Kejak appears to be the main branch. The united stream flows in a general westerly direction to a place well known as Shineh or Shinia (Doab)-Chiragdan, 9 miles west of Daulat Yar. Here it unites with the Sar-i-Jangal stream to form the Hari Rud.

LALA KALA   لالاقلعه
34-26 70-17 m. A village in the Jalalabad district, situated on the left bank of the Surkhab river, about 5 miles west of its junction with the Kabul. Inhabitants: Ghilzais. (Jenkyns.)

LALAKHEL   لالاخيل
34-49 67-51 G. Two villages in the Bamian valley. Inhabitants: Tajiks. (Maitland.) Another place with this name is located in the Nawa-i-Khoda-i-Dad, southwest of the Dasht-Nawer in Ghazni province at 33-13 67-35 m. (LWA)

LALAM PIARI KHEL   لالم بياري خيل
A village in the Ghazni district with a fort, situated between Mansur Karez and Kala Arzbegi. (Broadfoot.)

LALANDAR   للندر
34-23 69-1 A. A collection of villages situated on both banks of the Kabul river, the most eastern portion of the township being about 10 miles southwest of Kabul, at the southern base of the Korogh mountain. (I.B.C.)

LAL BEG   لال بيگ
A section of Jirghai Hazaras.

*LALCHAK   لعلچك
33-20 67-15 m. A village located west of Bughra and south of Ajrestan in western Ghazni province.

*LALI   لالي
33-26 67-27 m. A village located near Kapash on the Nawa-i-Belawghu in Ghazni province.

LALIDAR Or LULIDAR   لالدر
A ravine passed on the road from Bilut to the Lakarai pass. (Gordon.)

LALIZAI   لاليزئي
33-10 69-50 G. A village in the Ghilzai country 20 miles south of Kala-i-Abdul Rahman belonging to the Taraki Ghilzais. (Broadfoot.)

LALMA   للمه
35-11 69-13 m. A village of 20 houses in the Salang Dara, about 7 miles above Parwan. (I.B.C.) A village with this name is located near Ada, south of Jalalabad in Nangarhar province, at 34-21 70-28 m.

*LALMAI   للمي
34-1 70-50 G. A village located about 22 miles northwest of Anar Qala in Shinwar, Nangarhar province.

LALPUR Or LALPURA   لعل پوره
34-15 71-3 A. Lalpur is a village and an alaqadari in Nangarhar

province. The alaqadari comprises an area of 530 square kilometers and has an agricultural population that has been estimated at from 5,555 to 7,890. The alaqadari is bounded in the northwest by Goshta and in the northeast and east by Pakistan, in the south and west by Mohmand Dara. Lalpur has about 11 villages, 6 of which have more than 500 inhabitants. The villages are listed in the PG as follows: Lalpur, Kama-i-Lalpur, Ziarate Mela (Bela), Gul Dag, Chaknur, Sahebzadah Gano Kalay, Chanknur Ulya, Chaknur Sufla, Gerdabi (Gerdani), Sada-i-Lalpur, Shakotay, and Mar Sangi. (LWA) In 1914 the area was described as follows:

Elevation 1,450 feet. A village in the Jalalabad district, 47 miles from Peshawar. It is situated on the left bank of the Kabul river, immediately opposite Loe Dakka. It is the chief village of the Mohmand tribe and includes the minor villages of Sada and Malikhana. There is a ferry of boats between Lalpura and Dakka and a difficult ford when the river is low; a bridge of boats also is maintained in the cold weather, but is usually either dismantled or washed away when the melting snow causes the river to rise in the spring.

Muhammad Akbar Khan, Mohmand, was, until lately, Khan of Lalpura, but he has been summoned to Kabul where he now (1906) lives under surveillance, and no successor to the Khanship has up to date been appointed.

About 1 mile to the east of the village of Lalpura is the cantonment of the same name, with a garrison of 2 battalions infantry and 500 khasadars. In addition to these troops it is said that the Amir intends to station a battery of artillery and a regiment of cavalry here. (Jenkyns, Wanliss, I.B.C.)

LAMA KHEL لمه خيل
A tribe, probably Mangals, said to inhabit a tract to the north of the road between Dre Kala and the Shutur Gardan pass. (I.B.C.)

LAMATAK لمتك
34-44 71-2 G. A village in Laghman, on the right bank of the Alingar river, about 1 1/2 mile north of Mandrawar. It consists of the following hamlets, inhabited by Dehgans:
    (1) Banda-i-Musa Dado
    (2) Fakiran
    (3) Ziarat-i-Pir Sabz Baba. (Warburton.)

LAMATAK لمتك
34- 70-. A village on the right bank of the Kunar river above Shewa. It contains about 60 houses. (Masson.)

LAMATI SHIAK لمتی شیك (شیخ ؟)
A village in Laghman containing the following hamlets:
    (1) Kala-i-Sohrab
    (2) Sadar Bin
    (3) Banda-i-Bawar
    (4) Beyat Badru.
Inhabitants: Dehgans, Ghilzais, and mixed tribes. (Warburton.) Shiak should probably read Shaikh. (LWA)

LAMGHAN See LAGHMAN لمغان

LANDA See LANDHA لنده

LANDABUCH لنده بوچ (بوح ؟)
34- 70-. A village in the Kama division of the Jalalabad district, about 3 miles northeast of Deh-i-Ghazi. Inhabitants: Arabs, Parachas, and Sahibzadas. (Jenkyns.)

LANDAR SADIK لندرصادق
A river of Khost which joined to the Shamil, forms the Kaitu. It has the following villages on its banks: Zambar Mali Tarizi, Ali Shera, Aram Khel. (Muhammad Haiat.)

LANDAY See LANDI لنډی

LANDEH لنډه
33- 70-. A village in Khost, on the left bank of the Shamil stream, 3 miles to the south of Kadam. (I.B.C.)

LANDHA لنډه
33- 70-. A village in Khost, 14 miles southwest of the Shabak pass and about 13 1/2 miles due east of Matun. It is situated on the left bank of the Kaitu or Shamil river, at the junction with the latter of the Landha stream. There is ample space for camping ground with water from the river which here has low banks and a sandy bed. (I.B.C.)

*LANDI Or LANDAY لنډی
34-13 70-14 m. A village located some 3 miles northwest of Pachire Agam and southwest of Jalalabad in Nangarhar province. Other places with this name are located a few miles south of Ghanikhel on the way north to the Kabul river, at 34-9 70-48 m.; in the Khairaspan area, southwest of Zurket in Paktia province, at 33-28 69-42 m.; about 5 miles south of Chamkani in eastern Paktia province, at 33-44 69-49 m.; south of Tani on the way to Matun in Paktia province, at 33-11 69-50 m.

*LANDI KHEL لنډی خیل
34-12 70-16 m. A village located near Pachiro Agam on a tributary of the Kabul river in Nangarhar province.

LANDI WAM لنډی وام
33-49 69-39 m. A village on the right bank of the Kurram river and southeast of Dabuzai. Inhabitants: Ahmad Khel Jajis, capable of turning out 200 fighting men. (I.B.C.)

*LANGAK لنگك
34-6 67-14 m. A village near Pitaoqol, on the Helmand river in southern Bamian province.

LANGAR لنگر
34-49 69-11 m. A village in the Koh Daman, 24 miles north of Kabul. It contains 60 houses. (Masson.)

LANGAR لنگر
34-2 68-46. The name of the stream which, on its junction with the Shiniz, becomes the Logar river, about 3 miles south of Shaikhabad. The valley of Langar is fertile; but the cultivation does not extend far on either side of the water. Eastwards it is very contracted, partaking a good deal of the character of the Tangi Wardak. The Langar stream flows through Shaikhabad, and there are the remains of a masonry bridge over it, which has been destroyed by floods. Usually, however, the water is of little depth. From this point the village of Ambo Khak is distant 5 1/2 miles to the west, and Kala-i-Abdul Ghafur is 2 1/2 miles further on. The latter is the principal place in the Langar valley. (I.B.C.)

*LANGAR لنگر
34-9 68-41 m. A village near Girdab and west of the Ghazni-Kabul highway in Maidan province. Other places with this name are located northeast of Kalakan and west of the Kabul-Charikar road in Kabul province, at 34-49 69-12 m., and 3 miles south of Rukha, Panjshir, at 35-15 69-25 G.

LANGAR See SHIMILTU لنگر

LANGAR لنگر
A village in the Surkhab valley, or rather on one of the small streams rising in the northern slopes of the Safed Koh to the west of Sikaram, which together form the Surkhab river. Inhabitants are Gehar Mangals. (I.B.C.)

LANGAR لنگر
A Taraki Ghilzai village in Katawaz, forming the ninth stage on the road from Domandi (Gumal valley) to Ghazni, from which it is distant about 66 miles. There are two forts here containing about 80 houses. The larger fort is a square of 100 yards; the mud walls, 20 feet high and 6 feet thick are flanked by towers; there is no ditch, and the gate is uncovered. This is one of the strongest forts in Katawaz. (Broadfoot, I.B.C.)

LANGAR لنگر
35- 69-. A fort in the upper Panjshir glen, about 5 miles above Anaba. Langar Khan son of Gulzar Khan, Chief of Lower Panjshir, resided there in 1886. Outside the fort there are some 10 huts of the Khan's retainers. The width of glen is here from 600 to 700 yards. (Shahzada Taimus.)

LARGAR See KOH-I-BABA لنگر

LARGI لرگی
A village 48 miles southwest of Ghazni. (Thornton.)

*LAR KALAI لرکی
32-51 67-35 m. A village located some 8 miles north of Aghojan and west of Mukur in Ghazni province.

*LARO لارو
34-18 67-30 m. A village located on the Helmand river in Bamian province.

*LASHKARI KHEL لشکری خیل
34-9 69-5 m. A village located some 5 miles north of Kolangar on the road to Kabul in Logar province.

LASHKAR RAH لشکرراه
An easy kotal crossed by the main Kabul-Hazarajat-Daulat Yar road, about 8 1/2 miles southeast of Daulat Yar. The kotal forms the boundary at this point between the provinces of Kabul and Herat. (Wanliss.)

*LASHKO لشکو
33-18 68-19 m. A village located northeast of Kalakhel on the highway to Ghazni in Ghazni province.

LATABAND لتهبند
34-30 69-34 A. Elevation 7,950 feet. A pass in the Karkacha hills,

between Seh Baba and Butkhak. It is 19 miles distant from Kabul. A post was established at this point during the Afghan war of 1879-80, and during the investment of Sherpur by the Afghans, it was held by Colonel Hudson with less than 1,000 men, and heliographic communication was therefore available between the beleaguered garrison and the outer world as often as the sky was sufficiently clear. The presence of this body at Lataband, together with the Jagdalak garrison, was the means of keeping in check the Tezin Ghilzais, and the only time Lataband was attacked, the enemy was driven off easily, and with loss.

Before Kabul was evacuated by the British an excellent cart-road was contructed over the pass. This however has since fallen altogether into disrepair. (I.B.C.)

LEHWAN   لیوان (لهوان)
33- 69-. A village about 10 miles from Gardez, on the road thence to the Altimur Kotal, situated just at the point where the road enters the hills. Inhabitants: Amazai Ghilzais. (I.B.C.)

LEHWANAI Or LAR LEWANI   لرلیونی
33-57 69-48 m. A village on the right bank of the Karaja river, about 4 to 5 miles west of the Paiwar Kotal, and inhabited by Jajis. It is a collection of detached hamlets, each consisting of three or four fort-like houses, either situated in retired or sheltered hollows between the hills, or else perched on the summit of some commanding eminence. Almost every house is furnished with a tower for purposes of observation or defence. (Bellew, Lumsden.)

*LEWAN   لیوان
33-35 69-3 m. A village located near Dinarkhel and west of Gardez in Paktia province. Other places with this name are located 4 miles north of Gardez on the highway to Kabul in Paktia province, at 33-39 69-14 m.; a few miles east of Kota-i-Ashro in Maidan province, at 34-27 68-50 m.; north of Sarobi on the road to Kabul, at 34-36 69-43 m.

*LEWANKHEL   لیوان خیل
33-33 69-50 m. A village located some 4 miles north of Karezuna in Paktia province.

LIAS KHAN   لیاس خان
33- 69-. A village in the upper or southern portion of the Logar valley, situated on the right bank of that river, about 3 miles south of Hisarak, and forming one township with Patkao-i-Shahana. The inhabitants in 1880 numbered 260 families, including three hamlets of Sayyids (50 houses), and one of Ahmadzais (12 houses), the remainder of the residents being Astanazai Ghilzais and a few Mohmands. (Euan Smith, Clifford.)

*LICH   لیچ
34-54 69-42 m. A village located about 5 miles northeast of Tagab in Kapisa province.

LICH KOL   لیچ قول
35-3 68-47. A glen draining southwards from the main range of the Hindu Kush into the Ghorband valley which it joins at Chahardeh.

LINA See ARIOH   لینه

LODA Or LODI لوده (لودی)
A few families of this tribe exist in the Jalalabad district, chiefly in Kama. They state that they are the descendants of a Ghilzai father and a Sayyid mother. From their female ancestor being a Sayyid, a certain odour of sanctity attaches to the Lodis. Probably they do not number more than 40 families. (Jenkyns.) N.B. See "Lohani." A village with this name is located on a tributary of the Arghandab river in Ghazni province at 33-13 67-29 m. (LWA)

*LODAM لودم
34-55 71-4 m. A village located on a tributary of the Kunar river, northwest of Asadabad in Kunar province.

LODRAKH لودرخ
33- 69-. A village on the right bank of the Karaia river. In the same group are the villages of Ali Khel and Mama Khel, the three together supporting 200 fighting men. (I.B.C.)

LOE BARU See BARU-I-KALAN لویه برو

LOE DAKKA See DAKKA لویه دکه

LOE NAN لویه نان
33- 69-. A ravine running northwards and falling into the Hazardarakht stream opposite Karatiga. (I.B.C.)

LOGAR لوگر
34-33 69-17 A. A river which, according to the second edition of this Gazetteer, "rises about 1 mile above Azdhaha in the east slopes of the Paghman range, at an elevation of not less than 10,500 feet. Here the springs issue from a large verdant expanse of bog, not far from which the stream has a subterranean passage for about 200 yards, when it re-appears in a small lake or cavity, of about 80 yards in circumference. Here it turns two watermills and again disappears for about 500 yards, in which distance it passes under Azdhaha and issues east of it. Hence its course is unimpeded, and it flows a small but clear stream through a verdant valley, and traversing the Hazara districts (and receiving the waters of the Majab Dara through its right bank?), crosses at Shaikhabad the valley leading from Kabul to Ghazni, 50 miles from its source. "Azdhaha" is probably the same as Kala Hashtdar, a place in the Besud country passed on the road leading north from Ghazni. But the "east slopes of the Paghman range" is somewhat vague, seeing that the river is believed to be formed by the junction of the Khawat and Simila streams, both draining east from the high range which divides the Helmand and Arghandab drainage on the west from that going east to the Kabul river.
At Shaikhabad the river has an elevation of 7,473 feet. At this point it is crossed by a bridge, but it is fordable for guns though the banks require sloping down. At Doaba, 3 miles below Shaikabad, it is joined by the Shiniz; from this it flows east for 30 miles, when it turns north and joins the Kabul river, 10 miles below Kabul. At Hisarak, 3 miles below its last north bend, it is crossed by a bridge, and is here a narrow sluggish stream of no great depth, with a firm pebbly bed, and fordable at most parts of its course. During the rains, however, the volume of the river becomes greatly increased and it also flows with more than usual rapidity owing to the numerous freshets it receives from the hills around. It is also crossed by a bridge a few miles above its confluence with the Kabul river, and here it is deep and rapid, and about 50 yards in width.

From Shaikhabad to its junction with the Kabul river is 100 miles, and the difference in elevation is about 1,000 feet only, thus making the fall about 10 feet percent.

Before its junction with the Shiniz it seems to be generally known as the Langar.

This river is only used for purposes of irrigation and the district watered by it is one of the most fertile and populous in Afghanistan.

Between Shaikhabad and Hisarak the Logar is crossed at numerous points by rustic native bridges, and is everywhere fordable in April with an average depth of not more than 2 feet deep. (Masson, Griffith, Hough, Havelock, Bellew, Lumsden.)

LOGAR لوگر
34-6 69-3. A province in eastern Afghanistan which comprises an area of 4,409 square kilometers and an agricultural population estimated at from 112,579 to 172,704. The province is bounded in the west by Maidan, in the north by Kabul, in the east by Nangarhar, and in the south by Paktia provinces. Logar is divided into the wolewalis of Azru, Muhammad Agha, Baraki, and Pul-i-Alam, and into the alaqadaris of Khushi and Charkh. The capital of the province is the city of Pul-i-Alam. For woleswali lists from the Department of Statistics of the Ministry of Agriculture and Irrigation see the following six tables. (LWA) In 1912 the area was described as follows:

A district consisting of the valley of the Logar river from its northward bend to its junction with the Kabul river. The present Hakim is said to be one Abdur Rasul Khan. One of the roads from Ghazni to Kabul traverses the whole length of the Logar valley proper and in 1880 was made practicable for wheeled artillery. The Kurram route to Kabul also runs through the Logar district from Kushi as far as Safed Sang. The elevation of the district ranges between 8,000 and 5,000 feet, Kushi is 7,829 feet, Kala Amit 6,440 feet, Hisarak 5,148 feet, and Baraki Rajan 6,550 feet. The following is a report drawn up in 1880 by Major Euan Smith C.S.I., and to it is attached a report by Surgeon-Major Johnston, M.D., on the geology, botany, etc. of the Logar valley:—"The Logar valley may be roughly described as extending from Amir Kala in the southern Safed Sang in the north, and for convenience sake might be nominally divided into three portions:

"I. The Upper Logar, extending from Amir Kala to the other side of the pass lying between Saidan and Hisarak, called Tangi-Hisarak. This is by far the most populous and prosperous part of the valley, containing, as it does, the very large and flourishing groups of villages known, respectively, as Baraki-Rajan, Baraki-Barak, Patkao-i-Roghani and Patkao-i-Shahana, under one of which names almost every one of the villages enclosed within the great area of cultivated and irrigated land is grouped for revenue purposes, and it is this portion of the valley that may be looked upon as constituting the real granary of Kabul.

"II. The Middle Logar, extending from Tangi-Hisarak, inclusive of the Tangi-Waghjan. This portion of the district is much more sparsely populated and cultivated. The villages and cultivation lie almost exclusively along the banks of the river, and the irrigation canals are much fewer and less extensive than in the Upper Logar. The principal groups of villages are Hisarak, Kulangar, and Dadu Khel.

"III. The Northern Logar, comprising from the Tangi-Waghjan to the Safed Sang pass at the entrance to the Charasia district, near Kabul. This portion of the valley is thickly cultivated on both sides of the river, but is quite barren at a short distance from the

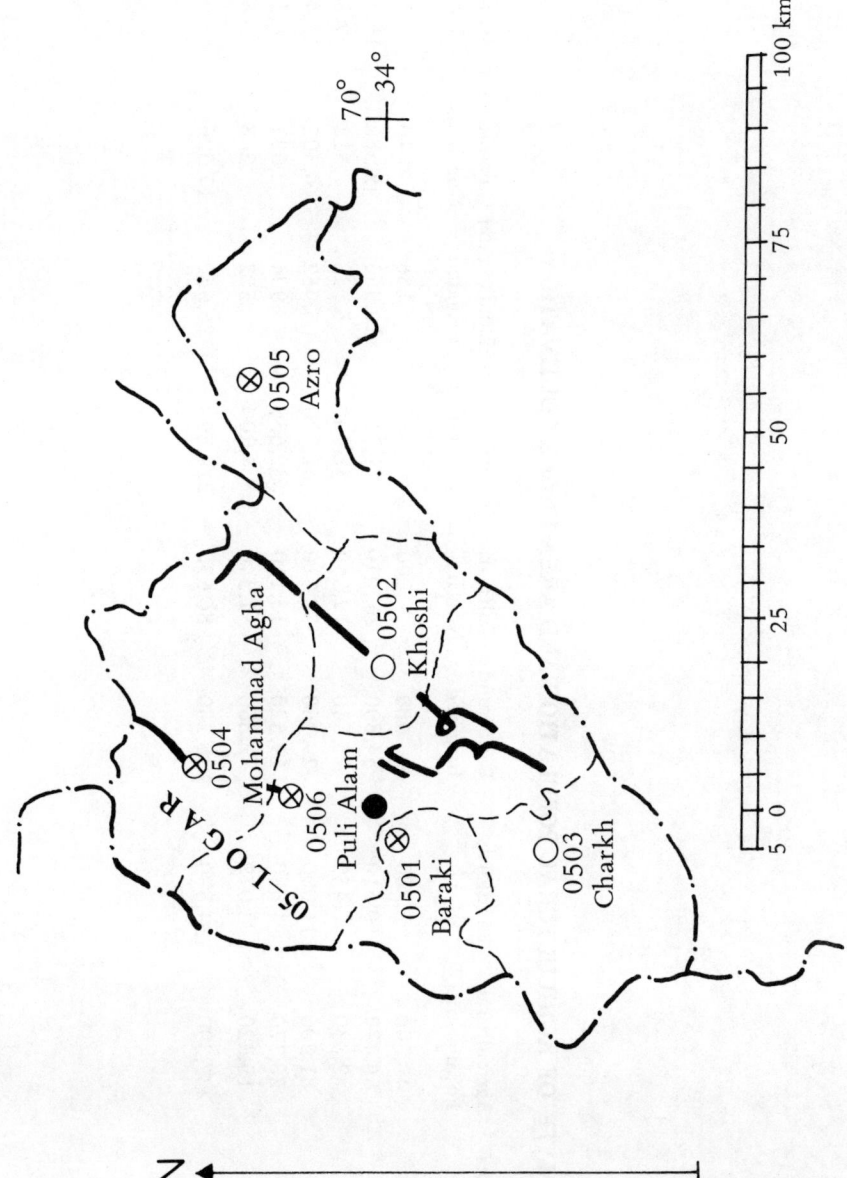

Administrative Divisions of Logar Province

ESTIMATE OF AGRICULTURAL POPULATION AND AREA UNDER CULTIVATION

	Villages	Agricultural Population	Landlords	Lands under Cultivation in Jaribs			Lands under Cultivation in Hectares		
				Irrigated	Non-Irrig.	Total	Irrigated	Non-Irrig.	Total
AZRO	29	43,000	5,780	680	200	880	136	40	176
KOLANGAR (PUL-I-ALAM)	76	66,470	9,510	54,800	26,910	81,710	10,960	5,382	16,342
MOHAMMAD AGHA	37	2,830	450	25,640	12,560	38,200	5,128	2,512	7,640
BARAKI	47	81,000	11,000	29,760	32,510	62,270	5,952	6,502	12,454
CHARKH	59	28,770	4,080	19,520	13,110	32,630	3,904	2,622	6,526
KHOSHI	17	15,320	4,070	2,860	1,340	4,200	572	268	840
TOTAL	265	237,390	34,890	133,260	86,630	219,890	26,652	17,326	43,978

STATISTICAL ESTIMATE OF LIVESTOCK BY WOLESWALIS AND ALAQADARIS

	Sheep	Karakul Sheep	Goats	Cattle	Buffaloes	Camels	Horses	Donkeys	Mules	Poultry
AZRO	2,765	—	800	2,052	—	5	70	3,000	—	5,610
KOLANGAR (PUL-I-ALAM)	16,055	—	1,400	10,690	—	15	780	8,350	—	35,340
MOHAMMAD AGHA	4,155	—	—	3,350	—	25	110	4,870	200	10,480
BARAKI	3,732	—	300	5,560	—	3	80	6,720	300	26,010
CHARKH	6,306	—	470	7,104	—	5	100	9,000	50	38,020
KHOSHI	4,277	—	550	2,924	—	7	—	1,850	50	13,820
TOTAL	37,290	—	3,520	31,680	—	60	1,140	33,790	600	129,280

PRODUCTION OF AGRICULTURAL CROPS—IN KABULI SEERS

	Grains			Vegetables	Other Crops		Fruits
	Irrigated	Non-Irrig.	Total		Industrial Crops	Other Temp. Crops	
AZRO	28,400	2,400	30,800	23,200	—	38,400	28,800
KOLANGAR (PUL-I-ALAM)	1,735,200	117,720	1,852,920	1,008,680	—	1,490,400	389,760
MOHAMMAD AGHA	768,000	75,840	843,840	483,990	—	720,000	595,200
BARAKI	1,039,600	206,880	1,246,480	839,990	34,200	537,600	249,600
CHARKH	585,200	100,680	685,880	368,350	—	324,000	602,880
KHOSHI	79,600	16,080	95,680	37,980	—	62,400	130,560
TOTAL	4,236,000	519,600	4,755,600	2,762,190	34,200	3,172,800	1,996,800

LAND UNDER IRRIGATION AND SOURCES OF IRRIGATION

	Area in Jaribs					Number of Sources			
	Canals	Springs	Karez	Wells	Total	Canals	Springs	Karez	Wells	Water Mills
AZRO	562	118	—	—	680	16	33	—	—	26
KOLANGAR (PUL-I-ALAM)	49,022	—	5,518	260	54,800	50	25	39	15	152
MOHAMMAD AGHA	19,300	—	6,000	340	25,640	20	25	32	14	105
BARAKI	21,184	—	8,066	510	29,760	31	26	15	50	56
CHARKH	17,368	662	1,450	40	19,520	31	36	24	5	68
KHOSHI	1,884	60	866	50	2,860	6	24	14	7	26
TOTAL	109,320	840	21,900	1,200	133,260	154	169	124	91	433

TOTAL CULTIVABLE LAND, BY CROP—IN KABULI JARIBS

	Grains			Vegetables	Industrial Crops	Other Crops	Fruits	Total Cultivated Land
	Irrigated	Non-Irrig.	Total					
AZRO	710	200	910	100	—	160	150	1,320
KOLANGHAR (PUL-I-ALAM)	43,380	9,810	53,190	4,780	—	6,210	2,030	66,210
MOHAMMAD AGHA	19,200	6,320	25,520	2,290	—	3,000	3,100	33,910
BAKARI	25,990	17,240	43,230	3,980	950	2,240	1,300	51,700
CHARKH	14,630	8,390	23,020	1,740	—	1,350	3,140	29,250
KHOSHI	1,990	1,340	3,330	170	—	260	680	4,440
TOTAL	105,900	43,300	149,200	13,060	950	13,220	10,400	186,830

TOTAL CULTIVABLE LANDS—IN KABULI JARIBS

	Total	Pastures	Forests	Under Cultivation	Fallow Lands
AZRO	37,790	21,210	15,700	880	530
KOLANGAR (PUL-I-ALAM)	106,380	24,670	–	81,710	22,290
MOHAMMAD AGHA	87,350	49,150	–	38,200	15,860
BARAKI	111,020	48,750	–	62,270	18,460
CHARKH	50,870	18,240	–	32,630	9,920
KHOSHI	11,380	7,180	–	4,200	2,890
TOTAL	404,790	169,200	15,700	219,890	69,950

bed of the stream. Its principal districts are Deh-i-Nao, Muhammad Agha, Gumran, Zahidabad, Kuti Khel and Zargan Shahr, the last named being situated 4 miles from the right bank of the river, and entirely dependent for its water-supply on the karez that have been dug from the district of Surkhao to the east.

"On every side Logar is completely shut in by high, barren hills, with passes leading to the south and southeast into Kharwar, Zurmat, and Musai, and on the west and southwest into Wardak, Maidan, and Chardeh. Two excellent bridle roads traverse the valley on both sides of the river, which latter is moreover fordable at almost all points, owing to the quantity of water that is diverted into the irrigation canals.

"The three principal outlying districts of Logar are Surkhai, the district belonging to the Ghilzai Chief, Padshah Khan, situated 7 miles to the east of Zargan Shahr; Kushi, an exceedingly prosperous Tajik district, situated some 10 miles east of Hisarak and near the entrance to the Shutur Gardan pass, of which Rahmatulla Khan, the head Malik, is a staunch friend of the English; and Charkh, situated some 12 miles southeast of Baraki Rajan, through which passes the road leading into Kharwar.

"With the exception of those three districts the cultivation in Logar is continuous, and the villages are closely situtated one to another. During the ripening of the harvest the Upper Logar presents to the eye an immense unbroken surface of waving corn. Where the cultivation ceases, the desert commences on either side of the river and continues so right up to the hills.

"Land tenure. There are three classes of land in Logar, depending partly on the water available for irrigation, partly on the ability or otherwise of the owners to manure the ground; fields which lie a distance from villages not being supposed to be manured at all. The Tajiks, Kizilbashis, and other Parsiwans are taxed at an extraordinary disadvantage to their Afghan neighbours. On land of the best class the rate fixed is from 12 to 22 seers Kabuli per jarib, the general rate per jarib being 15 seers. Land of the average sort pays 8 seers, and of the worst description 5 seers. A Kabuli seer weighs, roughly speaking, 16 lbs., and a jarib (in Logar) consists of 20 biswas, a biswa being a plot of ground twenty paces square. These paces are, however, short, and the biswa may be calculated as 15 yards square. The jarib is accordingly found to be 4,500 superficial yards, or about a quarter of a rood less than an English acre. Reduced therefore to English weights and measures, it will be seen that first class land pays an average of 2 1/4 cwt. per acre, second class land rather more than half that amount, and the worst land a third of it. First class land of the above description will yield if well cultivated (and the cultivation in Logar is extremely good), about 24 maunds per jarib. This gives the rate of taxation of such land to be about 12 1/2 per cent of the produce, which does not appear to be excessive. But it is only the classes above named who pay these rates; Afghans, according to a land settlement of a very old date, known as Kalandar Khan's settlement, pay but 1 1/4 Kabuli seer per jarib, i.e., less than 22 lbs, per English acre, though land purchased by them from Parsiwans is assessed at the rates paid by the latter. It may be imagined how greatly this difference of taxation affects the value of land in Logar, and how it tends to keep up that feeling of superiority which the Afghans claim to exercise over their less powerful neighbours. Many attempts have been made to equalise the taxation by raising the rates paid by Ghilzais, but no Amir has as yet been powerful enough to do this, and it need hardly be said the Parsiwans and others cannot get their taxes reduced.

"Rotation of crops. First class land is cultivated every year, that of the second class every second year, while the worst description is allowed to lie fallow or under clover for two years. The rotation of crops on the best land is as follows: barley or wheat is sown from the middle of August to the beginning of November, and reaped in June and July; clover seed is then sown, which is grazed down by cattle late in autumn. It grows up again the following spring, and is cut once or twice. In May or June the land is ploughed for rice or Indian-corn, which are fit for cutting in September or October. After the land has been well manured wheat is again sown.

"If the land be poor, the clover is allowed to grow for three or four cuttings, i.e., till the autumn, when the ground is ploughed for wheat or barley sowing.

"Rice is sown broadcast and allowed to grow where it springs; it is not transplanted by hand as in Kurram and Khost, though a thick crop may occasionally be thinned.

"Fodder for cattle. In an ordinary winter snow does not lie on the ground in Logar for more than 10 days; should it remain for three weeks the season is called extremely severe. At such time the scarcity of fodder for cattle is so great that bhusa has been known to sell for its weight in grain. Besides bhusa, dry clover and lucerne and a thorny shrub called gowan, which grows on low hills, are used as winter fodder for cattle and camelthorn for sheep and goats when snow prevents their grazing. Both the camelthorn and gowan require to be beaten small before animals are fed on them.

"Health. The Logar valley appears to be on the whole healthy, though deaths are common in the late summer months and autumn from remittent fever, the worst form of which is called in Pushtu chakai, and in Persian damana. Natives say that it is accompanied by extreme pain in the back and limbs. On the fourth day the patient generally becomes insensible. If perspiration cannot be induced by the seventh to the ninth day, the disease generally proves fatal. Diseases of the eye and small-pox are also common. Cholera appears every two or three years. Last year it made great ravages, commencing early in May; it lasted till late in September, and was of a very severe type. Many of the older residents are skilled in dressing wounds, and have a slight knowledge of the properties (or supposed properties) of certain herbs and drugs, but there is no one in the valley whose sole profession is that of a doctor. If such a man is required, he has to be brought from Kabul.

"Prices. In ordinary times wheat is sold in Logar at from 20 to 24 seers English per rupee Kabuli; barley and Indian-corn at about 35 seers English. The high prices prevalent owing to the presence of the English army were however, equalled in 1867-68 during the civil war consequent on the struggles of Muhammad Afzal Khan and Sher Ali Khan for the throne.

"Land, wood, cattle, grain, etc., are all paid for in cash; the sole exception seems to be in the purchase of dried mulberries, for which equal weight or double the weight of other grain is ordinarily given.

"Irrigation. The distribution of the water-supply for purposes of irrigation is, as elsewhere, a frequent source of strife. The period, to which each village community is entitled to the flow of the river watercourse or of the stream from the karez has been handed down traditionally from generation to generation, so that the authors of the distribution have been quite forgotten. Disputes on the subject are usually settled either by the Hakim in person, or by some one deputed by him.

"Tribes. On the whole, however, the residents of Logar appear to live in tolerable harmony with each other, not from a community of feeling, but because the Afghans (Astanaza, Ahmadzai, and Adramzai Ghilzais) are more powerful than the Parsiwans, who are Tajiks, Hazaras, and Kizilbashis. The Tajiks of Kushi are mostly Shias, but Kushi is somewhat isolated, and the inhabitants keep to themselves.

"There are about 150 Hindu families in Logar, viz.100 in Baraki Rajan, about 30 families in Charkh, and a few scattered about Amir Kala, Kulangar, Guvra, etc. These men do not appear to be much oppressed by their Muhammadan brethren. They are, generally speaking rich, and are very useful as money-lenders, their charges for such accommodation being usually 20 per cent per annum.

"Historical. The Ghazni Field Force marched into Logar on the 30th April 1880 in two brigades. One brigade with the guns and heavy artillery moved from Saiyidabad by the Zumburak pass, on which the sappers had been engaged for some days to make it practicable for artillery, and the other brigade marched from Shaikhabad by the more direct road through the Tangi Wardak. The march was accomplished without accident, and the two brigades encamped for the night at Amir Kala and Baraki Barak, respectively. Thence they moved down by easy marches, and established permanent camps at Kala-i-Jabir and Hisarak, the headquarters of the division, with General Hughes in command, being established at the latter place.

"On the 31st May the division struck camp and marched to the other side of the valley, encamping on the slopes of the high hills which overlooked the village of Deh-i-Mughalan, from which a magnificent view of the rich expanse of varied cultivation could be commanded.

"The near approach of Sardar Abdur Rahman to Kabul and the increased excitement visible in the capital rendered it advisable to collect the British forces in the neighbourhood of that city; so on the 18th June the entire Ghazni force marched to Charasia, but, on arrival there, it became apparent that the commissariat could not feed it, and it was obliged to return ot the Logar valley, where a permanent camp was formed at Zargan Shah.

"On the 22nd July Sardar Abdur Rahman was formally recognised by the British Government as Amir of Afghanistan, whereupon the Ghazni division marched from Logar to Kabul, arriving there on the 3rd August 1880. (See Official Account of the Second Afghan War.)

"At the time of the entry of the British force into the Logar valley, the general attitude of the inhabitants was inoffensive and even friendly. They made no difficulty about furnishing the necessary supplies, and were soon re-assured and relieved of any fear that they might have entertained as to our intentions by observing the good conduct of the troops. This friendly attitude, however, was not universal, and intelligence soon reached camp that the inhabitants of Zurmat and Kharwar had taken alarm at our approach, and were in a restless and disturbed condition.

"It was, therefore, deemed advisable to send a reconnaissance to the summit of the Altimur pass leading into Zurmat through the hills, which overlooked General Barter's camp to the west of Kala-i-Jabir; and Colonel MacLean was accordingly despatched with this object, having under his command a mixed force. General Barter at the same time entrenched his camp at Kala-i-Jabir, so as to be protected against any sudden or night attacks.

"Colonel MacLean succeeded in pushing his reconnaissance as far as Shahwas, beyond which point his instructions did not allow him to proceed. On return he reported the inhabitants of Zurmat as being in a considerable state of excitement and prepared for hostilities, and his retirement from this pass was the signal for its occupation in force by the Zurmat tribesmen, who at once commenced to throw up sangars. The appearance of our cavalry at the summit of the Altimur

defile had caused great alarm, and was looked upon as significant of our intentions to occupy the Zurmat valley. The tribesmen declared that they would oppose any such movement by force. Every night the summits of the hills were ablaze with their watch-fires, and on more than one occasion General Barter reported that his camp had been fired into at night. No damage was, however experienced.
"On the 10th May 1880 Major-General James Hills, C.B., V.C., was appointed to the command of the Ghazni Field Force in Logar, and he accordingly took up his appointment on the 15th of the same month, relieving General Hughes at Hisarak.
"On the 17th May Major Euan Smith resumed his duties with the force as Political Officer. Major Lance returned to regimental duty, and Major Clifford again took up his old appointment as Political Officer, with the 2nd Brigade.
"On the 19th May the head-quarters and cavalry brigade moved from Hisarak to Kala-i-Jabir. General Hughes remained encamped with his brigade at the former place.
"On the 21st May 1880 Major Euan Smith, accompanied by Major Lance and escorted by 100 sabres, visited Charkh, a fertile district, situated in a cul-de-sac, some 12 miles southeast of Kala-i-Jabir.
"Charkh is a most fertile little place, well-wooded, and with an abundant suply of water, and inhabited entirely by Tajiks. These Tajiks are divided into two parties, who have been at deadly enmity with one another ever since the memory of man. The English officers were, on the occasion of this visit, well received by both the contending factions, who though living close to one another, will not enter each other's houses or villages. Both were profuse in their expression of friendship towards our Government, and every one disclaimed any participation or sympathy in the proceedings of Ghulam Haidar Khan. The inhabitants declared that they had been very severely treated by the late Amir Sher Ali Khan, and that the taxation imposed upon them was more than they could bear. It is the case, I believe, that the exceptional fertility of Charkh (which, with its gardens and orchards, is a very tempting spot) has, from time to time, exposed it to exceptional demands from the Kabul authorities. Nevertheless, the inhabitants had a well-to-do and prosperous appearance. They had not paid any revenue for two years, and seemed to regard with dismay the probability of a return to any settled form of government, which should render such payment unavoidable.
"On the 31st May 1880 the division struck camp and marched to the othe side of the valley, encamping on the slopes of the high hills which overlooked the village of Deh-i-Moghalan, and from which a magnificent view of the rich expanse of varied cultivation could be commanded.
"At this time the country all around, with the exception of the Logar itself, was in a most disturbed state. Wardak had been excited at the news of the deportation of the Mustaufi Habibulla to India, Zurmat and Kharwar were kept in a state of restlessness by the machinations and intrigues of Muhammad Jan, and on the Maidan side Abdul Ghafur, Akhunzada, was doing his best to stir up the people to mischief. The prime cause of all this unsettled feeling was, of course, to be found in the uncertainty which reigned at the movements and intentions of Sardar Abdur Rahman Khan. Men had not yet made up their minds whose cause to expouse, and were everywhere ripe for any mischief that might turn up. The probabilities of a hostile demonstration against the English force in Logar seemed each day to become more probable.
"Under these circumstances General Hills constructed a complete series of defences for the division against night attacks. The

villages in front of the camp were ordered to be evacuated each day at sunset, and sangars were erected on the summits of the commanding hills for the protection of the picquets. The position was thus rendered nearly impregnable.

"The near approach of Sardar Abdur Rahman Khan to Kabul, and the increasing excitement visible in the capital, having rendered it advisable to collect the English forces in the neighbourhood of that city, orders were received on the 16th June that the Ghazni Field Force should without delay move towards Charasia. The entire force accordingly marched from their respective camps at Hisarak and Dehi-Moghalan on the 18th June, and on the same day rendezvoused at Dadu Kala. Previous to leaving, the maliks of Logar were all summoned by Major Euan Smith, and the meaning and object of this sudden move explained to them. They were told that it was more than probable that the English troops would return to Logar, and as it was certain that our departure would be the signal for the Zurmatis and malcontents to descend with mischievous objects into the valley, they were warned not to give these men countenance or support, or to assist them in any way in their hostile intentions towards ourselves. In reply, the maliks one and all declared that they would keep aloof from any combination against us. They said that we had treated them well and liberally, and that they had no quarrel with us, and that we should have no cause of complaint against them. It is worthy of note that, with the single exception of General Faiz Muhammad Khan of Baraki Rajan, the maliks of Logar subsequently acted in a manner entirely consistent with the promises that they then made, though it is impossible not to remember that the absence of Amin Muhammad from their councils had undoubtedly a great effect in confirming them in this praiseworthy line of conduct.

"As was anticipated, the departure of the troops from the Logar valley was immediately followed by the descent of the insurgent Zurmatis and other tribes, who quartered themselves upon the various villages and levied contributions upon the inhabitants, requesting them at the same time to join in arising against the English. This naturally led to constant disputes, the Logar is resolutely declining to join the proposed ghaza, and the insurgents insisting on having all their wants supplied. The only serious inconvenience which, as was foreseen, resulted from our departure from Logar regarded the important question of supplies, which daily became one of greater urgency. The grain stock of the preceding seasons had been all consumed, and the harvest in the ground was not yet ripe for the sickle. Until the third week in July, it was certain that there would be great difficulty in obtaining all that was requisite. "This was especially the case in the neighbourhood of the capital, where the demand had been so incessant, and such high prices had been obtained, that the districts of Chardeh Maidan, Musai, etc., etc., had parted with all their reserve stock. For some time past the rich and fertile provinces of Logar and Wardak had been the main source of supply, and our departure from Logar and the consequent impetus given to the designs of the insurgent leaders of Musa Khan's party in the south, at once closed the steady supply which had been hitherto coming in from it and the southern provinces.

"It therefore became apparent shortly after the arrival of the troops at Charasia that the commissariat could not feed them, and a return movement in the direction of Logar was thus unavoidable, being at the same time rendered politically feasible by the growing certainty that Abdur Rahman had no intention of engaging in active hostilities against the English.

"The troops halted for three days at Charasia, and this afforded all ranks an opportunity of visiting the city and the objects of interest in the neighbourhood, which was embraced with special eagerness by the native troops of all creeds. On the 26th June, the division marched back to Zahidabad, and in the course of four days reached Zargan Shahr, where a permanent camp was formed until the 27th July.

"The movement of the troops from Charasia was the signal for the hasty breaking up of all the rebel bands that had assembled in the Logar valley. The leaders and their followers again took to the summits of the hills and waited for events. These developed themselves shortly in a manner which, as regards these men, was equally unpleasant and unexpected.

"On the 30th June, news was received at Zargan Shar that Sardar Muhammad Husain Khan, who had been very active in fomenting the hostile feeling against us, had arrived at the large village of Patkao-i-Shahana, some 12 miles south of Zargan Shahr, accompanied by some 1,000 horse and foot, which were intended to form the nucleus of a much larger hostile gathering, and possibly to act in concert with Sardar Muhammad Hashim Khan.

"On receipt of this intelligence, General Hills at once decided on sending out the cavalry brigade to reconnoitre, and if a favourable opportunity offered, to atack and disperse the enemy; and, accordingly, on the morning of the 1st July, General Palliser, C.B., accompanied by the 1st Punjab Cavalry under Colonel Maclean, the 2nd Punjab Cavalry under Colonel Kennedy, C.B., and the 19th Bengal Lancers succeeded in coming up with some 800 men, who had nearly reached the safe cover of the hills, and of whom they killed some 200 with a comparatively slight loss on our side. The cavalry returned to camp in the evening, having been for fifteen hours uninterruptedly in the saddle and having ridden over 40 miles.

"The effect of this action was excellent; the hostile combination against us was entirely broken up, and Logar was at once freed from the presence of the ghazis. So great however was the terror caused by the sudden action of our troops, that immediate measures were necessary to prevent the inhabitants of Logar taking flight en masse. Reassuring letters were accordingly sent out the same evening, telling the inhabitants that they had nothing to fear, and praising them for their past abstention from joining the ghaza. As all the men engaged had come from Zurmat, and none of the Logaris were implicated, these letters had the desired effect, and the people remained quietly in their homes, and on the next day recommended sending supplies into our camp and into Kabul, where great distress was prevalent on account of the scarcity of food, which this suply from the Logar tended materially to alleviate.

"From the 1st July until the 27th of the same month, General Hills' division remained encamped at Zargan Shahr, and nothing of any importance occurred.

"On the 1st August the division encamped at Indaki in the Chardeh valley and on the 3rd August reached Kabul."

Supplies. With regard to the all-important question of supplies, it may perhaps be sufficient briefly to notice here that the supplies obtainable in the Logar valley are, to all intents and purposes, practically inexhaustible, and that an army could be maintained there for a very long period and find no difficulty whatever in supplying itself with all the necessaries of life both for man and beasts. The yearly crop of grain and of cereals of various kinds is immense; the grazing for camels is illimitable; and the supply of green forage and bhusa is ample for the supply of a very large force. (This is probably a somewhat exaggerated view of the resources of the Logar district, but there is no doubt that large quantities of supplies can be obtained there.) During the three months that the Ghazni division remained in Logar, there was never any real difficulty about supplies, though circumstances sometimes occasioned a brief temporary inconvenience. The inhabitants, however, reassured by the excellent behaviour of the troops and punctual payment for whatever was brought in, were ready to supply all that was necessary, save only at such times as they were restrained from doing so by the fear of surrounding ghazis. Their appreciation of the way in which they had been treated by us, and of the many advantages they had derived from our presence in the province, was evinced by their absolute refusal to join the ghazis when they assembled in the valley after our departure from Deh-i-Moghalan and previous to the action at Patkao-i-Shahana, and they acknowledged with gratitude the consideration and kindness which had been shown them.

"It must be remembered that the year 1880 was one of unusual dryness in Logar as in other parts of the country. Much land that was ordinarily cultivated was left untilled on this account, and a considerable quantity of the crops only produced half their yield owing to the impossibility of affording them sufficient irrigation. Notwithstanding this, supplies of all sorts were always forthcoming."

"Water. The water of the Logar river is excellent, and the irrigation canals drawn from the river distribute it all over the province. There is capital fishing in the river, and fish over 4 lbs. in weight were taken out of it with hook and line.

VILLAGES IN THE UPPER LOGAR (SOUTHERN DIVISION)

GROUPS OF VILLAGES.

1. BARAKI RAJAN -
   Contains 1,000 families, including the outlying hamlets. Inhabitants mostly Tajik.

2. BARAKI BARAK -
   500 families, Tajik.

3. PATKAO ROGHANI -
   100 families, mostly Tajik.

4. SHAH MAZAB -
   250 families, Stanazai branch of Ghilzais.

5. YUSUF KALA -
   200 families, Stanazai.

6. JABIB KALA
   200 families, Stanazai.

7. and 8. PATKAO-I-SHAHANA and KALA LIAS KHAN
   260 families, including 3 hamlets of Saiyids (50 houses, and one of Ahmadzais (12 houses), remainder of residents are Stanazais, Tajiks, and a few Mohamands.

9. MANGO KHEL and
10. FATEH KHEL   100 families, Stanazais.

11. UNI SAIYIDAN
    250 families and Saiyids and Tajiks.

12. HISARAK
    In village itself are 100 families of Tajiks and Liai Khels (a branch of the Stanazais). Attached to Hisarak are -
    4 hamlets of Liasi Khels -   45 families.
    2   "   " Tajiks -   20   "
    1   "   " Kizilbashis -   15   "
    3   "   " Popalzais -   40   "

13. MUGHAL KHEL
    50 families, Stanazai.

14. WAZIR KAREZ
    40 families, Hazara.

15. KALA-I-YAKUB   Are Government property,
16. KALA-I-HAKIM and   110 families, all Hazaras.
17. KHALLABAD

18. JUYAK
    40 families, Kizilbashis, and a few Afghans of various tribes.

19. PAIO KHEL and   25 families, Stnazai, and
20. TATTOR   Saiyid.

21. CHALOZAI
    250 families, Sulaiman Khel.

22. MOKHAND
    40 families, Mohmands.

Abstract of above.

Twenty-two village groups, containing approximately 3,535 families. All the above are included in the Southern Division of the Upper Logar. Notes. - To south of Logar proper, but included in the Kabul revenue accounts, lies -

CHARKH -
1,000 families of Tajiks occupying 4 villages, viz. -
    1. Kala-i-Nao   3. Garmawa
    2. Pingram   4. Nao Shahar.

VILLAGES IN THE UPPER LOGAR (NORTHERN DIVISION)

Groups of villages	Forts or Hamlets	of Families	Tribes
Kulangar Group	41	180	Khwajas
		60	Sayyids
		80	Tajiks
		10	Afghan
		30	Kizilbash and Hazaras
Purak Group	17	175	Astanazai (Ghilzai)
		15	Nasir "
		6	Tokhi "
Uni Sifla	2	20	Hotak "
Deh-i-Nao Amin al-Mulk	3	50	Parsiwan
Babus	2	120	Painda Khel, Sulaiman

Karez-i-Bashir	2	10	Khel	
Shulok	1	30	Gadai Khel, Ghilzai.	
Karez-i-Piaro Khel	1	30	Piaro Khel, Sulaiman Khel	
Karez-i-Mirwal	1	10	Ahmadzai, Ghilzai.	
Dadu Khel	2	100	" "	
Kar-ez-i-Saiyidaun	1	8	Saiyids.	
, TOTAL	93	934		
Add Southern Division	...	3,535		
GRAND TOTAL	...	4,469		

Families in Upper Logar, i.e., in the portion of the valley south of the defile called Tangi Waghjan, but exclusive of Charkh and Amir Kala and its vicinity.

VILLAGES IN THE LOWER LOGAR, i.e., NORTH OF THE TANGI WAGHJAN

VILLAGES	TRIBES	NUMBER OF FORTS OR HAMLETS	NUMBER OF FAMILIES	REMARKS
Zargan Shahar	1/3 Tajik 2/3 Ahmadzai	9	250	On direct road between Kushi and Kabul. Watered by karez.
Burg	Ahmadzai	4	100	To east of river Logar and close under the Koh-i-Sultan range of hills, watered by karez.
Surkhao	Ditto	8	120	
Mazgin	Tajik	1	30	
Karez-i-Daulat	Niazi and Ahmadzai.	1	10	Half-way between Zargan Shahar and Mirza Khel.
Kala-i-Nazir	Niazi	1	20	Between Karez-i-Daulat and Deh-i-Nao
Kala-i-Rahim Khan	Tajik		10	Close to Tangi Waghjan on left bank of Logar.
Waghjan	Ditto	1	20	On left bank of Logar.
Mughal Khel	Stanazai	7	70	On left bank of Logar.
Karez-i-Alam	Stanazai	1	10	On left bank of Logar.
Sukhbad	Hazara	1	40	On left bank of Logar.
Shahghasi	Ahmadzai and Hazara	1	10	On left bank of Logar.
Bagh-i-Sultan	Tajik	1	50	On right bank of Logar.
Deh-i-Nao	Tajik	4	150	On right bank of Logar.
Kala-i-Wazir	Hazara,	4	80	On right bank of

	Ahmadzai,	4	20	Logar.
	Tajik	2	30	
Mirza Khel	Ahmadazi	5	200	On left bank of Logar.
Kala-i-Kishin	Hazara	1	41	On left bank of Logar.
Muhammad Agha	Tajik	3	200	On right bank of Logar.
Kala Hafizulla	Stanzai	1	4	On right bank of Logar.
Kuti Khel	Stanzai	12	300	Ditto
Sher Afghan	Adramzai and	4	50	On left bank of Logar.
	Tajik	2	40	
Zahidabad	Miscellaneous	14	150	On both sides of Logar.
Gumran	Adramzai	1	20	On right bank.
Sangar Khel	Stanazai	3	100	On left bank.
Safed Sang	Tajik	1	5	On right bank.
Rahmatabad	Tajik	8	102	
Aubazak	Sahak			West of river Logar, in a valley towards Maidan. Karez water.
Auparan	Ahmadzai	5		East of river Logar and close under the hills. Karez water.
Dashtak	Hasankhel	5	40	On right bank of river Logar off the main road.
Shadkhana	Astanzai	1		Ditto
Kata Sang	Astanzai	2		
Musai Bala	Arab and Tajik	4	10	On left bank off the direct road to Kabul.
Musai	Ahmadzai	23	40	A continuation of valley of river Logar. Hamlets on both sides of the river off the Kabul road and out of sight of it.
	Hasankhel	23	160	
	Popalzai	23	250	
Kala-i-Nishan	Tajik	1	3	On west of Kabul road.
Nonias	Tajik	5	60	On west of Kabul road.
TOTAL HAMLETS		144	2,554	Families in Lower Logar.

Extract from Surgeon-Major Johnston's Chips from the Logar Valley.

"Regarding the domestic animals, although shepherds with the majority of their flocks migrate to Kurram and allied valleys in winter, a proportion are domiciled in the villages. The lambing season is from mid-March to mid-April. The farmers reckon that a ewe and she-goat carry five months, a cow ten, a mare eleven, and camel twelve months. The dumba are the sheep of the valley. They have a short flat tail and small ears. The mutton is good. They lamb in spring. The Hazara is a short-tailed variety. They never thrive in the

Logar, all getting out of condition from 'rot' or 'liver-fluke.' In Hazara the ewe is reputed to lamb in April and October, the dumba fattens in the Hazara hills, but only carries in spring. The Kuchi, Kohistan, or Turkistan sheep is very large, frequently carrying massive horns. The fibre of the muscle is coarse and the flesh rammy. The fat is deposited as a biped lobe in the caudal appendage. It has really no tail. The Ghilzai mountain sheep has a flat but small tail with long pendulous ears. The mutton is sweet and superior to the Hazara. Neither the Kuchi, Hazara, nor Ghilzai fatten in the valley. The last two are well set up, the fat chiefly depositing, as in the English sheep, around the kidney and along the flank.

"The cattle are small in stature, and the meat poor in quantity. The average yield of milch kine is four seers of milk daily; the specific gravity being 1026.

Ewes are regularly milked; their daily average is 10-5 chittaks specific gravity 1033.

"Goats. Both the large valley, and small hairy mountain, goats are excellent milk-producers giving an average of 10-3 chittaks daily, specific gravity 1029-6 (ninety-three observations).

"Mules of good transport qualities, although rather small, are occasionally bred; the mare is invariably the dam. A jenny is never covered, so there are no 'jennettes.'

"The ass is abundantly bred. They are small sturdy creatures with wonderful carrying ability.

"Horses are mostly galloways and ponies. The latter are excellent for baggage purposes.

"Camels are hardy and hairy, with broad forehead and narrow rat-like jowl. They are all well ribbed up and easily carry six maunds. Their hair yields 'pashm;' from the milk krut is prepared, while their droppings are stacked for fuel.

"Fowls. Much of the poultry is beautifully feathered and pencilled. From February to June, again in August and September, they usually lay two days on end with a bye-day following. In July they moult, and eggs are scarce. From October to January only an odd fowl or two lays. There are many varieties of fowl, resembling in size and taste the Dorking; the digits however differ. It produces a brownish egg quite equal to the large English fowl. The more ordinary small hen lays with the persistency of the Hamburgh, which it resembles. The Bantam is unknown. The game-cocks are very plucky and fight until victorious or exhausted.

"Dress. In summer a light cotton blouse, shirt, wide pyjamas, skull cap, pagri, and shoes are worn in the Logar. A wide blue skirt and pyjamas are affected by the women. Girls wear a long blue (sometimes adorned with gold stripes) short-bodied cotton gown.

"In winter a Kabul or Ghazni postin, Pyjamas of burzu (black barak from Kohistan), and a pair of long thigh leather snow boots made of cow or camel skin, and lined with felt, are universally worn.

"Neither the Kandahar felt kosai, the camel hair barak Hazara choga, nor the short lacing boots, so much patronised in Southern Afghanistan, are utilised.

"Manufactures. These are few. Pottery as surais, coarse felt rags, and blankets. Socks are made from sheep's hair only. Goats'skins are in the untanned state exclusively used for kidgi tents.

"Ethnology. There are two chief racial elements in the Logar valley, representing the Indo-Germanic and Mongolian Ettunic families. Of the Indo-Germanic, we have the Afghan, Tajik, and Kizilbash. The Hazara is of Mongolian origin.

"There has been considerable inter-crossing between the original

Persic Kizilbash and the Afghan. The Tajik is mostly Persic. Mongolian hybrids abound. In them the oblique eye is evanescent.

"The Afghans are the most numerous. They are subdivided into five sects—Ahmadzais, Adramzais, Kutikhels, Kharotis, and Mushwanis. The two first are chiefly small crafters and farm labourers. During the winter many of them prefer a migratory life in a more congenial clime living mainly by theft. The Kuti Khels are shepherds and drovers. The Kharotis are merchants and camel-breeders, while the Mushwanis are merchants and crafters.

"The Tajiks are the chief carriers and the Hazaras mostly farm servants.

"The Kizilbashis are mostly landed proprietors, who retain Hazaras, Ahmadzais or Adramzais as servants. They live on their estates, or serve the Crown as cavalry soldiers.

"Climatology. Time is reckoned from Mussulman New Year's Day (20th March). From mid-February to middle of April it rains incessantly; thence to 15th July clear weather with an occasional cloudy day is the rule; then comes a short sub-tropical summer of a month's duration, followed by two month's fair but sometimes very cloudy weather, during which the early morning hours are very cold; but the sun is still a warm orient ray.

"Snow falls by the end of October, and clothes the ground 3 to 5 feet deep until February. Heavy northerly winds scour the valley curling snow wreaths many yards in height. Throughout even the warmest months the nights are ever cool.

"Careful thermometric observations were recorded during May, June, and July, the result is summarised:

	Maximum	Minimum	Daily Range
May	90 F.	33 F.	80-2 F.
June	100 F.	51	6 F.
July	97 F.	51	87-3 F.

"The maximum thermometer was slung in a Kabul pal tent, opened on all sides, 3 feet from ground.

"The minimum was placed on a board in the open air.

"Earthquakes are common enough in March and April. They run across, never along, the valley, and are locally ever regarded as the precursor of misfortune.

"Thunder-storms are frequent during these months, hail-stones fall as large as pigeon's eggs seldom injuring man or beast. Both are betimes killed by lightning.

"Dust-whirls were very frequent during our three months' tour in the valley. They were remarkable for their impetuosity and columnar length. The electric drift was invariably from right to left.

"The atmospheric air was in June remarkably pure. The heliographic flash was read at 50 miles distance in a bee-line.

"The economic crops grown in the valley are:

Ajwain	Maize
Bean, field	Madder
Barley	Melons, water, two varieties,
Buckwheat	large turbooz, long thin.
Clover	" " Musk
Cabbage, blue drum-head	" " Rock
Cauliflower, large	(Pumpkin) bottle-necked
Carrots	" " round
Coriander	Mustard, three varieties
Cummin (scarce).	Onion, blue and white
Cucumber	Poppy
Dill	Raddish
Dalls	Rice

Egg-plant	Rye?
Flax, linseed	Sag, pot-herbs.
Fennel	Tares
Garlic	Tobacco, broad leaf
Gram, white	" " narrow leaf
Jowar, large millet	Turnip
Lettuce	Vines
Lucerne	Wheat
Leeks	

"The rotation of crops is well understood. Cereals and grass are grown on the same fields at an interval of two years. They manure with human dejecta and horse droppings. Cow and camel excreta are chiefly used for fuel. No field within the pale of irrigation lies fallow. Vines, the gandana leek and madder are topdressed before the snow falls. Their agricultural system may be thus summarised: The ground is ploughed, manured, watered; ploughed a second time. The seed is then sown, and from its briaring until it ripens water is plentifully irrigated through the crops.

"Wheat and allied grains are not, as in England, artificially desiccated. Irrigation is cut off and the piercing solar ray hardens and dries the grain in the ear.

"Farmers reckon on two principal crops—the spring, bari; and winter termai—corresponding, allowing for climatic influence, with the kharif and rabi of Hindustan.

"The spring crop is sown about 30th March and harvested in July. The winter sown about 20th October, and is also cut in July. An intermediate crop consisting chiefly of succulent vegetables, rice, and fodder for cattle, is sown early in June, and reaped about mid-October. The root of the madder does not ripen until it has been four years in the ground. Fennel attains a herbaceous character, and yields four years.

"Garlic, onions, moth and dall grow equally as spring and winter crops.

"The gandana leek is really an onion which has been trained as a perennial producer. The corm is left in the ground and the leafage used as leeks. The old corm shoots out cormlets and from these fresh leeks annually spring.

"There is a species of barley called jaodar which resembles rye so very closely that I am at present unable to detect any difference. It may possibly be a hybrid. The farmers tell me it is cultivated on arid soil by the poorer classes. The grain is dark outside, whitish internally. The flour and chapaties made of it are black. Jaodar is reputed to have originally grown of its own accord among the wheat-fields.

"Lucerne yields eight crops annually: the autumn one is twisted into ropes of hay, and stored."

LOGAR LAM   لوګرلم

A village in Laghman, consisting of the following hamlets occupied by Jabar Khel Ghilzais:

  (1) Kotlaha-i-Afzal Khan
  (2) Kala-i-Afzal Khan
  (3) Kala-i-Sikandar Khan
  (4) Kala-i-Mir Alam Khan.   (Warburton.)

LOHANI Or LOHANA   لوهانی (لواڼه)

Is the name now commonly given to a large number of Powindah tribes. As stated by certain of those tribes themselves, it includes not

only the descendants of Laharnai or Nuharnai, as he was also called, but all the descendants of his great-grandfather Ibrahim, and one still hears of Niazis and Dotanis and others being called Lohanis.
The similarity in the names of the Lohanis and Lowanas has, until quite recently, been the cause of much confusion in the minds of writers on border tribes and these two tribes have been confused not only with each other but with the Ghilzais. In the second edition of this Gazetteer, Part II, we find under heading "Lohani":
"The name which the Afghans give to the tribes who trade with Afghanistan and other countries, generally called by us Powindahs, such as the Nasirs, Sulaiman Khel, Kharoti, Daftiani, Maizak, Mia Khel, Mulla Khel, Andari, and Taraki."
As will be seen from Captain McMahon's note on the Ghilzais, five of the tribes given above are not Lohanis, but Ghilzais, i.e., the Nasirs, Sulaiman Khel, Kharotis, Andaris, and Tarakis. Again, in very recent maps we find the country of the Lowanas named Lohana, and in the "Gazetteer of the North-West Frontier" of 1886-87 we find the following:
"Their (Lohana) country is shown in the most recent survey map as situated at the head of the Khwandar (Kundar) valley immediately north of the Saran Kakars, southeast of the Nasirs and south of the Sulaiman Khel."
Now this country, so defined, belongs to Lowanas, and not Lohanis.
It may be mentioned that the correct name of the Lowanas is Lawunrs or Lowunrs. Owing to the extensive trade carried on by this tribe in salt, it was at one time supposed that this name was connected with "lun," the word commonly used by Punjabis for salt.
The following brief notes by Captain McMahon will suffice to explain how these tribes are in no way connected with each other:
Lohanis or Lowanas. "It has been shown above in the note on the Ghilzai tribe, that the Ghilzais are the descendants of Ghalzoe, the illicit son of Shah Husain, a Tajik, chief of Ghor, and Bibi Mato, the daughter of Bait or Baitani from whom the present Batanni (Bhittani) tribe claim descent. After the birth of Ghalzoe, a second son was born, named Ibrahim, and to distinguish him from his so-called illegitimate brother, his mother is said to have called him "Loedai," which would here mean 'he is the greater son.' From Loedai come the Lodis, who played an important part in the history of India. The following tree, according to Raverty, shows the descendants of Ibrahim:

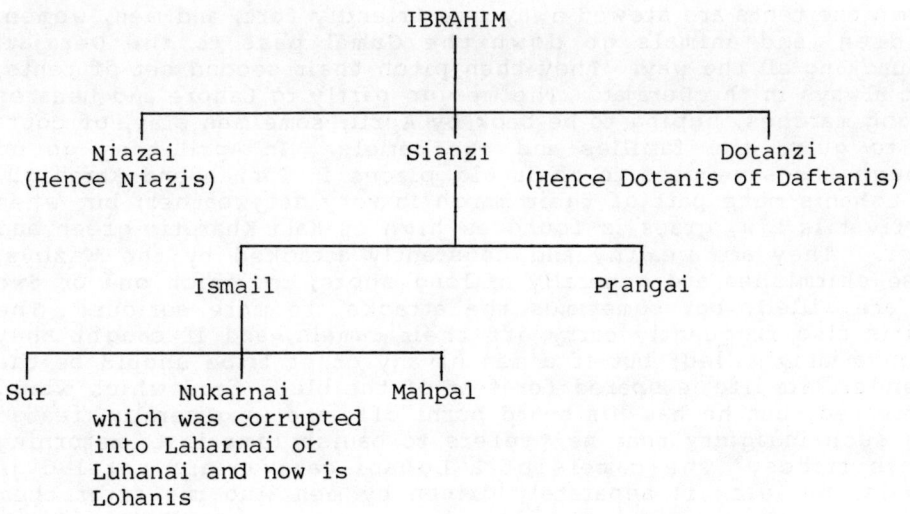

"The descendants of Nuharnai comprise the Maya Khel (Mia or Myan Khel), Tators, Marwats, Daulat Khel and others, and these therefore are the only sections who can rightly be called Lohanis. I have been given various genealogical trees by members of these tribes and in some of these Niazai is shown as a son of Laharnai. It is difficult now to ascertain the truth as the tribe seem to know very little regarding their descent. One hears them talking of other tribes such as the Mechan Khel, Isa Khel Kundis and others as Lohanis.

Luwanas. "As above noted the name of this tribe should more correctly be written Lowunr or Lawunr. The genealogical tree given below shows their descent from Kaiz-i-Abdur Rashid and proves that they are Parnis and have therefore no connection with the Lohanis:

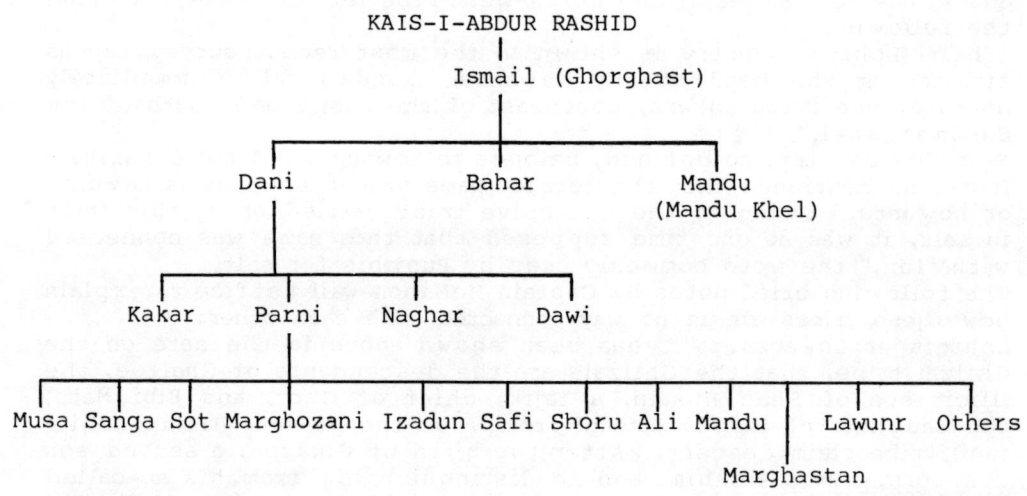

"In summer the Lohanis are said to live in fine large khizdi tents of felt near Pannah and Karabagh. The men are partly away in Bokhara and Samarkand trading, or buying and selling at Kabul. The women and children with a sufficient guard live in the tents. In autumn the tents are stowed away in a friendly fort, and men, women, children, and animals go down the Gumal pass to the Derajat, bivouacking all the way. They then pitch their second set of tents, kept always in the Derajat. The men go partly to Lahore and Benares by long marches, hoping to be back by April; some men stay, of course, to guard the families and the camels. In April they go up through the same pass to their old places in Pannah and Karabagh. The Lohanis make part of their march in very hot weather; but when the river is low, grass is found as high as Kala Kharoti; green and sweet. They are wealthy and constantly attacked by the Waziris; these skirmishes are generally at long shots, by which one or two men are killed, but sometimes the attacks are more serious. The Waziris also frequently carry off their camels, and if caught they are invariably killed; but if a man of any other tribe should be the offender, his life is spared for fear of the blood feud which would be created, but he has his beard burnt off, and is generally treated with such indignity that he prefers to banish himself to returning to his tribes. The camels of a Lohani caravan are not led in strings, but each is separately driven by men who run after them with heavy sticks and deep shouts of has! ha! ha! It is said they go quicker, as much as three miles an hour, by this method of driving them.

The Lohanis show their wealth by braiding the hair of their children with gold coins, and ornamenting their women with massive ear-rings, and covering their horses with expensive trappings. Young brides are carried on cushions of silk on the backs of camels most gorgeously hung with tassels, coins, and bells. The older married women are balanced against each other in kajawahs. On arriving at the ground they help to unload the camel, the girls draw water, and the men graze the camels. Their women seldom scold, and the men never, though they sometimes quarrel and fight. Their horses are peculiarly fine, generally 15 hands and upwards. Their arched crest, deep chests, and broad quarters are like those of the English horse. The heads small and well put on, but the legs are light for the weight, though by all accounts they never fail. The mares are kept for breeding, but the horses are sold for high prices to Hindu Rajas.

Generally there is not much order kept in their line of march, but when near the Waziris they keep more together. Parties of horsemen go before and behind, and the young men scour the hills as flanking parties."

(Broadfoot, Lumsden, Masson, McMahon, Benn.)

LOI KOI   لوی کوی

A valley passed through on the Tubbi route from Shutur Gardan to Jaji Thana. It is rather over 3 miles long, and in some places, is so rugged that horses can be led with great difficulty along the path, which is here and there blocked with boulders. The bed of the stream is only a few yards wide. The valley begins at the 3rd mile from the Shutur Gardan pass and ends at the 6th mile. (Spratt.)

LOKAR   لوکر

34-55 70-22 m. A village in Laghman. Inhabitants: Arokis. (Warburton.) The village is some 6 miles north of Alingar.

LOKHAI   لوخی

34-40 69-55 m. A village in the Khugiani country, about 10 miles east of Gandamak. It lies on the left bank of the Wazir Rud, and is a common halting place for kuchis. It was in this immediate neighbourhood that the Khugianis were defeated on the 2nd April 1879 (see "Official History of the Second Afghan War."). (Massey, I.B.C.) The village is northeast of Sarobi. Another village with this name is about 3 miles north of Chapriar, at 34-19 70-21 m. A pass with this name is located 34-21 69-52 G.

*LOKHAK   لخك

34-28 67-44 m. A village near Chargusha, about 4 miles north of the Helmand in Maidan province.

LOLA   لوله

33-40 68-34 m. A village northeast of Ghazni and about 6 miles west-southwest of Khwaja Khalan in Ghazni province.

LOLING   للنگ

The name applied to the lower part of the Turkoman Dara stream. At Kala Doab, the boundary at this point between the Ghorband district proper and Shaikh Ali country, the Loling river issues from a deep, narrow, rocky gorge on the right side of the valley called Tangi

531

Loling, and is as large as the Ghorband river. The latter above this point is about 20 feet wide and 2 feet deep; but below the juction becomes 20 yards wide and 3 feet deep, even over the shallows, while at most places it is much deeper and full of holes, 8 feet deep. The joint stream is very swift, and even in October is only passable at the occasional shallows, while with a very slight rise it becomes an impassable torrent. One bank is generally shelving gravel, and the other steep clay cliffs, 10 to 15 feet high.
A good camel road runs up the Tangi Loling, and at the upper end of the road divides into three branches. One leads to Dahan-i-Turkoman, the right one to Kotandar in Paghman, and the left to Parsa. The first of these joins the main Kabul-Hazijak road at Siah Sang, and is said to be a good and fairly level road. (Peacocke.)

LOMAN لومان
33-23 67-16 G. A locality in the Jaghuri Hazara country. (See Military Report on Hazara, Part II.)

*LONDI لوندی
34-54 69-45 m. A village located on a tributary of the Tagab, about 10 miles northeast of Tagab in Kapisa province.

LON KAD لونقد
Said to be a village 136 miles from Jalabad, on the Alingar river, and to consist of 5,000 houses of "Wamar" Kafirs. (Leech.)

LUCHA KHAN لچه خان
34-44 69-8 m. A village in the Koh Daman of Kabul, containing 80 houses. (Kinloch.) Recent maps show the spelling Lochakan. (LWA.)

*LUDIN KALAI لودین کی
32-7 67-28 m. A village located near Sherzai Kalai, north-northwest of Shinkai Ghar in Ghazni province.

LUJI See LAJI لجی

*LUKH لخ
34-33 67-27 m. A village located near Talkhak, north of the Dara-i-Shorshori in Bamian province.

LUKHAI لخی
34- 69-. Elevation 4,700 feet. A spot on the road between Gandamak and Jagdalak, about 9 miles from the former. Here, at about 1-1/2 miles from the right bank of the Surkhab, some level fields afford a good camping ground, and about 1 mile further west, near the old Pezwan post, room could be found for 2 brigades by scattering units. An ample water-supply is afforded by two streams, and a spring to the northwest of the post would provide good drinking water for 1,000 men. The position of this pring is well marked by a path of green grass on the black hillside. Supplies are only to be got with difficulty, if at all. Grass is procurable from the Hisarak valley; fuel is scarce. (Malleson.)

LUKHAI Or PEZWAN لخی (پیزوان)
34-21 70-52 G. Elevation 5,180 feet. A pass on the road between Gandamak and Jagdalak, being about 11 miles from the former and 10 from the latter. It affords a most commanding position, and from here heliographic communication can be maintained with Gandamak, Jagdalak fort and any other station that may be chosen in the Karkacha hills.

At about 1-1/2 miles from the crest, on the Gandamak side, are the ruins of a post built by us during the second Afghan war, which was usually garrisoned by about 500 men.

The name Pezwan is now (1907) unknown locally, though it was recognized by the Ghilzai camel-drivers who accompanied the Dane Mission to Kabul in 1905. The pass itself, and the whole country in its neighborhood, is now known as Lukhai. (Malleson.)

LUKI   لوکی
34- 70-. A plain in the Jalalabad valley, at the foot of the hills, south of the Kabul river, affording good pasturage. The pastoral Ghilzais come down with great flocks of camel and sheep in autumn to graze. (MacGregor.) Recent maps show the spelling Lokhay, at 34-19 70-21 m. (LWA.)

*LUKU   لوکو
34-42 69-2 m. A village located northwest of Haji Payk in Kabul province.

LULIDAR See LALIDAR   للیدر

LULUK   لولك
One of the chief settlements in the Skorigul in Kafiristan, consisting of a scattered hamlet of houses indifferently built. (Robertson.)

LUNI   لونی
A section of the Jaji tribe, who have eight forts, with 200 houses, and can muster 400 fighting men. This is probably the same as Lumsden's Lehwanas section. (Agha Abbas.)

LUTDEH See BRAGAMATAL   لوتده
35-40 71-21 m.

*MABATKHEL   مابتخیل
33-44 69-3 m. A village located north of the Spin Kamar and southwest of the Gardez-Kabul highway in Paktia province.

MACHALGU   مچلغو (مچلگو)
33-47 69-23 m. A village in Zurmat. It lies about 17 miles northeast of Gardez, on the road from that place to Kurram via the Mirzakai Kotal. The inhabitants are Khwazaks. It is a large and fertile place, the principal village being surrounded by forts and hamlets. (I.B.C.)

MACHALGU   مچلگو
33- 69-. A range of hills, an offshoot of the western Sulaiman system, which, running in a southwesterly direction from the Shutur Gardan pass, divides the Logar valley and Kharwar from Zurmat. (I.B.C.)

MACHIMMA   مچمه
Elevation 3,370 feet. A shaikh village in the Narigul, a tributary of the Kunar, consisting of nine houses and some sheds, enclosed by a square wall. It is built 200 feet above the Narigul main stream, on a long, low, narrow spur, which separates the main valley from the ravine leading to Arombrom in the Arundugul (Arnawai). Both above and below the village there is cultivation, but most of the fields are in the ravine leading up to Arombrom. (Robertson.)

MADA KHEL مده خیل
A subdivision of Chakmanis. A village with this name is located some 4 miles south of Chamkani on the Gabrtoi stream, at 33-46 69-48 m. (LWA.)

MADARDAND مدردند
34- 70-. A place in the Jalalabad district between Pezwan and Jagdalak. A column was encamped at this place in June 1880, to protect the road from marauding bands, as petty raids and the destruction of the telegraph line between the two posts were of constant occurrence. (I.B.C.)

MADAR-I-WAZIR مادر وزیر
34- 69-. A fort included in Allah-ud-din in the Chardeh valley of Kabul; thirty families of Gadi Hazaras. (I.B.C.)

MADINUI, AB-I مدینوی
A tributary of the Helmund.

MADOK-BAROK مدوك بارك
34-8 70-36 G. A village in the Kot division of the Jalalabad district, between Kamal Khel and Andarani-i-Bala. Inhabitants. Tirais. (Jenkyns.)

*MADRASA مدرسه
33-7 68-32 m. A village located southeast of the Jarkana Ghar and northwest of Mushkhel in Ghazni province.

MADUGAL مدگل
A tribe of Siahposh Kafirs who inhabit the short tract of country between the Kam and the Katirs of the Bashgul valley. They are collected into three villages, viz., Bagalgrom or Muman, Sasku, Mungul. They possess also a few Hamlets. Robertson.)

*MADU KACH مدوکچ
33-5 68-55 m. A village located near Jabbar Khel on the way northwest to the city of Ghazni.

*MAGAR مگر
32-53 69-16 m. A village located on the Kizwak stream, southeast of Urgun in Paktia province.

MAGAS مگس
33- 69-. A village in Khost, said to be eight miles north of Matun, and to contain 120 houses. Overlooking the village is said to be an old fort, in the ruins of which ancient coins are frequently found. (I.B.C.)

*MAGHAK مغك
34-26 67-48 m. A village on a tributary of the Helmand, northwest of Behsud in Bamian province.

MAHIGIR ماهی گیر
34-57 69-14 m. A village in the plain of Bagram, on the canal of the same name. The canal was made by Timurlang, and it is taken from the Ghorband river at the point where it issues from the hills, and has a course of ten miles, irrigating the lands of Baian and Mahigir. (Masson.)

MAHIPAR ماهيپر
34-39 69-42 A. The name given to a waterfall in the Tangi Gharu, where the combined waters of the Kabul and Logar rivers plunge bodily over a height of 90 feet. (Malleson.)

*MAHMUD RAQI محمود راقی
35-0 69-21. Mahmud Raqi is a loye woleswali in Kapisa, now Parwan province. The woleswali comprises an area of 121 square kilometers and has an agricultural population that has been estimated at from 9,928 to 10,999. The woleswali is bounded in the east by Nejrab, in the south by Kuh-i-Safi, in the west by Baghram and Charikar, and in the north by Kuhestan. Mahmud Raqi includes some 64 villages, of which one has more than 500 inhabitants. The villages are listed in the PG as follows: Ashur Khel, Kol Gai, Ataullah Khel, Haroki Sufla, Khanan Khel, Khodayar Khel, Khum-i-Robah, Dawud Khel, Darba Fan, Dangar Khel, Deh Bali, (Deh Babi), Nasrat Khel (Ezat Khel), Deh Baba Ali, Rahman Khel, Qala Afghanan, Taj Mohammad Khel, Rasul Khel, Sar Band, Sor Ghal, Abdullah Khel, Shukhi, Shahbaz Khel, Qala Sayed Khan, Saifuddin Khel, Ibadullah Khel (Abdullah Khel), Alam Sher Khel, Ali Khel, Sabah Khel, Ghazi Khel, Ghani Khel, Qazi Khel, Qorotak, Qazak, Qalacha, Qala-i-Safed, Kakari, Imam Khel, Jolayan, Surghondi, Zaghgir, Qala-i-Sher Khan, Qala-i-Malik, Qol-i-Babur, Qol-i-Shaghasi, Kaka Khel, Kalota, Korataz, Mohammad Omar Khel, Mahmud Khel, Morad Khwaja, Molla Khel, Molla Zada Khel, Molla Faqir Khel, Sayad, Sayed Mir Khel, Nazar Khel, Nauabad, Wali Khel, Hazara, Ado Khel, Haroki Ulya, Yaro Khel, Jamchi, Shabaz Khel, Qarya-i-Kochiha, Qala-i-Mokher Ahmad, Changagi, Moshwani, an Shahi Khel.

MAHREZ ماهريز
34- 70-. A village in the Hisarak subdivision of the Jalalabad district, about 6 1/2 miles south-southwest of Mazina, on the stream of that name. From here two tracks lead over the Safed Koh into Kurram, one by the Papin, and the other by the Orgaz pass. (I.B.C.)

MAI BOLAK مای بلاق
A village in the Ghazni district, inhabited by about 500 Andaris. (Broadfoot.)

MAIDAN Now WARDAK ميدان (وردك)
34-27 68-48. A province in east-central Afghanistan which comprises an area of 9,699 square kilometers and an agricultural population estimated at from 113,812 to 148,517. The province is bounded in the west and northwest by Bamian, in the north by Parwan, in the east by Kabul and Logar, and in the south by Ghazni. Wardak is divided into the woleswalis of Behsud 1 and 2, Chak-i-Wardak, Sayyidabad, and Maidan Shar, and into the alaqadaris of Jalriz, Nerkh, Dai Mirdad, and Jaghatu. The capital of the province is Kota-i-Ashro. For woleswali lists from the Department of Statistics of the Ministry of Agriculture and Irrigation see the tables below. (LWA)
In 1914 the province was described as follows;
The district of Maidan consists of the upper part of the valley of the Kabul river and extends to within 20 miles of Kabul city. It is bounded on the south by the Wardak valley belonging to the Ghazni district, on the west and north by Besud and Shaikh Ali Hazara country, and on the east by the Kabul and Logar districts. The district is well irrigated and richly cultivated, and it is studded with numerous forts and villages. Large quantities of supplies of all kinds for man and beast are procurable form Maidan, in excess of the requirements of its population, and camel forage is plentiful.

Administrative Divisions of Maidan (Wardak) Province

میدان ولایت

04—MAYDAN

- 0401 Maydan Shar
- 0402 Jalrez
- 0403 Nerkh
- 0404 Chake Wardak
- 0405 Day Mirdad
- 0406 Markaze Behsud (1)
- 0407 Behsud Part 1 (2)
- 0408 Sayyidabad
- 0409 Jaghatu

509

ESTIMATE OF AGRICULTURAL POPULATION AND AREA UNDER CULTIVATION

	Villages	Agricultural Population	Landlords	Lands under Cultivation in Jaribs			Lands under Cultivation in Hectares		
				Irrigated	Non-Irrig.	Total	Irrigated	Non-Irrig.	Total
MARKAZ-I-BEHSUD	14	43,960	3,380	21,100	—	21,100	4,220	—	4,220
BEHSUD 2 (GARDANDEWAL)	36	90,210	7,320	51,330	5,420	56,750	10,266	1,084	11,350
CHAKE-I-WARDAK	23	50,130	3,020	6,670	—	6,670	1,334	—	1,334
SAYYIDABAD	43	75,960	4,600	9,000	3,400	12,400	1,800	680	2,480
MAIDAN SHAR	10	20,130	3,290	6,490	—	6,490	1,298	—	1,298
JAGHATU	17	21,180	1,290	6,680	—	6,680	1,336	—	1,336
JALRIZ	12	32,790	3,070	6,130	—	6,130	1,226	—	1,226
DAI MIRDAD	14	26,190	980	5,090	—	5,090	1,018	—	1,018
NERKH	14	22,190	2,480	15,520	250	15,770	3,104	50	3,154
TOTAL	183	382,740	29,430	128,010	9,070	137,080	25,602	1,814	27,416

STATISTICAL ESTIMATE OF LIVESTOCK BY WOLESWALIS AND ALAKADARIS

	Sheep	Karakul Sheep	Goats	Cattle	Buffaloes	Camels	Horses	Donkeys	Mules	Poultry
MARKAZ-I-BEHSUD	68,990	—	4,300	10,600	—	130	—	6,490	—	29,330
BEHSUD 2 (GARDANDEWAL)	112,500	—	8,140	24,780	—	260	—	16,840	—	32,900
CHAKE-I-WARDAK	2,430	—	2,670	3,290	—	—	—	1,280	—	46,760
SAYYIDABAD	4,330	—	3,440	7,360	—	—	—	3,620	—	49,450
MAIDAN SHAR	1,800	—	920	1,870	—	20	—	2,070	—	22,990
JAGHATU	3,560	—	970	3,210	—	—	—	3,090	—	33,500
JALRIZ	4,320	—	—	3,360	—	30	—	3,760	—	34,370
DAI MIRDAD	5,570	—	4,870	2,060	—	—	—	3,150	—	26,230
NERKH	3,850	—	4,290	3,390	—	10	—	2,260	—	17,820
TOTAL	207,350	—	29,600	59,920	—	450	—	42,560	—	293,350

PRODUCTION OF AGRICULTURAL CROPS—IN KABULI SEERS

	Grains			Vegetables	Other Crops		Fruits
	Irrigated	Non-Irrig.	Total		Industrial Crops	Other Temp. Crops	
MARKAZ-I-BEHSUD	711,200	–	711,200	465,300	–	377,200	150,880
BEHSUD 2 (GARDANDEWAL)	1,828,000	34,970	1,862,970	1,132,560	–	460,000	371,680
CHAKE-I-WARDAK	249,600	–	249,600	67,320	–	55,200	46,000
SAYYIDABAD	324,800	21,710	346,510	150,480	3,500	144,900	51,520
MAIDAN SHAR	203,600	–	203,600	285,120	1,750	55,200	92,000
JAGHATU	250,400	–	250,400	146,520	–	20,700	46,000
JALRIZ	193,600	–	193,600	269,280	–	105,800	42,320
DAI MIRDAD	174,800	–	174,800	156,420	–	41,400	57,040
NERKH	540,000	1,820	541,820	342,540	1,750	276,000	42,320
TOTAL	4,476,000	58,500	4,534,500	3,015,540	7,000	1,536,400	899,760

LAND UNDER IRRIGATION AND SOURCES OF IRRIGATION

	Area in Jaribs					Number of Sources			
	Canals	Springs	Karez	Wells	Total	Canals	Springs	Karez	Wells	Water Mills
MARKAZ-I-BEHSUD	16,950	4,150	—	—	21,100	39	37	—	—	121
BEHSUD 2 (GARDANDEWAL)	26,540	24,790	—	—	51,330	124	142	—	—	283
CHAKE-I-WARDAK	2,370	2,190	2,110	—	6,670	73	18	32	—	69
SAYYIDABAD	4,120	2,400	2,480	—	9,000	122	136	144	—	89
MAIDAN SHAR	6,470	20	—	—	6,490	27	2	—	—	42
JAGHATU	—	5,430	1,250	—	6,680	46	77	104	—	53
JALRIZ	5,670	330	130	—	6,130	46	15	5	—	55
DAI MIRDAD	1,610	1,680	1,800	—	5,090	62	28	10	—	63
NERKH	10,910	2,480	2,130	—	15,520	50	64	41	—	47
TOTAL	74,640	43,470	9,900	—	128,010	589	519	336	—	822

TOTAL CULTIVABLE LAND, BY CROPS—IN KABULI JARIBS

	Grains Irrigated	Grains Non-Irrig.	Total	Vegetables	Industrial Crops	Other Crops	Fruits	Total Cultivated Land
MARKAZ-I-BEHSUD BEHSUD 2 (GARDANDEWAL)	17,780	—	17,780	2,350	—	1,640	820	22,590
CHAKE-I-WARDAK	45,700	2,690	48,390	5,720	—	2,000	2,020	58,130
	6,240	—	6,240	340	—	240	250	7,070
SAYYIDABAD	8,120	1,670	9,790	760	100	630	280	11,560
MAIDAN SHAR	5,090	—	5,090	1,440	50	240	500	7,320
JAGHATU	6,260	—	6,260	740	—	90	250	7,340
JALRIZ	4,840	—	4,840	1,360	—	460	230	6,890
DAI MIRDAD	4,370	—	4,370	790	—	180	310	5,650
NERKH	13,500	140	13,640	1,730	50	1,200	230	16,850
TOTAL	111,900	4,500	116,400	15,230	200	6,680	4,890	143,400

TOTAL CULTIVABLE LANDS—IN KABULI JARIBS

	Total	Pastures	Forests	Under Cultivation	Fallow Lands
MARKATZ-I-BEHSUD	84,250	63,090	60	21,100	4,220
BEHSUD 2 (GARDANDEWAL)	161,590	104,840	—	56,750	12,940
CHAKE-I-WARDAK	19,620	12,950	—	6,670	1,330
SAYYIDABAD	26,850	14,350	100	12,400	3,500
MAIDAN SHAR	20,840	14,350	—	6,490	1,300
JAGHATU	20,460	13,770	10	6,680	1,330
JALRIZ	20,490	14,330	30	6,130	1,220
DAI MIRDAD	20,020	14,930	—	5,090	1,020
NERKH	29,760	13,990	—	15,770	3,240
TOTAL	403,880	266,600	200	137,080	30,100

A peculiar kind of grain called "bakuli" grows in abundance, which resembles the Arabian horse-bean, and when crushed makes excellent food for horses. The average elevation of the inhabited portion of the district may be taken at 7,500 feet. The inhabitants are chiefly Umar Khel Ghilzais. At the eastern end of the Maidan valley proper, where it is very narrow and well calculated for defence, is an old fort, called Sar-i-Sanga. Hough thought this the strongest ground between Ghazni and Kabul, the heights affording a most commanding position, while the ground to the rear is not good for cavalry. However, a column advancing by the right could get in the rear of the position and then ascend the hills. Here on the 16th September 1842 General Nott defeated Shams-ud-din Khan, who with a force of 12,000 had taken up a succession of strong mountain positions to intercept his march on Kabul.

To the south of the main valley is a small branch valley known as Nirkh. It is entered from the east, and is surrounded by hills on its other sides. It was visited by our troops in 1879, and some of its villages were destroyed.

During the Afghan campaign of 1879-80, the Maidanis were conspicuous for their hostility to the British, and Muhammad Jan was able to raise a large contingent from amongst the inhabitants, when he advanced to Sherpur in December of the former year. (Masson, Hough, Havelock, Moorcroft, Campbell, I.B.C.)

"Maidan contains about 9,000 houses occupied by the following sections of the Ghilzai tribe, of which the Umar Khel section predominate:

"Amar Khel, Ismail Khel, Ibrahim Khel, Piaru Khel, Painda Khel, Chinzais, Rustam Khel, Ismail Khel. There are also three Tajik villages in the district of Maidan, viz., Zalred, Takana, Sarichasma, containing in all about 1,000 families. The revenue of Maidan amounts to two lakhs of Kabuli rupees." (Molloy.)

The Kabul-Bamian road, via the Unai pass, traverses Maidan from east to west. It is practicable for all arms, but would require some work on it before it is fit for wheeled traffic. The Kabul-Ghazni route passes through from north to south. It was traversed in 1880 by heavy artilery. Faiz Muhammad, nephew of General Ghulam Haidar Khan, is Hakim of Maidan at the present time. (I.B.C.)

The name Maidan is also applied to the Kabul river valley from Kot-i-Ashru down to the head of the Lalandar gorge. (Wanliss.)

*MAIDAN   میدان
34-42 70-14 G. A village about 4 miles northeast of Tirgari in Laghman province.

MAIDAN-I-KHUNI   میدان خونی
Elevation 11,830 feet. A halting place in the Kaoshan glen, 17 1/2 miles above its junction with the Ghorband valley, on the road leading over the Kaoshan pass into the Khinjan valley. There is no village at Maidan-i-Khuni; it is simply a small plateau between the road and the stream. There is room for a brigade to bivouac here, with a good and abundant water-supply; fuel probably sufficient for cooking purposes; supplies available in small quantities from lower down the glen. The place is said to have derived its name from the fact of a detachment of troops having once perished here in a snowstorm.

One mile above Maidan-i-Khuni the Kaoshan glen is joined from the northwest by the Chagalawez glen. (I.B.C.)

MAIDAN-I-PAI KOTAL   میدان پای کوتل
34- 67-. Elevation 10,200 feet. The name locally applied to a

halting place on the main Kabul-Hazarajat-Daulat Yar road, 101 1/4 miles from Kabul and 130 1/4 miles from Daulat Yar.

*MAIDAN SHAHR ميدان شهر
34-27 68-48. Maidan Shahr is a woleswali in Maidan (Wardak) province. The woleswali comprises an area of 351 square kilometers and has an agricultural population that has been estimated at from 6,708 t 14,057. The woleswali is bounded in the west and northwest by Jalriz, in the north and east by Paghman, and in the south by Muhamad Agha and Nerkh.
Maidan Shahr includes 110 villages. The villages are listed in the PG as follows: Piyaro Khel, Qala-i-Abdul Rashid, Qala-i-Ismail, Belal Khel, Qala-i-Sikander, Qala-i-Abul Wadud, Qala-i-Lalo Khel, Mohammad Khel, Qala-i-Abdul Aziz, Jani Khel, Ibrahim Khel, Qala-i-Farzail, Qala-i-Yar Mohd, Mashi Khel, Gul Ahmad Khel, Qala-i-Kashmiri, Qala-i-Haji Mohd. Akbar, Qala-i-Akhundzada, Qala-i-Abdul Wadud, Qala-i-Mohammad Rahim, Qala-i-Mohd. Osman, Qala-i-Malik, Qala-i-Ziyarat, Qala-i-Mohammad Omar, Qala-i-Mohammad Ayub, Qala-i-Ahmad Jan, Qala-i-Akhundzada, Qala-i-Chinzai, Qala-i-Nazar Khel, Qala-i-Bahadur, Qala-i-Delawar, Khudaye Nur, Shirindel, Qarya-i-Deh Afghanan, Qala-i-Zainulabeddin, Qala-i-Kuhna, Qala-i-Shahbaz, Qala-i-Mohamad Siddiq, Qala-i-Deh Afghanan, Qala-i-Malik Mohd. Hashim, Qala-i-Kochiha, Qarya-i-Zebdagh, Qala-i-Sayed Alem, Nahr-i-Folad, Qala-i-Pahlawan, Qala-i-Malik Nur Mohd., Qala-i-Ghulam Jan, Qala-i-Lashkar, Rustam Khel wa Charka, Qarya-i-Nayeb Qubad, Qala-i-Ashrat, Wala-i-Taslim, Qala-i-Abdul, Qala-i-Nur Khan Khel, Qala-i-Osman, Qala-i-Abdul Jalil, Qala-i-Haji Khangul, Qala-i-Shahbaz, Qala-i-Akhund Khel, Qala-i-Kota-i-Ashro Khel, Qala-i-Mulla Khel, Mami Khel, Landi Khel, Maro Khel, Sangar Khel-i-Charka, Qala-i-Laghmani Kharuti, Qala-i-Mohmand, Qala-i-Omara Khan, Qawm-i-Ido Khel, Kuhna Khumar, Qarya-i-Abdul Jabar, Ganda, Qala-i-Burj, Dara-i-Alimi , Qala-i-Kuhna, Qala-i-Gul Muhd. Qala-i-Fateh, Qala-i-Ahangaran, Qala-i-Nau, Qarya-i-Amar Khel, Qarya-i-Ghulam Haidar, Qarya-i-Akhundzada, Badin Khel, Qala-i-Mohammad Hashim, Qala-i-Khan Shirin, Qala-i-Maulawi, Qala-i-Sayyid Ghulam, Qala-i-Nasuzai, Qala-i-Welayat, Busraq-i-Charaka, Char Qala, Qala-i-Karez, Qala-i-Noman-i-Nur Khel, Qala-i-Nau, Qala-i-Sher Khan, Qala-i-Khwaja khel, Qala-i-Abdul Hakim, Qala-i-Negan, Qala-i-Bazi, Qarya-i-Ahmad Khan, Ker Lori Khel, Qala-i-Mirakai, Qala-i-Haji Mushko, Qala-i-Siyah Pitab, Qala-i-Mohammad Sarwar, Qala-i-Asad Khan, and Awal Khel.

MAIMAI مای مای
A settlement of the Qaraqul-daghi section of Sehpai Dai Zangi Hazaras.

MAIMAI, AB-I See UJARISTAN مای مای

MAJAB مجاب
A dara draining northeast through the Dai Mirdad district to the Logar river.

MAJARIN مهاجرین
A term applied in Afghanistan to refugees who have settled in the country. (Peart.) The proper spelling is Muhajirin. (LWA)

MAJIL مجل
A village in the Alishang valley, 88 miles from Jalalabad, on the road to Farajghan. It contains 300 houses of "Pashais." (Leech.)

MAKANAK مكنك
A section of the Polada Hazaras.

MAKHBIL See MUKHBIL مخبل

*MAKHDUM مخدوم
34-8 68-31 m. A vilage located on the Dara-i-Jelga in the Chak-i-Wardak area of Maidan province.

MAKNI See PANJSHIR مكنی

MAKSUD مقصود
A subsection of the Besud Hazaras.

MAKU ماكو
One of the principal mountains in the range to the west of Ghazni. (Mastings.)

*MAKULA ماكوله
34-54 68-39 m. A village located on a tributary of the Ghorband, about 2 miles south of Surkho Parsa in Parwan province.

MALAZAI ملازی
35-6 69-22 G. A village in the upper Panjshir glen, on the right bank of the stream, half a mile below Anaba, containing twenty housed of Tajiks. Here the road down the glen turns to the left to cross the stream, on the farther side of which it ascends the Gardan Chatha--See "Firaj."
In October 1886 the stream at this point was 60 yards wide and 2 feet deep, with a stony, but not rocky, bottom. The banks are low and easy, and artillery could cross without difficulty. (Shahzada Taimus.)

MALIKDAN ملكدان
A halting place in the Shakin Algad in Birmal, on the road form Shakin to Urgun and about ten miles from the former. There is (1896) a temporary village of about 20 Saifali houses here. Fuel, water and grazing are obtainable here but there is no cultivation. (I.B.C.)

MALIK DOST ملك دوست
A fort in the Chardeh valley of Kabul, included in the township of Allah-ud-din. Inhabitants: Gadi Hazaras; 50 houses, 4 towers. (I.B.C.)

*MALIK KHEL ملك خیل
34-11 68-41 m. A village located on a stream 2 miles north of Langar and west of the Ghazni-Kabul road in Maidan province. Other places with this name are located a few miles east of Kolangar in the Zarghun Shahr area in Logar province, 34-6 69-9 m.; on the Ghazni-Kabul highway, about 30 miles northeast of Ghazni, at 33-55 68-40 m.; southeast of Mukur in Ghazni province, at 32-48 67-49 m.; near Janikhel in Ghazni province, at 32-46 68-25 m.

MALIK MIANDAD ملك میانداد
A fort in the Mangal country. It contains 30 houses, and can turn out 100 fighting men. There is continually rain in this place. (Agha Abbas.)

545

*MALIMA ملیمه
   35-19 69-38 m. A village located on a tributary of the Panjshir, southeast of Astana in (Kapisa) Parwan province.

MALISTAN مالستان
   33-18 67-10 A. Malistan is a woleswali in Ghazni province. The woleswali comprises an area of 1,930 square kilometers and has an agricultural population that has been estimated at from 20,226 to 47,166. The woleswali is bounded in the east by Jaghori, in the north by Nawar, in the west by Ajrestan and Oruzgan, and in the south by Dai Chupan. Malistan has about 141 villages, of which about 21 have more than 500 inhabitants. The villages are listed in the PG as follows: Julga-i-Malang, Siyah Khak, Nahor-i-Qozi, Qajnaghtu, Mala Kasha, Shoghla, Khar Qol, Kekak, Maidan, Jasha, Shina Ghorjak, Siyah Qol, Moradina, Qol Adam, Mulki, Abdana, Pul-i-Haji Bashir, Godal, Qarya-i-Kamarak, Bocha, Siyah Shaghal (Siyah Shaghai), Madar Qol, Kor Sang (Kalo-Sang), Charshanba, Kosh Dad (Munduk), Sang Roz Wa Khosh Roz (Komov Mazur), Baloghu, Surkh Joye, Khordak Zayedah, Qafzai, Hasan Baluch, Bad Ulum, Nau Deh, Sabzak, Ulum-i-Benafshan (Belqishan), Kundali, Siyah Khasha, Lal Chak-i-Mulki, Alqublan, Bughra, Ghaighantu, Muridi, Jambud, Pul-i-Pain, Shina Deh, Shina Ya Pushta-Khana, Balagha, Nezar, Sabz Darah, Shatu, Sokhta-i-Sabz Darah, Bacha Lal, Ghar Sang, Dahba, Kohna Deh, Miyan Gul, Moye Tu, Monda Darakht, Oli, Takrak, Seh Paye, Chehel Baghtu, Qarya-i-Sar Nawah, Qarya-i-Miyana, Madak, Quldi Ulya Jaka (Awly-Pashi), Qandi Jaka (Tala-Qandi), Dewana Bulagh, Kalani Zaida, Kalan-ti Kamri, Konda Bed, Jow Shu, Mushyana Khana, Ahan Kushta, Sadak (Zardak), Tughlu, Nurak, Aspa, Wardah Malang, Sang Darah, Shaghal Dara, Nasi (Bashi), Khar Bed Bashi, Rubat Bashi, Qol-i-Khoshi, Laghar Joye, Kosha, Qol-i-Yahya, Talkhak, Mobad, Naizar, Suka, Dayzi, Ghaighantu, Paye Julga, Jana (Jaka Pashi), Khoshhal, Gul Koh, Reg Joy-i-Nawah, Dahan Dawrah, Nawah Julga, Shah Tapa, Qalak, Shab Bakhair-i-Nawah Julga, Archa, Aye Barka, Siyah Sang, Qarya-i-Haji, Shabar, Godal-i-Mir Ahmad, Sham Qol, Nawah Jelga Shela, Sher Dagh (Jani Sher-Dagh), Gul Koh, Yar Say, Ghulam Haji (Ghulam Ji), Jorah, Jakmatur, Bocha, Kamarak, Jawzi, Qarya-i-Tamta, Qab Joye, Qab Joye-i-Ulya, Qab Joy-i-Pushta, Jangal, Kadu, Oligak, Ligai, Sar Bed, Dadi, Zangar, Dai Baraka, Qarya-i-Dala (Saya-Khana), Qorughchi, Ghamquli-i-Mir Ahmad (Qarya-i-Mir Ahmad), Baghar-i-Mir Ahmad, and Ghaighantu-i-Mir Ahmad.

MALLIZAI ملی زی
   32-47 68-32 G. A main division of the Nasirs. Also a village with this name. (LWA)

MALU KHEL ملوخیل
   A village on the right bank of the Karaia river, in the Jaji country between Zabardast Kala and Ali Khel. (Lumsden.)

*MAMA ماما
   33-31 67-57 m. A village located on the Qol-i-Surkhab and east of the Dasht-i-Nawar in Ghazni province.

*MAMAGUL KHWAR ماماگل خوار
   34-43 70-42 m. A village located northeast of the Dara-i-Nur and north of the Kunar river in Kunar province.

MAMAKA ماماکه
   A section of the Dai Kundi Hazaras.

MAMA KALA ماماقلعه
A fort in the Wazikhwah district of the Ghilzai country, on a road from the Kundar to Kandahar, 12 miles from Khan Taraki, and some 32 miles from Mukur. The fort contains stables and lines for a horse and foot garrison, and has two shops and two wells inside. It has three gateways, and outside is a karez. (Broadfoot.)

MAMA KHATUN ماماخاتون
34-42 69-8 G. A pass over the range of hills separating the Kabul plain from the Koh Daman. It is crossed by a road leading from Kabul to Ziarat-i-Shahid and thence to Charikar its summit being reached at about 18 miles from Kabul. It is difficult, though practicable, for mule transport. (Masson, I.B.C.)

MAMA KHEL ماماخیل
34-15 69-59 A. A village in the Khugiani country, five miles south of Gandamak, situated on the Nian Rud. The different hamlets composing this village can furnish about 600 fighting men. The neighbourhood abounds in fruit trees and vineyards.
This place was occupied by a detachment of irregulars under Captain Gerard in December 1841. On the rebellion he was ordered to evacuate and retire on Jalalabad. This order was carried out with great difficulty, owing to the bad conduct of the Khaibari auxiliaries. But Lieutenant Cunningham, of the Engineers, before retiring, with great galantry, managed to blow up two bastions of the fort. The loss of the party on this occasion was 38 killed and 41 wounded. Lieutenant Dawson, of the Jazailchis and the Native Commandant, Haidar Ali Khan, behaved exceedingly well on this occasion, as did Risaldar Jawahir Sing of the Shah's 2nd Cavalry.
On the occasion of General Pollock's advance on Kabul, he was met here by the enemy under Haji Ali and Khairulla Khan, on the 23rd August 1842, whom he defeated with some loss, sustaining a loss himself of seven killed and 49 wounded. The fort and village of Mama Khel were then burnt.
With Mama Khel is coupled for revenue purposes the village of Manuzai; The inhabitants of both are Sherzad Khugianis. (Gerard, Pollock, I.B.C.)

MAMA KHEL ماماخیل
A village near (below ?) the junction of the Hariob and Hazardarakht streams, on the right bank and close to the river. The inhabitants are Ahmad Khel Jajis. (Stewart.)

MAMA KHEL ماماخیل
34-26 70-49 G. A village in the Kama division of the Jalalabad district, about midway between Bazid Khel, and Mayar-i-Akbar Khan. Inhabitants: Mohmands and Wardaks. (Jenkyns.)

MAMAKI See MAMUKA مامکی

MAMI مامی
A pass in Kafiristan, leading from the Upper Pech to the Upper Bashgul.

MAMO GHANDI ماموغندی
33-42 69-45 G. A village in the Chakmani valley, belonging to the Gabar Mangals. (I.B.C.)

MAMOZAI ماموزی
33-30 69-8 A. A village about three miles beyond the Mirzakai Kotal on the road from Kurram to Gardez. (I.B.C.)

*MAMRAI ممری
 33-32 69-10 m. A village on the Gardez river, some seven miles southwest of Gardez.

MAMUKA Or MAMAKI مکی (مامکی)
 34-27 68-44 m. Two Ghilzai villages on the left bank of the Kabul river, about six miles below Jalrez. The name Mamuka is also applied to the valley of the Kabul river in this neighbourhood.

*MAMUNA مونه
 33-9 69-31 m. A village located on a tributary of the Tangai, about 6 miles south of Spera in Ghazni province.

*MAMUNDA ماموندا
 34-42 71-6 m. A village located near the Pakistan border, about 8 miles south of Sarkani in Kunar province.

*MAMURKHEL مامورخیل
 32-47 68-28 m. A village located east of Janikhel and south of Khair Kot in Ghazni province.

*MANA منه
 34-1 69-35 m. A village located near Jab-i-Kalai, some ten miles south of Azro in Logar province. Another place with this name is located on a tributary of the Tangai, about three miles south of Spera in Paktia province, at 33-8 69-31 m. (LWA)

*MANAI منی
 34-5 69-17 m. A village located southeast of Zarghunshahr in Logar province.

MANANGUL منانگل
 A stream draining southwest to the Upper Bashgul—see "Manjam."

*MANDAGAL KHOLEH مندگل خوله
 35-28 71-17 m. A village on the Kantuz Rud, some 6 miles northwest of Urmul. Nearby is Mandagal Sufla, at 35-17 71-19 m.

MANDAL مندل
 35- 71-. Elevation 15,300 feet. A difficult pass over the Hindu Kush leading from the Bashgul valley to Minjan in Badakshan. Minjan traders with yabus heavily laden with hides and other merchandise make light of this pass, but it is really impracticable for horses. Approaching from Ahmad Diwana, altitude 8,530 feet, the road crosses the Bashgul stream at Imra's shrine, and keeps to the left bank. It is easy, the ascent being very gradual. At five miles it passes a lake through which the river flows silently. Two miles further on there is an expanse of water of considerable size where the river, bordered by a fringe of willow jungle, insinuates itself among a number of tiny lakes. At 10,250 feet wood ceases, and fuel must be carried up to a "sangar" at 11,000 feet where a small camp may be formed. Distance from Ahmad Diwana eight miles. Thence the road (1st June 1891) ran over trackless snow until at 7 1/2 miles the summit of the pass was reached. The valley runs at first north and south and then it turns to the left, so that the pass itself looks east and west. At first the gradient is easy for 1,500 feet, it then becomes more severe, but is nowhere of extreme difficulty except for the last 400 feet, when the incline is that of a house

roof. Surgeon-Major Robertson's party startd at 4 A.M. and the sun was shining strongly as they reached the knife-edge summit. The snow consequently gave way at every footstep. On the Minjan side of the pass there is an extremely steep descent for 500 feet, and it continues fairly severe for three-quarters of a mile. It then becomes easier being a succession of more or less level expanses with rather steep descents intervening. When the snow ceases, at about 13,000 feet, the track runs over boulders at the edge of the stream (the upper Kokcha?), which has to be frequently crossed and recrossed. The valley is narrow and winding, and impracticable for horses. At 14 1/2 miles it broadens out into a wide plain covered with willow and birch jungle, elevation 11,500 feet, where a camp may be formed. This plain is closed in, except at the upper part, where the narrow upper valley begins, and at the lower end, where the numerous water channels are collected again into one stream and flow round the end of a rounded hill barrier which stretches across the plain. The road then runs above and on the left bank of the river, now become a torrent, and descends over boulders and rough ground to the stony fields surrounding the hamlet of Pip or Peip, 19 1/2 miles, or 27 1/2 from Ahmad Diwana. (Robertson.)

MANDAWAR See MANDRAWAR   مند راور

*MANDI   مندی
34-22 67-6 m. A village located on the Darazqol, southeast of Panjao in Bamian province.

MANDRAWAR Or MANDAWAR   مند راور
34-33 70-13 A. One of the principal villages in Laghman, situated on the right bank of the Alingar-Alishang river, five miles above its junction with the Kabul. Mandrawar is composed of the following hamlets:
        1.) Dipi
        2.) Kismishabad
        3.) Kala-i-Kazi
        4.) Kala-i-Khwaja Muhammad
        5.) Abdul Rahim Khel
The population is almost entirely Tajik. There is a large Hindu trading community in Mandrawar. Supplies and water are plentiful here, but a camping ground would be difficult to find owing to the extensive cultivation and numerous grave-yards.
Two roads cross at Mandrawar, one going from Jalalabad up the Alishang valley and the other from Kala Asmatula Khan via Goudi to Nagalu. (Holdich, Warburton, I.B.C.)

MANDU KHEL See LOHANI   مند وخیل

MANDUL   مند ول
A tribe of Siahposh Kafirs who dwell in a portion of the valley of Kanda-i-Nil. They formerly dwelt in the Shamakat valley lying to the west of Laghman and containing 14 small glens, but they were driven from this locatlity as lately as the reign of the Emperor Jahangir. (Raverty.)
N.B. — This may be the same tribe as Madugal.

MANDUZAI   مند وزائی
The largest section of the Shinwaris.

*MANDUZAI   مند وزائی
33-18 69-47. Mandozai is an alaqadari in Paktia province. The

alaqadari comprises an area of 112 square kilometers and has an agricultural population that has been estimated at from 24,970 to 27,180. The alaqadari is bounded in the west and northwest by Nader Shah Kot, in the south by Tani, in the southeast by Gurbuz, and in the east by Khost. Mondozai has about 36 villages, 23 of which have more than 500 inhabitants. The villages are listed in the PG as follows: Delfori (Delpori), Khozi Khel, Omar Kalai (Omar Gul), Pastina, Manbo Kalai, Gedal Kalai, Bar Khan Khel, Dadwal, Matta Khan, Kabul Khel, Shamshi Khel, Ziray Terkha, Tsarbanai, Warza Lewan Khel (Warza-Sun Khel), Dray Koti, Chandar Khel (Chandi Khel), Payendah Khel, Hasan Mohamad, Dur Namay, Bahram Khel, Hasanzai, Shaddal, Darwi Khel, Ali Wat, Degan Wa Mangal, Kacha Khel, Shabi Khel, Sun-i-Sarakh (Tani-i-Sarakh), Musha Khana, Ali Khan Khel, Tur Khel, Ar Khel, Khani Khel, Melani, Abdul Karim-i-Miran, Haidar Khel, and Tar Khel.

*MANGAL منگل
32-51 69-16 m. A village located south of Pir Koti and southeast of Urgun in Paktia province. Another village with this name is located north of Kamdesh, Kunar province, at 35-29 71-18 G. (LWA.)

MANGAL منگل
34-8 69-43 A. A village twelve miles form Bilut towards Hisarak. It contains 400 houses. Inhabitants: Ghilzais. Wood and water plentiful; supplies procurable. There are 30 khasadars quartered here. (I.B.C.)

MANGAL منگل
A tribe which inhabits the southern and upper portion of the Kurram valley, and also part of Zurmat. their principal divisions are Miran Khel, Khajuri, Gabar, Marghai, and Kamal Khel. Of these the Miran Khel is the most powerful and their chief is head of the whole tribe. This clan has provided the present Amir and his sons with three wives. The Mangals are said to possess 250 forts and 500 black tents, and can muster 8,000 men.
The Mangals are said to be very thievish in their propensities; they hold a tower on the Paiwar Kotal, whence they levy a tax on all travellers frequenting the route, robbing the unprotected and skulking from the strong; acting as guides, and exacting safe-conduct money from Turis proceeding to Logar or the Kabul valley.
In April 1858, Muhammad Azim for the first time for twenty years collected the revenue of Chakmani. He was strongly opposed, and lost a number of men in doing so. It seems they paid their revenue shortly after the arrival of the troops with little demur; but being driven to desperation by the acts of the Aghan soldiery, they fought for the honour of their children.
The account given by Agha Abbas agrees in many particulars with the above account, but he does not say anything of the Mangals in Zurmat, which accounts for his small estimate of their strength, viz., 3,000.
This tribe caused a good deal of anxiety on the Kurram line during the Afghan war of 1878-80, and from time to time annoyed the posts and attacked convoys. On the 13th of December 1878 the rear guard of a column under Sir Frederick Roberts, exploring the country towards Kurram from Ali Khel via the Sapri pass, was attacked and suffered some loss, including one British officer (Captain Goad) mortally wounded; but the Mangals were soon driven back and lost many men.
The tribe appear to be perpetually in a state of rebellion against the Afghan Governors of Khost and Hariob, whose authority they recognise only to a very small extent. From time to time large

numbers of them migrate into British territory to escape from the oppression of their Afghan rulers. (Lumsden, Agha Abbas, Donald, I.B.C.)

*MANGAL KHEL CHINA   منگل خیل چینه
33-28 69-11 m. A village located between Zurmat and Gardez in Paktia province.

MANGAL MANZIL   منگل منزل
34- 69-. A place on a seldom-used route between Tutu, in the Khugiani country, and Ali Khel, via Petla, Nargasi, Sao, and across the Surkhab river. (I.B.C.)

*MANGARA TOY   منگاره توی
32-45 69-1 m. A village located about 5 miles southwest of Sarobi in southern Paktia province.

MANGASAK TAGAO   مندسك تگاو
A deep ravine draining draining northward into the Helmand.

MANGASTURA   منگستوره
A valley on the north of the Safed Koh range west of Mahmand, or Mahman, Dara. It is exceedingly fertile, and rears most of the pomegranates imported into Hindustan. (Moorcroft.)

MANGIAR KHULA   منگیار خوله
An affluent of the Karaia stream, which it joins at Kharkai. Up this nala a track leads over the Sapri pass to Ali Khel. (I.B.C.) A village called Mangiar is in Chamkani, Paktia province, at 33-50 69-47 G. (LWA)

MANGINA   منگینه
A village in the Hisarak valley, containing 300 houses of Shinwaris. (MacGregor.)

MANGROTAI See BIRMAL   منگروتی

MANGU   منگو
34-53 70-23 m. A cantonment in Laghman. The garrison of Mangu consists (1906) of one squadron cavalry, two mountain guns, hundred sappers and miners and two battalions infantry. (I.B.C.) The village is northeast of Alingar. (LWA)

MANGU KHEL   منگو خیل
33-59 69-2 m. A village on the right bank of the Logar river, 12 miles south of the Tang Waghjan. Inhabitants: Astanazai Ghilzais. In 1880 Mangu Khel and its adjoining village Fateh Khel contained one hundred families. (Euan Smith, Clifford.)

*MANJAKA   منجكه
33-26 69-36 m. A village located between Khairaspan and Janikhel, northwest of Khost in Paktia province.

MANJAM   منجام
35- 71-. Elevation 13,450 feet. A pass in Kafiristan, crossed by a road leading from the head of the Pittigul to the Bashgul. From the village of Pittigul altitude 5,000 feet, the valley ascends, curving slightly to the northwest. Surgeon-Major Robertson made two short marches to the foot of the Manjam, which was then 1 1/2 or 2 miles distant. The third day he crossed the pass and camped half-way down

551

the valley at a "pshal" on a rather high plain. The fourth day he marched down the valley to the point where it falls into the Manangul torrent, crossed the later to its right bank, and so on to Bragamatal. The total distance by road is probably not more than 24 miles, and is easy throughout. (Robertson.)

MANJAN منجان
A village in Laghman. Inhabitants: Kohistanis. (Warburton.)

*MANJARKHEL مانجرخیل
34-2 68-21 m. A village located between Mirzabek and Kot in southern Maidan province.

MANJOR or MANJADOR منجدار
35-26 69-40 m. A village on the left bank of the Panjshir stream, situated at the mouth of the Manjahor Dara, two miles above Bazarak, and inhabited by 80 Tajik families. (Shahzada Waimus.) Recent maps show the spelling Manjador. (LWA)

MANJU منجو
A hamlet in the Dai Zangi district of Lal; ten houses.

MANJUNI منجونی
A village in the Jalalabad district, about four miles southwest of Batikot. Inhabitants: Tirais. (Jenkyns.)

MANSUR KAREZ منصور کاریز
32-32 67-49 G. A village in the Ghazni district, 91 miles from Ghazni, 205 miles from Quetta, on the southwest corner of the Ab-i-Istadah, belonging to Taraki Ghilzais and consists of six forts. Water is procurable from some aqueducts. It is the first stage in the country of the independent Ghilzais from the north. Here four roads meet, viz., from Mukur, Margha, Zurmat, and Katawaz. (Campbell, Outram, Broadfoot.)

MANU منو
34-15 70-19 m. A village said to be situated at the head of the valley north of the Badpakht pass. (Young.) Other places with this name are near Kamkai, southwest of Alingar in Laghman province, at 34-46 70-14 m., and on the Kunar river, northeast of Chakai, at 34-44 70-55 m. (LWA.)

MANUGAI منوگی
34-14 70-2 G. A village close to Mama Khel, five miles south of Gandamak, and associated with it for revenue purposes.
Inhabitants: Sherzad, Khugianis. (Jenkyns.) Recent maps show the spelling Mankai at 34-15 70-7 m. (LWA.)

*MANU KALA مانوکلا
34-39 69-54 m. A village located northeast of Sarobi, near Lokhai, in Kabul province.

MANU-O-MAHURA مانو و مهوره
34-15 70-18 m. A village composed of two hamlets in the Chapriar division of the Jalalabad district, about four miles south of Hadia Khel. Mahura stands on the right and Manu on the left bank of the Chapriar stream. Inhabitants: Khugianis and Sahibzadas. (Jenkyns.)
N.B.--These places are probably the same as the Mano and Maora of map.

MANUZAI See MAMAKHEL (1) مانوزی

MANZINA
34- 69-. A village in Hisarak, Jalalabad, containing 300 houses of Shinwaris. (MacGregor.) A place with this name is located at 34-13 70-29 m.

MAORA See MANU-O-MAHURA ماوره

MARAK مرك
One of the ten dastas or subdistricts of Besud.

MARA KHEL ماره خیل
34- 69-. A village 55 miles east of Kabul, on the route by the Karkacha pass to Jalalabad. (Thornton.)

MARAN SAH مران ساه
33- 69-. A small summer shelter for cattle and herdsmen, passed at the 5th mile from Ali Khel towards the Paiwar pass. (Collett.)

*MARAO KOT مراو کوت
32-39 69-14 m. A village located on the Margha Rud, southeast of Sarobi in southeastern Paktia province.

MARAWARA مروره
34-53 71-11 m. Nearly opposite Chigha Sarai, in the Kunar Valley, is the large village of Marawara at the mouth of the dara of that name, by which a pass (probably about 8,000 or 9,000 feet) leads to Bajaur. It is inhabited by Mamunds, and from this point to near Asmar, on the left bank of the river, the Afghans have very little hold on the country. So much is this the case that a gathering from these villages fired on an Afghan escort while the Boundary Mission was at Nashagam. (Coldstream.) Another place with this name is near Jagdalak, at 34-29 69-45 G. (LWA)

*MARBULAQ مربولاق
34-1 67-49 m. A village located on the Daria-i-Sagan and southwest of the Band-i-Doab in northern Ghazni province.

MARDKUSH مردکش
34-40 66-52 G. A fort village at the mouth of the Bakkak glen; 20 houses of Takana Hazaras. (Maitland.)

MARGH See ZAK مرگ

MARGHA مرغه
32-47 69-20 m. A village in Birmal, west of Waziristan. It is a square walled village, containing about 300 houses. It is the principal settlement in Birmal, and belongs to the Kabul Khel Utmanzai Waziris, principally the Saifali and Paipali sections. Water good and plentiful from springs and stream. Sheep, fowls, ata, ghi, rice, etc., plentiful. (McNair.)
This place is an important stage on the route from British territory through the Drwar valley to Ghazni. It is 9 miles from Urgon (or Wargin according to Waziris). (McLean.) Another place with this name is located at 34-19 63-56 A. (LWA.)

MARGHA مرغه
32-49 69-22 m. A stream in Birmal which, joining the Mastoi at Dwo Toi, forms the Tochi river.

MARGHA مرغه
33-2 69-13 m. A village about 65 miles east of Kalat-i-Ghazni, situated in a plain. It has some cultivation, and water is procured from springs and karez. (Lumsden.)

MARGHAI مرغی
A division of the Mangal tribe.

*MARGHAKAI مرغه کی
32-8 68-10 m. A village near Jabbar Kalai and west of Wazakhwa in southern Ghazni province.

MARGHI مرغی
34-58 66-31 m. Elevation 7,355 feet. A small village and fort in the west of the Yakh Walang district, situated on a nala of the same name, which comes from the southwest and enters the Band-i-Amir valley at a point some 45 miles (by road) below Firozbahar. Dahan-i-Marghi and Nobala Margha together contain about 100 families, chiefly Hazaras. Nobala is Hazara for glen, and Nobala Marghi would therefore appear to mean the hamlets scattered about the Marghi glen, whilst Dahan-i-Marghi is doubtless the name of the village at the mouth of the glen. Maitland says:
"Marghi is a glen, entering from the left, abrest of the village. Beyond it is a high rocky spur, Koh-i-Marghi. The hills on both sides of the valley are lofty, and mostly inaccessible, or nearly so.
"Dahan-i-Marghi is the residence of Mehdi Beg, chief of the Kham-i-Aba district, which includes Sabz Dara; the Alkanis proper boundary being the spur southeast of that place. Medhi Beg has now little or no authority. Last year (1884), or the year before, he chose to rebel, but finding that troops would be sent against him, he fled to Sardar Isak Khan. The Sardar wrote to the Amir to get him off, on the ground that he was an old servant of his father. The Amir accordingly forgave him, but ordered that every place should pay its own revenue direct to the Governor of Bamian, thus depriving Mehdi Beg of his power and influence. I should rather like to have seen Mehdi Beg, but he was said to be away shikaring.
"This is a great place for the manufacture of Hazara carpets, long things of staring pattern and harsh texture. They are valued at Kabul for their wearing qualities, and would make good floor cloths for corridors and passages. There is a certain amount of trade done in these carpets, kurzins of the same material, and numdahs; and as well as in barak, ghi, sheep, etc." (Maitland.)

MARHEZ مرهز
34- 69-. A village in the Hisarak division of the Jalalabad district, about two miles south of Yahiband. Inhabitants Shinwaris. (Jenkyns.)

MARIAM مریم
34-40 70-11 G. A village in Laghman, on the left bank of the Alishang river, about 5 miles northwest of Tirgarhi. The following is a list of the forts and hamlets composing the place:

(1) Muhammadpur
(2) Kala-i-Mulla Afzal
(3) Kala-i-Mir Badshah
(4) Kala-i-Nasim
(5) Kala-i-Sufian
(6) Kala-i-Malik Lang

(7) Kala-i-Mullayan
(8) Banda-i-Malik Shuja
(9) Malik Jan Muhammad

Inhabitants: Dehgans. (Warburton.)

MARIAZ مریز
34- 70-. A fort in the Shinwari country, 15 miles from Jalalabad. The approach to it from Jalalabad is over very broken and difficult country with frequent ascents and descents. It hangs over a narrow valley on the right hand, which is generally under water from irrigation of the rice crops. It was destroyed on the 27th July 1842, by a party of the 31st Regiment, under Major Skinner. (Stocqueler.)

*MARID مرید
35-9 71-17 m. A village located northwest of Bargan on a tributary of the Kunar.

*MARIGAT مریگت
33-17 68-44 m. A village located on a tributary of the Rud-i-Julga-i-Janubi, southeast of Sardeh Band in Ghazni province.

MARISTAN See ISARAK مرستان

MARKA مرکه
A subsection of the Yanghur clan of Dai Zangi Hazaras.

MARKADAM مرکدم
A section of the Khatai Hazaras of the Bamian District.

MARKANDI مرکندی
34- 71-. A village of 40 houses on the left bank of the Pech river, 8 miles above Chigha Sarai. Supplies are plentiful. (I.B.C.)

*MARKHANA مارخانه
33-22 67-19 m. A village located northeast of Lalchak near Bolagha in Ghazni province. Another place with this name is located southwest of Nerkh in Maidan province, at 34-21 68-43 m.

MARKHANA مارخانه
34-20 67-31 G. A small village in the west of the Besud country, on the Kabul-Hazarajat-Daulat Yar main road. Ruins with this name are located 34-24 67-35. (LWA.)

MARKHANA مارخانه
34- 67-. The name given to the lower stretches of the Khawas.

MARKHOL مارخول
33- 68-. A pass over the Gulkoh range from Ghazni to the valley of Jarmatu. It is one of six passes said to be all of the same nature as the Gulbauri. (Broadfoot.) Recent maps show the spelling Marqul at 33-40 68-19 m. (LWA.)

MARKI KHEL مرکی خیل
34-8 70-1 m. A village 7 miles south Gandamak, on the right bank of the stream of the same name. The inhabitants are Sherzad Khugianis. The surrounding country is well cultivated with vines and cereals. A road to Kurram passes through the village.
The Marki Khel stream (which is also very commonly known as the

Hashim Khel, from the name of a village a few miles lower down) rises in the southern slopes of the Safed Koh and falls into the Surkhab about 5 miles north of Gandamak. Where crossed by the main Peshawar-Kabul road it is spanned by a stone and wooden bridge, built in the time of Dost Muhammad. This bridge was originally constructed entirely of masonry, but the arches have since been repaired with wood. It was found to be in a very ricketty condition in 1905, but transport carts crossed it in safety; it is doubtful if it would be fit for guns. The bridge is 120 yards long and 18 feet wide; the stream at this point was found in August to be 9 feet wide and 1 foot deep, flowing in a very stony bed about 100 yards across with banks 10 feet high. (Malleson; Wanliss, I.B.C.)

MARKOH ماركوه
34-15 70-49 G. A hill situated west of Basawal, so called on account of the number of snakes found in it. It is the end of a spur from the Safed Koh which runs down west of the Mahman Dara. (Masson.)

MARNU مرنو
34- 70-. A glen in the Safed Koh, south of Balabagh, inhabited by pastoral Afghans. (Masson.)

MARTAZA See MURTAZA مرتضی

*MARU
33-50 68-31 m. A village located northeast of Jaghatu-i-Wardak and west of the Ghazni-Kabul road in Ghazni province. Another place with this name is south of the Shinkai Ghar and northwest of Wazakhwa, at 32-16 68-8 m.

MARWAR مرور
35- 71-. A Madugal hamlet of 8 or 10 houses high up on the right bank of the Bashguls river, several hundred feet above the water, and near the Katir hamlet of Sunru on the opposite bank. (Robertson.)

MARWAT مروت
A section of the Lohanis. A village with this name is in Hesarak at 34-16 69-47 G. (LWA)

MARZ OR VOMARZ مرز (ومرز)
35-22 69-38 A. A group of villages in the upper Panjshir glen, 84 miles from Kabul, together containing 200 Tajik families. (Shahzada Taimus.)

*MARZAK مارزك
33-21 69-12 m. A village near Shahikot and southeast of Zurmat in Paktia province.

MASHAKI (or MUSHAKI) موشکی
33-14 68-13 A. Elevation 6,900 feet. A collection of villages on the Kandahar-Ghazni road, 192-1/2 miles from the former and 29 miles from the latter. The land is irrigated from two karez and is fertile. The following villages are included in the Mashaki group.

1. Khah Mashaki
2. Haji Musa
3. Kala-i-Meri   All inhabited by Andaris.

4. Akhund Khel
5. Kala-i-Murchi
6. Sayyid Musa   Inhabited by Sayyids.
7. Kala-i-Durani   Inhabited by Duranis.

On Sir Donald Stewart's reaching this place in April 1880, all the villages were found deserted, but supplies were brought into his camp by Hazaras.
The encamping ground is on an open sandy plain, about 1-1/2 miles in length. Water is abundant and supplies should be procurable in large quantities; fuel, however, is scarce.
A road from Quetta joins the Kandahar-Ghazni road at Mashaki. (Gaselee, I.B.C.)

*MASHI KALAI ماشی کلی
33-10 70-1 m. A village north of Gholamkhan Kalai and south of Sargali in Paktia province.

MASHU KHEL ماشوخیل
34-21 68-55 m. A village in the Taitamur valley, in the Kabul district, on the left bank of the Kabul river. It has a population of 20 families of Sohak Ghilzais. (Combe.)

MASHURI مشوری
32-12 68-21 m. A fort in the valley of Wazikhwah. (Broadfoot.)

MASHWANI مشوانی
34-46 69-6 G. A small walled village on the right bank of the Kabul river, about 9 miles west of Basawal. It lies some 300 yards to the north of the main road to Jalalabad. It contains 60 families of Mashwanis, possessing (in 1904) about 300 head of cattle, 500 sheep and goats and 50 buffaloes. The annual production of wheat and barley averages about 5,500 Indian maunds. (Wanliss.) Another village with this name is ten miles east of Miali Sahib at 34-20 70-43 G. (LWA.)

MASKA مسکه
The largest of the subdivisions of the Ata clan of Jaghuri Hazaras.

MASKANI مسکنی
33- 69-. A village of the Mangal country, at the head of the Kurram valley, and about 11 miles from Paiwar. (Agha Abbas.)

MASTALI مستعلی (؟)
34- 70-. A village in the Kama division of the Jalalabad district, about a mile north of Deh-i-Tahir. Inhabitants: Dehgans and Hindkis. (Jenkyns.)

MASTI KHEL مستی خیل
34-26 60-18 G. A village in the Surkhab Division of the Jalalabad district. Inhabitants: Ghilzais. (Jenkyns.)

MASTOI or MASTI LGAD مستی لگد
32-53 69-26 A. A stream which drains east and joins the Margha at Dwa Toi, the two thus forming the Tochi river. The lower part of the Mast valley is narrow and difficult. From Dwa Toi a track runs up it for 5 miles to Lag Kala, whence it goes by a very steep and difficult ascent over the hills to the open ground called Lwara, at the head of the Kazha valley. From Lwara there is a road down the

Dangar Algad, a branch of the Mastoi, striking the latter near a Paipali village and then going up the stream to Pir Koti. This is said to be easy for camels throughout and to be the best road from the Dawar country to the Pir Koti. (Douglas.)

MATAH متا
35-27 69-45 A. A village in the upper Panjshir glen, 7 miles above Marz, containing 50 houses of Tajiks. (Shahzada Taimus.)

MATAK See GHORBAND متك

MATA KALA متا قلعه
A village in the Hazarajat.

*MATA KHAN متاخان
33-16 69-52. Mata Khan is an alaqadari in Paktia province. The alaqadari comprises an area of 431 square kilometers and has an agricultural population that has been estimated from 5,190 to 8,255. The alaqadari is bounded in the south by Sarhawza, in the east by Orma, in the north by Zormat, and in the west by Sharan and Dehyale. Mata Khan has 27 villages, none of which has more than 500 inhabitants. The villages are listed in the PG as follows:
Tatorai, Koti Khel, Irahimzai, Shah Qala, Shor Kacha (Shor Kaja), Laghar, Karez Ibrahim (Qarya-i-Ibrahim), Shinkai, Gunbat, Aka Khel, Marjan Khel, Maryani, Dado Khel, Paikar, Bahram Kalai, Faqir Kalai, Saido Kalai, Polad Khel, Chawni, Karsu, Mullayan, Landiwal, Omar Khel, Gerdi, Chowal Khel, Toda China, Aw Gudar, Khar Dewal, Tor Khel, Jamali, Petkai, Lat Khel, Timor Khel, Kamkai Jamali, Hazar Khel, Surkai, Qala-i-Gul and Gulran.

MATUN Or KHOST متون
33-22 69-57 A. The principal town and a woleswali in Paktia province. See Khost for a description of Khost woleswali. (LWA) In 1914 the area was described as follows: Elevation 3,892 feet. The principal place in Khost, and the residence, except in summer, of the Governor of that district. It consists of a large group of villages lying on both sides of the Matun river which issues from the Ghalang Dara in the Mangal Hills.
There are two small forts at Matun, one of which is garrisoned by a regiment of cavalry and the other by a battalion of infantry. Besides these troops there are also in Matun 2 other battalions of infantry, 27 guns (12 mountain, 11 field and 4 machine), and 600 Khasadars. The machine guns are described in 1905 as having been "formerly mounted on the walls of the fort, but now lying on the ground." The whole of the troops mentioned above form the normal garrison of Matun, but they nearly all move up to Gabar Mangal in the hot weather, as also does the Governor of Khost. (I.B.C.)
For operations in, and around, Matun in 1879, see "Official History of the Second Afghan War."

MATUNGI متونگی
34-35 69-43 G. Elevation 12,700 feet. A mountain in the Hariob, 8 miles southwest of Lakhari Kotal, and 6 miles north of Ali Khel. (Gordon.)

MATWAR متور
33- 69-. A village in the Mukhbil valley, about 1/2 mile from the point where the Mukhbil ravine joins the Kurram river. South of the village the ground is very much cut up by watercourses. (I.B.C.) This is probably the same as below.

*MATWARKH متورخ
33-47 69-53 m. A village located some 6 miles east of Chamkani, halfway to the Pakistan border in Paktia province.

MAULANA مولانا
33- 68-. Elevation 9,140 feet. A kotal leading over the hills north of Kharwar. It is said to be an easy route. It is in reality only the westernmost branch of the Kotal-i-Kalam. (Griesbach.)

MAYA KHEL مياخيل
A section of the Lohanis. Also called Mia or Mian Khel. A village with this name is located about 2 miles south of Charasiab, at 34-21 69-10 G. (LWA)

MAYAR-I-AKBAR KHAN مياراكبرخان
34- 70-. A village in Kama, Jalalabad district, 2 miles north of the Kabul river, opposite Girdi Kats. The inhabitants are Mohmands. (Jenkyns.)

MAZANG Or MOZANG د مهزنگ
34- 69-. Deh Mazang is a village 1 mile west of the city of Kabul, at the entrance to the gorge on the Ghazni road. Inhabitants: Tajiks and Kizilbashis. On the retreat of the cavalry and horse-artillery from the Chardeh valley on the 11th December 1879, this village was held by 200 men of the 72nd Highlanders sent out from Sherpur, and the Afghan advance was checked. (I.B.C.) This village is now part of Kabul. (LWA)

MAZAR مزار
A river which flows down from the country of the Kafirs and joins the Kunar on its west bank. (Masson.)

*MAZAR مزار
33-13 68-31 m. A village located southwest of the Sardeh Band and southeast of Shahjoy in Ghazni province. Another place with this name is located east of the Tor Band and southwest of Lalchak in Ghazni province, at 33-16 67-9 m.

MAZAR مزار
34-39 70-45 G. A subdivision of the Jalalabad district. It contains the following villages:

Banda-i-Zabardast with	12	houses of the Barakzai clan
Mir	50	"
Shah Nur	50	Simzai
Khushi	20	"
Kala-i-Gai	50	"
Kala-i-Madad	20	Barakzai
Kala-i-Gada	60	Simzai
Deh-i-Sarawal	80	"
Gumchandu	15	Tajik
Kala-i-Faiz	30	Barakzai
Gurwah Nundalam	200	Simzai
Ghaziabad	300	Mixed
Shorabad	50	Barakzai
Kala-i-Gai	20	"
Kala-i-Shah Nur	20	"
Kala-i-Mahiaz	20	"

Kala-i-Akhun	20	"
Kala-i-Miru	30	"
Baris	15	"
Fari		"
Khund		Gurbaz
Kalan		"
Baz		Kandahari

(No authority quoted in first edition.)

*MAZARKHEL   مزار خیل

33-27 69-3 m. A village located northwest of Zurmat on the road to Gardez in Paktia province.

MAZGIN   مزگین (مزغین)

34-8 69-12 m. A village in the Logar valley, 5 miles northeast of Zargan Shahar, and forming with Surkhao a township under the authority, in 1880, of Padshah Khan, Ahmadzai. The inhabitants are Tajiks, of whom there were 30 families in 1880. The land in the neighbourhood is well cultivated and is watered by the Surkhao stream and by karez. (Euan Smith, Clifford, I.B.C.)

MAZID   مزید

A subsection of the Besud Hazaras. A village with this name is south of Mushaki in Ghazni province, at 33-2 68-13 m. (LWA.)

MAZINA   مازینه

34-13 70-29 m. Elevation 4,000 feet. A village in the Jalalabad district, on the right bank of the Hisarak Rud. It lies 15 miles southeast of Jalalabad and about the same distance southwest of Barikao. It is inhabited by Sayyids and Dehgans, and contains numerous mud forts, surrounded by cultivation and orchards. Supplies are plentiful.

Here, on the 27th July 1842, a British force, under Brigadier Monteath destroyed 35 forts belonging to the Shinwaris as a punishment for their marauding. The loss on the British side was Lieutenant MacIlveen, of the 31st Foot, and 2 men killed, and 23 men wounded.

Mazina was also the scene of an engagement in May 1880, in which the Mulla Fakir was defeated by Brigadier-General Gib. For details of this action see "Official History of the Second Afghan War." (I.B.C.)

*MEHMAN KALAI   مهمان کلی

32-18 68-24 m. A village near the Loy Ziri Ghar, 7 miles north of Mashuri in Ghazni province.

MEHRBAN KALA   مهربان کلا

34-28 68-37. A village on the right bank of the Kabul river, about two miles west of Jalrez. Inhabitants: Tajiks. (Wanliss.)

*MEHTERLAM   مهترلام

34-39 70-12. Mehterlam is a woleswali in Laghman Province. The woleswali, which comprises an area of 534 square kilometers, has an agricultural population that has been estimated at from 15,678 to 31,062. It is bounded in the north by Alishing and Alingar, in the east and south by Qarghai and in the west by Sarobi woleswalis. The woleswali contains about 79 villages, 44 of which have more than 500 inhabitants. The villages are listed in the PG as follows:
Tirgari, Sangturah, Chardehi, Dopi-i-Sufla wa Shamana, Dopi-i-Ulya, Qala-i-Haider Khan, Begh-i-Mirza, Gan Ahu, Kalakot, Omarzai, Ashak

Aghashi (Shaghasi), Alakozai, Kunj, Tandi, (Mawzo-i-Omarzai), Baghal, Shirgar, Dendah, Pashai, Torkotor Sultan-Ghazi Agha, Deh Malakh, Gomin, Deh Baghalak, Charqala-i-Wardakiya, Sehsadah (Sehsadrah) Qala-i-Safi, Joy-i-Saraj, Shamati Wa Kachur, Chehil Matai, Khadiya, (Shorawai), Qala-i-Ghulam Khan, Qala-i-Purdel, Kapla, Alishing, Karenj-i-Alighing, Qarya-i-Maryam, Deh Ziyarat, Dewah Tandai, Naudam Pur, Bazid Khel, Shamangul, Nurah, Akhundabad (Hakimabad), Harmal, Qala-i-Min, Nalawi, Nolam, Nolam Abusah Khel, Kandah Nolam, Tajgalai, Gulkari, Mashikhel (Mosha Khel), Doba-i-Qala-i-Nau, Chandok wa Khwaja Sahib, Padshah Khel, Saya Kandah, Shala Tak, Badish, Maskorah (Maskowa), Kutal, Maidani, Kachur-i-Shamati, Abizai, Nilawati, Moh'd Khel wa-Shorabah, Ali Khel, Basram, Badiabad, Ahmadzai, Landa Khel, Tabikunj, Dud-Kochi, Qarya-i-Daraki-Panjpaye, Qarya-i-Jugi, Muhammad Pur, Andlo, Galoch, Nawabad-i-Machan Khel, Chaparha, Mazkurah, Bela, Baluch Kalai, Baghalak, Bacha Khel, Ahmadzai and Kutal (Maidani-Kutal).

MELANAI ميلنى
33-12 68-30 m. A village 30 miles southeast of Ghazni, on the left bank of the Ghazni river in the Shilghar district of the Ghilzais. It consists of a cluster of forts inhabited by Andaris. (Outram, Broadfoot.)

MERGROM ميرگرام
32-20 71-24 G. A village on the left bank of the Bashgul river, and mainly built on the right bank of its own mountain stream. It has 33 houses, reached from the right bank of the Bashgul by a peculiarly ricketty bridge. Up the Mergal there is a difficult mountain track to the Saratgul. The inhabitants of Mergrom include a large number of outcasts, which makes it a kind of city of refuge for the Kam tribe. (Robertson.)

MESH, AB-I See MADINUI آب ميش

MESHA ميشه
34-44 66-55 G. A half-ruined, but inhabited, fort in the Yakh Walang district, 6 miles west of Ferozbahar (Kala Miana), situated on a conspicuous isolated rock on the left bank of the Rud-i-Band-i-Amir. (Maitland.)

MEST مست
32-58 68-33 m. A village in the Ghilzai country, between Dand and Mishkhel, at the bottom of the Katasang hill in Katawaz. Here are a few forts of the Sulaiman Khel Ghilzais, and water is procurable. (Broadfoot.)

*METAR ميتر
33-26 68-42 m. A village located northeast of the Sardeh Band and southeast of Ghazni in Ghazni province. Other places with this name are located north of Jaghatu and west of Saidabad in the Wardak area of Maidan province, at 33-59 68-28 m.; a tributary of the Helmand, north of Pitaokol in Bamian province, at 34-9 67-10 m.

*MIANA ميانه
34-2 67-33 m. A village near Safidab in southern Bamian province. Other places with this name are located northwest of Jelga, at 33-11 67-1 m.; in the Bughra area, east of Lalchak, at 33-19 67-19 m.; near Sangdah, west of the Dasht-i-Nawer, at 33-32 67-35 m.; on the Nawa-i-Khoda-i-Dad, northeast of Pai Tangi, at 33-16 67-35 m.; and near Saghana, northwest of Ghazni, at 33-44 68-6 m.; all of them in Ghazni province.

MIANA KALA ميانه قلعه
A fort near Ferozbahar in the Yakh Walang district. Altogether there are three forts in this part of the valley, and all are on the left bank. The most westerly is Rash; the centre one is Safedak, or Kala Miana; the name of the third is not known. They have a population of 20 to 30 families of Hazaras. (Maitland.) A village with this name is two miles west of Chamkani at 33-47 69-44 G. (LWA)

MIANDAD ميانداد (میاداد)
33-36 68-30. A village about 6 miles northeast of Ghazni, on the road to Kharwar. (I.B.C.)

MIANI See POWINDAH میانی

MIAN-I-DO-KOH ميان دوكوه
34-37 67-22 m. The name applied to the upper portion of the Sar-i-Bulak valley leading up to the Zard Sang pass over the Koh-i-Baba range. About 4 1/2 miles south of this pass is the small hamlet of Mian-i-Do-Koh, containing some 10 houses of Besud Hazaras. Just below the village there is a small maidan about 1/2 mile long where 2,000 troops could encamp, but no supplies are to be had and there is little fuel. (I.B.C.)

MIANKHEL See LOHANI مياخيل (ميان)
A village with this name is about 5 miles southeast of Qala Saraj in Laghman, at 34-36 70-14 G. (LWA)

MIAN NISHIN ميان نشين
A subdivision of the Dai Chopan Hazaras.

MIAN UMAR ZIARAT ميان عمر زيارت
About 27 miles northeast of Gardez, on the road thence to the Mirzakai kotal. (I.B.C.)

MICHIN KHEL See POWINDAH ميچين خيل

MINZAI See ALI KHEL مينزى

*MINZAI مينزى
32-36 68-1 m. A village near Dila in Ghazni province. Other places with this name are located west of Wazakhwa, at 32-10 68-16 m.; and northeast of Wur, at 32-9 68-41 m., both in Ghazni province.

MIR ADINA مير ادينه
A section of the Polada Hazaras.

*MIRAGUL KALAI ميراگل کلی
32-59 69-11 m. A village located some 4 miles north of Urgun in Paktia province.

MIRAK ميرك
A section of the Muhammad Khwaja Hazaras.

MIR AKHOR AGHA JAN ميرآخور آغجان
34- 69-. A fort in Chardeh, Kabul, in the Allah-ud-din township. Inhabitants: Kizilbashis and Gadi Hazaras. 6 towers, 18 houses. (I.B.C.)

MIR AKHOR ALI MUHAMMAD KHAN میرآخورعلی محمدخان
34- 69-. A fort in the Chardeh valley of Kabul, on the right bank of the Kabul river between Riskhor and Kala-i-Fathu. Inhabitants: Tajiks and Gadi Hazaras. 4 towers, 20 houses. (I.B.C.)

*MIR ALAM میرعلم
33-15 68-19 m. A village located northeast of Mushakai, east of the highway to Ghazni.

MIRAMUR See DAI KUNDI میرامور

*MIRAN میران
34-13 68-18 m. A village located on the Dara-i-Jelga in Maidan province. Another place with this name is located on the Lador Kholeh, northwest of Zurkot, at 33-35 69-37 m.

MIRAN KHEL میران خیل
A section of Jazis, who have 6 forts of 30 houses each and can turn out 30 fighting men. (Agha Abbas.)

MIRAN KHEL میران خیل
A division of the Mangal tribe.

MIRAN SHAH میران شاه
33-15 70-4 G. A village in the upper Panjshir glen, about 1 1/2 miles below Anaba, inhabited by 40 families of Tajiks. About a mile lower down is Zamankor, 12 houses. (Shahzada Taimus.)

MIR BACHA میر بچه
A subsection of the Yanghur clan of Dai Zangi Hazaras. A village with this name is 2 miles north of Panjpai, Maidan, at 34-28 68-13 G. (LWA)

MIR BACHA میر بچه
A section of the Daulatpai Besudis.

MIR BACHA میر بچه
A subsection of the Bul Hasan Besudis.

*MIR BACHA KOT میر بچه کوت
34-41 69-5. Mir Bacha Kot is a woleswali in Kabul province. The woleswali comprises an area of 63 square kilometers and has an agricultural population which has been estimated at from 12,500 to 15,120. The woleswali is bounded in the west and south by Shakar Dara, in the north by Istalef and Kalakan, and in the east by Deh Sabz. Mir Bacha Kot includes about 28 villages, 17 of which have more than 500 inhabitants. The villages are listed in the PG a follows: Marki, Qulugh, Deh Mir, Qala-i-Akhund, Qanat-i-Zulfi, Qurban Sultan, Dakoye Sufla, Deh Saqi-Sufla, Lochakan, Sarai Khwaja, Guzar-i-Mewa Khatun, Guzar, Shaikhan-i-Baqabeg, Laghmani Kola (koka), Bala Ab, Qala-i-Khanan, Khwaja Gia, Baba Quchqar, Baladeh Luchakan, Zamin Aghor, Daku-i-Ulya, Arazi, Shaikhan, Sayab wa Charmgar, Kharoti, Sofian, Deh Saqi-i-Ulya, and Joy Bar.

MIR CHAPPAR See CHARKHIL میر چپر

MIRDAD میرداد
Dai Mirdad is a division (or "tappa") of the district of Ghazni, bounded as follows: north and west, Hazara Besud; south and east, Wardak.

563

The inhabitants are chiefly Wardaks, but there are also Hazaras and Kizilbashis.

The tappa is enclosed by hills east and west, and the valley thus formed is irrigated by a stream bearing the same name as the tappa, and is well-cultivated. The valley from north to south is a long one. Wheat is the staple crop. There is a lead-mine in the hills on the west, but it is not now worked. In Amir Sher Ali's time an establishment was kept up, and the outturn of lead was said to be 4 kharwars, or 64 maunds, per annum.

The estimated land revenue amounts to about Rs. 15,358 a year. The jambast system of assessment prevails. (Hastings.)

MIR DEH میر ده
A village of 20 houses of Besud Hazaras, situated in the Dara Ali of the Yakh Walang district. (A.B.C.)

MIRGA BELA میرگه بیله
34-26 70-30. A village in the Besud division of the Jalalabad district, situated on the left bank of the Kabul river, about 2 miles above the point where the Kunar river runs in. Inhabitants: Tajiks and Arabs. (Jenkyns.)

MIR GHAZAB میرغصب
A village in the Ghilzai country, 120 miles south of Ghazni. It consists of only four families, but has a spring of water. The inhabitants are Nasir Khels. (Broadfoot.)

MIR GHAZAB میرغصب
34- 69-. A fort in the Chardeh of Kabul, between Gaokhana and Kala-i-Kazi. Water from karez and from a stream from the Korogh mountain. 6 towers, 18 families. (I.B.C.)

MIR GHULAM میرغلام
35-0 70-35 G. A village located about 19 miles northwest of Chegha Sarai in Kunar province. (LWA.) See Military Report on Hazarajat, Part II for another place with this name.

MIR GULAB میرگلاب
34- 69-. A village in the Koh Daman, north of Kabul, containing 10 houses. (I.B.C.)

*MIR HASAN میرحسن
32-2 68-55 m. A village near Sanga and east of Mamai in southern Ghazni province. Another place with this name is northeast of Chamkani near the Pakistan border, at 33-52 69-53 m.

MIR HAZAR میر هزار
A large section of the Dai Kundi Hazaras.

MIR HAZAR میر هزار
A Darghan Hazara village of 15 families in the Kalu glen, about 13 miles above Zohak. (Amir Khan.) Recent maps show the name Mir Hazari southwest of Nerkh, at 34-21 68-45 m. (LWA.)

MIR-I-ALI میرعلی
A subsection of the Besud Hazaras.

MIRJI KALA میرجی قلعه
A village in the Hisarak division of the Jalalabad district, about two miles northeast of Mazina. Inhabitants: Sayyids. (Jenkyns.)

*MIRKHANKHEL میرخان خیل
35-2 69-44 m. A village near Lukakhel, northeast of Nejrab in Kapisa province. Another place with this name is north of the Ghorband valley in Parvan province at 35-4 68-49 m.

MIRKOT میرکوت
32-28 67-23 G. A village 125 miles on the road from Kandahar to Ghazni. It is so cold here in the winter that Foster mentions that water suspended in a copper vessel at the end of October, was frozen into a solid mass during the night. (Foster.)

MIR LALA KALA میرلالاقلعه
34- 70-. A village in the Kama division of the Jalalabad district. Inhabitants: Sayyids. (Jenkyns.)

MIRZA AHMAD KHAN میرزا احمدخان
34- 69-. A fort in the Chardeh valley of Kabul, included in the village of Sarasia, and a little up stream from the latter. Inhabitants: Tajiks and Baluchis; 12 families of the former and 3 of the latter. (I.B.C.)

*MIRZA ALI میرزاعلی
32-53 67-51 G. A village located about 5 miles east of Mukur in Ghazni province. Nearby is another place with this name, at 32-57 76-52 G.

MIRZA ALIBAD میرزاعلی آباد (؟)
34- 70-. A village in the Surkhab division of the Jalalabad district, about 2 miles southwest of Mirzayan. Inhabitants: Tajiks. (Jenkyns.)

MIRZA GHIAS میرزاغیاث
34-33 69-13. A walled village in the Kabul district, 2 miles east of Bemaru. Inhabitants: Tajiks. It is square, with 100 yard faces. (I.B.C.)

MIRZA GHULAM NABI میرزاغلام نبی
34- 69-. A small village in the Kabul district, situated between Khwaja Rawash and the Wazirabad lake. It is surrounded by trees and cultivation reaching to the border of the lake. (I.B.C.)

MIRZA GHULAM SADIK میرزاغلام صادق
34- 69-. A fort in the Chardeh valley of Kabul, included in the village of Sarasia, situated between that place and Kala-i-Mirza Ahmad Khan. Inhabitants: Tajiks. (I.B.C.)

MIRZA HABIB میرزاحبیب
34- 69-. A small fort in the Kabul district. It stands on the right bank of the Maidan stream, near Deh-i-Bori, where the Ghazni road crosses the stream (Maidan). (I.B.C.)

MIRZA HASHIM میرزاهاشم
34- 70-. A village in the Jalalabad district, on the right bank of the Surkhab river, about 3 miles east of Balabad. The inhabitants are Kizilbashis. (Jenkyns.)

MIRZAI میرزی
34- 70-. A village in the Kama division of the Jalalabad district. Inhabitants: Ghilzais and Lodias. (Jenkyns.)

MIRZA JAFIR ميرزاجعفر
34- 69-. A fort in the Chardeh valley of Kabul, between Deh-i-Dana and Riskho. Inhabitants: Gadi Hazara. (I.B.C.)

MIRZA JAWAT ميرزاجوات
34- 69-. A fort in the Chardeh valley of Kabul, between Kala-i-Jafir Jan and Aoshar. Inhabitants: Kizilbashis and Gadi Hazaras. 15 houses. (I.B.C.)

*MIRZA KALA ميرزاقلعه
32-49 68-57 m. A village located a few miles north of Saidkhel in Paktia province.

MIRZA KHEL ميرزاخيل
34-13 69-8 m. A village in the Logar valley, 1-1/2 miles east of the right bank of that river, and 8 miles north of Zargan Shahar. Inhabitants: Ahmadzais. In 1880 the village, which consisted of 5 hamlets, contained 80 families. (Clifford, Euan Smith.) Another place with this name is in Nangahar province, at 34-30 70-40 G. (LWA.)

MIRZAKAI Or SURKHAI ميرزاكى كوتل
33-10 69-20 G. Elevation about 9,000 feet. A pass over the Mangal hills on the road from Karlachi to Ghazni and via the Altimur pass, to Kabul. The summit of the pass lies 4-1/2 miles from Karlachi and 93-1/2 from Ghazni. The road over the pass is easily practiable for camels and it is said that it could without difficulty be made fit for wheeled traffic. It is said never to be blocked by snow.
On the kotal is an Afghan post held by a detachment of 200 regular infantry. At the western foot of the pass, one mile from the summit, is the small village of Mirzakai Karez; this would be the best place for a brigade to encamp, forming the third stage from Karlachi; water from a karez. (I.B.C.)

MIRZAKKA ميرزكه
33-47 69-28 m. A village in a well-watered plain between Ambar and Gwamangal Kala, on the road from Ali Khel to Ghazni. Water is plentiful throughout the year. Fodder for about 800 animals for one day and about 500 maunds of unground grain may be collected within 5 miles of the village. Fuel also is obtainable. (Creagh, Johnston.)

MIRZA MUHAMMAD ALI ميرزامحمدعلى
34- 69-. A small square village, 50 yard faces, in the township of Yakatut, on the left bank of the Kabul river and to the east of Sherpur. The inhabitants are Kizilbashis. (Kennedy.)

*MIRZAWAL ميرزاوال
33-22 68-18 m. A village located some 3 miles west of Mustaufi and 15 miles southwest of Ghazni in Ghazni province.

MIRZAYAN ميرزايان
34- 70-. A village in the Surkhab division of the Jalalabad district, about 2 miles southeast of Zulmabad. Inhabitants: Ghilzais. (Jenkyns.)

MISH KHEL ميش خيل
A village 40 miles southwest of Ghazni. (Thornton.)

MIS KHEL مس خیل
A Sulaiman Khel Ghilzai village in Katawaz.

MISKIN مسکین
35- 69-. A village in the Kohistan of Kabul, between Baian Daolana. One fort, 120 houses. Inhabitants: Tajiks. The land is very fertile, grain of every sort, including rice, being grown; and vines and mulberries among the fruit trees. Water from the Charikar stream by a cut. (I.B.C.)

MISKIN مسکین
35- 69-. A village in the Chardeh valley of Kabul, between Indaki and Ghaib. Fifty houses of Tajiks. The inhabitants are all gilkar, i.e., people employed in building with clay (not bricks), mud-plastering, etc. (I.B.C.)

*MITA میته
33-19 69-26 m. A village loacted on a tributary of the Saidkhelo Lgad south of Waze in Paktia province.

MITHAI میتی
33- 69-. A stream which joins the Laladar stream from the west, at a point on the road to the Lakarai pass, at 3 miles north of Belut. The two streams enclose a large open, grassy space about half a mile long and a quarter of a mile broad. Hills on either side low but steep. (Collett.)

*MITRANI میترانی
34-11 70-38 m. A village located some 6 miles southeast of Shahikot in Nangarhar province.

MITTA KHEL میته (میتا) خیل
A sulaiman Khel Ghilzai village in Katawaz. There are two villages with this name, one southwest of the Ab-i-Istada, at 32-14 67-51 m., and at 32-50 68-28 G. (LWA.)

MIYALA SAHIB KALA میاله صاحب قلعه
34-22 70-39 G. A small village on the Peshawar-Jalalabad road, east of Ali Boghan. Here is a shrine famous for its power of healing lunatics. (Kabul Mission, 1905.)

MIZAH میزا (؟)
A main section of the Besud Hazaras.

MOGHAT موغت
34-33 69-10 G. A hamlet, consisting of three detached portions, on the southern shore of the Wazirabad lake, north of Sherpur. Inhabitants: Kizilbashis. (Kennedy.)

MOHAR BARDAK مهاربردک
A village in the Ghazni district, on the road towards Kandahar. Inhabitants: Andar Ghilzais. (Hastings.)

MOHBAT KALOZAIDA محبتکلوزیده
A subdivision of the Polada Hazaras.

MOHIN KALA مهین کلا
A village 45 miles from Kalat-i-Ghilzai on the Ghazni road. (Bellew.)

MOHMAND
    For a description of this tribe see "N.W.F. Gazetteer."

MOHMAND
    34- 69-. A village in the Logar valley, south of the Tangi Waghjan. The inhabitants are Mohmands, and in 1880 they numbered 40 families. (Clifford, Euan Smith.)

MOHMAND OR MAHMAN
    34-14 69-54. A stream of Jalalabad, which rises in a valley from which it takes its name and which is situated among the inner ranges of Safed Koh; it flows past the Nazian valley and the Shinwari forts of Pesh Bolak, and branches into two streams, near Basawal; the larger one falls into the Kabul river at Basawal and the smaller one flows in the direction of Hazarnao, and exhausts itself on the cultivation of that place. This valley is celebrated for the grapes produced in it. The following is Jenkyns' list of villages in what he styles the Rud-i-Mohmand Dara in 1879:

Name of Village	Inhabitants	Name of Village	Inhabitants
1. Siahchob	Dehgans	9. Ambar Khana	Mohmands
2. Zakhel	Mohmands	10. Girdi Sirkani (including Girdabai, Marsingai Landi, and Deh-i-Ziarat).	"
3. Kala-i-Inayatulla Khan	"		
4. Gulahi	"		
5. Pesh Bolak	Dehgans	11. Dakka	"
6. Kalajat-i-Shinwari	Shinwaris	12. Lalpura (including Sada and Malikana)	"
7. Basawal	Mohmands	13. Kuchian	Kuchis
8. Hazarnao	"		

N.B. Add to Rud-i-Mohmand the following villages of the Sipai Shinwaris, viz., Chalgazi, Maidanak, Girdai, Bahramkhel, Battan, Daonai, Asadkhel, Tangai, Makranas, Margha, Landai, Trelai, Sunduk, Kostal, Achin, and Dassar Kulba.
Add also the following villages of the Sangukhel Shinwaris, viz., Sarobai, Lakkar Shaikhan, Sholgar, Kasoba, Chenar, and Sisobi.
Add also Dehsarak, a village of the Alisherkhel Shinwaris. (Moorcroft, McGregor, Jenkyns.)

MOHMAND
    A locality occupied by Jaghatu Hazaras. One place with this name is located at 34-25 71-15 A. (LWA.)

*MOHMAND
    34-16 69-55 m. A village located near Pishdari and south of Ashpan in Nangarhar province.

*MOHMAND DARAH
    34-15 70-52. Mohmand Darah is a woleswali in Nangarhar province. The woleswali comprises an area of 281 square kilometers and has an agricultural population that has been estimated at from 13,280 to 15,450. The woleswali is bounded in the north by Goshta Khwaja Zemar and Lalpur, in the east by Pakistan, in the south by Dar Baba and Loye Shinwar, and in the west by Bati Kot. Mohmand Darah has about 11 villages, 6 of which have more than 500 inhabitants. The villages are listed in the PG as follows: Basol Kalai, Khar Kanai, Hazar Naw, Kando Ghazgai (Kando), Ghazgai Kalai, Gerdi Ghaus, Landikalai, Mila Basol, Daka Ulya, Daka Sufla, and Chaknur.

MOR مور
An affluent of the Panjao. It is a narrow winding tagao of no importance. (Muhammad Akbar Khan.)

MORU مورو
A village 25 miles from Ghazni, on the Kabul road. (Thornton.)

MOSHAN مشان
34- 69-. A village 5 miles east of Kabul, between it and Khurd Kabul. (Masson.)

MOSHUN مشون
A section of the Dai Kundis.

MOZANG See MAZANG مزنگ

MUBAT موبت
A section of the Polada Hazaras of Ujaristan.

MUCHI KHEL مچی خیل
A village in Kharwar; 60 houses of Ghilzais. (Griesbach.)

MUDKI مدکی
A hamlet on the road from Ali Khel to Ghazni, between Sulimi and Andoa. (Creagh.)

MUGHAL KHAN مغل خان
34- 70-. A village 106 miles northwest of Jalalabad, on the Alingar road, consisting of 300 houses of Adoke Afghans (?). (Leech.)

MUGHAL KHEL مغل خیل
34-9 69-3 m. A village of 70 houses on the left bank of the Logar, 2 miles north of Tangi Waghjan. (Clifford, Euan Smith.)

MUGHAL KHEL مغل خیل
34- 69-. A village in the Logar valley, south of the Tangi Waghjan. The inhabitants are Astanazai Ghilzais, and in 1880 they numbered 50 families. (Clifford, Euan Smith.)

*MUGHAL KHEL مغل خیل
34-44 69-40 m. A village located on the Tagab river some 10 miles south of Tagab in Kapisa province.

MUGHAL KHEL-I-AFGHANI مغل خیل افغانی
A village in the Surkhab division of the Jalalabad district. The inhabitants are Ghilzais. (Jenkyns.)

MUGHAL KOT مغل کوت
34-3 68-20 G. A village in the Khawat valley, about 44 miles northwest of Ghazni. There is room for a brigade to camp here with sufficient water. (I.B.C.)

MUHAMMAD AFZAL KHAN محمد افضل خان
34-38 69-13. A village in the Kabul district 3-1/2 miles north of the Paiminar Kotal on the road to Charikar. (I.B.C.)

MOHAMMAD AGHA محمد آغه
34-13 69-6. Mohammad Agha is the name of a village and a woleswali in the Logar province. The woleswali comprises an area of 1,017

square kilometers and has an agricultural population which has been estimated at about 20,900. The woleswali is bounded in the southwest by Puli-Alam, in the west by Nerkh, in the north by Charasiab and Khak-i-Jabbar, in the east by Azro, and in the south by Khoshi. Mohammad Agha includes about 73 villages, of which about twelve have more than 500 inhabitants. The villages are listed in the PG as follows: Qarya-i-Gomran, Qala-i-Anwar, Neyazi, Dawran Khel, Ghundi, Shir Afghan, Mirgai Khel, Nazar Khel, Hossen Khel, Ghulam Haider Khan, Qala-i-Khanjan, Qarya-i-Sheraza, Kandwala, Qarya-i-Kabkh, Kamal Khel, Nazar Khel, Qarya-i-Deh Nau, Bagh-i-Sultan, Dewalak, Shakarti Khel, Surkhabad, Qala-i-Shaikhak, Wazirestan, Qawm-i-Hazarah, Hazarah, Shadi Khan, Weghjan, Zargun Shahr-i-Ali Khel, Qala-i-Dalil, Qala-i-Shahi, Qala-i-Dawlat, Mohammad Agha, Mirza Khel, Kutub Khel, Qala-i-Jarnel, Qandahari, Khwaja Dakhel, Gotagi, Guli Khel, Khadokhel, Keshni, Shaghassi, Ghazni Khel, Qala-i-Wazir, Salam Khel, Seya Koh, Moghul Khel, Shekar Qala, Zaidabad, Dashtak, Qarya-i-Ainak, Abparan, Ahmadzai, Sayed Mir-i-Qala-i-Ahmadzai, Sangar Khel Geran, Taj Khan, Bahadur Khel, Safed Sang, Ab Bazak, Tari Gut, Seya Bini, Qala-i-Nazer, Qarya-i-Qoli, Langar, Ghal Dara, Karez, Surkh Ab, Dara-i-Surkh Ab, Qala-i-Kohna-i-Surkh Ab, Rahimabad, Qanat-i-Malik, Sher Afghan, and Bini Shir Afghan. (LWA) In 1914 the village was described as follows: A village in the northern portion of the Logar valley, and on the left bank of that river. It is 8 miles north of the Tangi Waghjan and about 23 miles south of Kabul. It consists of three detached portions, and in 1880 the inhabitants, who were Tajiks, numbered 200 families. The land in the neighborhood is very richly cultivated, and the apples of Muhammad Aga are said to be finest in Afghanistan. (Euan Smith, I.B.C.)

*MUHAMMADAK   محمدك
   33-9 67-25 m. A village located on a tributary of the Arghandab, southwest of the Dasht-i-Nawer in Ghazni province.

*MUHAMMAD ALI   محمدعلی
   32-43 68-18 m. A village located about half way between Khoshamand and Janikhel in Ghazni province.

MUHAMMAD ALI KHAN   محمدعلی خان
   34- 69-. A small walled village in the Kabul district, 1-1/2 miles from the Bala Hissar on the east side of the Kabul-Charasia road. It was burnt by the British on the 13th of December 1879. (I.B.C.)

*MUHAMMAD AMIN   محمد امین
   32-42 68-22 m. A village located some 8 miles east of Khoshamand and southwest of Janikhel in Ghazni province.

*MUHAMMAD DIN KALAI   محمد دین کی
   32-46 68-47 m. A village located about 5 miles north of Maryani in southern Ghazni province.

*MUHAMMAD DOST   محمد دوست
   32-50 68-29 m. A village located a few miles southeast of Khair Kot in Ghazni province.

*MUHAMMAD HASAN   محمد حسن
   32-48 68-28 m. A village located northeast of Janikhel and south of Khair Kot in Ghazni province.

MUHAMMAD HUSAIN محمد حسین
34- 70-. A fort in the Jalalabad district, situated 15 miles from Jalalabad.

MUHAMMAD IRAKI Or MAHMUD RAQI محمد عراقی (محمود راقی)
35-0 69-21. A township southeast of Ushtargiran in the Charikar district, south or southeast of Karezi, another large township south or southeast of Kham-i-Zardgar. Muhammad Iraki is said to consist of Murad Khwaja, Sayyid Khan, Malikji Baba Ali, Muhammad Umar Khel, Kalotar, Badi, Kalacha, Kazi Khel, Sayyidani, Soghal, Purdil Khan Shahbaz Khel, Sher Khan, Jamchi, Saifuddin Khel, Khudayar Khel, Mulla Fakir Khel, Wali Khel, Mulla Khel, Ali Khel, Mulla Zat Khel, Ali Khel (2), Hashur Khel, Malik Ahmad Khan, Ghani Khel, Sarban, Kazah, Kham-i-Robah, and Rahman Khel. Total 2,000 houses of Safis. There are orchards round the villages. (Shahzada Taimus.)

MUHAMMAD KARIM KHAN محمد کریم خان
A fort included in Deh-i-Murad Khan, Chardeh valley. Four towers and a large house over the gate which faces the river. Inhabitants: Tajiks, 15 houses. (I.B.C.)

*MUHAMMAD KHAN KALAI محمد خان کلی
32-42 68-59 m. A village on the Zawar Lgad in Paktia province another place with this name is between Marjana and Wazakhwa in Ghazni province, at 32-10 68-18 m.

*MUHAMMAD KHEL محمد خیل
32-19 67-51 m. A village located west of Nawa and south of the Ab-i-Istada in Ghazni province.

MUHAMMAD KHWAJA محمد خواجه
A main section of the Hazaras. A village with this name is in the Gulbahar area in Parwan, at 35-6 69-16 G. (LWA)

MUHAMMAD KICHAH See ZARSANG محمد کچاه

MUHAMMAD SADIK KHAN محمد صادق خان
34- 70-. A village in the Kama division of the Jalalabad district. Inhabitants: Hindkis and Tajiks. (Jenkyns.)

MUHAMMAD SHAH KHAN محمد شاه خان
34- 70-. A village in the Jalalabad district, 13 miles west of Gandamak; it lies on the left bank of the Surkhab river and forms one of the Hisarak group of villages in the Ghilzai country. The inhabitants are Jabar Khel Ghilzais. (I.B.C.) A pass with this name is located north of Jabalussaraj, at 35-18 69-7 G. (LWA)

MUHAMMAD SHAH KHAN محمد شاه خان
34-29 69-15. A small village in the Kabul district, on the left bank of the Logar river, between Bini Hisar and Bagrami. Inhabitants: Tajiks. (I.B.C.)

MUHAMMAD UMAR محمد عمر
34- 69-. One of the Rishkhor forts in the Chardeh valley of Kabul. (I.B.C.)

MUHAMMAD USMAN KHAN محمد عثمان خان
34- 69-. A small village in Chardeh valley, 1 mile west of Deh-i-Mozang on the Ghazni road. Inhabitants: Kizilbashis. (I.B.C.)

MURMARG مومرگ
    A place in the Besud country. (Maitland.)

*MUIN KALAI معین کلی
    32-56 69-23 m. A village located south of Giyan and east of Urgun in Paktia province.

MUKADAM مقدم
    A subsection of the Yanghur clan of Dai Zangis.

MUKASHRAK کشرق
    33-30 68-25. A village 4 miles south of Ghazni, on the road of Kandahar. (Thornton.)

MUKHBIL Or MAKHBIL مقبل
    33-50 69-56. A valley on the right bank of the Kurram river, about 17 miles west of Kurram fort. It runs down to the river in a north-westerly direction. A range of hills separates it on the west from the Chakmani valley. It contains the villages of Matwar, Hasan Khel and Woraki. The following is a reconnaissance report on the valley by Lieutenant Kane, date 9th June 1879:
Party consisted of Major-General Roberts, C.B., V.C., and staff, with an escort of 200 sabres 12th Bengal Cavalry.
From the right bank of the Kurram river, about 17 miles above the Kurram fort, this valley runs southeast. The river is here easily fordable, its depth not more than 2 1/2 feet, bottom of rough stones. After heavy rain the increased depth and force of the torrent (always very rapid) would render crossing dangerous.
1st mile. The path ascends from the river along the base of the hills on the west, and, crossing the valley, descends into a dry nala, some 200 yards wide; its banks are very steep, about 30 feet in height.
A party moving along this nala cannot be seen from the ground above. The outlet of this nala is not very clearly defined; south of the village of Matwar the ground is much broken, by reason of its softer nature, deeply fissured by the dry channels of rain torrents.
Abreast of and beyond the village, the valley has a width of some 1,500 yards; to the west of the nala for a distance of about 1,000 yards from the steeper slopes of the projecting spurs, the ground falls gradually towards the center of the valley; the surface is covered with short, coarse, dry grass the folds of the ground alone affording cover; the space of a similar character to the east is but 300 yards wide. Cavalry and infantry can move in any formation, guns making use of the nala as a road.
2nd mile. In the center long grass and scanty bushes cover the bed of the nala. Above it the glacis-like ground, now narrowing to about 500 yards, is clothed with holly scrub, many bushes as much as 10 feet in height, which obstruct all view; the surface is still smooth, and the scrub is not sufficiently thick to hinder the passage of troops of all arms.
On the left the hills now overhang the edge of the nala.
3rd mile. The width of the nala gradually decreases; from it a deep ravine runs in a southeasterly direction, its sides covered with scrub.
4th and 5th miles. The nala opening out now bifurcates, the wider branch running into the Musa Khel country, the narrower preserves the name of Mukhbil. On the left the hills slope directly down to the bank; on the right they recede to some distance; the intermediate space is very broken and covered with scrub.

6th mile. Above the nala on the right, but unseen from it, is a broad level patch of well-cultivated ground, and its further border is the village of Hasan Khel; the ground beyond is very broken.

7th mile. From the main nala a very narrow and tortuous ravine runs east; its banks are about 20 feet high, the bottom of fine gravel forms a good path, which leads to the miserable village of Woraki. Its situation commands a good view of the valley to the southeast. Water is of bad quality and very scarce; a large piece of ground already tilled lies waiting for its fertilising influence.

Return route. This lay partly over the high ground and through the flourishing village of Hasan Khel; it calls for no special remark.

Deduction. The passage of this portion of the Mukhbil valley for troops of all arms is easy and safe, provided that the precautions, usually taken on the line of march, are observed. The country in all directions can be effectually scoured by cavalry. Distance, approximately, from the Kurram river to Woraki village, 7 miles.

In reference to the above Mr. J.S. Donald, on special duty in Kurram, says:

"This (the Mukhbil valley) must be the Zegar valley in which these villages are located. The principal valleys inhabited by the Mukhbils are those of Ghozghari and Zegar. By the recent demarcation Ghozghari is now on the British side of the frontier."

The Mukhbils are subdivided thus:

    Musa Khel   Sultak
    Hasan Khel   Ahmad Khel
              Bobaki

It is important to note that the Ahmad Khel and Bobaki sections live in Ghozghari, the remaining sections are Afghan subjects. (Kane, Donald.)

*MUKHTAR   مختار

32-53 68-34 m. A village located southwest of Yahyakhel and northeast of Khair Kot in Ghazni province.

MUKUR   مقر

32-52 67-47 A. Mukur is a woleswali in Ghazni province. The woleswali comprises an area of 815 square kilometers and has an agricultural population that has been estimated at from 9,087 to 21,340. The woleswali is bounded in the west by Jaghori, in the southwest by Gilan, in the southeast by Kila, in the east by Ab Band, and in the north by Qarabagh. Mukur has about 80 villages, 14 of which have more than 500 inhabitants. The villages are listed in the PG as follows: Rabo Khel, Akhund Khel, Qala-i-Abul, Akhtar Khel, Afzal Khel, Ana Khel, Bazid Khel, Buzak, Bahawuddin, Tayef Khel, Tangi, Jani Khel, Jojha (Hajum Jaja), Char Deh, Chambar-i-Mahmud, Chambar-i-Mulla Sultan (Chambar-i-Sayed Khan), Chambar-i-Mulla Tur, Chori Khel, Qala-i-Khudaye Nazar Khan, Hamed Khel, Qala-i-Khudada-i-Gada Khel, Diwalak, Qala-i-Rahmani, Sar Chashma, Qala-i-Tokhi, Setar-i-Gada Khel, Qarya-i-Baz Moh'd, Nanga-i-Dolana Sangar (Nanga-i-Doland), Sulaimanzai, Samand Ya Rahman (Qala-i-Samand), Shali Khel, Seh Ganili, Saido Khail, Seh Gacha, Shah Alam Khel, Shah Moh'd Khel Larga, Shabnam, Shamak Khel, Qaya-i-Abdul Majid, Qala-i-Ezat, Alam Khel-i-Moh'd Khel, Ridel Khel, Eesa Khel, Mana Khel, Ati Khel-i-Gada-Khel, Azghar Khel-i-Bala, Bahrah Khan Khel, Qala-i-Abbas, Shamo Khel-i-Chambar-i-Zaman, Qala-i-Namdar, Qandahari, Qala-i-Qamaruddin, Qarya-i-Gala, Gul Khel-i-Bala, Gul Khel-i-Payin, Qala-i-Gudam, Gado Khel, Shabnam Largha, Lalam, Qarya-i-Manak, Ahmad Khel, Chambar-i-Moh'd. Gul, Chambar-i-Mado, Moqarab Khel-i-Larga, Malang Khel (Mana-Khel), Mala Khel, Momin Khel, Qala-i-Musa Jan, Mirza Khel, Nazer

Khel, Qarya-i-Nau Khuni, Nau-Ruzi, Chambar-i-Hashim, Helal Khel, Qala-i-Yar Beg, Azghar Khel-i-Shamali (Azghar Khel-i-Pain), Khana Dar-ha, Nauabad, Qarya-i-Dogha, Chaga, Ahmad Khel, Babu Qala, Khudzai, Dolant, Mulla Khel, and Lalan. (LWA) In 1914 the area was described as follows:

"The district of Mukur," says Molloy, "lies between the following points: On the north the territory of the Jaghur Hazaras and a little east of it Obah, on the southern boundary are Kala-i-Murtaza Khan and Gari, west are Shinkai and Ao Ghojan, and on the east Badam Kecha and the territory of the Suhail Khel Ghilzais. In Mukur itself and its immediate vicinity are settled the Ali Khel and Khudzai section of Sulaiman Khel Ghilzais; in the district the villages are chiefly those of the Taraki Ghilzais. The revenue of Mukur amounts to Rs. 40,000, and it contains between 4,000 to 5,000 houses." The elevation of the centre portion of the district averages about 6,500 feet. Mukur itself is 6,561 feet, Karez-i-Obah in the north of the district is 6,986 feet, while Murtaza on its southern boundary is 6,369 feet. Mansur Khan is Hakim at the present time (1895).

The headquarters of the district is Mukur; grass and forage are said to be procurable here in abundance. Wheat and barley are principally cultivated; goats, sheep, cattle, etc., are said to be kept in large numbers; but as the villages in 1880 were all deserted, neither supplies nor live-stock were obtainable for our troops. The Kandahar-Kabul main road runs through the centre of this district. The road, which as far as Mukur follows the valley of the Tarnak, was traversed by wheeled artillery both in the first Afghan war and in the 1879-80 campaign. Mukur is said to be a well-cultivated district; its appearance, however, is not attractive owing to the deficiency of trees. (Molloy, I.B.C.) Also see "Taraki."

MUKUR

32-52 67-47 m. Elevation 6,561 feet. The chief place in the Mukur district, distant 64 miles from Ghazni, 70 miles from Kalat-i-Ghilzai, and situated on the right bank of the Tarnak. Grass and forage are procurable here in great abundance, as well as grain of all kinds, goats, sheep and cows, and the river is famous for fish. Some 10 or 12 miles to the west of Mukur is Shinkai, where Amir Abdur Rahman established a small cantonment the garrison of which consists of 1 squadron cavalry, 2 or 3 battalions infantry, 4 mountain guns and 600 khasadars.

Near the village is a high rock, at the base of which is a pool of water supplied by six or seven springs, which are the source of the river Tarnak. On the borders of the pool is a thick clump of willow and ash trees, under the shade of which is a shrine dedicated to the memory of Shaikh Muhammad Rawani, a celebrated saint of this place who died some centuries ago. (Elphinstone, Bellew, Broadfoot, I.B.C.)

MULAGORI

A few families of this tribe live with the Sangu Khel Shinwaris. See "Shinwari." A description of the Mulagoris is given in the N.W.F. Gazetteer.

MULAIMPUR

A village in the Surkhab division of the Jalalabad district. Inhabitants: Ghilzais. (This place is also known as Kala-i-Khalikdad.) (Jenkyns.)

MULKABAD

A village in the Logar district, 45 miles south of Kabul. Thence there is a road into the Kharwar district. (Outram.)

MULKI
    A section of the Polada Hazaras.

ملکی

MULKYUB
    "Three thousand families of Nasir Powindahs live in the Mulkyub hills," was a statement made to General Chamberlain by some Powindahs. These hills are not noticed by any other authority.

ملکیوب

MULLA ABBAS KALA
    34- 68-. A small fortified hamlet in the Shibar valley, about 4 1/2 west of the Shibar Pass. At this point the road leading into the Birgalich Dara and over the Jalmish Kotal, branches off from the main Shibar-Bamian road. (I.B.C.)

ملاعباس قلعه

*MULLA AGHAJAN
    32-51 67-53 m. A village about 7 miles northeast of Mukur and east of the highway to Ghazni in Ghazni province.

ملاآغه جان

MULLA AYAN
    A village in the Bamian valley. (Maitland.)

ملااعیان

MULLA BASHIR
    A village in the Surkhab division of the Jalalabad district, at the confluence of the Rud-i-Kambu and Kabul river. Inhabitants: Dehgans. (Jenkyns.)

ملابشیر

MULLA GHAFUR
    34- 69-. A village in the Chardeh valley, Kabul district, 2 miles west of Aoshar. (I.B.C.)

ملاغفور

MULLAKHA
    A village 90 miles southwest of Ghazni, on a route to Kandahar. (Thornton.)

ملاخوا

MULLA KHEL See POWINDAH

ملاخیل

*MULLA KHEL
    34-23 71-1 m. A village located in the Nazarkhel area, north of Lalpura in eastern Nangarhar province. Other places with this name are located 1 mile west of Kota-i-Ashro on the Maidan river in Maidan province, at 34-27 68-46 m.; southeast of Sarobi, south of the road to Kabul, in Kabul province, at 34-29 69-39 m.

ملاخیل

MULLA KHEL
    33-10 68-6 G. A village in the Pannah district, Ghilzai country. It is inhabited by Andar and Taraki Ghilzais mixed. Water is found near it, but supplies are scarce. (Broadfoot.)

ملاخیل

MULLA MUHAMMAD GUL
    A village in the Surkhab division of the Jalalabad district. Inhabitants: Ghilzais. (Jenkyns.)

ملامحمدگل

MULLA MUHAMMAD GUL
    34- 70-. A village in the Chapriar division of the Jalalabad district. Inhabitants: Ghilzais. (Jenkyns.)

ملامحمدگل

MULLA YAKUB
    34- 69-. A large village in the Chardeh valley, 2 miles west of

ملایعقوب

Deh-i-Mozang and 1/2 mile north of the Ghazni road. Inhabitants: Tajiks. (Kennedy.) A pass with this name is located at 34-24 67-43 A. (LWA)

*MULLAYAN ملایان
34-20 69-25 m. A village located south of the Khurkabul and southwest of Khak-i-Jabbar in Kabul province. Other places with this name are located some 3 miles southwest of Sarobi, on the road to Kabul, in Kabul province, at 34-33 69-43 m.; 3 miles north of Maryan Marjan and southeast of Ghazni in Ghazni province, at 33-19 68-50 m.; some 12 miles west-southwest of Gardez and north of Haibatkhel in Paktia province, at 33-33 69-2 m.

MULLA ZARIB KHAN ملاظریب خان
34-29 69-15. A small village on the left bank of the Logar river, between Bagrami and Bini Hisar, in the neighborhood of Kabul. Inhabitants: Parsiwans. (Kennedy.)

*MUMA موه
33-14 67-23 m. A village located near Gosha and southeast of Aimaytu in Ghazni province.

MUMAK مومك
35- 69-. A village 4 miles north of the Bazarak pass over the Hindu Kush, consisting of 33 houses of men of Bazarak. (Leech.)

MUMAN See MADUGAL مومن

MUMARAK مومرك
34- 67-. A fort village in the Bamian district, situated on the shallow, gravelly stream which drains the Shahidan glen. On the opposite bank is the small fort of Alaf. The two together contain 40 families of Hazaras. (Maitland.)

MUMRAK ممرك
A section of Kaptasan Besud Hazaras.

MUNAL مونل
A fort in the Chardeh valley of Kabul between Aosar and Kala-i-Haji Yusuf. Forty families of Tajiks and Barakzais. Nine towers. Water from a karez. (I.B.C.)

*MUNARA مناره
34-47 67-46 m. A village located some 5 miles southwest of Bamian and northeast of Qazan in Bamian province.

MUNGUL منگل
A Madugal Kafir village of 40 houses in the nala of the same name, some distance from, and out of sight of, the right bank of the Bashgul river. (Robertson.)

MURAD BEG مراد بیگ
34-39 69-5 m. A village in the Koh Daman, 2 miles west of the Mama Khatun Kotal. It contains 100 houses, and is celebrated for its pottery, in which commodity there is a considerable trade. Kafilas usually make this the first stage (12 1/2 miles) from Kabul on the road to Badakhshan via the Khawak pass. (Kinloch, I.B.C.)

*MURAD KHAN مرادخان
33-48 68-16 m. A village located northwest of Babur and west of Jaghatu in Ghazni province.

MURAD KHAN مرادخان
34- 69-. A village in the Chardeh valley of Kabul, on the left bank of the river between Guzargah and Deh-i-Dana. Inhabitants: Barakzais and Tajiks. There are about 2000 houses in the place and four forts, viz:
        (1) Kala-i-Muhammad Karim Khan (Barakzai)
        (2) Kala-i-Sukar-Ullah Khan (Barakzai)
        (3) Kala-i-Malik Kurban (Tajik)
        (4) Kala-i-Janai (Tajik)   (I.B.C.)

MURAD KHANI مرادخانی
34-29 69-15. A small village in the Kabul district, 2 miles east of Bini Hisar, and close to the left bank of the Logar river. The inhabitants are Kizilbashis. (Kennedy.)

MURCHA KHEL مورچه خیل (مرچه)
A village in Laghman. Inhabitants: Tajiks. It contains the following hamlets:
        (1) Kala-i-Mian Sahib
        (2) Andarwan.   (Warburton.)

*MURCHAL مرچل
34-3 70-45 m. A village on the road north to Ghanikhel and the Torkham-Jalalabad road in Nangarhar province.

MURGH GIRAN مرغ گیران
34-28 69-1 m. A village in the Kabul district, on the northern slope of the Korogh mountain, about 3 miles south of Kala-i-Kazi. Inhabitants: Adramzais. (I.B.C.)

MURKI KHEL See MARKI KHEL مرکی خیل

MURSAL Or JILGA مرسل
33- 68-. A village on the road between Ghazni and Dawar, and immediately between Kala-i-Nazar Khan and Band. The village Jilga is commonly called Mursal from the pyramidal rock of that name said to have been thrown on to the village site by Ali. (McLean.)

MURTAZA مرتضی
Elevation 6,369 feet. A village between Pumba and Mukur, 12 miles from the latter and about 60 from the former. (I.B.C.)

MURTI مرتی
A section of the Polada Hazaras.

*MUSA DARA موسی دره
35-12 67-26 m. A village located about 3 miles west of Ergana and some 15 miles west of Saighan in northern Bamian province.

MUSAI موسئی
34- 69-. A small village in Logar district, on the left bank of the Logar river, about 13 miles from Kabul. Inhabitants: Husain Khels. (I.B.C.)

*MUSA KALAI موسی کلی
32-37 68-5 m. A village located some 10 miles southwest of Khoshamand and a few miles northeast of Dila in Ghazni province.

*MUSA KHEL موسی‌خیل
   33-7 68-17 m. A village located southeast of Batur in the Sardeh Rud valley of Ghazni province. Other places with this name are located on the Lazha Khwar, some 6 miles south of Lazha in Paktia province, at 33-41 69-37 m.; about 5 miles south of Mukur in Ghazni province, at 32-45 67-47 m.

*MUSA KHEL موسی‌خیل
   33-33 69-44. Musa Khel is a woleswali in Paktia province. The woleswali comprises an area of 410 square kilometers and has an agricultural population that thas been estimated at from 12,513 to 21,937. The woleswali is bounded in the west by Sayed Karam, in the south by Qalandar, in the southeast by Khost and Nader Shah Kot, in the east by Saroti and in the north by Jani Khel and Lajmangal. Musa Khel has some 72 villages, 11 of which have more than 500 inhabitants. The villages are listed in the PG as follows: Patak, Girnai (Mulla Matkai, Mulla Tangai), Ayebe Alang (Ibe), Yorukai, Margha Ghalang, Tarka (Tarkai), Kharlotai, Kombarai, Waya (Warya), Sur (Surkalai), Tsaparai (Khaparai), Tangai, Sandai, Khojol Lasti, Loy Chestun (Chestun-i-Ulya), Kamkai Chestun (Chestun-i-Sufla), Narai Moti (Mashrai Mati), Paru Khel (Pacha Khel), Kharkai, Zenda Mela, Shegai (Shaga), Khosmand, Prang Khola, Ayub Khel, Shenai, Khiyali Kala, Kaho Khola, Mewah Kahol, Hawas Kahol, (Yahosh Kahol), Adam Kahol, Maram Kahol Laja, Dray Khan Kahol (Darya Khan Laja), Zar Kahol, Mugag, Bechi Kot, Saydali Kahol (Sayd Kahol), Gerdi Khola, Sitkai, Lador Khola, Lakarai, Zhawrah (Paidah Zhawarah), Sotkan (Sur Kanai), Sur Lador, Yarghamalay (Arghamal), Zol Kot, Kossin Khola, Palah, Khirai, Mador (Marawar), Khan Kahol, Woreshmina (Warshina), Chakarai, Tamke, Mana Kahol, Zerirah (Zerirai), Kezha Kai (Kagai Deza), Woch Perrai, Ghozak, Manzi Kalai, Ghoyba, Miran, Kamkai Mazghor, Loy Mazghor, Shakhal, Khoshhal, Lowarah, Babti-i-Mina Khel, Khodkai (Ayub Khel-i-Bala), Gizha, Mirzah Kahol, Gharray Kalai, Gulag Golza, Narai Meti, Ein Qala, Mir Zaki, Kogai, Salim Kahol, Khwashidak, and Esmat Zhuwar.

MUSA KHEL موسی‌خیل
   A subdivision of the Sohak Ghilzais. (Kane.)

MUSA KHEL موسی‌خیل
   33-22 68-11 A. A village between Pannah and Kala Kharoti. It belonged to Mehtar Musa, a Ghilzai chief who threatened the British camp before the fall of Ghazni in 1839. He afterwards submitted to Outram, who visited this place. (Broadfoot.)

MUSAL موسل
   34- 69-. A village in the Chardeh valley, 5 miles west of Kabul city and close to Jangalak. Inhabitants: Tajiks. (I.B.C.)

MUSHAK See SHIBAR مشک
   33-49   69-38 A.

*MUSHAK مشک
   34-25 67-36 m. A village located on the Darra-i-Kalankhana, north of a series of ruined towers in Bamian province.

MUSHAKI See MASHAKI مشکی
   33-14   68-13 A.

*MUSHKHEL موش خیل
33-5 68-41 m. A village located some 7 miles south of Sharan woleswali seat and northeast of Yusufkhel in Ghazni province.

MUSHKHEL موش خیل
33- 68-. A village in Zurmat, at the third stage from Gardez towards Katawaz. Inhabitants: Sulaiman Khel Ghilzais. There are said to be 600 houses in the place, which is surrounded by a wall and ditch, with only one entrance. It stands on high ground. (I.B.C.)

MUSHTAN مشتان
35-5 69-1 G. A straggling village with a large square fort, in the Kaoshan glen, about 4 miles above its junction with the Ghorband valley. The village is surrounded with orchards. (I.B.C.)

MUSHUNGI مشنگی
A village 5 miles north of the Paiwar Kotal, on the road to the Lakarai pas. (Gordan.)

MUSTAUFI-ATA-MUHAMMAD مستوفی عطا محمد
34- 69-. A small fort in the Chardeh valley, 1 mile west of Deh-i-Mozang, on the Ghazni-Dawar road. The inhabitants are Andar Chilzais. (McLean.) A village with this name is located at 33-48 68-24 G. (LWA)

MYAN KHEL See LOHANI میان خیل

NABI نبی
34- 68-. A Ghilzai village on the left bank of the Kabul river, about 4 miles below Jalrez. (Wanliss.)

*NABI نبی
34-16 67-10 m. A village located on a tributary of the Helmand, near Naogiro and southeast of Panjao in Bamian province.

*NABI KALA نبی قلعه
32-28 69-12 m. A village located on the Zaura Lgad in the Shkin area, a few miles west of the Pakistani border in Paktia province.

NADAK ندك
A settlement of the Miramur clan of Sehpai Dai Zangi Hazaras.

NADIR DEH نادر ده
A village on the road from Ghazni to Shall. (Thornton.)

*NADIR SHAH KOT Or BATI KOT نادرشاه کوت
33-32 69-44. Nader Shah Kot is an alaqadari in Paktia province. The alaqadari comprises an area of 405 square kilometers and has an agricultural population that has been estimated at from 10,150 to 20,135. The alaqadaris is bounded in the west by Jadran and Shamal, in the south by Sperah and Tani, in the southeast by Mandozi, in the easty by Khost and in the north by Musa Khel and Qalandar. Nadir Shah Kot has some 38 villages, 15 of which have more than 500 inhabitants. The villages are listed in the PG as follows: Lora (Lola), Kuz Almarah, Bar Almarah, Pogai, Kikha (Kikhi), Nawi Kot, Bar Nawi Kot, Kuz Nawi Kot, Nader Shah Kot, Kaprai, Malwai (Milwai), Geda Wara, (Gedar Wala), Shambawat (Shabawat), Polisi, Kani, Tor Zawa, Spinkai Kalandar, Zangai, Aspirakai, Dawa Manda, Manzaka, Glorga (Shin Group), Spikan (Spikanzai Khel), Tamboka, Mir Goli (Mir

Goray), Spar Kai (Chaparai), Bogh Zeni Khel (Bagh Aka Khel), Soway Joyezai Khel, Mukbel (Bagh Muqbel), Sholgar, Badal, Wom, Shan (Khan), Shin Kalam, Meshkana (Mashkan, Shkun), Inzarkai (Kambarkai), Ghoreshtai (Sulemangul, Suleman Khel), Charmir, Khanwan, Em Toy, Gowaye, Ghanai and Shashi Ghar.

NAGHLU نغلو
34-37 69-44 A. A village in Laghman, on the left bank of the Kabul river, opposite Sarobi. The kafila road from Jalalabad to Nijrao and Kohistan passes through this village and there is an excellent camping ground here. The village lies close to the river and commands the ford across to Sarobi, but it is of no strength in itself. (Holdich, I.B.C.)

*NAGHAR KALAI نغرکی
32-19 68-26 m. A village located on the Baghlang Mandeh, east of the Loy Zeri Ghar in Ghazni province.

NAGHARAK-O-TAJIK نغرك وتاجك
34- 70-. A village in the Surkhab division of the Jalalabad district, situated on the right bank of the Kabul river, about 2 miles below Zulmabad. Inhabitants: Tajiks. (Jenkyns.)

NAHAR-I-FAULAD نهرفولاد
34- 68-. A village in Lower Maidan, on the left bank of the Maidan stream and lying southwest of the Korogh mountain. (I.B.C.)

NAHAR-I-MASI نهرماسی
34- 70-. A villge in the Besud division of the Jalalabad district, situated on the left bank of the Kabul river opposite Kala-i-Babari. Inhabitants: Dehgans and Tajiks. (Jenkyns.)

NAHAR-I-SHAHI نهرشاهی
34- 70-. A village in the Surkhab division of the Jalalabad district. Inhabitants: Dehgans, Tajiks, and Arabs. (Jenkyns.)

NAIB KALA نائب قلعه
34- 69-. A small square fort, close to the eastern end of Sherpur. In 1880, after the Afghan army had dispersed from before Sherpur, this place was occupied by a portion of the 67th Foot. (I.B.C.)

NAI KALA نی قلعه
A locality in the country of the Chahar Dasta Hazaras.

NAIMAN نیمان
A section of the Shekh Ali Hazaras.

NAIRUN نیرون
A locality in the country of the Jaghuri Hazaras.

NAITAK نیطاق
34-46 66-45 A. A wide and cultivated glen in the Yakh Walang district, which descends northeast to the Band-i-Amir valley. There is a small village in the middle, where the river route from Firozbahar crosses it (21 miles below the latter place), and a walled one on the opposite side. To the left of, that is above the latter, where a small hollow joins the glen, is a fort on the edge of a plateau. Above this again, and also on the further side, is another hamlet. (Maitland.)

*NAJARAN نجاران
   34-39 70-35 m. A village located on a tributary of the Kunar river, about 3 miles north of Darrah Nur in Nangarhar province.

*NAJI نجی
   33-24 68-33 m. A village located some 12 miles southeast of Ghazni in Ghazni province.

NAJIL نجیل
   34-53 70-7. A district in the valley of the Alishsang river, which is hence sometimes called the Najil river. It is situated about the centre of the valley, about 12 miles above the village of Alishang. It is inhabited by Nimcha Kafirs, who, though Muhammadans in religions, have retained most of the manners and customs of their Kafir neighbours. They pay revenue to the Afghan Governor of Laghman. (Masson.)
   Note.-- Only one Najir is given on the map of 1880, and that is apparently the place treated of above; but, in his list of the Laghman villages. Warburton mentions Najil, inhabitants: Tajiks. See next article.

NAJIL DARA نجیل دره
   34-53 70-7 m. A village in Laghman containing 12 forts and hamlets, viz.

   1. Sih Khandeh.   7. Daratui
   2. Kalwata   8. Shahi
   3. Kala-i-Ata Muhammad   9. Dakawato
      (consisting of 3 forts)
   4. Kotah   10. Dwa Shakh
   5. Kaswak   11. Naora and Ulwak
   6. Mandul   12. Dun Kroh

The inhabitants are Tajiks. Dara-i-Najil stands on the road from Ghaziabad to Farajghan. (Warburton.)

*NAK نک
   33-56 68-24 m. A village located in the Wardag o Jaghatu area, northeast of Sarsang in southern Maidan province.

*NAKAM ناکام
   33-2 68-11 m. A village near Manki and some 6 miles east of Qurbankhel in Ghazni province. Other places with this name are located some 10 miles south of Ghazni, at 33-24 68-29 m.; in Karezuna area, northeast of Matun in Paktia province, at 33-29 69-59 m.; near Khushamand in Ghazni province, at 32-25 68-13 m.; southwest of Yahyakhel and northeast of Zarghunshahr in Ghazni province, at 32-54 68-36 m.

*NAKHIL ناخیل
   32-29 67-39 m. A village located near Buri, west of the Ab-i-Istada in southern Ghazni province. Another place with this name is about 4 miles north of Mukur in Ghazni province, at 32-51 67-46 m.

*NALA ناله
   34-2 67-21 m. A village near Ajar on a tributary of the Helmand in Bamian province. Other places with this name are located near Mushak and west of Kharqol, at 34-26 67-37 m.; near Adamkhel in Maidan province, at 34-4 68-30 m.; on the Arghandab river in the Jaghuri

581

area in Ghazni province, at 33-9 67-27 m.; near Daru and west-southwest of Ghazni, at 33-29 68-10 m.

*NALAI or NARAI نری (نامی)
35-13 71-3. Nalai is an alaqadari in Kunar, now Nangarhar, province. The alaqadari comprises an area of 377 square kilometers and has an agricultural population that has been estimated at from 2,415 to 4,668. The alaqadari is bounded in the west by Kamdesh and Bar Kunar, on the south be Dangom, and in the east by Pakistan. Nalai has about 27 villages, none of which has more than 500 inhabitants. The villages are listed in the PG as follows: Barikot, Dokalan, Pashingar (Pashing), Incha Gul, Khun Nokass, Qarya-i-Nali, Liwafi, Dangpur, Suna Kala (Guna Kala), Machmana (Fanjaba), Kuchi Gul, Batas, Sehra Gul-i-Ulya, Chehrah Gul-i-Ulya, Azir Gul(Reza Gul), Shabili, Shergul Khul, Shergul, Saw (Sahmaw), Shah Mir, Zangar Gosha, Sawkhol (Nawkhol), Shalikot (Shai Kot), Shal Bandah, Shaklit, Shinagar, Badani, Qashang, Dolai Khor, Pul Saw, and Khonano Kass. For the village of Narai before 1914, see Nalai.

NALA SHERA ناله شیره
34- 68-. A village in the Shahidan glen, in the Bamian district, containing 20 families of Yanghur Hazaras. (Maitland.)

NALGIS Or NARGIS نرگس
A tagao in the Dai Zangi country. A pass with this name is located at 34-23 66-52 A. (LWA)

NAMADAK نمدك
A vilage in the Yakh Walang district, near the Firozbahar villages, inhabited by 20 families of Hazara Sayyids. (A.B.C.)

NAMATZAI نعمتزی
33- 68-. A village 30 miles southeast of Ghazni. (Thorton.) A place called Namati is located at 33-37 68-49 G. (LWA)

NAN نان
33- 69-. A village 15 miles north of Matun, on the road to Jaji Maidan by the Duni Kotal. (Carr.)

NANABAD نان آباد
34- 70-. A village in the Surkhab division of the Jalalabad district. Inhabitants; Ghilzais. (Jenkyns.)

NANACHI نانچی
34- 69-. A village 2 1/2 miles west of Kabul. Here are a succession of large forts surrounded by poplar and fruit trees. Shah Shuja halted here prior to his triumphal entry into Kabul in 1839. Inhabitants: Kizilbashis. The Nanachi pass leads from the Kabul plain into the Chardeh valley. (Havelock, I.B.C.)

NANAI نانی
32- 68-. A village about 42 miles southeast of Ghazni and near Dand, consisting of a group of four forts of Andar and Sulaiman Khel Ghilzais. Water is procurable. (Broadfoot.)

NANAI GHUND نانی غوند
32-57 68-17 m. A village at the first stage on the road south of Pannah, 37 miles south of Ghazni to the later place. There is a fort of the Shaki Khel Ghilzai near, and water and camel forage are procurable. (Broadfoot.)

*NANGA نانگ
   32-28 67-49 m. A village located west of the Ab-i-Istada on the road from Nawa north to Muqur in Ghazni province.

*NANGALAM Also see NIMGALAM ننگلام
   34-59 70-55 m. A village located on the Darra-i-Pich, a few miles south of Lalm Kats in Kunar province.

*NANGARHAR ننگرهار
   34-26 70-27. A province in eastern Afghanistan which comprises an area of 18,636 square kilometers and an agricultural population estimated at about 469,600. The province is bounded in the west by Kabul, in the north by Laghman and Kunar, and in the east and south by the State of Pakistan. Nangarhar is divided into the woleswalis of Kamdesh, Bar Kunar, Pich, Asadabad, Sirkanai, Chawki, Khas Kunar, Kauz Kunar, Kama, Goshta, Jalalabad, Surkh Rud, Hesarak, Khugiani, Deh Bala, Rudat, Achin, Shinwar, Nazian, and Mohmand Dara, and into the alaqadaris of Bargai Matal, Chapa Dara, Dangam, Marawara, Narang, Nur Gul, Behsud, Shirzad, Chaparhar, Pachir Aqam, Bati Kot, Lalpur, and Dorbaba. The capital of the province is the city of Jalalabad. For woleswali lists from the Department of Statistics of the Ministry of Agriculture and Irrigation see the tables below. For information prior to 1914, see Ningrahar.

*NANGIKHEL ننگی خیل
   34-52 69-10 m. A village located near the road from Kabul to Charikar in northern Kabul province.

*NANGRAHAR See NANGARHAR and NINGRAHAR ننگرهار

NANI نانی
   33-23 68-21. A village in the Shilghar district of the Ghilzai country, 12 miles from Ghazni. It is a large place, and there are several other forts in the vicinity inhabited by Andar Ghilzais. Grass and forage for camels are plentiful, and water is abundant and good from a karez. The village is surrounded by a plain, for the most part sandy, but there is a good deal of cultivation. At Nani the Gomal route from Dera Ismail Khan joins the Kabul-Kandahar road. (I.B.C.) A place called Nani Ghund is located at 32-57 68-17 A.

NANI نانی
   32-59 68-11 G. A group of 4 or 5 fortified hamlets about 55 miles south by west of Ghazni. Inhabitants: Sulaiman Khel and Andari Ghilzais. Water procurable. (I.B.C.)

NANI KHEL نانی خیل
   A village in the Gandamak division of Jalalabad, containing 300 houses of Wazir Khugianis.

*NAOABAD نو آباد
   34-21 66-47 m. A village located southeast of Asgharat in eastern Bamian province. Other places with this name are located south of Chahikhel on a tributary of the Tagab river in Kapisa province, at 34-57 69-48 m.; north of Ahmadzai on the road to Kabul in Logar province, at 34-18 69-8 m.; on the Kunar river near Jalalabad in Nangarhar province, at 34-26 70-31 m.; west of Nani and southwest of Ghazni, at 33-23 68-18 m.

583

Administrative Divisions of Nangarhar Province

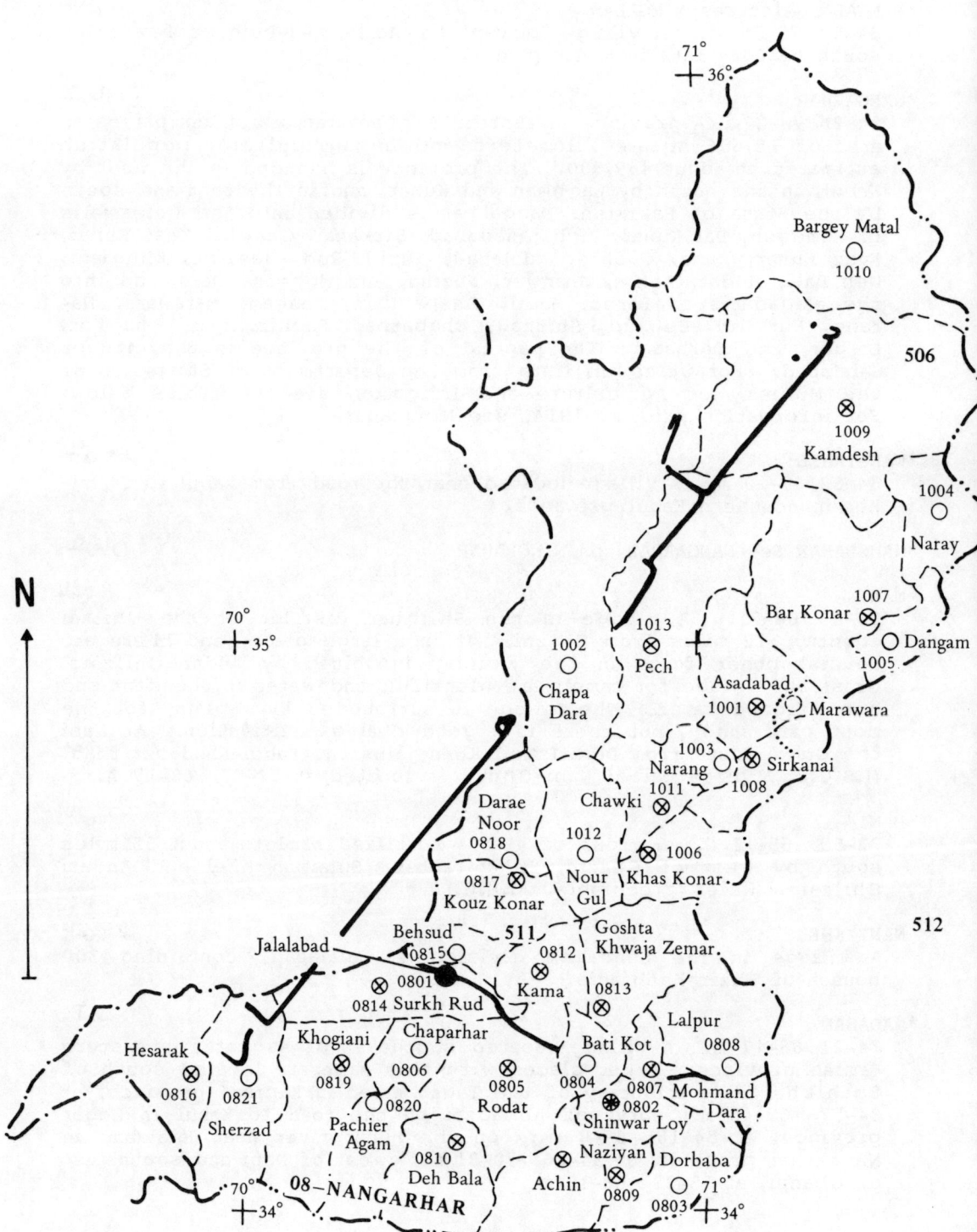

ESTIMATE OF AGRICULTURAL POPULATION AND AREA UNDER CULTIVATION

	Villages	Agricultural Population	Landlords	Lands under Cultivation in Jaribs			Lands under Cultivation in Hectares		
				Irrigated	Non-Irrig.	Total	Irrigated	Non-Irrig.	Total
ACHIN	27	47,980	5,530	12,910	18,490	31,400	2,582	3,698	6,280
HESARAK	49	27,990	2,660	8,380	11,780	20,160	1,676	2,356	4,032
KHUGIANI (KAGA, KAZA)	82	99,820	10,290	20,980	280	21,260	4,196	56	4,252
DEH BALA	33	24,640	6,140	11,050	3,030	14,080	2,210	606	2,816
SURKH RUD	51	43,340	6,870	26,170	300	26,470	5,234	60	5,294
SHINWAR	5	19,490	1,360	2,700	1,040	3,740	540	208	748
NAZIAN	6	9,490	280	10,050	–	10,050	2,010	–	2,010
RUDAT (SHAHI KOT)	43	39,280	6,180	15,970	26,100	42,070	3,194	5,220	8,414
MOHMAND DARA	8	18,450	1,100	7,860	540	8,400	1,572	108	1,680
KAMA	42	47,930	2,760	10,550	6,020	16,570	2,110	1,204	3,314
KAUZ KUNAR (SHEWA)	18	49,840	2,120	12,780	3,200	15,980	2,556	640	3,196
BATI KOT (NADAR SHAH KOT)	9	24,500	6,800	17,850	800	18,650	3,570	160	3,730
BEHSUD	33	13,790	3,560	8,820	2,200	11,020	1,764	440	2,204
DORBABA	23	15,980	1,390	1,140	1,320	2,460	228	264	492
DARA-I-NUR (DARA-I-KAUZ KUNAR)	20	26,340	1,850	8,630	630	9,260	1,726	126	1,852
PACHIR/AGAM (WAGAM)	17	17,970	2,710	8,920	–	8,920	1,784	–	1,784
CHAPARHAR (CHAPLEYAR)	25	26,840	2,160	10,170	–	10,170	3,034	–	3,034
SHERZAD	19	49,390	12,050	12,220	9,270	21,490	2,444	1,854	4,298
LALPUR	9	19,590	730	2,630	200	2,830	526	40	566
GOSHTA (KHWAJA ZEWAR)	12	18,250	1,220	1,950	5,450	7,400	390	1,090	1,480
TOTAL	531	640,900	77,760	211,730	90,650	302,380	43,346	18,130	61,476

STATISTICAL ESTIMATE OF LIVESTOCK BY WOLESWALIS AND ALAKADARIS

	Sheep	Karakul Sheep	Goats	Cattle	Buffaloes	Camels	Horses	Donkeys	Mules	Poultry
ACHIN	2,360	—	3,790	18,670	1,690	30	50	2,270	2,850	21,770
HESARAK	3,850	—	3,490	9,470	100	—	—	3,000	800	12,720
KHUGIANI (KAGA, KAZA)	8,900	—	3,460	14,890	50	240	30	4,890	620	32,500
DEH BALA	4,890	—	2,400	9,600	150	—	160	1,300	240	9,830
SURKH RUD	3,490	—	1,500	6,720	180	50	60	1,010	560	13,140
SHINWAR	6,250	—	4,200	6,290	70	30	80	1,990	950	2,650
NAZIAN	1,390	—	1,240	460	260	—	—	230	440	2,240
RUDAT (SHAHI KOT)	8,890	—	2,500	8,900	500	20	60	1,450	—	14,380
MOHMAND DARA	1,200	—	—	5,380	450	—	—	1,350	—	8,000
KAMA	1,360	—	—	9,190	650	—	—	2,280	—	7,160
KAUZ KUNAR (SHEWA)	1,400	—	340	9,500	50	70	—	1,990	—	8,970
BATI KOT (NADER SHAH KOT)	930	—	1,460	3,700	160	—	60	980	—	3,100
BEHSUD	3,360	—	590	6,620	650	50	30	1,590	650	7,340
DORBABA	1,180	—	1,590	1,760	390	230	80	1,800	7,000	3,680
DARA-I-NUR (DARA-I KAUZ KUNAR)	5,510	—	9,450	9,320	2,690	300	70	950	430	17,550
PACHIR/AGAM (WAGAM)	2,630	—	1,750	4,190	90	—	—	1,800	540	11,700
CHAPARHAR (CHAPLEYAR)	400	—	650	9,680	160	100	—	720	—	5,340
SHERZAD	1,720	—	2,480	4,290	—	—	90	1,900	940	3,080
LALPUR	—	—	1,420	4,900	800	—	—	1,980	—	3,280
GOSHTA (KHWAJA ZEWAR)	1,620	—	800	4,850	480	—	—	1,300	—	4,900
TOTAL	61,330	—	43,110	148,380	9,570	1,120	770	34,780	16,020	193,380

PRODUCTION OF AGRICULTURAL CROPS—IN KABULI SEERS

	Grains			Vegetables	Other Crops		Fruits
	Irrigated	Non-Irrig.	Total		Industrial Crops	Other Temp. Crops	
ACHIN	960,500	106,800	1,067,300	280,800	28,350	751,200	122,880
HESARAK	488,000	69,240	557,240	152,100	28,350	480,000	541,440
KHUGIANI (KAGA, KAZA)	1,659,000	1,680	1,660,680	924,300	505,640	28,800	514,560
DEH BALA	796,500	16,800	813,300	173,160	—	72,000	207,360
SURKH RUD	1,332,500	1,800	1,334,300	358,020	532,980	734,400	393,600
SHINWAR	198,000	12,000	210,000	126,360	181,440	655,200	13,440
NAZIAN	939,000	—	939,000	432,900	—	48,000	38,400
RUDAT (SHAHI KOT)	830,500	98,280	928,780	390,780	1,139,670	672,000	76,800
MAHMAND DARA	599,000	2,040	601,040	175,500	—	895,200	23,040
KAMA	118,500	34,800	153,300	109,980	170,100	873,600	599,040
KAUZ KUNAR (SHEWA)	818,000	18,000	836,000	425,880	340,200	480,000	288,000
BATI KOT (NADER SHAH KOT)	1,810,000	4,800	1,814,800	367,380	572,670	26,400	—
BEHSUD	637,000	8,400	645,400	273,780	295,840	28,800	28,800
DORBABA	95,500	7,200	102,700	—	—	36,000	—
DARA-I NUR (DARA-I-KAUZ KUNAR)	887,000	1,560	888,560	—	238,140	48,000	94,080
PACHIR/AGAM (WAGAM)	912,000	—	912,000	229,320	572,670	520,800	145,920
CHAPARHAR (CHAPLEYAR)	990,000	—	990,000	231,660	368,550	72,000	136,320
SHERZAD	1,152,000	126,120	1,278,120	624,780	—	724,800	263,040
LALPUR	156,000	1,320	157,320	226,980	221,130	655,200	5,760
GOSHTA (KHWAJA ZEWAR)	151,000	32,760	183,760	119,340	—	48,000	—
TOTAL	15,530,000	543,600	16,073,600	5,623,020	5,195,730	7,850,400	3,492,480

LAND UNDER IRRIGATION AND SOURCES OF IRRIGATION

	Area in Jaribs					Number of Sources			
	Canals	Springs	Karez	Wells	Total	Canals	Springs	Karez	Wells	Water Mills
ACHIN	—	8,910	4,000	—	12,910	—	18	64	—	104
HESARAK	4,200	1,180	3,000	—	8,380	15	19	45	—	66
KHUGIANI (KAGA, KAZA)	12,480	3,300	5,180	20	20,980	23	39	83	4	166
DEH BALA	9,540	1,350	160	—	11,050	5	32	1	—	48
SURKH RUD	24,170	2,000	—	—	26,170	16	8	—	—	126
SHINWAR	—	—	2,700	—	2,700	2	2	43	—	13
NAZIAN	8,000	—	2,050	—	10,050	6	5	3	—	17
RUDAT (SHAHI KOT)	7,790	2,490	5,690	—	15,970	43	13	84	—	96
MOHMAND DARA	4,250	—	3,600	10	7,860	8	4	41	3	10
KAMA	10,000	550	—	—	10,550	29	8	—	—	49
KAUZ KUNAR (SHEWA)	12,780	—	—	—	12,780	17	1	—	—	26
BATI KOT (NADER SHAH KOT)	16,300	220	1,550	—	17,850	4	3	25	—	34
BEHSUD	8,290	220	300	10	8,820	11	4	11	4	46
DORBABA	280	660	200	—	1,140	12	17	3	—	—
DARA-I-NUR (DARA-I-KAUZ KUNAR)	3,730	—	4,900	—	8,630	10	12	10	—	42
PACHIR/AGAM (WAGAM)	8,920	—	—	—	8,920	14	8	3	—	42
CHAPARHAR (CHAPLEYAR)	3,020	1,150	6,000	—	10,170	30	3	58	—	43
SHERZAD	4,300	—	7,920	—	12,220	13	11	21	—	62
LALPUR	2,620	—	—	10	2,630	8	—	—	2	7
GOSHTA (KHWAJA ZEWAR)	1,940	—	—	10	1,950	8	3	—	2	4
TOTAL	142,610	21,810	47,250	60	211,730	274	210	495	15	1,001

TOTAL CULTIVABLE LAND, BY CROP—IN KABULI JARIBS

	Grains Irrigated	Grains Non-Irrig.	Total	Vegetables	Industrial Crops	Other Crops	Fruits	Total Cultivated Land
ACHIN	19,210	8,900	28,110	1,200	50	3,130	640	33,130
HESARAK	9,760	5,770	15,530	650	50	2,000	2,820	21,050
KHUGIANI (KAGA, KAZA)	33,180	140	33,320	3,950	890	120	2,680	40,960
DEH BALA	15,930	1,400	17,330	740	—	300	1,080	19,450
SURKH RUD	26,650	150	26,800	1,530	940	3,060	2,050	34,380
SHINWAR	3,960	1,000	4,960	540	320	2,730	70	8,620
NAZIAN	18,780	—	18,780	1,850	—	200	200	21,030
RUDAT (SHAHI KOT)	16,610	8,190	24,800	1,670	2,010	2,800	400	31,680
MOHMAND DARA	11,980	170	12,150	750	—	2,730	120	15,750
KAMA	2,370	2,900	5,270	470	300	3,640	3,120	12,800
KAUZ KUNAR (SHEWA)	16,360	1,500	17,860	1,820	600	2,000	1,500	23,780
BATI KOT (NADER SHAH KOT)	36,200	400	36,600	1,570	1,010	110	—	39,290
BEHSUD	12,740	700	13,440	1,170	520	120	150	15,400
DORBABA	1,910	600	2,510	—	—	150	—	2,660
DARA-I-NUR (DARA-I-KAUZ KUNAR)	17,740	130	17,870	—	420	200	490	18,980
PACHIR/AGAM (WAGAM)	18,240	—	18,240	980	1,010	3,170	760	24,170
CHAPARHAR (CHAPLEYAR)	19,800	—	19,800	990	650	300	710	22,450
SHERZAD	23,040	10,510	33,550	2,670	—	3,020	1,370	40,610
LALPUR	3,120	110	3,230	970	390	2,730	30	7,340
GOSHTA (KHWAJA ZEWAR)	3,020	2,730	5,750	510	—	200	—	6,460
TOTAL	310,600	45,300	355,900	24,030	9,160	32,710	18,190	439,990

TOTAL CULTIVABLE LANDS—IN KABULI JARIBS

	Total	Pastures	Forests	Under Cultivation	Fallow Lands
ACHIN	116,160	11,970	72,790	31,400	11,760
HESARAK	195,540	13,300	162,080	20,160	7,790
KHUGIANI (KAGA, KAZA)	107,960	22,700	64,000	21,260	3,550
DEH BALA	22,740	8,660	—	14,080	3,750
SURKH RUD	96,260	19,230	50,560	26,470	5,150
SHINWAR	5,920	2,180	—	3,740	2,010
NAZIAN	101,300	1,260	89,990	10,050	3,530
RUDAT (SHAHI KOT)	97,390	3,330	51,990	42,070	15,560
MOHMAND DARA	9,520	1,120	—	8,400	2,030
KAMA	19,050	2,480	—	16,570	3,820
KAUZ KUNAR (SHEWA)	17,910	1,930	—	15,980	4,090
BATIKOT (NADER SHAH KOT)	49,840	6,750	24,440	18,650	3,540
BEHSUD	46,730	35,710	—	11,020	2,650
DORBABA	58,110	5,040	50,610	2,460	1,410
DARA-I-NUR (DARA-I-KAUZ KUNAR)	56,950	47,690	—	9,260	2,200
PACHIR/AGAM (WAGAM)	97,980	6,770	82,290	8,920	2,070
CHAPARHAR (CHAPLEYAR)	13,040	2,870	—	10,170	2,110
SHERZAD	22,280	790	—	21,490	6,960
LALPUR	4,450	1,620	—	2,830	1,070
GOSHTA (KHWAJA ZEWAR)	34,950	2,000	25,550	7,400	2,600
TOTAL	1,174,080	197,400	674,300	302,380	87,650

NAOABAD نوآباد
34-49 71-7. A ferry over the Kunar river on the Nawa Pass route to Chigha Serai, about two miles above Sarkani. Men and kit are ferried across on a raft consisting of a wooden frame supported on inflated skins, capable of carrying 12 men, but not animals, which have to be swum across. There is no rope, but the raft is rowed across by three men. There is only one raft ready, but more can be made at Sarkani without delay as everybody owns a "shinaz,' or inflated skin. The river here is about 100 yards wide and somewhat swift. There is a guard at the ferry of four sepoys to inspect travellers. (N.I.)

NAOABAD نوآباد
34-49 71-7 m. A small village on the right bank of the Kunar river five miles below Chigha Serai. (N.I.)

NAO BORIDA نوبریده
34-20 67-8 G. A low kotal crossed by the main Kabul-Hazarajat-Daulat Yar road about 6 miles east of Panjao serai.

NAO BURDA See NAO BORIDA نوبریده

NAODA MORA نوده موره
34- 70-. A village in Laghman, on the right bank of the Alingar river, near its junction with the Kabul. Inhabitants: Jabar Khel Ghilzais, Mohmands, and other tribes. The following is a list of the hamlets comprised in this place:
  1. Kabil-i-Sarbuland Khan   4. Kabil-i-Nasiri
  2. Kohna Lara Mora   5. Ziarat Babaji.
  3. Mashina   (Warburton.)

NAO DEH نوده
34- 69-. A village in the valley of the lower Logar, on the right bank of that river 5 miles northwest of Zargan Shahar, and 3 miles north of the Tangi Waghjan. The inhabitants are Tajiks. The village contained 150 families in 1880. (Clifford.)

*NAO DEH نوده
34-57 69-15 m. A village near Jamgadam in southern Parwan province. Other places with this name are located near Qara at the northwest corner of the Dasht-i-Nawer in Ghazni province, at 33-44 67-44 m.; north of Luman and southwest of the Dasht-i-Nawer, at 33-15 67-29 m.; north of Matun and southeast of Zorkot in Paktia province, at 33-29 69-55 m.

NAO DEH نوده
34- 69-. A walled village of considerable size in the Chardeh valley, 2 miles west of Deh-i-Mozang, to the north of the Kabul-Ghazni road. Inhabitants: Tajiks. (Kennedy.)

NAO-I-AMIN-UL-MULK نو امین الملك
A village in the valley of the upper Logar. Inhabitants: Parsiwans. In 1880 it consisted of three hamlets, containing 50 families. (Clifford, Euan Smith.)

NAO JU نوجو
34- 66-. A glen descending north to the Kirman valley, in the Dai Zangi country.

*NAO JUI نوجوى
    33-12 67-2 m. A village located near Shinia in the Sabzdara area in Ghazni province. Other places with this name are located on a tributary of the Band-i-Amir, southeast of Nashar in Bamian province, at 34-40 67-5 m.; northeast of Mianabad and southwest of Shahr-i-Khawat in Bamian province, at 34-1 67-49 m.

*NAO KALA Or NAWQALA نو قلعه
    33-59 68-2 m. A village located near Kamar in northern Ghazni province.

NAO KALA نو قلعه
    34-4 68-4 A. One of the four villages of Charkh, in the upper portion of the Logar valley. Inhabitants: Tajiks. (Clifford.)

NAO KALA نو قلعه
    33-37 68-24 G. A village about 6 miles north of Ghazni, containing 60 houses of Tajiks. Here also, on the opposite side of the road, is Chaharburja, 20 houses. (Muhammad Akbar Khan.)

NAO KALA نو قلعه
    A fortified hamlet on the left bank of the Helmand.

NAO KALA نو قلعه
    35-7 71-22. A village on the right bank of the Kunar river, close to the junction with the latter of the Pargan dara, 8 1/2 miles above Asnar. (I.B.C.)

NAO KALA نو قلعه
    34- 67-. Two villages in the Khawat valley, in Besud.

NAO KALA See ZARI نو قلعه

NAO NIAZ نیازنو
    34- 69-. A village in the Kabul district, between Chehil Dukhtaran and Aobazak, and 1 1/2 mile west of the Kabul road. It contains about 300 families inhabited by Tajiks. Fuel, fodder, grain, sheep and goats are easily procurable in the neighbourhood. Water is abundant. (Johnston.)

*NAORAK نورك
    33-26 68-1 m. A village located near Talkhak southwest of Ghazni. Other places with this name are located northeast of Takht and east of the Kuh-i-Diwalak in western Bamian province, at 34-8 66-44 m.; east of Asgharat in western Bamian province, at 34-23 66-59 m.; on the Naw-i-Binigaw in western Bamian province, at 34-17 66-49 m.; on a tributary of the Helmand in the Surkhabad area, at 34-17 67-39 m.; on a tributary of the Qol-i-Tsoitaman in Bamian province, at 34-15 67-13 m.

NAORAK نورك
    A village in the northwest of the Besud country.

NAORAM نورام
    A village in Laghman. Inhabitants: Tajiks. It contains three hamlets, viz.:
        1. Hajiabad   2. Duburja   3. Krandali
                        (Warburton.)

NAOROZ نوروز
    A large section of the Besud Hazaras.

592

*NAOROZI نوروزی
34-44 67-44 m. A village located on a tributary of the Bamian river, southwest of Bamian. Another place with this name is located near Helalkhel, southeast of Luman in Ghazni province, at 33-2 68-51 G.

NAO SHAHAR نو شهر
33-47 68-51 G. One of the four Tajik villages composing the township of Charkh.

NARANG نارنگ
34-45 71-3 A. Narang is an alaqadari in Nangarhar province. The alaqadari comprises an area of 164 square kilometers and has an agricultural population that has been estimated at from 5,796 to 7,705. Narang is bounded in the west by Pech and Chawki, in the east and southeast by Sirkanay, and in the north by Asadabad. Narang has about 28 villages, one of which has more than 500 inhabitants. The villages are listed in the PG as follows: Narang-i-Ulya and Sufla (Narhang), Sufla, Char Qala, Kado, Sharlo, Kala Mar, Ghando, Lamtak, Kotgai, Qala-i-Nau Badil (Qala Wana Badil), Soba Ghundi (Choba Ghundi), Kozah Ghundi, Qala-i-Wana, Amir Khan, Amluk Mina, Shino Kalai (Pashto Kalai), Qarya-i-Luchak, Lewat, Kozalai (Kozah Dai Banday), Khushal Bandah, Khudah Gash, Ahmad Khan Mina, Bajgul, Qarya-i-Qarghan, Kuchiano Bela, Adwal (Atwall), Khalatak, Ghazi Khan Ghundi and Qarya-i-Buzurg. (LWA) In 1914, the area was described as follows: Elevation 2,600 feet. Narang, or Bar Narang, consists of two villages on the right bank of the Kunar, 47 miles from Jalalabad. The valley here is wide, about 3/4 miles of flat ground on either side of the river. The Kuz Narang villages are situated some 3 miles lower down the stream. (Coldstream.)

NARGIS See NALGIS نرگس
34-23 66-52 A.

NARGOZAI نارگوزائی
34-15 69-52 G. A village in the Khugiani country, about 9 miles southwest of Gandamak. On the 6th July 1880, this place was taken and burnt by two bodies of troops moving in concert from Pezwan and Safed Sang, under the orders of Lieutenant-General Bright. Fifty-eight of the enemy were killed, and the lesson proved a salutary one in keeping the road free from petty raids. (I.B.C.)

NARI ناړی
34- 69-. A village in the Hisarak division of the Jalalabad district. Inhabitants: Shinwaris. (Jenkyns.) A village with this name is located at 35-13 71-32 G. (LWA)

*NARI Or NARAI ناړی
33-43 69-58 m. A village located southeast of Chamkani near the Pakistan border in Paktia province.

NARI Or NASRAT, NALAI ناړی
35-13 71-31 m. Elevation 3,000 feet. A village on the left bank the Kunar river, lying some 150 feet above its level, 8 miles below Arnawai. It contains about 100 houses, and is built on the pattern of Birkot, except that the lanes between the houses are somewhat broader. Rough bridges of boughs lead across them. The village parapet on the contiguous roofs is in some places 6 feet high, but in 1891 had mostly fallen into decay; certain portions of it have

large loop holes. Immediately to the north of the village is a square fort of the usual Chitrali type built by the late Mehtar Aman-ul-Mulk in 1891. It subsequently fell into the hands of Umra Khan of Jandol, but now lies within the limits of Afghanistan. There is a strong wooden bridge across the Kunar river, immediately opposite the village; this bridge is fit for pack animals and over it goes a road leading to Birkot, on the right bank, and thence up the Bashgul valley. From Nari a path goes up the Nari Gul and the Dolai dara, past the village of Machmana, and over the Dolai pass into Baraul. (Robertson, I.B.C.) This village is not the center of the alaqadari of Nalai or Narai. See Nalai. (LWA)

NARIJABAR ناړی جبار
A village 4 miles west of Gandamak, in the Khugiani country. (I.B.C.)

NASAR Or NASIR ناصر
34-26 69-54 A. A Powindah clan who "claim," says McMahon, "to be a Ghilzai tribe and to belong to the Turan division of that tribe. The Ghilzais deny their claim and say that their founder, Nasir or Nasar, was only a hamsayah of the Tokhis.

"According to some authorities, Nasir, or Nasar, had three sons, Tarakai, Spinkai and Surkai, from whom the Tai, Spin and Sur, i.e., the Black, White, and Red Nasirs, are descended. It is however, extremely difficult now to otain any authentic information as to the origin of these divisions, and as to which of them the various present sections and subsections of the tribe belong.

"I am inclined, after much enquiry, to think that the following genealogy of the tribe is approximately correct. It will be seen that the tribe comprises three main divisions, i.e., the Mallizais, Umarzais and Nasirzais.

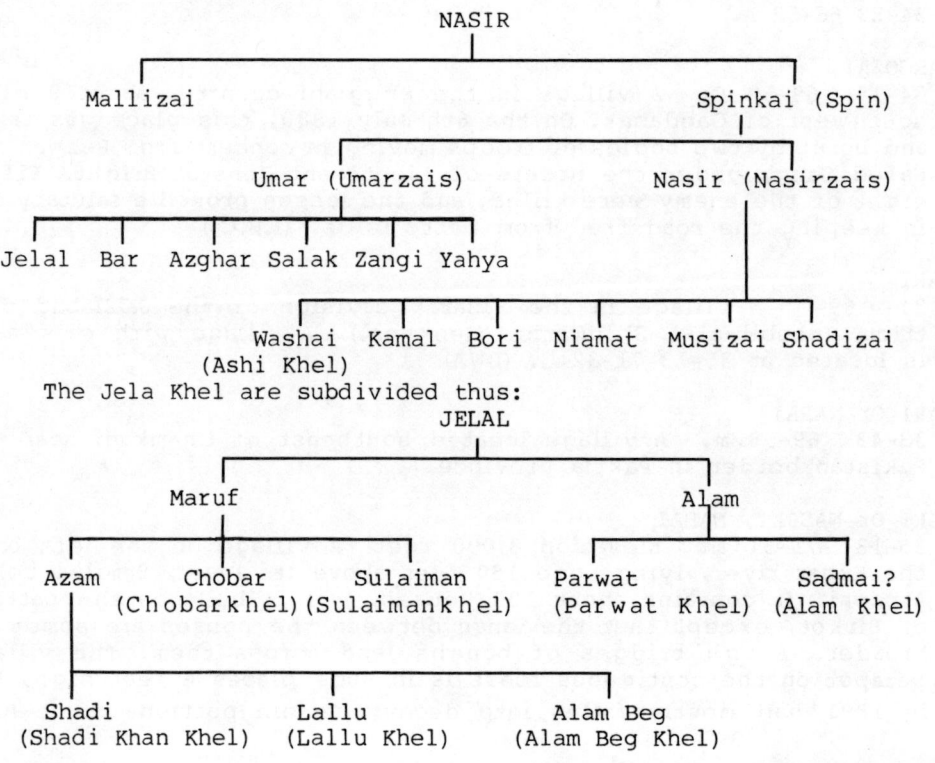

"The headman of the Jelal Khel is Abdulla Khan, Shadi Khan Khel. He is also the Chief of the Nasir tribe. The tribe numbers about 600 men.

"The Lallu Khel and Alam Khel live near the Ab-i-Istada in summer and in the Kulachi tahsil of Dera Ismail Khan in the winter.

"The Shadi Khan Khel live in Tirwah and near Ab-i-Istada in summer and near Chaudwan in winter.

"The Alam Beg Khel summer at Ab-i-Istada and Keshatu; winter in the Derajat Kachi.

"The Chobar Khel go with the Shadi Khan Khel.

"The Sulaiman Khel go half with Lallu Khel and half with the Shadi Khan Khel.

"The Parwat Khel summer at Zangala and winter at Zarkunni in the Derajat

"The Bar Khel are subdivided into the
(1) Babakar Khel   (2) Bariam Khel   (3) Sarwar Khel.

"They amount to about 400 men. They own no land. In former times they dwelt in the neighbourhood of Nawar and Ab-i-Istada, but since the Ghilzai rebellion, they live, during the summer months, between Keshatu and Tirwah and visit the Derajat in the winter. The present headman of the tribe is Ahmad Khan, Babakar Khel. They now own no land, but formerly cultivated Wano, Spin, Gulkach, etc.

"The Azghar Khel are said to number about 160 men and live with the Jelal Khel.

"The Salak Khel number about 300 men. They also live with the Jelal Khel.

"The Zangi Khel are subdivided into the following subsections:
(1) Sur   (2) Khairi Khel   (3) Saru Khel   (4) Ibrahim Khel
          (5) Khwaja Muhammad Khel.

"They number about 400 men. They spend the summer at Ghundghaz near Dochina and Chinjezam and Tirwah, and all go to Zerwani on the Kulachi border, Dera Ismail Khan, in the winter. They own lands and two karezes at or near Ghundghaz, but own no land elsewhere.

"The Yahya Khel are said to number about 600 men. They live near Ghundan in summer and in the Derajat in the winter.

"The Ashi Khel number about 400 men. Headman Pir Muhammad.

"They visit Mukur and the Lowana country in summer and Draband in the Dera Ismail Khan district or Sibi in the winter.

"The Kamal Khel summer in Zhob and Pishin and in winter some go to Draband, others to Sibi, Thal-Chotiali and Dera Ghazi Khan.

"The Bori Khel summer in Zhob and Pishin and in winter some go to Draband, others to Sibi, Thal-Chotali and Dera Ghazi Khan.

"The Niamat Khel summer in Zhob and Pishin and in winter some go to Draband, others to Sibi, Thal-Chotiali and Dera Ghazi Khan.

"The Musizais summer at Zangala and winter in Draband.

"The Shadizais spend the summer in Pishin and winter in Draband.

"The Daud Khel are not mentioned in the above genealogy. They are said not to be originally Nasirs but only hamsayahs. They call themselves 'Raghmai.' They own more land than any section of the Nasir tribe. Their lands are situated in Ghundghaz."

Lumsden says the Nasirs number only 1,850 families, and are divided into the following divisions:

	Tents
Jalal Khel (chief section)	200
Bar Khel	100
Alam Beg Khel	70
Chula Khel	80
Banu Khel	100
Yahya Khel	80
Zangi Khel	150

Kamal Khel (1)	200
Kamal Khel (2)	50
Ush Khel	200
Daud Khel	250
Musizai (1)	100
Musizai (2)	60
Saro Khel	60
Niamat Khel (1)	70
Niamat Khel (2)	80

The Nasirs are one of the strongest as well as one of the wealthiest of the Powindah clans, and the chief of the Jelal Khel section is generally acknowledged chief of the whole fraternity. Lumsden, as above stated, estimates their numbers at 1,850 families. Broadfoot thinks they number 5,000, Elphinstone places them at 12,000, while the "North-West Frontier Gazetteer" says "there are between 3,000 and 4,000 tents in the whole Nasir tribe, probably some 8,000 souls. Also see under "Powindah."

The Nasirs are said to pay a tribute of Rs. 3,000 annually to the head of the Turan Ghilzais at Margha for the right of pasturage; this sum they divide over encampments, according to the number of cattle, camels, sheep, and goats belonging to each. The poorer members of this clan, who possess not more than half a dozen camels each, club together and carry on a trade in salt which they bring from the Bahadur Khel mines to Ghazni, or the Kala-i-Ghilzai district, and barter it against grain, receiving three or four loads of the latter for every one of salt, according to the market value of the mineral on the spot at the time.

The Nasirs do not trade so much as the other Powindah clans, but depend almost entirely on their flocks and herds; the fleeces of their sheep supply the materials for their tents, their carpets and the sacks which hold their flour; their postins and some other articles are made of sheepskins; the milk of the ewe affords the cheese, butter and curd, which is their usual diet, and its flesh is their only luxury.

The produce of their sheep, and the hire of their camels, also furnish the means of obtaining the few articles they require from without; and the carriage of their tents and other property, which is so material to wandering people, is entirely performed by the camels. Their sheep and camels are extremely numerous, and every part of their economy is adapted to the moving life which is necessary to feed such a number of animals; their tents are small and light; their whole property is a suit or two of clothes, a few sacks of flour, with half a dozen earthen pots, and one or two of brass.

In their persons they are small, black and ugly; they are barbarous in their manners, and rude and squalid in their general appearance. They are, however, a remarkably honest and harmless people.

They leave the Derajat in March when the Gumal is flooded, their reason being that their sheep are with young, and lambs born in the Derajat are smaller and weaker than those born in Khorasan.

Elphinstone's account of their march, if somewhat coloured, is certainly most graphic: "The tribe marches through the hostile country of the Waziris in two divisions, and it is settled by the Khan and the Maliks which is to march first. The rendezvous for each division is at Kanzur on the Gumal, to which place all the hordes direct their march from their different camps in the Ghilzai country. In the beginning of this march they pass through barren wilds, where they see nobody but their own companions; but as they approach Kanzur the roads are choked with other hordes flocking from various and different stations to the rendezvous. Great confusion now arises; two hordes which are at war are often crowded together in one narrow valley, and new quarrels are also occasioned by the impatience of different parties to get first through the pass in the hills. At last they join the confused mass of tents, men, and cattle which are heaped together at Kanzur.

"The whole assemblage amounts to more than 30,000 people, with all their numberless flocks and herds of camels, and indeed with all their possessions. The bustle and disorder of such a throng may well be conceived. During the day they issue forth in swarms to search for forage and firewood; and at nightfall these unfrequented valleys resound with the confused voices of the multitude, the beating and lowing of their flocks and herds, the hoarse roar of the camel, and the shouts and songs of the Nasirs.

"When the whole division is assembled, Chiefs are appointed, and they renew their progress towards the Derajat. The Waziris in the meantime are preparing for their reception with all the caution and secrecy of savage war; their clans are assembled in the depths of the mountains, and a single scout, perhaps, watches on the brow of a rock, and listens in the silence of that desolate region for the hum of the approaching crowd, till at length the Nasirs are heard, and the valleys are filled with the stream of men and flocks that pours down the bed and the banks of the Gumal. The word is then passed round to the Waziris, who hasten to the defiles by paths known only to themselves, and attack the disorderly crowd, or lie in ambush to cut off the enemies. During this time of danger, which lasts a week or ten days, the Nasirs are in an unusual state of preparation; the power of the Chiefs suppresses all feuds, and arranges the order of march and the means of defence. The whole division moves in a body; parties of chosen men protect the front, the flanks, and the rear, while the other Nasirs drive on the sheep and camels, and hold themselves ready to repel any attack that may be made by their enemies. They had need, indeed, to be prepared, for the predatory disposition of the Waziris is sharpened by long enmity, they give no quarter to any Nasir that falls into their hands. (This state of things has undergone a considerable change since the Waziristan expedition of 1894-95.) At length they reach the pass of Zirkani, issue out into the plains, and are spread over the whole of Daman from the frontier of Upper Sind to the hills of the Marwatis. Each horde has a particular tract, where it is accustomed to encamp and round which it ranges as the supply of forage requires. They encamp in circles, within which they shut up their cattle at night. Their life is now idle and unwearied. The women do all the labour, pitch the tents, gather the wood, bring in water, and cook the dinner; the men only saunter out with the sheep and camels, and for this labour a very few men suffice. The rich hire out their cattle during their long halts, but the owner makes over the duty of accompanying them to some poor man, who gets a third of the hire for his labour. The women are never concealed, but they are said to be chaste and modest. When the snow has melted on the Takht-i-Sulaiman, the Chiefs of the Nasir camps send to the Khan of the whole to fix a time for a council; on the appointed day they all repair to his camp, determine their route, again appoint Chiefs, and soon after break up their camps and commence their return."

The Nasirs were in the habit of paying to the Sikhs, not only the customs dues for the goods they brought, but also a grazing-tax for liberty to pasture their camels during winter and spring in the Derajat. In 1848, when Major Edwardes was visiting the Kulachi border, it was brought to his notice that one Shahzad Nasir, Chief of the Nasirs, refused to pay anything at all, and from this cause arose a dilemma from which Edwardes extricated himself with his accustomed decision. He determined to attack the Chief in the midst of his clan and try to carry him off. To do this he started from Kulachi in the night with about 300 cavalry, Duranis and Sikhs; on arrival near the camp he found that of this number only 70 or 80 were present, the rest having remained behind on one pretence or another. He, however, determined to go on with the work in hand and led his men round ot the rear of the Nasir camp, and calling on them to follow charged down on the camp; but of the 70 or 80 only 15 followed him. Edwardes, however, got through, though with some danger, and finding a herd of Nasir camels on the other side, he drove them off and sold them in satisfaction of the grazing-tax which the Chief Shahzad had said he would never pay to the dogs of Sikhs and Faringis.

In March 1858, Captain Coxe, Deputy Commissioner, Dera Ismail Khan, reported that a party of the Nasirs and Kharoti Powindahs, who had sustained considerable loss at the hands of the Waziris during and after the passage through the hills from Khorasan, thinking a favourable opportunity offered for reimbursing themselves from the flocks and herds of the lower Waziris, moved into their country and succeeded in driving off some cattle.

On receipt of this intelligence Captain Coxe had intended to call on Shahzad Khan, to recover the whole of the property; but the thanadar of Kulachi previously on his own responsibility sent three Nasirs he had captured to troopers of the 5th Punjab Cavalry. Unused to deal with these men, and annoyed at the proposed interference, the Nasirs took the bold step of carrying the whole party off into the hills and removing themselves from British territory. The troopers were, however, soon released through the agency of Juma Khan, Zangi Khel Nasir, and the property given up without further demur.

Captain Coxe, in reporting the end of this affair, remarked with reference to the relation of the two parties to ourselves. "From the Waziris we experience nothing but annoyance and hostility. The long lists of acts of violence, thefts, and cruel murders, which are periodically submitted, will show that we owe them but little grace or favour. The Nasirs, on the other hand, have done us good and loyal service. To their watchfulness over many of the passes we owe much of our comparative immunity from petty raids on the centre portion of the frontier; and in 1855, when a serious attack was apprehended on Tank from the Waziris, the Nasir tribe furnished a large body of armed men for the defence of the frontier; and they would at any time render us similar aid when called upon." (Elphinstone, Broadfoot, Lumsden, Edwardes, Coke, McMahon.)

*NASAR ناصر
34-4 69-2 m. A village located near Kamalkhel on the Logar river in Logar province.

*NASDARA نسدره
34-53 69-28 m. A village located on a tributary of the Panjshir river south of Alikozai in Parwan province.

NASHAGAM Or NISHAGAM نشاگام
35-8 71-23 m. A village on the right bank of the Kunar, distant 85 miles from Jalalabad. (Coldstream.)

*NASHAR نشر
34-41 67-3 m. A village located on a tributary of the Daria-i-Band-i-Amir in Bamian province.

NASIR MUHAMMAD نصیر محمد
34- 68-. A village passed on the first march from the Lakarai Kotal towards Gandamak. It is situated on an affluent of the Surkhab river. (Collett.)

NASRAT See NARI نصرت

NAUROZ BEG نوروزبیگ
A section of the Kaptasan Besud Hazaras.

NAWA ناوه
A small village in the Daraz Kol, in the Dai Zangi country. A place called Nawa Nadak is located at 33-38 66-56 A. (LWA)

*NAWA ناوه
32-19 67-53 Nawa is a woleswali in Ghazni province. The woleswali comprises an area of 2,554 square kilometers and has an agricultural population that has been estimated at from 6,424 to 20,280. The woleswali is bounded in the east by Wazakhwa, in the northeast by Dila, in the northwest by Gilan, in the west by Shahjui, and in the south by Shinkai and Shemalzai. Nawa has about 53 villages, 10 of which have more than 500 inhabitants. The villages are listed in the PG as follows: Ikhtiyar Khel, Qarya-i-Andi, Bakol Khel, Burj-i-Rahman, Ibrahim Shah Khel (Bahram Shah Khel), Powati, Petab, Petab-i-Malik Din. Tor Kotsay (Targosh), Qarya-i-Talkhani, Tangi Chadar, Qarya-i-Akhund Saheb, Qarya-i-China, Qarya-i-Hasan Khel, Qarya-i-Khwaja Khel, Khoshhal (Khoshani), Dada Khel (Dado Khel), Zarin Khel, Sayed Khel, Qarya-i-Saleh, Sur, Hawli Khel (Ulya-Khel), Ghaizogai, Ghaybi Khel, Qasem Khel, Qala-i-Khan, Qarya-i-Moh'd Sarwar, Qarya-i-Mod'd Aziz, Qarya-i-Kalo Khel, Kamis Khel, Qarya-i-Kala Khan, Qarya-i-Garah, Qarya-i-Gajiyan, Qarya-i-Garaw Jan, Qarya-i-Gawranda, Mota Khel, Moh'd Khel, Qarya-i-Mansur, Qarya-i-Nanga, Jamal Khel, Karawoddin, Babri-i-Kalan, Babri-i-Khurd, Qarya-i-Haji Alwan, Qarya-i-Salimak (Yalmak), Qarya-i-Sakirah, Qarya-i-Laili Zai, Qarya-i-Zala (Qarya-i-Kohna), Qarya-i-Qahat-i-Safi, Qala-i-Rahman, Qala-i-Burj, Qala-i-Hawsi, Kanak Jamal (Kanak), Lal Moh'd Khel, Ango, Bazel Khel, Khan Khel, Babuli, Tarhi, Sado Khel (Shadu-Khel), Saifuddin Khel, Faiz Moh'd, Howli Khel, Harun, Qala-i-Moh'd Anwar, Jalo Khel, Hotak, Tangi, Zala, and Sekandar Khel.

*NAWA ناوه
34-49 68-8 m. A village located on a tributary of the Ghorband, about 2 miles south of Charkata. Another place with this name is southeast of Narang, near the Pakistan border in Kunar province, at 34-44 71-9 m.

NAWA AGHA See NAOGHAI ناوه آغه

*NAWAB نواب
32-39 68-52 m. A village located on the Gomal river, some 12 miles north of Gomal in Paktia province.

NAWAB KALA نواب قلعه
34- 68-. A village on the left bank of the upper Kabul river, about 4 miles west of Jalrez. (Wanliss.)

NAWACH See NAOCH نوچ

NAWAGI ناوه گی
34- 70-. A village in the Kama division of the Jalalabad district, situated close to and north of Landabuch. Inhabitants: Sayyids (of Kunar.) (Jenkyns.)

NAWA-I-RAHIM ناوه رحیم
A village in the Kishrao subdivision of the Dai Zangi district of Lal.

NAWAK See PARIAN ناوک
A pass with this name is located in Parwan, at 35-46 70-2 G. (LWA)

NAWALICH ناوه لیچ
35-21 69-33. A village in the upper Panjshir glen, situated on the right bank of the stream 3 miles above Bazarak. 20 houses of Tajiks. (Shahzada Taimuss.)

NAWAR ناور
A large valley in the Hazarajat.

NAWAR (NOAR) ناور (نوار)
33- 70-. A village in Khost, about 15 miles north-by-east of Matun. There is a good dry camping ground near the village. No grass is procurable, but there is plenty of bhusa; water is plentiful, but fuel is scarce. (I.B.C.) Recent maps show the name Nar, at 33-30 70-1 m. (LWA)

NAWAR LAM ناورلام
34-39 70-10 A. A village in Laghman, about 2 miles southeast of Alishang, on the left bank of the river. It is inhabited by mixed tribes. (Warburton.)

NAWA UJARISTAN See HAZARAS ناوه اجارستان

NAWI نوی
34- 68-. Kala Kazi Nawi is in the Ghorband valley, half a mile below Bin-i-Sehwak, 10 houses. Below Kala Kazi Nawi the valley opens out to a breadth of 1 1/2 miles, and is well cultivated, with numerous villages and gardens. This broad portion is called Nawi. (Peacocke.) Other places with this name are located at 34-4 68-4 and 34-56 68-29. (LWA)

*NAWUR Or NAWAR ناور
34-33 67-16 m. A village located near Panqash in Bamian province. Another place with this name is on a tributary of the Ghorband, northeast of Shaikh Ali in Parwan province, at 34-59 68-33 m.

*NAWUR Or NAWAR ناور
33-50 67-45. Nawur is a woleswali in Ghazni province. the woleswali comprises an area of 5,816 square kilometers and has an agricultural population that has been estimated at from 25,711 to 39,108. The woleswali is bounded in the west by Shahristan and Waras, in the north by Behsud, in the east by Dai Mirdad and Jaghatu, and in the south by Qarabagh, Jaghori and Malestan. Nawur has about 282 villages, of which about 198 have more than 500 inhabitants. The major villages listed in the PG are as follows: Abdara-i-Qar Nala, Altan, Almaqsud (Almaqsud-i-Burjagai), Wasi Muhammad, Barik Joye, Bariki (Baraki), Najara (Gardan Najara), Barik Aw, Sayed Pir Nazar, Bori Bahram (Bori Baran), Bahai (Bai), Tar Bulaq, Top Garmak, Jiska, Qarya-i-Joshan, Hesarak-i-Nahur, Khater Khosh (Qoriya-i-Khater

Khosh), Khar Murdah, Mehr Ali, Qarya-i-Du Abi, Dani Joshi (Dani Yakhshi), Dahan Barikak, Zard Regin-i-Kata Qala (Zard Regin), Sabz Nala, Shahjui, Deh Jan Beg, Shina, Joye Qol, Katar, Tughan, Wagha Jam, Deh Sikander, Sarpaye, Shaghna, Surkh Dewar (Surk Dewal), Qarya-i-Sardkoh, Sanginak-i-Mehr Ali, Sokhta Jangal, Siyah Reg, Shamaltu, Qar Nala, Karezak (Karezak Wa Tangi), Kutak-i-Sabz Ab (Sabz Ab), Kak-i-Shahr Khwab (Katok--Shahr Khawat), Korla(Karola-i-Khawat), Koh-i-Murdah-Sadan (Gaw Murda Wa-Siyah Reg), Garm Ab, Ghariba (Gharibi-Ali Panah), Garmak, Miyana Bed, Marid (Mazid), Mir Bacha, Nau Joye Bed, Gardan Altan, Neka, Wagh, Warchno, Wakak (Okak), Yakhshi, Sar Bed, Qarya-i-Emran, Qarya-i-Bator (Qarya-i-Jelga Badur), Qarya-i-Dosa (Dosa Jurghi), Qarya-i-Shurtur Murdah, Qarya-i-Pand Ali (Pendali Khawat), Dawlat Beg, Khashi Burjaki, Aludani, Khawat, Cheragh Sang-i-Nawur, Dang Aqa Beg, Dahan Suba, Anri, Sar Qala-i-Abdar, Shamaki, Shamak, Qala-i-Nader Khan, Qala-i-Nawa, Qala-i-Nau Pashya, Qobi, Qotan, Qalai-i-Chobi-i-Asyab, Kamokh, Ko-chi, Mashota Qala, Momarak, Qaracha, Sar Qala-i-Abdar, and Qarya-i-Hajat Bargali.

NAYAK نیک
34-44 66-57. Two fort villages, Nayak-i-Bala and Nayak-i-Pain, in the Band-i-Amir valley, both situated on the left bank of the stream 4 1/2 miles below Friozbahar, and together containing 70 families of Hazara Sayyids. (Maitland.)

NAYAK نیک
34- 66-. A small glen in the Yakh Walang district, running south of, and parallel to, that leading up to the Bakkak pass. (Maitland.)

*NAYAK نیک
34-5 67-34 m. A village located on the Garmab stream, near Geruqol in Bamian province. Other places with this name are located on a tributary of the Ghorband, south of Surkh o Parsa in Parwan province, at 34-51 68-37 m.; on a tributary of the Helmand, one mile north of Bum in Maidan province, at 34-27 68-5 m.

NAZARABAD نظرآباد
34-28 70-21 m. A village in the Surkhab division of the Jalalabad district, on the right bank of the Kabul river, near its junction with the Surkhab. Inhabitants: Tajiks and Dehgans. (Jenkyns.)

*NAZARKHEL نظرخیل
32-48 67-44 m. A village located about 3 miles southwest of Mukur in Ghazni province.

NAZIAN نازیان
34-7 70-48 A. Nazian is a woleswali in Nangarhar province. The woleswali comprises an area of 91 square kilometers and has an agricultural population that has been estimated at from 2,485 to 4,600. The woleswali is bounded in the north by Loye Shinwar, in the east and south by Dar Baba, and in the west by Achin. Nazian has about 6 villages, 3 of which have over 500 inhabitants. The villages are listed in the PG as follows: Surobi (Kurobi), Tarkha, Murchal, Kharmukhi or Sharmukhel, Bara Khel, and Landi (Landi Kalai). (LWA) In 1914 the area was described as follows:
A valley in the Jalalabad district, south of Basawal. It is aobut 8 miles in length, and is studded with forts from one extremity to the other, some of which are formidable positions. Towards the south it contracts to a narrow defile, lined with forts in many parts, con-

fined to the bed of the nala, with precipitous rocky sides. It is inhabited by the Sangu Khel section of Shinwaris, and there is a force of 300 khasadars quarterd in the valley.
During the early British occupation of Afghanistan, a force under General Shelton moved out from Jalalabad, to punish the Sangu Khels; 84 forts were taken in the course of the operations, with a loss of about 50 killed and wounded; among the former were Lieutenant Pigou, of the Engineers, and Captain Douglas, A.A.G. (Shelton, I.B.C.)

NAZIR ناظر
34- 69-. A small village in the valley of the lower Logar, between Deh-i-Nao and Karez-i-Daulat. Inhabitants: Niazis. In 1880 this hamlet contained 20 families. (Clifford, Euan Smith.) Recent maps show the name Nasar, at 34-4 69-3 m. (LWA)

NAZIR ABDUL WAHAB ناظر عبد الوهاب
34- 69-. A square fort in the Kabul district, 1 mile south of Aoshar, inhabited by Tajiks. It is surrounded by gardens and cultivation. (Kennedy.)

NAZIR ALI MUHAMMAD ناظر علی محمد
34- 69-. A small Tajik village in the Chardeh valley near Kabul. It is close to Baghwana, and has 30 houses. (I.B.C.)

NAZIR KHAN ناظر خان
33- 68-. A village 12 miles from Ghazni, on the road to Bannu via Dawar; 25 houses. Inhabitants: Andaris. Supplies abundant, except wood and grass, which are scarce. Water from karez plentiful and good. (McLean.)

*NAZUK نازوك
34-23 67-52 m. A village located some 6 miles northwest of Behsud in Maidan province.

*NAZUKKHEL نازوك خیل
34-13 68-28 m. A village located in the Dara-i-Jelga, west of Miran, in Maidan province.

*NEKA نکه
33-11 69-16. Neka is an alaqadari in Paktia province. The alaqadari comprises an area of 179 square kilometers and has an agricultural population that has been estimated at from 2,610 to 5,397. The alaqadari is bounded in the west by Sarhawza and Orma, in the northeast by Jadran, in the southeast by Zeluk, and in the south by Urgun. Neka has about 19 villages, 2 of which have more than 500 inhabitants. The villages are listed in the PG as follows: Sadeq, Bazak, Janat Khel, Sepai (Shapi-Khel), Fateh Khan Kalai, Khwaja Khel, Ashraf Khel, Nurakai, Tori (Torah) Khel, Zarbai, Barimi, Tori Khel-i-Mangal, Srah Qala, Sur Kot, Khalai, Mana, Andal Khel (Andar Khel), Miradak, Sayed Jan Kalai (Gul Jan Kalai), Oshakai, and Miradak.

NEKA نکه
A subdivision of the Bacha-i-Ghulam clan of Dai Zangi Hazaras.

*NEKAKHEL نکاخیل
34-56 69-24 m. A village located on the Panjshir river, opposite Giyaskhel in Kapisa province.

*NEKBAL نیکبل
33-19 69-44 m. A village located a few miles east of Nadirshahkot, on the road to Matun in Paktia province.

NEKPAI نیکپای
A small section of the Shaikh Ali Hazaras. Some 250 families of this section live in the Dara Kalan and at Dahana, both of which places are in the Ghori district of Badakhshan. (Maitland.)

NEKPAI KOL نیکپای قول
A lead mine in the Hazara mountains to the east of the Logar. Antimony in a metallic state is also said to exist in the same neighbourhood.

NESTI KOT نیستی کوت
33-40 69-16 m. A village about 6 miles northeast of Gardez, on the road thence to the Mirzakai kotal. The inhabitants are Amazai Ghilzais. (I.B.C.)

NIAN See ANIAN نیان
A stream with this name is located at 34-16 70-0 A.

NIASI نیاسی
34- 69-. A small village on the Kabul-Charasia road, near Bini Hisar. Inhabitants: Ghilzais. (I.B.C.)

NIAZAK نیازك
33- 69-. A village in the Chakmani valley, about 3 miles from its mouth. (Kane.)

*NIAZGUL نیازگل
34-14 69-12 m. A village located on a tributary of the Logar river, southeast of Narai Kot in Logar provinces.

*NIAZI نیازی
33-9 68-44 m. A village located near Sharan woleswali seat, northeast of Mushkhel in Ghazni province. Other places with this name are located near Kharoti, southwest of Nirkh in Maidan province, at 34-18 68-41 m.; on the Logar river, opposite Narai Kot in Logar province, at 34-16 69-8 m.; at 34-5 69-3 G. and 34-28 69-13 G.

NIAZI نیازی
A clan of Powindahs which numbers about 600 families and is subdivided into four sects, viz.:
Manrez Khel   150 tents   Musaud Khel   160 tents
Nurkhan   200 tents   Alikhel   80 tents.
The remainder of this clan is located in the vicinity of Isakhel in the Bannu district. They are British subjects and belong to the agricultural class. According to McMahon the Niazis are descended from the same stock as the Lohanis (q.v.). (Lumsden.)

NIAZI نیازی
33-45 69-6 m. A village in the Altimur pass. It consists of two hamlets. The inhabitants are Sayyids. The slope on which this village stands is within 2,000 yards of the top of the pass on the north side, and guns posted here could be used with good effect on the pass itself, as well as on the last 500 yards of road up to it. On the other hand, if the heights above Niazi were held, the forcing of the pass would be a difficult undertaking from the Logar side. (McLean, Bishop.)

NIAZI نيازى
A tribe inhabiting a portion of the valley of the Alingar. The Niazi Dara is a tributary glen towards the south. (Masson.)

NIAZI KHEL نيازى خيل
34-47 70-19 G. A village in Laghman, situated on the left bank of the Alingar river, about 2 miles northeast of Akinabad. The inhabitants are Ghilzais. The following is the list of hamlets contained in the place:

(1)	Kala-i-Ghulam Jan	(2)	Kala-i-Sayyid Ahmad
(3)	Kala-i-Amir Muhammad	(4)	Kala-i-Mir Muhammad
(5)	Kala-i-Azundin	(6)	Kala-i-Painda Gul
(7)	Kala-i-Tingawar	(8)	Kala-i-Hazrat Nur
(9)	Kala-i-Malik Zahid	(10)	Kala-i-Tak
(11)	Kala-i-Fakir Muhammad Akhzun	(12)	Kala-i-Sharfuddin
(13)	Kala-i-Hasan	(14)	Banda-i-Sharfuddin
(15)	Kala-i-Sharfudin	(16)	Kala-i-Ahmad Khan
(17)	Kala-i-Umra	(18)	Kala-i-Malik Adam

(19) Kala-i-Abdul Kadir
(Warburton.)

NIAZ KALA نياز قلعه
33- 68-. A village in the Ghazni district, between Ghazni and Kala-i-Nazir Khan. (McLean.)

*NIAZKHEL نيازخيل
34-53 69-42 m. A village located on a tributary of the Tagab river, about 5 miles northeast of Tagab in Kapisa province.

*NIAZULLAH نيازالله
33-19 68-16 m. A village located some 8 miles northeast of Mushakai on the road to Ghazni in Ghazni province.

NICHINGUL نچنگل
35-24 71-12 m. A valley which joins the right of the Bashgul near the village of Kamdesh in Kafiristan. A path leads up it to the Kungani pass and so on to the Presun or Pech river. Kashtan is passed at 3 miles, and a mile beyond the valley narrows greatly. At 13 miles the Mungilah Gul comes in from the north; up it is said to run a road to the Madugal country. From 8 to 20 miles the rise is 3,000 feet; the hills are bare save for grasses and shrubs. A good camping place at 20 miles. Elevation 11,600.
The road now begins to ascend steeply to the Kungani pass, but apart from the severity of the gradient there is no difficulty. At 20 1/2 miles the two Aramguls are passed, up both of which there are said to be roads which lead over passes into Waigul. The summit of the Kungani is reached at 23 miles elevation 14,600 feet. Rise in last 3 miles 3,000 feet. The descent west is by the Uzhamzhalgul, the first 1,300 feet being very steep. The Presun, or Wezgul, as it is now called, is reached at 6 miles from the crest of the pass, i.e., 29 miles from where the Bashgul is quitted. (Robertson.)

NIJRAO Or NIJRAB نجراو (نجراب)
34-58 69-34. Nijrab is a woleswali in Parwan province. The woleswali comprises an area of 58 square kilometers and has an agricultural population that has been estimated at from 25,986 to 28,652. The woleswali is bounded in the west by Mahmud Raqi, in the northwest by Durnama, in the north by Panjshir, in the southeast by Alasai, in the south by Tagab and Kohe Safi. Nijrab includes about 159 villages, of which 17 have more than 500 inhabitants. The

villages are listed in the PG as follows: Ibrahim Khel, Keki, Ibrahim Khel Pachghan, Abi Khel, Arbab Khel, Zarshoi, Jangal Bagh, Qala-i-Sarbeland, Eshno Dara Pota, Lala Khel (Allah Khel), Omba, Roza Khel, Ahangaran, Eskili, Babi Khel, Bakhana(Bakhan), Baqer Khel, Bazid Khel, Bagh-i-Aman, Bala Deh, Baba Sayad (Bala Hesar), Badakhi, Loka Khel Pachghan, Par Yad, Yasinzai, Khwaja Ghar, Khwaja Ghaus, Dachi Khel, Delyar, Dost Beg Khel, Doghabad, Dawlat Khan Khel, Do Qawmi, Pajen, Pasha-i-Pachghan, Pasha-i-Kharej Dara, Pand Waras, Tajekan, Taruri, Turchiyan, Tuman Khel, Jan Baba Khel, Jer-i-Feroz, Jamjugh (Jambogh), Jolayan, Jurghal, Char Safha (Chad Safha), Chasht Kohi, Deh Ghawchak, Aghaz, Laghman, Turnak, Dara Jay, Chakanda, Cocha Khel, Haji Khel, Hajian, Husain Khan Khel, Haider Khel Afghania, Arsalah Khel, Kando Khel, Tor Khel, Haider Khel Farukhsha, Khusrow Khel, Dara Kalani, Deh Khaki, Deh Qazi, Deh Lashi, Deh Pachkam, Deh Malo, Deh Nau, Mulla Khel, Ab Cheshma, Askini Dara Pata (Rashkin), Zekria Khel, Zendah Ghin, Sabat, Serghi, Shagheri (Seghri), Juma Khel, Sultan Shah Khel, Loka Khel Dara Pata, Nau Joi, Sayyidum Khel (Sirum Khel), Shoja Khel, Sharif Khel, Shafi Khel, Shaikhan, Sher Khan Khel, Sher Wani Sufla, Sher Wani Ulya, Salah Khel, Tula (Taka), Zuhri, Abdul Khel, Kurah, Alin, Omer Khel Dara Farukhshah, Wali Khel, Baba-i-Khel, Ayar Khel Sufla, Zolm Khel, Ayar Khel Ulya, Deh Rawan (Deh Ghori), Ghazi Beg Khel, Ghachulan, Ghundara, Ghin Pachgan (Ghani Bachakhan), Ghojan, Ghora (Ghorah), Farrukh Shah Khel, Baba-i-Khel, Wali Khel, Qer Ghash, Qalacha, Qala-i-Ghani, Qala-i-Khanjer, Qala-i-Khwaja, Qubad Khel, Kaka Khel, Kamsar, Qaylai, Kulhud, Gomman Garan, Kamanduk, Kurma, Gul Ko Khel, Galhin, Lik-i-Lama, Matan, Mohammad Khan Khel (Mohammad Jan Khel), Mazur Khel, Mulla Ghash (Mulla Ghani), Mir Khan Khel, Mir Khwaja Khel, Ferozai, Malik Khel, Namol (Nalon), Nakhchicha, Naghari, Nalkha, Waqsar (Wamiqsar), Weshar, Wehar, Homayun, Hura (Hoda), Yasin Khel, Aspa Khel, Spin Kundi, Pachi Khel, Farz Khel, Nawakhan, Kiligai, Shah Ka Khel, Sehdeh, Khozertan, Tapa-i-Ahmad Beg, Dawlat Khan Khel, Baborki Khel, Yahya Khel,Torkhan, Pasha Deh, and Soka Khel. (LWA) In 1914 the area was described as follows: A valley between Tagao and Panjshir. It is understood to form one of the four subdivisions of Kohistan; but very little is known about it, and it has never been mapped.

The waters of the Nijrao fall into the Panjshir near the Kora Kandao, the pass which connects the Nijrao with the head of the Tagao valley. A little above this the long valley of Pachigan joins it from the right, up which is the most direct road to Farajghan. Further up the Nijrao stream, about 10 miles, is the village of Kandi, at which branch off four different valleys. The easternmost one again separates into two glens, each leading to Farajghan. The three others lead into Panjshir.

The valley is very populous and has, according to Molloy, a population of about 4,000 Tajiks and 3,000 Safi families. Persian is chiefly spoken by all the Tajiks, but those of the Pachigan valley talk the "Pashai" language. Jalal-ud-din Khan, a nephew of Ghulam Haidar Khan, Sipah Salar, is said to be hakim at the present time (1895).

The Nijraois had always been independent of the rulers of Kabul previous to the reign of Sher Ali and it was only in the last two years of his rule that they were forced to own allegiance to him. He appointed Governors and obtained revenue. The first Governor, Mir Agha, was supposed to have enriched himself handsomely during his tenure of Governorship, paying ony a small portion of the revenue to the Government. The second Governor Mir Akbar, was unpopular, and was obliged to fly the country; and Abdul Karim, the third Governor, left the valley on the defeat of the Amir's troops at Ali

Masid, after which the people became again independent, or nearly so.

It is said that, in the time of Nadir Shah, the Nijraois so far submitted to that monarch that they each gave a wooden peg as a mark of allegiance, but they paid no revenue.

The whole valley is well watered and highly productive. Mulberries, wheat, rice, maize and barley, are the chief products. It is said to exceed in fertility the whole of the numerous valleys of Afghanistan. Merchants from the Koh Daman and Kohistan make large purchases from Nijrao of all kinds of grain. The hills and the upper ends of the branching glens are covered with pine trees. The chilghaza, or edible pine, is plentiful, as also are walnuts.

A considerable trade is carried on by Kuchis, who bring goods from Peshawar, avoiding Kabul and the severe taxations of that route. The kafilas branch off from Jalalabad to Laghman, and going by the Badpakht pass reach Nagulu on the Kabul river and proceed up the Tagao valley to Nijrao and the Kohistan.

A trade is also carried on with Farajghan. The people there are mostly in want of powder, lead, copper, dyes and cotton cloths, which they exchange for ghi, sheep, and gilims, or carpets of goats' hair. The people of Nijrao are said to be hospitable and more simple than the other inhabitants of the Kohistan, and they contrast favourably with the Panjshiris, who are always at enmity one with the other. There is said to be great mineral wealth in the Nijrao valley. (Steward, Molloy.)

NIKARA نكاره
34- 70-. A large village in the Alingar valley, said to contain 5,000 houses (?). Here there is a gigantic figure of the god "Gulshor." Nikara can be reached in thirteen days from Chitral, by the Kalash and Bashgul route. (McNair.) Recent maps show the name Nengarao, at 34-56 70-22. (LWA)

NIL نيل كوتل
34-48 67-22 G. Elevation 11,610 feet. A kotal crossed in the 3rd stage of the Bamian-DaulatYar main road. It presents no difficulty; the total rise from Karghanatu, 4 3/4 miles, being 950 feet. The descent is only about 85 feet. (Maitland.) This pass is about 12 miles west of Shahidan in Parwan province. (LWA)

NILAK, KOH-I نيلك كوه
A local name for the Koh-i-Kirghui.

*NILAO نيلاو
35-13 70-17 m. A village located on a tributary of the Pashal, northeast of Nawakzung in Laghman province.

*NILAY or NILI نلى
34-47 69-32 m. A village located on a tributary of the Panjshir river, southwest of Tagab in Kapisa province. Another place with this name is souteast of Nauruzi in Ghazni province, at 33-1 67-48 m.

NILI نلى
33-43 66-8 A. A locality in the country of the Dai Kundis.

NIMAKAO نمك او
35-1 68-57 A. A glen draining southwards from the Hindu Kush to the Ghorband valley which it joins at about 17 miles above Tutam Dara. It is traversed throughout its length by a road leading from Ghor-

band, over the Walian pass at the head of the glen, into the Khinjan valley. A considerable stream runs down the glen; it is said to be unfordable in summer in the lower part of its course. The road, however, keeps to the left bank the whole way, at times running up into the hills to avoid crossing the stream. At about 14 miles from its mouth the Nimakao glen is joined, from the east, by a ravine called the Dara Nao, or Kondilan; up this ravine a track, said to be practicable for horsemen and Afghan camels, leads over the Pech-o-Pech kotal and down the glen of the same name to the Kaoshan glen, which it joins at about 11 miles south of the Kaoshan pass. This forms an alternative approach to the Kaoshan pass when the road in the lower part of the Kaoshan glen is impassable owing to the swelling of the stream in spring. (I.B.C.)

NIMGALAM Or NANGALAM ننگلام
34-58 70-55 m. A village of 80 houses in Kafiristan. It is situated on the left bank of the Pech river near the junction with the latter of the Waigul. There is a good wooden bridge across the Waigul just above the junction of the two rivers. Supplies are plentiful at Nimgalam. (I.B.C.)

NIMLA نمله
34-18 70-6 A. Elevation 3,550 feet. A village in the Jalalabad district 5 1/2 miles east of Gandamak. It contains some 200 families of Khugianis. The inhabitants possess about 900 head of cattle, 500 sheep and goats, and 50 horses. There are about 700 jaribs of land under cultivation, yielding an average annual produce of about 44,500 Indian maunds. Rice, cotton and various kinds of pulse are also grown. Fodder enough for 4,000 animals for one day can be collected from Nimla and neighbourhood. Fuel is procurable from the neighbouring hills. There is good grazing ground for camels. Land-tax is assessed at the rate of 4 krans in cash, and 5 Kabuli maunds of wheat in kind, per jarib. The total revenue is said to amount to 18,000 krans.
There is a very fine old garden at Nimla, said to have been made by Shah Jehan; it is full of very old plane and cypress trees. In many cases the trunks of these trees are quite hollow from age, but they have been filled with cement under the Amir's orders to preserve the memory of their planter. Water enters at the top of the garden and flows throughout its length in succession of 4 masonry reservoirs each 10 feet wide, with a fall of 6 feet between each. The garden is about 400 yards by 375 in extent and is surrounded by a high wall; this wall was put into a thourough state of repair by Amir Abdur Rahman when he visited the garden in 1885. In the centre of the garden is a platform about 75 yards square, raised to a height of 8 feet above the ground. Fruit and flowers of all sorts abound.
A new sarai was built in 1905 about 400 yards west-southwest of the garden. Both the garden and the sarai lie in a hollow commanded on the east, south and west by the edges of the Nimla plateau. A good camping ground exists on the southern slopes of this plateau, with an ample supply of good water. (Malleson, Wanliss, I.B.C., Johnston.) Recent maps show the spelling Memla. (LWA)

NINGRAHAR Or NANGRAHAR Also See NANGARHAR ننگرهار
34-15 70-30 A. A province in eastern Afghanistan. For information on the period prior to 1912, see Nangarhar. In 1912 this area was described as follows: The old name of the Jalalabad valley, and still commonly applied to the southern portion of that district; the tract now known by this name is bounded roughly as follows: on

607

the west and north by the Surkhab and Kabul rivers, and on the east
and south by the Indo-Afghan frontier. The name is popularly supposed to signify "the land of nine rivers" (though the tract of
country described above cannot be said to contain that number), and
is explained by a combination of the Persian nuh, or nine, and the
Arabic nahar, or river. Bellew, however, states that it is really a
word of much more ancient origin, derived from the Sanskrit nau
vihara, or nine monasteries, the valley having been a very flourishing centre of Buddhism as late as the 5th century.
The following description is given of the inhabitants of Ningrahar:
"The Ningrahari wears a shortish coat, buttoned at the shoulder, and
a pagri without a kullah. He talks Pushtu, slightly differing from
our Frontier dialects, but most nearly resembling that spoken in the
Yusafzai district. He is distinctly more of a fighting man than his
neighbours the Laghmani and the Kunari."
Ningrahar appears to be one of the granaries of Kabul, and should be
able to furnish supplies for a large force anywhere on the line
between Dakka and Jalalabad. Quantities of wheat, barley, Indian
corn, etc., are exported to Kabul, and in the summer of 1903, whilst
the whole of the rest of Afghanistan was suffering from famine,
Ningrahar itself was not affected. The northern portion of the
district is watered by irrigation from the Kabul river and the
southern by means of Karez. (I.B.C.)

NIRKH نرخ
34-22 68-48. Nirkh is an alaqadari in Wardak province. The alaqadari comprises an area of 480 square kilometers and has a population that has been estimated at from 7,728 to 10,187. The alaqadari
is bounded in the west by Day Mirdad, in the north by Jalriz and
Maydan Shar, in the east by Muhammad Agha, and in the south by Puli-Alam, Sayed Abad, and Chak-i-Wardak. Nirkh includes 70 villages,
of which 5 have more than 500 inhabitants. The villages are listed
in the PG as follows: Deh Hayat, Karimdad, Markhana, Omar Khel,
Qala-i-Ismail Khosraw, Qala-i-Tatur, Tashluq, Qala-i-Tawa, Qala-i-
Pirdad, Qalai-Ghulam Haidar, Joy Asyab, Bajawri, Odah Khel, Khwaja
Boland, Wala-i-Wakil-i-Abdul Salam, Qala-i-Mohammad Alam, Qala-i-
Khairo, Qala-i-Ismail-i-Khoraw Khel, Qala-i-Awal Khel, Dadel, Qala-
i-Shah, Qala-i-Dadel, Qala-i-Mirza Khel, Qala-i-Allah Yar Khel,
Qala-i-Qol-i-Musa, Qala-i-Belal Khel, Qala-i-Zeyarat, Qala-i-Bocha,
Qala-i-Ghundi, Qala-i-Baluch Khel, Qala-i-Nandar Khel, Qala-i-Kul
Khel, Qala-i-Ghazi Khel, Qala-i-Darwiz Khel, Qala-i-Yaqub Khel,
Qala-i-Masum Khel, Sad Murda, Chinzai, Qala-i-Surkh, Rustam Khel,
Shamshir, Ab Khana, Haji, Azimuddin Watpur, Pachak, Qala-i-Kharoti-
i-Tokarak, Qala-i-Sultan, Qala-i-Abdul Rahman, Qala-i-Aqchi, Deh
Bochi, Qala-i-Kotagi, Qala-i-Khiyali, Qala-i-Acha Khel, Qala-i-
Aslam, Deh Kherqa, Ismail Khel, Amer Khel, Qala-i-Sad Barg, Aqchi,
Qala-i-Mohammad Akbar, Qala-i-Mohammad Shah, Qala-i-Jamal, Qala-i-
Aqa Gul, Qala-i-Sayed Khan, Kan-i-Ezat, Deh Muslem, Shah Kabul,
Shahabuddin, Tai Tamur, Chaghar, Awal Khel, Chashma Khel, Andar,
Durani, Qala-i-Awal Khel Omar Khel, Niazi Tokarak, Qala-i-Tir, Deh
Parak Deh Khurdak, Qarya-i-Nehak, and Chino. (LWA) In 1914 this
area was described as follows: A large, well cultivated valley,
with its head in the main Koh-i-Baba range, draining north and
debouching into the Ghorband valley 1 mile below Bin-i-Seewak. A
camel road leads up it to the Nirkh Kotal for Karezak (?). (Peacocke.)

NIRKH نرخ
34- 68-. A tributary of the Kabul river which, rising in the Sadmarda range, flows in an easterly direction and joins the Kabul

river about 6 miles below Kota-i-Ashru. The Nirkh valley, which is included in the Maidan district, is highly cultivated and is said to contain many villages. The inhabitants of the valley are Ghilzais. (Wanliss.)

NISADGUL نثادگل
35- 71-. A small camping ground in the Bashgul valley, in Kafiristan, 9 miles above Kirkot (Arnawai). (I.B.C.)

*NISHAGAM نیشه گام
35-8 71-23 M. A village located on the Kunar river near Bargam in Kunar province.

NISHAHAR نی شهر
33- 68-. A village at the head of the Charkh valley. (McLean.)

NISHAN نشان
34- 69-. A village in the valley of the lower Logar (Northern division), situated on the west of the Kabul road. The inhabitants are Tajiks, and in 1880 there were only three families inhabiting the place. (Clifford, Euan Smith.)

*NIZAMKHEL نظام خیل
32-50 69-24 m. A village located on the Margha Rud, some 4 miles from the Pakistan border in Paktia province.

NOACH Or NAWACH نوچ
35-13 69-13 A. A village in the Salang dara, 1 mile above Parwan. There is room for two battalions to encamp here on a stony and gravelly flat, and further space is available at Kalata, 1 1/4 miles higher up the valley. There is grass here on the hill-sides, and scattered bushes for fuel. Close by is the village of Shangol. (I.B.C.)

NOAR See NAWAR نوار

NOBALA نوبالا
34-19 67-12 G. A small village of 6 houses in (1904) on the left bank of the Siah Dara, about 10 miles east of Panjao serai. (Wanliss.)

*NODAL نودل
34-13 68-22 m. A village located a few miles east of Miran in Maidan province.

NOWALA نواله
35- 69-. A Tajik village in the Charikar district, situated under the hills left of the Panjshir stream, between Bazarak and Anada (Anaba?), 20 houses of Tajiks. (Shahzada Taimus.)

*NUKA نوکه
33-13 67-41 m. A village in the Nawa-i-Barik, northeast of Luman in Ghazni province.

NUKDARI نوکدری
A tribe mentioned by Babar as living west of Kabul. (Babar.)

NUKUR KHEL نکور خیل (نوکر)
34-15 70-3 G. A village in the Khugiani division of the Jalalabad district, about 3 miles southwest of Gandamak. Inhabitants: Kharbun Khugianis. (Jenkyns.)

Chutar, Linar, Sidur, Achgor, Pasanto (Pesta), Gul Neshan, Gadwal, Gazin Pacha (Pacha-Paicha), Poshal, Nalu, Atrara (Atalra), Jani Khel

*NUM RIZAY نوم ریزی
31-56 68-53 m. A village on the Helal Nikeh Mandeh in southern Ghazni province.

NUR See DARA-I-NUR نور

*NURA نوره
34-56 70-5 m. A village on the Alishang river, 2 miles north of Kusuk in Laghman province.

NURDI نوردی
Elevation 2,500 feet. A hamlet of six or seven houses only, also called Upper Bailam, on the right bank of the Kunar valley, just below the Garbar village of Palasgar. It stands on the right bank of the Viligul or Chugrikor Nala, which separates it from the fields of Palasgar. It is about 1,000 yards up-stream from the village of Bailam. Its inhabitants are Afghans and Shaikhs. (Robertson.)

*NUR GUL نورگل
34-36 70-45. Nur Gul is an alaqadari in Nangarhar province. The alaqadari comprises an area of 370 square kilometers and has an agricultural population that has been estimated at from 7,426 to 17,620. The alaqadari is bounded in the west by Dara-i-Nur and Kauz Kunar, in the south by Kama and Goshta Khwaja Zemar, in the east by Khas Kunar and Chawki, and in the north by Chapa Dara. Nur Gul has about 18 villages, 8 of which have more than 500 inhabitants. The villages are listed in the PG as follows: Nur Gul-i-Ulya, Nur Gul-i-Sufla, Patan, Siyah Qala (Miya Qala), Dara-i-Mazar, Tora Tizha (Siyah Sang), Sinzai Mazar, Lodlam (Lotgeram), Warina, Mashud (Masud-i-Ghazibad), Wazir, Wadir Ghazibad (Ghazibad), Shamasut (Shamash), Bela, Mama Gul, Shawat (Sholat), Garbuz-i-Ghazibad (Awrak-i-Ghazibad), Bal Nasrai (Bal Zai), and Qarya-i-Arit (Adit).

NURGUL نورگل
34-36 70-45 A. The Nurgul villages are situated on the right bank of the Kunar, 26 miles from Jalalabad. There is a great deal of cultivation and plenty of ground for camping but the latter is irrigated, and would be unsuitable after much rain. (Coldstream.)

NURI نوری
A section of the Daulatpai Besud Hazaras. A village with this name is located at 33-17 66-22 G.

NURISTAN نورستان
34-55 70-22. Nuristan is a woleswali in Laghman province. The woleswali, which comprises an area of 3,637 square kilometers, has an agricultural population that has been estimated at from 11,330 to 22,478. It is bounded in the north by Panjshir and Keran o Munjan, in the east by Chapa Dara and in the south by Alingar and Alishing, and in the west and southwest by Daulatshah and Panjshir. The woleswali contains about 77 villages, 16 of which have more than 500 inhabitants. The villages are listed in the PG as follows:
Wad Hu, Mamo, Kundi Sila, Shamgal (Letgal), Bachra (Lara), Pashagar (Pashgar), Noka, Shama, Chayel, Bagh-i-Tarang, Janya (Joniya), Chandaldari (Jangal Dari), Kandu, Piyar (Taipar), Dahan-i-Piyar, Gambata, Shotra Gambata, Khander Gambatra, Palosi, Guraj, Iskando (Skando), Bandal, Anish, Ko-Yesht, Duni, Awposh, Dahan Koyesht, Mandol,

(Jana Khel), Shakar Nal, Bala Murghab, Shalidur, Deh Sokhta, Lashtagam, Tai Kamar, Potla, Nilab, Mashwak (Shawak), Korgal, Pala Gal, Bachagal (Bajagal), Kori, Parkdari, Korna, Chatakwar (Shadis), Mashwi (Maswi), Malik Minok, Dara Falak, Jawajam-Kot, Koltan, Kora (Gora), Tatin, Deba Kalai, Pando (Pandaro), Kelem, Shakur, Monawar (Mangor), Goriz (Gorbuz), Malil, Mashfa, Nakrah, Kulcha Khel-i-Kaltan, Shamkal Gujar-ha, Balgosh Qawm-i-Gujar, Nangaraj, Saray, Kushan, Rumonar, Gudar, Tita, Yurnul, Deh Kalan, Shaqa, and Tabta.

NURI URDI   نوری اردی
A tribe mentioned by Wood as inhabiting the district of Yurt and the valley of Siah Sang.

NUR KADEH   نورکده
A low kotal between the Diwal Kol and Badasia valley.

NURKAH   نورکه
A section of the Dai Zangi Hazaras.

NUR KHAN   نورخان
33- 69-. A village 3 1/2 miles northeast of the Mirzakai kotal, on the road to Kurram. (I.B.C.)

NUR KHEL   نور خیل
A village in the Besud division of the Jalalabad district. Inhabitants: Dehgans and Tajiks. (Jenkyns.)

NUR MUHAMMADA   نور محمده
A small section of the Muhammad Khwaja Hazaras.

NUR-UL-ISLAM   نورالاسلام
The name which the Amir, in 1906, ordered to be adopted for Kafiristan (now called Nuristan).

NURZAI-O-USHTURI   نورزائی و اشتری
A village in the Besud division of the Jalalabad district. Inhabitants: Tajiks and Arabs. (Jenkyns.)

OBA   اوبه
32-59 67-54 G. A village on the road from Kandahar to Ghazni, 14 miles from Mukur and 12 miles from Jamrud. The village is marked by a large tree, near which a stream of clear water runs out from a karez. Across this stream (going from the high road) is the encamping ground on an open, waste plain. The following are the villages in the neighbourhood: (1) Piari Khel, (2) Bazak, (3) Laram, (4) Sekecha. Inhabitants: Taraki Ghilzais. The camping-ground, known as Oba Karez, was occupied by both Sir Donald Stewart and Sir Frederick Roberts on their respective marches to and from Kabul in 1880. The surrounding country is highly cultivated, and supplies of all kinds are abundant--grain, sheep, and fodder. Madder is grown and exported in great quantities. (I.B.C.)

OCHAK   اوچک
34-20 67-25 G. The sixth halting place on the old Kabul-Hazarajat road.

OCHAR   اچر
A subdivision of the Daichopan Hazaras.

OGHAZ Or UGHAZ اوغز
33-58 70-24 A. Elevation 7,000 feet (about.) A village in the Hisarak subdivision of the Jalalabad district. It lies amongst the low forest and grass-covered hills at the northern base of the Safed Koh, about 8 miles north of the pass, to which it gives its name. Water, wood and fodder are plentiful, but other supplies would have to be procured from villages lower down. (I.B.C.) Recent maps show the name Orghaz Kandao. Another place with this name is at 34-4 70-28 G. (LWA)

OGHAZ PASS اوغز کوتل
33-58 70-24. Elevation 13,000 feet. A pass in the Safed Koh, the summit lying about 8 miles south of the village of the same name. Over the pass a road said to be practicable for mules in summer, leads from the Hisarak valley in the Jalalabad district to the Kirman dara and Kurram. (I.B.C.)

OKI اکی
A section of the Jaghuri Hazaras.

OLIPUR الیپور
35- 70-. A valley north of Laghman and south of Kafiristan. Griffiths considers that its natural characteristics strongly resemble those of the valleys of the Himalaya, especially in the abundance, large growth, and excellence of its timber trees. The bottom of the valley which is about 3,000 feet above the sea, produces very fine oaks, and thick forests of these extend up the sides of the enclosing mountains to the height of about 4,500 feet above the same level. At that elevation commence the forests of zaitun, or wild olive, which clothe the mountains for a farther height of 2,000 feet. The deodar cedar grows in great abundance above this to the elevation of 10,000 feet. The timber used at Kabul being of bad quality and high price, it would be very desirable for that place that favourable means should be found for transporting thither the produce of these fine forests. This, however, is impracticable on account of the intervening difficulties; but the timber of Olipur could certainly be floated to the river of Kabul down the stream which flows through the valley and is described by Griffiths as a large torrent. Once afloat on the Kabul rivr, there would be no insurmountable obstacles to its passage as far as the ocean. (Griffiths.)

*OLMA Or ORMA اورمه
33-18 69-2. Olma is an alaqadari in Paktia province. The alaqadari comprises an area of 507 square kilometers and has an agricultural population that has been estimated at from 3,120 to 7,740. The alaqadari is bounded in the west by Mata Khan, in the south by Sarhawza, in the east by Neka and Jadran, and in the north by Zormat. Olma (Orma) has some 12 villages, two of which have more than 500 inhabitants. The villages are listed in the PG as follows: Gidzai Sur Dewar (Surkh Dewar), Dandak, Orma-i-Jadran, Gardid Khwah, Shaikh Malai, Asalat, Surkai (Tarkai), Shahi Kot, Kot Kala, Charwazai, Wocha Orma, Marzak, and Seway.

*OMNA اومنه
32-54 68-47. Omna is an alaqadari in Ghazni province. The alaqadari comprises an area of 464 square kilometers and has an agricultural population that has been estimated at from 1,526 to 7,436. The alaqadari is bounded in the west by Sultan Khel, in the south by Jani Khel, in the north by Sharan, and in the east by Sarhowza and

Gomal. Omna has about 27 villages, 10 of which have more than 500 inhabitants. The villages are listed in the Pg as follows: Ahmad Wal, Ata Khuna, Pas Khati, Bandar Khel, Sadozai Khadel, Sadat Wal, Shalo Khel, Qarar Khel, Qala-i-Abdurrahman, Lalam, Mirak Wal, Sayyid Khel, Spina, Zawaka, Qarya-i-Feroz Khan, Warroki, Bangi Wal, Taraki, Chahar Dewar, Dawlat Khanay, Sotiyan, Koliyan-i-Denar-Khel, Luqman Khel, Dangi, Maspiki, Garwal, and Dewalgai.

OPIAN اپیان
A village west of Charikar, in the plain of the Koh Daman. 300 Families of Tajiks. (Shahzada Taimus.)

ORFAN عرفان
A village in Kharwar, also known also as Urfan. 20 houses of Gada Ghilzais. (Griesbach.)

ORM اورم
33- 69-. A village on the righ bank of the Kurram river to the east of Landi wam. The inhabitants are Ahmed Khels, who can turn out 100 fighting men. (I.B.C.)

ORMA See OLMA اورمه

OSHLAN اشلان
33- 68-. Two forts in the Ghazni district, with 20 families. The ground around is completely void of brushwood and no supplies are procurable. It is on the left bank of the Ghazni river. (Broadfoot.)

OTLA See AGHAOJAN اتله

OULAGUL اولاگل
35- 71-. A Katir village built on the right bank of the torrent of the same name in Kafiristan, and a short distance from the left bank of the Bashgul river. It consists of 50 houses piled up on the end of a rocky spur. There is a good plank bridge over the Oulagul torrent. Up the valley there is a mountain track leading over into the Pittigul valley and to the Manjam pass. (Robertson.)

OUZHAK اوزك
35-48 71-16 G. A Katir settlement in the Skorigul in Kafiristan. In 1891 it was a hamlet of about a dozen houses, formed in the style of Luluk, and similarly surrounded by cultivation. (Robertson.)

PACHIGAN پچیگان
35- 69-. A long valley, running from the northeast into the Nijrao valley. The most direct road to Farajghan is said to lie through the Pachigan valley. The inhabitants speak the "Pashai" language. (Stewart.)

*PACHIGRAM پچیگرام
35-45 71-12 m. A village located on the Chapadara, southwest of Pazhgam in Kunar province.

PACHIR پچیر
34-8 70-17 m. Two villages, upper and lower (bala and pain), about 17 miles southeast of Gandamark. Inhabitants: Wazir Khugianis. (Jenkyns.)

*PACHIR O AGAM پچیر و اګام
   34-12 70-17. Pachir o Agam is an alaqadari named after the two
   major villages in Nangarhar province. The alaqadari comprises an
   area of 358 square kilometers and has an agricultural population
   which has been variously estimated at from 6,588 to 17,170. The
   alaqadari is bounded in the west by Khugiani, in the north by
   Chaparhar, in the east by Deh Bala, and in the south by the state of
   Pakistan. Pachir o Agam includes about 16 villages of which 5 have
   more than 500 inhabitants. The villages are listed in the PG as
   follows: Sabar-i-Sufla (Chapar-i-Sufla), Landi Khel, Zemar Khel,
   Morgai, Sabar-i-Ulya (Chapar-i-Ulya), Bami Khel, Khan Kalai (Khan
   Qala), Tangi-i-Sulaiman-Khel, Pachir-i-Ulya, Gari Khel (Gudi Khel),
   Mirza Bagh, Pachir-i-Sufla, Pankzai, Murgha, Lorrah Mina, Bangzar
   (Bang-i-Sarwar), and Mir Khani Khel.

PADKAU ROGHANI See PATKAO-I-ROGHANI   پادکو

PADSHAH KALA   پادشاه قلعه
   A fort at the entrance of the Dara-i-Nur glen, in Kunar, built by a
   former Governor of Jalalabad for the coercion of the neighbouring
   tribes. (Masson.)

PADSHAH KHANA   پادشاه خانه
   A village in the Logar district. It is noted from the excellence of
   its manufacture of porous water goblets, which are carried from this
   place to Kabul in great numbers. (Bellew.)

*PADSHAHKHEL   پادشاه خیل
   34-21 68-55 m. A village located on the Maidan river, southeast of
   Nirkh in Maidan province.

PAGHJUR   پغجور
   35- 69-. A village 15 miles south from the top of the Khawak pass.
   It has 200 houses of Tajiks. (Leech.)
   N.B. This may be the same as Sangpar (see "Khawak.).

PAGHMAN   پغمان
   34-35 68-57 m. Paghman is a town and a woleswali in Kabul province.
   The woleswali comprises an area of 413 square kilometers and has an
   agricultural population which has been variously estimated at from
   17,880 to 51,650. The woleswali is west of Kabul. Paghman includes
   about 35 villages, of which 18 have more than 500 inhabitants. The
   villages are listed in the PG as follows: Murghgiran, Kaj Darah,
   Isa Khel, Qala-i-Ada, Nader Khel, Qurban Khel, Lochka, Zarshakh,
   Tawalat, Kunjak, Bektut, Chandal Bai, Nalab wa Chalak, Parachi,
   Arghandi Sufla, Karezak, Pashai Paghman (Uria Khel), Khwaja Lakan,
   Khaldari, Arghandi Ulya, Chel Tan, Qala-i-Malik wa Pushta, Dara-i-
   Zargar, Samuchak, Qala-i-Hakim, Alabila, Khwaja Musafer (Khwaja
   Muzafar), Qargha, Deh Arbab, Deh Punbah, Doda Mast, Kushkak-i-Ulya
   wa Sufla, Kamangar, Muhammad Khel, Deh Uryan, Nabat, Najoy and
   Khwaja Mohammad Qargha. (LWA) In 1914 the area was described as
   follows: An important spur thrown off by the Sanglakh range. The
   summer palace of the Amir, which is situated on the eastern slopes
   of the Paghman range is connected with Kabul by a broad carriage
   road, 12 miles long. (I.B.C.)

PAIA KHEL   پایمخیل
   A village in Laghman. Inhabitants: Tajiks. (Warburton.)

PAIAN KHEL پائین خیل
34-31 70-9. A village in Laghman, on the left bank of the Kabul river, opposite Khairo Khel. Supplies are said to be fairly plentiful. (Young.)

PAI JEZKA پای جزکه
A locality in the Besud Hazara country.

PAI KOL پای قول
A small valley in the Besud country.

*PAI KOTAL پای کوتل
34-46 67-41 m. A village on the Dara-i-Syalayak, some 10 miles southwest of Bamian in Bamian province. Another place with this name is east of Badkhaneghar and south of Miran, at 34-5 68-19 m.

PAI KOTAL See SHIBAR 34-54 68-14 A. پای کوتل

PAI KOTAL See JALMISH پای کوتل

PAI KOTAL پای کوتل
34-22 66-37 G. A village on the main Kabul-Hazarajat-Daulat Yar road.

PAI KURKH See AKZARAT (1) پای کرخ

PAIMINAR پای منار
34-36 69-12 m. A pass over the low hills 6 miles north of Kabul. When seen in 1905 a cart-road over the pass had apparently been aligned but never completed, and the pass was crossed by a rough stony track, difficult even for single horsemen. To the north of the pass lies the village of Paiminar and to the south is the Wazirabad lake. (Kabul Mission, 1905, I.B.C.) Recent maps show Monar. (LWA)

PAIMURI پای موری
34-48 68-1 m. A village in the Bamian district, situated in the Kalu glen, 12 houses of Darghan Hazaras. (Amir Khan.)

*PAINDA پاینده
33-56 68-9 m. A village located southwest of Shinia and south of the Koh-i-Yakhaghan in northern Ghazni province.

PAINDA KHAK پاینده خاک
34- 71-. A small post in the Khaibar pass, 6-1/2 miles from Landi Kotal and about the same distance from Dakka. It is completely commanded at short range by hills on the northwest, and appeared to be in bad repair when seen in 1904. The Garrison consists of 50 khasadars armed with Lee-Metfords.
Frequent raids occurred here during the second Afghan War from a fairly easy path leading through a gap in the higher hills on the west to the village of Darband and thence over an open plain, westwards to Pesh Bolak in Ningrahar, or southwards, by the Sisobi pass, into the Bazar valley. In the spring of 1879 convoys used to be fired into almost daily when passing Painda Khak. At last a careful reconnaissance showed the value of this spot and a company of Gurkhas being posted there daily, all annoyance ceased almost immediately. One reason for this being such a favourite place for raiders was probably the fact of there being a small spring, called Gurrakki Obah, about halfway up the Darband pass on the western

side. This is the only water procurable, at any rate in a dry season, between Landi Khana and Haft Chah and though the supply is bad and very scanty, it was sufficient to prove of great value to the Gurkha picquet and, no doubt, to the raiders before them. Water might be led for miles down an old ruined irrigation channel on the left bank of the nala. (Malleson, I.B.C.)

PAINDA KHEL   پاینده خیل
    34-44 69-40 A. A Sulaiman Khel Ghilzai village in Katawaz.

PAIO KHEL   پایوخیل
    A village in the southern division of the Logar valley. 25 families of Ghilzais and Sayyids. (Clifford, Euan Smith.)

PAIPALI See SAIFALI 32-50 69-27 G.   پای پلی

*PAITAB   پیتاب
    34-33 68-40 m. A village located on a tributary of the Maidan river, some 6 miles north of Jalriz (Jaliz.)

*PAIWAND   پیوند
    34-13 68-31 m. A village located on the Dara-i-Jelga, some 8 miles north of Chamri in Maidan province.

PAIWAR   پیوارکندو
    33-58 69-52 A. Elevation 8,531 feet. A pass in the range of hills running southwestwards from Sikaram peak, in the Safed Koh, and separating the Hariob valley of Kurram. The summit of the pass lies about 11 miles from Ali Khel, in Hariob, and 16 miles from Parachinar, in Kurram. There is an Afghan post, called Wucha Margha, on the kotal; it lies some distance to the north of the road and is not visible from it; it is garrisoned by a company of regular infantry. Over the pass runs one of the great lines of communication between India and Afghanistan.
    The Paiwar Kotal was stormed and captured by Sir Frederick Roberts on the 2nd December 1878. For details of this action, see the "Official History of the Second Afghan War." (I.B.C.)

PAJA   پاجه
    35-12 69-13 m. A village 22 miles south of the Bajgah pass, 20 houses. (Sayyidulla.)

*PAKA CHINA   پاک چینه
    34-47 69-42 m. A village located near Daramdaram, southeast of Tagab in Kapisa province.

PAKATANGI   پکاتنگی
    34- 70-. A village in the Kunar valley, 10 miles from Jalalabad, consisting of a few scattered huts. (Leech.)

PAKHAGHAI See ZANGAKHAN   پخه غی

*PAKHA MINA   پخه مینه
    34-4 70-55 m. A village located near Sholgar on the way to Ghanikhel in Nangarhar province.

*PAKTIA   پکتیا
    33-35 69-13. A province in eastern Afghanistan which comprises an area of 17,772 square kilometers and an agricultural population estimated at from 432,285 to 569,537. The province is bounded in

Administrative Divisions of Pakthia Province

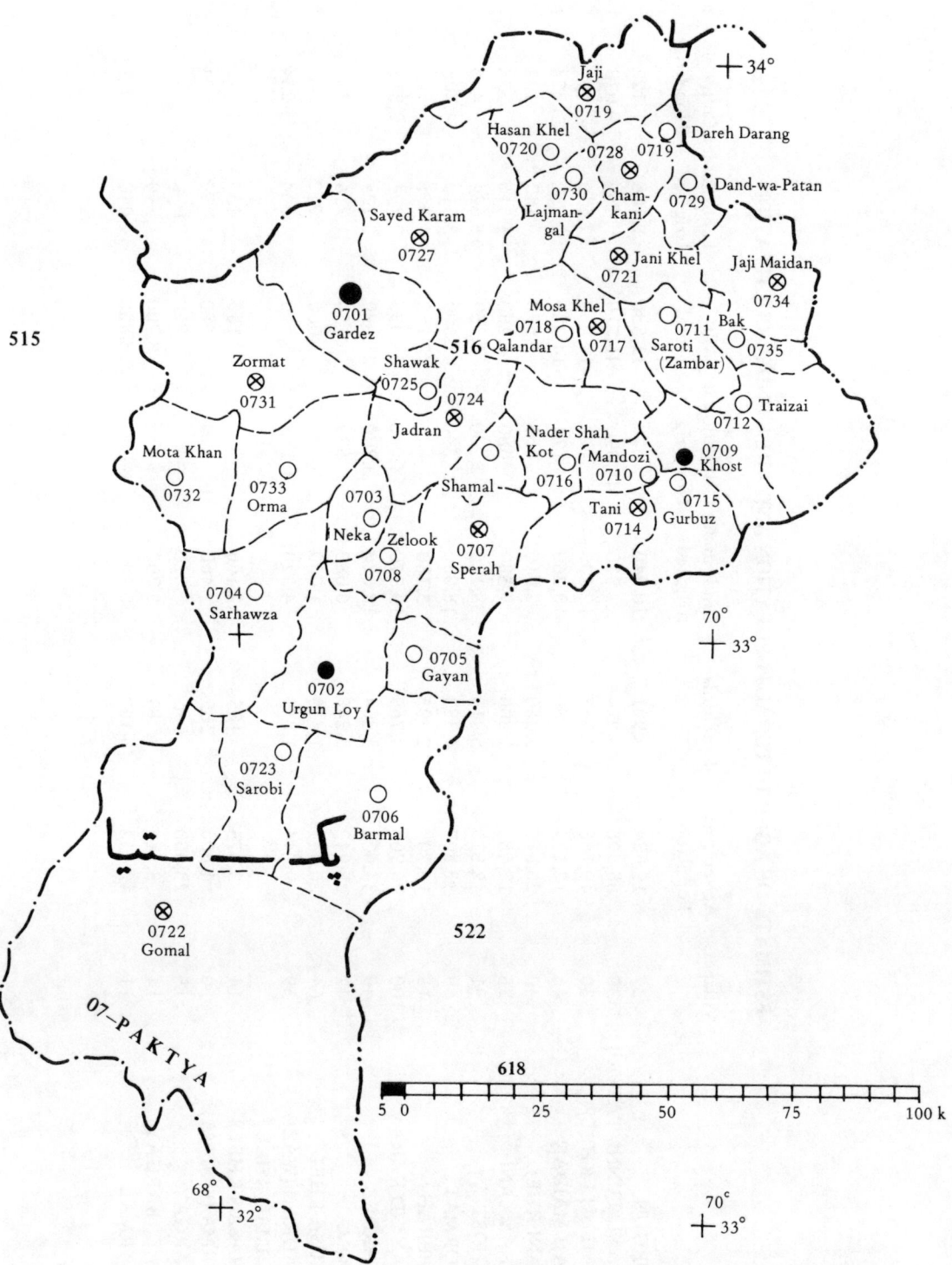

ESTIMATE OF AGRICULTURAL POPULATION AND AREA UNDER CULTIVATION

	Villages	Agricultural Population	Landlords	Lands under Cultivation in Jaribs			Lands under Cultivation in Hectares		
				Irrigated	Non-Irrig.	Total	Irrigated	Non-Irrig.	Total
URGUN	37	19,624	2,921	10,940	610	11,550	2,188	122	2,310
TANI (TUNNI, TAYOU)	30	86,228	5,014	1,320	45,390	46,710	264	9,078	9,342
JAJI (ALI KHEL)	30	49,166	4,847	12,230	—	12,230	2,446	—	2,446
JAJI MAIDAN	46	12,174	2,780	10,260	4,120	14,380	2,052	824	2,876
JANI KHEL	40	20,617	2,280	2,910	660	3,570	582	132	714
CHAMKANI	25	12,681	1,800	7,580	680	8,260	1,516	136	1,652
KHOST	91	42,579	5,915	78,120	2,230	80,350	15,624	446	16,070
ZORMAT	69	32,807	4,383	18,060	23,540	41,600	3,613	4,708	8,321
SPERAH	18	15,709	2,505	3,180	—	3,180	636	—	636
SAYYID KARAM	100	26,705	4,769	13,970	14,060	28,030	2,794	2,812	5,606
GARDEZ	49	34,632	3,364	18,620	3,200	21,820	3,724	640	4,364
GOMAL	47	25,942	3,248	6,080	670	6,750	1,216	134	1,350
MUSA KHEL	64	20,947	1,439	1,060	—	1,060	212	—	212
JADRAN (WAZI)	39	9,244	1,839	4,320	1,170	5,490	864	234	1,098
AHMAD KHEL (HASAN KHEL)	14	3,075	485	2,160	—	2,160	433	—	433
ORMA (WOLMA)	10	4,806	385	460	120	580	92	24	116
BARGAY	15	23,060	996	820	—	820	164	—	164
BAK (BARGAY)	14	8,117	1,281	8,700	—	8,700	1,740	—	1,740
BARMAL	11	42,432	5,160	20,200	8,600	28,800	4,040	1,720	5,760

ESTIMATE OF AGRICULTURAL POPULATION AND AREA UNDER CULTIVATION

	Villages	Agricultural Population	Landlords	Lands under Cultivation in Jaribs			Lands under Cultivation in Hectares		
				Irrigated	Non-Irrig.	Total	Irrigated	Non-Irrig.	Total
PATAN (DAND)	11	3,461	411	940	730	1,670	188	146	334
TRAYZAI (ALISHER)	24	10,766	1,641	11,910	3,220	15,130	2,382	644	3,026
DAREH DARANG	4	2,974	300	290	—	290	58	—	58
ZELUK	16	19,987	2,161	2,930	20	2,950	586	4	590
SAROBI	16	7,981	1,498	4,970	1,820	6,790	994	364	1,358
SARHAWZA (SULTANI)	15	19,309	2,859	1,680	430	2,110	336	86	422
SHAWAK	15	10,170	379	320	—	320	64	—	64
SABARI (SAROTI, ZAMBAR)	55	24,016	3,317	6,830	35,970	42,800	1,366	7,194	8,560
QALANDAR	12	2,851	225	30	—	30	6	—	6
GURBUZ (GURIZ)	27	21,566	2,138	880	3,150	4,030	176	630	806
GIYAN	14	14,663	2,650	3,740	—	3,740	748	—	748
LAJA	13	3,317	355	530	—	530	106	—	106
MATA KHAN (MATA KHEL)	22	12,903	871	4,580	100	4,680	916	20	936
MANDOZAI	20	38,970	3,449	16,000	5,960	21,960	3,200	1,192	4,392
NADER SHAH KOT	19	17,110	1,166	4,210	390	4,600	842	78	920
NEKA	5	4,101	560	870	—	870	174	—	174
TOTAL	1,037	704,690	79,400	281,700	156,840	438,540	56,340	31,368	87,708

STATISTICAL ESTIMATE OF LIVESTOCK BY WOLESWALIS AND ALAKADARIS

	Sheep	Karakul Sheep	Goats	Cattle	Buffaloes	Camels	Horses	Donkeys	Mules	Poultry
URGUN	3,299	—	5,817	5,431	—	258	87	1,569	—	12,580
TANI (TUNNI, TAYOU)	14,200	—	3,060	24,090	—	—	—	10,535	—	87,270
JAJI (ALI KHEL)	3,629	—	6,450	3,712	—	327	—	1,015	1,122	7,935
JAJI MAIDAN	3,364	—	15,334	11,223	286	36	65	1,126	1,048	8,557
JANI KHEL	1,150	—	5,861	4,110	5	240	—	458	—	9,286
CHAMKANI	1,648	—	9,864	5,044	71	677	2	1,062	1,034	6,190
KHOST	37,459	—	4,069	26,678	3,079	105	108	6,080	—	36,839
ZORMAT	6,840	—	2,796	7,664	265	12	130	3,288	—	14,488
SPERAH	928	—	3,999	1,703	—	199	22	167	—	5,698
SAYYID KARAM	6,462	—	3,504	10,518	794	295	126	1,065	1,195	22,355
GARDEZ	2,186	—	598	3,647	—	—	5	1,506	—	7,000
GOMAL	14,334	—	24,286	6,061	—	868	—	1,314	—	16,615
MUSA KHEL	20	—	14,320	5,178	—	1,779	—	920	—	13,110
JADRAN (WAZI)	2,724	—	5,998	694	—	848	—	390	—	9,170
AHMAD KHEL (HASAN KHEL)	1,431	—	820	2,504	78	180	17	272	1,140	1,414
ORMA (WOLMA)	628	—	—	1,200	—	—	—	1,887	—	3,050
BARGAY	10	—	3,550	400	—	67	—	57	—	7,660
BAK (BARGAY)	1,224	—	4,299	5,721	742	—	74	1,069	—	2,245
BARMAL	3,130	—	16,200	7,560	—	1,326	—	1,434	—	12,620

STATISTICAL ESTIMATE OF LIVESTOCK BY WOLESWALIS AND ALAKADARIS

	Sheep	Karakul Sheep	Goats	Cattle	Buffaloes	Camels	Horses	Donkeys	Mules	Poultry
PATAN (DAND)	410	—	1,080	785	25	954	6	1,085	2,118	1,400
TRAYZAI (ALISHER)	5,185	—	3,251	8,733	494	90	57	241	1,322	6,697
DAREH DARANG	102	—	1,645	340	—	155	—	16	—	1,060
ZELUK	—	—	10,020	12,568	—	368	—	1,061	—	8,350
SAROBI	3,732	—	3,427	1,628	—	249	—	811	317	3,390
SARHAWZA (SULTANI)	441	—	1,800	1,256	—	36	5	1,069	24	4,415
SHAWAK	20	—	—	180	—	—	—	704	—	3,942
SABARI (SAROTI, ZAMBAR)	14,004	—	2,733	12,520	921	4	98	1,793	20	13,661
QALANDAR	170	—	860	400	—	90	—	68	—	1,713
GURBUZ (GURIZ)	6,871	—	550	6,280	—	115	—	1,564	—	11,769
GIYAN	—	—	57,710	4,725	—	1,562	83	984	—	11,980
LAJMANGAL (LAZA)	211	—	2,508	408	—	198	—	291	40	2,339
MATA KHAN (MATA KHEL)	4,849	—	578	2,718	—	43	35	1,155	—	6,495
MANDOZAI	5,270	—	7,582	2,738	150	90	90	1,173	—	76,550
NADER SHAH KOT	1,026	—	923	1,358	—	49	—	395	—	4,797
NEKA	211	—	1,568	645	—	140	—	336	—	2,550
TOTAL	147,170	—	227,060	190,420	6,910	11,390 11,360*	1,010	47,960	9,380	395,190

PRODUCTION OF AGRICULTURAL CROPS—IN KABULI SEERS

	Grains			Vegetables	Other Crops		Fruits
	Irrigated	Non-Irrig.	Total		Industrial Crops	Other Temp. Crops	
URGUN	378,450	3,450	381,900	119,700	—	92,000	120,000
TANI (TUNNI, TAYOU)	51,300	312,300	363,600	—	—	—	129,600
JAJI (ALI KHEL)	430,650	—	430,650	107,730	3,500	50,000	83,200
JAJI MAIDAN	351,000	27,450	378,450	94,050	—	86,000	92,800
JANI KHEL	99,900	4,500	104,400	25,650	—	30,000	36,800
CHAMKANI	262,350	4,500	266,850	68,400	136,500	80,000	75,200
KHOST	2,672,100	14,850	2,686,950	713,070	—	1,140,000	200,000
ZORMAT	581,400	307,200	888,600	263,340	—	150,000	467,200
SPERAH	119,250	—	119,250	—	—	14,000	22,400
SAYYID KARAM	506,250	95,550	601,800	128,250	—	58,000	166,400
GARDEZ	231,750	4,200	235,950	—	—	6,000	9,600
GOMAL	697,050	21,000	718,050	—	—	194,000	22,400
MUSA KHEL	37,350	—	37,350	11,970	—	6,000	8,000
JADRAN (WAZI)	156,600	5,700	162,300	—	—	48,000	100,800
AHMAD KHEL (HASAN KHEL)	81,450	—	81,450	22,230	—	12,000	16,000
ORMA (WOLMA)	16,650	900	17,550	—	—	8,000	6,400
BARGAY	30,150	—	30,150	—	—	10,000	6,400

PRODUCTION OF AGRICULTURAL CROPS—IN KABULI SEERS

	Grains			Vegetables	Other Crops		Fruits
	Irrigated	Non-Irrig.	Total		Industrial Crops	Other Temp. Crops	
BAK (BARGAY)	315,000	–	315,000	32,490	–	72,000	41,600
BARMAL	731,700	36,150	767,850	184,680	–	–	728,000
PATAN (DAND)	32,400	4,950	37,350	8,550	–	16,000	12,800
TRAYZAI (ALISHER)	407,250	15,450	422,700	218,880	–	48,000	107,200
DAREH DARANG	10,350	–	10,350	6,840	–	8,000	3,200
ZELUK	100,350	150	100,500	27,360	–	30,000	35,200
SAROBI	175,950	12,150	188,100	47,880	–	42,000	48,000
SARHAWZA (SULTANI)	50,400	2,700	53,100	17,100	–	12,000	17,600
SHAWAK	11,700	–	11,700	–	–	2,000	4,800
SABARI (SAROTI, ZAMBAR)	278,550	238,050	516,600	64,980	–	56,000	80,000
QALANDAR	1,350	–	1,350	–	–	–	–
GURBUZ (GURIZ)	32,850	21,600	54,450	–	300	10,000	9,600
GIYAN	14,850	–	14,850	5,130	–	4,000	3,200
LAJA	140,850	–	140,850	–	–	34,000	–
MATA KHAN (MATA KHEL)	169,650	750	170,400	34,200	–	20,000	22,400
MANDOZAI	600,300	39,750	640,050	58,140	–	68,000	155,200
NADER SHAH KOT	112,050	2,700	114,750	15,390	–	18,000	46,400
NEKA	28,800	–	28,800	10,260	1,400	8,000	9,600
TOTAL	9,918,000	1,176,000	11,094,000	2,286,270	141,700	2,432,000	2,888,000

LAND UNDER IRRIGATION AND SOURCES OF IRRIGATION

	Area in Jaribs					Number of Sources			
	Canals	Springs	Karez	Wells	Total	Canals	Springs	Karez	Wells	Water Mills
URGUN	7,440	—	3,500	—	10,940	9	2	31	149	45
TANI (TUNNI, TAYOU)	630	590	100	—	1,320	11	3	—	—	3
JAJI (ALI KHEL)	12,010	220	—	—	12,230	18	18	3	30	79
JAJI MAIDAN	4,610	5,650	—	—	10,260	4	17	—	48	47
JANI KHEL	2,290	350	270	—	2,910	22	12	15	11	26
CHAMKANI	6,160	660	760	—	7,580	16	8	8	63	46
KHOST	75,620	560	1,940	—	78,120	46	2	3	—	37
ZORMAT	7,250	900	9,910	—	18,060	44	7	—	66	52
SPERAH	2,820	360	—	—	3,180	14	—	—	—	8
SAYYID KARAM	10,120	3,700	150	—	13,970	50	191	335	23	181
GOMAL	4,870	1,170	40	—	6,080	39	8	1	—	25
GARDEZ	15,520	2,500	600	—	18,620	24	10	19	108	75
MUSA KHEL	940	110	10	—	1,060	46	9	5	—	57
JADRAN (WAZI)	4,050	—	270	—	4,320	34	1	2	—	74
AHMAD KHEL (HASAN KHEL)	1,660	500	—	—	2,160	5	6	—	31	28
ORMA (WOLMA)	260	140	60	—	460	10	14	—	23	18
BARGAY	670	150	—	—	820	12	4	—	—	—
BAK (BARGAY)	8,700	—	—	—	8,700	5	2	—	12	27
BARMAL	18,200	500	1,500	—	20,200	6	—	1	—	16

LAND UNDER IRRIGATION AND SOURCES OF IRRIGATION

	Area in Jaribs						Number of Sources			
	Canals	Springs	Karez	Wells	Total	Canals	Springs	Karez	Wells	Water Mills
PATAN (DAND)	880	—	60	—	940	7	2	1	25	12
TRAYZAI (ALISHER)	9,080	930	1,900	—	11,910	14	6	17	35	31
DAREH DARANG	290	—	—	—	290	3	4	—	—	8
ZELUK	970	1,960	—	—	2,930	15	3	2	—	28
SAROBI	4,470	—	500	—	4,970	7	—	16	8	4
SARHAWZA (SULTANI)	1,040	640	—	—	1,680	8	7	—	41	62
SHAWAK	230	90	—	—	230	15	10	1	5	7
SABARI (SAROTI, ZAMBAR)	6,660	100	70	—	6,830	22	8	14	35	27
QALANDAR	30	—	—	—	30	16	1	1	11	17
GURBUZ (GURIZ)	440	—	120	320	880	3	—	—	61	1
GIYAN	630	950	2,160	—	3,740	20	3	13	—	27
LAJA	420	—	110	—	530	6	3	5	11	9
MATA KHAN (MATA KHEL)	2,380	—	2,200	—	4,580	22	3	23	2	8
MANDOZAI	13,400	—	2,600	—	16,000	15	1	3	—	51
NADER SHAH KOT	3,490	260	450	10	4,210	32	24	8	2	35
NEKA	470	400	—	—	870	5	3	1	—	—
TOTAL	228,700	23,390	29,390	330	281,700	625	392	528	800	1,171

TOTAL CULTIVABLE LAND, BY CROP–IN KABULI JARIBS

	Grains			Vegetables	Industrial Crops	Other Crops	Fruits	Total Cultivated Land
	Irrigated	Non-Irrig.	Total					
URGUN	8,410	230	8,640	700	—	460	750	10,550
TANI (TUNNI, TAYOU)	1,140	20,820	21,960	—	—	—	810	22,770
JAJI (ALI KHEL)	9,570	—	9,570	630	—	250	520	10,970
JAJI MAIDAN	7,800	1,830	9,630	550	100	430	580	11,290
JANI KHEL	2,220	300	2,520	150	—	150	230	3,050
CHAMKANI	5,830	300	6,130	400	—	400	470	7,400
KHOST	59,380	990	60,370	4,170	—	5,700	1,250	75,390
ZORMAT	12,920	20,480	33,400	1,540	—	750	2,920	38,610
SPERAH	2,650	—	2,650	—	—	70	140	2,860
SAYYID KARAM	11,250	6,370	17,620	750	—	290	1,040	19,700
GOMAL	5,150	280	5,430	—	—	30	60	5,520
GARDEZ	15,490	1,400	16,890	—	—	970	140	18,000
MUSA KHEL	830	—	830	70	—	30	50	980
JADRAN (WAZI)	3,480	380	3,860	—	—	240	630	4,730
AHMAD KHEL (HASAN KHEL)	1,810	—	1,810	130	—	60	100	2,100
ORMA (WOLMA)	370	60	430	—	—	40	40	510
BARGAY	670	—	670	—	—	50	40	760
BAK (BARGAY)	7,000	—	7,000	190	—	360	260	7,810
BARMAL	16,260	2,410	18,670	1,080	—	—	4,550	24,300

TOTAL CULTIVABLE LAND, BY CROP–IN KABULI JARIBS

	Grains			Vegetables	Industrial Crops	Other Crops	Fruits	Total Cultivated Land
	Irrigated	Non-Irrig.	Total					
PATAN (DAND)	720	330	1,050	50	—	80	80	1,260
TRAYZAI (ALISHER)	9,050	1,030	10,080	1,280	—	240	670	12,270
DAREH DARANG	230	—	230	40	—	40	20	330
ZELUK	2,230	10	2,240	160	—	150	220	2,770
SAROBI	3,910	810	4,720	280	—	210	300	5,510
SARHAWZA (SULTANI)	1,120	180	1,300	100	—	60	110	1,570
SHAWAK	260	—	260	—	—	10	30	300
SABARI (SAROTI, ZAMBAR)	6,190	15,870	22,060	380	—	280	500	23,220
QALANDAR	30	—	30	—	—	—	—	30
GURBUZ (GURIZ)	730	1,440	2,170	—	10	50	60	2,290
LAJMANGAL (LAZA)	330	—	330	30	—	20	20	400
GIYAN	3,130	—	3,130	—	—	170	—	3,300
MATA KHAN (MATA KHEL)	3,770	50	3,820	200	—	100	140	4,260
MANDOZAI	13,340	2,650	15,990	340	—	340	970	17,640
NADER SHAH KOT	2,490	180	2,670	90	—	90	270	3,120
NEKA	640	—	640	60	40	40	60	840
TOTAL	220,400	78,400	298,800	13,370	4,050	12,160	18,030	346,410

TOTAL CULTIVABLE LANDS—IN KABULI JARIBS

	Total	Pastures	Forests	Under Cultivation	Fallow Lands
URGUN	98,030	7,970	78,510	11,550	3,090
TANI (TUNNI, TAYOU)	53,180	4,870	1,600	46,710	21,120
JAJI (ALI KHEL)	59,980	4,320	43,430	12,230	3,370
JAJI MAIDAN	31,670	2,950	14,340	14,380	4,520
JANI KHEL	1,116,820	2,520	1,110,730	3,570	1,050
CHAMKANI	54,600	2,270	44,070	8,260	3,260
ZORMAT	51,500	9,900	—	41,600	5,720
KHOST	93,680	1,770	11,560	80,350	22,090
SPERAH	112,770	3,500	106,090	3,180	840
SAYYID KARAM	31,690	3,660	—	28,030	10,040
GOMAL	22,620	1,790	14,080	6,750	2,780
GARDEZ	24,330	1,990	520	21,820	6,250
MUSA KHEL	263,290	41,630	220,600	1,060	190
JADRAN (WAZI)	52,540	1,070	45,980	5,490	11,655
AHMAD KHEL (HASAN KHEL)	3,750	1,200	390	2,160	500
ORMA (WOLMA)	8,340	5,400	2,360	580	250
BARGAY	7,730	6,170	740	820	220
BAK (BARGAY)	12,560	640	3,220	8,700	2,230
BARMAL	102,820	3,330	70,690	28,800	9,030

TOTAL CULTIVABLE LANDS—IN KABULI JARIBS

	Total	Pastures	Forests	Under Cultivation	Fallow Lands
PATAN (DAND)	62,850	2,440	58,740	1,670	570
TRAYZAI (ALISHER)	55,340	19,920	20,290	15,130	4,340
DAREH DARANG	270,330	150	269,890	290	70
ZELUK	7,690	—	4,740	2,950	700
SAROBI	23,880	12,090	5,000	6,790	2,110
SARHAWZA (SULTANI)	39,670	10,200	27,360	2,110	450
SHAWAK	2,220	90	1,810	320	80
SARABI (SAROTI, ZAMBAR)	60,570	1,940	15,830	42,800	18,250
QALANDAR	58,220	2,730	55,460	30	—
GURBUZ (GURIZ)	19,750	13,360	2,360	4,030	1,440
LAJMANGAL (LAZA)	250,970	12,710	237,730	530	140
GIYAN	6,610	—	2,870	3,740	990
MATA KHAN (MATA KHEL)	18,930	14,250	—	4,680	50
MANDOZAI	26,850	4,890	—	21,960	6,840
NADER SHAH KOT	18,000	1,540	11,860	4,600	1,260
NEKA	214,960	10,640	203,450	870	240
TOTAL	3,338,740	213,900	2,686,300	438,540	144,730

the west and south by Ghazni, and in the north by Logar provinces and in the east by the State of Pakistan. Paktia is divided into the wolewalis of Gomal, Urgun, Sperah, Zurmat, Gardez, Jadran, Sayyid Karam, Tani, Jaji, Musa Khel, Chamkani, Jani Khel, Jaji Maidan, and Khost, and into the alaqadaris of Sarobi, Barmal, Sarhowza, Gian, Neka, Orma, Mata Khan, Shawak, Zeluk, Shamal, Nadir Shah Kot, Hasan Khel, Mandozai, Gurbuz, Lajmangal, Darah Darang, Dand-wa Patan, Saruti, Bak, and Traizai. The capital of the province is the city of Gardez. For woleswali lists from the Depart-ment of Statistics of the Ministry of Agriculture and Irrigation see tables.

*PALA پله
33-36 69-38 m. A village located on the Lador Kholeh, northeast of Miran, in Paktia province.

PALAN or MURAD ALI پلان
A subsection of Daikhitai Hazaras.

*PALAO پلاو
32-57 68-37 m. A village near Ghaibkhel and northwest of Yahya Khel in Ghazni province.

PALASGAR پلسگر
Elevation 2,500 feet. Is the lowest of the five Gabar villages (see "Gabar"). It stands high on the right bank of the Kunar river, about 250 feet above it, and a very short distance below the point where it is joined by the Dungul torrent. It contains about 20 houses, arranged in the form of a square, as at Birkot. In 1891 they were in a dilapidated condition. (Robertson.)

PALT or SARAFZAI پلت
A stream in Zurmat, watering Paltanai. (McLean).

PALTANAI or PATANAI پتنی
33-21 68-52 G. A village in Zurmat, between Band and Sultanai, 11 miles from the former and 15 from the latter. People: Tajiks. Supplies of all kinds to be procured, but fuel is scarce. Ground open and level; urial and deer plentiful. The Jilga river is not far off. Water good from springs and the river, Palt or Sarafzai. (Broadfoot, McLean.)

PALTU پالتو دریا
32-31 68-2 A. A river which rises in the pass of that name, and runs through Katawaz to the lake Ab-i-Istada; in its course it becomes slightly brackish; its banks are never above 4 feet high, and it has a stream about 20 feet wide and 1 foot deep. The pass of Paltu is said to be difficult, and runs among craggy mountains from Zurmat to the Kharoti country and the source of the Dwa Gumal---(See "Kotanni"). (Broadfoot.) Recent maps show the name Putay Shilah. (LWA.)

PALU پالو
34-59 68-1. A kotal leading over a spur of the Ghandak Koh, in the Bamian district. It is of some importance, for by using this track pressure on the worst part of the Bamian-Ak Robat main road may be relieved, though guns would probably not be able to go this way. The track takes off near the Ziarat of Khwaja Ali, 6-1/2 miles above Kala Sarkari, and ascends the hills on north side and leads to Chashma Palu, from which it joins the ordinary main road at the top

of the Tangi Mushan, 3-1/2 miles south of the southern Ak Robat Kotal. (A.B.C.)

PALUN پلون
Said to be a valley west of Ujaristan.

*PAMI پامی
34-23 68-5 m. A village located on a tributary of the Dara-i-Jelga, east of Shika in Maidan province.

*PANAGIR پناگیر
32-39 68-13 m. A village located a few miles southwest of Khushamand in southern Ghazni province.

PANAH or PANNAH پناه
33-6 68-19 m. A village in the Ghazni district, inhabited by about 500 Andari Ghilzais. Supplies for a small force could be obtained. Among the hillocks here are camps of shepherds and Lohani merchants who emigrate in winter. There is a supply of water from a karez (Broadfoot.) Another place with this name is on the Sardeh Rud, south of Ghazni, at 33-17 68-31 m. (LWA.)

PANAH, KOL-I پناه
A glen in the Besud country, occupied by Burjigai Besud Hazaras.

*PANDAK پندک
34-51 68-48 m. A village south of the Kuh-i-Yakhdara on a tributary of the Ghorband in Parwan province.

PANDANAO See ZARSANG پنده نو

PANDIT پندت
A village in Kafiristan, on the Kunar frontier, said to be situated on the ridge of a table-land at the extremity of a valley, and to contain 1,000 houses. (Masson.)

PANDU پندو
A tribe of Siahposh Kafirs, who formerly occupied the valley of "Pohan," and now hold the east portion of the valley of Mel (Alishang). Here they have several villages, viz., Mukiwati, Nioli, Teiliu, Pandu, Parmahwal. A very few of this tribe have become converts to Islam. (Raverty.)

*PANJAB Or PANJAO پنجاو
34-23 67-1. Panjab is the name of a woleswali in the Bamian province. The woleswali comprises an area of 1,526 square kilometers and has an agricultural population which has been estimated at from 11,619 to 15,239. The woleswali is bounded in the west by Lal wa Sarjangal, in the north by Yakowlang, in the northeast by Bamiam, in the east by Deh Behsud, and in the south by Waras. Panjab has about 27 villages, 13 of which have more than 500 inhabitants. The villages are listed in the PG as follows: Akhzarat, Piyazan, Tar Bulaq, Tagab-i-Barg-i-Sufla, Tagab-i-Barg-i-Ulya, Khordak Takhta, Kham-i-Marga (Marga-i-Sufla), Daraz Qol, Ghar Ghari, Tara Pus, Gandab, Marga-i-Ulya (Marka-i-Ulya), Miyan Kawak, Guhdar, Narges, Nilqol (Negol), Tukhak, Anak-i-Neqol, Hesarak-i-Neqol, Sang-i-Mashaf, Sewak-i-Neqol, Miyana Deh, Kerani, Sar-i-Neqol, Targhi, Sadiz (Sagdiz), Paye Bun, Godar, Khum, Qarya-i-Jan Muhammad, and Sar-i-Darakhtan.

PANJAO پنجاو
A large valley in the Dai Zangi Hazara country. There are 2 villages with this name, located at 34-22 67-1 A. and 34-15 66-52. (LWA.)

PANJAO پنجاو
Elevation 9,200 feet. A halting place, with a sarai, in the Dai Zangi Hazara country.

PANJASIA پنج اسیاب
A village on the right bank of the Helmand. This is probably Panj Asiab, located at 34-21 68-7 G. (LWA.)

PANJFILAN پنج فیلان
A pass over a high spur of the Koh-i-Baba, crossed by a road leading from the Kalu glen to the Bamian valley. The ascent to the kotal from Gumbat is not very steep, but the pass is higher than the Hajigak. The descent is much steeper than the ascent, but otherwise the road is tolerably good, and practicable for camels. Panjfilan village, 5 miles from Gumbat, contains 15 houses of Tajiks. From Gumbat to Kala Topchi, in the Bamian valley is 10 miles. (Ata Muhammad.)

PANJPAI پنج پای
A section of the Polada Hazaras of Ujaristan.

PANJPAI پنج پای
34-29 68-13 G. A village in Kharwar, 80 houses of Yusuf Khel Ghilzais. (Griesbach.)

*PANJPAI پنج پای
34-39 70-18 m. A village located in the Alingar valley, east of Tarakhel in Laghman province.

PANJPAI See UTPUR پنج پای

PANJSHIR پنجشیر
35-30 69-51. A valley drained by the river of the same name, which rises in the southern slopes of the Hindu Kush in the vicinity of the Khawak pass. After being joined by numerous streams, chief of which are the Ghorband and Shakar Dara the river falls into the Kabul. The upper part of the valley is described as a glen varying in width from 200 yards to 1-1/4 miles. There are numerous villages and a good deal of wheat, barley, cotton, and rice cultivation, while dense orchards of apricot, mulberry, and walnut trees surround almost every village. These orchards form an obstacle to the passage of baggage animals.
Though limited in range, the scenery of Panjshir is soft and beautiful. Its rugged, red-tinged surface is dotted over with castellated dwellings, whose square corner towers and solid walls rising on every knoll are relieved by the smiling foliage of fuit trees and the lively green of the garden-like fields which surround them.
The Panjshiris have the reputation of being good soldiers. Subsequent to the time of Timur Lang they were for a long time independent of the many rulers who successively occupied the Kabul throne, and the valley frequently became a scene of tubulence and unnatural warfare. They acknowledged Dost Muhammad as their ruler, but added nothing to his exchequer. Their arms are the musket and the long knife-like sword of the Afghans.
The Panjshiris, like the bulk of the Kohistanis, are chiefly Tajiks.

They are Sunni Muhammadans, and not being very old in the faith, are the more violently bigotted. Before Babar's time they are said to have been Kafirs.

There are a few weavers amongst them, but their clothing is principally procured from the Bazar of Kabul. The Panjshiris, while they speak Persian, also understand the "Pashai" language.

Masson mentions that formerly there was a silver mine in this valley.

The passes leading from Panjshir over the Hindu Kush to the Andarab valley are the Khawak, Rejak, Til, Zuria, Shoba, Parandev, and Arzu. From the Parian glen a branch dara at the head of the Panjshir, there are said to be five roads: (1) Northwest over the Chunduk Kotal to Khost; (2) up the glen to the Nawak Kotal, and over this to Anjuman: (3) up the Chamar glen, and over the mountains into Kafiristan; (4) from Chahardeh of Parian, roads lead into Kafiristan by the Wariaj Kotal; and (5) by the Arioh.

The road down the Panjshir was not fit for laden camels in 1886, but mules could use it; since that date it has probably been improved as the Khawak pass is now said to be practicable for wheeled traffic. (Maitland, Shahzada Taimus, Wood, Masson, Leech.)

The following list of villages in the valley and its branch glens, from its head down to the vicinity of the point where it is quitted by the Charikar road, is taken from Shahzada Taimus's report:

Name of Village	No. of families	Inhabitants
Chapchi Kani	20	Tili Hazaras
Khawak	12	Saiyid Khel Ghilzais
Parian glen	300	Tajiks
Til (eastern)	90	Tili Hazaras
Haodak	5	"
Dasht-i-Rewat	130	"
Ghanchu	20	"
Safedjir	150	"
Matah	50	"
Khinj	100	"
Jarwesh	10	"
Burjyman	20	"
Kharu	60	"
Push	12	"
Pashghur	100	"
Marz	200	"
Shahbah	12	"
Hazara Dara	{ 510	"
	310	Hazaras
Barak	20	Tajiks
Aru	15	"
Sanganah	50	"
Astana	80	"
Watkol	30	"
Mulaspur	40	"
Nawalich	20	"
Jangalak	10	"
Manjakor	80	"
Dada Khel	30	"
Sata	30	"
Parandev glen	53	"
Yakub Khel	30	"
Deh Malah	40	"
Bazarak, or Kachu	40	"

Laghana	20	"
Khaniz	60	"
Farubal	80	"
Parakh	50	"
Ghiji	40	Saiyids
Nolawa	20	Tajiks
Kot Dara	180	"
Isarak Dara	120	"
Dar Khel	2	"
Bakshi Khel	100	"
Kala-i-Fathulla	20	"
Piawash Dara	112	"
Shaikhan	30	"
Bangi	12	"
Baram Khel	12	"
Kabazan	200	"
Gulistan	30	"
Pachinar	40	"
Deh Khwaja	30	"
Aodawa	12	"
Alok	15	"
Kala Langar	10	"
Tawak Dara	240	"
Ab Dara	300	"
Anaba	150	"
Malikan	20	"
Faraj Dara	200	"
Miran Shah	40	"
Zamankor	12	"
Koraba	35	"
Pufdam	15	"
Sanjan	150	"
Aramghia	15	"
Bolaghain Dara	300	"
Kohna Deh	100	"
Nimazjai	30	"
Gulbahar	300	"
Mazulla Khel	15	"
Mir Baba	18	"
Ushtargiran	500	"
Jamal Aka	500	"
Kishiktan	100	"
Deh Raisan	40	"
Chinaki	60	"
Kham Zardgar	500	"
Karezi	1,500	"
Muhammad Iraki	2,000	"
Aruki	100	"
Badam Ali	30	Ghilzais
Shokhi	50	"
TOTAL	11,194	families

*PANJSHIR Or ROKHA پنجشیر

35-15 69-28. Panjshir is a woleswali in Parwan province. The woleswali comprises an area of 706 square kilometers and has an agricultural population that has been estimated by various Afghan sources at from 25,254 to 31,457. The woleswali is bounded in the west by Kapisa and Salang, in the north by Andarab, in the east by Char Qarya and Dara Hazara, and in the south by Durnama and

Kuhistan. Panjshir includes about 52 villages, of which 20 have more than 500 inhabitants. The villages are listed in the PG as follows: Astana, Dostam Khel Faraj, Onaba, Oluk, Dashtak, Bazarak-i-Khas, Bad Qul, Borja Khel, Bakhshi Khel, Parakh, Parshar-i-Abdara, Piyawesht, Paye Chenar, Tawakh, Jangalak, Hessarak-i-Shast, Khaniz-i-Bazarak, Khwaja, Dawa Khel, Talakan, Darband-i-Faraj, Dur Khel, Rahman Khel, Zaman Kor, Satai Bazarak, Sanguna, Shast Rukha, Shofa-i-Abdara, Shaikhan, Ghalback (Ghelbalak), Ghuchi Dar Khel, Farach, Qabezan, Tulkha-i-Bazarak, Qalacha-i-Faraj, Gim Abdara, Kunda wa Kot, Kango Abdara, Kuhna Abdara, Garwashi, Gulistan, Gir-i-Abdara, Koraba, Mala Bazarak, Ferobal Bazarak, Mulla Khel, Manjahur, Nolaba, Nolich wa Malaspa, Waro wa Barak, and Mareshtan-i-Bazarak.

PANNAH See PANAH پناه

*PANQASH پنقاش
34-32 67-16 m. A village located near Qash, south of the Kuh-i-Baba in Bamian province.

PAPIN-I-KALAN پاپین کلان
34-7 70-24 m. A village in the Hisarak division of the Jalalabad district, situated at the foot of the Siah Koh range, about 5 miles south of Yaghiband. Inhabitants: Mians. (Jenkyns.)

PAPIN-I-KHURD پاپین خرد
34- 70-. A village in the Hisarak division of the Jalalabad district, about a mile north of Papin-i-Kalan. Inhabitants: Mians. (Jenkyns.)

PAPIN PASS پاپین کوتل
Elevation 13,000 feet. A pass over the Safed Koh leading from the Hisarak valley in the Jalalabad district to the Kirman Dara in Kurram. The pass lies at the head of the Papin, or Hisarak, river, and about 5 miles west of the Oghaz pass. It is reported to be practicable for mules in the summer. (I.B.C.)

PAPIN RIVER See HISARAK RUD پاپین رود

PARACHA پراچه
A people settled in Afghanistan, and chiefly in the province of Kabul. They originally emigrated from the Punjab, and are Sunni Muhammadans. Their total number throughout Afghanistan is said to be 4,000 souls. They may possibly be identical with the Paranchehs. (IB.C.)

PARAKH پراخ
35-33 69-30. A village on the right bank of the upper Panjshir stream, 2 miles below Bazarak. It has 50 houses of Tajiks. There is an open level space here called the Maidan-i-Margha from a fight which occurred near at some former time. The road is good and the width of the glen is from 600 to 700 yards, of which the bed of the stream occupies about 150 yards. It lies under the hills on the left hand. The water is in several channels, and shallow. The hills on both sides are high, those on the left being very steep. (Shahzada Taimus.)

PARAM پرام
A tribe of the Chahar Dasta Hazaras.

PARANCHEH or PIRANCHA پرانچه
A race of Hindkis who are scattered in various parts. Of their descent nothing is known, though Masson says they can hold converse with the Siah-posh Kafirs, their dialect to some extent coinciding with that of the Kafirs. There are a few families of them in the lower Panjshir valley. Raverty also mentions that the only traders found at the head of the Swat valley are Paranchehs. They are also found to inhabit British territory, being found in the Bannu district in Peshawar, in Kohat, and in Hazara, besides a number in the Rawal Pindi division. Their dialect is not unlike Hindi, and it is possible they may be the same race as the Kafirs.
Alimulla also mentions that Paranchehs are traders in Swat, and the caravans which go through the Khaibar are mostly conducted by them. They are much trusted by and receive great pecuniary assistance from rich chiefs and bankers of the Punjab.
Regarding the Paranchehs of the Jalabad district, Jenkyns remarks:
The origin of the name is said to be "farashan," or chamberlains. In this district they occupy the village of Sarai (part of Sangar Sarai--Sangar being Afghan), and some are found in Landabuch.
In Sarai, which is in Kama, on the banks of the Kabul river, the Piranchas number 200 families. In Landabuch, also in Kama, there are 20 families. They are not found in any other part of the district.
The Piranchas state that they came originally from Khushan in the Punjab. They speak Hindustani among themselves. Their avocations are shoe-making, dyeing, cloth-selling, etc., etc., and they also engage in agriculture. (Jenkyns, Elphinstone, Masson, Raverty, Alimulla, Punjab Report, Munphool.)

PARANDEV or PARANDEH پارنده
35-23 69-26 m. A dara springing from the Hindu Kush and running in a southeasterly direction down to the Panjshir valley which it joins about 1 mile above Kachu. It is described as a narrow glen varying in width from 40 to 100 yards, and bounded by precipitous cliffs. The hills on either side are destitute of trees, and small bushes only are available as fuel; there is, however, plenty of grass to be found on the hillsides in spring and summer. There are patches of cultivation in the bottom of the glen, and also on the hillsides.
At about 4 miles above its junction with the Panjshir the Parandev is joined, from the south, by another large ravine, known as the Tul Dara, in which there is some cultivation.
The following villages, all inhabited by Tajiks, lie in the Parandev Dara: Kalat, Dangana, Kaltari, Godaran, Daolana, and Kund.
At the head of the Parandev Dara, 13 miles from Kachu, is the pass over the Hindu Kush known as the Parandev pass. A road leads up the Parandev Dara and over the pass at its head. (I.B.C.)

PARANDEV or BAZARAK پارنده
35-25 69-24 A. A pass over the western Hindu Kush, leading from the Panjshir into the Andarab valley. It lies at the head of the dara of the same name, about 13 miles from Kachu in Panjshir. It forms the best communication (except the Khawak pass) between the two valleys, and from native reports seems to be a fairly easy pass for Afghan camels. The Amir Sher Ali is said to have taken guns over this pass on camels in 1864 and it is probable that he improved the road then and that nothing has been done to it since. The pass is closed by snow from about the middle of November to the middle, or end of April.
The Hindu Kush is said to be known about here as the Talab-i-Ab; the

lower slopes and spurs on the northern side of the pass are well wooded, but the main range itself is bare, and snow lies on it in places all the year round. The Parandev pass is also known as the Bazarak. (I.B.C.)

*PARCHA پارچه
33-9 68-24 m. A village located in the Sardeh Rud valley, northeast of Bar Metakhan in Ghazni province.

*PARCHAO پارچاو
34-16 71-7 m. A village located on the Kabul river near the Pakistan border, northeast of Lalpura in Nangarhar province.

PARGAM Or BARGAM پارگام
35-8 71-23 A. A village with a great deal of cultivation on the right bank of the Kunar river, 7-1/2 miles above Asmar. (I.B.C.)

PARIAN پریان
35-38 70-1 m. A glen descending from the main range of the Hindu Kush and running southwest to the head of the Panjshir valley, which it joins about 11 miles above Dasht-i-Rewat. It contains several villages, the highest of which is Pir Guzar. Then come Mazar and Kirpitao (Kur Pitab). In these three, which are collectively known as Kirpitao, are 200 houses. Below Kirpitao are the Chahardeh settlements of Jista, Kuchan, Kala-i-Sujah, Shahnuz, and Parian proper, having collectively 100 houses. Thus in all Parian there are 300 houses, the inhabitants being exclusively Tajiks. There is a good deal of cultivation, but not many fruit trees. Supplies for a battalion for one or two weeks could be collected. The width of the glen is said to be on an average 200 yards, and there is room to camp troops.

"From Kirpitao there are said to be three roads. That to left (northwest) over the Kotal Chunduk leads to Khost, and is a bad road, said to be unfit for baggage animals. The second (north) leads up the glen to the Kotal-i-Bubak (more often called the Kotal Nawak) and over this into the Anjuman glen, and so to Badakhshan (Faizabad). Above Pir Guzar the road crosses a small kotal (over a spur?) known as the Kotal-i-Kalatak. Formerly there was a fort and village of Kalatak near here, but it has been abandoned. The ascent of the Nawak Kotal is said to be good. The descent is not so easy, and is 10 miles long into Anjuman. There is water on the road, but no habitations. This route is said to be practicable for camels, though the descent is trying. (The existence of this route from Faizabad to the head of the Panjshir is important from a strategical point of view.) The third road leads to the right (east) up the Chamar glen (Darrah-i-Chomar) and over the mountains into Kafiristan. It is a difficult road. The Chamar ascends considerably and is enclosed by high hills. It is not very narrow, and there are places where a few troops might encamp. The track is said to be only a footpath and impractcable for horses. The people of Parian get their fire-wood from Chamar, where there is an abundance of willow. The distance from Kirpitao to the Kotal-i-Chamar is said to be 10 miles. The descent is down a similar glen equally difficult. At 14 miles the first Kafir settlement is reached. It is called Atati. The next is Poshal, then Lashta Gham, and then Larha Pachha. The latter is a fort said to have been built by Amir Timur (-i-Lang). Below Pachha are Gadu, Chatur and Mandul. At the latter place the eastern Arioh and eastern Wariaj glens unite.

"From Chahardeh in Parian there are two roads into Kafiristan, the Waraz and Arioh. Both go up glens of those names and descend by other glends having the same names. The Arioh road is the best. Horses have been taken over it. The Wariaj path is used by salt traders. Those from the Panjshir side take the salt halfway to the kotal (about 5 miles?), and are there met by the Kafirs, who barter for it. The Wariaj is said to be very similar to the Chamar road. The kotal is on the Koh-i-Surkhshal, which has a high peak. The peak northeast of the kotal is Mir Ismail. The Arioh Kotal is southwest of the Surkhshal peak. Wakhe peak is on the other side of it.

The distance from the Wariaj Kotal to the first settlement of Kafirs is said to be the same as the corresponding distance on the Chamar road, that is, about 14 miles. The first village is Lina (Linar?) then Purang. The two contain 250 houses of Koreshi Kafirs (so called from the name of the place, which was once inhabited by Koreshi Arabs.) There is cultivation, and also orchards. The glen is 200 yards wide, with a narrow bottom and sloping sides. There is a place lower down called Dasht-i-Ayar where troops might encamp. Below this the glen becomes a defile called Mukhim Kadao. Lower still is another, Lina, with steep high hills on both sides.

The Arioh road is said to be the best of the three from Parian, and laden yabus can be got over it, though with difficulty. It resembles the others more or less. Some 5 or 6 miles up the western Arioh glen was formerly a village called Arioh, but having been constantly attacked by the Kafirs, it has been abandoned. The Arioh Kotal is said to be 15 miles from Chahardeh, and the first Kafir village is the same distance beyond. It is now deserted like Arioh, and for a like reason; that is, because it is too exposed to the attacks of Panjshiris." (Shahzada Taimus, from native information.)

PARI DARA See JAGDALAK

PARJAK
34-44 67-1 m. A village located on the Daria-i-Band-i-Amir in Bamian province.

PARJINA
34-19 69-51 m. A village in the Jalalabad district, on the left bank of the Surkhab river, 3 miles southwest of the bridge (Surkhpul). Inhabitants: Khugianis. (McNair.)

*PARK
33-3 68-43 m. A village located about 2 miles southeast of Mushkhel in Ghazni province.

PARPIT
35- 71-. Elevation 13,500 feet. A pass leading from the head of the Pittigul valley in Kafiristan to Bomboret in Chitral. Both ascent and descent are very steep, and quite impracticable for mules. (Robertson.)

PARSA
34- 68-. A steep, narrow valley which debouches into that of Ghorband at Chahardeh. A camel road leads up it to the crest of the Paghman range, and so to the Kabul-Charikar main road. It is understood to be inhabited by Shaikh Ali Hazaras, but practically nothing is known of the glen or its inhabitants. (Peacocke.)

*PARSHAR
35-13 69-25 m. A village located on a tributary of the Panjshir, east of Anawa, in Kapisa province.

PARSIWAN See Volume 5. پارسیوان

*PARUM پروم
35-20 70-9 m. A village located on a tributary of the Nurestan river, near Bala Murghab, in Laghman province.

*PARWAN پروان
35-0 69-10. A province in east-central Afghanistan which comprises an area of 11,367 square kilometers and an agricultural population estimated at from 281,941 to 305,031. The province is bounded in the west by Bamian, in the north by Baghlan and Takhar, in the east by Laghman and Kabul, and in the south by Kabul and Maidan (Wardak). The province now also includes the former province of Kapisa. Parwan (and Kapisa) is divided into the woleswalis of Ghorband, Jabal al-Saraj, Bagram, Mahmud Raqi, Kohistan, Panjshir, Nejrab, and Tagab, and into the alaqadaris of Shaikh Ali, Shinwar, Koh-i-Safi, Alasai, Durnama and Panjshir 1 and 2.
The capital of the province is the town of Charikar.
For woleswali lists from the Department of Statistics of the Ministry of Agriculture and Irrigation see the following six tables. (LWA)

PARWAN Or CHARIKAR پروان
35-15 69-30 A. A large village at the mouth of the Salang glen, some 49 miles due north of Kabul. It is, in fact, two villages on either side of the stream which descends south from the Bajgah pass. There are at least 1,500 houses in the two. The stream joins the Ghorband at about 4 miles south of Tutamdara. Parwan Dara has attained a very unpleasant notoriety to the British from an action which took place on the 2nd November 1840, when General Sale's force came up with the remnants of Dost Muhammad's army, who finding himself pressed, faced about and came down to the charge. The matchless gallantry of the officers, Captains Fraser and Ponsonby, Lieutenants Crispin and Broadfoot, and Dr. Lord was not seconded by the men under their command, who fled, followed by the enemy's cavalry. Captains Fraser and Ponsonby were desperately wounded, and Lieutenants Crispin and Broadfoot and Dr. Lord were killed. (Wood, Kaye, Sayyidulla.) Parwan is now the name of a province, the village of Parwan is presently called Charikar. (LWA)

*PASATIAN پساتیان
34-21 68-40 m. A village located on a tributary of the Maidan river, some 10 miles west of Nirkh in Maidan province.

*PASDEH پسده
34-51 68-44 m. A village located on a tributary of the Ghorband river, south of Dahana Kharbid in Parwan province.

*PASHAD پشد
34-43 71-1 m. A village located on the Kunar river, about 4 miles southwest of Narang in Kunar province.

PASHAGAI پشه گی
A tribe of Siahposh Kafirs who formerly held the valley of Saikal, a portion of which containing the large villages of Dumian, Kandla, Paramdol, and Taru, it continues to retain. The people of these places have become Muhammadans. Of the remainder of the tribe, who follow their ancient religion, some dwell in the country of the Siahposh and some to the north in the valley of Mel. (Raverty.)

639

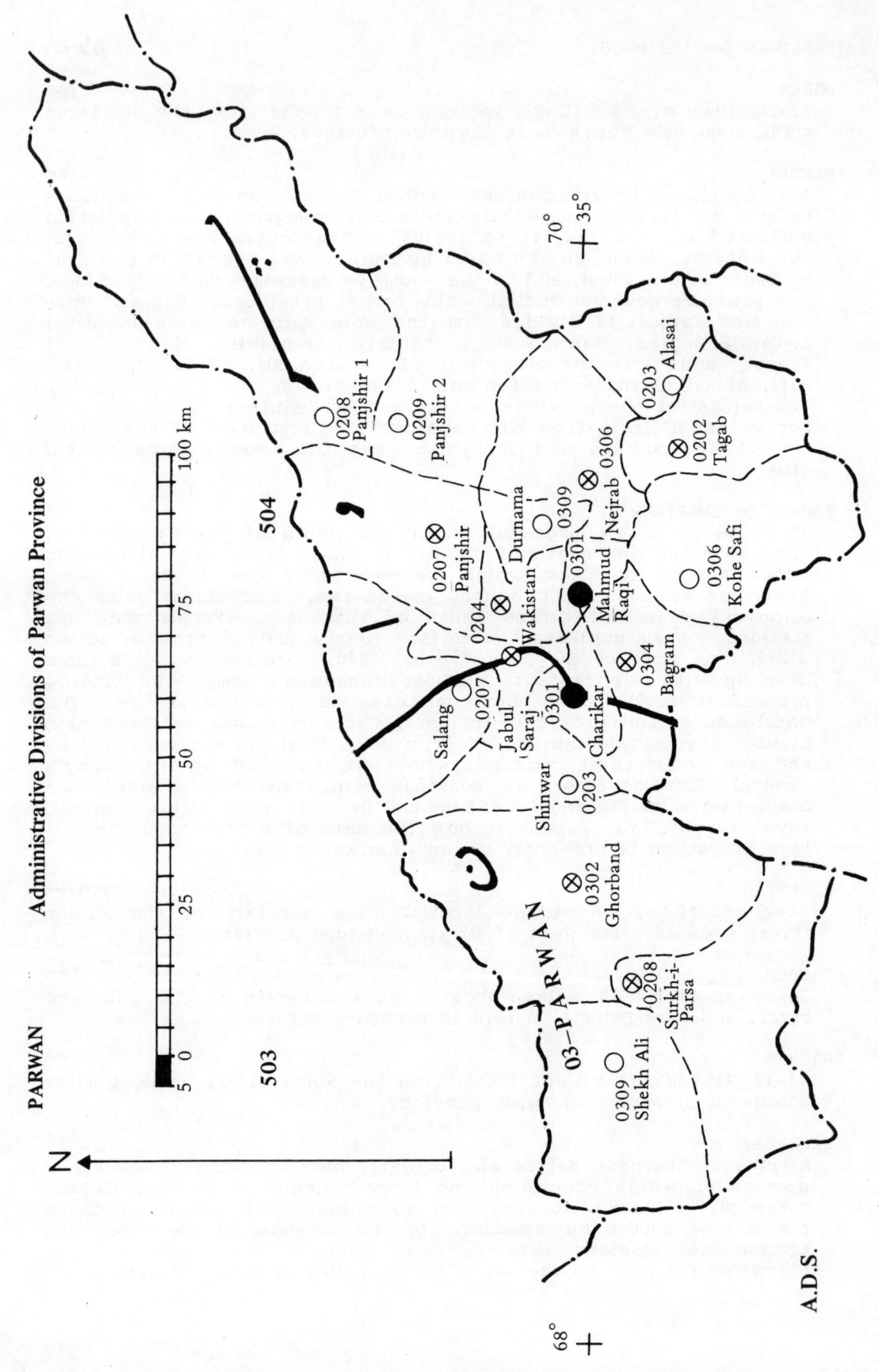

ESTIMATE OF AGRICULTURAL POPULATION AND AREA UNDER CULTIVATION

	Villages	Agricultural Population	Landlords	Lands under Cultivation in Jaribs			Lands under Cultivation in Hectares		
				Irrigated	Non-Irrig.	Total	Irrigated	Non-Irrig.	Total
BAGRAM	52	84,430	11,530	25,000	55,000	80,000	5,000	11,000	16,000
JABUL SARAJ	86	79,340	7,670	39,390	–	39,390	7,878	–	7,878
CHARIKAR	33	61,860	12,650	36,390	4,230	40,620	7,278	846	8,124
SURKH PARSA	37	58,050	7,990	26,680	–	26,680	5,336	–	5,336
GHORBAND	37	86,300	11,850	21,530	3,400	24,930	4,306	680	4,986
SALANG	23	40,460	4,040	7,020	–	7,020	1,404	–	1,404
SHENWARI	13	31,430	3,940	12,360	1,150	13,510	2,472	230	2,702
SHAIKH ALI	27	33,160	1,860	5,490	3,150	8,640	1,098	630	1,728
KOH-I-SAFI	37	18,690	2,170	1,840	1,030	2,870	368	206	574
TOTAL	345	493,720	63,700	175,700	67,960	243,660	35,140	13,592	48,732

STATISTICAL ESTIMATE OF LIVESTOCK BY WOLESWALIS AND ALAKADARIS

	Sheep	Karakul Sheep	Goats	Cattle	Buffaloes	Camels	Horses	Donkeys	Mules	Poultry
BAGRAM	6,600	—	1,980	9,880	—	270	70	2,130	—	29,920
JABUL SARAJ	5,420	—	2,260	14,470	—	—	50	1,070	—	44,120
CHARIKAR	2,670	—	1,850	9,740	—	—	40	3,300	—	32,170
SURKH PARSA	15,120	—	7,550	7,120	—	—	10	2,140	—	20,770
GHORBAND	11,050	—	7,390	5,280	—	—	20	4,940	—	18,700
SALANG	7,380	—	9,070	1,180	—	—	170	910	—	9,890
SHENWARI	14,600	—	8,810	3,840	—	70	70	1,400	—	11,440
SHAIKH ALI	14,000	—	16,740	6,300	—	—	40	1,690	—	9,900
KOH-I-SAFI	350	—	12,370	3,100	—	130	20	1,430	—	10,910
TOTAL	77,190	—	68,020	60,910	—	470	490	19,010	—	187,820

PRODUCTION OF AGRICULTURAL CROPS—IN KABULI SEERS

	Grains			Vegetables	Other Crops		Fruits
	Irrigated	Non-Irrig.	Total		Industrial Crops	Other Temp. Crops	
BAGRAM	1,238,500	322,320	1,560,820	801,000	38,500	275,000	1,896,000
JABUL SARAJ	1,524,500	—	1,524,500	945,000	45,500	780,000	1,526,000
CHARIKAR	762,000	28,800	790,800	2,373,750	98,000	600,000	2,682,000
SURKH PARSA	1,143,500	—	1,143,500	497,250	—	667,500	1,308,000
GHORBAND	952,500	24,000	976,500	436,500	—	542,500	1,390,000
SALANG	291,000	—	291,000	—	—	380,000	438,000
SHENWARI	571,500	7,200	578,700	326,250	—	227,500	338,000
SHAIKH ALI	286,000	18,000	304,000	108,000	—	247,500	200,000
KOH-I-SAFI	145,500	6,480	151,980	38,250	—	145,000	146,000
TOTAL	6,915,000	406,800	7,321,800	5,526,000	182,000	3,865,000	9,924,000

LAND UNDER IRRIGATION AND SOURCES OF IRRIGATION

	Area in Jaribs				Number of Sources			
	Canals	Springs	Karez	Wells	Total	Canals	Springs	Karez	Wells	Water Mills

	Canals	Springs	Karez	Wells	Total	Canals	Springs	Karez	Wells	Water Mills
BAGRAM	19,000	2,000	4,000	—	25,000	4	3	15	—	12
JABUL SARAJ	38,460	930	—	—	39,390	30	3	—	—	122
CHARIKAR	25,320	11,070	—	—	36,390	8	7	—	—	203
SURKH PARSA	13,680	12,640	360	—	26,680	23	33	4	—	84
GHORBAND	20,580	950	—	—	21,530	32	5	—	—	119
SALANG	4,020	3,000	—	—	7,020	3	8	—	—	86
SHAIK ALI	3,880	1,610	—	—	5,490	12	10	—	—	53
SHENWARI	9,890	2,470	—	—	12,360	8	4	—	—	43
KOH-I-SAFI	—	980	860	—	1,840	—	20	15	—	34
TOTAL	134,830	35,650	5,220	—	175,700	120	93	34	—	756

TOTAL CULTIVABLE LAND, BY CROP—IN KABULI JARIBS

	Grains			Vegetables	Industrial Crops	Other Crops	Fruits	Total Cultivated Land
	Irrigated	Non-Irrig.	Total					
BAGRAM	24,770	26,860	51,630	3,560	1,100	1,100	9,480	66,870
JABUL SARAJ	30,490	—	30,490	4,200	1,300	3,120	7,630	46,740
CHARIKAR	15,240	2,400	17,640	10,550	2,800	2,400	13,410	46,800
SURKH PARSA	22,870	—	22,870	2,210	—	2,670	6,540	34,290
GHORBAND	19,050	2,000	21,050	1,940	—	2,170	6,950	32,110
SALANG	5,820	—	5,820	—	—	1,520	2,190	9,530
SHENWARI	11,430	600	12,030	1,450	—	910	1,690	16,080
SHAIKH ALI	5,720	1,500	7,220	480	—	990	1,000	9,690
KOH-I-SAFI	2,910	540	3,450	170	—	580	730	4,930
TOTAL	138,300	33,900	172,200	24,560	5,200	15,460	49,620	267,040

TOTAL CULTIVABLE LANDS—IN KABULI JARIBS

	Total	Pastures	Forests	Under Cultivation	Fallow Lands
BAGRAM	133,300	53,300	—	80,000	25,350
JABUL SARAJ	42,960	3,570	—	39,390	12,290
CHARIKAR	41,960	1,340	—	40,620	9,840
SURKH PARSA	53,330	25,340	1,310	26,680	6,340
GHORBAND	34,060	9,130	—	24,930	4,420
SALANG	12,520	5,500	—	7,020	3,680
SHENWARI	24,460	10,950	—	13,510	3,250
SHAIKH ALI	36,230	26,500	1,090	8,640	2,080
KOH-I-SAFI	3,140	270	—	2,870	1,790
TOTAL	381,960	135,900	2,400	243,660	69,040

PASHAI پشه ئی
A race which formerly was more numerous, but is now obscure and nearly forgotten. Leech says they inhabit the districts of "Mundal," "Chitela," "Parina," "Kundi," and "Seva Kulman." Masson says we are enabled to trace a people of this name throughout the whole country from Panjshir to Chitral. In Nijrao are still a few Pashai families; in Laghman, a village at the foot of Koh-i-Karinj, preserves the appellation of Pashai; in Kunar, the actual village of Pashat retains a nominal memento of the Pashai race, as in Bajaur does the village of Pashgram. The inhabitants of Panjshir and Nijrao, speaking the Pashai dialect, although now calling themselves Tajiks, may not unreasonably be supposed to be of Pashai descent; and the same remark may apply to the Safis of Tagao and the Dara-i-Nur, etc., and to the inhabitants of Laghman. (Leech, Masson.)
N.B. A number of people calling themselves Pashais are found in the Andarab valley.

PASHAI پشه ئی
34- 70-. A village in Laghman on the left bank of the Alishang river, 1-1/2 miles above its junction with the Alingar. The following are the hamlets composing the place:
(1) Deh-i-Malokh (2) Deh-i-Hashim (3) Banda-i-Fakiran.
The inhabitants are Tajiks. (Warburton.)

PASHAI پشه ئی
A subsection of the Jaghuri Hazaras.

*PASHAI پشه ئی
34-34 68-55 m. A village located a few miles southwest of Paghman in Kabul province. Other places with this name are located on a tributary of the Tagab, some 10 miles northeast of Nejrab in Kapisa province, at 34-59 69-42 m.; in the Nawabad area, southwest of Reza Kohestan in Kapisa province, at 35-4 69-24 m.; on the Tagab river, southeast of Bazar-i-Badakhshi in Kapisa province, at 35-1 69-37 m.; on a tributary of the Tagab, west of Lokakhel in Kapisa province, at 35-1 69-42 m.

PASHAIAN پشیان
A village east of Charikar; 500 families of Tajiks. (Shahzada Taimus.)

PASHAK پشك
A village in the Dai Zangi district of Lal.

*PASHAKARI پشكری
34-49 69-40 m. A village located on the Tagab river, about 3 miles south of Tagab in Kapisa province.

PASHAR پشر
A village in the Ab Dara.

PASHAT Or PASHAD پشد
34-43 71-1 m. An old town in the Kunar district, on the left bank of the river about 43 miles from Jalalabad. It was the residence of the kings of Kunar, and the royal palace and garden, though rather delapidated, are still in existence. A ferry crosses the river to the most northerly of the Kotgai villages. From Pashat there are apparently two passes over the Kabul Sapar range. A force of 100 khasadars is quartered here.
During the First Afghan War a mixed force was sent to take Pashat

under Colonel Orchards. Lieutenants Pigou and Tytler made a gallant but unseccessful (owing to the damp) attempt to blow in the gate, and the Sayyids evacuated the fort soon after. Our loss was 65 killed and wounded. (Orchard, Mulla, Coldstream, I.B.C.)

PASHE
پشه
A subdistrict of the Jaghuri Hazara country.

PASHGHUR See PUKH
پاش غور
35-24 69-42 A. A village in Panjshir, northeast of Rakha.

*PASHKI
پشکی
35-20 70-53 m. A village on the Darrah-i-Paron, some 10 miles south of Ashtiway (Eshtiwi) in Kunar province.

PASHKIGROM Or PUSHKIGROM
پشکی گرام
35-20 70-54 m. A Siahposh village in the Parun portion of the Pech, or Presun, valley in Kafiristan. It is the most important village in the valley, and is situated at some little distance from the right bank of the river, at about 71 miles above Chigha Sarai. Nearly opposite the village, on the left bank of the river, is a narrow valley leading to Bargul, the highest of the Wari villages. The village consists of about 150 houses and a fort, in which live the hakim of Parun and 40 Khasadars. The fort is 50 yards square, with a tower at each corner, with the four walls loopholed. The village is situated on the hill side. A good supply of water comes down from above the village. The houses are built of round baulks of timber with little or no masonry in betwen. In shape they resemble the Bashgul houses, but are provided with the peculiar wide chimney structures characteristic of Presungul; they have no verandahs. The "Pshals" are clustered all round the base of the slope in the usual way. There is a good cantilever bridge of two spans over the river here. The centre pier, of rough stone masonry bounded with layers of branches, stands in the water. The best place of a camping-ground is on the left bank. Supplies of all sorts are procurable. (Robertson, I.B.C., Peart.) Recent maps show the spelling Pashki. (LWA)

*PASHOK
پشوک
35-8 70-34 m. A village located at the source of the Kolatan Darrah, near the Koh-i-Watyali in Laghman province.

PASHTO
پشتو
A subsection of the Polada Hazaras.

PAS-I-KOH
پسی کوه
33-43 67-7 G. A mountain located east of Chakmak in the Dai Kundi area.

*PASQAD
پسقد
33-20 67-20 m. A village located near Bughra and east of Lalchak in western Ghazni province.

*PASTAI
پستی
34-18 68-13 m. A village located a few miles west of Kot-i-Asho and north of the Koh-i-Khwaja Bahadur in Maidan province.

*PATA
پاته
33-12 68-15 m. A village located southeast of Mushakai in Ghazni province.

*PATAK پتك
33-47 69-39 M. A village located on the Lazha Khwar, near its junction with the Kurram river in Paktia province.

*PATAN پتان
33-28 68-54 m. A village located about 3 miles north of Kolalgu in Paktia province. Another place with this name is located on the Kurram river, near Kharlachi and the Pakistan border, some 8 miles east of Chamkani in Paktia province, at 33-49 69-57 m.

PATAN پتان
34-36 70-47 G. A small village in the Kunar valley, 27 1/2 miles from Jalalabad. Half a mile above the village there is a pari of the usual type, i.e., a steep rocky spur running down to the river, and surmounted by a khasadar post. These posts are always square towers of dry stone masonry bonded together by layers of ballis and branches at intervals of two or three feet. Just below this point is a flying bridge (a raft working on a rope) across the river. From the Patan Pari a good view of the opposite side of the valley across the river, which here widens out into a basin of several square miles area, is obtained. The spurs of the Kabul Sapar range form the back and sides of this basin, which is heavily cultivated and contains some four or five villages, all apparently known as Kunar. (Coldstream.) Another place with this name is located at 33-11 68-48 A.

PATANAI See PALTANAI پتنی

PATAR پتار
One of the four tributary glens of the Nijrao valley. It is inhabited by "Pashais" and Tajiks. (Leech.)

PATHAN Or PATTAN پتان
33-49 69-57 m. A village on the right bank of the Kurram river, about 1 mile on the Afghan side of the frontier. Half a mile east of the village are two posts, called Pathan and Dand (Danda), each held by 100 khasadars. (I.B.C.)

*PATIRAI پتیری
34-18 70-19 m. A village located on the Kambu Khwar, some 15 miles southwest of Jalalabad in Nangarhar province.

PATKAO-I-ROGHANI پادخواب روغانی (پاتکاو)
33- 69-. A village in the southern division of the Logar valley, on the right bank of the river, an 2 miles southeast of Baraki Barak. Inhabitants: Tajiks and Sayyids. Supplies, water and fuel are all plentiful. At Patkao-i-Roghani a road from Gardez, via the Altimur pass, joins the Logar valley road from Kabul to Ghazni. (I.B.C.)

PATKAO-I-SHAHANA Or PADKHWAB-I-SHANA پادخواب شانه
33-57 69-4 m. A village in the southern division of Logar valley, and on the right bank of the river. It is 6 miles northeast of Patkao-i-Roghani and 12 miles southwest of Zarghun Shahar. For revenue purposes Patkao-i-Shahana is included in one township with the neighbouring village of Lias Khan.
It was in the neighbourhood of this place that Brigadier-General Palliser, C.B., attacked and totally defeated a large gathering of ghazis from Zurmat on the 1st July 1880. For details of this action see the "Official History of the Second Afghan War."

پتخه

PATKHA
33-33 69-11 m. A village on the Gardez Rud, some 5 miles southwest of Gardez in Paktia province.

پتکن (پچکیون)

PATKUN
35-27 71-37 A. Elevation 8,400 feet. A pass leading over the eastern watershed of the Bashgul valley from Gourdesh (Gowhardesh) to Utzun and so on to Kala Drosh.
From the village of Gourdesh, altitude 4,130 feet, the road runs up the left bank of the torrent of that name for a quarter of a mile, where it crosses to the right bank by a particularly dubious bridge. Two hundred yards further is a convenient camping place. Thence the track runs over fields near the water's edge, and at 1 1/2 miles passes a Shaikh hamlet of six houses. At 3 miles the valley divides into two, the one running to the Patkun pass, the other leading to Pittigul. The road to the Patkun is up a narrow gul thickly clothed with pine trees. At first the ascent is gradual, and with the exception of one or two rocky bits the path is fairly easy. The stream has to be crossed and recrossed two or three times. The road finally keeps to the right bank high above the water, and gets easier and steeper. The last few hundred feet are very steep. The top of the pass is probably 8 miles from Gourdesh. Thence the road descends through a pine forest at a very severe gradient to a rough stony channel, in which it continues till Utzun is neared, when it keeps to the slopes on the left bank of the stream. Opposite Utzun it crosses a torrent from the Pittigul direction, by means of a fair bridge, and reaches the foot of the isolated conical rock on which Utzun, 40 houses, is perched amidst cornfields and in an amphitheatre of hills. From the foot of the Patkun to Utzun is probably 4 miles, giving the whole length of the march form Gourdesh as 12-1/2 miles. Plenty of room to camp. (Roberson.) Recent maps show the name Pachkiun Kandaw. (LWA)

پتره

*PATRA
32-52 68-6 m. A village located on a tributary of the Ghazni river, near Spina Kala in Ghazni province.

پتسا (پتخه)

PATSA
Biddulph says: "There is also a small slave population existing among the Bashgulis, who speak their language and seem to differ from them in no respect, except in social position. They are called Patsas and are probably descendants of captives taken from other tribes in war. They bear arms, and identify themselves in every way with their masters in all contests with external enemies. They are distinguished by their tunics having no sleeves, very narrow edgings, and a coloured badge sewn on to the back. Their women are not allowed to wear the head-dress with horns like the other Bashguli women."
Robertson's report on Kafiristan contains the following: "They (the Patsas) are not slaves. They have no flocks nor herds of their own, merely a little land which their wives cultivate. It is from this class that the shepherd or patsa is chiefly obtained. During the winter months he takes care of the goats, and receives for the whole winter one animal for every 20 in his charge. He often attaches himself to an important man as a hench-man, and performs all the duties of a servant without receiving that title." (Biddulph, Robertson.)

پتان

PATTAN See PATHAN

PATU پاتو
A place in the Jaghuri Hazara country.

PAWINDAH See POWINDAH پاونده

PAZGIRAN Or PEZGARAN پزگران
35-17 69-39 m. A village in Panjshir. See "Hazara Dara."

PAZHINGAR Or PASHANGAR پاشنگر
35- 71-. A Shaikh hamlet of 9 houses on the right bank of the Kunar river, situated near the mouth of the Kuntgul stream between Birkot and Nari. A few hundred yards to the west are the ruins of houses. An old Kafir informed Robertson that in his time the place was inhabited by Kam Kafirs, who were driven away by Musulmans who settled at Pazhingar in considerable numbers, but who were all eventually killed by the Kam. In 1891 the hamlet was inhabited by Shaikhs; i.e., by Kafirs become Muhammadan. (Robertson.) A mountain with this name is located at 35-22 71-31 m. (LWA)

PEANI پیانی
33- 68-. Elevation 9,140 feet. A pass on a road from Kharwar to Ghazni. It leads from Aman Khel to Zanakhan, and is supposed to be the best route to that valley. (Griesbach.)

*PECH (پچ) چ
34-58 70-54. Pech is a woleswali in Nangarhar province. The woleswali comprises an area of 1,121 square kilometers and has an agricultural population that has been estimated at from 11,230 to 22,243. The woleswali is bounded in the west by Chapa Dara, in the south by Chawki and Narang, in the east by Asadabad and Bar Konar, and in the north by Kamdesh. Pech has about 38 villages, 16 of which have more than 500 inhabitants. The villages are listed in the PG as follows: Manogai, Nangalam, Garaw, Wardesh, Kandahari, Wadigram (Warigam), Bacha Lam (Lacha Lam), Sinzai, Shamund (Shamur), Sundari, Kundagul, Kolak, Barkundi-i-Ulya wa Sufla, Mangai (Sanagi), Shorik, Kulangul (Kand Gul-i-Ulya), Waigul-i-Ulya, Waigul-i-Sufla, Warness (Arness), Hamsoz (Masoz-Mandas), Neshai (Neshagi), Shingul, Qala Gul, Konal Kalai (Kan Kalai), Qala Gul (Qala-i-Gul-i-Sufla), Jama Mesh, Lotalam, Nati Gram, Khalq Lam, Matin, Emar, Kor Bagh, Dargai, Gandila, Hel Gul, Sawki, Kalmo, Zarmundi, China, Emshaza, Qala-i-Siddiq, Dumsoz, and Bar Kandai.

PECH DARA پیچ دره
34-52 71-9 A. A river believed to rise in the southern slopes of the Hindu Kush, and flowing in a general southerly direction to the Kunar at Chigha Sarai. It is variously designated by the Kafirs as the Presungul or Tsarogul, and it is referred to by Bellew and Lumsden as the Kamah, a very good name inasmuch as one of its branches flows from the important Kamah pass, Pech is, however, a fairly well-known name, and it will be convenient to adhere to that appellation.
The river is formed by the Wezgul drainage which includes that of the pass leading to Skorigul, that of the Mami pass which leads to the Baprok valley, and that of the Uzhamezhalgul, up which is the Kungani pass road. Just below the Uzhamezhalgul junction it is joined by the considerable Shidgul stream up the valley of which there is no road. At the village of Shtevgrom the main stream is joined by the Kamahgul, and then flows placidly down the valley through land set aside for the service of Imra, and past all the other Presun villages. After passing the last, Pushkigrom, it makes an abrupt turn, which was the limit of Dr. Robertson's journey, and

enters the Tsaro country. Some little distance lower down it receives on its right the Kti river. The village of Tsaro is on the right bank, and nearly opposite it the Amzhi valley of Waigul empties its drainage into the main stream. The latter is also said to be joined by the two Ashkun streams the upper falling into the Kti, the lower, which drains the Ashkun valley, joining the Pech direct. Regarding the road down the valley, Robertson remarks:

"Of the routes (in Kafiristan) with which I am acquainted, or partially acquainted, perhaps the most interesting is that from the Munjan valley over the Kamah pass to the village of Shtevgrom, thence through a charmingly easy valley rich in flocks and herds, and containing six large and populous villages. It follows the course of the Pech or Kamah river round the bend below Pushkigrom, where my personal knowledge of it ends as abruptly as the river turns, and so on to Chigha Sarai. If we argue by analogy it is probable that from the bend mentioned to Chigha Sarai the road is extremely difficult. But if this is not so, and if the Munjan portion of the road is of an average kind, this route from Badakhshan to Chigha Sarai ought to be a good one, for in the Presun valley there are large tracts of grass lands, and considerable quantities of supplies could be obtained. Wood is scarce at the upper part of the valley, but plentiful lower down near Pushkigrom."

The Presuns, also called Virun by their Muhammadan neighbours, are probably a very ancient people. They are entirely different from the Siaposh tribes of Kafiristan on the one hand and from the Wai and Ashkun people on the other. They are remarkable for their more peaceful disposition, and their inefficiency as fighting men. "Indeed," says Robertson, "it seems improbable that the Wai, provided that the Pushkigrom men remained neutral and the Siahposh tribe did not interfere, could do very much as they liked in Presungul, for the only act in the way of reprisal of which the Presuns could boast during the tree years the war (between the Presuns and Waigulis) had lasted was the murder of a Wai girl." The Presuns have six villages:-- Shtevgrom, Prontzgrom, Diogrom, Kstigigrom, Satsumgrom, Pushkigrom. Their numbers are estimated at 5,000 souls.

Further information regarding this river, collected from native information, is as follows: Looking north from Shtevi two branches of the river are seen, one flowing down a valley from the north and the other from the northeast. The latter has considerably more water and appears to be the main stream. At the head of the northeast valley is the pass leading to Paprok (or Saprok) in Bashgul, sometimes known as the Paproki Pass. These two branches unite about two miles above Shtevi. Just below Shtevi the main river is joined by a small stream flowing from the lake at the foot of the Weram or Kamar (or Kamah)--Bida Pass.

The principal tributaries on the right bank are the Kantiwa, Kurdwar and the Chappa streams, whilst on the left bank the Waigal and the Katar-Gambir are the principal affluents.

The valley is known by various names by the inhabitants at different portions of its course of which the main divisions are:

1. Parun, from Shtevi to the Kurdar Nala. The lower stretch of this portion, from Atakund Nala, 12 miles below Pashki, to the Kurdar, is also sometimes known as Wama; 2. Pech, from below the Kurdar to Matina; and 3. Chigha Serai, from below Matina to its junction with the Kunar river. In addition to this the Kafir portion of the valley is called Jadid ul-Islam.

The upper portion of the Parun valley is comparatively wide, but from the Atakund Nala downwards it becomes a narrow gorge flanked by high precipitous hills with bare needle-like peaks. The hills are wooded wherever the slopes admit of trees growing.

The river through this protion is a rapid.
These conditions continue into the Pech portion to a few miles above Gosalak, below which the valley widens and is richly cultivated with rice. Here the hills are well wooded, the villages are close together and the river flows gently.
In the Chigha Serai portion the valley is still wider and is well cultivated, chiefly with rice.
The hills become easier and are well wooded.
From Simartan to Kamchi it is known as Bar Chigha Serai and from below this to Dam Killi as Kuz Chigha Serai.
The Parun is inhabited by Siah Posh Kafirs who are now all Mussalmans, and in each of their villages is a mulla who draws Rs. 20 a month from the Amir. He is in charge of the village school and in addition, does duties similar to those of a lumbardur in British India. All the boys have to attend school regularly, where their instruction is confined to religious books. Some of them however can talk Persian fairly fluently. The pupils go to Asmar to be examined by the Brigadier there. The Siah Posh appear happy and contented and Islam is popular with the young generation. They are treated very leniently by the Afghan officials, and the only revenue they have to pay is Rs. 2 (Kabuli) per house irrespective of the amount of land held or numbers of flocks maintained. The Hakim of Parun lives at Pashki. He is an Afghan and both he and the Hakim of Pech are under Hakim Sayid Kadir Jan of Kunar, who lives at Pashat. The people keep sheep and goats in large numbers, but no transport animals, and they do not go in for trade of any kind. All available land is under cultivation and the soil appears good, wheat and barley being the chief crops whilst apricots and walnuts are also grown. Salt is obtained from Munjan in exchange for wool and hides. Villages appear to be always built on the hillsides, whatever level ground there is being kept for cultivation: The houses are clustered together, one above the other, the higher ones being reached over the roofs of the ones below. The roofs of the houses, which are all one-storyed, also do duty as courtyards. A separate portion of the village is reserved for cattle and flocks. The people all wear white clothes. The men appear to be all unarmed. The chief villages are Pashki and Wama.
The people of Pech are Safis who now speak Pushtu among themselves. Their houses are three-storeyed and, being built up one against the other, the backwalls of the outer houses form a continuous wall to the village which, as a rule, has only one entrance gate. The people are poor as there is no outlet for their spare grain. They keep sheep and goats, but have no transport animals. Every man carries a dagger, but they were not noticed to carry any other arms. The chief villages of Pech are Ningalam and Rachalam. In the winter the Kuchis from Jalalabad come here with their camels for grazing.
The inhabitants of Chigha Serai are mostly Dehganis, who are considered of lower caste than the Safis. Their houses are clustered together and sometimes walled. They do not appear to have any arms. (N.I.)
There is a regiment of cavalry quartered in the Pech valley. (Robertson, I.B.C.)

PECH-O-PECH   پچ و پچ
A large ravine which joins the Kaoshan glen from the west, 11 miles south of the Kaoshan pass. Up this ravine a track, said to be practicable for horsemen and Afghan camels, leads over the Pech-o-Pech kotal and descends the Dara Nao to the Nimakao glen, which it joins just below Khurd Barg. This route may be used to avoid the

lower part of the Kaoshan glen route when the latter is rendered impassable by the swelling of the Kaoshan stream in spring. (I.B.C.)

PEIWAR See PAIWAR
33-58 69-52 A.

*PENAR
34-55 70-41 m. A village located on a tributary of the Darra-i-Pech, between Bolak and Ghundai in Kunar province.

PERISTAN
A subsection of the Daikundi Hazaras.

PEROWAR See PIRAWAR

*PERUZI
34-41 70-9 m. A village on the Alishang, some 4 miles northwest of Tirgari (Mehterlam) in Laghman province.

PESH BOLAK
34-12 70-48 A. A group of 6 ot 7 Dehgan villages in the Jalalabad district, about 5 miles south-southwest of Basawal, the largest of the group containing about 400 houses. There is a fortified post here with a garrison of 2 squadrons of cavalry and 2 (in summer 3) companies of infantry. During the first Afghan campaign there was a detachment of jazailchis here under Captain Ferris. On the 13th November 1841, the detachment, which then consisted of 300 infantry and 25 cavalry, was attacked by a small party of insurgents. These, on the 15th, had increased to upwards of 5,000 men, principally composed of Sangu Khel Shinwaris, Pesh Bolakis, Kuchis, etc, etc., who attacked the fort with some vigour. On the 16th it was found that the ammunition of the detachment was nearly exhausted, so it was determined to cut a way through the rebels. This operation was effected with the loss of some 16 killed and 25 wounded, and the detachment arrived at Girdao, where they were protected by Turabaz Khan, chief of the Mohmands. All public and private property had to be left behind, including among the former Rs. 38,000 belonging to Government. (Ferris, Limond, Jenkyns.)

*PESHGHUR
35-24 69-41 m. A village located on the Panjshir river, a few miles northeast of Zenya in Kapisa province.

PETLA
34-15 69-53 m. Elevation 4,760 feet. A village in the Khugiani section of the Jalalabad district. It is situated 4 miles west of Tulu, and 5 miles south of the Surkhab bridge (Surkhpul). The inhabitants are Khugianis of the Sherzad subdivision. (Jenkyns.)

PEZWAN See LIKHAI (2)

*PIADARA
34-1 67-33 m. A village located a few miles southeast of Safidab in southern Bamian province.

PIADARA
33- 68-. A kotal leading over the hills north of Kharwar. It is only passable for footmen. The east flank of the pass is formed by the conspicuous Koh-i-Piadara. (Griesbach.) A village with this name is west-southwest of Ghazni, at 33-30 68-6 m. (LWA)

PIAWASH پیاوش
35-17 69-26 G. A glen descending southeast from the Hindu Kush to the Panjshir valley. It contains two villages: Piawash, which has 100 houses; and Chamal Dara, 2 miles further, with only 12 houses. All Tajiks. From Chamal Dara lies the road over the Arzu Kotal to Andarab. (Shahzada Taimus.) Recent maps show the spelling Pyawusht. (LWA)

PINGRAM پندگرام
33-47 68-56 G. A large and important village at the head of the Charkh valley, south of the Logar district. It is surrounded by walled enclosures and vineyards, and is capable of offering a stout resistance. The inhabitants are Tajiks. (McLean, Euan Smith.)

*PIRA پیره
34-23 67-19 m. A village located on the Darazqol, southwest of the Koh-i-Chaharband in Bamian province.

PIRA KHEL پیراخیل
A village 23 miles southwest of Jalalabad. The inhabitants belonging to the Wazir section of the Khugianis. (Jenkyns.)

*PIRAKHI پراخی
33-58 68-2 m. A village located about 2 miles south of Bokan on the Okak stream in Ghazni province.

PIRANCHA See PARANCHEH پرانچه

PIRAWAR پیراوار
34-25 70-32. A village in the Besud division of the Jalalabad district, situated on the right bank of the Kunar river, about 2 miles above its junction with the Kabul. Inhabitants: Arabs. (Jenkyns.)

*PIRDAD پیرداد
34-22 68-43 m. A village located on a tributary of the Maidan, some 8 miles west of Nirk in Maidan province.

PIRDAD پیرداد
A village in the west of the Bamian district.

PIR GUZAR See PARIAN پیرگذر

PIR HUSAIN پیر حسین
A section of the Bul Hasan Besud Hazaras.

*PIR KALAI پیرکلی
33-48 69-47 G. A fort located north of Chamkani in Paktia province.

PIR KAMAL BABA ZIARAT پیرکمال بابا زیارت
34-16 70-48. A small shrine on the main Peshawar-Kabul road, 6 1/2 miles west of Basawal. At about 100 yards from the shrine is a ruined Buddhist tope, situated on a steep isolated hill some 250 feet above the plain. In 1880 the crest of this hill was fortified and held by 150 infantry, while at the foot was an enclosure for 60 sowars. There is room for a force of any size to encamp here, with a plentiful supply of water from the Kabul river, 1 mile to the north; grass is easily obtainable, and fodder also if warning is given. The valley to the north of the river is fertile. (Malleson.)

PIR KOTI پیرکوتی
32-56 69-15 A. A village in Birmal, on the road from Ghazni to Dawar, 12 miles from Shahtorai; 400 houses. All suplies, including forage and fuel, plentiful. Water good.(McLean.)

PIR KULI پیرقولی
A section of the Dai Zangis.

PIR NAZAR پیرنظر
A section of the Bul Hasan Besud Hazaras.

PIR SARAI پیرسرای
33-48 69-49 A. A halting-place 13 miles from Kharlachi on the road thence to Ghazni, via Gardez. There is ample room for a brigade to encamp here with good facilities for water; at certain amount of bhusa is usualy procurable. (I.B.C.)

PIRU KHEL پیروخیل
34-8 69-3. A village in the Logar district, 5 miles northwest of Babus. (Hervy.)

*PISHBAND پیش بند
34-25 66-40 m. A village located a few miles north of Asgharat in eastern Bamian province.

*PITAO پیتاو
34-3 66-50 m. A village located southeast of the Koh-i-Chasht and east of Espighaw in southwest Bamian province. Other places with this name are locatd south of the Koh-i-Baba range and east of the Koh-i-Sare Ghar in Bamian province, at 34-34 67-48 m.; northeast of the Koh-i-Safi and southwest of Tagab in Kapisa province, at 34-44 69-28 m.; on a tributary of the Kabul river, north of Torkani, near the Kunar-Nangarhar border, at 34-31 70-57 m.; on the Hindu stream, a tributary of the Kunar, southeast of Cheghasarai in Kunar province, at 34-51 71-14 m.; in the Aimaitu area of Ghazni province, at 33-14 67-22 m.; and in the Sikander Khel area, southwest of the Ab-i-Istada in Ghazni province, at 32-18 67-41 m.

PITAO پیتاو
A fort village in the Dai Zangi country.

PITAWA پیتاوه غربان
The name by which the Panjao valley appears to be known below the junction of the Binigao tagao. See Panjao (1). A village called Pitawa-i-Ghurban is located at 34-22 70-31 G. (LWA)

PITLA پیتله
34- 69-. A Jaji village about 1 mile northwest of the Lakarai Kotal. (Barton.)

PITTIGUL Or PITIGAL پتی گل
35-28 71-32 m. Elevation 5,000 feet. A village in Kafiristan, consisting of 50 houses and much cultivation. The Pittigul valley descends from the Parpit pass in a south-southwesterly direction and debouches into the Bashgul after a course of some 10 miles. Its affluents on the right bank are the Tramzhigul, Loshalgul, Karatgul, and Sazaillaigul, while on the left are the Wogul, Papomligul, and Ditongul. A very difficult track from Bomboret in Chitral crosses the Parpit pass and then leads down the Pittigul to the Bashgul. (Roberts.)

*PODIN پدین
33-18 68-54 m. A village located on the road from Metakhan to Gardez in Paktia province.

*PODINA پدینه
34-26 67-8 m. A village located on the Dara-i-Mur, some 10 miles northeast of Panjao in Bamian province. Another place with this name is west of Panj Pitao Ghar in northwest Ghazni province, at 34-3 68-5 m.

*POHENDA پهندا
34-54 69-6 m. A village located north of Istalif and west of Khwajakhel in northern Kabul province.

POJAWA See HAZARA DARA پوجاوه
A village with this name is located northeast of Malima, at 35-19 69-39 m.

*POKA پوکه
34-29 68-22 m. A village located on the Helmand river, northeast of Qala Sayyid in Maidan province.

POLADA پولاده
A main section of the Hazaras.

*PORUNS پرونس
35-25 70-55 m. A village located on the Dara-i-Parun, about 4 miles south of Ashtiwai (Eshtiwi) in northern Kunar province.

POSTINDOZA پوستین دوزه
34- 69-. A village between the Siah Sang hill and the city of Kabul, 1/2 mile from the latter. It is a small straggling place. Inhabitants: Tajiks. (I.B.C.)

POWINDAH Or PAWINDAH پاونده
This name in the Derajat is applied to all those migratory Pathan tribes who come down to British teritory at the beginning of the cold weather, returning, as summer approaches, to the highlands of Afghanistan. The derivation of the term "Powindah," or "Pawindah," is somewhat obscure. Bellew says it is derived from the Persian "parwinda" - a bale of merchandise - which signifies their occupation as packmen, mercantile travellers, etc. Raverty is of opinion that the word is derived form the Persian verb, pawidan, to wander; while according to "Paget and Mason" the term is probably from the same root as the Pushtu word for "to graze." About 50,000 of these traders enter the Dera Ismail Khan district every year by the Gumal and adjoining passes between the 20th of October and the 15th of December, and return between the 20th of March and the 10th of May. They may be classified as follows:

Nasir	15,000	Sulaiman	12,000
Mian Khel	7,000	Kharoti	6,500
Dotani	1,000	Miscellaneous	8,500

The last are composed of different tribes, such as the Mithi, Kundi, Miani, Niazi, Mulla Khel, Michin Khel, Andari, Taraki, and others. The following general description of the Powindahs is given in the second edition of this Gazeteer:

"The Powindahs are pastoral in their mode of life. During the autumn months they proceed down the Zhob passes, and, leaving their families to graze the spare cattle in the Derajat, a portion of the tribe goes on with goods to Delhi, Cawnpore, etc., and arranges so as to be back about the commencement of March, when the clans again pick up their families and worldly goods and move up the passes to the Ghazni and Kalat-i-Ghilzai districts, sending on caravans to Kabul, Bokhara, Kandahar, and Herat (the Kharoti division carry on most of the trade with the latter place), the whole returning in time to accompany the tribe down the passes again.

"To any one commonly familiar with the internal divisions of Afghanistan, a glance at the map of Central Asia will suffice to convey a just notion of enterprise these merchants have voluntarily undertaken and successfully accomplished. They sell to the luxurious Muhammadan at Delhi the dried fruits of Bokhara, and buy at Calcutta English calico and muslin for the soft harems of Herat and the savage tribes of Turkistan; while midway in their path lie the rugged mountains of Sulaiman, whose snows and torrents are friendly in comparison with the unappeasable Waziris who live amongst them, and carry on against the merchants war to the knife, year after year and generation after generation.

"To meet the opposition that awaits them at this part of their road, the Powindahs are compelled to move in large bodies of from five thousand to ten thousand, and regular marches and encampments are observed, under an elected Khan or leader, exactly like any army moving through an enemy's country.

"A day's march in the Waziri hills seldom passes without a skirmish in van or rear, the cutting up of some stragglers, or the plundering of some cattle. Occasionally there is a regular pitched battle of the most bloody character, when any particular event has occurred to exasperate the hatred on both sides. The merchants have more than once attempted to come to a compromise with their enemies, and arrange for an unmolested passage on payment of a fixed 'blackmail' but the Waziri Council has invariably and nemine dissentiente, refused the offer of peace. (Since the Waziristan Expedition of 1894-95 the Powindahs, relying on the protection of the Government of India, have relaxed their old precautions, and now pass through the Gumal in small parties of 2 or 3 men accompanied by valuable property and animals. W.R.R.)

"The consequence is that the Powindahs are as much soldiers as merchants. They are always heavily armed, even while pasturing their flocks and herds in the Derajat, though they pay the British Government the compliment of going unarmed into India. In appearance, with their storm-stained Afghan clothing, reckless manners, and boisterous voices, they are the rudest of the rude; and though the few individuals who are deemed sufficient to conduct the caravans into India show a cunning quite commercial in their mild and quiet conduct, never taking the law into their own hands, and always appealing to the justice of the magistrates, yet when united in large bodies, as they are throughout the winter and spring, in the plain of the Indus, they are, or fain would be, utterly lawless, and succumb only to superior force. They paid heavy custom dues to the Sikh authorities on the Indus, because there was no help for it, as their caravans would otherwise have been seized in the Punjab; but beyond that the Sikhs never ventured to interfere with them, though they committed all sorts of depredations on the lands under the skirts of the hills."

Edwardes says: I hardly ever saw a Powindah who had not one or more wounds on his body; and the loss of an eye, broken noses, scored skulls, lame legs, and mutilated arms are almost as common as freckles in England."

The following acount of the Powindah tribes, by Mr. H. St. G. Tucker, appeared in the Dera Ismail Khan Settlement Report published in 1883:

"From time immemorial, the Powindahs have traded between India and Khorasan. They bring down long strings of camels laden with the goods of Bokhara and Kandahar, and carry back in exchange the products of Hindustan and the manufactures of Wilayat. Many of the poorer Powindahs, instead of trading, engage in the local carrying trade of the Derajat, while others subsist on the profit which they derive from their flocks and herds."

"The Powindahs may be roughly divided into three classes:

"1st. Those who bring their families and establish themselves in fixed camping-grounds known as kiris (camp villages), a portion perhaps going off to trade."

"2nd. Those who come down with caravans (kafilas), but without their families, and who have no fixed camping-grounds."

"3rd. Those who have no belongings and come down as labourers. These latter are known by the name of charra folk. They wander about, sometimes in gangs, sometimes by twos and threes, through the towns and villages of the Derajat. They are ready for rough work of any sort, such as stone-breaking, road-making, clearing jungle (butimari), and any sort of job where energy and strength are more necessary than professional skill. They are industrious and economical, saving all that they earn to take back with them to Afghanistan, and subsisting while here mainly on what they gain by begging in the evening after the day's work is over.

"The mass of the Powindahs enter the district by the Gumal pass. Most of the trading Powindahs take this route; but a certain number, mostly sheepowners, prefer the branch road that goes by the Zam pass and debuches at Zarkani. The total number of Powindahs entering the district, according to an enumeration made at the mouths of the passes during the cold weather of 1877-78, amounted to 76,403. Of these the details are as follows:

Men		35,439
Women		9,128
Children;	boys	25,422
	girls	6,414
Total		76,403

"The number of men given is probably fairly correct. The figures for women and children are not so reliable. Another enumeration for 1879 gives the number of fighting men belonging to kiris (i.e., those who bring their families) as 14,133. Allowing an average of two women and children to each man, the total number of kiri folk should be 42,399. The number of the kafila charra folk is given at 15,300 fighting men, which would raise the total number to 57,699, of whom 29,433 are fighting men. In the cold weather of 1880-81 it was found that 49,392 Powindahs entered the district of whom 32,219 were males. The numbers of the kiri folk remain tolerably constant; but the number of charras is liable to great fluctuations, seasons of scarcity driving down large numbers of men, who in ordinary years remain at their homes. The people of each Powindah kiri have a fixed camping ground of their own, which they seek as soon as they arrive in the plains and where they pitch their tents for the season. The same camping ground is resorted to year after year, and though a kiri may for special reasons move to a new location, yet such changes are rare. The women, children, and arms are left in the kiri. Two-thirds of the men also generally remain behind, while the remaining third go off with the laden camels and merchandise to Hindustan. Although the Powindahs appreciate the railway and such as wish to be early in the market use it largely, the bulk of them still adhere to their old practice, and take their camels to Delhi, Cawnpore, Benares and even to Patna."

"There are no very reliable statistics as to the extent of the Powindah trade. The following figures are the best estimate obtainable of the principal articles of import and export:

Imports:

	Rs.
Fruits, dried and fresh	7,00,000
Madder	6,00,000
Raw silk	5,00,000
Wool	1,50,000
Charras (an intoxicating drug extracted from hemp)	1,02,000
Horses	65,000
Hing (asafoetida)	50,000
Tobacco	30,000
Total Imports	21,97,000

Exports:

	Rs.
Indigo	6,00,000
Manufactured cotton goods (English)	5,00,000
Manufactured cotton goods (country)	6,00,000
Tea	1,00,000
Shoes and leather	40,000
Salt	20,000
Sugar	20,000
Metal goods	20,000
Crockery and earthenware	7,000
Total Exports	19,07,000

"The centres of the Powindah trade in Khorasan are Bokhara, Kabul, Kandahar, and Ghazni. The following are the principal articles of merchandise brought from each:
Bokhara: Silk, charras; gold and silver thread (kalabatin), and furs.
Kabul: Almonds, pistachio nuts, raisins, dried fruits, and wool from the Kakar country.
Ghazni: Madder, wool, ghi, tobacco, and asafoetida.
"I must now give a brief account of the leading Powindah tribes.
"These are the Nasirs, Sulaiman Khels, Kharotis, Mian Khels and Dotanis; tribes of less importance are the Niazis, Mulla Khels, Mithis, Kundis, Tarakis, Tokhis, and Andars."
"The Nasirs are the least settled of all these tribes; they have no country of their own. They winter in the Derajat and summer in the Ghilzai country; they pay Rs. 3,000 (nandrami) to the Turan Ghilzais for the right of grazing in their country. The Nasirs live principally by their herds and flocks. They own about 33,000 camels and some 1,30,000 sheep and goats, their wealth consisting mainly in their herds and flocks; their kiris are scattered along the skirts of the hills from the Zarkani pass in the Gumal valley to Kot Tagga

below Chandwan. They probably number, with their women and children, 20,000. They are divided into a number of important sections, but the more popular division of the Nasirs is into camel folk, ox and ass folk, and sheep folk. Of the camel folk, or Ushwals, the poor ones come down first. They engage principally as carriers, taking goods to and from Bannu. They bring salt from the Kohat mines, Multani matti from the hills, and grain from Marwat. They are also much employed in cutting and selling fuel. The well-to-do men come later, and generally bring merchandise, grapes, almonds, and madder. The kiris of the camel folk are usually situated away from the hills, at Saggu, Iriniman, Paniala, Potah, and in the Kahiri ilaqa. The ox and ass folk (Gaiwals and Kharwals) own only oxen and donkeys. They are generally engaged in doing jobs, carrying earth, bricks, etc., in the towns. They have no kiris of their own. They arrive at the end of September, and return about the beginning of April. The sheep folk (Gosfandwals) arrive during October, and return about the end of April. They occupy the country along the foot of the hills. Some of them encamp at Paniala, but these generally take their flocks for part of the season into the Bhakkar Thal. The Nasirs are for the most part short, sturdy men. On the whole they are a well-behaved tribe, though a little inclined to be overbearing in their treatment of the villagers in whose neighbourhood they encamp. Their cattle not unfrequently trespass on to the cultivated fields, and attempts on the part of the proprietors to seize and impound them are sometimes opposed by force. They are a rough-and-ready lot, who would probably, but for the advent of British rule, have treated the Mian Khels and other tribes, who have been enervated by long residence in the plains, much as the forefathers of these latter treated the Suris and the Pabbis, driving them out and appropriating their lands. (For further information regarding the Nasirs and other tribes here mentioned, see under their respective headings)."

"The Kharotis are a tribe occupying the hills near the sources of the Gumal and the district of Arghun (Urgun) to the west of the Sulaiman Khel country. They generally arrive in the plains towards the end of November and depart in May. They have sixteen kiris. These are located near Tank, Mulazai, and Paharpur. They are a poor tribe, and have been nearly ruined by a long and unequal contest with the Sulaiman Khels. This feud, though allowed to rest during their stay in Hindustan, breaks out afresh as soon as they re-enter the hills; though attempts have latterly been made by the Deputy Commissioner, with some success, to bring the two tribes to terms. Most of the Kharotis engage as labourers and carriers like the Nasirs. A large proportion of them are charra folk. Some are merchants, and trade in dried fruits and madder. The Kharotis own four or five thousand camels, which they bring down with them to the plains. They leave their flocks in their own country."

"The Sulaiman Khels are the most numerous and powerful of all the Powindahs, the name covering not only the Sulaiman Khels proper, but a number of allied clans all belonging to the great Ghilzai tribe. The Sulaiman Khels occupy a great extent of country stretching from Pishin and Kalat-i-Ghilzai nearly as far as Jalalabad, though most of them who come down into British territory reside for the most part in the hills lying east of Ghazni. The number of these probably averages about 12,000. Most of them are charra folk, and they own altogether only about 4,000 camels. They bring but little merchandise with them, but great numbers of them go down country, especially to Calcutta, where they act as go-betweens, or dalals, buying goods from the merchants there and selling them to the Powindahs. They bring back their profits for the most part in cash.

Those who stop in the district work as labourers. They generally come and go about at the same time as the Kharotis, but a few days before or after, on account of the feud already mentioned. The Sulaiman Khels are fine, strong men. They have the character of being rather a set of rascals, though on the whole they behave themselves very fairly while in British territory. They have nine kiris located at Amakhel, Mulazai, and in the neighbourhood of Tank and Kulachi, but the population attached to them is not a third of the whole number of Sulaiman Khels who enter the district. One of these kiris has now disappeared, the men belonging to it having been nearly all killed in a fight between them and our troops during the suppression of the late disturbance in Tank (January 1879)."

"The Mian Khels are the richest of the Powindahs. Most of the valuable trade with Bokhara is in their hands. Their kiris are situated near Draband and Musazai, at Kat Malana and Shalu, and in the Miran ilaqa. They have fourteen kiris in all, and number about 4,500 men. They own from 4,000 to 5,000 camels. They are closely related to the plain Mian Khels. During the summer their kiris are stationed in the hills near Panah and Karabagh. They generally arrive here in November and leave in May."

"The Dotanis inhabit the Wano valley and the country between the Waziri hills and the Gumal. Their lands are comparatively fertile, growing rice and cereals. They are on good terms with the Waziris. They are a small tribe numbering only some 700 fighting men. They are well-to-do, and carry on a profitable trade with Bokhara. They bring down postins, chakmas, and charras. They have three kiris in our territory, near Kat Malana and in the Kahiri ilaqa. About a third of them are kafila folk and have no kiris. They own about 3,500 camels. They leave their flocks behind in the hills. They come and go along with the Mian Khels, though forming separate caravans."

"The Niazis number only some 400 men. They have three kiris at Mandra and in the Kahiri ilaqa. They trade to Kandahar, bringing down dried fruits and madder. They have some 3,000 camels, but no flocks."

"The Mianis are allied to the plain Mianis of the Gumal valley, near whom they reside during the winter. They number some 400 men. They have four kiris, and own about 800 camels and some 8,000 sheep and goats."

"The Mithis are another small tribe; they have three kiris in the Paharpur ilaqa. They number some 300 men, and own about 1,250 camels."

"The Mulla Khels, Kundis, Zamranis, and Guranis are small tribes, not requiring separate mention, whose kiris are scattered about the Paharpur ilaqa. They number some 600 men in all, and own some 350 camels. The Mulla Khels also own some 3,500 sheep."

"The Tarakis, Tokhis, Andars, and Daulatzais are all Ghilzai clans occupying tracts near Ghazni and Kalat-i-Ghilzai. Those of them who visit this district are kafila folk and leave their families behind. Between them they number some 6,000 fighting men, and own about 11,000 camels."

"The different Powindah tribes are sometimes supposed to come down to the plains in regular order -- Nasirs, Sulaiman Khels, Kharotis and Mian Khels -- and at one time this may have been the case. There is now, however, no fixed rule. This year (1878-79), for instance, the Mian Khels came first and the Nasirs last."

"The statement on next page shows the numbers of the different tribes accompanying and the cattle owned by each in tabular form: The following report by Mr. L. W. King, Deputy Commissioner, Derajat on the Powindah force (torah) which assembled in the autumn of 1894 with the object of attacking the Wano Ahmadzais and the Mahsuds, furnishes some interesting information:

"To understand the relations between the two parties that gave rise to the torah it will be necessary to go back a little in the history of the tribes chiefly concerned. In by-gone times the Wano Valley was in possession of the Dotanis, who were and are still under the protection of the powerful Sulaiman Khel tribes. Some 50 years ago the Ahmadzais, who were then a nomad tribe, moved from their settlements in Margha and Birmal to Wano and obtained a footing in the valley, partly by force and partly by occupying land in the capacity of mortgages. In the course of time almost the whole valley had come into their hands. Some 30 years ago the Dotanis with the aid of the Sulaiman Khels, who themselves claimed grazing right in Wano, made a desperate attempt to recover possession of the valley. A fierce fight ensued in which the invaders were worsted and lost heavily. The scene of the fight, old Dotani Kot, has been a ruin ever since. After this there was a chronic dispute between the Ahmadzais on the one hand and the Dotanis and Sulaiman Khels on the other, about the possession of landed and grazing rights in Wano. In the beginning of last cold weather a dispute arose between the Ahmadzais and Dotanis respecting the right to a certain "karez" or water course known as Mir Khan. In the fight which ensued the Ahmadzais killed a number of Dotanis and demolished their fortified village (new Dotani Kot).

In consequence of this the Dotanis and Sulaiman Khels determined to make a joint attack on the Ahmadzais of Wano on their way back to their summer quarters in Khorasan. On receiving information of this the civil authorities in Dera Ismail Khan summoned a jirga of Sulaiman Khel, Dotani and Ahmadzai Maliks with a view to preventing reprisals and bringing about, if possible, an amicable arrangement between the hostile tribes. The Ahmadzais ultimately agreed to pay blood-money or compensation for the Dotanis they had killed and to rebuild the village they had demolished. On receiving a satisfactory assurance of this the Dotanis and Sulaiman Khels promised to refrain from further hostilities. In the beginning of last hot weather, however, the Dotanis were again attacked by Ahmadzais at Totoi on the Toi, where they had halted on their return to their summer quarters. In this raid the Dotanis lost seven men killed and had 120 cows looted as well. The Dotanis thereupon determined to exact revenge for this unprovoked attack, and accordingly approached their allies, the Sulaiman Khels, with a view to their taking joint action against the Wanowals during the cold weather.

"The Sulaiman Khels not only agreed to suport them, but determined to get up a coalition of all the Powindah tribes for the purpose. With this end in view the leading Sulaiman Khel Maliks, Muhammad Akram Khan, Khan Khan, Kate Khan, Sultan Muhammad and Allahyar Khan, with a small following, arrived in Shalgar in September last and summoned the Mian Khel Maliks to meet them there. The Maliks Nawab Khan, Sayyid Muhammad, Sher Ali, Yar Muhammad and Atagul were sent to Shalgar to represent the Mian Khel tribe. An agreement was come to between the two tribes to collect a joint torah against the Mahsuds. The Mian Khels declined, however, to join in an attack on the Wano Ahmadzais, with whom they had concluded a treaty of peace. It was settled that when the Mian Khel kiris were on their way to the plains (they getting the last of the Powindahs to go down) they would join forces with the Sulaiman Khels against the Mahsuds. The Sulaiman Khels then sent a message to the Dotani Maliks Ghulam Haidar, Shahab-ud-din, Ghulam Sadiq and Sad Rahmat, who agreed on behalf of the tribe to be in readiness to join the torah at the appointed time. Finally the Kharoti Maliks, Zarif Khan, Roshan Khan, Wali Khan and Azim Khan were summoned to the meeting, and they also agreed to join in the torah. They however first made the Sulaiman Khel Maliks subscribe to an oath that they would not accept a bribe from the Mahsuds to settle the matter amicably. It was at the same time decided by the representatives of the four leading tribes that all the kuchi (nomad Powindahs) would also join the torah at Warshak on their way to the plains. All the nomad Powindahs (including their families) according to this agreement were to engage in the torah, but only the fighting men from the settled sections. It appears from this that only the Sulaiman Khels and Dotanis were to attack the Wanowals, but that the whole strength of all the Powindah tribes would be exerted against the Mahsuds, at whose hands they had suffered severely from time to time.

"The torah collected at Warshak in the middle of October with the intention of ravaging Wano and then attacking the Mahsuds. The allied army of the Powindahs advanceed as far as Miran, where the Commissioner's letter was received in which he warned them against committing hostilities against Wano, which was under our protection and would shortly be occupied by our troops. The attack on the Wano Ahmadzais was accordingly checked and the hostile gathering began to break up. On the arrival of the Delimitation Escort, however, in Wano a deputation of Sulaiman Khels, Dotani and Kharoti Maliks waited on the Commissioner and requested his permission to invade the Mahsud country. This request was peremptorily refused and the Maliks informed that hostilities between the Amir's subjects and the Waziris who were under our protection could on no account be allowed. The Maliks, though not altogether pleased at the ill success of their mission, accepted the inevitable with a good grace, and the torah shortly afterwards finally dispersed.

"A jirga of the leading Darwesh Khel Maliks was subsequently convened at the request of the Dotanis to settle their long-standing dispute with the Wano Ahmadzais. This jirga only took up the question of blood-money and decided, with the consent of both parties, that a sum of R 400 should be paid on this account by the Wano Ahmadzais to the Dotanis, viz., R 200 within a month and the remainder on the return of the latter to their summer quarter in Khorasan."

PRESUNGUL   See PECH   پراسون گل

PRONTZGROM   پرونسگرام
34- 70-. Elevation 8,530 feet. A Kafiristan village in the Presungul. It is built in a rudely defensive irregularly oblong form on the right bank of the river, and about 100 yards from its margin. In general construction it resembles Shtevgrom. The back wall of contiguous houses forms the west wall of the village, while on the east the village wall is separated from the dwelling houses by a sloping bank covered with long coarse grass. The interior is packed with houses, the greater part of which are underground. The lanes between the houses are exceedingly narrow. (Robertson.) The stream with this name is located at 34-52 71-9 A. (LWA)

PSHU or PESHAWUR   پشاور
35-50 71-21 m. A fort village in the Katir part of the Bashgul (Katigal) valley. It has proved too small for its inhabitants, and in 1891 a three-sided enclosure of houses was being added to its east wall. It numbers 150 houses. In siege time it can draw its water supply from the left bank of the Bashgul river, on the brink of which it stands. From Pshui there is a horse track, it is said, to Drusp in the Lutkho valley. (Robertson.)

PTSIGROM Or PACHIGRAM پچیگرام
35-45 71-12 m. Is the chief settlement in the Shorigul, in Kafiristan, and the furthermost from the Bashgul valley. In 1891 the village was being built in the usual oblong defensive form of a Katir village when on the plain. It is on the left bank of the Shorigul river, and probably contains 60 houses or more. (Robertson.)

*PUFDAM پفدم
35-9 69-21 m. A village located about 3 miles northeast of Reza Kohestan, near the Koh-i-Sangriz in Kapisa province.

PUKH پخ
35-26 69-44 G. A village on the right bank of the upper Panjshir stream, 3 miles above Marz. Twelve houses of Tajiks. One mile lower down is Pashghur with 100 houses of Tajiks. (Shahzada Taimus.)

PUL-I-CHARKHI پل چرخی
34-33 69-21 A. A village of 200 houses, with a sarai, 4 miles north of Butkhak, on the right bank of the Kabul river. Inhabitants: Sohak, Ghilzais and Tarakhel Shahghasis. The river used to be crossed here by a bridge; wooden platform on stone piers unfit for guns, but suitable for cavalry. The action of the current, however, has cut away the alluvial soil on the right bank and the bridge now (1904) ends in the air. Fodder for about 4,000 animals and about 400 maunds of unground grain may be collected in neighbourhood. Fuel is procurable and there is good ground for encampment. (I.B.C., Johnston) This village is now the site of Afghanistan's major modern jail. (LWA)

PUL-I-FARINGI پل فرناگی (فرنگی)
34-54 67-40 G. A rude wooden foot-bridge over the Bamian river, 9 1/4 miles above Kala Sarkari. It has replaced one of stone said to have been erected during the British occupation of 1839, and is therefore known as the Pul-i-Faringi. (Maitland.)

*PUL-I-RUSTAM پل رستام
35-34 71-19 m. A village located about 2 miles south of Chapo on the Kantoz Rud in Kunar province.

PULWARI پلوری
A fort in the Kunar valley, on the right bank. (Masson.)

PULWATA پلواته
34-41 70-9. A village in Laghman situated on the right bank of the Alishang river about 1 mile below Ghanjawan. Inhabitants: Tajiks. It contains a fort called the Kala-i-Uhdadar. (Warburton)

*PUNBAR پونبار
35-9 71-30 m. A village located south of Narai and about 2 miles southeast of Shangah in Kunar province.

*PUNGA پنگه
33-28 69-37 m. A village in the Khairaspan area, southwest of Zorkot and northwest of Matun in Paktia province.

PURAK Or PURAKH پورك
34-7 96-4. A group of 17 forts and hamlets in the Logar valley, on the right bank of the river and 2 miles south of the Tangi Waghjan. Fodder for 5,000 animals for one day and about 600 maunds of un-

665

ground grain may be collected from these villages. The following was the population of Purak in 1880:

Astanazai Ghilzais	175	families
Nasir	15	families
Tokhi	6	families
Total	196	

(Clifford, Euan Smith, Johnston.)

PURDIL KHAN پردل خان
33-38 68-32 G. A village about 9 miles northeast of Ghazni, on the road thence to Kharwar. (I.B.C.)

*PURSHAKHEL پرشاخیل
34-7 70-32 m. A village located a few miles east of Haska Mina and near Laghjuri in Nangarhar province.

PURSTAM Or PUL-I-RUSTAM پرستم (پل رستم)
35-34 71-19 m. Is one of the lowest Katir villages in the Bashgul valley. It comprises 40 houses, built on the face of a steep rock, inaccessible on every side except straight up the face. Although at Purstam the river widens considerably and throws out a supplementary stream, which curves round towards the lowest houses, which are built close to the water, it is yet overshadowed in the morning by the high cliff on the left bank of the river. Apart from the houses on the rock there is a group of four or five houses down stream, a couple of hundred yards or so. The Purstam bridge is just below. Near it is a large collection of "pshals" which may readily be mistaken for another village especially as there are several small temples among them. (Robertson.)

*PUSHAL پوشال
35-26 70-20 m. A village located on the Nuristan river, opposite Jeshpal and some 5 miles southwest of Atati in Laghman province.

PUSHKI GROM See PASHKIGROM پشکی گرام

*PUSHTI Or PUSHTEY پشتی
32-58 69-13 m. A village near Sultanai and about 5 miles northeast of Urgun in Paktia province.

PUSHT-I-HAJI KHAK پشت حاجی خاک
34-38 68-5. A pass over the main ridge of the Koh-i-Baba, south of the Hajigak pass. It is a better road than either that of the Irak but can only be traversed by caravans in July, August, and September. (Wood.)
N.B. This is evidently the Kafzar pass.

*PUSHT-I-WAZ پشت واز
35-16 67-28 m. A village on the Dara-i-Murghan, northwest of Saighan in Bamian province.

*PUTWAL پتوال
33-4 68-14 m. A village located about 1 mile north of Rustamkhel on the Sardeh Rud and some 10 miles south of Mushakai in Ghazni province.

RABAT, AB-I رباط
A stream of about 12 miles flowing into the Helmand.

RABAT رباط
34- 69-. A village in the Kohistan of Kabul, between Chaikal and Karabagh. About 400 houses of Tajiks, about 100 houses of Mishwani Ghilzais, and a few of Hindu traders. Water from the Charikar canal. Much cultivation; wheat, cotton, etc.; no rice. (I.B.C.)

RABAT رباط
33- 68-. A village in the Shilghar district of the Ghilzai country. It contains about 150 houses inhabited by Tajiks. There is a pass from Shilghar to Kharwar, which starts from this village, and is thence known as the Rabat Kotal. See "Robat" (1). (Broadfoot.)

*RABAT رباط
33-34 68-42 m. A village located some 5 miles northeast of Ramak and about 14 miles east of Ghazni in Ghazni province. Other places with this name are located some 5 miles south of the above, at 33-31 68-42 m.; about 6 miles northwest of Gardez in Paktia province, at 33-38 69-10 m.; and at 34-48 67-53 G., 34-59 68-51 G., 34-59 69-10 G.

RAFAK ZINBARDAR رفاق زنبردار
35- 71-. A village in the Kunar valley, on the left bank of the river at the junction of a large tributary of the Kunar called the "Bash Ghalok," and 80 miles above Jalalabad. (Davies.)

*RAGAI رگی
33-13 69-32 m. A village located on the Tangai river, some 8 miles southwest of Nadirshahkot in Paktia province.

*RAGHEH راغه
32-57 69-22 m. A village located south of Gian and east of Urgun in Paktia province.

RAHAN راهان
34-43 70-8 G. A village in the Alishang valley, 41 miles from Jalalabad. Supplies and water plentiful. (I.B.C.)

*RAHESHT راهشت
34-55 69-6 m. A village near Kabuli, about 8 miles north of Istalif in southern Parwan province.

RAH-I-BADI راه بادی
A small village, in the west of the Besud district on the Kabul-Hazarajat main road, and situated in the Isfi Sang Tagao. (Twenty houses) (Muhammad Akbar Khan.)

*RAH-I-RAMA راه رامه
33-3 67-15 m. A village located on a tributary of the Helmand, in the area of Baba in Ghazni province.

RAH-I-GOSFAND راه گسفند
34- 69-. The name of a gorge leading from Kabul, via the Koh Daman, to Charikar. This has been pronounced by far the best route by Kinloch, who reconnoitred it in 1880, and found it practicable for wheeled artillery. At the present time (1895) the main road is believed to go by the Khirskhana Kotal. (Kinloch, I.B.C.)

RAH-I-MALIK راه ملك
Said to be a large valley in the Hazara Yaghistan.

RAHIM KHAN رحیم خان
34- 69-. A village in the valley of the lower Logar (northern division), close to the Tangi Waghjan on the left bank of the Logar. In 1880 the place contained 10 families, the inhabitants being all Tajiks. (Clifford, Euan Smith.)

RAH-I-REG راه ریگ
The ninth halting-place on the Kabul-Chahardar pass route to Mazar-i-Sharif. It is merely an open Chaman on the left bank of the stream 10 1/4 miles north of the pass. "Rah-i-Reg" is a very steep footpath leading west, up a stony ravine. (Drummond.)

*RAH KOL   Also see RAQOL راه قول

RAH KOL راه قول
34-20 67-51 A. In the Sar-i-Kol subdistrict of Yakh Walang. It contains only 15 houses of Dai Zangis. (A.B.C.)
The valley descending south from the Jalmish Kotal. Recent sources show the name Sar-i-Raqowl. (LWA)

RAH KOL راه قول
A valley in the Besud Hazara country.

RAH KOL راه قول
Elevation 9,800 feet. Two villages, and a serai, on the right bank of the stream of the same name, just east of where the latter is crossed by the main Kabul-Hazarajat-Daulat Yar road. A mountain with this name is located south of Paghman at 34-33 68-51 G. (LWA)

RAHMAK رحمك (رامك)
A village 15 miles east of Ghazni. (Thornton) Recent maps show the name Ramak at 33-31 68-37 A. (LWA)

RAHMAN BEG رحمن بیگ
A village in the Dai Zangi country.

*RAHMAN KALAI رحمن کلی
32-30 67-40 m. A village located between Shahjoy and the Ab-i-Istada in Ghazni province.

*RAHMAN KHEL رحمن خیل
32-19 67-37 m. A village located southwest of the Ab-i-Istada and north of the Botakhel area in Ghazni province.

RAHMAN KHEL See KACHU رحمن خیل

RAHMATABAD رحمت آباد
A village in the Burjistan glen, a tributary of the Turkoman Dara. It contains about 10 families of Hindustanis.

RAHMATABAD رحمت آباد
34-19 69-6 m. A hamlet in the Logar valley, on the right bank of the river and to the north of the Tangi Waghjan. The inhabitants are Tajiks. In 1880 the place contained only 5 families. (Clifford, Euan Smith.)

*RAIKHOSHI ریخوشی
34-1 69-2 m. A village located in the Logar valley, some 5 miles south of Kolangar in Logar province.

RAJAI راجی
34- 70-. A village in Laghman, about 5 miles northeast of Badiabad. The inhabitants are Arokis, and it contains the following hamlets:
(1) Kala-i-Shiggi (3) Kala-i-Shahi (5) Kala-i-Kukkur Mangai
(2) Kala-i-Kokhi (4) Kala-i-Sakhra (6) Banda-i-Shahdad.
(Warburton.)

*RAJAN راجان
34-14 69-27 m. A village located east of Sangdar-i-Ghar, on a tributary of the Kabul river in Logar province.

RAKIAN See ROKIAN راکیان

RAKMAK رکمک
33- 68-. A village in the Shilghar district of the Ghilzai country. It contains 150 houses inhabited by Tajiks. (Broadfoot.)

*RAMAK رامک
33-31 68-37 m. A village located north of Tenfer and west of Ghazni in Ghazni province.

RAMA TALA رامه تاله
34- 68-. A tributary of the Helmand which, rising in the Sanglakh range north of the Unai pass, joins the Helmand about 5 miles northeast of Jaokul. A road runs up the Rama Tala Tagao and crosses the Sanglakh range by the Baghar kotal. (Wanliss.)

RAMGUL رام گل
35- 70-. Understood to be the name applied to the main western valley of Kafiristan, inhabited by the Ramgul branch of the Katirs. Its river after being joined by the Kulam from the left is known as the Kao or Aligar.
The Ramgulis are roughly estimated at 18,000 souls, and they are said to possess 24 villages. (Robertson.) A pass with this name is located at 35-41 70-33 A., and a stream is located at 35-6 70-18 G. (LWA)

RAMUZ راموز
A section of the Besud Hazaras.

*RAMZI رمزی
34-17 68-3 m. A village on the Dara-i-Jelga, at the Maidan-Ghazni border. Another place with this name is located on a tributary of the Dara-i-Garmab, in southern Bamian province.

*RANDAKHEL رانده خیل
34-13 69-23 m. A village located northeast of Kolangar and southeast of Kabul in Logar province.

RANGAR رنگان (رنگر)
A village in the Ghorband valley, situated near the mouth of the Kipchak glen. (Peacocke.) Recent maps show the name Rangan at 35-0 68-49 m. (LWA)

RANGUL رانگل
35-43 71-22 G. A hamlet in the Bashgul valley in Kafiristan, 4 miles above Bragamatal. (I.B.C.) There is also a pass with this name at 35-41 70-33, and a stream, also spelled Ramgul, at 35-6 70-18 A. (LWA)

RAQOL راقول
A stream draining into the Helmand, from the south, in Besud. A village with this name is located at 34-20   67-51 A.

*RAQOL راقول
34-17 66-41 m. A village located on the Nawa-i-Sagdiz, southeast of Asgharat in western Bamian province. Other places with this name are located nearby at 34-18   66-45 m.; a few miles north of Espighaw in Bamian province, at 34-5   66-55 m.; on a tributary of the Helmand in Bamian province, at 34-17   67-14 m.; at the Band-i-Doab, southwest of Behsud in Bamian province, at 34-9   67-49 m.; on a tributary of the Maidan river, north of Jaliz in Maidan province, at 34-34   68-42 m.; in Sardkoh area, west of Garmab in Bamian province, at 33-58 67-20 m.; and in the Korala area, north of the Dasht-i-Nawer in Ghazni province, at 33-52   67-45 m.

RASANA راسانه
A pass leading to the Jaghuri Hazara country. See "Ghazni." A village with this name is located at 32-46   67-15 G.   (LWA)

*RASHAK رشك
34-26 66-43 m. A village located on a stream, some 8 miles northeast of Asgharat in western Bamian province. Other places with this name are located near Dara-i-Mur, northeast of Panjao in Bamian province, at 34-27   67-6 m.; some 8 miles south of Behsud in Maidan province, at 34-15   67-54 m.; on a tributary of the Helmand, north of Behsud in Maidan province, at 34-31   67-53 m.; on a tributary of the Bamian river, some 8 miles south-southwest of Bamian in Bamian province, at 34-44   67-48 m.

*REGAK ريگك
34-31 68-14 m. A village located on a tributary of the Helmand, southeast of Siasang in Maidan province.

REGAK ريگك
35- 69-. A pass in the Hindu Kush about 4 miles south of the Khawak pass. It is closed by snow during part of the year but as long as it is open the shortest route as also the best for laden animals, from Dasht-i-Rewat to the Khawak pass lies up the Sar-i-Lang ravine, over the Regak pass at its head, and then northwards to the Khawak. (I.B.C.)

REGAN See ROGUN رگان

REG-I-RAWAN ريگءروان
A hill 40 miles north of Kabul, which is thus described by Burnes: "Two ridges of hills, detached from the rest, run in and meet each other; at the apex of this a sheet of sand, as pure as that on the sea-shore, with a slope of about 40, forms the face of a hill to its summit, which is about 400 feet high. When this sand is set in motion by a body of people who slide down it, a sound is emitted. On the first trial we distinctly heard two loud hollow sounds such as would be given by a large drum. On two subsequent attempts we heard nothing, so that perhaps the sand requires to be for a time settled before the curiosity is displayed. There is an echo in the place, and the inhabitants have a belief that the sounds are only heard on Friday when the saint of Reg-i-Rawan, who is interred hard by, permits! The locality of the sand is remarkable, there being none

other in the neighbourhood. Reg-i-Rawan faces the south, but the wind of Parwan (Bad-i-Parwan) blows from the north for the greater part of the year, and has probably deposited it by an eddy. Such is the violence of this wind that all the trees in the neighbourhood bend to the south, and a field, after a few years, requires to be cleared of the pebbles and stones which the loss of soil lays bare. The mountains here are generally composed of granite or mica, but at Reg-i-Rawan we had sandstone, lime, slate, and quartz.

"Reg-i-Rawan is seen from a great distance, and the situation of the sand is so curious that it might almost be imagined the hill had been cut in two, and that it had gushed forth as from a sand-bag, though the wind could have brought it together. Convulsions of nature, however, are exceedingly common in this part of the world." (Burnes.)

N.B. There is another "Reg-i-Rawan" in the Herat province -- see Volume 3.

*REGJOY ریگ چوی
33-15 67-23 m. A village located near Almaitu, southwest of the Dasht-i-Nawer in Ghazni province.

REHAN ریحان
A village in Laghman. Inhabitants: Safis. (Warburton.)

*RIGA ریگا
34-5 67-22 m. A village located on a tributary of the Helmand, 2 miles south of Sewak in Bamian province.

RIKA ریکا
A people found in Kabul, Jalalabad and Laghman. In Kabul city they have a quarter called the Rikakhana, near the Lahori gate and they are said to number 1,000 families in the capital, and in the villages in its neighbourhood.

Their headman, Sultan Aziz, was hanged at Kabul for the part taken by him in the massacre of Sir Louis Cavagnari and his companions and escort in September 1879. (I.B.C.)

Jenkyns says:

"Very few representatives of this tribe are now found in Jalalabad. There are not, probably, more than twenty persons in this district, but in Kabul they are said to number 2,000 families.

"By origin they are Kurds, and were brought from Kurdistan by Taimur Lang, at the same time as the Arabs were introduced. The villages where they are found are Kala-i-Charbagh, Bahrabad, Bakhtan, Shamsapur, and Girdikach.

"The Rikas are divided into four classes, viz.:
    1. Murkri   2. Boumri   3. Moghadam   4. Ardalani.

"Of these only the Mukris are represented in Jalalabad.
"They are Sunni Muhammadans."

RIKA ریکا
34- 69-. A village in the Kabul district between Shewaki and Bagrami, on the left bank of the Logar river. (I.B.C.)

RIKABASHI رکاب باشی
34- 69-. A fort 1 mile south of Bemaru, and about 3/4 mile from the southeast bastion of Sherpur. This place was destroyed in December 1879 by the British. (I.B.C.)

RIKAGAN ریکاگان
    34-32 70-15. A village in Laghman, containing three hamlets, situated between Mandrawar and the Junction of the Alingar and Kabul rivers. The inhabitants are Rikas and the Mian Khel. The following are the forts and hamlets belonging to the place:
        (1) Kala-i-Baluchabad   (2) Kala-i-Abdul Rahman
           (3) Banda-i-Baz Gul.   (Warburton.)

RISHKHOR-I-BALA رشخور بالا
    34-26 69-8 A. A village in the Chardeh valley of Kabul, on the right bank of the river, about 8 miles southwest of the city, and separated from the Charasia plain by an off-shoot from the Takht-i-Shah mountain. Inhabitants: Tokhi Ghilzais. (I.B.C.)

RISHKHOR-I-PAIN رشخور پائین
    34- 69-. A village in the Chardeh valley of Kabul, about 12 miles north of Rishkhor-i-Bala, and 1 mile south of Kala-i-Pathu. It is separated from Rishkhor-i-Bala by a spur of no great height. Inhabitants: Tajiks, Kizilbashis and Barakzais, each of whom have a fort of their own. There is said to be a stone bridge over the Kabul river between the two Rishkhor villages. (I.B.C.)

*RIWA ریوا
    35-4 68-57 m. A village located on the Jar-i-Namakao, a tributary of the Ghorband in Laghman province.

*RIWKAK ریوک
    34-3 67-6 m. A village located in the Waras area, southwest of Pitaoqol in Bamian province.

ROBA روباه (؟)
    A pass over the Gulkoh Range, between Ghazni and the valley of Jarmatu. It is similar in its character and appearance to the Galbauri pass over the same range. (Broadfoot.)

*ROBAT Also See RABAT رباط

ROBAT رباط
    33- 68-. A drainage of southwestern Kharwar, from the slopes of the Koh-i-Robat, Koh-i-Sar, and Koh-i-Gurbed, forms a wide valley into which a number of side ravines open from both sides. At the head of the valley three routes lead into Shilghar; they are:
(1) From Gurbed to Robat, see "Gurbed;" (2) and (3) Kotal-i-Satarnai and Kotal-i-Arda, both passable for horses and very similar to the Gurbed. (Griesbach.) A village with this name is located at 33-34 68-42 m. (LWA)

ROBAT رباط
    34- 69-. A collection of villages, southeast of Charikar, containing 2,000 Tajik families. (Native information.)

ROBAT See ZAK رباط

*RODAT رودات
    34-15 70-34. Rodat is a woleswali in Nangarhar province. The woleswali comprises an area of 661 square kilometers and has an agricultural population that has been estimated at from 33,180 to 34,410. The woleswali is bounded in the north by Surkh Rud, and Kama, in the east by Bati Kot and Shinwar, in the south Achin and Deh Bala and in

the west by Parchir Agam and Chaparhar. Rodat has about 49 villages, 13 of which have more than 500 inhabitants. The villages are listed in the PG as follows: Kan-i-Mohmand, Hesar-i-Shahi, Bazar, Chachi Qala, Qala-i-Miran, Chaghari, Qala-i-Murji, Koza Qala, Qarya-i-Diwan, Qarya-i-Zakhel, Zarbacha, Barbalu, Banda, Zeno, Kamar, Roghani (Roghali), Qarya-i-Sare Pay (Seh Pay), Mazina (Narta), Sangar (Sangar Bero), Metrani, Dushah, Gazwabi (Gazwani), Maduh, Banduk, Hindrani Ulya, Hindrani Sufla, Laghar Joy, Farukhshah Khel, Sayed Ahmad Khel, Terili (Karili), Kandigan, Zango Kach, Qala-i-Jaba, Haidar Khel, Saadatmand (Qara-i-Saadat), Qala-i-Ata Khan (Changira), Khatwanai, Manzanai, Kheder Khali, Hesarak, Koz Balu, Kadai, Shayesta Khel, Tawus Khel, Anar Khel, Qarya-i-Dawani, Bara Khel, Tatang, Katraghi, Qawai, Qarya-i-Nadar, Qara-i-Shahed-Khel, Qala-i-Jaber, Sipaya, Parsha Khel, Spola, Kadra, Akhundzada, Kambalo, and Kaihan.

*ROGHANI
34-14 70-32 m. A village located on a tributary of the Kabul river, about 3 miles southwest of Shahi Kot in Nangarhar province.

ROGHANI GARDAN
34-38 66-43 G. Elevation 11,700 feet. A pass leading over the Band-i-Amir--Hari Rud watershed, and crossed by a road leading from Sar-i-Jangal to Yakh Walang. From Khwaja Josh, a village in Sar-i-Jangal, the road ascends the main valley (called Garmao above this village) and then, according to Maitland, who traversed this route in October 1885, passes the rocky mouth of the Dahan-i-Surkh Guli, and after three quarters of a mile reaches Kohna Deh.
Here is a small rude fort, surrounded by the huts of a Hazara village. It is situated at the end of a low projection from the hills on the north side of the valley, and has a detached tower overlooking the stream. It is the residence of Kasim Ali Beg, Chief of Garmao. A little beyond Kohna Deh, and on the opposite (south) side of the valley, is the mouth of the Takhta glen.
From Kohna Deh the road runs along under the hills on the north side of the valley which is 200 to 150 yards wide. There is a little cultivation and a good deal of willow-scrub. The hills on the north are steep and high. On the other side, the hills immediately abutting on the valley are easier, being spurs of higher hills behind. The road is narrow in places, where the stream cuts in, to rather over 1 mile, but might easily be widened. A path, seen ascending the hills on the south, was said to go to Shaharistan.

ROGUN Or ROJAN, REGAN
34- 69-. A Ghilzai village on the road from Belut to Khurd Kabul, about 15 miles from the latter place. (I.B.C.)

ROJAN See ROGUN

ROKIAN Or RAKIAN, RUQYAN
33-59 69-40 m. A village in the Kurram valley, 4 miles from Ali Khel, and 165 miles from Kohat on the road to Ghazni. The valley here narrows to 1/2 mile, with precipitous commanding peaks upon each side, clad with pine forests. It contains about 30 houses, and consists of many scattered houses surrounded by a few fruit trees and cornfields. The main portion is situated at the entrance of the Hazardarakht defile, and is overhung by the abrupt shoulder of a towering rocky spur of the Safed Koh. Honey is produced here in abundance, almost every house possessing its bee-hives. (Lumsden, Bellew.)

ROSHAN روشان
A small section of the Chahar Dasta Hazaras.

*ROSHANA روشانه
33-12 69-42 m. A village located southwest of Tani and south of Nadirshahkot in Paktia province.

ROSHAN BEG روشان بیگ
A section of the Dai Kundi Hazaras.

ROZA Or RAWDZA روضه
33-35 68-27 m. A village about 2 miles northeast of Ghazni situated among the ruins of the old city, destroyed in the middle of the twelfth century by the Prince of Ghor. Amidst the destruction which overtook nearly all besides, the conqueror spared the tomb of the renowned Mahmud of Ghazni.
This has been suffered to dwindle away into ruins, and broken figures of marble lions, with other fragments, along attest the former beauty of its courts and fountains.
The tomb is a rude and humble structure, consisting of an oblong chamber, 36 feet long and 18 wide, with a mud cupola. The grave stone is of marble, covered with inscriptions and highly polished, the result of being handled by numerous visitors during several centuries. The interior is hung with large ostrich-eggs, peacock-feathers, and other trumpery. The apartment in which repose the relics of the "mighty victor" was, previously to the British invasion, closed by the gates which it is believed he triumphantly removed from the temple of Somnath in Guzerat. These gates are of sandal-wood, 18 feet high, each 5 feet broad and 3 inches thick, very beautifully carved in tasteful arabesques. As Mahmud is said to have removed these gates in 1024, they must, in this view, be nearly 900 years old, yet they are still in perfect preservation. In 1842, when the British, under General Nott, dismantled Gazni, they carried off these gates, with the view of restoring them to their original place in the temple in Guzerat. (It is now acknowledged that they are not the gates of Somnath. They may be seen in the Fort at Agra.) The mace asserted to be that of "the destroyer," the name under which Mahmud is familiarly designated in oriental history and tradition, has been usually exhibited by the priest who officiates at his tomb, and it is, as might be expected of one assigned to the use of so mighty a hero, too ponderous to be wielded by any of the present race of men.
Previous to the capture of the place by the British, it had been removed so that it might not fall into their hands. The building is environed with luxuriant gardens and orchards, watered by an aqueduct discharging an abundant supply of fine water; and this delightful suburb is hence denominated roza, or the garden. The houses of the village have an antique appearance.
The ruins of the old city consist of a vast extent of shapeless mounds. The only remains of its former splendour are two minarets, 400 yards apart, which are said to mark the limits of the bazar of the ancient city. They are of brick, above 100 feet high and 12 in diameter.
They are usually ascribed to Sultan Mahmud. They are, however, due to the period when Cufic characters were in use, for the bricks of which they are constructed are so disposed as to represent Cufic inscriptions and sentences. One of them has a winding staircase within, and inclines considerably over its base. That buildings so easily demolished should have been spared in the destruction of the

old city by the Prince of Ghor, may perhaps have resulted from some religious feeling with which they were associated. (Thornton.)

ROZABAD Or KALA-I-ARSALA KHAN روزآباد
34-24 70-16 G. A village 12 1/2 miles from Jalalabad, on the road to Gandamak. There was a British detachment of varying composition at this place in the campaign of 1879-80, and a commissariat depot in the fort and pleasure garden, 7/8 mile north of the high road. These latter were constructed by the Ghilzai Chief Arsala Khan out of the profits made by him from the contract for building the fort at Dakka. The fort was destroyed by the present Amir in 1885; His Highness objecting to leave standing a fort belonging to a person who was the object of his dislike. (I.B.C.)

ROZANAI روزنی
A ridge lying to the west of the Turkani Nawa plain in the Ghilzai country, dividing it from Sarmargha. It is about 1,000 feet above the plain, but not very steep and inhabited by Muhammadzai Tokhi Ghilzais. (Broadfoot.)

*RUDAKAI رودکی
31-44 68-47 m. A village located 2 miles northwest of Mariani in Ghazni province.

*RUDBAR رودبار
34-44 69-50 m. A village located on the Wuzbin Khwar, some 12 miles northeast of Sarobi in Kabul province.

RUD-I رود
Places and rivers the names of which begin with the word Rud followed by the Persian izafat, are described under the second word of their designations.

RUKA Or ROKHEH روکه (رخه)
35-16 69-28 A. A village in the Panjshir valley, about 2 miles below Bazarak. There is a force of 150 khasadars stationed here. Kafilas going from Kabul over the Khawak pass usually make this their 5th stage. (I.B.C.)

RUSTAM رستم
A section of the Dai Zangi Hazaras.

RUSTAM KHEL رستم خیل
34-27 68-46 G. A village 25 miles west of Kabul, on the Bamian road east of the Isphak pass. There is a small district attached to it on the Kabul river, the valley of which is here not more than 12 miles in width, but it is finely watered, and a considerably portion of its surface is under cultivation. A little rice is raised, but barley and wheat are the principal crops. No wood is found on the hills, but grass is plentiful. The produce amounts to 2,100 kharwars. The inhabitants are Sunni Afghans, but it is not clear to what clan they belong. (Wood.)

*RUSTAM KHEL رستم خیل
33-3 68-13 m. A village located near Putwal in the valley of the Sardeh Rud in Ghazni province.

*RUSTO رستو
35-21 70-14 m. A village located on the Nuristan (Pashal) river, about 2 miles northeast of Gadwal in Laghman province.

SAADATMAND سعادت مند
34- 70-. A village in the Kot division of the Jalalabad district, about 1 mile north of Kamal Khel. Inhabitants: Tirais. (Jenkyns.)

SABARI Or ZAMBARI صبری
33-34 69-52. Sabari is an alaqadari in Paktia province. The alaqadari comprises an area of 313 square kilometers and has a population that has been estimated at from 16,108 to 22,245. The alaqadari is bounded in the west by Musa Khel, in the south by Khost, in the east by Trayzai, and Bak, and in the north by Jani Khel. Sabari has some 60 villages, 12 of which have more than 500 inhabitants. The villages are listed in the PG as follows: Levaneyo Kalai (Lewan Khel), Zavar Kalai (Saidan Khel), Husain Kalai (Saydan Khel), Baryaqubi (Saryaqubi Kalai, Yaqubi Khord), Kuz Yaqubi Kalai (Yaqubi Khord), Orri Kalai, Khori Kalai, Guldak Kalai (Guldak Khel Mal), Sabza Kalai, Mad Khel (Mangat Khel Mal), Umumi Zambar (Umum Zambar), Rahim Kohol, Abo Khel, Okbi (Aqbi), Lakari (Lori Kalai), Pari Khel, Toda, Guldar Kalai, Sabari, Kalai Karez, Laghar Kota (Laghar Kot), Muchi (Mahi Kalai), Bad Khana, Lewan Khel (Lewal Khel), Sorwi Pan, Zambar (Nada Kalai), Zardar Kalai (Zar Darah), Nori Kalai, Nakam Kalai, Sahra Kalai, Khatkad, Wos Kai Khanda (Khoskai Danda), Gulam Kalai (Gulnam Kalai), Mirzadin Kalai (Nasapa Kalai), Tor Tangi, Musa Kot, Khal Busat, Sor Landi (Sorlandi Sayedan Khel), Gedel (Ledor Kale), Pesho Kalai (Pesho Kalai Meli), Toti Kalai, Karr Do (Kroro Gheljai, Shaykh Madi Baba, Dela Zara (Repal Razar Kala), Gorchak Kalai (Kochak), Pir Jan Kalai, Pira Gul Kota, Pirata Ghundai Mangal, China Kalai (China Kale Khalsat), Faqiran (Faqir Abad Khel), Qasem Qala (Kala-Sam), Sorobi Kalai (Sorobi Kalai Mirai), Tor Kadar (Doki Kadi), Kotkai, Sayyid Abbas Kalai (Haji Sayed Abbas), Faqir Jan Abad Kalai, Mulla Kota (Mullayan), Tsapari Sabri, Maskh Kota, Majlesa, Karezi-Bahram, Piri Kalai, Haji Nurullah Khan Kalai, Dokai, Ahmad Qol and Karolo (Karo). (LWA) In 1914, the village of Sabari was described as follows: a village in Khost 12 miles north of Matun. The neighbourhood is well watered, and the ground is cultivated close up to the village. (Kennedy.)

SABAR-I-BALA صبر بالا
34-13 70-18 m. A village in the Jalalabad district about 2 miles north of Agham, on the left bank of the Chapriar stream. Inhabitants: Khugianis and Tajiks. (Jenkyns.) Recent maps show the spelling Sabre. (LWA)

SABAR-I-PAIN صبر پائین
34- 70-. A village about 1 mile north of Sabar-i-Bala. Inhabitants: Khugianis and Tajiks.

*SABIKHEL سابی خیل
34-57 69-18 m. A village located in the Dasht-i-Bagram area, in Parwan province.

SABZ سبز
A low kotal crossed by the road leading east from the Shibar pass--see "Ghorband."

SABZ سبز
34-50 66-39 G. A narrow dara in the Yakh Walang district which descends northeast and joins the Sachak glen, the united streams forming a large watercourse which debouches into the Band-i-Amir valley through a gorge known as the Dahan-i-Guli. Here are a number

of hamlets collectively known as Kiligan, and containing about 30 families fo Kirigu Kham-i-Aba Hazaras. There is a small fort on the left bank of the Dahan-i-Guli watercourse, and a number of caves used for storing grass, corn, etc, and as cow houses.

The Sabz Dara is crossed by the Firozbahar-Mazar-i-Sharif road at 27 miles from the former place, and at about 3 miles above its junction with the Sachak, while the latter is crossed at a point some 4 miles further on. There is a fairly good track down each of these glens to their junction and thence through the Dahan-i-Guli to Kiligan in the main valley. Maitland, who ascended the Dahan-i-Gul from Kiligan, gives the following description of it and the Sabz and Sachak glens:

"Having turned to the right at 6 miles (from Chihilburj ravine), followed road through cornfields, for half a mile, to the entrance of the defile. It turns to the right. Width about 30 yards, with inaccessible walls of rock on either hand. A hardly distinguishable path up its stony bed. After a mile (7 miles) the gorge divides into narrow defiles, turning abruptly to right and left. Down these comes the drainage of Sachak, and Sabz Dara, respectively.

"We turned up the Sabz Dara defile, to see the Sang Nawishta or inscribed stone, which I had been told existed there. The gorge is only some 15 yards wide, enclosed by lofty perpendicular cliffs, much honeycombed and occasionally worn into strange shapes by the action of water. After a quarter of a mile the guide stopped and pointed to a place on the left hand side about 8 or 10 feet up the rock. By looking closely, we could discern characters which, with some little trouble we made out to be a short inscription. I could see no trace of the inscription having been any longer, nor could I myself see that there had been any letters in a gap in the middle of the writing but my dafadars were of opinion that such formerly existed. As it stands, the writing may mean Jung Ataluk, 'the Ataluk's fight,' but it is not sufficiently ancient to be of any importance. Altogether it was a disapointing inscription.

The road up the defile is pretty good, and less rough than below. It is evidently much used.

"Returned and proceeded up the Sachak gorge. Tolerable path. After about half a mile, the defile opens out into the lower end of the Sachak valley. Here the lesser hollow comes in from the left. There is a hamlet at the junction. After another half mile (2 miles from Kiligan), the valley is over 200 yards wide, and the breadth gradually increases. It is grassy here, and there is some low scrub.

"Continued up valley for a mile and half, passing several hamlets, to our camp on the stream where the main road crosses."

The villages in the Sabz glen are given under "Bamian (district)." (Maitland.)

SABZAB سبزاب
A pass leading over the Koh-i-Baba from Besud to Bamian—see "Jolah." There is a village with this name located at 34-42 67-59 G.

SABZAB سبزاب
34- 68-. A small village in the Bamian district, situated in the Kalu glen. Five houses of Hazaras. (Amir Khan.)

SABZABAD سبزآباد
34- 70-. A village in the Jalalabad district, situated on the right bank of the Kabul river, between Zulmabad and Nagharak. Inhabitants: Ghilzais. (Jenkyns.)

*SABZAK سبزك
    34-53 67-39 m. A village located in the Dara-i-Sabzak, some 12 miles northwest of Bamian in Bamian province.

SABZAL See TABARGHAN (KOL-I) سبزل

*SABZANG سبزسنگ
    33-6 67-31 m. A village located near the Chub-i-Busid and southeast of the Arghandab in Bamian province.

SABZ DEH سبزه
    34-38 69-19 m. A range separating the Kabul plain on the east from the rough uneven plateau through which the river runs down to Laghman. (Holdich.) Recent maps show the name Dehsabz Dagh. (LWA)

SABZ DEH سبزه
    34- 69-. A village 12 miles northeast of the city of Kabul, on a feeder of the Panjshir river. (Thorton.)

*SABZJOY سبزجوی
    34-10 66-55 m. A village located near Wakilan and south of Waras in Bamian province. Another village with this name is located north of the Koh-i-Baba and northwest of Sar-i-Qol in Bamian province, at 34-40 67-6 m.

SABZ KALA سبزقلعه
    A village on the eastern daman of the Paghman range, 42 miles north of Kabul. (Maitland.)

SABZ, KOL-I قول سبز
    A village of 120 houses of Andari Ghilzais in the Kharwar district. (Griesbach.)

SACHAN See SABZ سچان

*SADA سده
    34-15 71-1 m. A village located on the Kabul river, about three miles west of Lalpura in Nangarhar province.

*SADAK سدك
    34-46 69-26 m. A village located north of the Koh-i-Safi, about one mile east of Shami in Kapisa province.

SADBAR صدبار
    34- 68-. A glen which falls into the Kalu glen 11 1/2 miles above Zohak. (Amir Khan.)

*SADBARG صدبرگ
    35-11 69-46 m. A village located west of the Koh-i-Ferengal and on a tributary of the Panjshir in Kapisa province.

SADDA-I-GHULAM JAN سده غلام جان
    34- 70-. A village in the Kama division of the Jalalabad district situated between Gaj and Nawaji. Inhabitants: Sayyids of he Kunar Padshah's family. (Jenkyns.)

SADMARDA صدمردا
    35-40 67-14 A. A section of Shaikh Ali Hazaras living in the Dara Jalmish. They are Sunnis. (Peacocke.) There are two villages with this name, one at 35-40 67-14 A., the other at 34-20 68-41 G.

SAD MASTI صدمستی
   34-49 67-53 G.   Two fort-villages in the Bamian valley.   60 families of Tajiks. (A.B.C.)

SADOZAI سدوزی
   See Volume 5.

SADU سدو
   A tribe inhabiting the base of the Paghman hills. They are not Afghans, but are probably originally of Hindu extraction, now converted to Muhammadanism. They very much resemble gipsies in their habits and modes of life, and are well known as fortunate tellers and thieves. (Bellew.)

SADULLA سعدالله
   35-4 69-14 A. A village near Tutamdara. 50 Tajik houses. (Shahzada Taimus.)

*SADWAR سدوار
   34-59 68-53 m. A village located on the Ghorband river, about two miles east of Siagird in Parwan province.

SAF صاف
   A valley in the Hazarjat.

SAFARAK KALA سفرك كلا
   34-30 66-33 G. Elevation 9,650 feet. The 16th stage on the Kabul-Daulat Yar road, 44 miles east of the later. There is now a fort with this name.

SAFARAK TAGAO See SURKH سفرك تگاو

SAFDAR ALI KHAN صفدرعلی خان
   34- 69-. One of the forts in the Rishkhor township, Kabul district, 15 houses of Gadi Hazaras. The place was confiscated from the original owner (Safdar Ali Khan, Governor of Kandahar, for Amir Sher Ali) by Amir Abdur Rahman Khan. (I.B.C.)

*SAFEDAK سفیدك
   34-21 66-44 m. A village north of Surkhqoli and southeast of Asgharat in Bamian province. Another village with this name is near Damurda, on a tributary of the Helmand in Bamian province, at 34-9 67-22 m.

SAFED BINI سفید بینی
   34- 70-. A village in the Jalalabad district, situated on the left bank of the Kabul river, about 1 mile above Girdao. Inhabitants: Mohmands. (Jenkyns.)

*SAFED DIVAR سفید دیوار
   34-8 68-14 m. A village near the Qol-i-Zangi, southwest of Miran in Maidan province.

SAFED JIR سفید جیر
   35- 69-. A village in the upper Panjshir valley, 8 miles above Marz. It contains 150 families of Tajiks. Kafilas going from Kabul over the Khawak pass are said to halt here in preference to Dasht-i-Rewat, 3 miles further on. From Safed Jir a track is said to lead up the Zuria dara, over the Zuria kotal, to Kala Ahingaran in the Andarab valley. It is impracticable for camels. (I.B.C.)

SAFED KALA سفيد قلعه
34- 69-. A small village in the Shakar Dara valley, Koh Daman of Kabul. (Masson.)

SAFED KALA سفيد قلعه
34-26 68-28. A fortified village 5 miles east of the Unai pass on the main Kabul-Herat road. It contains (in 1904) some 30 families of Timuris possessing about 50 head of cattle and 80 sheep and goats. The annual production of wheat and barley averages about 370 Indian maunds. The Unai, or Sar-i-Chashma, as the upper Kabul river is here called, is crossed at Safed Kala by a kacha stone bridge, of 10 feet span and 10 feet roadway, the actual stream, being (in July) 6 feet broad and 6 inches deep. (Wanliss.)

*SAFEDKECH سفيد كيچ
34-11 67-17 m. A village near Khushqol on the Helmand in Bamian provinc.e

SAFED KHAK سفيد خاك
34-27 68-51 G. Elevation 8,330 feet. A pass over a spur of the Paghman mountains, between the village of Maidan. It is crossed by the main Kabul-Herat road at about 20 miles from Kabul. The ascent from the west is somewhat steep up a rather stony path; the descent is similar. The pass is passable for artillery, but with difficulty. Safed Khak was continually occupied by disaffected Afghans, who also held the Kotal-i-Takht in 1880, thereby stopping supplies from coming into Sherpur or the city of Kabul from the west and south-west. (I.B.C.)

SAFED KOH Or SPIN GHAR سفيد كوه
33-58 70-25 A. A lofty range of hills, forming part of the Sulaiman mountain system and separating the basin of the Kabul river from that of the Kurram.
The highest point of the main range is at its western extremity and is known as the Sikaram peak. This peak lies about 5 miles north of the Paiwar Kotal and reached a height of 15,620 feet. From this point the main range runs nearly due east for a distance of some 60 miles to the head of the Bazar valley in Tirah; here it splits into two branches, one, under the name of the Surghar range, running southeast between the Bazar and Bara valleys of Tirah, and the other running northeast down to the valley of the Kabul river which it reaches in the neighbourhood of the Khaibar Pass.
The main range throws off many spurs both southwards into the Kurram valley and northwards into Ningrahar; its most important offshoot, however, is that which runs down from the Sikaram peak, in a south-westerly direction, to the Shutur Gardan pass where it connects with the Machalgu hills, which are in turn a continuation of the Sanglakh range and, thus, of the Hindu Kush. This is of the utmost importance from a geographical point of view as forming the last connecting link in the great watershed formed by the Hindu Kush, the Sanglakh and western Sulaiman ranges, which divides the Iranian plateau from the river system of India.
The only other offshoots of the Safed Koh which require notice here are those which, projecting northwards towards the Kabul river, separate the Surkhab, Jagdalak, Tezin and Logar valleys. These spurs (which may be spoken of collectively as the Siah Koh and the Karkacha hills) running as they do at right angles to the main Peshawar-Kabul road form sucessive positions for opposing an advance in either direction.

The passes over the main Safed Koh range are all high and difficult, the only one of any military importance being the Agam pass. This is the lowest point in the main range but even it reaches a height of 11,766 feet and is closed for several months in the year.
The lower spurs of the Safed Koh are bare and rocky in the extreme but the higher spurs and the main range itself up to a height of about 12,000 feet, are thickly wooded with pines, deodars and other timber trees, while the valleys lying between the various spurs are, as a rule, very fertile and full of orchards, etc. (I.B.C.)

SAFED POSH   See KAFIRISTAN   سفید پوش

SAFED SANG   سفید سنگ
Elevation 4,500 feet. A place in the Khugiani country, on the right bank of the Marki Khel stream and about 2 1/2 miles east of Gandamak. There was a British fortified post and encampment here in the second Afghan war. The old post is now unoccupied and in ruins, but the remains of the walls would still (1904) form a fairly good defence for an entrenched camp. The Marki Khel stream is here spanned by an old bridge, built in the time of Dost Muhammad. There is unlimited space for camping ground with ample good water from the stream and also from a spring near the old post, above the stream. Supplies are only at times availabe. The climate is cool in summer and very cold in winter. The position commands the country on all sides except towards Fatehabad (N.E.).
At Safed Sang a road and tracks from the Paiwar and Lakarai kotals, join the main road from Jalalabad. (Maleson, Wanliss, I.B.C.)

SAFED SANG   سفید سنگ
34- 69-. A village in the Logar valley on the left bank of the river and north of the Tangi Waghjan. The inhabitants are Tajiks, and in 1880 numbered 100 families. Safed Sang is 19 miles south of the city of Kabul, and 2 miles north of Zahidabad. (Clifford, Euan Smith.)

SAFED SANG See ISFI SANG   سفید سنگ

SAFI   صافی
A race of people inhabiting the hills to the north of the Mohmands. They occupy the valleys of Barkot and Daminj, adjoining the Dara-i-Nur, and also all the valleys opening into the Kunar valley on the right bank of the river up to Chigha Sarai. Some are found on the Fajaur side of the Kunar river. They also have villages in Laghman, both in the Alishang and Alingar valleys, and large numbers dwell in Tagao and the other valleys running down to the left bank of the Kabul river.
Masson describes them as a straightforward, manly race, with florid complexions, light eyes and hair. They have many peculiar customs, and retain many vestiges of ancient arts; for instance they have bee-hives, unknown to the inhabitants of the plains. Their valley is most celebrated amongst their neighbours as being the native soil of the narcissus. The hills of the inhabitants yielding grapes, quantities of wine and vinegar are made by them.
The Safis adjoining Jalalabad, although they understand the Pushtu language, speak among themselves a peculiar language which may be called the Kohistani dialect. It is a language of Sanskrit origin, resembling the language of the Siahposh Kafirs. There can be little doubt that the Safis were originally Kafirs, and have been converted

to Muhammadanism during the last four centuries. The name Safi has been plausibly supposed to imtimate that fact, being derived from saf, meaning pure. This tribe is according to Jenkyns, divided into two sections, viz:

       1. Gurbuz   2. Wader

The Gurbus are subdivided into
(a) Badinzai (b) Gagizai (c) Khadikhel (d) Sulaimanzai
The Wader are subdivided into
(a) Kandahari (Including Amroi) (b) Musawad (c) Barizai
(d) Sinzai

Merk gives the following information regarding the Safis:
1. The Kandaharis are subdivided into Sipah, Kamal Khel, Mirza Khel, and Amroi.
Their villages are: Waidansha, Karel, Chingai, Kundo Kuhai, Amroi Chinarai. These are known collectively as Sarkamar.
2. The Gurbuz live in Taraki Tangi, Lakarai, Kamar Kala, Katasar (not the Gandao Katasar). Their subdivisions are: Badinzai, Sulaimanzai, Shahzada Kor, Katasar.
3. The Musawad consist of Shamsho Kor, Aba Khel, Madur Kor, and Ghilzai Kor. They occupy Chinarai, Ziarat, Khazina, Kokpan.
4. The Wader section lives on the northern slopes of the range south of the Kunar river beyond Mitai.
The Kandahari Safis joined in Mulla Khalil's attack on our communications near Dakka in January 1880. Merk says they number 1,500 fighting men, and that the whole clan musters under 3,000 men. (Jenkyns, Merk, Masson.)

SAFRA Or JAFRA   سفره
35-15 69-12 G. A village of 40 houses in the Salang Dara, about 13 1/3 miles above Parwan. (I.B.C.0

SAGDAO   سگداو
34- 67-. A village in the Sar-i-Kol subdivision of Yakh Walang. 15 houses of Yanghur Hazaras. (I.B.C.)

*SAGHANA   سغنه
33-44 68-6 m. A village near Miana, on a tributary of Dara-i-Yusuf in Ghazni province.

SAGPAH   سگ پاه
A tribe of Hazaras.

SAGPAR   سگپر
34- 68-. A large valley which joins that of Ghorband 9 1/2 miles above Bin-i-Sehwak. It is inhabited by about 60 families of the Dai Malan taifa of Shaikh Ali Hazaras. A road leads from it and over the kotal of the same name on the main Koh-i-Baba range to Gulak (in the Dara Turkoman?). At Gulak there are 50 resident families of Turkomans. The road is difficult, but camels use it going to Kabul. The Sagpar Kotal can also be reached by the Dark (Dara) Kojak, a glen joining the Ghorband valley 2 miles below that of Sagpar. This road is said to be much used by local camel kafilas as the ordinary communication with Kabul. (Peacocke.)

SAHAK See SOHAK   سهاك
33-32 69-3 A.

*SAHIB   صاحب
34-47 70-3 m. A village located on a tributary of the Alishang, west of Alishang in Laghman province.

SAHIBZADA-I-ARABAN صاحب زاده عربان
A village in the Surkhab division of the Jalalabad district. Inhabitants: Tajiks. (Jenkyns.)

SAHIBZADA UZBIN صاحب زاده اوزبین
A tribe who inhabit the Usbin valley, between Laghman and Tagao. (Masson.)

SAHLAO ساهلاو
34-46 70-4 G. A village in Laghman, inhabited by Dehgans and containing the following forts and hamlets:
1. Kala-i-Alaram
2. Kala-i-Shah Nur
3. Kala-i-Halim
4. Banda-i-Muhammad Azim, Akhunzada
5. Tangi
6. Kotki
7. Dakian
8. Dhundi-i-Barakzai
9. Sharbat Khel

In the Sketch-map of Jalalabad, Laghman, and Kunar, compiled in 1810, the course of a tributary of the Alishang river is indicated by dots as running from the northwest under the name of Salao dara and falling into the Alishang at Deh-i-Ghazi, about 8 miles northwest of the village of Alishang.
Warburton does not define the position of his Dara-i-Sahlab, which, instead of being a village, as he says, is more likely to be the valley of this northwestern stream. The map, however, shows none of the hamlets and forts stated by Warburton to be contained in the place. (Warburton.)

SAI سای
A dara debouching from the south into the Ghorband valley, 13 miles above Chahardeh. A road leads up it by the Sai Kotal to Loling and the Turkoman Dara. It is said to be easy. (Peacocke.)

SAIANDA ساینده
A strong walled village in Logar, about 55 miles from Ghazni and 63 miles from Kabul on the banks of the Logar. (Lusden.)
This is not to be identified with any village in Logar noted in the occupation of 1880. (I.B.C.)

*SAID BABA سید بابا
35-11 67-35 m. A village located in the Saighan Dara, about four miles west of Saighan in Bamian province.

*SAIDIKHEL صیدی خیل
34-15 69-56 m. A village located southeast of Ashpan in Nangarhar province.

*SAIDKHEL سیدخیل
34-24 69-13 m. A village located on the Logar river, southwest of Bagrami in Kabul province.

SAIFALI سیف علی
One of the three main sections of the Kabul Khels, Maimai and Paipal being the other two. They inhabit Birmal and other localities on the Indo-Afghan frontier - see "N.W.F. Gazetteer."

SAIGAN Or SHAIGO سیگان
A place in the Jaghuri country.

683

*SAIGHAN سيغان

Saighan is the name of an alaqadari in Bamian province, The alaqadari comprises an area of 1,652 square kilometers and has an agricultural population which has been variously estimated at from 4,821 to 5,142. The alaqadari is bounded in the west by Yakowlang, in the north and east by Kahmard, and in the south by Shibar and Bamian. Saighan has about 21 villages of which 3 have more than 500 inhabitants: The villages are listed in the PG as follows: Eshan (Khwaja-ha), Bayani, Chiraghdan, Ghorab Shah-i-Muhammad Beg, Ghorab-i-Kogada, Khargin-Baigal, Ab Dara-i-Baigal, Goshak-i-Abdara, Khudadad Khel, Khwaja Ganj, Deh Iman, Deh Nola, Sokhta Chenar, Sayidabad, Ghorab, Ghor Wachi, Qurghan, Quruna, Qara Khawal, and Koh Gadai.

SAIJADAN سيجدان

A village of 500 Tajik houses, east of Charikar. (Shahzada Taimus, from native information.)

SAI KAZI See ZAK ساى قاضى

*SAIYID Properly SAYYID سيد

SAIYID سيد

There are several Saiyid tribes in Afghanistan, the principal being the Wardak. The designation "Sayid" means a descendant of the Khalifa Ali, son-i-law of Muhammad.

SAIYID سيد

A subdistrict of Yak Walang--See "Bamian (district)."
This name is applied to the Band-i-Amir valley for some distance below Firozbahar. (A.B.C.)

SAIYIDABAD سيدآباد

34- 67-. A long glen descending north from the Koh-i-Baba and debouching into the Bamian valley 2 miles below Kala Sarkari--see "Bamian (district)." There is a pass at the head of the glen, called the Dokan, which leads over the main range. (Maitland.)

SAIYIDABAD سيدآباد

33-59 68-43. Sayyidabad is the name of a woleswali in Wardak province. The woleswali comprises an area of 1,033 square kilometers and has an agricultural population which has been veriously estimated at from 20,352 to 25,353. The woleswali is bounded in the west by Jaghatu and Chak-i-Wardak, in the north by Nerkh, in the east by Pul-i-Alam, Baraki, Charkh, and in the south by Zina Khan and Khwaja Omri. Sayyidabad woleswali includes about 147 villages, of which about sixteen have more than 500 inhabitants. The villages are listed in the PG as follows: Hakim Khel-i-Onkhi, Fazel Khel, Hasan Beg, Musa Khel, Yami Khel, Badam Khel, Chenar, Ferang, Hashim Khel, Dag Baghri, Duab Tangi, Hasan Khel, Bini Safed, Qala-i-Amir, Haider Khel, Taj Begi, Kaj Qala, Aman Khel-i-Takyah, Shadi Khel, Todah China, Salar, Salar Takyah, Salar-i-Siyah, Patan, Sarwar Khel, Sultan Khel, Chardehi, Dandoki, Haft Asyab, Awez, Kodi Hasan Beg, Jang Jai, Lowara, Baber Khel, Mehro, Sandawar, Shaikhi, Gogar, Shash Qala, Yusuf Khel, Mashin Qala, Khwajatup, Khalyan, Zankhan, Abdul Muhyuddin, Guli Khel-i-Tangi, Mamal-i-Ulya, Mamal-i-Sufla, Barat Khel, Sar-i-Qol, Baghak, Muli Khel, Badur Khel, Changi-i-Baghak, Badogak, Mangali,Karez,Busak, Hasan Khel-i-Shaniz, Baker Khel, Khar Lowarah, Lala Gul Khel, Aka Khel-i-Takya, Mir Khan Khel, Zarak Khel, Zarak Khel-i-Haft Asyab, Alam Khel, Mulla Khel, Gulab Khel, Qala-i-Mulla Shah Mohd, Ramzi Khel, Babu Khel, Lachi Khel, Shahgul, Mushak

Khel, Qabchi Khel, Kamran Khel, Qala-i-Allah Dad, Jan Mohd Khel, Zamuch, Burhani Khel, Timur Khel, Kot, Sisi, Kodlak, Seyah Chub, Qala-i-Surkh, Qala-i-Sadudin, Shater, Allah Yar Khel, Arab Khel, Bulandi, Hamza Khel, Payenda Khel, Larum, Sadullah Khel, Shir Khel, Ishaq Khel, Badak Khel, Khwaja Gharamban, Larum-i-Sufla, Tarah Khel, Mado Khel, Karo Khel, Utri Takya, Qala-i-Nau-i-Haft Asyab, Ghazi Khel, Hakim Khel, Zangor, Nasir Khel, Mohd Azim Khel, Musa Khel, Allah Yar Khel, Jarchiyan, Mohabat Khel, Barak Khel, Chori Khel, Alam Khel, Rahim Khel, Ghaibak Khel, Latu Khel, Bandah Khel, Gadaye Khel, Barikak Khel, Chawni, Saikh Azam Baba, Nasrat Khel, Mir Yahya Khel, Shirak, Abdarah, Landah Khel, Jan Mohd Khel, Gadaye Khel, Cheshma-i-Kaka, Shamshi, Qutub Khel, Azad Khel, Patak Khel, Buland Qash, Kharyan, Pirak Khel, Abdara-i-Khurd, Abdara-i-Kalan, Patak Khel-i-Chardehi, Dasht-i-Tup-i-Shekh Abad, Shadi Puch, Qala-i-Guldin, Baraki Hasan Beg, Hasan Beg, Dawlat Khel, Hurjan, Takya, Qarya-i-Sayed, Shaikhabad, Dasht-i-Am, and Tarwati Khel.

SAIYIDABAD سیدآباد
33-59 68-43 m. Elevation 6,950 feet. A village in the Shiniz valley, about 38 miles north of Ghazni. It is a cluster of hamlets belonging to the Khawaja Rasul Saiyids. Signalling communication with the Sher Dahan Kotal can be maintained from a hill just west of this village. At Saiyidabad the Maidan and Logar valley roads from Kabul to Ghazni join.
The best camping ground is on the left bank of the Shiniz river. Supplies must be collected from the various villages in the Shiniz and Unkai valleys, both of which are well cultivated and fertile.
Near this village, in November 1841, Captain Woodburn, proceeding to Kabul with 108 invalids, was attacks by an overwhelming force of Ghilzais and he and his whole party were killed.
During the year 1880, Saiyidabad was used as a halting place by Sir Donald Stewart on his march from Kandahar to Kabul, and by Sir Frederick Roberts on his march from Kabul to Kandahar. Saiyidabad was in that year a collection of scattered buildings of no importance. The best place for an encampment was then found to be on the opposite, or right bank, of the Shiniz river. Due east of the village a path leads by a gradual ascent to a pass 3 miles distant, from which the Logar valley is visible, and by which it can be reached. This route, however, is difficult. There are two alternative good routes from here to Kabul, one by Maidan and Arghandi, the other by the Tangi Wardak and Logar valley. (Campbell, Lumsden, I.B.C.)

SAIYIDABAD Or ZAHIDABAD سیدآباد
34- 69-. A large village, surrounded by cultivation, on the left bank of the Logar river, about 2 miles south of Safed Sang. The inhabitants are Tajiks and Adramzai Ghilzais. There is a small square fort here, built about 1875, by a Wardak chief named Baz-ud-Din, and there is a bridge here over the Logar river, practicable for laden animals. Fodder for 4,000 animals and about 300 maunds of unground grain is obtainable from Saiyidabad and its neighbourhood. (I.B.C., Johnston.)

SAIYIDABAD سیدآباد
34-47 69-6 G. A village in the Koh Daman of Kabul, between Istalif and Baba Kushkar. Water from a karez. There are said to be only 16 houses (Tajiks) in the village itself, and about the same number among the three forts outside the place, and belonging to it. (I.B.C.)

SAIYID AHMAD سیداحمد
34- 70-. A village in the Besud division of the Jalalabad district, situated on the left bank of the Kabul river, about 3 miles down from Jalalabad. Inhabitants: Arabs. (Jenkyns.)

SAIYIDAN سیدان
34- 68-. A dara descending north from the Paghman range to the Ghorband valley. It is traversed by the road leading over the Kachan Kotal.
Peacocke, who calles this the Dara Koishki, says:
"In the Dara Koishki live 3,000 families of Koishki Afghans, owning 50 flocks, 5,000 cattle, 30 watermills, and 2,100 gardens. They also own a number of asses, and act as carriers. The surface of the Koishki valley is broken into irregular terraces on each side of the sunken trough of its stream. The trough of the stream is about 200 yards wide, and both it and the terraces are covered with villages, gardens, and orchards, and the branch valley which runs up to Parsa is of similar description." (Peacocke.)
A well with this name is located at 35-5 67-51 G., and a village at 33-35 69-6 G. (LWA)

SAIYIDAN-I-ARABI سیدان عربی
34- 70-. A village in the Jalalabad district, situated on the right bank of the Surkhab river, about a mile southwest of Saiyidan-i-Fauladi. In this place are included Kala-i-Arsala Khan and Bazid Khel. Inhabitants: Tajiks and Ghilzais. (Jenkyns.)

SAIYIDAN-I-FAULADI سیدان فولادی
34- 70-. A village in the Jalalabad district, situated on the right bank of the Surkhab river, about two miles above Wattapur. Inhabitants: Tajiks and Ghilzais. (Jenkyns.)

SAIYID GHARIB سیدغریب
34- 70-. A village 23 miles from Jalalabad, on the Kunar river, consisting of 60 houses of Tajiks. (Leech.)

SAIYID GHULAM سیدغلام
33-45 68-21 G. Elevation 8,140 feet. A fortified village on the left bank of the Barikao, and just to the right of the Ghazni-Besud road. The inhabitants are Sayyids of whom there are some 20 houses. There is a bridge over the Barikao stream about 1/2 mile above the village.
There is ample room for camping ground on the left bank of the stream, and supplies for a mixed brigade for 2 or 3 days are said to be easily obtainable. (I.B.C.)

SAIYID GUL KUSHTA See SAR-I-BULAK سیدگل کشته
A village with this name is located at 34-33 67-26 G.

*SAIYID-HA-I-ACHOKHAN سیدهای اچوخان
33-36 68-3 m. A village located on the Dara-i-Yusuf, about 2 miles north of Babur and some 20 miles west of Ghazni in Ghazni province.

SAIYID HUSAIN سیدحسین
34- 69-. A village in the Koh Daman, 2 miles south of the Rah-i-Gosfand pass. (Kinloch.)

SAIYIDI سیدی
A village apparently in the Jaji country, containing 80 houses, and able to turn out 300 fighting men. (Agha Abbas.)

SAIYID KALA سید قلعه
34- 68-. A small village on the left bank of the Helmand, about three miles northeast Jaokul. It contains about 10 families of Saiyids and is surrounded by a considerable amount of cultivation. (Wanliss.)

SAIYID KANDA سید کنده
34- 70-. A village in Lagman, probably in the neighbourhood of Kanda. Inhabitants: Ghilzais (Warburton.)

SAIYID KARAM سید کرم
33-41 69-21. Saiyid Karam is a woleswali in Paktia province. The woleswali comprises an area of 938 square kilometers and has an agricultural population that has been estimated at form 16,454 to 20,709. The woleswali is bounded in the southwest by Gardez, in the south by Shawak, in the south east by Musa Khel, in the east by Lajmangal and Hasan Khel, and in the north by Jaji. Saiyid Karam has some 115 villages, 55 of which have more than 500 inhabitants. The villages are listed in the Pg as follows: Mirzaka, Andwam, Khalilan-i-Mirzaka, Jandel Kala, Azad Khol, Haji Hamid Kalai, Rud Ahmadzai, Srah Kala, Salam Khel, Dawlat Khel, Azak Khel, Sahbaz Khel, Pahlawan Khel, Sayed Khel, Sham Shir Abad, Shah Alam Khel, Qader Khel, Moh'd. Ali Khel, Padshah, Torah Khel, Khwaja Khel, Mali Khel, Gandawi, Shato Kalai (Sato Khel Kale), Rahmanulla Kalai, Ashraf Khel, Patiyan, Jangi Khel, Miya Khel, Qala-i-Khandan (Tandan Qala), Husain Khel, Khanak Kala (Nanak Qala), Kamal Khel (Esa Khel), Najaran, Afzal Khel, Gamrani Khel, Feroz Khel, Qala-i-Mahmud, Hemat Khel, Marbutat-i-Tuti Khel, Khawresh, Shah Nur-Khel, Khawr Kayan, Kod Mangal, Kundar Khel, Kotaki, Spina Husain Khel, Najo Kala, Nano Kala, Wazir Khel (Wali Khel), Jar Nel-Kala, Bazid-i-Karez, Masak Karez, Dado Kala, Niyazo Haji, Galak Khel, Ali Khel, Ghani Khel, Salah Khel, Koz-Wazir Khel, Sultan Khel, Wazir Khel-i-Bala, Baraki Machalghu, Hasan Kala, Mamand, Mulla Khel, Taru Khel, Shato Khel, Bazo Khel, Godiyan, Akhund Khel, Salam Khel, Dezendah Khel (Spina Kala), Kuz Nura-Khel, Nurak Khel, Lewal-i-Akhund-Khel, Khwaja Dad Khel, Ghalak, Ghalak-i-Khusk, Gurgi Khel, Ramak KHel, Zendi Khel, Tsaplai, Alef Khel, Kossin, Kalgar Kossin, Khan Jan-Khel, Kossin-i-Sufla, Miya Gul Kala, Shakar Khel, Khedri Kala, Akbar Khel, Dam, Khajori-Kalai, Kelkin Khola, Garandai-Khula, Nasti Kot, Mohamadzai (Momozai), Feroz Khel, Zargul Kalai (Zol Kalai), Ghundai Kalai, Khano Khel, Kuz Senjak, Osman Khel, Ghoreza, Much (Mush), Koshhal-Khel-i-Chini (Chino), Chorlagai, Ghunzai, Karezgai, Ashpan, Nura China, Tarai (Taraijangai), Mansur Khel, Gul Khel, Sadat Khel, Tandan, Mazarzai, Rafiqan, Srah Khel-Khula, Bandah Bin-Khel, Qala-i-Pirak, Guldin Kalai, and Muntazer Khel.

SAIYID KHEL سید خیل
35- 69-. A township of about 300 Tajik houses, on the Kabul-Khawak pass road, northeast of Charikar. It includes the villages of Kamangar, Chora, Haziram, Chukur Khel, Aziz Khel, Abdu Khel, Chinaki Pain, Shinwari, Musha Khel, Harif Khel, Ushturhar, Rasuldad Khel, Khwajagi, and Ibrahim Khan. (Shahzada Taimus.)

SAJAWAN سجاون
33-54 68-45 G. A pass over the spur from the Safed Koh which separates the Logar valley from Zurmat. The road is fit for footmen and mules, and the pass turns that of the Sher Dahan. (I.B.C.)

SAKA KALA ساکی قلعه
34- 69-. A large village in the Kabul district, on the right

bank of the Logar river, and close to the northern entrance of the Sang-i-Nawishta defile. Inhabitants: Afghans of the "Saka" tribe. (I.B.C.) A village with this name is located at 34-33 68-58 G.

SAKAWA سقاوه
34-29 66-17 m. Elevation 9,200 feet. A village on the right bank of the Lal stream. A fort with this name is located at 34-30 66-15 G.

SAKHA See CHAHAR DEH (1) ساخه

SAKH KHAN ساخ خان
A village in Laghman, on the right bank of the Kabul river, 10 miles west of Ismatullah Khan's fort. It is a small, unimportant place built at the end of a sandstone spur which extends from the Siah Koh down to the river. (Holdich.)

*SAKINI سکنی
33-38 68-11 m. A village located a few miles south of Dara-i-Yusuf, and about 14 miles west-northwest of Ghazni in Ghazni province.

SALAB سلاب
A village in Laghman. Inhabitants: Kohistanis. (Jenkyns.)
N.B.-- This is probably the same as Sahlao.

*SALAKHEHL صلاح خیل
34-48 69-2 m. A village located some 3 miles south of Istalif and west of Kalakan in Kabul province.

*SALAMI سلامی
34-53 71-1 m. A village located near Aybat and west of Asadabad (Chaghasarai) in southern Kunar province.

*SALAMKHEL سلام خیل
34-26 69-40 m. A village located northwest of Jagdalak and north of the Surtai Ghar in Kabul province.

SALANG سالنگ
35-12 69-13. Salang is a village and an alaqadari in Parwan province. The alaqadari comprises an area of 688 square kilometers and has an agricultural population that has been estimated at from 8,450 to 13,242. The alaqadari is bounded in the west by Shinwar, in the north by Khenjan and Andarab, in the east by Panjshir, in the south by Jabul Saraj. Salang includes 40 villages, of which 13 have more than 500 inhabitants. The villages are listd in the PG as follows: Aghel Khel-i-Agh Ali Khan, Ahangaran, Anamak, Awrati, Ahangarha-i-Awrati, Seyahchub Sar-i-Awrati, Takht-i-Awrati, Nau Bahra-i-Awrati, Sambolak Awrati, Tutumzar Awrati, Anarzar Awrati, Deh Awrati, Segha-i-Awrati, Audak Awrati, Shaghal Kunda-i-Awrati, Tanha Khak-i-Awrati, Lalma Sabzak, Tughak, Aulang, Ijan, Baba Shungul, Bagh-i-Lala, Bini Nawach, Paja, Gumzen wa Peshi-Raj, Jafarak, Charikarak (Charikarak Duab), Deh Yek, Kotah, Wawa, Surnai Kacha, Taghma, Salah Khan, Qala-i-Tak, Lewan, Nawuch-i-Ulya wa Sufla, Hunarwa-i-Bala wa Pain (Handuwa), Nau Tut Waltarzum, Kohna Deh, Qala-i-Baqi, Chilakta, and Salang. (LWA) In 1912 the area was described as follows:
A valley running southwards from near the Bajgah pass in the Hindu Kush past the village of Parwan, and joining the Ghorband valley about 4 miles below Tutamdara. A road leads up the Salang Dara, over the Bajgah pass, into the Andarab valley. (I.B.C.)

Regarding the Salang Dara and its inhabitants, Maitland says, "The Salangis are a numerous race, accounted Tajiks. They speak Persian. The glen is narrow, but wherever a field can be placed there is cultivation. There are many orchards in this glen, the trees being mostly mulberries.
The Salangis are carriers. They buy salt, oil of til (sesamum?), rice and wheat in the Andarab and Khinjan districts, and carry them to Kabul. The salt is from Chal but the Salangis do not go for it. They buy it from the Andarab people. There is also a stream with this name at 35-4   69-14 A., and the famous Salang Tunnel, located at 35-19   69-2 m.   (LWA)

SALANGAI Or WALANGAI   سالنگی
35-22   69-4 A. A pass over the Hindu Kush. It lies at the head of the Ejan Dara on a direct road from the Panjshir to the Khinjan valley. It is open longer than either the Kaoshan, or the Walian kotals. The road over the actual pass is fully practicable for camels. (I.B.C.)

*SALAR   سالار
33-54   68-40 m. A village located near Malikhel on the Ghazni-Kabul road in Maidan province.

*SALAW   سالاو
34-51   70-16 m. A village located some 6 miles west of Alingar in southern Laghman province. Another place with this name is a few miles southwest of Alishang and southeast of Feradoli in Laghman province.

SALEH KEH   صالح که
A village 10 miles northwest of the Abi-i-Istada, on the direct route from Ghazni-Quetta. (Thornton.)

SALEH KHAN   صالح خان
33-   69-. One of the two mud forts (Shalim being the other) which dominate the mouth of the Chakmani valley at a distance of about 1/2 mile from the junction of the Gobarak stream with the Kurram river. In June 1879 this fort was found to be in good order, of rectangular shape and with flanking defence provided by two towers 35 feet high, and a third of smaller dimensions, each placed at an angle of the walls, about 20 feet high, the whole loop-holed for musketry fire. Attached to the west face was an orchard, encircled by a mud wall, 7 feet high. The valley here is about 700 yards wide. (Kane.)

SALIM   سليم
32-12   66-28 A. A village in the Khugiani country, 2 miles south of Fatehabad, and the same distance from Fort Battye. It is a small walled place. (I.B.C.)

SALOH   سلوه
One of the tribes of Kafiristan. In former times it held the valley of Ranakot or Salao, but for very many years past it has been dwelling in that part of the centre of Kafiristan watered by the Shunah river, towards the highest ranges of Hindu Kush, and called the Shunah valley. It lies to the west of the "Katihi" country, north of Laghman and east of the valley of Kanda-i-Nil. Robertson makes no mention of such a tribe. Masson mentions a place, called Saloh Ranakat, about 8 miles southwest of Alishang, where there are two or three modern forts and, it is said, some ancient vestiges. From a spring here it is also asserted that fragments of rubies are

ejected, and that parcels of them are collected and sold to the Kabul druggists as medicaments. (Raverty, Masson.)

*SAMADI صمدی
34-45   67-4 m.   A village located some 8 miles northeast of Yakawlang and north of the Koh-i-Shorakarak in Bamian province.

SAMAJIL سمجیل
A tribe of Kafiristan, who, in ancient times, dwelt in the Shamakot and its contiguous valley along with the Manduls, and at the present day occupy a portion of the valley of Kand-i-Nil, with the Manduls, and 'Katihis.' (Raverty.)

*SAMANDAR سمندر
34-22   68-35 m.   A village located on a stream some 12 miles west of Nerkh alaqadari seat in Maidan province.

*SAMANDUR سمندر
35-1   70-19 m.   A village located some miles west of the confluence of the Pshal and Kolatan streams in Laghman province.

SAMAR KHEL   See ALI BOGHAN سمرخیل

SAMAR KHEL سمرخیل
34-   70-.   A village containing about 100 houses in the Jalalabad district, lying about 1 miles to the north of Ali Boghan and included in the latter. Fair camping ground. Inhabitants: Duranis. (Jenkyns, Johnston.)

SAMBALA سنبله
A village situated on a cross road between the valleys of Ghorband and Parwan Dara. It is scattered along the bottom of a deep dale. (Wood.)

SAM GOKH سم کوخ
A valley passed on the road from Matun, in Khost, to Hazara Pir, about 8 miles from Zer Kamar. (I.B.C.)

SAMUCH MULLA UMAR سموچ ملاعمر
34-   69-.   Elevation 5,900 feet. The name given to the camping ground at the western end of the Lataband pass. It lies in a hollow surrounded on three sides by hills and is about 5 miles from the summit of the Lataband and two miles from the right bank of the Kabul river. Room might be found for a division to encamp here by scattering units. There is a very good and plentiful water-supply from the Lataband stream and from many springs; it is thus not liable to be cut off nor is it affected by the season of the year. Fuel is abundant, but bad; no supplies are procurable. A sarai was built here in 1905 and there is a garrison of one squadron of cavalry and one company of infantry. (Malleson, Wanliss, I.B.C.)

*SAMUSI سوسی
34-5   70-9 m.   A village located north of the Spin Ghar and south of Miyagan in Nangarhar province.

*SANAQ سناق
35-6   67-34 m.   A village located on a tributary of the Saighan river, some 8 miles southwest of Saighan in Bamian province.

SANBULAK   سنبولاق
   34-21   67-54 G.   A village of 14 families in the Besud Hazara country, about 1 1/2 miles northeast of the Diwal Kot Kotal.

*SANDUQ   صندوق
   34-6   70-42 m.   A village located about 2 miles north of Achin and 10 miles southwest of Ghani Khel in Nangarhar province.

SANGANAH Or SANGUNAH   سنگونه
   35-21   69-34 m.   A village in the Panjshir glen, 6 miles above Bazarak. It contains 50 houses of Tajiks. (Shahzada Taimus.)

SANGANDAO   سنگ انداو
   34-   68-.   A kotal on a southern spur of the Koh-i-Jaolanga, the westernmost eminence of the Hindu Kush proper. The prolongation of this same spur forms the watershed of the Shibar Kotal, and the Sangandao Kotal is a communication between the Dara Birgilich and the Ghorband valley. The noticeable white cliffs adjoining it can be distinguished easily from the Shibar Kotal. On the west a difficult hill track leads to it from the Kotal-i-Jalmish, and a good, easy road leads to it also from Birgilich up the open valley in which Kala Faiz is situated. This latter road could easily be rendered practicable for guns as far as the kotal; but the decent down the Dara Sangandao into the Ghorband valley is difficult for anything but pack animals. This road is of some importance, as by it the Shibar Kotal can be turned. (Peacocke.)

*SANGAR   سنگر
   34-16   70-39 m.   A village located near Baru and south of the Jalalabad-Torkham road and about 4 miles east of Shahikot in Nangarhar province. Another place with this name is on the Kunar river, some 8 miles southwest of Asadabad in Kunar province, at 34-46 71-6 m.

*SANGAR KHEL   سنگرخیل
   34-26   69-48 m.   A village located on the Maidan river, near Kota-i-Ashro in Maidan province.

SANGAR KHEL   سنگرخیل
   34-16   69-8 m.   A village in the Logar valley, on the right bank of the river, 1/4 mile east of Zahidabad. The inhabitants are Astanazai Ghilzais, of whom the village contained 20 families in 1880. (Clifford, Euan Smith.)

SANGAR SARAI   See SANG-I-SARAI   سنگرسرای
   A village with this name is located at 34-24   70-38 A. (LWA)

SANG DARA   سنگ دره
   34-19   66-38 G.   A defile leading from Burg, in the Logar valley, to the Abkhor defile.
   The following is a report on it by Captain Gaselee:
   From 1 to 10 miles--On leaving south end of Zargun Shahr cultivation cross barren level plain fit for all arms, bearing 108 degrees. At 6 miles pass the village of Burg, about 1 1/2 miles to left, lying in low hills unconnected with range of hills to east.
   10 to 12 1/2 miles--At about 10 miles strike a track which leads from the village of Burg, and at 10 1/2 miles turns sharp to the north into the Sang Dara pass.
   For two miles the track through the pass is easy; the hills to the east are about 3 miles distant, with spurs and under features running from them. At about 1 mile on the right, immediately after

entering pass, is the small hamlet of Darkot with four or five houses.
At about 1 1/2 miles the village of Nasarai is met; about 30 houses. There is a good deal of land cultivated in terraces, running close up to the slope of the main range to the east.
About 1 mile beyond the village reach a low kotal, or saddle-back, by which the main range on east and small range on west are connected. The hills on both sides are easy, and up to this point troops would encounter no difficulty, and it would be practicable to make a road for wheeled guns in short time.
12 1/2 to 15 miles.—Here, however, the character of the pass changes, and immediately on leaving the kotal, the track descends rapidly into a defile with precipitous masses of black rock on both sides.
The surface of the rock is very hard, and at present the track is so narrow that horsemen can only pass singly.
After about 1 mile reach the bed of a nala with a very hard stony bottom; the width of this nala is from 20 to 30 yards, the hills on both sides maintaining their precipitous nature.
Infantry could move along the crest of the hills on the west; but it would be difficult to occupy those on the east, as they could only be gained by descending first to the bed of the nala above mentioned.
At about 15th mile reach the Abkhor defile, which runs east and west from the Koh-i-Sultan to the Surkhao Tangi. (Gaselee.)

SANGHAR سنغر
A village and fort in the Kunar valley, on the left bank of the river, about 55 miles above Jalalabad, containing 100 houses. (Muhammad Amin.)

*SANGIKHAN سنگی خان
35-15 69-47 m. A village located on a tributary of the Panjshir in Kunar province. Nearby is another village with this name, located at 35-14 69-41 m. (LWA)

*SANG-I-LAKHSHAN سنگ لخشان
35-13 69-17 m. A village on the Dara-i-Shotul, a tributary of the Panjshir river, north of Gulbahar in Parwan province.

SANG-I-MASHA سنگ ماشه
33-8 67-27 A. A plain in the Arghandab valley. A village with this name is located at 33-15 67-7 G. (LWA)

SANG-I-MEKH سنگ میخ
A well-known peak in Takht.

*SANGIN سنگین
34-2 68-25 m. A village northwest of the Katagai Ghar, near the village of Bulagh, in Maidan province.

SANGINA See KOTGAI-O-SANGINA سنگینه
A village with this name is located at 34-14 70-20 G. (LWA)

SANG-I-NAK سنگ ناك
An easy kotal crossed by the main Kabul-Hazarajat-Daulat Yar road.

*SANGINAK سنگینك
34-35 67-35 m. A village located on a tributary of the Helmand, near Qash and south of the Koh-i-Baba in Bamian province. Other

places with this name are located near Garmak and south of the Band-i-Doab in Ghazni province, at 34-5 67-54 m.; on a tributary of the Bum-i-Yakhak in Bamian province, at 34-29 67-24 m.; on a tributary of the Qol-i-Khesh in Parwan province, at 34-47 68-24 m.   (LWA)

SANG-I-NAWISHTA سنگ نوشته

34- 69-. A defile 5 miles south of Kabul and extending southwards for rather more than a mile, where it debouches on the Charasia plain. Through this defile the Logar river runs northwards. The sides of the gorge are precipitous, and it formed an important feature in the action of Charasia on Sir Frederick Roberts' advance on Kabul in October 1879.

A new bridge over the Logar river was built near the head of this gorge in 1904. (I.B.C.)

SANG-I-NAWISHTA See BULOLA سنگ نوشته

SANGINIA سنگینیه

34- 68-. A low kotal northwest of the Unai Kotal, crossed by the Kabul-Bamian road, from the hamlet of Jaokul, about 4 miles northwest of the Unai, the road crosses to the far side of the Jaokul valley; thence it ascends to the Kotal-i-Aboband (not to be confused with that of the same name southwest of Gardan Diwal), the summit of which is reached at 3 3/4 miles. Descent is about a furlong and a half in length and is easy. A dry nala, 200 yards wide, is next crosssed, and there is then a gentle rise of one furlong to the Kotal Sanginia. From here the road descends easily for half mile, where it enters a narrow defile, about 10 yards wide, and enclosed by lofty cliffs. After 2 miles the defile is quitted, and the Helmand crossed by an easy ford. The sarai of Gardan Diwal lies beyond the river. (Muhammad Akbar Khan.)

N.B. --The above distances are probably underestimated by about 2 miles.

SANG-I-SARAI سنگ سرای

34-24 70-38 A. A large village in the Kama subdivision of the Jalalabad district; it lies on the left bank of the Kabul river, 5 miles northeast of Ali Boghan on the other bank. (Wanliss.) Recent maps show the spelling Sangar Sarai.

SANG-I-SHANDA سنگ شانده

34-15 67-43. A large plain to the South of Besud.

SANG-I-SHANDA سنگ شانده

34-15 67-43. A small subdistrict of the Besud country. There is also a village with this name at 34-15 67-43 m. Another village with this name is located at 33-2 67-30 m. (LWA)

SANG-I-SHANDA سنگ شانده

A valley in the Besud country draining eastward.

SANG-I-SULAKH سنگ سولاخ

A small village in the Zari sub-division of the Yakh Walang district. 15 houses of Khwajadad Takanas. (Maitland.)

SANG-I-SULAKH سنگ سولاخ

A place in the Hazara country.

SANG-I-SULAKH سنگ سولاخ

33- 69-. A small fort in the Logar valley, some 7 miles south of

Patkao-i-Shahana, to the north of Aucha Khan. There are only four or five houses of Ahmadzais in the fort, but in spring it is a favourite resort, for six weeks, of Kuchis from Zurmat, principally Gabar Mangals, who bring their camels and sheep here to graze. There is a fine spring of water rushing from the hillside, which affords a good supply at all seasons.   (I.B.C)

SANG-I-SURAKH سنگ سوراخ
34-28 68-32 m. A tagao draining south into the Kirman valley, which it joins at 1 mile east of Komaghai village. It is only about 50 yards wide at its mouth but 1/4 mile higher up it opens out to form a chaman about 300 yards square with excellent grazing. There is also plentiful camel grazing in the form of a small plant, somewhat like a thistle, known as Khar-Safed. A road runs up this tagao and joins the Bamian road near Siakkhagi. (Wanliss.) There is also a village with this name at the above location.   (LWA)

*SANG-I-TAWUS سنگ طاوس
34-59 67-55 m. A village located east of Kangur on a tributary of the Shikari Dara in Bamian province.

SANG-I-ZARD سنگ زرد
34-35 66-2 A. A village in the Sar-i-Jangal valley, 17 miles above Daulat Yar.

SANGLAKH سنگلاخ
34-32 68-40 A. The Sanglakh range may be said to have its origin near the junction of the Hindu Kush and the Koh-i-Baba and is really an offshoot of the former running in a general southwesterly direction and dividing the Kabul river basin from that of the Helmand. It is of the utmost importance in considering the physical geography of Afghanistan, as it forms the link which connects the Safed Koh (and consequently the Sulaiman mountains also) with the main Hindu Kush range, which is, in turn, an offshoot from the great central upland of Asia known as the Pamirs.
Immediately after leaving the Hindu Kush, the Sanglakh range throws off an important spur known as the Paghman range which runs in a northern direction and forms the watershed between the Ghorband and Shakar Dara tributaries of the Panjshir river. It overhangs the west of the Koh Daman plain, north of Kabul, and on its eastern slopes is situated a summer palace of the Amir. It is crossed by the Parsa, Kachan (12,000 feet), Istalif and Sinjit kotals as well as by others of minor importance. The highest peak in this range is known as the Takht-i-Turkoman which reaches a height of 15,447 feet. The Sanglakh range proper only extends as far as the Unai pass, after crossing which it resolves itself into two branches which, at first, may be said to run east and west. Between its points of origin and the Unai pass it is crossed by no pass of any importance except, perhaps, the Kotal-i-Baghar, about 6 miles north of the Unai pass, which, though difficult in places even for single horsemen is of value as affording a means of completely turning the Unai pass itself. The elevation at the crest of the Kotal-i-Baghar is over 11,000 feet.
South of the Unai pass, taking first the western of the two branches mentioned above, we find it known at first as the Buland-i-Kash and, as such, running in a south-westerly direction and separating the Badasia plain from the Kajao tagao. It then, under the name of Koh-i-Daman, turns almost due west as far as the Surkh Sang kotal where it is crossed by the Ghazni-Bamian road. Here is turns southeast and, encircling the headwaters of the Logar river and separating its

basin from that of the Ghazni river, reaches the main Kabul-Ghazni road, where it is crossed by the Sher Dahan kotal at an elevation of 8,500 feet. From here it turns almost due east for about 30 miles to the Altimur pass (9,600 feet) whence under the name of the Machalgu hills, it turns northeast to the Shutar Gardan pass, thus completing the conection with the Sulaiman mountain system.

To return to the point of division of the main range south of the Unai pass; the eastern branch referred to in paragraph 3 above runs in a general southeasterly direction for a distance of about 25 miles forming the watershed between the Khawat and upper Kabul rivers. It is crossed by the Tawa Kotal and terminates in a peak, 13,067 feet high, immediately above the village of Beni Badam on the main Kabul-Kandahar road. At about 15 miles southeast of the Unai pass it throws off to the north an important spur called the Sadmarda range, which, curving round to the east, divides the upper Kabul river from its tributary the Painda Khel Nirkh and terminates, just to the west of the junction of the two, in a peak known as the Koh-i-Beg; the height of the Koh-i-Beg is 10,184 feet. Here, on the northern slopes, is a white marble quarry from which is obtained all the white marble used in the Kabul workshops. (I.B.C.)

*SANGLAKH سنگلاخ
34-49 69-6 m. A village located a few miles east of Istalif and south of Mahala in Kabul province.

SANGLAKH DARA سنگلاخ دره
34-29 68-37. A tributary of the Kabul river which, rising in the Sanglakh range, flows south-southwest and, after a course of about 20 miles joins the Kabul river at Jalrez. It is spanned immediately above this junction by a wooden bridge, 20 feet long and 12 feet broad, over which goes the main Kabul-Herat road. At the point of junction the Sanglakh contains a larger volume of water than the Kabul river, being here (in July) 20 feet broad and 2 feet deep. The Sanglakh valley is said to be exceedingly fertile. (Wanliss.)

SANG NISHANDEH سنگ نشانده
A district in the Hazarajat.

SANGOTA سنگوته
34- 69-. A village in the Hisarak division of the Jalalabad district, about 1/2 mile southwest of Marhez. Inhabitants: Shinwaris. (Jenkyns.)

SANGPAR See KHAWAK سنگپر

SANGRA سنگره (سنگراه؟)
A place mentioned by Leech in a route from Jalalabad to Kashkar, 216 miles from Jalalabad, on the river Alingar, 114 miles form Kashkar, on the other side of a snowy pass and containing 6,000 houses of Kafirs. (Leech.)

SANG SURAKHI سنگ سوراخی
34- 68-. A pass in the upper Helmand valley over a western spur of the Paghman range.

SANG TODA سنگ توده
34- 69-. A place on the road between Jagdalak and Kata Sang, 5 miles from the former. Here the Pari Dara track joins the high road

to Kabul. As its name implies, Sang Toda is a cairn of stones, some ancient landmark. There are no habitations in the neighbourhood. (Thompson, Young.)

SANGU KHEL سنگوخیل
A subdivision of the Shinwaris. A village with this name is located at 34-9 70-49 G. (LWA)

*SANGUNA سنگونه
35-21 69-34 m. A village located on the Panjshir river, about 8 miles southwest of Zenia in Kapisa province.

SANJAN سنجان
35-9 69-22 m. A village on the daman of the hills northeast of Charikar. 150 houses of Tajiks. (Shahzada Taimus.)

SANJIT DARA سنجت دره
A village in the Koh Daman of Kabul 30 miles north of Kabul. It is situated on the banks of a rivulet, and is surrounded with gardens. The soil around is too rocky to be turned to great profit, and prevents the cultivation of the vine to any extent. The orchards are principally stocked with mulberry and walnut-trees. (Masson.) Shahzada Taimus gives the population of "Sinjit Dara" on the daman of the Paghman range, as 1,000 families of Tajiks.

SAO ساو
35-10 71-28 A. A village in the Khugiani country, on the right bank of the Surkhab river, 5 miles west of Gandamak. The inhabitants are Maruf Khel Ghilzais. (MacNair.)

SAO ساو
A village of Laghman, according to Warburton, whose inhabitants in 1880 were Kohistanis.
The people are said to be Nimcha Kafirs. (Warburton, I.B.C.)

SAO Or SAW ساو
35-10 71-28 m. A fort and small hamlet on the left bank of the Kunar river, about 14 miles below Arnawai, and 89 miles from Jalalabad. The fort appears to be a strong place, 80 yards square, with walls about 20 feet high and several towers. There is a wooden bridge over the Kunar river at Sao; the roadway is only about 3 or 4 feet wide and the bridge sways considerably. Horses and mules can be led over it, if quiet, but it is impossible for camels. There is a considerable amount of cultivation to the north of Sao. (I.B.C.)

SAOKAD سوقد
A village in the Alingar valley, 136 miles from Jalalabad, on a road to Kashkar. It is said to consist of 5,000 houses of "Wanierbafars." (Leech.)

*SAOROSU سورسو
34-29 67-22 m. A village located near Diwal, north of Chaharband, in Bamian province.

*SAOSANG سوسنگ
34-31 67-44 m. A village located on the Dara-i-Zirtag, a tributary of the Helmand, and south of the Koh-i-Sar-i-Ghar in Bamian province.

SAOSANG سوسنگ
34-48 69-8 G. A village said to be about 4 miles to the northeast of Istalif. About 100 houses of Daudzai Ghilzais. Water from the Istalif canal and also from karez; much cultivation. The inhabitants are camel-breeders, and hire their animals out on an extensive scale. (I.B.C.)

SAOSANG سوسنگ
A place in the Jaghuri Hazara country inhabited by the Haidar section. (I.B.C.)

SAOZAK سوزك
35- 69-. A small village on daman of the Paghman range, 4 1/2 miles northeast of Charikar. (Maitland.)

SAOZAK سوزك
34-53 67-39 m. A village in the Bamian valley, 1 mile below Pul-i-Faringi. 15 houses of Besud Hazaras. (Sahibdad Khan.)

SAOZAL سوزل
34- 67-. A village of 15 houses in Yakh Walang, 3 miles up the Tabarghan Kol. (Muhammad Akbar Khan.)

SAOZ-I-KAH SEPAI سوزكاه سپی
A sub-section of the Besud Hazaras.

*SAPIBUM سپیبوم
34-8 67-12 m. A village located on a tributary of the Helmand, east of Shahi in Bamian province.

SAPRI Or TSAPARAY سپری منگل (څپری)
33-55 69-43 m. A village in Hariob, 4 miles south of Ali Khel, or about 5 1/2 miles by the Karmana route. It is situated on an elevated plateau, and is approached from the Hazardarakht stream at Karmana by a narrow glen, thickly wooded with pine trees. The village gives its name to this defile and also to a pass to its east leading into the Kurram valley, which is unsuited for the passage of convoys, or troops with camel carriage. Infantry and mountain guns could traverse this route, although the natural features would make it difficult to force a passage, if the defile were held by an enemy.
On the 13th December 1878, Sir Frederic Roberts, marching from Ali Khel towards Kurram, had his rear-guard attacked by a mixed body of Mangals and Jajis (and some fugitives from the Afghan army defeated at the Paiwar Kotal on the second of the month) in descending the southern slope of this pass. On that occasion Captains Goad and Powell were mortally wounded, and 3 sepoys were killed and 11 wounded of the 5th Gurkhas. The enemy was, however, driven off without the loss of any of our baggage or transport animals. (Cane, I.B.C.)

*SARAB سراب
33-11 67-34 m. A village in the Nawa-i-Khodaidad, northeast of Jaghuri in Ghazni province. Another place with this name is near Belandi in Ghazni, at 33-3 67-38 m.

SARACHA سراچه
34-22 70-32 G. A village in the Jalalabad district, 5 1/2 miles east of Jalalabad. It contains from 60 families of Tajiks possessing (in 1904) about 140 head of cattle. The annual production of wheat

and barley at Saracha averages about 3,000 Indian maunds. (Wanliss.)

SARAFSAR سرافسر
33-7 68-54 G. A large group of villages in the Kharoti Ghilzai country, about 22 miles northwest of Urgun and 8 miles northwest of the Kotauni Narai. It contains about 800 houses of Kharoti and Sulaiman Khel Ghilzais. There is much cultivation round about, and water and supplies of all sorts are available, as is also a large amount of camel transport. Sarafsar is the second stage on a route from Urgun to Gardez and here another route branches off which forms a direct route from Urgun to Ghazni. Sarafsar is also known as Sarafzai, Shah Saruf, Sarfaraz and Sarup Sher. (I.B.C.)

SARAFZAI   See SARAFSAR سرافزی

SARAI سرای
34- 69-. A large village in the Koh Daman, about 20 miles north of Kabul, on the left bank of the Shakar Dara, and inhabited principally by Hindus. (Masson.)

*SARAI سرای
34-52   69-49 m. A village near Kunda and east-northeast of Tagab in Kapisa province.

SARAJ سراج
34-57 69-48 G. A dara descending south and joining the Ghorband valley 11 miles above Chahardeh. A path leads up it to the Band-i-Warsandan; but it is little used and little known. (Peacocke.)

SARA KALA سره قلعه
33-59 69-25 G. A halting-place on the Gandamak to Basawal road, about 8 1/2 miles east of the former. Water is plentiful from springs in a ravine 1/2 mile to the west; suplies, and also a good number of camels, are procurable from the villages of Argach, one mile to the north and Kaja, or Kaggu, 2 miles to the south. (I.B.C.)

SARANDIA سراندیا
34-19 69-53 G. A village on the left bank of the Surkhab river, 8 miles west of Gandamak and 1 1/2 miles southwest of the Surkhpul bridge. (I.B.C.)

*SARAO سراو
34-13 69-54 m. A village located about 3 miles southeast of Jakan in Nangarhar province. Another place with this name is near Amro, north of the Dasht-i-Nawer in Ghazni province.

SARASIA سراسیاه
34- 69-. A village in the Chardeh valley, on the left bank of the Kabul river, between Thiba and Rishkhor. It has 10 small forts round the place, which contains 120 houses of Tajiks.
  The forts are as follows:
  1. Kala-i-Shamsud-din Khan (Barakzai)
  2. Kala-i-Mirza Ahmad Khan (Baluch)
  3. Kala-i-Mirza Ghulam Sadik (Baluch)
  4. Kala-i-Khwaja Khan (Tajik)
  5. Kala-i-Malik Taj (Tajik)
  6. Kala-i-Nur Gul (Tajik)
  7. Kala-i-Haji Muhammad (Tajik)
  8. Kala-i-Mahmud

```
        9. Kala-i-Mir Akhor Kasim (Barakzai)
       10. Kala-i-Khwaja Ahmad (Tajik).      (I.B.C.)
```

SARAT سرات
35- 71-. A Kam village of Kafiristan, situated on the Saratgul, which torrent falls into the Bashgul through its left bank. 40 houses. Paths lead from Sarat to the Pittigul and into all the neighbouring guls. (Robertson.)

SARAZ سراز
A section of the Sulaiman Khel.

SARAZGHUMI   See BIRMAL سرازغومی

*SARBAND سربند
34-29 67-47 m. A village located on a tributary of the Helmand, northwest of Behsud in Bamian province. Other places with this name are located on the Kunar river across from Chaperi and northeast of Shewa in Nangarhar province, at 34-36 70-44 m; on the Kabul river, one mile northwest of Loya Daka in Nangarhar province at 34-13 71-2 m.

SARBULAK سربولاق
34-36 67-24 A. Two small villages in the Yak Walang district, situated in the Dara Ali; 40 houses of Sayyids and Neka Hazaras. (A.B.C.)

*SARBULAQ سربولاق
34-53 68-47 m. A village located on a tributary of the Ghorband, west of the Koh-i-Yakhdara in Parwan province.

SARDARA سردره
35-54 66-1 A. A pass over the Hindu Kush, lying at the head of the Salang valley between the Bajgah pass on the west and the Arzu pass on the east. It is crossed by a road leading into the Khinjan valley, at about 27 miles north of Charikar. The ascent from the south is exceedingly steep and is difficult even for yabus; the descent on the northern side is impassable for animals of any description owing to a cliff which has to be clambered down. (I.B.C.)

SARDAR MUHAMMAD AMIN KHAN سردار محمد امین خان
A fort in the Chardeh valley, between Gaokhana and Deh-i-Mozang.

SARDEH سرده
A division of Zurmat. It is a narrow strip between the lower end of Takri and the hill Spinsak. It has seven or eight forts of Andaris, comprising about 1,000 souls. The ground is covered with tamarisk bushes, and cut up by a ravine running into the Jilgu. Opposite Mursal there is an easy pass into Shilghar over the lower end of Takri; there are others lower down; a guide can show several easy passages through the ravines. (Broadfoot.)

SAR DEHI سردهی
A small tribe, inhabiting Sardeh, southeast of Ghazni. They are Tajiks. (Elphinstone.)

SAREGUL سرگل
35- 71-. A hamlet in the Kunar valley, situated near the mouth of a branch valley whose stream falls into the Nari torrent about 3 miles above Nari fort. (Robertson.)

SARFARAZ   See SARAFSAR سرفراز
   A village with this name is located at 32-56 68-2 G. (LWA)

SARGIN سرگین
   A section of the Dai Kundis.

SARGO سرگو
   A defile 80 miles southeast of Ghazni and 60 miles from the Kotal-i-Sarwandi over the Sulaiman range. It commences 11 miles from Kala-i-Langar, and is a ravine cut by water down the west of the range, winding in easy curves. Its width is never less than 30 yards, and is often 100. The ascent is scarcely perceptible, and the hills on either side are easily ascended; the bottom is sometimes rough and heavy, but two hours' work would make it an excellent road. There are some scattered huts of Tokhi Ghilzais near, standing in hamlets of 20 and 30 in the midst of cultivation. (Broadfoot.)

*SAR GOZAR سرگذر
   35-1 68-41 m. A village located a few miles south of Otapur and north of the Ghorband in Parwan province.

SARHAWZA سرحوضه
   33-3 69-2. Sarhawza is an alaqadari in Paktia province. The alaqadari comprises an area of 725 square kilometers and has an agricultural population that has been estimated at from 11,115 to 16,760. The alaqadari is bounded in the west by Sharan and Omna, in the north by Mota Khan and Orma, on the east by Neka and Urgun, and on the south by Sarobi and Gomal. Sarhawza has about 14 villages, 5 of which have more than 500 inhabitants. The villages are listed in the PG as follows: Sultani, Sarawza, Mazak (Marzak), Surkot, Liyaki (Layaki), Goralddin (Kulalddin), Kazhakai, Shah Turai, Mir Darang (Maydanak), Sundur Khel, Tab Dobi, Madokats, Jabar Qala, and Qatari.

SAR-I-AB سرآب
   A glen in the Besud country. A village with this name is located at 33-36 68-2 A. (LWA)

SAR-I-AB سرآب
   33-36 68-2 A. A stream which appears to have its source in Muhammad Khwaja Hazara country.

*SAR-I-AOPUSH سراوپوش
   34-46 68-21 m. A village located on a tributary of the Qol-i-Khesh, a few miles northwest of Khurdakza in Parwan province.

SAR-I-ASIA سراسیا
   35-33 67-34 A. A village of 20 Tajik houses in the Bamian valley. (A.B.C.)

*SAR-I-BID سربید
   33-59 67-47 m. A village located on a stream in northern Ghazni province. Another place with this name is located on the Shila-i-Tabjoi, northeast of Qabjoi in Ghazni province, at 33-10 67-13 m. (LWA)

SAR-I-BULAK سربولاق
   34- 68-. A large village in the Bamian district, passed on the road leading from the Aodara to the Jalmish Kotal. (Peacocke.)

700

SAR-I-BULAK   Also See SARBULAK   سربولاق
   34- 67-.   A small district in the northwest of the Besud country.

SAR-I-BULAK-I-TARGAI   سربولاق ترگی
   34- 67-.   An important stream in Besud draining into the Khawas,
   which in turn flows into the Helmand.

SAR-I-BUM   سربوم
   35-33   67-14 m.   A village in the Dai Zangi country. The village is
   on the Daimirdad, about 8 miles north of Safidkhak. (LWA)

*SAR-I-CHAL See KALU   سرچل
   A village with this name is about 2 miles southeast of Shash Burja,
   Bamian province, at 34-39.

SAR-I-CHASHMA   سرچشمه
   34-25   68-31.   A valley at the head of the Kabul river, running
   eastwards from the Unai pass and included, for purposes of administration, etc., in the Maidan district. The Sar-i-Chashma, as also
   the Dara-i-Baghar and other side valleys draining into it, is inhabited by Taimuris, this being the only part of the Kabul province
   where any members of this tribe are to be found. They are said to
   have been located here for over 200 years and number about 600
   families. Their headman is (1904) Daulat Muhammad; this man was
   formerly a partisan of Amir Sher Ali and for some time after the
   accession of Abdur Rahman lived as a refugee in Quetta, but was
   subsequently permitted to return to his native country. About 1904
   his only son was murdered by a Ghilzai as the result of a quarrel
   and he was unable, at any rate for a long time, to obtain any
   redress. It is therefore not unlikely that he may be disaffected
   towards the present Amir Habibulla. He can talk Hindustani.
   The valley is studded with villages the houses of which are substantially built, giving to the whole neighbourhood an air of
   prosperity. The river banks are lined with poplars and the whole of
   the valley is richly cultivated. Not an inch of land is ever left
   fallow and a strictly scientific rotation of crops is practised,
   clover or beans being always interpolated between two crops of corn,
   to allow the land to recuperate. The principal crops are wheat and
   barley besides which red clover, shaftal (a kind of lucerne) and
   horse beans are largely grown. The flour of these beans is mixed
   with wheat flour and eaten by the poorer classes.
   At Sar-i-Chashma village the main valley is joined by the Dara-i-
   Dastgin from the south and by the Dara-i-Baghar from the north, both
   of which contain (in July) a certain amount of water. The valley at
   this point is about 3 miles across. (Wanliss, Dobbs.) A village
   with this name is southeast of Jaliz, at 34-25   68-31 m.

SAR-I-CHASHMA   سرچشمه
   34-25 68-31 m. Elevation 8,850 feet. (Also called Hauz-i-Mahya, from
   some tanks close by which are fed by copious springs and contain
   some large fish.)
   A village with a sarai in the valley of the same name about 8 1/2
   miles east of the Unai pass. The village contains about 100 families of Taimuris; headman (1904)   Daulat Muhammad. The inhabitants
   possess 150 head of cattle and 200 goats. The annual production of
   wheat and barley averages about 1,650 Indian maunds. It would be
   difficult to find a good camping ground here as nearly all the
   ground is under cultivation but, by scattering units, room could be
   found for a brigade of infantry. Supplies are obtainable in fairly

large quantities and lucerne is very plentiful. There is an ample water-supply from the river. (Wanliss.) A village with this name is near Qala-i-Hasht, Behsud, at 34-10 67-49 G.

SAR-I-CHASHMA   سرچشمه
32- 67-. A village between Oba and Mukur, near which is the source of the Tarnak river. (Masson.)

SAR-I-CHASHMA   سرچشمه
33- 68-. A Besud Hazara village in the Sar-i-Ab glen.

SAR-I-DARIA   سردریا
A place in Nawar. A place with this name is about 50 miles northwest of Ghazni, at 33-47 67-50 G. (LWA)

SAR-I-GARMAO   سرگرم او
In the Besud country; 150 families of the Jirghai section. (A.B.C.)

SAR-I-JANGAL   سرجنگل
34-33 66-23 m. It has its rise at Kasim Ali Beg, where there is a large spring. One of the two streams which form the head of waters of the Hari Rud, the Lal being the other. It runs in a westerly direction from the Roghani Gardan Kotal, and after a course of about 70 miles joins the Lal about 9 miles below Daulat Yar. The upper part of the valley is called Garmao, Sar-i-Jangal proper being considered to begin at Khwaja Josh. Between the latter place and Daulat Yar the valley has not been explored, but a road is said to continue down it to Daulat Yar. Further information is given under "Dai Zangi." (A.B.C.)

SAR-I-JULGAI RAOTI   سرجلگه روتی

SAR-I-KEJAK See KEJAK   سرکجك
A village with this name is northwest of Mushak, at 34-29 67-30 m.

SAR-I-KHAWAT See KHAWAT   سرخوات (شهر خوات)
34-4 67-59 m. Recent maps show the name Shahr-i-Khawat. (LWA)

SAR-I-KOL   سرقول
34-39 67-9 m. A glen running down north from the Koh-i-Baba to the Band-i-Amir valley near Firozbahar. A road leads up it for the Khak-i-Chagir Kotal, and so to Tagao Barg and Panjao. A second road runs by Siah Bumak to the Gul-i-Robat pass. For detail of villages, etc., see "Bamian (district)."

SARIKOT   سرکوت
A village on the road from Belut to Jalalabad by the Lakarai pass, situated on the northern slope of the latter, on a tributary of the Surkhab river. Inhabitants: Mangals. (I.B.C.)

SAR-I-NASAR   سرنصر
34-30 70-13. A village in the Laghman district, on the right bank of the Kabul river, 10 miles west of the Darunta pass. It stands at the foot of a low, stony spur from the Siah Koh range, which would if held prove a formidable obstacle, as it is impossible to turn it by the river-side and difficult to turn it to the south. The village itself is small and open, without towers. (Young.)

SAR-I-ROQOL See KOH-I-SHAITUS   سرروقول

SAR-I-SANG سرسنگ
34- 68-. A fort in the Maidan valley, 22 miles from the Kabul, on the Ghazni road. It is built of stone, and is situated on a hill which completely commands the road. (Thornton.) Villages with this name are located on a tributary of the Dara-i-Mur, at 34-31 67-6 m.; on the Garmab, at 34-4 67-34.; and some 8 miles east, at 34-4 67-37 m.

SAR-I-SANG-I-SHANDA   See KOH-I-SHAITUS سرسنگ

SAR-I-TAL سرتل
34- 67-. A small fort and village in the Dai Zangi country.

*SAR-I-TALA سرتاله
34-34 66-38 m. A village located on a tributary of the Hari Rud, about 5 miles east of Shinya and north of Asgharat. Other villages with this name are located on a tributary of the Qol-i-Khesh, at 34-42 68-29 m.; and east of Naudeh and north of Luman, Ghazni, at 33-15 67-40 m. (LWA)

SAR-I-TANUR   See KOH-I-SHAITUS سرتنور

SAR-I-TARGAN سرترگان
A place in the Jaghatu Hazara country.

SAR-I-UCHAK   See KOH-I-SHAITUS سراوچک

SAR KANAI   Or SARKANAY سرکنی
34-47 71-6. Sar Kanai is a village and a woleswali in Nangarhar province. The woleswali comprises an area of 299 square kilometers and has an agricultural population that has been estimated at from 5,020 to 15,288. The woleswali is bounded in the west by Asadabad, Chawki, and Narang, in the south by Khas Konar, in the north by Marawaro, and in the east by the State of Pakistan. Sar Kanai has about 33 villages, 19 of which have more than 500 inhabitants. The villages are listed in the PG as follows: Sarkani, Da Khani Baba Kalai, Do Nahr (Do Nahi), Sangar, Pashad (Qushad), Qaland, Bahrabad (Barbad), Qala Pali (Nangar Kala Perai), Naulai, Kotkai, Nawah, Ganjgal, Barogai (Bahrogai), Dara-i-Marwarah, Changai, Tango, Totnaw Kalai, Gala, Chenar, Warghala, Mulla Gorah, Dara-i-Shingali, Mahay, Khadi Khel-i-Garbuz, Sobagi, Sulaimanzai, Baddinzai, Gargo Kalai, Kandaharo Kalai, Bagh Kalai, Tangi, Ghokhtankai, Qarya-i-Qala, Wacha Hurah, Bandah, Shakal, and Sarah Lam (Sharah Lam). (LWA) In 1912, the village was described as follows: A large village on the left bank of the Kunar river, about 8 miles below Chigha Serai. A battalion of regular infantry and 200 Khasadars are quartered here. (I.B.C.)

SARKARI KALA سرکاری قلعه
34-39 67-49. Now the site of the town of Bamian. For a recent description of the area, see Bamian. (LWA) In 1912 the area was described as follows: Elevation 8,350 feet. A place in the Bamian valley, 98 1/2 miles from Kabul on the road to Mazar-i-Sharif. It is the residence of the Governor of Bamian and lies almost opposite to the famous carved-rock idols of Bamian.
There is a bazar of some 30 or 40 shops here and two sarais, one old and one new. The latter is built up against a hillside, which forms one of its walls, and is about 600 yards from the old one. There is also a small kacha fort situated on a low hill about 1,000 yards

from the new sarai. The garrison consists of 1 battery (6 mountain, 4 field and 4 machine guns), 2 companies of infantry and 300 khasadars. Tarvellers' passports, or rahdaris, are subject to inspection at Sarkari Kala.

About a mile to the west there is room to encamp a brigade on cultivated ground on the right bank of the river. Supplies are procurable at Sarkari Kala. The valley is here about 1/2 mile across and is entirely taken up with cultivation; there are many fruit trees, also chinars and willows.

There is really no town or open village in the Bamian valley, but only a succession of small fortified hamlets. The inhabitants are Tajiks. (I.B.C.)

SARMA KOL سرماقول
34- 66-. A glen in the south of the Yakh Walang district. It drains to that of Kanak.
The word "Sarma" is said to be Tatar for cold, and "Kol" is of course the common word for valley or glen. Sarma Kol, therefore, means the cold glen. It contains 4 villages, with a total population of about 50 families of Hazaras. (Maitland.)

SARMARGHA سرمرغه
32- 68-. A district of the Ghilzai country, to the east of Kalat-i-Ghilzai, from which it is divided by a range of hills. It is the home of the Muhammadzai Tokhi Ghilzais. There is a place of this name west by a little south of Shakin. (Broadfoot.)

SARMAST KHANA سرمست خانه
34-5 69-48. A peak in the Safed Koh range, which appears to be situated a little to the west of the Lakarai pass. (I.B.C.)

SAR MUHAMMAD سرمحمد
34- 68-. Elevation 8,051 feet. A village on the Ghazni and Kabul road, between Shaikhabad and Maidan. (Hough.)

SAROBI Or SORUBAY سروبی
34-36 69-45 m. Sarobi is a town and a woleswali in Kabul province. The woleswali comprises an area of 1,159 square kilometers and has an agricultural population which has been variously estimated at from 9,145 to 12,445. The woleswali is in the east of Kabul province, bordering on Nangarhar and Laghman provinces.
Sarobi includes about 42 villages, of which about 14 have more than 500 inhabitants. The villages are listed in the PG as follows: Qala-i-Kalan wa Zamin, Laker Lam, Naghlu, Yakhdand, Salam Khel, Marwarah, Torkanai, Jagdalek, Narghundi, Farmanbeg, Dabili, Chasma-i-Duka, Husain Khel, Kabaltu, Ibrahim Kel, Gaz, Gogamundah, Shapol-Baba, Chashma-i-Ismail, Chashma-i-Nasrat, Sasbobi, Kotagai, Waka, Ispar Kundi, Angur Tak, Chenar, Rodbar, Qaria-i-Sarobi, Hut Khel Sarobi, Tezini-i-Khas, Julubi, Sayed Mia Rasul Baba, Abdurrahim (Chapar Sia Koh), Murghi Chasma-i-Karam Qol, Ahangaran, Shamak-i-Mulla Khel, Qala-i-Hasan, Zarandah, Gerdi Murgha, Qala-i-Janan Jaroy, Jarobi, Shirab, and Tastin. (LWA) In 1912, the area was described as follows:

A group of villages on the left bank of the Tezin stream, near the junction of the latter with the Kabul river. There is room for a large force to encamp here with plentiful water from the Tezin stream and from springs, but supplies are scarce. Fodder for about 1,000 animals for one day and about 100 maunds of unground grain may with difficulty be collected from the neighbourhood. Fuel is plentiful. There is a public sarai in the place.

At Sarobi the river route from Jalalabad to Kabul crosses the route from Seh Baba to Nagalu and Charikar. By this latter route the Kabul river is crossed opposite Sarobi by a V-shaped ford, the apex of the V lying upstream. The bed of the river here is of pebbles and gravel, and the ford is practicable for laden animals. (I.B.C., Johnston.)

SAROBI سروبی
34-7 70-48 m. A village in the Shinwari country, south of Pesh Bolak. A force of 20 khasadars is quartered here. (I.B.C.) The place is southwest of Basawal.

*SAROBI سروبی
32-48 69-5m. Sarobi is an alaqadari in Paktia province. The alaqadari comprises an area of 411 square kilometers and has an agricultural population that has been estimated at from 3,838 to 5,125. The alaqadari is bounded in the west and south by Gomal, in the north by Sarhawza, and Urgun and in the east by Barmal. Sarobi has some 21 villages, 3 of which have more than 500 inhabitants. The villages are listed in the PG as follows:
Nawi Kala Pasani, Pastolay, Zala Pasani, Rubat, Mastoy, Abbas Khel, Nawai Lanchi Khel, Zala Lanchi Khel, Taus Khel (Kaus Khel), Nawi Babo Khel, Khani Qala, Haybati, Zala Babo Khel, Sodan Khel (Shoran Khel), Bas Nas Khel (Shabi Nash Khel), Ezai, Mangro Toye (Mongor Joye), Tor Khel, Tabut Hayat Khel, Tabut Babo Khel, and Haji Sadozai.

SAROBIA سروبیه
32- 68-. A village in the Kharoti country. It has a ruined fort with a few houses near the sources of the Dwa Gumal river. (Broadfoot.)

SARUN سارون
A section of the Dai Kundis.

*SARUNKHEL سارون خیل
32-4 68-16 G. An area in Katawaz. Also, a village about 6 miles west of Alikhel, at 33-57 69-40 G; recent maps show the name Sernikhel. (LWA)

SARUP SHER   See   SARAFSAR سروپ شیر

SARWAI TANGI سروی تنگی
33- 69-. A defile in the Upper Kurram valley, between Nur Ghasi and the Laji ravine. The general width of this defile is from 70 to 80 yards. (Kane.)

SARWANDI سروندی
32-36 68-41 A. Elevation 7,500 feet. A pass over the Sulaiman range at the head of the Gumal river. The ascent from Shintsa on the west side is gradual for 3 miles, passable for guns. There is then an ascent of 20 yards, the angle of the slope being about 11 degrees then it ascends very gradually through a ravine 30 to 40 yards wide, winding among hills, steep on the north and rounded on the south. From this point it descends at a slope of about 3 degrees. The hill is covered with bushes and the road lies down a small rivulet. (Broadfoot.)

SARWANI KHEL سروانی خیل
33- 69-. A fort apparently in the Jaji country, but the authority

is here not very clear. It contains 50 houses, has numerous apricot gardens, and can turn out 100 fighting men. (Agha Abbas.)

SATARNAI   See ROBAT (1)

SATSUMGROM OR (TETSEMGROM) ستڑنی
سڅم گرام (تڅوڅم گرام)
35-20   70-55 m.   A small Presun village in Kafiristan. It is built on a steep slope on the right bank of the Pech or Presun river about 74 miles above Chigha Sarai, and between the villages of Kstigrom and Pashkigrom. It contains some 30 houses and is unfortified. Just below the village there is a good bridge provided with folding doors at the end further from the village. (Robertson, I.B.C.) This may be the same as Tsotsum (Cocum), at 35-21 70-55 m. (LWA)

SEH BABA سه بابا
34-   69-.   Elevation 4,600 feet.   A shrine in the Tezin valley, 10 miles from Jagdalak, and nearly the same distance from the Lataband pass. The inhabitants in the neighbourhood are Ghilzais.
During the war of 1879-80 there was a post and commissariat depot at this place, from which there is an alternative route to Kabul by Tezin. The Tezin river-bed is at this point particularly rough and difficult for the passage of baggage animals, especially camels. Supplies are procurable with difficulty from Tezin and Sarobi.
A good stream of water flows past Seh Baba in winter, but it is all taken off for cultivation in the Tezin valley in the summer months. (I.B.C.)

*SEH DIWAR سه دیوار
34-59   68-49 m.   A village located on a tributary of the Sekari, about 2 miles northwest of Sukhta.

SEHKAM سه کم
A subsection of the Besud Hazaras.

SEHPAI سه پای
A section of Dai Zangi Hazaras.

SEHPAI Or SIPAI سی پای
A main section of the Shinwaris. A village with this name is near Dusha, at 34-10 70-37 G. Recent maps show the name Sipia at 34-8 70-34 m. (LWA)

*SEHQALA سه قلعه
34-35   68-43 m.   A village located on a tributary of the Maidan river, about 15 miles north of Jaliz.

SEHTARH سه ترح
34-49   71-7.   A ferry across the Kunar river, near a town of the same name. The latter stands on the left bank of the river, 7 miles below Chigha Sarai. The valley here narrows down to a gorge about 300 yards wide and the river flows in one channel. (I.B.C.)

SEHWAK سیوك
A village in the Dai Zangi district of Lal. A village with this name is located at 34-21 66-28 m. (LWA)

SEKANDARI سکندری
A small section of Hazarajat.

*SERKANI   See   SARKANI   سرکنی

SHABAH   See   SHAHBAH   شاهباه

SHABAK   Or   BATAI   KANDAO   شبك
33- 69-. Elevation 4,126 feet. A pass leading from the neighbourhood of Manduri in Kurram to the Shamil, or Kaitu, valley in Khost. Though steep in places it is practicable for camels and could easily be made fit for wheeled guns. There is an Afghan khasadar post about one mile to the west of the summit. (I.B.C.)

SHABI   شبی
34-7   70-23 A. A village in the Hisarak division, Jalalabad district, containing 100 houses of Khugianis. (MacGregor.)

SHADI BEG   شادی بیگ
A section of Kaptasan Besud Hazaras.

SHAD KHANA   شادخانه
34-20 69-11 m. A village in the northern division of the Logar valley, i.e., north of the Tangi Waghjan. It is situated on the right bank of the river, and at the southern extremity of the Musai township. The inhabitants are Astanazai Ghilzais, who in 1880 only numbered 10 families. (Clifford, Euan Smith.)

SHAH ALAM-I-AFGHANI   شاه علم افغانی
34- 70-. A village in the Kama division of the Jalalabad district near Mayar, and under the headman of the place. Inhabitants: Mohmands. (Jenkyns.)

SHAH ALAM-I-TAJIKI   شاه علم تاجکی
34- 70-. A village in the Kama division of the Jalalabad district, situated between Mayar and Sangar Sarai. Inhabitants: Tajiks. (Jenkyns.)

SHAHAR   شهر
34-39   66-24 A. A village in Sar-i-Jangal, 40 miles east of Daulat Yar.

SHAHAR-I-AFGHAN   شهر افغان
34- 69-. A village in the northern division of the Logar valley, on the right bank of the river. It consists of four hamlets, whose inhabitants, numbering in 1880 fifty families are Adramzais and Tajiks. (Clifford, Euan Smith.)

SHAHAR-I-BARBAR   شهر بربر
35- 67-. The remains of an ancient city of the Koh-i-Baba, standing on the higher rugged and scarped hill between the streams of Firozbahar and Band-i-Amir just above their confluence. There is nothing in the ruins to repay any one but an archaeologist for the trouble of going up to them. The city is traditionally said to have been the capital of a kingdom which comprised the greater part of what is now the Hazarajat. The people were called Barbar, and were probably Tajiks of the same race as those now inhabiting the small states on the Oxus. When the country was peopled by the ancestors of the present Hazaras, after the Tatar invasion, the remnant of the Barbars appears to have been absorbed by them, for which reason, or from their inhabiting the old Barbar country, the Hazaras are still known as Barbari. The word Barbar is said to be old Arabic for

"mountaineer." It is no doubt the same as that we are familiar with under the form "Berber," the pronunciation being exactly similar. (Maitland.)

SHAHBAH Or SHOBA شهبا (شوبه)
35-24 69-10. A pass over the Hindu Kush leading from the Panjshir into the Andarab valley, its summit lying about 6 miles northeast of the Parandev pass. The road over the Shahbah pass is said to be difficult, but practicable for laden yabus. It leaves the Panjshir valley at the village of Astana, 5 1/4 miles above Kacha. (I.B.C.)

SHAHBAZJAN شهبازجان
34-29 69-3. A small fort in the Kabul district, situated close to Kala-i-Kazi and inhabited by Hazaras. (I.B.C.)

*SHAHBID شاه بید
34-13 66-56 m. A village on the Nawa-i-Surkhjoy, south of the Koh-i-Sar-i-Ghar, southwest of Bamian province.

*SHAHBIDAK شاه بیدك
34-47 66-40 m. A village located about 2 miles south of Mantiq in western Bamian province. Another village with this name is some 14 miles west of Ghazni, at 33-33 69-10 m.

SHAH BOBO شاه بوبو
34-29 69-13. A small square fort 1/2 mile north of Bini Hisar on the west side of the Kabul-Charasia road. (I.B.C.)

SHAH BUNYAD شاه بنیاد
A village in the Yakh Walang district.

SHAHGHASI شاه غاسی
34-6 69-4 m. A village in the Logar valley, on the left bank of the river, 2 1/2 miles north of the Tangi Waghjan. Inhabitants: Ahmadzais and Hazaras. In 1880 there were 10 families in the place. (Clifford, Euan Smith.) The village is near the Kalangar woleswali seat. (LWA)

SHAHGUM BEG شهگم بیگ
A section of Takana Dai Zangi Hazaras.

*SHAHI شاهی
34-38 66-39 m. A village on the Hari Rud, west of Siahchashma, Bamian province. Other villages with this name are on a tributary of the Helmand, at 34-8 67-10 m.; on the Alishang River, some 12 miles north of the Alishang river, at 34-55 70-5 m.; and about 15 miles southwest of Nawa-i-Kharwar in Logar province, at 33-38 68-12 m.

SHAHI شاهی
A subsection of the Dai Zagi Hazaras.

*SHAHID شهید
34-59 71-5 m. A village located one mile north of Katar on a tributary of the Kunar river.

SHAHIDAN شهیدان
34-31 70-1 m. A village in Laghman, on the right bank of the Kabul river, at its junction with the Alingar.

The following are the hamlets composing the village:

        1. Kala-i-Kamardin
        2. Banda-i-Muhammad Islam
        3. Banda-i-Shahabuddin
        4. Deh-i-Dur Muhammad

The inhabitants are Kuchis. (Warburton)

SHAHIDAN   شهیدان
34- 68-. A glen which decends form the Koh-i-Baba to the Bamian valley, debouching into the latter about 10 miles above Kala Sarkari.
It runs from southwest to northeast and is about half a mile wide where entered by the Bamian road to Daulat Yar. It is very fertile here, and there are five forts and villages near the point where the road crosses. Above are three others. Above them the valley narrows and runs up under high hills. The largest village is Kala Bakar Beg. The people of Shahidan are Yanghur Dai Sangis, according to their own statement. See "Bamian (District)."
There is a road up the Shahidan over the Jiria Khana Kotal to Besud. It appears to join the Siah Beg road from Polada. Below the Bamian road crossing the Shahidan becomes a defile. (Maitland.)

SHAHI-KALA   See MAIDAN-I-PAI-KOTAL   شاهی قلعه

SHAHI-KALA   See TATANG-I-JABAR   شاهی قلعه

*SHAHI KHEL   شاهی خیل
34-57 68-51 m. A village on a tributary of the Ghorband in Parwan province.

*SHAHI KOT   شاهی کوت
34-16 70-34 m. A village southeast of Jalalabad and east of Chaparhar in Nangarhar province.

SHAH-I-MARDAN KUL   شاهی مردان غل
34- 69-. A fort in the Chardeh valley of Kabul, between Gaokhana and Kala-i-Mir Ghazab. Water from a karez. Inhabitants: Tajiks and Barakzais; 25 families. (I.B.C.)

SHAH-I-MASHAD   شاه مشهد
Is said to be a well-known place in the Dai Kundi country.

SHAH MASID   شاه مسید (مسجد؟)
A subdivision of the Bacha-i-Ghulam clan of Dai Zangi Hazaras.

*SHAHIN   شاهین
34-7 69-31 m. A village on the Azra Dara, some 6 miles southwest of Azra in Logar province.

SHAHIN   شاهین
34- 66-. A village in the upper part of the Sar-i-Jangal valley. A village with this name is located at 34-38 66-39 m. Recent maps show the name Shahi.

SHAHKI   شهکی
35-9 69-7. A fort in Kohistan, situated at the entrance to the Nijrao valley, 10 miles northwest of Tutamdara. (Pottinger.)

SHAHMAK شاهمك (شامق)
34-58 69-8 m. A village of 50 houses of Tajiks in Kohistan, 2 miles south of Charikar. The inhabitants are agricultural, and the village has an excellent canal near it. (Masson, Shahzada Taimus.) Recent maps show the spelling Shamaq. (LWA)

SHAH MAZAR شاه مزار
33-52 68-56 G. A village in the Logar valley on the left bank of that river, 4 miles southeast of Baraki Rajan. Inhabitants: Astanazai Ghilzais, of whom there were 150 families in 1880. (Clifford, Euan Smith.)

SHAH MUHAMMAD شاه محمد
A fort containing 50 houses and able to turn out 200 fighting men. It is not clear where this fort is, but this authority seems to infer it is in the Jaji country. (Agha Abbas.)

*SHAHQALA شاه قلعه
34-49 68-57 m. A village on the Pengram stream, about halfway between Nawa-i-Kharwar and Baraki Barak in Logar province.

SHAHRISTAN شهرستان
34-22 66-47 A. A halting place on the main Kabul-Hazarajat-Daulat Yar road, 15 miles west of Panjao Sarai. Other villages with this name are located at 34-34 66-31 m., and near the Band-i-Amir, Bamian province, at 34-47 67-13 m. (LWA)

SHAHRISTAN See ZAR SANG شهرستان

SHAH SAROF See SARAF شاه سراف

SHAHTORI Or SHATURI شاتوری
33-1 69-14 A. A Kharoti settlement on a stream of the same name (which falls into the Tochi) on the road from Ghazni to Dawar, five stages from the former. There are 20 to 30 houses. Ata, ghi, and rice plentiful. Water from springs good, but not abundant. Fuel and forage in fair quantities. The distance of this place, on native information, is estimated at 69 miles from Ghazni. (McLean.) Another village with this name is located at 33-1 69-4 m. (LWA)

SHAHTU Or SHATU شاتو
34-35 66-58 m. A difficult pass leading over the Koh-i-Baba from the Helmand valley to that of the Band-i-Amir. The road leaves the Kabul-Hazarajat main road at Panjao, and reaches Pai Kotal-i-Shahtu at 17 miles, Shewa Anda at 32 miles, and Tagao Zari at 46 miles. (Native information.)

SHAHTUS شاتوس
33- 68-. One of the principal mountains to the west of Ghazni. (Hastings.)

SHAHTUT شاه توت
34-23 69-5 m. A small village in the Lalandar valley of Kabul. (Dutton.)

SHAHU شاهو
A section of the Muhammad Khwaja Hazaras.

SHAIGO See SAIGAN شیگو

SHAIKH شیخ
A subsection of the Besud Hazaras.

SHAIKHA شیخه
A section of the Khatai Hazaras. (See "Bamian".)

SHAIKHABAD شیخ آباد
34-5 68-45. A village in Wardak, 46 1/2 miles from Kabul, on the Ghazni road. It stands on the right bank of the Logar stream, opposite Kheri Taisang, which is included in it. It was from this village that Outram started in pursuit of Dost Muhammad in 1839 by a cross-road leading over the Paghman hills to Yurt. It was last visited by British force in 1880, in which year General Ross encamped here in April and Sir Frederick Roberts a few weeks later, the latter on the occasion of his returning to Kabul from Logar. It possesses a good fort.
A masonry bridge is (1906) being built here over the Logar river and there is also a strong temporary wooden bridge; the Logar is usually fordable here.
There is ample space for camping ground at Shaikhabad; rice and jowar are plentiful; wheat scarce; fuel in small quantities; grass and clover abundant. (I.B.C.) Another place with this name is located at 34-20 69-44 m.

*SHAIKH ALI شیخ علی
34-57 68-30 m. Shaikh Ali is an alaqadari in Parwan province. The alaqadari comprises an area of 908 square kilometers and has an agricultural population that has been estimated at from 7,887 to 9,677. The alaqadari is bounded in the west by Shibar, in the north by Tala wa Barfak, in the east by Ghor Band, and in the south by Surkh-i-Parsa. Shaikh Ali includes 27 villages, of which 6 have more than 500 inhabitants. The villages are listed in the PG as follows: Qarya-i-Babur, Sangariyan, Rubat, Darwaz, Bini Sayuk wa Mohammad Yar (Benisayuk Surkh), Bed (Bed Deh Kalan), Kotak Deh Kalan, Dara-i-Nerkh, Dahan-i-Nerkh, Tuchi-Nerkh, Jerf, Kajak, Sang Par, Khwajaka (Awlang-i-Khwajaka Koh), Nawi, Khak-i-Ghulam Ali, Torgich (Torich), Butiyan, Sang Andab, Bad Qol (Bedel Qol), Gandab, Pawaz, Jangalak, Jaw Qol, Dektor, Khum-i-Qarghana, and Tana Bed Deh Kalan.

SHAIKH ALI HAZARAS شیخ علی هزاره
The following article has been taken from a report by Colonel Maitland, compiled from information collected by the Intelligence party, Afghan Boundary Commission, including Captain Peacocke's diary:
The Shaikh Ali Country
"General Description. The country, inhabited by Shaikh Ali Hazaras, lies on both sides of the southwestern end of the Hindu Kush which is locally known as the Koh-i-Warsandan. It is thus situated in three provinces and forms part of half-a-dozen different districts. South of the range the Ghorband river is formed by the junction of two streams, one of which rises at the Shibar watershed, and flows eastwards through a valley called Dara Shaikh Ali; the other comes from Khesh and the Helmand watershed north of the Gardan Diwal, and runs through the Dara Turkoman, joining the Shaikh Ali stream at Doab-i-Loling, about 23 miles from the Shibar Kotal. South of the Dara Turkoman rises the lofty Koh-i-Paghman, rivalling the Hindu Kush itself: between the Dara Turkoman and the Dara Shaikh Ali is the eastern end of the Koh-i-Baba, which appears to be called the Koh-i-Darwaz, though possibly this name is only applied to its termination. Then between the Dara Shaikh Ali and the Surkhab river,

whose narow valley and deep lateral glens are almost entirely peopled by Shaikh Alis,is the above mentioned Koh-i-Warsandan, so that the Shaikh Ali not only occupy the Surkhab and its glens as far as Doshi, where the river turns northwards, but they extend all up the western side of Ghori, and also continue along the north side of the Hindu Kush, where they almost exclusively populate the small district of Khinjan, and are not wanting in Andarab.

"The Shaikh Ali country may be divided into three parts. First, in the Kabul province there is what appears to be called the Shaikh Ali district, which consists of the Dara Shaikh Ali and the Dara Turkoman, together with the Parsa glen, whose mouth is below Doab-i-Loling. Then, on the other side of the Koh-i-Jalmish and Dahan-i-Jalmish are Shaikh Alis. Below Dahan-i-Jalmish are Tajiks, who are succeeded at Doab-i-Mekhzari by Tatars. But Shaikh Alis commence again below Doab-i-Mekhzari, and extend to Shutar Jangal, Jalmish is in the Bamian district, which belongs to the Kabul province, but the rest is in the Afghan Turkistan district of Doab. Thirdly, there are the Shaikh Ali Hazaras of Ghori, Doshi, Khinjan, and Andarab, all of which are in the province of Badakhshan.

"Character and proclivities. The Shaikh Alis have no chiefs except local headmen, arbabs of taifas (sections) and the like. They have a very bad reputation, and it appears to have been necessary to repress them continually, which no doubt accounts in a great measure for their present broken and disorganized condition. Not long ago, in the time of Amir Sher Ali, the Shaikh Alis continually plundered travellers on the Kara Kotal, and almost stopped traffic on the Turkistan kafila route. Even as late as 1883 they plundered a caravan; but for this they seem to have been promptly and effectually punished, troops and levies being despatched against them from three sides. They were made to pay a heavy fine and partly disarmed. It was the Shaikh Alis of the Surkhab who appear to have been mostly responsible for these outrages, and Dilawar Khan, the Tatar Chief of Doab, in whose district they are, appears to have had an allowance, or remission of revenue, to keep them in order. The Shaikh Alis of Doshi, Khinjan, etc., also appear to have been given to plundering, and we noticed when passing through those districts in 1886 that the name appeared to be as it were prescribed, all the Hazaras we met declining to allow they were Shaikh Alis, and calling themselves Khinjanis. Since Abdur Rahman Khan's accession, the Shaikh Alis, like other troublesome tribes, have been reduced to complete submission and made to pay revenue. When the parties of the Boundary Commission passed through them, they appeared to be quiet and hardworking cultivators. No doubt they actually resemble most other Hazaras in being industrious and not specially warlike. It was the inaccessibility of their settlements on the Surkhab and the strength oftheir fastness in the glens of the Hindu Kush which enabled them for so long to carry on their evil practices. Lately, that is during Ishak Khan's rebellion of 1888, the Shaikh Alis made some sort of a rising. It appears that Dilawar Khan, the Chief of Doab, declared for the Sardar, and induced the Shaikh Alis in his district to turn out. The Amir on his way to Turkistan took the Surkhab route, and Dilawar Khan who had been taken prisoner, or surrendered himself, was put to death at Dasht-i-Safed. Nothing was done to the Shaikh Alis, who had become quiet enough, but the Amir significantly remarked that he would deal with them when he returned.

"Physique and arms. The Shaikh Alis are for the most part a fine, hardy-looking race, and are good mountaineers, as might be expected. They are badly armed--that is to say, they have no rifles, and probably not many firearms of any sort. Those of the Surkhab would not admit to Peacocke that they possessed any weapons at all; and as they had been compelled to give up one gun and one sword per family as part of the punishment for plundering the kafila above alluded to, it is not likely they should have many left. Peacocke makes no remarks as to the dress of the Shaikh Alis of the Surkhab and Dara Shaikh Ali, but it was noticed that those of Doshi and Khinjan rarely wore the distinctive Hazara cap, and could hardly be distinguished at first sight from Tajiks.

"The feeling of the Shaikh Alis towards the Afghans is perhaps rather more inimical than that of the Hazaras in general, none of whom love their masters. Peacocke thinks that in case of Russian troops advancing into their country they would remain neutral, as they do not expect much amelioration in their condition from the advent of these people.

"Elevation and climate. The Shaikh Ali country, being one of great mountain ranges, divided by deep valleys, possesses a considerable variety of climate. South of the Hindu Kush most of the Hazaras settlements in the Dara Shaikh Ali and elsewhere are between 7,000 and 8,000 feet in elevation. North of the main range they are between 3,000 and 5,000 feet. The Hindu Kush rises to a height of 16,000 feet and over, and down to 12,000 feet is covered with snow for nearly half the year. But in the valleys there is little snow, and the comparatively small amount of land available for cultivation produces all the cereals, including rice in Doshi and Khinjan, also pulses, vegetables, and fruit. However, it will be better to give a brief description of each portion of the Shaikh Ali country separately.

"Roads. Numerous paths lead over the three principal ranges, the Paghman, the Koh-i-Darwaz (Koh Baba) and the Koh-i-Warsandan (Hindu Kush). Many of these, however, though used for local traffic, are mere rugged footpaths, or practicable only (and with difficulty) for the bullocks, donkeys, and surefooted yabus of the country. At the same time there are some very important routes which lead through the country of the Shaikh Alis. Beginning from the east, there is the Kaoshan pass road which leads to Khinjan. This was the old main route to Badakhshan and Turkistan. Next is the Chahardar pass road, the present main route over the Hindu Kush. Thirdly, there is the road running the whole length of Ghorband and the Dara Shaikh Ali to the Shibar Kotal, and so to Bamian. Fourthly, there is the Surkhab road.

"The Shibar pass, an open watershed connecting the western end of the Hindu Kush with Koh Darwaz, is specially important as being open all year round, and thus forming the only communication between Kabul and the provinces of Badakhshan and Turkistan during the winter months.

I. Shaikh Ali District (which is adjacent to, but distinct from, Ghorband.) (Almost the whole of the following is from information recorded by Peacocke, who passed through the district in October 1886.)

"The Shaikh Ali district is understood to comprise: (1) the Dara Shaikh Ali; (2) the Dara Turkoman; and (3) the Parsa glen of the Paghman range.

"The Dara Shaikh Ali. From the foot of the Shibar Kotal (Pai Kotal-i-Shibar) to the junction of the Dara Turkoman stream which issues from the Loling defile just above Kala Doab is about 21 miles. The valley is of very variable width. It averages about four hundred yards down to Bini Sehwak. Afterwards, at Nawi, it is a mile and a half across for a short distance. Again, at Gazar Chaman it is three-quarters of a mile wide. Soon after this, however, it becomes a defile, which continues to Doab-i-Loling. The wider parts of the valley are well cultivated, and contain numerous villages surrounded by orchards. The mouths and lower portions of the numerous affluent glens, some of them of large size, are also well cultivated.

"Besides wheat and barley, jowar is largely grown. Altogether considerable quantities of grain are procurable, and it is said that Ghilzais from Shaikh Dara (on south side of the Paghman) come over in numbers to buy the surplus.

"The district contains many sheep and also cattle. Riding horses are scarce, but there are a certain number of pack yabus. Bullocks are also much used for transport.

"According to Peacocke, snow rarely lies to a depth greater than 2 feet at Pai Kotal, and it is of course, less lower down the valley. The climate is therefore, not very cold even in winter.

"The following is a detail of the people:

Shaikh Ali Hazaras of Dara Shaikh Ali

Section	Location	Families
Karam Ali (Shiahs?)	Pai Kotal (10) Dara Shingarian (50)	60
Dai Kalan (Shiahs); headman Asadulla	Upper Dara Shaikh Ali (600), Dara Sagpur (60)	660
Naiman (Shiahs); headman the same Asadulla.	Dara Shaikh Ali, below Dai Kalan (300), Bed Kol (60), Kala Kazi Nawi (10)	370
Karluck or Kalluk (Sunnis); headman, Mirza Akbar.	Dara Shaikh Ali, below the Naiman (500), Dara Taori (60).	560
Ali Jam (2/3 Shiahs, 1/3 Sunnis)	Dara Shaikh Ali, below the Kalluk	30
Babar (Sunnis)	Dara Behuda	60
Nekpai (Shiahs)	Koh-i-Khurd and Kol-i-Lech (or Luch). Both these lateral glens are understood to be in the Ghorband district.	100
	TOTAL	1,840

"Peacocke mentions several other sections, as the Sadmarda, Hasht Khoja and Daulat Beg. But the first named are in Jalmish, and the Hasht Khoja on the Surkhab, while the Daulat Beg (or Pai) are a division of Besud Hazaras. There may be a few of each of these and of others living in the Shaikh Ali district, but their location is not knwon.

"The Shaikh Alis are cultivators and also own a considerable number of sheep and cattle. The numbers are given by Peacocke as under:

Dai Kalan	150 flocks	1,200	head of cattle
Naiman	40 "	600	" "
Karluk	200	700	
Ali Jam	10	200	
Babar	10	200	
TOTAL	410	2,900	

"The number in each flock is not stated, but the average is not likely to be less than 200 head. Even this would not give the large total of 82,000 sheep belonging to the Dara Shaikh Ali alone.

"The people of the Dara Shaikh Ali are partly Sunnis, the only instance, with the exception of the Kala Nao tribe, of Hazaras holding the orthodox form of the Mussalman faith. The sunnis, as may be gathered from the table just given, are those living in the lower part of the valley, while the whole of the upper part is still Shiah. From this it may be inferred that the Sunni Shaikh Alis have become so under pressure from their Afghan neighbours, and that they are still (in all probability) Shiahs at heart like the Hazaras of Kala Nao.

"The Shaikh Alis of the Dara Shaikh Ali appear to be on the whole very well-to-do. They are also (perhaps in consequence) the quietest and best behaved of the race.

"The Dara Turkoman and Parsa glen.--The Dara Turkoman is a very large valley between the Koh-Darwaz, the eastern extension of the Koh-i-Baba, and the Paghman range. At its head is the small district of Kesh, consisting of some half dozen minor glens, which are inhabited by Besud Hazaras, and belong to the Besud district. The Dara Turkoman was described to Peacocke as a beautiful, fertile, and well-wooded valley. It appears to be the main source of fuel in this part of the country, and the wood used for smelting the ore at Farinjal lead mines is taken from it.

"The Dara Turkoman does not lie parallel to the Dara Shaikh Ali, but, starting from the Kotal-i-Lakshan on the watershed of the Helmand, it runs about northeast for some 80 miles and then turns north, contracting to a narrow defile at, or below, the village of Loling. Issuing from this defile, the stream joins that of the Dara Shaikh Ali just above Kala Doab, as already stated.

"The people of the Dara Turkoman were originally Turkomans, refugees from their own country, but have long been settled in their present location. They are so much intermarried and mixed with the Hazaras as to be themselves Hazaras to all intents and purposes. And this was the case so far back as the time of Babar, who attacked and plundered the Turkoman Hazaras after crossing the Shibar pass on his winter march from Herat to Kabul (1506-7). Little is known of these people, but they seem to be numerous. Dafadar Amir Khan says there are 3,000 families in three sections--Shadi Beg, Mansuri, and Ali Madat. According to Peacocke's information, there are 4,000 families, and they have four taifas--Bacha Shadi, Mansur, Khidar, and Surkh. The last-mentioned figure seems a large estimate, but it doubtless includes the 300 families of Shaikh Alis, who live, as Drummond was informed, at Darwaz. Possibly also the 500 families of Parsa Hazaras located, according to the same authority, in the Parsa glen, a lateral valley of some size, which runs down from the Paghman range and opens into the Ghorband valley at Chahardeh, several miles below Kala Doab. Practically nothing is known of the Parsa glen or of its inhabitants. According to existing information, it would appear safe to put down the population of the Dara Turkoman and Dara Parsa together at 4,000 families. Though not exactly Shaikh Alis, they must be reckoned with them for present purposes.

"The total population of the Shaikh Ali district may, therefore, be estimated at about 6,000 souls.

"The Hakim in 1886 was Mir Sultan, a Kandahari Afghan, who was also Kotwal (Naib Kotwal?) of Kabul city. It is not known what the revenue of the district may be, but it is no doubt regularly assessed and paid.

"Roads.-- Besides the main road which runs along the whole length of the Dara Shaikh Ali, and goes over the Shibar Kotal to Bamian--there are numerous tracks over the high range to north and south, leading in the former direction to the Surkhab, and in the latter to the Dara Turkoman. With regard to those northward over the Band-i-Warsandan (Hindu Kush), Peacocke declares they are, as a rule, very bad and difficult footpaths on the north side of the range, but are frequently practicable for pack bullocks in the glens leading up from the Dara Shaikh Ali on the south. (The Kaoshan and Chahardar pass roads previously mentioned do not start from the Dara Shaikh Ali, but from Ghorband.) The gradients on that side must, however, be much greater than those going down to the Surkhab on the north.

The best of these paths is that up the Dara Robat, over the Zak Kotal and down the Dara Murgh, but it is difficult. There appear to be at least half a dozen tracks leading southward over the Koh-i-Darwaz into the Dara Turkoman and Kesh. They are less difficult than the Hindu Kush paths, some even being practicable for camels of the country. According to Peacocke, the track up the Sagpar glen, and over the Sagpar Kotal to Gulak, is the principal route for local traffic to Kabul, but whether it goes from Gulak up the valley and over the Lakshan Kotal to Gardan Diwal, or over the Paghman range into the Koh Daman, is uncertain.

"According to Peacocke, there is a good camel road from Kala Doab up the Tangi Loling. At the upper end of the defile it divides into three. The right-hand branch goes up the Dara Turkoman, and again divides one road going through Khesh to the Kotal Irak; the other by the Lakshan Kotal to Gardan Diwal. The middle branch of the original three goes (up the Dara Surkh?) to Kotandar in Paghman, while the left hand branch leads into the Parsa glen.

"Supplies. Supplies of grain, grass, bhusa and garden produce are procurable throughout the Dara Shaikh Ali, and probably also in the Dara Turkoman. Fuel is scarce in the former, but abundant in the later. Camel grazing is scanty in the Dara Shaikh Ali, but is said to be good up the lateral valleys.

II.--Surkhab and Jalmish.

"From the Shibar Kotal westwards the country is occupied by the Darghan, or Khatai, Hazaras, who cover all the eastern part of Bamian, and will be found described under the head of 'Bamian Proper.' These Darghan Hazaras extend up the Birgilich and other glens to the north watershed of the Dara Bulola, but beyond the watershed the Shaikh Alis recommence, and in particular occupy the Jalmish glen which runs west-northwest to the defiles of the Bamian stream locally known as the Aodara.

"Jalmish itself is in the Aodara. The main valley for a short distance up and down, and the mouth of the glen, is known as Dahan-i-Jalmish. Here there is cultivation and a small population, but above and below Dahan-i-Jalmish the Aodara is an impassable gorge, and without inhabitants as far down as Baghak, where there are Tajiks. West of the Aodara, the Zarsang glen, joining at Baghak, is also Tajik, but on the east the long glen called the Dara Purkaf is Shaikh Ali. The boundary of Bamian runs northwest from the Koh Jaolangah along the watershed between the Aodara and the Dara Purkaf. Turning west and southwest it includes Baghak and the Dara Zarsang. Below Baghak is Daob-i-Mekhzari, where the Kamard stream joins. Daob-i-Mekhzari is in the district of Doab which belongs to Afghan Turkistan. The people of Doab are Tatars, who are not exactly Hazaras though closely akin. (They will be found mentioned under "Doab" in Volume 4.)

"Four or five miles below Doab-i-Mekhzari the road on the left bank of the river (now become the Surkhab) crosses a couple of spurs by the Karimak Kotal. Here Shaikh Alis re-commence and continue down the river to Doshi. They also inhabit all the affluent glens on both sides. But the Doab district ceases at Shutar Jangal, where is the boundary between the provinces of Afghan Turkistan and Badakhshan. From Shutar Jangal onwards, therefore, the Shaikh Alis are included in the next part. (See Volume 1.)

"The Dara Jalmish is a glen with nothing very remarkable about it except the ruins of two ancient castles called Kala Khak-i-Sabur. It is rather thickly populated, and there is a road through it which will be further referred to.

(A description of the Surkhab from Doab-i-Mekhzari downwards is given under "Surkhab" in Volume 1.)

"Roads.--The road along the Surkhab is of importance, being a part of the winter road from Kabul to Badakhshan and Turkistan. It was the Amir's intention in 1886 to have this made into a gun road, but not much appears to have been done to it. He travelled by it himself in the spring of 1889 with his whole camp and an escort of troops, and Mr. Griesbach reports that it was hastily improved day by day as he advanced. The road through Jalmish is noteworthy. It is the direct road from the Shibar Kotal to Doab-i-Mekhzari, and therefore, to Kamard, etc. It goes up the Birgilich glen crosses the Jalmish Kotal, which is practicable for mules, but not for camels, and descends the Dara Jalmish to Dahan-i-Jalmish. Crossing the stream three times by easy fords, it goes westward up the Muhammad Kichar ravine to the Kotal-i-Pandanao, on a spur of the Ghundak mountain, and, passing over it, drops into the Dara Zarsang. All this piece, and a bit lower down in the glen, is bad. It is no doubt frequently travelled by yabus of the country and by bullocks, but is hardly practicable for troops with mule carriage. Two more kotals are crossed before reaching the Saighan valley at Dahan-i-Peshang. The descent from the second is difficult for mules. Thence the road crosses the Kalich Kotal to the Lower Kamard valley two miles above Doab-i-Mekhzari. The Kalich Kotal is high and steep, although the road on the whole is good.

"There are a number of branch tracks from the Surkhab valley up the glens on either side. Those leading to the crest of the Hindu Kush are all rocky and so difficult in places as to be practically impassable by any troops. Those going up in the opposite direction towards the Surkh Kala valley and Doab-i-Shah Pasand are generally much easier, but none are of any great importance.

"Supplies.--It is not to be supposed that any but small quantities of supplies could be obtained in the Surkhab valley, though Tala might furnish some. However, grass, grazing, and fuel appear to be abundant. Peacocke says a considerable amount of supplies would be procurable in Jalmish, with abundance of fuel, while dried grass is found stored in every hamlet.

Shaikh Ali Hazaras of Jalmish and Surkhab.

Section	Location	Number of Families	Remarks
Sadmarda	Dara Jalmish & Dahan-i-Jalmish (in the district of Bamian).	1,000	Were over 1,600 families, but many moved in the summer of 1886 on account of the locusts.
Karamali	Barfak (40) Dara Margh (40)	80	These are in the Doab district of Afghan Turkistan. Ashraf Khan, Saiyid Hazara appears to have been the principal man in 1886. He lived at Tala.
Ali Jam	Tala (1,000), Tangi Anarbata (15), Ashraf & Paindeh (40).	1,055	
Hasht Khoja	Daman-i-Khilar (15), Dara Wadu (300).	315	
Tarmush (Saiyida)	Dara Tarmush, just above Shutur Jangal.	100	
	Total	2,550 families.	

"Peacocke also mentions the Gaohi, Gadhi, and Kalluk sections. The two former are no doubt the Gawi and Koh-i-Gadi of Doshi and Khinjan; the latter are in the Dara Shaikh Ali.

"As before mentioned, it was these Shaikh Alis of the Surkhab who formerly plundered travellers on the Kara Kotal, and rendered the Bamian kafila route unsafe. The Doab district in 1886 was under Dilawar Khan, the Tatar chief of Doab-i-Shah Pasand. He was put to death in 1889 for participating in Sardar Ishak Khan's rebellion. Ashraf Khan appears to have been local head of the Shaikh Alis, responsible to Dilawar Khan. A guard of 70 Khasadars was maintained in the fort of Tala, and 40 more at Barfak. These men were Panjshiris (Kohistani Tajiks), and struck Peacocke by their magnificent physiques. The Shaikh Alis are also fine, hardy-looking fellows, and are capital mountaineers. They are at enmity with the Tatars, but the small force of khasadars was sufficient to keep order. As already stated the Shaikh Alis have been partially disarmed. Their dress is that of other Hazaras.

"According to Peacocke, the Shaikh Alis of the Surkhab are all Shiahs. They are in fact followers of Aga Khan of Bombay, whose representative Sayyid Jafar, formerly resided among them; but he was imprisoned by Amir Abdur Rahman shortly after his accession, and sent to Mazar-i-Sharif, where he is said to have been still in confinement in 1886.

"It is not known what revenue is paid by the Shaikh Alis of the Surkhab. In the time of the late Dilawar Khan, Chief of Doab, the revenue of his district was remitted—that is to say, he levied what he pleased for his own benefit, but it was less than the usual Government demand. Subadar Muhammad Husain says the Shaikh Alis are assessed at a low rate, which is different in different places.

"The Shaikh Alis of the Surkhab do not leave their country to seek employment at Kabul or elsewhere.

"We may now recapitulate the population of the whole country occupied by the Shaikh Alis:

I.	Shaikh Alis of the Dara Shaikh Ali	1,840 families
	Hazaras of the Dara Turkoman & Dara Parsa	4,000 families
II.	Shaikh Alis of Jalmish in the Bamian district	1,000 families
	Shaikh Alis of the Surkhab in the Doab district of Afghan Turkistan	1,550 families
III.	Shaikh Alis and other Hazaras of Ghori, Doshi, Khinjan, and Andarab in the province of Badakhshan.	4,600 families
	Total	12,990 " "

(Maitland.)

SHAIKHAN شیخان
33-38 68-43 m. A village in Kharwar, about 23 miles northeast of Ghazni. (I.B.C.)

SHAIKHAN شیخان
34-40 69-23. A village in the Koh Daman, about 2 miles southeast of Baba Kush Kar, on the left bank of the Shakar Dara stream. Inhabitants: Tajiks. It is a place of some 200 houses, and has numerous gardens. (I.B.C.) Other places with this name are located at 34-19 70-2 m. and 34-14 69-53 m. (LWA)

SHAIKHAN شیخان
35-16 69-29. A village in the upper Panjshir glen, 6 miles above Anaba. 30 houses of Tajiks. (Shahzada Taimus.)

SHAIKHAN شیخان
32-53 69-9 m. A village of 50 houses and 1/2 mile southeast of Urgun. (I.B.C.) Recent maps show the name Qarya-i-Shaikh-ha. (LWA)

SHAIKH BANDA شیخ بنده
34- 69-. A hamlet at the foot of the northern slope of the Lakarai Kotal, on the road to Jalalabad. (Collett.) Recent maps show the name Shaikhan in this area. (LWA)

SHAIKH KALA شیخ قلعه
34- 70-. A village in the Chapriar division of the Jalalabad district, about a mile northeast of Kala-i-Surkh. Inhabitants: Arabs (Khwajazadas). (Jenkyns.)

SHAIKH-MIRAN, AB. -I See BAGHAL-I-KANDU شیخ میران

SHAIKH MIRAN شیخ میران
A place in the Dai Kundi country. A place with this name is located at 34-3 66-14 A. (LWA)

*SHAIKHU شیخو
34-16 66-51 m. A village on the Nawa-i-Binigao, northwest of Binigao village.

SHAISTA KHEL شایسته خیل
34- 70-. A village in the Kot division of the Jalalabad district, about 2 miles west of Madok Badok. Inhabitants: Tirais. (Jenkyns.)

SHAITANA شیطانه
34- 68-. A village in the upper valley of the Helmand.

SHAITAN GUM شیطان گم
A place in Laghman, east of the Badpakht pass, and north of the road from the latter to Tirgarhi. No road passes through this place, and it is only celebrated for a story which relates how a Laghmani succeeded in cheating the devil here in a bargain over the produce of some fields claimed by both. Shaitan Gum is full of foxes, which the people course with grey hounds, and antelopes are also said to be found in the neighbourhood. (I.B.C.)

SHAITUS See KOH-I-SHAITUS شایتوس

*SHAKAR شکر
33-16 67-29 m. A village near Sangjoy, west of Koh-i-Charagah in Ghazni province.

SHAKAR DARA شکر دره
34-56 69-27 A. A stream running northeastwards from the Paghman range into the main waters of the Koh Daman. It appears to join the united Ghorband-Panjshir stream some 15 miles southeast of Charikar. (Kinloch.) Recent maps list the name Barikaw. (LWA)

SHAKAR DARA شکر دره
34-41 69-1 A. A village about 17 miles northwest of Kabul, on the north slope of the low ridge which separates Koh Daman from the plain of Kabul. It is a delightful village surrounded with gardens, grassy slopes, and groves of stately walnut trees. (Kinloch, A.B.C.)

*SHAKAR DARA شکر دره
34-41 69-0. Shakar Dara is a woleswali in Kabul province. The woleswali comprises an area of 418 square kilometers and has an agricultural population which has been estimated at about 23,500. The woleswali is north of Paghman and northwest of Kabul. Shakar Dara includes about 59 villages, 37 of which have more than 500 inhabitants. The villages are listed in the PG as follows: Deh Nau-i-Guldara, Rast Dara, Qala-i-Yunus, Marghzar, Qala-i-Ahmad-Shah Khel, Jangalak, Payenda Khel, Maidanak, Chap Dara, Qala-i-Lali, Kochkin (Kochki Qala-i-Wazir), Dulana, Khwaja Wujud, Qala-i-Ezat, Gawhar Tani, Qala-i-Murad Beg, Qala-i-Dasht, Qala-i-Danishmand, Alghoi, Haji Bakhshi, Seyab Quli, Bedak-i-Guldara, Qala-i-Akhundzada, Jalwanoi (Chalwarani), Deh Balai Guldarah, Dara Guldara, Qarya-i-Behzadi, Qarya-i-Lako (Lahko), Deh Yaqub, Sahra-i-Behzadi, Syasang, Saleh Khel, Sana Khel, Jangi Khel, Fateh Khel, Deh Boyazar, Qala-i-Khwaja Azizuddin, Karez-i-Ulya wa Sufla (Karez Mir), Bala Karez, Alghoy, Anjirak, Baye Lal Khel, Aqa Ali Khwaja, Haji Payk, Deh Naseri, Aqa Ali Shaikho, Qarya-i-Janshah, Qala-i-Safed, Qala-i-Ahmad, Qarya-i-Sulaiman, Turkman, Qarya Surkh Belandi, Shahi Khel, Deh Chuqurak, Qala-i-Yadgar, Qarya-i-Mumen, Qarya-i-Eltefat, Qarya-i-Ghaza, Qalam Andaz-i-Aqwam Kochi (Naseri), and Bech Khel.

SHAKH شاخ
A section of the Khatai Hazaras.

SHAKHA شاخه
A section of the Jaghatu Hazaras.

*SHAKH-I-SAHIB شاخ صاحب
33-35 68-29 m. An area located a few miles northeast of Ghazni. (LWA)

SHAKH-I-BARANTA شاخ برنتی
34-25 69-12 G. A sharp-pointed hill northeast of Charasia, on the right bank of the Logar river, the eastern slopes of which run to the Khurd Kabul defile. (I.B.C.)

SHAKH SANG شاخ سنگ
34-22 66-40 m. A village in the Dai Zangi country. The village is south of Shina and southeast of Asgharat in Bamian province. (LWA)

SHAKI KHEL شاکی خیل
32-59 68-9 m. A Sulaiman Khel Ghilzai village in Katawaz.

SHAKIN Or SHKIN شاکن
32-32 69-16 m. Elevation 6,900 feet. A village in Sulaiman Khel country, south of Birmal. (I.B.C.) Recent maps show the spelling Shkin. (LWA)

SHAL شال
35-5 71-22 m. A large village in the Kunar valley, on the left bank of the river, 48 miles above Jalalabad, having a fort with 200 houses. (Muhammad Ali.)

SHALEZ شالیز
32-28 68-28 m. A village in the Ghazni district, 6 miles southeast of the town of Ghazni and 1/2 mile south of Arzu. (Hastings.)

SHALIM شلیم
33-47 69-48. One of two mud forts (Saleh Khan being the other)

which dominate the mouth fo the Chakmani valley at a distance of 1/2 mile from the junction of the Gobarak stream with the Kurram river. (Kane.)

*SHAMAKA شمکه
34-27 67-51 m. A village located on a tributary of the Helmand, northwest of the Behsud in Maidan province.

SHAMAL شمال
A main division of the Sulaiman Khel.

SHAMAL Or BARGY شمال
33-19 69-33 m. Shamal is an alaqadari in Paktia province. The alaqadari comprises an area of 156 square kilometers and has an agricultural population that has been estimated at from 5,772 to 6,625. The alaqadari is bounded in the west by Jadran, in the south by Sperah, and in the east by Nader Shah Kot. Shamal has some 15 villages, 5 of which have more than 500 inhabitants. The villages are listed in the PG as follows: Baragay, Sayed Khel, Alo Khel, Sawi Kot, Qarya-i-Allahuddin, Ganda Khola, Khelwati, Koti Khel, Kamal Khel, Dawi Khel, Zakarah, Khwaji Koat, Dangar Kalai, Star Kas, Arm Kot, Zamji Koti Khel, and Zamji Saiyed Khel.

*SHAMALKHEL شمال خیل
34-15 69-59 m. A village located in the east of Chakan in Nangarhar province.

SHAMANGAL شاه منگل
34-38 70-14 m. A village in Laghman on the left bank of the Alingar river, 1 mile above the junction of the latter with the Alishang. Inhabitants: Tajiks and Jabar Khel Ghilzais. (Warburton.)

SHAMATI See SHAMTI شمتی
34-40 70-15 m.

SHAMAZAR شمه زار
33-54 68-58. A village in Logar, about 4 miles south of Baraki Rajan. It is situated in a valley, open and well cultivated, though watered only by karez. (I.B.C.)

SHAMBAPUR شمبه پور
34- 70-. A village in the Surkhab valley, Jalalabad, containing 200 houses of Tajiks. (MacGregor.)

SHAMBOL, Or SHUMBAL See JOLAH شمبول

SHAMIL شمیل
The united streams of the Khost district become the Shamil river east of Matun. A village with this name is near Chuki, Kunar, at 34-43 70-53 G.

SHAMSHAPUR شمشه پور
34-25 70-17 G. A village in the Jalalabad district, situated on the left bank of the Surkhab river, about 6 miles above its junction with the Kabul. Inhabitants: Tajiks. (Jenkys.)

SHAMSHER SANG See BAKKAK (1) شمشیر سنگ
A pass with this name is located at 34-38 66-46 G. (LWA)

SHAMSI KHEL شمسی خیل
A village in Laghman, consisting of the following hamlets, viz.:
  1. Watangatu   2. Nalu   3. Krandali.
Inhabitants: Dehgans. (Warburton.) A village with this name is located at 34-45 70-7 G. (LWA)

SHAMS-UD-DIN KHAN شمس الدین خان
34- 69-. A fort in the Chardeh valley of Kabul, included in the village of Sarasia. Inhabitants: Tajiks, about 20 families. (I.B.C.)

SHAMS-UD-DIN KHAN شمس الدین خان
34- 70-. A village in the Surkhab division of the Jalalabad district. Inhabitants: Tajiks and Ghilzais. This village is under the same headmen as Sultanpur-i-Bala. (Jenkyns.)

*SHAMS-UD-DIN شمس الدین
33-35 67-59 m. A village and a dara in Ghazni province.

SHAMTI Or SHAMATI شامتی
34-40 70-15 m. A village in Laghman on the left bank of the Alingar river, 2 1/2 miles above its junction with the Alishang. This is one of the principal places in Laghman, and is composed of the following hamlets. Inhabitants: Shamsher Khel and Khan Khel Ghilzais:

1.	Nilawat	6.	Kala-i-Jalal Khan
2.	Banda-i-Fateh Khan	7.	Kala-i-Yar Muhammad
3.	Ghandi Taria Khel	8.	Banda-i-Mamo Khan Kachu
4.	Deh-i-Sahibzada	9.	Hakimabad
5.	Lakar-i-Akhunzada	10.	Bela-i-Par-i-Daria.

(Warburton.)

SHAMU KHEL شمو خیل
33-59 69-39 G. A village in Upper Kurram, on the Hazardarakht river, about 13 miles west of the Paiwar Kotal. There is a slope near this village on which a considerable force could be encamped. Water is abundant from the above river. (Lumsden.)

*SHANASHI شانشی
34-23 67-17 m. A village located on the Darazqol, southwest of the Koh-i-Chaharband in Bamian province.

SHANGOL See NOACH شانگل (شین)
A village called Shingol is located at 35-13 69-39 G.

SHANUR شنور
34-46 70-18. A village in Laghman, on the right bank of the Alingar river, 3 miles southwest of Badiabad, and giving its name to a small district. (Warburton, Dutton.)

SHAOKRI شوکری
34- 70-. A valley of the Jalalabad district. It contains the following villages:

	Inhabitants		Inhabitants
Mamugai	Kandaharis	- Daodhai	Gurbuz
Mullagarhi	"	- Hazarnao	"
Khan Dara	"	- Kubandi	"
Wakhtinkai	Masuwids	- Sabazai	"
Deh-i-Garbar	Kandaharis	- Maya	Musawids
Shikhal	Gurbuz	- Gargi	Banuzai

which have in all 1,000 houses. (MacGregor.) (This division of the district is not to be identified now. I.B.C.)

*SHAR شار
34-28 67-4 m. A village on a tributary of the Dara-i-Mur, some 7 miles north of Panjao in Bamian province.

*SHARAH شاراه
34-49 67-26 m. A village located a few miles northeast of Qarghanatu in Bamian province. Another village with this name is located at 34-29 67-20 m.

SHARAK KUSHTA See AKZARAT (1). شرك كشته

*SHARAN شرن
33-10 68-44. Sharan is a woleswali in Ghazni province. The woleswali comprises an area of 580 square kilometers and has an agricultural population that has been estimated at from 11,022 to 13,012. The woleswali is bounded in the north by Deh Yak, in the west by Andar, in the southwest by Yusuf Khel, and in the east by Mota Khan and Sarhowza. The woleswali has about 104 villages, 6 of which have more than 500 inhabitants. The villages are listed in the PG as follows: Islam Khel, Asghar, Amni Khel, Barakat Khel, Patt Khel, Tazi Wall, Tati Wall, Tarukai, Jabar Khel, Zadran, Chagan, Chardeh, Chakan, Chambar-i-Zamir, Haji Payendah Moh'd, Khanak Wall, Khachi, Khanigai, Khahu, Khalak, Khwaja Khel-i-Mirak, Khwaja Dur-Khel, Sala, Dagaray, Dalu, Dandak, Zawali, Sulaiman Zai, Surkai Khel, Sayed Ahmad Khel, Shatori, Sharan Khushk, Shehabuddin-Batan, Sher Khanai, Safun, Ambar Khel, Emran Khel, Ata Gul, Algai Khel, Ghuhdai, Fatema Khel, Qala-i-Haji-Ahmad Khan, Qala-i-Haji-Amir, Qala-i-Khal, Qala-i-Surkh, Qala-i-Mirza, Qamarruddin, Kakai, Kashi Wall, Kanawah Khel, Kotwal, Kari, Godal-i-Moh'd Khel, Godal-i-Mamai, Gula Wal, Lat Wal, Mahamad Khel, Godal Kati, Madad Khel, Muqarab Khel, Malekan, Malkakai, Maswass, Moli Wall, Mahraban, Mullayan, Nazar Khan, Niyazi, Haibat, Yaro Wall, Haji Yar-Wall, Shar Ali-Patan, Mulla Patan, Patwall-i-Khohna, Gul, Fut Khel, Haji Dadai, Mohamad Satar, Qartanan, Gada Khel, Mizak, Momen, Khozun, Khudaye Dost, Hanif, Nawabkhel, Qala-i-Fakhruddin, Khalqan, Qala-i-Hazar, Qala-i-Tobi, Hazar Khel, Shahr-i-Kuhna, Azamat, Baz Qala, Sabad Khel, Sultan, Shahnawall-i-Ulya, Shahnawall-i-Sufla, Hafri, Jabar Khel-i-Andar, Karri Khel, Najar, Burj-i-Patan, Chambar-i-Haji Rozhan, Taraki Khel-i-Sharan, Babu Khel, Nazuk Wall, Haji Khel, Haji Khel-i-Kuchi, and Kok Khel.

SHARFAK شرفك
A tagao in Yakh Walang. See "Bamian (District)."

SHARGUL شرگل
35-11 71-29. A Shaikh hamlet in Kafiristan, consisting of 8 poor-looking houses, which, with cattle-sheds, are enclosed by a square wall. It is only a few hundred yards from the left bank of the Kunar, but is invisible from the road. It stands on the left bank of the Shargul torrent, and is about half-way between Nari and Sao. (Robertson.)

*SHARIFKHEL شريف خيل
34-17 69-37 m. A village on a stream, north of Azro and 2 miles southwest of Lahuri in Nangarhar province.

SHARSHAHI شهر شاهی (شاهی کوت)
34-16 70-34 m. A group of villages on the left bank of the Papin river, about 21 miles southeast of Jalalabad. The largest of the villages contains about 300 houses and has a bazar of some 20 shops. The road from Sharshahi to Jalalabad is said (1906) to have been made fit for wheeled traffic. There is a good camping ground here and supplies are plentiful. Fodder for 8,000 animals for one day and about 1,600 maunds of unground grain are obtainable in the village and neighbourhood. Fuel is also procurable. Donkeys of good stamp are available here in large numbers. (I.B.C., Johnston.) This appears to be the present Shahi Kot. (LWA)

SHARSHARI شرشری
35- 67-. A group of hamlets in the Walang valley, 50 houses of Takanas. (Maitland.)

SHARZA KHAN شرزه خان
34- 70-. A village in the Surkhab division of the Jalalabad district, about 2 miles northwest of Ghaurhak. Inhabitants: Tajiks. (Jenkyns.)

SHASHBURJA شش برجه
34- 68-. A hamlet of 12 houses in the Kalu glen, 4 1/4 miles northwest of the Hajigak Kotal. (Amir Khan.)

SHASHBURJA شش برجه
A group of hamlets in the Besud country.

SHASHGAO شش گاو
33-45 68-33 m. Elevation 8,184 feet. A walled village 13 miles from Ghazni and 5 miles north of the Sher Dahan pass. It is situated on the Shiniz stream and is surrounded by a considerable amount of cultivation and numerous forts. An open plain affords a site for a good camping ground, the hills to the east being about 1 mile distance. Suplies and forage are procurable for a large force and a moderate amount of camel-grazing and lucern for horses; water is supplied by 11 karez. The whole of the Kabul-Kandahar Force (10,000 fighting men with followers) camped here on the 14th August, 1880. (I.B.C.)
Hough calls the Sher Dahan pass by this name. (Campbell, Lumsden, Hough, Havelock.)

*SHAST-I-ZAIDABAD شست زید آباد
34-15 69-7 m. A village on the Logar river, about 10 miles north of Kolangar in Logar province.

SHATKHEL شات خیل
A Sulaiman Khel Ghilzai village in Katawaz.

SHATUR KALA شاتور قلعه
34- 69-. A square fort with bastions and high walls, on the right bank of the Logar river, between Bagrami and Kabul. (Kennedy.)

SHAUNKARAI شاون کاری
34- 70-. A pass in the Kabul Tsappar range over which a footpath leads from Pashat in the Kunar valley to the Muhmand valley of Mitai. (I.B.C.) Recent maps show the name Shamkar. Other sources show the name Shaunkanrai for a dara, at 34-40 70-59 m. (LWA)

SHAWAK   شواك
33-25 69-23. Shawak is an alaqadari in Paktia province. The alaqadari comprises an area of 129 square kilometers and has an agricultural population that has been estimated at from 6,530 to 9,950. The alaqadari is bounded in the west by Zurmat, the northwest by Gardez, in the south and east by Jadran, and in the north by Sayed Karam. Shawak has some 24 villages, 4 of which have more than 500 inhabitants. The villages are listed in the PG as follows: Ghalkai, Shabak Khel, Loch Khel, Jani Kot, Tamar Kot, Shamshiri Kalai, Naway Kot, Mazari Kach, Khwajadad Khel, Ibrahim (Baraim), Kar Khel, Musa Khel, Arab Khel, Akhter Khel, Marachan, Nazar Gul (Nazar Kot Shawak), Goran, Sarwar Khel, Lambaly, Sur Gul Khan, Gunday, Sapar Khan, Guldaray, Khoji Khel, and Zor Khel.

SHAWAL   شول
35- 71-. Elevation 14,030 feet. A pass over the eastern watershed of the Bashgul valley, northeast of the Manjam. Over the Shawal pass a footpath leads to Ayun in the Chitral valley. (I.B.C.)

SHAWAZ   شواز
33-48 69-5. A pass leading from Logar into Zurmat, about 3 miles northwest of the Altimur pass, and said to be much more difficult than the latter. (Gaselee, Bishop.)

SHAWAZ   شواز
33- 69-. A village near the pass of the same name, 2 miles southeast of the latter. (Gaselee, Bishop.)

*SHEKARI   شكاری
34-54 68-2 m. A village on the river of the same name, about 8 miles northwest of Shibar in Bamian province.

*SHERABAD   شیرآباد
34-14 71-1 m. A village on the Kabul river, near Lalpur, Nangarhar province.

SHER AHMAD   شیر احمد
A sub-section of Daikhitai Hazaras.

*SHERAI   شیری
34-48 67-48 m. A village on a tributary of the Bamian river, a few miles southwest of Bamian.

SHERAKAI   شیركی
35-6 68-59. Elevation 7,495 feet. A group of hamlets in the Kaoshan glen, about 10 miles above its junction with the Ghorband valley, on the road leading over the Kaoshan pass into the Khinjan valley. There is room for only a small detachment to camp here, on some small fields; there is a good and abundant water-supply, and sufficient fuel for cooking purposes; supplies are available in small quantities, principally from Tajiks. There are several small orchards and patches of terraced cultivation here.
From Sherakai tracks lead eastwards into the Kol-i-Yer, and westwards, up the Husain Dara, into the Nimakao glen. (I.B.C.)

SHER ALI KHAN   شیرعلی خان
34- 70-. A village in the Surkhab sub-division of the Jalalabad district. Inhabitants: Ghilzais. (Jenkyns.)

SHERAN, AB-I   See BAGHAL-I-KANDU   شیران

SHER ANDAZ شیرانداز
33- 68-. A village in the Ghazni district, between Gazni and Kala-i-Nazar Khan. (McLean.)

SHERDAD شیرداد
A section of Daulatpai Besud.

SHERDAGH شیرداغ
A valley in the Jaghori Hazara country.

SHERDAGH شیرداغ
A sub-section of the Jaghori Hazaras.

SHER DAHAN شیردهان
33- 68-. Elevation 8,300 feet. A pass in the hills between Shashgao and Ghazni. It is the highest spot on the road between Kabul and Kandahar.

SHER DARWAZA شیردروازه
34- 69-. Elevation 7,166 feet. The name given to the southern heights of the gorge through which the Kabul river runs to the northern side of the city of Kabul. These heights are the end of a spur running northwards from the Takht-i-Shah, and are, faced from the north by the Asmai hill.

*SHERDOSH شیردوش
34-40 67-15 m. A village in the Koh-i-Baba, east of Sar-i-Qol, in Bamian province.

SHERGARH شیرگړ
34-27 70-37 m. A village in the Kama division of the Jalalabad district, about 1/2 mile north of Kamal Khel. Inhabitants: Tirais. (Jenkyns.) Another place with this name is located near Ghanikhel, Nangarhar, at 34-12 70-47 m. (LWA)

SHERGARH شیرگړ
34- 71-. The name given to the fort built by Sher Ali at Dakka, Jalalabad district, and occupied by the British in 1878, 1879 and 1880. (I.B.C.)

SHERGARH شیرگړ
34- 70-. A village in the Kot Division of the Jalalabad district, about 1/2 mile north of Kamal Khel. Inhabitants: Tirais. (Jenkyns.) Recent maps show the name Shegay, at 34-11 70-39 m. (LWA)

SHERI JAN GUL شیری جان گل
A section of the Chahar Dasta Hazaras.

SHER MUHAMMAD شیرمحمد
34- 68-. A village 30 miles southwest of Kabul, near the south entrance of the Maidan valley and on a feeder of the Kabul river. (Thornton.)

SHER PAO شیرپاو
A section of the Ghilzai clan, who have mixed with the Tajiks in the Koh Daman of Kabul, and along the north bank of the Kabul river, as far as the east border of the Ghilzais.
They number about 6,000 families and are said to be the superflous population of the other clans of Ghilzais, who emigrated from Kandahar long before the rest of the tribe. (Elphinstone.)

SHERPUR
شیرپور

34-32 69-10 A. Elevation 5,781 feet. The cantonment built by Amir Sher Ali, 1 mile to the north of Kabul city, and in which the British army, under Sir Frederick Roberts, was beleaguered in December 1879. Sherpur is said to be connected with the Amir's palace at Paghman by an underground passage, repaired in 1902. (I.B.C.)

SHERZAD Or MAMA KHEL
شیرزاد

34-15 70-0. Sherzad (Mama Khel) is an alaqadari in the Nangarhar province. The alaqadari comprises an area of 583 kilometers and has an agricultural population that has been estimated at from 12,251 to 35,370. The alaqadari is bounded in the west by Hesarak, in the north by Sarobi, in the east by Khugiani and Surkh Rud, and in the south by Pakistan. Sherzad (Mama Khel) has about 23 villages, 11 of which have more than 500 inhabitants. The villages are listed in the PG as follows: Gharra Koti Khel, Samar Khel (Shorwala Khel), Mama Khel, Khadi Khel-i-Ulya Taw Taw, Khadi Khel-i-Sufla Taw Taw, Surkh Pul, Gar Khel-i-Taw Taw, Laghman Khel-i-Taw Taw, Tormi Marki Khel, Marki Khelha (Kher Marki Khelha), Koti Khel (Katbi Khel), Kundai-i-Taw Taw, Narai Jaba-i-Taw Taw, Kotgai Gandumak (Koatgai), Patla, Ishpan, Wadisar-i-Margi Khel (Wayshar), Gandomak, Shewa (Shawah), Zangzai, Chapar Margi Khel, Sadah Khel-i-Taw Taw, Sangar Khel-i-Taw Taw, and Mar Khel.

SHESNAK
شسنك

33- 69-. A group of villages 12 miles from Tashnak on a road from Kurram to Gardez. There is room here to encamp half a brigade with guns, with sufficient water from a small stream. (I.B.C.)

SHEWA
شیوه

34-34 70-34 m. At 8 miles from Jalalabad the road to Chitral "leaves the hills and runs up the Kunar valley parallel to and about 1/2 mile from the river, through a thickly populated and well-cultivated country, cut up by water channels fed from a small canal, which for a few miles runs alongside the road. This canal is crossed in places by small bridges of tree trunks laid across from bank to bank. For loads heavier than gun-mules or camels they would have to be strengthened. Shortly after entering the valley the first of the numerous Shigai (Shewa?) villages is passed. The Shewa villages are reached at the 14th mile. The latter portion of the road, which lies in the Kunar valley, is very good and shaded by avenues of mulberry trees. At Shewa water and fuel are abundant, and there is enough good ground for a division to encamp between the hills and the river."

The Shewa villages are all fortified with high walls and towers, and a force of 200 regular cavalry and 50 khasadars is quartered here. (Coldstream, I.B.C.) Another place with this name is located on the Ghorband a few miles east of Abgerd in Parwan province, at 35-0 68-59 m. (LWA)

*SHEWAK
شیوك

34-4 66-57 m. A village located a few miles northeast of Spighaw (Espighaw) in southwest Bamian province. Other places with this name are located on a tributary of the Dara-i-Mur, northeast of Panjao in Bamian province, at 34-25 67-10 m.; on a tributary of the Helmand, east of Pitaoqol, in Bamian province, at 34-5 67-21 m.; and on the Logar river, a few miles southwest of Bagrami in Kabul province, at 34-27 69-13 m., the latter is also called Shiwaki.

SHEWAKI شيوکی
34-27 69-13 m. A village on the right bank of the Logar river, 4 miles from Kabul, and connected with Deh-i-Yakub by a bridge.
The road from Kabul, after crossing the river here, branches into two, one road leading to the Sang-i-Nawishta defile, the other going to Butkhak along the foot of the Siah Sang. Inhabitants: Tajiks. There are some 150 or 200 houses in the place. (Kennedy, I.B.C.)

*SHIBAR شیبر
34-23 66-43 m. A village on a stream, some 6 miles east of Asgharat in eastern Bamian province. Other places with this name are located on a tributary of the Band-i-Amir, northeast of Siahdara in eastern Bamian province, at 34-33 66-47 m.; on a tributary of the Dara-i-Mur, some 10 miles north of Panjao in Bamian province, at 34-30 67-2 m.; and a few miles south of Lalchak in Ghazni province, at 33-17 67-14 m.

*SHIBAR شیبر
34-53 68-9. Shibar is the name of an alaqadari in Bamian province. The alaqadari comprises an area of 1,076 square kilometers and has an agricultural population which has been variously estimated at from 8,212 to 9,410. The alaqadari is bounded in the west by Bamian and Saighan, in the north by Kahmard, and the province of Baglan, in the east and south by the provinces of Parvan and Maidan. Shibar has about 56 villages about 4 of which have more than 500 inhabitants. The villages listed in the PG are as follows: Kalo, Piri Kalo, Kuhna Kalo, Khaki Kalo, Tajak Kalo, Mir Bacha Kalo, Pusht-i-Mazar, Miya Mardah, Jawzar, Qol-i-Mirak, Jan Mohammad (Kalo), Jandargul Kalo, Jaw Qol-i-Kalo, Mirka Kalo, Jalmesh, Daki (Daki Shebar), Ghulam Ali Shibar, Shah Qadam Shibar, Sar-i-Shebar, Noka-i-Sar Shibar, Zard Sang, Opar Ghundak (Ghundak), Abdal Khel, Zehburan-i-Pain (Zebaram-i-Pain), Ze Mohammad-i-Pain, Malzar Beg (Hazar Beg), Mardum Belal, Mardum Zehram (Mardum Zehram-i-Bala), Ziyashem (Zehyasim), Quchangi, Khuk Kushta, Dahana-i-Ghundak, Chahar Gunbad, Siyah Khak, Wata Pur, Gorbandak, Bargalech, Bulola wa Shekari, Bulola, Paye Muri, Khaki, Shina Kalo, Ghaibat Ali Kalo, Taraqchi Kalo, Ayam-i-Shebar, Shunbul, Abpar, Welayatak, Ghujorak, Adal Shibar, Iraqi Sufla, Toti Keshta, Iraq-i-Ulay, Qoryak (Noka-i-Qoryak-i Shebar), Keshi Shebar, Jola, Kafsh Andaz-i-Bulola, Abdara-i-Hanif, Jawari Shebar, Sayyid Parak, Sar-i-Jander Gul, Khar Qadam, Madar Qol, Kangor, Toghi, Mohammad Kacha, Baghak, Baldarghan, Sar Khoshk, and Qambari.

SHIBAR شیبر
34- 68-. Elevation 9,800 feet. A pass leading from the head of the Ghorband valley into the Bamian valley. It crosses an open, and rather flat, watershed which connects the western end of the Hindu Kush with the Koh-i-Baba range; it is of special importance as being open practically all the year round, thus forming almost the only communication, the Khawak pass excepted, between Kabul and the provinces of Turkistan and Badakshan during the winter. A road over th Shibar pass forms an important lateral communication between the Chahardar an Hajigak routes following it the high passes on the latter two routes are avoided. (I.B.C.) A village with this name is located at 34-54 68-14 A.

SHIBARAK شیبرک
34-28 67-20 A. A hamlet in the Dai Zangi district of Lal.

728

SHIBARTU شيبرتو قول
34-44 67-27 m. A long glen which descends north from the Koh-i-Baba to the Bamian valley. Where entered by the main road from Yak Walang to Bamian 6 miles from Karghanatu, the Shibartu is about a mile wide, and is bounded on both sides by low hills, its direction being from west-southwest to east-northeast, or thereabouts. There are several villages up it, about a mile to the right of where the road enters. About the same distance below, the valley contracts like the Karghanatu, and its stream escapes through a defile to join that from the last-named valley. Shibartu is part of the Shahidan subdistrict (see Bamian).
The road turns down the valley a little way, and then crosses it diagonally. The lower part of it, like Karghanatu, is barren, and the ground is soft and salty. It is intersected by boggy little streams, and the road is consequently by no means good. ("Shibar" is Uzbaki for mud, and "tu" is the possessive.) It would be difficult to get guns across here, and the best way would probably be to enter the valley higher up, near the villages, where the crossing is said to be better. (Maitland.) A village with this name is located at 34-47 67-29 m. (LWA)

SHIDGUL Or SHUDGUL شدگل
35-42 71-20 m. A Katir village on the right bank of the Bashgul river, a short distance above Bragamatal. 140 houses. (Robertson.)

SHIDGUL شدگل
35- 71-. A fine valley in Kafiristan, which descends south and joins the upper Pech just below the Wezgul-Uzhamezhalgul confluence. It has its head in the main range which separates it from Minjan, and is said to be a cul-de-sac. (Robertson.)

SHIGAI شیگی
34-32 70-34 m. A small district between the Besud division of Jalalabad and Kunar, on the right bank of the Kunar river below Shewa. Its inhabitants are Zakhels and Arabs. The district contains a good many forts of the Kazi Khel Arabs, and is under the Hakim of Jalalabad. (I.B.C.)

SHIGAL شیگل
35-2 71-15 m. A collection of villages in the Kunar valley, 68 miles from Jalalabad; they are numerous and are in and near the mouth of the Shigal Dara. The camping ground of the Boundary Mission (1894-95) was just inside the mouth of the dara, but a better camp for troops would be the corn-fields just below the mouth, where there is plenty of room. There is a good deal of cultivation which extends far up the dara and for 1 1/2 mile below and about 1 mile above the mouth of the dara. The people are Shinwaris. A road leads up the hills on the south side of the Shigal stream over the range into the Katar and Dewaz daras.
On the left bank of the river a little above Shigal are the Shurtan villages (Mamunds and Salarai) at the mouth of the Shurtan Dara, the scene of the fight between the Afghans and the Mamunds reinforced by Bajauris. Since then the inhabitants of these villages have indulged in occasionally sniping at travellers across the river. From Shurtan a road leads up the Shurtan valley over a low pass into the Tangi branch of the Asmar Dara, which joins the Asmar Dara at Dangam. On leaving the camping ground at Shigal the Shigal stream is crossed by a wooden bridge. This bridge can be ridden over, as it is rigid. The abutments look hardly strong enough to resist the rush of the water in summer; the approaches to the bridge, especially that at the

north end, are bad, but could be very easily improved. For the next half mile are the ruins of old sangar walls erected as a shelter for travellers in the event of the Mamunds across the river shooting at them. About 1 1/2 miles from Shigal there is a khasadar post called "Khushk Obo." From this point to near Asmar the road, though fairly good otherwise, crosses several small nalas and descends and ascends a good deal. (Coldstream.) Recent maps show the name Shigal Khwar.

SHIGANU شیگنو
32- 68-. A village on the road from Ghazni to the Gumal pass, between Dand and Mishkhel. It consists of a few forts of the Sulaiman Khel and, with Mest, is the only watering-place on this part of the road. (Broadfoot.)

SHIKARI شکاری
34-54 68-2 m. A village in the Bamian valley, situated at the mouth of the Bulola glen. (Peacocke.)

SHILGHAR شلگر
33-23 68-25 m. A district of the Ghilzai country, south of Ghazni, and lying between the Ala Koh and Takri ranges and the river of Ghazni. The population are Andar Ghilzais, with the exception of the Tajik villages, Rahmak and Robat, each of about 150 houses. It contains about 340 square miles, and a population of about 20,000. The west part is well cultivated with wheat, barley, lucerne, and clover, and partly suplies Ghazni. The country is flat and easily passed in all directions. Water is abundant, and troops would be well supplied.

According to Molly, "the boundaries of Shilghar are approximately as follows: On the north are Kharwar and Ghazni, on the south Katawaz about Kharbin to Jamrud. East of it lies Zurmat; Kalalgu, a Tajik village, and Khwaja Khel, a Sohak village, are situated on the border line in this direction. On the west are the Jaghatu and Karabagh Hazaras. It is inhabited by Andari Ghilzais, of whom I have the following sub-divisions:

1. Lakkan Khel
2. Jalalzai
3. Ibrahimzai
4. Musa Khel
5. Marjan Khel
6. Pir Khel
7. Bazid Khel
8. Rana Khel

"The Rana Khel are found between Chahardeh and Mashaki; east of them are the Jalazais. On the west of Nani in Waghaz are the Musa Khel, whose western borders adjoin that of the Jaghatu Hazaras. On the east of Nani are the Bazid Khel. There are Tajik villages in this district on the east side of, and not far from, Ghazni, viz., Rahmak, Tahsan, and Robat. The Andaris are computed at 2,000 families, and their revenue amounts ot Rs. 1,20,000." (Broadfoot.)

SHIMILTU شملتو
34- 67-. Elevation 11,000 feet. A kotal in Hazarajat crossed by the Band-i-Amir Ghazni road, said to be closed from the beginning of December to the end of March.

SHIMRAM شمرام
A village in Laghman, inhabited by Kohistanis. (Warburton.)

SHINAGAM شینه گام
A tributary of the Kunar river, joining on its right bank. (Masson.)

*SHINA شینه
34-26 66-49 m. A village near Panjshanbeh in western Bamian province. Other villages with this name are located some 4 miles east of Asgharat in eastern Bamian province, at 34-23 66-41 m.; on the Helmand river, some 8 miles north of Behsud in Bamian province, at 34-26 67-54 m.; on the Dara-i-Sialayak, about 5 miles southwest of Bamian, at 34-47 67-44 m.; on a tributary of the Helmand, one mile north of Sherqol in Bamian province, at 34-33 67-48 m.; and on a tributary of the Ghorband, a few miles south of Shaikh Ali in Parwan province, at 34-53 68-31 m.

SHINA KALA شینه قلعه
34-31 69-17 m. Two large Parsiwan villages in the Kabul district, situated on the left bank of the Logar river, 2 miles north of Bagrami, and surrounded by cultivation. (Kennedy.) Recent maps show the name Shina. (LWA)

SHINBUTY شین بوتی
33- 68-. A village in the Ghazni district. It has a fort, and is inhabited by nomadic Ghilzais. A spring of water issues from a hillock near this. (Broadfoot.)

SHINGARIAN See ZAK شنگریان

SHINIA شنیه
34- 67-. An easy kotal crossed by the Kabul-Hazarajat main road about 3 miles southeast of where the latter crosses the Helmand.

SHINIA شنیه
34-23 66-41 m. Two small villages on either side of the Akzarat valley.

SHINIA شنیه
33- 66-. A small glen tributary to the Shorkol. In its upper part it is known as the Haoz Tagao, and is entered by the Bamian-Daulat Yar main road at 1/2 mile after crossing the Kotal-i-Haoz. There is a small hamlet at its mouth. (Pana Khan.)

SHINIA شنیه
A village about 14 miles from Daulat Yar on the main Daulat Yar-Hazarajat-Kabul road.

*SHINIA شنیه
34-35 66-49 m. A village located on a tributary of the Band-i-Amir, southwest of Yakawlang in Bamian province. Other places with this name are located some miles north of Spighaw (Espighaw) in southern Bamian province, at 34-7 66-54 m.; on a tributary of the Hari Rud, north of Asgharat, at 34-34 66-36 m.; on a tributary of the Band-i-Amir, south of Yakawlang in Bamian province, at 34-37 66-59 m.; near Dobuka at the Dara-i-Shibar in Bamian province, at 34-28 67-16 m.; northeast of Behsud in Bamian province, at 34-23 67-57 m.; on a tributary of the Garmab, south of Kamarak in Bamian province, at 34-8 67-36 m.; on the Qol-i-Khesh, some 15 miles southwest of Asheq in Parwan province, at 34-42 68-22 m.; and northeast of Lalchak in Ghazni province, at 33-22 67-25 m.

SHINIA (IN SIAH DARA) See BAGALAK KALA شنیه

SHINIA-I-LALAK, AB-I شنیه لالک
34- 67-. An important stream flowing into the Helmund from the north in Besud.

SHINIA MAKHBUL شنیه مخبل
A small valley in the northwest of the Dai Kundi country.

SHINIA TAKHT شنیه تخت
34- 66-. A village in the Talkhak valley, Dai Kundi country.

SHINIZ شنیز
34- 68-. A river which rises in the Sher Dahan pass, north of Ghazni, and, running northeastwards, joins the Langar stream at a place known as the Do-aba in the Tangi Wardak, 2 1/2 miles south of Shaikhabad. The united waters are henceforward styled the Logar river. (Dutton.)

SHINKAI شینکی
33-57 69-19 m. A pass in the hills between the Shutur Gardan and the Logar plain. The ascent to it commences about 2 miles beyond the village of Dobandi, and is only 500 yards in extent, very steep, and a severe trial for baggage animals. The descent to Kushi is very gradual, and is 5 1/2 miles long. The Babar Ghilzais have a tower on the Kushi side of this pass, about 500 yards from the crest, which marks their boundary. (Kennedy.)

SHINKAI شینکی
32-18 68-10 m. A ridge in the Ghilzai country which divides the plain of Margha from the district of Wazikhwa. It is a western spur of the Sulaiman range, and is probably the same range that was crossed by the Charder pass by the Bombay division going from Ghazni to Quetta. (Broadfoot.)

SHINKAI شینکی
32-47 67-37 m. A place situated some 10 or 12 miles west of Mukur, near Aghao Jan. Here, at Shinkai, the present Amir has established a small cantonment. (I.B.C.)

*SHINKAI شینکی
34-20 69-15 m. A village located some 5 miles east of the Logar river in Logar province.

SHINKAI شینکی
33- 68-. Elevation 9,090 feet. A pass which leads from southern Kharwar to Zurmat. It is easy for animals to ascend to the top, but the descent down on the Zurmat side is slightly difficult. A second kotal, about a mile southeast of the Shinkai, is also easy. (Griesbach.)

SHINKORAK شین کروك (کورك)
34-56 71-15 m. A small village and fort on the right bank of Kunar, 7 miles below Chigha Sarai.

SHINPAD شین پاد
A village on the southern slopes of the Siah Koh range, 3 miles northwest of the Pezwan Kotal. (I.B.C.)

SHINTSA شینده
32- 68-. A halting place 3 miles west from the Kotal-i-Sarwandi over the Sulaiman range. There are no houses, the cultivation being migratory, but a little watch-tower commands the cultivation, and water is plentiful from a spring. Grass is scanty, but there is an

abundance of thorny bushes and low trees for fuel. The inhabitants are Ghilzais, who only remain here in summer. (Broadfoot.)

SHINWAR شنوار
34-11 70-48. Shinwar is a Loye woleswali in Nangarhar province. It comprises an area of 179 square kilometers and has an agricultural population that has been estimated by various Afghan sources at from 6,900 to 9,400. The woleswali is bounded in the west by Achin, on the north by Bati Kot and Mohmand Dara, in the east by Darbaba and in the south by Naziyan. Markaz-i-Loye Woleswali Shinwar has about 10 villages, 5 of which have populations of more than 500 inhabitants. The villages are listed in the PG as follows:
Gulai, Ghani Khel, Anar Bagh, Za Khel, Shirgar (Sergar), Katali, Daga (Daga Ser), Lokhi, Chehil Gazi, and Tor Largai (Siyah Chob).

*SHINWAR شنوار
34-20 69-36 m. A village near the Karkacha Ghar in Kabul province.

SHINWARI شنواری
Where not otherwise mentioned, the information contained in this article has been taken from a paper supplied to the Intelligence Branch by the Foreign Department, September 1888. The paper was compiled from the second edition of this Gazetteer, Jenkyns' pamphlet on Jalalabad, Kaye's "Afghan War, 1839-43," and the remainder from private information.
Boundaries, etc.
The Shinwaris are a tribe who inhabit the country between the Khugianis of the Jalalabad district on the west and the Afridis of the Khaibar range on the east, as well as the valleys running northwards from the Safed Koh and westwards from the western crests of the Bazar valley, between the above two limits; or taking a different view of their boundary, this may be said to commence a few miles east of the Khugiani village of Agam, and runs due southwards to the crest of the Safed Koh, and then follows that ridge in an easterly direction to the head of the Bazar valley; it then curves a little northwards to the Thabai pass, past the Panr Peri hill to the Tsatsobi pass, and onwards to the hill due west of Khargali. It then takes a curve eastwards up to the crest of the hill that forms the northern boundary of the Bazar valley, and then northwards by Loe-Charwazi to the western limits of Laka Sar on the Tartara range; from here it runs to Tor Tsappar, leaving the Kam Shilman valley to the north. The last portion of this tract embraces the Landi Kotal plateau, which belongs to a section of the Alisher Khel Shinwaris, who, since the signature of the Treaty of Gandamak, have come under the political charge of the British Government. Spurs from this plateau run down westwards towards Tor Khan, Haft Chah, Tangi. The land is claimed by the Shinwaris up to these places, but the boundary has not been finally demarcated or disposed of with the Afghan Government. Another branch of the Shinwari tribe resides in the Kunar valley, and on the borders of Bajaur; but although we have heard of these people, we have never been able to get any information regarding them.
The summit of the Safed Koh, which forms the southern limit of the Shinwari country, varies from 12,000 to over 15,00 feet in height, and is densely wooded for a considerable distance downwards with pine and walnut and other trees that grow at this altitude in a mountainous region. Ridges then descend northwards till they meet the plains, forming plateaux and exquisite valleys, with bold scarp sides filled with fruit trees of all descriptions. The view from the hill above Band Kaddi Roghani southwards up the Rud-i-Hisarak

towards the Safed Koh, is one of the prettiest sights to be seen in Afghanistan: well watered, full of forts with massive towers as far as the eye can see, fruit trees in profusion, and in the background the Safed Koh covered with snow, showing black, dark patches where the forests abound. In the Sangu Khel country the hills are not so lofty, nor so well covered with timber, the highest peak not being more than 6,000 feet in altitude. It is more rugged in its nature, and portions of it produce nothing but rock and stone.

The principal daras, or water-courses, with the villages near them are: First, the western, the Agam or Chapriar Dara, which is joined by a lesser stream known as the Kambo. The villages are Kambo, Pachir, Agam, Chapriar, and Daulatzai, the last three being each composed of twenty to thirty forts or enclosed hamlets. Second, the Papin or Mazina Dara; villages Papin, Hisarak, Mazina, Shershahi, in all composed of not less than one hundred forts. Third, the Kot Dara; villages: Kot, Shash Khel, Jaba, Trelai, about hundred forts. Fourth, the Mahman Dara; villages: Mahman, Maidanak, Chalgazi, Zerbacha, composed of forty to fifty forts. Fifth, the Pesha or Pekha Dara, joined at Deh Sarak by the Nangas and Bandan Daras, and at Pesh Bolak by the Nazian Dara; villages: Pesha, Kashtal, Sandak, Nangas, Bandan, and Nazian, containing not less than 150 to 200 forts. The forts are generally about 100 yards long and broad, entered by a strongly-made gateway and flanked by towers at each corner, the towers rising to 25 and 30 feet, the walls being 12 to 15 feet.

Between the Nazian Dara and the western watershed of the Bazar valley and the Khaibar, a breadth of about fifteen miles, the country is very different. A mass of intricate, barren, treeless hills, with a few small hamlets and cave-dwellings here and there--very difficult, yet twice traversed and re-traversed by General Tytler's column in 1878-79. It contains the hamlets of Chinar, Kasoba, and Tsatsobi between Nazian and Bazar, and above Landi Khana three or four hamlets known as Khargali. Khargali belongs to the Alisher Khel clan." (N. W. F. Gazetteer)

Routes. The communications between the Bazar valley and Sangu Khel Shinwari country is by means of five passes. The most northern is called Tsatsobi, then comes the Thabai, after that Mazuri or Mazrui, the fourth is called Dabbar, and the fifty Shinghai Ghakha.

The Tsatsobi lies near to the Khusrogi cave hamlets at Khwar in the Bazar valley, and is said to be the best pass between this valley and the Jalalabad district. The ascent is by a steep zig-zag about two miles in length, which leads to the crest of the kotal, 1,000 feet above Bazar, and descends in a similar manner down steep, oak-covered slopes, at the bottom of which a well-cultivated valley descends gently to the Tsatsobi villages, where there is water and room to encamp. From here the road runs northwest for 3 1/2 miles to the village of Chinar, from which tracks diverge to Basawal and Dakka. This route is practicable for laden camels. The Tsatsobi pass is historical, as being the route by which Nadir Shah, the Persian conqueror, turned the Khaibar in his invasion of India, when he was unable to advance from Landi Khana to Landi Kotal owing to the resistance of the combined forces of Orakzais, Afridis, and Shinwaris. During 1878-79, it was twice traversed by British flying columns engaged in the Bazar expedition.

The Thabai pass is also said to be practicable for laden camels. In 1878, General Tytler, with two mountain guns and 700 men, forced this route on his way from the Bazar valley, in face of a large gathering of hostile Afridis. The crest of the pass is about 1,000 feet about the village of Nekai, and the path leading up to it is winding, steep, and difficult for mules, its length being 1 1/4 miles, shaded by trees, and overhung on the left by inaccessible cliffs. From the crest there is a similar descent for about 3 miles, the road then enters a narrow gorge 5 or 6 feet wide, along which runs a stream. A mile beyond the plains are reached, and a sort of road leads to Pesh Bolak and onwards to Basawal.

The Mazuri (or Mazrui) leads from Khusrogi in the Bazar valley in an almost westerly direction to the Nazian valley, to the village of Feroz-Sangu Khel. This road is said to be clear in some places, but frequent hillocks are to be met. It is not suitable for laden camels, horses or mules but lightly loaded mules and bullocks can venture along it. Water is very scarce here. The entire length of the pass and road from Bazar to the Sangu Khel hamlet is about 9 1/2 miles; in some places it is very narrow, and enclosed by precipitous cliffs.

The fourth pass, called by the natives Dabbar, commences from Nekai and leads to Dur Baba's Ziarat, and from thence to Kosaba, a village of the Tar Khel Mulagoris. From Kasoba it proceeds to Gado Kandao, and from thence to the village of Suragha in the Nazian valley. From Nekai to Dabbar the road is very difficult, and can only be used by footmen; distance 2 miles; very narrow, with water in two localities; trees abundant. From Dabbar westwards the road is clear; water abundant; and can be traversed by laden camels, mules, ponies, etc. From Dabbar to Suragha the distance is about 10 miles.

The fifth pass, Shingai Ghakha, leads from the proximity of China in the Bazar valley to the village of Gul Muhammad, Karmu Khel, in the Nazian valley. The road seems to be clear and can be used by laden animals. In Bazar limits water is scarce along this route, but further on it is found in abundance. Near a spot named Mari a hillock is met, up which the road leads. Entire length of this route is about 18 miles, tolerably broad, but at places its width is diminished to 9 feet.

The passes from Bara and Rajgul, leading northwards to the Shinwari country, are named Sandana, Tordara, Tanara Morgha, taken in the order going from east to west.

The Sandana leads from Bara, from the ziarat of that name, which lies close to the hamlet of Kazi Sipah, and proceeds to the village of Gul Muhammad, Karmu Khel, in the Nazian valley. This road is said to have been a difficult one, and can only be used by footmen, unladen animals like bullocks, mules, donkeys, sheep, goats, but not camels or horses. It is densely covered with trees and thickets, which in places bar the road. Water can be had in abundance. Length of the entire route about 15 miles, but its breadth in certain localities is very narrow, being limited to 3 or 4 feet.

The Tordara also leads from Bara, and goes to the village of Sapri in the Nazian valley. The road is good and clear; can be used by laden animals of all descriptions, although two or three hillocks have to be faced. In spite of its ascents and descents, this road is said to be the best of all in these parts. Water found in abundance. Length about 20 miles, and its narrowest part 12 feet. Generally used by Afridis going to the Nazian valley.

The Tanara Morgha route begins at the northern limit of Rajgul and leads to the Bandan Dara village Ganzoban, inhabited by the Alijer Khel Shinwaris. This road is represented to be very difficult; can be used by unladen bullocks, mules, donkeys, sheep, goats but not by either camels or horses. Its entire length is said to be about 30 miles, and is very narrow in certain parts.

Other passes giving access to Shinwari country from the south are the Mahman, Oghaz, Papin, and Agam.

Subdivisions. The Shinwaris, as we know them, are divided into four tribes, viz., (1) Manduzai, (2) Sangu Khel, with whom are included their hamsayahs the Mullagoris, (3) Alisher Khel, (4) Sipai. The Manduzai lie west of all, adjoining the Khugianis, and occupy some 16 villages and hamlets. East of these lie the Alisher Khel of Deh Sarak, the Sipai, and last of all the Sangu Khel. Of these four tribes the Manduzai have the reputation of being the best behaved and somewhat tamer than the other sections. The remainder are turbulent and riotous to a degree. Of course the Alisher Khel of Landi Kotal are not included in this category, as now they have no connection with the Amir's Government, and for ages have been engaged in trade and carrying goods for merchants between Peshawar and Jalalabad, which has got rid of a great part of the turbulent nature that they once had in common with their brethren of Deh Sarak. The Mirjan Khel section of the Sangu Khel, who in their origin were Ghilzais, are amongst the most notorious robbers of that country; and in their unholy work cannot be surpassed by any section in Afganistan. During the year 1879-80 there were some good elders amongst these tribes, notoriously Yar Muhammad (Maghdud Khel) of the Manduzais, Umra Khan and Azim Khan of Chalgazi (Sipai), and Yar Muhammad Khan, Sangu Khel of Kilajat. But since 1882, trouble has come upon them all. Yar Muhammad, Manduzai, is dead, and his son has been driven away from his home by the Amir's soldiery. Azim Khan went to Mecca on a pilgrimage and died there in 1882. Umra Khan was arrested by orders of Amir Abdur Rahman Khan and died a captive at Kabul. Yar Muhammad Khan, Sangu Khel, also disappeared from this world during 1880; so that now only the young generations of the old maliks are in existence, who have all the faults of their fathers with only a few of their good qualities. The Shinwaris are always supposed to have numbered about 13,000 fighting men: whether this is an exaggerated estimate or not it is impossible to say. This number might be thus divided:

Manduzai	4,000
Sangu Khel	3,000
Alisher Khel	3,000
Sipai	3,000
	13,000

According to "Paget and Mason," the Shinwari tribe numbers between 11,000 and 12,000 fighting men. The Alisher Khel number from 2,000 to 3,000 of whom about 1,250 come under British protection; the majority of this section live at and about Deh Sarak. During the attack on that place by General Tytler in 1879 the total number of assailants, collected in less than six hours, was certainly not less than 5,000 men from the villages between Maidanak and Nazian alone. The N. W. F. Gazetteer gives the total strength of the tribe as probably not less than 25,000 souls. It is probably greater.

Manduzais. The Manduzais live in the Rud-i-Hisarak; their most northerly village on this stream is known as Fakir Khel. From here their country extends southwards to the Oghaz Dara (valley of walnuts) and up it to the crest of the Safed Koh. Two villages in this limit are inhabited by Mians, called Papin-i-Kalan and Papin-i-Khurd.

The Manduzais have, or had, no less than some 120 forts, or large substantial enclosures, in their country, named after the following elders and grey-beards: Osman, Saiyid Amir, Bashar, Gul Mir Khan, Kewas Khan, Shakar, Zamanai, Iran, Malkae Maddo Azam Khan, Saiyid Rasul, Ajab Mir Narai, Gulyar Khan, Badshah Gul, Mauladad Zarif Khan, Kamran, Muhammad Gul, Paidin-Painda Gul, Hajat Sanna Gul,

Saiyid Gul, Hazrat Gul, Ilam Gul, Gandar Khan, Lukman Shah Rasul, Mirs Hasan, Taj Muhammad, Sadulla Khan, Adam Sher Ali, Saiyid Nazim Ali, Baz Kalandar, Bahadur Khan, Dad Muhammad, Jamal Mazae, Gullo, Amaldin, Jamaldin, Saihdin, Gul Asan, Amanat Raza Khan, Sherza Khan, Feroz, Pakol, Baz Rohil Khan, Mia Shahnam, Ghulam Sadik, Amir Shah, Muhammad, Mirdin Amira Khan, Izat Khan, Amira Khan (2), Sarbuland, Khalil, Taus Khan, Saibal, Kaim, Muhammad Amir, Bustan Shah, Zaman, Abdulla, Azimo, Jafar Husain Khan, Ambargul, Rahmat, Bazai, Yar Muhammad Khan, Sarbaz Amirgul, Khangul, Afghan, Majid Khan, Pir Dad, Danran, Mandez, Sher Khan, Sikandar Khan, Asad Khan, Sherin Khan, Purdil Khan, Afridai, Samaldin, Sherdil, Maryon, Mehrmuddin, Ainulla Khan, Habibulla Khan, Naib Khan, Dah Ali, Gul Salam, Gul Sanam Daud Khan, Aslam Khan, Nazak, Lalzad, Mahut, Salam, Dilbar, Jassin, Mirzal, Hamidulla, Khairadin, Salamdin, Tazamir, Sulaiman, Hakim, Sikandar Khan (2), Manowar Shah, Purdil Khan (2), Ganjbir Muhammad Amir, Bastan Khan, Adil Khan, Muhammad Saiyid, Muhammad Amin, Sadik Lukman, Miangul Akhundzada. The Hisarak valley is about 12 to 13 miles in length and its breadth about 400 yards.
Sangu Khels. The forts of the Sangu Khels will be taken under the following headings:
(1) The Ghani Khel of Kilajat near Pesh Bolak.
(2) The Kachkal Khel of Sarobi, which are included with the Tsalorplara, Karmu Khel, Khani Khel, Haidar Khel, who occupy the whole Nazian valley.
(3) The Mirjan Khel of Shaikhan, Kasoba and Chinar between Sarobi and Tsatsobi
(4) The Mullagoris of Tsatsobi, Kasoba and Pakha Mena
(5) Mai Khel.
Ghani Khel: Jenkyns includes the Adil Khel of Nangas Dara amongst the sections of the Sangu Khel, but later inquiries disclose the fact that the residents of Nangas Dara are Alisher Khel Shinwaris. The forts in this valley are therefore entered amongst the Alisher Khel. Forts named after Muhammad Gul Khan, Khanai, Bahraman, Mir Kala, Yar Muhammad Khan, Shergul, Mir Zaman, Mir Muhammad, Haji Walli, Nurulla, Dama Khan, Nur Khan, Shakar, Mir Zaman (2), Hajadzara Kala, Faraz, Saiyida Gul, Multa Khan, Jelan, Kundul, Mulul Nawab Gud (lame), Nasim, Abdul Nabbi, Faruk, Nasim (2), Hajo Kala, Muran Kala, Matro, Matro (2), Sala Khan, Samad Aka Nawasai. This quarter in which the Ghani Khel forts lie is about two miles in length, and its breadth varies in places from a mile to a stone's throw.
Kachkal Khel, Tsalor-plara, Karmu Khel, Khani Khel and Haidar Khel, in the Nazian valley and Sarobi: Yardin, Shamshal, Mir Khush Haidar, Fakir, Aslam, Mahbub, Samand, Ikbal, Rahim, Niazmir, Guddai, Nurai, Fakir (2), Abdul Majid, Lalgul, Mir Alam Zaman, Razai, Kamran, Sahib Gul, Hamidulla Mohmand, Ali Gul, Sazokai, Parang. Zaman (2), Shah Mir, Abdur Rahman, Khairdad, Bazdin, Lalai, Ambar, Nekai, Naib, Umar Shah, Jinabul, Ali Gul (2), Samundar, Sahib Nur, Zaman Shah, Shalmo, Shattak, Taj Gul, Atmin, Gulai, Majan. Zakka Khel, Jalanbad, Hafiz, Hazrat Mir, Bahram Khan, Azad Khan, Kahyasta Khan, Ahmad Shah, Jamai, Saiyid Muhammad, Gulab Shah, Saiyid Baz, Azghar, Yarukai, Bistaradin Muhammad Hasan, Afghan, Shahnam, Saiyid Jan, Sarbaz, Roshan, Faiz Talab, Gul Man, Sadi Muhammad, Zarif, Daim, Gul Rair. Gul Dost, Pacluk, Omargul, Muhammad Amir, Agha Jan, Ahmad Shah (2), Hasan, Gul Sher, Sadulla, Baz, Muhammad, Ahmad Sher, Ghulam Rasul, Sultan, Sarkai, Mir Ali, Ghazai, Kharai Mad Bag, Gul Baz, Medyuns. Baz Muhammad, Khanokai, Dostai, Gulnam, Yusuf, Sohrab, Gullak, Bahadur, Nurai, Sherdil, Mirwal, Jamadar, Narai, Ali, Nur Ali, Jamal Madassar, Mehradin, Rahmdin, Razgul, Gul Muhammad, Saleh Mir Hasan, Zurmati, Ali Mast, Mir Afzal, Daridai, Sher Khan, Bazo,

Saidal, Kamil, Mir Azar, Saiyid Hasan, Zalla Khan, Agha Jan, Ali Gul, Kashmir, Sher Muhammad, Ahmad Nur Gul Mat, Bashakai, Kabul, Shah Zaman, Gud, Akhbar Shah, Ghulam, Zaman, Naim, Shah Murad, Yar Mir, Mughal, Hazrat Nur, Ganjali, Mirjan, Fakir Jan, Bangai Nazar Ali, Sahib Khan; about 450 forts belonging to men of note.
Mirjan Khel: Lal Baz, Shah Baz, Sahahdad, Muhammadji, Anwar, Shaikh Mia Kadir, Shaikh Manulla, Shaikh Muhammad Afzal. These eight forts belong to the descendants of Dur Baba.
Saidokai, Nasir (Mirjan Khels), Saiyid Ali Mullagori.
Mullagoris: Tab Khan, Mahmad, Alam, Fazal, Nadir, Saiyid Shah, Gul Shah Mihrban, Mira Khan, Aoghan, Lal Khan, Kajir, Lalai, Bahadur Shah: 14 forts belonging to the Mullagoris.
Maik Khel: Mashai, Zalla Khan, Karim Shah, Ghulam Janai, Ata Khan, Akbar Sherdil, Tor Gul-Da Khan, Dad Ali.
Sikandar, Jamal Din, Fakir, Sijat Khan, Torai, Tajai Sherdil, Abdulla Khan, Mirjan, Tor Jan, Lawang Gul Shah, Narai, Kuchai, Rahman, Aslam.
Alisher Khel. The Alisher Khel have also been divided for ready reference into (i) those of Landi Kotal and Loargai, (ii) of Bandan, (iii) Deh Sarak, (iv) Pekha, (v) Nangas Dara.
The Landi Kotal or Loargai plateau is so well known now that a further description of the same is hardly necessary. The following sections have their forts located on this plateau:
Shaikhmal Khel on the northeast corner of the plateau.
Piro Khel on the north between the Khuga Khel and the Shaikhmal Khel.
Khuga Khel on the western portion.
Sayyid Khel of Khargali on the plateau due south of Landi Khana.
The forts held by these four sections number 59.
Alisher Khel of Bandan: Forts of Shahdad, Shah Muhammad, Taza, Khan, Walai, Lal Mir, Saifulla, Amir Shah, Raz Gul, Amir, Karimdad, Naoroz, Mohim Khan, Ghazo, Nazim, Zardad, Shahzada Abdur Rauf, Hazarat Shah, Alam, Lal Mir (2), Sahib Nur, Shaz Khan, Zatalla, Sarkai Zaman, Sultanai, Khan Mir, Malakh, Mullukutah, Ganzuban, Lal Din, Senai, Maizal, Guldast, Mastanai, Nur Gul, Sahibjan, Darwezai, Dad Mir, Porchakai, Fadil. (40)
Alisher Khel of Deh Sarak: Mulla Kadir (Pa Khel) Mirdil, Madghalli, Mosam, Haidar (Shaikhmals), Mombarak Shah, Saiyid Ali, Mir Zaman (Khuga Khel), Sahibdin (Shaikhmal Khel), Naib, Majid, Shergul (Ash Khel), Shazai, (Khuga Khel), Khana, Khwaja Mir (Shaikhmal Khel). A ravine intervenes and separates the above forts from those that now follow.
Mero (Khwaja Khel), Naib Mirza (Ash Khel), Kala-i-Akhundzadagan, Izat Khan (Ash Khel), Khan Mir (Shaikhmal Khel), Lal Zad, Saiyid Ali (2) (Khuga Khel), Zainulla Khan, Taib (Shaikhmal Khel), Darwazai, Hazarat Mir, Mobarak Shah, Sultan Mir, Zainulla, Rahmat, Azam Khan, Sahib Shah, Sardar (Khuga Khel), Dad Muhammad, Badshah (Ash Khel), Kahai, Samundar, Dehgano Mir Kalan, Akbar Shah, Gulzar, Miran, Nurai, Lal Shah (Piro Khel), Rahmat (Mirdad Khel), Rahman, Guldin, Kalandar, Jala (Piro Khel), Haidar, Sahibdin, Yar Khan (Shaikhmal Khel), Kala-i-Akhundzadagan (2), Azmat Khan, Saiyid Muhammad, Isa Khan (Khuga Khel), Niaz Mir and Muhammad (Akhundzadas). (57)
Alisher Khel of Pekha: The forts in this valley are Abdur Rahman (Piro Khel), Lal Muhammad (Khuga Khel). Haji (Shaikhmal Khel), Naib, Ghulam Shah, Gul Mast (Piro Khel). Mulla Mino, Imam of the Masjid, Ajar Khan, Hazrat Shah (Piro Khel), Lal Beg, Sargand, Mad Hissam (Pa Khel), Mardan, Ahbat, Yaro, Sagnai Muhammad Amir, Lal Muhammad (Khuga Khel), Shah Khan Mir Ghulam (Piro Khel), Mia Jan (Khuga Khel), Naukar, Bahram Muhammad Amir, Amir (Piro Khel), Mohsin, Shahi, Yardin, Yar Muhammad, Mir Muhammad, Mir Juma Khan, Naib, Mir

Ahmad (Piro Khel), Ibrahim, Mosam Khan (Shaikhmal Khel), Samand (Khuga Khel), Shah Mir, Zamin (Piro Khel), Mushaduddin and Iram, Abdur Rahman, Jan Baz, Mira Khan, Alfai, Shahshak, Azad, Nasir, Zafaran (Piro Khel), Saiyid Ghulam, Sahibdin, Osman, Zobar, Amir Shah. (54)

Alisher Khel of Nangas Dara: Alisherzai, Shahzai, Mulko. Mahmud, Langar, Ghazal, Shahnak Mir, Ullus Mir, Zazai, Ganjai, Alam Khan, Admir, Yadmir, Hazrat Mir, Malik Mir, Barai, Shahwali Dagai, Yadmir (2), Rahim Khan, Paiao, Ganjai (2), Mulla Sikandar, Kamran, Shaz Khan, Uzbak, Shah Murad, Nurai, Rahmatulla, Purdil, Mirdil, Niaz Mir, Ghaljai, Durani, Langar (2). (36) The Alisher Khel therefore have in all about 246 forts spread over the country held by them.

The Sipais. The Sipai appear not to be so well provided with fortresses as the rest of the Shinwaris. These will be noted as they appear in certain quarters of their country, recognised by the local names given to the tract or quarter.

In Chalgazi they have forts of Umra Khan, Azim Khan, Sher Muhammad Khan, Badruddin, Lal Mir, Sultan Ujjam.

In Maidanak. Tor. Khanzada, Ghaumbaz, Torkaka, Shahi Khan.

In Girdai. Samand, Muhabbat Khan, Khairo.

In Baltan. Bostan, Ganjai, Azim Bai Khan, Alam Khan, Akbar Khan, Muhammbat Khan.

In Tanga. Lala, Nazim, Shakir, Naimdar.

In Makranai. Alidad, Bazai, Bostan, Lal Mir, Yad Mir.

In Dawarai. Shakar (2), China.

In Morgai. Lal Mir, Sultan Jan, Kagi Mir, Alam Khan, Saiyid Amir.

In Bagh. Mirjan, Sadulla Zardad Khan.

In Tangi. Daim, Muhammad Gir, Rahim Khan.

In Achine. Afghan, Muhammadji, Khaipul, Bostan Mia Gul, Kano Khan.

In Trelai. Khwas Khan, Mansur, Saifal, Samundar.

The following tables show the subsections and their subdivisions, places of residence, etc., as they existed in 1888:

MANDUZAI

No.	Section	Subdivision	Residence
1	Hamza Khel	1. Ahmad Khel	Deh Bala / Narai
		2. Maghdud Khel	Gagra / Faqir Khel / Marhez / Gaijana
2	Ilias Khel	1. Kuki Khel	Deh Bala
		2. Daulat Khel	Deh Bala
		3. Kotwal	Nari / Charwazi
3	Hasan Khel	1. Umar Khel	Yaghaiband / Tarnao / Tsandalai
		2. Musi Khel	Shpola / Narai
		3. Da Oghaz Kandi	Aka Khel / Gurguri / Oghaz

SANGU KHEL

1	Ghani Khel, incl. Ghaus Khel	1. Baba Nmasi	Kilajat
		2. Dada Nmasi	"

		3.	Akan Nmasi	"
2	Kachkal Khel	1.	Hazarmia Nmasi	Sarobi
		2.	Sahib Khan Nmasi	"
3	Tsalor-plara	1.	Zarin Nmasi	They occupy the lower end of the Nazian Dara
		2.	Kandi Khel	
		3.	Bara Khel	
		4.	Mazid Khel	
		5.	Mirki Khel	
4	Karmu Khel	1.	Azara Nmasi	They live in the Nazian Dara above Tsalor-plara
		2.	Walak Nmasi	
		3.	Shah Wali Nmasi	
5	Khani Khel	1.	Khwajun Nmasi	In Nazian Dara above Karmu Khel
		2.	Malun Nmasi	
		3.	Janun Nmasi	
6	Haidar Khel	1.	Badia Nmasi	In the top of Nazian Dara
		2.	Bazai Nmasi	
7	Mirjan Khel	1.	Darbaba Nmasi	Shaikhan
		2.	Wari Nmasi	In Kasoba and Chinar between Sarobi & Sisobi
		3.	Ana Nmasi	
7	Mirjan Khel	4.	Sanzi Nmasi	
		5.	Bangin Nmasi	
		6.	Godin Nmasi	
8	Mullagoris *	1.	Par Khel	They occupy Tsatsobi, Kosoba & Pakhamena
		2.	Tar Khel	
		3.	Kamal Khel	
9	Mai Khel	1.	Ata Khan party	Dadghara or Sholgar.
		2.	Masha's party	
10	Adil Khel (said to be Alisher Khel, not Sangu Khel)	1.	Usman Khel	In Nangas Dara adjoining the Pekha Rud.
		2.	Kuru Khel	

* The origin of the Mullagoris is not clear; and they are not acknowledged by either Shinwaris, Mohmand or Afridis. Merk is of opinion that they are remnants of the Dilazaks.

ALISHER KHEL

1	Khuga Khel	1.	Fatima Nmasi	Loargai, Deh Sarak, Pekha
		2.	Basai Nmasi	Loargai, Deh Sarak
		3.	Ashrapai Nmasi	Loargai, Deh Sarak
		4.	Alam Khan Nmasi	Pekha, Loargai
2	Shekhmal Khel	1.	-------	Deh Sarak and Pekha
		2.	Ghani Nmasi	Loargai
		3.	Talib Khel	"
3	Piro Khel	1.	Mat Khel	" Deh Sarak, and Pekha
		2.	Shudan Khel	Loargai, Deh Sarak
4	Piset Khel	1.	Shamu Khel	Darband, Khargali
		2.	Rostam Khel	Loargai
5	Mirdad Khel	1.	Tirai Nmasi	"
		2.	Ganjun Nmasi	"
		1.	Shahmad Nmasi	"

6	Ash Khel	2.	Alijan Nmasi	------
		3.	Kamal Nmasi	Deh Sarak
		1.	Badia Nmasi	------
7	Otar Khel	2.	Nur Gholam Nmasi	
		3.	Kadir Nmasi Nil	------
8	Pa Khel		Nil	Pekha Rud

SIPAI

1	Haidar Khel	1.	Nimidar	Trelai and Maidanak
		2.	Mama Khel	Landal, Maidanak Trelai, Dannai
		1.	Lala Nmasi	Sunduk, Achim Battan
		2.	Ata Nmasi	Chalgazi, Battan Tanga
2	Babar Khel	3.	Aka Nmasi	Rushkai
		4.	Fatima Nmasi	Battan
		1.	Mamai Khel	Chalgazi and other villages
3	Rahimdad Khel	2.	Aka Khel	------
		3.	Ya Khel	------

* Hastings subdivides the Alisher Khel as follows:

Sections	Fighting men	Villages
Khwaja Khel	800	Loargai and Deh Sarak
Shaikhmal Khel	600	Ditto
Ash Khel	200	Ditto
Pirwal Khel	800	Loargai and Pekha
Pa Khel	20	Deh Sarak
Shaikhai	100	Bandar
Kali Khel	300	Bandar and Deh Sarak
Past Khel	300	Loargai, Khargali, Darband, Bagh and Bandar

(The word "Nmasi" used in the above table is the plural of the Pushtu word "Nmasi," signifying a grandson. It is used by the tribe and denoting offspring or descendants generally.)

History

The origin of the Shinwari tribe is shrouded in gloom. They say that the ancestor of the tribe was a Pathan or Afghan, whose very name they are unacquainted with; that he married the daughter of a Saiyid, and that this accounts for the indomitable bravery and courage their tribesmen have always displayed; and that, being descended from a Saiyid on the mother's side, they were respected by all rulers of Afghanistan, except Amir Abdur Rahman Khan, who alone raised his sword and the hand of oppression against the descendant of Saiyids.

The ancient home of the tribe was in Ghora Margha, wherever that locality may be. In all probability the Shinwaris figured in the excursions of Mahmud of Ghazni, and gradually occupied the country they now live in after the same had been conquered. We can put aside the traditions of the past centuries, and deal with what we have seen and noticed regarding them in our times, for which we have some tangible, and perhaps a little clearer, data to go upon.

The British Government was first brought into contact with the Shinwari tribe during th Afghan War of 1839-42. A post of 250 men under command of Captain Ferris was located at Pesh Bolak, with the object of keeping the communications open between Jalalabad and Peshawar via the Khaibar pass. The unsettled feeling which existed all over Afghanistan against the occupation of their country by us gradually extended to the Shinwaris, although Pesh Bolak did not belong to them at all. On the 13th November 1841, a party of Mohmands from Gulahi, assisted by Shinwaris, numbering in all 2,000 men, attacked our picquets, and the whole party were compelled to take shelter in a dilapidated fort. The assailants were then joined by the Sangu Khel from Nazian and other quarters, and the Alisher Khel of Deh Sarak, until their numbers reached 5,000. The ammunition of the garrison running short, Captain Ferris withdrew it with little loss, and eventually reached Peshawar on the 21st November 1841. When General Pollock had forced the Khaibar and reached Jalalabad, it was deemed advisable to punish the Shinwaris and men of Gulahi, who had captured 18,000 to 20,000 rupees in cash, and secured a gun which was retained in Deh Sarak. A brigade under General Monteath moved out to execute these orders in the month of June. On the 20th he moved to Gulahi, and the work of destruction commenced; 35 forts were burnt or blown up; the fruit trees were ruined and destroyed; 10,000 rupes in cash and some other property were recovered as well as the gun; and the expedition having moved to Mazina, returned to Jalalabad on the 3rd of August, having lived entirely on the produce of the country during the time they were in it.

After 1842 our dealings in every form and shape ceased with the Shinwaris of the Jalalabad district; and it was not till the last war against Afghanistan had commenced again that we came in contact with them once more. The Alisher Khel of Maidanak had fired on a party of our officers and men who had gone into their country on the 18th March 1879; and, to punish them for their conduct, a force under Brigadier-General J. Tytler, C.B., V.C., proceeded to Maidanak on the 24th March: and in the engagement that ensued 200 Shinwaris are said to have been killed and wounded. On the night of the 24th December 1879 a party of Manduzai Shinwaris came down and cut up some 20 kahars who were being invalided to India from Jalalabad, and who, having permitted the escort to proceed onwards, had stopped for the night at Chorgali, in spite of all remonstrances, instead of going on to Barikao. The Manduzais were said to have been sheltered and fed at the Durani village, Banda Kaddi Roghani in the Rud-i-Hisarak. At the end of December a party of 200 infantry, 120 cavalry and two field guns, under command of Colonel Mackenzie, C.B., Commandant 3rd Bengal Cavalry, were sent against this village: its headmen were secured and conveyed prisoners to Jalalabad.

Owing to the exertions of Yar Muhammad Khan of Mahrez, and his son Armia Khan, who remained with the Chief Political Officer at Jalalabad, the Manduzais continued peaceful and remained quiet for several months. But certain changes and the preachings of Mulla Fakir again stirred them up during the following May; and on the 18th of that month a force of 715 rifles, 245 sabres and four guns, all under command of Brigadier-General Gib, advanced against Hisarak and Mazina. In the action that insued the enemy were defeated with a loss of 120 killed, 200 wounded, whilst three of their flags fell into our hands. The troops returned to Pesh Bolak on the 22nd May 1880. With the evacuation of Eastern Afghanistan that year our connection with the Ningrahar Shinwaris also ceased, and their dealing remained in the hands of Amir Abdur Rahman Khan.

During the period that we occupied the country between Landi Khana and Dakka, we found that the Ningrahar Shinwaris claimed certain portions of the road, and this claim being admitted, the tribes were called upon to locate chokidars at them, and for this they were paid by our Government. Thus the Sipais had their post at Tor Kham, 2,000 yards west of Landi Khana; the Manduzais at Painda Khak and Darband Sar, whilst the men of Deh Sarak held Jirga, near Haft Chah. Beyond this the land belonged to the Mohmands, and they were answerable for the safety of the road. When Amir Abdur Rahman Khan took the management of this road in his own limits, he determined to keep it open by the employment of Mohmand khasadars, and ignored in toto all and every claim of the Shinwaris to any share or allowances in the same. The result was obvious and the Shinwaris, finding redress impossible, resorted to arms and took the matter into their own hands.

These troubles commenced in earnest about the month of October 1882 although the bubblings of discontent amongst the four Shinwari tribes were apparent some time even before this period. The Sangu Khel held consultations amongst themselves as to the procedure they should adopt to secure their lawful rights. Their example was followed by the Alisher Khel, the Sipai and the Manduzai. It was resolved unanimously to take united action, and to set aside private and tribal quarrels; but before resorting to arms it was decided that a united jirga should be sent to Kabul, with the object of representing their right to the Amir, and to solicit redress of their grievances. The jirga went in October, and having gained nothing, returned to their homes in December 1882, greatly dissatisfied at the treatment they had received. After this the Khan of Lalpura summoned a jirga to meet him at Basawal; these were secured and sent on to Kabul, where a number of them were executed, and the remainder cast into prison. At Basawal, whilst trying to escape, one of the Shinwaris named Ashraf was wounded by a rifle shot.

Instigated by Sardar Muhammad Hasan Khan and Mir Bacha, who had taken shelter in their country, the Sangu Khel commenced raiding into the Amir's limits and at the same time moved their families into safer localities in their hills. Letters were also forwarded to the Loargai Shinwaris and the Zakka Khel soliciting assistance from them, as their jirga had been arrested and sent on to Kabul in contravention of the usual custom, which held that the persons of all such members sent in by a tribe were always considered sacred, and whose liberties should not be interefered with. About the commencement of January 1883 news was received that the Sangu Khel had commenced collecting in large numbers. On the 4th January a party of 70 Sangu Khel attacked a convoy between Landi Khana and Dakka, escorted by 15 sowars, who fled at the first shot. One camel was killed, three were wounded, as well as a pony; two loads were carried off; and the rear of the kafila fled back to Dakka. Another convoy proceeding from Landi Khana to Dakka was attacked on the 6th January; but this time, the guard being ample, the raiders were easily driven away. On the 11th January a large gathering of Sangu and Mirjan Khel having collected at Painda Khak, the convoy was not permitted to proceed onwards lest it should receive severe injuries at the hands of the raiders. The Sangu Khel then moved on Khargali and boldly attacked the Khan of Lalpura's men, and a free fight took place; the road beyond Landi Khana towards Dakka remained closed for days; at last want of provisions, and finding they could do no ultimate good, induced the tribesmen to disperse to their homes. On one occasion the raiders secured some thousands of rupees from some Shikarpuri Hindus; but although they had dispersed, their offences towards Basawal and Paindeh Khak continued at intervals until 1885, when Sartip Muhammad Husain, Ghilzai, was appointed to the command of the khasadars, their numbers regularly organised, and Malik Lahor nominated their Sad-Bashi. After that the road between Landi Khana and Dakka was rendered tolerably safe.

Amir Abdur Rahman Khan arrived at Jalalabad from Kabul on the 2nd February 1883. His Highness had determined to thoroughly punish the Shinwaris for their numerous offences, and during the latter end of March he had induced all the Shinwari tribes to send to him hostages from their different sections, who were required to be men of good families. These hostages, with all their women and children, were located at Kala-i-Shahmard Khan and in Besud. Each man was allowed one Kabuli rupee daily for the family expenditure. After a few day's residence the whole of them managed to escape to their country. The Sangu Khel outrages not having yet been disposed of, the Amir took a fresh step and determined to make all the Shinwari tribes pay up yearly seh-kot revenue; i.e., a third of the annual produce of all their hands, which was quite contrary to the rule under which the former rulers of Afghanistan had dealt with the tribesmen of the Safed Koh. The Shinwaris held meetings and determined to oppose this measure in every way.

During the month of April 1883 the Amir sent Ghulam Haidar Khan, Orakzai (who had lately come from the Mangal country, where he had crushed that tribe and been raised to the rank of General for his services), at the head of two regiments of infantry, one of cavalry, and about six guns to Pesh Bolak to attack the Shinwaris. The troops were assisted by local levies under the different Mohmand Khans of Lalpura, Baro, Shershai, Girdao, etc., and the headmen of the Khugianis. Ghulam Haidar Khan having reached Pesh Bolak, moved on to Maidanak, where all the Shinwaris had collected to oppose him. In the encounter that followed the Amir's troops were victorious, suffering merely a loss of 14 to 15 killed. The Shinwaris could make no stand against the artillery fire; and a number of the Adil Khel, who are reported to be their bravest clan, took shelter in the fort of Khan Mir, which was near at hand. The guns were then turned on this fort, its gate was set on fire, and the Adil Khels rushing out were nearly all killed or made prisoners. The Shinwari loss was about 150 to 200 killed, whilst 50 of their number were captured. The heads of the slain were despatched to Jalalabad, where they were exposed in the plain between the fort and Shahmard Khan's garden. Ghulam Haidar destroyed as many forts as he was able to do, as well as their standing crops. The Shinwaris then dispersed to their hills. After traversing several valleys and doing the utmost damage, Ghulam Haidar returned to Jalalabad with the bulk of his troops in May 1883, leaving only one troop of cavalry, 300 khasadars, and four guns as a guard over Pesh Bolak.

Sardar Muhammad Hasan Khan and Mir Bacha, after the Shinwari defeat recorded above, fled to Tirah, and tried to stir up the Afridis and Orakzais to give aid to the Shinwaris in the time of their trouble.

The Amir left Jalalabad on the 10th June for Mama Khel, and after spending two months and a few days there, proceeded onwards to Kabul. After his departure no further movements took place against the Shinwaris. The tribal jirgas were called in to pay revenue, to dispose of the dispute, and to induce them to become law-abiding subjects of the Amir; but it was of no avail. Matters remained thus till the month of May 1887, when Sardar Nur Muhammad Khan (Son of Wali Muhammad Khan, halfbrother of Amir Sher Ali. Nur Muhammad accompanied his father to India in 1880, and resided with him at Peshawar till March 1887, when he fled across the border to Tirah and Shinwari country, and there joined in the rebellion against the Amir.), and Sardar Baz Muhammad Khan and others appeared amongst the

Sangu Khels, and the insurrection in that quarter commenced afresh. We will now turn to the Manduzais, whose homes lie in the Rud-i-Hisarak, at its southern extremity, and extending up to the crest of the Safed Koh. The fixed assessment for the whole tribe in the Amirship of Sher Ali Khan was Rs. 9,035, with Rs. 833 Mehmani and Rs. 446 as Rasum-i-daftar. But this assessment was seldom realised, as it was considered better by the Kabul Government to forego the amount, and secure the good will of a powerful tribe, and in this way win them over. Their headman, Yar Muhammad Khan, was a man of good position and power in the tribe, and could be made very useful, and this revenue was given to him in jagir; and he was also faojdar for the Manduzai tribe. His son, Armia Khan, was also a good man.

When Amir Abdur Rahman came to Jalalabad on the 2nd February 1883, he made up his mind to stop the Manduzai jagir allowances, and realise the full assessment. This decision was communicated to Yar Muhammad Khan, who had attended to make his salaams to the Amir. Yar Muhammad replied that he would go to his tribe, consult them, and then forward their decision. He went, assembled his tribal elders, consulted their wishes, and they in a body declined to pay revenue. This decision was communicated to the Amir, and Yar Muhammad Khan further said "that although his tribe had declined to pay revenue, he himself was willing to attend whenever his presence was required." The Amir's answer was characteristic: "If you are unable to restrain and coerce your tribe, what good do I derive by your coming in to me." The Amir then ordered a post to be built at Deh Bala, and located khasadars in the same. During 1883 various rumours were brought in that the Manduzais were ready to rise, and that troops would be despatched against them, but these rumours subsided again for some time. During June 1884 a force from Jalalabad moved to Hadda, Mazina, and ultimately Mahras, where upon the Manduzais left their villages and with their families took shelter in their hills. They then made preparations to attack the Amir's troops that had occupied their country. Messengers were repeatedly sent to the other sections asking them to render aid at this period. The Sipah Salar, Ghulam Haidar Khan (Ghulam Haidar Khan, Charkhi, who had meanwhile relieved Ghulam Haidar Khan, Orakzai), then sent the Mirs of Trelai, whose exhortations induced some of the Manduzais to return to their homes. The force returned, and at last Armia Khan himself accompanied by 50 men, paid a visit to the Sipah Salar at Jalalabad. This visit ended in nothing. Afterwards numerous jirgas were sent for by Ghulam Haidar; they came; the Amir's wishes were explained to them; they then returned to their homes, and the result was nil. Onthe 18th April 1887, matters came to a climax, the 100 khasadars at Deh Bala were attacked by the Manduzais, three of their number were killed, five wounded, their arms taken away, and the rest were told to return to Jalalabad. On receipt of this news, and under orders from the Amir, a force moved up from Jalalabad to Deh Bala under command of Ghulam Haidar. The Shinwaris had burnt Deh Bala and fled. Several encounters took place, but the Sipah Salar resolutely held his ground, built a very strong fort there, cut down fruit trees, and destroyed everything belonging to the recalcitrant Shinwaris that he could lay hands upon. He succeeded in the end. Yar Muhammad Khan and Armia Khan had later on taken shelter in Muhammad (Mahman?) Dara, where the former died in 1887. Some of the Shinwaris returned to their country, but were not permitted to occupy their houses or cultivate their lands. The remainder continued in revolt, scattered about in diverse hill localities.

Referring back to the other Shinwaris, it has already been briefly noticed that in spite of jirgas being sent for and dismissed, followed by messengers and release of certain prisoners, the Sipah

Salar was as far as ever from gaining his object with them, till the time that Sardar Nur Muhammad Khan and his party of Sardars appeared amongst them during the commencement of May 1887. Muhammad Sadik Khan, former Khan of Lalpura, was then sent to the Deh Sarak and Sangu Khel Shinwaris, advising them to pay up revenue, which they refused to do. Later on they were asked to receive a Kazi and Hakim of the Amir in their country, which was also declined. Raids commenced afresh, and the Amir's postal runner was waylaid near Girdi Kach, and the mail bags taken away from him. During August 1887 all the Sangu Khel, Alisher Khel and Sipai Shinwaris, who were up in arms, decided to assist Sardar Nur Muhammad Khan if he came down to attack Pesh Bolak, where there were one troop of cavalry, 300 khasadars, and four guns under command of a Risaldar. The Sardar, instead of attacking these troops, moved first to the Nazian valley; after that to Nangas Dara, and stopped with the Adil Khel Shinwaris. During September 1887 the Sipah Salar intimated that he had received the Amir's orders to build forts at Achin and Sarobi. In the same month he summoned the Sangu Khel jirga, through Ghulam Jan, and presented them with khilats; they were then dismissed and asked to turn out Sardar Nur Muhammad Khan. On the 7th of this month the Amir's mail bags were again carried off by Shinwaris from between Basawal and Jalalabad, and handed over to Sardar Nur Muhammad Khan. The year 1887 closed without the Sipah Salar having come to any understanding with the tribe, and without his having persuaded them to carry out a single order of his.

The Amir arrived at Jalalabad about the 13th January 1888. Whilst at Nimla some of the Shinwari elders came to salute him at this place, and another party did the same at Sultanpur. His Highness was greatly pleased at this, gave them presents, and fed them. After giving them good advice they were dismissed to their homes. Seeing what had been done for their brethren, other Shinwaris also came in to visit the Amir, and were treated in the same spirit. Sardar Nur Muhammad Khan on this moved up to Tirah.

At the close of January 1888, however, raiding by Shinwaris commenced again. The officer in command of the Amir's troops at Pesh Bolak retaliated and carried off some 550 sheep belonging to the people of Sarobi. After this the Amir sent the Alisher Khel of Deh Sarak and the Sangu Khel of Nazian to the Shinwaris of Pekha and Mahman Dara, inviting them to come in and assuring them that they had not the slightest reason to fear any danger. Their efforts were unsuccessful. It would be a waste of time to relate here all the different intrigues that went on at Jalalabad with the object of inducing the Shinwaris to carry out entirely what the Amir wished. The revenue was to be reduced from one-third to one-tenth of the annual produce, but even this was not accepted. The Amir then left Jalalabad about the 14th April 1888, and as he had failed on every point, the future settlement of the Shinwari question was left in the hands of Sipah Salar Ghulam Haidar Khan.

The Shinwaris had given a semi-assent to the Amir and Sipah Salar that they would receive four Hakims and four Kazis in their country, viz., at Kilajat, Maidanak, Chalgazai, and Oghaz. In conformity with this compact these men were sent in charge of certain Shinwari elders to take up their, abodes at their several posts. With the exception of the two men for Kilajat, the remainder were all turned back and directed to return at once to Jalalabad as the tribesmen had declined to receive them in their country, and the elders who had brought them so far declined to be answerable for their safety. These officials found themselves in an unhappy predicament. Death and outrage faced them in the Shinwari country and if they returned to Jalalabad they had to stand the anger of the Amir, who would have demanded the reason they vacated their stations without receiving first His Highness's permission. Sardar Nur Muhammad Khan also turned up in the Shinwari country after a few days' absence in Tirah.

Ghulam Haidar Khan's patience was not exhausted, as he found that both the Amir and himself had been tricked by Shinwari elders. All the khilats and feeding and kind treatment had ended in nothing. He therefore moved with all his available troops from Jalalabad to Chalgazai and summoned other regiments to be forwarded to his assistance. From Chalgazai he marched to Deh Sarak and halted there with the object of concentrating his tropps at that place. These eventually assembled to the number of:

```
4 1/2   regiments of infantry
3       regiments of cavalry
18      guns
14      elephants
300     khasadars
```

The above does not include the local Mohmand Khans and others who followed in his footsteps with their tribal levies. The number of these men could not be correctly ascertained.

The Shinwaris were taken by surprise at the Sipah Salar's unexpected and rapid movements. Their spring crops had been gathered in and were lying in their villages. They had had no time or warning to remove their families, cattle, and crops to the hills, and had made no preparations for a defence. They were caught unprepared and must suffer for the same. The Sipah Salar remained nearly the whole of June at Deh Bala, and during this period of his soldiery lived on the Shinwaris and plundered them at leisure. Their women were unable to leave their houses and remained inside with closed doors. Like a swarm of locusts the troops and levies cleared out everything in their immediate neighbourhood. Some of the Shinwari sections on this gave in and promised to pay the following sums annually:

	Rs.
Shinwaris of Pekha Rud	17,000
Shinwaris of Deh Sarak	4,000
Adil Khel	1,400
Bandan Shinwaris	3,200

The Sangu Khel and men of Sarobi declined to pay a farthing, and, incited by Sardar Nur Muhammad Khan, who advanced them funds, parties of them turned out repeatedly at night and fired into the Sipah Salar's camp, wounding men and horses.

At the commencement of July 1888, Ghulam Haidar evacuated Deh Sarak, and moved with all his troops and following to Baltan, which lies more towards the Manduzais and away from the Sangu Khel. After his departure a great many of the Shinwaris who had given in and promised to pay revenue removed themselves with their families and property to the hills.

About the middle of July the Shinwaris of Pekha made a treacherous attack on a jirga sent to them by Ghulam Haidar, and many of the maliks were killed. The country remained in a very disturbed state throughout the year, but the defeat of Nur Muhammad by the Afghan Commander-in-Chief gave some respite. It may be mentioned here that Nur Muhammad returned to India in 1892, and was allowed to live with the ex-Amir, Yakub Khan.

In 1889 operations dragged on with no decisive results. Ghulam

Haidar constructed a fort and cantonment at Kahi, but though the tribe seemed tired of opposition they did not make complete submission. In 1890 the Sangu Khel continued to raid villages in their vicinity, to harass convoys, and to attack the Afghan outposts. In the following year no change took place, Ghulam Haidar being still unable to bring this refractory section under proper control, and raids were continued as heretofore. In 1892, however, the tribe as a whole settled down, but recently signs of lawlessness have begun to reappear in consequence probably of the large importation of arms from the Persian Gulf. (N.W.F. Gazetteer, Hastings, I.B.C.)

SHINWARI شنواری
35-2 69-1. Shinwari is an alaqadari in Parwan province. The alaqadari comprises an area of 359 square kilometers and has an agricultural population that has been estimated at from 7,758 to 9,863. The alaqadari is bounded in the west by Ghorband, in the north by Salang and Khinjan, in the east by Charikar and Jabal Saraj, and in the south by Bagram.
Shinwari includes about 25 villages, of which 10 have more than 500 inhabitants. The villages are listed in the PG as follows: Ab Khanah Ushtur Shahr, Astana, Afghania Ushtur Shahr, Afghania Kafshan, Tajika Kafshan, Borj Gul Jan, Sufi Khel, Dahan Kafshan, Bulandi, Tajika Ushtur Shahr, Daraz Gerd, Ser Dara-i-Ushtur Shahr, Shewa, Qashal, Khak Angur (Sangu), Surkh Sang, Qai Kamar, Mullaqi, Kajakan, Bagh Afghan, Heir, Ab Gerd, Qalacha, Chenar Dara, Namak Ab, and Wiwila.

*SHINWARI شنواری
34-34 69-29 m. A village on the Kabul river, north of the Kabul-Jalalabad highway in Kabul province.

*SHIRAZI شیرازی
34-52 68-38 m. A village located on a tributary of the Ghorband river, south of Surkho Parsa, Parwan province.

*SHIRBAZKHEL شیربازخیل
34-43 68-58 m. A village near Qala Lalay to the north of Paghman in Kabul province.

SHIRIN شیرین
A section of the Chahar Dasta Hazaras.

SHISTAR ششتر
33- 69-. A village on the right bank of the Kurram river, 1 1/2 miles distant from it. It lies in a well-cultivated valley a few miles west of the point where the Karaia stream joins the Kurram. This valley is commanded and surrounded on all sides, except the west, by low bare hills. The inhabitants are Ahmad Khel Jajis, and can turn out 500 fighting-men. (I.B.C.)

SHOBA See SHAHBAH شهباه

SHOGHLA شغله
33-25 67-27 G. A place in the Jaghuri Hazara country.

SHOLANA شلنه
34- 70-. A village in the Chapriar division of the Jalalabad district, about 2 miles northeast of Hadia Khel. Inhabitants: Tajiks and Dehgans. (Jenkyns.)

SHORIGUL Or SKORIGUL شوکوریگل
35- 71-. A valley, or gul, in Nuristan which drains northeast and debouches into the Bashgul at a point about half-way between Ahmad Diwana and Pshui. It is about 17 miles by road from the mouth of the Shorigul to its upper end, where there are three branches; that to the south leads over a high pass into the Wezgul, the other two to the west leading over passes to villages in Minjan. All the nalas running down to the left bank of the Shorigul are said to have difficult roads up them, which cross a range of mountains (the main Hindu Kush?) and descend into Minjan.
The Shorigul is a fine valley, with much cultivation in the great bays formed by the hills. About 3 miles from its mouth is the hamlet of Luluk; the hamlet of Ouzhak is 10 miles, and Ptsigrom village, which was being built in the ordinary square fort shape in August 1891, is about 15 miles. There are in addition tiny settlements and watch towers sprinkled all over the district. The road lies up the left bank throughout, and is fit for horses. There is little or no cultivation along the right bank, and the hill slopes in most places run steeply right down to the stream. The Shorigul acts as an overflow reservoir for the population of the Katir part of the Bashgul valley, and has representatives from all the Katir villages. It is very prosperous looking. (Robertson.) Recent maps show the name Chapdara. (LWA)

SHORKACH شورکچ
33- 69-. A small Ghilzai village of 30 houses situated in a large plain about 9 miles south of Gardez. There are many villages close by; water and grazing are available here. (I.B.C.)

SHORKOL شورقول
34- 66-. A large glen descending north through a long defile to the Sar-i-Jangal valley.

SHPOLA شپوله
34-11 70-29 m. A village in the Hisarak division of the Jalalabad district, about 3 miles northeast of Yaghiband. Inhabitants: Shinwaris. (Jenkyns.) A village called Shpoli Baba is located at 34-34 69-32 m.

SHTEVGROM شتوی گرام
35-27 70-56 A. Elevation 8,920 feet. A Kafir village of 100 houses, situated on the right bank of the Presungul, or upper Pech, stream, near the head of the valley. It is built in the shape of an irregular square, more or less convex on the river side. From under the priest's house a tunnel through which a man can crawl on all fours, leads to the water's edge, which is 100 to 150 yards distant. Most of the houses are extremely low; they are closely packed together, and have underground rooms. The top room is semi-subterranean, and there are two apartments underneath it, the one below the other. The village wall is built with great economy of wood, and has a coping of dried shrubs kept in position by large stones. It is strengthened by two small towers, while there is a third amidst the houses, which forms the citadel of the place. There is no parapet or banquette except where housetops or irregularities of the wall accidentally produce them. Many of the housetops are flush with the wall, which is nowhere more than 10 feet high. A road leads west to Minjan via the Kamah pass. Suplies are plentiful at Shtevgrom. (Robertson, I.B.C.) This appears to be identical to Shtevi. Another location is given at 35-13 70-51 G.

SHTEVI Or ESHTVI اشتی وی
35-27 70-56 m. The highest village in the Pech valley. It consists of 60 houses clustered together and not surrounded by a wall. The village has one tower. The houses are one-storeyed and have no underground rooms. (N.I.)

SHUDOSH شودوش
A village in the Sar-i-Kol subdistrict of Yakh Walang. 25 houses of Neka Hazaras. (A.B.C.)

SHUI شوی
35-51 71-22 A. A fortified village of 120 houses in the Bashgul valley in Kafiristan; about 11 1/2 miles above Bragamatal. From here a path leads over the Shui pass, about 12,000 feet, to Izh in the Lutkuf valley in Chitral. It is said to be practicable for horses. (Robertson, I.B.C.) Recent maps show the name Peshawur. (LWA)

SHUJAN شجان
33- 68-. A village north of the Sher Dahan pass. (Kennedy.)

SHUKUR-ULLA-KHAN شكرالله خان
34- 69-. A fort in the Chardeh valley of Kabul, included in Deh-i-Murad Khan, and closed to the latter. Inhabitants: Barakzais and Tajiks. About 30 families. (I.B.C.)

SHULUK Or SHULAK شولك
34-7 68-53 m. A village in the northern portion of the Logar valley, 4 miles northwest of Babus. Inhabitants: Gradi Khel Ghilzais, of whom there were 30 families inhabiting the place in 1880. (Clifford, Euan Smith.)

SHUMBAL See JOLAH شمبل
34-52 68-10 A.

SHUMIA شمیه
A village in Kafiristan, on the Kunar frontier, said to be situated on the edge of a table-land at the extremity of a valley, and to have 1,000 houses. (Masson.)

SHUNAH شونه
34-38 70-14. The proper name, according to Raverty, of the river, usually called Alingar above its junction with the Alishang.

SHURTAN See SHIGAL شرتن
34-58 71-21 A. Another name given is Lar Shotan.

SHUTUR GARDAN شترگردن کوتل
33-55 69-23 m. Elevation 11,200 feet. A pass over the western continuation of the Safed Koh, leading from the Hariob into the Logar valley. It is crossed by the Paiwar Kotal-Kabul road, its summit lying about 43 miles from the Paiwar Kotal. From the summit of the pass a grand and extensive view of the Logar valley is obtained. The ascent from the east is easy, with a general gradient of about 8 in 100 increasing slightly as the summit is approached; the descent on the west is more difficult, and though guns were got down by hand in 1879 it would be almost impossible to get them up with the road in the state it was in at that time. The soil is, however, of disintegrated rock and a fair road for wheeled traffic could be made without very much difficulty. There is no timber available near the summit. Regarding the Shutur Gardan pass Sir

Frederick Roberts, in balancing the respective advantages of the Kurram and Khaibar routes into Afghanistan, remarked as follows in 1880:

"The only period the Shutur Gardan is closed to the passage of troops is from the middle of December to the end of March, and though of course it is objectionable to have an army practically cut off from Kabul for from 3 1/2 to 4 months, still it must be remembered that during this period the plains of Kabul are more or less covered with snow, and that this season of the year would certainly not be selected for military operations in Afghanistan except under very pressing circumstances. But I think I may safely asert that, even in the depth of winter, were a move necessary, an enterprising commander would cross the Shutar Gardan. Practically, therefore, troops quartered in the upper portion of the Kurram valley are capable of being pushed on to Kabul all the year round."
For details of the operations in the neighbourhood of the Shutur Gardan pass in 1879, see the "Official History of the Second Afghan War." (I.B.C.)

SHUTUR MURDA   شترمرده
   34- 67-. A fort in the Besud country. A place with this name is located at 34-29 67-36 G.

SHUTURSHAHR or USTARSHAHR   شترشهر
   35-0 68-52 G. A large Shinwari village on the right bank of the Ghorband river, 18 1/2 miles above Tutam Dara. It lies at the mouth of the Shuturshahr ravine which here joins the Ghorband from the south. At Shuturshahr the road leading over the Walian pass into Khinjan leaves the main road to the Chahardar pass and, crossing the Ghorband river, leads up the Nimakao glen. The Ghorband is said to be bridged opposite Shuturshahr, but it is doubtful if this bridge really exists; the river, however, is probably easily fordable hereabouts; it certainly is so at several places both above and below Shuturshahr. (I.B.C.)

SIAB   سیاب
   34- 69-. A village in the Koh Daman of Kabul, about 1 mile south of Dakka. Its name, three waters, indicates its position near the confluence of the Kah Dara, the Shakar Dara, and the Karez-i-Mir streams; 300 houses of Tajiks and Kharotis. (I.B.C.)

*SIAHBANDI   سیاه بندی
   34-58 71-24 m. A village located a few miles southwest of Dangam in Kunar province.

SIAH BINI   سیاه بینی
   34- 68-. A pass over a spur from the Paghman range leading into the Koh Daman of Kabul from the southwest. It lies 1 1/2 mile to the northwest of the Surkh Kotal. This is an easy pass, but with no well-defined road; it is, however, practicable for all arms, except wheeled artillery, and for baggage mules and ponies. (Kinloch.)

SIAH BUMAK   سیاه بومك
   34-39 67-9. Appears to be the name applied to the upper part of the Sar-i-Kol glen.

SIAH BUMAK   سیاه بومك
   34-37 67-13 m. Elevation 10,375 feet. A village in the Dai Zangi

district of Lal, situated in a large tagao which enters the Kirman valley from the south. Other places with this name are located at 34-29 67-0 m., 34-16 67-3 m., and 34-12 66-40 m. (LWA)

SIAH CHASHMA سیاه چشمه
34- 66-. A fort village of the ordinary type, situated in the Talkhak sub-division of the Dai Zangi district of Lal. Other villages with this name are located at 34-38 66-43 m., 34-21 66-23 G, 34-30 66-17 G, and a well at 34-37 66-43 G.

*SIAHCHO سیاه چو
34-25 68-59 m. A village on the banks of the Maidan, south of the Koh-i-Qorugh in Kabul province.

SIAH CHOB سیاه چوب
34- 70-. A village in the Mahman Dara division of the Jalabad district. Inhabitants: Dehgans. (Jenkyns.) Places with this name are located at 34-10 70-44 m.; about 4 miles northwest of Doaba, Maidan province, at 34-3 68-42 m.; and northeast of Ghazni, at 33-43 69-36 m. (LWA)

SIAH DARA سیاه دره
34-21 67-1. A glen in the Dai-Zangi country, tributary to the Panjao. A village with this name is located at 34-21 67-13 G. (LWA)

SIAH DARA سیاه دره
34-31 66-45 m. A very populous glen which descends northeast to the Zari valley in Yakh Walang. See "Bamian (District)."
A road appears to lead up it and over the Kharkol or Gandao Kotal on the Koh-i-Baba, and so to Akzarat. (A.B.C.) A village with this name is located at 34-55 66-30 m. (LWA)

SIAH DARA سیاه دره
34-37 66-53 G. A glen which runs north and joins the Band-i-Amir valley in the northwest of Yakh Walang. The village at its mouth contains 20 houses. (Maitland.)

*SIAH DASHT سیاه دشت
34-29 67-4 m. A village on a stream, some 10 miles north of Panjao in Bamian province.

*SIAHDEH سیاه ده
33-30 67-25 m. A village on the Nawa-i-Quchangatu, east of the Koh-i-Qada-i-Barik in Ghazni province.

SIAHGIRD سیاه گرد
35-0 68-52 M. Elevation, 6,270 feet. Four fort villages on the left bank of the Ghorband stream and the village of Chahar Burjak on the right bank constitute Siahgird proper; distance 7 1/2 miles below Chahardeh. They contain in all 200 families of Tajiks, with a sprinkling of Ghilzais. There is good camping ground on the right bank above Siahgird; supplies procurable. The Dara Findukistan, which here joins on the right, is a broad valley, with population of 500 families of Tajiks, owning some 700 gardens. A road leads up it to the Kotal Istalif on the Paghman range. This kotal is said to be difficult for pack animals, but is occasionally crossed by lightly laden camels.
The Dara Wazghar joins on the left, and about its mouth are a number of small villages. Here and up the dara live 500 families of Tajiks owning 400 gardens.

At Siahgird, opposite the mouths of these two daras, the main valley opens out to a width of 5 to 6 miles, and a broad, gravelly dasht on the right bank slopes down from the foot of the Paghman range to the river through, abutting on it in gravel cliffs 150 feet high. The river trough itself is 1 mile wide, and is crowded with trees and gardens. (Peacocke.) Another village is located at 34-59 68-53 m. (LWA)

SIAHKHAGI سياه خاگى
34-33 66-32 A. Elevation 10,585 feet. A group of five villages in the Dai Zangi district of Lal, about 50 miles east of Daulat Yar.

SIAH KHAK سياه خاك
34-26 68-29 m. A village in the Sar-i-Chashma valley, 6 miles east of the Unai pass. It contains (in 1904) 40 families of Taimuris; headman, Ghulam Nabi. The inhabitants possess about 60 head of cattle and 100 sheep and goats. The annual production of wheat and barley averages about 600 Indian maunds. (Wanliss.)

SIAHKHAK سياه خاك
34- 66-. In the Sar-i-Kol subdistrict of Yakh Walang. See "Bamian (District)." Recent maps show the village Siahkhaki at 35-1 67-5 m. (LWA)

SIAH KHARAK سياه خرك
A locality in the Dai Kundi country. A pass and a village with this name are located at 34-13 67-5 m. 35-4 68-40 m. (LWA)

SIAHKHAWAL سياه خوال كوتل
35- 67-. A place in Yakh Walang, 26 miles north of Kala Jafir, situated in the Dara Siah Khawal. No inhabitants. A road runs down the dara to the Kamard valley; in fact, the dara appears to be the head of the Kamard river. (Amir Khan.) A dara and a pass with this name is located at 35-10 67-7 m. (LWA)

SIAH KHOLA سياه خوله
34-33 66-13 G. A glen running north to the Sar-i-Jangal valley.

SIAH KOH Or TOWR GHAR سياه كوه (تور غر)
34-27 70-13 A. A spur of the eastern Safed Koh mountains, which starts from the parent range south of Jagdalak, forms the watershed between the Tazin and Surkhab rivers and, on arriving east of Jagdalak, turns due east to the junction of the Surkhab with the Kabul river. It is in the last part of its course that the above name is more specially applied. It separates Laghman from Jalalabad. The principal passes over this range from the Kabul valley to the valley of the Surkhab are the Darunta and the Waragali. (Masson, Holdich.) Another mountain with this name is located at 34-24 69-51 G., and a village with this name is located at 33-57 68-57 G. (LWA)

SIAH LIAK Or LAYAK سياه لايك
34-44 67-38. Elevation 10,500 feet. A pass on the Bamian-Daulat Yar main road, crossed at 38 miles from the former. From a low elevation to the north of the road a good view is obtained. The country is a mass of ridges and undulations, running northward from the main range on the south, and forming part of the great plateau north of the Koh-i-Baba. The latter is intersected by hollows, which are not unfrequently rocky gorges. Its general aspect is that of a brown, stony or gravelly and treeless waste. There is little or no grass, except in the hollows, but low scrub; apparently good camel

grazing exists everywhere. The ascent to the kotal is rather stiff, but could easily be improved; the descent is slight. The head of the Siah Liak ravine is crossed by the road before the kotal is reached. This ravine runs away north, the road from Firozbahar to Band-i-Amir descending into the lowest part of it. (Maitland.) There is also a village and a stream with this name in this area. (LWA)

*SIAH NAO سیاه نو
    34-24 67-12 m. A village on a tributary of the Darazqol, northeast of Panjao in Bamian province.

SIAH NUR Or (RAH KOL) سیاه نور
    34- 67-. A kotal in the Besud country.

SIAH NUR سیاه نور
    34- 67-. A village in Besud.

SIAH POSH See KAFIRISTAN سیاه پوش

*SIAHQOL سیاه قول
    34-2 67-1 m. A village southwest of Pitaoqol; other places with this name are northeast of Pitaoqol, at 34-7 67-17 m., and nearby at 34-10 67-26 m.

SIAH REG سیاه ریگ
    34-40 67-57. A pass leading over the Koh-i-Baba from the Helmand valley to that of Bamian, and the next pass west of the Hajigak. The descent is so difficult that Masson mentions most of his party dismounted to lead their horses. On reaching "Siah Sang," the road takes a west direction, and crosses two long passes, and descends into the Kalu valley. (Masson.)
    N.B.: This would appear to be identical with the Kafzar. It cannot well be the same as the Siah Reg mentioned under "Jiria Khana." There is a Siah Sang 10 miles south of the Irak Kotal. Villages with this name are located at 33-25 67-9 m., 33-56 68-11 G., and 34-2 66-32 m. (LWA)

SIAH SANG سیاه سنگ
    34-36 68-7 A. A valley tributary to the Helmand near its source.

SIAH SANG سیاه سنگ
    34- 67-. A group of villages in the northeast of the Besud country. One village with this name is located at 34-6 67-33 m. (LWA)

SIAH SANG سیاه سنگ
    34-31 69-14 A. An isolated hill lying between the city of Kabul and the confluence of the Kabul and Logar rivers. Its crest is about 2 miles long, interrupted by several dips, and its slopes are gentle, except on the western side, which is steep. (See "Kabul City.")

SIAH SANG سیاه سنگ
    34-49 69-29 m. A village in the Koh Daman; 50 houses. (Kinloch.)

SIAH SANG سیاه سنگ
    33- 68-. A place near Ghazni. Another place with this name is located at 33-12 67-29 m. (LWA)

*SIAH SANGAK سیاه سنگک
    34-40 67-58 m. A village on a stream, some miles northwest of Qala Sangak in Bamian province. Other villages with this name are

located a few miles south of the Dahana-i-Shurab in Ghazni province, at 34-1   68-2 m., and on a tributary of the Ghorband, southeast of Asheq and some 15 miles south of Surkho Parsa in Parwan province, at 34-46   68-39 m.

SIAH SANGI سیاه سنگی
A subsection of the Daulat Pai Besuds.

*SIBAK سیبك
34-14 67-14 m. A village on the Qol-i-Tsuitamman in Bamian province. Another place with this name is located on a tributary of the Ghorband south of Surkho Parsa in Parwan province at 34-49 68-37m.

SIKANDAR سکندر
A village of Besud Hazaras.

SIKANDAR KHEL سکندرخیل
33-53 69-40 m. A village of the Hasan Khel Tajiks, 1 mile south of Karmana on the right bank of the united waters of the Karaia and Hazar Darakht streams. The village consists of 60 houses. Cultivation extensive and running a considerable distance up the valley to the west. (Khane.) Other places with this name are located at 33-53 69-51 G. and 34-13 66-44 m. (LWA)

SIKARAM or SITARAM سکرم
34-2 69-54 m. Elevation 15,620 feet. The highest point in the Safed Koh range. Bellew, who calls it Sitaram, says: "Towards its base Sitaram is thickly covered by a dense growth of oaks and olives, which, together with other trees, extend over its lower heights. On the ridges above these are splendid forests of pines and yew trees, and above them projects in wild grandeur the bare mountain rock, presenting here and there massive boulders that overhang in threatening attitude craggy precipices of fearful depth; whilst rising above all is a huge snow-covered mass, whose summit towers aloft in a conical point, which is surrounded by pure, white, fleecy snow, clouds and vapours, whose particles sparkle like diamonds in the sunlight as they float calmly round the pinnacle of Sitaram." (Bellew, Holdich.)

SILMAN See DAI MIRDAD سیلمان(سلیمان؟)

*SINABOLAQ سنه بلاق
34-21 67-52 m. A village in the Behsud area in Maidan province.

SINI سینی
34- 68-. A small village in the south of the Bamian district, 2 miles west of the Hajigak Kotal. Near it is the hamlet of Siah Khak. (Amir Khan.) A place with this name is located at 34-38 68-2 G. (LWA)

SINJIT سنجت
34- 69-. A kotal leading over the northern end of the Paghman range. A track takes off west from the Kabul-Charikar main road 7 1/2 miles before reaching the latter place, and leads up the Sinjit Dara to the kotal, distant about 10 miles, and thence down to Kala Amir Ali in Kakshal. This route is difficult, but said to be practicable for camels. Sinjit proper, a large place at the mouth of the dara, is said to contain 1,000 Tajik families. (I.B.C.)

SINJIT (DAHAN) سنجت
A place in the Dai Kundi country.

*SINJITAK سنجتك
34-10 67-14 m. A village on the Helmand a few miles northeast of Pitaoqol in the Bamian province.

*SINZA'I سنزی
34-36 70-27 m. A village near Dogar north of Jalalabad.

SIPAH SALAR سپاه سالار
34-36 69-13. A small fort in the Kabul district, east of and close to the Paiminar pass. Inhabitants: Kizilbashis. (Kennedy.)

SIPAI سه پای
34- 70-. A village in the Kot division of the Jalalabad district, a little to the west of Kamal Khel (about 1/2 mile). Inhabitants: Tirais. (Jenkyns.) A place with this name is located at 34-10 70-37 G., another - spelled Sipia - is at 34-8 70-34 m. (LWA)

SIPAI Or SEHPAI سه پای
One of the four main divisions of the Shinwaris.

*SIPIAO سی او
34-16 70-44 m. A village on the Jalalabad - Torkham road, about 8 miles west of Basawul in Jalalabad province.

SIRACHA-I-ALI KHAN سراچه علی خان
34- 70-. A village in the Surkhab division of the Jalalabad district. Inhabitants: Dehgans and Tajiks. (Jenkyns.) One village with this name is located at 34-22 70-32 G. (LWA)

*SIRAK سیرك
33-55 68-37 m. A village located a few miles west of the Ghazni - Kabul road, near Malikhel in Maidan province. Another village with this name is located on the Jar-i-Antak, south of Koh-i-Baba, in Bamian province, at 34-34 67-52 m.

SIRANGAN سیرنگان
A settlement of the Kara-kul-daghi clan of Sehpai Dai Zangi. (Peart.)

SIRANGAN, AB-I   See UJARISTAN آب سیرنگان

*SIRDAK سرداق
34-37 66-54 m. A village located on a tributary of the Band-i-Amir, southwest of Yakawlang in Bamian province.

SIRGUL سرگل
A village in Hariob, between Belut and Zabardast Kala. (Collet.)

SIRKAI سرکی
33-47 69-30 m. A pass between the Shutur Gardan and Karatiga, about 3 miles from the former. In 1879 a British detachment of 1 officer and 50 men was stationed on this pass in a block-house, on which a futile attack was made in the month of September by a band of Mangals and Ghilzais. In the same month the approaches to the pass were much improved by the Sappers and Miners. (McLean, I.B.C.) Another place with this name is located at 33-8 69-44 G. (LWA)

SITARAM   See SIKARAM ستړم

*SIWAY سيوى
34-0 69-38 m. A village near Tsaparay about 10 miles south of Azraw in Paktia province.

SKORIGUL   See SHORIGUL شوکوریگل

*SOBAT سوبت
34-14 67-7 m. A village located on a tributary of the Helmand southeast of Panjao in Bamian province.

SOFIAN صوفيان
34-38 69-22. A village in the Koh Daman, 3 miles south of Baba Kush Kar. It stands on the left bank of the Shakar Dara stream, and in 1880 it contained 30 houses. (Kinloch.)

*SOFIKHEL صوفى خيل
34-1 68-32 m. A village in the Wardak area south of Lwara, in Maidan province.

*SOFI SAHIB KOHI صوفى صاحب کوهى
34-28 70-56 m. A village located on a tributary of the Kabul river, northeast of Goshta, in Nangahar province.

SOHAK سهاك
A branch of the Burham division of the great Ghilzai clan. They number about 5,000 or 6,000 families; one-third of them live in Kharwar; the rest are in Paghman, west of Kabul, and resemble the other Ghilzais in that neighbourhood. We have little dealings with them, but a few come into the Zhob and Thal Chotiali districts in the winter. (McMahon, Elphinstone.)

SOJAWAN سجاون
33- 68-. A pass leading from Baraki Rajan in the Logar district to the Shiniz valley. A village with this name is located at 33-54 68-45 G. Recent maps show the name Sejrawand at 33-54 68-48 m. (LWA)

SOKHTA سوخته
33- 68-. A valley at the head of the Ghazni river, inhabited by Wardaks, and so called from its burnt-up look. It produces several fine veins of lead, the ore evidently being very pure by the ease with which it is worked. Small quantities of iron have been found. A shrub on the hills around, like a fern, bears a medicinal gum smelling like turpentine. (Broadfoot.) Villages with this name are located on a tributary of the Maidan a few miles southwest of Sarchashma in Maidan province, at 34-24 68-28 m.; on a tributary of the Ghorband northeast of the Koh-i-Sokhta, in eastern Bamian province, at 34-45 68-5 m.; on a tributary of the Garmab, northeast of Safidab, in southern Bamian province, at 34-4 67-34 m.; on a tributary of the Shekari, north of Bamian, in Bamian province, at 34-59 67-51 m.

SOKHTA CHINAR سوخته چنار
34- 69-. A pass over the Karkacha range north of the Tezin pass. It is not difficult, being used by caravans. (Masson, Wood.)
N.B. The Sokhta Chinar would appear to be identical with the Iro Mangal, while the Tezin is perhaps the same as the Karkacha. A village with this name is located at 35-7 67-41 m. (LWA)

*SOKHTAGI سوختگی
34-56 66-36 m. Elevation 7,950 feet. A collection of hamlets on the Band-i-Amir river.

SOKHTA JANGAL سوخته جنگل
A place in the Besud country.

SOKHTA KALA سوخته قلعه
A village in the Dai Zangi country.

SOKHTA KOL سوخته قول
A name applied to the lower Tarbulak.

SOLANAK سلانک
35- 69-. A pass over the Panjshir ridge, on the road between Kabul and Farajghan between the villages of Barakzai and Zarshoi. It is said to be so narrow in some places as only to admit a single horseman. (Leech.)

*SOTAN سوتن
34-43 70-37 m. A village located on a tributary of the Kunar, some 8 miles north of Dara-i-Nur in Nangarhar province. A place called Shotan is located at 33-35 68-40 m.

SPERAH سپیره
32- 69-. A range of hills running south from Birmal to the Gumal at Domandi. (I.B.C.) A place with this name is located at 33-12 69-31 A. (LWA)

SPERAH سپیره
33-12 69-31. Sperah is a village and a woleswali in Paktia province. The woleswali comprises an area of 513 square kilometers and has an agricultural population that has been estimated at from 10,053 to 12,775. The woleswali is bounded in the west by Zeluk, in the southwest by Urgun, in the south by Gayan, in the east by Tani and the State of Pakistan, in the north by Nadar Shah Kot and Shamal. Sperah has some 43 villages, 6 of which have more than 500 inhabitants. The villages are listed in the PG as follows: Dwah Mandah, Sarwikani, Dargai, Shaddal, Espi (Wazipa Kalai), Zendah Tiga, Dandakai, Sperah, Khor Gorai, Khair Kodai, Warma (Ghorma), Wasti, Bazi, Laka Tiga, Sarkoh (Sura Kakh), Mina Darah (Mana), Tani Khel, Kotkai (Qala), Kala, Torwah, Yar Afzal (Afzal Khel), Kashmir Kot, Zandar Garre, Tut Kalai, Bir Khel, Lawori (Babori), Atsal Khel, Tor Mandah, Dand, Tari, Shami Khola, Khang, Mandata, Ghojarah (Ghosbara), Bazi Kana (Bazigan), Kana, Kata Sar Khel, Khost Khel, Mulki, Tang-i-Sultan-Khel (Tanisultan-Khel), Bakhmala, Islam Khan, Talib Khel, Kheder, Sur Kakh, and Balali.

*SPIDAR سپیدر
34-46 70-50 m. A village located about 10 miles northwest of Tsawkae on a tributary of the Kunar in the Kunar province.

SPIDAR NARAI سپیدر نری
32-41 69-2 A. A pass in Birmal over the watershed between the head waters of the Shakin and Urgun algads. It lies about 15 miles south of Urgun, and is said to be easy for camels at all times of the year. (I.B.C.)

SPIGA سپی گاه
A valley west of the Sulaiman range, which drains into the Ghazni

river. (Elphinstone.) A stream with this name is located at 33-33 69-4 G. (LWA)

SPINATIGA سپینه تیره
An alternative name for the Narki Khel stream in the Khugiani country south of Gandamak. (Stewart.)

SPINGAWAI سپین گوی
33- 69-. A pass about 2 1/2 miles northeast of the Paiwar. On this point the left flank of the Afghan army rested in the action of the Paiwar Kotal, 2nd December 1878.

SPIN GUND سپین گوند
The white faction of the Khostwals. (I.B.C.)

SPINKAI سپینکی
One of the two main divisions of the Nasirs.

*SPIN KALAY سپین کی
34-5 68-34 m. A village located about 4 miles northeast of Lwara in Maidan province. A place called Spina Kala is located at 34-10 68-55 m.

SPIN SAK سپین ساک
The name of a portion of the range which, coming from the Sher Dahan hills, runs between the Shilghar and Zurmat districts. (Broadfoot.)

*SRA سره
34-14 69-38 m. A village located north of Azraw in eastern Nangarhar province.

STAGHAI See STIGAI ستگی (ستغی)

STANIZAI or ASTANAZAI ستانیزی
Said to be a section of the Sulaiman Khel Ghilzais, but McMahon does not show them as such. See "Sulaiman Khel."

STERKUAL سترکول
33- 70-. An affluent of the Shamil river which it joins from the northeast, 1 mile below Kadam, on the opposite bank. (Spratt.)

STIGAI or STAGHAI ستگی
A halting place on the Gumal, 34 miles from the source of that river. It is a dry plain 300 yards wide. Water has to be brought from a spring nearly 1 mile distant up a ravine on the north. Grass is here abundant. Between Ahmadsi Kats, 10 miles above this halting place, and Betsul, 14 miles below, a road goes over the hills on the left bank, avoiding the bed of the river. At 1 1/2 miles is the kotal of Stigai: this is a low ridge crossed by three paths all equally good. The ascent is about 150 yards by a broad, level road, not at all steep; the descent is easy and down a ravine to the Gumal. (Broadfoot.)

STIR KALA ستیر کلا
34- 69-. A village 6 miles from the crest of the Lakarai pass on its north-eastern side. Here there is a deep narrow ravine, crossed by a rough wooden bridge. The inhabitants are Mangals, and their malik, Mulaim, Akbar Khel Ghilzai, was killed in an attack on the British post at Jagdalak December 1879. (I.B.C.)

SUBAH سوبه
A pass at the head of the Sadbar glen leading into the Ahingaran glen.

*SUFI See SOFI صوفی

*SUKHTA Also see SOKHTA سوخته

SUKHTA سوخته
A valley in the Allahuddin country of the Jaghatu Hazaras.

*SUKHTA JANGAL سوخته جنگل
33-57 67-57 m. A village located some 8 miles north of Okak in northern Ghazni province.

SULAIMAN KHEL سلیمان خیل
The Sulaiman Khel are the largest and most important of all the Ghilzai tribes, while they and the Ali Khel are the most important of the Burhan division. The Sulaiman Khel live chiefly in Mukur, Katawaz, and west of Waziristan, and annually migrate in large numbers via the Gumal to the Dera Ismail Khan district. (See "Powindah.")
According to McMahon they are divided into the following main sections and sub-sections:

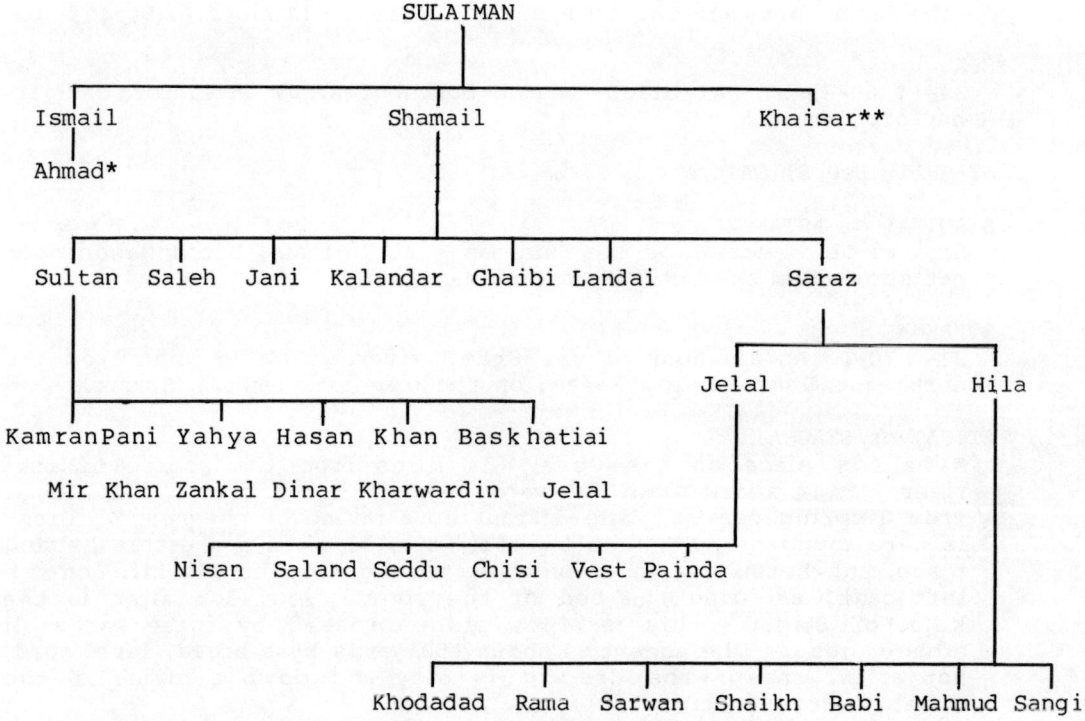

*The Ahmadzais, the main branch of the Sulaiman Khel tribe, reside in the neighborhood of Spega and Bahlol, Logar.

**The sons of Khaisar are said to be: Adan, Nao, Satur, Kajhkai, Mamur, Mitha, Begh, Mallai, Mallu, Sahibdin, Hanzkai, Gul, Batin.

"The Chief of all the Sulaiman Khels was Ismatulla Khan, Jabar Khel

Ahmadzai (see "Jabar Khel"). He and his eldest son, Muhammad Hashim, were killed by the present Amir. Two other sons are said to be in Kafiristan, and the fourth and youngest, Abdur Rahman Khan, is with other Afghan refugees in Rawal Pindi.

"We are brought into contact chiefly with the following sections of the Sulaiman Khels, and but little with the rest of the tribe, i.e.:
Bahlolzais. "A few of the Landaizais cross the border yearly under Malik Dina, while the following Sultan Khel subsections yearly visit the Girdao and Zarmelan plains and other tracts within the British border under the following headmen:

Kamranis	Mir Hazar Khan
Mir Khan Khel	Azan Khan, Mirza Khan
Pani Khel	Dilai
Zankais	Pahlwan Khan
Yahya Khel	Muhammad Akram Khan
Dinar Khel	Kattai Khan
Jelal Khel	Mammai Khan

"Of the remaining subsections of the Sultan Khel the Hasan Khan Khel and Baskhattais live throughout the year in Umnai and the Kamardid Khel in Katawaz.
Saraz. "Of these we have little to do with any but the Hilazais of which the Sheikh Khel and Mahmud Khan Khel sub-sections yearly cross our border.
"Their present headmen are:

Sheikh Khel	Kalwat Khan
Mahmud Khan Khel	Muhammad Yar Khan,
	Neku Khan

Khoedad Khel, etc. "The Khoedad Khel, Rama Khel, Sarwan Khel, Shaikh Khel and Mahmud Khel have, until quite recently, had no dealings with the Afghan Government and reside in the Pierak range under their Chief Shahabuddin Khan. The Babi Khel and Sangin Khels reside in Katawaz.
"The Saraz recognise the chiefship of Shahabuddin Khan who, until the last two or three years, held an independent position on the Afghan border and denied the Amir's authority. He has since admitted the Amir's sovereignty and has given his daughter in marriage to one of the Amir's younger sons. The Bahlolzais have two headmen:
"Muhammad Akram Khan, Yahya Khel, and Muhammad Azim Khan."
The second edition of this Gazetteer says: "The inhabitants of Mukur are mostly of the Ali Khel section of the Sulaiman Khel," but the Ali Khel would appear to be a separate branch of the Ghilzai--see McMahon's table given under "Ghilzai." Hastings mentions Tappa Ali Khel as a portion of the Ghazni district as follows:
"Tappa Ali Khel.--This tappa is known by two names, viz., Ali Khel and Mukur, the chief town, which, on the watershed system, is the boundry line between Kandahar and Kabul.
"The name of the clan who inhabit this tappa is 'Ali Khel.' The boundaries are said to be as follows:
North.--Jah-i-Murad, in Andari.
South.--Tokhi, in the Kalat-i-Ghilzai district and Arghandab.
East.--Taraki
West.--Jaghuri in Hazara
There are celebrated places or large villages in this tappa.
There are from 80 to 100 forts.

The inhabitants are Ghilzais, they are split up into main subdivisions (1) Khudozai, (2) Ali Khel.
"The chief men of the Khudozai section are Maliks Azam Khan and Shadi Khan. Painda Khan is the chief of the Ali Khel section.
"The Khudozais own about 3,000 houses in the district. The Ali Khel population is more numerous and also more powerful. They number but a few Kuchis.
The district is in parts level and elsewhere hilly; the hilly portion occupies a larger area than the level portion. None of the hills in the district are large.
Irrigation is by means of the karez system fed from springs.
There is one karez of note, called Sadozai. It is Government property and lands watered by it are khalsa."
The above has been allowed to stand, but judging from McMahon's information it would evidently be more correctly placed under "Ali Khel."
In April 1880, when Sir Donald Stewart marched from Kandahar to Ghazni the villages in the Mukur district were completely deserted, and a considerable number of those who opposed him at Ahmad Khel were Sulaiman Khel. (Hastings, McMahon, I.B.C.)

SULAIMAN KHEL سليمان خيل
A subdivision of the Chakmanis. A village with this name is located at 32-16 68-30 G. (LWA)

SULAIMAN RANGE سليمان
The name which has been applied by geographers, for purposes of geographical description, to the most southerly portion of the great watershed which divides the drainage system of the Helmand from that of the Indus. The name Sulaiman, as applied to this range, is quite unknown locally and no doubt owes its origin simply to the fact that it passes for a considerable distance through country inhabited by the Sulaiman Khel Ghilzais.
Starting from the neighbourhood of the Shutur Gardan pass it runs at first in a south-southeasterly direction and, under the names of the Mangal, and Jadran hills, separates the headwaters of the Gardez, or Jilga stream from those of the Kurram and Kaitu. This section contains several peaks of from 11,000 to 12,000 feet in height, and is crossed by a difficult track leading from Matun in Khost to Gardez in Zurmat.
At about 35 miles from the Shutur Gardan pass the range turns sharply to the west for a short distance and then continues in a southwesterly direction for about 60 miles to the Sarwandi Narai. In this section it is variously known as the Kotanni, Koh-i-Nak and Sarwanid range and separates the Kharoti Ghilzai country and Birmal on the east from the Katawaz district on the west. It is crossed by two easy passes, the Kotanni Narai (8,000 feet) and the Sarwandi Narai (7,500), over which run roads from the Tochi and Gomal to Ghazni and Mukur respectively. The higher peaks in this section are still over 10,000 feet but beyond the Sarwandi Narai they decrease in height and the range becomes insignificant.
From the Sarwandi Narai the range continues in a southwesterly direction for about 45 miles under the name of the Wazi Khwa; it then turns sharply southwards and, now almost undefined except as a water-parting, enters British territory near Surzangal. From here it continues under the name of Khwaja Amran and, passing to the west of Quetta, terminates in the Sarlat range just north of Nushki.
For purposes of geographical description only the mountain system just described is sometimes spoken of as the Western Sulaiman range, and in this case the Eastern Sulaiman range is held to be the

Succession of hills along whose crest runs the Indo-Afghan boundary from the Paiwar Kotal to Domandi (see Introduction). These hills throw off a number of spurs to the east but as these all lie within British territory they need not be treated of here. (I.B.C.)

SULIJ Or SOLECH سلج
35-3 66-26 A. A hamlet in the Band-i-Amir valley, some 57 miles below Firozbahar, and near the boundary line of the Kabul-Turkistan provinces. There is said to be space enough to camp a battalion. (A.B.C.)

SULTAN AHMAD سلطان احمد
A subsection of Daikhitai Hazaras.

SULTAN BAGH سلطان باغ
33-20 68-36 A. A village of Ander Ghilzais, between Ghazni and Kala-i-Nazar Khan, the first stage towards Darwar. (MacLean.)

SULTAN BAKAR سلطان بکر
33- 67-. A fort in Sang-i-Masha.

SULTAN BAKAR, KALA-I- Or KALA-I-NAU سلطان بکر
33- 67-. A Jahuri village situated about one mile to the west of Sang-i-Masha.

SULTAN BURJ سلطان برج
34- 69-. A village on the left bank of the Surkhab river, on the road from Gandamak to Kabul by the Karkacha pass. It is near the village of Yaghiband and, like it, belongs to the Maruf Ghilzais. Supplies are not procurable, but fuel is abundant. There is no camping ground. (Stewart, Johnston.)

SULTANI سلطانی
33-4 68-58 m. A village situated at the entrance of Zurmat and Katawaz from the Dwa Gumal river. (Broadfoot.) Other places with this name are located at 34-20 68-1 m., and 34-2 67-18 m. (LWA)

SULTAN JAN سلطان جان
34-30 69-3. A fort in the Chardeh valley of Kabul, included in the village of Inchu, and close to it. About 30 families of Tajiks. It belonged formerly to Sardar Sultan Jan (Barakzai), who died in confinement at Herat in the days of Amir Dost Muhammad Khan. His son Abdulla Khan was killed at Kandahar in 1881. (I.B.C.)

SULTAN KHEL سلطان خیل
33-52 68-38 G. A village 26 miles northeast of Ghazni, on the road to Kabul. Other places with this name are located at 34-18 68-42 m. and 34-18 69-13 m. (LWA)

*SULTAN KHEL سلطان خیل
32-56 68-38. Sultan Khel is an alaqadari in Ghazni province. The alaqadari comprises an area of 394 square kilometers and has an agricultural population that has been estimated at from 2,605 to 4,959. The alaqadari is bounded in the west by Katawaz, in the south by Jani Khel, in the east by Omna, and in the north by Yusuf Khel. Sultan Khel has about 36 villages, 2 of which have more than 500 inhabitants. The villages are listed in the PG as follows: Ghaibi Khel, Yahya Khel, Atalan, Muruwat Khel, Khalat, Naw-i-Khalat, Zala Khalat, Allayar, Waluki (Mughul Waluki), Mughal Khel, Zanki,

Terwi-i-Zanki, Malakh Zanki, Karawuddin, Mehtargai, Ghaz-i-Achmar, Osman-i-Ghani, Godal-i-Shamalzai, Moh'd Afzal, Haji Alam, Mulla Gagh, Marzakan, Muchan, Mata Khel, Palaw, Spin Sar, Balu Godali, Gulwal, Qazla-i-Asghar, Qala-i-Shin-Marakan, Marezkan, Qala-i-Kashmir, Koriyan, Karim Khan, Pa Yaw-i-Jalal-Khel, Somuy Qala, Borakai, and Zartagai.

SULTANPUR BALA سلطان پور بالا
34-25 70-19 m. A village in the Jalalabad district, on the right bank of the Surkhab river, about 10 1/4 miles southwest of Jalalabad. There is a sarai here and there is room to encamp a division with plentiful supplies, and water from irrigation channels. Camel grazing is scanty. (Wanliss.) Recent maps show the spelling Sultanpure. (LWA)

SULTANPUR PAIN سلطان پور پائین
34-24 70-17. A village in the Jalalabad district, about 1 1/2 miles southeast of Sultanpur Bala. It is surrounded by cultivation irrigated from the Surkhab. It contains (in 1904) some 1,000 families of Tajiks possessing about 1,200 head of cattle; the annual production of wheat and barley averages about 22,000 Indian maunds, the area of land under cultivation being 800 jaribs. Land-tax is assessed at the rate of 16 krans per jarib on cultivated land and 24 krans per jarib on orchards. There is a great deal of weaving done here. (Wanliss.)

*SUM صم
34-44 66-48 m. A village located on the Band-i-Amir, some 10 miles west of Yakawlang in western Bamian province.

SUMARA سمره دره
34-49 67-53 G. A large glen inhabited by Tajiks, descending north from the Koh-i-Baba and debouching into the Bamian valley about 4 1/2 miles below Kala Sarkari. According to Amir Khan the villages in it are:

	Families
Kala Murad Ali	6
Kala Akram	4
Kala Ramzan	15
Kala Fatehulla	20
Kala Faizullah	7
Kala Sumara	15

(Amir Khan.)

SUMBALAK سمبلك
35-18 69-3. A branch of the Bajgah pass over the Hindu Kush. The road to it goes from Tutamdara in the Kohistan, and thence by Sumbalak and "Alang" in 38 miles to the top of the pass, whence it is about 10 miles to Khinjan. (Leech.)
N.B.--This is probably the same as the Salang.

SUM-I-DULDUL سم دلدل
34-2 68-44. A low pass in the Logar valley over which the Kabul road runs. It is 2 1/2 miles north of Zahidabad, and has an almost imperceptible ascent and descent. The print of the hoof of Dudul (the favorite horse of Ali, the Prophet's son-in-law) is pointed out on a rock at the summit, hence the name. (I.B.C.) A village with this name is located at 34-9 69-7 G. (LWA)

*SUMUCHAK سمچك
34-51 68-44 m. A village near Pasdeh on a tributary of the Ghorband in Parwan province. Other places with this name are located a few miles northeast of Paghman in Kabul province, at 34-37 69-0 m., and on a tributary of the Helmand in Maidan province, at 34-31 67-50 m.

SUMUK سمك
Is said to be a valley west of Ujaristan, and to be inhabited by the Kolian tribe. (Maitland.)

*SUNBULAGH سون بولاغ
34-3 67-20 m. A village near Hajigak on a tributary of the Helmand in Bamian province.

SUNRU سنرو
35- 71-. Elevation 4,610 feet. A place on the left bank of Bash-gul, in Madugal territory. (I.B.C.)

SURAKH سوراخ
33-40 69-11 G. A village 12 miles from Gardez, on the road thence to the Altimur kotal. The inhabitants are Amazai Ghilzais. (I.B.C.)

SURBI سربی
A village near the junction of the Kohistan (Panjshir?) with the Kabul river. (Masson.)

*SUR DAG سورداغ
34-19 70-13 m. A village located a few miles south of Didawan on a tributary of the Surkhrud in Nangarhar province.

SURKAI سرکی
33-56 69-27 m. Elevation 10,200 feet. A kotal about 3 miles east of the Shutur Gardan on the Paiwar-Kabul road. It is passable for wheeled guns though the road would require some improvement in places as it has some very sharp turnings. A well-aligned road could easily be made as the soil is soft. (I.B.C.) Another village with this name is located at 32-5 67-15 A. (LWA)

SUR KALAY سورکلی
34-2 70-55 m. An area near Dur Baba in southern Nangarhar province.

SURKH See AKZARAT سرخ

SURKH سرخ
33- 66-. Elevation 10,020 feet. A kotal crossed by the Daulat Yar-Bamian main road at about 43 miles from the former place, and 8 3/4 miles west of Sakawa. It forms at this point the boundary between the Hazara districts of Lal and Kirman.

SURKH سرخ
34- 68-. A pass on the main road from Arghandi to the Koh Daman. It is about 1 1/2 miles southeast of the Siah Bini pass. It is practicable for all arms except wheeled artillery. (Kinloch.)

*SURKH سرخ
35-7 69-27 m. A village located southwest of Tsapdara and east of Reza Kohestan in Kapisa province.

SURKHAB Or SURKHRUD سرخاب (سرخرود)
24-23 70-7 m. A river which rises in the Safed Koh range to the west of the Lakarai Kotal, and runs north-eastwards until it falls into the Kabul river, 4 miles northwest of Jalalabad, receiving in its course numerous shall tributaries from the northern slopes to the west of Sikaram, and giving its name to a subdivision of the Jalalabad district. The Surkhab river is crossed by an ancient bridge, 7 miles northwest of Gandamak, which is known as Surkhpul, or the "red bridge." The bridge, which is of brickwork and masonry, consists of one arch of about 60 feet span and 30 feet above the water, and was in good repair when seen in 1905. It is including approaches, 170 yards long by 5 yards broad. There is a good and permanent ford just below it. The Surkhab is here a fine stream, 60 feet in breadth, running (in October) about 3 miles an hour. Fodder for about 8,000 animals for one day and about 1,500 maunds of unground grain may be collected in the neighborhood of Surkhpul. Fuel also is ample. (Stewart, Wanliss, Johnston, I.B.C.)

According to Jenkyns, the Rud-i-Surkhrud, or Surkhab, sub-division comprises a strip on both banks of the river between the Siah Koh range and Kabul river on the north, and the Khugiani, Chapriar, and Hisarak subdivisions on the south, and includes the town of Jalalabad.

The following is Jenkyns' list of the villages contained in Surkhab in 1879:

Village	Inhabitants
1. Tatang-i-Sihkoti	Ghilzais
2. Tatang-i-Wazir	Dehgans, Khugianis Ghilzais
3. Kankarak-i-Afghani	Ghilzais (Astanazai)
4. Kankarak-i-Tajiki	Tajiks
5. Baghwani	Ditto
6. Balabagh	Ditto
7. Barina	Ghilzais (Astanazai)
8. Fatebabad	Tajiks
9. Lakh-i-Tajiki	Khugianis
10. Kukukkhel	Ghilzais
11. Kotapur-i-Afghani and Kota Muhammad Shah	Ditto
12. Kotapur-i-Tajiki	Tajiks and Ghilzais
13. Tatang-i-Jabar	Ghilzais, Tajiks, and Dehgans
14. Shamsapur-i-Bala	Tajiks
15. Shamsapur-i-Pain	Ditto
16. Mughalkhel-i-Afghani	Ghilzais
17. Kala-i-Lula	Ditto
18. Kala-i-Dara	Ditto
19. Baghal-i-Afghani	Ditto
20. Khairabad (alias Tatang-i-Usman Khan)	Ghilzais, Tajiks, and Dehgans
21. Kushkak	Tajiks
22. Sahibzada-i-Araban	Ditto
23. Kalan-Mirza Hashim	Kizilbash
24. Saidan-i-Arabi and Kala-i-Arsala Khan and Bazidkhel	Tajiks and Ghilzais
25. Sultanpur-i-Bala	Tajiks
26. Sultanpur-i-Pain	Ditto
27. Saidan-i-Fauladi	Tajiks Ghilzais
271/2. Banda-i-Mir Akram	Sahibzadas
28. Wattapur, alias Kala-i-	Ghilzais

	Shukur Khan	
29.	Khudpur	Ditto
30.	Malaimpur, alias Kala-i-Khalikdad Khan	Ditto
31.	Mastikhel	Ditto
32.	Kala-i-Shamsuddin Khan	Tajiks, Ghilzais
33.	Kala-i-Sardar Muhammad Yusuf Khan	Tajiks, Gbilzais
34.	Kala-i-Sher Ali Khan	Ghilzais
35.	Kala-i-Iwaz	Ditto
36.	Deh-i-Ballo	Tajiks
37.	Deh-i Walid	Tajiks, Ghilzais
38.	Amarkhel-i-Afghani	Ghilzais
39.	Sabzabad	Ditto
40.	Nazarabad	Tajiks, Dehgans
41.	Mirzaian	Ghilzais
42.	Kala-i-Jamadar	Tajiks, Ghilzais
43.	Mirza Aliabad	Tajiks
44.	Nagharak-o-Tajik	Ditto
45.	Zulmabad	Ghilzais
46.	Nanabad	Ditto
47.	Kala-i-Sharga Khan	Tajiks
48.	Swati	Ditto
49.	Kala-i-Mulla Muhammad Gul	Ghilzais
50.	Banda-i-Hajian	Hindkis
51.	Charbagh	Tajiks
52.	Kala-i-Agha Jan	Rikas
53.	Kala-i-Haji Shakur	Ditto
54.	Kala-i-Bakhtan	Tajiks, Dehgans
55.	Baladeh	Tajiks
56.	Bagrami	Tajiks, Dehgans
57.	Chiknaori	Ditto
58.	Kala-i-Mulla Bashir	Dehgans
59.	Ghanchak	Tajiks, Dehgans
60.	Zerani	Ditto
61.	Jahannuma, alias Kasaba-i-Pain (including Kala-i-Alikhel, Kala-i-Babari, Kala-i-Arbabha, Kala-i-Fazil Beg.)	Tajiks, Mughals, Kashmiris, Arabs
62.	Jalalabad	Dehgans, Tajiks, Kashmiris
63.	Karezha-i-Shahmand Khan	Dehgans, Afghans
64.	Karez-i-Ghulam Muhammad Khan	Barakzais
65.	Kasaba, alias Banda-i-Ambar Shah and Mufti Sultan	Tajiks, Dehgans, Kizilbash
66.	Nahar-i-Shahi	Dehgans, Arabs, Tajiks
67.	Kush Gumbaz	Dehgans, Tajiks
68.	Karez-i-Malik Lala	Arabs
69.	Siracha-i-Ali Khan	Dehgans, Tajiks
70.	Samarkhel, alias Ali Boghan	Duranis (weavers)
71.	Girdikach-i-Bala	Dehgans
72.	Girdikach-i-Pain	Ditto
73.	Sultanpur-i-Bala wa Kushkak-i-Afghani	Tajiks
74.	Imlak-i-Shahidar Surkhrud	Tajiks, Ghilzais, Dehgans
75.	Imlak-i-Shah Paiwasta-i-Jalalabad	Dehgans, Arabs, Tajiks
76.	Imlak-i-Arbabha	

77. Zakhel-i-Girdikach　　　　　Tajiks, Dehgans, Kuchis

SURKHABAD　　　　　　　　　　　　　　　　　　　　سرخ آباد
34-11 69-4 m. A village in the Logar valley, on the left bank of the river, 5 miles north of the Tangi Waghjan. The inhabitants are Hazaras, of whom there were 40 families in 1880. (Clifford, Euan Smith.) Another place with this name is west of Divaqol in Bamian province, at 34-19 67-40 m. (LWA)

SURKHAI　See MIRZAKAI　　　　　　　　　　　　　　سرخی

SURKHAK　　　　　　　　　　　　　　　　　　　　　سرخك
34-37 66-45. A village on the Bamian-Daulat Yar main road, 3 miles west of the Bakkak Kotal. Recent maps show the name Surkhak-i-Shivna. Another place with this name is located at 34-42 68-8 G. (LWA)

SURKHAK　　　　　　　　　　　　　　　　　　　　　سرخك
34-20 66-22 A. A kotal leading over the Band-i-Doakhan from the Lal valley to the Talkhak glen. It is approached from the north by the Sakawa glen, which is of some size, and is said to be practicable for camels. (Maitland.)

SURKHAK　　　　　　　　　　　　　　　　　　　　　سرخك
A small fort village in the Dai Zangi country. A village with this name is located at 34-36 67-14 m. (LWA)

SURKHAK　See KHESH　　　　　　　　　　　　　　　سرخك

*SURKHAN　　　　　　　　　　　　　　　　　　　　سورخان
34-38 70-31 m. A village located in the mountains northwest of Shiva and southwest of Najaran in Nangarhar province.

SURKHANDAO　　　　　　　　　　　　　　　　　　سرخ انداو
34-4 69-47. A small saddle, 1/2 mile from the crest of the Lakarai pass towards Belut. (I.B.C.)

SURKHAO　　　　　　　　　　　　　　　　　　　　　سرخاو
34-7 69-7. An outlying district of Logar, 6 miles east of Zargan Shahar, and inhabited by Ahmadzai Ghilzais, whose Chief, Padshah Khan, gave some trouble to the British in 1879-80. As a punishment to this chief, his towers were blown up by Sir Frederick Roberts in May 1880. The district takes its name from the stream which flows through it from the east, and which, by an extensive system of karez, supplied Zargan Shahar and other villages towards the Logar river with water. (Clifford, Euan Smith.)

SURKH BEDAK　　　　　　　　　　　　　　　　　　سرخ بیدك
34- 68-. A pass leading from the Logar into the Maidan valley, 8 miles northwest of Shuluk. It is practicable for all arms until within 300 yards of the crest, when it becomes too steep for field-guns. The soil is easily worked, and there would be no difficulty in making a good road over it. (Gaselee.)

SURKH BUM　　　　　　　　　　　　　　　　　　　سرخ بوم
34-26 66-36 m. The name applied to a portion of the upper Kirman valley which is, in turn known lower down as the Lal valley. Villages with this name are located at 34-28 66-35 G. and 34-37 66-33 G.

SURKHDAR سرخ در
34-51 67-45 m. The name applied to the upper part of the Bamian valley. Recent maps show a village with the name Sughdar. (LWA)

SURKH DEH سرخ ده
35-36 67-0 G. Two forts and a village in the Yakh Walang subdistrict, containing 70 houses of Hazaras. (Maitland.) A village with this name is near Bidqol, southwest of the Dasht-i- Nawer in Ghazni province, at 33-24 67-27 m. (LWA)

SURKH DEHYAK سرخ دهیک (دیک)
A place in the Besud country. A village with this name is at 34-8 67-1 m. (LWA)

SURKH DENKOR سرخ دنکور
34- 70-. A plain in the Jalalabad valley, between Ali Boghan and Chardeh. It is a wide, barren and stony desert, and in the months of April and May the deadly simoon blows over it. It has a breadth of 9 miles. (Hough.)

SURKH DIWAL سرخ دیوال
34-22 70-42. A low range of hills in the Jalalabad district occupying the whole of the angle formed by the northward bend of the Kabul river between Lachipur and Ali Boghan. It is also known as the Ali Boghan or Samar Khel range. (Wanliss.) A village with this name is located at 33-57 67-57 G. (LWA)

SURKH-DIWAL سرخ دیوال
34- 67-. An important stream flowing from the north into the Helmand in Besud country. It flows from the Kohi-i-Baba through the Pusht-i-Jambud-Bebud country. A village with this name is located at 34-3 67-51 m. (LWA)

*SURKHGAH سرخ گاه
34-1 67-12 m. A village near the Band-i-Takhak in Bamian province.

SURKHJUI, AB-I سرخ جوی آب
34-15 66-55 m. A tributary of the Helmand in the Hazarajat. It joins that river from the north after a course of 30 miles. It is always fordable. Two places with this name are located at 33-47 67-14 G., and 33-25 67-1 G. (LWA)

SURKHJUI سرخ جوی
A locality in the Jaghuri Hazara country. (Maitland.)

SURKH KALA سرخ قلعه
34- 69-. A fort in the Chardeh valley of Kabul, between Rishkhor and Sarasia, and included in the latter. Inhabitants: about 20 families of Tajiks. (I.B.C.) A fort with this name is located at 34-16 68-59 G. (LWA)

SURKH KALA سرخ قلعه
33-41 68-59. A village, 1 mile from Ispidar, towards Zana Khan, on the road from Guda in Kharwar to Ghazni. (Gaselee.)

SURKH KALA سرخ قلعه
34- 70-. A village in the Chapriar division of the Jalalabad district, situated about midway between Hafizan and Kala-i-Shaikh. Inhabitants: Ghilzais. (Jenkyns.)

SURKH KOL
سرخ قول
    33- 68-. A village in the Ghorband valley, situated 10 1/2 miles above Farinjal, and 33 miles from the head of the valley. It has 600 houses of Hazaras. (Leech.)

*SURKHKUCHA
سرخ کوچه
    34-36 67-3 m. A village located in the Kuh-i-Baba range, southwest of Sar-i-Qol in Bamian province.

*SURKHO PARSA See SURKH PARSA
سرخو پارسا

*SURKH PARSA
سرخ پارسا
    34-55 68-39 m. Surkh Parsa is a village and a woleswali in Parwan province. The woleswali comprises an area of 949 square kilometers and has an agricultural population that has been estimated from 16,338 to 23,289. The woleswali is bounded in the west by Behsud, in the northwest by Shaikh Ali, in the northeast by Ghorband, in the east by Paghman, and in the south by Jalriz. Surkh Parsa includes 42 villages, of which 21 have more than 500 inhabitants. The villages are listed in the PG as follows: Baqi Pir Sultan, Qatander (Qatander-i-Surkh), Khedri, Paiwand Surkh, Lulanj, Khwaja Parsa, Rahman Quli Ulya, Rahman Quli Sufla, Abdal Parsa, Wand Parsa, Amertak, Gulak wa Kafzar, Ab Push, Dastarzan, Khakrez, Ghujur, Dahan Ghar, Ghazal, Kariz Dahani, Kariz, Dahan Kariz, Bakhshenda, Ata wa Jamil, Sumuch, Shadman, Wahid, Bangi, Lala, Sangenak, Jami, Daulat Khani, Suruki Surkh (Saidoki), Paye Roki, Beghamak, Khajam Aman, Meyana Ja-i-Surkh, Shina, Fazel, Pir Sultan, Kalan Tala, Sharak (Shadak), and Dahan Qamar wa Ali Khani.

SURKHPUL See SURKHAB
سرخ پل

SURKHRUD
سرخ رود
    34-25 70-18. Surkh Rud is a woleswali in Nangarhar Province. The woleswali comprises an area of 383 square kilometers and has an agricultural population that has been estimated at about 22,800. The woleswali is bounded in the north by Kats Aziz Khan and Behsud, in the east by Kama, in the south by Rodat, Chaparhar, and Khogiani, and on the west by Sherzad. Surkh Rud has about 64 villages, 30 of which have more than 500 inhabitants. The villages are listed in the PG as follows: Chaknuri, Sultan Pur-i-Ulya, Shaikh Mesry, Qala Dand, Deto Khel, Deh Ghawchak, Naghzak (Naqrak), Qala-i-Jumadar, Khairabad, Qala-i-Sardaran, Masti Khel, Char Bagh-i-Safa, Qala-i-Hazrat Sahib, Qala-i-Azim Khan, Mohd. Rahim-Pur, Akhund Qala, Darunta, Seyah Sang, Lokhi, Qala-i-Amanullah, Bazid Khel, Deh Walid, Bagh-i-Bala, Shamsa Pur, Tatang-i-Qala-i-Shahi, Zirani, Wata Pur, Ahmadzai, Mulayem Pur, Sultan Pur-i-Sufla, Sayedan-i-Foladi, Bakhtan, Keshkalik, Sayedan-i-Arabi, Fatehabad, Kata Pur, Tatang-i-Nawab-i-Jabar Khen, Banda-i-Mir-Alamji, Deh Balu, Amar Khel, Bimaran, Baghbani, Qala-i-Haji Sahib, Kankarak, Kakrah, Ganda Chashma, Nazarabad, Banda-i-Bibi-Said, Swati, Qarya Haji-Pir Sahib, Shah Naser, Qala-i-Abdul Wahed, Mirzayan, Qala-i-Nau, Miyagan, Mirane Qasimi Yaka, Bala Deh, Zulm Abad-i-Mirzayan, Bagrami, Qala-i-Maruf, Mirza Ali Abad, Kako Khel (Barkakokhel), Sherabad-i-Mirzayan, Khanowa Baba-Khasal, Banda Bibi Shablo, and Ganbagak.

SURKHRUD See SURKHAB
سرخ رود

SURKH SANG
سرخ سنگ
    34-13 67-45 m. Elevation about 11,000 feet. A group of 5 fortifified villages 13 1/2 miles south of Maidan-i-Pai Kotal on the road

770

from Ghazni to Yakh Walang. A village with this name is located at 34-29 67-13 m. (LWA)

SURKH SANG سرخ سنگ
34- 67-. Elevation 11,730 feet. A kotal on the watershed between the Helmand and Kabul river basins. It is crossed by the Ghazni-Yakh Walang road at about 62 miles from Ghazni and 15 miles south of Maidan-i-Pai Kotal.

*SURKHSAR سرخ سر
34-44 67-20 m. A village located on a tributary of the Band-i-Amir, southwest of Qarghanatu, in Bamian province.

SURKHURGAI سورخرگی
32-35 68-41. A halting-place at the foot of the Kotal-i-Sarwandi over the Sulaiman range, on the Gumal route. Fuel, water, and camel forage are abundant. (Broadfoot.)

SURKI سرکی
33- 69-. A stream falling into the Kurram river, about 10 miles below Ali Khel; near the confluence is situated on both sides of the Surkhi stream, a large settlement of Ahmad Khel Jajis. (Kane.)

SURKIA سرکی (؟)
33-56 69-27. A valley to the east of the Shutur Gardan, on the road to Jaji Thana. It is open and easy, and is connected to eastward with the Loi Koi valley. (Spratt.) Recent maps show the spelling Surkay. (LWA)

SURMA See BIHAR-I-ULYA سرمه

SUROKOT سورکوټ
33- 69-. A Kharoti Ghilzai village of 80 houses about 21 miles south of Gardez. It lies in a large plain on the left bank of a branch of the Ghazni river. Wood, water and grazing are available and supplies could be collected from villages near by. (I.B.C.) Recent maps show Shahi Kot in this area at 33-22 69-12 m. (LWA)

SURWANI KHEL سروانی
33-46 69-6 m. The principal village in the Altimur pass, the other and the smaller collection of hamlets being Niazi. (Bishop.) Recent maps show the spelling Sarwankhel. (LWA)

SUSKU Or CHASHKU سسکو (چاشکو)
35-28 71-19 m. A Madugal village of 70 houses in the Bashgul valley, in Kafiristan, about 5 miles above Kamdesh. The village is built high up above, and some distance from, the left bank of the river and cannot be seen from the road in the valley. (I.B.C., Robertson.)

SWARA سواره (سپاره)
33- 68-. A village in the valley of the Shiniz, 22 miles north of Ghazni. There is a good deal of cultivation, and at the end of May the hills around are covered with majoram and prangos, which the natives dry, mix, and use as fodder for their horses and cattle, storing large quantities of it in the winter. (Bellew.)

SWATI سواتی
34- 70-. A village in the Laghman district, situated on the left bank of the Alingar river, about 2 miles west of Charbagh. The

inhabitants are Nasiri Ghilzais. In Swati are included 12 forts and hamlets, viz.:

1. Kala-i-Abdul Hamid
2. Banda-i-Kazi
3. Daulatabad
4. Ghundi
5. Kala-i-Malik Rustam
6. Kala-i-Muhammad Yusuf
7. Deh-i-Muhammad Amin
8. Banda-i-Mian Nur
9. Kala-i-Muhammad Azim Khan
10. Deh-i-Saiyid Ahmad
11. Kala-i-Arab Khan
12. Kala-i-Sherdil.
(Warburton.)

SWATI سواتی
34- 70-. A village in the Surkhab subdivision of the Jalalabad district, 1 mile southwest of Charbagh. Inhabitants: Tajiks. (Jenkyns.)

*TABAKHSAR تبخسر
33-16 67-19 m. A village near Warchaghu and southeast of Lalchak in Ghazni province.

TABARGHAN KOL تبرغان قول
34- 67-. A glen in the southeast of Yakh Walang district. It drains west along the northern foot of the Koh-i-Baba for several miles, and then turns north to the Band-i-Amir valley, into which it debouches near Kala Jafir. A road leads down, or roughly parallel to, the glen to Kara Khawal, and thence to Kala Jafir. It appears to be called Saozal or Sabzal in the lower part of its course. (Muhammad Akbar Khan, Maitland.)

*TABARKHEL تبارخیل
34-23 68-43 m. A village located about 6 miles west of Nerkh in Maidan province.

TABBI تبی (طبی)
33- 69-. A pass 2 miles west of Jaji Thana on the road to the Shutur Gardan from which it is distant 6 miles. One village with this name is located at 34-1 70-55 G., another - also spelled Tabay - is located at 33-59 69-31 m. (LWA)

TABUT تابوت
A settlement of the Kara-Kut-Daghi clan of Sehpai Dai Zangi Hazaras. A village with this name is located at 33-50 67-20 G. (LWA)

TADEOLI تدیولی
34-20 67-42 G. A village on the Ghazni-Band-i-Amir road, about 4 miles from the left bank of the Helmand.

TAG تگ
34-54 70-18 m. A village in Laghman. Inhabitants: Kohistanis. (Warburton.)

*TAGAB تگاب
35-51 69-39. Tagab is a woleswali in Parwan province. The woleswali comprises an area of 485 square kilometers and has a population that has been estimated at about 16,600. The woleswali is bounded in the east and southeast by Alasai and Sarobi, in the west by Kohe Safi, and in the north by Nejrab. Tagab has about 54 villages, of which about 7 have more than 500 inhabitants. The villages are listed in the PG as follows:

Adizai, Aka Khel, Almas Khel, Baba Khel, Bahadur Khel, Payenda Khel, Pashagari, Tapadar wa Mulla Khel, Babar Khwaja, Tatar Khel, Jalu Khel, Joybar, Hesa-i-Awal-i-Miya Khel, Wali Khel, Deh Mukhi, Shani Khel, Sultankhel, Laghmani, Shaturi, Shahi Khel, Moshwani, Shakot, Shankai, Seddiq Khel, Sinzai-i-Ulya, Sinzai-i-Sufla, Seddiq Khel Ulya, Omer Khel, Ghazi Khan Khel, Qorghol, Ghani Khel, Ghani Khel Ulya, Qala-i-Saleh, Karam Khel, Kamush, Naliyan, Korah, Gada Khel, Ezat Khel, Sofiyan, Gandah Chashma, Daram Daram, Shaluti, Landa Khel, Mirah Khel, Nawroz Khel, Isa Khel, Khan Dawrah, Hamzah Khel, Saqi Khel, Seh Padar, Anar Joy, Brutiyan, and Jangal.

TAGAO تگاو

34-45 69-40 m. A valley lying to the west of the Laghman district, and between Laghman and Nirjrao. The Tagao stream rises in the mountains bordering on Nuristan, and joins the Kabul river somewhere to the northeast of Lataband. Very little, however, is known of the geography of this region, which has not been visited by any European. Tagao is believed to form one of the four subdistricts of Kohistan, and at the present time (1895) is said to be under one Ismail Khan.

The inhabitants are more agricultural than pastoral, and cows are their chief live-stock. Grass is cheap and plentiful. The houses are flat-roofed, and timber is easily procurable in most places, as is fuel from shrubs or branches of trees. Provisions are cheap. Some sheep are bought from the Ghilzais. Besides provisions, some pomegranates and other fruits are sent to Kabul before they come in season there, and this district is distinguished by making a little silk. The crops are irrigated with few exceptions, and the quantity of rabi which is sown and grown is but little. Within the district bullocks are the chief carriage. The climate is different in various places, but on an average is a temperate one.

Leech says Tagao contains 9,000 families of Safis, all independent. Many vestiges of an ancient race having inhabited Tagao have been found, as well as many coins; but Masson makes no mention of the nature of those relics.

The revenue of Tagao is said by Molloy to amount to Rs. 40,000.

The following is an extract form a report on the valley of Tagao and Nijrao, drawn up in 1880 by Lieutenant-Colonel Stewart, of the Guides:

"This is a region into which no European traveller has penetrated, and very little is known of its geography. The maps are therefore very imperfect and the routes and distances to many places in the remote valleys are incorrect.

Whilst with the column under Colonel Jankins last year in Laghman, I was able to find out correct distances in that valley as far as Tirgarhi, and from enquiry of men of Farajghan, I ascertained the route to the latter place from Jalalabad, and pointed out in a report that it was not at the head of the Tagao valley, as mentioned on the authority of Major Leech, but at the head of the Alishang river. From enquiries made here of inhabitants of the Nijrao valley I learn the same fact. (This is correct, LWA.)

The Tagao valley, far from being a long valley, running north to Farajghan, is a comparatively small valley, meaning, as the name implies, the lower water, it being situated below the Nijrao and Alasai valleys. Tah in Persian means 'under' or 'below' and 'Ab' water. Tahab is easier pronounced Tagab or Tagao, by either of which names it is now called.

The valley runs north and south. The lower end is inhabited by Ghilzais and the upper portion by Safis. It is said to contain 8,000 houses of Safis, who are all independent. Their chief, Usman Khan, was killed in the late rising of the tribes against the British. The people are chiefly agricultural and the valley is tolerably productive." (Raverty, Irwin, Masson, Leech, Stewart.)

TAGAO-I تگاو
Places the names of which begin with the word Tagao followed by the Persian izafat, will be found described under the second word of their designation.

TAGAO LUR تگاولر
A settlement of the Khushamadi clan of Sehpai Dai Zangi Hazaras.

TAGAO LUR And AB-I-ULQAN تگاولر
A stream about 30 miles in length flowing into the Helmand from the north after draining Chukshar, Waragha, Ushu, Janz and Tagao Lur.

TAGHAN تغان
34-6 69-44 G. Elevation 8,500 feet. A village between the crest of the Lakarai Kotal and Hisarak, 5 miles from the former. The inhabitants are Mangals, vassals to the Ghilzais. (Collet.)

TAGHARI تغری
34- 68-. A village in the Sar-i-Chashma valley, about 10 miles east of the Unai pass and close to another village called Takhana. The two together contain some 140 families of Tajiks possessing (in 1904) about 140 head of cattle and 150 sheep and goats. The annual production of wheat and barley averages about 1,450 Indian maunds. About 1 1/2 miles below the village of Taghari the main Kabul-Hazarajat-Daulat Yar road crosses the stream by a wooden bridge of 20 foot span and 12 foot road-way, the actual stream being, in July, about 15 feet broad and 2 feet deep. (Wanliss.)

*TAGHIBEG تاغی بیگ
34-30 68-13 m. A village near Chalak on the Helmand river in Maidan province.

TAGHMA تغمه
35-11 69-13 m. A village of 200 houses in the Salang dara, about 6 1/2 miles above Parwan. (I.B.C.)

*TAHANA تهانه
33-23 68-42 m. A village located west of Tapor in the Tapor Dasht, southeast of Ghazni.

TAHBUTI تابوتی
34- 67-. A village in the Bamian valley, containing 40 houses of Tajiks. (Maitland.)

TAHIR طاهر
34- 70-. A village in the Kama division of the Jalalabad district, nearly opposite Girdi Kats. The inhabitants are Dehgans. (Jenkyns.)

TAIBAR See UTPUR تیبر

*TAIBUM تییوم
33-55 68-12 m. A village located on the Shimiltu stream about 2 miles south of Shinia in northern Ghazni province.

TAIDU KUL تید وقول
A tangi in the Ghorband valley--see "Ghorband."

*TAI RASHAK تی رشک
34-31 66-56 m. A village near Rashak and southwest of Shatu in Bamian province.

TAITAMUR تیتامور
34-20 68-53. A village on both banks of the Kabul river, 5 miles southwest of Lalandar, giving its name to the most northern pass leading from the Logar valley into Maidan. The path is only suitable for foot traffic. (Kennedy.)

*TAJ تاج
35-17 69-7 m. A village near Kalari, a few miles east-southeast of the Salang Tunnel in Parwan province.

TAJDIN See ZARSANG تاج دین

TAJIK تاجک
The Tajiks, or, as they are sometimes called, the Parsiwans, constitute a numerous and widely spread portion of the inhabitants of Afghanistan, from whom they differ in language, internal government, manners and customs. The designation Parsiwan, however, is more particularly applied to Persian-speaking people of Iranian origin who inhabit the Kandahar and Herat provinces. In the latter province both Parsiwans and Tajiks are further spoken of as "Heratis." As regards to so-called Tajiks, "they are," says Bellew, "the representatives of the ancient Persian inhabitants of the country, as the Afghans are of its ancient Indian inhabitants. It would appear that, as the Afghan (whose true home and seat are in the neighbourhood of Kandahar) mixed and intermarried with the Indian people whom they conquered, and gave their name to the mixed race, so the Arabs, who did the same with the Persian people whom they conquered, left their name as the national designation of their mixed posterity, that is the name by which they were called by the Persians. The term Tajik, it is said, is derived from the ancient Persian name for the Arab, the ancient Persian writers distinguishing their hereditary enemies on the north and south respectively by the terms Turk and Taz or Taj. And hence it is that the term Taz applied to the Arab in Persia; and everything connected with him, or proceeding from him, was called by the Persians Tazi or Tajik, which are the same as Taji or Tajik."
By some, however, the term is said to signify "Persian," and there isalso reason to believe that the Taochi of the Chinese is the same word as the modern Tajik. If so, and this latter appears to be the correct version, the former explanation must be rejected, and Tajik held to be merely the ancient name for the Persian peasant. The word in fact, being a Persian one, is restricted to the territories which formerly owned the Persian sovereignty. Hence its absence from India, and its presence in Turkistan.
As stated at the beginning of this article, the name is applied now-a-days in a very loose way, and is often made to include all the Persian-speaking people of the country who are not either Hazara, Afghan, or Saiyid.
The Tajiks of Badakhshan are divided into distinct communities, who for long centuries maintained their independence, though they are now subjects of Afghanistan. They are, as a rule, professedly Mussalmans of either the Sunni or Shiah sect, claim to be descendants of Alexander the Great and his Greek soldiers, differ in appearance, as well as in some of their manners and customs, from the Tajiks of the plain country, and speak different dialects of Persian. They are known as the Badakhshi, the Wakhi, the Shigni,

etc., and in this respect differ from the Tajik of the plains, who has no such subdivisional distinction but is simply a Tajik, whether of Herat, Kabul, or elsewhere.

As a race the Tajiks of the plains are a handsome people, of tall stature, and robust frames. They are of a peaceable disposition, industrious, and frugal in their habits, and fond of social gatherings and amusements. They occupy a subordinate and, to some extent, servile position among the inhabitants of the country, and have no voice in its Government or politics. In the rural districts they are entirely devoted to agriculture and gardening, either settled in village communities of their own, or scattered about as farm servants. In the towns they furnish the several industrial and mechanical trades with their handicraftsmen. They possess naturally many estimable qualities but being a subject and down-trodden people, they are suspicious of their rulers, and meet force with deception. Bellew estimates the numbers of Tajiks in Afghanistan at 500,000 souls. Elphinstone, however, estimates them at 1,500,000 souls. The latter is probably the more correct figure. Owing to the indiscriminate use made of the word Tajik it would be useless to attempt to give any further statistics, and it will be sufficient to add that Tajiks are most numerous about the towns, forming the principal part of the population around Kabul, Kandahar, and Herat; while the inhabitants of Badakhshan proper and the Upper Oxus provinces are so-called Tajiks, as are those of most of the districts on the north of the Hindu Kush, such as Khost Andarab, Khinjan, etc. (Bellew, I.B.C.)

*TAJIKAN
35-8 69-14 m. A village in the Salang valley, some 10 miles northeast of Charikar in Parwan province. Other places with this name are near Matan, some 24 miles northeast of Tagab in Kapisa province, at 35-3 69-40 m., and north of Zirat on a tributary of the Helmand in Bamian province, at 34-29 67-51 m. (LWA)

TAJIKIA GUNKAR
A village in Laghman. Inhabitants: Tajiks. It contains one fort, viz., Kala-i-Mansur Khan. (Warburton.)

TAJI KOH
34-23 67-40 m. A small hamlet on the right bank of the Helmand, containing 5 houses of Besud Hazaras.

TAJ-I-SARETI See BAJGAH

TAJKHAN KALA
34-30 69-18. A ruined fort in the Kabul district, between Butkhak and Bagrami. No one lies in the place, but in spring Kuchis pitch their tents by it. The land belongs to some Tajiks of Shina. (I.B.C.)

TAJ MUHAMMAD KHAN
34-33 69-13. A village in the township of Yakatut, Kabul district, situated 1 1/2 miles east of Bemaru. The place is square, with bastions, and the inhabitants are Duranis. (Kennedy.)

TAKAGHAL
A village in the Dai Zangi district of Lal.

TAKAGHAL
34-30 66-16. A glen running south to the Lal valley, which it joins near Sakawa.

*TAKALGHU تكلغو
33-12 67-13 m. A village located north of the Koh-i-Nala and southwest of Aimaitu in Ghazni province. (LWA)

TAKANA تكانه
A main section of the Dai Zangis.

TAKANA تكانه
A Tajik village in Maidan (Molloy).

*TAKATU تكتو
34-32 68-17 m. A village located on a path leading from Siasang to the Helmand river at Sar-i-Olum in Maidan province.

TAKAWEZ تكه ويز
35- 69-. The name applied to that part of the Panjshir glen lying between the mouth of the Rewat and the mouth of the eastern Til. (Shahzada Taimus.)

TAKHCHI تاخچی (تخشی)
A section of Chahar Dasta Hazaras. A village with this name is located at 35-14 66-29 m. (LWA)

TAKHT تخت
34-5 66-37. A district in Dai Zangi country, about which very little is known.

TAKHT تخت
34- 68-. Elevation 7,600 feet. A pass on the Kabul and Ghazni road, 18 miles southwest of the former. During the British occupation of Kabul in 1880, this pass was frequently closed by bands of marauders, who from time to time were thus able to stop supplies from coming into Kabul from the southwest. (I.B.C.) A village with this name is located at 34-6 68-17 m. (LWA)

TAKHTA تخته
34- 66-. A glen debouching into the south side of the Sar-i-Jangal valley, a little above Kohna Deh.

*TAKHTAK تختك
33-46 68-55 m. A village located on the Pengram stream, about 5 miles northeast of Nawa-i-Kharwar in Logar province. (LWA)

TAKHT-I-SHAH تخت شاه
34- 69-. Elevation 7,530 feet. A mountain to the south of Kabul, with which the Sher Darwaza heights are connected by a narrow ridge, nearly precipitous on the western side. This is the most commanding point in the immediate vicinity of Kabul. It was seized by the Afghans on the 11th December 1879, and captured by the British on the 13th after an unsuccessful attempt on the previous day.
The summit is supposed to have been the site of an ancient king's palace, hence its name. (I.B.C.)

TAKHT-I-TURKMAN تخت تركمن
34- 68-. Elevation 15,300 feet. A peak in the Paghman range, about due west of Kabul. Near this point the Helmand and Kabul rivers take their rise. (Holdich.)

TAKIAH تکیه
    33-55 68-41 m. The name given to the portion of the valley of the Shiniz around Haidar Khel, 34 miles north of Ghazni. (Campbell.)

TAKRI تکری
    33- 68-. A ridge in the Ghilzai country, a portion of the spur of the Sher Dahan range which divides Shilghar from Zurmat. It is described as a rocky ridge, about 1,000 feet above the plain, 18 miles long, steep in the centre, and easily passed at either end. (Broadfoot.)

TALA تاله
    A settlement of the Kara-Kul-Daghi clan of Sehpai Dai Zangi Hazaras.

TALA BEGUM تاله بیگم
    33-36 68-3 A. A village on the Sar-i-Ab, probably the highest place on the stream which is inhabited by Jaghatu Hazaras.

TALAB-I-AB تالاب آب
    35-24 69-9. A name said to be locally applied to the Hindu Kush in the neighbourhood of the Parandev pass. (See Parandev.)

*TALABKHEL طلب خیل
    33-8 69-22 m. A village located near the source of the Tangay stream, southeast of Ziruk, in Paktia province.

TALA DEH تاله ده
    A village of 10 houses in the Besud country.

TALAKUL تاله کول
    34- 66-. A village in the Dai Zangi country, on the Kabul-Hazarajat main road.

TALATU تلتو
    34-34 66-28 m. A village in the Dai Zangi district of Lal, situated in the Kirman valley.

TALATU تله تو
    34-33 66-28 G. Elevation 10,830 feet. A pass leading across the watershed between the Lal and Sar-i-Jangal valleys.

TALIA تلیه
    33- 68-. A village 9 miles north of Ghazni.

TALKHA GUZAR تلخه گذر
    33-37 68-27. A plain in the Ghazni district, 2 miles north of Roza, towards the Sher Dahan pass. It is noted as being an asylum for outlaws and bad characers of all sorts. It is said to be 6 miles broad. (I.B.C.)

TALKHAK تلخك
    35-10 68-56 m. A ravine draining southeast into the Nimakao glen. (See " Zalikan.")

TALKHAK تلخك
    34-26 67-40 m. A place in the Besud country.

TALKHAK تلخك
    33- 68-. A place some 20 miles northwest of Chahardeh on the Kandahar-Ghazni road.

TALKHAK تلخك
    34-18 66-15 m. A valley descending in a general southwesterly direction from near the Akzarat Kotal, and running roughly parallel to the south side of the Band-i-Duakhwan.

*TALKHAN تلخان
    33-46 69-20 m. A village in the Mechalghu area some 15 miles northeast of Gardez in Paktia province. (LWA)

*TALKHANA تلخانه
    35-17 69-32 m. A village located southeast of the Panjshir river, and southwest of Astana in Kapisa province. (LWA)

TALPECH See TALKHAK (VALLEY) تال پیچ
    34-18 66-12 m.

TAMAKI تمکی
    A section of the Chahar Dasta Hazaras. A village with this name is located at 33-12 67-40 G. (LWA)

TAMAZAN تمزان
    A place in the Dai Kundi country.

*TAMBEKA تمبکه
    33-25 69-35 m. A village in the Janikhel area, northwest of Matun, in Paktia province. (LWA)

*TAMQOL تام قول
    33-6 67-38 m. A village north of the Koh-i-Tamqol and southwest of Luman in Ghazni province. (LWA)

*TANA تانه (تنه)
    33-51 69-45 m. A village located northwest of Chamkanni and southeast of Ali Khel in Paktia province. (LWA)

TANACHOB تانه سبز چوب
    33-18 67-8 G. A place in the Maska subdistrict of the Jaghuri Hazara country.

*TANDA تنده
    33-43 69-54 m. A village on a tributary of the Zambar Toy in Paktia province. Nearby is another village at 33-43 69-55 m. (LWA)

TANDAN تندان
    33-44 69-9 m. A village on the southern side of the Altimur pass, 16 miles from the village of Altimur. The inhabitants are Amazai Ghilzais. There is a sarai here and room for a brigade to encamp with ample water from springs.

*TANGAY See TANGI تنگی

TANGI تنگی
    32-58 67-45 m. Deh Tangi Bala and Deh Tangi Pain are two villages about 7 and 10 miles, respectively, south of the Chahardar pass, on the road from Kabul to Haibak. They contain some 60 families between them. Water and fuel are plentiful at Deh Tangi Bala, and there is room for a battalion to encamp here though the ground is narrow and cramped. Other places with this name are located at 33-42 70-2 m.,

34-30 70-41 m., 34-49 68-40 m., 34-5 70-27 G., 34-10 70-15 G., 33-13 69-25 G., 34-57 69-52 G.; an area at 33-12 69-26 m., and a stream at 33-13 69-33 m. (LWA)

TANGI GHARU تنگی غارو

34-34 69-30 A. The name of a gorge on the Kabul river through which runs a route alternative to the main Jalalabad-Kabul road, thus avoiding the Lataband pass, the summit of which reaches a height of 7,950 feet, and is covered with deep snow in winter.

The gorge extends from a point about 5 miles below Pul-i-Charkhi to just above the village of Gogamand, or for about 9 1/2 miles in all, though there is a short break about 2 miles from the lower end.

The Kabul river is crossed by three well-built bridges at about 2, 6 1/2 and 8 1/2 miles, respectively, from the western, or upper, entrance to the gorge. The first of these bridges is made of wood and the other two of brick.

As mentioned above, the gorge opens out slightly between the second and third bridges but elsewhere its width is nowhere more than 100 and, in places, not more than 20 yards, the cliffs on either side towering up, at times almost perpendicularly, to a height of some 5,000 feet above the river. The fall of the river in the gorge is generally very steep and, in one stretch of little over a mile, is not less than 1,000 feet. This is just above the second bridge, and it is in this stretch that the "Mahipar," or "Fish-Leap," waterfall occurs, where the river plunges bodily over a height of about 90 feet.

The road all through the gorge has been constructed for wheeled traffic, but it is in bad repair in parts. Afghan kafilas, however, invariably make use of this route in winter in preference to that over the Lataband Pass. A battery of artillery, two squadrons of cavalry and a battalion of infantry are reported to have marched from Jalalabad to Kabul by this route in April 1906. (I.B.C.) There is now an excellent road which has completely replaced the Lataband route. (LWA)

TANGI KHARUM تنگی خروم (غارو؟)

34-34 69-30. A gorge through which the Kabul river flows between the end of Siah Koh and the Tagao hills. (Evidently identical with the preceding place.) (Masson.)

TANGI-LECH تنگی لچ (لش)

34-27 68-33 G. A village of 50 houses on the left bank of the Kabul river, 11 3/4 miles east of the Unai pass. The inhabitants are Tajiks possessing (in 1904) about 60 head of cattle and 80 sheep and goats. The annual production of wheat and barley averages about 720 Indian maunds.

The Kabul river here runs in a narrow gorge about 60 yards wide and is spanned by a wooden bridge of 20 foot span and 12 foot roadway over which runs the main Kabul-Herat road. A few hundred yards above the village the Tang-i-Lech stream falls into the Kabul river; the road crosses this stream just above the junction by a wooden bridge of 10 foot span and 8 foot roadway; this bridge would carry field artillery. (Wanliss.)

TANGI SAR-I-CHASHMA تنگی سر چشمه

34- 69-. A narrow and precipitous defile joining the Abkhor defile (southeast of Zargan Shahar in Logar) from the northeast. A stream of excellent water runs through the defile, up which a track is said to lead to Chakari, which is very difficult for horsemen.

In the Tangi Sar-i-Chashma are situated the villages of Aghajan and Tariki. (Gaselee.)

*TANG-I-SAYYIDAN تنگ سیدان
34-25 69-6 m. A village on the Maidan river in the Charasiab area, Kabul province. (LWA)

TANGI-I-SHAKHTAKA See UJARISTAN تنگی شاخ تکه

TANGI TURKI تنگی ترکی
34- 69-. A pass east of Khurd Kabul on the south route over the Karkacha range between Kabul and Jalalabad, 18 miles southeast of Kabul. (Eyre, Thornton.)

TANGI WAGHJAN See WAGHJAN تنگ وغجان

TANGI WARDAK تنگ وردك
34- 68-. A defile leading from the Wardak country into the Logar valley, its northern mouth being near Shaikhabad, and it southern near Amir Kala. (Kennedy.)

TANI تنی
33-15 69-49 A. Tani is a woleswali in Paktia province. The woleswali comprises an area of 439 square kilometers and has an agricultural population that has been estimated at from 35,210 to 51,060. The woleswali is bounded in the west by Sperah and Nadar Kot, in the north by Mandozai, in the east by Gurbuz, and in the south by the State of Pakistan. Tani has about 49 villages, 27 of which have more than 500 inhabitants. The villages are listed in the PG as follows: Daragai, Landai, Utman (Lotman), Kotakai Utman, (Kotakai Latman), Sangari, Narizai, Alam Khel, Sur Kot, Faqiran, Landi, Warzala, (Istar Kalai), Chari Pakhi, Tsaprah Aw Mana, At Khel, Tandai Kalai, Tirah Tiga, Wolizai; Warghal, Rashunah, Mirzagai, (Mirzogai), Tar Khel (Tor Khel), Matak, Khesrai Kalai, Damburai Kalai, Stergai Lota, Manza, Neshpa, Dabar (Babur), Kochan (Kochman), Khandakai Senarak, Hesarak, Lagholi Piran, Gokha, Dakhi, Lalmi Kotkai, Landai Kotkai, Kotkai Tur Khel, Kotkai Dargai, Der Malika, Lezhay Kotkai, Kotkai Piran Lalmi, Utmanzai, Gandi Kalai, Isa Khel, Srah, Shabi Khel, Zendah Khel, Khasirai, Shinkai, and Kotgai Lali Darah.

TANI تنی
A section of the Khostwals.
The following account of the Tanis and their country is taken from information, collected in 1892 from native sources, by Mr. Anderson, at that time Political Officer in the Tochi valley.
"The Tani country is situated in the southwestern corner of the Khost valley. It is bounded on the north by the Ismail tappa of Khost, while on the south lie Upper Dawar and the hill tracts occupied by the Gurbaz and Saidgais. It is said to be 8 km. in length and 6 km. in breadth; it is partly hill-country and partly plain, the former lying to the south and the latter to the north.
The Tanis and Dawaris are reputed to be of one line of descent, Tani and Dawar having been brothers. The Tanis eat the same food and wear nearly the same dress as the Dawaris but they are more hardy and warlike than the latter. They are divided into three main sections, the Sinaki, Mari Khel and Arevzai.
The chief village of the Tanis is Daraggi, or Dargeh, which belongs to all three sections; it is said to contain 500 houses and to be able to turn out 1,000 armed men. It is situated in the plains. The hilly portion of the Tani country consists of a semi-circular range

of hills, called Chehla or Mana, and is said to be difficult of access; it contains four main villages, vis: Gokha, to the west near the Zadran border; Hisarak and Tarakhi, to the south of Gokha; and Utman in the eastern portion of the hill-country. Besides these there are many small hamlets scattered through the hills. The chief products of the plain are chenna, wheat and kankani, while tobacco and wheat are grown in the hills. Tobacco is said to be largely exported from the Tani country to Bannu. The Tanis are computed to number 10,000 souls; they belong to the Spin, or white, faction in politics and are bitterly opposed to the Ismail Khel Khostwals, who are of the Tor faction. They pay, nominally, Rs. 1,000 in annual revenue to the Governor of Khost, of which sum Rs. 200 is repaid in allowances to their own Maliks. They always resist the attempt of the Amir's officials to collect this revenue in cash, preferring to make up the amount due in horseshoes, woolen belts, bullocks, mats, etc." A village with this name is located at 33-14 69-49 m. (LWA)

TANUR تنور
34-29 68-10 m. A stream flowing into the Helmand from the south in the Besud country. A place with this name is located at 33-50 67-14 G. (LWA)

*TANURAK تنورك
34-53 68-56 m. A village on a tributary of the Ghorband about 8 miles southeast of Siagerd in Parwan province. (LWA)

TANURAM تنورم
34- 68-. A village on the left bank of the Helmand; it lies close to the junction with the latter of the Tanuram tagao, about 1 1/3 miles above Farakhulam serai. This may be the Tanur above. (LWA)

TAORI Or TURI توری
35-8 68-26 G. A dara joining the Ghorband valley on the left, 11 1/2 miles above Chahardeh. There is also a pass with this same name. (LWA)

TARAI تری
A village in the Dai Zangi country. A village with this name is located at 33-3 68-2 m. (LWA)

TARAKAI تره کی
34- 69-. A lofty spur lying between the Marki Khel and Mama Khel (Nianrud) valleys running northwards from the Safed Koh into the Khugiani country. The slopes are very steep towards the north in the direction of the Gandamak plain, and rise to a height of about 8,300 feet; but after reaching this elevation, the whole character of the spur becomes changed. The top is of comparatively level formation, consisting of rounded knolls, gently sloping and gradually increasing in height, until they ultimately join the rugged and snowy slopes of the Safed Koh proper, beyond the zone of vegetation. (Stewart.)

TARAKAO ترکاو
34- 69-. A defile leading from Tezin to Khurd Kabul on the southern road from Gandamak to Kabul. (I.B.C.)

TARA KHEL تره خیل
34-36 69-15. A collection of hamlets in the Kabul district, lying to the east of the Paiminar pass and south of Deh-i-Yahiya, close to the latter. A low ridge from the Paiminar hill runs eastward through the place, part of which lies on the north, or Deh-i-Yahiya

side, the principal portion, however, being on the south side. There are 300 houses, inhabitants all Afghans, and there is a great deal of cultivation. On the north side there is a walled place called the Kala-i-Pul-i-Sang. (Kennedy.) Another place with this name is on the Alingar, a few miles north of its junction with the Alishang in Laghman province, at 34-39 70-15 m. (LWA)

TARAKI نره کی
32-30 67-45. A tappa, or division of the Ghazni district. It is bounded on the north by Jamrud; on the south by the country of the Tokhi Ghilzais in the Kalat-i-Ghilzai country; on the east by the Katawaz district (Sulaiman Khel Ghilzais); on the west by the country of the Jaghuri Hazaras. The principal villages are said to be Nawa Taraki, Gilan, Oba, Aoband, Saga, Aghao Jan, and Gandao. The following is an extract from Hastings' report (1880) on the Ghazni district regarding this place, from native information:
"In this tappa there is an extensive lake or marsh, called the Ab-i-Istada, measuring 6 km. in length and 4 in breadth. Three streams fall into the lake, called:
    1. The Rud-i-Ghazni   3. The Rud-i-Karabagh
    2. The Rud-i-Sardeh
"There is an island in the middle of the lake where wild fowl breed in great numbers. When the lake is frozen over in the winter, shikaris are said to shoot the wild fowl in large quantities. This lake is in the Nawa Taraki valley, near the village of Nawa Taraki.
"The inhabitants of this tappa are chiefly Taraki Ghilzais; they are divided into 6 clans:
    1. Feroz Khel, who live in the village of Nawa Taraki
    2. Gurez Khel, who live in Gilan
    3. Soel Khel, who live in Oba
    4. Badin Khel, who live in Aoband
    5. Saki Khel, who live in Saga
    6. Nakhel, who live in Aghao Jan and Gandao
"The Kuchis of this tappa are numerous, and they chiefly belong to the Badin Khel, who in the winter months take their flocks to Kandahar and to Nawar in the Ghazni district. They pay a tax to the Governor of Ghazni for the pasturage of their cattle. The Sarmardi tax is levied; they pay more per head than the Andar tribe. They are said to number 20,000 souls.
"This country is surrounded on all sides by hills, but there is much level land under cultivation, and the villages are mostly in the Nawa valley. This valley commences in the Katawaz country of the Sulaiman Khel, and runs down to the Bata Khel Tokhis in the Kalat-i-Ghilzai district. The valley is 30 km. in length, and in the middle of it is the Ab-i-Istada. There are no hills with any known names in the tappa, nor are there any large rivers. There are three streams, but they do not irrigate the country, which is chiefly dependent on rain and artificial irrigation by means of karez. The village of Nawa Taraki is watered by karez.
"The revenue, inclusive of the Sarmardi tax, amounts to 1 1/2 lakh of (Kham) Kabuli rupees." (Hastings.)
The district above described is apparently none other than that which we know as Mukur, and is said to be under the same Hakim, namely, Mansur Khan. The name Taraki is probably taken from the inhabitants Tarakis.

TARAKI نره کی
34-19 70-25. A village in the Jalalabad district, situated on the right bank of the Chapriar stream, about 1 1/3 miles north of Deh-i-Gaz. Inhabitants: Ghilzais. (Jenkyns.)

TARAKI ترهکی

A main section of the Burhan branch of the Ghilzias. They inhabit Mukur and the country around it extending to the south as far as the south border of the Ghilzais. They are estimated to number 12,000 families, many of them are pastoral, and of those some move in winter into the Durani country, while others wander as far as Daman. (Elphinstone.)

*TARAKI ترهکی

33-19 68-21 m. A village located about 2 miles south of Mustaufi on the Moqur-Gazni road in Ghazni province. A pass with this name is at 33-38 69-49 A., another at 34-2 69-50 G. A stream with this name is located at 33-36 69-50 m., and villages at 33-36 69-50 m., 34-11 69-56 G., and 34-22 69-26 G. (LWA)

TARAKI TANGI ترهکی تنگی

34- 69-. About 11 miles from Tezin, is a halting place for kafilas. No habitation. Water obtainable from springs throughout the year. No supplies available. Fair camping ground. Fodder for 800 animals for one day and unground grain about 150 maunds can be collected from Chakari, a village four miles south of Taraki Tangi. A road branches off from here to Butkhak which is about six miles. (Johnston.)

TARA KOH   See FIRAJ تره کوه

*TARAN تاران

34-29 70-35 m. An area located north of Kama in Nangarhar province. (LWA)

TARBULAK تربولك (بولاق)

34- 66-. A valley descending southeast from the Sharak Kushta Kotal, which afterwards, it is believed, turns south-west and joins the Talkhak. A gorge with this name is located at 34-22 66-33 G., and a village at 34-7 67-46 m. (LWA)

*TARGHAY ترغی

34-3 67-44 m. A village northwest of the Koh-i-Mir and southwest of Barikjoy in Bamian province. (LWA)

TARGUNAK ترگنك

34- 67-. A tributary of the Helmand which, rising in the Band-i-Baba and flowing in southerly direction, falls into the Helmand about 4 miles east of Maidan-i-Pai-Kotal. A village with this name is located at 34-24 67-43 G. (LWA)

TARISTAN ترستان

A section of the Dai Kundis.

TARKHANA   See TAGHARI ترخانه

TARLAKI ترلکی

A section of the Jajis who inhabit a valley and three forts containing 80 houses, and who can turn out 120 fighting-men. Tarlaki is probably the name of a village in the Jaji country. (Agha Abbas.)

TARNAO ترنو

34- 70-. A village in the Hisarak division of the Jalalabad district. Inhabitants: Shinwaris. (Jenkyns.)

*TARNAWA ترناوه
    34-49 67-48 m. A village located on a tributary of the Bamian river, southwest of Bamian in Bamian province. (LWA)

TAROAI Or TARVI تروی
    34-36 69-45. A village at the junction of the Tezin river with the Kabul river. This is evidently meant for Sarobi. (Hough.) Another village with this name is located at 31-49 68-25 A. (LWA)

TASHNAK تشنك
    33-43 69-37 m. A village of 100 houses in the Lajha (Lazha) nala. It lies 12 miles above the junction of the Lajha nala with the Karaia stream, on an alternative route from the Karaia valley to Gardez. There is room here to encamp half a brigade with guns. (I.B.C.)

*TASAN تاسن
    33-29 68-35 m. A village located west of Tenfer and southeast of Ghazni in Ghazni province.

*TATANAK تتنك
    33-29 69-1 m. A village near Kolikhel, a few miles west of the road to Gardez in Paktia province.

*TATANG تتنگ
    34-10 68-38 m. A village on the Badqol stream, about 2 miles southeast of Badqol in Maidan province. An other place with this name is located at 34-25 70-15 G.

TATANG-I-JABAR Or KALA-I-SHAHI تتنگ جبار
    34-25 70-15 m. A village about 11 miles west-by-south of Jalalabad on the left bank of the Surkhab river from which it is distant about 1 mile. It lies about 3 miles from Bawali (Baghwani) sarai on a bearing of 317 1/2 degrees.
    The village is State property and consists practically entirely of a powder factory and of the houses of the men employed therein. The site of the factory is surrounded by extensive willow-groves, the wood of which furnishes the charcoal used in the factory. There are two mills, in each of which four wooden tilt-hammers pound the ingredients in holes sunk in the floor; these hammers are worked by waterpower. After being thus pounded for 24 hours the mixture is further treated by hand in a pestle and mortar, and is then dried and passed through a sieve. The two mills are said to be able to turn out about 15 1/2 Indian maunds daily. The powder, when ready, is stored in a magazine in the center of the enclosure and is sent to Kabul as required. A smaller factory is said to exist at the village of Amar Khel, near the Darunta Gorge. (Malleson, I.B.C.)

TATANG-I-SEH KOTI تتنگ سه کوتی
    34- 70-. A village on the left bank of the Surkhab river, opposite to, and about 1/2 mile from, Tatang-i-Wazir. (I.B.C.)

TATANG-I-WAZIR تتنگ وزیر
    34-21 70-3 G. A village on the right bank of the Surkhab river, about 10 miles southwest of Tatang-i-Jabar. (I.B.C.)

TATTOR تتور (تاتور)
    A village in the Logar valley close to Paio Khel, being indeed

reckoned as one and the same for revenue purposes. (I.B.C.) A village with this name is located at 35-33 67-49 A. (LWA)

*TATUMDARA   See TUTAMDARA   توتم دره

TAWA   ناوه
35- 68-. A pass leading over the Hindu Kush from the Ghorband valley to that of the Surkhab. The ascent from the south is by the Dara Farinjal, a narrow cramped valley issuing from among very broken hills, and debouching into the Ghorband 5 miles above Chahardeh. The summit of the pass is reached at 18 or 20 miles from the mouth of the Dara Farinjal. The descent is by the Ashraf Dara for Tala. This road is said to be easy for pack animals on the south side of the range, but to be very difficult on the north side; the pass can, on the whole, be considered practicable for men on foot only. (Peacocke, I.B.C.)

TAWAK Or TAWAKH   ناواخ
35-15 69-24 m. A village 1 mile up a dara which debouches into the right of the upper Panjshir valley 3 miles above Anaba. It contains 240 houses of Tajiks. (Shahzada Taimus.)

TAZ   تاز
A village 152 miles from Jalalabad, 176 miles from Kashkar, consisting of 150 houses inhabited by Kohistanis, surrounded by a good deal of jungle. Water is procurable from a stream, the Alingar. (Leech.)

TEBA Or THIBA   تبه (تیبه)
34- 69-. A village in the Chardeh valley of Kabul, at the northeastern base of the Korogh mountain, about 1 1/2 miles from Deh Dana. There are about 500 houses of Tajiks in the place. Water from a canal from the Kabul river. Much cultivation, including wheat, barley and rice; and many peach and apple trees. There is a shrine here, Ziarat-i-Sultan-Ghazi, to which the people of Kabul and of the Chardeh villages repair for devotion and amusement once a month, summer and winter. In summer the amusement consists in cockfighting; in winter they have a sport resembling "montagne russe," in which an average of ten to twelve people are said to lose their lives annually. (I.B.C.)

*TEBAZAR   تبزار
35-6 69-18 m. A village located south of Rezakohestan in Parwan province. (LWA)

TIRGARHI Or TIGRI   Now called MEHTERLAM   تیرگهی (مهترلام)
34-39 70-13 m. One of the principal villages in Laghman, on the left bank of the Alishang river, 2 miles above its junction with the Alingar. In Tirgarhi are included 16 forts and hamlets, the inhabitants of which are all Tajiks. The following is a list of the forts and hamlets that go to make up the township of Tirgarhi:

    1. Bagh-i-Bibi Sahiba   9. Banda-i-Abdul Ahmad
    2. Shiggi   10. Kala-i-Shah Baz
    3. Kala-i-Jaji   11. Sang Toda
    4. Kala-i-Sher Muhammad   12. Deh-i-War
    5. Kala-i-Hasan   13. Deh-i-Sultan Muhammad
    6. Kala-i-Khala Khel   14. Mariam Kora
    7. Deh-i-Ziarat   15. Kala-i-Muhammad Khan
    8. Deh-i-Sherulla Khan   16. Kala-i-Wali

Tirgarhi is surrounded by cultivation, and supplies and water are plentiful here. The camping-ground used by the British in 1880 lies some 1/4 mile to the west of the village. (Warburton, I.B.C.)

*TEKAR تکر
34-46 67-43 m. A village near Zakaria, southwest of Bamian in Bamian province.

*TELGAR تلگر
33-25 69-48 m. A village near Badal Kalay, northwest of Matun, in Paktia province.

TERAH تیره
33-45 69-10 A. An alternative name for the Altimur pass.

TETSEMGROM   See SATSUMGROM   څوښم گرام (سڅم گرام)

TEZAK تیزك
A section of Daulatpai Besud Hazaras. A village with this name is located at 34-12 68-4 G. (LWA)

TEZAO تیزاو
A place in the Jaghuri Hazara country. A village with this name is located at 34-47 66-46 G. (LWA)

TEZIN تزین
34-21 69-35 m. A large group of villages near the head of the valley of the same name, about 10 miles southwest of Jagdalak. There is room to encamp a considerable force here with an abundant water supply, but supplies are scarce. Fodder for 1,000 animals for one day and about 150 maunds of unground grain may be collected from the Tezin valley within four miles. Fuel is abundant and there is fair ground for encampment. There is a company of infantry quartered at Tezin. (I.B.C., Johnston.)

TEZIN تزین
34-36 69-46 m. A stream which rises in the Safed Koh and, flowing nearly due north, falls into the Kabul river at Sarobi, 40 miles below Kabul, after a course of about 40 miles.
Masson describes it as a picturesque valley with much cultivation on either bank of the rivulet, and with forts and gardens of various Ghilzai chiefs, the owners of the valley, scattered about, especially towards the south. Hough, however, says it is not above 1,000 yards broad, and is barren, with the exception of a few patches of cultivation, a few bushes of holly and some stunned shrubs among the rocks being all the vegetation visible. To the south the valley is shut in by the Safed Koh, which is wooded from its base to its summit and to the west of north and to the east there are other mountains. There are many indications of copper in the rocks in the hills which bound the valley. The cultivation consists of wheat and rye.
Brigadier Sale, retiring from Kabul to Jalalabad in 1841, with a force of 1 field battery, 1 mountain battery, 1 squadron, 5th Light Cavalry, 1 squadron the Shah's 2nd Cavalry, Broadfoot's Sappers, Her Majesty's 13th Regiment and the 35th Native Infantry, encountered and defeated on the 22nd October 1841 a body of hostile Afghans at this place, with the loss on his side of 5 killed and 19 wounded. The details of the action are thus described by that officer: "From the valley of Tezin, another vale stretches out towards the southeast and on the sides and summits of the mountains which enclose the latter were posted, in every quarter, bodies of the insurgents,

whilst another portion of their force, consisting of foot, led on by Sardars on horseback, and their mounted followers, showed a determination to dispute the possession of a conical hill, which partially closes the entrance of the branching valley, and barred our approach to Muhammad Afzal's fort a large work backed by gardens, which the rebels still garrisoned. From this eminence, the advance guard under Colonel Monteath drove them by a combined attack, and I then directed the 13th Light Infantry and a portion of Captain Abbott's battery to advance under Lieutenant-Colonel Dennie, and assault the fort itself. The insurgents, however, abandoned it after directing from it a feeble fire."

On the 11th January 1842, the remnant of the British force retreating from Kabul, consisting of 4,500 men, including followers (out of a total of 16,400 who had left Kabul three days before), arrived at Tezin, saved so far by the persevering energy and unflinching fortitude of General Shelton, who had commanded in the rear with a few of the 44th Foot. Their bivouac at Tezin was happily not disturbed, and they were thus enabled to collect their numbed energies for the dreadful miles yet before them--miles which were not ended ere all had been destroyed.

When General Pollock was advancing on Kabul in 1842, he halted at Tezin for a day, on the 12th September 1842, to recruit his cattle; this halt the enemy imagined to be the result of hesitation, and in the afternoon attacked the picquets on his left flank, and became so daring that it was "considered necessary to send Lieutenant Colonel Taylor, with 250 men of Her Majesty's 9th Foot, to drive them back; some sharp fighting took place, and the enemy were driven up the neighboring hills from the crests of which they kept up a heavy fire. Lieutenant-Colonel Taylor, however, with a small party, crept up one end of the hill unperceived by the enemy, who were hotly engaged in their front, and lay concealed until joined by a few more of his men, when rushing upon the flank of the astounded Afghans, he inflicted a severe lesson pouring in a destructive fire upon them as they fled down the hill. The enemy remained inoffensive on the left flank in consequence of this very well-planned and gallant affair of Lieutenant-Colonel Taylor's and withdrew to the right where they commenced a furious attack upon a piquet, consisting of 80 men of the 66th Regiment Native Infantry, commanded by Lieutenant Montgomery, who sustained the assault with great resolution until reinforcements reached him when the enemy were beaten off; in this attack the picquet had four killed, Lieutenant Montgomery and 17 men wounded; the enemy came so close that frequent recourse was had to the bayonet. Their attemps on the piquets continued throughout the night, but were invariably unsuccessful.

"On the morning of the 13th, it was perceived that the Afghans had occuppied in great force every height not already crowned by our troops; and General Pollock commenced his march towards the mouth of the Tezin pass, where he left two guns, two squadrons of Her Majesty's 3rd Light Dragoons, a party of the 1st Light Cavalry and 3rd Irregular Cavalry. The enemy's horse appeared in the valley, with the intention of falling upon the baggage, but the dragoons and native cavalry (Regular and Irregular) made a most brilliant charge, and with such effect that the whole body of the enemy's force was completely routed, and a number of them cut up.

"The pass of the Tezin affords great advantage to an enemy occupying the heights, and on the above occasion Muhammad Akbar neglected nothing to render its natural difficulties as formidable as numbers could make it. The British troops mounted the heights, and the Afghans, contrary to their general custom, advanced to meet them, and a desperate struggle ensued; indeed, their defence was so obstinate, that the bayonet in many instances alone decided the contest. The Light Company of Her Majesty's 9th Foot, led by Captain Lushington, who was wounded in the head, ascending the hills on the left of the pass, under a heavy cross fire, charged and overthrew their opponents, leaving several horses and their riders, supposed to be chiefs, dead on the hill. The slaughter was considerable, and the fight continued during a great part of the day, the enemy appearing resolved that the British should not ascend the Haft Kotal; but one spirit seemed to pervade all, and a determination to conquer overcame the obstinate resistance of the enemy, who were at length forced from their numerous and strong position, and the British troops mounted the Haft Kotal giving three cheers when they reached the summit." There were about 16,000 men in the field opposed to General Pollock, a considerable portion of whom were cavalry; Muhammad Akbar Khan, Muhammad Shah Khan, Amin Ulla, and many other chiefs with their followers were present. The General thus gained a complete victory, and his enemies suffered severely, having several hundreds killed, losing their guns and three standards, one of which was taken from the enemy's horse by the 1st Light Cavalry.

THIBA   See TEBA

TIGRI   See TIRGARHI

TIL
35-36 69-44 A. Elevation about 11,700 feet. A pass in the Hindu Kush, leading from the Panjshir valley into the Andarab valley of Badakshan. The summit of the Til pass lies about 7 miles southwest of the Khawak pass. It is crossed by a route which is said to be sometimes used by salt kafilas, though it is not generally considered to be fit for camels; being much shorter than the route over the Khawak pass, however, travelers with yabus frequently make use of it. From the eastern foot of the pass a stream runs in an easterly direction and joins the Sar-i-Lang stream, which flows down from the Regak pass. This stream is sometimes spoken of as the Eastern Til, as opposed to the stream of the same name which flows down the western side of the pass to the Andarab valley. (I.B.C.)

TIL
35-34 69-51 m. A village on the right bank of the Eastern Til, or Sar-i-Lang stream, about 7 miles west of Dasht-i-Rewat. It is said to contain about 90 houses. The stream here is said to be (in October) 24 feet wide and 6 inches deep. (I.B.C.) This is also called Til-i-Panjshir. (LWA)

TIMRAM
A place in the Dai Kundi country. A mountain with this name is located at 33-44 66-50 G. (LWA)

TIMURI SHAH
34- 69-. A village in the Tagao valley, 16 miles from Farajghan, consisting of 50 houses of "Pashais." (Leech.)

TIRAHI
A small tribe in the Jalalabad district.
"They occupy the Rud-i-Kot. Naib Khan, who in 1879 was the chief man in the tribe, stated that they were originally transported (by Taimur Lang probably) from Tehran in Persia, and located on the plateau of Tirah. The name Tirahi may be derived from Tehran, or

from Tirah, most probably the latter. After residing for some time in Tirah, they were expelled by the Afridis and Orakzais. They then descended into the plains of Ningrahar, and driving out the Dilazaks, who then occupied the Rud-i-Kot, took possession of the country. Since then the Tirahis have not changed their place of residence. They are engaged entirely in agriculture.
The Tirahis are divided into three sections:
  1. Shabadwani 2. Sipai 3. Lartoi
"The Shabadwani occupy Farukhshahkhel, Hidwani, Iddurkhel, Shayastakhel, Kalajat, Kala-i-Saadatmand, etc., and are sub-divided into three families, viz:
  1. Farkukhshahkhel (including Haibatkhel)
  2. Shayastakhel
  3. Andarani
"The Sipai contain the following subdivisions:
  1. Sandwani (in Manzuni, Batikot, and Sipai.)
  2. Guzwani (in Dosha, etc.)
  3. Zarkani (in Changar, Jabba, Mitrani, etc.)
"The Lartoi are not subdivided; they occupy Lagharju, Khidarkhani, Batikot, Madok Badok, Kamahkhel, etc.
"The highest village in the Rud-i-Tangi is held by Utmanzai Mohmands, and at the lower end of the Rud the village of Zerbacha is occupied by Saiyids; but all the rest of the Rud is in the hands of the Tirahis.
"It is probable that the Tirahis were originally Shias, and, indeed, a portion of them, called Dupa, who still remain among the Orakzais, are Shiahs; but now all the Tirahis in this district, like the other Muhammadans of Jalalabad, are strict Sunnis.
"They number about 3,000 souls.
"Naib Khan has for several years held the Kot villages in farm, and has been Naib Hakim under the Governor of Jalalabad.
"The Tirahis speak the Pushtu language, but it is said that they have a peculiar language of their own, which they talk in their homes. I have not had an opportunity of discovering the nature of this language, but from one or two words that I have heard, it would seem to be one of the Indian family of languages." (Jenkyns.)

TIRALAI-I-MIRAN   تریلی میران
34- 69-. A village in the Hisarak division of the Jalalabad district, about 3 miles south of Barikao. Inhabitants: Saiyids. About 200 maunds of unground grain and fodder for 2,000 animals for one day is obtainable. Fuel also may be procured in small quantities. (Jenkyns, Johnston.)

TIRALAI Or TRELAI   تریلی
34-20 70-25 m. A village in the Jalalabad district, about a mile north of Taraki, on the left bank of the Chapriar stream. Inhabitants: Mohmands. (Jenkyns.)

TIRIAK   تریک
34- 67-. A village in the Besud Hazara country, about 6 1/2 miles east of the Dewal Kol kotal. One village with this name is located at 34-35 67-22 m. (LWA)

TIRKHANA   تیرخانه
34-27 68-37. The name of the valley of the Kabul river between Jalrez and Sar-i-Chashma. There are numerous villages and forts scattered about, usually constructed of stones, with generally the stock of winter provender on the roofs. The inhabitants are Tajiks and Afghans, with some Hazara cultivators. (Masson.)

TOBAGI توبگی
34- 69-. A pass in the Karkacha range, by which Chakari is reached from the eastern portion of the Logar valley. (I.B.C.)

*TOBAK توبك
34-15 67-13 m. A village near Chah, on a tributary of the Helmand in Bamian province. Another place with this name is about 2 miles southwest of Miran in Maidan province, at 34-12 68-18 m. (LWA)

TOCHI توچی
A section of Muhammad Khwajo Hazaras.

*TOGHA توغه
32-58 69-22 m. A village near Giyan, east of Urgun, in Paktia province.

TOHAK توحك
A place in the Ghorband valley, where there are abundant petrifying springs; in one place the beds cut through by the torrent show a thickness of 50 feet, the individual layers not exceeding 1 to 3 inches. (Lord.)

TOI MUHAMMAD توی محمد
A Darghan Hazara village of 20 families in the Kalu glen.

TOKCHI تکچی
34- 70-. A village in the Besud division of the Jalalabad district situated about 2 miles north of Bininga, on the right bank of the Kunar river. Inhabitants: Tajiks and Barakzais. (Jenkyns.)

TOKHI See Volume 5. تخی

TOKH WIRDI توخ ویردی
A village between Parwan and Charikar. It contains about 400 houses of Tajiks, and there are 8 families of Hindu traders. Water from a canal known as the Nahar-i-Mahi-Gir, which comes from the Ghorband river. Much cultivation, chiefly a kind of dal and cotton. (I.B.C.)

TOP توپ
34-9 68-47 A. Elevation 7,400 feet. A small district on the Kabul and Ghazni road, between Kala Durani and Saiyidabad. There is plenty of space for encamping, and a good supply of water from a stream. The Sher Dahan is not visible from here, but it can be seen from the hills close by. (Montgomery.) Recent maps show the name Top Kalay, at 34-10 68-47 m. (LWA)

TOP توپ
A village on the right bank of the Kajao stream, about 11 miles southeast of Diwal Kol. Villages with this name are located at 34-34 67-46 m., 34-13 67-10 m., and 34-20 67-33 m. (LWA)

TOPCHI توپچی
34-49 67-57 m. Two forts in the Bamian valley, together containing 100 families of Tajiks. Topchi Bala is on the north side of the valley, nearly opposite the mouth of the Panjfilan glen, 7 miles below Kala Sarkari. Topchi Pain is on the opposite side of the valley, about 1 1/2 miles lower down. (Maitland.)

TOPCHI BASHI   توپچی باشی
34- 69-. A ruined fort a short distance west of Kabul. It still possesses some fine plane trees near it and an excellent spring of water. It is usual for kafilas going west to collect here. (Masson.)

TOP DARA   توپ دره
34- 69-. A group of 8 or 9 forts and villages on the daman of the Paghman range, 4 miles south of Charikar. (Maitland.) A village with this name is located 34-59 69-8 G. (LWA)

*TORA   توره
34-6 70-57 m. A village near caves, southeast of Ghanikhel in Nangarhar province.

TORACHINA   توره چینه
34- 69-. A place between the Karkacha range and Tezin, on the southern road from Gandamak to Kabul. (I.B.C.)

TOR GUND   تورگند
The black faction of Khostwals--see "Khost."

*TORKHEL   تورخیل
34-56 69-37 m. A village located on the Tagab river, some 6 miles north of Tagab in Kapisa province.

*TRAIZAI Or TERIZAI (ALI SHER)   تیری زائی (علی شیر)
33-26 70-4. Terizai (Ali Sher) is a village and an alaqadari in Paktia province. The alaqadari comprises an area of 484 square kilometers and has an agricultural population that has been estimated at from 6,302 to 15,315. The alaqadari is bounded in the west by Khost and Saroti, in the north by Bak, and in the east and southeast by the State of Pakistan. Terizai (Ali Sher) has some 42 villages, 10 of which have more than 500 inhabitants. The villages are listed in the PG as follows: Abu Khan, Belawat (Belawut), Kadam, Tor-Abo, Derabo-Kalai, Ster Kalai, Shakarai, Landar, Jadrano Kalai, Zakar Khel, Kotgai, Dabgai, Mata Khel, Akhgarai, Jono Ghundai, Khwaja Moh'd Kalai, Siddiq (Sadeq), Tatarai, Yuri Kalai (Yur Kahol), Sawaki, Tarakai, Koza Tarakai, Mirzajan-i-Tarakai, Kerghadi, Kats (Kach), Kabal Kalai, Fakiran, Matani, Khorami, Zela Ghondai, Liwano Kalai, Kharkai, Harun Khel, Shebi Kalai, Shaikh (Shaikh Madi), Masud Kalai, Mira Jan Kalai, Sahra Kalai (Gheljeyo Kalai), Gan Terizi, Mamajan Kalai, Talwal, Mullayano Kalai (Molayan), Tar Kani, Terizai, Danai Terizai, Ali Sher, Kuz Kalai, and Hazer Makay.

TRELAI See TIRALAI   تیرلی

TSAGAI   څاګی
34- 69-. A Kuchi encampment lying in a hollow among the hills to the south of Lataband, and three hours' march from the top of the pass. There is plenty of good water and grass here, and some fuel. The Kuchis who frequent this spot are Mian Khel Ghilzais. From Tsagai easy paths run in several directions. One to the east leads to Seh Baba, another southeast to Tezin (distant 6 or 7 miles), another to the south leads direct to the front over a low ridge and down to the Tezin and Khurd Kabul road (joining it near the Haft Kotal, at a place called Balutak), a fourth path leads to the southwest, over the same ridge towards Khurd Kabul, passing, at 1 mile from the ridge, the southern end of the Chinari pass. (Young.)

TSANDALAI
A village in the Hisarak division of the Jalalabad district. Inhabitants: Shinwaris under the headman of Yaghiband. (Jenkyns.)

TSARO   See PECH

TSRANU   See WAMA

TUBU
A village in the Gandamak valley, Jalalabad district, containing 300 houses of Sherzad Khugianis. (McGregor.)
(This is probably intended for Tutu.)

*TUCHI
33-42 68-0 m. A village near the Khak-i-Sayyid Ziarat, east of the Dasht-i-Nawer in Ghazni province. (LWA)

TULAKSHA   See DAI MIRDAD

TUL DARA   See PARANDEV

TULKHAH   See KACHU

TULU   See DAI MIRDAD

*TUMQUL
33-16 67-37 m. A village located southwest of the Koh-i-Chehelbuz in Ghazni province. See also Tamqol. (LWA)

TUNDI
34- 69-. A village in Laghman. Inhabitants: Tara Khel Ghilzais. This place is probably on the Alishang river, not far north of its junction with the Alingar. (Warburton.)

*TUNDKHUY
35-16 69-38 m. A village near Pezgaran, on a tributary of the Panjshir river, in Kapisa province.

TUNKHANA
A pass over the Hindu Kush--see "Zak".

TUPAKAL
A tribe of Kafir Siahposh, who inhabit the valley of Inkar which they have held some centuries past. They are nearly all Muslims by profession, but are nevertheless considered by their neighbors of that faith to be worse than the Kafirs generally. (Raverty.)

TURAN
One of the two main divisions of the Ghilzais.

TURGAN
33- 68-. A glen draining west to the Ghazni river.

TURKER
33- 69-. A village of the Ahmad Khel Jajis, situated on the right bank of the Kurram river, south of Ali Khel.

TURKOMAN DARA   See SHAIKH ALI HAZARAS

TUTAMDARA
توتم دره

35-5 69-12 m. Elevation 5,270 feet. A large village situated at the northeast corner of the great plain of the Koh Daman, 46 miles north of Kabul, and consisting of a compact group of about 100 houses. The road leading down the Ghorband valley crosses the stream by a wooden bridge near this village. The span is 35 feet, and the bridge can take field guns and laden camels. The volume of the river is here much reduced by the four large canals, which take off from the right bank near the mouth of the valley. The road after leaving the bridge crosses three of these canals, each 15 feet wide and 6 feet deep, and lined with spoil banks, and then ascends a rise of 75 feet on to the daman at the Tutamdara village, where it crosses the fourth canal, which runs along just inside the top of the rise.

There is a very good site for a camping ground on the daman near the village but well clear of the village water supply from the canal. Supplies and camel-grazing are plentiful.

The top of the rise on to the daman affords an excellent position to close the exit from the valley. On the 29th September 1840, a British force under General Sir Robert Sale encountered here a party of Kohistanis who were friendly to the cause of Dost Muhammad Khan. "On arriving in front of Tutamdara, he found the enemy posted in a very strong position. A village surrounded by garden walls, defended by a small fort and several detached towers, commanded the undulating ground below the high and steep hills which bound the 'Ghorband' pass to the south, and a chain of their detached forts within musket range, respectively of the village and each other, extended to the eastward of the village; one of these forts, a hexagonal structure with towers at the angles, was of considerable strength. The rear, or north of the position, was defended by a deep canal carried along the high ground above the Ghorband river, the vale below was entirely covered with gardens, beyond which again rose the rocky hills to the north of the pass.

"A party of the enemy was drawn up in front of the village protected by a mound, a second occupied the face of the hill to the west of the village, and the towers and forts were garrisoned by matchlockmen, who opened a brisk fire on the party of cavalry sent in advance to reconnoitre.

"The Grenadier Company of the 37th Native Infantry, a party of Her Majesty's 13th Light Infantry, Shah Shuja's 2nd Cavalry, and two 6-pounder guns, under Lieutenant Warburton, were directed to clear the hill to the left, and then to take the position of the enemy flank, and cooperate with the other parties engaged in clearing the village.

"Two companies of Her Majesty's 13th Light Infantry were detached to the right to take possession of two of the small detached forts, in which operation they were supported by three 9-pounder guns under Captain Abbot. The fire from these guns was also, as opportunity offered, directed on the towers and other defenses of the village, with the view of dislodging the enemy from their advantageous position, and facilitating the advance of the infantry. These operations were crowned with complete success.

"The principal column of attack, consisting of the remainder of Her Majesty's 13th Light Infantry, two companies of the 27th Native Infantry, and the Light Company of the Native Infantry, was then ordered to advance and moved on the village at a rapid pace. The enemy continued their fire till the heads of the companies were within 50 paces of the walls, when they fled with precipitation across the river, and over ground where they could not be followed by the cavalry.

The garrison of the large fort seeing the position both to their right and left thus in the possession of our troops, and Captain Abbot's guns in battery opposite the gate, abandoned the post and escaped through a wicket which, opening to the south, was covered from the fire of the detachment."
The loss on this occasion was slight as to numbers, but really great from the fact that it included the brilliant and talented officer, Captain Edward Connolly, who was here shot through the heart. (Leech, Masson, Sale.)

TUTU توتو
Elevation about 5,100 feet. A large collection of forts and hamlets in the Jalalabad district and in the Khugiani subdivision of that district. It lies about 6 miles southwest of Gandamak. There is much cultivation here and water is usually abundant. The inhabitants are Sherzad Khugianis, and the place is celebrated for the excellence of the knives it produces. Some of the British captives of the old war were quartered in Tutu and the maliks of the place produced, during the campaign of 1879-80, some relics and certificates from these captives. (I.B.C.)

*UBAGAK ابه گک
34-28 68-7 m. A village near Pasinaqol on the Helmand river in Maidan province.

UBAZAKA   See AO BAZAK ابازک

UD KOL   (AOKOL) اوقول
A place in the Jaghuri Hazara country.

UGHAZ   See OGHAZ اغاز

UJARISTAN اجرستان
33-4 66-13 G. A valley in the center of the Hazarajat.

UKORI اکوری
A village in the Ghilzai country, about 30 miles north of lake Ab-i-Istada. (Outram.) A place with this name is located at 32-52 67-53 G. (LWA)

ULAB-I-GARDAN الاب گردن
A place in the Besud country.

ULAMA علماء
A section of Daulatpai Besud Hazaras.

*ULANG اولنگ
33-9 67-8 m. A village on a tributary of the Jangali Rud, at the foot of the Koh-i-Khushqul, in Ghazni province.

ULANGASH اولنگش
34- 67-. A village in Bamian, situated in the Saiyidabad Tagao.

ULUMBULUKSANG الوم بلوک سنگ
33- 67-. A locality in Malistan.

ULYAR الیار
In the Dai Kundi country.

UMAR KHAN عمرخان
33- 68-. A village in Kharwar, containing 20 houses of Ghilzais. (Griesbach.)

*UMARKHAN KALAY عمرخان کلی
34-37 70-27 m. A village near Dogar, some 10 miles west-northwest of Shiwa in Nangarhar province.

*UMARKHEL عمرخیل
34-46 69-40 m. A village on the Tagab about 6 miles south of Tagab in Kapisa province.

*UMAY اومی
33-48 68-51 m. A village north of Nawa-i-Kharwar and west of Charkh in Logar province.

UMKI امکی
A village near Saiyidabad, on the Kabul and Ghazni road. Supplies plentiful, especially in the way of live-stock. (Montgomery.)

UMRAZ Or MARZ ومرز
35-22 69-38 A. A village in the Panjshir valley, 17 miles from the crest of the Khawak pass over the Hindu Kush. It contains 300 houses of the Zamarat Khel tribe. (Leech.)
(This is probably the same as Marz, but the latter is about 300 miles from the Khawak.)

UNAI اونی
34-27 68-22 A. Elevation about 11,000 feet. A pass over the watershed between the Helmand and Kabul river basins; it is crossed by the main Kabul-Herat road at about 49 miles west of the former place. The ascent from the east is rather steep and slippery in wet weather and the road is obstructed by fallen stones and granitic boulders. The whole of the road over the pass is, however, practicable, with very slight improvement for field artillery. The descent on the west is gradual and consists of a succession of 2 or 3 kotals. The hills for about a mile on either side of the road are practicable for infantry. (I.B.C., Wanliss.) A village with this name is located at 34-26 68-25 G. (LWA)

UNAMAK انامک
35- 69-. A group of hamlets in the Salang Dara, about 16 3/4 miles above Parwan. They contain some 150 houses in all and have thick and extensive orchards. (I.B.C.)

UNCHI See INCHU انچی

UNI SAIYIDAN اونی سیدان
33-58 69-1. A village in the Logar district and on the left bank of that river, 2 miles southwest of Hisarak. The inhabitants are Saiyids and Tajiks, and in 1880 the place contained 250 families. (Euan Smith.)

UNI SUFLA اونی سفلی
34- 69-. A village in the Logar valley, to the south of the Tangi Waghjan. Inhabitants: Hotak Ghilzais. In 1880 the place consisted of two forts, and contained 20 families.

UNKAI اونکی
34- 68-. A village 54 miles southwest of Kabul and 4 miles west of the road to Ghazni. (Thornton.)

*URDU اردو
    34-11 68-37 m. A village near Badqol and the stream of the same name in Maidan province.

URDU SHAH اردوشاه
    A section of the Dai Kundi Hazaras.

URETI ارتی
    35- 69-. A small dara draining into the Salang Dara, which it joins from the west at about 23 miles above Parwan. Near the junction of the two daras is the small village of Bagh-i-Dala, containing 30 houses, many orchards and a tank. (I.B.C.)

URGUN ارگون
    32-54 69-9. Urgun is a woleswali in Paktia province. The woleswali comprises an area of 574 square kilometers and has an agricultural population that has been estimated at from 12,458 to 17,575. The woleswali is bounded in the west by Sarhawza, in the north by Zeluk, in the east by Sperah and Gayan, and in the south by Barmal and Sarobi. Urgun has some 36 villages, 11 of which have more than 500 inhabitants. The villages are listed in the PG as follows:
    Sayed Hasan, Ahangaran, Ghundai, Manda Sayedan, Qala-i-Khwaja Hasan, Bahadur Khel, Changalai, Qala-i-Murgha, Farari, Gulak, Bandi, Mushki, Khandar, Dahana, Barakat, Hamborwan (Ambarwan), Faqiran, Chana Khor, Urgon-i-Kalan, Melati-Kalan, Qara Khel, Dara-i-Urgon, Shenkai-i-Khurd, Shenkai-i-Kalan, Sarkhat, Pushti-i-Jadran, Qala-i-Mufti, Balesh-i-Kalan, Kamran, Khaleqdad, Nasrullah, Pir Koti, Hesa-i-Dowom-i-Pirkoti, Qala-i-Musa, Janai, Shaikha, Galarddin, Chankho Kalai, and Qala-i-Bondi. (LWA) In 1912 this area was described as follows: A large fortified town and civil station in Birmal, and the residence of the Governor of that district. It has a very mixed population of about 1,000 families in all, the inhabitants being mostly Tajiks who are said to be largely occupied in smelting iron; there are also a large number of Hindu shop-keepers. It lies on a direct road from Bannu to Ghazni at about 63 miles from the latter place. There are said to be 2 powder and 3 flint lock factories here. A large maidan affords a good site for a camping ground; supplies of all sorts are available in large quantities, and ample water from karez.
    The garrison of Urgun consists of 2 squadrons of cavalry, 6 mountain guns, 3 battalions of infantry, and 900 khasadars. Flour for the troops is said to be brought from Zurmat, there being little cultivation in the neighborhood of Urgun. Urgun itself, and the country for a few miles around it, appears to be occupied by Tajiks but all the surrounding country outside is in the hands of the Kharoti Ghilzais. (I.B.C.)

URMIR Or URMUL اورمر (اورمول)
    35-25 71-19 m. A Kafir village on the right bank of the Bashgul, near the junction of the Nichingul, It is the Kam frontier village towards the Madugal country and contains 20 houses. The bridge over the Nichingul, over which goes the road up the main valley, is some 200 or 300 yards from Urmir. (Robertson.)

*URMUL See URMIR اورمول

URMUR اورمر
    34- 70-. A village in Laghman, on the right bank of the Kabul

river, about 18 miles west of the Darunta pass. It consists of two hamlets, viz.
      1. Banda-i-Bahawaldin   2. Banda-i-Din Muhammad
The inhabitants are Mamozais. (Warburton.)

URT   See YURT   اورت

URZA   ورزه
35- 69-. A pass which leads from Umraz in the Panjshir valley over the Hindu Kush. It is seldom free from snow, and on that account is not passable for animals. (Leech.)
Supposing Umraz to be the same as Marz, the Urza pass is probably identical with the Zuria.

USBIN Or WUZBIN   اوسبین
34-44 69-50 m. A river which, rising in the spur of the Hindu Kush between the valleys of the Tagao and Alishang, joins the Kabul river nearly north of Jagdalak, about 50 miles above Jalalabad. It has a short course, and its valley is inhabited by Ghilzais. (Elphinstone.) A village with this name is located at 34-44 69-47 G. (LWA)

USGUNAJAI   See WAZGHUNAJUI   وسگونه جای

*USHAY   اوشی
35-1 71-19 m. A village on the Kunar river, about 2 miles southwest of Asmar in Kunar province.

USHTARGIRAN   اشترگیران
35-7 69-18 m. "A township, or group of villages, on the left bank of the Panjshir, comprising altogether 500 houses of Tajiks. The different villages are Sher Khan Khel, Izzat Khel, Panah Khel, Baku Khan, Tabazar, Shekaj Khel, Latif Khel, Toghak and Jamal Aka. The orchards are extensive, and so is the cultivation. Charikar is 10 miles southwest of Baku Khan." (Shahzada Taimus.)

*USMANKHEL   عثمان خیل
33-38 69-12 m. A village south of Tutakhel, about 10 miles northeast of Gardez in Paktia province. Another village with this name is on the Azraw Dara about 2 miles west of Azraw in Logar province at 34-10 69-35 m.

USTAM   استم
A village in Daraz Kol.

USTAR SHAHR   See SHUTUR SHAHR   استر شهر

UTAHDARI   اوتهدری
A clan of the Kam Kafirs.

UTAK Or ATAK   هوتك (اتك)
33-1 67-59 m. A large fort in the Jamrud district of Ghazni, 249 miles from Quetta and 46 miles from Ghazni by the direct road. The inhabitants are Popalzai Duranis, and there are some villages near. (Campbell.)

UTARMA Or VATERMEH   اوترما
34-17 66-9 A. An ordinary fort of some size in the Talkhak valley.

UTIPURI-GHULAK   اوتی پر غولك
34-44 66-48 G. A village in Yakh Walang, 7 1/2 miles northwest of

Zari, near to the road leading thence down the Band-i-Amir valley. (Maitland.) A village called Utpur is located at 34-36 68-10 m., another called Utapur is at 35-3 68-40 m. (LWA)

UTKHEL Or WUTKHEL اتخیل
34- 69-. A village in the Kabul district, near the junction of the Kabul and Logar rivers, on the left bank of the former. There are 200 houses in the place; inhabitants all Ghilzais. Much cultivation. (Kennedy.) Villages with this name are located at 34-38 69-42 A., and 34-32 69-17 m. (LWA)

UTPUR اتپر
34-29 68-12 G. A fortified hamlet on the left bank of the Helmand, about 4 miles above Farakhulm sarai.

*UZBAGH ازباغ (ازبگ)
34-34 70-40 m. A village on the Kunar, some 5 miles east of Shiwa in Nangarhar province.

UZBIN See USBIN اوسبین

UZHAMEZHALGUL ازمژل گل
35- 70-. One of the main heads of the Pech river--see "Nichingul."

VIRUN ویرون
The name given to the inhabitants of the Presungul by their Muslim neighbors--see "Pech."

WADAT ودت
34-23 69-45 G. A hamlet of six houses, inhabited by Maruf Khel Ghilzais, on the road between the Jagdalak and Karkacha passes. (Stewart.)

*WADAWU ود او
34-57 70-21 m. A village near Nengara in the Alingar-Kolatan Dara in Laghman province.

WADER See SAFI وادر

WADIHU ود هو
A Kafir clan inhabiting the valley of Inkar. A few of them are Muslims. (Raverty.)

*WADQOL واد قول
35-20 69-33 m. A village on the Panjshir river, about 3 miles northeast of Bazarak in Kapisa province. Another place with this name is about 1 mile northeast of Wadkhol at 35-21 69-34 m.

WAGA JAN See WAGHJAN واغجان

WAGH واغ
A place in the Muhammad Khwaja Hazara country.

WAGHJAN Or WAGA JAN واغجان
34-9 69-5 m. A Tajik village in the Logar district, to the north of the ridge separating the upper from the lower portion of the valley. This ridge is pierced by a defile, known as the Tangi Waghjan, through which the Logar river runs. The village stands on the left bank of the river, close to Kala-i-Rahim Khan. It contains about

500 houses. Water abundant. Fodder for 4,000 animals for one day and 400 maunds of grain is procurable within 5 miles of this village. Fuel also is obtainable. The best route for all arms passing from Kabul to the Upper Logar, or vice versa, is to Zargan Shahar or by the Dado Khel defile just above Zargan Shahar, both being used for a large force, as the plains north and south are broad and admit of the march of parallel columns. The road through the tangi is fit for cavalry, infantry, and baggage animals, on both sides of the river, but very difficult for wheeled guns. (I.B.C., Euan Smith, Clifford, Johnston.)

WAHID DEH وحیدده
34- 67-. A village of 40 Tajik houses in the Bamian valley. (A.B.C.)

*WAIGALAK ویگلک
35-10 70-21 m. An area on the Dara-i-Kolum in Laghman province.

WAIGUL وایگل
A tribe of Kafirs who live in the Waigul and Amzhi valleys, tributaries of the lower Pech. They speak a language quite different from that spoken in Presungul--the upper Pech--or by the Siahposh, and are a brave, high spirited race, remarkable for their hospitality, and for their proneness to quarrel. At present it seems that there is no very strong tribal feeling amongst the Wai, for they are perpetually fighting amongst themselves. They are roughly estimated at 5,500 souls and are said to own ten villages, of which the names given to Robertson were as follows: Runchi, Nizhai, Jamma, Amzhi, Chimion, Kegili, Akun or Akum, Mildesh, Bargul and Prainta. Nizhai, near the Pech river, is believed to be the residence of a very energetic Mulla who has either converted the people to Islam, or keeps them steadfast in their new faith.
Barrow's "Gazetteer of the Eastern Hindu Kush" contains the following regarding the Waigulis:
They are subdivided into 18 clans. In the Dara-i-Nur are converted Waigulis, who have abandoned the national costume and adopted cotton clothes. Biddulph notices the following peculiarities in their dress: "On their feet they wear rude sandals of goat-skin, with a tuft of hair on the instep as a decoration. The women wear long sack-like garmets of black woven goat's hair with long loose sleeves and a coloured cotton scarf bound tightly over the shoulders. Their hair they wear plaited in a number of thin plaits, which are coiled away under the head dress." (Robertson, Masson, Raverty, Biddulph.) The stream with this name is located at 34-59 70-54. (LWA)

WAKHE KOH   See DASHT-I-REWAT واخه کوه

WALANG   Also see WOLANG ولنگ
35-16 69-6 m. A name sometimes applied to the Salang Kotal--see Salang.

WALANG ولنگ
35-17 67-7 A. A grassy camping ground, about 300 yards wide, at the head of the Ejan Dara, about 15 miles from the point where the latter joins the Salang Dara. There is some cultivation here, and the place is much resorted to in spring and summer. There is plenty of water, and grass is abundant till fairly late in the year; fuel is scanty and consists of small shrubs only. (I.B.C.)

WALANGAK ولنگک
   34-43 67-18 m. A small valley descending north from the Koh-i-Baba to Karghanatu. This is also spelled Wolangak. (LWA)

WALIAN وليان
   35-36 68-52 A. A pass over the Hindu Kush. It lies at the head of the Nimakao glen, between the Kaoshan pass on the east and the Chapdara on the west. It is crossed by a road leading from the Ghorband valley to that of Khinjan. There are really two kotals at the summit, and of these the more westerly (on the left going towards Khinjan), is the Walian proper; it is said to be practicable for Afghan camels. The other kotal, called the Loani, or Loahani, is a short-cut impracticable even for yabus. At the top of the pass is a stream which runs for a short way down the northern slope; in places it runs underground but water is said to be easily obtainable in any part of the watercourse by scraping away the shingly surface. A little way below the summit, on the Khinjan side, a footpath strikes off to the east; this leads over the watershed to the head of the Changalawez glen and then down the latter to the Kaoshan glen which it joins near Maidan-i-Khuni. (I.B.C.)

WALID وليد (والد)
   34-27 70-22. A village in the Surkhab division of the Jalalabad district, situated on the left bank of the Surkhab river, 2 miles above its junction with the Kabul and nearly opposite Deh-i-Balo. Inhabitants: Tajiks and Ghilzais. (Jenkyns.)

*WALIKHEL ولى خيل
   34-45 69-40 m. A village on the Tagab river, about 7 miles south of Tagab in Kapisa province.

WALI MUHAMMAD ولى محمد
   34-14 69-15. A fort in the Kabul district, situated to the east of Bini Hisar, on the left bank of the Logar river. Sides of this square fort 50 yards long. (Kennedy.)

WAMA وامه
   A Kafir tribe who inhabit the Inkar valley. Some few of them have become Muslims. They are also called Sanu Kafirs, or Lal Kafirs, and are described as a merry, jovial people. According to Tanner, they live in the upper end of the Pech Dara, but Stewart places them on the east side of the Alingar river, and reckons them at about 4,000 fighting men. (Raverty, Tanner, Stewart.)

WAMA Or TSRANU وامه
   35-7 70-45 m. A Siahposh village of about 200 houses in the Pech valley in Nuristan about 55 miles above Chighar Serai. This portion of the valley is known as Parun. The village is on the right bank of the river where the river is fordable as well as bridged over. The houses are clustered together in a very strong natural position, perched high above the river. On its south side is a 500 feet cliff, while on the riverside the spur on which it stands drops perpendicularly to the water's edge. The hills behind are unscaleable, and the village is reached by a narrow path which climbs up a "chimney" on the northeast side. The village is not walled. This name is also applied to the valley a short distance above and below the village. A company of sappers is camped here in summer to repair the roads and superintend the floating of timber down the river.
   Kafilas camp here on the river banks. Supplies are plentiful from the village. (I.B.C., N.I)

*WAND
وند
    34-46 68-50 m. A village near Ushturmurda, on a tributary of the
    Ghorband in Parwan province.

WARAGALI Or LAKHI
وره گی
    34-21 70-8 G. Elevation 4,400 feet. A pass over the Siah Koh range
    between Khairo Khel, on the river route from Jalalabad, and Fateha-
    bad, or Fort Battye, on the Jalalabad-Gandamak road. It is practic-
    able, though difficult in places, for mules and hill camels.
    (I.B.C.)

*WARAS
ورس
    34-13 66-54 A. Waras is a woleswali in the Bamian province. The
    woleswali comprises an area of 2,845 square kilometers and has an
    agricultural population which has been estimated at from 23,362 to
    33,940. The woleswali is bounded in the west by Da-i-Kundi and Lal
    wa Sarjangal, in the north by Panjab, in the east by Behsud and
    Nawer, and in the south by Shahristan. Waras has about 69 villages,
    35 of which have more than 500 inhabitants. The villages are listed
    in the PG as follows:
    Abdal (Abdal-i-Surkh Joy), Acha Sar Asp, Khar Push, Sang-i-Sukhta,
    Surkh Joy, Qala-i-Beg-i-Sokhta, Shubat (Shobat Surkh Joy), Qawm-i-
    Sultan, Bar Qol, Safed Kich, Miyana Deh, Bad Rawak, Lakhak (Talkhak-
    i-Bad Qol), Qol-i-Haidar, Buz Girak, Bani Gaw, Pitab Joy, Pilan
    (Plan), Panja Dur (Pajandur), Sakhawi (Takhawi), Sarab-i-Waras,
    Tagab-i-Ghor (Tagab-i-Ghar), Bastuk (Sutrak), Tagab-i-Shinaw (Tagab-
    i-Shewi), Qonak-i-Shinaw (Qonak-i-Takht), Jaw Qol, Chambar, Chah
    Chin-i-Waras, Qawm-i-Barfi), Chachin (Chachin wa Sura Soy-i-Surkh
    Joy), Khalachak wa Borlak-i-Waras, Dola, Baragh Sang-i-Dola, Shamin-
    i-Obe (Shina-i-Obe), Surkh Gawak, Safed Ghoy-i-Sufla, Niqol, Chijan,
    Reg-i-Safed Gho, Safed Ghu-i-Ulya, Sultan Robat, Sil Burda, Shahi-i-
    Surkh Joy, Shanuk (Shuyaki-i-Surkh Joy), Fatu-i-Surkh Joy, Tagab-i-
    Sha, Qawm-i-Khudi, Qawm-i-Mirza, Gal Qol-i-Surkh Joy, Gambatak-i-
    Surkh Joy, Ligan-i-Waras, Nayespatan (Nayestan), Warasgin-i-Surkh
    Joy, Warzang, Qawm-i-Yari, Qarya-i-Takht, Ulyatak, Qayaghak-i-Arga-
    nak, Sar-i-Takht, Qulba-i-Toy-i-Takht, Qara Ghajur-i-Takht, Surkh
    Sang, Isparmak, Sang-i-Naweshta, Sokhta Qol, Manda-i-Ulyat-i-Takht,
    Sarghawchak-i-Takht, Khak-i-Bibi-i-Takht, Reg Joy-i-Qawm-i-Khoshi,
    Sawalyu-i-Surkh Joy, Qawm-i-Isa, Malik (Mulk), and Bagh-i-Sang. (A
    district in the Dai Zangi country.)

WARAS-I-NAZRULLA KHAN, AB-I
ورس نصرالله خان
    A tributary of the Helmand, from the north, in the Hazarajat.

WARDAK
وردك
    A tribe of Saiyids holding a narrow strip of country which runs from
    the Hazara portion of the Ghazni district to the western portion of
    the Logar valley, and includes the Tangi Wardak defile. The people
    are quiet, hospitable and industrious, and their country is well
    cultivated. The present headman of Wardak, including Tangi Waghjan
    and Tangi Wardak, is Nazir Muhammad Ismail Khan.
    The founder of the tribe was Ward. He had four sons--1, Mayar; 2,
    Nuri; 3, Mirkhel; 4, Gudai--and the four sub-divisions of the War-
    daks are called after the above.
    The most prominent members of the tribe in recent years have been
    Mustaufi Habibulla Khan, General Ghulam Haidar Khan and Muhammad
    Jan, notorious for his opposition to the British in 1879-80, and who
    was afterwards put to death by Amir Abdur Rahman's orders.

Molloy says of this tribe: "The Wardaks are subdivided as follows:
1. Mayar   2. Mir Khel   3. Nuri
"In their territory are the following places--Shashgao, inhabited by the Mir Khel and Mayar sections; Shaikhabad, in which are the Mayars. Between Shashgao and Shaikhabad is the Dara-i-Shiniz, where all three sections are found. The Dara-i-Unkhai belongs to the Nuri section. The Dara-i-Tangi to the Mir Khel section; whilst both the Mir Khel and Mayar sections are found in the Dara-i-Khawai. Jaghalie is a Mayar village with a few of the Mir Khel section interspersed among its inhabitants. Gardan-i-Masjid is another Mayar village. In Deh Mirdad all three sections are found. The Wardaks are computed at 20,000 families, and they pay one lakh of rupees in revenue." (Bellew, Hastings, I.B.C.) Places with this name are located at 34-15 68-0 m., and 34-40 70-10 G. (LWA)

*WARGHA   ورغه
33-22 69-53 m. A village located northeast of Matun in Paktia province.

*WARGUR   ورگور
33-50 69-48 m. A village north of Chamkanni in Paktia province.

WARIAJ   See ARIOH   وریج

WARKHAN   See MADINUI   ورخان

WARNATA   ورنته
34- 70-. A village in Laghman. It is reckoned as one township with Adar. Inhabitants. Arokis. (Warburton.)

WARSANDAN   ورسندان
The name applied to the western end of the Hindu Kush.

WARSANDAN   ورسندان
An alternative name for the Tun Khana pass over the Hindu Kush--see 'Zak'.

WASIL   واصل
34- 69-. A fort in the Kah Dara division, Koh Daman, northwest of Kabul. (Masson.)

WASTAZI   وستزی
32- 68-. A village 88 miles south of Ghazni, on the road to the Kundar and Gumal valleys. It is situated in a hilly and partially cultivated country; the water is brackish, from wells. (Lumsden.)

WATKOL   Or WADQOL   واد قول
35-20 69-33 m. A village in the Upper Panjshir valley, on the left bank of the stream, 4 miles above Bazarak. 30 houses of Tajiks. (Shahzada Taimus.)

WATTAPUR   وته پور (کته پور)
34- 70-. A village in the Surkhab department of the Jalalabad district. It is sometimes called Kala-i-Shukar Khan, and its inhabitants are Ghilzais. It is situated 5 miles west of the junction of the Kabul and Surkhab rivers, on the right bank of the latter. (Jenkyns.) The place may also be called Utapur. A village with the name Katapur is located at 34-24 70-14 m. (LWA)

WATTI JABAR KHEL واټ جبارخیل
34- 70-. A village in Laghman. Inhabitants: Jabar Khel Ghilzais. (Warburton.)

WATTIPUR واتی پور
34- 70-. A village in Laghman, close to the junction of the Kabul and Alingar rivers, and between them both. (Warburton.) Probably the same as Wattapur. (LWA)

WAWAK Or WEYWAH واوک (ویوه)
35-18 69-10 m. A village in the Salang Dara, about 20 1/4 miles above Parwan, and close to another village called Arzani. They lie at the junction with the Salang of a small dara which comes in from the west; up this dara a road is said to lead to Walang, a halting-place at the head of the Ejan Dara. The Salang stream is here about 20 feet wide; there is a good ford immediately above the village, and just below is a foot-bridge, 5 or 6 feet wide. The road bearers are of white poplar and the bridge is probably strong enough for pack animals, but the roadway is not good. (I.B.C.) Recent maps show the spelling Wiwa. (LWA)

WAZGHAR See SIAHGIRD وازغر
A village with this name is located at 35-3 68-52 m. (LWA)

WAZGHUNAJUI وژگونه جوی
Elevation 9,045 feet. A subdivision of the Dai Zangi district of Lal.

WAZA KHWA, WAZIKHWA Or MASHURAY وازه خواه
32-12 68-21 m. Waza Khwa is a woleswali in Ghazni province. The woleswali comprises an area of 3,551 square kilometers and has an agricultural population that has been estimated at from 4,211 to 8,320. The woluswali is bounded in the west by Nawa, in the east by Gomal and Wol-Mamay, in the north by Jani Khel, in the northwest by Dila. Waza Khwa has about 82 villages, 19 of which have more than 500 inhabitants. The villages are listed in the PG as follows: Haji Adam Khel, Akram Khan, Andai, Bazid, Batta Khel, Burj, Buzai, Patnai, Khwajer, Ashuq, Qabat, Mulla Karo, Tarwah, Tarwakai, Tanga-i-Najaf, Tor Tangai, Torwam, Nur Murgha, Spina Khama, Chashma-i-Azad Khan, Chashma-i-Sar Qalam, Hayat Khel, Khargah, Khezer Khel, Khaira-bad, Warabni, Zang Khel, Zarghun, Sperki, Shabi Khel, Shukur Khel, Shinko Wall, Sha Khel, Shahnawaz, Shahin, Shergul Tarkha, Omar Khel (Omaran Khel), Ashuq Khel, Abdul Matin, Abdul Jalil-i-Petaw, Qala-i-Mehman wa Zafar, Karez-i-Petaw, Kudali, Kamkai Wazkhwah, Kach Khor-i-Mulla Shah Moh'd, Kotsak, Gul Shah Gari, Gulabi, Lalizai, Landi, Qala-i-Moh'd Khan, Mashwarrai, Marjan, Manzai, Mullayan, Najaf, Wassel Khel, Qala-i-Haji Raz Moh'd, Mankai, Sangin, Arab Shakhil, Maryani Pataw, Goshta, Aka Khel-i-Tawgari, Tolai, Jani Khel, Chatak, Chali, Chenargai, Khud Kundi, Haji Dosti, Shah Mardan, Ghat (Ghash), Gada Geram-i-Jalalzai, Gerdawi (Gorawi), Gadaywal-i-Jalalzai, Nag-har, Nangar Khel, Wuch Khwarah, Din Omar, Wali, and Atum Khel. (LWA) In 1912 this area was described as follows:
A locality inhabited by Sulaiman Khel Ghilzais, and lying west of the Sulaiman range. According to native information obtained by Lieutenant Benn, the Taraki Tirwah-Ghazni road reaches the Wazikhwah plain at about 19 miles, and then crosses it through cultivation and Sulaiman Khel villages until camp at Marjan is reached at 26 miles. Water good and plentiful; supplies of every kind obtainable, also bhusa. No grass, fuel scarce, camel-grazing good. From Wazikhwah three main roads lead off to Ghazni: (1) by the Shinkai Kotal and

Oban; (2) by Sara Kala; (3) by Patanai and Oban. There are many villages in the vicinity, inhabited by Tarakis and Sulaiman Khels. (Benn.)

*WAZIRI وزیری
33-2 68-1 m. A village located a few miles off the Kandahar-Ghazni road in Ghazni province.

WAZIRABAD وزیرآباد
34-33 69-10 G. A large straggling village, one mile northwest of Sherpur, near Kabul. The inhabitants are Kizilbashis. The place gives its name to the lake lying to its north. This lake is 4 1/2 miles long, and on an average 1/2 mile broad. (Kennedy.) Another village with this name is located at 34-27 70-22 G. (LWA)

WAZIRBAGH وزیرباغ
34-25 70-28. The name of a garden and palace of the Amir lying about 1 mile to the west of Jalalabad.

WAZIR KALA وزیرقلعه
34- 69-. A village on the right bank of the Logar river, in the lower or northern portion of the valley. It is about a mile south of Muhammad Agha. The village consists of two hamlets, inhabited by Ahmadzais, Hazaras, and Tajiks. In 1880 there were only 20 families in the place. (Clifford, Euan Smith.) A village with this name is located at 34-0 69-4 G. (LWA)

WAZIR KALA وزیرقلعه
34-27 68-24 m. A village at the eastern foot of the Unai pass on the main Kabul-Herat road. It contains some 20 families of Taimurs, headman (in 1904) Daulat Muhammad. The inhabitants possess some 50 head of cattle and 100 sheep and goats. The annual production of wheat and barley averages about 430 Indian maunds. (Wanliss.) Recent maps show only the name Wazir. (LWA)

WAZIR KAREZ وزیرکاریز
34-3 69-3. A village in the Logar district, 3 miles northeast of Hisarak, on the right bank of the river. The inhabitants are Hazaras, and in 1880 they numbered 40 families. (Euan Smith, Clifford.)

WAZIR RUD وزیررود
34- 70-. A tributary of the Surkhab river, rising in the northern slopes of the Safed Koh and joining the Surkhab just above Bawali (Rozabad). It is a perennial stream and is occasionally impassable in spring as much as 15 miles above its junction with the Surkhab. (I.B.C.)

WERAN See KAMAHBIDA وران
There is a valley with this name, at 35-35 70-50 and a pass at 35-28 70-52 A. (LWA)

WESHAR ویشر
A place on the road between Kabul and Farajghan, 154 miles from the latter. (Stewart.)

WEYWAH See WAWAK ویوه

WEZGUL وزگل
35-30 70-58 m. One of the main heads of the Presungul or Pech river.

WILAYATI ولایتی
34- 69-. A village in the Jalalabad district, in the Besud department. The inhabitants are Arabs. The village is surrounded by cultivated land, watered by irrigation channels from the Logar river. There is a plentiful supply of water from these channels, and from the river itself. (Jenkyns, I.B.C.)

WILAYATI ولایتی
34-28 69-12 m. A small village in the Kabul district, about 1 mile southwest of Bini Hisar and 1/2 mile north of the Logar river. Inhabitants: Ghilzais. (Kennedy.)

*WOL MAMAI ورومعی (ورمه می)
32-5 68-41. Wol Mamai is an alaqadari in Ghazni province. The alaqadari comprises an area of 3,272 square kilometers and has an agricultural population that has been estimated at from 3,440 to 5,195. The alaqadari is bounded in the west by Wazakhwa, in the north by Gomal, in the east and south by the State of Pakistan. Wol Mamai has about 38 villages, 3 of which have more than 500 inhabitants. The villages are listed in the PG as follows:
Ahmad Khel, Akhtar Dad, Shah Sekandar, Akhtar Denar Khel, Ispasit, Manzai, Alokozai, Terkha, Jabar Khel, Khezer Khel, Danar Khel Wal, Danar Khel-i-Arta Ghbarga, Faiz Moh'd Danar-Khel, Duchina, Dawlat Sharak, Landi, Rahmat (Chawar Khel), Rui, Sangar Khel, Sayed Khan Khel, Mad Zar, Shahbaz Khan Khel, Ghulam Rasul, Qandil, Guli Khel, Moh'd Jan, Jalalzai, Masum Khel-i-Mir Dal, Masum Khel-i-Karim, Mamai, Niyazi, Wasel Khel-i-Ismail Khan, Wasel Khel-i-Ghulam Raza, Lalo Khel, Nakand, Safed Rish-i-Jalad, Sayyid Khan Khel-i-Surkai, Ahmad Khel-i-Surkai, and Mahmud Khel.

WORAKI ورکی
33- 69-. A small village at the southeastern extremity of the Mukhbil valley. (Kane.)

WUCH ALGAD وچ الگد
34-14 69-57. A small valley in a northern spur from the Safed Koh range, which runs down to the Kudi Khel and Mama Khel villages in the Khugiani country, south of Gandamak. Lieutenant-Colonel Stewart, of the Guides, who visited it in May 1879, writes of it as follows:
"The road lay up this valley, called in Pushtu the 'Wuch Algad', or dry ravine. Why the name has been given cannot be ascertained, for it is anything but dry, and contains a good volume of water, sufficient to support considerable cultivation." (Stewart.)

WUJAI وجی
A small valley tributary to the Helmand near its source.

*WURGAR ورگار
33-42 69-45 m. A village on the Gabrtoy, some 8 miles southwest of Chamkanni in Paktia province.

*WURGHALAY ورغالی
34-42 71-7 m. A village located a few miles southeast of Sherkani near the Pakistan border, Kunar province.

WUTKHEL See UTKHEL اوت خیل

YADGAR KALA یادگار قلعه
34- 68-. A village in the Birgalich Dara, at the point where the

latter is entered by the road leading from the Shibar valley over the Jalmish Kotal. Yadgar Kala is about 6 1/2 miles from the Jalmish Kotal and the valley is here about 200 yards wide, with plenty of grass. (I.B.C.)

YAGHIBAND یاغی بند
34-10 70-27. A village in the Jalalabad district, 4 miles southwest of Mazina. Inhabitants: Shinwaris. (Jenkyns.)

YAGHIBAND یاغی بند
34- 69-. A village on the road from Gandamak to Tezin, southwest of Jagdalak fort, and due west of the Pezwan Kotal. (Kennedy.)

YAHIA یحیی
34-36 69-15 m. A village 8 miles north of Kabul, 2 miles northwest of Tara Khel, and 1 1/2 miles east of Paiminar. Inhabitants: Tajiks. (I.B.C.) Another village with this name is located at 31-50 68-8 A. (LWA)

YAHYA KHEL یحیی خیل
A section of the Kharotis. A village with this name is located at 32-56 68-39 A. (LWA)

YAKATUT یکه توت
34- 69-. A collection of villages lying to the east of Sherpur (Kabul district), and about 2 miles from it. It stands on both banks of the Kabul river, and contains the following villages:
1. Kala-i-Mirza Muhammad Ali (Kizilbash)
2. Abdul Majid (Tajik)
3. Mirza Ghaias (Tajik)
4. Ali Mardan (Tajik)
5. Ismail (Tajik)
6. Kala-i-Jurab (Tajik)
7. Kala-i-Miru Khel (Tajik)
8. Kala-i-Kadir Khan (Durani)
9. Taj Muhammad Khan (Durani)   (Kennedy.)

YAKAWLANG Or YAKH WALANG یکاولنگ
34-44 66-58. Yakawlang is the name of a woleswali in the Bamian province. The woleswali comprises an area of 6,628 square kilometers and has an agricultural population which has been estimated by various Afghan sources at from 18,820 to 30,349. The woleswali is bounded in the west by Ghur and Jawzjan, in the north by Samangan provinces, in the east by Kahmard, Saighan, and Bamian, and in the south by Panjab districts. Yakawlang has about 116 villages of which about 21 have more than 500 inhabitants. The villages are listed in the PG as follows: Baraka, Baghalak (Bafalakha), Band-i-Amir, Div Khana, Sang-i-Surakh, Bedak-i-Siya Dara-i-Sufla, Bedak wa Juy-i-Nau, Bidak, Pudinato, Tajekan, Shina Dara-i-Ali wa Tano, Shina, Taghak-i-Otapur, Tang-i-Safidak (Sang-i- Safidak), Chahar Dewar wa Safid Rah, Chahardeh, Chehel Burj, Chaman-i-Chardeh (Chaman-ighor), Chashma-i-Pahlu, Barkhaha, Zardiga, Zamin-i-Rajab, Siya Khak, Dahan-i-Zurlich wa Sar-i-Sorlich, Zurlich, Sabzil, Sar Reg, Sartarnuk wa Showha, Sartarnuk, Sabz Dara, Seh Pakhsa-i-Chel Gaw, Sagduw, Sokhtagi, Sarma Qol, Siya Bamak, Kargah (Garga), Sarbazan, Safed Barah (Safed Dara) Sar Murghi, Kushkak, Halwa Qawm, Khak-i-Do-i-Sufla, Khak-i-Do-i-Ulya, Khurjin Bulaq-i-Ulya wa Sufla, Khak-i-Chighal, Kharestan (Khamistan), Band-i-Kakruk-i-Amir, Kham-i-Astana, Ghunda Sangine (Ghunda Sang), Jushang-i-Sar-i-Qol, Dara-i-Chesht, Dara-i-Ali, Do Burja, Dahan-i-Murghi, Ra Qol (Sar Qol), Anda wa

Shatoye, Sabz Nau, Zarin, Yeslach, Kharestan (Sharistan), Sachak (Sarchak), Shor Shirin Kin-i-Bala (Shahr Shirin Bagnila), Shamsuddin-i-Dasht Nek (Shamrin-i-Dasht Neka), Shir Dosh was Juy Nau, Gharak, Firoz Bahar, Qurghan, Qalandaran, Kata Qala, Kochagak, Koh Kanak, Kaligan, (Qawmabad), Gamab, Gazak-i-Sharshari, Miyana Deh-i-Sharshari, Gard Bid-i-Dahr Chi, Deh Turachi, Garan Ghabar (Gardan Ghabr), Kalta Tup-i-Sulfa, Kalta Tup-i-Ulya, Tubak, Kafalzak (Taghalzak), Lilorha, Larnozan (Mirbazan), Mohammad Sharaf-i-Rustam (Mohd. Sharif), Mush Khana, Sargich (Bargich), Baghalak wa Surkh Qala, Dahan-i-Kamar Kuch wa Royaha, Rustam, Sardagh (Sirdagh), Minar, Menda Yak, Namadak-i-Sulfa, Namadak-i-Ulya, Naitaq, Na-Yak, Bazar-i-Yakawlang, Nauabad. Nauabad-i-Deh Surkh, Olangak, Hazar Chashma, Duzdan Chashma, Dahan-i-Kanak, Deh Surkh, Dahan Tawa, Bid Mushkin wa Gerd Bid (Bed-i-Mushki), Gunbadi, Akhundan, Shatughan, Jarukashan, Qala-i-Jafar, Sar Bulaq, Zarsang wa Razag, Sarkanak, Gurgin-i-Hawza Shah, Siyah Dara-i-Ulya, Sachak-i-Qawm-i-Hasan, and Isperah. (LWA)

In 1912, this area was described as follows: a subdistrict of Bamian inhabited chiefly by Dai Zangis. It lies west of Bamian proper, and is drained by the head-waters of the Band-i-Amir river. On the north it is bounded by the Dara Yusuf and Balkh-Ab districts of Afghan Turkistan, on the west and south by the Dai Zangi country proper and the Koh-i-Baba. It covers an area of about 2,800 square miles, a part of which, however, is barren and uninhabited, except by people grazing their flocks in summer.

The source of the Rud-i-Band-i-Amir is in the curious lakes called Band-i-Amir; from the lakes to Sulij, the deep valley of the river, though generally speaking more than 8,000 feet above the sea, is fairly populated and fertile. Below Sulij the road down the valley is quite impracticable for baggage animals. See "Band-i-Amir."

The Bamian-Daulat Yar road runs across the district from east to west, via the Bakkak Kotal, and meets the Kabul-Hazarajat road near Kala Safarak.

The Ghazni road having crossed the Koh-i-Baba by the lofty Zard Sang Kotal, leads to Band-i-Amir, whence it runs via Dara Yusuf to Tashkurghan.

Information regarding population, supplies, etc., is given under Bamian (district).

YAKH DARA يخ دره
35-1 68-51. A valley which leads out of the Ghorband valley, 1/2 mile from the entrance to the Chahardar pass. (Leech.)

YAKHNAO يخ نو
35-3 69-4. A large glen joining that of Kaoshan about 5 1/2 miles south of the Kaoshan Kotal.
It comes from the northeast, its head being probably close to the kotal, and joins the main glen just below Maidan-i-Khuni. There is said to be no road up it. (Maitland.)

*YAKH WALANG See YAKAWLANG يخاولنگ

*YAKUB يعقوب
33-22 68-23 m. A village located some 10 miles south of Ghazni, left of the Highway to Ghazni.

YAKUB DEH يعقوب ده
34-28 69-14. A large village 4 miles southeast of Kabul, and 1 1/2 mile from Bini Hisar. It stands on the left bank of the Logar river, and is connected with the village of Shewaki, on the right

bank, by a bridge 90 feet long by 8 feet broad, composed of wood supported on crates filled with stones as piers; no parapets. The village contains 80 or 90 houses, and is surrounded by orchards, gardens and cultivation. Inhabitants: Muhammadzais, Tajiks and Utkhels. (Kennedy, I.B.C.)

YAKUBI يعقوبی
34-27 69-59 m. A village in Khost about 9 miles north by east of Matun. There is room for a small camp on the right bank of the stream which flows just north of the village. The inhabitants are Lewan Khel, Jajis. (I.B.C.) Another village with this name is located at 34-21 71-3 G. (LWA)

YAKUB KHEL يعقوب خيل
35-20 69-31. A village in the upper Panjshir glen, situated on both banks of the stream, about one mile above Bazarak. Thirty houses of Tajiks. (Shahzada Taimus.)

YANGUR ينگور
A main section of the Dai Zangi Hazaras.

YAR AHMAD ياراحمد
A village in the Jaghatu Hazara country.

YARGHATI يارغتی
33- 68-. A village 18 miles south of Ghazni. It is situated in a singularly dull and dreary looking country, quite bare of trees and even brushwood. (Bellew.)

YAR MUHAMMAD يارمحمد
34- 69-. A village near Kabul, on the right bank of the Logar river, between Kala-i-Sak and the bridge at Bagrami. Inhabitants: Muhammadzai Afghans. (I.B.C.)

YASIN ياسين
34- 69-. Elev. 8,000 feet. A fort 33 miles southeast of Kabul, on the route from Kabul to Jalalabad by the Karkacha pass. (Thornton.) A village with this name is located at 34-52 69-33 G. (LWA)

*YERGANA يرګنه
33-38 68-47 m. A village located southwest of Kharwar in Logar province.

YER KOL or QOL-I-HER هيرقول
35-7 69-3. A glen draining southwards from the Hindu Kush, about 4 miles to the east of and parallel to, the upper portion of the Kaoshan glen. It joins the Kaoshan about two miles above the point where the latter debouches into Ghorband. It is of considerable size and up it there are villages and cultivation belonging to the Shinwaris, but at, and just above, its junction with the Kaoshan it is a defile with high rocky sides. The stream of the Koh-i-Yer has to be crossed by the road leading from the Kaoshan pass down to the Ghorband valley. It is nearly as large as the Kaoshan stream itself. (Maitland.)

YURT يورت
34- 68-. Two small villages lying about 4 miles west of the Unai pass. (See Military Report on Hazarajat, Part II.)

YURT   يورت
   34- 68-. Elev. 9,000 feet. A plain situated on the crest of the
   Paghman range, 56 miles from Kabul, being an elevated table-land
   about 8 miles broad, at an elevation of 9,000 feet. It has an
   uncongenial climate and a poor soil. The chief crop is barley, but
   enough can never be raised for the inhabitants, who consequently
   emigrate in great numbers in the winter to Kabul. The only fuel
   obtainable on it is the buta bush, and grass is plentiful. (Wood.)

YURT   يورت
   34- 67-. A tributary of the Helmand, from the south, in the Besud
   country. (See Military Report on Hazarajat, Part II.)

YUSUF KALA   يوسف قلعه
   A village in the Logar district, southern division. In 1880 the
   place contained 200 families of Astanazai Ghilzais. (Euan Smith,
   Clifford.)

YUSUF KHEL   يوسف خيل
   33-40 68-53 G. A village in Kharwar, about 22 miles northeast of
   Ghazni. (I.B.C.) Another village with this name is located at 33-3
   68-39 A. (LWA)

*YUSUF KHEL   يوسف خيل
   33-3 68-39. Yusuf Khel is a village and an alaqadari in Ghazni
   province. The alaqadari comprises an area of 550 square kilometers
   and has an agricultural population that has been estimated at from
   5,780 to 6,130. The alaqadari is bounded in the west by Giru, in
   the southwest by Katawaz, in the southeast by Sultan Khel, in the
   northeast by Sharan and in the northwest by Andar. Yusuf Khel has
   about 11 villages, 4 of which have more than 500 inhabitants. The
   villages are listed in the PG as follows: Barat Khel, Bokhan Khel,
   Jar Kana-i-Ulya wa Sulfa, Zmarai Kot, Khar Bin, Madrasa-i-Khar Bin,
   Khazan, Mast, Malakh, Yusuf Khel, and Kochi-i-Landizai.

ZABAR DAST   زبردست
   33- 69-. A village in the Jaji country, 25 miles from Kurram fort,
   situated above the Karaja stream. No supplies are procurable, and
   forage of all sorts is scarce. Water is plentiful. There is plenty
   of open ground to the north suitable for encamping.
   This village would be better described as situated in the Hariob
   valley, 8 miles northeast of Ali Khel. (Lumsden, I.B.C.)

ZAFAR KHAN   ظفرخان
   34- 70-. A fort in the Jalalabad district, situated on a low, stony
   ridge, about 4 miles south of Fort Battye, 5 east of Nimla, and 9
   southwest of Rozabad. In 1880 the fort was in good preservation,
   with high mud walls and towers, and was surrounded by mulberry
   trees. Good water from a ravine southwest of the place. Fair
   camping ground at foot of ridge. (Masson.)

ZAHIDABAD See SAIYIDABAD   زاهدآباد
   A village with this name is located at 34-16 69-7 G. (LWA)

ZAHIK See GAHIK   زاهك

ZAHO   زاهو (زاوه)
   34- 70-. A village described as situated beyond Gardez Zurmat. A
   force under Captain Hay is said to have gone there in September 1841

to punish a chief, but finding it much stronger than was supposed, reinforcements were sent out under Colonel Oliver to destroy the forts. There seems to be no mention of it except in Lady Sale's book. (Sale.) A place with this name is located at 34-10 70-5 G. (LWA)

ZAIDAM زیدم
A subdivision of the Dai Zangi Hazaras.

ZAIMANI زایمانی
34-28 68-40 G. Two Ghilzai villages on the main Kabul-Herat road, 3 1/4 miles east of Jalrez. The name Zaimini is also applied to the Kabul river valley for about 5 miles below Jalrez. (Wanliss.)

*ZAINAL زینل
35-4 68-45 m. A village located on a tributary of the Ghorband, about 4 miles from its junction with the latter, in Parwan province.

ZAINO زینو
34- 69-. A village on the Hisarak division of the Jalalabad district. Inhabitants: Duranis. (Jenkyns.)

ZAK زاك
35- 68-. A pass leading over the Hindu Kush from the Ghorband to the Surkhab valleys. It can be reached from the south by either the Robat of Shingarian Dara. The former is a narrow ravine debouching through broken, barren clay hills four and a half miles below Bin-i-Sehwak. The Shingarian is a similar ravine joining the main valley 3 miles higher up. The track up it leads to the village of Sari Kazi, and there divides. The left branch crosses the main range by the Kotal-i-Tun Khana (or Warsandan), and descends by the Dara Narkoh to the Surkhab valley, a little above Barfak. The right branch crosses the main range by the Kotal-i-Zak, and leads down the Dara Margh to Tallah on the Surkhab. All these roads are said to be very difficult, and only practicable for bullocks and yabus, and may be disregarded as possible routes for troops. The Kara Malli taifa inhabits the Dara Shingarian. (Peacocke.)

*ZAKAR ذكر
33-28 68-36 m. A village near Tasan, some 10 miles southeast of Ghazni.

ZAKHEL زاخیل
34- 70-. A village 15 miles from Jalalabad, on the Kunar river, consisting of 80 houses of Tajiks. (Leech.)

ZAKHEL-I-GIRDI KACH زاخیل گردی کچ
A Kuchi village in the Jalalabad district, Surkhab department. (Jenkyns.)

ZAKHEL-I-ZULFIKAR-KHAN زاخیل ذوالفقار خان
34-24 70-33 m. A village in the Jalalabad district, Kama department. It is situated on the left bank of the Kunar, at its confluence with the Kabul. The inhabitants are Hindkis, Arabs, Mohmands and Dehgans. (Jenkyns.)

ZAKHEL See ZANGO KATS زاخیل

ZAKHO KHEL زاخوخیل
A section of the Kharotis. A village with this name is located at 33-19 70-3 G. (LWA)

ZALIKAN زالكان
35-8 68-56. A ravine which joins the Nimakao glen from the north-west at about 8 miles above where the latter debouches into the Ghorband valley. At Dahan-i-Zalikan (the junction of the Zalikan and Nimakao), there is said to be room for a large camp; the ground is partly cultivated and there is a certain amount of grass in summer. Some large bushes and small trees are available for fuel, but no supplies are to be had nearer than the Ghorband valley. Up the Zalikan ravine a road runs to the head of the Waghur, or Wadaghur, a glen lying between, and parallel to, the Nimakao and Deh Tangi glens.
Nearly opposite Dahan-i-Zalikan the Nimakao glen is joined from the east by the Talkhak ravine; up this ravine a track, said to be easily practicable for horsemen and Afghan camels, leads over the Chashma Husain kotal and down the Husain ravine into the Kaoshan glen, which it joins just below Sherakai. (I.B.C.)

ZAL RED زل رید
A Tajik village in Maidan. (Molloy.)

ZAMANI زمانی
34- 68-. A beautiful valley which comprises a portion of the Kabul river, near its source, below Jalrez and Sar-i-Chashma. (Masson.)

ZAMAN KALA زمان قلعه
35- 70-. A village east of Charikar, inhabited by 100 families of Tajiks. (Shahzada Taimus.)

ZAMAN KHAN زمان خان
34- 69-. A fort included in Alla-ud-din, Chardeh valley of Kabul; 15 families of Gadi Hazaras and Kizilbashis. (I.B.C.)

ZAMBURAK زمبورك
33-59 68-46 G. A pass in Wardak country, leading into the Logar valley. The following is a report on the pass by Captain Larminie, R.E., attached to the Ghazni Field Force, on its march to the Logar valley on April 1880:
"On the morning of the 29th April, the upper portion of the Logar valley between Shaikhabad and Tangi Wardak having been declared impracticable for guns, a reconnaissance of the Zamburak pass was ordered with a view to crossing them there.
"The Zamburak pass is situated near the end of the range of hills in the angle formed by the junction of the Shiniz and Logar rivers. The slopes on the Saiyidabad, or western side, were found to be very easy and requiring but little work to reach the top of the pass without difficulty; but on the side towards Tangi Wardak the fall was very abrupt, in some places almost precipitous. The hills were on this side composed chiefly of mica schist, the strata being tilted up at various high angles.
"An examination showed that a narrow track existed for three-fourths of a mile leading down into a wide, sandy nala, which afforded an easy road along its bed for the remainder of the distance down to the Logar river, near Tangi Wardak. It appeared probable that, with large working parties, this path with improvements and a change of direction at the lower portion, might be made passable for guns by the 2nd of May; but as it was considered desirable that at least one battery of artillery should cross on the 1st, orders were issued to commence work upon the path with a view to improve it as far as time

would allow of, whilst a position for a gun-slide was decided upon. Scarcely had the work commenced, when a second report arrived, declaring the Logar valley route practicable, upon which work on the pass was stopped, and a third and careful reconnaissance made of the valley resulted in the pass being decided upon as the least hazardous method of getting guns to Tangi Wardak.

"Work on the pass was accordingly recommenced at daylight on the 30th. The gun-slide was laid out down a spur somewhat to the right of the existing path, the upper half of which had a slope of about 1 in 2 and the lower about 1 in 3.

"A wire cable was in course of preparation to run the guns down the entire distance, about 1,100 feet, into a small nala, the way was being prepared, when, at this stage, the Officer Commanding detachment sappers and miners, who had been working vigorously at the road, reported that, having found the rock much softer and more easily worked than had been anticipated, he would probably be able to make a track practicable for guns by 10 o'clock the following morning.

"With the permission of the Brigadier-General Commanding, who was on the pass at the time, the work on the gun-slope was stopped, and the working parties transferred to the road, the result being that at 8 on the following morning the battery of Horse Artillery commenced the descent. The entire battery, guns and wagons, was drawn up in the bed of nala already mentioned three hours and forty minutes from the time of starting.

"Considerable improvements were made in the road during the day, and these, combined with the better arrangement resulting from the experience of the first day, enabled the second battery, G-4th Royal Artillery, to accomplish the same feat on the morning of the 2nd of May in exactly two hours.

"The guns and wagons were on each occasion taken down by hand for the greater part of the way, limbered up, with drag ropes attached, manned by working parties of 25 men to each gun or wagon; the shoe or dragchain was used whenever considered necessary.

"At the lower portion of the road, where it ran along a small nala, it was found practicable to use the horses.

"No accident occurred to either battery during the descent, and all the mules and ponies of the batteries, as also those of the Ordnance Park, Engineers' Field Park, and entire baggage of two companies sappers and miners were enabled to cross without any hitch."

ZANA KHAN زنه خان
33-40 68-36. Zana Khan is the name of an alaqadari in the Ghazni province. The alaqadari comprises an area of 258 square kilometers and has an agricultural population which has been estimated at 3,350. The alaqadari is bounded in the west by Khwaja Omri, in the north by Sayyidabad and Charkh, in the east by Charkh, in the south by Deh Yak, and in the southwest by Ghazni. Zana Khan includes some 34 villages, none of which has more than 500 inhabitants. The villages are listed in the PG as follows: Azam Wal, Aman Khel, Bashagi, Bayani, Payendah Khel, Pur Del, Chagi, Khacha Khel, Khwaja Khel, Khushab Del, Daddo, Dadak, Dur Khan Khel, Rahat Khel, Rashid Khel, Zarak, Qala-i-Surkh, Sar-i-Qol, Safedar, Sang Ab, Shaykhan, Alam Khel, Ewaz Khan, Farid, Faqir, Mamush (Qala-i-Mamoshi), Qala-i-Moh'd-Hasan, Gadol, Gogar, Lola, Mullayan, Yasin Khel, Shahi, and Haibat Khel. (LWA) In 1912 the area was described as follows: A small valley, and a pass of the same name, leading from Ghazni into Kharwar, the summit of the pass lying about 19 miles northeast of Ghazni. The road over the pass is fit for Indian camels but would

require some improvement for wheeled artillery, especially on the eastern side which is the more difficult of the two. (I.B.C.)

ZANGAL زنگل
35-5 68-59 G. A village in the Kaoshan glen, about 6 1/4 miles above its junction with the Ghorband valley. It lies concealed in a mass of thick orchards terraced down to the stream. (I.B.C.)

ZANGO KATS Or ZAKHEL زنگوکڅ
34- 70-. A village of 300 houses in the Jalalabad district; it is situated in a ravine of the same name 10 miles south-southwest of Ali Boghan. The inhabitants are Mohmands. There is a plentiful supply of water here. (I.B.C.)

ZANGUL زنگول
34- 70-. A village in the Jalalabad district, 3 miles southeast of Besud. The inhabitants are Arabs, and in 1879 the headman was Saiyid Arab. (Jenkyns.)

ZAOLI زولی
A subsection of Daikhitai Hazaras.

ZARAK زرك
33- 69-. One of the Ahmad Khel villages on the right bank of the Kurram river, southeast of Ali Khel. The place is said to be able to turn out 200 fighting men. (I.B.C.) Villages with this name are located at 33-14 69-23 A. and 33-19 68-1 m. (LWA)

ZARA KHUNDI زره خندی
34- 69-. The name given to a short route from Belut in the Hariob valley to Gandamak, through the Khugiani country. This begins by a difficult path from the Lalidar ravine up the precipitous sides of the Safed Koh. See "Lakarai." A fort with this name is located at 34-2 69-59 G. (LWA)

ZARDAK زردك
A locality in the Jaghuri Hazara country.

ZARDALU زردآلو
A section of Chahar Dasta Hazaras. A village with this name is located at 33-11 67-51 A. (LWA)

ZARDALU KAK زردآلوكك
35-6 68-40 G. A hamlet in the glen descending south from the Chahardar pass, from which it is distant about 9 miles.
There is ample room for a battalion to encamp on some level strips of cultivated ground on the left bank of the stream which flows in the glen, and further space is available a little way up and down the valley.
The water supply is good and abundant, and there is plenty of fuel; supplies in small quantities, are procurable from adjacent villages. Zardalu Kak is a most convenient halting-place for the 4th stage from Charikar on the road from Kabul to Haibak. (I.B.C.) A dara with this name is located at 35-5 67-35 G. (LWA)

ZARDGAH OR ZARD-I-GAO زردگاه
35-1 67-9 m. A village in Yak Walang, 17 miles (by road) north of Kala Jafir. In 1886 it was deserted on account of the locusts. The ordinary inhabitants are Takana Hazaras. Five miles southeast is the Kotal-i-Zardgah (10,500 feet). The ascent and descent are both

easy, over gentle slopes, and quite practicable for guns. The Kotal and ground on both sides of it are open dasht, cultivated in patches, and capable of being crossed in any direction. (Amir Khan.)

ZARD-I-GAO   See ZARDGAH   زرد گاو
A place with this name is located at 34-57 67-15 A. (LWA)

ZARD SANG   Or SHAHRISTAN   زرد سنگ
34- 66-. A tagao descending south to the head of the Kirman valley. A village with this name is located at 34-29 66-9 m. (LWA)

*ZARD SANG   زرد سنگ
33-56 68-6 m. A village located on a tributary of the Shimiltu, some 3 miles west of Payenda in Ghazni province. Another village with this name is located at 34-41 67-17 G., a mountain, at 34-22 66-40 G., and a dara at 35-12 67-58 G.

ZARD SANG   زرد سنگ
34-39 67-1 A. Elevation about 13,310 feet. A pass over the Koh-i-Baba range at the head of the Sar-i-Bulak Valley leading into the valley of the Band-i-Amir.

ZARD SANG   زرد سنگ
34-39 67-1 m. Elevation 10,820 feet. A village on the Maidan-i-Pai Kotal -- Mazar-i-Sharif road, about 4 miles north of the Zard Sang pass in the Koh-i-Baba range.

ZARD SANG   زرد سنگ
A village of about 10 houses in the east of the Dai Zangi country, on the left bank of the Siah Dara stream.

*ZARGAR   زرگر
33-29 68-22 m. A village located some 6 miles southwest of Ghazni, west of the road to Kandahar, in Ghazni province.

ZARGARAN   زرگران
34- 69-. A village in the Koh Daman, situated on an eminence south of the river Farza and about 24 miles northwest of Kabul. (Masson.) A village with this name is located at 32-42 67-18 A.

ZARGHUN SHAHR   زرغون شهر
34-7 69-9 m. A large village in the Logar valley; it lies on the Paiwar Kotal-Kabul road at about 33 miles from Kabul. It consists of 9 hamlets, and in 1880 had a population of 250 families, half Tajik and half Ahmadzai. There is room here for a very good and unlimited camping ground with an excellent water supply from karez. The surrounding land is very fertile, being watered by karez. Grain, fodder and fuel obtainable in great quantity. There is a shrine here of Khwaja Sadar-i-Aolia.
At Zargan Shahr the Paiwar Kotal-Kabul road meets the Logar valley route from Kabul to Ghazni.
It was from this village that Major-General Hills defeated, with his cavalry, the Zurmatis at Patkao-i-Shahana on the 1st July 1880, see the "Official History of the Second Afghan War." (I.B.C.)

ZARGHUN SHAHR   زرغون شهر
32-51 68-27 m. A village in the Katawaz district, about 56 miles south of Ghazni, 8 miles from Kala-i-Langar. It has a fort with about 50 houses of Sulaiman Khel Ghilzais, and about 500 acres of

cultivation, of which, however, much is fallow. (Broadfoot.)

ZARGRI زرگری

A narrow glen running south into the Gurzah tagao just east of the junction of the latter with the Akzarat valley.

ZARI زاری

34-40 66-53 m. Elevation 8,625 feet. Zari, otherwise known as Kala Nao, is situated at the junction of the Zari and Bakkak glens, 6 1/2 miles northeast of the Bakkak Kotal. Another place with this name is located at 35-57 66-42 A. (LWA)

ZARINKALA Or ZARIBKALA زرین کلا (زریب)

34-37 69-14 m. A small fort in the Kabul district, 3 miles northeast of the Paiminar Kotal. (I.B.C.) Recent maps show the name Zarin Kala. (LWA)

ZARKAWAL زرکوال

33-35 68-28. A village 4 miles northeast of Ghazni, on the road thence to Kharwar. (I.B.C.)

ZARSANG زرسنگ

35-13 67-58. A dara which drains north to the Saighan stream.
Starting from Nagara Khana at the junction of the Saighan and Bamian rivers, the road to Jalmish leads up the Saighan valley for about a mile and then runs up the narrow Pishang Dara. It is good, and fit for guns as far as the foot of the Salati Kotal. Here the track bends sharply to the left, and climbs the steep side of the valley. The ascent is 3/4 mile long, and the total rise is 1,012 feet. The ascent is very steep, as much as 1 in 3 for the last 1/4 mile, and the soil of the hillside is clay and loose gravel, affording rather precarious foothold on the final zig-zags. There is only a narrow foot track, and laden mules ascend with difficulty. To make even a good camel track would require some days. At the top of the kotal there is no descent, but the track almost at once strikes the bed of the Dara Kaftar Khana. Here a track branches to the left to Baghak in the Aodara.
The Kaftar Khana Dara is a shallow ravine about 30 to 50 yards wide, and its bed is level and good going for all arms over small grassy chamans, with many springs, for the next 3 miles. At 3 1/4 miles (mileage from the Salti Kotal), about a quarter mile short of the deserted fort of Kala Kaftar Khana, the road ascends over a gentle slope up the rise bordering the ravine on the left to the Kotal-i-Khawaja Tajdin. Altitude of the top of the kotal, 7,453 feet.
Here the track descends a drop of 700 feet into the Dara Zarsang. Its general gradient is 1 in 8, but steep portions occur at 1 in 6 to 1 in 4. There is a good track practicable for laden camels down the open hillside, and it could easily be improved.
The Dara Zarsang as far as Khawaja Kashmir, 6 1/4 miles, is fairly open. It is cultivated in patches; and though stony in places, there is a good camel track up it. For its first 1 1/4 miles above the foot of the descent from the Tajdin Kotal the fields are continuous. Portions of the surrouding hillsides are also cultivated. This portion is called Mandao, and there are two miles and some few scattered habitations. The Zarsang valley was inhabited and cultivated by the Tajiks of Baghak until 1886, but on account of the locusts they then emigrated to the Dara Yusuf. Two or three seminders still remain at Baghak; but the Zarsang valley is quite deserted. There is no wood, except an occasional large mulberry tree in the valley.

The Zarsang joins the Aodara at Baghak, and becomes very narrow and rock-bound in its lower portions. It is divided into the following small districts:

1. Mandao
2. Khawaja Kashmir
3. Tai Kandi
4. Saiyidan
5. Khawaja Ghar

Good camping ground at Mandao or at Khawaja Kashmir. No grass or fuel, but in ordinary years supplies would be procurable.

Altitude of Khawaja Kashmir 7,900 feet. Heavy snow falls in the Dara Zarsang, and lies for the three winter months.

Above Khawaja Kashmir the Dara Zarsang becomes a tortuous rocky defile shut in by lofty cliffs for three-quarters of a mile, and the track is very rocky and difficult for laden mules. It then opens out to a breadth of 250 yards; its bed becomes smooth, and the side slopes less rocky, and in some places smoothly rounded. Here the track is very easy and good, and runs through fields or small grassy chamans.

At 8 1/4 miles Kala Tai Kandi and a cluster of deserted hovels; 10 1/4 miles Saiyidana; and at 11 1/4 miles Khawaja Ghar.

At Khawaja Ghar the head of the valley is reached under the foot of a lofty serrated ridge. Here a track branches to the right to Ghandak and Bamian only passable by men on foot; and the track to Jalmish leaves the valley and bends to the left up an open hillside to the Kotal-i-Pandanao. The rise from Khawaja Kashmir to Khawaja Ghar is 1,850 feet. The top of the Pandanao Kotal is reached at 12 3/4 miles. Altitude 11,260 feet. Rise from Khawaja Ghar 1,500 feet. The ascent of the kotal, owing to its length (1 1/2 miles), is trying for baggage animals. There is, however, a good, but stony zig-zag path up the hillside of a general gradient of 1 in 7. The hillside is open; and there is no necessity to adhere to the pathway, and the gradient can easily be reduced by increasing the number of the returns. The descent is much steeper; it winds down a smooth bare spur; clay soil with loose stones. There is a rough pathway 4 feet wide; but the gradient is steep (1 in 8 to 1 in 4) and a false step would be fatal to any laden baggage animal. The foot of the descent is reached at 14 miles. Main descent from kotal is a fall of 1,400 feet.

Then there is a good path with easy gradient down a small open valley to 15 1/4 miles, as far as the small hamlet of Muhammad Kichah. The hamlet is situated at the junction of another tributary valley, both of these head valleys being bordered by lofty ridges thrown out from the main Ghandak mountain. In both of these head valleys, and for 2 miles below the hamlet, there is a considerable extent of cultivation (wheat) in terraces; and the ordinary population of the hamlet is thirty families, Tajiks of Ghandak.

The valley rapidly contracts between lofty rocky ridges, and rocky and difficult to its mouth, which is reached at 19 3/4 miles. The last 2 1/2 mile becomes a narrrow rocky gorge, and the track is throughout that distance as bad as it well could be, and is quite impracticable for any laden animals, except lightly laden mules and bullocks, and difficult even for them. At one place the bed of gorge is only 5 feet wide; at another it is only 10 feet wide between lofty cliffs, and the bed of the watercourse is the only means of passage. Down the watercourse one has to clamber often over sheet rock, over which a strong mountain torrent is flowing, and led horses make the descent with difficulty.

The path on meeting the Aodara fords the river Bamian, and runs up the right bank, re-crossing to the left bank to the principal hamlet of Jalmish, which is reached at 21 1/4 miles. Altitude 6,630 feet.

(Peacocke.) A village with this name is located at 34-4 68-43 m., and a mountain is at 34-39 67-1 A. (LWA)

*ZARSHAKH   زرشخ (شاخ)
34-35 69-1 m. A village located a few miles northwest of Qargha Lake in Kabul province.

ZARSHO   زرشو
A village 54 miles from Kabul, 69 miles from Farajghan, consisting of 100 houses of Safis. Water is abundant, from a stream. (Leech.)

ZARSHO-I-ARBABHA   زرشو اربابها
34- 70-. A village in the Kama department of the Jalalabad district. Inhabitants: Moghals. (Jenkyns.) A village with this name is located at 34-54 69-32 G. (LWA)

ZARSHO-I-JALALUDDIN KHAN   زرشو جلال الدين خان
34- 70-. A village in the same district as the foregoing. Inhabitants: Hindkis, Arabs, Mohmands and Dehgans. (Jenkyns.)

ZARYAFT   زريافت
34-25 67-48 G. A village in the Besud Country.

ZARYAFTA   زريافته
34- 66-. A village in the Dai Zangi district of Lal.

ZARYAFTA   See ROGHANI GARDAN   زريافته

ZAWA   زاوه
34-10 70-5 G. A village in the Jalalabad district, about 16 miles southeast of Gandamak. The inhabitants belong to the Kharbun section of the Khugianis. (Jenkyns.)

ZAWAR   زور
32-26 69-11 m. A stream which flows south along the west foot of the Spera range, and joins the Gumal at a point some 7 miles above the Kundar-Gumal confluence at Domandi. (I.B.C.) Recent maps show the spelling Za'ura Lgad. A village with this name is located at 32-42 69-20 G. (LWA)

ZEBBUDAK   زيبدك
34- 68-. A village on the Kabul river, near its source below Jalrez, whence this portion of the valley is sometimes called the district of Zebudak. It is entirely inhabited by Rustam Khel. Wheat and rice are produced in large quantities in the valley. (Masson.)

ZERANA   زيرانه
34- 70-. A village in Laghman on the left bank of the Kabul river, about 8 miles from its junction with the Alingar. Inhabitants: Kohistanis. The following hamlets are included in Zerana:
  1. Kotha-i-Azam   3. Banda-i-Mura Khan
  2. Banda-i-Abdulla Khan   4. Banda-i-Mulla Khan
      5. Kaj Mian Khan   (Warburton.)

ZERANI   زيرانی
34- 70-. A village 4 miles west of Jalalabad. The inhabitants are Tajiks and Dehgans. (Jenkyns.) Recent maps show the name Ziranj, at 34-31 70-8 m. (LWA)

ZERBACHA زربچه
34-13 70-41 m. A village in the Jalalabad district, about 3 miles south of Batikot. (Jenkyns.)

ZERU زيرو
A range of mountains described as "the end of the ridge which, coming from the Sulaiman range, divides Zurmat from Katawaz, and ends in the Ab-i-Istada lake." (Broadfoot.)

*ZERUK See ZILUK زيروك

ZIARAT زيارت
34-40 70-10. A village in Laghman, on the right of the Alishang river, 4 miles above its junction with the Alingar. It contains the following hamlets:
    1. Banda-i-Wali Muhammad
    2. Banda-i-Shekhan
    3. Banda-i-Sadulla Khan
The inhabitants are Sohak and Shaikhan Ghilzais. (Warburton.) Another village with this name is located at 34-13 70-58 G. (LWA)

ZIARAT-I-MEHTAR LAM زيارت مهترلام
A shrine in the Alishang valley, Laghman district, on the right bank of the river. It is supposed to be the tomb of Lamech, Noah's father, to whom some ascribe the origin of the name Laghman. (Holdich, Young.)

ZIARAT-I-PEWA زيارت پيوه
34- 70-. A halting place 8 miles from Sharshahi. Water plentiful. Supplies not procurable. Good camping ground. (Johnston.)

ZIDIG See AHMAD DIWANA زيدگ (صديق)

*ZIKRIAKHEL زكرياخيل
35-2 69-44 m. A village near Mirankhel, on a tributary of the Tagab, in Kapisa province.

*ZILUK Or ZIRUK زيروك
33-9 69-18. Ziluk is an alaqadari in Paktia province. The alaqadari comprises an area of 241 square kilometers and has an agricultural population that has been estimated at from 9,140 to 11,810. The alaqadari is bounded in the west by Neka, in the south by Urgun, in the east by Sperah, and in the north by Jadran. Ziluk has some 16 villages, 7 of which have more than 500 inhabitants. The villages are listed in the PG as follows: Salam Khan-i-Kesham, Bakhmala Kesham (Feroz Khan), Kheder Khel (Koti Khel), Sar Maidan, War Jana (Wurzana Ali Khan-Khel), Bali Wurzana (Wurzana Khel-i-Bali), Sharmai, Madakai, Sar Mast, Surai, Khudkai, Alamai, Dabai-i-Sultan-Khel, Tang-i-Sultan-Khel, Tolub Khel-i-Kesham, and Dalai.

ZIMMA زمه
34-43 69-11 m. A village in the Kabul district, 10 miles north of the Paiminar pass, on the left bank of the Ju-i-Bar stream. This village gives its name to a pass into Koh Daman. (Kinloch.)

ZIMMA زمه
34-43 69-11. A pass leading from the plain north of Kabul into the Koh Daman. Several roads from Kabul converge at the village of Zimma, southeast of the pass, where there are easy approaches over open ground to Baba Kush Kar, Ak Sarai, etc. It was by this pass

that Brigadier-General Baker entered the Koh-Daman in December 1879, in order to destroy the fortified villages belonging to Mir Bacha. (I.B.C.)

ZINA KHAN زینه خان (زنه)
33- 68-. A village said to be about 16 miles from Ghazni, towards Kharwar. The inhabitants are Wardaks; 100 houses; water from karez; some cultivation. The route on which this place stands is said to be quite impracticable for wheeled artillery, and supplies are probably very scarce on it. (Scott.) This is apparently the same place as Zanakhan. (LWA)

ZINDAN زندان
A valley mentioned by Babar in his memoirs, as lying to the west of Kabul. It is probably one of the valleys of the Hazarajat. (Babar.)

ZINDAWANA زنده وانه
34- 69-. A village between the Siah Sang ridge and the city of Kabul. It is a small straggling place on the right bank of the river, close to Postindoza. Inhabitants: Tajiks. (Kennedy.)

ZINTEGA زینتگه
33- 68-. Elev. 9,150 feet. A pass leading over the hills south of Kharwar to Kalalgu and Shilghar. The road from Mani Khel is very good and reaches the kotal by a scarcely perceptible ascent. Descent on south side is also very easy, and might with some trouble be used by wheeled artillery. This pass is one of the principal routes leading south from Kharwar. (Griesbach.)

ZIRAK زیرك
34-53 68-17. A difficult and high pass leading over the Koh-i-Baba, said to be only fit for pack yabus and bullocks. It is approached from the north by a track leading up the Bedkul valley. The latter joins the Ghorband valley 3 miles east of the Shibar Kotal, is two hundred yards wide at its mouth, and is cultivated and inhabited. Another track leads to Kotal-i-Zirak by the Shumbal Dara. (Peacocke.)

*ZIRAY Or ZHIRAI زیری
34-25 70-50 m. A village located on the Injer Khwar, about 5 miles northeast of Goshta, in Nangarhar province.

ZIRMALA   See ZURMAT زیرمله

ZIRUK   See ZILUK زیروك

ZIWALAT زی ولایت
34-28 68-41 m. A group of four Ghilzai villages on the left bank of the Kabul river, about 5 1/2 miles below Jalrez. (Wanliss.) Recent maps show the spelling Zaywalayat. (LWA)

ZIZHGAI زیژگی (خیبوگی)
33- 68-. A village in the Ghilzai district, near Pannah, inhabited by Audar and Taraki Ghilzais mixed. There is a peak of this name on the range which divides Zurmat from the Shilghar district. (Broadfoot.)

ZOAR زور
A village on the north slopes of the Safed Koh, and south of Gandamak. It is famed for the multitude of its vineyards and orchards. (Masson.)

ZOHAK زهاك (ضحاك)

34-49 67-58 A. An extensive ruin near the debouchure of the Paimuri (Kalu) glen into the Bamian valley, 95 1/2 miles from Kabul by the Irak pass and 1 1/2 miles from Kala Sarkari. Maitland, who visited this place in November 1884, says:

"The ascent to Zohak is a few hundred yards up the Paimuri, on the right hand. A steep zig-zag road, rather narrow and out of repair, but which can still be ridden up, is defended all the way, on the outer side, by a line of battlemented walls and towers, still fairly perfect. The walls are of sun-dried brick, the bricks being made of the tough reddish clay of the hill. They are arranged in open patterns towards the top of the walls and towers. These outer fortifications are the most striking of the whole. They looked to me to be of later date than the place itself. Some of the towers here are octagonal, and some of the arches are distinctly pointed, though flat. But the majority of the arches are round-headed. Besides the line of walls and towers covering the road, towers are placed in several places on knolls, or the shoulders of spurs, and connected by curtains with the other works. As seen from below, the general effect is picturesque, and even impressive: nothing can altogether overcome the meanness of aspect inseparable from the mud-brick buildings; and the colour of the walls and towers is so nearly that of the steep broken slopes behind, that they are almost lost against it. I make these remarks, as a previous traveller has written of Zohak in a style calculated to give an altogether false idea of its appearance. Apart from their antiquity and associations neither this place, nor Ghulghulah, are worth going a quarter of a mile to see and as architectural remains are absolutely insignificant beside the magnificent forts, palaces and tombs, which abound in India.

"Two gateways are passed through, near the foot of the ascent, and above the second the road is tunnelled, for a few yards, through soft rock. I think the ascent is about a quarter of a mile, perhaps more.

"At the top of the hill, the upper parts of two or three ravines, running to the main valley, have been enclosed by lines of walls and towers radiating from a loftily placed citadel, whose southern face appears to overhang the precipitous side of a deep and narrow ravine running at right angles to the Paimuri glen. Mindful of Talbot's advice, I did not go up there. There are many large chambers along the lines of wall, square in plan and with domed roofs, the square being converted into an octagon in exactly the same way as the caves. In fact the interior detail of many of the caves is so remarkably similar to that of these domed chambers of raw brick, that one would imagine the former had been hewn out in careful imitation of the latter, were it not certain that the caves existed long before the ruins.

"The interior walls, though of the same sun-dried brick throughout, are of somewhat ruder construction than those of the other defenses, and there is no attempt at ornamentation. They are by no means high, about 18 feet where perfect. The citadel walls may be higher, but I did not see them. The foundations here, as at Ghulghulah and elsewhere, are of rough round stones bedded in clay. This rubble is continued a foot or two above the ground. The interior spaces of the lower portion of the fortress are almost empty. I saw some half cave dwellings in one of the hollows, and no doubt habitations of a superior sort existed at the top of the hill. But the place appears to have been intended rather to shelter a large number of warriors

in time of war than for permanent occupation by an ordinary population. In fact the latter would have been much incommoded by the want of a convenient water supply. As a strategic fortress Zohak is well placed, commanding the exits of the three principal passes into the valley from the west, practically all the roads from Kabul."
(Maitland.)

ZUKHAGAK زوخگک

A pass leading over the hills north of Kharwar from Orfan to the Shiniz valley. It is a very difficult track and only passable by men on foot, or sheep. (Griesbach.)

ZULICH زولچ

34-55 66-34 m. A small dara descending north to the Bandi-i-Amir, in the west of the Yakh Walang district. There are 10 houses of Hazaras at Dahan-i-Zulich. (Maitland.) The village is located at 34-53 66-31 m. (LWA)

ZULMABAD ظلم آباد

34- 70-. A village in the Jalalabad district, on the right bank of the Kabul river, close to its junction with the Surkhab. The inhabitants are Ghilzais. (Jenkyns.)

ZURIA زوریه

35-31 69-43. A track over the Hindu Kush, which appears to leave the Panjshir valley at Safed Jir, about 8 miles above Marz. Here is the mouth of the Dara Zuria, in which is a hamlet with some trees. The road to the Zuria Kotal is believed to lead up this dara. After crossing the kotal, the road descends the Arzia or Zuria Dara, which runs in a general northerly direction down to the upper Andarab valley. The route is considered a bad one, and is said to be only practicable for laden bullocks and donkeys. It can hardly be more than a mere footpath, and is of little military importance, though it might be used by infantry without baggage, either to turn the Khawak and Til passes, or to relieve pressure in event of a movement by those roads. (A.B.C.)

*ZURKALA زورکلا

34-27 70-52 m. A village located some 8 miles northeast of Goshta in Nangarhar province.

*ZURKOT See MUSA KHEL زورکوت

ZURMAT زرمت

33-25 69-7 m. Zurmat is a woleswali in Paktia province. The woleswali comprises an area of 917 square kilometers and has an agricultural population that has been estimated at from 20,217 to 42,841. The woleswali is bounded in the south by Mata Khan and Orma, in the east by Shawak, in the northeast by Gardez, in the north by Charkh, and in the west by Zena Khan and Deh Yak. Zurmat has some 129 villages, 23 of which have more than 500 inhabitants. The villages are listed in the PG as follows:
Bekwal-i-Orya Khel, Mazar Khel, Qala-i-Alef, Maroz Khel, Gorjai, Husain Khel, Shah Karez, Makawa-i-Ulya, Makawa-i-Dawlatzai (Miyadad Khel), Char Kala, Omar Khel, Nek Nam, Naway Kadus, Kados-i-Kohna (Zal Kadus), Hawas Khel, Gandir Khel, Sardi Khel, Kohigar, Mangal Khel, Khurdah-i-Malikan, Malikan, Spin Takht, Paye Loch, Guldad Khel, Hazar Khel, Khandak, Hayat Khel, Ghola Khel, Bator, Dirai (Zoya Khel), Dawlat Khan, Dawlatzai, Nazar Khel, Shakar Khel, Babakar Khel, Mulla Shamolzai (Madiwal), Mira Jan-i-Mamozai (Bangiyan),

Baki Khel, Shadidar, Khader Khan, Janak Khel-i-Mamozai, Mattkai Khel, Zapar Khel, Omar Khel, Turah Baz Khel, Fateh Khel, Lak Dewal, Astogan, Khwaja Fatehulla, Kuli Khel, Mado Khel, Ghani Khel, Shaikhan, Khwajagan, Jalalzai, Bahram Khel, Alozai, Timur Khel, Haibat Khel, Ali Jan Khel, Shah Gum Khel, Adam Khel (Adram Khel), Madwal, Adhundzadah Khel (Tsarai wa Mullayan), Mullayan-i-Shabaka, Khair Mast, Sarmast Khel, Chini, Menjawor, Chalozai, Shaikh Nur, Mullah Khel, Nakam, Dawlat Khan (Dawlat Khel), Zol Kohi (Kohi Kohna), Godal, Khuni Baghcha (Hawz-i-Baghcha), Kharashai, Joma Gul Kala, Adin Khel, Mushak, Mastak, Darya Khan, Sepaye, Patan Khel, Gandah Khel, Ashkawi, Matwarkh, Azmat Khel, Barat Khel, Ashok Khel, Surkai, Zotni Khel, Khwaja Dad Khel, Khudi Khel, Alim Khel, Sholgad, Haidari Kala, Ibrahim Khel, Jan Moh'd Khel, Shamulzai, Khoji Khel, Babakar, Mullah Kala, Kandai Kala, Hayat Khel, Rahman Khel, Kaki Kala, Najarano Kala, Jeba, Shah Sahib Kala, Shahbaz Khel, Imni Khel, Mukarab Khel, Shabak, Kaliyan, Kulalgo, Mullayan, Sar-i-Jar, Seray, Jaghatiyan, Payendah Khel, Zarghun Shahr, Nawai Kohi, Konbi Khazak, Luchi Khel, Salih Khel, Lalo Khel, Mimizai Ahangaran, Baro Khel, Maraye Khel-i-Mamozai, Miyadad Khel, Kambad, Torsaye, Babat Khel, Mirza Khel, Qala-i-Surkh, Tata Nak, Qala-i-Alozai, Tani Khel, Zarin Khel, Sahak, Worya Khel, Koti Khel, and Panj Paye. (LWA) In 1914 the area was described as follows: A district separated from Logar by a south-western branch of the Safed Koh range, by the Altimur pass. Southwest of the district, and bordering on it, is Katawaz. Its eastern boundary is formed by spurs from the Jadran hills. Very little is known of Zurmat, and no survey of the country exists. It is said to be a plain 40 miles long by 20 across, and is watered by a stream running from Kalalgu, and also by one from the Altimur pass. The principal place is Gardez, which used to be the residence of the Ghilzai Governor, Arsala Khan, and is now one of the great centers of the Ghilzai tribe. Molloy says: "The inhabitants of Zurmat belong in the main to the following sections of the Sulaiman Khel Ghilzais, viz.

    1. Sohak   3. Tuta Khel
    2. Ahmadzai   4. Minzai
                  5. Mamozai

There are also some Tajiks and Kharotis settled in Zurmat. The following are some of the villages owned by the different sections: Gardez, Tajiks; Koshin, Sohak; Chara and Machalgar, both Ahmadzai; Robat, Tajik; Sohak, a village inhabited by Sohaks. In the town of Zurmat itself are Sulaiman Khel, Minzai and Mamozai sections. Kalalgu is a Tajik village; Urgan is another Tajik village. Khwaja Khel belongs to the Sohak section; Sarafzai is an independent village in the possession of the Sulaiman Khel section. This must be one of the largest places in Zurmat; it is said to contain as many as 2,000 houses. In the district of Katawaz most of the inhabitants are said to be independent, whilst a few are subject, but in Zurmat the majority prefer to be raiats, whilst the minority are independent. The total families in Zurmat are computed at from 25,000 to 30,000, and they pay 1 1/2 lakhs of rupees in revenue. But this is rarely realized in either Zurmat or Katawaz until forcible steps are taken to exact it."

The present Hakim of Zurmat is one Muhammad Aslam Khan.
There are said to be four principal routes in Zurmat, viz:
                1. To Kabul via the Altimur pass
                2. To Kurram via the Chakmani valley
                3. To Ghazni via Kalalgu
                4. To Mukur via Shilghar
Little or nothing is known of the nature of these roads with the exception of the first one--see "Altimur." In September, 1838, a

force, including artillery and cavalry, visited Zurmat, and again in September, 1841 troops were sent into the district to reduce it to order, and the forts, which were found deserted, were all destroyed. The latter expedition consisted of 200 men of Her Majesty's 44th Foot, 5th Infantry, Anderson's Horse, 6th Shah's Infantry, Captain Backhouse's mountain train, four guns of No. 6 Battery, two 8-inch mortars, two iron 9-pounders, and three companies of Shah's Sappers. This force crossed the Altimur on the 3rd and 4th October 1841. Captain Abbott (from whose journal these details are taken) described the Zurmat valley as well watered and susceptible of great fertility, but the inhabitants were few in number, and not above half the available land was cultivated annually, the other half remaining fallow. The hills were sprinkled with stunted firs, resembling the juniper in foliage. He described Gardez as a remarkable object in the valley, being built on an isolated hill, about 40 feet above the plain, having a sort of citadel on a natural mound rising 20 or 30 feet higher.

During the British occupation of the Logar valley in the summer of 1880, the Zurmatis and their neighbors of Katawaz assembled in some force on the Altimur pass, and made occasional descents to annoy the troops and to molest the people friendly to the latter. The notorious Wardak leader, Muhammad Jan, fomented the excitement from a distance, and at last a large body of the tribesmen committed themselves to an advance down the valley as far as Patkao-i-Shahana. At this latter place they were encountered on the 1st July by Palliser's brigade of cavalry, and utterly routed.

In the Pushtu language the district is called Zirmala, but Zurmat is the name recognized generally. (Abbott, Broadfoot, Molloy, I.B.C.)

Glossary of Terms

Ab	آب	Water, also a stream or river.
Abdan	آبدان	Used in northern Afghanistan for reservoir or cistern.
Aftab	آفتاب	The sun.
Ahingar	آهنگر	A blacksmith; ahingaran, blacksmiths, is a common name for a village.
Ahu	آهو	Deer; the big deer of the Oxus is called gawaz; kurk-i-ahu is "kurk" made of deer's "pashm"; a gazelle.
Ailak	ایلاق	A summer camping ground or village, in contradistinction to kishlak, winter camp.
Aimak	ایماق	This word means simply nomad; chahar-aimak the four nomad tribes; dowazda-aimak, the twelve nomad tribes, kibchaks.
Ak	آق	White; ak-sakal, white beard, the head man of a village.
'ak	ك	A diminutive suffix, as bazarak, meaning a little bazar; saraiak, a little sarai.
Akhor, or Aokhor	آخور آوخور	A drinking trough, a cylindrical mud trough from which horses eat their bhusa; otherwise a manger; mirakhor, master of the horse, head groom.
Alaf	علف	Grass.
Alakadari	علاقه داری	A district, subdivision.
Alaman	اله مان	A raid, particularly a Turkoman raid; also a party of raiders; rah-i-alaman, a track followed by raiding parties.
Alkhani, or Ulkhani	الخانی	See Ilkhani.
Alparghan or Altarghan	الپرغان	A small bush with a yellow flower, very similar to Iskich.
An	آن	Pass.

Anbar	انبار	A store or granary.
Angur	انگور	Grapes.
Anguri	انگوری	Revenue on fruit trees and vines.
Anjir	انجير	Figs.
Aokhor	آوخور	See Akhor.
Aolia	اوليا	A ziarat or shrine.
Aorez	آب ريز اوريز	A stream of water.
Araba	عرابه	A cart.
Aral	آرال	Island; the Aral Sea is said to be so called, because it is full of islands.
Arbab	ارباب	The headman of a village (among Tajiks, and other Persian-speaking peoples).
Archa	ارچه	The juniper tree, "obusht" in Pushtu.
Arg, or Ark	ارگ	Citadel or keep.
Arik	آرق	Canal; yang-arik, the new canal.
Arzan	ارزن	Millet.
Asia	آسيا	Watermill; bad-asia, a windmill.
Asp	اسپ	Horse; maidan-i-asp; used as a vague measure of distance, meaning about a quarter, or half, a mile.
Azhdaha	اژدها	Dragon, often met with as the name of a locality in connection with some legend.
Azwaji	ازواجی	Revenue on arable land.
Bad	باد	Wind; badasia, wind-mill; badgir, a ventilator; bad-i-sad-o-bist roz, the wind of 120 days, famous in Sistan and Herat.
Bagh	باغ	Garden or orchard; chahar-bagh, a common name.
Baghat	باغات	The orchard suburbs of a town or village.
Bai (Boi in some dialects)	بای	A title applied to any well-to-do Usbak or Turkoman. It implies an owner of flocks.

Bairak	بيرق	Literally a standard; a company of khasadars.
Baital	بيتال	Mare.
Bala	بالا	High, in contradistinction to "pa'in" low; bala hisar, the high fort, is used indifferently with "ark" for citadel.
Bam, or Bum	بام	Terrace, roof, any flat place or plateau on the top of a cliff; apparently also the cliff or scarp itself. The name Bamian is probably Bam-mian, "between cliffs or terraces."
Band	بند	Literally a dam, fequently used for range.
Bandar	بندر	Road; never used in the sense of market or port.
Barak	برك	Soft cloth woven from sheep's wool and undyed. Superior barak is called "kurk."
Barkhan	برخان	Sand dunes.
Bash	باش	Head; bashi, the headman of anything, as sad-bashi, chief of 100, a captain of khasadars; mingbashi, chief of a 1,000, was a leader of local levies in northern Afghanistan; karawalbashi, chief of outposts.
Bast	بست	Closed or enclosed; diwal bast, surrounded by a wall.
Baz	باز	Hawk; jangal-i-baz, hawk, wood.
Bazgar	بزگر	A tenant cultivator.
Bed	بيد	Willow.
Beg	بيگ	A common title among all Turki-speaking peoples; a beg is a more important person than a "bai;" begler begi, the beg of begs, a high title.
Beghami	بيغمى	See Tahwil pago.
Bel	بيل	A spade.
Bel	بيل	This word is a synonym of "kotal" or "gardan," pass.

Bhusa	بهوسه	Chopped straw. The straw is naturally broken small by the process of threshing with bullocks.
Bini	بینی	Nose; applied to the spur of a hill.
Birinj	برنج	Rice.
Bolak	بلاق	Spring.
Bolak, or Buluk	بولوك	Sub-division of a district, a taluk.
Borida	بریده	Pierced or cleft; sang-borida, the pierced rock.
Bum	بام	See "Bam."
Bunnu	بنو	A kind of grass.
Buriabaf	بوریا باف	Mat or basket-work. Weaver.
Burj	برج	A tower, or bastion.
Burkhan	برخان	A ridge of sand, formed by the winds action into the shape of a wave.
Burna	برنا	High; same as "bala."
Buta	بته	Small brushwood.
Buzghunj	بزغنج	The gall of the pista, pistachio, tree; it is produced in alternate years with the berry.
Chah	چاه	Well.
Chaharbagh	چهار باغ	See "Bagh."
Chaharmagz	چهار مغز	Walnuts; literally "four kernels."
Chakao	چکاو	A waterfall.
Chaman	چمن	Any grassy place; turf.
Chapchal	چپچل	A road cut in rock.
Chargo	چارگو	½ of a pago.
Chashma	چشمه	Common word for a spring, but applied to a small stream.
Chehildukhtar	چهل دختر	Forty daughters; a common name of locality.

Chim	چم	A clod of earth or sod of turf.
Chinar	چنار	Plane tree.
Chir, or Chil	چير	Pine.
Chob	چوب	Wood; or piece of wood; a pole, stick, or club.
Chol	چول	Turkish for a desert; common in Afghanistan, and always applied to a sandy waste.
Chopan	چوپان	Shepherds.
Chughur	چقور	Deep.
Dahbashi	ده باشی	Head of ten; sergeant or havildar.
Dagh, or Tagh	داغ تاغ	Range or hill.
Dahan	دهن	Mouth; commonly applied to the lower part of a glen, valley, ravine, or stream.
Dahana	دهانه	A place at the mouth of a valley, glen, or a stream.
Daima, or Daimi	ديمه	Cultivation not dependent on irrigation; same as "lalmi."
Daqq	دق	Marsh.
Dara, Darrah	دره	Properly a valley; generally applied to a narrow rocky glen or defile; especially with a stream flowing through.
Darakht	درخت	Tree; yak-darakht, one tree; ming-darakht, a thousand trees.
Darband	دربند	A gorge or defile.
Daria	دريا	A river; Amu Daria, the Oxus.
Darwaza	دروازه	Literally a door; also applied to a gap between hills or short defile.
Dasht	دشت	A gravelly or stony plain or open space; often applied to flat, gravelly plateaux of small size.
Dast	دست	Hand or fist.

Davan	دوان	Pass.
Deh	ده	Village; dehat, populated country; suburbs or a town.
Dehkan	دهگان (دهقان)	An agricultural tenant or laborer.
Dev	ديو	Demon or supernatural being; occurs in names, as Dev Kala, Dev Hisar.
Diwal	ديوال	Wall.
Dongaz	دونگز	Understood to be Turkoman for sea or lake.
Dost	دوست	A friend.
Duzd	دزد	Robber; duzdan, robbers; chashma duzdan the robbers' spring; rah-i-duzdan, a robbers' road implying a difficult, out-of-the-way path.
Duz	دز	Salt.
El	ايل	This word is of Turkic origin, meaning large or big; ellai (see "Bai"), a man of importance, a large sheep-owner; elband, the great range or dam, said to be the real name of the Helmand river-Rud-i-Elband, the river of the great range, or great dam.
Farash	فرش	Spread out; sang-i-farash, sheet rock.
Farsakh	فرسخ	Parasang, a measure of length varying from 3¼ to 4 miles, but always called 12,000 paces; farsakh-i-gurg, or wolf's farsakh, is anything from 7 to 10 miles. Also, 18,000 feet.
Fasl	فصل	Harvest. Season.
Gah	گاه	Place; kadam-gah, a footprint; shikargah, hunting ground.
Gallah	گله	A flock, a number, also "in kind."
Gandum	گندم	Wheat.

Gao	گاو	A cow; post-i-gao, cow skin; occurs more than once as the name of a place said to have been measured with a cow's skin cut in strips, a hide of land.
Gao, or Gai	گاو گای	Oxen or bullocks.
Gardan, Gardana	گردن	A low neck, or an easy kotal, where a low place in hill or ridge is crossed.
Garm-sel	گرمسیل	A low-lying, hot, country.
Gawaz	گوز	The large deer of the Oxus.
Gaz	گز	A yard or pace (varies considerably).
Gaz	گز	Tamarisk or manna tree.
Ghami, or Ghani Pago	غنی پگو	A small gang of men organised as a unit for agricultural labour. It differs from a tahwil pago in being liable for State service, vide Khash.
Ghar	غار	A cave; this common word is used for an animal's den in Hazarajat; mountain range.
Gilim	گلیم	A long narrow carpet.
Gosfand	گوسفند	Sheep; rah-i-gosfand, a sheep track, often a well marked road, but when known as a "rah-i-gosfand" is impracticable.
Gowd	گود	Depression.
Gumbaz, or Gumbad	گنبذ	A domed building; a tomb or shrine.
Gurg	گرگ	Wolf; gurg-farsakh, a long farsakh.
Guzar	گذر	A crossing place; a ford; a ferry; used by Turkomans for a place where the banks of a river are practicable, and animals can go to drink; a watering place.
Ghrunah	غرونه	Mountains, mountain range.
Haidara	هدیره	Graveyard.
Haizum	هیزم	Firewood.
Hakim	حاکم	Governor of a province or district.

Hakim	حکیم	Doctor.
Hamai	حمی	"Hing," the asafoetida plant.
Hamsaya	همسایه	Neighbor; client.
Hamun	هامون	Literally the sea; any large piece of water or place where water collects, especially the lakes of Sistan.
Hamwar	هموار	Level smooth.
Haram-sarai	حرم سرای	See "Sarai."
Hashar	هشار	A gang of labourers who make canals.
Hauz	حوض	An artificial reservoir for water; it may be an open pond, or a brick-built cistern.
Hinduwana	هندوانه (تربوز)	Watermelon.
Hing	هنگ	The asafoetida, or angoza, plant.
Hisar	حصار	A fort; dev-hisar, the demon's castle.
Hotpur, or Utpur	هاتپر اوتپر	A tower.
Ikhrajat	اخراجات	Land revenue.
Ikhtiar	اختیار	A title among Hazaras and Chahar Aimak tribes; an ikhtiar is generally the headman of a village, kul ikhtiar is a higher rank, and sahib ikhtiar higher still, probably a chief of some importance.
Ilbai, or Ilbegi	ایل بیک	See "El."
Ilband	ایل بند ایل بای	See "El."
Ilkhani	ایلخانی	A title of honour; the head of tribe.
Ishan	ایشان	A Turkoman, or Uzbak, sayyid.
Iskich	ایسکیچ	A small, spreading bush, very common in the Hazarajat, Taimani country, etc. It is poor firewood, but rope is said to be made of the fibres.
Ispust	ایسپوست	Lucerne.

Istikbal	استقبال	A party sent out to do honour to a distinguished person on arrival at a place; a guard of honour.
Izbashi	ایز باشی	A title among Hazaras.
Jaidad	جایداد	Land given by way of payment for military service.
Jageer	جاگیر	A fief, pension.
Jala	جلا	A raft.
Jam	جام	Cup.
Jangal	جنگل	Forest.
Jao	جو	Barley.
Jar	جر	A ravine; a small tagao; in Turkistan, a hollow; a stream.
Jarib	جریب	A measure of land (not a thing to measure with as in India).
Jawal	جوال	Bag.
Jazira	جزیرة	Island.
Jehil	جهیل	Lake.
Jowar, or Jowari	جوار جواری	Millet.
Juft	جفت	A pair (of oxen), i.e., a plough land — see "Kulba."
Jui	جوی	Irrigation canal or stream.
Julga, Jilga	جلگه	A glen.
Kabal, or Kabul	کابل کابل	Sheep-fold.
Kadam	قدم	Pace; kadam-gah, a footprint.
Kadim	قدیم	Ancient.
Kadkhoda	کدخدا	Headman.
Kafila	قافله	A number of animals carrying merchandize or baggage; baggage train.
Kagh	کاغ	See "Kak."

833

Kah	كاه	Grass, dried grass, or hay; kah-i-safed is bhusa.
Kaiak	قايق	A small boat.
Kafir	كافر	Infidel; places called Kafir Kala are innumerable; at least 50 per cent, of the old ruins in the country are called "Kafir Kala."
Kak	كاك	An open reservoir, or cistern; several places beginning with khak should really have kak.
Kal	كل	A hollow or ravine.
Kala	كلاء قلعه	Fort.
Kalacha	قلعچه	A little fort.
Kalama	كلمه	Reed; a reed pen.
Kalan	كلان	Great.
Kaldar	كلدار كلاه دار	Kallahdar, from kallah, cap or head – Indian money so called on account of the head on the obverse.
Kalgir or Kalgirkhar	كالگیر	A term supplied to village land given to poor relations of the headman, or to bazgars (labourers) which they are allowed to cultivate for their own benefit.
Kaljao	كلجو	An inferior, thin-husked, species of barley, grown in the higher portions of the Hazarajat. Animals, as a rule, take sometime to get accustomed to 'kaljao,' and do not eat it readily at first.
Kam (Kaum)	قوم	Section of a tribe.
Kam	كم	Few.
Kamar	كمر	Cliff; kamar kulagh, crow's cliff.
Kaman	كمن	Bow, bend, loop; kaman-i-bihisht, bow of paradise, the name of a place.
Kandao, Kandaw	كندآو	Pass.

Karez	كاريز	An underground water channel.
Karkana	كركنه كاركانه	Word used in Turkistan for the low brushwood elsewhere called "iskich."
Karwan	كاروان	Caravan or "kafila;" also a halting place for caravans; a karwan-sarai or caravan-sarai.
Kaus	كوز	Arc.
Kavir	كوير	Marsh.
Keshtegar	كشتگر	Tenant farmer.
Khaima, or Khima	خيمه	Tent.
Khak	خاك	Ashes or clay; any clayey soil. See also "Kak."
Khakistar	خاكستر	Graveyard; ashes.
Khakmah	خاكمه	Camel's hair cloth.
Kham	خام	Raw; also means "in kind."
Kham, or Kaj	خم كج	Bent. Used for the bend, or reach, of a river.
Khan	خان	Title of honor; In Herat local governors (hakims) are called Khans of such a place; khan khel, the chief's family in a tribe.
Khana	خانه	Place; rud-khana, river bed; sar-khana, house or family tax; siah-khana, black tents, also the people who live in them; safed-khana is sometimes used for people living in houses.
Khandak	خندق	A rock cistern; literally ditch.
Khar	خار	Thorn; khar-i-shutur, camel thorn.
Khar	خر	Donkey; khargor, wild ass.
Kharabeh	خرابه	Ruin(s).
Kharaj, or Kharach	خراج	Toll; kharaj giri, toll bar.

Kharwar	خروار	Literally an ass load, about 10 maunds in Herat and 16 in Afghan Turkistan.
Kharbuza	خربوزه	Melon.
Khargah, or Khirgah	خرگاه	The ordinary felt tents called by most travellers "kibtika." In Turki it is "oweh."
Kharif	خریف	Crops reaped in autumn.
Khasadar	خاصه دار	Irregular foot soldier; the police of the country; tribal militia.
Khawal	خوال	A natural cave.
Khima, or Khaima	خیمه	Tent.
Khinjak	خنجك	Pistacia cabulica, a common tree.
Khishti	خشتی	Brick; khisht pukhta is burnt brick.
Khum, or Kum	خم	The sandy soil of the "chol."
Khuni	خونی	Blood guilty, also deadly; barf-i-khuni is said to be an expression for "fatal snow."
Khush	خوش	Pleasant.
Khushk	خشك	Dry.
Khwaja	خواجه	Descendent of a saint or holy man, not necessarily a sayyid.
Khwar	خور	Stream.
Kila	كله	Synonymous with Kulba.
Kiri	کیری	A low hill.
Kirta	کرته	A kind of grass suitable for horses.
Kishlak	قشلاق	Any permanent village or settlement; a winter camp as opposed to ailak, a summer camp.
Kishti	کشتی	Boat.
Kizil	قزل	Red.
Koh, or Kuh	کوه	Hill, or mountain, Kohistan, hill country.

Kohna	کهنه	Old.
Kol	قول	Glen, wide hollow, or valley.
Kotal	کوتل	Common word for a pass or "col" on a range.
Kowl	کول	Lake.
Kran	قران	A coin worth four pence.
Kro	کرو	A kas, one and a half to two miles.
Kruman	کرومن	½ a sang man.
Kucha	کوچه	Literally a lane, applied to a narrow defile, or gorge.
Kulach	قلاج	Fathom, 6 feet.
Kulba, or Zauj	قلبه زوج	A plough land, i.e., as much of one plough with one pair of oxen can cultivate in a year; generally about 30 acres.
Kum	خم کم	See "Khum."
Kund	کند	Day.
Kundal	کندل	A kind of grass' food for horses.
Kurghan	کرغان	Fort.
Kurk	کرک	A superior kind of barak, or fine soft cloth woven from the under-wool of the sheep.
Kush	کوش	A pair.
Kush (Kushta)	کش کشته	Death place.
Kushk	کوشک	Elevated; a place.
Kupruk	کپروک	A bridge; in Turkoman Turki, kupru or kukru.
Lab	لب	The edge; lab-i-ab the river side.
Lag-lag	لك لك	Stork.
Lak	لاك	A word used instead of "kotal" in Baluchistan.

Lalmi	للمی	Cultivation not dependent on irrigation.
Lang	لنگ	A ford or passage.
Langar	لنگر	A place of sacrifice or devotion.
Langar	لنگر	The area a pago or plough can sow in one day.
Lar	لار	Pass.
li, or lik	لق لك لی	A locative suffix; Khorasanli, people from Khorasan; pistalik, a tract where the pista tree abounds.
Lig-lig	لیگ	Trot.
Lurga	لرګه	A ridge.
Lut	لوت	A waterless tract; a stony desert, or "dasht," without water.
Ma'dan	معدن	Mine.
Maidan	میدان	Plaine; maidan-i-asp, an indefinite measure of distances, about a quarter, or half, a mile.
Mal, Maldar	مال مالدار	Livestock; maldar, owner of live stock, a flockmaster.
Malakh	ملخ	Locusts.
Malik	ملك	The headman of a village, or of a tribal section (among Pathans).
Maliya, or Maliyat	مالیه مالیات	Taxes in general.
Man	من	A maund.
Manda	مانده	Stream.
Mar	مار	Snake; marpich, zig-zag or winding like a snake's track.
Mash and Mung	ماش منگ	Sorts of dhal or pulse.
Mashk	مشك	A sheep-skin filled with air to serve as a float for crossing rivers. A number of such skins are often combined to ferry men and livestock across rivers.

Mazar, or Mizar	مزار	Shrine; a ziarat.
Mehman	مهمان	A guest; mehmandar, a person who has charge of guests.
Mehtar	مهتر	Hazara title of honour; a tribal chief.
Mi		A measure of water for irrigation purposes.
Mingbashi	منگباشی	Literally head of a thousand the chief of a local levy in Turkistan.
Mir	میر	Chief; mir section the chief's own clan or family, the "khan khel" of a tribe; mirakhor, master of the horse; mirabashi, the divider of water for irrigation, often an important official.
Mirigan, or Mirgan	میرگن	Shikari, or matchlockman; any footman armed with a gun.
Mawajib	مواجب	Literally pay; the allowance of a chief or "hakim."
Motabar	معتبر	Headman.
Munj	منج	Fibre, rope.
Munshrif	منشریف	A man usually a khassadar who looks after the crops to see that the Government gets its share.
Nahr	نهر	Canal; irrigation canal; used in northern Afghanistan as the equivalent of "jui."
Naju	ناجو	The tree resembling a Scotch fir (pinus religiosa?), often seen at ziarats in the Herat province, particularly at Karokh.
Nakhchir	نخچیر	Game (shikar).
Nala	ناله	Small river, canal.
Namad	نمد	Felt.
Nao	نو	New; nao-roz, new year's day, the 21st March.
Narai	نری	Pass.

839

Nawa	نوا	Ravine or nala; stream.
Nawar	ناور	Tank, lake, intermittent lake.
Neh	نی	Reed; naizar reed beds.
Nihang	نهنگ	Crocodile; Kafir-nihang, the faithless or unbelieving crocodile, the name of a river.
Nimaksar	نمکسار	A place where salt is obtained; a salt bed, or salt mine.
Nipta	نپته	In line with, the same as barabar.
Nobala	نوبالا	Glen or ravine.
Obah	اوبه	A Turkoman camp in the chol.
Oeh, or Oweh	اوی	Felt tent of the Turkomans; a khirgah or kibitka.
Ow	او	Stream.
Padah, or Patoh	پاداه	The padah tree; populus euphratica.
Pago	پاگو	A team of six men organized for agricultural purposes. One works the plough and five work with hoes. The team has a pair of oxen. See Lash Juwain for information about the pago system.
Pai	پای	Foot; pai-band, foot of a range; pai-kotal, foot of a kotal; pai Duldul, foot print of Duldul (a celestial horse).
Pa'in	پائین	Low or lower, in contradistinction to Bala, high.
Pal	پل	A ridge or small range.
Palas	پلاس	Canvas; palasnishin, tent dwellers, nomads, living in huts made of wicker frames of tamarisk wood.
Palez or Faliz	پالیز فالیز	Garden crops, melon-ground.
Pam	پام	A flat place.
Pashakan	پشه کان	A tree.

Pat	پت	A flat clay plain, or desert, without water.
Patah	پته	See "Padah."
Pech	پیچ	A bend or winding; marpech, zig-zag like the track of a snake.
Pir	پیر	A holy man.
Pista	پسته	The pistachio tree; the pistachio berry.
Pitao and Geru	پیتاو	Sunny and shady sides, as of a hill; also pitao and sori.
Post	پوست	Skin or hide.
Pukhta	پخته	Literally cooked; answers to the Indian pakka.
Pul	پل	Bridge.
Pul	پول	Money.
Puz	پوز	Nose; puzak, spur of a hill or promontory.
Qabrestan	قبرستان	Cemetary.
Qal'a	قلعه	Fort.
Qolla	قله	Peak.
Rabi		Crops reaped in spring and early summer.
Rah	راه	Road; rah kalan, a high road; rah-i-gosfand, a sheep track; rah-i-duzd, a robber's path. The last two imply a bad road.
Rai'at	رعیت	A subject, also peasant.
Rama	رمه	Flock of sheep.
Reg	ریگ	Sand; registan, country of sand — i.e., a sand desert.
Rishka	رشقه	Lucerne.
Rishta	رشته	Guinea worm.

Robat	رباط	A caravansarai; also sometimes a village.
Rud	رود	River; rud-khana, river-bed.
Sabz	سبز	Green; sabz-barg, autumn crops.
Sadbashi	صد باشی	Head of 100; a captain of khasadars.
Safed	سفید	White; safed barg, spring crops; safed rish, grey beard, a headman or leader; safed khana, people who live in houses, in contradistinction to "siah-khana," black tents.
Safeda, or Safedal	سفیده	White poplar.
Sai	سی	A ravine; saiat appears to mean cultivation and habitation in a ravine. There are several villages so called in northern Afghanistan.
Sailab	سیلاب	Flood.
Saiyid, Sayyid	سید	A descendant of the Prophet, ishan in Turki.
Sakht	سخت	Hard: used for steep, difficult.
Sal	سال	A raft of wood tied on four pumpkin floats.
Salsola		A plant with dark leaves which grows on salt encrusted land.
Samuch	سموچ	Plural of "Sum": caves; a cave village or settlement.
Sanduk-i-daulat	صندوق دوله	A locked box into which petitions may be dropped. One is supposed to be set up in every bazar.
Sang	سنگ	Stone; sang-i-sulakh, pierced stone; sangtoda, a heap of stones.
Sang	سنگ	A farsakh in Turkistan; it is 12,000 paces.
Sang kharwar or Khir	سنگ خروار	About 15 Indian maunds.
Sang Man	سنگ من	Equivalent to 13 lbs. of wheat and 12 lbs. of other grain.

Sangreza	سنگریزه	Gravel.
Saur	ثور	The name of a month.
Sar, or Nok	سر نوك	Head or peak of a hill.
Sarai	سرای	A house or building; more particulary a public resting place for travellers; Haram-sarai, the private house of a governor or person of importance. In most towns there is a sarai which is state property, and all officials of rank, and distinguished visitors, put up there when passing through.
Sarband	سربند	Watershed.
Sard	سرد	Cold; sardaba, a covered brick cistern (this word, though Persian, is used only in Turki).
Sarhad	سرحد	Boundary or frontier; also any country of moderate height which is neither hot nor cold.
Sarhang	سرهنگ	In Persia a major, or lieutenant-colonel. In Afghanistan the leader of three "bairaks" of khasadars.
Sarma	سرما	Cold.
Shaft-alu	شفتالو	Peach.
Shakh	شاخ	A branch, whether of a road, a ravine or a tribe.
Shamal	شمال	Literally north wind, but used apparently for a strong wind from any quarter.
Sartip	سرتیپ	In Persia a colonel or general. In Afghanistan the leader of 6 or more, "bairaks" of khasadars. It appears to be in reality an honorary title.
Seh	سه	Three.
Selsela	سلسله	Mountain range.
Sev, or Sib	سیب	Apple.

Sharif	شريف	Noble.
Shela	شيله	A hollow or valley; applied to the entire valley of a stream the wider parts of which may be "tagaos" of various names.
Shewagi	شيوه گی	A descent; from shev, low.
Shibar	شيبر	Mud.
Shikan	شكن	Breaker; dandan-shikan, tooth-breaker.
Shikast	شكست	Broken; shikasta, broken ground.
Shinia	شينيه	Juncture of two streams (do-ab).
Shinai	شنای	Pistacia cabulica, the "khinjak" of Persia.
Shirkhisht	شيرخشت	Manna.
Shirin	شيرين	Sweet.
Shor	شور	Salt; also salt mud, saltmarsh, or a ravine with salt water; stream.
Shutur and Ushtar	شتر اشتر	Camel.
Siah	سياه	Black; siah khana, black tents; applied also to the dwellers in them.
Sipah-salar	سپه سالار	Commander-in-chief; really the commander of the troops in a province, not the commander-in-chief of the whole army.
Sokhta	سوخته	Burnt.
Spin	سپين	White.
Sulakh	سولاخ سوراخ	Pierced.
Sultan	سلطان	A title given to chief of clans among some Hazaras, and also among certain other Persian-speaking tribes.
Sum	سم	Cave (excavated, not natural); samuch, caves; a cave village.
Sur and Surkh	سور سرخ	Red.
Tababa		A group of villages.
Tabistan	تابستان	Summer.

Tagao	تگاو	A hollow, valley, or ravine; generally grassy. Stream.
Taghaz	تغاز	A kind of tamarisk with a white bark whose foliage is suitable for camel grazing.
Tahwil	تحویل	A small gang of men organised as a unit for field labour. They are not liable for state service, and are taxed by the head man of the district for his own remuneration instead of by the State, vide Khash.
Ta'ifa	طائفه	A tribal sub-division, or section.
Taimus	تاموس	Summer.
Tairna	تیرنه	Lower, as opposed to burna, upper.
Takht	تخت	Any flat place; a seat; a throne; takht-i-rawan, a horse litter.
Tal	تال	A hollow, pit, or small basin.
Tawa	تاوا	Camel.
Talkh	تلخ	Bitter.
Tanab	تناب	A measure of land, same as a jarib.
Tang	تنگ	Gorge.
Tanga	تنگه	A coin; one-third of a Kabuli rupee.
Tangi	تنگی	Defile.
Taoki	تاوکی	A name applied in Sistan to Baluch tribesmen who are not "asil," i.e., noble, or of pure descent; it means bondsmen or dependants.
Tapa, tappa	تپه	A mound; pronounced by Turkomans, also by Persians, "tepeh."
Tash	تاش	Stone or brick.
Tikan	تیکان	"Buta;" small shrubs or brushwood used for fuel.
Tir	تیر	An arrow; tirband, a path along the crest line of a range.

Tirkh	ترخ	A herb growing into a small bush, common all over Afghanistan, and grazed on by camels and sheep.
Tirma, or Tirima	تیرما	Autumn.
Tokrak, or Toghrak	تکرک	Straight.
Tor	تور	Black.
'tu	تو	A possessive suffix: shibar-tu, a muddy or clayey place; badam-tu, a place where there are almonds.
Tufang	تفنگ	A matchlock; any firearm.
Turbat	تربت	A shrine, ziarat.
Tursh	ترش	Pungent.
Uch	وچ	Dry.
Ulang, or Walang	ولنگ والنگ	Grassy place.
Ulan	اولان	Death place.
Umed	امید	Hope; dasht-i-na-umed, the plain of hopelessness, a bad desert.
Urdu	اردو	Camp of troops.
Ush	اوش	Camel.
Ushtar	اشتر	Camels.
'Ushar	عشر	Land revenue.
Viala	ویاله	A water channel.
Wadi	وادی	Stream, riverbed.
Wali	والی	A hereditary governor.
Walang, or Ulang	والنگ	A grassy place; a natural meadow.
Wasuli	وصولی	Ordinary revenue
Wazifa	وظیفه	Land, the revenue of which is given as an endowment to a shrine; or, to the descendants of a mint.
Welayat	ولایت	First-order administrative division.

Woleswali	ولسوالی	A district, administrative subdivision of a welayat.
Yabu	یابو	Pony.
Yaghi	یاغی	Rebellious or independent; Yaghistan, independent country.
Yang	ینک	New; yang kala, new fort; yang-arik, new canal.
Yarim	یارم	A half; yarim padshah, Turki for a viceroy or governor of a province.
Yurt	یورت	A village, a semi-permanent settlement.
Zakat	زکوة	Cattle-Tax.
Zamistan	زمستان	Winter.
Zauj	زوج	Same as "kulba," that is, a "plough land," as much as can be cultivated by one plough with a pair oxen in one year.
Zar	زر	Gold.
Zard	زرد	Yellow.
Zardak	زردك	Carrot.
Zardalu	زردآلو	Apricot.
Ziarat	زیارت	A shrine, generally a grave or tomb.

MAP SECTION

MAP SECTION

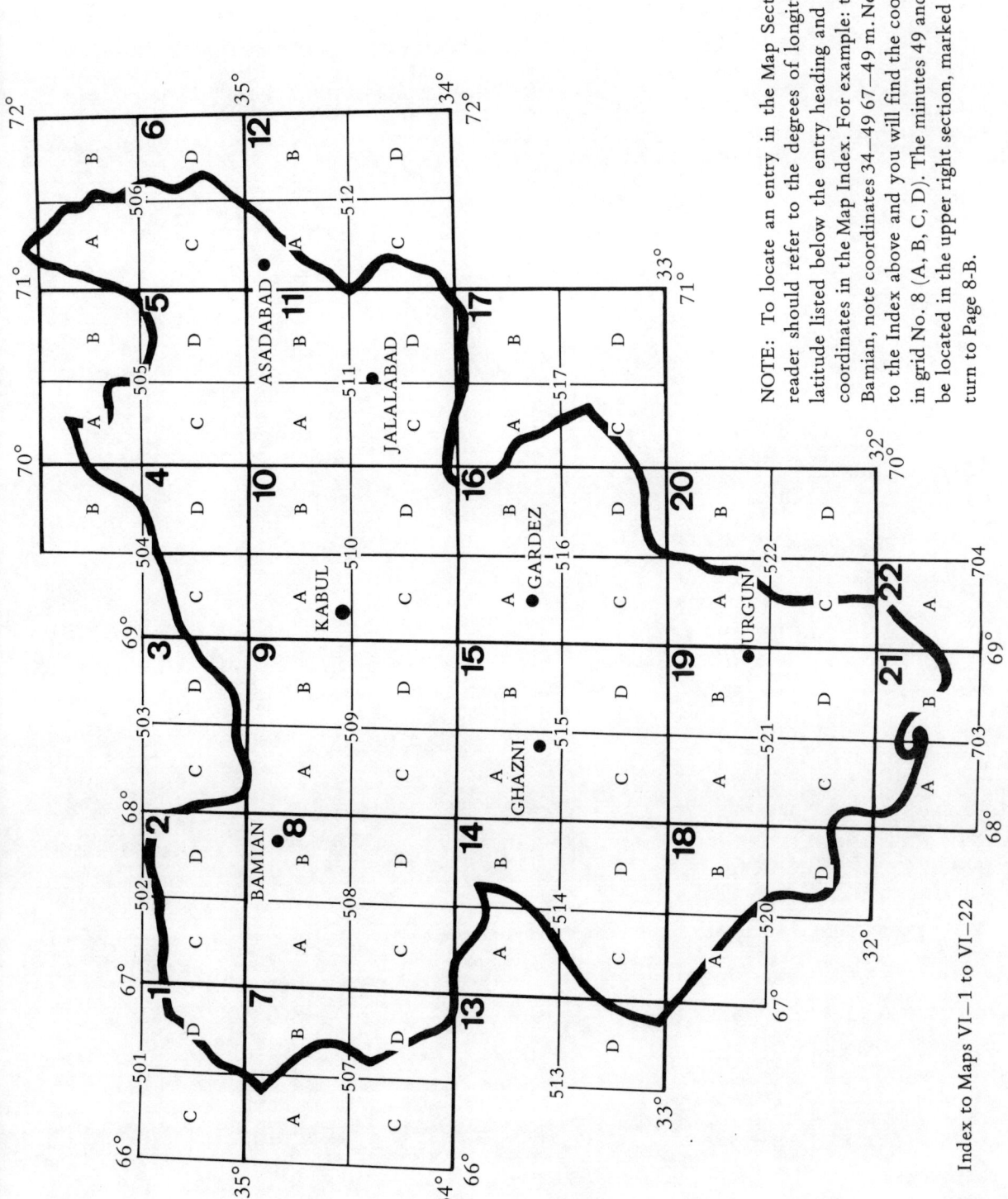

Index to Maps VI–1 to VI–22

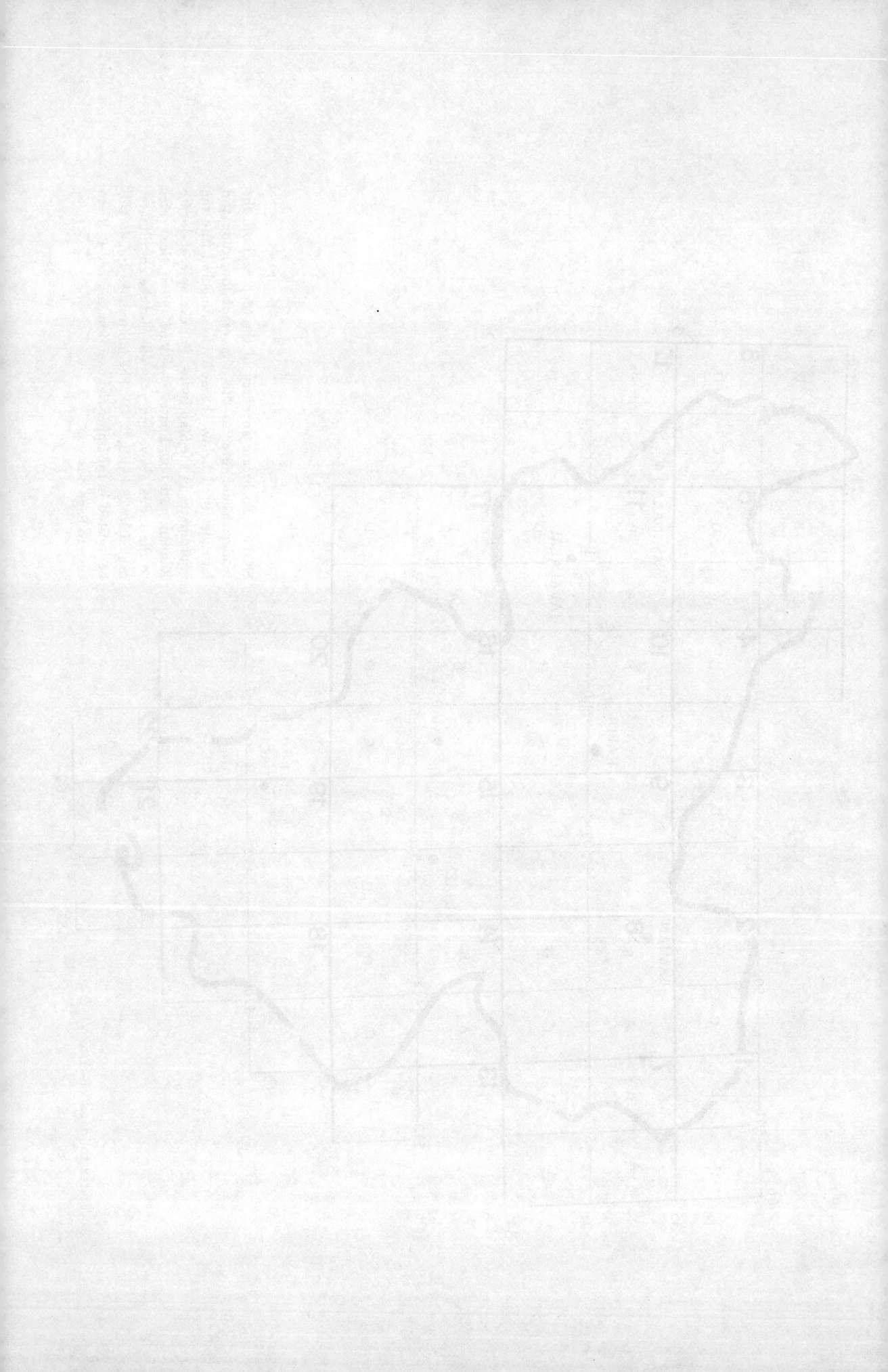

System of Transliteration
(Compiled by Muzaffarud Din Yaqubi)

1. Signs for Letters

English Equivalents (in capital letters)	Examples English	Pashto/Farsi	Letters Roman	Pashto/Farsi	No.
At, Out, Eye	Alefbā	اَلِفْبَا	a	ا	١
Bank	Band	بَنْد	b	ب	٢
Pull, Push	Pašto	پَښْتُو	p	پ	٣
T with the top of the tongue against the upper teeth	Ṭel	تَلْ	ṭ¹	ت	٤
Tomb	Tōl	تُولْ	t²	ټ	٥
THree	Sābet	شَابَتْ	s̄	ث	٦
DZāy	Jāy	جْنَایْ	j̄	څ	٧
JudGE	Jazirah	جَزِیرَه	j	ج	٨
TSānga, yachTSman	Cānga	څَانګَه	c	څ	٩
CHeek	Čāh	چَاه	č	چ	١٠
A sound between H and KH	Hamīd	حَمِیدْ	ḥ	ح	١١
KHān	Khwāja	خْوَاجَه	Kh	خ	١٢
D with the tip of the tongue against the upper teeth	Dīn	دِینْ	d̄	د	١٣
Doubt	Dōday	ډُوډَی	d	ډ	١٤
THat, THus	Ẕalīl	ذَلِیلْ	z̄	ذ	١٥
As Spanish 'r'	Rahmat	رَحْمَتْ	ṛ	ر	١٦
Road, fiRst	Lamray	لَمْرَی	r	ړ	١٧
Zenith	Zūza	زُوزَه	z	ز	١٨
aZure	Žāla	ژَالَه	ž	ژ	١٩
meaSure	Kaẓ̌a	کَږَه	ẓ̌	ږ	٢٠
Spread	Salām	سَلَامْ	s	س	٢١
SHore	Šōṛaw	شُورَاوْ	š	ش	٢٢
A sound between SH and KH	Ṣ̌āṛ	ښَارْ	ṣ̌	ښ	٢٣

853

English Equivalents (in capital letters)	Examples English	Pashto/Farsi	Letters Roman	Pashto/Farsi	No.
SWim	Ṣamad	صَمَدْ	ṣ	ص	٢٤
FayDZābād	Fayḍzābād	فَيْضْ آبَادْ	ḍz	ض	٢٥
THWāleb	Ṭāleb	طَالِبْ	ṭ	ط	٢٦
MoZWaffar, ZWālemi	Moẓaffar	مُظَفَّرْ	ẓ	ظ	٢٧
As ''Ayn' in Arabic.	'Ālem	عَالِمْ	'	ع	٢٨
GHazni	Gholām	غُلَامْ	Gh	غ	٢٩
Finish	Fatḥ	فَتْحْ	f	ف	٣٠
———	Ya'qūbi	يَعْقُوبِي	q	ق	٣١
Can, Kit	Kārēz	كَارِيزْ	k	ك	٣٢
Get, Good	Gata	گَتَه	g	گ	٣٣
Guard	Goẕar	گُذَرْ	g	گ	٣٤
Latitude	Laylā	لَيْلَى	l	ل	٣٥
Meat	Muḥtaram	مُحْتَرَمْ	m	م	٣٦
Number	Nuqrah	نُقْرَه	n	ن	٣٧
———	Manay	مَانَهى	n	ن	٣٨
What	Wali	وَلِىْ	w	متحرك	٣٩
OUt	Palāw	پَلَاوْ	w	ساكن و	
flOOr	Tōr	تُورْ	o	مجهول	
shrEWd	Kabūd	كَبُودْ	ū	معروف	
Hamper	Hamdam	هَمْدَمْ	h	ه	٤٠
———	Ra's	رَاْسْ	'	ساكن ء	
———	Čašma-i-Kamōna⁴	چَشْمَهٔ كَمُونَه	-i-	متحرك	٤١
marrY	Wādi	وَادِىْ	i	ساكن كوتاه	٤٢
Yoke	Yaman	يَمَنْ	y	متحرك	
mAIn	Kārēz	كَارِيزْ	ē	مجهول ى	
bEEt, mEAt	Šarīf⁴	شَرِيفْ	ī	معروف	
spUY	Spay	شپِىْ	y	تاءنشى	
bItE	Zaynab	زَيْنَبْ	ay	ملينه	

2. Signs for Vowel Sounds

English Equivalents (in capital letters)	Examples Transliteration	Pashto/Farsi	Vowel Sounds Transliteration	Pashto/Farsi	No.
mAn, bAt, thAt	Bâr 'Andâr	بَـرْ	â	طویل	
fUnd, bUt	Band	بَـنْدْ	a	فتحه کوتاه	۱
———	Māndeh, Bəl	مَانْدَهْ بَلْ	ə, ě	زورکی	۲
AInu, IcE	Jazira-i-Darqad	جَـزِیْرَهٔ دَرْقَـدْ	–i–, e[5]	اضافی	
agrEssive	Kohe Babā	کُوهِ بَابَا			
bEt, sEt, mEt	Selsela	سِلْسِلَه	e[6]	خفیف	۳
pEOn	Syāh	سِیَاهْ			
It, sIt	Hindu	هِـنْدُوْ	i[7]	سریع	
hollO	Moqur	مُـقْـرْ	o	خفیف	٤
pUt			u[8]	سریع	
someONE	Mašalan	مَشَـلاً	an		
mEN	Jadden	جِـدِّ	en		۵
intONate, yON	Hukmun	حُـکْـمٌ	un		
suDDen	Mohammad[9]	مُـحَـمَّـدْ	Letter doubled	شد	٦
AlkAli	Ahmad	اَحْـمَـدْ	a	با فتحه کوتاه	
dwArf	Bālā	بَـالاَ	a	با فتحه طویل	
tOp	Doāb	دُوآبْ	ā	با مد	
bOUGHt	Sarāsyāb	سَرَاسْیَابْ			
sEt, IEt	E'dām	اِعْـدَامْ	e	کوتاه	
AId, AtE	Ešan-Ewri-Dara	اِیشَانْ اِیوْری دَرَهْ	ē	با کسرهٔ خفیف طویل	
tIn, bIt	Istālef	اِسْتَالِفْ	i	کوتاه	
EAt, bEEt	Īnjā	اِیـنْـجَـا	ī	با کسرهٔ سریع طویل	
Obey, Obedient	Obē	اُبـِی	o	باضمهٔ خفیف کوتاه	
OAr, OAt	Ōr	اُورْ	ō	طویل	
Othman, Uzziel, Osram	Uzbak	اُزْبَـكْ	u	" " سریع کوتاه	
EWE	Ūzgad	اُوزْکَـدْ	ū	طویل	
WOrd	Wardak	وَرْدَكْ	w	کوتاه با فتحه	
WAsh	Wādi	وَادِی		طویل	

English Equivalents (in capital letters)	Examples Transliteration	Pashto / Farsi	Vowel Sounds Transliteration	Pashto / Farsi	No.
WEld	Welāyāt Wĕṛsak	ولایَتْ وَرْسَكْ	w	بازورکی با کسره	
WhErE	Wyālay⁶	وِیَالَیْ	w		
	Weštĕh	وِښْتَه			
WAIting	Wēwāya	وِیـوَایَه			
WInter	Wino; Winu	وِیْنُوْ وِیْنُوْ	w	با کسره	
WEEd	Wīšt	وِیْشْتْ			
WEAry	Wiyaīnām	وِیَتْنَامْ			۸
WOmen	Woli;	وُلِـیْ			
	Wowāya	وُوَایَـه			
mOrE	Ṛāwōr;	رَاوُوْرْ	w	با ضمه	
	Dwo	دْوُوْ			
WOrn	Wulwala	وُلْـوَلَه			
WOOl	Šowūnkē	شوُوْنْكِىْ			
YAma	Yakawlang¹⁰	یَـکَـوْلَنْګْ	ya	کوتاه	
YAhoo	Yāsin	یَاسِـیـنْ	yā	طویل	
YEt	Tangī Sayedān	تَنْگِی سَیـْدَانْ	ye	باکسره خفیف کوتاه	
YAlE	Byāyēd	بْیَایِـیـدْ	yē	طویـل	
bUOY (bui)	Nabiyi	نَـبِیـیْ	yi	سریع کوتاه	
YEAst	Šayin-Āyin	شَایِـیـنْ آیِـیـنْ	yī	با کسره طویـل	۹
YIEld	Qāšūrī Bālā	قَاشُورِی بَلَا	see notes 4 & 5	با کسره اصافی	
gEOcentric	Yoma	یَـمَه	yo		
YOke, YOlk	Yōgh	یُـوغْ	yō		
gEOstatic	Yughlān	یُـغْلَانْ	yu	با ضمه	
YOU, YOUth	Yūm	یُـوْمْ	yū		
	Aybak	اَیْـبَكْ			
sIGHt	Aynabak	اَیْنَـبَكْ	ay	کوتاه	
mInE	Byānzāy	بِیَانْ زَایْ	āy	طویـل	۱۰
AIda	Yanamāyi	یَـنَه مَایـیْ	āyi	طویـل و دبل یا	

English Equivalents (in capital letters)	Examples Transliteration	Pashto / Farsi	Vowel Sounds Transliteration	Pashto/Farsi	No.
————	Mānay	مَانَسى	əy	زوركى ياسى	11
rAIn, fAll	Rēg	رِيگ	e	مجهول	
bIngo	Jinaw	جِنَوْ	i		12
copY	Māhi	مَاهِى	i	ضمه معروف كوتاه	
	Jehĭl	جِهِيْل	ī	كسره يا ـ ى معروف	12
mEAl, mEEn	Ā'in	آئِيْنْ		طويل	
bOY, OYster	Boyāra	بِيَارَه	oy	با ضمهٔ خفيف	
	Jōy	جَوْى	ōy	با واو مجهول	
————	Wuy	وُى	uy	با ضمهٔ سريع	13
bUOY (būi)	Mūy, Būy	مُوْى بُوْى	ūy	با واو معروف	
fOUnd	Mamakaw	مَمَكَوْ	aw	فتحه كوتاه	
thOUsand	Azāw	ازَاوْ	āw	زور طويل	14
————	Aležgrew	اَلِـژگِرِوْ	ew	خفيف كوتاه	
LEO	Dēw, Sēw	دِيْو سِيْو	ēw	طويل باياى مجهول	
————	Niwal	نِيْوَلْ	iw	طويل كوتاه	15
New York	Nĭw Yārk	نِيْوْ يَارْك	ĭw	طويل سريع	
dOrmitory, Opinion	Koh, Pašto	كوه پَشْتوْ	o¹¹	باياى معروف مجهول كوتاه	
flOOr	Tōr, Ghōri	تَوْر غَوْرِى	ō	طويل	
tWO	Jaghatu	جَغَتُوْ	u	معروف كوتاه	16
mOOn	Čehel Sotūn	چِهَلْ سَتُوْنْ	ū¹²	طويل	
	Ra'san,	رَأسًا	'	ساكن	
————	Be'sa,	بِئْسَ	'		
	Mu'men	مُؤْمِنْ	'	متحرك	17
————	Mo'assesa	مُؤَسِّسَه	'		
————	Čašma-i-Šafā	چَشْمهٔ شَفَا	-i-	اضافى	

857

3. Explanatory Notes

1 In some cases a Roman (English) letter has been used three times in order to express different (although similar) letters of the Pashto and Farsi alphabet. Distinction of the pronunciation is expressed by adding a bar over or under the letter. The bar has been placed over the letter the first time it appears in the sequence of the Pashto/Farsi alphabet. The second time it appears it carries no diacritic, and the third time it is used a bar is placed under the letter. Example: t̄,t,ṯ.

2 Letters in the Pashto/Farsi alphabet which are pronounced similar to their corresponding letters in the Roman (English) alphabet are always transliterated by a plain letter without any diacritic.

3 The following three points are to be considered on the letter 'h':

a. Whenever 'h' comes after the composite forms 'kh' and 'gh' and after 'k' and 'g', (as may happen when forming the plural of a word by adding the syllable 'ha') the 'h' has to be separated from the 'kh', 'gh', 'k' and 'g' by a hyphen. Example: Šaykh–hā; bāgh–hā: tāk–hā: sang–hā.

b. Whenever 'h' appears after any other consonant it is pronounced separately. Example: Qal'a–i–Faṯh; aylāqhā.

c. Excepting the cases in which 'h' appears after the composite forms 'kh' and 'gh', the 'h' is never doubled. For instance, a word ending on 'h' will get its plural form by adding 'ā' only, not 'hā'. Example: Šāh, Šāhā; māh, māhā.

4 The 'ee' –sound (yā–i–ma'rūf) is written with 'i' whenever the vowel is short and by 'ī' whenever the vowel is long, as explained in the following:

a. The 'ee'–sound (yā–i–ma'–rūf) at the end of a word is always pronounced short and will always be expressed by 'i'. Example: Wali, Wāli.

b. An 'ee'–sound in the middle of a word followed by a syllable is also always pronounced short and will be expressed by 'i'. Example: Jaziṟa.

c. An 'ee'–sound followed by a consonant only is pronounced long and is expressed by 'ī'. Example: Ta'mīr.

d. A word in its original form transliterated according to rules (4 a,b,c) above, when appearing in a different grammatical form, which makes the 'yā–i–ma'rūf' sound longer or shorter, will not be made subject to any changes in the transliteration of the 'yā–i–ma'rūf'. Examples: Mirānšāh Kalay – Miṟšāh Kalay; Amīr – Amīri.

5 The 'kasṟa-i-edẕāfi' is transliterated as explained in the following:

a. It is expressed by adding an 'e' to the generic term whenever the term ends with a consonant. Example: Koh, Kohe Bābā.

b. Whenever the generic term ends with a vowel (including 'hamza' but excluding 'yā-i-ma'rūf') the 'kasṟa-i-edẕāfi' is expressed by inserting '-ī-' between the generic term and the proper noun. Examples: Jazīra, Jazīra-i-Darqad; Ḏarakhtha, Ḏarakhtha-i-Munfaṟeḏ; Ḏarya, Ḏaryā-i-Kabul.

c. If the 'kasṟa-i-edẕāfi' is to be expressed immediately after a 'yā-i-ma'rūf', it is simply transliterated by adding a bar over the 'yā-i-ma'rūf' ('i'). Examples: Wádi, Wādī Helmand; Ghundi, Ghundī Ya'qūb.

6 'Kasṟa-i-khafīf' is always expressed by 'e', except in the cases where the next letter would be the transliterated letter 'y'. Since the 'kasṟa-i-khafīf'-sound is fully covered by the 'y', the 'e' will be omitted in this case. Example: Senjeḏ; Myān.

7 'Kasṟa-i-edẕafi' "sounds like the short 'ya-i-ma'rūf'" and is expressed by 'i'. Example: Sinkay. (See note 4–a,b).

8 The 'ḏzamma' is expressed by 'o' if the sound is smooth and by 'u' if the sound is sharp. The rules are as follows:

a. A 'ḏzamma' immediately followed by a syllable will usually be pronounced smoothly and is transliterated by 'o'. Example: 'Omaṟ('O-mar); Moḥammaḏ(Mo-ḥammaḏ).

b. A 'ḏzamma' immediately followed by one or more consonants will usually be pronounced sharply and is expressed by 'u'. Examples: 'Us̄mān('Us̄-mān); 'Ulyā('Ul-yā); Muhṟ (Mu-hṟ).

c. A word, in its original form transliterated according to rules 8—b or 8—a above, when appearing in a different grammatic form which makes the 'dzamma' sound smoother or sharper, will not be made subject to any change in the transliteration of the 'dzamma'. Example: Pul, Pule Khumri. Moghul, Moghulāne Bālā. De Haji Mullā Golān Kalay, De Haji Mullā Gol Kalay.

9 Numerous cases exist in which the transliteration requires the use of double letters (e. g. the double 'm' in 'Mohammad'). However the letters 'w' and 'y' are never doubled, even though the pronunciation of a word might lead one to think it should. Example: Awal, qowah; Qayūm, Molayena.

10 When a geographic name is composed of more than one word and a stress appears only in one of them, the name shall be written as one word, e. g. Yakawlang; if a stress appears in more than one of the words, then each word having a stress shall be written separately, e. g. Čehel Sotūn.

1 : 300 000

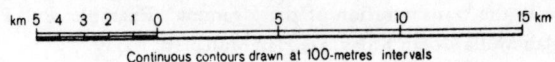

Continuous contours drawn at 100-metres intervals

LIST OF CONVENTIONAL SIGNS

	Motor gravel roads 1. Width of a metalled (gravelled) part of the road 2. Width of the road between the ditches
	Motor gravel roads under construction
	Unmetalled motor roads with ditches 1. Bridges 10- carryig capacify of a bridge in tons
	Unmetalled motor roads primary
	Unmetalled motor roads secondary
	Pack tracks and paths 1. Parts of paths on artificially made corniccs rafak
	Telephone and telegraph lines
	Embankments and cuttings with markings of height and depth
	1. Block 2. Habitable or not habitable buildings 3. Single habitable buildings
	Ruins
	1. Mosques 2. Mazars 3. Monuments
	1. Single graves 2. Cemeteries
	1. Aerodromes 2. Airfields
	Power stations
	1. Radio stations 2. Meteorological stations
	1. Factories or works 2. Brick-kilns
	Permanent camps of nomads
	1. Water mills 2. Wind mills
	Gasolene or oil tanks
	Ancient historical walls
	Saltworks
	1. Tower type structures and buildings 2. Fortresses
	International boundaries
	Barrows and holes with markings of depth and height
	Lakes or ponds perennial
	1. Rivers 2. Streems perennial 3. Streams non-perennial
	Shoals
	1. Springs 2. Wells 3. Main wells ground height mark at the well / depth of well
	1. Irrigation canals with a bank and the height of the bank 2. Water distribution device. 3. Dams
	Weirs
	1. Water pipe lines 2. Karezes
	Landing-stages
	Contours at 100-mertes intervals

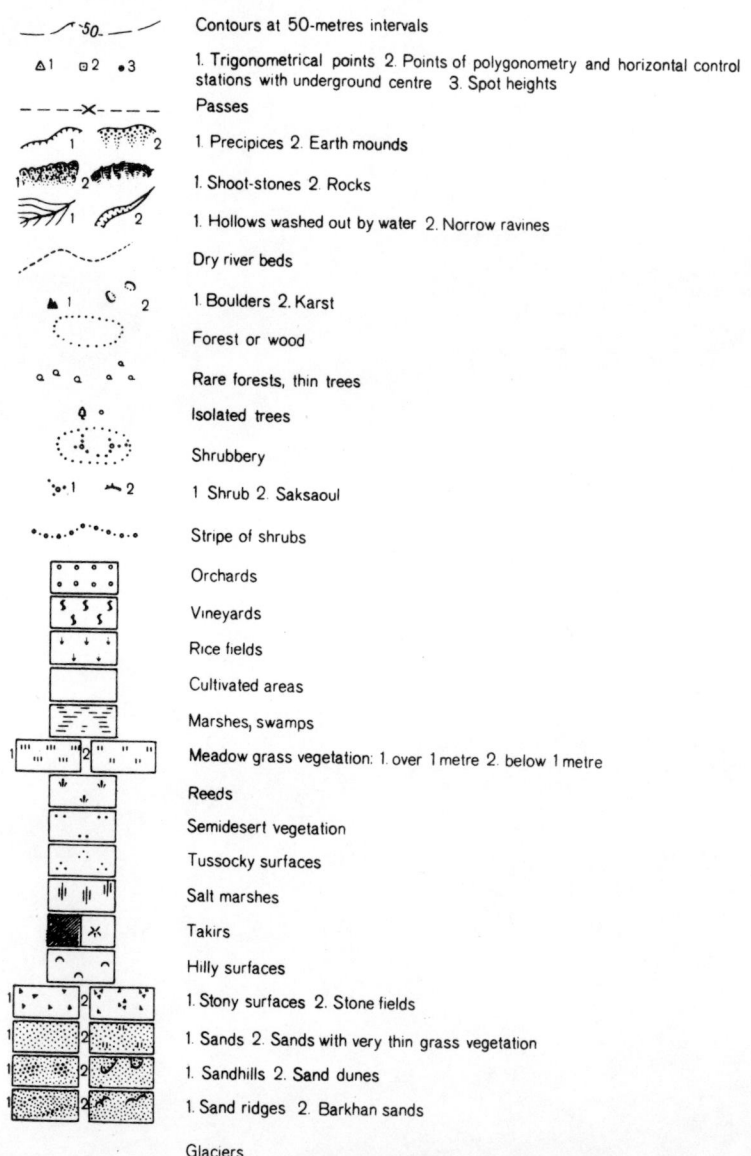

The boundaries shown in these maps are not, in some instances, finally determined and their reproduction does not imply any endorsement or recognition.

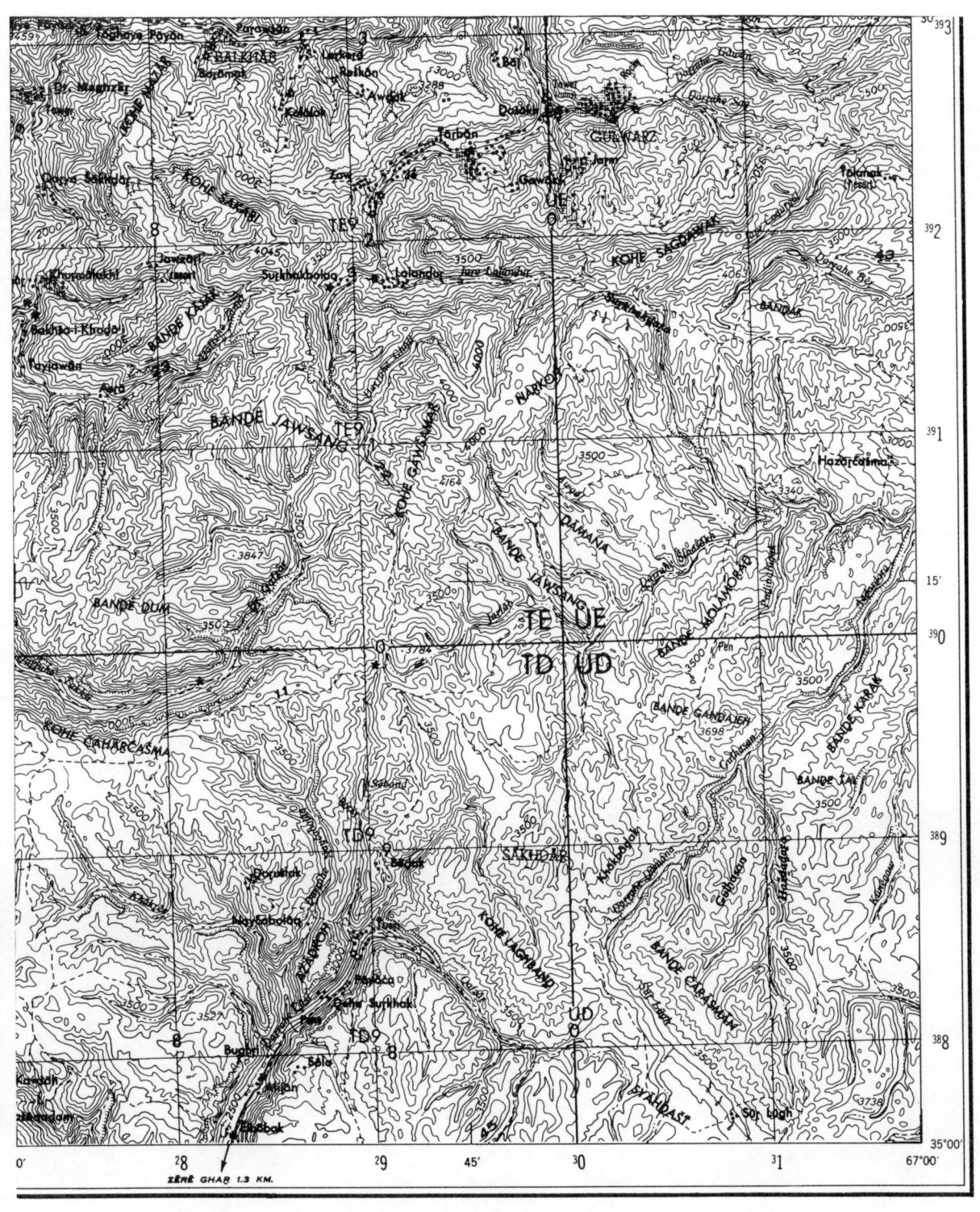

VI–2–C
See IV–14–C

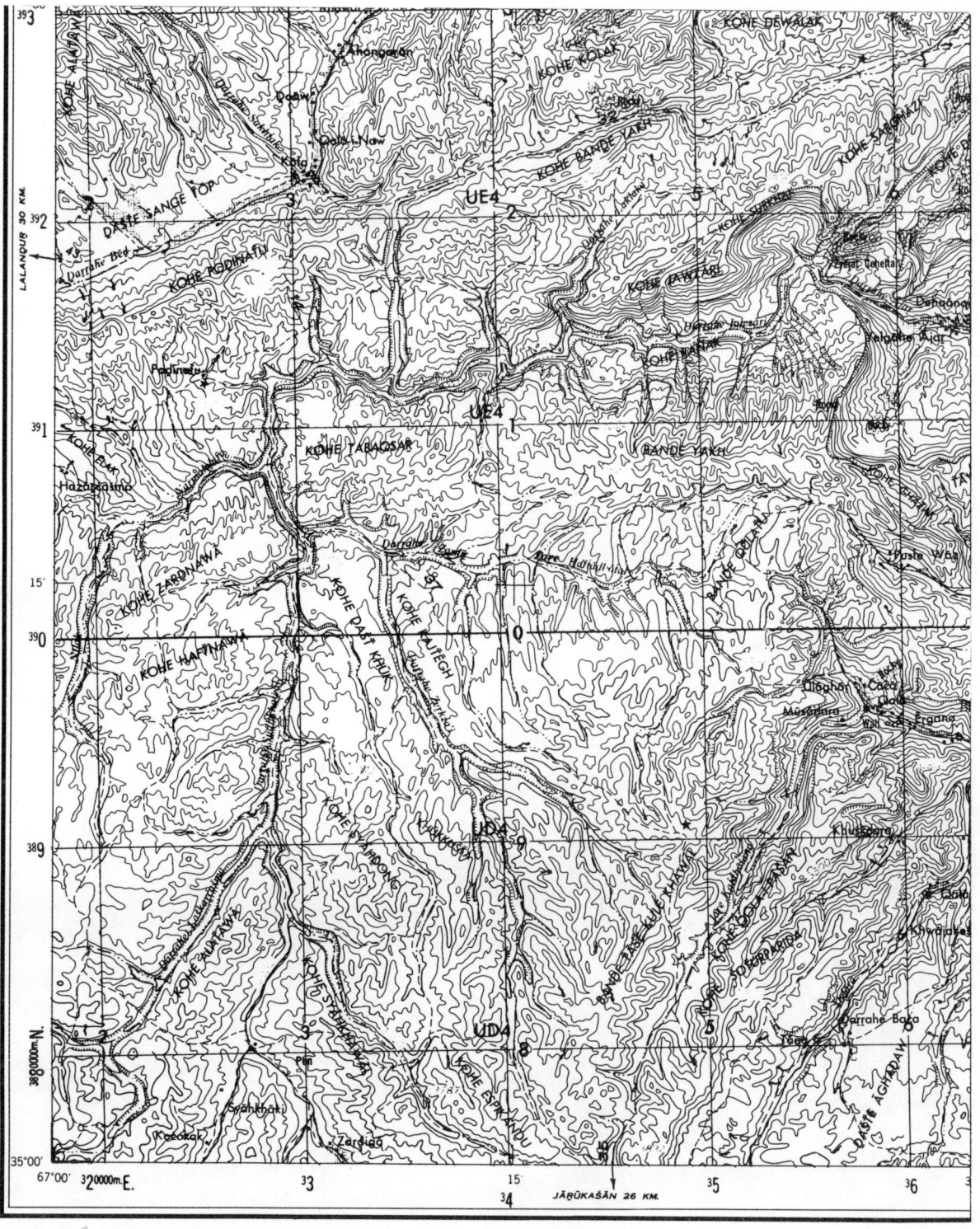

VI-2-D
See IV-14-D

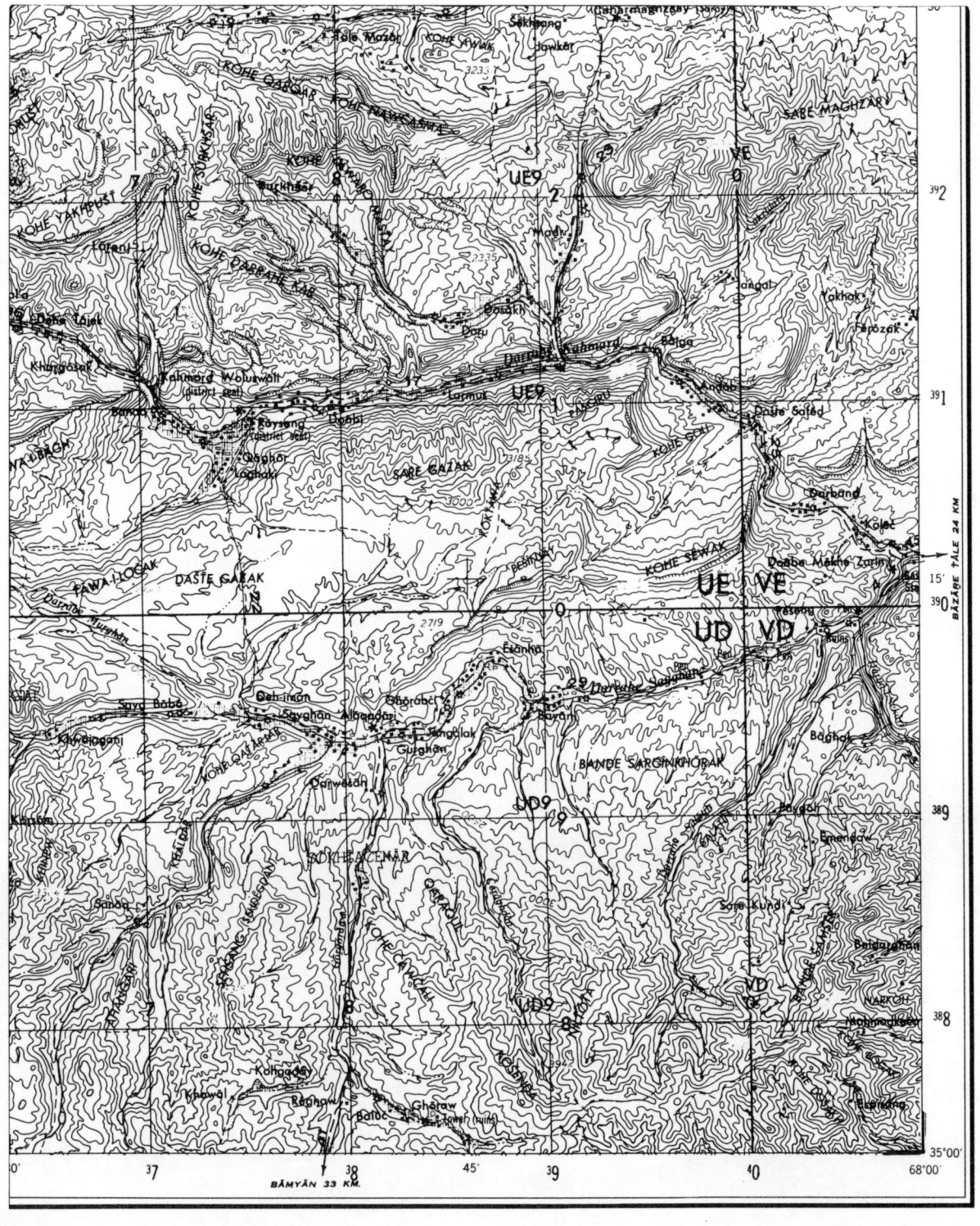

VI−3−C
See I−17−C

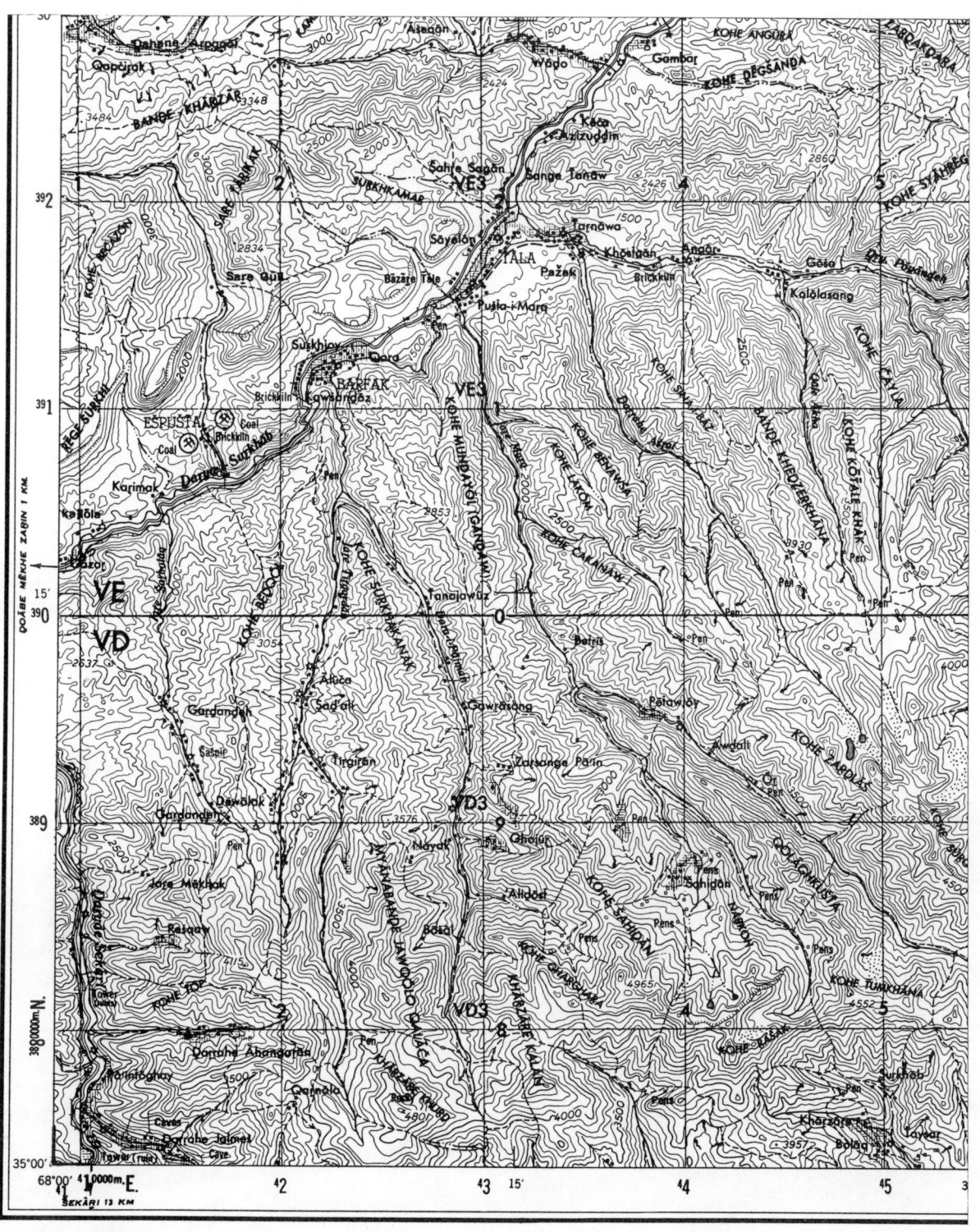

VI-3-D
See I-17-D

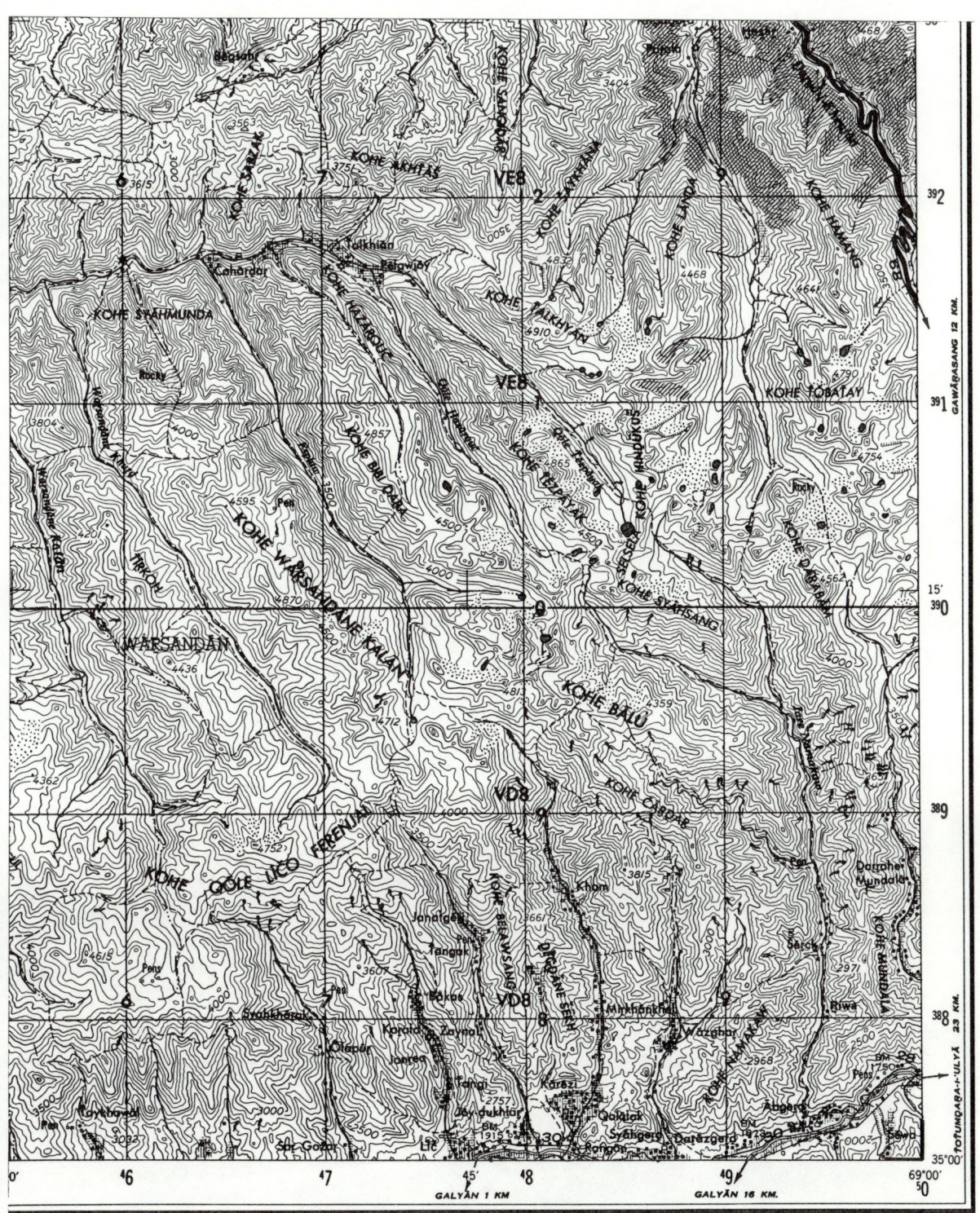

VI—4—B
See I—18—B

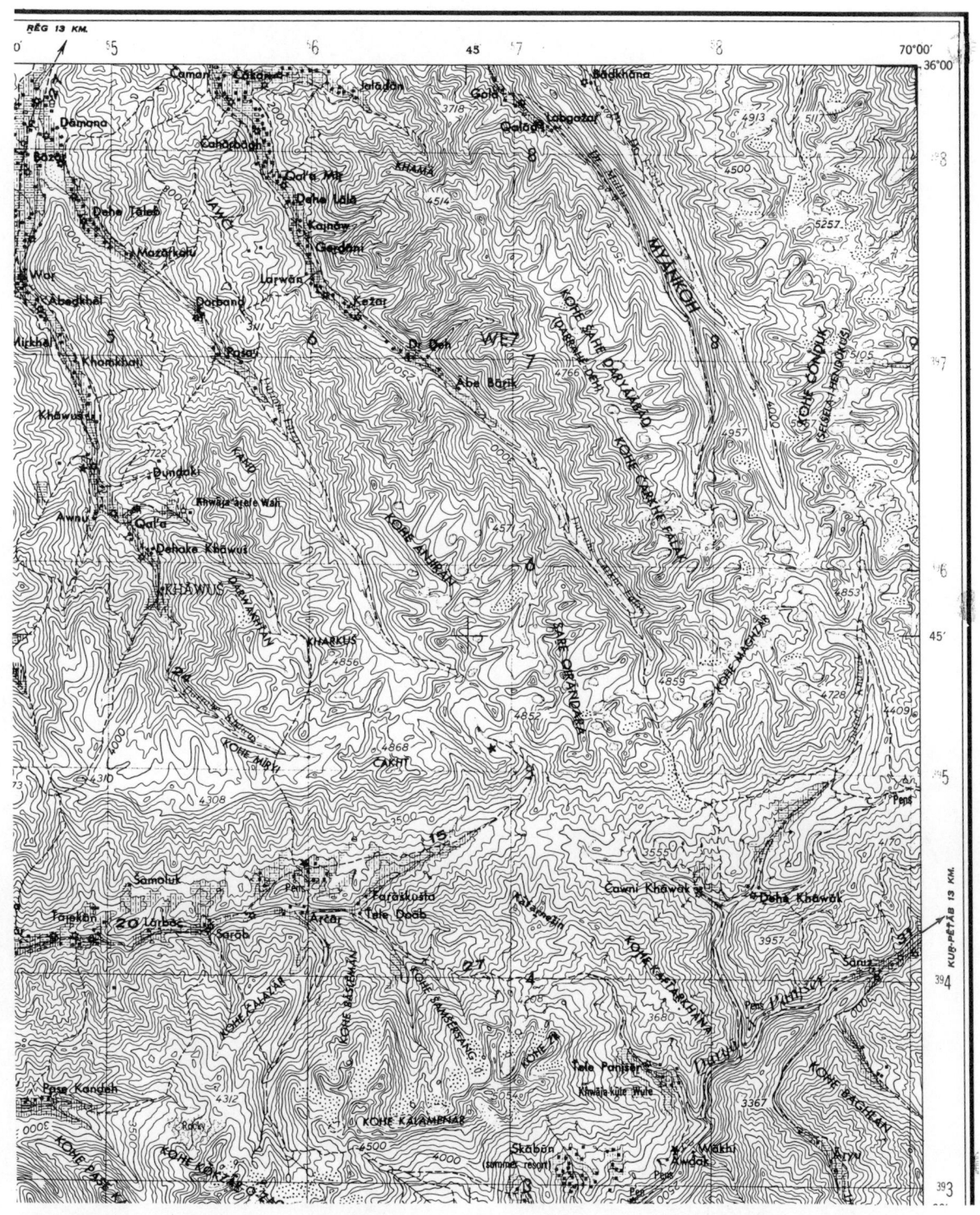

VI-4-C
See I-18-C

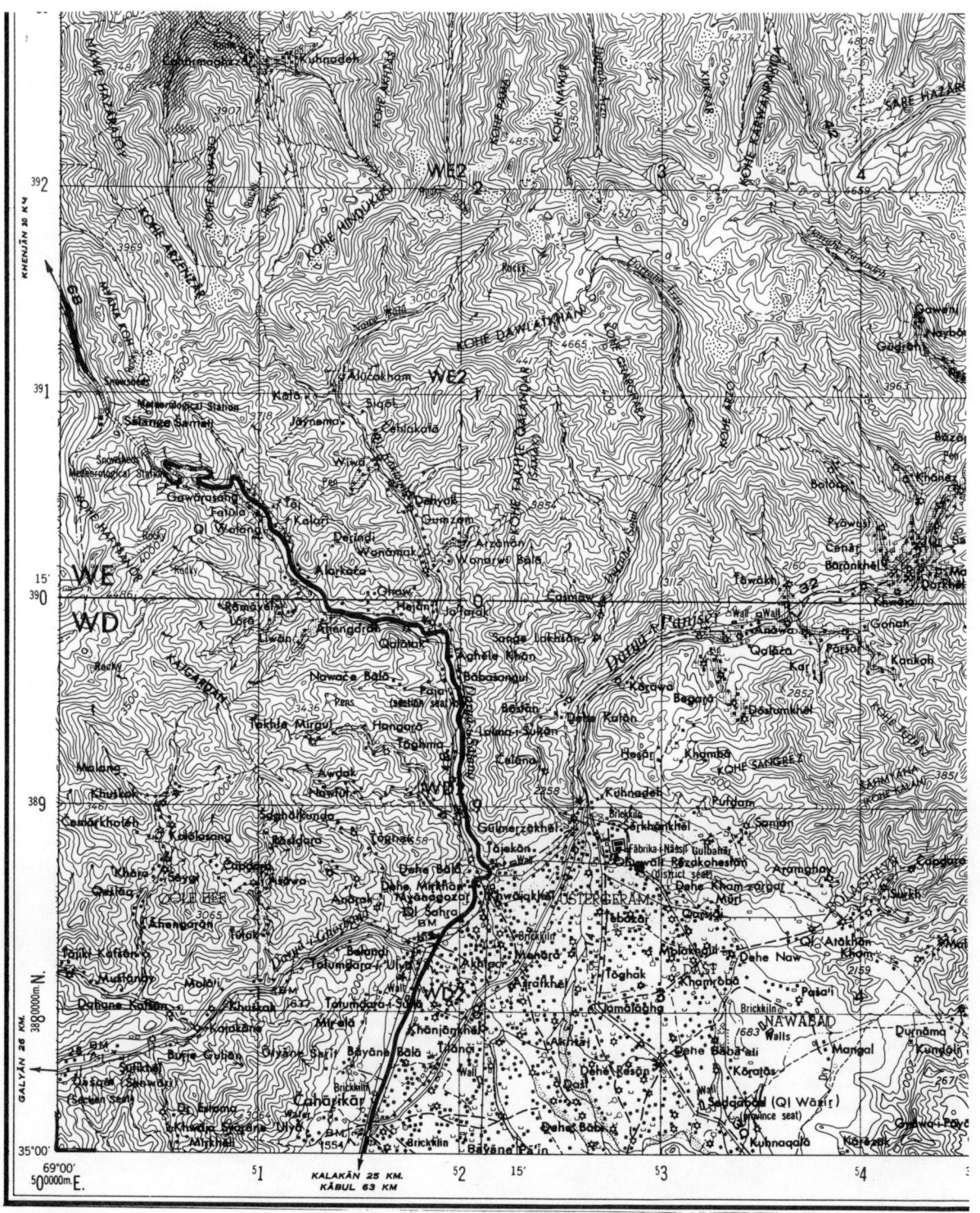

VI-4-D
See I-18-D

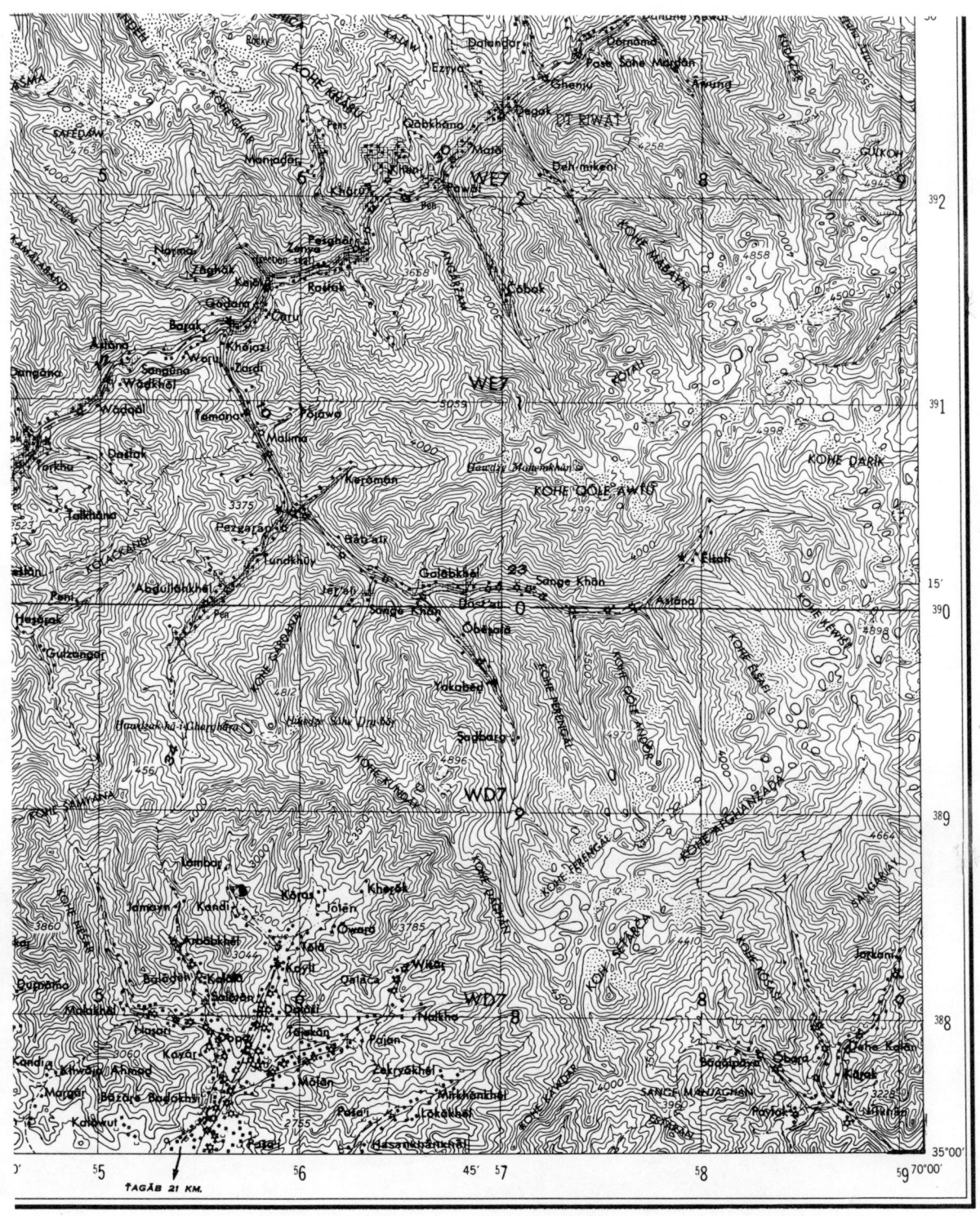

VI–5–A
See I–19–A

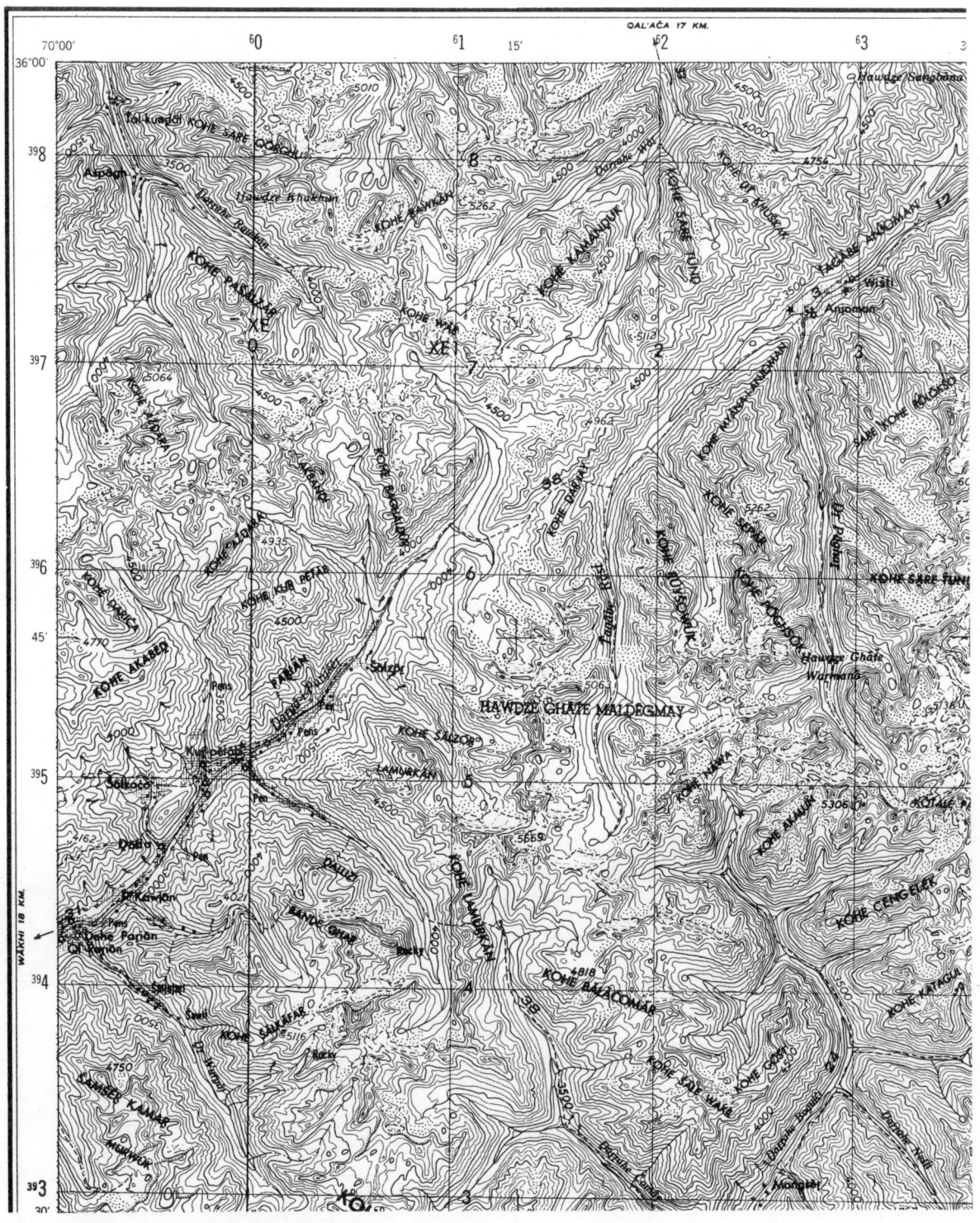

VI–5–B
See I–19–B

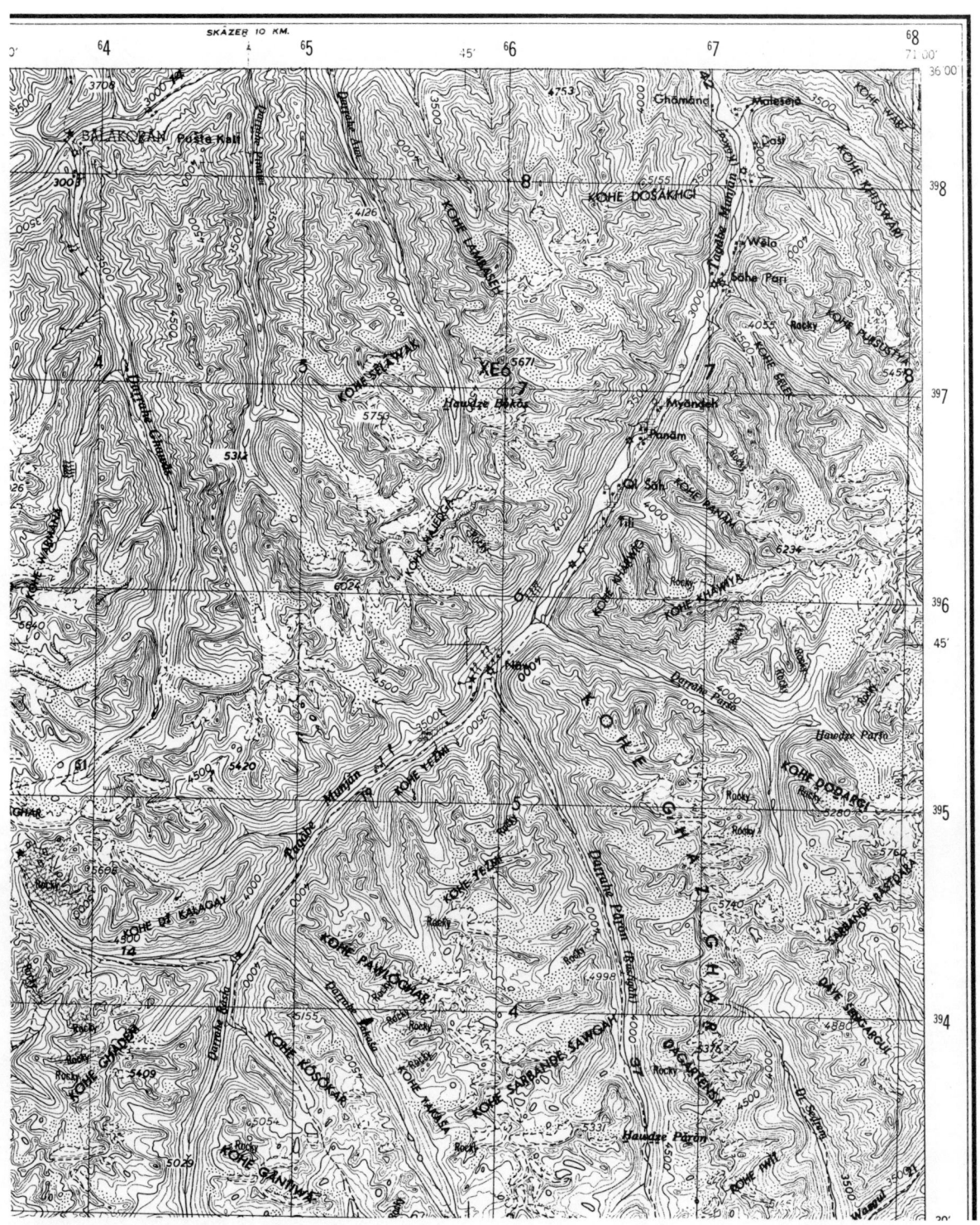

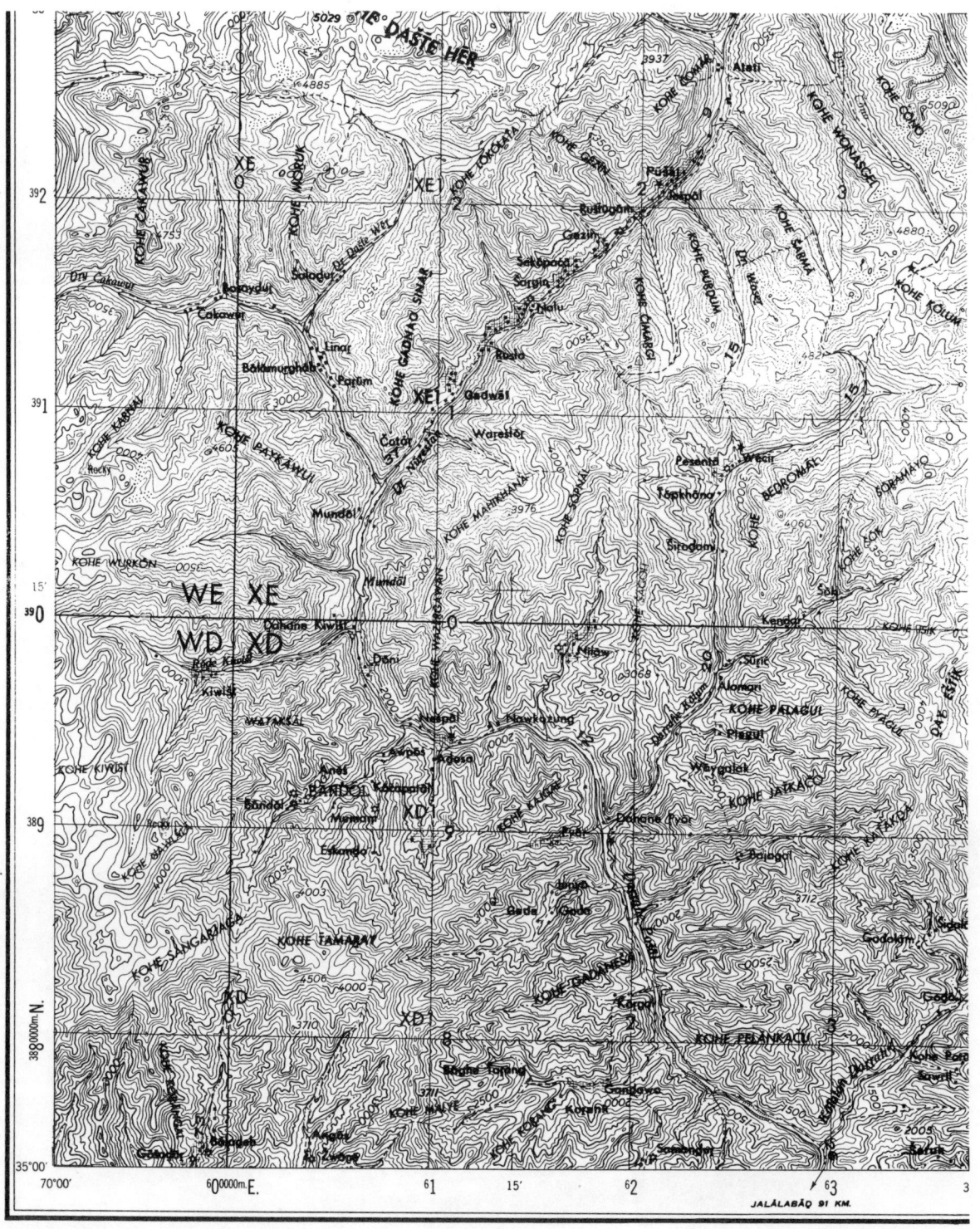

VI-5-D
See I-19-D

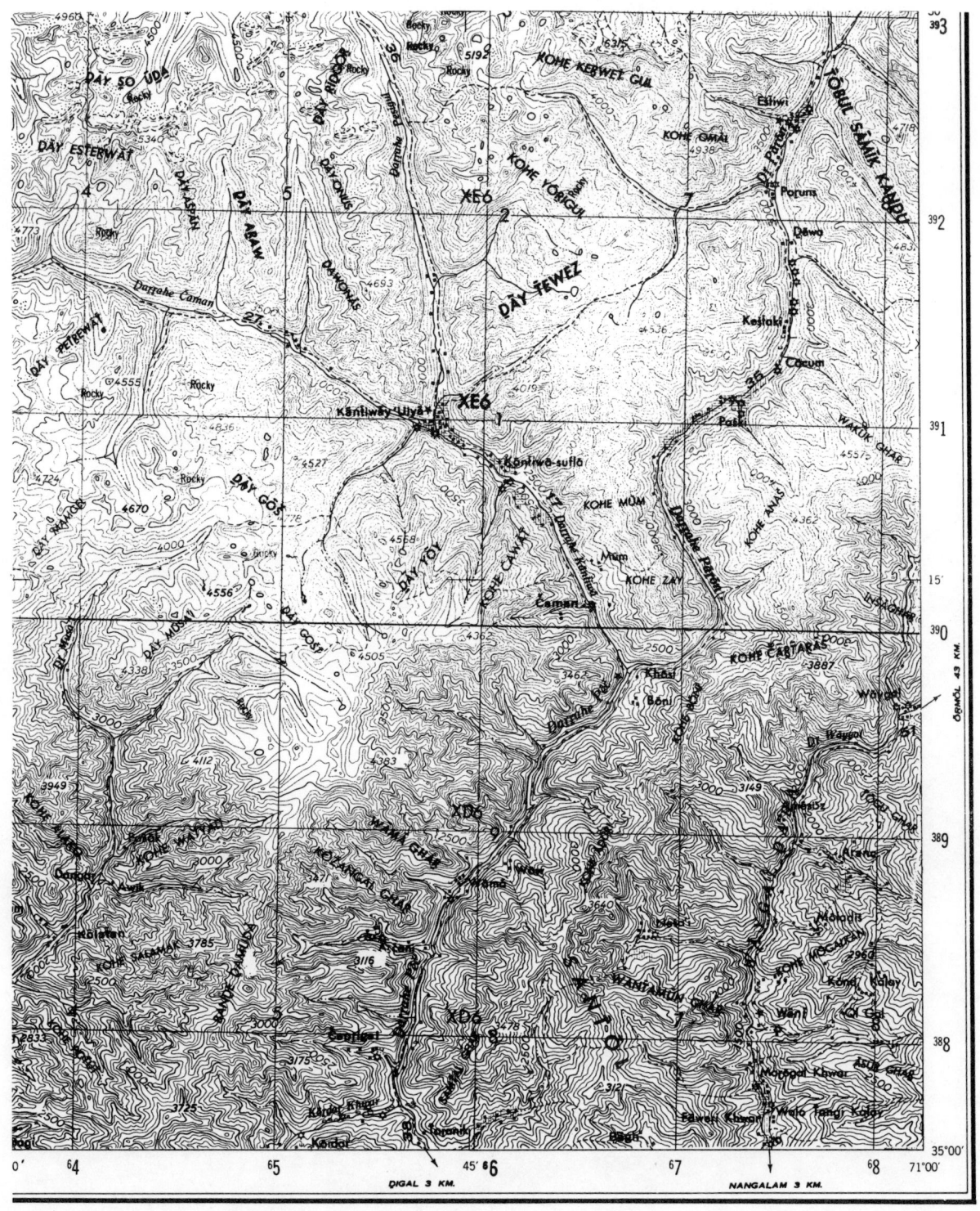

VI–6–A

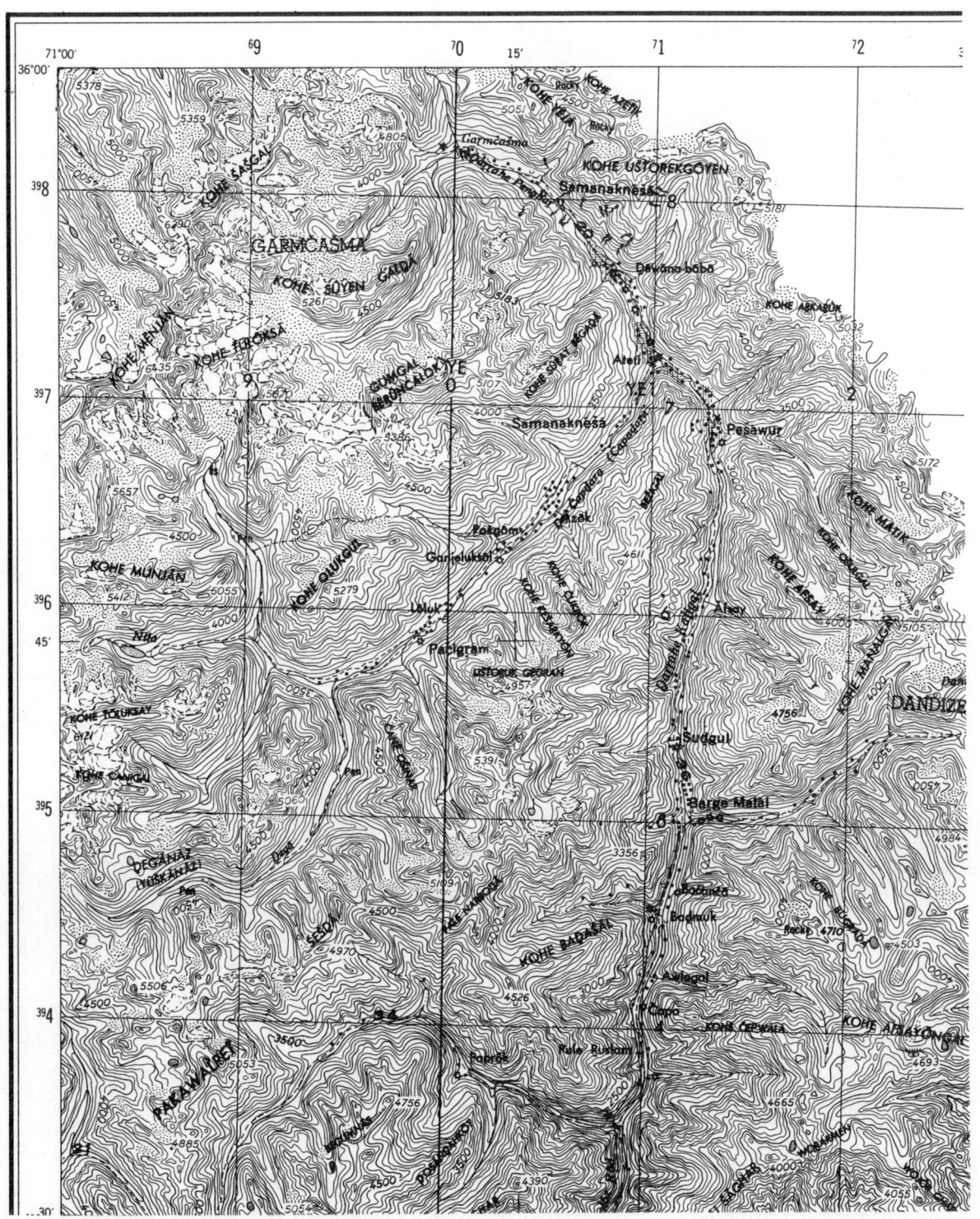

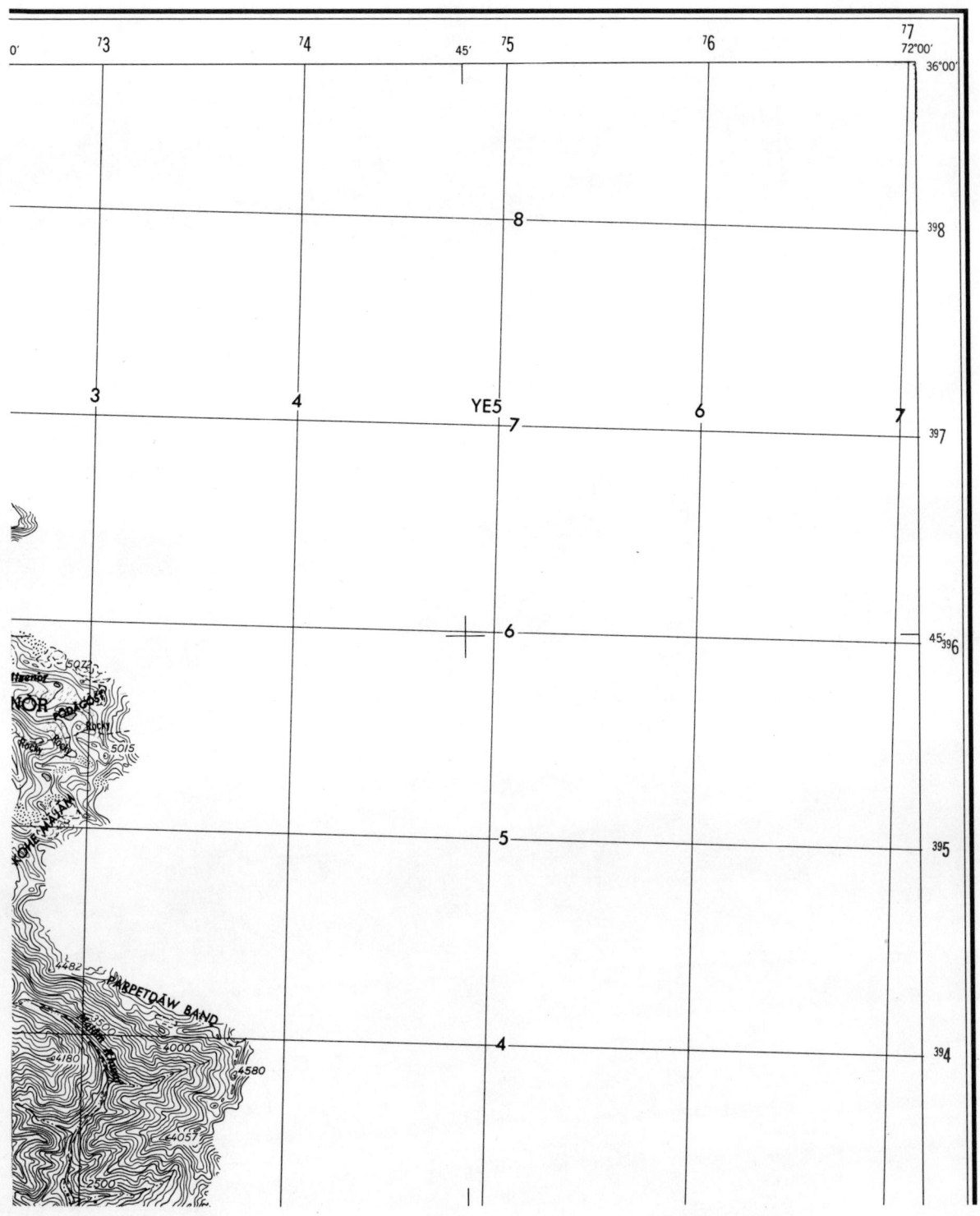

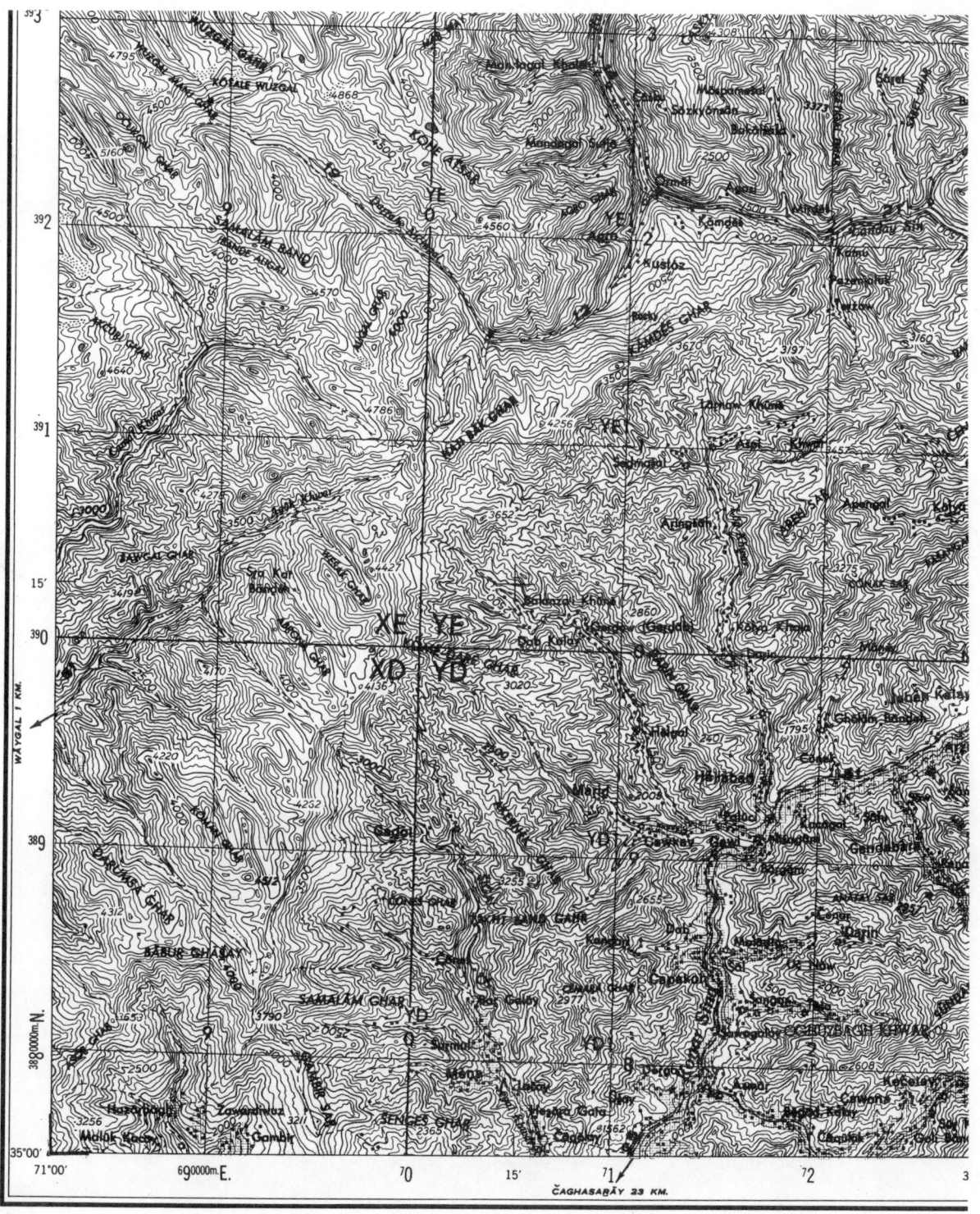

VI-6-D

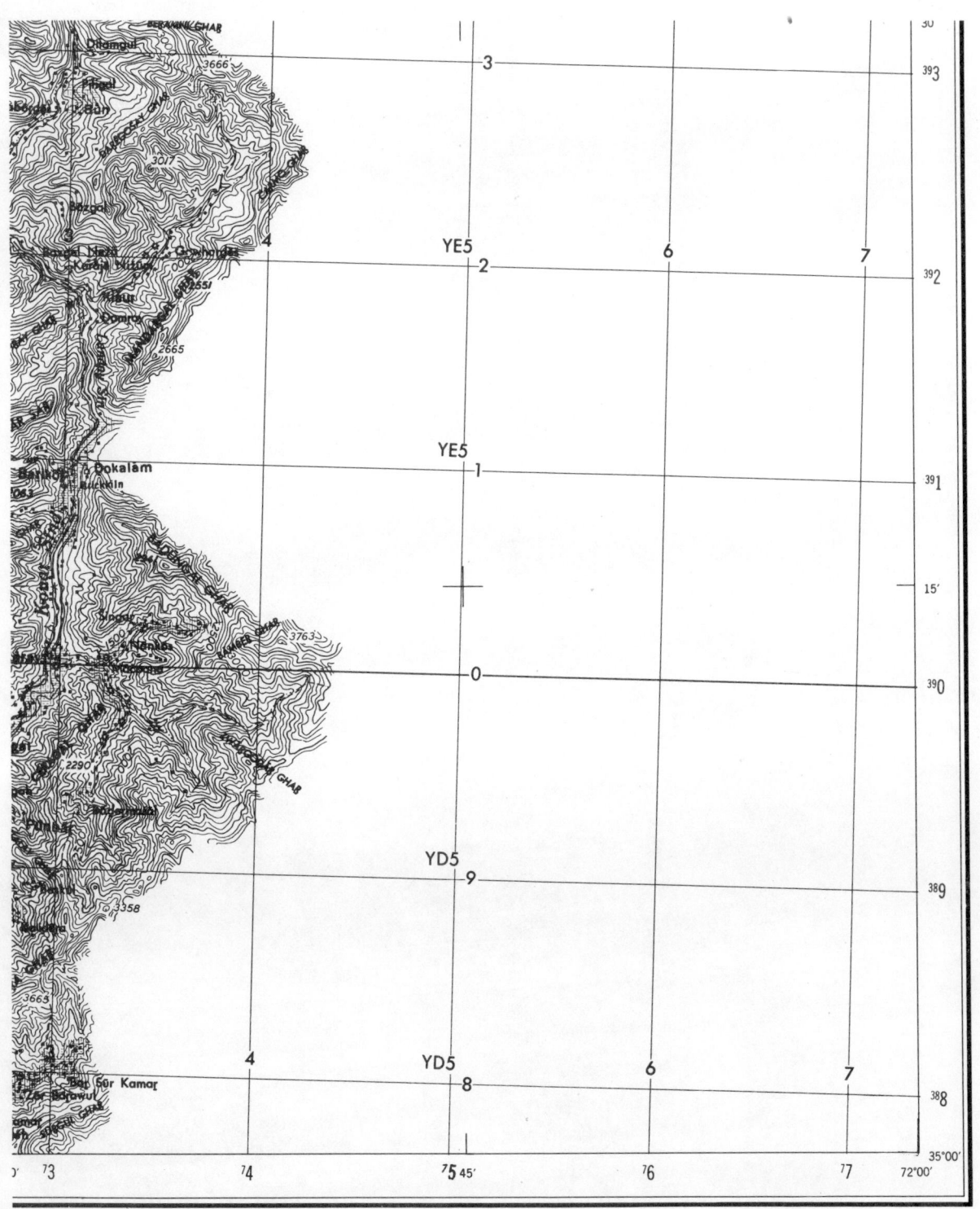

VI–7–A
See III–12–A and IV–16–A

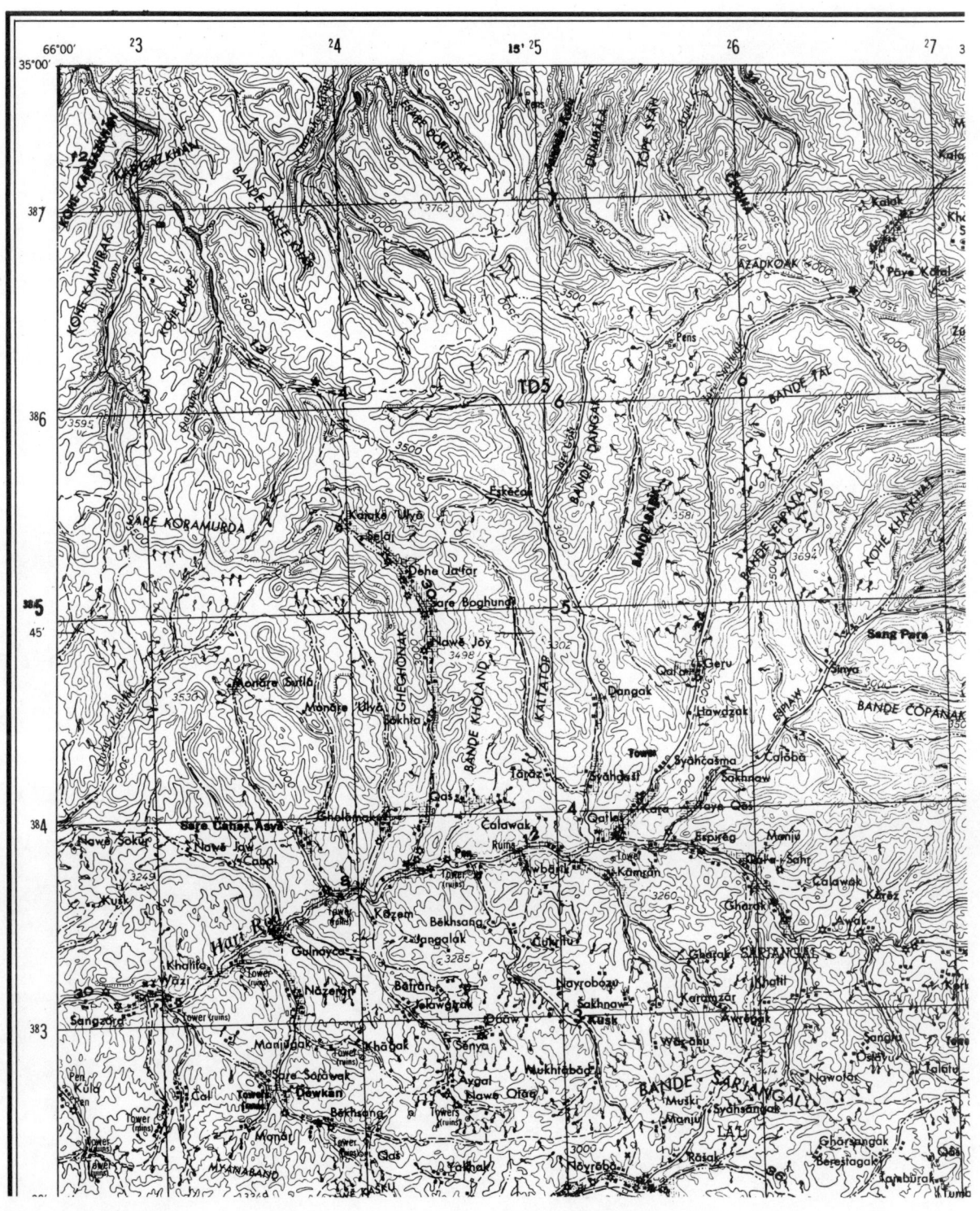

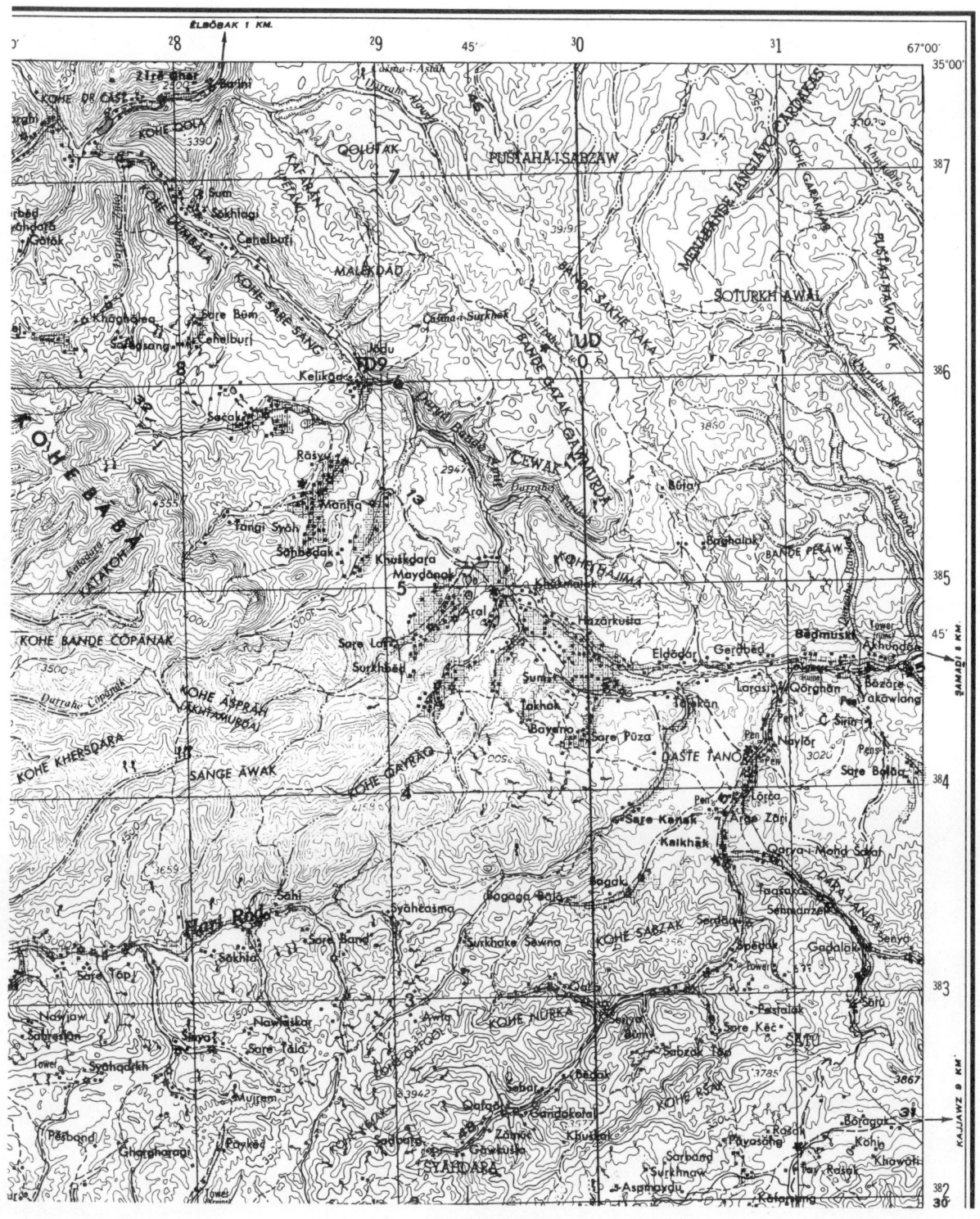

VI–7–D
See III–12–D and V–2–D

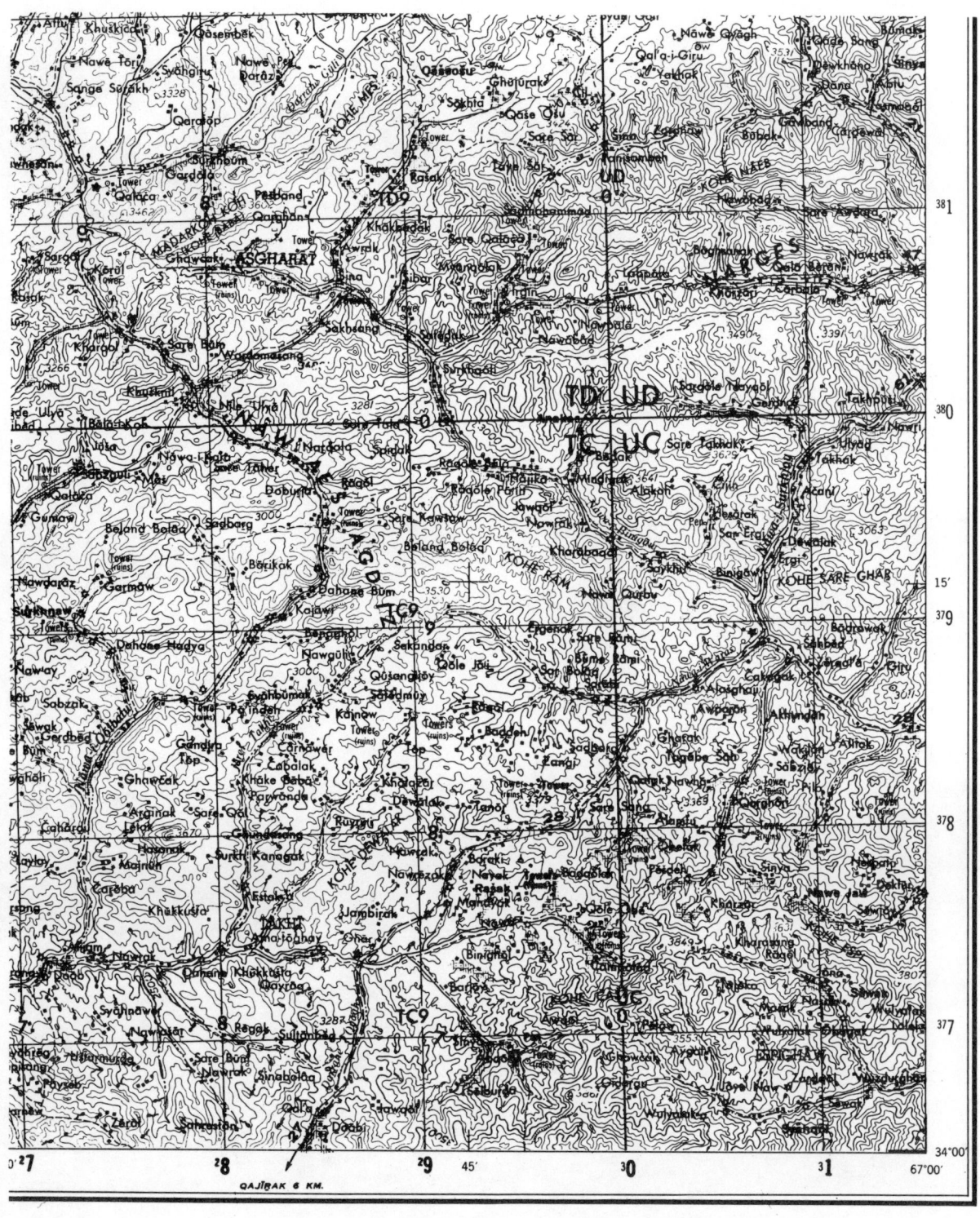

VI–8–A

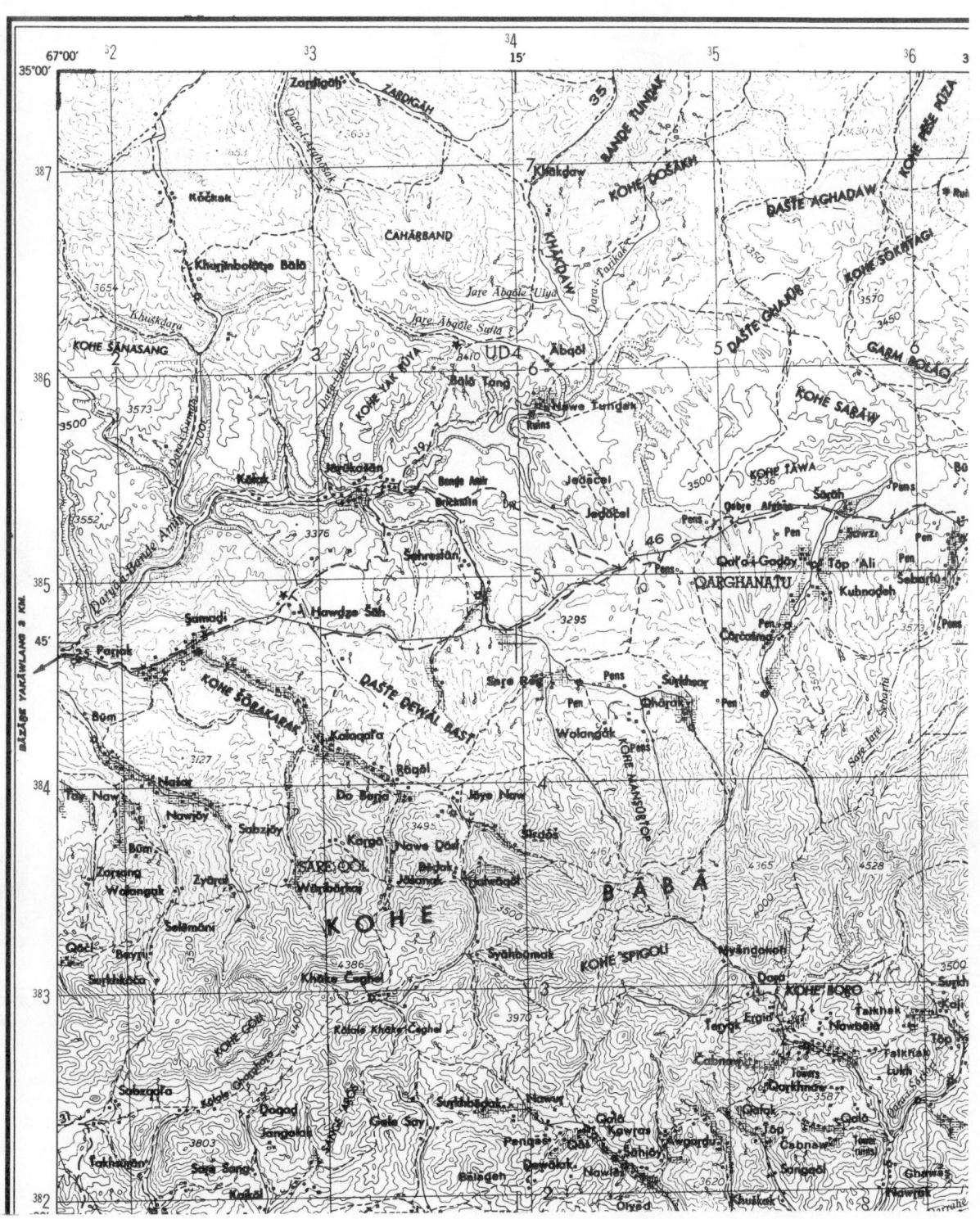

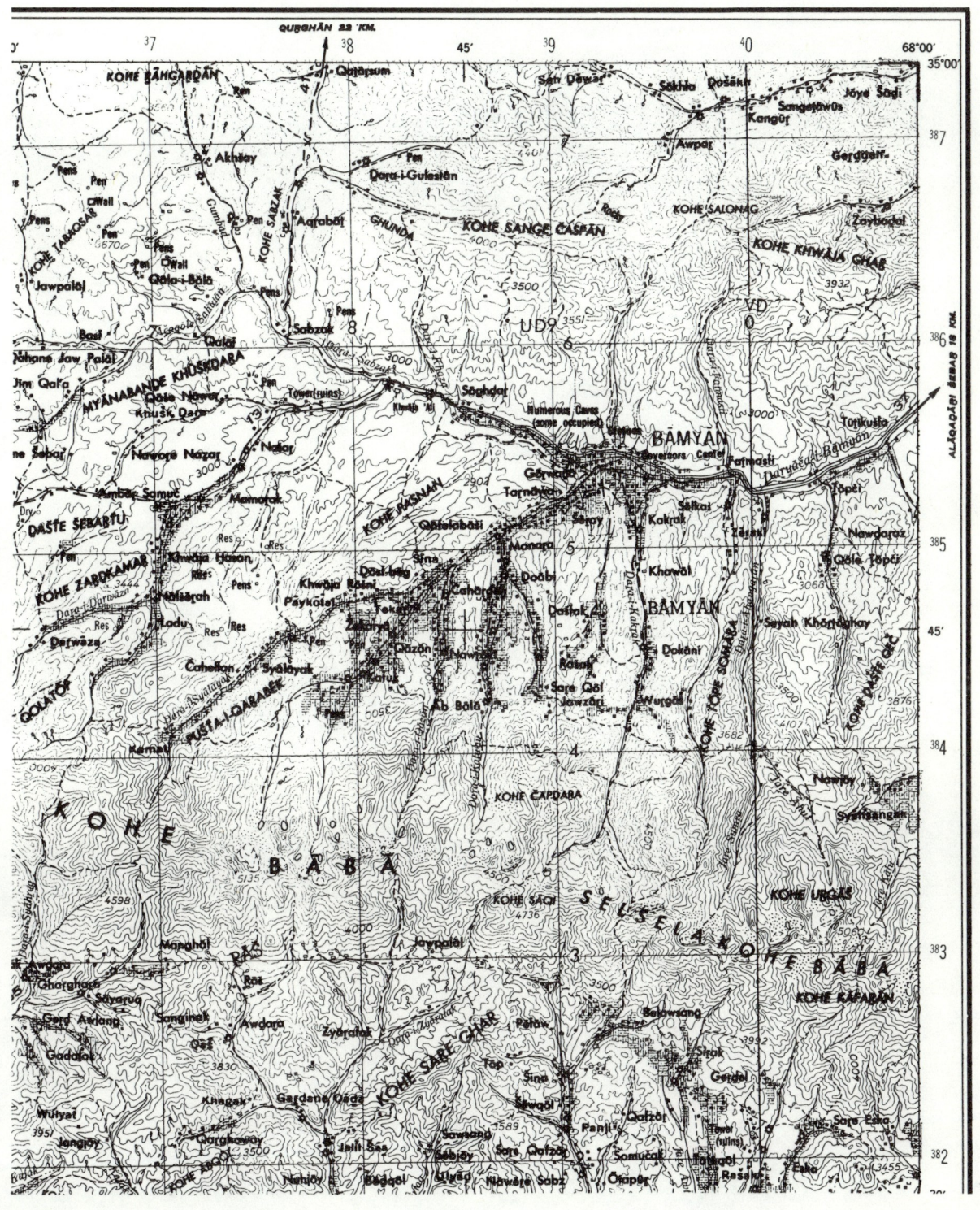

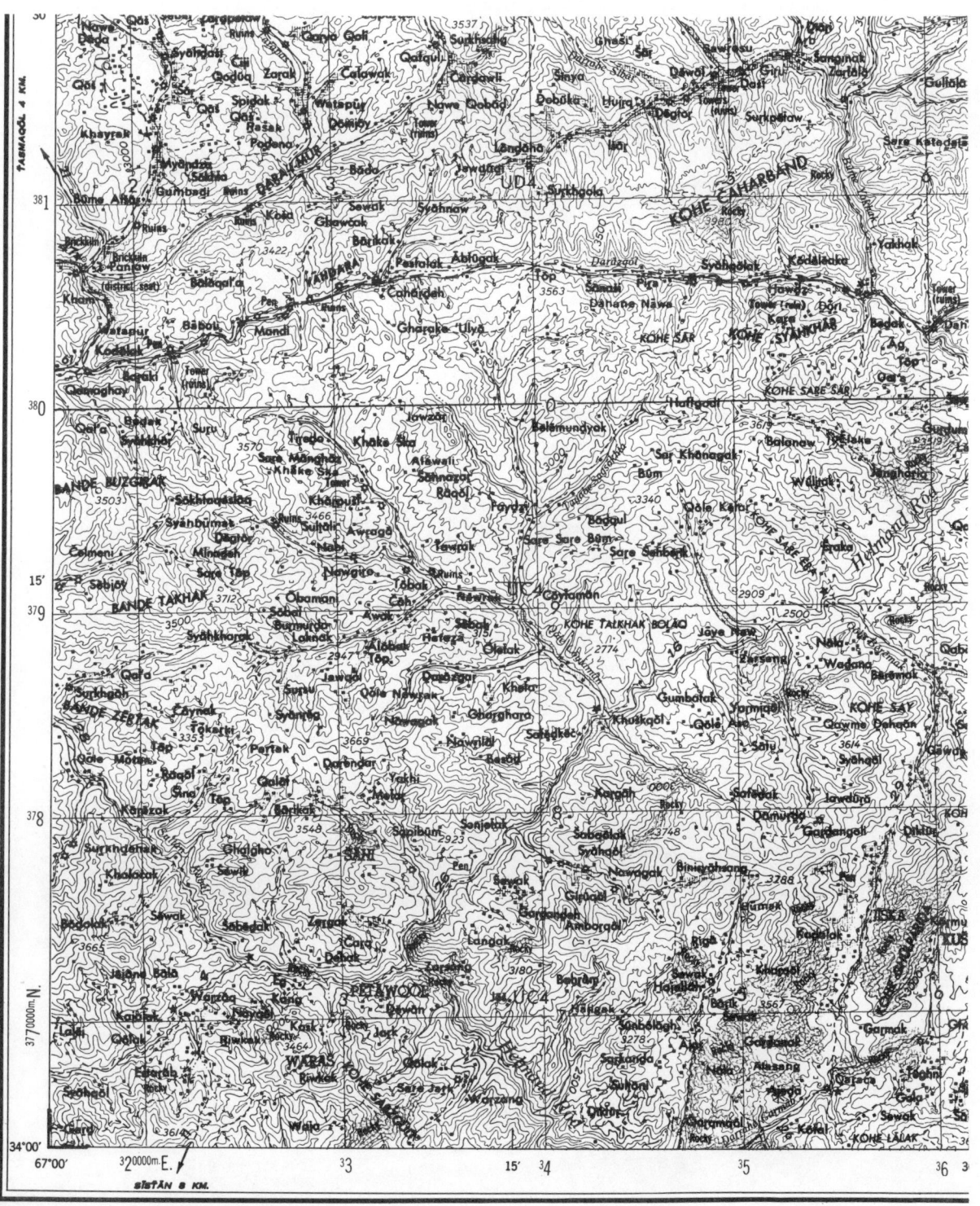

VI–8–D

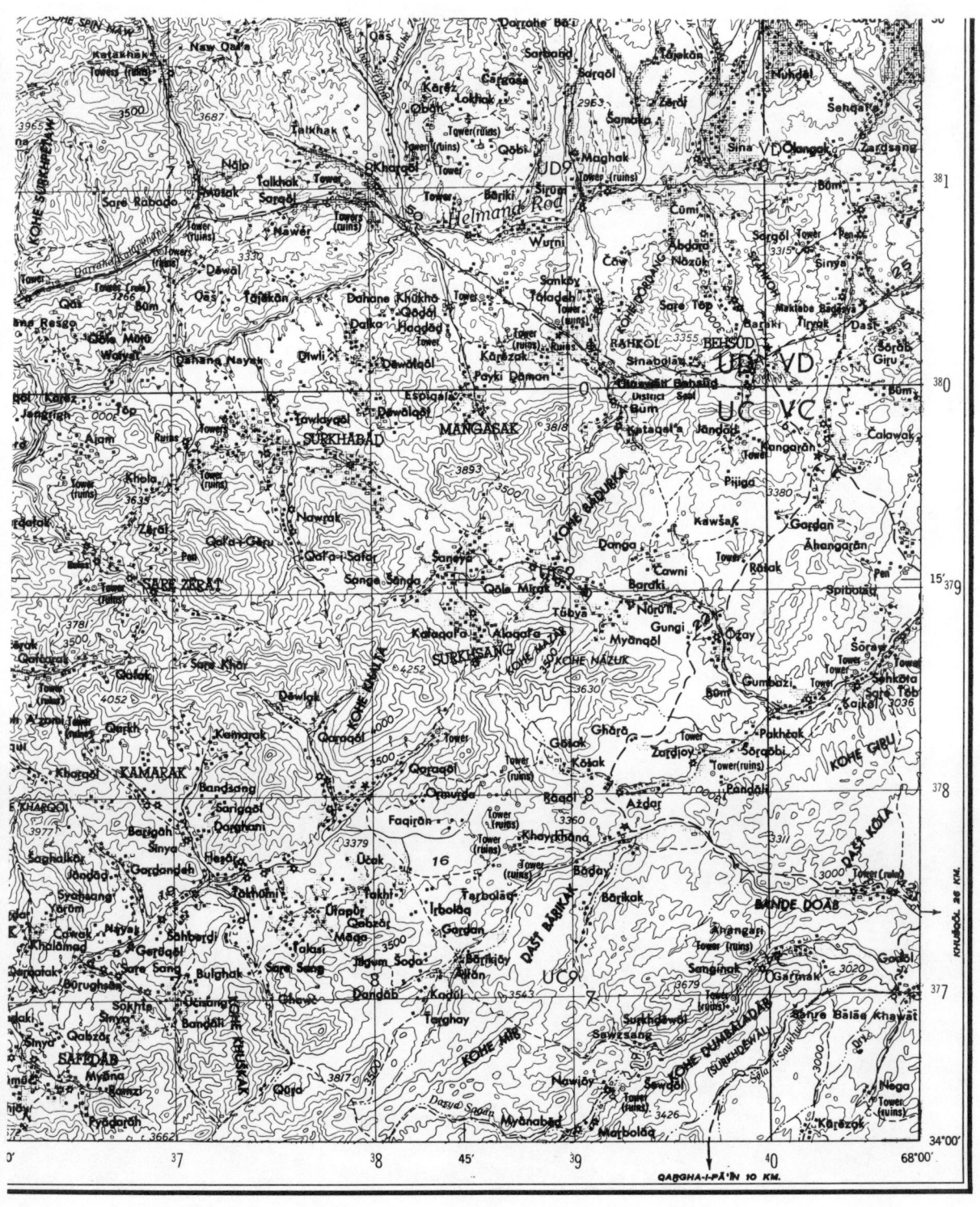

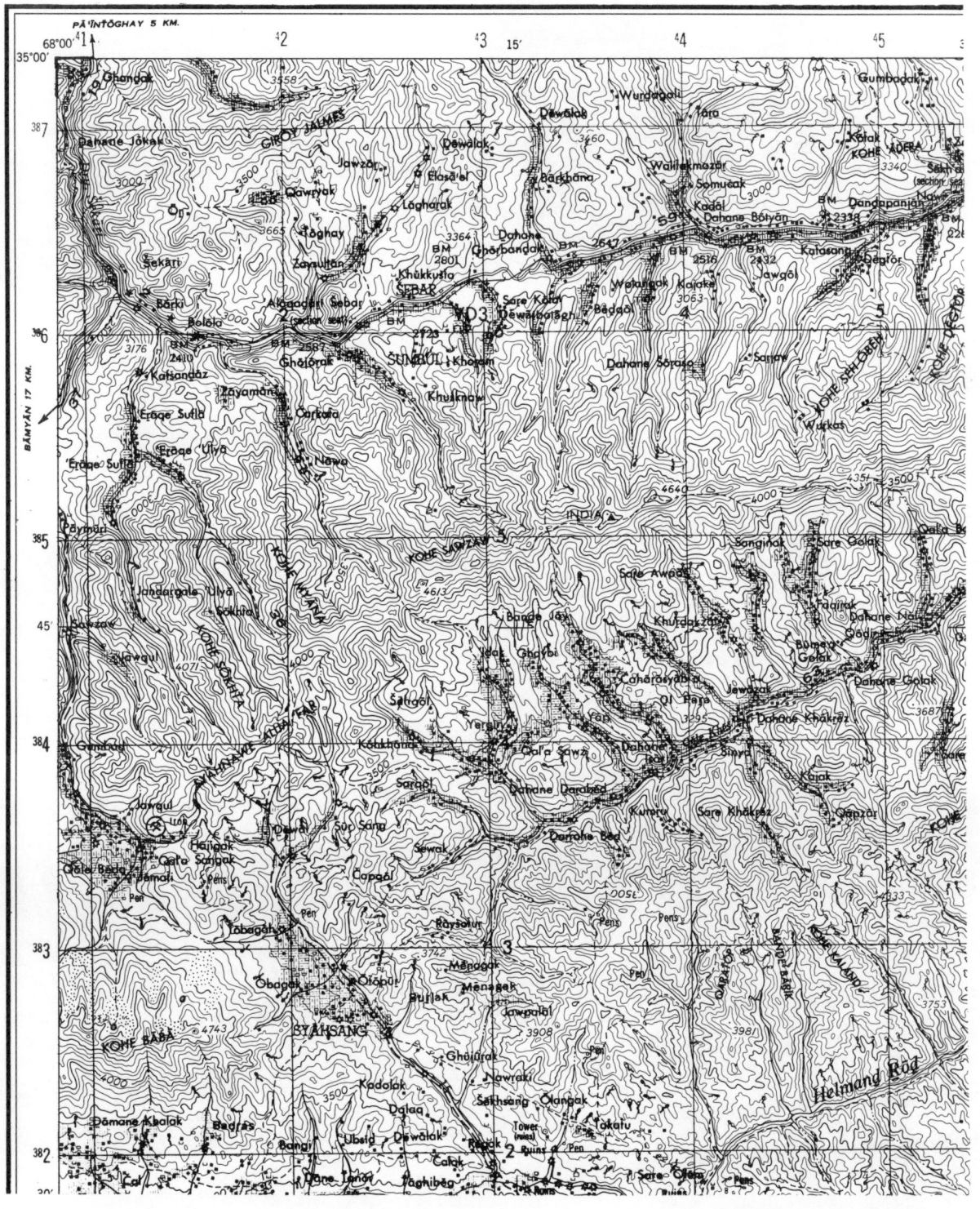

VI-9-B

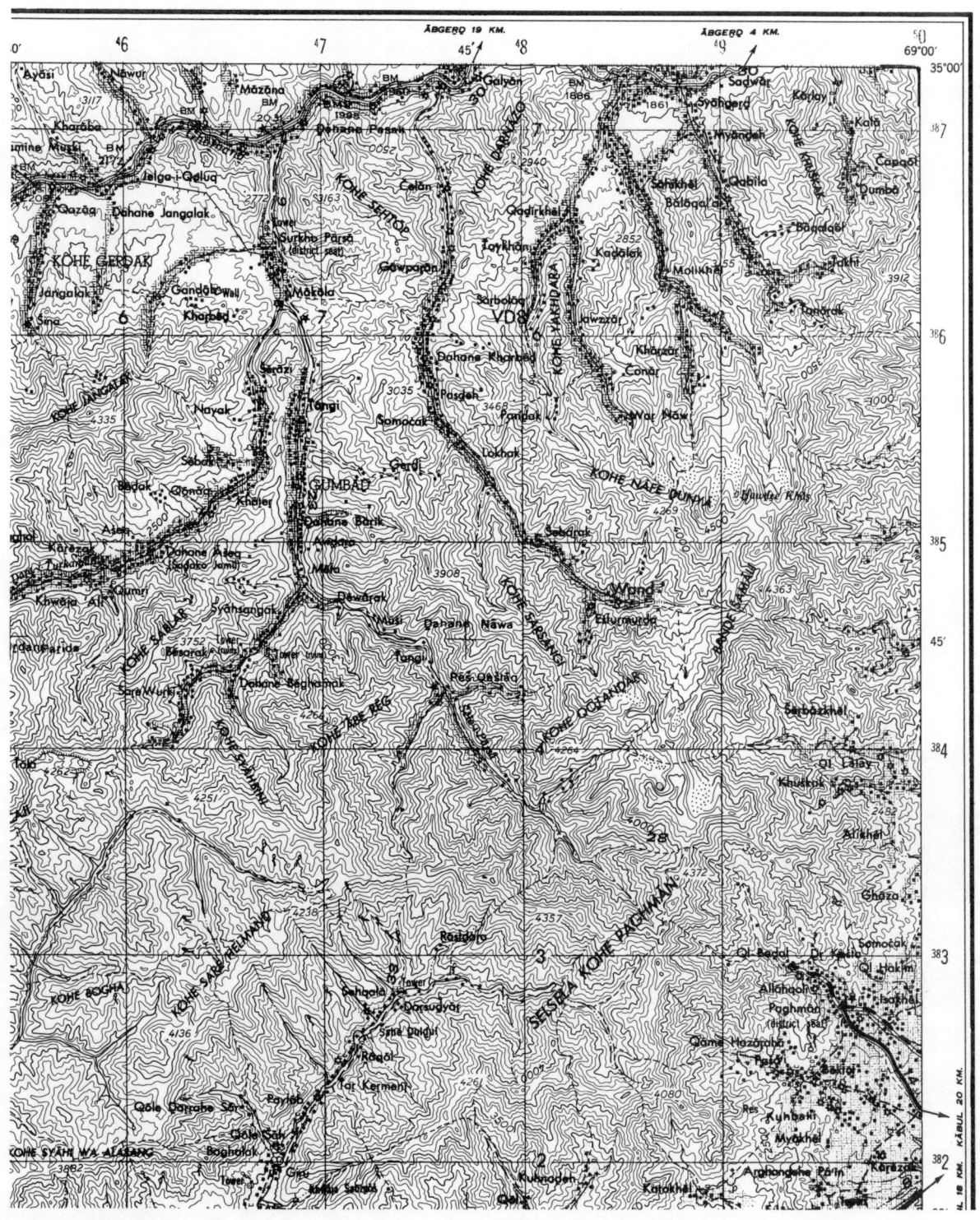

VI-9-C

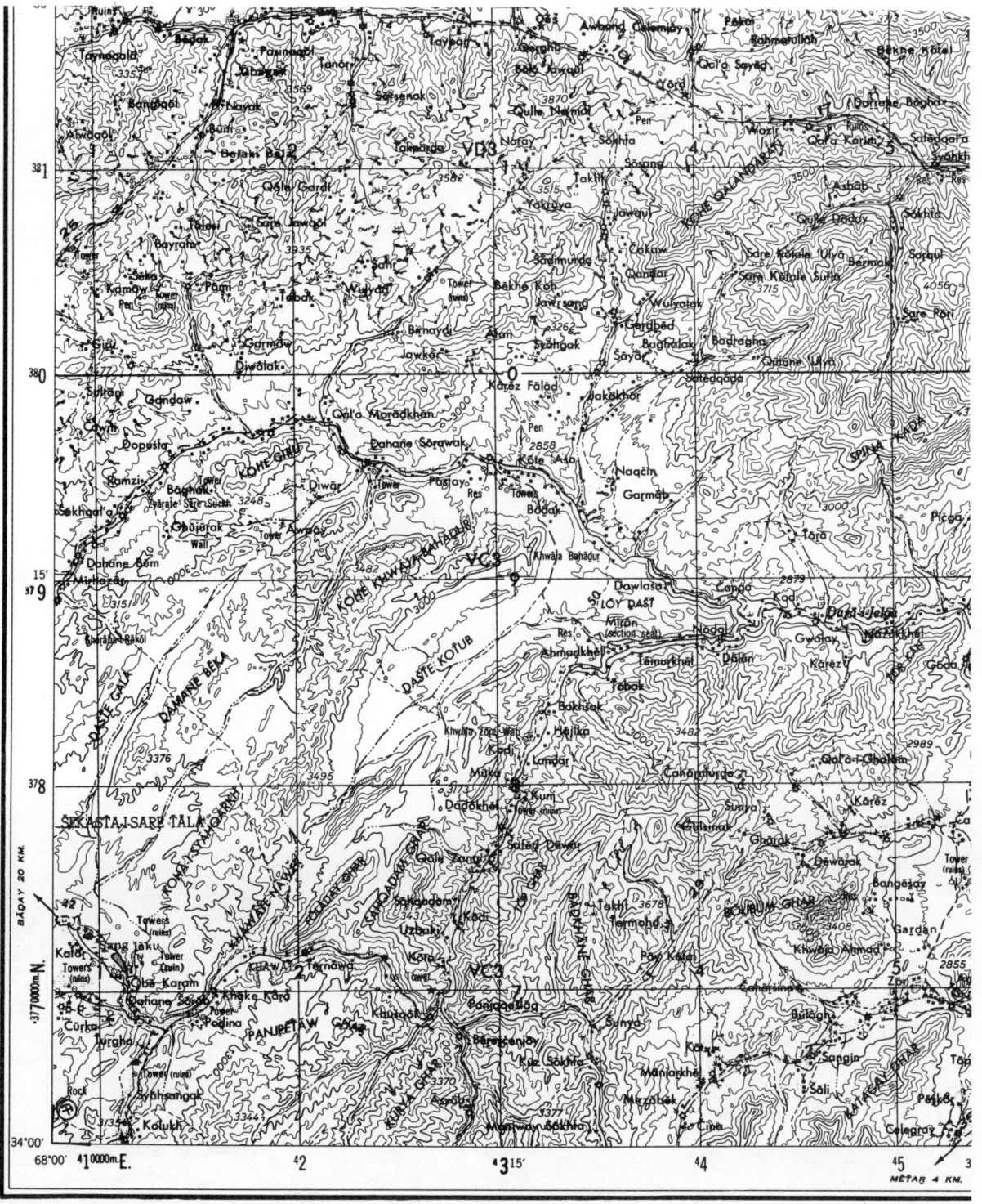

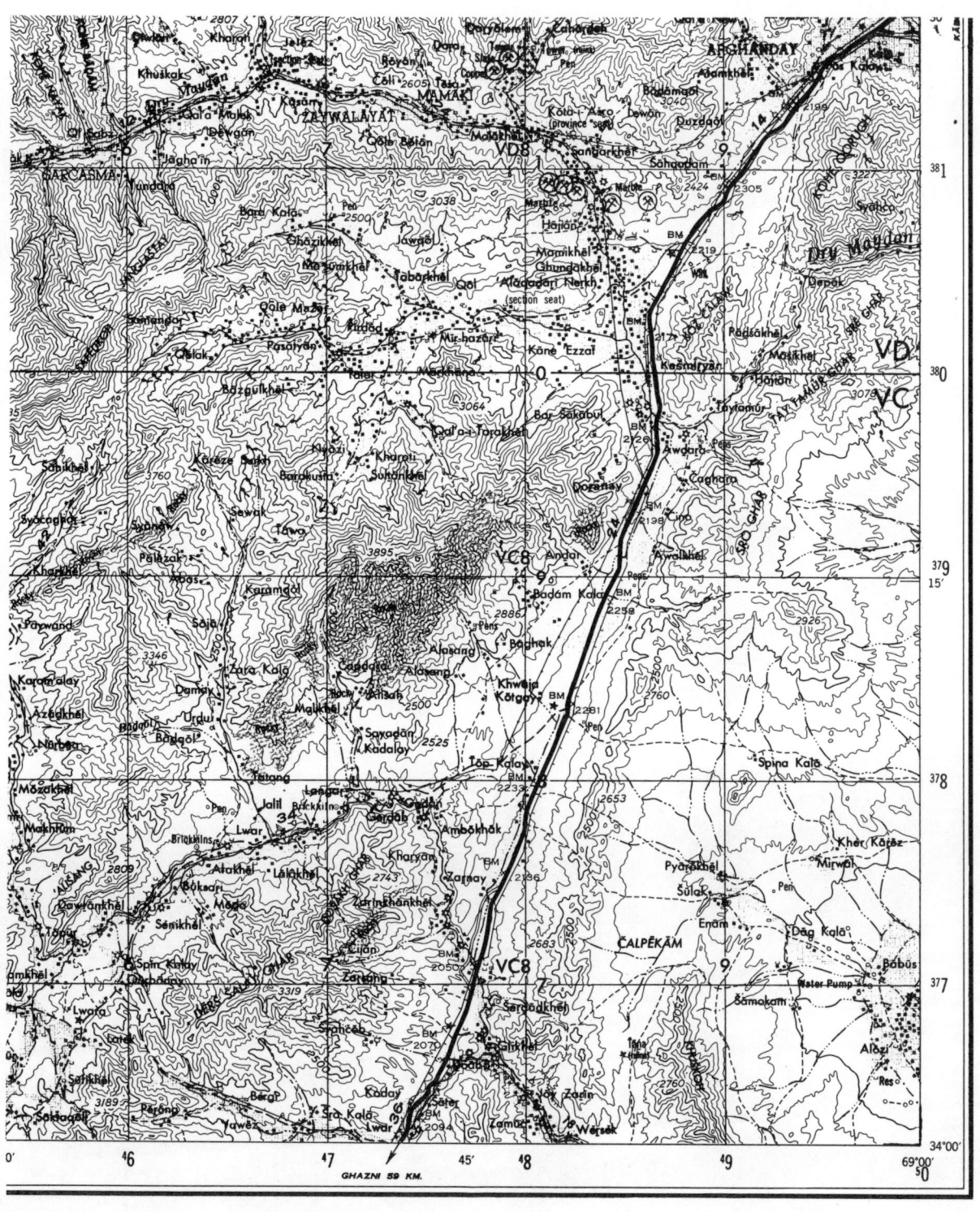

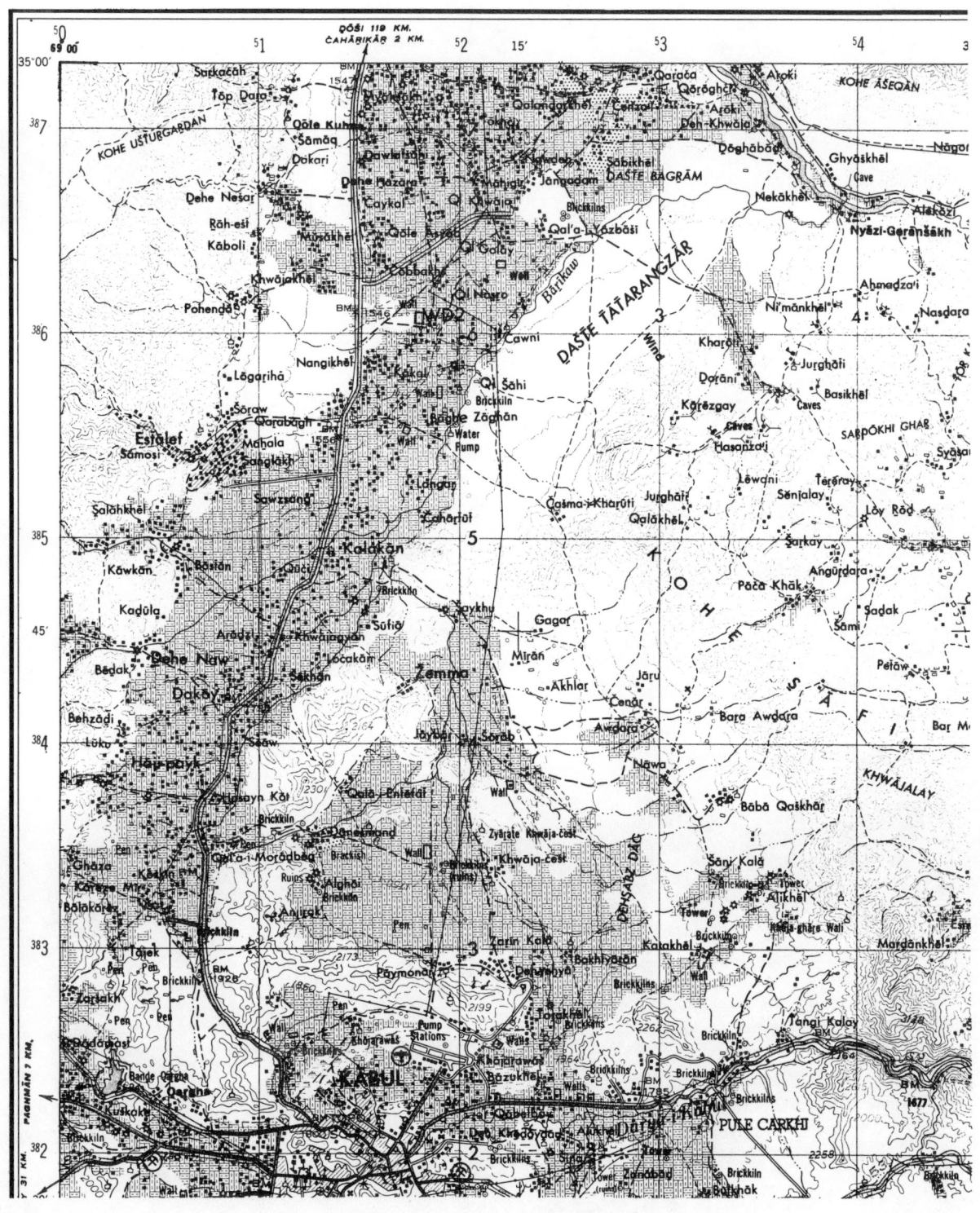

VI–10–A

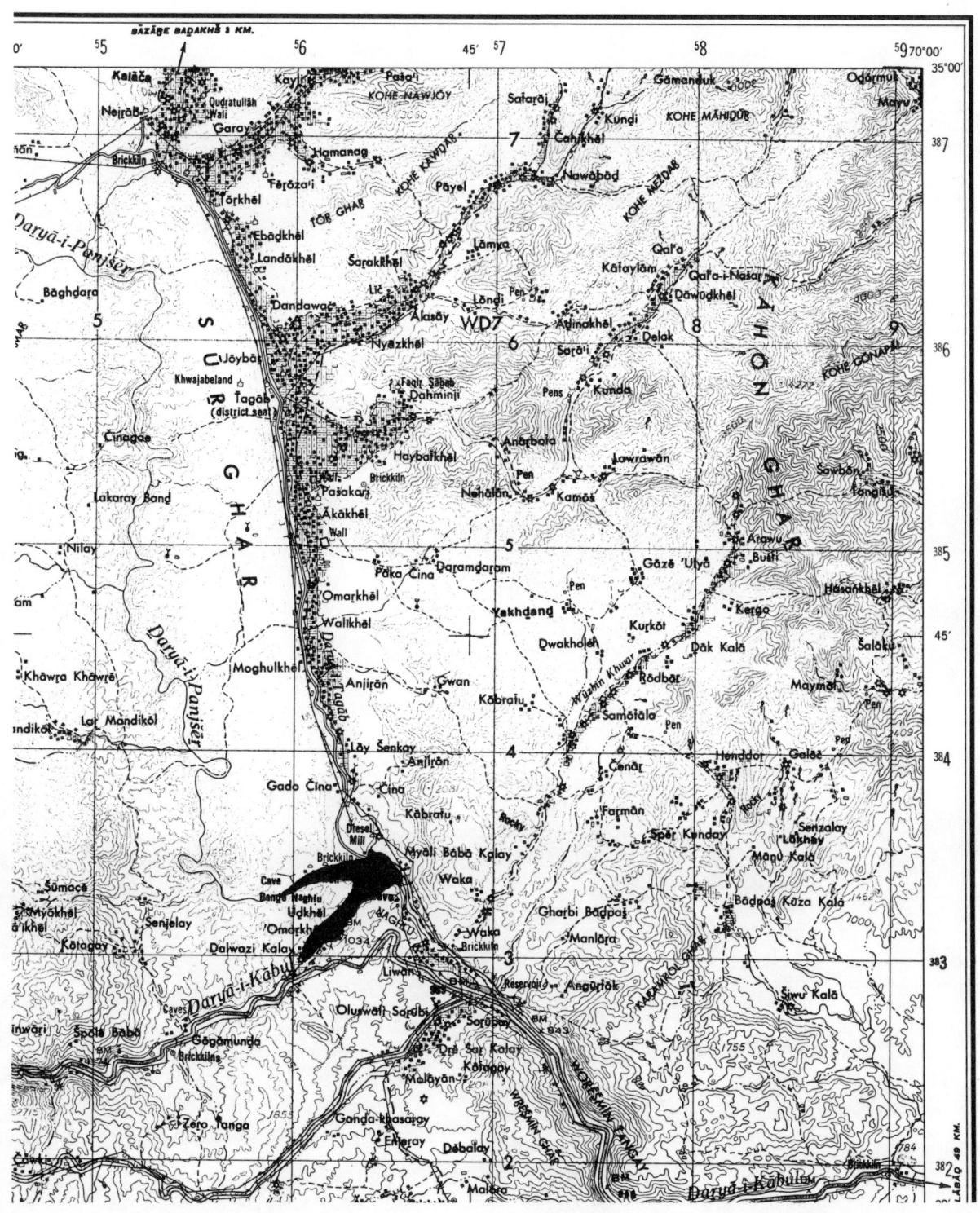

VI-10-B

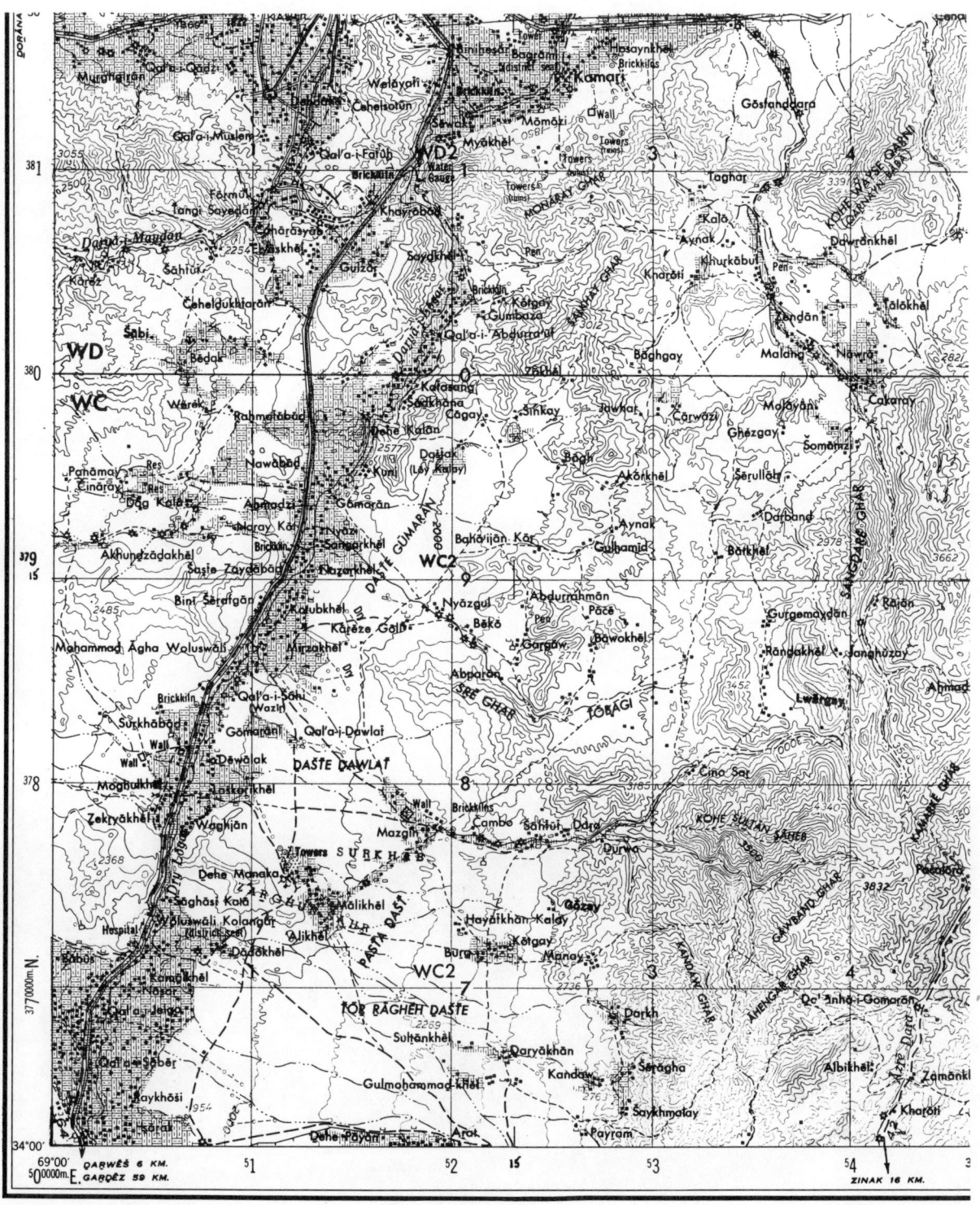

VI-10-D

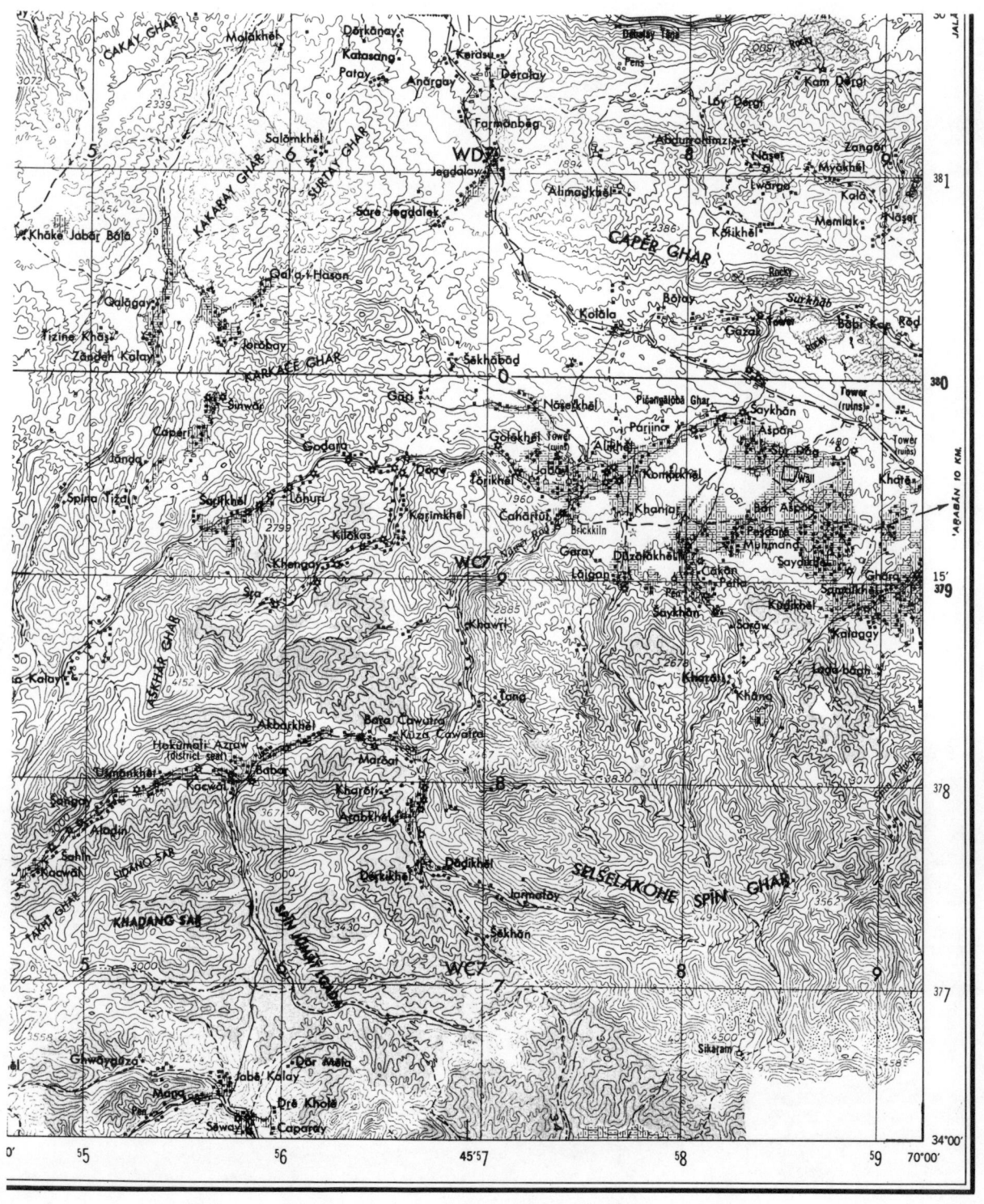

VI–11–A

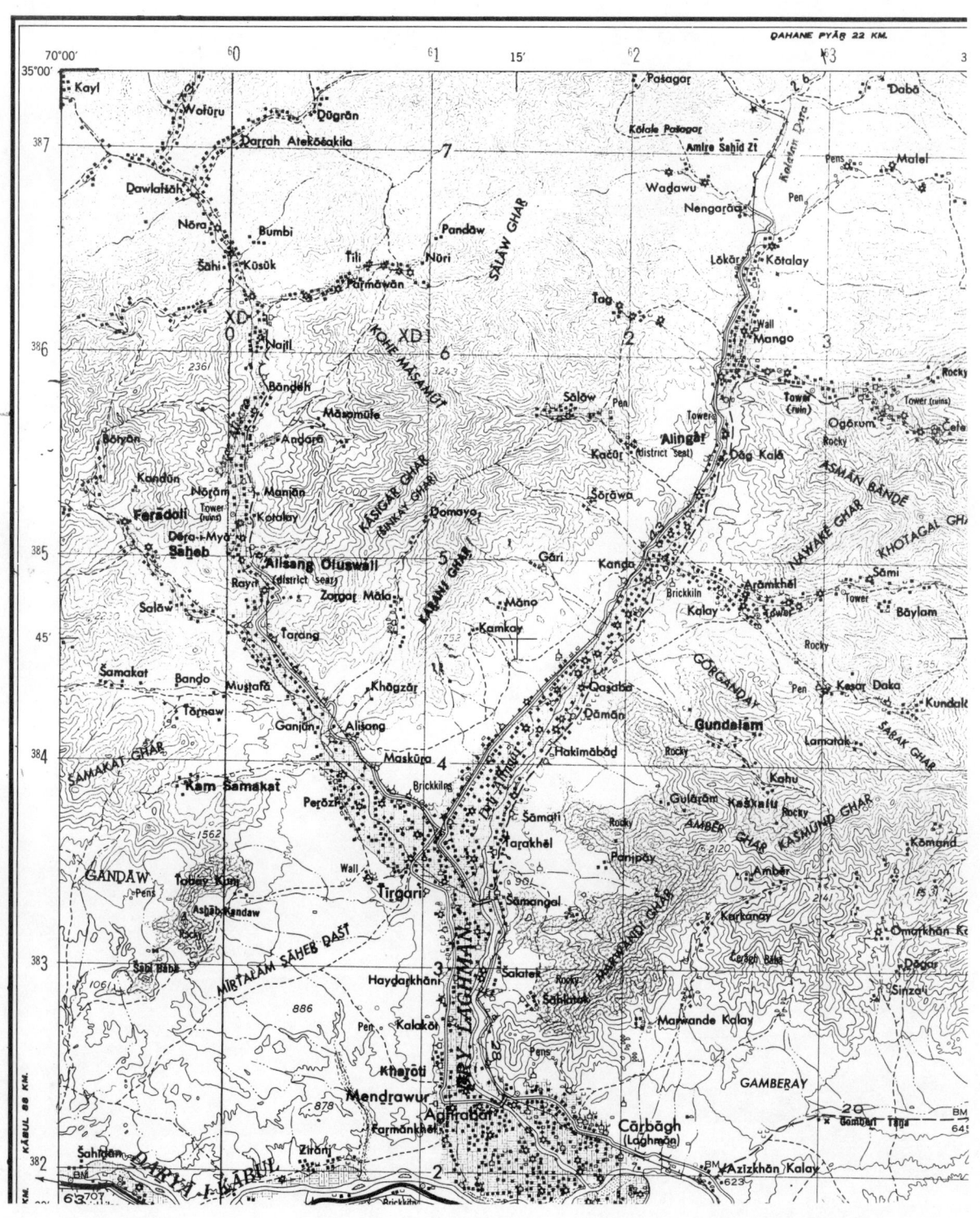

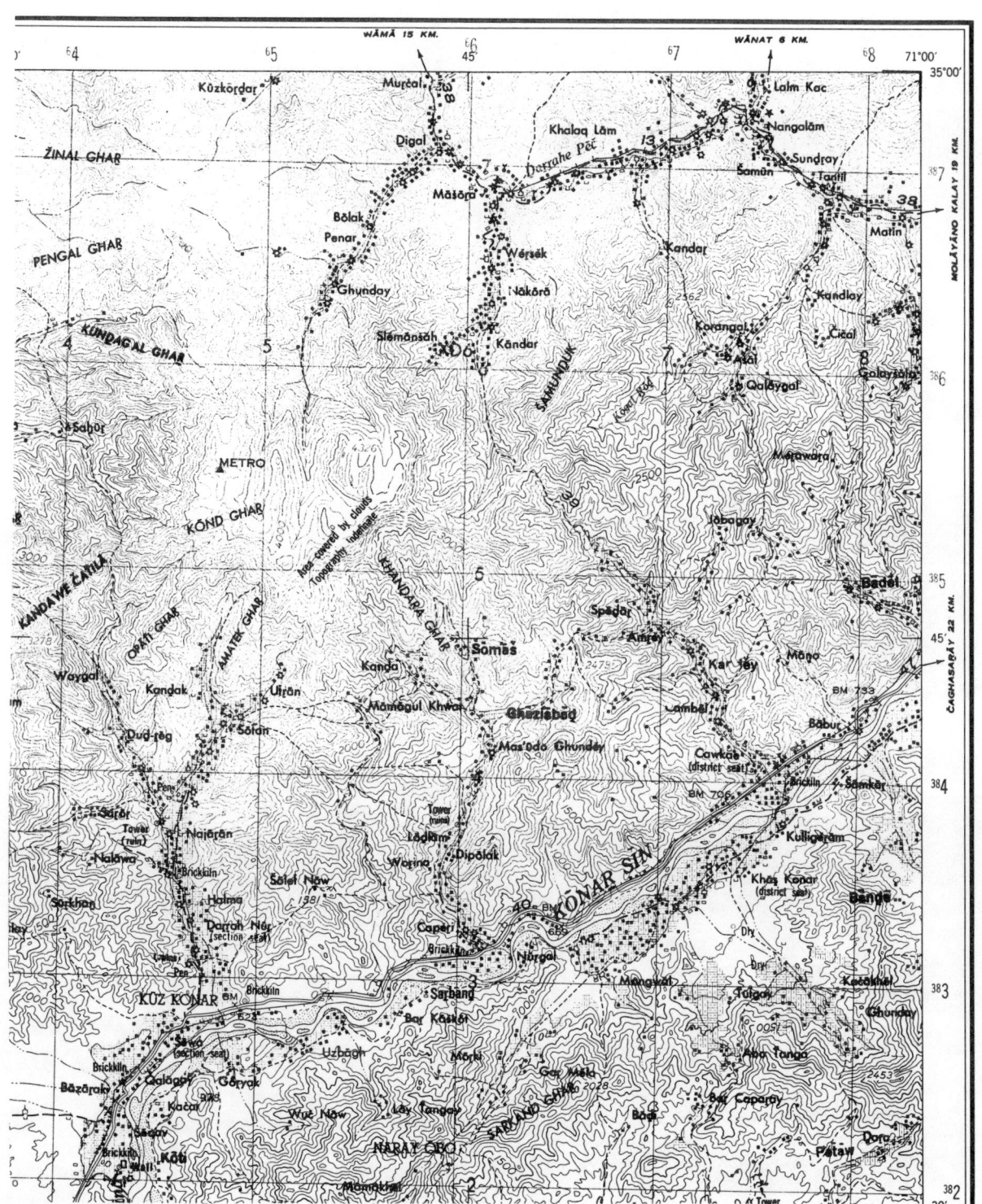

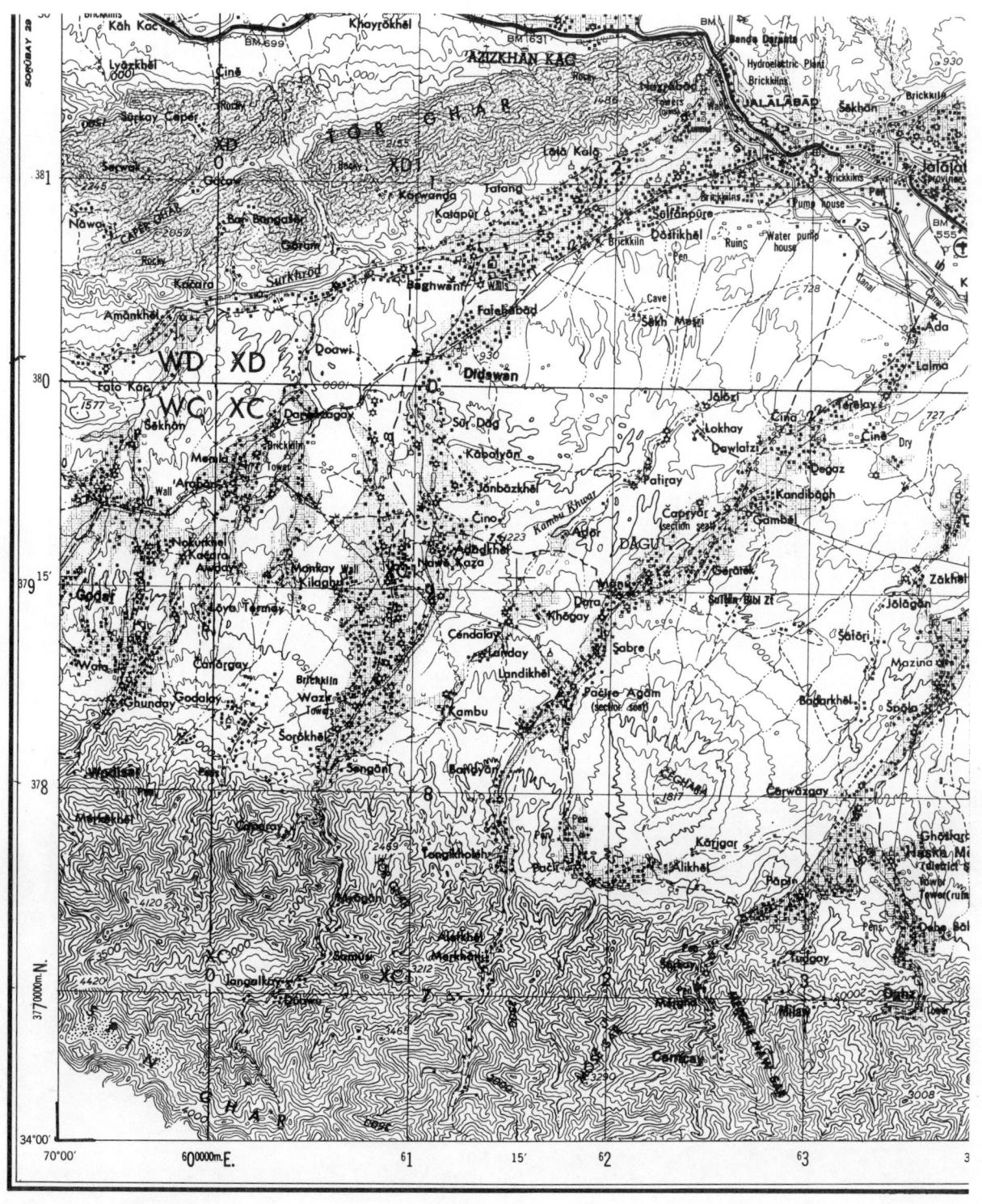

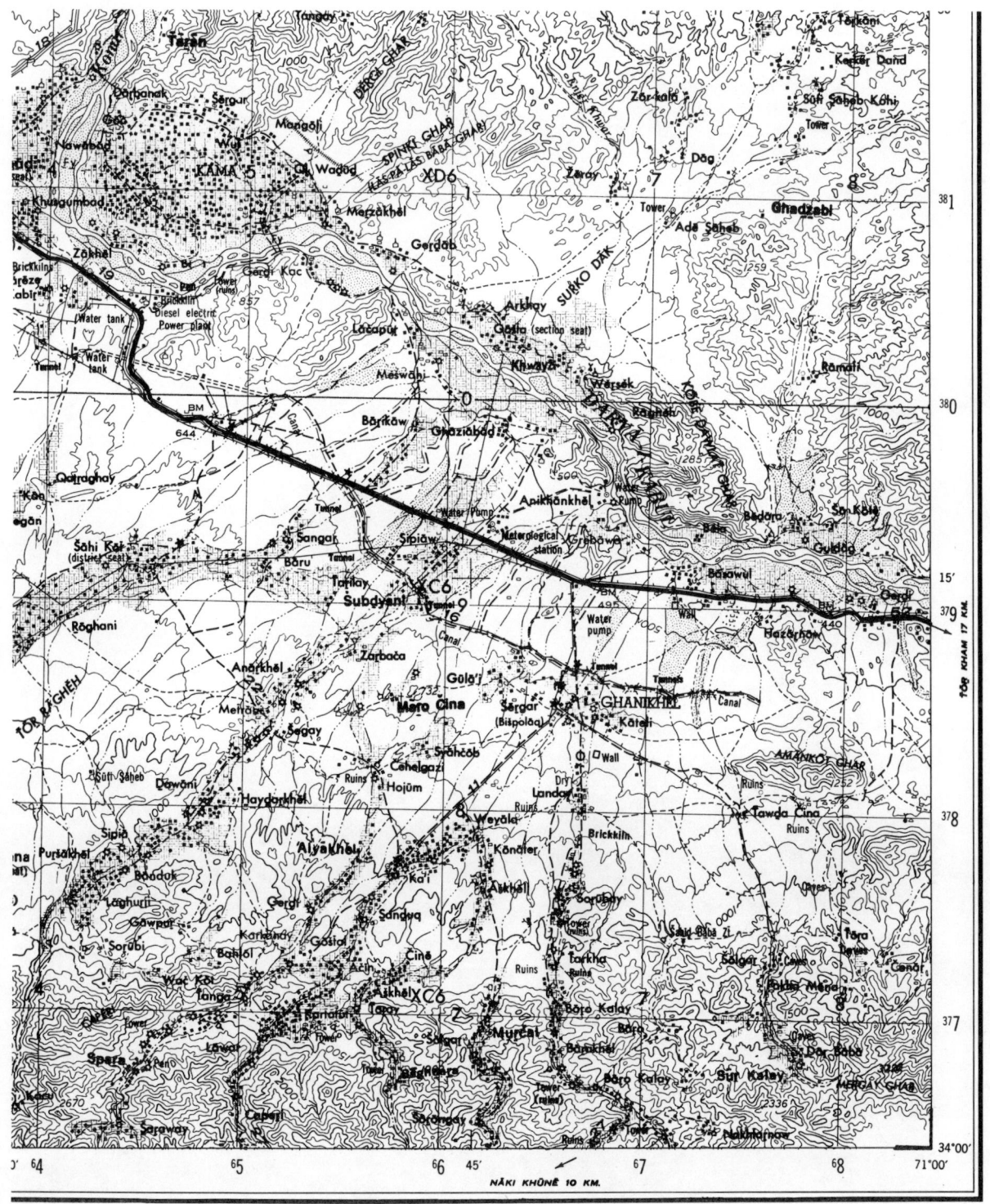

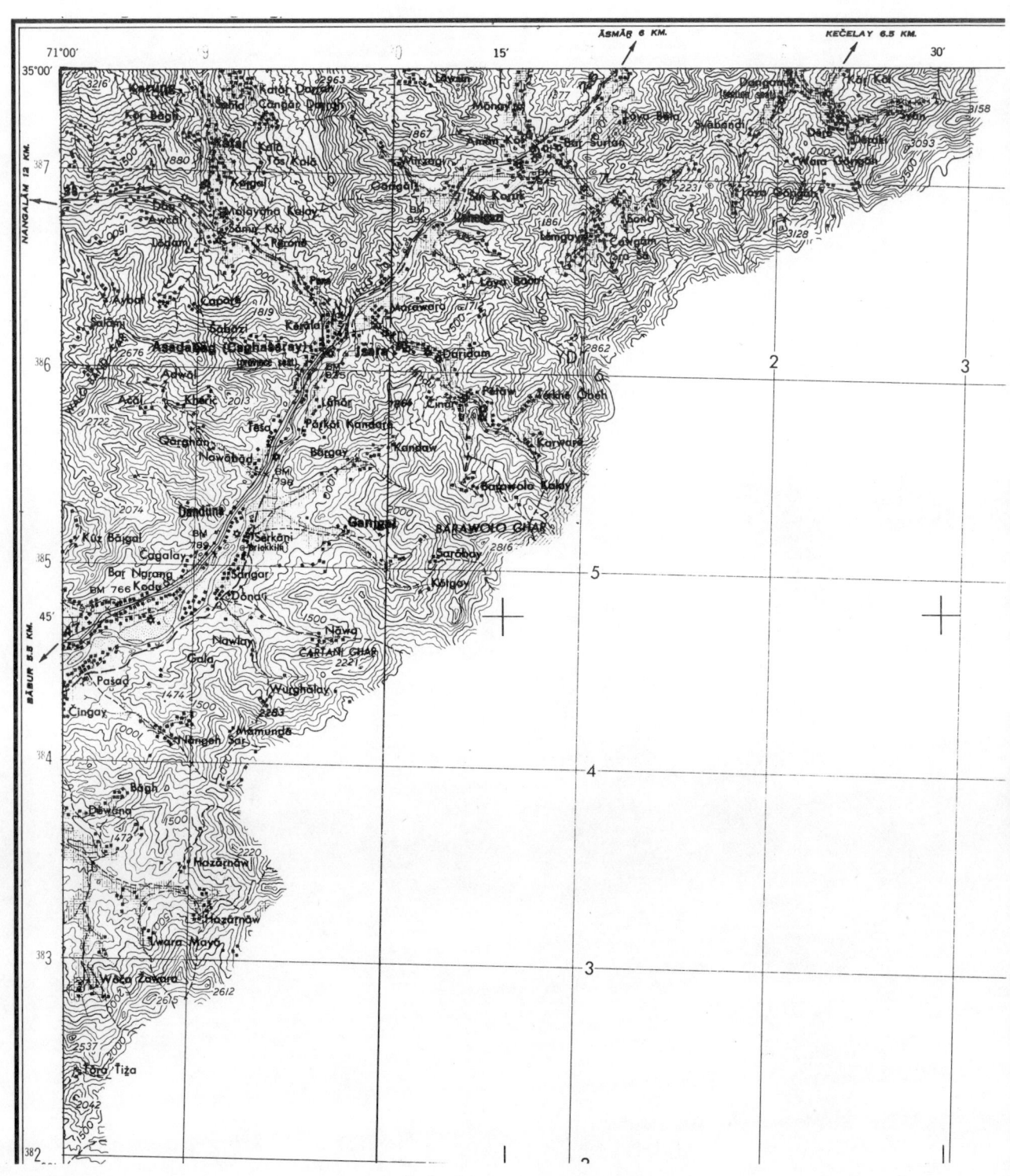

VI–12–C

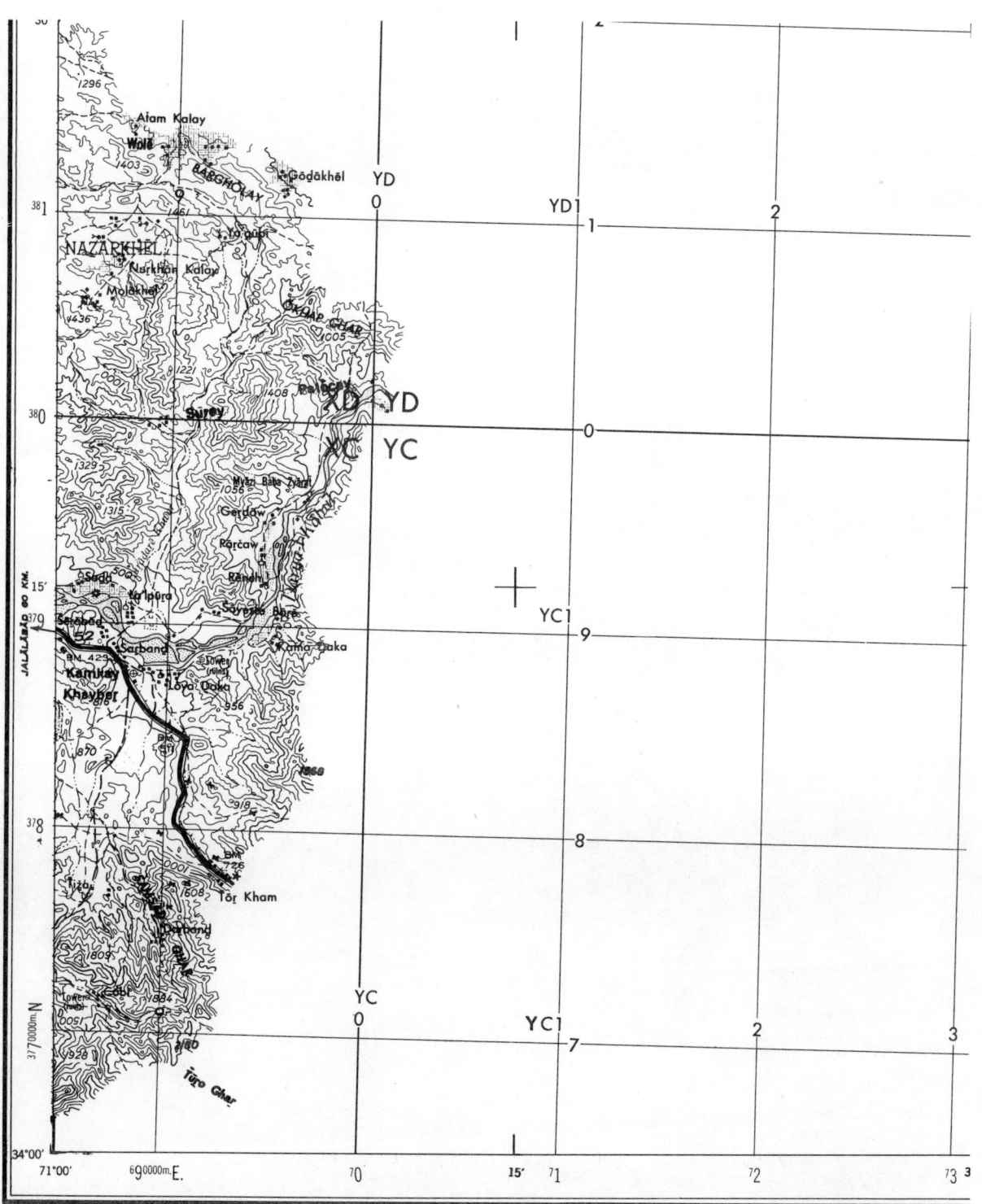

VI-13-D
See V-4-D

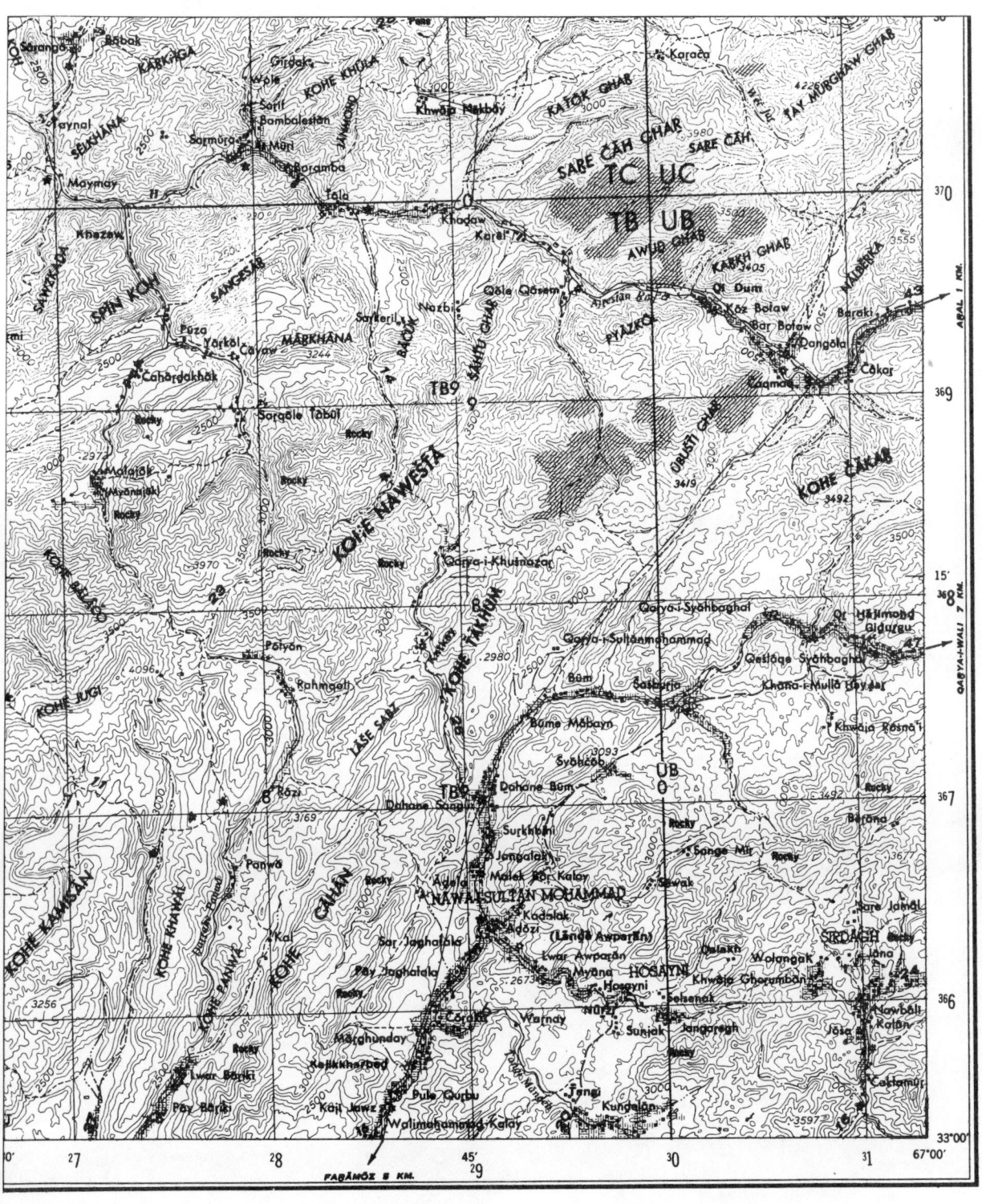

VI–14–A
See V–5–A

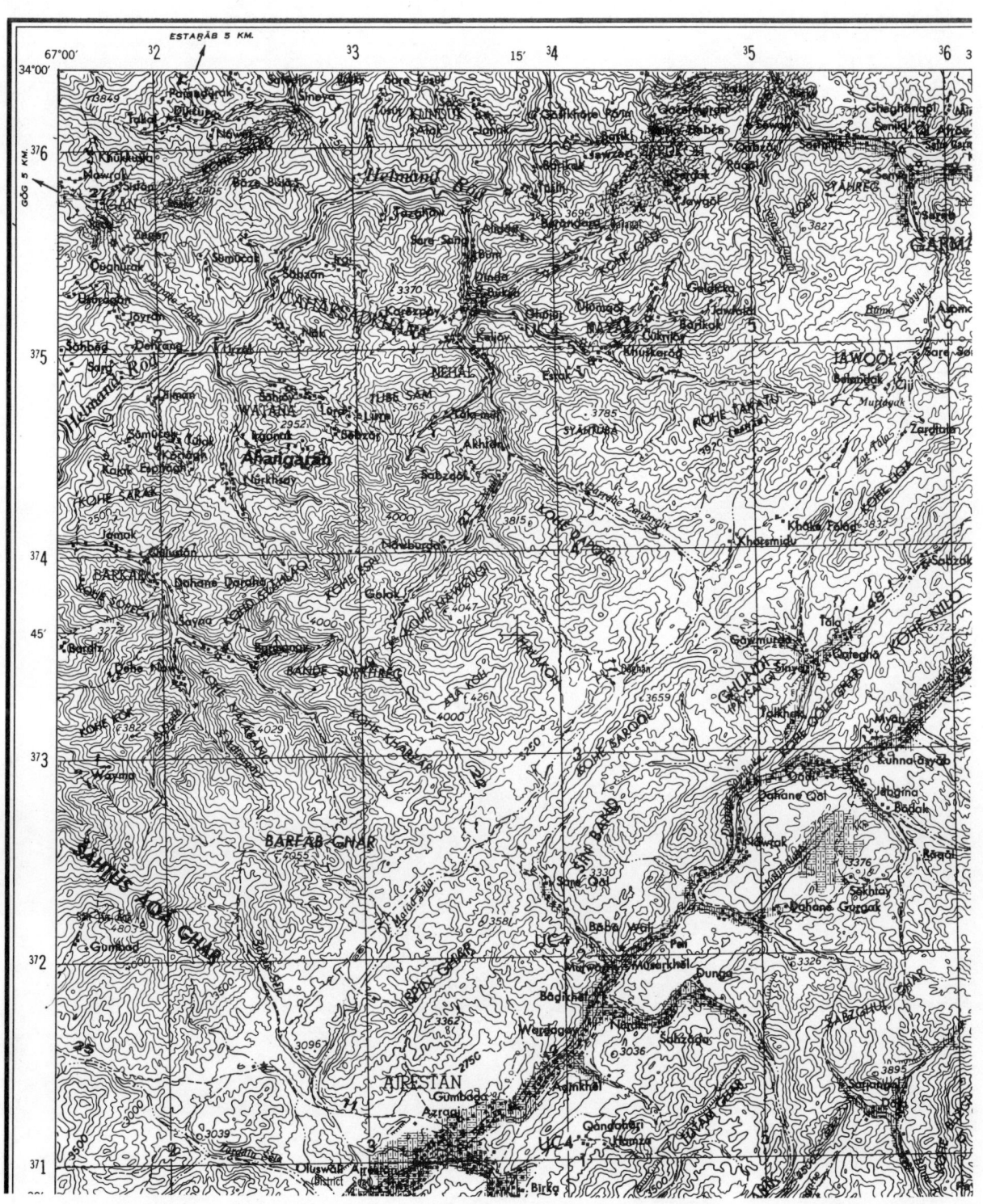

VI–14–B
See V–5–B

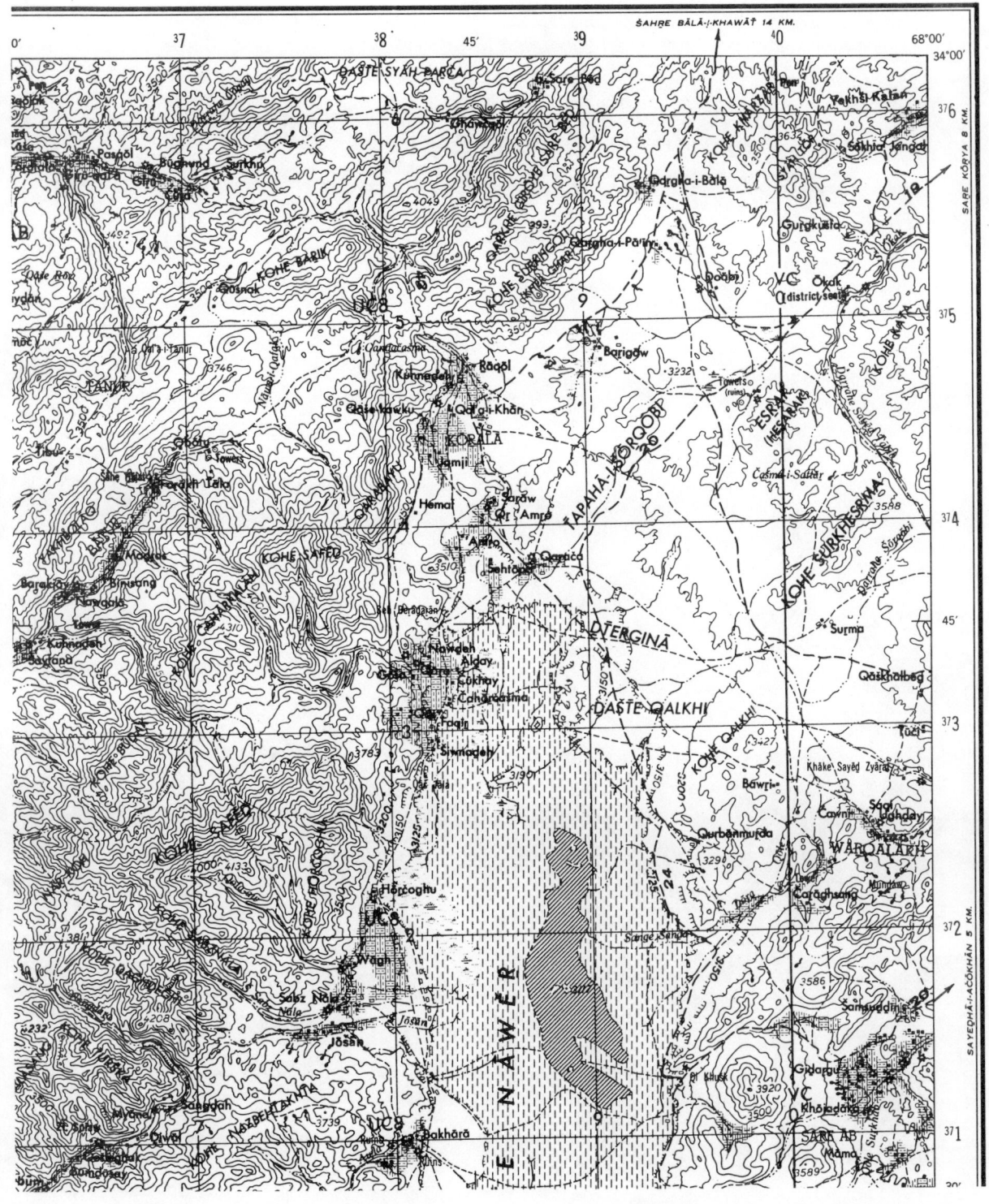

VI–14–C
See V–5–C

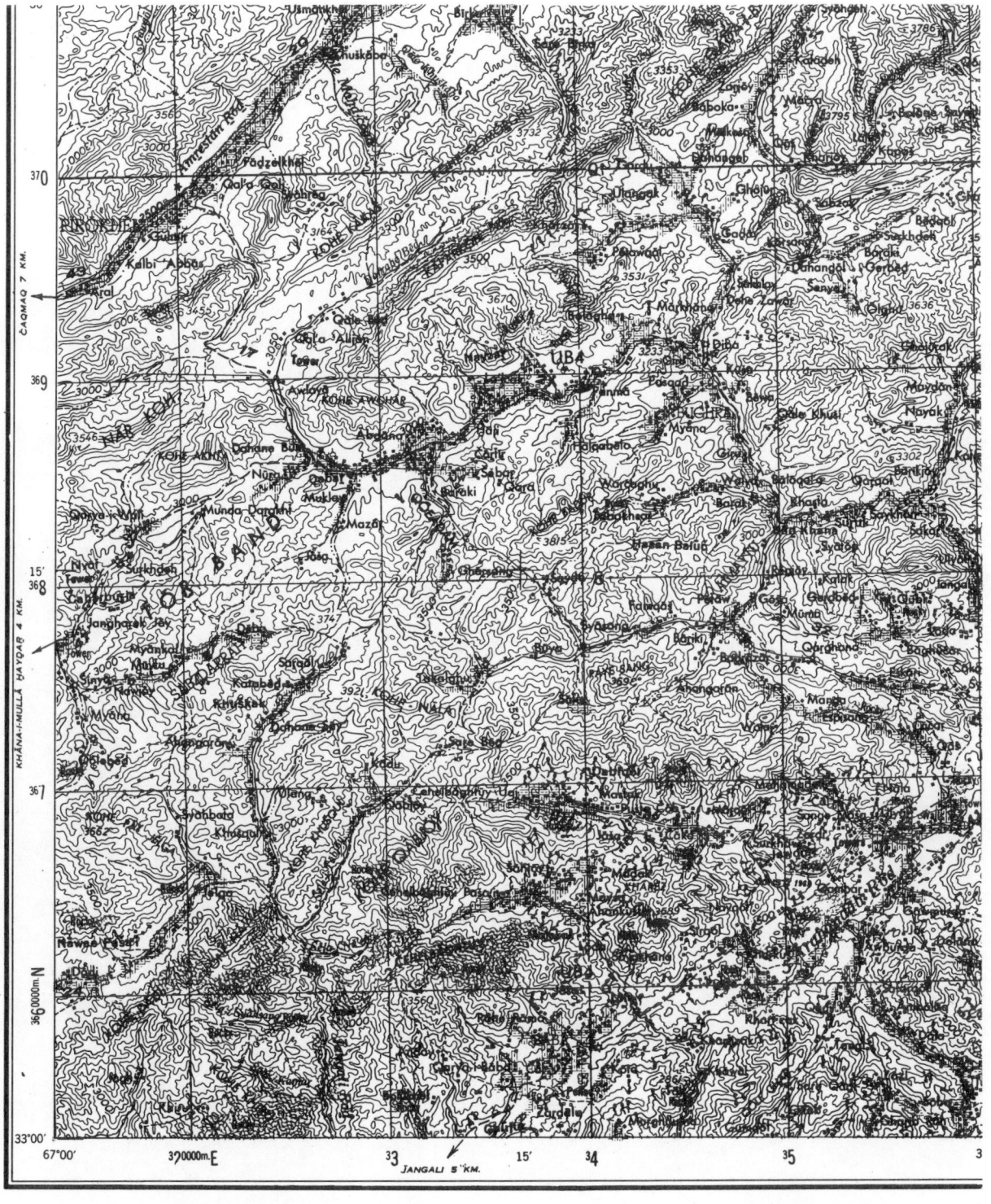

VI–14–D

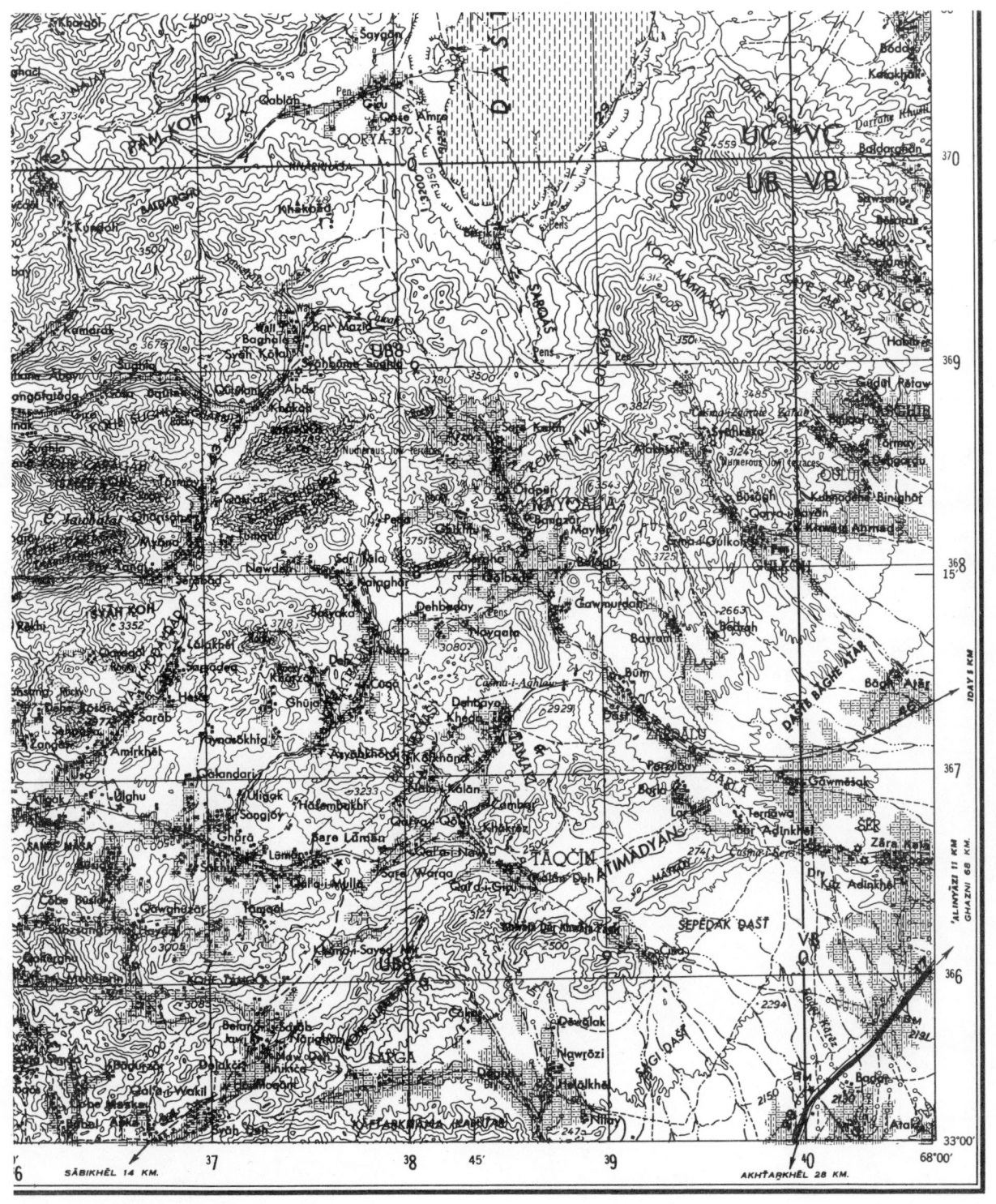

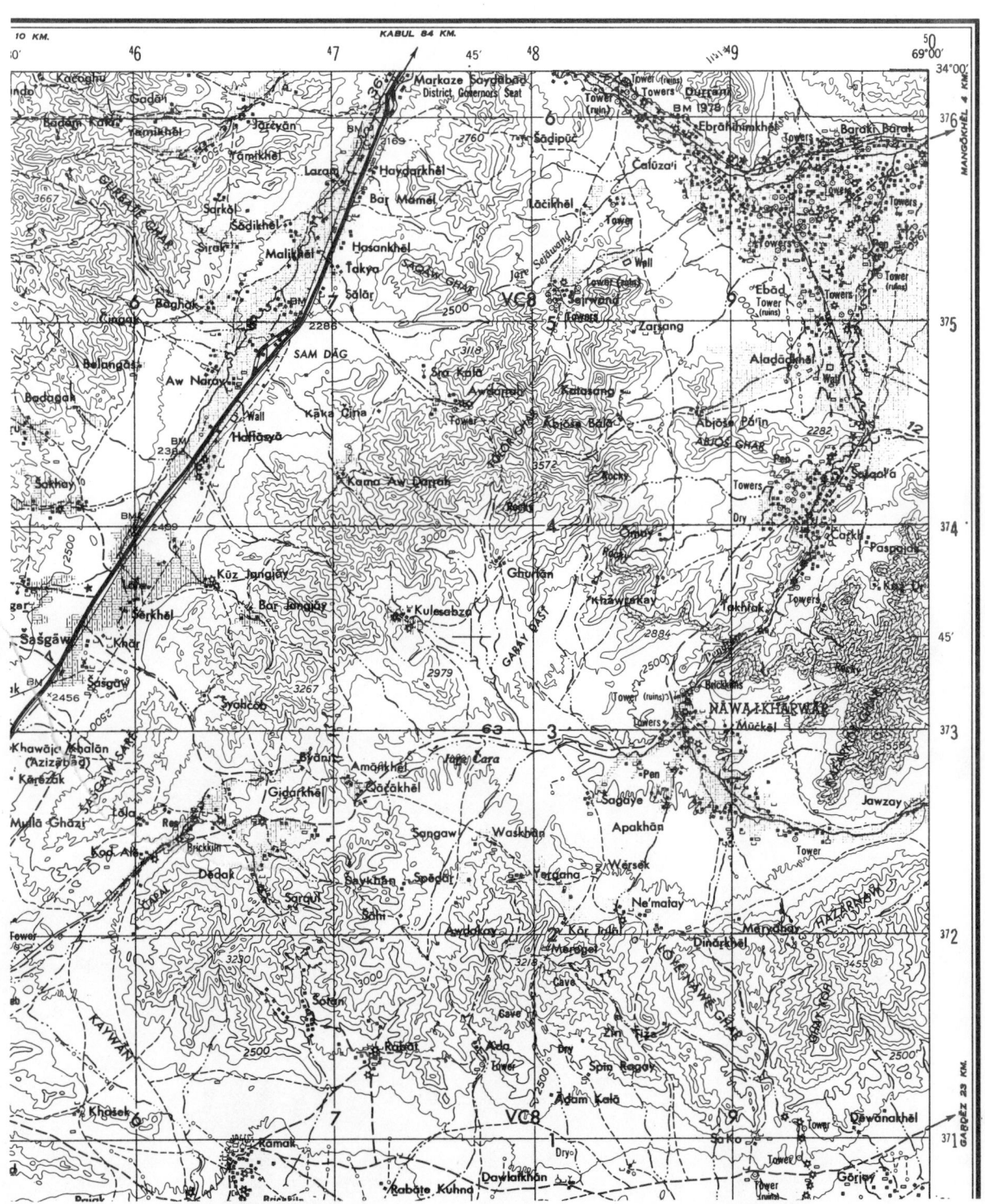

VI–15–A

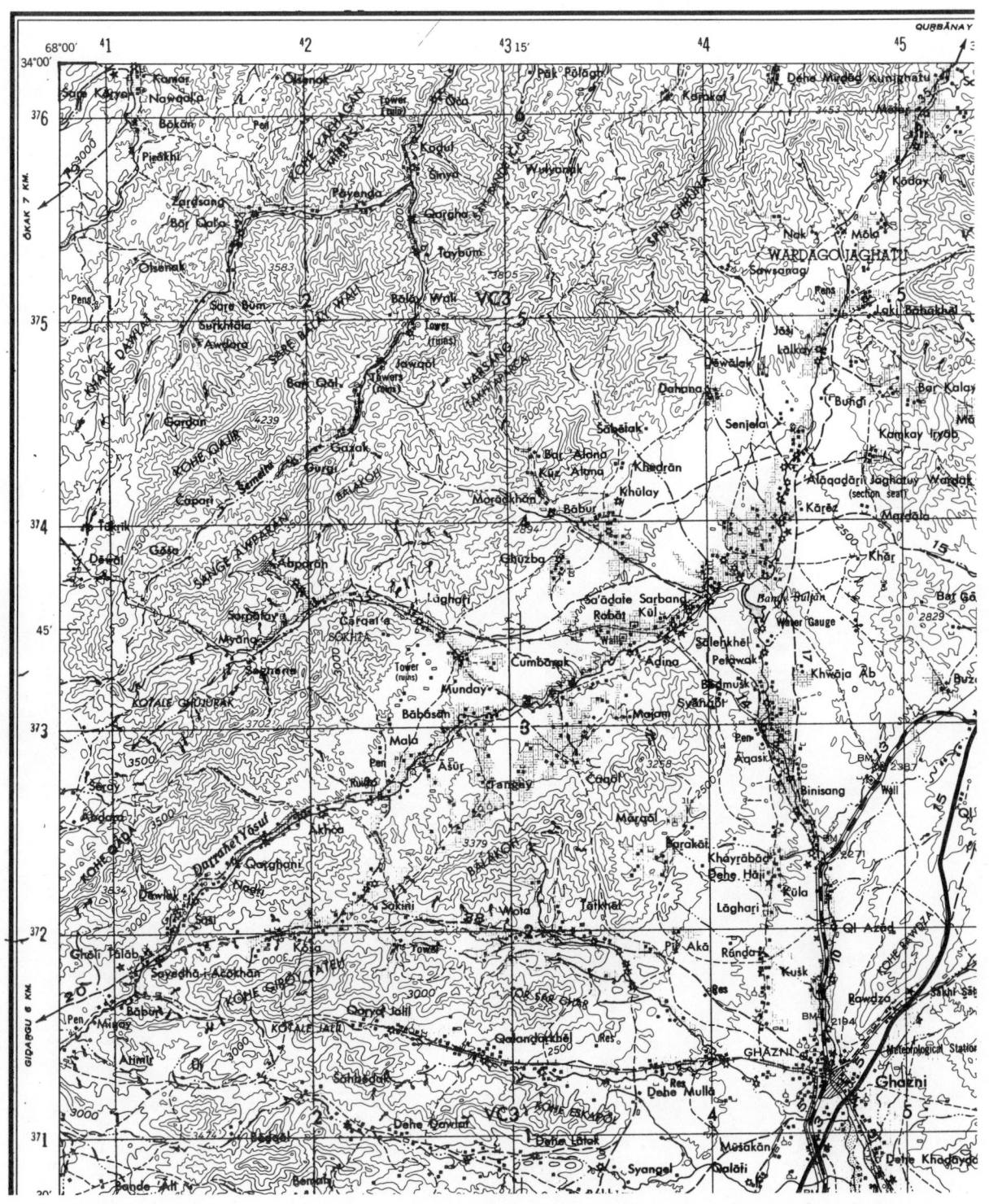

VI–15–C

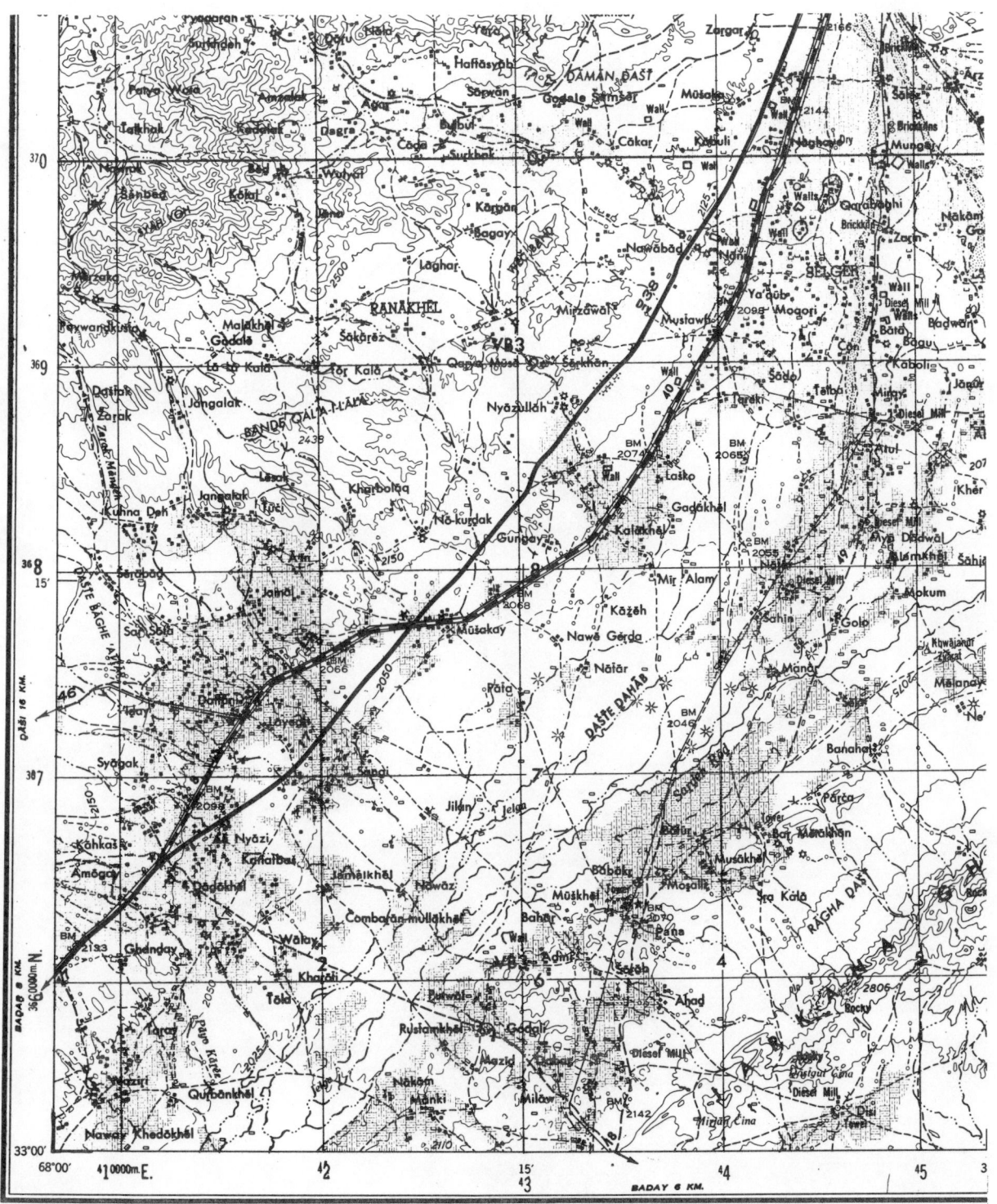

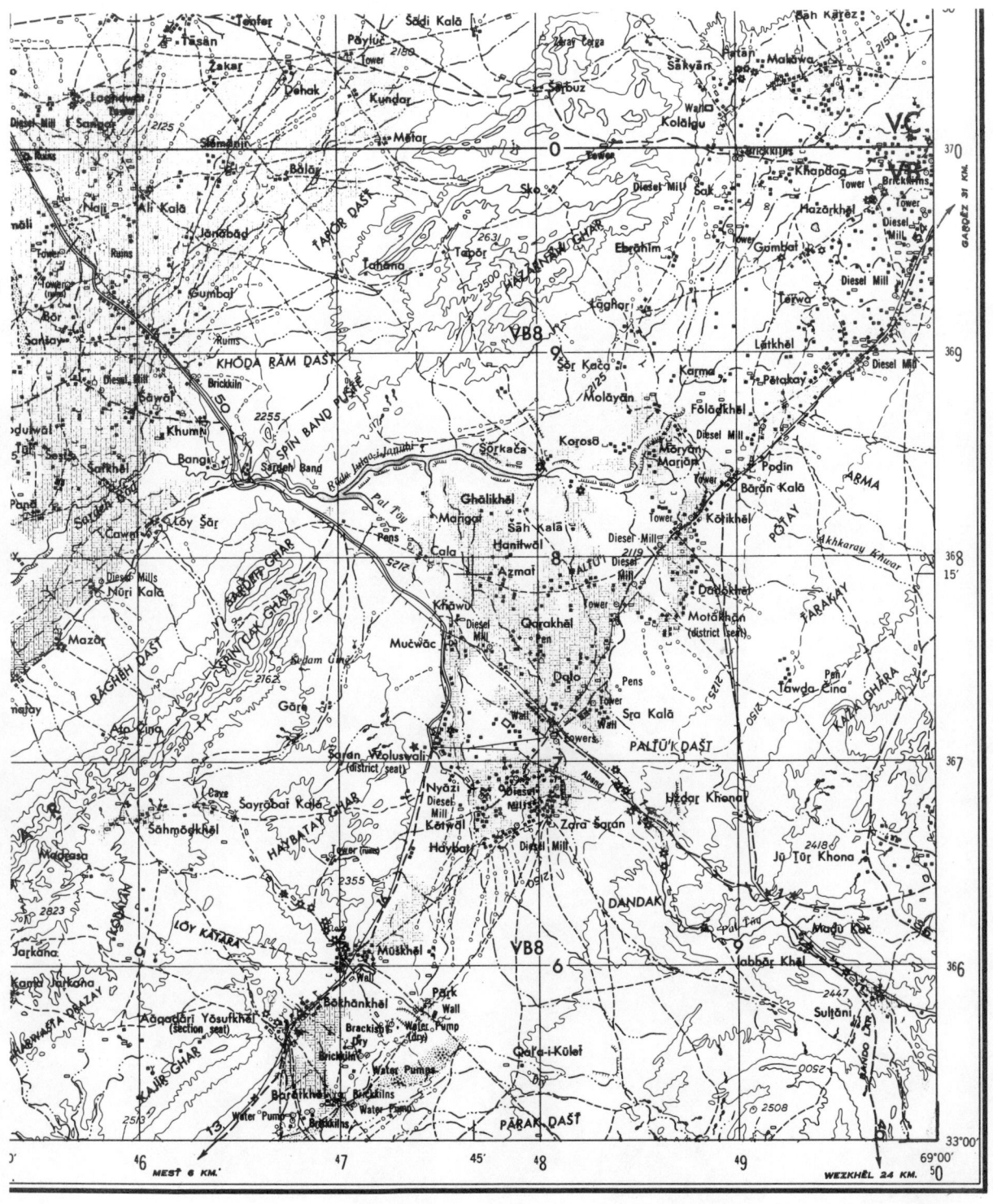

VI–16–A

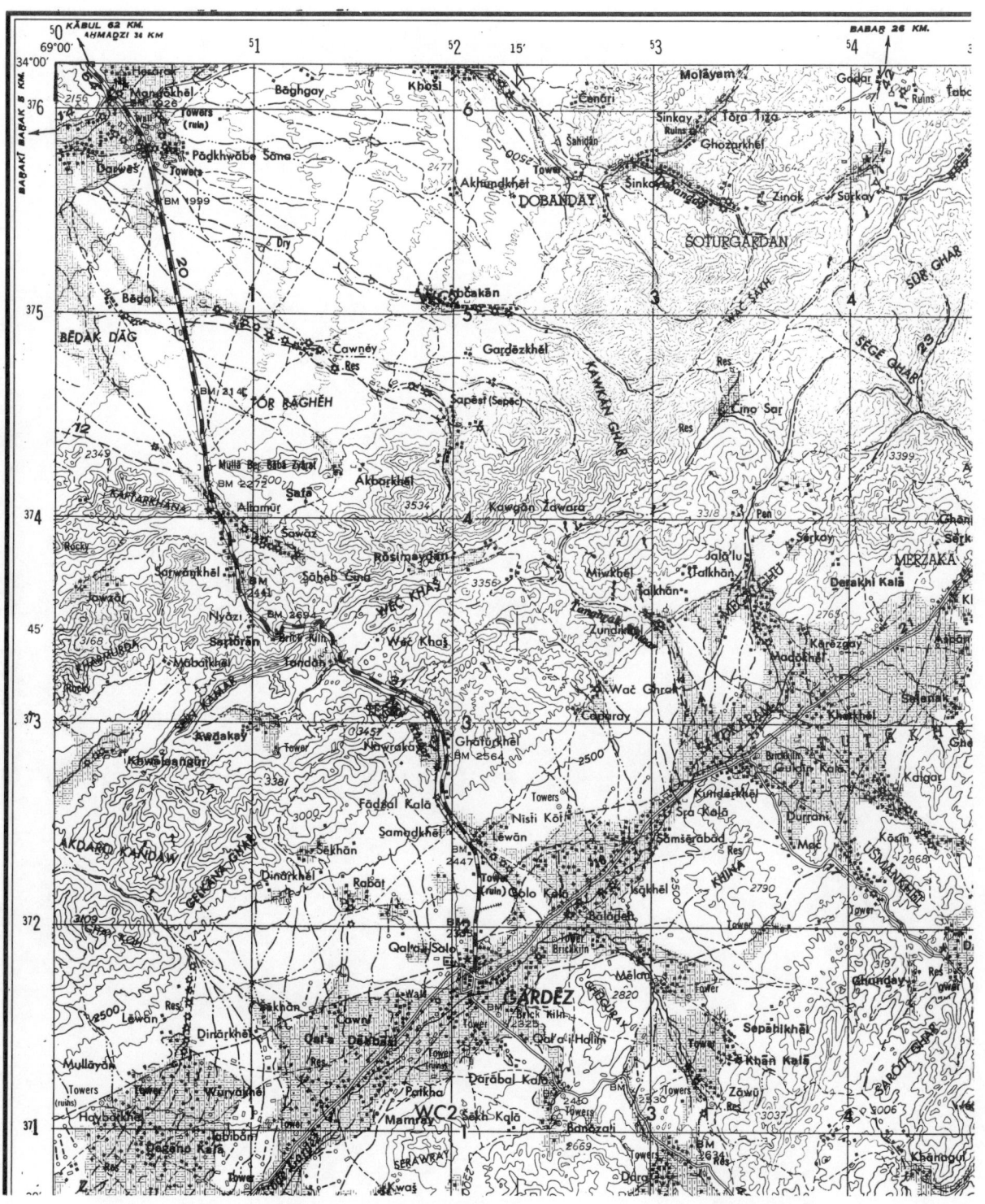

VI–16–B

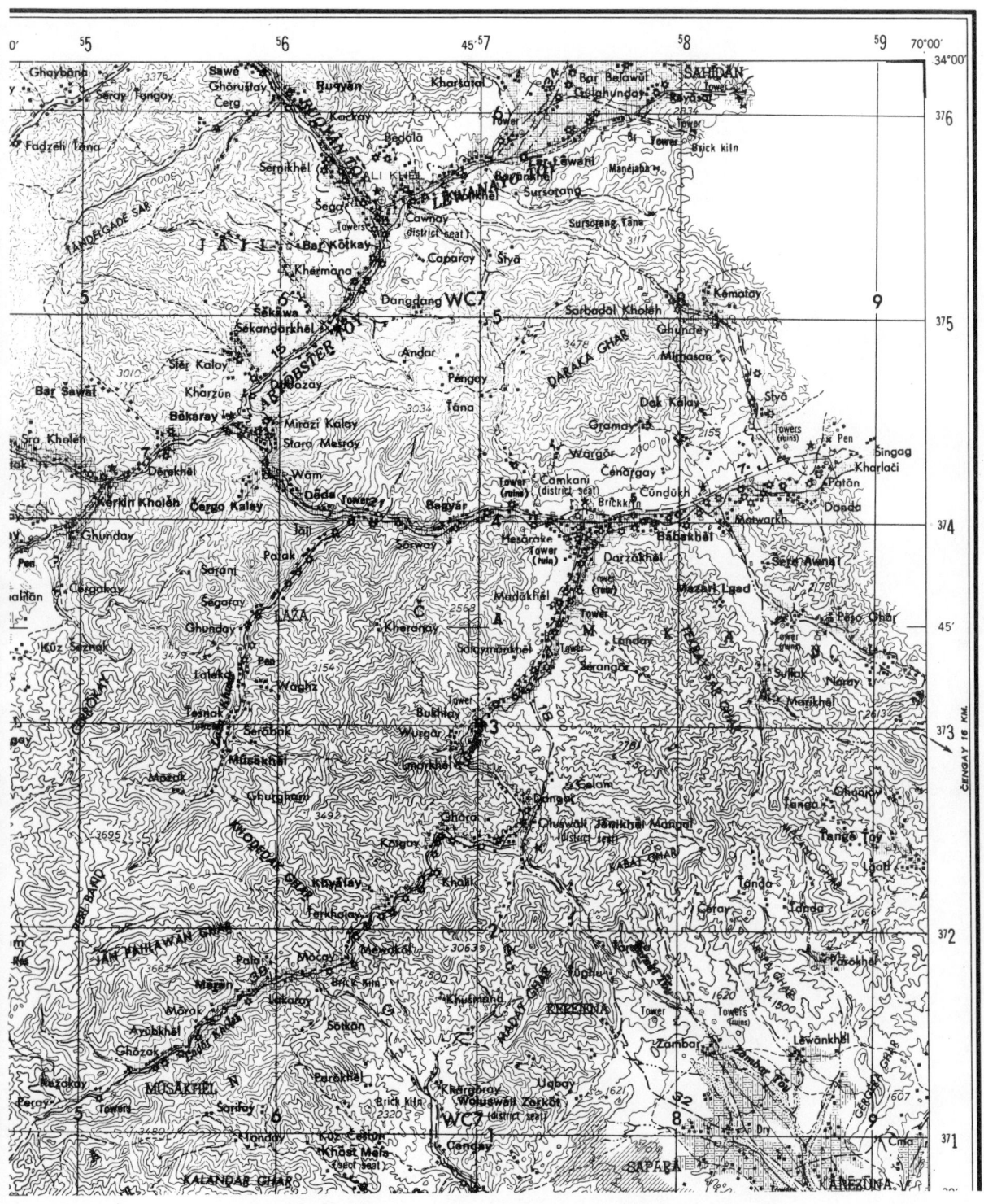

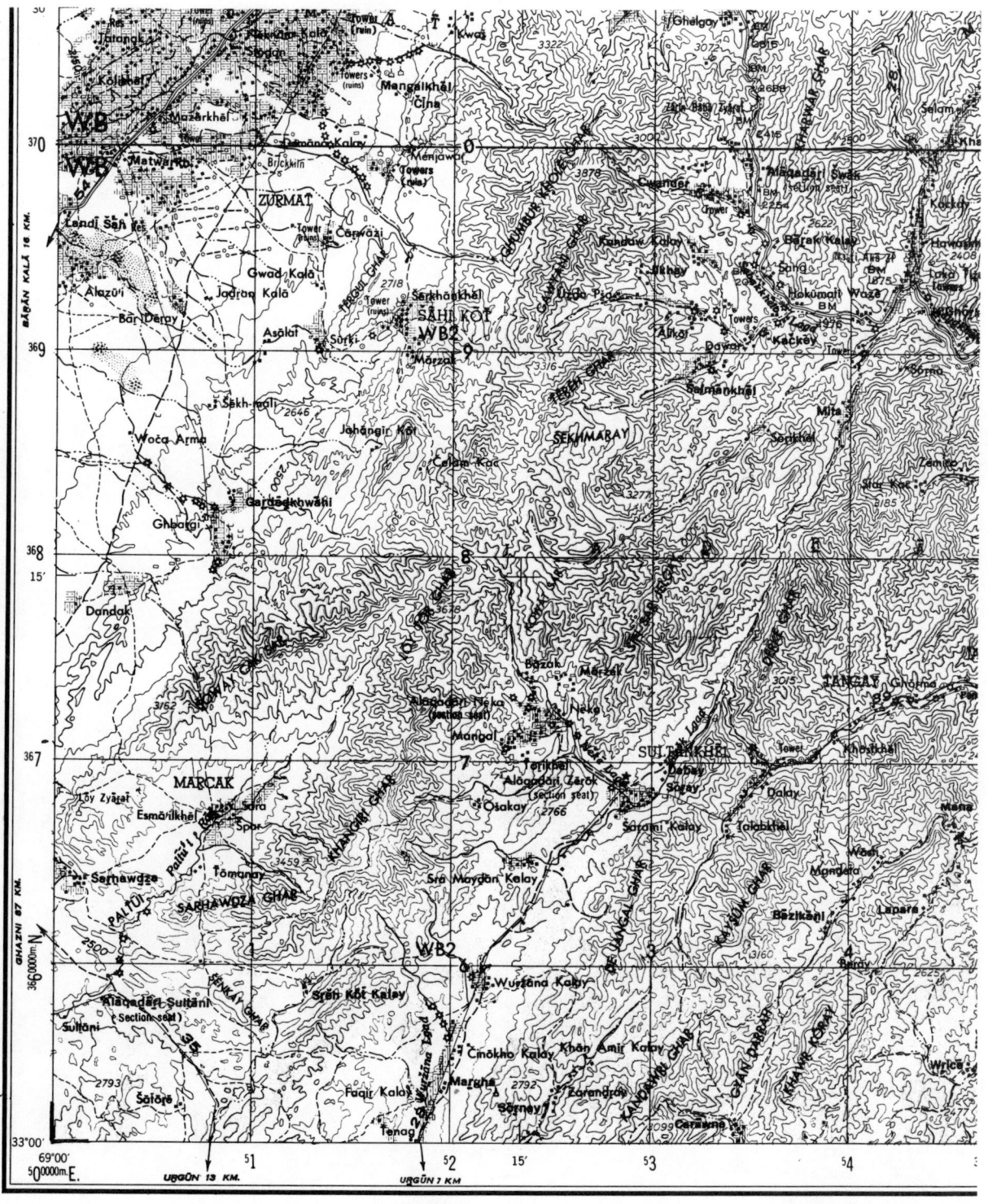

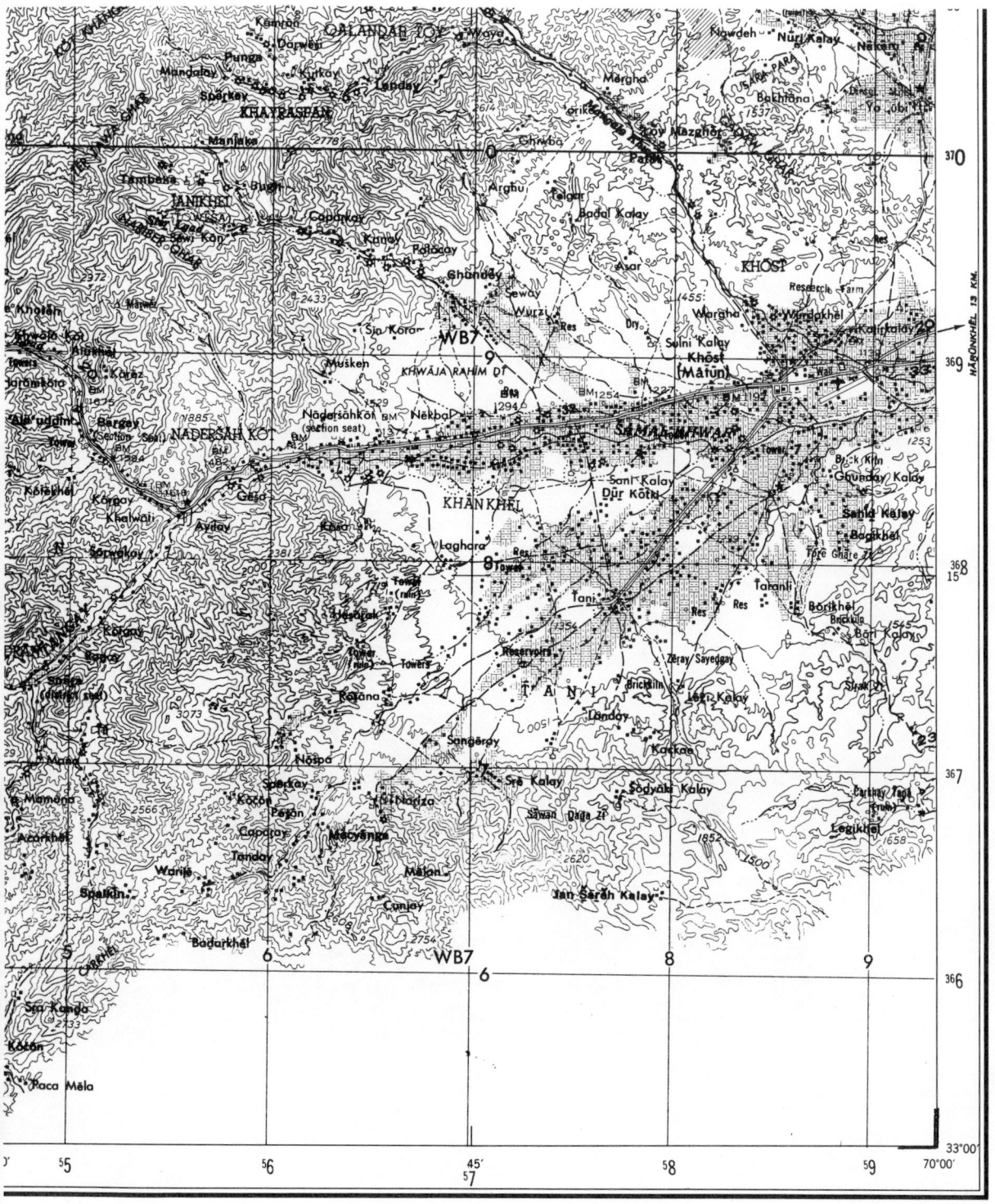

VI–17–A

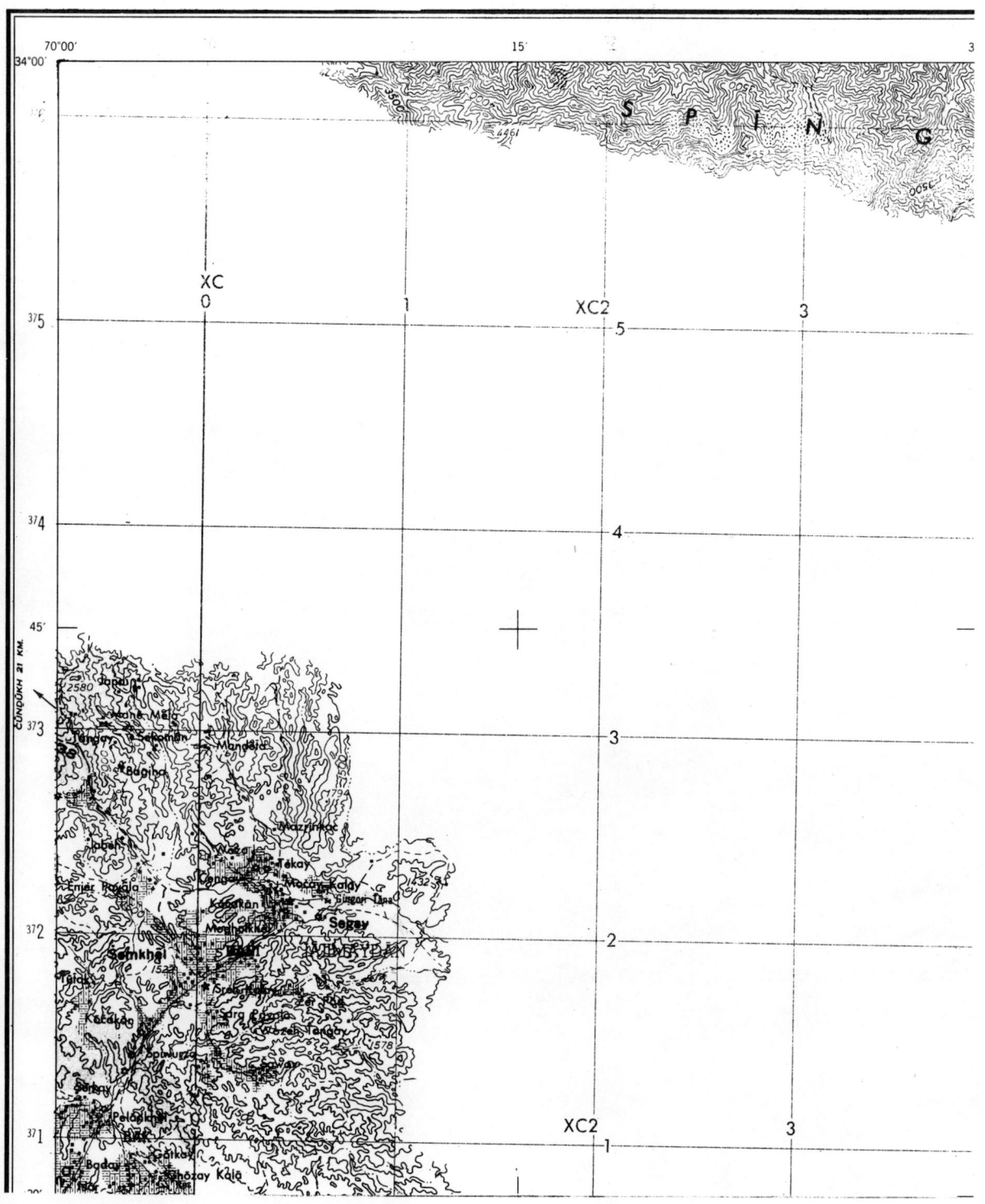

VI-17-B

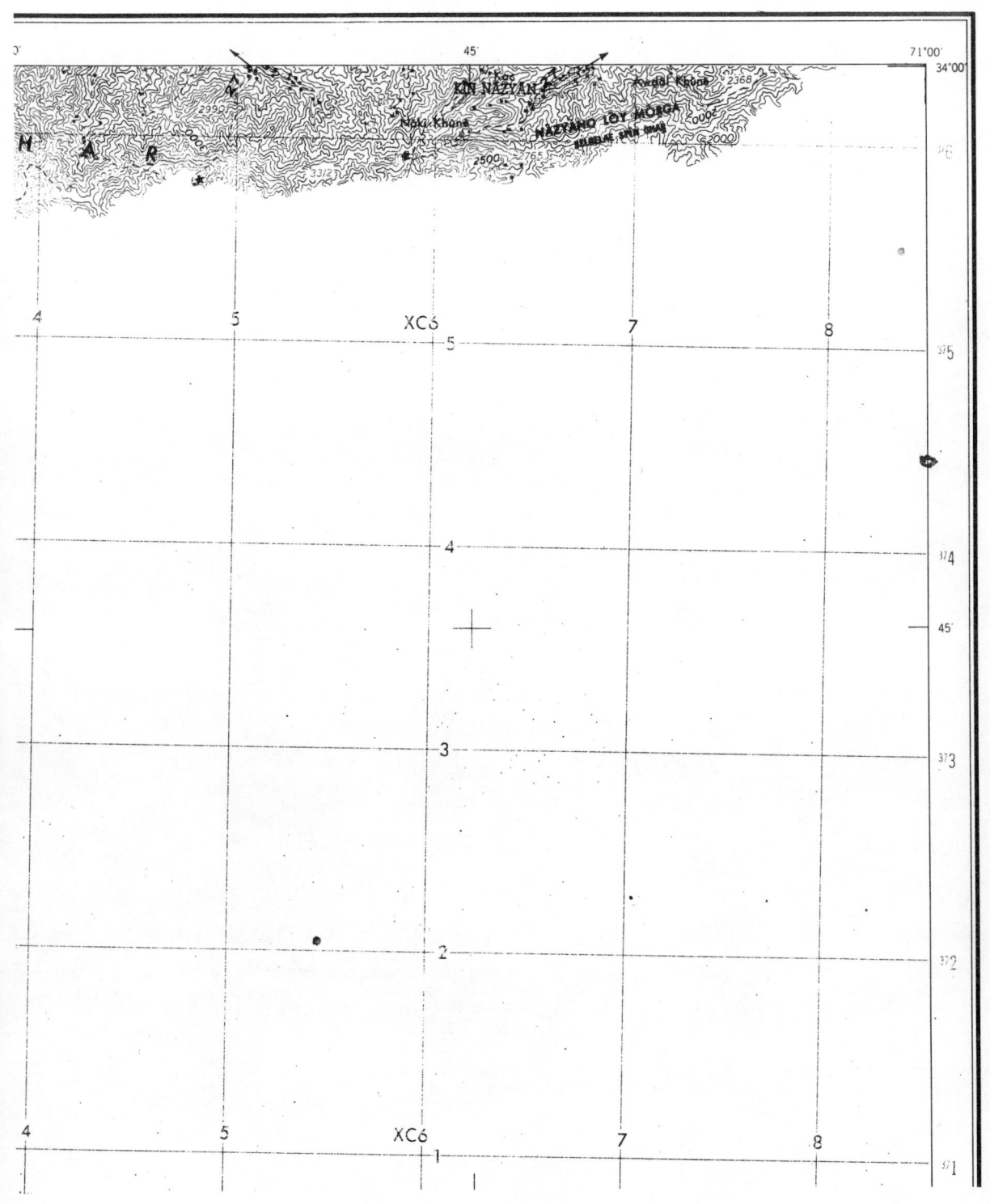

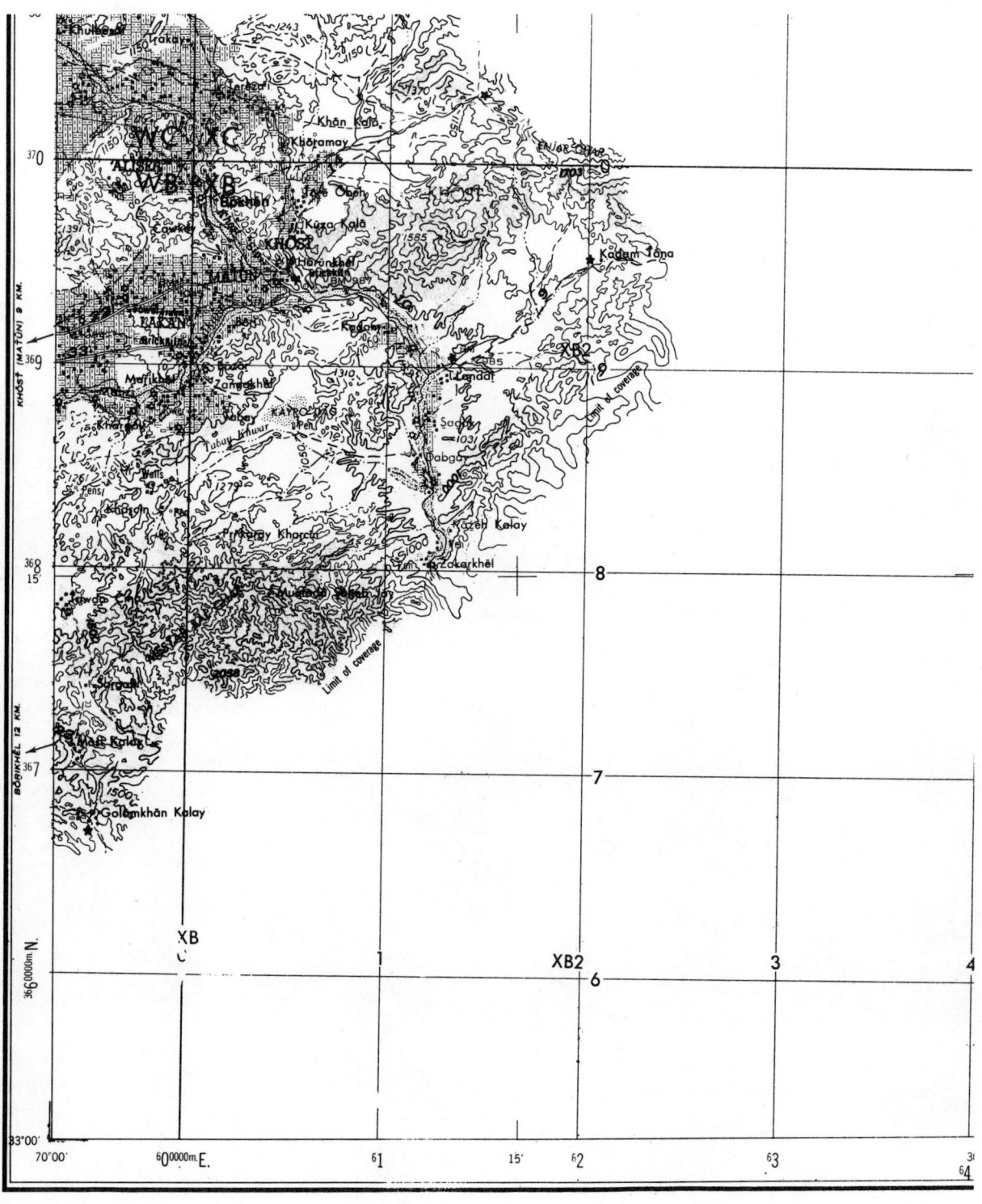

VI–18–A
See V–8–A

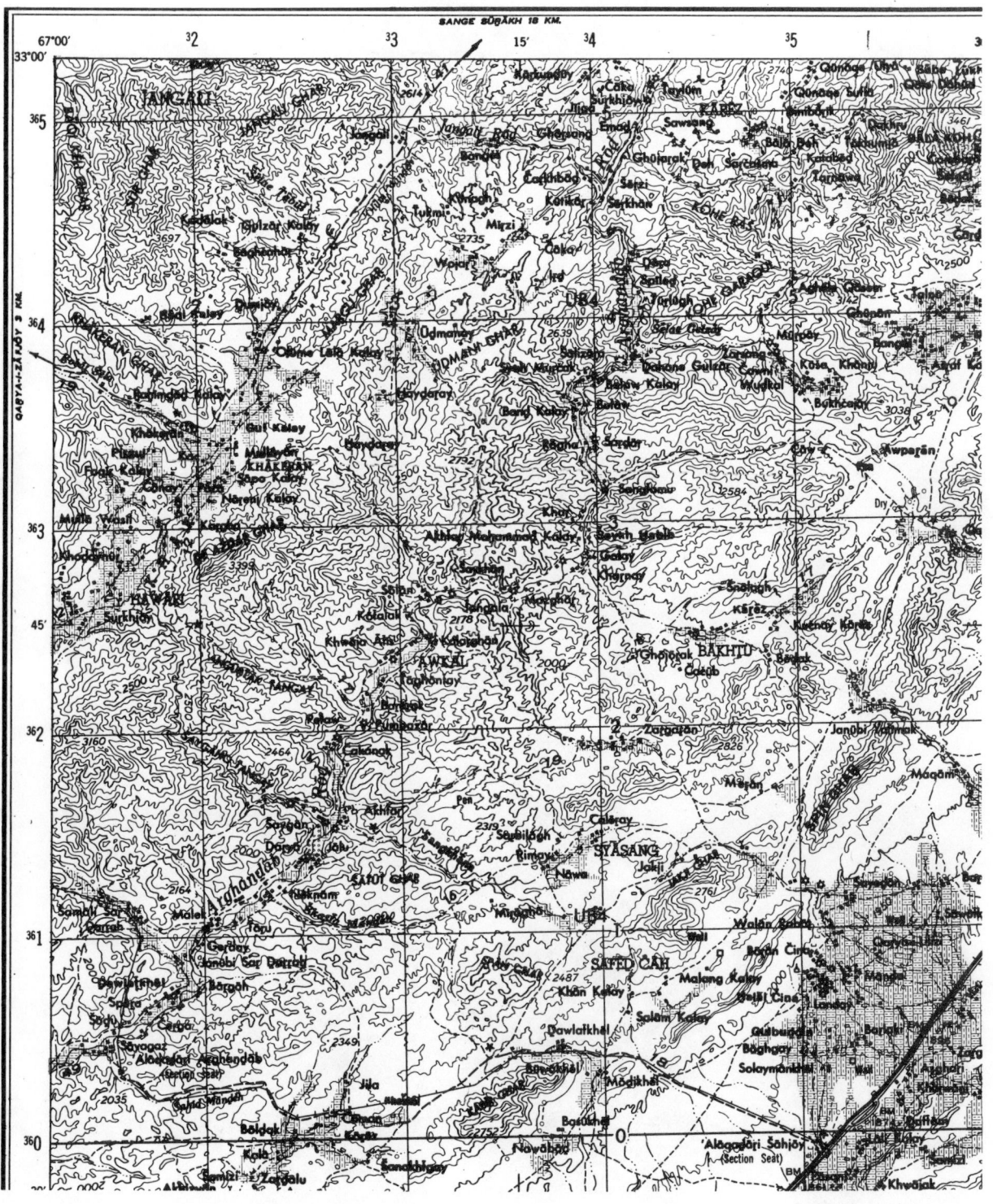

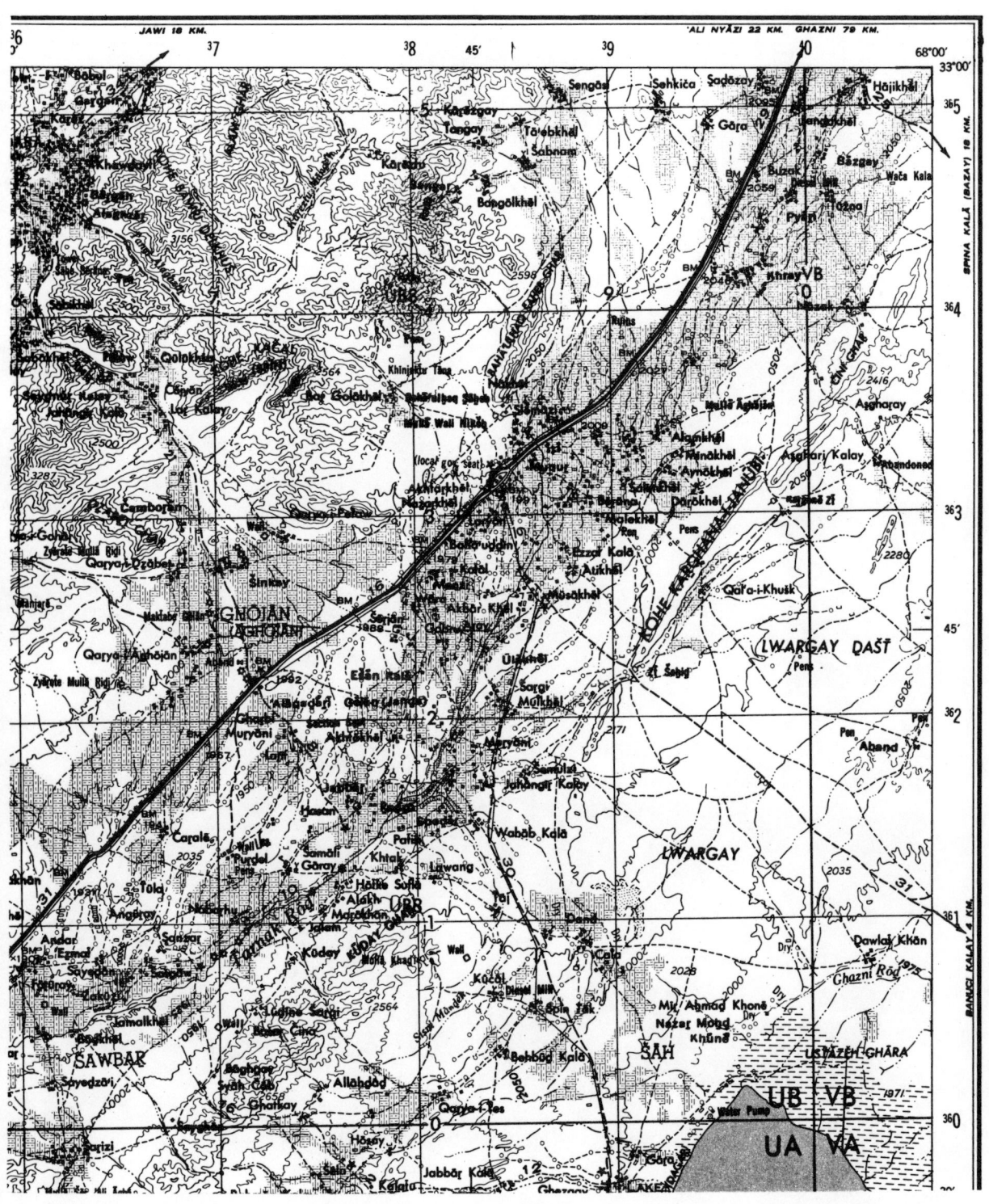

VI–18–D
See V–8–D

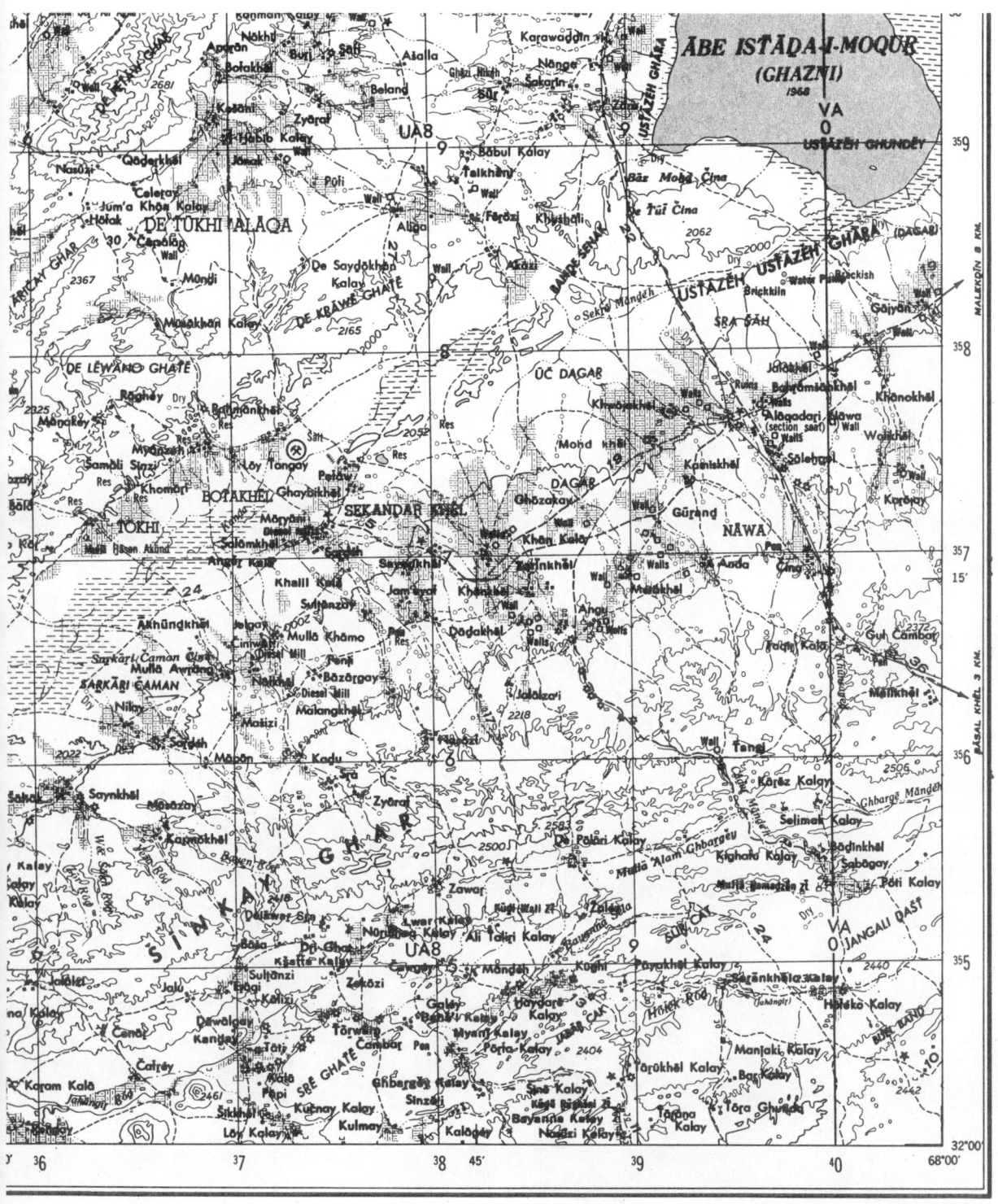

VI-19-A

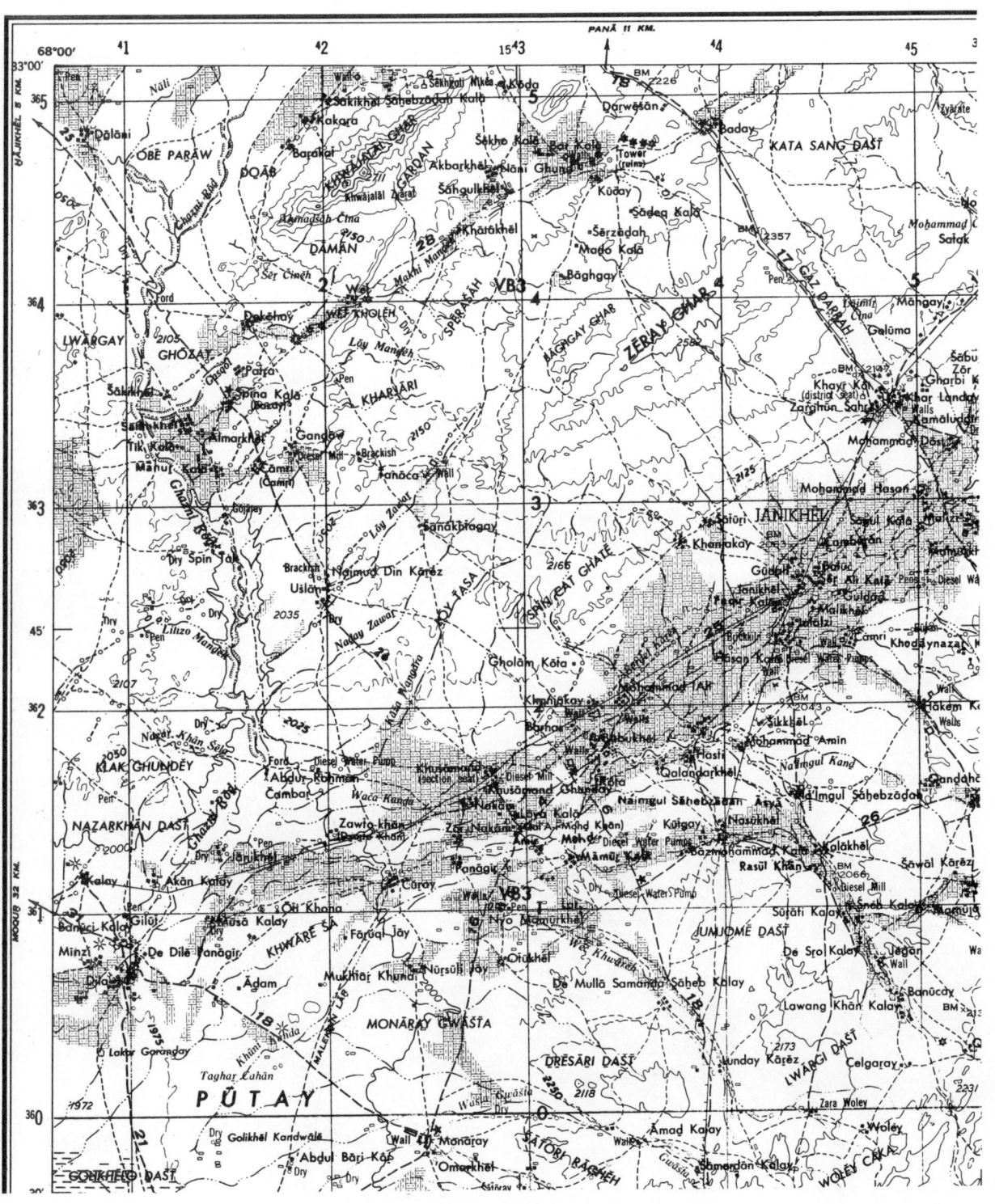

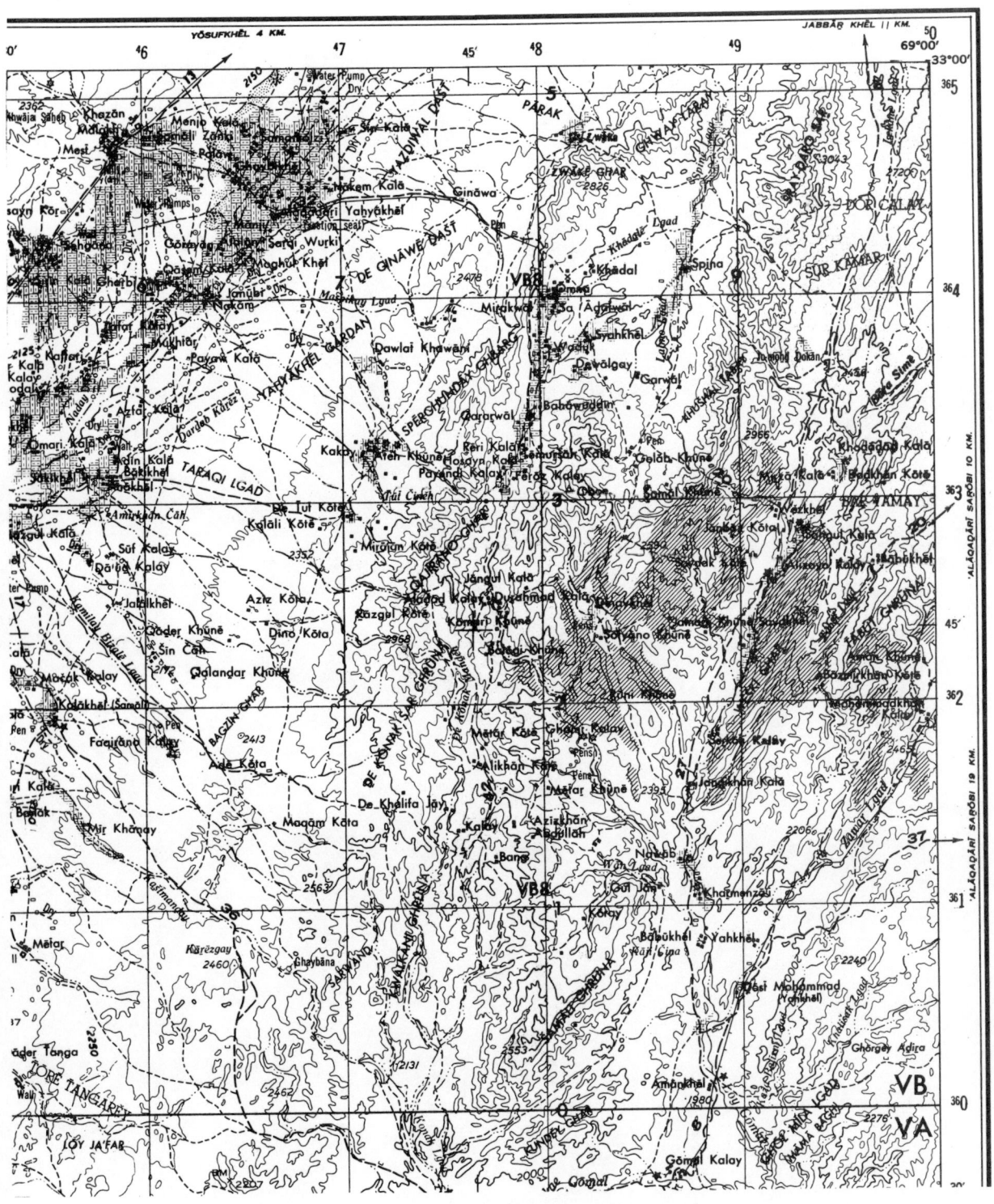

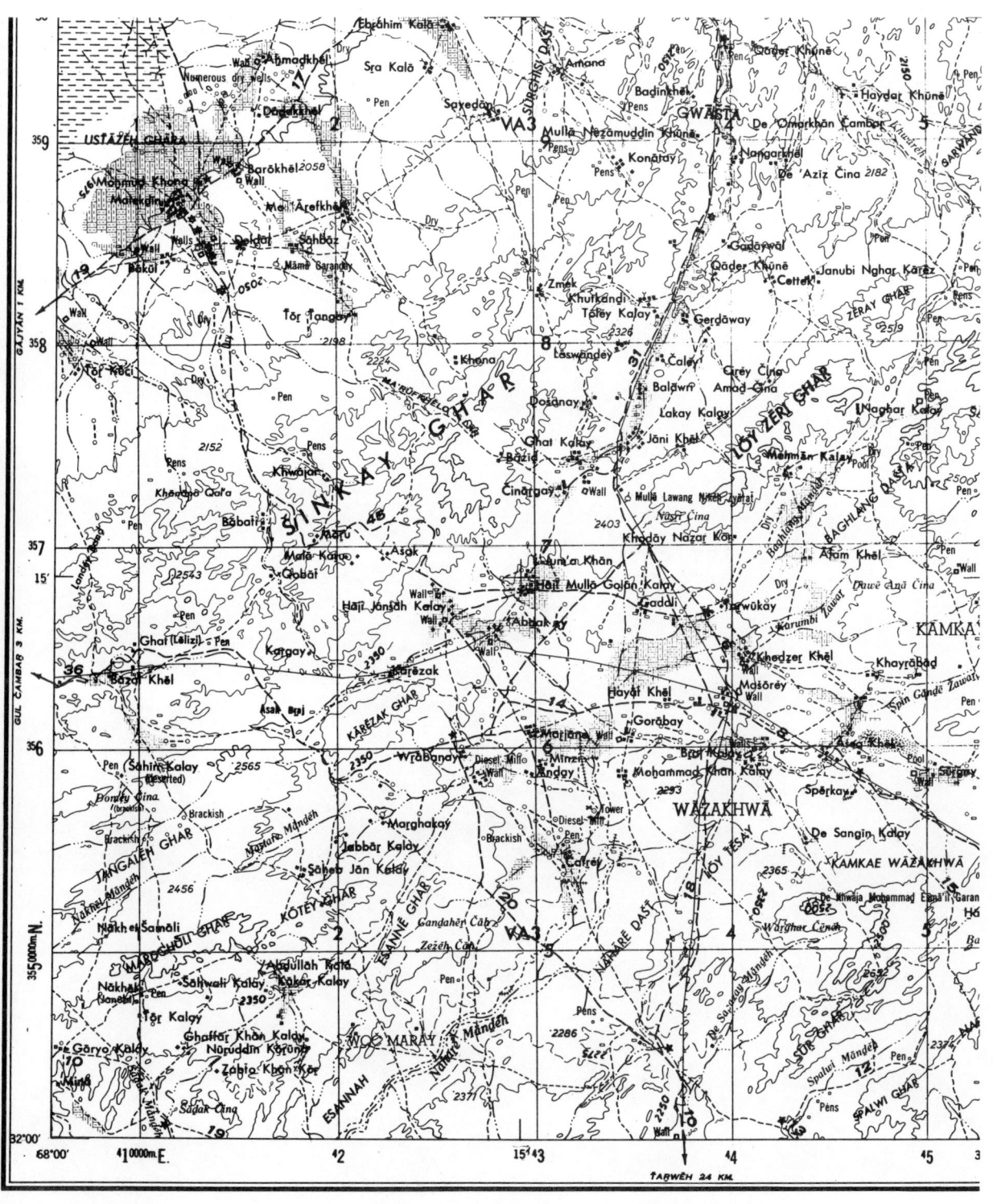

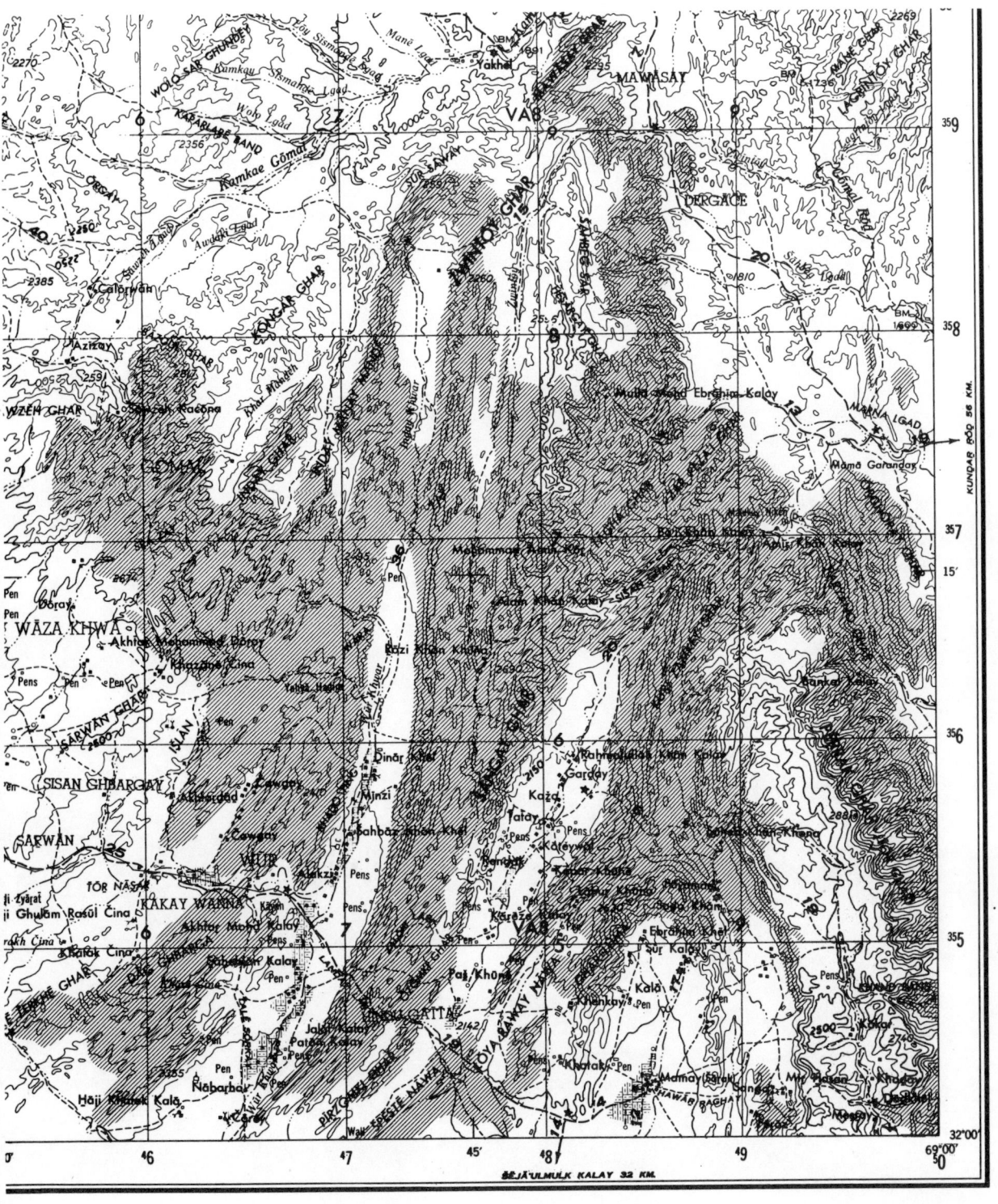

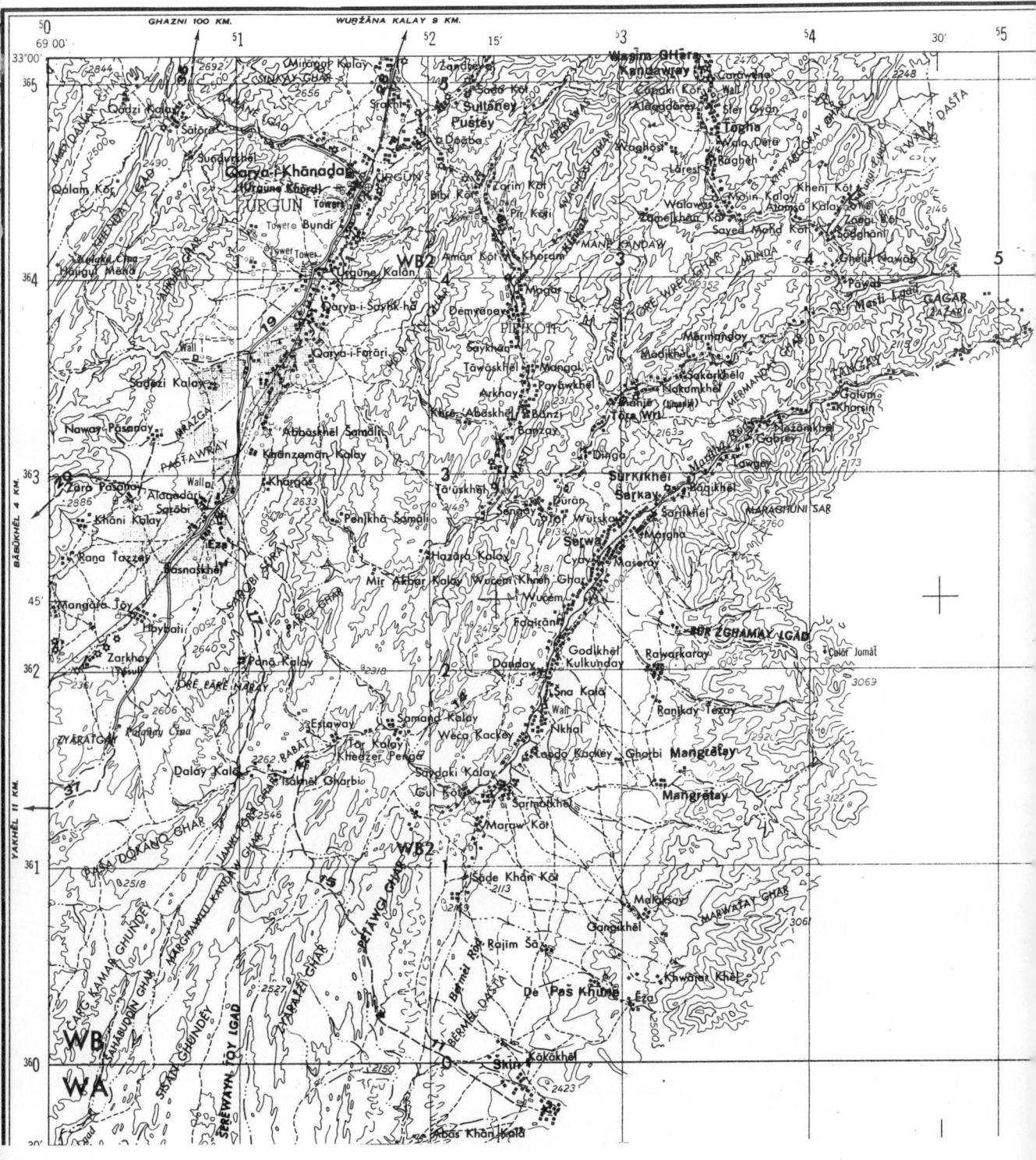

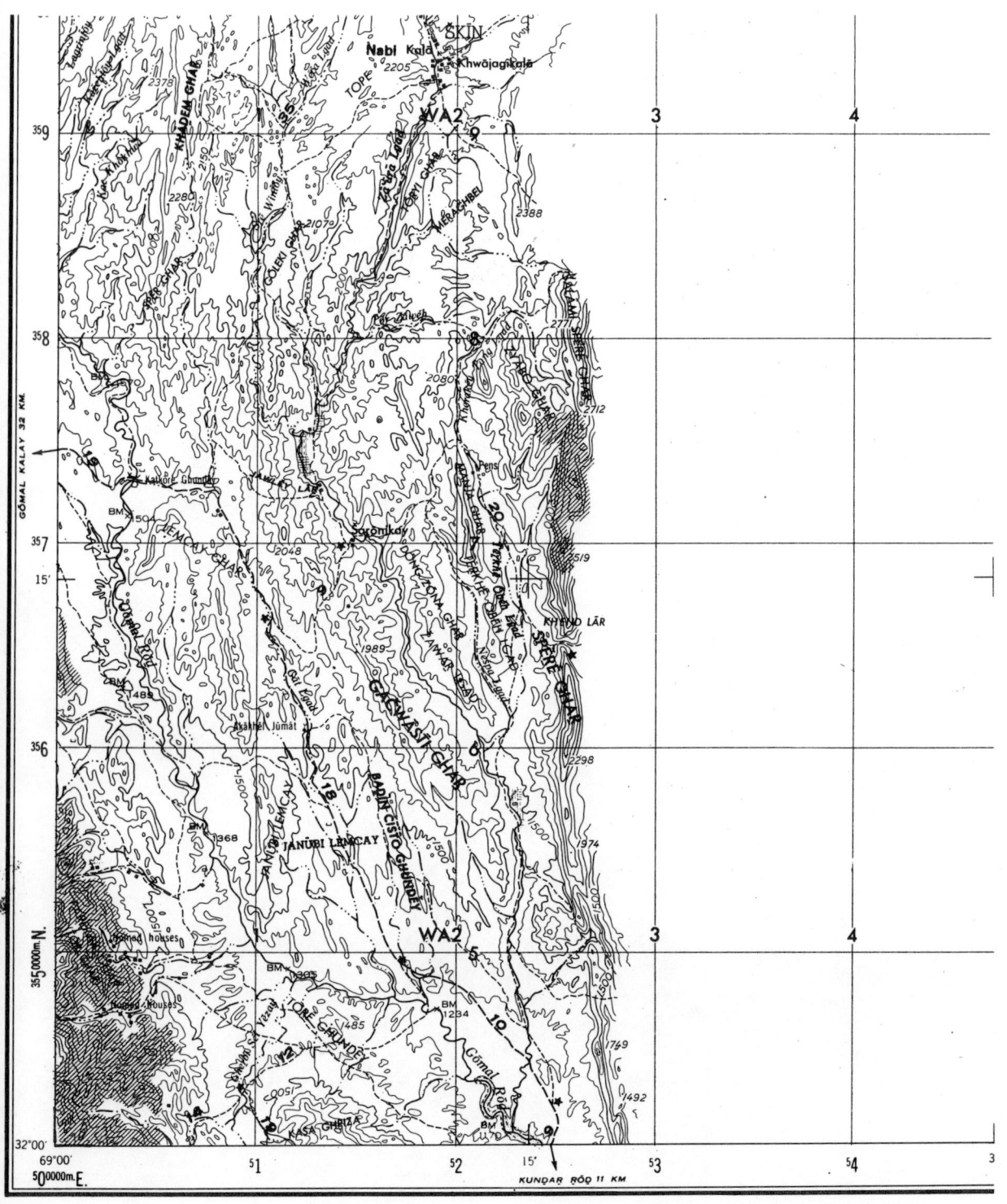

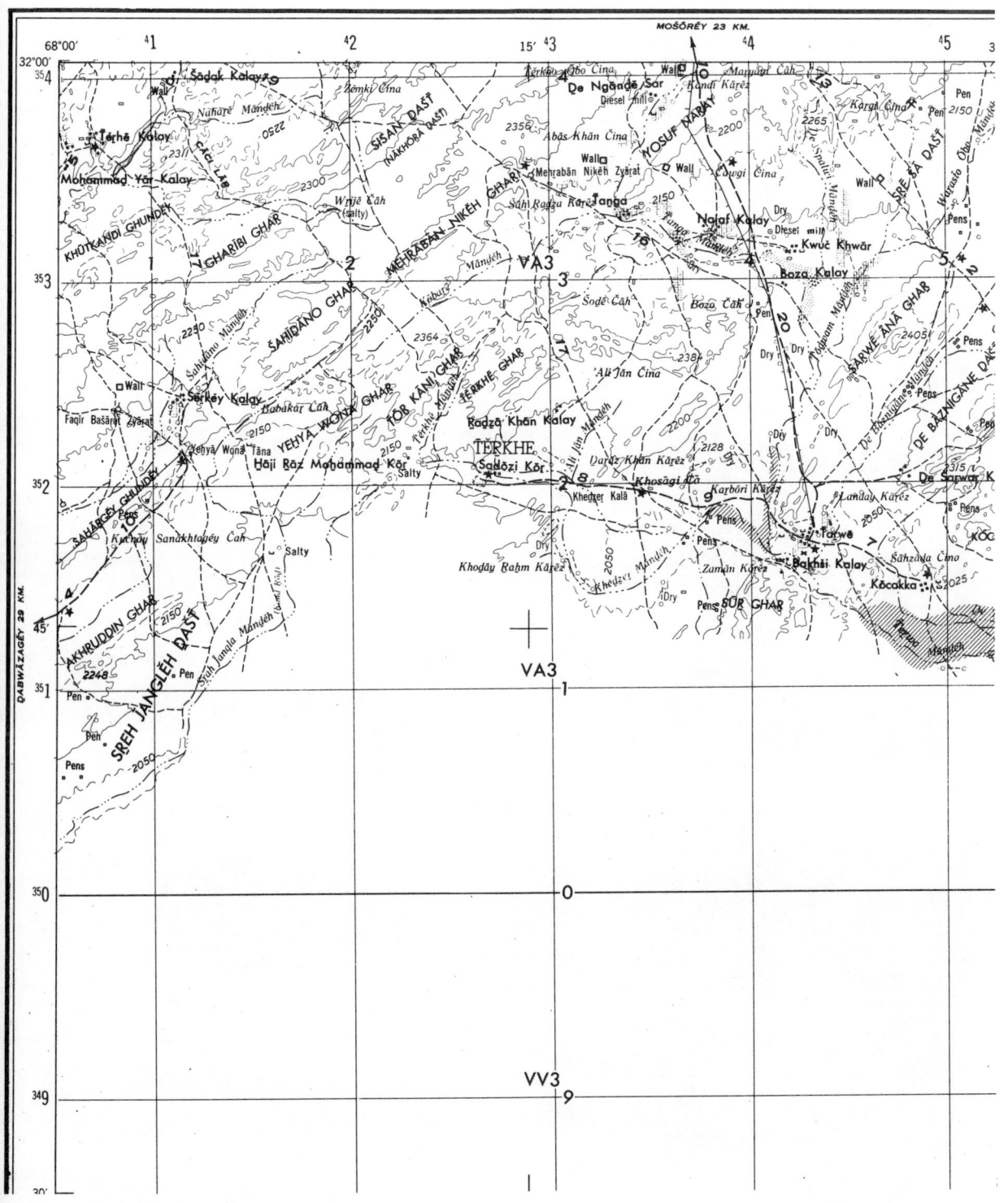

VI-21-B

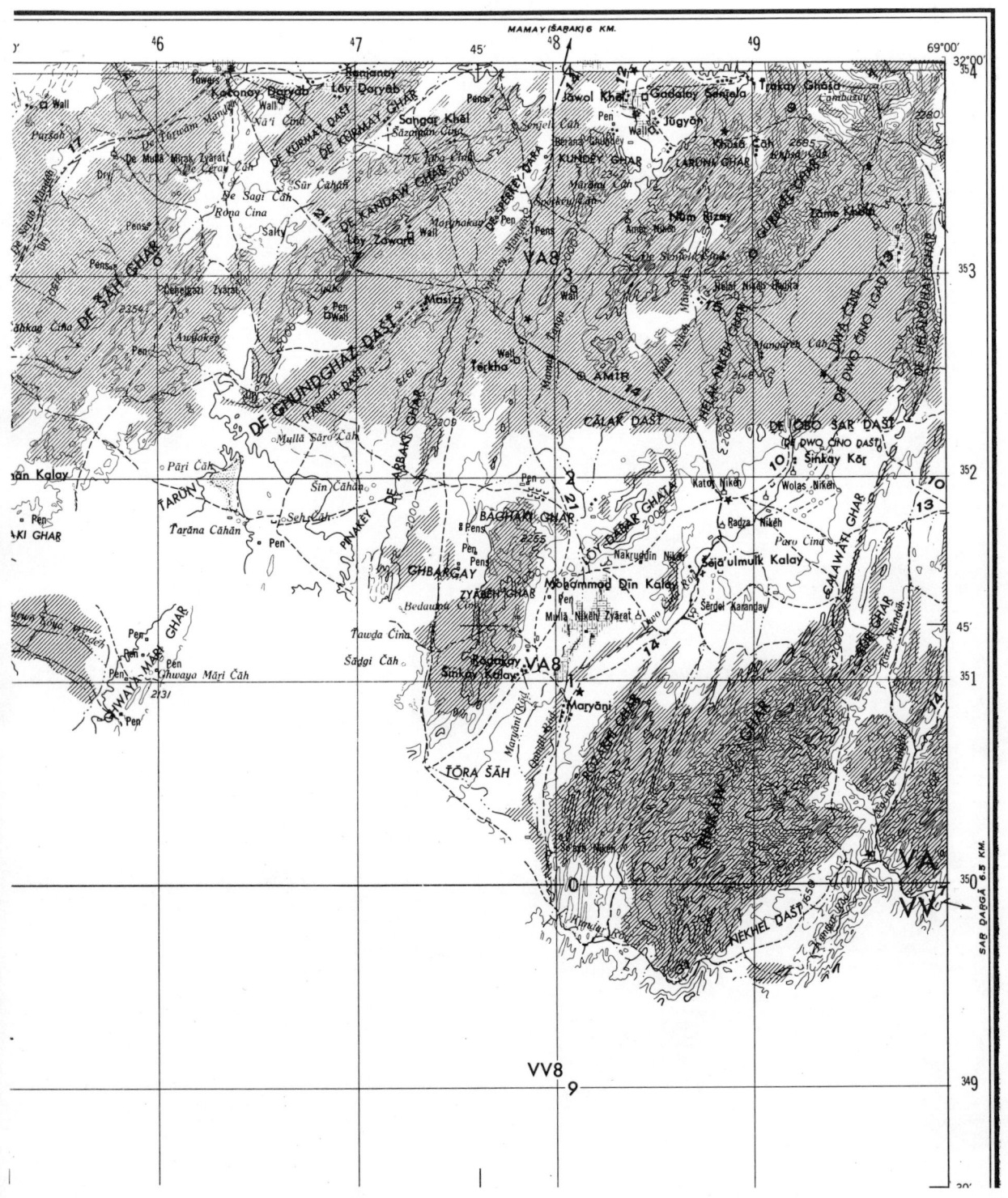

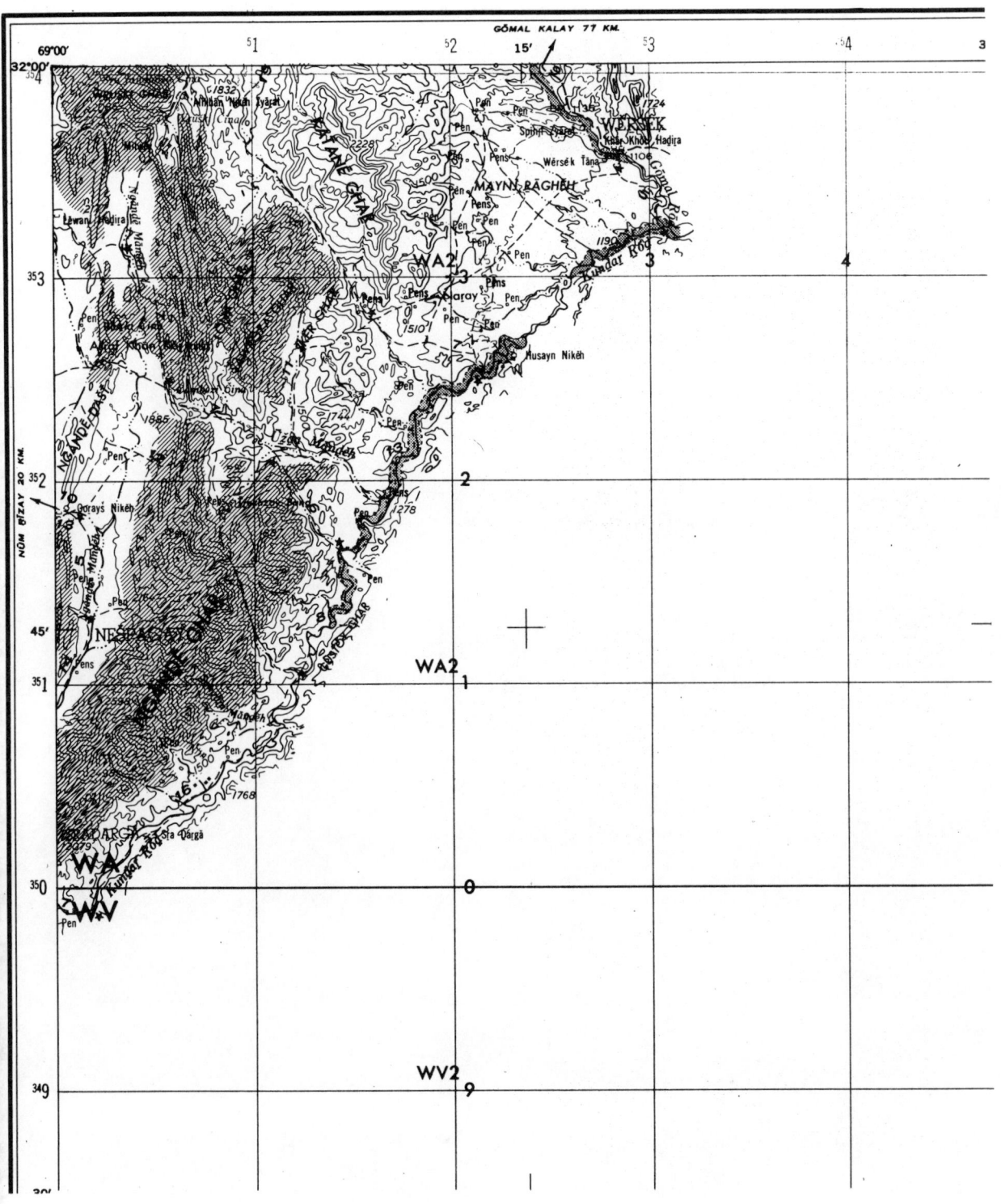